Longman Annotated English Poets

GENERAL EDITOR: F. W. BATESON

Plate 1 John Keats. Miniature by Joseph Severn
painted in 1818

THE POEMS OF

JOHN KEATS

EDITED BY

MIRIAM ALLOTT

LONGMAN

LONGMAN GROUP LIMITED
LONDON
*Associated companies, branches and representatives
throughout the world*

© Longman Group Ltd 1970

First published 1970
ISBN 0 582 48446 4

Printed in Great Britain by
William Clowes and Sons, Limited
London and Beccles

To
K. A.

Contents

POEMS

1*

APPENDICES

Illustrations

Note by the General Editor

This series has been planned to apply to the major English poets the requirements, critical and scholarly, that a serious reading of their poems entails today. Whereas editorial emphasis has recently been on what may be called textual refinements, sometimes carried to grotesque extremes, the Longman Annotated English Poets series concerns itself primarily with the *meaning* of the various texts in their separate contexts. With the aids provided in the table of dates, the headnotes and the footnotes, the modern reader should have all, or almost all, that he requires both for aesthetic appreciation and for proper emotional response to the whole poetic corpus of each poet represented.

Our ideal of comprehension, for the reader, combined with comprehensiveness, for the poet, has three logical consequences:

1. Since an essential clue to an author's intentions at any point is provided, on the one hand, by what he has already written and, on the other hand, by what he will write later, an editor will print his poems as far as possible in the order in which they were composed.

2. A poet writing in a living language, such as English, requires elucidation of a different kind from that suitable to the poet of a dead language, such as Sanskrit, Latin or Old English: with minor exceptions vocabulary and syntax can be taken for granted, but sources, allusions, implications and stylistic devices need to be spelt out.

3. Since the reader in any English-speaking country will tend to pronounce an English poet of the past (at any rate to Chaucer) as if he was a contemporary, whatever impedes the reader's sympathetic identification with the poet that is implicit in that fact–whether of spelling, punctuation or the use of initial capitals–must be regarded as undesirable. A modern pronunciation demands a modern presentation, except occasionally for rhymes (e.g. *bind-wind*) or obsolete archaisms (*eremite*, hermit).

Some exceptions have had to be admitted to the principles summarized above, but they have been few and unimportant.

F. W. BATESON

Preface

At present serious readers use according to their needs either Ernest de Selincourt's *The Poems of John Keats* (1905, fifth edition revised and enlarged 1926) or H. W. Garrod's *The Poetical Works of John Keats* (1939, second edition 1958) or both books. Selincourt's *The Poems of John Keats* is an annotated edition (although the annotation is somewhat limited in scope and is now in many particulars superseded). Garrod's *The Poetical Works of John Keats* is an excellent critical text. In agreement with the title of the series to which it belongs, the principal object of this new edition is of course annotation, but for a reason that has been noted by Garrod rather more attention has been paid to textual matters than in the case of some other poets. As Garrod says in the Introduction to his edition, 'The textual criticism of Keats studies, in fact, not so much to establish the text as to go behind it. Its primary concern is not the poet's *ultima manus*, but his first fingerings and gropings.' I have therefore included a substantial number of variant readings from Keats's manuscripts. Although my edition contains no new poems by Keats and brings to light few significant new readings, it is based on a fresh examination of the MSS and departs occasionally from Garrod's text. These departures occur for the most part in posthumously published work: one instance is *Otho the Great*, which is the product of collaboration and is preserved in MSS in Keats's hand and also in that of his collaborator, Charles Brown; other instances include poems of which there are transcripts, but of which no holograph MSS exist. A new look at the MSS was also needed before deciding on the permissible degree of modernization, notably in the matter of punctuation. Keats's punctuation was often erratic and by today's standards misleading, but to modernize it completely would in certain cases involve reconstruction that few readers would find acceptable.

Apart from textual comment the annotation consists primarily of information about the circumstances of composition; Keats's source materials; suggestions about probable influences and echoes; and some critical and explanatory material. The dating of Keats's poems presents comparatively few problems to the editor, since Keats's life is closely documented and there is good evidence to show when, where and in what circumstances many of the poems were written. When there is less evidence, conjecture in most cases can still be sufficiently well informed to avoid the likelihood of serious error. The question of 'influences' is more difficult. It is at the best of times a marshy area in literary study and is especially so in Keats's case since he was the most literary of poets, possessed an exceptionally retentive memory, and transmuted all that he read in a highly individual way by the complexity of the associations which he made between different parts of his reading. The editor, then, must tread with unusual care when deciding whether parallels are a matter of accident or design, whether echoes are conscious or unconscious, or whether an 'influence' has significantly affected the current of the writer's thinking and feeling. This must be said in order to explain the guarded phrasing of some references in the commentary, and also the omission from it of a few customary, and perhaps in some cases specially cherished, suggestions about sources and influences.

But an editor's principal difficulties in dealing with Keats lie in the fact that at the end of his brief writing career the poet was still struggling to determine not only what he thought and felt but also what the legitimate concerns of his thought and feeling should be. The annotator's task throughout is, in effect, to try to make out what Keats was trying to make out, and his work is not made easier by the forced expressions and looseness of style which are found in the earlier poems. Had Keats lived, it is probable that he would have rejected many of these early poems; and, if he had preserved them, he would almost certainly have gathered them in any collected edition under the defensive heading 'Juvenilia'. As it is, a modern editor must pay the early poems due attention without appearing to attach more importance to them than they really deserve. In the later poems, for example in the Odes or *The Fall of Hyperion*, the task of making out what Keats was making out, if still frequently perplexing, is nevertheless of an entirely different order.

In those parts of the commentary where an attempt is made at criticism or elucidation of meaning, as indeed elsewhere in my notes, I have drawn freely on the suggestions and ideas of Keats scholars over the past century and have had constantly in mind the vast accumulation of Keats studies since Selincourt's 1926 edition of the poems. This edition is thus deeply indebted to many more Keatsians than can possibly be named. As those who have worked closely on Keats know well, certain names identified with Keats scholarship are household words. Those of Ernest de Selincourt and H. W. Garrod have already appeared in this preface, and the names of other 'Presiders' recur throughout the commentary, but I must mention here Hyder E. Rollins, whose splendid editions of Keats's letters and of the correspondence of Keats's friends and associates are indispensable for any work on the poet; C. L. Finney, whose early study of Keats's poetic development did much useful spadework on the background and interpretation of the poems; and three recent biographers of Keats, W. J. Bate, Aileen Ward and Robert Gittings, from whose experience and hard work this edition is fortunate in being able to benefit. To Mr Gittings I am also indebted for his generous assistance in making available to me material gathered when he was preparing his biography of Keats.

I must also express gratitude to various institutions for permission to consult MS materials in their collections: namely the authorities of the Pierpont Morgan Library, New York; The Texas University Library, Austin; the University Library, Harvard; the University Library, Bristol; and Keats Memorial House, Hampstead. Among individuals who have similarly helped me I should especially like to thank Mrs June Moll of the Miriam Lutcher Stark Library, Texas, for providing me with photostats of *Otho the Great*; Miss Dorothy Withey of the Chaucer Head Bookshop, Stratford-upon-Avon, for sending me a photocopy of the MS of *Welcome joy and welcome sorrow* in her possession; Dr W. H. Bond of the Houghton Library for permission to reproduce Keats's MSS of *To Autumn* and *On First Seeing Chapman's Homer*; Mr William R. Maidment, Curator of Keats Memorial House, for his assistance in enabling me to procure numerous photocopies of Keats material; and Mrs Christina M. Gee, Assistant Curator of Keats Memorial House, for her kindness in facilitating my work on the MSS at Keats House and for her help in many other ways during my frequent visits to Hampstead. Her considerateness has continued the tradition of friendliness at Keats House with which I first became acquainted in the time of her predecessor, Miss Charlotte Lutyens, who assisted me in solving several problems in the early stages of my work on Keats.

Among others who at different times have come to my aid, it gives me special pleasure to thank Miss Mary Bennet of the Walker Art Gallery, Liverpool; Dr Gál István of Budapest; and many members of the academic staff of Liverpool University, including Professor A. R. Myers, Dr Robert Markus and Dr Henry Mayr-Harting of the Department of Medieval History, and my old friend Miss Lucrezia Zaina of the Department of Italian. I am, of course, especially grateful to my colleagues in the English Department at Liverpool, notably Professor Kenneth Muir, who lent me books, cuttings and photostats from his collection of Keatsiana and read over the commentary when it was nearing completion, and Mr R. T. Davies and Mr Vincent Newey with whom I discussed various points. My sincere thanks are also due to our Departmental Secretary, Miss Margaret Burton, who has devoted care and patience to typing the book in its successive stages of revision over several years.

My principal debts are owed to those who have given time and trouble to working over various drafts of the whole edition. I am under a deep obligation to Mr F. W. Bateson of Corpus Christi College, Oxford, the general editor of the Longman Annotated English Poets, on whose detailed criticism of my own commentary I have drawn freely for the final version, and to Mr J. C. Maxwell of Balliol College, Oxford, who has suggested many corrections and improvements and generously put at my disposal several findings of his own. It is difficult to express adequately my gratitude to Mr Bateson and Mr Maxwell, and I have a similar difficulty in acknowledging the assistance given to me by my husband, Kenneth Allott, who discussed each poem with me, spent many hours improving the style and substance of the commentary, and in fact did all that could be done to see that the usefulness of the book should not be too seriously impaired by its editor's shortcomings. Were these shortcomings less apparent, I should think it right to ask him to allow his name to appear with mine on the title-page. As things are, his initials appear elsewhere as those of the person to whom this volume is dedicated.

MIRIAM ALLOTT

Liverpool
July 1968

Chronological Table of Keats's Life and Chief Publications

1795 (*31 October*) Born at Finsbury, eldest child of Thomas Keats, head ostler at the Swan and Hoop, and Frances Keats (née Jennings).

1797 (*28 February*) Birth of George Keats.

1799 (*18 November*) Birth of Tom Keats.

1803 (*3 June*) Birth of Fanny (Frances Mary) Keats.
   (*August*) With George begins to attend the Rev. John Clarke's school at Enfield.

1804 (*15 April*) Death of his father.
   (*27 June*) His mother marries again. The Keats children move to the home of their grandparents, John and Alice Jennings, at Enfield.

1805 (*8 March*) Death of John Jennings. The Keats children move with Alice Jennings to Lower Edmonton.

1810 (*March*) Death of his mother from tuberculosis.
   (*July*) Alice Jennings appoints as guardians for the Keats children John Nowland Sandall and Richard Abbey. On Sandall's death in 1816 Abbey becomes their sole guardian.

1811 Leaves Enfield School and is apprenticed to Thomas Hammond, surgeon and apothecary of Edmonton. George Keats becomes a clerk in Abbey's counting-house where Tom joins him later.

1814 First known attempts at writing verse, including *Imitation of Spenser*.
   (*December*) Death of his grandmother, Alice Jennings. Fanny Keats moves to the Abbeys' home.

1815 (*2 February*) Writes a sonnet celebrating Leigh Hunt's release from prison.
   (*October*) Enters Guy's Hospital as a student, taking lodgings nearby.

1816 (*5 May*) The sonnet *O Solitude*, his first published poem, appears in Hunt's *Examiner*.
   (*25 July*) Qualifies at Apothecaries' Hall.
   (*August*) Visits Margate with Tom.
   (*October*) Writes the sonnet *On First Looking into Chapman's Homer*. Meets Hunt, Benjamin Haydon, John Hamilton Reynolds.
   (*November*) Writes a sonnet to Haydon ('*Great Spirits . .* '.).

Lodges with his brothers at 76 Cheapside, near Abbey's business house.

(*December*) Writes *Sleep and Poetry*. His life mask taken by Haydon. Mentioned with Shelley and Reynolds for his poetic promise in Hunt's *Examiner* article 'Young Poets'. This year makes the acquaintance of Joseph Severn.

1817 (*February*) Some of his poems shown by Hunt to Shelley, Godwin and Hazlitt.

(*March*) Moves to Hampstead with his brother.

(*1 or 2 March*) Sees the Elgin Marbles with Haydon.

(*3 March*) His first collection, *Poems*, published by C. and J. Ollier.

(*April–November*) *Endymion* composed.

(*April*) Visits the Isle of Wight and Margate. At Carisbrooke, I. of W., begins to study Shakespeare closely.

(*May*) Visits Canterbury and meets Isabella Jones at Hastings.

(*June*) Returns to Hampstead.

(*September*) Stays with Benjamin Bailey at Oxford; begins to read Milton's *Paradise Lost*.

(*October*) Visits Stratford-on-Avon with Bailey.

(*November*) Reads Shakespeare's *Poems* and Coleridge's *Sibylline Leaves*.

(*22 November*) Writes an important letter to Bailey ('I am certain of nothing but of the holiness of the Heart's affections and the truth of Imagination–What the imagination seizes as Beauty must be truth . . .')

(*15 December*) Sees Edmund Kean in Shakespeare's *Richard III* at Drury Lane.

(*21 December*) Discusses 'intensity' in art and 'Negative Capability' in a letter to his brothers.

(*28 December*) With Charles Lamb, Wordsworth and others at Haydon's 'immortal dinner' (Haydon's *Autobiography* ed. T. Taylor 1853, 1926 edn; i 269–71). This year makes the acquaintance of Charles Armitage Brown and possibly Richard Woodhouse.

1818 (*January–February*) Hears Hazlitt's lectures on English poetry, later published as *Lectures on the English Poets* (1818).

(*27 February*) Sets out his poetic 'Axioms' in a letter to John Taylor ('Poetry should surprise by a fine excess. . . . Its touches of Beauty should never be half way . . . if Poetry comes not as naturally as the Leaves to a tree it had better not come at all . . .').

(*March–April*) At Teignmouth with his brother Tom.

(*April*) *Endymion* published by Taylor and Hessey; writes *Isabella*.

(*3 May*) Writes an important letter to Reynolds containing his fragment of an *Ode to May*, his comparison of Milton and Words-worth and his simile of human life as 'a large Mansion of Many Apartments'.

(*c. 28 May*) Attends his brother George's wedding to Georgiana Wylie.

(*June–August*) Walking tour to the Lakes and Scotland with Brown, after seeing George and Georgiana Keats off to America from Liverpool. Tells Bailey 'You say I must study Dante–well the only Books I have with me are those three little Volumes [Cary's *Dante*, 1814].'

(*mid–August*) Breaks off his tour because of a sore throat and severe chill, and returns to London to find his brother Tom seriously ill.

(*September*) Meets Fanny Brawne. John Wilson Croker's un-favourable notice of *Endymion* in the *Quarterly Review*. Begins to compose *Hyperion* while nursing Tom.

(*6 October*) Reynolds's defence of *Endymion* appears in the *Alfred, West of England Journal*.

(*14 October*) Reynolds urges him to publish *Isabella* as a reply to hostile criticism.

(*24 October*) Meets Isabella Jones again.

(*27 October*) Writes an important letter to Woodhouse ('As to the Poetical character . . . that sort of which, if I am anything, I am a Member; that sort distinguished from the Wordsworthian or egotistical sublime . . . it is everything and nothing–It has no character–it enjoys light and shade. . . . It has as much delight in conceiving an Iago as an Imogen. What shocks the virtuous philosopher, delights the camelion Poet . . .')

(*1 December*) Death of Tom Keats. Moves into Brown's half of Wentworth Place, Hampstead.

(*25 December*) Dines with Mrs Brawne and her daughter Fanny; arrives at an 'understanding' with Fanny Brawne.

1819   (*January*) Visits Chichester and Bedhampton with Brown; writes *The Eve of St. Agnes*.

(*February*) Writes *The Eve of St. Mark*.

(*April–May*) Writes *La Belle Dame Sans Merci* and the major odes, except *To Autumn*; abandons *Hyperion*. Discusses the world as a 'vale of Soul-making' in his journal-letter of February–May 1819.

(*3 April*) Mrs Brawne becomes Charles Dilke's tenant in the other half of Wentworth Place.

(*9 June*) In a letter to Sarah Jeffrey distinguishes Boiardo, 'a noble Poet of Romance', from Shakespeare, 'a miserable and mighty Poet of the human Heart'.

(*June–August*) Stays at Shanklin, I. of W., working at *Otho the Great, Lamia* and *The Fall of Hyperion*.

(*mid-August–early October*) At Winchester. Writes the ode *To Autumn* (19 September) and probably the *Bright Star* sonnet; abandons *The Fall of Hyperion* as too Miltonic; studies Italian.

(*November*) At Wentworth Place. Writes *King Stephen, The Cap and Bells* and tinkers again with *The Fall of Hyperion*.

(*17 November*) Writes to Taylor outlining his plans for future work ('I wish to diffuse the colouring of St Agnes eve throughout a Poem in which Character and Sentiment would be the figures to such drapery–Two or three such Poems . . . written in the course of the next six years . . . would nerve me up to the writing of a few fine Plays–my greatest ambition . . .').

(*December*) Unwell with a recurrence of his sore throat.

(*25 December*) Becomes engaged to Fanny Brawne after an unsuccessful attempt to 'wean' himself from her in the autumn.

1820 (*January*) George returns from America to raise funds. *Otho the Great* rejected by Covent Garden (after its earlier acceptance for future performance at Drury Lane and subsequent withdrawal by the authors). The *Ode on a Grecian Urn* appears in James Elmes's *Annals of the Fine Arts*.

(*February*) Suffers a severe haemorrhage which leaves him weak and confines him to the house for the rest of the month. Offers to break off his engagement to Fanny Brawne.

(*May*) Moves to Kentish Town when Brown lets Wentworth Place and goes to Scotland.

(*10 May*) *La Belle Dame Sans Merci* published in Hunt's *Indicator*.

(*22 June*) Has an attack of blood-spitting.

(*end of June–mid-August*) At Leigh Hunt's house to be better looked after.

(*July*) *Lamia, Isabella, The Eve of St Agnes, and other Poems* published by Taylor and Hessey. Ordered to Italy for the winter by his doctor.

(*August*) Returns to Wentworth Place and is nursed by Fanny Brawne and Mrs Brawne; receives Shelley's invitation to stay with him in Italy; makes his will. Francis Jeffrey's sympathetic notice of *Endymion* and *1820* appears in *The Edinburgh Review*.

(*23 August*) Hunt prints lines from *The Cap and Bells* in the *Indicator*.

(*18 September*) Sails from Gravesend for Italy with Severn.

(*28 September*) Lands at Portsmouth and visits Bedhampton.

(*c. 1 October*) Writes out the *Bright Star* sonnet for Severn in his copy of Shakespeare's *Poems*.

(*21–31 October*) Arrives at Naples. The ship is held in quarantine for ten days.

(*15 November*) Arrives in Rome with Severn and takes lodgings on the Piazza di Spagna.

(*30 November*) Writes his last known letter (to Charles Brown).

1821   (*23 February*) Dies at 11 p.m.

(*26 February*) Buried in the English Cemetery at Rome near the tomb of Caius Cestius.

Abbreviations

1817	*Poems* (1817).
Endymion	*Endymion: A Poetical Romance* (1818).
1820	*Lamia, Isabella, The Eve of St. Agnes, and other Poems* (1820).
Galignani (1829)	*The Poetical Works of Coleridge, Shelley and Keats.* Published by A. and W. Galignani, 1 vol. (Paris 1829). Contains *1817, Endymion, 1820*, four additional poems ('In drear-nighted December . . .', 'Four seasons fill . . .', 'On a Leander Gem', 'To Ailsa Rock') and a memoir probably derived from Leigh Hunt's *Lord Byron and some of his Contemporaries* (1828).
1848	*Life, Letters and Literary Remains of John Keats*, ed. Richard Monckton Milnes, 2 vols (1848).
1876	*The Poetical Works of John Keats*. Aldine edition, ed. Richard Monckton Milnes (1876).
Forman (1883)	*The Poetical Works and Other Writings of John Keats*, ed. H. Buxton Forman, 4 vols (1883).
Forman (1890)	*Poetry and Prose by John Keats*, ed. H. Buxton Forman (1890). Supplement to *Forman* (1883).
Forman (1938–9)	*The Poetical Works and Other Writings of John Keats*, ed. H. Buxton Forman, revised M. Buxton Forman, 8 vols (Hampstead Edition 1938–9)
Colvin (1915)	*The Poems of John Keats*, ed. Sidney Colvin (1915).
de Selincourt	*The Poems: John Keats*, ed. E. de Selincourt (1926). A revision of the 1905 edn.
Garrod	*The Poetical Works of John Keats*, ed. H. W. Garrod (1958 edn).
Baldwin	'Edward Baldwin' [W. Godwin], *The Pantheon: or Ancient History of the Gods of Greece and Rome* (1806).
Bate (1963)	W. J. Bate, *John Keats* (1963).
Colvin (1917)	Sidney Colvin, *John Keats; his Life and Poetry, his Friends, Critics and After-fame* (1917).
Finney	C. L. Finney, *The Evolution of Keats's Poetry* (1936).

Gittings (1954)	Robert Gittings, *John Keats: The Living Year* (1954).
Gittings (1956)	——, *The Mask of Keats* (1956).
Gittings (1958)	——, *John Keats* (1968).
Harvard	The Houghton Library, Harvard University.
Huntingdon Library	The Henry E. Huntingdon Library, California.
KC	*The Keats Circle: Letters and Papers 1816–1879*, ed. H. E. Rollins, 2 vols (1965). Combines H. E. Rollins's *The Keats Circle: Letters and Papers 1816–1878* (1948) and his supplementary volume, *More Letters and Poems of the Keats Circle* (1955).
KShJ	*Keats-Shelley Journal.*
L	*The Letters of John Keats 1814–1821*, ed. H. E. Rollins, 2 vols (1958).
Lemprière	J. Lempriere, *A Classical Dictionary* (1788).
Lowell	Amy Lowell, *John Keats*, 2 vols (1925).
Morgan Library	The Pierpont Morgan Library, New York.
Murry (1925)	J. M. Murry, *Keats and Shakespeare* (1925).
Murry (1930)	——, *Studies in Keats* (1930).
Murry (1949)	——, *The Mystery of Keats* (1949).
Murry (1955)	——, *John Keats* (1955)
Pettet (1957)	E. C. Pettet, *On the Poetry of John Keats* (1957).
Reassessment (1958)	*John Keats: A Reassessment*, ed. K. Muir (1958).
Cowden Clarke	Charles and Mary Cowden Clarke, *Recollections of Writers* (1878).
Reynolds	J. H. Reynolds's copy (now in the Bristol Central Library) of *The Literary Diary; or Improved Commonplace Book* (1814), dated on the title-page, 'Augt. 1816.'. Contains transcripts in an unidentified hand of seventeen poems written by K. between 1817–19 (including 'The Fall of Hyperion' ll. 1–326).
Ridley	M. R. Ridley, *Keats's Craftsmanship: a Study in Poetic Development* (1933).
Sandys's *Ovid*	George Sandys, *Ovids Metamorphosis, Englished, Mythologizd and Represented in Figures* (1640 edn).
Spence's *Polymetis*	Joseph Spence, *Polymetis; or an Enquiry concerning the Agreement between the works of the Roman Poets and the Remains of the antient Artists . . .* (1747).
Sperry's *Woodhouse* (*1817*)	Stuart M. Sperry, Jr., 'Richard Woodhouse's Interleaved and Annotated Copy of Keats's Poems (1817)', *Literary Monographs 1*, ed. E. Rothstein and T. K. Denseath (1967).

Spurgeon	Caroline F. Spurgeon, *Keats's Shakespeare, a Descriptive Study* (1928).
Ward (1963)	Aileen Ward, *John Keats, The Making of a Poet* (1963).
Woodhouse 1	Richard Woodhouse's transcripts of thirty-six poems written by K. between 1814–19 copied into *The Literary Diary; or Improved Commonplace Book* (1811).
Woodhouse 2	A second volume of MSS belonging to Woodhouse, dated at the beginning 'Nov. 1818' but containing transcripts of poems by K. written before and after this date. Includes copies of the poems in *Woodhouse* 1 with thirty-seven additional poems written by K. between 1814 and 1819; a record of K.'s alterations to *Endymion* when preparing the poem for the press; and transcripts of K.'s original Dedication and Preface for *Endymion*.
Woodhouse 3	A third volume of MSS belonging to Woodhouse (now in the Morgan Library). Contains transcripts of letters exchanged by members of the Keats circle; transcripts of some twenty poems already included in *Woodhouse* 1, 2; and transcripts of six additional poems attributed to K., of which the authorship of at least two is doubtful (see 'Doubtful Attributions and Trivia', pp. 744, 745 below).

The location of MSS throughout, unless otherwise stated, is the Houghton Library, Harvard University.

GENERAL

JEGP	*Journal of English and Germanic Philology*
MLN	*Modern Language Notes*
MLR	*Modern Language Review*
N & Q	*Notes and Queries*
OED	*The Oxford English Dictionary*
PMLA	*Publications of the Modern Language Association of America*
PQ	*Philological Quarterly*
RES	*Review of English Studies*
TLS	*The Times Literary Supplement*

THE POEMS

THE POEMS

1 Imitation of Spenser

Probably written early 1814: see Charles Brown, 'Though born to be a poet he was ignorant of his birthright until he had completed his eighteenth year [31 Oct. 1813]. . . . It was *The Faery Queen* that awakened his genius . . . enamoured of the stanza, he attempted to imitate it and succeeded. This account . . . I first received from his brothers, and afterwards from himself. This, his earliest attempt, the "Imitation of Spenser", is in his first volume of Poems' (*KC* ii 55–6). K.'s lake and island diffusely recall the isle of Mirth and the Bower of Bliss in *The Faerie Queene* ii Cantos 6 and 12, but his models include the eighteenth-century Spenserians (who were much influenced by Milton), especially perhaps Thomson in *The Castle of Indolence* (1748), Beattie in *The Minstrel* (1771–74) and Mary Tighe in *Psyche* (1811). On K.'s early enthusiasm for Beattie and Mary Tighe see *To Some Ladies* 20 *n* (p. 19 below) and on the versification of the poem *Bate* (1945) 189–91. K. did not use the Spenserian stanza again until *The Eve of St. Agnes*. The single transcript by Tom Keats is undated. For accounts of Spenser's influence on K. see also Cowden Clarke, 'A few memoranda of the early life of John Keats' (*KC* ii 148–9) and *Cowden Clarke* 125–6. Published *1817*.

> Now Morning from her orient chamber came,
> And her first footsteps touched a verdant hill,
> Crowning its lawny crest with amber flame,
> Silvering the untainted gushes of its rill,
> 5   Which, pure from mossy beds, did down distil,
> And after parting beds of simple flowers
> By many streams a little lake did fill,
> Which round its marge reflected woven bowers
> And, in its middle space, a sky that never lowers.
>
> 10   There the king-fisher saw his plumage bright
> Vying with fish of brilliant dye below,
> Whose silken fins and golden scalës' light
> Cast upward, through the waves, a ruby glow.

¶ 1. *3. with amber flame*] Echoes Milton, *L'Allegro* 60–1,

> When the great Sun begins his state
> Rob'd in flames and Amber light . . .

K. probably borrowed 'lawny' in this line from Thomson. See, for example, Thomson's *The Seasons* (1730), *Summer* 53,

> . . . opens all the lawny prospect wide . . .

On Hunt's encouragement of this type of epithet in K. see *Calidore* 10 *n* (p. 37 below).
12. scalës'] *scalès Tom Keats MS.*

There saw the swan his neck of archèd snow,
15   And oared himself along with majesty;
        Sparkled his jetty eyes; his feet did show
        Beneath the waves like Afric's ebony,
And on his back a fay reclined voluptuously.

        Ah! could I tell the wonders of an isle
20   That in that fairest lake had placèd been,
        I could e'en Dido of her grief beguile,
        Or rob from agèd Lear his bitter teen;
        For sure so fair a place was never seen,
        Of all that ever charmed romantic eye.
25   It seemed an emerald in the silver sheen
        Of the bright waters; or as when on high,
Through clouds of fleecy white, laughs the cerulean sky.

14–15. From Thomson's imitation of Milton; *The Seasons* (1730) *Spring*
778–81,
                        ... The stately-sailing swan
                Gives out his snowy plumage to the gale,
                And, arching proud his neck, with oary feet
                Bears forward fierce ...
and *Paradise Lost* vii 438–40,
                            ... the Swan, with Arched neck
                Between her white wings mantling proudly, Rowes
                Her state with Oarie feet ...
K.'s marking of this passage in his copy of Milton at Hampstead probably
belongs to a later date.
21–2. Indications of K.'s early reading. For his knowledge of Virgil see
Cowden Clarke, '[K.'s] classical attainment extended no further than the
Aeneid; with which epic, indeed, he was so fascinated that before leaving
school he had *voluntarily* translated in writing a considerable portion' (124).
22. teen] Grief. A Spenserian archaism. Woodhouse cites the use of the
word in *The Tempest* I ii 64, *Richard III* IV i 96, *Venus and Adonis* 808
(Sperry's *Woodhouse (1817)* p. 45).
24. Cp. Beattie's *The Minstrel* (1771–74) i lviii,
                        ... whate'er of beautiful, or new,
                Sublime, or dreadful, in earth, sea, or sky,
                By chance, or search, was offer'd to his view,
                He scann'd with curious and romantic eye ...
27. K.'s vocabulary derives from Milton and his eighteenth-century imi-
tators. Cp. the description of the moon in *Il Penseroso* 72,
                Stooping through a fleecy cloud ...
and Thomson's adaptation of it in *The Seasons* (1730), *Autumn* 1096–7,
                Now through the passing cloud she seems to stoop,
                Now up the pure cerulean rides sublime ...

And all around it dipped luxuriously
Slopings of verdure through the glossy tide,
30   Which, as it were in gentle amity,
Rippled delighted up the flowery side;
As if to glean the ruddy tears it tried,
Which fell profusely from the rose-tree stem.
Haply it was the workings of its pride,
35   In strife to throw upon the shore a gem
Outvying all the buds in Flora's diadem.

36. Flora] For Flora see *Sleep and Poetry* 102 *n* (p. 73 below).

2 On Peace

Probably written *c.* April 1814 to celebrate the end of the war with France:
the sonnet echoes the tone of Leigh Hunt's articles in the *Examiner* April–
May 1814 at the time of Napoleon's deposition by the allies and exile to
Elba. For K.'s familiarity as a schoolboy with the *Examiner* and its influence
on his political views see headnote to *Written on the Day that Mr. Leigh Hunt
left Prison* (p. 11 below).

    The poem is an irregular Shakespearian sonnet (*abab cdcd ddedee*) influenced
stylistically by sonneteers of the later eighteenth century, and with some
reflection of Wordsworth's manner in *Sonnets dedicated to Liberty* (1807) and
Coleridge's *Sonnets to Eminent Characters* (1797). The other early sonnets use
a form of Petrarchan rhyme scheme; thereafter with few exceptions K.
adopts the Shakespearian form–see headnote to *When I have fears* (p. 296
below). On K.'s dissatisfaction in spring 1819 with both the Petrarchan and
the Shakespearian rhyme schemes see headnote to *If by dull rhymes* (p. 521
below). Commentaries on K.'s early sonnets include those in Finney 39–42,
L. J. Zillman's *John Keats and the Sonnet Tradition* (1939) and Bate (1945)
191–6. The three transcripts of the poem, including those by Woodhouse
(*Woodhouse* 2, 3), largely agree.
Published *N and Q* 4 Feb. 1904; repr. *de Selincourt* (1905).

O Peace! and dost thou with thy presence bless
    The dwellings of this war-surrounded isle,
Soothing with placid brow our late distress,
    Making the triple kingdom brightly smile?
5 Joyful I hail thy presence; and I hail
    The sweet companions that await on thee.
Complete my joy–let not my first wish fail:
    Let the sweet mountain nymph thy favourite be,

¶ *2. 8. sweet mountain nymph*] An echo of Milton, *L'Allegro* 35–6,
          And in thy right hand lead with thee,
          The Mountain Nymph, sweet Liberty . . .

With England's happiness proclaim Europa's liberty.
10   O Europe! let not sceptred tyrants see
That thou must shelter in thy former state;
Keep thy chains burst, and boldly say thou art free;
Give thy kings law—leave not uncurbed the great.
So with the honours past thou'lt win thy happier fate.

9. A free rendering of the inscription forming part of the peace decorations on Somerset House, London, 'Europa Instaurata, Auspice Britanniae / Tyrannide Subversa, Vindice Libertatis'. The inscription is quoted in Hunt's account of the celebratory illuminations in London (*The Examiner* 17 April 1814, 255–6). The line has seven feet.
12. thou art] Scanned as a monosyllable.
13. The new French constitution was ratified April 1814 and Louis XVIII returned to Paris May 1814. Hunt remarked in *The Examiner* 1 May 1814, 'That he [Louis XVIII] will not have power to play the tyrant like some of his predecessors, his subjects will take care, if they remain true to their new charter' (273).
14. An alexandrine.

3 'Fill for me a brimming bowl'

Written Aug. 1814 (after briefly catching sight of an unknown woman at Vauxhall according to Woodhouse) and so dated in K.'s holograph MS (Morgan Library). For K.'s later celebrations of the same woman see *When I have fears* 9 *n* and *To*—['*Time's sea*'] (pp. 297, 306 below).
    The parallel with Byron's *To a Beautiful Quaker* (1807) is probably more than a coincidence, but K.'s use of octosyllabic couplets derives chiefly from Milton's *L'Allegro* and *Il Penseroso* and eighteenth-century imitations of these poems, such as Dyer's *Grongar Hill* (1726).
Text from K.'s MS (Morgan Library) with some variants noted from the two transcripts in *Woodhouse* 3, which largely agree.
Published *N and Q* 4 Feb. 1905; repr. *de Selincourt* (1905).

> *What wondrous beauty! From this moment I efface from my mind*
> *all women.*   TERENCE [*Eunuch* Act 2 sc. 4]

Fill for me a brimming bowl,
And let me in it drown my soul;
But put therein some drug, designed

¶ *3. Motto.* Cp. Terence, *Eunuchus* II iii 296, *O faciem pulchram! deleo omnis dehinc ex animo mulieres.* K. may have read the play in Latin, but for various English translations of Terence currently available see *Finney* 50. The motto, with Scene 4 for Scene 3, appears in K.'s MS but not in the four known transcripts.

To banish Woman from my mind.
5   For I want not the stream inspiring
       That heats the sense with–lewd desiring;
       But I want as deep a draught
       As e'er from Lethe's wave was quaffed
       From my despairing breast to charm
10   The image of the fairest form
       That e'er my revelling eyes beheld,
       That e'er my wandering fancy spelled.
       'Tis vain–away I cannot chase
       The melting softness of that face,
15   The beaminess of those bright eyes,
       That breast, earth's only Paradise.
       My sight will never more be blessed,
       For all I see has lost its zest;
       Nor with delight can I explore
20   The classic page, the Muses' lore.

6. *Woodhouse* 2, 3 have 'That fills the mind with fond desiring . . .' Woodhouse's copy of the poem was taken from Mary Frogley (*Woodhouse* 3) for whom K. probably watered down his original line. See headnote to *To Mary Frogley* (p. 29 below).

7–8. Cp. Thomas Moore's translation of *Anacreon* (1800), Ode 62 1–2,

    Fill me, boy, as deep a draught,
    As e'er was fill'd, as e'er was quaff'd . . .

8. *Lethe's wave*] Lethe in classical mythology was a river which had the power of making the souls of the dead 'forget whatever they had done, seen, or heard before' (*Lemprière*). Of K.'s various references to Lethe the best known appears in *Ode to a Nightingale* 4 (p. 525 below), 'Lethe-wards had sunk'.

9. *breast*] heart *Woodhouse* 2, 3.

12. *spelled*] Enchanted.

13–18. Cp. Byron, *To a Beautiful Quaker* (1806) 1–8,

    Sweet girl! though only once we met,
    That meeting I shall ne'er forget;
    And though we ne'er may meet again,
    Remembrance will thy form retain;
    I would not say, 'I love', but still,
    My senses struggle with my will:
    In vain to drive thee from my breast,
    My thoughts are more and more represt . . .

20. *classic page . . . Muse's lore*] Poetic commonplaces. See, for example, Byron, *Childish Recollections* (1807) 111,

    With him for years, we searched the classic page . . .,
and Thomson's *The Castle of Indolence* (1748) i 42,
    Cheered the lone midnight with the muse's lore . . .

Had she but known how beat my heart,
And with one smile relieved its smart,
I should have felt a sweet relief,
I should have felt 'the joy of grief!'
25   Yet as the Tuscan 'mid the snow
Of Lapland thinks on sweet Arno,
So for ever shall she be
The halo of my memory.

24. '*the joy of grief*'] A quotation from Campbell's *The Pleasures of Hope*
(1799) i 182,
And teach impassioned souls the joy of grief . . .
27. *So*] Even so *Woodhouse* 3.

4 'As from the darkening gloom a silver dove'

Written Dec. 1814 on the death of K.'s grandmother, Alice Jennings, who
was buried 19 Dec. 1814: '1816' in Woodhouse's three transcripts, but see
his note of 7 Feb. 1819, '[K] said he had written it on the death of his grandmother, about five days after . . . he had never told anyone, not even his
brother, the occasion on which it was written; he said he was tenderly
attached to her' (*Woodhouse* 3).
Published *1876*.

As from the darkening gloom a silver dove
    Upsoars and darts into the Eastern light
    On pinions that naught moves but pure delight;
So fled thy soul into the realms above,
5   Regions of peace and everlasting love,
    Where happy spirits, crowned with circlets bright
    Of starry beam, and gloriously bedight,
Taste the high joy none but the blessed can prove.

¶ 4. *1–5*. Cp. Mary Tighe's *Psyche* (1811) iii st. 30,
Meantime the dove had soared above their reach
                    . . .
Conspicuous mid the gloom its silver plumage shone . . .
and see also Chatterton's elegy *On the death of Mr. Phillips* (1803) 79–80,
Peace, decked in all the softness of the dove,
    Over thy passions spread her silver plume . . .
and 83–4,
Peace, gentlest, softest of the virtues spread
    Her silver pinions . . .

There thou or joinest the immortal quire
10   In melodies that even Heaven fair
Fill with superior bliss, or, at desire
        Of the omnipotent Father, cleavest the air
On holy message sent—What pleasures higher?
Wherefore does any grief our joy impair?

9. *quire*] The usual pre-1700 spelling. Here an archaism.
11–13. at desire . . . sent] Suggests a recollection of Milton's sonnet *When I consider how my light is spent* 12–13,
                . . . Thousands at his bidding speed
        And post o'er Land and Ocean without rest . . .
13] *pleasures*] The reading of *Woodhouse* 1, 3; 'pleasure's' in *Woodhouse* 2, *1876*.

5 To Lord Byron

Written Dec. 1814: so dated in *Woodhouse* 2. The sonnet reflects the popular taste for Byron whose oriental verse-tales were published 1813–14. For K.'s later feelings about Byron see headnote to *The Cap and Bells* and *The Fall of Hyperion* i 207–8 *n* (pp. 702 and 671 below). The form is regular Petrarchan, but the style reflects the polite idiom of such eighteenth-century elegiac sonneteers as Charlotte Smith (*Elegiac Sonnets*, 1784).
Text from *Woodhouse* 2.
Published *1848*.

Byron, how sweetly sad thy melody,
        Attuning still the soul to tenderness,
        As if soft Pity, with unusual stress,
Had touched her plaintive lute, and thou, being by,
5   Hadst caught the tones, nor suffered them to die.
        O'ershading sorrow doth not make thee less
        Delightful; thou thy griefs dost dress
With a bright halo, shining beamily;
        As when a cloud a golden moon doth veil,
10   Its sides are tinged with a resplendent glow,
Through the dark robe oft amber rays prevail,
        And like fair veins in sable marble flow.
Still warble, dying swan, still tell the tale,
        The enchanting tale, the tale of pleasing woe.

¶ 5. *7*. An eight-syllable line.
9–12. On K.'s early feeling for the moon see *I stood tip-toe* 116–24 *n* (p. 90 below).
9. a golden] the golden *1848*.
11. amber] Probably a Miltonic echo. See *Imitation of Spenser* 3 *n* (p. 3 above).

6 To Chatterton

Written early 1815: the sonnet is dated '1815' in *Woodhouse* 2, 3 and is
similar in form and style to others written in late 1814 and early 1815. For
K.'s admiration of Chatterton—an admiration shared by Wordsworth,
Coleridge, Shelley—see his dedication to him of *Endymion* (headnote p. 119
below) and his Sept. 1819 journal-letter, 'The purest English . . . is Chatterton's . . . I prefer the native music of it to Milton's' (*L* ii 212). Other
allusions to Chatterton appear in *L* ii 167 and *To George Felton Mathew* 56
(p. 26 below).
Text from Woodhouse's transcripts, which largely agree.
Published *1848*.

> O Chatterton, how very sad thy fate!
>   Dear child of sorrow—son of misery!
>   How soon the film of death obscured that eye,
> Whence genius wildly flashed, and high debate.
> 5 How soon that voice, majestic and elate,
>   Melted in dying murmurs! Oh, how nigh
>   Was night to thy fair morning! Thou didst die
> A half-blown floweret which cold blasts amate.
> But this is past; thou art among the stars
> 10 Of highest Heaven; to the rolling spheres
> Thou sweetly singest; naught thy hymning mars,

¶ 6. *1–3.* Chatterton committed suicide in 1770 at the age of seventeen in
a state of destitution. To the romantic poets he became a symbol of the
world's misunderstanding and neglect of the dedicated artist. For the controversy after his death over the authenticity and value of his *Rowley* poems
(1777) see E. H. Meyerstein's *Life* (1930) 449–500. The first collected edn of
his works was published by Robert Southey and Joseph Cottle 1803.
4. wildly] mildly *1848*. The 'high debate' in this line may refer to Chatterton's political contributions in the style of Junius to various periodicals.
6. murmurs] numbers *1848*.
7–8. Thou . . . amate] Probably a recollection of Coleridge's allusion to
Chatterton in *On observing a blossom on the first of February* (1796) 13–15,

> An amaranth, which earth scarce seem'd to own,
> Till disappointment came, and pelting wrong
> Beat it to earth . . .

The words 'amate' (destroy) and 'floweret' are poetic diction used by
Chatterton. See, for example, *Aella; a Tragycal Enterlude* (1777) 58,

> Thou doest mie thoughtes of paying love amate . . .

and 1235,

> So falles the fayrest flourettes of the playne . . .

9–11. Cp. Coleridge's similar but specifically religious tribute in *Monody on
the Death of Chatterton* 21–4,

Above the ingrate world and human fears.
On earth the good man base detraction bars
From thy fair name and waters it with tears.

Amid the shining Host of the Forgiven
Thou at the throne of mercy and thy God
The triumph of redeeming Love dost hymn
(Believe it O my Soul!) to harps of Seraphim . . .

Coleridge's poem was first published in *Rowley's* [i.e. Chatterton's] *Poems*, ed. L. Sharpe (1794).

12. ingrate] A poeticism for unfriendly, ungrateful. Used this once as an epithet by K.

7 Written on the Day that Mr. Leigh Hunt left Prison

Composed 2 Feb. 1815: Hunt was released 2 Feb. 1815 after serving a sentence of two years' imprisonment for a libellous article on the Prince Regent in *The Examiner*, 22 March 1812. Cowden Clarke records that K. gave him the sonnet when he was on his way to greet Leigh Hunt newly released from prison, and also notes, 'Leigh Hunt's *Examiner* – which my father took in and I used to lend to Keats – no doubt laid the foundation of his love of civil and religious liberty' (*Recollections* 127, 124). K. himself did not meet Hunt until Oct. 1816.

Published *1817*.

What though, for showing truth to flattered state,
   Kind Hunt was shut in prison, yet has he,
   In his immortal spirit, been as free
As the sky-searching lark, and as elate.
5 Minion of grandeur, think you he did wait?
   Think you he naught but prison walls did see,
   Till, so unwilling, thou unturn'dst the key?
Ah, no! far happier, nobler was his fate.
In Spenser's halls he strayed, and bowers fair,
10   Culling enchanted flowers; and he flew
With daring Milton through the fields of air;
   To regions of his own his genius true
Took happy flights. Who shall his fame impair
   When thou art dead and all thy wretched crew?

¶ 7. *9–11*. Hunt's admiration for Spenser and Milton is warmly expressed in *The Feast of the Poets* (1811).

14. wretched crew] Cp. *Nebuchadnezzar's Dream* 10–11 (pp. 289–90 below),
      . . . a most worthy crew
    Of loggerheads and chapmen . . .

8 To Hope

Written Feb. 1815: so dated in K.'s holograph MS. The verses express some
personal feeling but are chiefly an exercise in the elevated style of the
eighteenth-century ode with its personified abstractions to which K. had
been introduced by Cowden Clarke – see *To Charles Cowden Clarke* 62–3
(p. 56 below).
Published *1817*.

> When by my solitary hearth I sit,
>   And hateful thoughts enwrap my soul in gloom,
> When no fair dreams before my 'mind's eye' flit,
>   And the bare heath of life presents no bloom,
> 5   Sweet Hope, ethereal balm upon me shed,
>   And wave thy silver pinions o'er my head.

¶ 8. *1–4.* K.'s opening quatrain has the ring of a Shakespearian sonnet;
for example sonnet xxix 1–4,

> When in disgrace with fortune and men's eyes
>   I all alone beweep my outcast state,
> And trouble deaf heaven with my bootless cries,
>   And look upon myself, and curse my fate . . .

See K.'s letter of 11 May 1817 to Benjamin Haydon, '. . . truth is I have a
horrible Morbidity of Temperament which has shown itself at intervals'
(*L* i 142). There were few 'intervals' towards the close of his life; see his
letter of 1 Nov. 1820 to Charles Brown, 'o that something fortunate had
ever happened to me or my brothers! – then I might hope, – but despair is
forced on me as a habit' (*L* ii 352).

1. my solitary hearth] In the house of the surgeon, Thomas Hammond, at
Edmonton where K. had been living as an apprentice since summer 1811.
The Keats home at Edmonton was broken up Dec. 1814 on the death of
K.'s grandmother. Cp. ll. 19–20 below.

3. 'mind's eye'] Quoted from *Hamlet* I ii 185, 'In my mind's eye, Horatio . . .'.

4–5. Echoes Campbell's *The Pleasures of Hope* (1799) i 219–20,

> And call from Heaven propitious dews to breathe
>   Arcadian beauty on the barren heath . . .

5–6 (and *23–4, 29–30, 35–6, 47–8* below). K.'s couplet refrain with variations was probably inspired by Chatterton's *Eclogue the Second* (1777), for
example 1–2,

> Sprytes of the bleste, the pious Nygelle sed,
>   Poure owte yer pleasaunce onn mie fadres hedde . . .

and 81–2,

> Sprites of the bleste, and everich Seyncte ydedde,
>   Syke pleasures powre upon mie fadres hedde . . .

With 'silver pinions' (l. 6) cp. *As from the darkening gloom* 1–5 *n* (p. 8
above).

Whene'er I wander, at the fall of night,
    Where woven boughs shut out the moon's bright ray,
Should sad Despondency my musing fright,
10   And frown to drive fair Cheerfulness away,
        Peep with the moon-beams through the leafy roof,
        And keep that fiend Despondence far aloof.

Should Disappointment, parent of Despair,
    Strive for her son to seize my careless heart,
15 When, like a cloud, he sits upon the air,
    Preparing on his spell-bound prey to dart,
        Chase him away, sweet Hope, with visage bright,
        And fright him as the morning frightens night.

Whene'er the fate of those I hold most dear
20   Tells to my fearful breast a tale of sorrow,
O bright-eyed Hope, my morbid fancy cheer;
    Let me awhile thy sweetest comforts borrow;
        Thy heaven-born radiance around me shed,
        And wave thy silver pinions o'er my head.

25 Should e'er unhappy love my bosom pain,
    From cruel parents, or relentless fair,
Oh, let me think it is not quite in vain
    To sigh out sonnets to the midnight air!
        Sweet Hope, ethereal balm upon me shed,
30   And wave thy silver pinions o'er my head.

In the long vista of the years to roll,
    Let me not see our country's honour fade:
Oh, let me see our land retain her soul,

5. *ethereal*] Heavenly. On K.'s use of this word see R. T. Davies's discussion in *Reassessment* (1958) beginning, 'Keats uses ethereal in a variety of senses. When applied to physical things and actions it can mean "having the insubstantiality and rarity of *ether*, delicate, refined, volatile". It seems to be derived from Keats' medical studies in which he would have found ether contrasted with heavy spirits . . . Sometimes it means spirit-like, aerial, heavenly' (136).

15–16. An anticipation of *Ode on Melancholy* 11–12 (pp. 539–40 below),
        But when the melancholy fit shall fall
        Sudden from heaven like a weeping cloud . . .

19–20. K.'s sister Fanny (aged eleven) was living with Richard Abbey, the guardian of the Keats children, in his house at Walthamstow. Of his two brothers, George (aged eighteen) was living and working in Abbey's business house in Pancras Lane, and Tom (aged fifteen) was either still at Enfield School or had already joined George at Abbey's.

21. *morbid*] See 1–4 *n* above.

2*

Her pride, her freedom—and not freedom's shade.
35   From thy bright eyes unusual brightness shed;
Beneath thy pinions canopy my head.

Let me not see the patriot's high bequest,
Great Liberty—how great in plain attire!—
With the base purple of a court oppressed,
40   Bowing her head and ready to expire,
But let me see thee stoop from Heaven on wings
That fill the skies with silver glitterings!

And as, in sparkling majesty, a star
Gilds the bright summit of some gloomy cloud,
45   Brightening the half-veiled face of heaven afar,
So, when dark thoughts my boding spirit shroud,
Sweet Hope, celestial influence round me shed,
Waving thy silver pinions o'er my head.

43–8. Hope as a star is a commonplace, but cp. *The Pleasures of Hope* i 200,
                HOPE is thy star, her light is ever thine . . .
and Mary Tighe's *Psyche* ii st. 54,
                Hope like the morning star once more shall reappear . . .

9 Ode to Apollo

Written Feb. 1815: so dated in *Woodhouse* 2, 3. The poem is an early illustration of K.'s reverence for poetic achievement and of his individual reworking of influences from various literary sources, including Leigh Hunt's *The Feast of the Poets* (1811; repr. 1814, 1815 etc.) and various eighteenth-century odes, especially perhaps Gray's *The Progress of Poesy* (1757). On K.'s special feeling for Apollo and frequent references to him in his earlier poems see Ian Jack's *Keats and the Mirror of Art* (1967) 176–90.
Text from Woodhouse's transcripts, which largely agree.
Published *1848.*

In thy western halls of gold,
        When thou sittest in thy state,
Bards, that erst sublimely told
        Heroic deeds and sang of fate,
5   With fervour seize their adamantine lyres,
Whose chords are solid rays and twinkle radiant fires.

¶ 9. *1.* The golden light of sunset in the west. Cp. K.'s image of the poets
leaning from the evening sky in *To my Brother George* 3–4 (p. 48 below),

There Homer with his nervous arms
   Strikes the twanging harp of war,
And even the western splendour warms,
10   While the trumpets sound afar;
But, what creates the most intense surprise,
His soul looks out through renovated eyes.

Then, through thy temple wide, melodious swells
   The sweet majestic tone of Maro's lyre.
15   The soul delighted on each accent dwells—
   Enraptured dwells—not daring to respire,
The while he tells of grief around a funeral pyre.

'Tis awful silence then again;
   Expectant stand the spheres,
20   Breathless the laurelled peers,
Nor move till ends the lofty strain;
Nor move till Milton's tuneful thunders cease,
And leave once more the ravished heavens in peace.

          . . . the laurelled peers
    Who from the feathery gold of evening lean . . .
With the first three words quoted cp. l. 20 below and on K.'s identifying
gold with poetry see *On First Looking into Chapman's Homer* 1 *n* (p. 61
below).

5. *adamantine*] Diamond. The primary associations of 'adamantine' are
with hardness, but K. is thinking of the brilliance of the precious stone.

7. *There*] Here *1848*. The word 'nervous' in this line means vigorous. Cp.
Thomson's *Liberty* iv 153-4,

          . . . the storm of war,
    Ruffling, o'er all his nervous body frowns . . .

8. Homer strikes a harp rather than a lyre because its stronger resonance
seems to accord better with his vigorous style—cp. the choice of a lyre for
Virgil (l. 14). K. first knew Homer in Pope's translation—see headnote to *On
First Looking into Chapman's Homer* (p. 60 below).

12. Homer has recovered his sight in heaven. It is not clear why this should
be so surprising.

13-17. The stanza is a line short.

14. *Maro*] A common eighteenth-century way of referring to Virgil
(Publius Virgilius Maro).

17. Probably a reference to the burial of Misenus in Virgil's *Aeneid* vi
212-35, a book which K. knew well. See *Imitation of Spenser* 21-2 *n* (p. 4
above).

19. *spheres*] The planets. Cp. Dryden's *A Song for St. Cecilia's Day* 55-6,

    As from the pow'r of sacred Lays
    The Spheres began to move . . .

22. *Milton's tuneful thunders*] The characterization of Milton's poetry as

Thou biddest Shakespeare wave his hand,
25   And quickly forward spring
The Passions—a terrific band—
       And each vibrates the string
That with its tyrant temper best accords,
While from their Master's lips pour forth the inspiring
       words.

30   A silver trumpet Spenser blows,
       And, as its martial notes to silence flee,
From a virgin chorus flows
       A hymn in praise of spotless Chastity.
'Tis still! Wild warblings from the Aeolian lyre
35   Enchantment softly breathe, and tremblingly expire.

Next thy Tasso's ardent numbers
       Float along the pleasèd air,
Calling youth from idle slumbers,
       Rousing them from Pleasure's lair:—
40   Then o'er the strings his fingers gently move,
       And melt the soul to pity and to love.

---

organ-like was common by the beginning of the nineteenth century. Cp.
Leigh Hunt on Milton in *The Feast of the Poets* 493,

The organ came gath'ring and rolling its thunder . . .

24–9. Shakespeare is the master of all the passions. They are often personified in eighteenth-century poetry—see, for example, Collins's *The Passions.
An Ode for Music* (1746).

26. terrific] Terrifying.

30. Spenser frequently refers to the sound of heralding trumpets in *The
Faerie Queene*. Cp. Leigh Hunt, *The Feast of the Poets* (introducing Spenser)
498,

. . . the light-neighing trumpet leaped freshly on air . . .

K.'s choice of 'silver' as an epithet derives from Spenser. See, for example,
The Faerie Queene II xii 11,

The silver sounding instruments did meet
With the base murmure of the waters fall . . .

33. A reference to *The Faerie Queene* iii, 'Contayning the legend of Britomartis. Or, Of Chastitie'.

34. Aeolian lyre] A stringed instrument producing musical sounds as cur-
rents of air pass over it, frequently referred to by both eighteenth-century
and Romantic poets as an emblem of poetic inspiration. On its invention in
the seventeenth century and literary references to it from the time of its re-
invention by James Oswald in the early 1740s see G. Grigson's *The Harp of
Aeolus* (1947) 24–46.

36–7. On K.'s knowledge of Tasso see *On Receiving a Curious Shell* 8 *n*
(p. 20 below).

But when *thou* joinest with the Nine,
    And all the powers of song combine,
        We listen here on earth.
45 The dying tones that fill the air
    And charm the ear of evening fair,
From thee, great God of Bards, receive their heavenly
    birth.

42–7. Apollo and the nine Muses are the originators of all earthly harmony.
The 'dying tones' are the colours of the sunset – see l. 6 above where 'chords
are solid rays'. K.'s altered rhyme scheme in this stanza heightens the effect
of a hymn.

10 Written on 29 May
The Anniversary of the
Restoration of Charles the 2nd

Year of composition unknown, but probably not later than 1815 since the
lines are in keeping with K.'s other political allusions 1814–15. According
to Woodhouse, 'written probably when much in company with Leigh
Hunt' (*Woodhouse* 3), but K.'s political liberalism preceded the meeting
with Hunt in Oct. 1816. For the view that the poem was written 1814 at
the time of the restoration of Louis XVIII see *Gittings* (1968) 42.
Published *Lowell* (1925).

Infatuate Britons, will you still proclaim
    His memory, your direst, foulest shame,
        Nor patriots revere?
Ah, while I hear each traitorous lying bell,
5 'Tis gallant Sidney's, Russell's, Vane's sad knell,
        That pains my wounded ear.

¶ 10. *Title.* The other transcript in *Woodhouse* 3 has the fuller title: 'Written
on 29 May – the anniversary of Charles's restoration. – On hearing the bells
ringing.'
5. Sidney's, Russell's, Vane's] Whig heroes often mentioned in the literature
of the time and earlier in Thomson – see, for example, Thomson's *The
Seasons* (1730) *Summer* 1511 and 1522–3. Algernon Sidney (b. 1622) and
Lord William Russell (b. 1639) were executed in 1683 for complicity in the
Rye House Plot; Sir Henry Vane (b. 1613) was executed for treason in
1662. K. alludes to Sidney again in *Oh, how I love* 10 (p. 46 below) and in
his journal-letter of 14–31 Oct. 1818, '. . . the motives of our worst Men are
interest and of our best Vanity – we have no Milton, no Algernon Sydney'
(*L* i 396).

11 To Some Ladies

Presumably written summer 1815 since it is in response to the gift of a shell
from the Mathew sisters on holiday by the sea; '1815' in K.'s holograph
MS (Christian University, Fort Texas) and see Woodhouse's note, 'The
verses . . . were sent to the Misses Mathew . . . then at Hastings' (*Woodhouse* 3). The poem has the anapaestic metre and fanciful lyric style of Tom
Moore's early poems which K. temporarily admired (see following headnote).
Published *1817*.

> What though, while the wonders of nature exploring,
>   I cannot your light mazy footsteps attend,
> Nor listen to accents that, almost adoring,
>   Bless Cynthia's face, the enthusiast's friend.
>
> 5   Yet over the steep, whence the mountain stream rushes,
>   With you, kindest friends, in idea I muse—
> Mark the clear tumbling crystal, its passionate gushes,
>   Its spray that the wild flower kindly bedews.
>
> Why linger you so, the wild labyrinth strolling?
> 10 Why breathless, unable your bliss to declare?
> Ah! You list to the nightingale's tender condoling,
>   Responsive to sylphs, in the moonbeamy air.
>
> 'Tis morn, and the flowers with dew are yet drooping,
>   I see you are treading the verge of the sea.
> 15 And now! Ah, I see it—you just now are stooping
>   To pick up the keepsake intended for me.
>
> If a cherub, on pinions of silver descending,
>   Had brought me a gem from the fretwork of heaven,
> And smiles, with his star-cheering voice sweetly blending,
> 20 The blessings of Tighe had melodiously given,

¶ 11. *1. while . . . exploring*] While you are the wonders of nature exploring.
4. enthusiast's friend] The moon is loved by persons of poetic sensibility.
6. muse] rove *1817*. The final MS reading (over 'rove' cancelled) is required
by the rhyme.
8. its] In *K.'s MS*.
9. According to Woodhouse a cancelled false start was 'Ah! why do you
start, the wild to . . .' (Sperry's *Woodhouse (1817)* 143).
17. pinions of silver] See *As from the darkening gloom* 1–5 *n* (p. 8 above).
18. the fretwork of heaven] See *Hamlet* II ii 307, 'this majestical roof fretted
with golden fire'.

It had not created a warmer emotion
    Than the present, fair nymphs, I was blest with from
        you—
Than the shell from the bright golden sands of the ocean
    Which the emerald waves at your feet gladly threw.

25   For, indeed, 'tis a sweet and peculiar pleasure
        (And blissful is he who such happiness finds)
    To possess but a span of the hour of leisure
        In elegant, pure, and aërial minds.

20. *Tighe*] Mary Tighe, a popular Irish poetess whose *Psyche, or The Legend of Love* (1811), an allegorical poem in Spenserian stanzas was also admired by Tom Moore–see his *To Mrs. Henry Tighe, on reading her Psyche*. K. refers to his own early liking of her work in his journal-letter of 16 Dec. 1818–4 Jan. 1819, 'Mrs. Tighe and Beattie once delighted me–now I see through them and can find nothing in them' (*L* ii 18). For an exhaustive if exaggerated account of her influence on K. see E. V. Weller, *Keats and Mary Tighe* (1928).
24. 'Oh down by yon bank, where the waves gently flow'–cancelled version recorded in Sperry's *Woodhouse* (*1817*) 143.
28. *aërial*] Ethereal, i.e. refined, delicate: see *To Hope* 5 *n* (p. 13 above).

12 On Receiving a Curious Shell and a Copy of Verses from the Same Ladies

Written summer 1815 for George Felton Mathew, cousin of the Mathew sisters addressed in the preceding poem: Woodhouse's note, part quoted in preceding headnote, continues, 'The next copy of verses appear to be addressed to Mr. Mathew' (for K.'s friendship with Mathew see headnote to *To George Felton Mathew*, p. 24 below). The 'copy of verses' of the poem's title was Tom Moore's *The Wreath and the Chain* (1801); see note to title below. Moore's contemporary popularity is reflected in Leigh Hunt's *The Feast of the Poets* (1811) 515–18; K.'s later attitude to Moore is expressed in his Feb.–May 1819 journal-letter, 'The undersigned . . . doth not admire . . . Tom Moore' (*L* ii 69).
The present location of K.'s holograph MS is unknown, but its minor variants are given in *Garrod*.
Published *1817*.

¶ 12. *Title*. Entitled in George Keats's transcript: 'Eric. Written on receiving a copy of Tom Moore's "Golden Chain", and a Dome shaped shell from a lady.' 'Eric' is K.'s name for Mathew (see l. 41 below).

Hast thou from the caves of Golconda a gem,
    Pure as the ice-drop that froze on the mountain,
Bright as the humming-bird's green diadem,
    When it flutters in sunbeams that shine through a
        fountain?

5   Hast thou a goblet for dark sparkling wine,
    That goblet right heavy, and massy, and gold,
And splendidly marked with the story divine
    Of Armida the fair and Rinaldo the bold?

Hast thou a steed with a mane richly flowing?
10   Hast thou a sword that thine enemy's smart is?
Hast thou a trumpet rich melodies blowing?
    And wear'st thou the shield of the famed Britomartis?

What is it that hangs from thy shoulder, so brave,
    Embroidered with many a spring-peering flower?
15 Is it a scarf that thy fair lady gave,
    And hastest thou now to that fair lady's bower?

Ah, courteous Sir Knight, with large joy thou art
      crowned;
    Full many the glories that brighten thy youth.
I will tell thee my blisses, which richly abound
20   In magical powers to bless and to soothe.

On this scroll thou seest written in characters fair
    A sunbeamy tale of a wreath and a chain;
And, warrior, it nurtures the property rare
    Of charming my mind from the trammels of pain.

25 This canopy mark: 'tis the work of a fay;
    Beneath its rich shade did King Oberon languish,

1. *Golconda*] The old name for Hyderabad, once famous for its diamonds.
Cp. Thomson's *The Seasons* (1730) *Summer* 870–1,
                Deep in the bowels of the pitying earth
                Golconda's gems . . .
6. *massy*] Vast. A Miltonic word known to K. from *Il Penseroso* 158, 'With
antick Pillars massy proof . . .'
8. *Armida . . . Rinaldo*] Characters in Tasso's *Gerusalemme Liberata* (1581),
which K. had read in Fairfax's translation (1600); see headnote to *Isabella*
(p. 327 below).
12. *Britomartis*] The warrior heroine in *The Faerie Queene* iii. See *Ode to
Apollo* 33 *n* (p. 16 above).
24. *trammels*] fetters. On K.'s personal circumstances in 1815 see *To Hope*
1 *n* and 19–20 *n* (pp. 12, 13 above).
25. *This canopy*] The 'Dome shaped shell' sent to K. by the Mathew sisters.

When lovely Titania was far, far away,
    And cruelly left him to sorrow and anguish.

There oft would he bring from his soft-sighing lute
30   Wild strains to which, spell-bound, the nightingales
        listened;
The wondering spirits of heaven were mute
    And tears 'mong the dewdrops of morning oft glistened.

In this little dome all those melodies strange,
    Soft, plaintive and melting, for ever will sigh;
35 Nor e'er will the notes from their tenderness change;
    Nor e'er will the music of Oberon die.

So, when I am in a voluptuous vein,
    I pillow my head on the sweets of the rose,
And list to the tale of the wreath and the chain,
40   Till its echoes depart—then I sink to repose.

Adieu, valiant Eric, with joy thou art crowned;
    Full many the glories that brighten thy youth.
I too have my blisses, which richly abound
    In magical powers, to bless and to soothe.

26–30. K. would have known about Titania and Oberon from *A Midsummer Night's Dream*, but the allusion here is to William Sotheby's popular translation (1798) of Wieland's *Oberon* (1780), which gives a romantic emphasis to the pathos of Oberon's separation from Titania. On K.'s fondness for fairy lore 1815–16 see *Cowden Clarke*, 'He said . . . "the other day . . . during the lecture [at St. Thomas's Hospital], there came a sunbeam into the room, and with it a whole troop of creatures floating in the ray, and I was off with them to Oberon and fairyland" ' (131–2).
33–4. The sounds heard in the hollow shell are said to be Oberon's fairy music.
38. the sweets of the rose] Cp. Moore's *The Wreath and the Chain* 41–2,
        . . . the garland's brightest rose
      Gave one of its love-breathing sighs . . .

13 To Emma Mathew

Probably summer 1815 as similar in style to the two preceding poems, *To Some Ladies* and *On Receiving a Curious Shell* (pp. 18, 19, above).
Text from K.'s MS (Morgan Library), which has minor variants from Woodhouse's transcripts (*Woodhouse* 2, 3).
Published *Forman* (1883).

¶ 13. *Title.* So in *Woodhouse 2* (with 'Mathews' for 'Mathew'). The poem was probably addressed to one of the Mathew sisters; the name 'Emma', as

Oh, come, dearest Emma! The rose is full blown
And the riches of Flora are lavishly strewn.
The air is all softness and crystal the streams,
And the west is resplendently clothèd in beams.

5   We will hasten, my fair, to the opening glades,
The quaintly carved seats, and the freshening shades,
Where the fairies are chanting their evening hymns,
And in the last sunbeam the sylph lightly swims.

And when thou art weary, I'll find thee a bed
10 Of mosses and flowers, to pillow thy head;
There, beauteous Emma, I'll sit at thy feet
While my story of love I enraptured repeat.

So fondly I'll breathe, and so softly I'll sigh,
Thou wilt think that some amorous Zephyr is nigh;
15 Ah, no!—as I breathe, I will press thy fair knee
And then thou wilt know that the sigh comes from me.

Ah why, lovely girl, should we lose all these blisses?
That mortal's a fool who such happiness misses.
So smile acquiescence and give me thy hand,
20 With love-looking eyes and with voice sweetly bland.

de Selincourt suggests, may have been borrowed for the occasion in imitation of Wordsworth's use of it when referring to his sister Dorothy (see,
e.g., *It was an April morning: fresh and clear* (1807) 39). George Keats's transcript (British Museum) has 'Stanzas to Miss Wylie' and substitutes, at the
expense of the metre, Georgiana for 'Emma' throughout. He probably
used the poem when courting Georgiana Wylie (see *To Georgiana Augusta
Wylie*, p. 98 below).

14 'O Solitude, if I must with thee dwell'

Written *c.* Oct.–Nov. 1815 shortly after K. had left Edmonton to study
medicine in London. The poem is a regular Petrarchan sonnet expressing
K.'s distaste for his new city surroundings and is written in the polite sentimental style affected by George Felton Mathew (see following headnote).
The 'two kindred spirits' (l. 14) have been taken by some readers to be K.
and Mathew, but Woodhouse's note in his copy of *1817* that K. 'perhaps'
wrote the sonnet for George Keats's use (see *To my Brother George* 121 *n*,
p. 53 below) lends some support to the view that K. may be referring in
the sestet to the Mathew sisters and that the poem was perhaps intended 'for
George to send to them' (see *Gittings* (1968) 53).

Cowden Clarke correctly records that this is K.'s 'first published poem' (*Recollections* 127). Leigh Hunt printed it in *The Examiner* before meeting K. and 'without knowing more of him than any other anonymous correspondent' (Hunt's review of *1817*, *The Examiner* 1 June 1817; the review, continued in *The Examiner* 6, 13 July 1817, is repr. *Forman* (1883) i 331–2). The version in *The Examiner* and K.'s undated holograph MS (Morgan Library) both have minor variants from *1817*, some of which are noted below.

Published *The Examiner* 5 May 1816; repr. *1817*.

> O Solitude, if I must with thee dwell,
>   Let it not be among the jumbled heap
>   Of murky buildings. Climb with me the steep –
> Nature's observatory – whence the dell,
> 5   Its flowery slopes, its river's crystal swell,
>   May seem a span; let me thy vigils keep
>   'Mongst boughs pavilioned, where the deer's swift
>   leap
> Startles the wild bee from the foxglove bell.
> But though I'll gladly trace these scenes with thee,
> 10 Yet the sweet converse of an innocent mind,
>   Whose words are images of thoughts refined,
> Is my soul's pleasure, and it sure must be
> Almost the highest bliss of human-kind,
> When to thy haunts two kindred spirits flee.

¶ 14. 7. *'Mongst boughs pavilioned*] Where boughs make a pavilion. A favourite image in K.'s early poems. Cp. *To Hope* 8 (p. 13 above), 'woven boughs' and see the following poem *To George Felton Mathew* 48 (p. 26 below), 'sylvan roof'.

7–8. *where the deer's . . . bell*] Echoed by George Felton Mathew in his poem to K., *To a Poetical Friend* (see following headnote) 46–8,

> And let not the spirit of Poesy sleep
> Of Fairies and Genii continue to tell –
> Nor suffer the innocent deer's timid leap
> To fright the wild bee from her flowery bell . . .

Middleton Murry quotes the quatrain to support his argument that K.'s sonnet was addressed to Mathew; see *Murry* (1930) 4.

8. Perhaps a reminiscence of Wordsworth's sonnet, *Nuns fret not at their convent's narrow room* (1807) 5–7,

> . . . bees that soar for bloom
> High as the highest Peak of Furness-fells,
> Will murmur by the hour in foxglove bells . . .

K. probably acquired Wordsworth's *Poems* (1815 edn) in autumn 1815.

9. Ah! fain would I frequent such scenes with thee . . . *Examiner*.

10. *innocent*] elegant *K.'s MS*.

12. *pleasure; and it sure*] pleasure. It certainly *K.'s MS*.

13. Recalls the phrasing in *To Some Ladies* 26 (p. 19 above).

15 To George Felton Mathew

Written Nov. 1815: date attached to the poem in *1817*. The poem was sent as a verse letter to George Felton Mathew (*L* i 100–3) in response to Mathew's *To a Poetical Friend* (published in the *European Magazine* Oct. 1816). K.'s unstopped couplets recall William Browne (from whom K. takes his motto), but his general style is in correspondence with that of Mathew's poem. K.'s friendship with Mathew declined *c*. autumn 1816 when K. became intimate with Hunt. Mathew's *To a Poetical Friend* and his cool review of *1817* are reprinted in *Murry* (1930).
Published *1817*.

> *Among the rest a shepheard (though but young*
> *Yet hartned to his pipe) with all the skill*
> *His few yeeres could, began to fit his quill.*
>
> BROWNE [*Britannia's Pastorals*]

Sweet are the pleasures that to verse belong,
And doubly sweet a brotherhood in song;
Nor can remembrance, Mathew, bring to view
A fate more pleasing, a delight more true
5   Than that in which the brother poets joyed,
Who with combinèd powers their wit employed
To raise a trophy to the drama's muses.
The thought of this great partnership diffuses
Over the genius-loving heart, a feeling
10 Of all that's high and great and good and healing.

Too partial friend, fain would I follow thee
Past each horizon of fine poesy.
Fain would I echo back each pleasant note
As o'er Sicilian seas clear anthems float
15 'Mong the light skimming gondolas far parted,

¶ 15. *Motto.* William Browne's *Britannia's Pastorals* ii (1616), Song 3 748–50.
5. *the brother poets*] Beaumont and Fletcher, with whom K. compares himself and Mathew.
11. *Too partial friend*] See Mathew's *To a Poetical Friend* 21–4,
> . . . a Shakespeare–a Milton are ours!
> And who e'er sung sweeter, or stronger than they?
> As thine is, I ween was the spring of their powers;
> Like theirs, is the cast of thy earlier lay . . .
15. Gondolas are used on Venetian canals, not Sicilian seas.

Just when the sun his farewell beam has darted—
But 'tis impossible. Far different cares
Beckon me sternly from soft 'Lydian airs',
And hold my faculties so long in thrall
20   That I am oft in doubt whether at all
I shall again see Phoebus in the morning;
Or flushed Aurora in the roseate dawning;
Or a white naiad in a rippling stream;
Or a rapt seraph in a moonlight beam;
25   Or again witness what with thee I've seen—
The dew by fairy feet swept from the green
After a night of some quaint jubilee,
Which every elf and fay had come to see,
When bright processions took their airy march
30   Beneath the curvèd moon's triumphal arch.

But might I now each passing moment give
To the coy muse, with me she would not live
In this dark city, nor would condescend
'Mid contradictions her delights to lend.
Should e'er the fine-eyed maid to me be kind,
Ah, surely it must be whene'er I find
Some flowery spot, sequestered, wild, romantic,
That often must have seen a poet frantic;

17–18. Mathew records, 'when Keats wrote his Epistle to me . . . he was walking the hospitals' (*KC* ii 186). 'Lydian Airs' is a quotation from Milton's *L'Allegro* 135–6,

> And ever against eating cares
> Lap me in soft *Lydian Aires* . . .

21. Phoebus] Phoebus Apollo, the sun god.

21–2. morning . . . dawning] A Cockney rhyme. Cp. *To Mary Frogley* 38 *n* (p. 30 below).

22. Aurora] Goddess of the dawn.

23 (and *93* below). *naiad*] Water nymph. See *To Charles Cowden Clarke* 6 *n* (p. 54 below).

24. rapt] Enraptured. The phrase 'rapt seraph' derives from Pope, *Essay on Man* (1733) i 279, 'the rapt Seraph that adores and burns'.

26–8. Cp. *To a Poetical Friend* 1–2,

> O Thou whou who delightest in fanciful song,
> And tellest strange tales of the elf and the fay . . .

For K.'s enthusiasm for fairy-lore in 1815–16 see *On Receiving a Curious Shell* 26–30 *n* (p. 21 above).

33. this dark city] Cp. the preceding poem 2–3 (p. 23 above)

> . . . the jumbled heap
> Of murky buildings . . .

Where oaks, that erst the Druid knew, are growing,
40   And flowers, the glory of one day, are blowing;
Where the dark-leaved laburnum's drooping clusters
Reflect athwart the stream their yellow lustres,
And intertwined the cassia's arms unite,
With its own drooping buds, but very white;
45   Where on one side are covert branches hung,
'Mong which the nightingales have always sung
In leafy quiet; where to pry, aloof,
Atween the pillars of the sylvan roof
Would be to find where violet beds were nestling,
50   And where the bee with cowslip bells was wrestling.
There must be too a ruin dark and gloomy,
To say 'joy not too much in all that's bloomy'.

Yet this is vain—O Mathew, lend thy aid
To find a place where I may greet the maid,
55   Where we may soft humanity put on,
And sit and rhyme, and think on Chatterton,
And that warm-hearted Shakspeare sent to meet him
Four laurelled spirits, heaven-ward to intreat him.

---

39. Druid] Poet-priest. A commonplace of Pre-Romantic eighteenth-century poetry, often linking associated notions of poetry, nature, philosophic wisdom and liberty. See, for example, Collins's *Ode occasion'd by the death of Mr. Thomson* (1749) 1,

> In yonder grave a Druid lies . . .

43. cassia] A poeticism for a fragrant shrub or plant. Here the honeysuckle or woodbine.

47. aloof] i.e. close to the ground, at a distance from the branches of the trees.

50. cowslip bells] Suggested by Ariel's song in *The Tempest* V i 89, 'In a cowslip's bell I lie . . .', but cowslips are not found in woods.

51–2. Cp. Mathew's lines in his *Written in Time of Sickness and addressed to a Friend*,

> The ruin'd monastery, the waving woods,
> All show more gloomy in the doubtful light . . .

Mathew's poem was copied out by his sister in her album, *The Garland*; see *Gittings* (1968) 45, 57 *n*.

56. Chatterton] On K. and Chatterton see *To Chatterton* (headnote, p. 10 above).

58. four laurelled spirits] No specific allusion is intended. On the pseudo-specific numeral as a characteristic stylistic device in K. see *La Belle Dame Sans Merci* 32 *n* (p. 504 below). The word 'heaven-ward' may be owed to Chatterton's *Godwyn: A Tragedie* (1777) 146,

> I leave you to doe hommage heaven-were . . .

With reverence would we speak of all the sages
60　Who have left streaks of light athwart their ages,
And thou should'st moralize on Milton's blindness,
And mourn the fearful dearth of human kindness
To those who strove, with the bright golden wing
Of genius, to flap away each sting
65　Thrown by the pitiless world. We next could tell
Of those who in the cause of freedom fell:
Of our own Alfred, of Helvetian Tell,
Of him whose name to ev'ry heart's a solace,
High-minded and unbending William Wallace.
70　While to the rugged north our musing turns
We well might drop a tear for him and Burns.

Felton, without incitements such as these,
How vain for me the niggard Muse to tease.
For thee, she will thy every dwelling grace
75　And make 'a sun-shine in a shady place',
For thou wast once a floweret blooming wild

Chatterton's gloss on the last word quoted reads 'heaven-ward, or God-ward'.

60. streaks of light] The sages flash like comets across the darkness of their times.

62–5. And mourn . . . pitiless world] Cp. K.'s letter of 9 June 1819 to Sarah Jeffrey, 'One of the great reasons that the English have produced the finest writers in the world; is, that the English world has ill-treated them during their lives and foster'd them after their deaths. They have in general been trampled aside into the bye paths of life and seen the festerings of Society' (*L* ii 115).

67–9. Alfred . . . Tell . . . Wallace] K.'s admiration for such national heroes was fostered by Cowden Clarke. See *To Charles Cowden Clarke* 68–70 (p. 57 below),

You too upheld the veil from Clio's beauty,
And pointed out the patriot's stern duty;
The might of Alfred, and the shaft of Tell . . .

Romantic interest in William Tell as liberator of the Swiss from Austrian tyranny was stimulated by Schiller's play *Wilhelm Tell* (1804).

71. Burns] K.'s first reference to Burns (1759–96). The first collected edn of his works was published by J. Currie 1800 (8th edn 1820). K. links him here with other national heroes because of his Scottish patriotism and his zest for liberty and brotherhood.

75. Cp. *The Faerie Queene* I iii 4,

And made a sunshine in the shadie place . . .

K.'s marking of this line in George Keats's copy of Spenser is recorded in *Lowell* ii 553.

Close to the source, bright, pure and undefiled,
Whence gush the streams of song; in happy hour
Came chaste Diana from her shady bower,
80 Just as the sun was from the east uprising,
And, as for him some gift she was devising,
Beheld thee, plucked thee, cast thee in the stream
To meet her glorious brother's greeting beam.
I marvel much that thou hast never told
85 How, from a flower, into a fish of gold
Apollo changed thee; how thou next didst seem
A black-eyed swan upon the widening stream;
And when thou first didst in that mirror trace
The placid features of a human face;
90 That thou hast never told thy travels strange,
And all the wonders of the mazy range
O'er pebbly crystal and o'er golden sands,
Kissing thy daily food from naiad's pearly hands.

76–7. Mathew was once a flower growing near the springs of Helicon,
home of the Muses. On Chatterton's use of 'floweret' see *To Chatterton*
7–8 *n* (p. 10 above).
85–9. Mathew's transformations are inspired by Ovid's *Metamorphoses* and
anticipate K.'s inventions in *Endymion*.

16 'Give me women, wine and snuff'

Written between autumn 1815–autumn 1816, but possibly March 1816,
when K. was studying medicine at the United Hospitals of St Thomas's and
Guy's: see Henry Stephens's letter to George Felton Mathew, March(?)
1847, 'In my Syllabus of Chemical Lectures he scribbled many lines on the
paper cover. This cover has been long torn off, except one piece on which
is the following fragment of Doggrel rhyme' (*KC* ii 210). K. moved into
lodgings with Stephens Oct. 1815. R. Gittings suggests the influence of
Leigh Hunt's translation of Anacreon's Ode 54, published *The Examiner*
31 March 1816, 203 (but K. was already familiar with Tom Moore's
Anacreontics: see *Fill for me* 7–8 *n*, p. 7 above).
MS at Trinity College, Cambridge.
Published *Colvin* (1915).

Give me women, wine and snuff
Until I cry out, 'Hold, enough!'
You may do so sans objection
Till the day of resurrection;

¶ 16. 2. '*Hold, enough!*'] Cp. *Macbeth* V vii 63, '... damned be him that
first cries, "Hold, enough!" '

5   For, bless my beard, they ay shall be
       My belovèd Trinity.

17 To Mary Frogley

Written 14 Feb. 1816 as a valentine: so dated in three of Woodhouse's
transcripts: see *Woodhouse 2*, 'These lines were written by K. at his brother
George's request and sent as a valentine to a lady (Miss Frogley) . . . They
were afterwards altered for Publication'. Mary Frogley was a cousin of
Richard Woodhouse, who obtained from her several of K.'s early poems.
R. Gittings suggests (*Gittings* (1968) 59) that K'.s lines were affected by
William Hazlitt's essay 'On Beauty', *The Examiner* 4 Feb. 1816 (Works
ed. P. P. Howe IV 68–72).
Some of the variants in K.'s undated holograph MS and in the version
followed in three of Woodhouse's four transcripts (referred to as *Wood-
house*) are noted below.
Published *1817*.

           Hadst thou lived in days of old,
           Oh, what wonders had been told
           Of thy lively countenance,
           And thy humid eyes that dance
5   In the midst of their own brightness,
           In the very fane of lightness.
           Over which thine eyebrows, leaning,
           Picture out each lovely meaning.
           In a dainty bend they lie,
10   Like to streaks across the sky,
           Or the feathers from a crow,
           Fallen on a bed of snow.
           Of thy dark hair that extends
           Into many graceful bends,
15   As the leaves of hellebore

¶ 17. *3–36*. In place of these lines *Woodhouse* has,
                Of thy lively dimpled face
                And thy footsteps full of grace
                Of thy hair's luxurious darkling,
                Of thine eyes' expressive sparkling,
                And thy voice's swelling rapture,
                Taking hearts a ready capture.
                Oh! if thou hadst breathed then,
                Thou hast made the Muses ten . . .

15. hellebore] A botanical term for a class of plants often grown in English
gardens, perhaps used here for the Christmas rose (one of the best known
species).

Turn to whence they sprung before,
And behind each ample curl
Peeps the richness of a pearl.
Downward too flows many a tress
20   With a glossy waviness,
Full and round like globes that rise
From the censer to the skies
Through sunny air. Add, too, the sweetness
Of thy honeyed voice; the neatness
25   Of thine ankle lightly turned;
With those beauties, scarce discerned,
Kept with such sweet privacy
That they seldom meet the eye
Of the little loves that fly
30   Round about with eager pry,
Saving when, with freshening lave,
Thou dipp'st them in the taintless wave,
Like twin water-lilies born
In the coolness of the morn.
35   Oh, if thou hadst breathèd then,
Now the Muses had been ten.
Couldst thou wish for lineage higher
Than twin sister of Thalia?

21-2. Cp. Spenser, *Colin Clout's Come Home Againe* 608-11,
        . . . like the fume of Franckincence,
    Which from a golden Censer forth doth rise:
    And throwing forth sweet odours mounts fro thence
    In rolling globes up to the vauted skies . . .
29. little loves] *Putti*, or winged cherubs, frequently represented in Italian
Renaissance painting. Perhaps suggested here by Spenser's *Epithalamion*
(1595) 357-9,
        . . . an hundred little winged loves,
    Like divers fethered doves,
    Shall fly and flutter round about your bed . . .
K.'s special fondness for this poem is recorded in *Cowden Clarke* 125-6.
33-4. Cp. Spenser's *Epithalamion* 176,
        Her paps lyke lillies budded . . .
35-6. An Elizabethan conceit. See, for example, Drayton's *To the Celestiall
Numbers* (*Idea*, sonnet 18) 10,
    And my faire Muse, one Muse unto the Nine . . .
38. Thalia] The muse who 'presided over festivals, and over pastoral and
comic poetry' (*Lemprière*). See G. M. Hopkins's somewhat stringent use of
the line to illustrate one kind of 'unlawful' rhyme, '. . . the *r* is not trilled
bu tthe knowledge that it is . . . dormant in the one word and not in the
other is . . . offensive to a trained taste . . . the fault cannot be excused by

At least for ever, evermore,
40   Will I call the Graces four.

Hadst thou lived when chivalry
Lifted up her lance on high,
Tell me what thou wouldst have been?
Ah! I see the silver sheen
45   Of thy broidered floating vest
Covering half thine ivory breast,
Which—Oh, heavens!—I should see,
But that cruel destiny
Has placed a golden cuirass there,
50   Keeping secret what is fair.
Like sunbeams in a cloudlet nested
Thy locks in knightly casque are rested,
O'er which bend four milky plumes
Like the gentle lily's blooms
55   Springing from a costly vase.
See with what a stately pace
Comes thine alabaster steed—
Servant of heroic deed!
O'er his loins his trappings glow
60   Like the northern lights on snow.

Keats's authority' (*The Journals and Papers of Gerard Manley Hopkins*, ed.
H. House (1959) 286). For an earlier example of K.'s use of Cockney rhyme
see *To George Felton Mathew* 21–2 (p. 25 above).

39–40. Cp. Spenser's *The Shepheardes Calendar*, 'April' 112–13,

Wants not a fourth grace, to make the daunce even?
Let that rowme to my lady by yeven . . .

48–58. K. sees Mary Frogley as the chaste Britomartis of *The Faerie Queene*
iii. Cp. *On Receiving a Curious Shell* 12 (p. 20 above),

. . . wear'st thou the shield of the famed Britomartis? . . .

52. Thy hair in gilden casque is nested . . . *K.'s MS*.

54. gentle lily's] fleur-de-luce's *K.'s MS*.

55. costly] Indian *Woodhouse*.

56. pace] For the rhyme cp. *I stood tip-toe* 133–4 (p. 91 below),

Fair dewy roses brush against our faces
And flowering laurels spring from diamond vases . . .

K.'s pronunciation of 'vase' follows eighteenth-century and early nineteenth-century usage: see, e.g., Swift's rhyming the word with 'face' in
Strephon and Chloe (1731) 191, and Byron's rhyming it with 'place' and
'grace' in *Don Juan* (1823) VI xcvii.

57. alabaster] White. Frequently in Spenser, e.g. *The Faerie Quene* VI viii 42,

Her yvorie neck, her alabaster brest . . .

60. the northern lights] The Aurora Borealis.

Mount his back! Thy sword unsheathe—
   Sign of the enchanter's death,
   Bane of every wicked spell,
   Silencer of dragon's yell.
65   Alas! Thou this wilt never do—
   Thou art an enchantress too,
   And wilt surely never spill
   Blood of those whose eyes can kill.

62–3.   Sign of the Magician's death
                Bane of the Enchanter's spell ...   *Woodhouse.*
65–8. Omitted in K.'s MS.
68. Followed in *Woodhouse* by the lines:
                Ah me! whither shall I flee?
                Thou hast metamorphosed me.
                Do not let me sigh and pine,
                Prythee be my valentine.

18 To—['Had I a man's fair form']

Probably written *c.* 14 Feb. 1816 as a valentine for Mary Frogley: Woodhouse's note, part quoted in preceding headnote, continues later: 'There
were three valentines written by him on that same occasion.' The poem
appears as the second of the seventeen Petrarchan sonnets printed together
in *1817.* According to Woodhouse's comments in his copy of *1817* K. is
expressing the 'idea that the diminution of his size makes him contemptible
and that no woman can like a man of small stature' (Sperry's *Woodhouse*
(1817) 148). For the view that the speaker is a fairy see J. Burke Severs,
KShJ VI (1957) 109–13.
Published *1817.*

Had I a man's fair form, then might my sighs
   Be echoed swiftly through that ivory shell
   Thine ear, and find thy gentle heart, so well
Would passion arm me for the enterprize.
5   But ah! I am no knight whose foeman dies,
   No cuirass glistens on my bosom's swell;

¶ 18. *1. Had I a man's fair form*] K. is probably thinking of his lack of inches.
See his letter of 22 July 1818 to Bailey, 'I do think better of Womankind
than to suppose they care whether Mister John Keats five feet hight likes
them or not' (*L* i 342), and his joking reference to George and Georgiana
Keats's child in his Sept. 1819 journal-letter, 'When it is two feet in length
I shall not stand a barley corn higher. That's not fair—one ought to go on
growing as well as others' (*L* ii 213).

> I am no happy shepherd of the dell
> Whose lips have trembled with a maiden's eyes.
> Yet must I dote upon thee—call thee sweet,
> 10   Sweeter by far than Hybla's honeyed roses
> When steeped in dew rich to intoxication.
> Ah! I will taste that dew, for me 'tis meet,
> And when the moon her pallid face discloses,
> I'll gather some by spells and incantation.

10. Hybla] A mountain in Sicily famous for its flowers, bees and honey.
12–14. K. may mean that the dew from the roses will have the magical power to transform him. The lines suggest a recollection of the magic rites practised by Medea at the full moon in order to restore Aeson's youth; see Ovid's *Metamorphoses* vii 179–293 and *The Merchant of Venice* V i 12–14,

> . . . In such a night
> Medea gather'd the enchanted herbs
> That did renew old Aeson . . .

19 Specimen of an Induction to a Poem

Generally agreed to have been written *c.* Feb.–March 1816 as clearly inspired by Leigh Hunt's *The Story of Rimini* (Feb. 1816), a romantic narrative in heroic couplets. For Hunt's stylistic influence on K. see headnote to the following poem, *Calidore*, which is the 'Poem' of the title (p. 36 below). The single transcript by Tom Keats has minor variants from *1817*, some of which are noted below.
Published *1817*.

> Lo! I must tell a tale of chivalry,
> For large white plumes are dancing in mine eye.
> Not like the formal crest of latter days,
> But bending in a thousand graceful ways—
> 5   So graceful that it seems no mortal hand,
> Or e'en the touch of Archimago's wand,
> Could charm them into such an attitude.
> We must think, rather, that in playful mood

¶ 19. *2.* A reference to the knightly *panache*. See *To Mary Frogley* 52–3 (p. 31 above),

> Thy locks in knightly casque are rested,
> O'er which bend four milky plumes . . .

3. formal crest] The decoration on military helmets of K.'s day.
5. So graceful] On K.'s and Hunt's use of this phrasing see *Calidore* 11 *n* (p. 37 below).
6. Archimago] The wizard in *The Faerie Queene* I, II.

Some mountain breeze had turned its chief delight
10 To show this wonder of its gentle might.
Lo! I must tell a tale of chivalry,
For while I muse, the lance points slantingly
Athwart the morning air. Some lady sweet,
Who cannot feel for cold her tender feet,
15 From the worn top of some old battlement
Hails it with tears, her stout defender sent,
And from her own pure self no joy dissembling,
Wraps round her ample robe with happy trembling.
Sometimes, when the good knight his rest would take,
20 It is reflected clearly in a lake,
With the young ashen boughs 'gainst which it rests,
And the half-seen mossiness of linnets' nests.
Ah, shall I ever tell its cruelty,
When the fire flashes from a warrior's eye
25 And his tremendous hand is grasping it,
And his dark brow for very wrath is knit?
Or when his spirit, with more calm intent,
Leaps to the honours of a tournament
And makes the gazers round about the ring
30 Stare at the grandeur of the balancing?
No, no, this is far off! Then how shall I
Revive the dying tones of minstrelsy,
Which linger yet about long gothic arches,
In dark green ivy and among wild larches?
35 How sing the splendour of the revelries,
When butts of wine are drunk off to the lees?

12. *slantingly*] See *Calidore* 5 n (p. 36 below).
14. K.'s introduction of naturalistic descriptive detail into his romantic
narrative is anticipated by Hunt. See, for example, *The Story of Rimini* i
253–4,

> The princess . . . scarcely knows
> Which way to look . . .

Hunt praised K.'s line in his review of *1817* (see headnote to *O Solitude*,
p. 23 above).
17. And now no more her anxious grief remembering . . . *Tom Keats MS.*
Woodhouse notes the similar construction in *The Faerie Queene* II vi 14,
' . . . her sweet self . . . / She set beside . . .' and VI ii 41, 'And her sad self
with careful hand constraining / To wipe his wounds' (Sperry's *Woodhouse*
(*1817*) 142).
18. *trembling*] On K.'s use of participial nouns see *Calidore* 27 n (p. 38
below).
22. *mossiness*] See *Calidore* 7 n (p. 37 below).
35. *splendour*] grandeur *Tom Keats MS.*

And that bright lance against the fretted wall,
Beneath the shade of stately banneral,
Is slung with shining cuirass, sword and shield
40   Where ye may see a spur in bloody field?
Light-footed damsels move with gentle paces
Round the wide hall, and show their happy faces,
Or stand in courtly talk by fives and sevens,
Like those fair stars that twinkle in the heavens.
45   Yet must I tell a tale of chivalry—
Or wherefore comes that steed so proudly by?
Wherefore more proudly does the gentle knight
Rein in the swelling of his ample might?

Spenser, thy brows are archèd, open, kind,
50   And come like a clear sun-rise to my mind;
And always does my heart with pleasure dance
When I think on thy noble countenance,
Where never yet was aught more earthly seen
Than the pure freshness of thy laurels green.
55   Therefore, great bard, I not so fearfully
Call on thy gentle spirit to hover nigh
My daring steps; or if thy tender care,
Thus startled unaware,
Be jealous that the foot of other wight
60   Should madly follow that bright path of light
Traced by thy loved Libertas, he will speak

37. *that ... lance*] this ... spear *Tom Keats MS.*
38. *banneral*] Pennon. See *The Faerie Queene* VI vii, 26,
                    ... knightly bannerall ...
40. The knight's shield has a spur on a field gules.
44. *fair stars*] Constellations.
46. *steed*] *Tom Keats MS*; knight *1817*. K. substituted 'steed' for 'knight'
in a presentation copy of *1817* (*Forman* (1883) i 19).
51. Cp. Wordsworth's *To Daffodils* (1807) 23–4,
                    For then my heart with pleasure fills,
                    And dances with the daffodils.
For K.'s earliest probable echo of Wordsworth see *O Solitude* 8 *n* (p. 23
above).
57. *tender*] gentle *Tom Keats MS.*
58. For this metrical variation see *Calidore* 12 *n* (p. 37 below).
59. *other*] living *Tom Keats MS.*
61. *Libertas*] K.'s name at this time for Leigh Hunt because of his imprisonment—see headnote to *Written on the Day that Mr. Leigh Hunt left Prison*
(p. 11 above). Cp. *To my Brother George* 24 (p. 50 below),
                    For knightly Spenser to Libertas told it ...

And tell thee that my prayer is very meek,
That I will follow with due reverence
And start with awe at mine own strange pretence.
65 Him thou wilt hear. So I will rest in hope
To see wide plains, fair trees and lawny slope,
The morn, the eve, the light, the shade, the flowers,
Clear streams, smooth lakes and overlooking towers.

---

and *To Charles Cowden Clarke* 44–5 (p. 56 below),

The wronged Libertas, who has told you stories
Of laurel chaplets and Apollo's glories . . .

66. *lawny*] Grassy. For K.'s earlier use of this epithet see *Imitation of Spenser* 3 and *n* (p. 3 above).

20 Calidore

a fragment

Exact date of composition unknown, but probably *c*. Feb.–March 1816 as an unsuccessful attempt to tell the 'tale of chivalry' promised in the previous poem. K. took his hero's name from *The Faerie Queene* vi, 'The Legend of Sir Calidore, or, Of Courtesie'. The influence of Leigh Hunt's *The Story of Rimini* (1816) is apparent in the poem's diction, loose heroic couplets and sentimental eroticism, but description is substituted for Hunt's narrative energy. For discussions of Hunt's stylistic influence on K. see *de Selincourt* 602–5, W. J. Bate's *The Stylistic Development of John Keats* (1945) 9–19, 19–27, 192–6, 199–201, but some special features of this influence are singled out for mention in the notes below.
The single transcript by Tom Keats has minor variants from *1817*, some of which are noted below.
Published *1817*.

Young Calidore is paddling o'er the lake,
His healthful spirit eager and awake
To feel the beauty of a silent eve,
Which seemed full loth this happy world to leave,
5 The light dwelt o'er the scene so lingeringly.
He bares his forehead to the cool blue sky

¶ 20. 1. Modelled on the opening line of *The Faerie Queene*,
A Gentle Knight was pricking on the plaine . . .
5. *lingeringly*] K.'s fondness for adverbs formed from present participles derives from Hunt. Cp., for example, *The Story of Rimini* iii 594, 'together, thrillingly' and iv 34, 'gone smilingly'. For other instances of such adverbs in this poem see ll. 16, 31, 82, 149.
6. *cool*] clear *Tom Keats MS*.

And smiles at the far clearness all around,
Until his heart is well nigh overwound,
And turns for calmness to the pleasant green
10   Of easy slopes, and shadowy trees that lean
So elegantly o'er the waters' brim
And show their blossoms trim.
Scarce can his clear and nimble eye-sight follow
The freaks and dartings of the black-winged swallow,
15   Delighting much to see it half at rest,
Dip so refreshingly its wings, and breast
'Gainst the smooth surface, and to mark anon
The widening circles into nothing gone.

And now the sharp keel of his little boat
20   Comes up with ripple and with easy float,
And glides into a bed of water lilies:
Broad-leaved are they and their white canopies
Are upward turned to catch the heavens' dew.
Near to a little island's point they grew,
25   Whence Calidore might have the goodliest view
Of this sweet spot of earth. The bowery shore

7. *clearness*] K.'s frequent use of abstract nouns ending in '-ness' was encouraged by Hunt. See, for example, *The Story of Rimini* i 7, 'a crystal
clearness' and i 9, 'A balmy briskness'. For other instances in this poem see
ll. 9, 34, 48, 144.

8. *Well nigh overwound*] Wound up to the highest pitch by intense feeling.

10. *shadowy*] K.'s use of adjectives ending in '-y' formed from verbs and
nouns was encouraged by Hunt. Cp. *The Story of Rimini* i 22, 'with scattery
light', and iii 389, 'flamy heart's ease'. Other instances in this poem will be
found at ll. 26, 50, 139.

11. *So elegantly*] See W. T. Arnold on K. and Hunt, 'Both poets have a
curious way of using "so" . . . a sort of appeal to the reader, a tacit question
whether he has not noted the same thing, and felt the same pleasure from it'
(*The Poetical Works* of *John Keats* (1888) xxvii). Other examples at ll. 16,
130.

12 (and *72, 84, 92* below). The line of three stresses as a metrical variation
probably derives from K.'s enjoyment of Spenser's *Epithalamion*. For his
pleasure in this poem see *To Mary Frogley* 29 n (p. 30 above).

14. Cp. *The Story of Rimini* i 16–17,
        The birds to the delicious time are singing,
        Darting with freaks and snatches up and down . . .

20. *float*] K.'s habit of using verbs as nouns was encouraged by Hunt. Cp.
The Story of Rimini i 141, 'with stately stir', and i 177, 'a lightsome fit'.
Other instances in this poem are at ll. 69, 86, 139.

26. *bowery shore*] Cp. *The Story of Rimini* iii 473, 'by the waterside on
bowery shelves'.

3+K.

Went off in gentle windings to the hoar
And light blue mountains, but no breathing man
With a warm heart, and eye prepared to scan
30   Nature's clear beauty, could pass lightly by
Objects that looked out so invitingly
On either side. These gentle Calidore
Greeted, as he had known them long before.
The sidelong view of swelling leafiness,
35   Which the glad setting sun in gold doth dress,
Whence ever and anon the jay outsprings,
And scales upon the beauty of its wings.
The lonely turret, shattered and outworn,
Stands venerably proud—too proud to mourn
40   Its long lost grandeur; fir trees grow around,
Ay dropping their hard fruit upon the ground.
The little chapel with the cross above
Upholding wreaths of ivy; the white dove
That on the window spreads his feathers light
45   And seems from purple clouds to wing its flight.
Green tufted islands casting their soft shades
Across the lake. Sequestered leafy glades
That through the dimness of their twilight show
Large dock leaves, spiral foxgloves, or the glow
50   Of the wild cat's eyes, or the silvery stems

27. windings] Cp. the participial nouns in l. 14 above and ll. 113, 143 below.
For similar instances in Hunt see, for example, *The Story of Rimini* i 142,
'snortings proud', and i 195, 'purple smearings'.

28. mountains: but no] Mountains. But sure no *Tom Keats MS*.

30–45. Printed as quatrains in *1817*.

34–52. A Keatsian imitation of descriptive interludes in *The Story of Rimini*,
for example, iii 382 ff.

37. scales] Ascends.

40. fir trees] Laburnums *Tom Keats MS*.

41. And bow their golden honors to the ground . . . *Tom Keats MS*. The
revised version was praised by Hunt for its 'Greek simplicity' (review of
1817; see headnote to *O Solitude*, p. 23 above).

42–3. The little chapel . . . ivy] Cp. *The Faerie Queene* VI v 35,
        . . . nigh thereto a little Chappell stoode,
        Which being all with Yvy overspred,
        Deckt all the roofe, and shadowing the roode . . .

44. window] The reading follows *Tom Keats's MS*; *1817*'s reading 'windows' is probably a misprint. The dove is depicted in the stained glass of
the chapel window.

49. spiral] Tapering like spires.

50. cat's eyes] The speedwell or forget-me-not (OED).

Of delicate birch trees, or long grass which hems
A little brook. The youth had long been viewing
These pleasant things, and heaven was bedewing
The mountain flowers, when his glad senses caught
55   A trumpet's silver voice. Ah, it was fraught
With many joys for him! The warder's ken
Had found white coursers prancing in the glen.
Friends very dear to him he soon will see,
So pushes off his boat most eagerly,
60   And soon upon the lake he skims along,
Deaf to the nightingale's first under-song,
Nor minds he the white swans that dream so sweetly,
His spirit flies before him so completely.

And now he turns a jutting point of land,
65   Whence may be seen the castle gloomy and grand;
Nor will a bee buzz round two swelling peaches
Before the point of his light shallop reaches
Those marble steps that through the water dip.
Now over them he goes with hasty trip
70   And scarcely stays to ope the folding doors.
Anon he leaps along the oaken floors
Of halls and corridors.
Delicious sounds! Those little bright-eyed things
That float about the air on azure wings

55. *A trumpet's silver voice*] Cp. *Ode To Apollo* 30 and *n* (p. 16 above),
               A silver trumpet Spenser blows . . .
56. *The warder*] The soldier on watch in the castle mentioned in l. 65 below.
57. *found*] seen *Tom Keats MS.*
60. *upon*] across *Tom Keats MS.*
61. *under-song*] Accompanying refrain; frequently in Spenser. For K.'s
early allusions to the nightingale see *Endymion* i 828–31 *n* (p. 157 below).
65. The line is hypermetrical.
66. *two swelling peaches*] Perhaps suggested by *The Story of Rimini* iii 593–4,
        . . . their cheeks, like peaches on a tree,
      Leaned with a touch together . . .
67. *shallop*] Light skiff. Spenser has *The Faerie Queene* III vii 27,
              . . . with the ore
    Didst thrust the shallop from the floting strand . . .
69. *goes*] flies *Tom Keats MS.*
70. *stays*] stops *Tom Keats MS.*
73. *bright-eyed*] K.'s use of compound adjectives was encouraged by Hunt.
See, for example, *The Story of Rimini* i 95, 'the bright-eyed throng',
and ii 234,
        Boy-storied trees and passion-plighted spots . . .
For other instances in this poem see l. 14 above, ll. 73, 122, 127, 135 below.

75   Had been less heartfelt by him than the clang
      Of clattering hoofs. Into the court he sprang
      Just as two noble steeds and palfreys twain
      Were slanting out their necks with loosened rein,
      While from beneath the threatening portcullis
80   They brought their happy burthens. What a kiss,
      What gentle squeeze he gave each lady's hand!
      How tremblingly their delicate ankles spanned!
      Into how sweet a trance his soul was gone,
      While whisperings of affection
85   Made him delay to let their tender feet
      Come to the earth. With an incline so sweet
      From their low palfreys o'er his neck they bent,
      And whether there were tears of languishment,
      Or that the evening dew had pearled their tresses,
90   He feels a moisture on his cheek and blesses,
      With lips that tremble and with glistening eye,
      All the soft luxury
      That nestled in his arms. A dimpled hand,
      Fair as some wonder out of fairy land,
95   Hung from his shoulder like the drooping flowers
      Of whitest cassia, fresh from summer showers,
      And this he fondled with his happy cheek
      As if for joy he would no further seek—
      When the kind voice of good Sir Clerimond
100   Came to his ear, like something from beyond
      His present being. So he gently drew
      His warm arms, thrilling now with pulses new,
      From their sweet thrall, and forward gently bending
      Thanked heaven that his joy was never ending,

80–108. Cp. Hunt's sentimental style in the love scene between Paolo and Francesca, *The Story of Rimini* iii 591–604.

84. affection] Four syllables. The line is still a syllable short. Woodhouse inserted the word 'soft' before 'affection' in his copy of 1817 (Sperry's *Woodhouse* (1817) 143).

92. luxury] Pleasure. See, for example, Hunt's *The Story of Rimini* iii 515–16,
            . . . distant plash of waters tumbling o'er,
      And smell of citron blooms, and fifty luxuries more . . .
The word is frequently employed by K. in Hunt's manner 1816–17. On his individual use of it in later poems see further E. F. Guy's 'K.'s use of "luxury": a note on meaning' *KShJ* vol xiii (1964) 87–95.

96. Cassia] Honeysuckle. See *To George Felton Mathew* 43 *n* (p. 26 above).

99. Sir Clerimond] An invented name with a Spenserian flavour.

101. His] This *Tom Keats MS.*

103. gently] meekly *Tom Keats MS.*

105   While 'gainst his forehead he devoutly pressed
     A hand heaven made to succour the distressed,
     A hand that from the world's bleak promontory
     Had lifted Calidore for deeds of glory.

     Amid the pages and the torches' glare,
110   There stood a knight, patting the flowing hair
     Of his proud horse's mane. He was withal
     A man of elegance and stature tall,
     So that the waving of his plumes would be
     High as the berries of a wild ash tree,
115   Or as the wingèd cap of Mercury.
     His armour was so dexterously wrought
     In shape that sure no living man had thought
     It hard and heavy steel, but that indeed
     It was some glorious form, some splendid weed,
120   In which a spirit new come from the skies
     Might live, and show itself to human eyes.
     ''Tis the far-famed, the brave Sir Gondibert,'
     Said the good man to Calidore alert,
     While the young warrior with a step of grace
125   Came up—a courtly smile upon his face,
     And mailèd hand held out, ready to greet
     The large-eyed wonder and ambitious heat
     Of the aspiring boy, who, as he led
     Those smiling ladies, often turned his head
130   To admire the visor arched so gracefully
     Over a knightly brow, while they went by
     The lamps, that from the high roofed hall were pendent
     And gave the steel a shining quite transcendent.

     Soon in a pleasant chamber they are seated.
135   The sweet-lipped ladies have already greeted
     All the green leaves that round the window clamber
     To show their purple stars and bells of amber.
     Sir Gondibert has doffed his shining steel,
     Gladdening in the free and airy feel
140   Of a light mantle, and while Clerimond
     Is looking round about him with a fond
     And placid eye, young Calidore is burning

115. *Mercury*] The messenger of the gods. For his 'winged cap' see *I stood tip-toe* 24 *n* (p. 87 below).

119. *weed*] Dress. Frequently in Spenser.

122. *Sir Gondibert*] The name was suggested by Davenant's *Gondibert* (1651).

139. *airy*] easy *Tom Keats MS*. On K.'s use of 'feel' see *In drear-nighted December* 21 *n* (p. 288 below).

To hear of knightly deeds and gallant spurning
Of all unworthiness, and how the strong of arm
145   Kept off dismay and terror and alarm
From lovely woman; while brimful of this,
He gave each damsel's hand so warm a kiss,
And had such manly ardour in his eye,
That each at other looked half staringly—
150   And then their features started into smiles
Sweet as blue heavens o'er enchanted isles.

Softly the breezes from the forest came,
Softly they blew aside the taper's flame.
Clear was the song from Philomel's far bower;
155   Grateful the incense from the lime-tree flower;
Mysterious, wild, the far-heard trumpet's tone;
Lovely the moon in ether, all alone.
Sweet too the converse of these happy mortals,
As that of busy spirits when the portals
160   Are closing in the west, or that soft humming
We hear around when Hesperus is coming.
Sweet be their sleep. * * * * * * * *

146. brimful] A favourite image in K.'s early work; see *Endymion* iii 366 *n* (p. 221 below).

147. warm] sweet *Tom Keats MS.*

154–5. Perhaps suggested by Coleridge's *This lime-tree bower my prison* (1800: reprinted 1810); cp. *To one who has been long in city pent* 1 *n* (p. 45 below).

155. incense] A poeticism for the scent of flowers. Cp. Milton's *Paradise Lost* ix 194,

> ...Flours that breathd
> Thir morning incense ...

and Gray's echo of Milton's lines in *Elegy Written in a Country Churchyard* (1751) 17 (possibly K.'s source), 'incense-breathing morn'. The word is often used by K., the best known example of his associating it in later poems with his characteristic theme of transience being *Ode to a Nightingale* 42 (p. 528 below), 'soft incense hangs upon the boughs'.

157. The line suggests Wordsworth's influence, rather than Hunt's. See, for example, Wordsworth's *The Shepherd looking eastward* (1815) 2–6,

> 'Bright is thy veil, O Moon, as thou art bright!'
> Forthwith that little cloud, in ether spread
> And penetrated all with tender light,
> She cast away, and showed her fulgent head
> Uncovered ...

See *Specimen of an Induction* 51 *n* (p. 35 above).

159–60. busy spirits ... west] Perhaps the poets referred to in *Ode to Apollo* (p. 14 above).

21 'Woman ! When I behold thee flippant, vain'

Written *c*. March 1816: the poem is one of three Petrarchan sonnets printed together in *1817* celebrating women in the sentimental style of *Calidore*. The other two sonnets follow. For K.'s views on women see his letter to Bailey, July 1818, '. . . they fall . . . far beneath my Boyish imagination'. When I was a Schoolboy I thought a fair Women a pure Goddess (*L* i 341), and his Oct. 1818 journal-letter, '. . . the generality of women . . . appear to me as children to whom I would rather give a Sugar Plum than my time' (*L* i 404).
Published *1817*.

> Woman! When I behold thee flippant, vain,
>   Inconstant, childish, proud, and full of fancies,
>   Without that modest softening that enhances
>   The downcast eye, repentant of the pain
> 5   That its mild light creates to heal again—
>   E'en then, elate, my spirit leaps and prances,
>   E'en then my soul with exultation dances
>   For that to love, so long, I've dormant lain.
>   But when I see thee meek and kind and tender,
> 10   Heavens, how desperately do I adore
>   Thy winning graces! To be thy defender
>   I hotly burn – to be a Calidore,
>   A very Red Cross Knight, a stout Leander,
>   Might I be loved by thee like these of yore.

¶ 21. *12–13. Calidore . . . Red Cross Knight . . . Leander*] Examples of devoted love, of which the first two were familiar to K. from *The Faerie Queene*. He would have known about Leander's swimming the Hellespont to reach Hero from his early reading of various works of classical reference (see headnote to *Endymion*, p. 116 below) and from allusions encountered in his Elizabethan reading. The use of the epithet 'stout' faintly suggests a recollection of Spenser's *Hymne in Honour of Love* 231–2,
> Witness *Leander* in the Euxine waves,
> And stout *Aeneas* in the Troiane fyre . . .

22 'Light feet, dark violet eyes, and parted hair'

Written *c*. March 1816; see headnote to the preceding poem.
Published *1817*.

Light feet, dark violet eyes and parted hair,
 Soft dimpled hands, white neck and creamy breast,
 Are things on which the dazzled senses rest
Till the fond, fixèd eyes forget they stare.
5 From such fine pictures, heavens! I cannot dare
 To turn my admiration, though unpossessed
 They be of what is worthy, though not dressed
In lovely modesty and virtues rare.
Yet these I leave as thoughtless as a lark,
10 These lures I straight forget, e'en ere I dine
Or thrice my palate moisten. But when I mark
 Such charms with mild intelligences shine,
My ear is open like a greedy shark
 To catch the tunings of a voice divine.

¶ 22. *13. like a greedy shark*] As wide as the mouth of a greedy shark.

23 'Ah, who can e'er forget so fair a being'

Written *c*. March 1816; see headnote to *Woman! When I behold thee* (p. 43 above).
Published *1817*.

Ah, who can e'er forget so fair a being?
 Who can forget her half-retiring sweets?
 God! She is like a milk-white lamb that bleats
For man's protection. Surely the All-seeing,
5 Who joys to see us with His gifts agreeing,
 Will never give him pinions who intreats
 Such innocence to ruin, who vilely cheats
A dove-like bosom. In truth there is no freeing
One's thoughts from such a beauty. When I hear
10 A lay that once I saw her hand awake,
 Her form seems floating palpable and near;
Had I e'er seen her from an arbour take
 A dewy flower, oft would that hand appear,
 And o'er my eyes the trembling moisture shake.

¶ 23. *3–4.* Woodhouse notes, 'When Keats had written these lines he burst into tears overpowered by the tenderness of his own imagination' (Sperry's *Woodhouse* (*1817*) 145).
5. agreeing] Being pleased. Woodhouse notes (*loc. cit.*) the use of the word in Shakespeare's sonnet cxiv 11,
 Mine eye well knows what with his gust is 'greeing . . .
6. give him pinions] Admit him to heaven.

24 'To one who has been long in city pent'

Written June 1816: 'Written in the Fields–June 1816' (Georgiana Wylie's transcript). This and the two following sonnets record K.'s excursions into the countryside around London when he was studying medicine at St. Thomas's and St. Guy's 1815–16. The sequence owes something to Leigh Hunt's Hampstead sonnets (*Examiner* 1813–14; repr. *The Feast of Poets* 1814).

The two transcripts by Georgiana Wylie and George Keats are identical. Some of their variants from *1817* are noted below. Published *1817*.

> To one who has been long in city pent,
>   'Tis very sweet to look into the fair
>   And open face of heaven, to breathe a prayer
> Full in the smile of the blue firmament.
> 5   Who is more happy, when, with heart's content,
>   Fatigued he sinks into some pleasant lair
>   Of wavy grass and reads a debonair
>   And gentle tale of love and languishment?
>   Returning home at evening, with an ear
> 10   Catching the notes of Philomel, an eye
>   Watching the sailing cloudlet's bright career,
>   He mourns that day so soon has glided by,

¶ 24. *1. in city pent*] Milton, *Paradise Lost* ix 445–8,

>   As one who long in populous City pent,
>   Where Houses thick and Sewers annoy the Aire,
>   Forth issuing on a Summers Morn to breathe
>   Among the pleasant Villages and Farmes . . .

K.'s marking of this passage in his copy of Milton now at Hampstead probably belongs to a later date. Here the quotation was perhaps encouraged by Coleridge's echo of Milton in *To the Nightingale* (1796) 2,

>   Bards in city garret pent . . .

and *This Lime-tree Bower my Prison* (1800; reprinted 1810) 28–30,

>   . . . thou hast pined
>   And hunger'd after Nature, many a year,
>   In the great City pent . . .

4. blue] bright *Wylie, G. Keats MS.*
7. debonair] Pleasant, gracious. A common Spenserianism.
8. of love and languishment] Of yearning love.
9. home at evening] thoughtful, homeward *Wylie, G. Keats MSS.*
10. Philomel] The nightingale.
11. Following the wafted Cloudlet's light career . . . *Wylie, G. Keats MSS.*

3*

E'en like the passage of an angel's tear
That falls through the clear ether silently.

14. That droppeth through the Æther silently. *Wylie, G. Keats MSS.*

25 'Oh, how I love, on a fair summer's eve'

Written summer 1816: '1816' in the five transcripts, which largely agree. Published *1848.*

Oh, how I love, on a fair summer's eve,
    When streams of light pour down the golden west,
    And on the balmy zephyrs tranquil rest
The silver clouds, far, far away to leave
5   All meaner thoughts, and take a sweet reprieve
    From little cares; to find, with easy quest,
    A fragrant wild with Nature's beauty dressed,
And there into delight my soul deceive.
There warm my breast with patriotic lore,
10   Musing on Milton's fate, on Sidney's bier,
    Till their stern forms before my mind arise—
Perhaps on the wing of poesy upsoar,
    Full often dropping a delicious tear
        When some melodious sorrow spells mine eyes.

¶ 25. *7. wild*] Wilderness.
9–10. K.'s patriots are the Whig heroes of the Civil War and the 'glorious Revolution'. For Sidney see *Written on 29 May 5 n* (p. 17 above).
12. on the wing] on wing *1848.* The line foreshadows *Ode to a Nightingale* 33 (p. 527 below), 'on the viewless wings of Poesy'.
14. spells] Enchants. Cp. *Fill for me* 12 (p. 7 above),
            That e'er my wandering fancy spelled . . .

26 To a Friend who Sent me Some Roses

Written 29 June 1816: so dated in Tom Keats's transcript, which has the title, 'To Charles Wells on receiving a bunch of roses'. Wells (1800–79) was Tom's schoolfellow, a friend of Hunt and Hazlitt, and author of *Stories after Nature* (1822) and *Joseph and his Brethren* (1824); see Thomas Wade's Jan. 1845 letter to Milnes, 'Keats and he quarrelled about some trifle or other; the quarrel being ended by Wells' present of roses' (*KC* ii 115).

For K.'s later hostility to Wells over the latter's behaviour towards Tom
see *L* i 84, 192 *n.*, and ii 82, 90–1.

K.'s undated holograph draft and Tom Keats's transcript have minor
variants from *1817*, some of which are noted below.

Published *1817*.

> As late I rambled in the happy fields –
>> What time the sky-lark shakes the tremulous dew
>> From his lush clover covert, when anew
> Adventurous knights take up their dinted shields –
> 5 I saw the sweetest flower wild nature yields,
>> A fresh-blown musk-rose. 'Twas the first that threw
>> Its sweets upon the summer; graceful it grew
> As is the wand that queen Titania wields.
> And, as I feasted on its fragrancy,
> 10 I thought the garden-rose it far excelled.
> But when, O Wells, thy roses came to me,
>> My sense with their deliciousness was spelled;
> Soft voices had they, that with tender plea
>> Whispered of peace and truth and friendliness
>>> unquelled.

¶ 26. *1. rambled*] wandered *Draft*.
6. musk-rose] Frequently referred to by K. as one of his favourite flowers.
The most familiar reference is in *Ode to a Nightingale* 49 (p. 528 below),

> The coming musk-rose, full of dewy wine . . .

For other references in K.'s early poetry see *To my Brother George* 89, *Sleep
and Poetry* 5, *Endymion* i 19, iv 102 (pp. 52, 69, 121 and 249 below). K.'s
feeling for the musk-rose as a sign of early summer was probably heightened
by the allusions to it in *A Midsummer Night's Dream* II ii 52,

> With sweet musk-roses, and with eglantine . . .

and Milton's *Lycidas* 146,

> The musk-rose, and the well-attired Woodbine . . .

8. Titania] The queen of the fairies in *A Midsummer Night's Dream*.
12. spelled] Enchanted. See the preceding sonnet, *Oh, how I love* 14 *n* (p. 46
above).
14. Whispered of truth, Humanity and Friendliness unquell'd. *Tom Keats
MS*. The line is an alexandrine.

27 To my Brother George

Written at Margate Aug. 1816: so dated in George Keats's transcript. The
poem appears as the first of the seventeen Petrarchan sonnets printed together in *1817*, and is one of two poems written for George Keats during
K.'s first holiday by the sea.

K.'s holograph draft (Huntington Library) has variants from *1817*, some of which are noted below.
Published *1817*.

> Many the wonders I this day have seen:
>   The sun, when first he kissed away the tears
>   That filled the eyes of morn; the laurelled peers
> Who from the feathery gold of evening lean;
> 5   The ocean with its vastness, its blue green,
>   Its ships, its rocks, its caves, its hopes, its fears,
>   Its voice mysterious, which whoso hears
> Must think on what will be, and what has been.
> E'en now, dear George, while this for you I write,
> 10   Cynthia is from her silken curtains peeping
> So scantly that it seems her bridal night,
>   And she her half-discovered revels keeping.
> But what, without the social thought of thee,
> Would be the wonders of the sky and sea?

¶ 27. 3. *filled the eyes of morn*] trembled in the morning's eye *Draft* (*cancelled*). The phrase 'the laurelled peers' is repeated from *Ode to Apollo* 20 (p. 15 above).
4. *feathery gold*] Cp. Shelley's *Queen Mab* (1813) ii 16, 'far clouds of feathery gold'. The word 'feathery' is substituted for 'paleing' in the draft. On K.'s associating the sunset with poetry see *Ode to Apollo* 1 *n*, 42–7 *n* (pp. 14, 17 above).
6. *rocks*] Dangers *Draft* (*cancelled*).
7. *Its voice mysterious*] Cp. *On the sea* 1 *n* (p. 112 below),
>   It keeps eternal whisperings around . . .
8. *think on what will be*] muse on what's to come *Draft*.
10. *silken*] silver *Draft*.
11.   Giving the world but snatches of delight . . .
>   *Draft* (*uncancelled alternative*).
12. *revels*] Probably suggested by the title of Ben Jonson's play, *Cynthia's Revells* (1601).
13–14.   The Sights have warmed me but without thy love
>   What Joy in Earth or Sea or Heavn above?   *Draft* (*cancelled*)

28 To my Brother George

Written Aug. 1816 as a verse letter from Margate: so dated in *1817*. The poem is the second of K.'s three verse epistles in heroic couplets printed together in *1817* (the first being *To George Felton Mathew*, p. 24 above). K.'s familiar style in this and the following poem owes something to Leigh

Hunt's verse letters to Tom Moore and William Hazlitt (*Examiner* 30 June, 28 July 1816).

K.'s holograph letter and the transcript by George Keats have minor variants from *1817*, some of which are noted below.

Published *1817*.

> Full many a dreary hour have I passed,
> My brain bewildered and my mind o'ercast
> With heaviness, in seasons when I've thought
> No sphery strains by me could e'er be caught
> 5 From the blue dome, though I to dimness gaze
> On the far depth where sheeted lightning plays,
> Or, on the wavy grass outstretched supinely,
> Pry 'mong the stars, to strive to think divinely;
> That I should never hear Apollo's song,
> 10 Though feathery clouds were floating all along
> The purple west and, two bright streaks between,
> The golden lyre itself were dimly seen;
> That the still murmur of the honey bee
> Would never teach a rural song to me;
> 15 That the bright glance from beauty's eyelids slanting
> Would never make a lay of mine enchanting,
> Or warm my breast with ardour to unfold
> Some tale of love and arms in time of old.
>
> But there are times when those that love the bay
> 20 Fly from all sorrowing far, far away.
> A sudden glow comes on them, naught they see
> In water, earth, or air, but poesy.
> It has been said, dear George, and true I hold it

¶ 28. *4. sphery strains*] Music from the spheres. The epithet was probably suggested by Milton's *Comus* 1021, 'the Spheary chime'.

7–8. Cp. Hunt's feminine rhyme and use of 'divinely' in *The Story of Rimini* iii 135–6,

> . . . touched the music in his turn so finely,
> That all he did, they thought, was done divinely . . .

10–11. feathery clouds . . . purple west] Cp. the sonnet *To my Brother George* 4 (p. 48 above), 'the feathery gold of evening' and *n*.

11. streaks] strokes G. Keats MS.

12. dimly] faintly K.'*s MS*, G. Keats MS. Apollo's golden lyre was often in K.'s mind as an emblem of poetic achievement. Other references in *To Apollo* 2, *Endymion* iv 702, *Hyperion* iii 63 (pp. 111, 274 and 437 below).

17–18. K. is thinking of his unfinished poem, *Calidore* (p. 36 above).

18. time] times K.'*s MS*.

23. It has been said] Apparently by Hunt—see following line—but this may be K.'s invention since the context suggests a playful reference to *Calidore* (with ll. 25–6 cp. ll. 56–7, p. 39 above).

        (For knightly Spenser to Libertas told it),
25   That when a poet is in such a trance,
        In air he sees white coursers paw and prance,
        Bestridden of gay knights in gay apparel,
        Who at each other tilt in playful quarrel,
        And what we, ignorantly, sheet-lightning call,
30   Is the swift opening of their wide portal,
        When the bright warder blows his trumpet clear,
        Whose tones reach naught on earth but poet's ear.
        When these enchanted portals open wide,
        And through the light the horsemen swiftly glide,
35   The poet's eye can reach those golden halls
        And view the glory of their festivals:
        Their ladies fair, that in the distance seem
        Fit for the silvering of a seraph's dream;
        Their rich brimmed goblets, that incessant run
40   Like the bright spots that move about the sun;
        And, when upheld, the wine from each bright jar
        Pours with the lustre of a falling star.
        Yet further off are dimly seen their bowers,
        Of which no mortal eye can reach the flowers—
45   And 'tis right just, for well Apollo knows
        'Twould make the poet quarrel with the rose.
        All that's revealed from that far seat of blisses
        Is the clear fountains' interchanging kisses,
        As gracefully descending, light and thin,
50   Like silver streaks across a dolphin's fin
        When he upswimmeth from the coral caves,
        And sports with half his tail above the waves.

        These wonders strange he sees, and many more,
        Whose head is pregnant with poetic lore.

25. *trance*] Poetic reverie. See *Sleep and Poetry* 19 *n* (pp. 70–1 below).
37. *fair*] bright *K.'s MS*.
38. Shining like figures in an angelic dream.
40. Presumably the stars (cp. l. 42 below).
50–2. K. associates the dolphin with coral again in *To Homer* 4 (p. 352 below), 'dolphin-coral in deep seas'. His image of the dolphin sporting near the surface of the sea may be owed to *Antony and Cleopatra* V ii 88–90,
                                    . . . his delights
            Were dolphin-like, they show'd his back above
            The element they liv'd in . . .
The 'coral caves' also suggest a literary recollection, perhaps Milton's *Comus* 886, 'thy coral-pav'n bed'.
54. *pregnant*] Cp. Gray's *Elegy written in a Country Churchyard* (1751) 46,
            Some heart once pregnant with celestial fire . . .

55   Should he upon an evening ramble fare
       With forehead to the soothing breezes bare,
       Would he naught see but the dark, silent blue
       With all its diamonds trembling through and through?
       Or the coy moon, when in the waviness
60   Of whitest clouds she does her beauty dress,
       And staidly paces higher up, and higher,
       Like a sweet nun in holy-day attire?
       Ah, yes, much more would start into his sight—
       The revelries and mysteries of night.
65   And should I ever see them, I will tell you
       Such tales as needs must with amazement spell you.

       These are the living pleasures of the bard,
       But richer far posterity's award.
       What does he murmur with his latest breath,
70   While his proud eye looks through the film of death?
       'What though I leave this dull and earthly mould,
       Yet shall my spirit lofty converse hold
       With after times. The patriot shall feel
       My stern alarum, and unsheathe his steel,
75   Or in the senate thunder out my numbers
       To startle princes from their easy slumbers.
       The sage will mingle with each moral theme
       My happy thoughts sententious; he will teem
       With lofty periods when my verses fire him,
80   And then I'll stoop from heaven to inspire him.
       Lays have I left of such a dear delight

56. Cp. *Calidore* 6 (p. 36 above),
            He bares his forehead to the cool blue sky . . .
59. *waviness*] See *Calidore* 7 *n* (p. 37 above).
60. *does*] doth *K.'s MS.*
65–66. *you . . . you*] ye . . . ye *K.'s MS.*
66. *spell*] Enchant. Cp. *Oh, how I love* 14 *n* (p. 46 above).
72. *lofty converse*] Cp. Thomson's *The Seasons* (1730) *Winter* 432,
            And hold high converse with the mighty dead . . .
and Hazlitt's 'On Classical Education', 'By conversing with the mighty
dead we imbibe sentiment with knowledge' (*Examiner* 12 Feb. 1815, repr.
The Round Table 1817; *Works* ed. P. P. Howe 1930, iv 5).
78. *sententious*] Wise. The placing of the epithets is Miltonic—an unusual
effect in K.'s early poems.
81–8. Cp. Spenser's *Colin Clout's Come Home Againe* 640–4,
            And long while after I am dead and rotten:
            Among the shepherds daughters dancing rownd,
            My layes made of her shall not be forgotten.
            But sung by them with flowry gyrlonds crownd . . .

That maids will sing them on their bridal night.
Gay villagers, upon a morn of May,
When they have tired their gentle limbs with play,
85   And formed a snowy circle on the grass,
And placed in midst of all that lovely lass
Who chosen is their queen—with her fine head
Crowned with flowers purple, white, and red,
For there the lily and the musk-rose, sighing,
90   Are emblems true of hapless lovers dying;
Between her breasts, that never yet felt trouble,
A bunch of violets, full-blown and double,
Serenely sleep. She from a casket takes
A little book—and then a joy awakes
95   About each youthful heart, with stifled cries,
And rubbing of white hands, and sparkling eyes,
For she's to read a tale of hopes, and fears,
One that I fostered in my youthful years.
The pearls, that on each glistening circlet sleep,
100   Gush ever and anon with silent creep,
Lured by the innocent dimples. To sweet rest
Shall the dear babe, upon its mother's breast,
Be lulled with songs of mine. Fair world, adieu!
Thy dales and hills are fading from my view.
105   Swiftly I mount, upon wide spreading pinions,
Far from the narrow bounds of thy dominions.
Full joy I feel, while thus I cleave the air,
That my soft verse will charm thy daughters fair
And warm thy sons!' Ah, my dear friend and brother,
110   Could I, at once, my mad ambition smother
For tasting joys like these, sure I should be
Happier, and dearer to society.
At times, 'tis true, I've felt relief from pain
When some bright thought has darted through my brain;
115   Through all that day I've felt a greater pleasure
Than if I'd brought to light a hidden treasure.
As to my sonnets, though none else should heed them,
I feel delighted, still, that you should read them.
Of late, too, I have had much calm enjoyment,

---

86. Placing in midst thereof that happy lass . . . *K.'s MS.*
100. *With silent creep*] See *Calidore* 20 *n* (p. 37 above).
117. K. had written some fifteen sonnets by this time, though possibly **not**
yet *How many bards*, which was among the poems selected by Cowden
Clarke when introducing K.'s poetry to Hunt a few weeks after this (see
headnote, p. 59 below).

120 Stretched on the grass at my best loved employment
       Of scribbling lines for you. These things I thought
       While, in my face, the freshest breeze I caught.
       E'en now I'm pillowed on a bed of flowers
       That crowns a lofty clift, which proudly towers
125 Above the ocean-waves. The stalks and blades
       Chequer my tablet with their quivering shades.
       On one side is a field of drooping oats
       Through which the poppies show their scarlet coats,
       So pert and useless that they bring to mind
130 The scarlet coats that pester human-kind.
       And on the other side, outspread, is seen
       Ocean's blue mantle streaked with purple and green.
       Now 'tis I see a canvassed ship, and now
       Mark the bright silver curling round her prow.
135 I see the lark down-dropping to his nest,
       And the broad winged sea-gull never at rest,
       For when no more he spreads his feathers free
       His breast is dancing on the restless sea.
       Now I direct my eyes into the west,

121. scribbling lines for you] Woodhouse underlined the word *you* in his
copy of *1817* and noted marginally that *To Mary Frogley* and *To Georgiana
Wylie* (p. 29 above, p. 98 below) and 'perhaps' also *O Solitude, if I must
with thee dwell* (p. 22 above) 'were written *for* his brother' and that the
present epistle and the sonnets *To my Brother George* and *To my Brothers*
'were written *to* his brother'. See Stuart M. Sperry, 'Keats's first published
poem', *Huntington Library Quarterly* xxix (Feb. 1966) 193 and Sperry's
Woodhouse (1817) 146–7.

123–42. 'Written on the cliff at Margate'–K. in Isabella Towers's copy of
1817 (Garrod).

123. Cp. Leigh Hunt, *To Thomas Moore* 35,
       Even now while I write, I'm half stretched on the ground . . .

124. crowns . . . clift] crown . . . cliff *L*.

126. The blades of grass and the flower-stems cast a flickering pattern of
shadows on K.'s writing paper. The phrasing suggests that K. was combining recollections of Milton's *L'Allegro* 96, 'Dancing in the Chequered
shade', and Pope's *Windsor Forest* (1713) 135, 'the quivering shade'. See
also Pope's *Pastorals* (1709), *Summer* 4, 'a quiv'ring Shade'.

130. scarlet coats] Soldiers. See K.'s letter to Reynolds of 17 April 1817 from
Carisbrooke, 'On the road from Cowes to Newport I saw some extensive
Barracks which disgusted me extremely with Government for placing such
a Nest of Debauchery in so beautiful a place' (*L* i 131–2).

135. his] her *L*.

139. into] towards *L*.

140 Which at this moment is in sunbeams dressed—
Why westward turn? 'Twas but to say adieu!
'Twas but to kiss my hand, dear George, to you!

141. westward turn] George was westward in London.

29 To Charles Cowden Clarke

Written Sept. 1816 and sent as a verse letter from Margate: so dated in *1817*
and K.'s holograph copy (Huntington Library).

K.'s correspondent Charles Cowden Clarke (1787–1877) was the son of
the headmaster of the school at Enfield which K. and his brothers attended;
details of Cowden Clarke's friendship with K. and of his crucial influence
on K.'s early reading, both celebrated in this poem, are given in *Cowden
Clarke* and *KC* i lxxii–lxxiv, ii 146–53, 319–21.
K.'s MS has minor variants from *1817*, some of which are noted below.
Published *1817*.

Oft have you seen a swan superbly frowning
And with proud breast his own white shadow crowning.
He slants his neck beneath the waters bright
So silently, it seems a beam of light
5 Come from the galaxy; anon he sports,
With outspread wings the naiad Zephyr courts,
Or ruffles all the surface of the lake
In striving from its crystal face to take
Some diamond water drops, and them to treasure
10 In milky nest and sip them off at leisure.
But not a moment can he there insure them,
Nor to such downy rest can he allure them,
For down they rush as though they would be free,
And drop like hours into eternity.
15 Just like that bird am I in loss of time

¶ 29. *1–2.* Perhaps a recollection of Wordsworth's *Yarrow Unvisited* (1807)
43–4,

> The swan on still St. Mary's Lake
> Float double, swan and shadow ...

5. Come] Shot *K.'s MS*. The 'galaxy' is the Milky Way.
6. the naiad] A slip, as the swan here is masculine. K. knew from *Lemprière*
that Naiades were 'inferior deities who presided over rivers, springs, wells
and fountains. They are represented as young and beautiful virgins'; on
K.'s familiarity with *Lemprière* see headnote to *Endymion* (p. 116 below).
14. hours] time *K.'s MS*.
15–20. Cp. K.'s despondency about his lack of inspiration in *To my Brother
George* 1–18 (p. 49 above).

Whene'er I venture on the stream of rhyme.
With shattered boat, oar snapped, and canvas rent
I slowly sail, scarce knowing my intent,
Still scooping up the water with my fingers,
20 In which a trembling diamond never lingers.

By this, friend Charles, you may full plainly see
Why I have never penned a line to thee:
Because my thoughts were never free and clear,
And little fit to please a classic ear;
25 Because my wine was of too poor a savour
For one whose palate gladdens in the flavour
Of sparkling Helicon. Small good it were
To take him to a desert rude and bare
Who had on Baiae's shore reclined at ease,
30 While Tasso's page was floating in a breeze
That gave soft music from Armida's bowers,
Mingled with fragrance from her rarest flowers;
Small good to one who had by Mulla's stream
Fondled the maidens with the breasts of cream;
35 Who had beheld Belphoebe in a brook,
And lovely Una in a leafy nook,
And Archimago leaning o'er his book;
Who had of all that's sweet tasted and seen,
From silv'ry ripple up to beauty's queen,

17–18. *With shattered boat . . . sail*] Cp. *Endymion* i 46–7 (p. 122 below), 'I'll smoothly steer / My little boat', and see also the imagery of exploration and discovery in *On First Looking into Chapman's Homer* (p. 60 below). The phrasing here may owe something to Cowper's *On the Receipt of my Mother's Picture* (1798) 103,

      Sails ript, seams op'ning wide, and compass toss'd . . .

27. *sparkling Helicon*] Synecdoche. The spring Hippocrene, sacred to the Muses, is referred to by the name of the mountain in Boeotia where it is found.

29–30. A tribute to Cowden Clarke's knowledge of Tasso. '*Baiae's shore*' is the Bay of Naples, the home of Tasso (1493–1569). Tasso was born in Sorrento and brought up in Naples.

31. *Armida*] See *On Receiving a Curious Shell* 8 *n* (p. 20 above).

33–7. A tribute to Cowden Clarke's knowledge of Spenser.

33. *Mulla's stream*] The river near Spenser's home at Kilcolman in Ireland, frequently referred to in his poems.

34. *with breasts of cream*] Cp. Spenser's *Epithalamion* 175,

      Her brest like to a bowle of cream uncrudded . . .

35–6. *Una . . . Belphoebe . . . Archimago*] Characters in *The Faerie Queene* I, II.

40   From the sequestered haunts of gay Titania
     To the blue dwelling of divine Urania;
     One who, of late, had ta'en sweet forest walks
     With him who elegantly chats and talks—
     The wronged Libertas, who has told you stories
45   Of laurel chaplets and Apollo's glories,
     Of troops chivalrous prancing through a city,
     And tearful ladies made for love and pity,
     With many else which I have never known.

     Thus have I thought; and days on days have flown
50   Slowly or rapidly—unwilling still
     For you to try my dull, unlearned quill.
     Nor should I now, but that I've known you long,
     That you first taught me all the sweets of song:
     The grand, the sweet, the terse, the free, the fine;
55   What swelled with pathos, and what right divine;
     Spenserian vowels that elope with ease,
     And float along like birds o'er summer seas;
     Miltonian storms, and more, Miltonian tenderness;
     Michael in arms, and more, meek Eve's fair slenderness.
60   Who read for me the sonnet swelling loudly
     Up to its climax and then dying proudly?
     Who found for me the grandeur of the ode,
     Growing, like Atlas, stronger from its load?
     Who let me taste that more than cordial dram,

40. Titania] K. is probably thinking here of *A Midsummer Night's Dream* rather than Wieland's *Oberon* (see *On Receiving a Curious Shell* 26–30 *n*, p. 21 above).

41. Urania] The Muse of astronomy was known by this name, but K. may be thinking of Venus. See *Lemprière*: 'Urania, a surname of Venus, the same as Celestial. . . .'

44. wronged Libertas] Leigh Hunt. See *Specimen of an Induction* 61 *n* (p. 35 above). Cowden Clarke introduced K. to Hunt a few weeks after this poem was written.

46–7. Refers to the mounted procession through the streets in Hunt's *The Story of Rimini* i 147 ff.

52. I've known you long] i.e. since 1803, when K. first attended Enfield School.

57. Perhaps halcyons, birds traditionally associated with calm and ease. Cp. *Endymion* i 453–5 *n* (p. 140 below).

60–1. The description suggests a Petrarchan sonnet. On K.'s later dissatisfaction with both the Petrarchan and the Shakespearian sonnet forms see headnote to *If by dull rhymes* (p. 521 below).

63. The ode becomes richer as it widens the range of material enclosed.

65   The sharp, the rapier-pointed epigram?
     Showed me that epic was of all the king,
     Round, vast, and spanning all like Saturn's ring?
     You too upheld the veil from Clio's beauty,
     And pointed out the patriot's stern duty;
70   The might of Alfred, and the shaft of Tell;
     The hand of Brutus, that so grandly fell
     Upon a tyrant's head. Ah, had I never seen,
     Or known your kindness, what might I have been?
     What my enjoyments in my youthful years,
75   Bereft of all that now my life endears?
     And can I e'er these benefits forget?
     And can I e'er repay the friendly debt?
     No, doubly no—yet should these rhymings please,
     I shall roll on the grass with two-fold ease,
80   For I have long time been my fancy feeding
     With hopes that you would one day think the reading
     Of my rough verses not an hour misspent.
     Should it e'er be so, what a rich content!

     Some weeks have passed since last I saw the spires
85   In lucent Thames reflected—warm desires
     To see the sun o'erpeep the eastern dimness,
     And morning shadows streaking into slimness
     Across the lawny fields and pebbly water;
     To mark the time as they grow broad and shorter;
90   To feel the air that plays about the hills,
     And sips its freshness from the little rills;
     To see high golden corn wave in the light
     When Cynthia smiles upon a summer's night,
     And peers among the cloudlets jet and white,
95   As though she were reclining in a bed
     Of bean blossoms, in heaven freshly shed.

67. K. won Bonnycastle's *Introduction to Astronomy* (1807 edn) as a school prize at Enfield (Plate xv shows Saturn and its rings).

68. Clio] The Muse of history.

70–1. Alfred . . . Tell . . . Brutus] Cp. K.'s celebration of Alfred, Tell and Wallace in *To George Felton Mathew* 67–9 (p. 27 above).

72. a tyrant's head] Julius Caesar's.

84. Some weeks]. K. had been staying in Margate since August.

85. —warm desires] I had warm desires.

87. streaking] stretching *K.'s MS.*

88. lawny . . . pebbly] See *Calidore* 10 *n* (p. 37 above).

93–6. On K.'s feeling for the moon see *I stood tip-toe* 116–24 *n* (p. 90 below). The comparison of the clouds to bean-blossoms has the flavour of direct observation.

No sooner had I stepped into these pleasures
Than I began to think of rhymes and measures.
The air that floated by me seemed to say
100 'Write! thou wilt never have a better day.'
And so I did. When many lines I'd written,
Though with their grace I was not oversmitten,
Yet, as my hand was warm, I thought I'd better
Trust to my feelings and write you a letter.
105 Such an attempt required an inspiration
Of a peculiar sort—a consummation,
Which, had I felt, these scribblings might have been
Verses from which the soul would never wean
But many days have passed since last my heart
110 Was warmed luxuriously by divine Mozart,
By Arne delighted, or by Handel maddened,
Or by the song of Erin pierced and saddened,
What time you were before the music sitting
And the rich notes to each sensation fitting;
115 Since I have walked with you through shady lanes
That freshly terminate in open plains,
And revelled in a chat that ceasèd not
When at night-fall among your books we got,
No, nor when supper came, nor after that—
120 Nor when reluctantly I took my hat,
No, not till cordially you shook my hand
Mid-way between our homes; your accents bland

98. rhymes] Verse *K.'s MS.*
103. warm] in *K.'s MS.*
106. a consummation] Something consummate.
108. wean] Be weaned.
109 ff. K. is recalling the early days of his friendship with Cowden Clarke,
first at Enfield School and later during his apprenticeship as a surgeon at
Edmonton.
110–11. Mozart . . . Arne . . . Handel] Eighteenth-century composers whose
music Cowden Clarke played. Thomas Arne (1710–78) was a prolific
English composer famous for his settings of Shakespeare's songs; he also
wrote music for Milton's *Comus*, Addison's *Rosamond* and J. Thomson's
and D. Mallet's masque *Alfred* (containing the song, 'Rule Britannia!').
On K.'s feeling for Mozart see his Oct. 1818 journal-letter, '. . . she kept
me awake one Night as a tune of Mozart's might do' (*L* i 395).
113. the music] The pianoforte. For K.'s further recollection of Cowden
Clarke playing the piano at Enfield School see *The Eve of St. Agnes* 261 *n*
(p. 470 below).
122–6. Unliterary recollection. K. heard his friend's words when the sound
of his footsteps had faded. Sometimes the sound was lost and then picked

Still sounded in my ears, when I no more
Could hear your footsteps touch the gravelly floor.
125   Sometimes I lost them, and then found again;
You changed the footpath for the grassy plain.
In those still moments I have wished you joys
That well you know to honour: 'Life's very toys
With him,' said I, 'will take a pleasant charm;
130   It cannot be that ought will work him harm.'
These thoughts now come o'er me with all their might.
Again I shake your hand–friend Charles, good night.

up again as Cowden Clarke stepped from the hard path to the grass verge
and back.
128–9. Even the smallest happenings take a charm from his presence.

30 'How many bards gild the lapses of time'

Date of composition unknown, but conjecturally *c*. Oct. 1816: Cowden
Clarke records that this was one of the 'two or three' poems by K. which
he showed to Leigh Hunt and Horace Smith when visiting Hunt's home in
the Vale of Health, Hampstead, Oct. 1816–'. . . the visit ended with my
being requested to bring him [Keats] over' (*Recollections* 132–3). The poem
is generally dated March 1816, for which there is no authority; on the origin
of the error and the lack of evidence concerning the date see Sperry's *Woodhouse (1817)* 110–11.
Published *1817*.

How many bards gild the lapses of time!
  A few of them have ever been the food
  Of my delighted fancy–I could brood
Over their beauties, earthly, or sublime;
5   And often, when I sit me down to rhyme,
    These will in throngs before my mind intrude:
    But no confusion, no disturbance rude
  Do they occasion; 'tis a pleasing chime.

¶ 30. *1*. Poets brighten and enrich their times. On K.'s identifying gold and
poetry see *On First Looking into Chapman's Homer* 1 *n* (p. 61 below). The
word 'lapse' was common in the eighteenth century for a period of past
time. With the first three words of the line cp. Coleridge's *To the Nightingale*
(1796) 2,

        How many bards in city garret pent . . .

For an earlier echo of Coleridge's poem see *To one who has been long in city
pent* 1 *n* (p. 45 above).

So the unnumbered sounds that evening store:
10   The songs of birds, the whispering of the leaves,
The voice of waters, the great bell that heaves
    With solemn sound, and thousand others more
That distance of recognizance bereaves,
    Make pleasing music, and not wild uproar.

9–14. Cowden Clarke records that Horace Smith read the sonnet aloud and marked 'with particular emphasis and approval the last six lines' (*Recollections* 133).

11–12. The voice ... sound] Cp. Milton, *Il Penseroso* 74–6,
                    I hear the far-off *Curfeu* sound,
                    Over som wide-water'd shoar,
                    Swinging slow with sullen roar ...

13. 'What a well-condensed expression for one so young!'–Horace Smith's comment according to Cowden Clarke. The meaning is that the identity of individual sounds is lost by distance.

31 On First Looking into Chapman's Homer

Written Oct. 1816: so dated by Leigh Hunt in *The Examiner* 1 Dec. 1816. Cowden Clarke records, 'A beautiful copy of the folio edition of Chapman's translation of Homer had been lent me ... and to work we went, turning to some of the "famousest" passages, as we had scrappily known them in Pope's version ... it was in the teeming wonderment of this ... first introduction, that, when I came down to breakfast the next morning, I found upon my table a letter with no other enclosure than his famous sonnet. ... We had parted ... at day-spring, yet he contrived that I should receive the poem from a distance of, may be, two miles by ten o clock' (*Recollections* 128–30); in Oct. 1816 both men were in lodgings in London, K. at Southwark and Cowden Clarke at Clerkenwell.

K.'s imagery of exploration and discovery in the poem is drawn chiefly from William Robertson's *History of America* (1777), which he read in his schooldays (*Cowden Clarke* 124), with possibly some additional influence from John Evelyn's dedicatory poem prefacing Thomas Creech's 1683 translation of Lucretius. The merits of the sonnet were immediately recognized by K.'s friends; Hunt showed it to Godwin and Hazlitt and later reprinted it in his *Lord Byron and Some of his Contemporaries* (1828) 'as a remarkable instance of a vein prematurely masculine' (248). For detailed discussions of the poem's sources, structure and organization see *Murry* (1930) 15–33 and B. Ifor Evans, 'Keats's approach to the Chapman sonnet', *Essays and Studies of the English Association* xvi (1931).

K.'s draft (Morgan Library), fair copy and the version in the *Examiner* have variants from *1817*, some of which are noted below.
Published *The Examiner*, 1 Dec. 1816; repr. *1817*.

> Much have I travelled in the realms of gold,
>   And many goodly states and kingdoms seen;
>   Round many western islands have I been
> Which bards in fealty to Apollo hold.
> 5   Oft of one wide expanse had I been told
>   That deep-browed Homer ruled as his demesne;
>   Yet did I never breathe its pure serene
> Till I heard Chapman speak out loud and bold.

¶ 31 *Title. On the first . . . Fair Copy.*
1. realms of gold] The world of the imagination. Cp. Sidney, *A Defence of Poesie* (1595): '[Nature's] world is brazen, the poets only deliver a golden.' K. associates his discovery of Homer's 'realm of gold' with the discovery of the New World; see, for example, in Robertson's *History of America* (1792 edn) i 284–90, Balboa's emotion on discovering Peru and its wealth of gold.
4. in fealty] Poets are the feudal vassals of Apollo.
5. Oft] But *Examiner.*
6. deep-browed] low-browed *Draft (cancelled)*. With K.'s view of Homer as the ruler of a 'wide expanse' (l. 5) cp. his letter to Reynolds 3 Feb. 1818, 'Each of the moderns like an Elector of Hanover governs his petty state . . . the ancients were Emperors of vast Provinces' (*L* i 224). K. uses the word 'demesne' (dominion) again at *The 'Castle Builder'* 6, *Hyperion* i 298, *Lamia* ii 155 (pp. 390, 413 and 641 below).
7. Yet could I never judge what men could mean . . . Draft, Fair copy, Examiner. Cowden Clarke notes, 'he made an alteration in the seventh line . . . which he said was bald and too simply wondering' (*Recollections* 130). The phrase 'pure serene' derives from the Latin–*serenum* means a clear, bright or serene sky, as in Suetonius, *De Vita Caesarum*, 'Augustus' 5 *liquido et puro sereno*'–and was used by K.'s contemporaries. See, for example, Coleridge's *Hymn before Sunrise in the Vale of Chamouni* (1802) 72 (possibly K.'s source),
>   . . . glittering through the pure serene . . .
and Cary's translation (1814) of Dante's *Paradiso* xix 60–1,
>   . . . the pure serene
>   Of ne'er disturbed ether . . .
8. George Chapman (1559–1634), poet and dramatist, published his translation of Homer, *The Whole Works of Homer, Prince of Poetts . . .* in folio *c.* 1614, the edition read by K. and Cowden Clarke (first modern edn R. Hooper 1857). See Leigh Hunt, 'Chapman . . . stands upon no ceremony. He blows as rough a blast as Achilles could have desired to hear . . . K.'s epithets of "loud and bold" showed that he understood him perfectly' (*Lord Byron and Some of his Contemporaries*, 1828, 249).

> Then felt I like some watcher of the skies
> _10_   When a new planet swims into his ken;
> Or like stout Cortez when with eagle eyes
> He stared at the Pacific, and all his men
> Looked at each other with a wild surmise—
> Silent, upon a peak in Darien.

_9–10._ A reference to F. W. Herschel's discovery of the planet Uranus, 18 March 1781, as described in J. Bonnycastle's _Introduction to Astronomy_, which K. possessed—see _To Charles Cowden Clarke_ 67 _n_ (p. 57 above).

_11–12._ K. has conflated memories of Balboa's first sight of the Pacific from the isthmus of Darien (as recorded by Robertson) and of William Gilbert's account of the effect on a man of sensibility of seeing such natural wonders as the Pacific. See Robertson's _History of America_, 'Balboa . . . advanced alone to the summit. . . . As soon as he beheld the South Sea . . . he fell on his knees, and . . . returned thanks to God. . . . His followers . . . rushed forward to join in his wonder, exultation and gratitude' (i 289–90); and William Gilbert's commentary on his poem _The Hurricane_ (1796), 'when he . . . contemplates, from a sudden promontory, the distant, vast Pacific— and feels himself a freeman in this vast theatre . . . his exaltation is not less than imperial' (quoted by Wordsworth in _The Excursion_ (1814) iii 931 _n_). The substitution of Cortes for Balboa is the result of K.'s confusing Robertson's account of Balboa's emotion with his description of Cortes's feelings on first seeing Mexico City (_History of America_ ii 292–3). The confusion may have been encouraged by K.'s recollection of Evelyn's poem to Creech (see headnote) 16–21:

> Columbus thus, only discover'd Land,
> But it was Won by Great Corteze's hand:
> As with rich Spoils of goodly Kingdom's fraught,
> The immense Treasure to Iberia brought;
> So you the rich Lucretius (unknown
> To th' English world) bravely have made Your Own.

11. eagle] wond'ring _Fair Copy_. Commentators have consistently followed Leigh Hunt in associating the phrase 'eagle eyes' with a portrait of Cortes by Titian; see Hunt's _Lord Byron and his Contemporaries_ (1828) 249. No such portrait has survived, though there is an early engraving by Fernando Selma of a portrait of Cortes (reproduced in several biographies of Cortes, including F. A. Macnutt's _Letters of Cortes_ (1908) vol i) which is attributed to Titian.

14. a peak in Darien] 'The isthmus of Darien is not above sixty miles in breadth; but this neck of land, which binds together the continents of North and South America, is strengthened by a chain of lofty mountains, stretching through its whole extent' (Robertson's _History_ i 286). Hunt comments on the 'energetic . . . calmness' of the sonnet's ending (_loc. cit._ 248). Cp. K.'s description of the movement of a sonnet in the preceding poem, _To Charles Cowden Clarke_ 60–1 (p. 56 above).

32 'Keen, fitful gusts are whispering here and there'

Written Oct. or early Nov. 1816 after a visit to Leigh Hunt's cottage in the Vale of Health, Hampstead: K. first met Hunt between 9 and 27 Oct. 1816 – for the earlier date see K.'s letter to Cowden Clarke of 9 Oct. 1816, 'I can now devote any time you mention to the pleasure of seeing Mr. Hunt – 'twill be an Era in my existence' (*L* i 113); the later date is based on Benjamin Robert Haydon's being at Hampstead and frequently in Hunt's company *c*. 13–27 Oct. 1816, during which time he first met K. – see his letter to David Wilkie 27 Oct. 1816 (*Correspondence and Table Talk*, ed. F. W. Haydon 1876, i 309) and Haydon's *Autobiography* ed. T. Taylor (1853) 1926 edn. i 251.

Published *1817*.

> Keen, fitful gusts are whispering here and there
>   Among the bushes, half leafless and dry;
>   The stars look very cold about the sky,
> And I have many miles on foot to fare.
> 5 Yet feel I little of the cool bleak air,
>   Or of the dead leaves rustling drearily,
>   Or of those silver lamps that burn on high,
> Or of the distance from home's pleasant lair.
> For I am brimful of the friendliness
> 10   That in a little cottage I have found;
> Of fair-haired Milton's eloquent distress,
>   And all his love for gentle Lycid drowned;
> Of lovely Laura in her light green dress,
>   And faithful Petrarch gloriously crowned.

¶ 32. *1–4*. A recollection of the sharp night wind on the wintry heath at Hampstead – Cowden Clarke notes that the poem was written 'on the day after one of our visits' (*Recollections* 134). K. faced a walk of over five miles from Hunt's cottage at Hampstead to London where he lodged with his brothers (they lived together at Southwark *c*. 9 Oct.–*c*. 18 Nov. 1816, at Cheapside *c*. 18 Nov. 1816–*c*. 25 March 1817 and moved to Hampstead *c*. 25 March 1817).

3. Cp. *O thou whose face* 3 (p. 311 below), 'the freezing stars'.

8. home's pleasant lair] K.'s tranquil life with his brothers is recorded in *To my Brothers* (p. 65 below).

9. brimful] See *Endymion* iii 366 *n* (p. 221 below).

11–14. Topics discussed with Hunt at the cottage.

12. Lycid] Lycidas, Milton's name for Edward King.

13–14. Petrarch (1304–74) celebrated Laura in his *Rime in Vita e Morte di Madonna Laura*, a collection of odes and sonnets otherwise known as the *Canzoniere*. For the portrait of Petrarch and Laura in Hunt's cottage see *Sleep and Poetry* 389–91 (p. 85 below).

33 On Leaving Some Friends at an Early Hour

Probably written Oct.–early Nov. 1816 as one of the poems celebrating K.'s recent installation in Leigh Hunt's circle of friends at Hampstead. Woodhouse's uncompleted note on the poem runs 'Reynolds Hunt and [   ] in a hackney coach' (Sperry's *Woodhouse* (*1817*) 150).
K.'s undated draft (Morgan Library) has variants from *1817*, some of which are noted below.
Published *1817*.

>   Give me a golden pen, and let me lean
>   On heaped-up flowers, in regions clear and far.
>   Bring me a tablet whiter than a star,
>   Or hand of hymning angel when 'tis seen
> 5   The silver strings of heavenly harp atween.
>   And let there glide by many a pearly car,
>   Pink robes, and wavy hair, and diamond jar,
>   And half discovered wings, and glances keen.
>   The while let music wander round my ears,
> 10   And as it reaches each delicious ending
>   Let me write down a line of glorious tone
>   And full of many wonders of the spheres.
>   For what a height my spirit is contending!
>   'Tis not content so soon to be alone.

¶ 33. *1–4.*   Give me a golden pen and let me lean
                On heap'd up flowers in regions clear and calm
                Bring me a tablet whiter than the palm
                        Of a young Angel what time it is seen ... *Draft (cancelled)*
2. clear ... far] calm ... clear *Draft (cancelled)*.
4. hymning] young-eyed *Draft (cancelled)*. Cp. *The Merchant of Venice* V i 61–2,
                                    ... like an angel sings
                Still quiring to the young-eyed cherubins ...
7. Pink robes ... wavy ... diamond] Bright looks ... floating ... sapphire *Draft (cancelled)*. Thomas Hardy's suggested emendation for 'jar' in this line was 'tiar' (*Garrod*), but see K.'s reference to 'diamond vases' in *I stood tip-toe* 134 (p. 91 below) and note the rhyme in *Lamia* i 57–8 (p. 619 below),
                                    ... fire
                Sprinkled with stars, like Ariadne's tiar ...
8. discovered] seen *Draft (cancelled)*.

34 To my Brothers

Written 18 Nov. 1816 for Tom Keats's birthday: so dated in *1817* and see
the title in Tom's transcript, 'Written to his brother Tom on his Birthday'
(T. was born 18 Nov. 1799). K. and his brothers were probably in lodgings
at Cheapside by this date (see *Keen, fitful gusts* 1–4 *n*, p. 63 above). The
poem reflects the mood of Wordsworth four 'Personal Talk' sonnets
(1807), but is stylistically closer to Leigh Hunt's *Quiet Evenings*. *To Thomas
Barnes, Esq.* and *To T. M. Alsager, Esq.* (1815).

K.'s two fair copies and his pencil draft of ll. 1–8 (Huntington Library)
have minor variants from *1817*, some of which are noted below. For details
of the MSS see H. Rollins, *Harvard Library Bulletin* vi (Spring 1952) 161–3.
Published *1817*.

Small, busy flames play through the fresh-laid coals,
    And their faint cracklings o'er our silence creep
    Like whispers of the household gods that keep
A gentle empire o'er fraternal souls.
5 And while for rhymes I search around the poles,
    Your eyes are fixed, as in poetic sleep,
    Upon the lore so voluble and deep
That ay at fall of night our care condoles.
This is your birth-day, Tom, and I rejoice

¶ 34. *1. busy flames play*] flames are peeping *Draft*.
2. cracklings . . . creep] crackling . . . creeps *Draft*. One of K.'s two fair
copies has 'light' for 'faint'. Cp. Leigh Hunt's *Quiet Evenings* 10–11,
        Nought heard through all our little, lulled abode
        Save the crisp fire . . .
Hunt singled out K.'s line in his review of *1817*, third instalment, *Examiner*
13 July 1817, p. 443: see headnote to *O Solitude* (p. 23 above).
3. Like whisper of the household God that keeps *Draft*. The 'household
gods' are the Lares and Penates, tutelary deities of the home in Roman
mythology.
5. And while for rhymes I search] And while I am thinking of a Rhyme
Draft; And while I search for Rhyme *One of K.'s two fair copies*. K. searches
for his 'rhymes' like a discoverer voyaging over the world from pole to
pole.
6. fixed] fixéd *Draft*. Tom is absorbed in his books.
7. lore so] Pages *Draft*. The word 'voluble' was probably suggested by
Wordsworth's description of books and reading in his third 'Personal
Talk' sonnet, *Wings have we* 9–10,
        There find I personal themes, a plenteous store,
        Matter wherein right voluble I am . . .
8. condoles] Used transitively. See, for example, *Henry IV* II i 133,
        Let us condole the knight . . .

10   That thus it passes smoothly, quietly.
        Many such eves of gently whispering noise
            May we together pass, and calmly try
        What are this world's true joys, ere the great voice
        From its fair face shall bid our spirits fly.

13. the great voice] God (or perhaps death).

35 Addressed to Haydon

Written March–early Nov. 1816 before K. knew Haydon intimately: the
later date is suggested by the sonnet being less personal in tone than the
following poem, *Addressed to the Same* (p. 67 below), written after K.'s
initial visits to Haydon's studio 3 and 19 Nov. 1816; the earlier date is suggested by Wordsworth's celebration of Haydon's devotion to the cause of
art in *To B. R. Haydon* (*The Champion* 4 Feb. 1816, repr. *Examiner* 31 March
1816), and by the fact that in March 1816 a successful outcome had been
reached in the controversy over the Elgin Marbles—see ll. 11–12 n. For the
view that K. wrote the poem immediately after his first visit to Haydon see
Gittings (1968) 95.

  Benjamin Robert Haydon (1786–1846) had already gained a reputation
as a historical painter, notably with 'The Repose in Egypt', 'Dentatus' and
'The Judgment of Solomon'. He was working at this time on 'Christ's
Entry into Jerusalem' into which he subsequently incorporated portraits of
K., Wordsworth, Lamb and Hazlitt. For the ups and downs of his later
relationship with K. see *KC* i xc–xcii and *L* i 76–7, and for his influence on
K.'s interest in art, Ian Jack's *Keats and the Mirror of Art* (1967) 23–45.
The version of the poem in *Hood's Magazine* (1845) has minor variants from
1817, some of which are noted below.
Published *1817*.

        Highmindedness, a jealousy for good,
            A loving-kindness for the great man's fame,
            Dwells here and there with people of no name,
        In noisome alley, and in pathless wood.
5   And where we think the truth least understood,
            Oft may be found a 'singleness of aim'

¶ 35. *1–3* (and *9–10* below). K.'s reply to Wordsworth's *To B. R. Haydon* 8,
            . . . the whole world seems adverse to desert . . .

2. loving-kindness] Adoring kindness *Hood's Magazine*.

4. pathless] A word of which Shelley was fond, e.g. *Queen Mab* (1813, repr.
1816) ix 144, '. . . pathless wilderness' and *Alastor* (1816) 210, '. . . pathless
desert of dim sleep'.

6. 'singleness of aim'] A quotation from Wordsworth's *Character of the
happy warrior* (1807) 40,
            Keeps faithful with a singleness of aim . . .

> That ought to frighten into hooded shame
> A money-mongering, pitiable brood.
> How glorious this affection for the cause
> 10   Of steadfast genius, toiling gallantly!
> What when a stout unbending champion awes
> Envy and Malice to their native sty?
> Unnumbered souls breathe out a still applause,
> Proud to behold him in his country's eye.

11-12. A reference to Haydon's part in the controversy over the Elgin Marbles. Lord Elgin brought the Marbles from the Parthenon for his own collection 1803 and offered to sell them to the British Government 1811. Public debate about their authenticity, artistic merit and the rights and wrongs of keeping them in England ended early in 1816 when their purchase was recommended by a Government committee on the advice of a selected group of established British painters. Haydon was not among these, but won praise from friends for immediately recognizing and proclaiming the value of the Marbles, notably in his attack on Payne Knight for denying their authenticity, *Examiner* 17 March 1816 (see headnote to following poem, *Addressed to the Same*). On K.'s enthusiasm for the Marbles see *On Seeing the Elgin Marbles* (p. 104 below).

11. What when] What happens when.

36 Addressed to the Same ['Great Spirits']

Written 19 or 20 Nov. 1816: see K.'s letter to Benjamin Haydon of this date, 'Last Evening wrought me up and I cannot forbear sending you the following' (*L* i 117) and 21 Nov. 1816, containing another copy of the poem with a variant reading in l. 13 (*L* i 118-19); K. was at Haydon's studio on the evening of 19 Nov. 1816. Woodhouse records, 'The author had passed the evening in company with H. That night he could get no sleep. The next morning he sent Haydon this sonnet' (Sperry's *Woodhouse (1817)* 150). The poem is the second of K.'s three sonnets to Haydon (the third being *To B. R. Haydon*, p. 105 below) and echoes the exalted tone of Haydon's essay, 'The Judgment of Connoisseurs upon Works of Art . . . in reference . . . to the Elgin Marbles' (*The Examiner* 17 March 1816; repr. Tom Taylor's *Life of Benjamin Robert Haydon* (1853) 1926 edn i 332-40). K.'s holograph MS, dated 'Christ Day', and his two letters have minor variants from *1817*, some of which are noted below.
Published *1817*.

> Great spirits now on earth are sojourning:
>   He of the cloud, the cataract, the lake,
>   Who on Helvellyn's summit, wide awake,
> Catches his freshness from Archangel's wing;
> 5 He of the rose, the violet, the spring,
>   The social smile, the chain for freedom's sake;
>   And lo!—whose stedfastness would never take
> A meaner sound than Raphael's whispering.
> And other spirits there are standing apart
> 10   Upon the forehead of the age to come.
> These, these will give the world another heart
>   And other pulses. Hear ye not the hum
> Of mighty workings?——
>   Listen awhile ye nations, and be dumb.

¶ 36. *1. Great spirits*] The trio celebrated in the poem are Wordsworth (ll. 2–4), Leigh Hunt (ll. 5–6) and Haydon (ll. 7–8). Cp. Haydon's closing remarks in 'The Judgment of Connoisseurs . . .', 'I never enter among them [the Elgin Marbles] without bowing to the Great Spirit that reigns within them . . .'. The word 'now' is underlined in K.'s MS.
3. Helvellyn] The third highest mountain in the Lake District, rising at the head of Grasmere and often referred to by Wordsworth in his poems. See, for example, *To Joanna* (1800) 61,
> Helvellyn far into the clear blue sky . . .
5. Characterizing Hunt's poetry, as Wordsworth's is characterized in l. 2.
6. the chain for freedom's sake] A reference to Hunt's imprisonment for libel 1813–15. See headnote to *Written on the Day that Mr. Leigh Hunt left Prison* (p. 11 above).
7–8. Obscurely expressed, but K. means that Haydon is comparable with Raphael. Leigh Hunt celebrated Haydon as the successor of Michael Angelo and Raphael in his Oct. 1816 sonnet *To Benjamin Robert Haydon* 3–5,
> Fit to be numbered in succession due
> With Michael, whose idea austerely presses,
> And sweet-souled Raphael . . .
9. there are] *are there K.'s two letter copies. K.'s MS. agrees with 1817.*
10. forehead] Used only once again as a metaphor by K., *Endymion* i 801–2 (p. 155 below),
> . . . high
> Upon the forehead of humanity . . .
11–14. Cp. the prophetic ardour of Haydon's peroration in 'The Judgment of Connoisseurs . . .', for example: 'Such a blast will Fame blow of their grandeur, that its roaring will swell out as time advances . . . nations now sunk in barbarism, and ages yet unborn, will . . . be aroused by its thunder, and . . . refined by its harmony.'
13. Of mighty workings?——] Originally 'Of mighty Workings in a distant

Mart ?' (K.'s MS. and first letter), but altered at Haydon's suggestion. See
K.'s letter to him 21 Nov. 1816, 'My feelings entirely fall in with yours in
regard to the Elipsis and I glory in it' (*L* i 118).

37 Sleep and Poetry

Written after *c.* 9 Oct. (when K. met Hunt) and probably completed Dec.
1816: for the earlier date see *Cowden Clarke* 133–4, 'It was in the library at
Hunt's cottage, where an extemporary bed had been made up for him on
the sofa, that he [K.] composed the framework and many lines of the poem
. . . the last sixty or seventy being an inventory of the art garniture of the
room;' the later date is suggested by the resemblance in style to the following poem, *I stood tip-toe*. The poem, which is the last piece in *1817*, contains
K.'s first serious attempt to outline his poetic ambitions and represents his
most substantial achievement in longer poems up to this time. It was
enthusiastically received by K.'s friends, including Haydon (*L* i 125), Hunt
(review of *1817*) and Woodhouse, who composed a sonnet *To Apollo,
written after reading Keats's 'Sleep and Poetry'* (*Woodhouse* 3, Sperry's *Woodhouse* (1817) 152). Commentaries on the poem include those in Bridges's
introduction to *The Poems of John Keats*, ed. G. Thorn Drury (1896) xxxii–
ix; *Colvin* (1917) 114–29; *Murry* (1926) 17–26; and Ian Jack's *Keats and the
Mirror of Art* (1967) 130–40.
Text from *1817* (no MSS of the poem exist).
Published *1817*.

> As I lay in my bed slepe full unmete
> Was unto me, but why that I ne might
> Rest I ne wist, for there n'as erthly wight
> [As I suppose] had more of hertis ese
> Than I, for I n'ad sicknesse nor disese.
>
> CHAUCER

What is more gentle than a wind in summer?
What is more soothing than the pretty hummer
That stays one moment in an open flower
And buzzes cheerily from bower to bower?
5   What is more tranquil than a musk-rose blowing
In a green island, far from all men's knowing?

¶ 37. *Motto. The Floure and the Leafe* 17–21. On the attribution of this poem
to Chaucer and the edition used by K. see headnote to *Written on the blank
space of a leaf at the end of Chaucer's tale 'The Floure and the Leafe'* (p. 103
below).

1–10. A catalogue of Keatsian 'luxuries'. Cp. *I stood tip-toe* 27–8 (p. 87
below),

> . . . I straightway began to pluck a posy
> Of luxuries . . .

5. See *To a Friend who Sent me Some Roses* 6 *n* (p. 47 above).

4+K.

More healthful than the leafiness of dales?
More secret than a nest of nightingales?
More serene than Cordelia's countenance?
10   More full of visions than a high romance?
What, but thee, Sleep? Soft closer of our eyes!
Low murmurer of tender lullabies!
Light hoverer around our happy pillows!
Wreather of poppy buds and weeping willows!
15   Silent entangler of a beauty's tresses!
Most happy listener when the morning blesses
Thee for enlivening all the cheerful eyes
That glance so brightly at the new sun-rise!

But what is higher beyond thought than thee?
20   Fresher than berries of a mountain tree?
More strange, more beautiful, more smooth, more regal,
Than wings of swans, than doves, than dim-seen eagle?
What is it? And to what shall I compare it?
It has a glory, and naught else can share it.
25   The thought thereof is awful, sweet and holy,

11–18. The catalogue element in K.'s first tribute to sleep suggests an Elizabethan influence—see, for example, Sidney's *Come sleep! O sleep, the certain knot of peace, Astrophel and Stella* sonnet 39. K. may also have been influenced by Iris's address to Morpheus, the god of sleep, in Ovid's *Metamorphoses* xi 623–6,

> somne, quiese rerum, placidissime, Somne, deorum,
> pax animi, quem cura fugit, qui corpora duris
> fessa ministeriis mulces reparasque labori . . .

('O Sleep, thou rest of all things, Sleep, mildest of the gods, balm of the soul, who puttest care to flight, soothest our bodies worn with hard ministries, and preparest them for toil again' [Loeb edn].) K.'s other references to sleep include the well-known sonnet *To Sleep* (p. 510 below); see also *Endymion* i 453–64, ii 703–6 (pp. 140 and 193 below).

13–14. The sleep of the happy is light, but the grief-stricken sleep heavily as if drugged. The poppy is traditionally associated with Morpheus; see Ovid's description of his cave, *Metamorphoses* xi 605,

> ante fores antri fecunda papavera florent . . .

('Before the cavern's entrance abundant poppies bloom' [Loeb edn].) 'To wear the willow' is to be forsaken, as in *Much Ado about Nothing* II i 215–16, 'I offered him my company to a willow tree . . . to make him a garland, as being forsaken'.

16. Most happy listener!] Sleep, as he receives thanks from the morning for his healing gift to man.

19. The answer is poetry, which K. attempts to define in the subsequent lines. His association of sleep and poetry in this poem is in keeping with his frequent description of imaginative experience as a state of trance or reverie.

Chasing away all worldliness and folly,
Coming sometimes like fearful claps of thunder,
Or the low rumblings earth's regions under;
And sometimes like a gentle whispering
30 Of all the secrets of some wondrous thing
That breathes about us in the vacant air,
So that we look around with prying stare,
Perhaps to see shapes of light, aërial limning
And catch soft floatings from a faint-heard hymning,
35 To see the laurel wreath on high suspended
That is to crown our name when life is ended.
Sometimes it gives a glory to the voice,
And from the heart up-springs, 'Rejoice! Rejoice!'—
Sounds which will reach the Framer of all things,
40 And die away in ardent mutterings.

No one who once the glorious sun has seen,
And all the clouds, and felt his bosom clean
For his great Maker's presence, but must know
What 'tis I mean and feel his being glow.
45 Therefore no insult will I give his spirit
By telling what he sees from native merit.

O Poesy! For thee I hold my pen
That am not yet a glorious denizen
Of thy wide heaven. Should I rather kneel
50 Upon some mountain-top until I feel
A glowing splendour around about me hung,
And echo back the voice of thine own tongue?
O Poesy! For thee I grasp my pen
That am not yet a glorious denizen
55 Of thy wide heaven. Yet, to my ardent prayer,
Yield from thy sanctuary some clear air,
Smoothed for intoxication by the breath
Of flowering bays, that I may die a death
Of luxury and my young spirit follow

On traditional ideas concerning this state and K.'s individual experience of
it see J. R. Caldwell's 'The bardic trance' in his *John Keats's Fancy* (1945)
9–17.
28. rumblings] Altered to 'rumbleings' by Woodhouse in his copy of *1817*
with note '3 syllables' (Sperry's *Woodhouse (1817)* 153).
33. shapes of light, aërial limning] Spirits delicately limned or outlined.
48. denizen] 'An alien admitted to citizenship by royal letters patent, 1576'
OED).
58–9. die a death | Of luxury] Die of an excess of pleasure. On 'luxury' as a
term used by Leigh Hunt see *Calidore* 92 *n* (p. 40 above).

60   The morning sunbeams to the great Apollo
      Like a fresh sacrifice; or, if I can bear
      The o'erwhelming sweets, 'twill bring to me the fair
      Visions of all places. A bowery nook
      Will be elysium—an eternal book
65   Whence I may copy many a lovely saying
      About the leaves and flowers, about the playing
      Of nymphs in woods and fountains, and the shade
      Keeping a silence round a sleeping maid,
      And many a verse from so strange influence
70   That we must ever wonder how and whence
      It came. Also imaginings will hover
      Round my fire-side, and haply there discover
      Vistas of solemn beauty, where I'd wander
      In happy silence, like the clear Meander
75   Through its lone vales, and where I found a spot
      Of awfuller shade, or an enchanted grot,
      Or a green hill o'erspread with chequered dress
      Of flowers and, fearful from its loveliness,
      Write on my tablets all that was permitted,
80   All that was for our human senses fitted.
      Then the events of this wide world I'd seize
      Like a strong giant, and my spirit tease
      Till at its shoulders it should proudly see
      Wings to find out an immortality.
85   Stop and consider! Life is but a day;

66–7. *the playing / Of nymphs in woods and fountains*] A stock decorative flourish, but perhaps echoing here Milton's *Comus* 119–21,

       By dimpled Brook, and Fountains brim
       The Wood-Nymphs deckt with Daisies trim,
       Their merry wakes and pastimes keep . . .

69–70. Cp. Wordsworth. *To the Daisy* ('In youth from rock to rock . . .' 1807) 70–1,

       A happy, genial influence,
       Coming one knows not how, nor whence . . .

71–2. *imaginings will hover / Round my fireside*] See *To my Brothers* (p. 65 above).
74. *Meander*] Maeander, the name in classical antiquity for a river of Asia Minor flowing into the Aegean Sea and celebrated for its winding course.
77–9. Cp. K.'s similar description of himself writing on the hill-top overlooking the sea at Margate in *To my Brother George* 123–6 (p. 53 above).
81. Woodhouse notes, 'in order to describe them' (Sperry's *Woodhouse* (*1817*) 153).
82. *tease*] Tantalize; cp. *Ode on a Grecian Urn* 44 (p. 537 below),
       Thou, silent form, dost tease us out of thought . . .

A fragile dew-drop on its perilous way
From a tree's summit; a poor Indian's sleep
While his boat hastens to the monstrous steep
Of Montmorenci. Why so sad a moan?
90   Life is the rose's hope while yet unblown;
The reading of an ever-changing tale;
The light uplifting of a maiden's veil;
A pigeon tumbling in clear summer air;
A laughing school-boy, without grief or care,
95   Riding the springy branches of an elm.

Oh, for ten years, that I may overwhelm
Myself in poesy; so I may do the deed
That my own soul has to itself decreed.
Then will I pass the countries that I see
100   In long perspective, and continually
Taste their pure fountains. First the realm I'll pass
Of Flora and old Pan: sleep in the grass,

88–9. steep | Of Montmorenci] The falls of Montmorenci in Quebec. K.'s
source for this reference has not been identified.

96–154. A Keatsian recapitulation of the successive stages of personal development in Wordsworth's *Tintern Abbey* (1798), foreshadowing the
'simile of human life as far as I now perceive it . . . a large Mansion of
Many Apartments' described in K.'s letter to Reynolds 3 May 1818 (*L* i
280–1). According to Woodhouse, some of whose comments on the lines
are recorded below, the passage lists the different kinds of poetry K. planned
to write in the successive stages of his career (Sperry's *Woodhouse (1817)*
153–4).

99. 'Then I will apply myself in turn to all the species of poetry'–Woodhouse's gloss (*loc. cit.* 153).

101–21. The period of simple enjoyment in sensuous pleasure. Cp. K.'s
letter to Reynolds 3 May 1818, 'We no sooner get into . . . the Chamber
of Maiden-Thought than we become intoxicated with the light and atmosphere, we see nothing but pleasant wonders, and think of delaying there
for ever in delight' (*L* i 281). The pictorial imagery echoes in some details
William Browne's arcadian scenes in *Britannia's Pastorals* ii Song 3, but may
also owe something to Nicholas Poussin's painting 'L'Empire de Flore'.
For reproductions of this painting and discussion of its influence on K. see
Ian Jack's ' "The realm of Flora" in Keats and Poussin', *TLS* (19 April
1959) 201, 212 and his *Keats and The Mirror of Art* (1967) Frontispiece, 135–8.
101–2. Woodhouse notes, 'Pastoral . . . or rather rural poetry' (*loc. cit.*
153).

102. Flora . . . Pan] Flora was the 'goddess of flowers and gardens' (*Lemprière*) and Pan the god of universal nature. For K.'s 'Hymn to Pan' see
Endymion i 232–306 (pp. 130–33 below).

Feed upon apples red and strawberries,
And choose each pleasure that my fancy sees;
105   Catch the white-handed nymphs in shady places
To woo sweet kisses from averted faces,
Play with their fingers, touch their shoulders white
Into a pretty shrinking with a bite
As hard as lips can make it, till, agreed,
110   A lovely tale of human life we'll read.
And one will teach a tame dove how it best
May fan the cool air gently o'er my rest;
Another, bending o'er her nimble tread,
Will set a green robe floating round her head,
115   And still will dance with ever varied ease,
Smiling upon the flowers and the trees;
Another will entice me on and on
Through almond blossoms and rich cinnamon,
Till in the bosom of a leafy world
120   We rest in silence, like two gems upcurled
In the recesses of a pearly shell.

And can I ever bid these joys farewell?
Yes, I must pass them for a nobler life,
Where I may find the agonies, the strife
125   Of human hearts—for lo! I see afar,
O'ersailing the blue cragginess, a car

113–16. Cp. the pose of the central figure in Poussin's 'L'Empire de Flore'.
K. had probably looked at engravings of Poussin when in Hunt's company.
See Hunt, '. . . shall we *read* an engraving from Poussin. . . . ?' (*Indicator*
20 Oct. 1819) and Ian Jack's discussion of the importance of prints from old
masters for Hunt and his friends in *Keats and the Mirror of Art* 7–9.
122–54. K. follows Wordsworth in seeing individual development as a
progress from unreflecting delight in nature to a deeper understanding of
human life. Cp. *Tintern Abbey* 88–93,

> . . . I have learned
> To look on nature, not as in the hour
> Of thoughtless youth; but hearing often-times
> The still, sad music of humanity . . .

and see another passage in K.'s letter to Reynolds 3 May 1818 on the effect
of remaining in the Chamber of Maiden-Thought as 'sharpening one's
vision into the heart and nature of Man . . . convincing one's nerves that the
World is full of Misery and Heartbreak, Pain, Sickness and oppression. . . .
This Chamber of Maiden Thought becomes gradually darken'd. . . . We
feel the "burden of the Mystery" [see *Tintern Abbey* 38]. To this point was
Wordsworth come . . . when he wrote "Tintern Abbey" ' (*L* i 281).
123–4. 'Epic poetry'—Woodhouse's note (*loc. cit.* 154).

And steeds with streamy manes—the charioteer
Looks out upon the winds with glorious fear.
And now the numerous tramplings quiver lightly
130 Along a huge cloud's ridge, and now with sprightly
Wheel downward come they into fresher skies,
Tipped round with silver from the sun's bright eyes,
Still downward with capacious whirl they glide.
And now I see them on the green hill's side
135 In breezy rest among the nodding stalks.
The charioteer with wondrous gesture talks
To the trees and mountains, and there soon appear
Shapes of delight, of mystery, and fear,
Passing along before a dusky space
140 Made by some mighty oaks; as they would chase
Some ever-fleeting music on they sweep.
Lo! how they murmur, laugh, and smile, and weep—
Some with upholden hand and mouth severe;
Some with their faces muffled to the ear
145 Between their arms; some, clear in youthful bloom,
Go glad and smilingly athwart the gloom;
Some looking back, and some with upward gaze.
Yes, thousands in a thousand different ways
Flit onward—now a lovely wreath of girls
150 Dancing their sleek hair into tangled curls,

126-8. Perhaps suggested by details in Poussin's paintings 'L'Empire de
Flore' and 'La Vie Humaine', both of which show a chariot with four
horses being driven by Apollo across the sky. K. uses the image as a symbol
of the creative imagination. In the subsequent lines the charioteer descends
to earth and experiences his visions of 'delight . . . mystery, and fear . . .'
(l. 138) after a period spent in responding to nature.
127-8. the charioteer . . . fear] Woodhouse notes, 'Personification of the
Epic poet, when the enthusiasm of inspiration is upon him . . .' (*loc. cit.* 154).
131. wheel] Wheeling.
135. stalks] Woodhouse comments, 'poetical expression for trees' (*loc. cit.*
154).
137-8. there soon . . . a fear] Woodhouse notes, 'for him to describe' (*loc.
cit.* 154).
138-40. Shapes . . . oaks] Perhaps a half-recollection of Wordsworth's *Yew-Trees* (1815) 23-8,

> . . . beneath whose sable roof
>   . . . ghostly Shapes
> May meet at noon-tide; Fear and trembling Hope,
> Silence and Foresight; Death the Skeleton
> And Time the Shadow . . .

And now broad wings. Most awfully intent,
The driver of those steeds is forward bent
And seems to listen. Oh, that I might know
All that he writes with such a hurrying glow.
155 The visions all are fled—the car is fled
Into the light of heaven, and in their stead
A sense of real things comes doubly strong,
And, like a muddy stream, would bear along
My soul to nothingness. But I will strive
160 Against all doubtings and will keep alive
The thought of that same chariot and the strange
Journey it went.

                Is there so small a range
In the present strength of manhood, that the high
Imagination cannot freely fly
165 As she was wont of old? Prepare her steeds,
Paw up against the light, and do strange deeds
Upon the clouds? Has she not shown us all
From the clear space of ether to the small
Breath of new buds unfolding? From the meaning
170 Of Jove's large eye-brow to the tender greening
Of April meadows? Here her altar shone,
E'en in this isle, and who could paragon
The fervid choir that lifted up a noise
Of harmony, to where it ay will poise
175 Its mighty self of convoluting sound,
Huge as a planet, and like that roll round,

151–3. Most awfully . . . listen] Woodhouse notes, 'Here he is supposed to
write what he sees and hears' (*loc. cit.* 154).
157–9. A sense of real things . . . nothingness] A romantic reaction to the
difference between the ideal and the actual. Cp. *Endymion* ii 274–6 (pp.
174–5 below),

             . . . when new wonders ceased to float before
        And thoughts of self come on, how crude and sore
        The journey homeward to habitual self! . . .

162–229. K. turns to the development of English poetry—from the greatness of the Elizabethans and their seventeenth-century successors (ll. 171–80)
through a period of decline in the later seventeenth and the eighteen century
(ll. 181–206) to the renewed promise of his own times (221–9).
168. ether] The sky.
172. paragon] Surpass. An Elizabethan poeticism, e.g. *Othello* II i 61–2,

                . . . a maid
        That paragons description . . .

173–7. The poetry of the Elizabethans is seen as a planet which contributes
to the music of the spheres.

Eternally around a dizzy void?
Aye, in those days the Muses were nigh cloyed
With honours, nor had any other care
180   Than to sing out and soothe their wavy hair.

Could all this be forgotten? Yes, a schism
Nurtured by foppery and barbarism
Made great Apollo blush for this his land.
Men were thought wise who could not understand
185   His glories; with a puling infant's force
They swayed about upon a rocking horse
And thought it Pegasus. Ah, dismal souled!
The winds of heaven blew, the ocean rolled
Its gathering waves—ye felt it not. The blue
190   Bared its eternal bosom and the dew
Of summer nights collected still to make
The morning precious. Beauty was awake!
Why were ye not awake? But ye were dead
To things ye knew not of—were closely wed
195   To musty laws lined out with wretched rule
And compass vile, so that ye taught a school
Of dolts to smooth, inlay, and clip, and fit,
Till, like the certain wands of Jacob's wit,

178. cloyed] Surfeited. K.'s most familiar use of this word is in *Ode on a Grecian Urn* 29 (p. 536 below),

    . . . a heart high-sorrowful and cloyed . . .

180. soothe] sooth *1848*. K.'s regular spelling of the verb in all his early poems. The meaning here is 'smooth'. Cp. *Isabella* 403 (p. 347 below), 'calmed it's wild hair' and *The Eve of St. Agnes* 266 *n* (p. 471 below).

181–206. K.'s attack on the Augustan poets whom he sees as a body of schismatics who have cut themselves off from the central poetic tradition. The attack pleased Leigh Hunt (*Examiner* review of *1817*), but angered Byron.

186–7. A reference to the use of the heroic couplet by eighteenth-century poets. See Hazlitt on Milton, 'Dr. Johnson and Pope would have converted his vaulting Pegasus into a rocking horse' ('On Milton's versification', *Examiner* 20 Aug. 1815, repr. *The Round Table* 1817; *Works*, ed. P. P. Howe 1930, iv 40).

189–90. The blue / Bared its eternal bosom] Echoing Wordsworth, *The world is too much with us* (1807) 5,

    The Sea that bares her bosom to the moon . . .

198. The wands were from different kinds of tree, but were all partly stripped to reveal the white and were all used for the same purpose. For 'Jacob's wit', i.e. the stratagem by which he increased his wealth at the expense of Laban, see *Genesis* xxx 27–43.

4*

Their verses tallied. Easy was the task—
200 A thousand handicraftsmen wore the mask
Of Poesy. Ill-fated, impious race
That blasphemed the bright Lyrist to his face
And did not know it! No, they went about,
Holding a poor, decrepit standard out
205 Marked with most flimsy mottoes, and in large
The name of one Boileau!

                              O ye whose charge
It is to hover round our pleasant hills!
Whose congregated majesty so fills
My boundly reverence that I cannot trace
210 Your hallowed names in this unholy place,
So near those common folk—did not their shames
Affright you? Did our old lamenting Thames
Delight you? Did ye never cluster round
Delicious Avon, with a mournful sound,
215 And weep? Or did ye wholly bid adieu
To regions where no more the laurel grew?
Or did ye stay to give a welcoming
To some long spirits who could proudly sing
Their youth away, and die? 'Twas even so.
220 But let me think away those times of woe.
Now 'tis a fairer season. Ye have breathed
Rich benedictions o'er us, yet have wreathed
Fresh garlands, for sweet music has been heard
In many places. Some has been upstirred
225 From out its crystal dwelling in a lake,
By a swan's ebon bill; from a thick brake,

202. *the bright Lyrist*] Apollo.
206. *Boileau*] Nicolas Boileau (1636–1711), French poet and critic, whose
L'Art Poétique (1674) is the fullest expression of neo-classical principles.
206–7. *O ye . . . hills*] The poets. Cp. *Bards of passion and of mirth* 2 (p. 446
below),
                    Ye have left your souls on earth . . .
209. *boundly*] Either bounden or boundless. According to W. T. Arnold
(*The Poetical Works of John Keats* (1888) xliv) a coinage probably formed on
the model of the seventeenth-century use of adjectives ending in '——ly',
for example Browne's *Britannia's Pastorals*, Book i Song 4 663, 'about the
edges of whose roundly form . . .'.
218. *some lone spirits*] Woodhouse notes, 'alluding to H[enry] Kirke White
[1785–1806]–Chatterton [1752–70]–and other poets of great promise,
neglected by the age, who died young' (*loc. cit.* 155).
226. *By a swan's ebon bill*] Woodhouse notes, 'Wordsworth, who resides
near one of the lakes in Cumberland' (*loc. cit.* 155). See ll. 233–5 *n* below.

Nested and quiet in a valley mild,
Bubbles a pipe—fine sounds are floating wild
About the earth. Happy are ye and glad.

230   These things are doubtless. Yet in truth we've had
Strange thunders from the potency of song,
Mingled indeed with what is sweet and strong
From majesty, but in clear truth the themes
Are ugly clubs, the poets Polyphemes
235   Disturbing the grand sea. A drainless shower
Of light is Poesy; 'tis the supreme of power;
'Tis might half slumbering on its own right arm.
The very archings of her eye-lids charm
A thousand willing agents to obey,
240   And still she governs with the mildest sway.
But strength alone, though of the Muses born,
Is like a fallen angel. Trees uptorn,

226–8. *from a . . . pipe*] According to Woodhouse, 'Leigh Hunt's poetry is here alluded to, in terms too favourable' (*loc. cit.* 155).

230. *doubtless*] Beyond doubt.

231. Woodhouse glosses 'Allusion to Lord Byron, and his terrific style of poetry–to Christabel by Coleridge etc.' (*loc. cit.* 155). See following *n.*

233–5. *the themes . . . grand sea*] Modern poets are like Homer's one-eyed giant Polyphemus (*Odyssey* ix), they handle themes as roughly as Polyphemus handles his club. De Selincourt maintains probably correctly that K. is referring to Byron and 'the contrast which his stormy poetry affords with the serenity of Wordsworth or the cheerful chirping of Hunt' (for K.'s later mixed feelings about Wordsworth see his letter to Reynolds, 3 Feb. 1818, *L* i 223–4). K. may also, as Woodhouse suggests, have had Coleridge in mind; cp. Hunt's reading the lines in his review of *1817* as a comment on 'the morbidity that taints the productions of the Lake Poets' (*Examiner* 13 July 1817) and the review of Coleridge's *Christabel* in *The Examiner* 2 June 1816, 'There is something disgusting at the bottom of his subject, which is but ill glossed over by a veil of Della Cruscan sentiment and fine writing–like moonbeams playing over a charnel-house or flowers strewed on a dead body' (349).

236. *supreme of power*] Power barely exerted (cp. l. 240 below).

237. Possibly inspired by the Elgin Marbles, to which Woodhouse refers in his gloss (*loc. cit.* 155), but the phrasing suggests a recollection of Coleridge's *The Eolian Harp* (1796) 32–3,

> . . . the mute still air
> Is Music slumbering on her instrument . . .

239. Perhaps echoing Milton's sonnet *When I consider how my light is spent* 12, quoted in *As from the darkening gloom* 11–13 *n* (p. 9 above).

241–2. Woodhouse notes, 'alluding still to Lord Byron' (*loc. cit.* 155).

Darkness and worms and shrouds and sepulchres
Delight it, for it feeds upon the burrs
245 And thorns of life, forgetting the great end
Of Poesy, that it should be a friend
To soothe the cares and lift the thoughts of man.

Yet I rejoice; a myrtle, fairer than
E'er grew in Paphos, from the bitter weeds
250 Lifts its sweet head into the air, and feeds
A silent space with ever sprouting green.
All tenderest birds there find a pleasant screen,
Creep through the shade with jaunty fluttering,
Nibble the little cuppèd flowers and sing.
255 Then let us clear away the choking thorns
From round its gentle stem; let the young fawns,
Yeaned in after times, when we are flown,
Find a fresh sward beneath it, overgrown
With simple flowers; let there nothing be
260 More boisterous than a lover's bended knee;
Nought more ungentle than the placid look
Of one who leans upon a closèd book;
Nought more untranquil than the grassy slopes
Between two hills. All hail delightful hopes!
265 As she was wont, the imagination
Into most lovely labyrinths will be gone,
And they shall be accounted poet-kings

243–7. Darkness, and worms . . . delight it] A reference to the current taste for Byronic melancholy and Gothic sensationalism.
244–7. for it feeds . . . man] K. must mean that poetry of this sort feeds self-indulgently on the dark side of life. This would be in keeping with his statement in ll. 122–5 above, but his praise of Huntian poetry in ll. 248–69 leads to what seems to be an advocacy of simple escapism (see ll. 267–8).
246–7. a friend . . . of man] Poetry should console human suffering. Cp. *Ode on a Grecian Urn* 47–8 (p. 537 below),

Thou shalt remain, in midst of other woe
Than ours, a friend to man . . .

248–69. K.'s account of the promising elements in modern poetry reads like a tribute to Leigh Hunt.
249. Paphos] A city in Cyprus, celebrated for its temple to Venus.
257. Yeaned] Born or brought forth (used of sheep, goats and kids).
266. labyrinths] Intricacies of poetic thought. Cp. *To Georgiana Wylie* 4 (p. 99 below), 'the labyrinths of sweet utterance', and *On Receiving a Laurel Crown from Leigh Hunt* 2–3 (p. 109 below),

Nothing unearthly has enticed my brain
Into a delphic labyrinth . . .

Who simply tell the most heart-easing things.
Oh, may these joys be ripe before I die.

270 Will not some say that I presumptuously
Have spoken? That from hastening disgrace
'Twere better far to hide my foolish face?
That whining boyhood should with reverence bow
Ere the dread thunderbolt could reach? How?
275 If I do hide myself, it sure shall be
In the very fane, the light of Poesy.
If I do fall, at least I will be laid
Beneath the silence of a poplar shade,
And over me the grass shall be smooth-shaven,
280 And there shall be a kind memorial graven.
But off, despondence! Miserable bane!
They should not know thee, who, athirst to gain
A noble end, are thirsty every hour.
What though I am not wealthy in the dower
285 Of spanning wisdom; though I do not know
The shiftings of the mighty winds that blow
Hither and thither all the changing thoughts
Of man; though no great ministering reason sorts
Out the dark mysteries of human souls
290 To clear conceiving—yet there ever rolls
A vast idea before me, and I glean
Therefrom my liberty. Thence too I've seen
The end and aim of Poesy. 'Tis clear
As anything most true: as that the year
295 Is made of the four seasons; manifest
As a large cross, some old cathedral's crest,

270-311. K.'s confession of his own immaturity and high poetic ambitions.
276. Cp. *To Mary Frogley* 6 (p. 29 above),
                    In the very fane of lightness . . .
284-90. *What though I am not wealthy . . . clear conceiving*] K. is aware of the
limitations of his own intellect and also of the intellect itself as an instrument for penetrating truth. See *To J. H. Reynolds, Esq.* 74-6 (p. 324 below),
                    . . . Oh, never will the prize,
                High reason and the lore of good and ill,
                Be my award . . .
and K.'s letter to Benjamin Bailey 22 Nov. 1817, 'I am certain of nothing
but of the holiness of the Heart's affections and the truth of Imagination
. . . I have never yet been able to perceive how anything can be known for
truth by consequitive reasoning' (*L* i 184-5).
290-3. *there ever rolls . . . aim of poesy*] K.'s 'vast idea' is not defined, but his
ideal conception frees him from the sense of being fettered by his ignorance
and strengthens his belief in the importance of poetry.

Lifted to the white clouds. Therefore should I
Be but the essence of deformity,
A coward, did my very eye-lids wink
300   At speaking out what I have dared to think.
Ah, rather let me like a madman run
Over some precipice! Let the hot sun
Melt my Dedalian wings and drive me down
Convulsed and headlong! Stay! An inward frown
305   Of conscience bids me be more calm awhile.
An ocean dim, sprinkled with many an isle,
Spreads awfully before me. How much toil,
How many days, what desperate turmoil,
Ere I can have explored its widenesses.
310   Ah, what a task! Upon my bended knees,
I could unsay those—no, impossible!
Impossible!

For sweet relief I'll dwell
On humbler thoughts and let this strange assay
Begun in gentleness die so away.
315   E'en now all tumult from my bosom fades.
I turn full-hearted to the friendly aids
That smooth the path of honour: brotherhood
And friendliness, the nurse of mutual good;
The hearty grasp that sends a pleasant sonnet
320   Into the brain ere one can think upon it;
The silence when some rhymes are coming out;

302–3. Let the hot sun / Melt my Dedalian wings] Daedalus made wings for himself and his son Icarus so that they might escape from exile in Crete by flying through the air; Icarus fell from the sky when he soared too near the sun, which melted the wax securing his wings. The story is related in Ovid's *Metamorphoses* viii 183–235, but K. may have known it first from the version in *Lemprière*.

306–9. K. on the threshold of experience is like an explorer setting off into the unknown. Cp. the imagery of exploration and discovery in *On First Looking into Chapman's Homer* (p. 60 above).

306. 'The ocean of poetry'–Woodhouse's note (*loc. cit.* 157).

311. I could unsay those–] I could unsay those vows I have uttered.

313. assay] Attempt.

312–30. Familiar details of K.'s association with Hunt. For K.'s disenchantment with Hunt by spring 1817 see his letter to Haydon 11 May 1817, 'I could not be deceived in the Manner that Hunt is ... There is no greater Sin after the 7 deadly than to flatter oneself into the idea of being a great Poet–or one of those beings who ... wear out their Lives in the pursuit of Honor' (*L* i 143).

And when they're come, the very pleasant rout;
The message certain to be done tomorrow –
'Tis perhaps as well that it should be to borrow
325 Some precious book from out its snug retreat,
To cluster round it when we next shall meet.
Scarce can I scribble on; for lovely airs
Are fluttering round the room like doves in pairs,
Many delights of that glad day recalling
330 When first my senses caught their tender falling.
And with these airs come forms of elegance
Stooping their shoulders o'er a horse's prance,
Careless and grand; fingers soft and round
Parting luxuriant curls; and the swift bound
335 Of Bacchus from his chariot, when his eye
Made Ariadne's cheek look blushingly.
Thus I remember all the pleasant flow
Of words at opening a portfolio.

Things such as these are ever harbingers
340 To trains of peaceful images: the stirs
Of a swan's neck unseen among the rushes;
A linnet starting all about the bushes;
A butterfly, with golden wings broad parted,
Nestling a rose, convulsed as though it smarted
345 With over pleasure – many, many more,
Might I indulge at large in all my store
Of luxuries. Yet I must not forget
Sleep, quiet with his poppy coronet,
For what there may be worthy in these rhymes
350 I partly owe to him. And thus the chimes
Of friendly voices had just given place
To as sweet a silence, when I 'gan retrace
The pleasant day, upon a couch at ease.
It was a poet's house who keeps the keys

322. rout] Congratulatory clamour.
335–6. Bacchus . . . Ariadne] Bacchus, the god of wine and revelry, consoled
Ariadne, daughter of King Minos of Crete, after she had been abandoned
on the island of Naxos by Theseus (see Ovid, *Metamorphoses* viii 172–82).
K.'s description of Bacchus's 'swift bound . . . from his chariot' is based on
Titian's 'Bacchus and Ariadne' exhibited at the British Institution in 1816.
On K.'s enthusiasm for this painting see W. Sharp, *Life and Letters of Joseph
Severn* (1892) 32.
348. See 13–14 *n* above.
354–91. K.'s 'inventory of the art garniture' in Hunt's cottage in the Vale
of Health at Hampstead (see headnote). The various pictures and busts cannot be identified, but K.'s descriptions in ll. 360–80 suggest in some details

355   Of pleasure's temple. Round about were hung
      The glorious features of the bards who sung
      In other ages—cold and sacred busts
      Smiled at each other. Happy he who trusts
      To clear futurity his darling fame!
360   Then there were fauns and satyrs taking aim
      At swelling apples with a frisky leap
      And reaching fingers, 'mid a luscious heap
      Of vine-leaves. Then there rose to view a fane
      Of liny marble, and thereto a train
365   Of nymphs approaching fairly o'er the sward:
      One, loveliest, holding her white hand toward
      The dazzling sun-rise; two sisters sweet
      Bending their graceful figures till they meet
      Over the trippings of a little child;
370   And some are hearing, eagerly, the wild
      Thrilling liquidity of dewy piping.
      See, in another picture, nymphs are wiping
      Cherishingly Diana's timorous limbs;
      A fold of lawny mantle dabbling swims
375   At the bath's edge and keeps a gentle motion
      With the subsiding crystal, as when ocean
      Heaves calmly its broad swelling smoothness o'er
      Its rocky marge, and balances once more
      The patient weeds that now unshent by foam
380   Feel all about their undulating home.

      Sappho's meek head was there half smiling down
      At nothing; just as though the earnest frown
      Of overthinking had that moment gone
      From off her brow and left her all alone.

385   Great Alfred's, too, with anxious, pitying eyes,

Poussin's 'Bacchus and Ariadne' (ll. 360–3), Claude's 'Landscape with the
Father of Psyche sacrificing at the Milesian Temple of Apollo' (ll. 363–71)
and Titian's 'Diana and Actaeon' (ll. 372–80). For a discussion of paintings
possibly influencing these lines see Ian Jack's *Keats and the Mirror of Art* 132–3.
364. liny] Full of lines, veined. The word was normally used in the early
nineteenth century to mean 'resembling a line, thin, meagre' (*OED*).
376–80. The passage foreshadows K.'s more mature style.
379. unshent] Undisfigured.
381. Sappho's meek head] A bust of the Greek poetess (born Lesbos *c.*
612 B.C.).
383. overthinking] Thinking over or perhaps thinking too much.
385. Great Alfred] Alfred the Great. For K.'s earlier references to him see
To George Felton Mathew 67–9 *n* (p. 27 above).

As if he always listened to the sighs
Of the goaded world; and Kosciusko's worn
By horrid suffrance, mightily forlorn.

Petrarch, outstepping from the shady green,
390   Starts at the sight of Laura; nor can wean
His eyes from her sweet face. Most happy they!
For over them was seen a free display
Of out-spread wings, and from between them shone
The face of Poesy. From off her throne
395   She overlooked things that I scarce could tell.
The very sense of where I was might well
Keep sleep aloof, but more than that there came
Thought after thought to nourish up the flame
Within my breast, so that the morning light
400   Surprised me even from a sleepless night,
And up I rose refreshed and glad and gay,
Resolving to begin that very day
These lines; and howsoever they be done,
I leave them as a father does his son.

387. Kosciusko] For the Polish patriot Kosciusko (1746–1817) see headnote
to *To Kosciusko* (p. 99 below).
389–91. On Petrarch and Laura see *Keen, fitful gusts* 13–14 *n* (p. 63 above).

38 'I stood tip-toe upon a little hill'

Completed Dec. 1816: so dated in draft and fair copy. According to Leigh
Hunt the poem was 'suggested by a delightful summer-day, as [K.]
stood beside the gate that leads from the Battery on Hampstead Heath into
a field of Caen Wood' (*Lord Byron and some of his Contemporaries*, 1828,
249). The view that the first part of the poem was drafted spring–summer
1816 receives some support from the stylistic parallels in ll. 1–115 with
Calidore (p. 36 above), but K.'s descriptions of spring and early summer in
the poem are not confined to his 1816 experiences–there are recollections
of the countryside around Edmonton in ll. 61–106. K. referred to the poem
as 'Endymion' in his letter to Cowden Clarke 17 Dec. 1816, 'I have done
little to Endymion lately–I hope to finish it in one attack' (*L* i 121), and at
this time was obviously still thinking of expanding the summary treatment
of the myth in ll. 181–242. See also Haydon's letter to Wordsworth 31 Dec.
1816, '[K.] is now writing a longer sort of poem of "Diana and Endymion"
to publish with his smaller productions' (*Correspondence and Table Talk*, ed.
F. W. Haydon (1876) ii 30). But the descriptions in ll. 1–115–in which
fancy is less important than sensitive observation–constitute the most
valuable part of the poem. K. placed the poem first in *1817*.

Text from *1817*, with some variants noted from K.'s fair copy and his draft (on the location of the various fragments of the draft and their bearing on the composition of the poem see *Garrod* lxxxiv–lxxviii; for the fragment containing ll. 1–6, 19–23 – recorded as missing in *Garrod* – see *KShJ* x Winter 1962, 12–13).
Published *1817*.

> *Places of nestling green for poets made*
> *Story of Rimini*

I stood tip-toe upon a little hill,
The air was cooling, and so very still
That the sweet buds which with a modest pride
Pull droopingly, in slanting curve aside,
5   Their scantly leaved and finely tapering stems,
Had not yet lost those starry diadems
Caught from the early sobbing of the morn.
The clouds were pure and white as flocks new shorn,
And fresh from the clear brook; sweetly they slept
10 On the blue fields of heaven, and then there crept
A little noiseless noise among the leaves,
Born of the very sigh that silence heaves,
For not the faintest motion could be seen
Of all the shades that slanted o'er the green.
15 There was wide wandering for the greediest eye,
To peer about upon variety;
Far round the horizon's crystal air to skim,
And trace the dwindled edgings of its brim;
To picture out the quaint and curious bending
20 Of a fresh woodland alley, never ending;
Or by the bowery clefts and leafy shelves

¶ 38. *Motto.* Leigh Hunt's *The Story of Rimini* iii 430.
1. He who has lingered in a *Draft* (cancelled).
7. early sobbing of the morn] The morning dew. Cp. K.'s use of 'sobbing' in *Endymion* i 331 (p. 134 below), 'the sobbing rain'.
10–14. then . . . green] Cp. *Hyperion* i 7–9 (p. 397 below),
> . . . No stir of air was there,
> Not so much life as on a summer's day
> Robs not one light seed from the feathered grass . . .

10–12. there crept . . . leaves] '. . . a fancy founded . . . on a strong sense of what really exists or occurs' – Hunt's comment in his review of *1817*.
13. faintest] gentlest *Draft*.
17. Far round the crystal Horizon to skim *Fair copy*; To leap into the crystal Horison *Draft* (cancelled).
18. dwindled] little *Draft*.
21. Probably suggested by Leigh Hunt's *The Story of Rimini* iii 473 – see *Calidore 26 n* (p. 37 above).

Guess where the jaunty streams refresh themselves.
I gazed awhile and felt as light and free
As though the fanning wings of Mercury
25 Had played upon my heels; I was light-hearted,
And many pleasures to my vision started.
So I straightway began to pluck a posy
Of luxuries bright, milky, soft and rosy.

A bush of May flowers with the bees about them—
30 Ah, sure no tasteful nook would be without them—
And let a lush laburnum oversweep them,
And let long grass grow round the roots to keep them
Moist, cool and green; and shade the violets,
That they may bind the moss in leafy nets.

35 A filbert hedge with wild briar overtwined,
And clumps of woodbine taking the soft wind
Upon their summer thrones; there too should be
The frequent chequer of a youngling tree,
That, with a score of light green brethren, shoots
40 From the quaint mossiness of agèd roots,
Round which is heard a spring-head of clear waters
Babbling so wildly of its lovely daughters
The spreading blue-bells—it may haply mourn
That such fair clusters should be rudely torn
45 From their fresh beds, and scattered thoughtlessly
By infant hands, left on the path to die.

22. *refresh*] embower *Fair copy.* The word 'jaunty' is substituted for 'nestling' in the draft: Woodhouse's gloss is 'wandering' (Sperry's *Woodhouse* (*1817*) 141).

24. *the fanning wings of Mercury*] See *Lemprière*, '[Mercury] was presented by the king of heaven with a winged cap called *petasus* and wings for his feet called *talaria* . . .'.

25-7.   Had started to my heels – This pleasant Earth
             Is filled with loveliness of glorious birth
             Nor were it a bad task to pluck Posey . . . *Draft*

28. *luxuries*] See *Calidore* 92 *n* (p. 40 above).

30. *tasteful nook*] Cp. Hunt's *Politics and poetics* (1811; repr. *The Feast of the Poets* 1815) 72,

             Oh for a seat in some poetic nook . . .

31. *lush*] 'Deep coloured' – Woodhouse's gloss (Sperry's *Woodhouse* (1817) 141).

38. The patterned shadows cast by the branches of a sapling. Cp. K.'s use of 'chequer' in *To my Brother George* 126, quoted in l. 68 *n* below.

39. *a score of light green brethren shoots*] many of its light green peers *Draft* (cancelled).

46. *By infant hands*] By Urchin's Hand *Draft*.

Open afresh your round of starry folds,
Ye ardent marigolds!
Dry up the moisture from your golden lids,
50   For great Apollo bids
That in these days your praises should be sung
On many harps, which he has lately strung.
And when again your dewiness he kisses,
Tell him I have you in my world of blisses,
55   So haply when I rove in some far vale,
His mighty voice may come upon the gale.

Here are sweetpeas, on tip-toe for a flight,
With wings of gentle flush o'er delicate white,
And taper fingers catching at all things
60   To bind them all about with tiny rings.

Linger awhile upon some bending planks
That lean against a streamlet's rushy banks
And watch intently Nature's gentle doings—
They will be found softer than ring-dove's cooings.

47–8. The style and rhythm of K.'s invocation are suggested by Spenser's
Epithalamion, for example 204–5,

> Open the temple gates unto my love,
> Open them wide that she may enter in . . .

and 114–15,

> Set all your things in seemly good aray
> Fit for so joyfull day . . .

47. Come ye bright Marigolds *Draft (cancelled).*
49. from] of *Fair copy.*
52. A reference to the renewed promise of modern poetry–see *Sleep and
Poetry* 162–229 *n* (p. 76 above).
57.   Sweet Peas that seem on tip-toe for a flight . . . *Draft.*
The line is substituted in the draft for 'Sweet Peas with gentle flush o'er
delicate white . . .'. The sweetpeas are like butterflies.
59. taper fingers] slender hands *Draft (cancelled).* The tendrils of sweetpeas.
60. with tiny rings] with neat encircleings *Draft (cancelled).*
61–106. Wanting in the draft. According to Cowden Clarke, the passage
was inspired by 'the recollection of our having frequently loitered over the
rail of a foot-bridge that spanned . . . a little brook in the last field upon
entering Edmonton . . . [K.] . . . thought the picture correct and acknowledged a partiality for it' (*Recollections* 138–9)–K. left Edmonton *c.* Oct.
1815. For the view that the lines were written during K.'s stay in Margate
Aug.–Sept. 1816 see *Ward* (1963) 420–1.
64. Followed in the draft by

> The inward ear will ear [sic] her and be blest
> And tingle with a joy too light for rest . . .

The word 'her' is substituted for 'them' cancelled.

65   How silent comes the water round that bend,
      Not the minutest whisper does it send
      To the o'erhanging sallows; blades of grass
      Slowly across the chequered shadows pass—
      Why, you might read two sonnets ere they reach
70   To where the hurrying freshnesses ay preach
      A natural sermon o'er their pebbly beds,
      Where swarms of minnows show their little heads,
      Staying their wavy bodies 'gainst the streams,
      To taste the luxury of sunny beams
75   Tempered with coolness. How they ever wrestle
      With their own sweet delight, and ever nestle
      Their silver bellies on the pebbly sand.
      If you but scantily hold out the hand,
      That very instant not one will remain—
80   But turn your eye, and they are there again.
      The ripples seem right glad to reach those cresses
      And cool themselves among the emerald tresses.
      The while they cool themselves, they freshness give
      And moisture, that the bowery green may live:
85   So keeping up an interchange of favours,
      Like good men in the truth of their behaviours.
      Sometimes goldfinches one by one will drop
      From low-hung branches; little space they stop—
      But sip, and twitter, and their feathers sleek,
90   Then off at once, as in a wanton freak,
      Or perhaps, to show their black and golden wings,

67. *sallows*] Willows. Used again in *Endymion* ii 341, iv 392 and *To Autumn* 28 (pp. 176, 261 and 654 below).

68. *chequered shadows*] Cp. *To my Brother George* 126 and *n* (p. 53 above),
        Chequer my tablet with their quivering shades . . .

71. Cp. *As You Like It* II ii 16–17,
        . . . tongues in trees, books in the running brook,
          Sermons in stones . . .

74. *To taste the luxury*] That they may taste the warmth *Draft*.

82. *emerald*] amber *Draft (cancelled)*

87–8. *Sometimes . . . branches*] Woodhouse notes a parallel (Sperry's *Woodhouse (1817)* 141) in *The Floure and the Leafe* 89–90,
        Therein a goldfinch leaping pretile
        Fro bough to bough . . .
See *Sleep and Poetry*, note to *Motto* (p. 69 above).

90. Cp. *Calidore* 14 (p. 37 above),
        The freaks and dartings of the black-winged swallow . . .

91–2.   And as they come and go but mark their wings
          So lovely for their yellow flutterings . . . *Draft (cancelled)*.

Pausing upon their yellow flutterings.
Were I in such a place, I sure should pray
That naught less sweet might call my thoughts away,
95   Than the soft rustle of a maiden's gown
Fanning away the dandelion's down;
Than the light music of her nimble toes
Patting against the sorrel as she goes.
How she would start, and blush, thus to be caught
100   Playing in all her innocence of thought.
Oh, let me lead her gently o'er the brook,
Watch her half-smiling lips, and downward look;
Oh, let me for one moment touch her wrist;
Let me one moment to her breathing list;
105   And as she leaves me may she often turn
Her fair eyes looking through her locks auburn.
What next? A tuft of evening primroses,
O'er which the mind may hover till it dozes;
O'er which it well might take a pleasant sleep,
110   But that 'tis ever startled by the leap
Of buds into ripe flowers; or by the flitting
Of diverse moths, that aye their rest are quitting;
Or by the moon lifting her silver rim
Above a cloud, and with a gradual swim
115   Coming into the blue with all her light.
O Maker of sweet poets, dear delight
Of this fair world and all its gentle livers,
Spangler of clouds, halo of crystal rivers,
Mingler with leaves and dew and tumbling streams,
120   Closer of lovely eyes to lovely dreams,

96. Fanning] Sweeping *Draft.*
102. downward] A favourite word in K.'s early poems, e.g. *To Mary Frogley*
19, *Sleep and Poetry* 131, 133 (pp. 30, 75 above), *Endymion* i 584, ii 87, 526,
iii 673, iv 384 (pp. 146, 167, 185, 232, and 261 below). See further *To
Georgiana Augusta Wylie* 1 *n* (p. 99 below).
114. with a gradual swim] Cp. *On First Looking into Chapman's Homer* 10
(p. 62, above), 'a new planet swims into his ken'.
115.   Floating through space with ever loving eye
        The crowned queen of ocean and the sky . . . *Draft.*
The word 'crowned' is substituted for 'night' cancelled.
116–24 (and *184–210* below). Like all the Romantic poets K. responds with
special feeling to the moon's appeal to his imagination; Woodhouse records
Cowden Clarke's recollection that 'one of the earliest things J.K. wrote was
a sonnet to the moon' (note dated 21 Aug. 1823, *Woodhouse* 3). In these passages K. anticipates *Endymion* in celebrating the moon's peculiar power
over his poetic imagination.

Lover of loneliness and wandering,
Of upcast eye and tender pondering!
Thee must I praise above all other glories
That smile us on to tell delightful stories.
125 For what has made the sage or poet write
But the fair paradise of Nature's light?
In the calm grandeur of a sober line
We see the waving of the mountain pine;
And when a tale is beautifully stayed,
130 We feel the safety of a hawthorn glade;
When it is moving on luxurious wings,
The soul is lost in pleasant smotherings—
Fair dewy roses brush against our faces
And flowering laurels spring from diamond vases;
135 O'er head we see the jasmine and sweet briar,
And bloomy grapes laughing from green attire;
While at our feet the voice of crystal bubbles
Charms us at once away from all our troubles,
So that we feel uplifted from the world,
140 Walking upon the white clouds wreathed and curled.

122. Followed in the draft by the cancelled lines,

    Smiler on Lovers when they smile on thee
    Thee must I place among these pleasures
    Thee must I praise above all other things
    That give our thought a pair of little wings . . .

125-6. For unreflecting delight in nature as a stage in poetic development see *Sleep and Poetry* 101-21 *n.* (p. 73 above).
127-40. Art reflects nature's grandeur (ll. 127-8), tranquillity (ll. 129-30) and richness (ll. 131-40).
128. An image possessing a strong appeal for K. Cp. his invocation to Pan, *Endymion* i 260-2 (p. 131 below),

               . . . be quickly near,
    By every wind that nods the mountain pine,
    O forester divine . . .

129. *stayed*] Grave, sedate.
132. *smotherings*] Overwhelming delights.
134. *vases*] For K.'s pronunciation see *To Mary Frogley* 56 *n* (p. 31 above).
141-204. Myths and legends originate in imaginative response to the beauties of nature–K. singles out the legends of Eros and Psyche (ll. 141-50), Pan and Syrinx (ll. 157-62), Narcissus and Echo (ll. 163-80) and Endymion and Phoebe (ll. 181-204). The passage is influenced by Wordsworth's *The Excursion* iv 347-87, which suggests that the figures of Apollo, Diana and various rural deities were called into being by imaginative response to the sun, moon and various familiar natural objects–see Hazlitt's quotation of and commentary on this passage in his 'Observations on . . . *The Excursion*'

So felt he who first told how Psyche went
On the smooth wind to realms of wonderment;
What Psyche felt, and Love, when their full lips
First touched; what amorous and fondling nips
145   They gave each other's cheeks; with all their sighs,
And how they kissed each other's tremulous eyes;
The silver lamp–the ravishment–the wonder–
The darkness–loneliness–the fearful thunder;
Their woes gone by, and both to heaven upflown
150   To bow for gratitude before Jove's throne.
So did he feel, who pulled the boughs aside
That we might look into a forest wide
To catch a glimpse of Fauns and Dryades
Coming with softest rustle through the trees,
155   And garlands woven of flowers wild and sweet,
Upheld on ivory wrists or sporting feet:

(*Examiner* 21 and 28 Aug. 1814, *Works*, ed. P. P. Howe 1930, iv 114–15),
and on K.'s special fondness for the descriptions of Apollo and of the hunter
calling to the moon (*Excursion* iv 857–64) see M. Moorman's *William Wordsworth: The Later Years* (1965) 315–15. K.'s renewed interest in mythology at
the end of 1816 may also owe something to Leigh Hunt's current project
to retell Greek legends in the style of his *The Story of Rimini.*

141–50. The legend of Eros and Psyche was probably first known to K.
from classical reference books read at school–see headnote to *Endymion* (p.
116 below)–and later from allusions in Elizabethan writers and from Mary
Tighe's *Psyche* (see *To Some Ladies* 20 *n*, p. 19 above). For his later interest
in the legend see headnote to *To Psyche* (pp. 514–15 below).

141. first told] Marked by Woodhouse with the note 'Apuleius' (Sperry's
Woodhouse (*1817*) 141); cp. headnote to the *Ode to Psyche* (p. 514 below).

142. wonderment] Woodhouse notes, 'the concluding word of *Endymion*
[see p. 284 below]' (*loc. cit.* 141).

147–8. Dramatizes the contrast between Psyche's moment of delight when
she broke her vow and saw Eros for the first time by the light of her lamp,
and her desolation and fear when Eros abandoned her.

149–50. After many hardships Psyche was reunited with Eros and received
with him among the immortals.

151–2. Marked by Woodhouse with the note, 'Ovid' (*loc. cit.* 141).

153. Fauns and Dryades] Satyrs and nymphs of the woods. Satyrs were
country deities, half man and half goat, usually associated in classical mythology with Pan. See Wordsworth's account of the origin of Pan and the
satyrs, and of Naiads and Oreads (water nymphs and mountain nymphs), in
The Excursion iv 871–87.

156. Followed in draft by the lines,

> One Sunbeam comes the Solitude to bless
> Widening it slants arthwart the Duskiness

Telling us how fair trembling Syrinx fled
Arcadian Pan, with such a fearful dread.
Poor nymph, poor Pan – how he did weep to find
160 Nought but a lovely sighing of the wind
Along the reedy stream, a half-heard strain
Full of sweet desolation, balmy pain.

What first inspired a bard of old to sing
Narcissus pining o'er the untainted spring?
165 In some delicious ramble he had found
A little space, with boughs all woven round,
And in the midst of all a clearer pool
Than e'er reflected in its pleasant cool
The blue sky here and there serenely peeping
170 Through tendril wreaths fantastically creeping.
And on the bank a lonely flower he spied,

And where it plays upon the turfy Mould
There sleeps a Nest of Hair wavy and gold . . .

157–62. The legend of Pan and Syrinx is related in Ovid's *Metamorphoses* i
689–712.

159–62. Syrinx became a reed. Cp. Ovid's *Metamorphoses* i 705–8,

> *Panaque cum prensam sibi iam Syringa putaret,*
> *corpore pro nymphae calamos tenuisse palustres,*
> *dumque ibi suspirat, motos in harundine ventos*
> *effecisse sonum tenuem similemque querenti . . .*

('. . . and how Pan, when now he thought he had caught Syrinx, instead of
her held naught but marsh reeds in his arms; and while he sighed in disappointment, the soft air stirring in the reeds gave forth a low and complaining sound' [Loeb edn]).

161. a half heard strain] Substituted in the draft for the cancelled readings,

> 1. how desolate how wild
> 2. how desolate how lone

163–80. The legend of Narcissus and Echo is related in Ovid's *Metamorphoses* iii 339–510.

167–8. Woodhouse notes (*loc. cit.* 141) the similar construction in Thomson's *The Seasons* (1730) *Summer* 1300–01,

> Meantime, this fairer nymph than ever blest
> Arcadian stream . . .

171–4. Narcissus was transformed into a flower after he had died of despairing love for his own image reflected in the water. See Ovid's *Metamorphoses*
iii 509–10,

> *nusquam corpus erat: croceum pro corpore florem*
> *inveniunt foliis medium cingentibus albis . . .*

('his body was nowhere to be found. In place of his body they find a flower,
its yellow centre girt with white petals' [Loeb edn].)

A meek and forlorn flower, with naught of pride,
Drooping its beauty o'er the water clearness
To woo its own sad image into nearness.
175 Deaf to light Zephyrus it would not move,
But still would seem to droop, to pine, to love.
So while the poet stood in this sweet spot,
Some fainter gleamings o'er his fancy shot,
Nor was it long ere he had told the tale
180 Of young Narcissus, and sad Echo's bale.
Where had he been, from whose warm head out-flew
That sweetest of all songs, that ever new,
That ay refreshing pure deliciousness,
Coming ever to bless
185 The wanderer by moonlight? To him bringing
Shapes from the invisible world, unearthly singing
From out the middle air, from flowery nests,
And from the pillowy silkiness that rests
Full in the speculation of the stars.
190 Ah, surely he had burst our mortal bars,
Into some wond'rous region he had gone
To search for thee, divine Endymion!

171–3. Woodhouse (*loc. cit.* 141) quotes the similar image in Ronsard's
Amours Diverses xv, 'Amour tu me fis voir pour trois grandes merveilles'
10–11,

> ... semblait une fleur, voisine d'un ruisseau,
>
> Qui mire dans ses eaux ses riches vermeilles ...

For K.'s knowledge of Ronsard see *Translated from Ronsard* (p. 383 below).
173. watery clearness] deepness fair *Draft* (*cancelled*).
174. sad] fair *Fair copy.*
175. Zephyrus] One of the winds–usually the west wind. See *Lemprière*,
'The same as the Favonius of the Latins ... said to produce flowers and
fruits by the sweetness of his breath ... supposed to be the same as the west
wind.'
180. sad Echo's bale] Echo was spurned by Narcissus and pined away.
181–204. On K.'s sources for the legend of Endymion and Phoebe see
headnote to *Endymion* (pp. 116–17 below).
186. unearthly] delicious *Fair copy.* With 'Shapes from the invisible
world ...' cp. Wordsworth's *Excursion* iv 1144,

> Authentic tidings of invisible things ...

189–92.   Or slowly moves about the Heavens–where

> Where Had he been to catch a Thing so fair–
>
> Into what Regions was his spirit gone
>
> When he first thought of thee Endymion? ... *Draft.*

189. speculation] Sight. '[K.] almost always used the word ... with the
meaning ... of "contemplation" or "simple vision"' ('Keats' use of
"speculation"', *Murry* (1930) 93).

He was a poet, sure a lover too,
Who stood on Latmos' top, what time there blew
195 Soft breezes from the myrtle vale below,
And brought in faintness solemn, sweet and slow
A hymn from Dian's temple; while, upswelling,
The incense went to her own starry dwelling.
But though her face was clear as infant's eyes,
200 Though she stood smiling o'er the sacrifice,
The poet wept at her so piteous fate,
Wept that such beauty should be desolate.
So in fine wrath some golden sounds he won,
And gave meek Cynthia her Endymion.

205 Queen of the wide air! Thou most lovely queen
Of all the brightness that mine eyes have seen!
As thou exceedest all things in thy shine,
So every tale does this sweet tale of thine.
Oh, for three words of honey, that I might
210 Tell but one wonder of thy bridal night!

Where distant ships do seem to show their keels,

193–5. Crossed out in the draft.
194. Latmos] The mountain in Caria, Asia Minor, where the shepherd
Endymion was visited by Phoebe (Cynthia), the goddess of the moon. K.
describes it more fully in *Endymion* i 63–88 (p. 123 below).
199–204. The legend of Endymion and Phoebe was inspired by the thought
of the lonely beauty of the moon.
203. So from Apollo's Lyre a tone he won . . . *Fair copy.*
204. meek] bright *Fair copy.* On K.'s early fondness for the word 'meek'
when describing women see *Endymion* iii 46 *n* (p. 208 below). With its use
here cp. Wordsworth on the moon, *The Shepherd looking Eastward* (1815)
13–14,

> Who meekly yields, and is obscured – content
> With one calm triumph of a modest pride.

For K.'s probable earlier echo of Wordsworth's poem see *Calidore* 157 *n*
(p. 42 above).
205–42. K. begins his unfinished attempt to recreate the story of Endymion
and Phoebe by celebrating their wedding night, which he sees as a period of
universal happiness, health and love.
207. shine] Brightness. Woodhouse (*loc. cit.* 142) notes the use of the word in
Shakespeare's *Venus and Adonis* 488,

> As if from thence they borrow'd all their shine . . .

and 728,

> Cynthia for shame obscures her silver shine . . .

Phoebus awhile delayed his mighty wheels
And turned to smile upon thy bashful eyes,
Ere he his unseen pomp would solemnize.
215   The evening weather was so bright and clear
That men of health were of unusual cheer,
Stepping like Homer at the trumpet's call
Or young Apollo on the pedestal,
And lovely women were as fair and warm
220   As Venus looking sideways in alarm.
The breezes were ethereal and pure,
And crept through half-closed lattices to cure
The languid sick; it cooled their fevered sleep,
And soothed them into slumbers full and deep.
225   Soon they awoke clear-eyed, nor burnt with thirsting,
Nor with hot fingers, nor with temples bursting,
And springing up, they met the wondering sight
Of their dear friends, nigh foolish with delight,
Who feel their arms and breasts, and kiss and stare,
230   And on their placid foreheads part the hair.
Young men and maidens at each other gazed
With hands held back, and motionless, amazed
To see the brightness in each other's eyes;
And so they stood, filled with a sweet surprise,
235   Until their tongues were loosed in Poesy.
Therefore no lover did of anguish die,
But the soft numbers, in that moment spoken,
Made silken ties that never may be broken.
Cynthia! I cannot tell the greater blisses
240   That followed thine and thy dear shepherd's kisses:
Was there a poet born?—But now no more,
My wandering spirit must no further soar.

217. Stepping with such an elegance withall . . . *Fair copy; Draft.*
218. Or] Like *Fair copy; Draft.* The description of Apollo 'on the pedestal'
is a reference to the Apollo Belvedere–K. knew the full-page illustration in
Spence (Plate XI).
220. As Venus bending from her Car dove drawn . . .*Draft (cancelled).*
With the revised reading cp. Thomson on the Venus de Medici, *Liberty*
(1734–6) iv 177–8,

> Bashful she bends, her well-taught look aside
> *Turns in enchanting guise . . .*

221–30. Perhaps recollected from walking the wards at St Thomas's Hospital.
223. sleep] dreams *Draft (cancelled).*
227. And springing up, they] So up they sprang and *Fair copy.*
230. foreheads] temples *Fair copy.*

39 Written in Disgust of Vulgar Superstition

Written Sunday 22 Dec. 1816: '24 Dec. 1816' in Tom Keats's transcript but 24 Dec. 1816 fell on a Tuesday; Cowden Clarke records, '[K.] wrote [the sonnet] on Sunday morning as I stood by his side' (*KC* ii 154); K.'s undated holograph MS. is subscribed in another hand, 'Written by JK in 15 minutes'.
Published *1876*.

The church bells toll a melancholy round,
    Calling the people to some other prayers,
    Some other gloominess, more dreadful cares,
More hearkening to the sermon's horrid sound.
5   Surely the mind of man is closely bound
    In some black spell, seeing that each one tears
    Himself from fireside joys and Lydian airs,
And converse high of those with glory crowned.
Still, still they toll, and I should feel a damp,
10   A chill as from a tomb, did I not know
    That they are going like an outburnt lamp;
    That 'tis their sighing, wailing ere they go
    Into oblivion; that fresh flowers will grow,
And many glories of immortal stamp.

¶ 39. *Title*. From Tom Keats's transcript. K.'s MS is untitled.
3. Some other gloominess, more dreadful] To fill their breasts with fear and gloomy *K.'s MS (cancelled)*.
7. Lydian airs] Miltonic echo. See *To George Felton Mathew* 17–18 *n* (p. 25 above).
8. Echoing Thomson's 'converse with the mighty dead', *Winter* 432. See *To my Brother George* 72 *n* (p. 51 above).
10. tomb] sepulchre *K.'s MS (cancelled)*.
11. going] dying *Tom Keat's transcript*.

40 On the Grasshopper and Cricket

Written 30 Dec. 1816: so dated in K.'s holograph copy (Forster Collection) and *1817*. Woodhouse records, 'The author and Leigh Hunt challenged each other to write a sonnet in a Quarter of an hour. – The Grasshopper and Cricket was the subject. – Both performed the task within the time allotted' (Sperry's *Woodhouse (1817)* 151); according to Cowden Clarke, 'Keats won as to time' (*Recollections* 135). For other poems by K. written in

contests with Leigh Hunt see *On Receiving a Laurel Crown, On Seeing a Lock of Milton's Hair, To the Nile* (pp. 109, 292, and 307 below).
Published *1817*.

The poetry of earth is never dead.
    When all the birds are faint with the hot sun
    And hide in cooling trees, a voice will run
From hedge to hedge about the new-mown mead—
5   That is the Grasshopper's. He takes the lead
    In summer luxury; he has never done
    With his delights, for when tired out with fun
He rests at ease beneath some pleasant weed.
The poetry of earth is ceasing never.
10   On a lone winter evening, when the frost
        Has wrought a silence, from the stove there shrills
    The cricket's song, in warmth increasing ever,
        And seems to one in drowsiness half lost,
        The grasshopper's among some grassy hills.

¶ 40. *1*. 'Such a prosperous opening'–Hunt's comment recorded in *Cowden Clarke* 135.
10–11. *On a lone winter evening . . . silence*] 'Ah! that's perfect! Bravo Keats!'–Hunt's comment recorded in *Cowden Clarke* 136. Cp. Coleridge's *Frost at Midnight* (1798) 1–2,

> The Frost performs its secret ministry,
> Unhelped by any wind . . .

and 8–12,

> . . . so calm, that it disturbs
> And vexes meditation with its strange
> And extreme silentness.

41 To Georgiana Augusta Wylie

Written Dec. 1816 for K.'s future sister-in-law: date attached to Tom Keats's transcript. Georgiana Wylie (*c.* 1797–1879) married George Keats May 1818 and emigrated with him to America June 1818. K. probably wrote the sonnet at George's request (see *To my Brother George* 121 *n*, p. 53 above), but the poem obviously expresses K.'s own affection; see his letter to Benjamin Bailey 10 June 1818, 'I had known my sister in law some time before she was my sister and was very fond of her' (*L* i 293) and his Oct. 1818 journal-letter, 'If you were here my dear Sister I could not pronounce the words which I write . . . from a distance: I have a tenderness for you and an admiration . . . as great and more chaste than I can have for any woman in the world' (*L* i 392). Henry Stephens described Georgiana Wylie's appear-

ance as 'Rather short, not what might be called strictly handsome, but
looked like a being whom any man of moderate sensibility might easily
love' (*KC* ii 212). On the question of her age (probably nineteen) in late
1816 see *Gittings* (1968) 106. K.'s undated holograph MS largely agrees
with *1817*.
Published *1817*.

    Nymph of the downward smile and sidelong glance,
       In what diviner moments of the day
       Art thou most lovely? When gone far astray
    Into the labyrinths of sweet utterance,
5   Or when serenely wandering in a trance
       Of sober thought? Or, when starting away
       With careless robe to meet the morning ray,
    Thou sparest the flowers in thy mazy dance?
    Haply 'tis when thy ruby lips part sweetly
10   And so remain, because thou listenest—
    But thou to please wert nurtured so completely
       That I can never tell what mood is best.
    I shall as soon pronounce which Grace more neatly
       Trips it before Apollo than the rest.

¶ 41. *Title.* To Miss Wylie *K.'s MS.* To G.A.W. *1817.*
1. Cp. Thomson's *The Seasons* (1730) *Summer* 1280,
         In sidelong glances from her downcast eye . . .
On K.'s fondness for the word 'downward' see *I stood tip-toe* 102 *n* (p. 90
above).
4. labyrinths] See *Sleep and Poetry* 266 *n* (p. 80 above).
7–8. See *I stood tip-toe* 94–8 (p. 90 above),
         That naught less sweet might call my thoughts away,
         Than the soft rustle of a maiden's gown
         Fanning away the dandelion's down;
         Than the light music of her nimble toes
         Patting against the sorrel as she goes . . .

42 To Kosciusko

Written Dec. 1816: date attached to the poem in *The Examiner* 16 Feb. 1817.
Tadeusz Kosciusko (1746–1817), a Polish patriot admired by English liber-
als, fought as a volunteer in the United States army in the American War of
Independence and led his countrymen in their rising against Russia (1791–
94). Hunt kept a bust of him in his cottage–see *Sleep and Poetry* ll. 387–8 (p.
85 above)–and celebrated him in a sonnet (*Examiner* 19 Nov. 1815).
    This and the following poem appear as the last in the series of seventeen

Petrarchan sonnets printed together in *1817*. The version in *The Examiner*
largely agrees with *1817*.
Published *The Examiner* 16 Feb. 1817; repr. *1817*.

> Good Kosciusko, thy great name alone
>   Is a full harvest whence to reap high feeling;
>   It comes upon us like the glorious pealing
> Of the wide spheres—an everlasting tone.
> 5 And now it tells me that in worlds unknown
>   The names of heroes burst from clouds concealing
>   And change to harmonies, for ever stealing
> Through cloudless blue and round each silver throne.
> It tells me too, that on a happy day,
> 10 When some good spirit walks upon the earth,
>   Thy name, with Alfred's and the great of yore
>   Gently commingling, gives tremendous birth
> To a loud hymn, that sounds far, far away
>   To where the great God lives for evermore.

¶ 42. *3–4. glorious pealing | Of the wide spheres*] Cp. *To my Brother George* 4
and *n* (p. 49 above), 'sphery strains'.
7. And change] Are changed *Examiner*; And changed *1817*. The reading follows Woodhouse's emendation in his copy of *1817* (see Sperry's *Woodhouse*
(1817) 152).
8. and round] around *Examiner*.
11. Thy name, with Alfred's] See *Sleep and Poetry* 385–8 (pp. 84–5 above).

43 'Happy is England! I could be content'

Probably written winter 1816 as one of a series of sonnets produced by K.
at this time: see the four preceding poems, *Written in Disgust of Vulgar Superstition*, *On the Grasshopper and Cricket*, *To Georgiana Augusta Wylie*, *To Kos-
cuisko* (Nos. 39–42 above), all of which were written Dec. 1816. K.'s undated holograph MS agrees with *1817* except for minor variations in punctuation.
Published *1817*.

> Happy is England! I could be content
>   To see no other verdure than its own,
>   To feel no other breezes than are blown
> Through its tall woods with high romances blent.
> 5 Yet do I sometimes feel a languishment
>   For skies Italian, and an inward groan

¶ 43. *3–4.* For K.'s later expression of his romantic feeling for 'tall woods'
see *Hyperion* i 73–4 and *n* (p. 401 below).

To sit upon an Alp as on a throne,
And half forget what world or worldling meant.
Happy is England, sweet her artless daughters,
10   Enough their simple loveliness for me,
      Enough their whitest arms in silence clinging.
    Yet do I often warmly burn to see
      Beauties of deeper glance, and hear their singing,
And float with them about the summer waters.

7. *an Alp*] Woodhouse cites marginally (Sperry's *Woodhouse* (1817) 152)
Paradise Lost ii 620,

        O're many a Frozen, many a Fierie Alp . . .
and also *Endymion* i 665–6 (p. 149 below),
            . . . there was store
        Of newest joys upon that Alp . . .

44 'After dark vapours have oppressed our plains'

Written 31 Jan. 1817: so dated in *Woodhouse* 1, 2 and *1848*. Text follows the
transcripts and also *1848* (except for Milnes's correction).
Published *The Examiner* 23 Feb. 1817; repr. *1848*.

After dark vapours have oppressed our plains
    For a long dreary season, comes a day
    Born of the gentle South, and clears away
From the sick heavens all unseemly stains.
5   The anxious month, relievèd of its pains,
      Takes as a long-lost right the feel of May;
      The eyelids with the passing coolness play
Like rose leaves with the drip of summer rains.

¶ 44. *1–4.* Winter is seen as a sickness cured by Spring. Cp. *The Fall of
Hyperion* i 97–100 (pp. 663–4 below),
        When in mid-May the sickening east wind
        Shifts sudden to the south, the small warm rain
        Melts out the frozen incense from all flowers,
        And fills the air with so much pleasant health . . .
5. month, relievèd of] *Examiner*; mouth, relieved from *1848*. The reading
'mouth' might be justified by the context (cp. l. 7 below, 'eyelids'). *1848*
attempts to correct the unusual intransitive use of 'relieving'.
6. the feel of] Cp. *In drear-nighted December* 21 *n* (p. 288 below),
        The feel of not to feel it . . .

The calmest thoughts come round us; as of leaves
10   Budding, fruit ripening in stillness, autumn suns
Smiling at eve upon the quiet sheaves,
Sweet Sappho's cheek, a sleeping infant's breath,
    The gradual sand that through an hour-glass runs,
A woodland rivulet, a poet's death.

10. fruit . . . suns] Foreshadows *Ode to Autumn* 1–2 (p. 651 below),
                    Season of mists and mellow fruitfulness,
                    Close bosom friend of the maturing sun . . .
12. Sappho's cheek] Suggested by the bust of Sappho in Leigh Hunt's cottage: see *Sleep and Poetry* 381–4 (p. 84 above). The reading 'smiling' for
'sleeping' in *Examiner* is probably an error.
14. a poet's death] The references to autumn in ll. 9–11 suggest that K. was
thinking of Chatterton: cp. K.'s letter to J. H. Reynolds of 21 Sept. 1819,
'I always somehow associate Chatterton with autumn' (*L* ii 167). For Chatterton's early death see *To Chatterton* 1–3 *n* (p. 10 above).

45 To Leigh Hunt, Esq.

Written late Feb. 1817 as a dedication sonnet to Leigh Hunt for *1817* (published 3 March): see *Cowden Clarke*, 'on the evening when the last proof-
sheet [of *1817*] was brought from the printer, it was accompanied by the
information that if a "dedication to the book was intended it must be sent
forthwith" . . . [K.] withdrew to a side-table . . . in the buzz of a mixed
conversation, he composed . . . the Dedication Sonnet' (137–8).
Published *1817*.

    Glory and loveliness have passed away,
        For if we wander out in early morn
        No wreathèd incense do we see upborne
    Into the east, to meet the smiling day;
5 No crowd of nymphs soft-voiced and young and gay,
        In woven baskets bringing ears of corn,
        Roses and pinks and violets, to adorn
    The shrine of Flora in her early May.
    But there are left delights as high as these,
10   And I shall ever bless my destiny
    That in a time, when under pleasant trees

¶ 45. *1*. Perhaps echoing Wordsworth's *Ode on Intimations of Immortality*
(1807) 18,
            . . . there hath past away a glory from the earth . . .
5–8. Another scene perhaps suggested by Poussin's 'L'Empire de Flore'.
See reference in *Sleep and Poetry* 101–21 *n* (pp. 73–4 above).

Pan is no longer sought, I feel a free,
A leafy, luxury, seeing I could please
With these poor offerings a man like thee.

13. luxury] See *Calidore* 92 *n* (p. 40 above).

46 Written on a blank space at the end of Chaucer's tale 'The Floure and the Leafe'

Written 'Feb. 1817' (probably *c.* 27 Feb.): so dated by K. in Cowden Clarke's copy (now in the British Museum) of *The Poetical Works of Geoffrey Chaucer* (1782) xiii. Woodhouse dates Reynolds's answering sonnet '27 Feb. 1817.' See *Cowden Clarke* 139, 'the sonnet ... was an extempore effusion and without the alteration of a single word.' *The Floure and the Leafe*, five lines of which K. quoted as a motto to *Sleep and Poetry* (p. 69 above), though included in the early editions is not now attributed to Chaucer. Text from K.'s MS.
Published *The Examiner* 16 March 1817; repr. *1848*.

This pleasant tale is like a little copse.
　　The honeyed lines do freshly interlace
　　To keep the reader in so sweet a place,
So that he here and there full-hearted stops;
5　And oftentimes he feels the dewy drops
　　Come cool and suddenly against his face,
　　And by the wandering melody may trace
Which way the tender-leggèd linnet hops.
Oh, what a power hath white simplicity!
10　What mighty power has this gentle story!
　　I that for ever feel athirst for glory
Could at this moment be content to lie

¶ 46. 2. do] so *1848*.
5–6. Suggested by *The Floure and the Leafe* 122–3,
　　　　... the herber was so fresh and cold,
　　　　The wholsome savours eke so comforting ...
8. Suggested by *The Floure and the Leafe* 89–90,
　　　　Therein a goldfinch leaping pretile
　　　　Fro bough to bough ...
9. hath] has *Examiner, 1848*. K. refers to 'white simplicity' because *The Floure and the Leafe* celebrates chastity, the followers of the Leafe (Chastity) being dressed in white.

> Meekly upon the grass, as those whose sobbings
> Were heard of none beside the mournful robins.

13–14. A reference to the Babes in the Wood. See Addison, *Spectator* 85
7 June 1711: 'the old Ballad of the "Two Children in the Wood" . . . is
one of the darling Songs of the common People . . . the Circumstance of the
Robin-red-breast . . . is indeed a little Poetical ornament. . . .' The reference and the false rhyme suggest a recollection of Wordsworth's *The Red-
breast chasing the Butterfly* (1807) 3–5,

> Our little English Robin;
> The bird that comes about our doors
> When Autumn-winds are sobbing . . .

and 21–3

> That, after their bewildering,
> Covered with leaves the little children,
> So painfully in the wood . . .

47 On Seeing the Elgin Marbles

Written shortly before 3 March 1817 with the following poem after visiting
the Elgin Marbles at the British Museum in Haydon's company: see his letter to K. 3 March 1817, 'Many thanks My dear fellow for your two noble
sonnets' (*L* i 122). The Marbles were purchased for the nation 1816 (see
Addressed to Haydon 11–12 *n*, p. 67 above). For their effect on K. see W.
Sharp, '[K.] went again and again to see the Elgin Marbles, and would sit
for an hour or more at a time beside them rapt in revery' (*Life and Letters of
Joseph Severn*, 1892, 32) and for their influence on K.'s poems see Stephen
Larrabee's *English Bards and Grecian Marbles* (1943) 209–32 and Ian Jack's
Keats and the Mirror of Art (1967) 161, 163, 165–7. The poem expresses K.'s
reverence for artistic creativity and his sense of bafflement and physical op-
pression when struggling with his own creative imagination.
Published *The Examiner* and *The Champion* 9 March 1817; repr. *Annals of
the Fine Arts* April 1818, *1848*.

> My spirit is too weak—mortality
>   Weighs heavily on me like unwilling sleep,
>   And each imagined pinnacle and steep
> Of godlike hardship tells me I must die
> 5   Like a sick eagle looking at the sky.

¶ 47. *1. mortality*] The limitations of being human. 'Godlike' powers (cp.
l. 4) are required for the greatest imaginative creation.
2. unwilling sleep] Drowsiness when one wants to be active.
5. See Haydon's letter to K., 'I known not a finer image than the comparison of a Poet unable to express his high feelings to a sick eagle looking at the
Sky!' (*L* i 122). A healthy eagle can soar higher than all other birds.

Yet 'tis a gentle luxury to weep
    That I have not the cloudy winds to keep
Fresh for the opening of the morning's eye.
Such dim-conceivèd glories of the brain
10   Bring round the heart an undescribable feud;
So do these wonders a most dizzy pain,
        That mingles Grecian grandeur with the rude
Wasting of old Time, with a billowy main,
    A sun, a shadow of a magnitude.

6. *gentle*] pleasing *Woodhouse's MS* (reproduced Sperry's *Woodhouse* (*1817*) 160).

10. Cp. K.'s account of the relief afforded by poetic creation in his letter to Reynolds of 22 Sept. 1818, 'This morning Poetry has conquered . . . I feel escaped from a . . . threatening sorrow. . . . There is an awful warmth about my heart like a load of Immortality' (*L* i 370).

11. *dizzy*] On K.'s early use of this word see *Endymion* i 565 *n* (p. 145 below).

12–14. K. seeks to express the causes of his 'dizzy pain' through a rapidly associated series of images suggesting the vastness and splendour which defy both the passage of time and his own powers of expression. The lines foreshadow his concern with the permanence of art and human transience in *Ode to a Grecian Urn* (p. 532 below).

14. *shadow of a magnitude*] The conception of something so great that it can only be dimly apprehended.

48 To B. R. Haydon, with a Sonnet Written on Seeing the Elgin Marbles

Written shortly before 3 March 1817: see headnote to previous poem. Published *The Examiner* and *The Champion* 9 March 1817; repr. *Annals of the Fine Arts* April 1818, *1848*.

Haydon, forgive me that I cannot speak
    Definitively on these mighty things.
    Forgive me that I have not eagle's wings,
That what I want I know not where to seek;
5   And think that I would not be overmeek
    In rolling out upfollowed thunderings

¶ 48. 1. *Haydon, forgive me*] Forgive me, Haydon *K.'s MS* (in the copy of *1817* presented to Reynolds by K.).

3. Cp. l. 5 in the preceding sonnet, *On Seeing the Elgin Marbles*.

6. *upfollowed thunderings*] Poetic strains to parallel the glories of the Elgin Marbles.

Even to the steep of Heliconian springs,
Were I of ample strength for such a freak;
Think too, that all those numbers should be thine—
10   Whose else? In this who touch thy vesture's hem?
For when men stared at what was most divine
With browless idiotism, o'erwise phlegm,
Thou hadst beheld the Hesperian shine
Of their star in the East, and gone to worship them.

7. steep] sleep *K.'s MS, Champion, Annals.* With 'Heliconian springs' cp.
To Charles Cowden Clarke 27 *n* (p. 55 above).

8. freak] Used for the sake of the rhyme as a synonym for 'feat'. For
'strength' Woodhouse's MS has 'might' (Sperry's *Woodhouse (1817)* 160).

11–14. A tribute to Haydon's part in the controversy over the Elgin
Marbles; see *Addressed to Haydon* 11–12 *n* (p. 67 above).

12. o'erwise] o'erweening *K.'s MS.* Milnes substitutes 'brainless' for 'browless' in *1848.*

13–14. Haydon is like one of the Three Magi (*Matthew* ii 1–11).

49 On *The Story of Rimini*

Written March 1817: see K.'s letter to Cowden Clarke 25 March 1817, 'I have
written . . . a Sonnet on Rimini' (*L* i 127). Leigh Hunt's *The Story of Rimini*
(1816) was reprinted 1817. For its influence on K. see headnotes to *Specimen
of an Induction* and *Calidore* (pp. 33 and 36 above). The two transcripts
largely agree.
Published *1848.*

Who loves to peer up at the morning sun
    With half-shut eyes and comfortable cheek,
    Let him, with this sweet tale, full often seek
For meadows where the little rivers run.
5   Who loves to linger with that brightest one
    Of heaven, Hesperus, let him lowly speak
    These numbers to the night, and starlight meek,
Or moon, if that her hunting be begun.
He who knows these delights and, too, is prone
10   To moralize upon a smile or tear,
    Will find at once a region of his own,
        A bower for his spirit, and will steer

¶ *49. 11–12. a region . . . spirit*] Cp. K.'s reference to *Endymion* in his letter
to Benjamin Bailey Oct. 1817, 'Do not the Lovers of Poetry like to have a
little Region to wander in . . .?' (*L* i 170).

To alleys where the fir-tree drops its cone,
  Where robins hop and fallen leaves are sere.

13. Cp. *Calidore* 40–1 *n* (p. 38 above),
                    . . . fir-trees grow around
  Ay dropping their hard fruit upon the ground . . .

50 On a Leander Gem which Miss Reynolds, my Kind Friend, Gave Me

Probably written March 1817: the date 'March 1816' in K.'s holograph MS must be a slip as K. did not meet the Reynolds family until late 1816. The gift acknowledged in the poem was one of James Tassie's ten popular paste reproductions of gems engraved with classical scenes, in this case Leander swimming the Hellespont. For other devices on the gems see K.'s March 1819 letter to Fanny Keats (*L* ii 45–6) and Ian Jack's *Keats and The Mirror of Art* (1967) 100–5 (Plate IX b reproduces a 'Leander gem'). According to Woodhouse, '. . . it was once Keat's intention to write a series of . . . sonnets and short poems on some of Tassie's gems' (*Woodhouse* 2).
Text from K.'s MS.
Published *The Gem, A Literary Annual* 1829; repr. *Galignani* (1829), *Forman* (1883).

Come hither all sweet maidens soberly,
  Down-looking ay, and with a chastened light
    Hid in the fringes of your eyelids white,
  And meekly let your fair hands joinèd be.
5 Are ye so gentle that ye could not see,
    Untouched, a victim of your beauty bright
    Sinking away to his young spirit's night,
  Sinking bewildered 'mid the dreary sea?
  'Tis young Leander toiling to his death.
10   Nigh swooning, he doth purse his weary lips
      For Hero's cheek and smiles against her smile.
    Oh, horrid dream! See how his body dips
      Dead-heavy; arms and shoulders gleam awhile;
  He's gone; up bubbles all his amorous breath!

¶ 50. *5. Are ye so gentle*] As if so gentle *Gem, Galignani.*
6. untouched] Untearful *K.'s MS (cancelled).*
9. For K.'s earlier allusion to Leander see *Woman! When I behold thee* 12–13 *n* (p. 43 above).
11. against] In anticipation of.
13. Dead-heavy] Cp. the description of Odysseus, Chapman's *Homer, Odyssey* v 614, 'Dead wearie was he . . .' See *Cowden Clarke* 130, 'I could not fail to introduce to [K.] . . . the shipwreck of Ulysses [in Chapman's *Homer*] . . . and . . . had the reward of one of his delighted stares'.

51 To a Young Lady who sent me a Laurel Crown

Date of composition unknown, but perhaps March 1817 in reply to a 'young lady's' encouraging gesture on K.'s decision to abandon medicine for poetry (K. was listed as a certified apothecary Dec. 1816). His decision was probably associated with the publication of *1817* in March and his intention to write *Endymion*. The 'young lady' may have been K.'s future sister-in-law Georgiana Wylie, or one of the Reynolds sisters. For the view that the poem was written Oct. 1816 see ll. 11–12 *n* below. The four transcripts largely agree.
Published *1848*.

> Fresh morning gusts have blown away all fear
>   From my glad bosom; now from gloominess
>   I mount for ever–not an atom less
> Than the proud laurel shall content my bier.
> 5   No, by the eternal stars! Or why sit here
>   In the sun's eye, and 'gainst my temples press
>   Apollo's very leaves, woven to bless
> By thy white fingers and thy spirit clear.
>   Lo, who dares say, 'Do this'? Who dares call down
> 10   My will from its high purpose? Who say, 'Stand,'
>   Or 'Go'? This very moment I would frown
>   On abject Caesars, not the stoutest band
> Of mailèd heroes should tear off my crown—
>   Yet would I kneel and kiss thy gentle hand!

¶ 51. *1. Fresh morning gusts*] Cp. the similar opening phrases in the sonnets *Keen, fitful gusts* and *To my Brothers* (pp. 63 and 65 above).
9–11. Possibly referring to Richard Abbey's bullying behaviour. According to John Taylor, Abbey advised K. to 'commence Business at Tottenham as a Surgeon' and on hearing K.'s decision to dedicate himself to poetry, 'called him a Silly Boy and prophesied a speedy Termination to his inconsiderate Enterprise' (*KC* i 307–8).
10. high] own *Woodhouse 1, 2 (cancelled)*.
11. This very moment] This mighty moment *1848*. The word 'mighty' is omitted in the four transcripts, but *Woodhouse 1* has 'very' pencilled in. The *1848* reading is Milnes's attempt to compensate for the missing foot.
11–12. I would frown / On abject Caesars] Cp. Horace Smith's 'Addressed by the Statute of Jupiter, lately arrived from Rome, to his Royal Highness the Prince Regent' (*The Examiner* 27 Oct. 1816) 4,

> Caesars, whene'er I frown'd, stood petrified . . .

The parallel leads R. Gittings to suggest that K.'s sonnet was written Oct. 1816 (*Gittings* (1968) 93). Smith's sonnet does not otherwise resemble K.'s.

52 On Receiving a Laurel Crown from Leigh Hunt

Written before 18 April 1817 when K. began *Endymion*; see K.'s spring 1817 letter to George Keats referring apologetically to the incident recorded in the poem, 'I put on no Laurels till I shall have finished *Endymion*' (*L* i 170). According to Woodhouse, 'As Keats and Leigh Hunt were taking their wine together after dinner at the house of the latter, the whim seized them to crown themselves with laurel after the fashion of the elder Bards' (*Woodhouse* 2). The poem was a contribution to one of Hunt's poetry contests.

Text from K.'s MS.
Published *The Times* 18 May 1914.

> Minutes are flying swiftly, and as yet
>   Nothing unearthly has enticed my brain
>   Into a delphic labyrinth. I would fain
> Catch an immortal thought to pay the debt
> 5 I owe to the kind poet who has set
>   Upon my ambitious head a glorious gain,
>   Two bending laurel sprigs–'tis nearly pain
> To be conscious of such a coronet.
> Still time is fleeting, and no dream arises
> 10   Gorgeous as I would have it; only I see
> A trampling down of what the world most prizes,
>   Turbans and crowns and blank regality—
> And then I run into most wild surmises
>   Of all the many glories that may be.

¶ 52. *1* (and *9* below). For Hunt's setting a time limit in his poetry contests see headnote to *On the Grasshopper* (pp. 97–98 above).

3. delphic labyrinth] Poetic intricacy. See *Sleep and Poetry* 266 *n* (p. 80 above).

4. immortal] unmortal *Garrod*. The word is not clearly written in K.'s MS, but the reading given is generally accepted and has been confirmed by Hyder Rollins in *Harvard Library Bulletin* vi Spring (1952) 164.

5–7. the kind ... sprigs] Cp. K.'s description of Hunt in *To Charles Cowden Clarke* 44–5 (p. 56 above).

> ... Libertas, who has told you stories
>   Of laurel chaplets and Apollo's glories ...

6. gain] Prize.

13. wild surmises] Cp. *On First Looking into Chapman's Homer* 13 (p. 62 above), 'with a wild surmise'.

53   To the Ladies who Saw Me Crowned

Written spring 1817 immediately after the preceding sonnet: according to
Woodhouse, friends of Hunt called while K. and Hunt were still wearing
their bardic wreaths, '. . . Hunt removed the wreath from his own brows
. . . Keats however in his mad enthusiastic way, vowed that he would not
take off his crown for any human being: and . . . wore it . . . as long as the
visit lasted' (*Woodhouse* 2). The visitors were probably the Reynolds sisters –
see l. 3 *n*
Text from K.'s MS.
Published *The Times* 21 May 1914.

> What is there in the universal earth
> > More lovely than a wreath from the bay tree?
> > Haply a halo round the moon, a glee
> Circling from three sweet pair of lips in mirth;
> 5   And haply you will say the dewy birth
> > Of morning roses, ripplings tenderly
> > Spread by the halcyon's breast upon the sea –
> But these comparisons are nothing worth.
> Then is there nothing in the world so fair?
> 10   The silvery tears of April? Youth of May?
> > Or June that breathes out life for butterflies?
> > No – none of these can from my favourite bear
> Away the palm; yet shall it ever pay
> > Due reverence to your most sovereign eyes.

¶ 53. *3. three sweet pair of lips*] Probably those of Jane, Marianne and Charlotte Reynolds. For K.'s friendship with the Reynolds family early 1817 see
headnote to *On a Leander Gem* (p. 107 above); K. wrote out the poem in
John Hamilton Reynolds's presentation copy of *1817* (the poem's single
known autograph MS).
7. Halcyon] See *To Charles Cowden Clarke* 57 *n* (p. 56 above).
8. nothing worth] Echoing Shakespeare's sonnet lxxii 13–14,
> > . . . I am sham'd by that which I bring forth,
> > And so should you, to love things nothing worth.

54   To Apollo

Written spring 1817 after the two preceding poems as an apology: Woodhouse records that K. regretted '. . . the folly of his conduct . . . he was
determined to record it by an apologetic ode to Apollo. . . . He shortly
after wrote this fragment' (*Woodhouse* 2); see also K.'s spring 1817 letter to
George Keats, '. . . I hope Apollo is not angered at my having made a

Mockery of him at Hunt's'(*L* i 170). The poem's irregularly stressed twelve-line stanzas represent one of K.'s rare attempts at lyrical verse since Feb. 1816, his compositions in the interval having been chiefly Petrarchan sonnets and poems in five-stressed couplets.

Text from K.'s holograph MS (Morgan Library) with some variants noted from his draft.

Published *Western Messenger* (Louisville) 1 June 1836; repr. *Harbinger* (New York and Boston) 21 March 1846, *1848*.

God of the golden bow,
And of the golden lyre,
And of the golden hair,
And of the golden fire,
     5   Charioteer
Of the patient year,
Where, where slept thine ire,
When like a blank idiot I put on thy wreath,
Thy laurel, thy glory,
    10   The light of thy story?
Or was I a worm, too low-creeping for death?
O Delphic Apollo!

The Thunderer grasped and grasped,
The Thunderer frowned and frowned.
    15   The eagle's feathery mane
For wrath became stiffened. The sound
Of breeding thunder
Went drowsily under,
Muttering to be unbound.
    20   Oh, why didst thou pity, and beg for a worm?
Why touch thy soft lute
Till the thunder was mute,
Why was I not crushed—such a pitiful germ?
O Delphic Apollo!

¶ 54. *8. wreath*] Laurel *Draft (cancelled)*. The phrase 'blank idiot' derives from *The Merchant of Venice* II ix 54, 'the portrait of a blinking idiot'—the 'portrait' was the Prince of Aragon's reward for his self-esteem.

11. low-creeping] low crawling *Draft*.

13. Jupiter gripped his thunderbolt.

15–16. The eagle was one of Jupiter's emblems. The frontispiece in *Baldwin* shows Jupiter sitting half-astride an eagle and grasping a thunderbolt in his uplifted right hand.

20. and beg for a worm?] and for a worm *Draft*. An earlier attempt was 'and beg of thy father for a worm . . .?

23. I not] Not I *1848*.

25   The Pleiades were up,
                Watching the silent air;
            The seeds and roots in earth
                Were swelling for summer fare;
            The ocean, its neighbour,
30   Was at his old labour,
            When who, who did dare
        To tie, for a moment, thy plant round his brow
                And grin and look proudly,
                And blaspheme so loudly,
35   And live for that honour, to stoop to thee now?
                O Delphic Apollo!

25. *The Pleiades*] A constellation rising in the English sky in early spring.
27. *in earth*] in the earth *Draft.*
30. *his*] its *1848.*
32. *for a moment*] like a Madman *Draft.*

55 On the Sea

Written 17 April 1817 in the Isle of Wight on the day before beginning
Endymion: see K.'s letter of 17–18 April 1817 to John Hamilton Reynolds
from Carisbrooke, Isle of Wight, under 17 April, '. . . the passage in Lear–
"Do you not hear the Sea?" [see *King Lear* IV vi 4]–has haunted me intensely', and under 18 April, 'I had become all in a Tremble from not having written anything of late – the Sonnet over leaf did me some good. I slept the
better last night for it' (*L* i 132–3). K.'s last sonnet until Jan. 1818.
Text from *1848*; the variants in the *Champion* are noted below.
Published *The Champion* 17 Aug. 1817; repr. *1848*.

    It keeps eternal whisperings around
        Desolate shores, and with its mighty swell
        Gluts twice ten thousand caverns, till the spell
    Of Hecate leaves them their old shadowy sound.

¶ 55. *1*. See K. to Jane Reynolds 14 Sept. 1817, 'I have found in the
Ocean's Musick–varying (though selfsame) . . . an enjoyment not to be put
into words' (*L* i 158).
3. Gluts] Fills to repletion. For K.'s best known use of the word see *Ode on
Melancholy* 15 (p. 540 below),
            . . . glut thy sorrow on a morning rose . . .
With its use here cp. *The Cap and the Bells* 737–8 (p. 734 below).
            . . . the sea, at flow, gluts up once more
        The craggy hollowness of a wild reefed shore . . .
3–4. the spell | Of Hecate] K. is thinking of the moon's effect on the ebb and
flow of the tides. On Hecate see headnote to *Endymion* (p. 117 below).

5   Often 'tis in such gentle temper found
       That scarcely will the very smallest shell
       Be moved for days from where it sometime fell,
When last the winds of heaven were unbound.
O ye who have your eye-balls vexed and tired,
10   Feast them upon the wideness of the sea!
          O ye whose ears are dinned with uproar rude,
       Or fed too much with cloying melody,
             Sit ye near some old cavern's mouth and brood
Until ye start, as if the sea-nymphs quired!

7. *Be moved for days*] Be lightly moved *Champion*.
9. *ye who*] ye, that *Champion*.
11. *O ye whose ears are dinned*] Or are your hearts disturb'd *Champion*.
12. *cloying*] Surfeiting. See *Sleep and Poetry* 178 *n* (p. 77 above).
14. *as if the*] as the *Champion*.

56 'You say you love'

Date of composition unknown, but perhaps early summer 1817 after meeting Mrs Jones: the undated transcript in *Woodhouse 3* has 'From Miss Reynolds and Mrs Jones'–K. first met Mrs Isabella Jones at Hastings May–June
1817 (*L* i 402–3). For the possible influence of the Elizabethan poem *A Proper Wooing Song* (1594; repr. *Heliconia* 1814, ed. Thomas Park) see *Colvin*
(1917) 157–8.
Text from *Woodhouse 3*.
Published *TLS* 16 April 1914.

I

You say you love, but with a voice
    Chaster than a nun's who singeth
The soft Vespers to herself
    While the chime-bell ringeth–
5   Oh, love me truly!

II

You say you love, but then you smile
Cold as sunrise in September,

¶ 56. *1–5.* Cp. *A Proper Wooing Song* (headnote) 1–6,
             Maide will ye love me yea or no?
                tell me the trothe and let me go.
             It can be no lesse than a sinful deed
                trust me truly,
             To linger a lover that lookes to speede,
                in due time duly.
6. *then you smile*] Written above 'with a smile' (uncancelled) in *Wood-*

As you were Saint Cupid's nun
And kept his weeks of Ember.
10   Oh, love me truly!

III

You say you love, but then your lips
Coral-tinted teach no blisses
More than coral in the sea—
They never pout for kisses.
15   Oh, love me truly!

IV

You say you love, but then your hand
No soft squeeze for squeeze returneth,
It is like a statue's, dead—
While mine to passion burneth.
20   Oh, love me truly!

V

Oh, breathe a word or two of fire!
Smile as if those words should burn me,
Squeeze as lovers should—oh, kiss
And in thy heart inurn me!
25   Oh, love me truly!

---

house 3; with a smile *Reynolds, Woodhouse* 2. The reading is justified by the
context—see the phrasing in ll. 11, 16—and was probably taken by Woodhouse from K.'s version of the poem for Mrs Jones.
9. weeks of Ember] Periods of abstinence and fasting. 'Ember is the English
name for the four periods of fasting and prayer (Latin *quatuor tempora*) in
the four seasons of the year' (*OED*).

57 'Unfelt, unheard, unseen'

Probably written early summer 1817 with the preceding poem and certainly before 17 Aug. 1817 when John Hamilton Reynolds quoted
l.9 of the poem in *The Champion*.
Text from K.'s holograph fair copy (Morgan Library); some variants in the
draft (British Museum) are noted below.
Published *1848*.

Unfelt, unheard, unseen,
I've left my little queen,

Her languid arms in silver slumber lying.
Ah, through their nestling touch,
5   Who, who could tell how much
There is for madness–cruel, or complying?

Those fairy lids how sleek!
Those lips how moist! They speak,
In ripest quiet, shadows of sweet sounds;
10   Into my fancy's ear
Melting a burden dear,
How 'Love doth know no fullness nor no bounds'.

True, tender monitors!
I bend unto your laws—
15   This sweetest day for dalliance was born!
So, without more ado,
I'll feel my heaven anew,
For all the blushing of the hasty morn.

¶57. 3. *lying*] The words 'dying' and 'kissing' are cancelled in the draft
with nothing substituted.
4. And stifling up the Vale *Draft*. According to R. Gittings the draft version
and also l.17 below are examples of K.'s use of sexual slang; see 'Keats's use
of Bawdy', *Gittings (1968)* 453.
5–6. It is hard to imagine the passion which she can arouse by her resistance
or compliance when she is awake.
7–9. *Those . . . quiet*]   How sleek those faery lids
                            How moist that the lip that bids
                            E'en in quiet stillness . . . *Draft (cancelled)*

58 'Hither, hither, love'

Perhaps written in the spring or summer of 1817. K.'s holograph MS (in
private possession) is undated.
Published *The Ladies Home Companion* New York 1837; repr. *Lowell* (1925).

Hither, hither, love,
    'Tis a shady mead.
Hither, hither, love,
    Let us feed and feed!

5   Hither, hither, sweet,
        'Tis a cowslip bed.
    Hither, hither, sweet,
        'Tis with dew bespread!

Hither, hither, dear,
        By the breath of life,
Hither, hither, dear!
        Be the summer's wife!

Though one moment's pleasure
        In one moment flies,
Though the passion's treasure
        In one moment dies,

Yet it has not passed,
        Think how near, how near!
And while it doth last,
        Think how dear, how dear!

Hither, hither, hither
        Love this boon hath sent.
If I die and wither
        I shall die content.

10

15

20

59 Endymion: a Poetic Romance

Begun *c.* 18 April 1817 at Carisbrooke, Isle of Wight, and completed by 28 Nov. 1817 at Burford Bridge, Surrey: see K.'s letter to Reynolds from Carisbrooke 18 April 1817, '. . . I shall forthwith begin my *Endymion*' (*L* i 134) and statement on 10 May 1817 that he had begun the poem 'about a Fortnight since' (*L* i 139); Woodhouse notes in his copy of the first edition that K.'s first draft was dated at the end 'Burford Bridge, Nov. 28 1817'. For the composition of the individual books see headnotes to Books I, II, III, IV (pp. 120, 163, 205 and 244 below). On K.'s initial attempt to deal with the subject in late 1816 see headnote to *I stood tip-toe* (p. 85 above).

K. describes his intention in writing the poem in his letter to Bailey of 8 Oct. 1817, 'it will be a test, a trial of my Powers of Imagination and chiefly of my invention . . . by which I must make 4000 lines of one bare circumstance and fill them with Poetry' (*L* i 169–70). He met the legend of Endymion and Phoebe first in works of classical reference read at school–'The books that were his . . . recurrent sources of attraction were Tooke's *Pantheon*, Lemprière's *Classical Dictionary* which he appeared to *learn*, and Spence's *Polymetis*. This was the store where he acquired his intimacy with the Greek mythology' (*Cowden Clarke* 124)–and later in allusions encountered in his reading of Shakespeare, Spenser, Marlowe, Fletcher and other Elizabethans (for some of the best known of these allusions see *Colvin* (1917) 166–8, *de Selincourt* 414–16). He took material for some episodes from Drayton's *The Man in the Moone* (1606), which he read in his copy of John Smethwick's edition of Drayton, and from Ovid's *Metamorphoses*, which he knew both in the original and in Sandys's translation (1640 edn). (The suggestion that he was influenced by Drayton's earlier poem, *Endimion and Phoebe* (1595), which is discussed in *de Selincourt* 567–8, *Bate* (1963) 176–7, is unconvincing.) Endymion's encounters with the moon goddess on the earth (Book I) and his subsequent adventures below the earth (Book II), beneath the sea (Book III) and in the air (Book IV) have a loose resemblance to Endymion's journeys with Phoebe in *The Man in the Moone* and probably owe something to traditional notions of the moon's various spheres of influence: see, for example, *The Man in the Moone* 477–8 on the moon's different names, 'PHOEBE, DIANA, HECATE . . .', as indicating her 'Sovereigntie in Heaven, in Earth and Hell . . .' and cp. K.'s sonnet *To Homer* 14 (p. 353 below) 'Dian, Queen of Earth and Heaven and Hell'. K. probably took further hints for the 'wonders' of Endymion's journeys from contemporary narrative poems, including Landor's *Gebir* (1798) and Southey's *Thalaba the Destroyer* (1801) and *The Curse of Kehama* (1810); some pictorial details are also owed to Sandys's *Ovid*, Chapman's *Homeric Hymns*, *The Arabian Nights*, and possibly various paintings of classical scenes by Titian, Claude and Poussin. K.'s conception of the hero's dream-vision was, however, probably most strongly affected by recollections of Shelley's *Alastor* (1816), to which his own poem reads in certain respects as a reply. See, for example, A. C. Bradley's commentary:

'The hero, before the coming of the vision, has, of course, a poetic soul, but he is not self-secluded, or inactive, or fragile, or philosophic; and his pursuit of the goddess leads not to extinction but to immortal union with her. It does lead, however, to adventures of which the idea evidently is that the poetic soul can only reach complete union with the ideal (which union is immortality) by wandering in a world which seems to deprive him of it; by trying to mitigate the woes of others instead of seeking the ideal for himself; and by giving himself up to love for what seems to be a mere woman, but is found to be the goddess herself. It seems almost beyond doubt that the story of Cynthia and Endymion would not have taken this shape but for *Alastor*' (*Oxford Lectures on Poetry*, 1909, 241).

Endymion is written in the heroic couplets frequently used by K. in 1816, but its diction and imagery show an advance in concentration and power over the general style of *1817* (see especially the 'Hymn to Pan' i 232–306) and reflect the influence of his new close study of Shakespeare. His purchase in April 1817 of a copy of the Johnson and Steevens annotated edn (1814) of Shakespeare and the numerous markings in this copy are recorded in *Spurgeon* (1928). K. expresses his fresh enthusiasm for Shakespeare and his growing disenchantment with Leigh Hunt as a model in his letter to Haydon of May 1817, '. . . you had notions of a good Genius presiding over you–I have of late had the same thought. . . . Is it too daring to fancy Shakespeare this Presider? . . . I wrote to Hunt yesterday . . . I could not talk about Poetry. . . . I was not in humour with either his or mine' (*L* i 141–3). On K.'s growing familiarity with Milton in late 1817 see headnote to Book IV

(p. 244 below) and on the stylistic qualities of *Endymion* as indicating K.'s gradual movement towards a greater maturity of thought and feeling see R. Mayhead's *John Keats* (1967) 28–41. The poem met with a hostile reception from *Blackwood's Magazine* Aug. 1818, *The Quarterly Review* April 1818, *The British Critic* June 1818, but its poetic promise was acknowledged in 1820 by Jeffrey in *The Edinburgh Review* as it had been earlier by K.'s friends and associates, including Bailey and Shelley, some of whose comments are referred to in the notes. Reynolds published a defence of *Endymion* in the *Alfred, West of England Journal* 6 Oct. 1818 (reprinted by Hunt in the *Examiner* 11 Oct. 1818); Woodhouse compared it with Shakespeare's *Venus and Adonis* (*KC* i 54); Taylor found the faults 'numberless, but there are redeeming Beauties . . . and the faults are those of real genius' (*KC* i 68). Two protests against the injustice of the *Quarterly*'s attack were published in *The Morning Chronicle* of 3 Oct. and 8 Oct. 1818 under the signatures 'J.S.' and 'R.B.' respectively. For K.'s view of *Endymion* see his Preface and Appendix A (pp. 754–6 below). Subsequent readers of the poem have generally agreed about its importance for K. as an apprentice-piece, but have differed on its intrinsic value and, since the 1880s, on the extent to which K. intended it to be read as a sustained allegory. Matthew Arnold wrote severely to Sidney Colvin, 'What is good in *Endymion* is not, to my mind, as good as you say, and the poem as a whole I could wish to be suppressed and lost. I really resent the space it occupies in the volume of Keats's poetry' (letter of 26 June 1887, quoted in E. V. Lucas's *The Colvins and their Friends* (1928) 193), but Hopkins defended it to Patmore, comparing it with Shakespeare's early work, 'After all is there anything in *Endymion* worse than the passage in *Romeo and Juliet* about the County Paris as a book of love that must be bound and I can't tell what? [*Romeo and Juliet* I iii 81–94]' (letter of 20 Oct. 1887, *Further Letters of Gerard Manley Hopkins*, 1956 edn, 382). The view— first expressed by Frances Owen in her *John Keats* (1880) and subsequently supported by Bridges (whose analysis largely contradicts his statement that K. 'was not making an allegory, but using a legend'), Colvin, de Selincourt and some of K.'s more recent readers–that *Endymion* is to be read as a coherent allegory of the poet's search for ideal beauty is in my opinion unconvincing, but the poem obviously focuses some of K.'s central ideas in 1817 concerning the poetic nature and its conception of ideal happiness. Critical summaries of the principal allegorical interpretations appear in C. Godfrey's 'Endymion' in *Reassessment* (1958) 20–38; E. C. Pettet's '*Endymion* 1: Some preliminary considerations', *Pettet* (1957) 123–45; W. J. Bate's 'A trial of invention: *Endymion*', *Bate* (1963) 168–76; and N. F. Ford's studies of *Endymion* referred to in i 778–81 *n* below. Indications of influences from sculpture and painting on some of the descriptive passages are discussed by Ian Jack in his *Keats and the Mirror of Art* (1967) 143–60.

Text from *1818*, with some variants noted from K.'s fair copy (Morgan Library) and for Books II–IV from the draft variants recorded by Woodhouse in his copy of *1818* which are reproduced in *Garrod* from H. Buxton Forman's collation.

Published May 1818, with the following motto, dedication and preface; for the original preface and relevant correspondence see Appendix A (pp. 754–6 below).

'The stretched metre of an antique song'

Inscribed to the memory
of
Thomas Chatterton

Knowing within myself the manner in which this Poem has been produced, it is not without a feeling of regret that I make it public.

What manner I mean, will be quite clear to the reader, who must soon perceive great inexperience, immaturity, and every error denoting a feverish attempt, rather than a deed accomplished. The two first books, and indeed the two last, I feel sensible are not of such completion as to warrant their passing the press; nor should they if I thought a year's castigation would do them any good;—it will not: the foundations are too sandy. It is just that this youngster should die away: a sad thought for me, if I had not some hope that while it is dwindling I may be plotting, and fitting myself for verses fit to live.

This may be speaking too presumptuously, and may deserve a punishment: but no feeling man will be forward to inflict it: he will leave me alone, with the conviction that there is not a fiercer hell than the failure in a great object. This is not written with the least atom of purpose to forestall criticisms of course, but from the desire I have to conciliate men who are competent to look, and who do look with a zealous eye, to the honour of English literature.

The imagination of a boy is healthy, and the mature imagination of a man is healthy; but there is a space of life between, in which the soul is in a ferment, the character undecided, the way of life uncertain, the ambition thick-sighted: thence proceeds mawkishness, and all the thousand bitters which those men I speak of must necessarily taste in going over the following pages.

I hope I have not in too late a day touched the beautiful mythology of Greece, and dulled its brightness: for I wish to try once more, before I bid it farewell.

Teignmouth, *April* 10, 1818.

BOOK I

Begun *c.* April 1817 (see main headnote), but the date of completion is unknown. K. finished Book II at Hamsptead *c.* 28 Aug. 1817–see his Hampstead letter to Haydon conjecturally dated 21 or 28 Aug. 1817, 'I have
finished my second Book' (*L* i 149)–and during the period from 16 April
to *c.* 3 September was successively at Carisbrooke, Margate, Canterbury,
Hastings and London. He may have begun the 'Hymn to Pan' (*Endymion* i
232–306) at Margate 26 April 1817 (date attached by Woodhouse to this
part of the poem in the copy of *Galignani* given to him by Severn in 1832–
K. left Carisbrooke for Margate *c.* 24 April 1817). His restlessness and difficulty in making progress with this poem are expressed in letters written
10–16 May 1817, but no further records of the details of composition exist.

> A thing of beauty is a joy for ever:
> Its loveliness increases; it will never
> Pass into nothingness, but still will keep
> A bower quiet for us, and a sleep
> 5   Full of sweet dreams, and health, and quiet breathing.
> Therefore, on every morrow, are we wreathing
> A flowery band to bind us to the earth,

¶ 59. *Title*. Endymion, a Romance *K.'s rejected title (written out with the dedication quoted below as the heading for his rejected preface: see main headnote).*
Motto. From Shakespeare's Sonnet xvii, 'Who will believe my verse in time
to come' 12. K. quotes the line in his letter to Reynolds of 22 Nov. 1817 as
'a capital Motto for my Poem' (*L* 1 189).
Dedication. Inscribed / with every feeling of pride and regret, / and with 'a
bowed mind' / To the memory of / The most english of Poets except
Shakespeare, / Thomas Chatterton *Rejected dedication (see note to Title).* On
K.'s feeling for Chatterton see *To Chatterton* (p. 10 above).
Preface. The closing paragraph hints at K.'s intention to write *Hyperion*; see
Endymion iv 774 *n* (p. 276 below).
i 1. According to Henry Stephens, a fellow medical student with K., the
line originally read, 'A thing of beauty is a constant joy.' Stephens reported
the reading to Sir B. W. Richardson, who gives details in *The Aesculapiad*
(April 1884) 148–9: see further F. W. Bateson's *English Poetry a Critical Introduction* (1951) 47–8. K.'s opening celebration of beauty (i 1–33) may owe
something to Wordsworth's *Excursion* (1814), 'Prospectus' 42–7,

> –Beauty,–a living Presence of the earth,
> Surpassing the most fair ideal Forms
> Which craft of delicate Spirits hath composed
> From earth's materials–waits upon my steps;
> Pitches her tents before me as I move,
> An hourly neighbour . . .

In his letter to Haydon of 10 Jan. 1818 K. praises *The Excursion*, along with
Haydon's pictures and Hazlitt's 'depth of taste', as one of 'three things to
rejoice at in this Age' (*L* i 203).

Spite of despondence, of the inhuman dearth
Of noble natures, of the gloomy days,
10 Of all the unhealthy and o'er-darkened ways
Made for our searching—yes, in spite of all,
Some shape of beauty moves away the pall
From our dark spirits. Such the sun, the moon,
Trees, old and young, sprouting a shady boon
15 For simple sheep; and such are daffodils
With the green world they live in; and clear rills
That for themselves a cooling covert make
'Gainst the hot season; the mid-forest brake,
Rich with a sprinkling of fair musk-rose blooms;
20 And such too is the grandeur of the dooms
We have imagined for the mighty dead,
All lovely tales that we have heard or read—
An endless fountain of immortal drink,
Pouring unto us from the heaven's brink.

25   Nor do we merely feel these essences
For one short hour; no, even as the trees
That whisper round a temple become soon
Dear as the temple's self, so does the moon,
The passion poesy, glories infinite,
30 Haunt us till they become a cheering light
Unto our souls, and bound to us so fast
That, whether there be shine or gloom o'ercast,
They always must be with us, or we die.

i 8–9. *dearth* / *Of noble natures*] Especially in political life (cp. iii 1–21 and *n* below), but K. found some 'noble natures' in art and literature. See *Great spirits now on earth are sojourning* (p. 67 above) and also preceding *n*.

i 13–24. A Keatsian catalogue of 'luxuries'. For similar catalogues see *Sleep and Poetry* 1–10, *I stood tip-toe* 1–115 (pp. 69–70 and 86–90 above).

i 13. *From our dark spirits*] Followed in the fair copy by the cancelled passage,
> and before us dances
> Like glitter on the points of Arthur's Lances.
> Of these bright powers are . . . *Fair copy (cancelled)*

i 19. *musk-rose*] On K.'s special fondness for this flower see *To a Friend who Sent Me Some Roses* 6 *n* (p. 47 above).

i 21. *the mighty dead*] Echoing Thomson's *The Seasons* (1730), *Winter* 432, quoted in *To my Brother George* 72 *n* (p. 51 above). Haydon had recently quoted the line in his letter to K. of March 1817 (*L* i 124).

i 24. *Pouring unto us from*] Telling us we are on *Fair copy (cancelled)*.

i 25–33. Beautiful objects give immediate sensuous delight and also remain in the memory to sustain and cheer the human spirit. With K.'s use of 'essences' (i 25) cp. i 779 *n* below.

i 29. *The passion poesy*] And passion–poetry *Fair copy (cancelled)*.

Therefore, 'tis with full happiness that I
35   Will trace the story of Endymion.
The very music of the name has gone
Into my being, and each pleasant scene
Is growing fresh before me as the green
Of our own valley. So I will begin
40   Now while I cannot hear the city's din;
Now while the early budders are just new,
And run in mazes of the youngest hue
About old forests; while the willow trails
Its delicate amber and the dairy pails
45   Bring home increase of milk. And, as the year
Grows lush in juicy stalks, I'll smoothly steer
My little boat for many quiet hours,
With streams that deepen freshly into bowers.
Many and many a verse I hope to write
50   Before the daisies, vermeil-rimmed and white,
Hide in deep herbage; and ere yet the bees
Hum about globes of clover and sweet peas,
I must be near the middle of my story.
Oh, may no wintry season, bare and hoary,
55   See it half finished, but let autumn bold,
With universal tinge of sober gold,
Be all about me when I make an end.
And now at once, adventuresome, I send
My herald thought into a wilderness—
60   There let its trumpet blow, and quickly dress
My uncertain path with green, that I may speed
Easily onward, thorough flowers and weed.

i 36. *The very music of the name*] See K.'s reference to the legend of *Endymion*
in *I stood tip-toe* 182 (p. 94 above),

That sweetest of all songs . . .

i 39–57. *I will begin . . . end*] K.'s timetable for the composition of his poem,
which took longer than he had planned. See his letter to Haydon of 11 May
1817, 'I revoke my Promise of finishing my Poem by the Autumn which I
should have done had I gone on as I have done–but I cannot write while
my spirit is fevered in a contrary direction' (*L* i 142). K. worked 'about
eight hours a day' on the poem until 10 May (*L* i 141).

i 40. *din*] A word also used by Wordsworth and Coleridge. See iv 198 *n*
below.

i 50. *vermeil*] A Spenserian word for crimson frequently used by K. See, for
example, *The Faerie Queene* III i 46, '*a vermeill Rose*' and cp. i 696, iv 148
below.

i 63. *Latmos*] The mountain in Caria, Asia Minor, traditionally associated
with Endymion. See *I stood tip-toe* 194 *n* (p. 95 above).

Upon the sides of Latmos was outspread
A mighty forest, for the moist earth fed
65   So plenteously all weed-hidden roots
Into o'er-hanging boughs and precious fruits.
And it had gloomy shades, sequestered deep,
Where no man went, and if from shepherd's keep
A lamb strayed far a-down those inmost glens,
70   Never again saw he the happy pens
Whither his brethren, bleating with content,
Over the hills at every nightfall went.
Among the shepherds, 'twas believèd ever
That not one fleecy lamb, which thus did sever
75   From the white flock, but passed unworrièd
By angry wolf or pard with prying head,
Until it came to some unfooted plains
Where fed the herds of Pan—aye, great his gains
Who thus one lamb did lose. Paths there were many,
80   Winding through palmy fern, and rushes fenny,
And ivy banks—all leading pleasantly
To a wide lawn, whence one could only see
Stems thronging all around between the swell
Of turf and slanting branches. Who could tell
85   The freshness of the space of heaven above,
Edged round with dark tree tops, through which a dove
Would often beat its wings, and often too
A little cloud would move across the blue ?
Full in the middle of this pleasantness

i 71. *Whither*] To which *Fair copy (cancelled)*.

i 76. *pard*] Leopard. See iv 241 n below.

i 80. *palmy . . . fenny*] On K.'s use of epithets ending in '-y' see *Calidore* 10
n (p. 37 above).

i 86. *Edged round with dark tree tops*] Foreshadowing *Ode to Psyche* 54–5
(p. 520 below),

. . . those dark-clustered trees
Fledge the wild-ridgèd mountains steep by steep . . .

i 89–392. K.'s description of the festival of Pan may have been suggested in
the first place by the opening of Drayton's narrative in 'The Man in the
Moone' (1606) 5–8,

It was the time when (for their good Estate)
The thankefull Shepheards yerely celebrate
A Feast, and Bone-fires on the Vigills keepe,
To the great PAN, preserver of their Sheepe . . .

Pan, celebrated in classical mythology as the god of universal nature, is a
leading figure in Elizabethan pastoral poetry. K. probably took further hints
for his description of the festival and his 'Hymn to Pan' (i 232–306) from

90   There stood a marble altar, with a tress
      Of flowers budded newly; and the dew
      Had taken fairy phantasies to strew
      Daisies upon the sacred sward last eve,
      And so the dawnèd light in pomp receive.
95   For 'twas the morn. Apollo's upward fire
      Made every eastern cloud a silvery pyre
      Of brightness so unsullied that therein
      A melancholy spirit well might win
      Oblivion, and melt out his essence fine
100   Into the winds. Rain-scented eglantine
      Gave temperate sweets to that well-wooing sun;
      The lark was lost in him; cold springs had run
      To warm their chilliest bubbles in the grass;
      Man's voice was on the mountains; and the mass
105   Of nature's lives and wonders pulsed tenfold
      To feel this sunrise and its glories old.

          Now while the silent workings of the dawn
      Were busiest, into that self-same lawn
      All suddenly, with joyful cries, there sped
110   A troop of little children garlanded,
      Who gathering round the altar seemed to pry
      Earnestly round, as wishing to espy

his Elizabethan reading, including Ben Jonson's *Pan's Anniversarie* (1623);
Fletcher's *The Faithfull Shepherdess* (1610), in which the priest of Pan plays a
prominent part; and Chapman's Homeric *Hymn to Pan*, '. . . his favourite
among Chapman's "Hymns of Homer"' (*Cowden Clarke* 131).

i *94. dawnèd*] coming *Fair copy* (cancelled).

i *95. Apollo's upward fire*] The rays of the rising sun.

i *98–100. might win . . . winds*] Might forget himself in the beauty of the
scene before him. The phrasing suggests a recollection of *Hamlet* I ii 129–30,

          O! that this too too solid flesh would melt,
          Thaw and resolve itself into a dew . . .

K. echoes Shakespeare's lines again at i 501 below,

          Endymion's spirit melt away and thaw . . .

i *99. fine*] pure *Fair copy* (cancelled).

i *100. eglantine*] Sweetbriar. Cp. *Ode to a Nightingale* 46 and 46–9 *n* (p. 528
below), 'the pastoral eglantine'.

i *102–3. cold springs . . . in the grass*] Cp. *I stood tip-toe* 81–2 (p. 89 above),

          The ripples seem right glad to reach those cresses
          And cool themselves among the emerald tresses . . .

i *107–13. Now while . . . holiday*] Ian Jack suggests K.'s recollection of
Titian's 'The Worship of Venus' and Rubens's 'Sacrifice to Venus' or 'The
Feast of Venus' (*Keats and the Mirror of Art*, 1967, 149).

Some folk of holiday. Nor had they waited
For many moments, ere their ears were sated
115   With a faint breath of music, which even then
Filled out its voice, and died away again.
Within a little space again it gave
Its airy swellings, with a gentle wave,
To light-hung leaves, in smoothest echoes breaking
120   Through copse-clad valley—ere their death o'ertaking
The surgy murmurs of the lonely sea.

And now, as deep into the wood as we
Might mark a lynx's eye, there glimmered light
Fair faces and a rush of garments white,
125   Plainer and plainer showing, till at last
Into the widest alley they all passed,
Making directly for the woodland altar.
O kindly muse, let not my weak tongue falter
In telling of this goodly company,
130   Of their old piety, and of their glee,
But let a portion of ethereal dew
Fall on my head and presently unmew
My soul—that I may dare, in wayfaring,
To stammer where old Chaucer used to sing.

135   Leading the way, young damsels danced along,
Bearing the burden of a shepherd song,

i *114. sated*] Satisfied. A forced expression for the sake of the rhyme.
i *120–1. ere their death . . . sea*] The music's fading echoes mingle with the
sound of the sea. K. was living near the sea when writing this part of the
poem. See headnote to the whole poem and to *On the Sea* (pp. 116 and 112
above).
i *130. their old piety*] Cp. *Ode to Psyche* 40–1 (p. 518 below),

> . . . these days so far retired
> From happy pieties . . .

i *132. unmew*] Set free.
i *134.* Cp. K.'s letter of 16 May 1817, 'This Evening I go to Canterbury . . .
I hope the Remembrance of Chaucer will set me forward like a Billiard-
Ball' (*L* i 146–7).
i *135–74.* See Ian Jack, 'In these lines accounts of pagan festivals which [K.]
had read in books are brought to life with the help of images remembered
from paintings and prints . . . we are again in the country . . . of Poussin
and Claude' (*Keats and the Mirror of Art*, 150–1). Cp. *Sleep and Poetry*
354–91 *n* (pp. 83–4 above), *To J. H. Reynolds Esq.* 20–2 *n* (p. 321 below).
i *135. Leading the way, young*] In front some pretty *Draft (cancelled).*
i *136. shepherd*] mayday *Fair copy (cancelled).* 'Bearing the burden' means
singing the chorus; the phrasing has the effect of a pun.

Each having a white wicker over-brimmed
With April's tender younglings; next, well trimmed,
A crowd of shepherds with as sunburnt looks
140   As may be read of in Arcadian books,
Such as sat listening round Apollo's pipe,
When the great deity, for earth too ripe,
Let his divinity o'erflowing die
In music, through the vales of Thessaly;
145   Some idly trailed their sheep-hooks on the ground,
And some kept up a shrilly mellow sound
With ebon-tippèd flutes. Close after these,
Now coming from beneath the forest trees,
A venerable priest full soberly,
150   Begirt with ministering looks; always his eye
Steadfast upon the matted turf he kept,
And after him his sacred vestments swept.
From his right hand there swung a vase, milk-white,
Of mingled wine, out-sparkling generous light;
155   And in his left he held a basket full
Of all sweet herbs that searching eye could cull–
Wild thyme, and valley-lilies whiter still
Than Leda's love, and cresses from the rill.

i *137. having a white*] with a heavy *Fair copy* (*cancelled*).

i *138. younglings*] Young plants.

i *139. Sunburnt*] Cp. *The Tempest* IV i 134, 'Yon sun-burn'd sicklemen'.

i *140. Arcadian books*] Pastoral poetry, such as Virgil's *Eclogues*.

i *142–4.* Apollo's period of exile as a shepherd in Thessaly is recorded in Ovid's *Metamorphoses* ii 677–82. Other allusions to the legend known to K. appear in *Lemprière*, *The Faerie Queene* III xi 39, *The Winter's Tale* IV iii 29–31.

i *150. Begirt with ministering looks*] Surrounded by ready attendants.

i *153–4. vase . . . light*] milk white vase,
    Of mingled wines, and sparkling like the stars . . . *Fair copy* (*cancelled*).
On 'mingled wines' see Potter's *Antiquities of Greece* (1697–8), 'though sometimes mixed wine is mentioned at sacrifices . . . this mixture was not . . . wine and water, but . . . different sorts of wine' (i 251). On the compound 'out-sparkling' see Croker's review of *Endymion*, *Quarterly Review* xxxvii (April 1818, repr. *Forman* (1883) i 354), '. . . he has formed new verbs by the process of cutting off their natural tails, the adverbs, and affixing to their foreheads; thus, "the wine out-sparkled" . . . the multitude "up-followed" [i 164] . . . "night up-took" [i 561] . . . the "hours are down-sunken" [i 708] . . .'.

i *155–8.* See Potter's *Antiquities*, 'In the most ancient sacrifices . . . herbs and plants, plucked up by the roots, were burnt whole, with their leaves and fruit, before the gods' (i 248–9).

His agèd head, crownèd with beechen wreath,
160 Seemed like a poll of ivy in the teeth
Of winter hoar. Then came another crowd
Of shepherds, lifting in due time aloud
Their share of the ditty. After them appeared,
Up-followed by a multitude that reared
165 Their voices to the clouds, a fair-wrought car,
Easily rolling so as scarce to mar
The freedom of three steeds of dapple brown.
Who stood therein did seem of great renown
Among the throng. His youth was fully blown,
170 Showing like Ganymede to manhood grown,
And, for those simple times, his garments were
A chieftain king's; beneath his breast, half bare,
Was hung a silver bugle, and between
His nervy knees there lay a boar-spear keen.
175 A smile was on his countenance; he seemed
To common lookers-on like one who dreamed
Of idleness in groves Elysian.
But there were some who feelingly could scan
A lurking trouble in his nether lip,
180 And see that oftentimes the reins would slip

i *157–8. whiter still . . . rill*] An earlier attempt in the fair copy was,
                                        . . . white as Leda's
     Bosom, and choicest strips from the mountain Cedars . . .
'Leda's love' is Jupiter, who appeared to Leda in the form of a swan. See
Spenser's *Prothalamion* (1596) 40–4,
                    The snow which doth the top of *Pindus* strew,
                    Did never whiter shew,
                    Nor *Jove* himselfe when he a Swan would be
                    For love of *Leda*, whiter did appeare . . .
i *160. poll*] Used in the Elizabethan sense to mean 'the part of the head on
which the hair grows' (*OED*).
i *170. Ganymede*] The Phrygian youth who was carried up to Heaven by
Jupiter and became cup-bearer to the gods (Ovid's *Metamorphoses* x 155–61).
A standard reference in Elizabethan poetry.
i *172. chieftain king*] Endymion figures variously in classical mythology as a
prince of Elis and a Carian shepherd. See *Lemprière*: 'Some suppose that
there were two of that name, the son of a King of Elis and the shepherd or
astronomer of Caria.'
i *174. nervy*] Muscular Cp. *Ode to Apollo* 7 and *n* (p. 14 above), 'his nervous
arms'.
i *177. groves Elysian*] See *Lemprière*: 'Elysium or Elysii Campi, a place or
island in the infernal regions, where, according to the mythology of the
ancients, the souls of the virtuous were placed after death.'

Through his forgotten hands. Then would they sigh,
And think of yellow leaves, of owlets' cry,
Of logs piled solemnly. Ah, well-a-day,
Why should our young Endymion pine away?

185   Soon the assembly, in a circle ranged,
Stood silent round the shrine; each look was changed
To sudden veneration. Women meek
Beckoned their sons to silence, while each cheek
Of virgin bloom paled gently for slight fear.

190   Endymion, too, without a forest peer,
Stood wan and pale, and with an awèd face,
Among his brothers of the mountain chase.
In midst of all, the venerable priest
Eyed them with joy from greatest to the least,

195   And, after lifting up his agèd hands,
Thus spake he:
                    'Men of Latmos! Shepherd bands,
Whose care it is to guard a thousand flocks—
Whether descended from beneath the rocks
That overtop your mountains, whether come

200   From valleys where the pipe is never dumb,

i *182*. Emblems of autumn and winter perhaps suggested by *Macbeth* V iii
22–3,

                    . . . my way of life
          Is fall'n into the sear, the yellow leaf . . .

and *The Tempest* V i 90,

                    There I couch when owls do cry . . .

i *187*. *Women meek*] See iii 46 *n* below.
i *199*. *overtop*] Crown. Normally used to mean rise or tower above.
i *204*. *Nibble their fill*] Echoes *The Tempest* IV i 62,

          Thy turfy mountains, where live nibbling sheep . . .

The line is marked by K. in his copy of Shakespeare (*Spurgeon* 79). His recent close reading of *The Tempest* is recorded in his letter to Reynolds of
April 1817 (*L* i 133). For other echoes of the play see i 225 *n*, 394 *n*, 639–40
n, 747–9 *n*.
i *206*. *Triton*] A sea-deity, usually represented as half-man, half-dolphin
and blowing a shell. See Spenser's *Colin Clout's Come Home Againe* (1595)
244–5,

          . . . the shepheard which hath charge in chief,
          Is Triton, blowing loud his wreathed horne . . .

and Wordsworth's echo of Spenser's lines in *The world is too much with us*
(1807) 14,

          . . . hear old Triton blow his wreathed horn . . .

Or from your swelling downs, where sweet air stirs
Blue hare-bells lightly, and where prickly furze
Buds lavish gold; or ye, whose precious charge
Nibble their fill at ocean's very marge,
205   Whose mellow reeds are touched with sounds forlorn
By the dim echoes of old Triton's horn;
Mothers and wives, who day by day prepare
The scrip with needments for the mountain air,
And all ye gentle girls who foster up
210   Udderless lambs, and in a little cup
Will put choice honey for a favoured youth—
Yea, every one attend! For in good truth
Our vows are wanting to our great god Pan.
Are not our lowing heifers sleeker than
215   Night-swollen mushrooms? Are not our wide plains
Speckled with countless fleeces? Have not rains
Greened over April's lap? No howling sad
Sickens our fearful ewes, and we have had
Great bounty from Endymion our lord.
220   The earth is glad, the merry lark has poured
His early song against yon breezy sky
That spreads so clear o'er our solemnity.'
     Thus ending, on the shrine he heaped a spire
Of teeming sweets, enkindling sacred fire;
225   Anon he stained the thick and spongy sod
With wine, in honour of the shepherd-god.
Now while the earth was drinking it, and while

For an earlier recollection of Wordsworth's sonnet in K. see *Sleep and Poetry*
189–90 *n* (p. 77 above).

i *208. scrip with needments*] A satchel containing food etc. (cp. i 392 below,
'. . . their famished scrips . . .'). See *The Faerie Queene* I vi 35,

                    . . . eke behind,
   His scrip did hang, in which his needments he did bind . . .

Croker (*loc. cit.*) thought that 'needments' was one of the '. . . new words
with which, in imitation of Mr Leigh Hunt . . . [K.] adorns our language . . .'.

i *210. Udderless*] Motherless.

i *217. Greened over*] Cp. *Sleep and Poetry* 170–1 (p. 76 above),
             . . . the tender greening
       Of April meadows . . .

i *217–18. No howling . . . ewes*] Wolves have been kept away.

i *225. spongy*] Absorbent. Perhaps suggested by *The Tempest* IV i 64–5,
       Thy banks with peonied and lilied brims,
       Which spongy April at thy hest trims . . .

K. marked the passage in his copy of Shakespeare (*Spurgeon* 79). See i 203 *n*.

Bay leaves were crackling in the fragrant pile,
And gummy frankincense was sparkling bright
230 'Neath smothering parsley, and a hazy light
Spread greyly eastward, thus a chorus sang:

'O thou, whose mighty palace roof doth hang
From jagged trunks, and overshadoweth
Eternal whispers, glooms, the birth, life, death
235 Of unseen flowers in heavy peacefulness;
Who lov'st to see the hamadryads dress
Their ruffled locks where meeting hazels darken,
And through whole solemn hours dost sit, and hearken
The dreary melody of bedded reeds
240 In desolate places, where dank moisture breeds
The pipy hemlock to strange overgrowth,
Bethinking thee how melancholy loth

i 228–9. See the account of ancient Greek sacrifices in *Baldwin*, '... the whole temple was pervaded with the smell of fragrant woods, myrtle, cedar and sandal-wood, together with incense, burning on the altar' (25).

i 232–306. K.'s stanzaic 'Hymn to Pan' (see i 89–392 n) looks forward to the mature style of his major 1819 odes. Its 'promise of ultimate excellence' was recognized by Shelley (*1848* i 86), but not by Wordsworth: Haydon records that Wordsworth asked K. in Dec. 1817 '... what he had been lately doing, *I* said he has just finished an exquisite ode to Pan. ... I begged Keats to repeat it–which he did in his usual half chant, (most touching) walking up and down. ... Wordsworth drily said "a very pretty piece of Paganism"–This was unfeeling, and unworthy of his high Genius to a young Worshipper like Keats ... [K.] felt it *deeply*' (*KC* ii 143–4).

i 232–3. *whose mighty palace ... trunks*] The dense foliage of mountain-forests. See i 261–2 n.

i 234–5. Foreshadows *Ode to a Nightingale* 38–42 (p. 528 below),

　　　　　　　　　　　... here there is no light
　　Save what from heaven is with the breezes blown
　　Through verdurous glooms and winding mossy ways.

　　I cannot see what flowers are at my feet,
　　　　Nor what soft incense hangs upon the boughs ...

i 236. *hamadryads*] See *Lemprière*, '... nymphs who lived in the country, and presided over the trees, with which they were said to live and die'.

i 238. Foreshadows *To Autumn* 22 (p. 653 below),

　　Thou watchest the last oozings hours by hours ...

i 241. *the pipy hemlock*] Poison hemlock has tall hollow stems. See Virgil's *Eclogues* ii 37–8,

　　est mihi disparibus septem compacta cicutis
　　fistula, Damoetas dono mihi quam dedit olim ...

Thou wast to lose fair Syrinx—do thou now,
By thy love's milky brow,
245 By all the trembling mazes that she ran,
Hear us, great Pan!

'O thou, for whose soul-soothing quiet, turtles
Passion their voices cooingly 'mong myrtles,
What time thou wanderest at eventide
250 Through sunny meadows that outskirt the side
Of thine enmossèd realms. O thou, to whom
Broad-leavèd fig trees even now foredoom
Their ripened fruitage, yellow-girted bees
Their golden honeycombs, our village leas
255 Their fairest-blossomed beans and poppied corn,
The chuckling linnet its five young unborn
To sing for thee, low-creeping strawberries
Their summer coolness, pent-up butterflies
Their freckled wings, yea, the fresh budding year
260 All its completions—be quickly near,
By every wind that nods the mountain pine,
O forester divine!

'Thou, to whom every faun and satyr flies
For willing service, whether to surprise

('I have a pipe formed of seven uneven hemlock-stalks, a gift Damoetas
once gave me . . .' [Loeb edn].)

i *243. Syrinx*] On Pan and Syrinx see *I stood tip-toe* 157–62 and *n* (p. 93
above).

i *247. turtles*] Turtle-doves.

i *248. Passion*] Imbue with deep feeling. Often used by the Elizabethans to
suggest powerful grief, for example, *Two Gentlemen of Verona* IV iv 167–8,

    '. . . twas Ariadne passioning
    For Theseus' injury and unjust flight . . .'

and *Venus and Adonis* 1059,

    'Dumbly she passions . . .'

The word was objected to by Croker as one of K.'s 'new' expressions.

i *253. yellow-girted*] The past participle should be 'girt' or 'girdled'.

i *256. chuckling*] Clucking. So used in the later eighteenth century.

i *258. pent-up butterflies*] Butterflies still in chrysalis.

i *261-2.* The pine tree was a traditional emblem of Pan. See Sandys's commentary on Ovid's *Metamorphoses* iv, 'The browes of Pan are crowned with
Pine branches, because those trees adorne the tops of the Mountains' (Sandys's *Ovid* p. 267). The phrasing suggests a recollection of *Cymbeline* IV ii
174-5,

    . . . as the rud'st wind
  That by the top doth take the mountain pine . . .

265   The squatted hare while in half-sleeping fit;
     Or upward ragged precipices flit
     To save poor lambkins from the eagle's maw;
     Or by mysterious enticement draw
     Bewildered shepherds to their path again;
270   Or to tread breathless round the frothy main,
     And gather up all fancifullest shells
     For thee to tumble into naiads' cells,
     And, being hidden, laugh at their out-peeping;
     Or to delight thee with fantastic leaping,
275   The while they pelt each other on the crown
     With silvery oak-apples and fir-cones brown—
     By all the echoes that about thee ring,
     Hear us, O satyr king!

     'O hearkener to the loud-clapping shears
280   While ever and anon to his shorn peers
     A ram goes bleating; winder of the horn
     When snouted wild-boars routing tender corn
     Anger our huntsmen; breather round our farms
     To keep off mildews and all weather harms;
285   Strange ministrant of undescribèd sounds
     That come a-swooning over hollow grounds
     And wither drearily on barren moors;
     Dread opener of the mysterious doors
     Leading to universal knowledge—see,
290   Great son of Dryope,

i 265. *squatted*] An epithet derived from 'squat', used in the seventeenth century for the hare's form or lair.

i 268–9. Perhaps suggested by the satyr's obedience to Pan's orders in Fletcher's *The Faithful Shepherdess* III i 80–3,

> . . . Here must I stay
> To see what mortals lose their way,
> And by a false fire, seeming bright,
> Train them in and leave them right . . .

i 272. *For thee to tumble into*] To tumble them into fair *Fair copy* (*cancelled*). On 'naiads' see *To Charles Cowden Clarke* 6 n (p. 54 above).

i 285–7. See *Baldwin*, 'All the strange, mysterious and unaccountable sounds which were heard in solitary places, where attributed to Pan' (105).

i 288–9. *mysterious doors . . . to universal knowledge*] On Pan (Greek τὸ πᾶν, the all) as the god of universal nature see i 89–392 n above. Cp. K.'s simile for individual development in his letter to Reynolds of 3 May 1818, 'This Chamber of Maiden Thought becomes gradually darken'd and the same time on all sides of it many doors are set open' (*L* i 281) and also *Sleep and Poetry* 96–154 n, 102–21 n, 122–54 n (pp. 73–4 above).

The many that are come to pay their vows
With leaves about their brows!

'Be still the unimaginable lodge
For solitary thinkings–such as dodge
295   Conception to the very bourne of heaven,
Then leave the naked brain; be still the leaven,
That spreading in this dull and clodded earth
Gives it a touch ethereal, a new birth;
Be still a symbol of immensity,
300   A firmament reflected in a sea,
An element filling the space between,
An unknown–but no more! We humbly screen
With uplift hands our foreheads, lowly bending,
And giving out a shout most heaven-rending,
305   Conjure thee to receive our humble paean,
Upon thy Mount Lycean!'

i *290*. Classical mythology offers various accounts of Pan's parentage. K. follows Chapman's Homeric *Hymn to Pan* which represents Pan as the son of Dryope and Hermes.

i *293*. *lodge*] The place where solitary thinkings may lodge.

i *294–6*. *such . . . brain*] Imaginative conceptions not easy to express in words. De Selincourt notes a parallel with Marston's *Antonia and Mellida* (1602) IV i 18-22,

> . . . for when discursive powers fly out
> And roam in progress through the bounds of heaven,
> The soul itself gallops along with them,
> As chieftain of this winged troup of thought,
> Whilst the dull lodge of spirit standeth waste . . .

Marston's play was included in the second volume of C. Dilke's *Old English Plays* (6 vols. 1814–1816).

i *295*. *bourne*] Boundary. Frequently used by K. (for example at iii 31, iv 461 below). Probably suggested initially by *Hamlet* III i 79–80,

> The undiscover'd country from whose bourn
> No traveller returns . . .

i *298*. *ethereal*] Transcending the earthly. On K.'s various uses of this word see *To Hope* 5 and *n* (pp. 12, 13 above).

i *305*. *paean*] Song of praise (in Greek antiquity a hymn of thanksgiving to Apollo under the name Paean, physician of the gods).

i *306*. *Mount Lycean*] See *Lemprière*, 'LYCAEUS, a mountain of Arcadia, sacred to Jupiter . . . also sacred to Pan, whose festivals, called Lycaea, were celebrated there', and Ovid's *Metamorphoses* i 698–9,

> . . . *Redeuntem colle Lycaeo*
> *Pan videt hanc pinuque caput praecinctus acuta . . .*

('Pan saw her as she was coming back from Mount Lycaeus, his head wreathed with a crown of sharp pine-needles' [Loeb edn].)

6 + K.

Even while they brought the burden to a close,
A shout from the whole multitude arose,
That lingered in the air like dying rolls
310 Of abrupt thunder when Ionian shoals
Of dolphins bob their noses through the brine.
Meantime, on shady levels, mossy fine,
Young companies nimbly began dancing
To the swift treble pipe and humming string.
315 Aye, those fair living forms swam heavenly
To tunes forgotten, out of memory;
Fair creatures, whose young children's children bred
Thermopylae its heroes—not yet dead,
But in old marbles ever beautiful;
320 High genitors, unconscious did they cull
Time's sweet first-fruits. They danced to weariness,
And then in quiet circles did they press
The hillock turf, and caught the latter end
Of some strange history, potent to send
325 A young mind from its bodily tenement.
Or they might watch the quoit-pitchers, intent
On either side; pitying the sad death
Of Hyacinthus, when the cruel breath
of Zephyr slew him—Zephyr penitent,
330 Who now, ere Phoebus mounts the firmament,
Fondles the flower amid the sobbing rain.
The archers, too, upon a wider plain,
Beside the feathery whizzing of the shaft
And the dull twanging bowstring, and the raft

i *311. bob*] Woodhouse notes, 'The words *raise push* were suggested to the author: but he insisted on retaining *bob*' (*Woodhouse* 2).

i *318. Thermopylae*] Defended by the Spartans against Xerxes in 480 B.C.

i *319.* Perhaps suggested by the Elgin Marbles, although these depict Athenian, not Spartan, heroes.

i *320. genitors*] Progenitors. Other examples of aphaeresis for the sake of the metre at i 571, 808, 850 below.

i *326–31.* Hyacinthus was accidentally slain while playing a game of quoits with Apollo, who then transformed him into a flower. K. follows Lemprière in making Zephyr the cause of the accident (this is omitted in the version in Ovid's *Metamorphoses* x 162–219). Zephyr's grief (i 329–31) is K.'s own addition to the story, perhaps inspired by Apollo's lamentation over Hyacinthus in *Metamorphoses* x 185–215.

i *331. sobbing*] Cp. *I stood tip-toe* 7 *n* (p. 86 above), 'the early sobbing of the morn'.

i *334. raft*] Torn away. See *The Faerie Queene* I i 24,
He raft her hatefull head . . .

335   Branch down-sweeping from a tall ash top,
       Called up a thousand thoughts to envelop
       Those who would watch. Perhaps the trembling knee
       And frantic gape of lonely Niobe—
       Poor, lonely Niobe, when her lovely young
340   Were dead and gone, and her caressing tongue
       Lay a lost thing upon her paly lip,
       And very, very deadliness did nip
       Her motherly cheeks. Aroused from this sad mood
       By one, who at a distance loud hallooed,
345   Uplifting his strong bow into the air,
       Many might after brighter visions stare–
       After the Argonauts, in blind amaze
       Tossing about on Neptune's restless ways,
       Until, from the horizon's vaulted side,
350   There shot a golden splendour far and wide,
       Spangling those million poutings of the brine
       With quivering ore—'twas even an awful shine
       From the exaltation of Apollo's bow,
       A heavenly beacon in their dreary woe.
355   Who thus were ripe for high contemplating
       Might turn their steps towards the sober ring
       Where sat Endymion and the agèd priest

i *335. Branch*] The single syllable does duty for the initial foot.
i *337–43. Perhaps . . . cheeks*] Niobe was changed into stone after her children
were slaughtered by Apollo as a punishment for her arrogance. The story is
related in Ovid's *Metamorphoses* vi 165–312. Other references known to K.
appear in *Lemprière, Baldwin, Hamlet* I ii 149, *The Faerie Queene* IV vii 30.
On pictorial and sculptural representations of Niobe well known at the
time see Ian Jack's *Keats and the Mirror of Art* (1967) 152–3.
i *341. paly*] A recently revived Elizabethan poeticism. Used again at i 984
below and in *On First Seeing the Tomb of Burns* 5 (p. 357 below).
i *347–54.* The Argonauts sailed with Jason in the *Argo* in search of the Golden Fleece. Apollo does not appear in the versions of the story in *Lemprière,
Tooke, Baldwin* or Ovid's *Metamorphoses* vii 1–58, but see Apollonius Rhodius's *Argonautica* (Fawkes's translation ii 857–60),

>   To Thynia's neighbouring isle their course they bore
>   And safely landed on the neighbouring shore,
>   When bright Apollo show'd his radiant face,
>   From Lycia hastening to the Scythian race . . .

K. may have read Fawkes's lines in *Chalmers' English Poets* (1810) XX 271.
De Selincourt suggests that K. was told of the episode by Shelley who admired '. . . the Apollo so finely described by Apollonius Rhodius when the
dazzling of his beautiful limbs suddenly shone over the dark Euxine' (*de
Selincourt* 423–4).

'Mong shepherds gone in eld, whose looks increased
The silvery setting of their mortal star.
360   There they discoursed upon the fragile bar
That keeps us from our homes ethereal,
And what our duties there: to nightly call
Vesper, the beauty-crest of summer weather;
To summon all the downiest clouds together
365   For the sun's purple couch; to emulate
In ministering the potent rule of fate
With speed of fire-tailed exhalations;
To tint her pallid cheek with bloom, who cons
Sweet poesy by moonlight—besides these,
370   A world of other unguessed offices.
Anon they wandered, by divine converse,
Into Elysium, vying to rehearse
Each one his own anticipated bliss.
One felt heart-certain that he could not miss
375   His quick-gone love among fair blossomed boughs,
Where every zephyr-sigh pouts and endows
Her lips with music for the welcoming.
Another wished, mid that eternal spring,
To meet his rosy child, with feathery sails,
380   Sweeping, eye-earnestly, through almond vales—
Who, suddenly, should stoop through the smooth wind,
And with the balmiest leaves his temples bind,
And, ever after, through those regions be
His messenger, his little Mercury.
385   Some were athirst in soul to see again
Their fellow huntsmen o'er the wide champaign
In times long past; to sit with them and talk
Of all the chances in their earthly walk—

i *358. eld*] Old age.

i *363. Vesper*] The evening star, sometimes called Hesperus. See i 531 *n* below.

i *367. fire-tailed exhalations*] Comets. The word 'exhalations' has five syllables.

i *368. pallid*] pretty *Fair copy*. The correction may be owed to Taylor, who wrote the words 'pallid waning' on the opposite page in K.'s MS.

i *372. Elysium*] See i 177 *n* (above).

i *379. feathery sails*] Wings.

i *380. eye-earnestly*] With earnest eyes. A Keatsian coinage. The 'almond vales' are dales or valleys filled with almond trees.

i *386. champaign*] Expanse of open country (OED).

i *388.* See *The Book of Common Prayer*, 'All the changes and chances of this mortal life' (Collects after the Offertory 1).

Comparing, joyfully, their plenteous stores
390   Of happiness to when upon the moors,
Benighted, close they huddled from the cold,
And shared their famished scrips. Thus all out-told
Their fond imaginations—saving him
Whose eyelids curtained up their jewels dim,
395   Endymion; yet hourly had he striven
To hide the cankering venom that had riven
His fainting recollections. Now indeed
His senses had swooned off; he did not heed
The sudden silence, or the whispers low,
400   Or the old eyes dissolving at his woe,
Or anxious calls, or close of trembling palms,
Or maiden's sigh, that grief itself embalms;
But in the self-same fixèd trance he kept,
Like one who on the earth had never stepped.
405   Aye, even as dead-still as a marble man,
Frozen in that old tale Arabian.
      Who whispers him so pantingly and close?

i *392. famished*] Scantly supplied.
i *394.* Cp. *The Tempest* I ii 405 (marked by K. in his copy of Shakespeare: see *Spurgeon* 72),

> The fringed curtains of thine eye advance . . .

and *Pericles* III ii 99–101,

> Her eyelids, cases to those heavenly jewels
> Which Pericles hath lost,
> Begin to part their fringes of bright gold . . .

i *396. cankering*] Infecting and consuming like a canker.
i *401. close of trembling palms*] Nervous clasping of hands.
i *402. that grief itself embalms*] That makes grief itself fragrant.
i *405–6.* See 'The History of the Young King of the Black Isles' in *The Arabian Nights*, 'The sultan . . . saw a handsome young man, richly habited, seated upon a throne. . . . Melancholy was painted on his countenance . . . lifting up his robe, he shewed the sultan that he was a man only from the head to the girdle, and that the other half of his body was black marble' (1811 edn i 117–18). 'Frozen' is substituted for 'Sitting' in the fair copy.
i *407–12.*   Now happily, there sitting on the grass
> Was fair Peona, a most tender Lass,
> And his sweet sister; who, uprising, went
> With stifled sobs, and o'er his shoulder leant.
> Putting her trembling hand against his cheek
> She said: 'My dear Endymion, let us seek
> A pleasant bower where thou may'st rest apart;
> And ease in slumber thine afflicted heart:
> Come my own dearest brother: these our friends

Peona, his sweet sister—of all those,
His friends, the dearest. Hushing signs she made,
410   And breathed a sister's sorrow to persuade
A yielding up, a cradling on her care.
Her eloquence did breathe away the curse.
She led him, like some midnight spirit-nurse
Of happy changes in emphatic dreams,
415   Along a path between two little streams,
Guarding his forehead, with her round elbow,
From low-grown branches, and his footsteps slow
From stumbling over stumps and hillocks small,
Until they came to where these streamlets fall,
420   With mingled bubblings and a gentle rush,
Into a river, clear, brimful, and flush
With crystal mocking of the trees and sky.
A little shallop, floating there hard by,
Pointed its beak over the fringèd bank;
425   And soon it lightly dipped and rose, and sank
And dipped again, with the young couple's weight—

Will joy in thinking thou dost sleep where bends
Our freshening River through yon birchen grove:
Do come now!' Could he gainsay her who strove,
So soothingly, to breathe away a Curse? . . .

Fair copy (*cancelled*).

i *408. Peona, his sweet sister*] Chapman provides the hero with a sisterly con-
fidante in his continuation of Marlowe's *Hero and Leander*, but Peona's
healing powers (see i 436–42, iv 863–4 below) are K.'s invention. He may
have derived her name from Paeon, physician to the gods (Homer's *Iliad* v
401–2, 899–901). See *Lemprière*: 'Paeon . . . cured the wounds which the
gods received during the Trojan war. From him physicians are sometimes
called Poenii.' According to some traditions Peon was a son of Endymion
and Cynthia. See also i 305 *n* above.

i *411.* An unrhymed line, probably accounted for by the revision of i 407–
412.

i *413. midnight spirit-nurse*] An attempted correction in the MS was 'mid-
night-spirit nurse'; midnight spirit nurse *1848*. The expression is obscure,
but K. means that she is like a good spirit ministering in the depths of night
to a troubled sleeper and changing the course of his dreams.

i *414. emphatic*] Vividly convincing.

i *420. a gentle rush*] The phrasing follows Hunt. See *Calidore* 20 *n* (p. 37
above).

i *421. brimful*] See below iii 366 *n*.

i *422. crystal mocking*] Reflections in the water.

i *423. shallop*] See *Calidore* 67 *n* (p. 39 above).

Peona guiding, through the water straight,
Towards a bowery island opposite.
Which gaining presently, she steerèd light
430 Into a shady, fresh, and ripply cove,
Where nested was an arbour, overwove
By many a summer's silent fingering,
To whose cool bosom she was used to bring
Her playmates, with their needle broidery
435 And minstrel memories of times gone by.

    So she was gently glad to see him laid
Under her favourite bower's quiet shade
On her own couch, new made of flower leaves
Dried carefully on the cooler side of sheaves
440 When last the sun his autumn tresses shook,
And the tanned harvesters rich armfuls took.
Soon was he quieted to slumberous rest,
But, ere it crept upon him, he had pressed
Peona's busy hand against his lips,
445 And still a-sleeping held her finger-tips
In tender pressure. And as a willow keeps

i *428. a bowery island*] Cp. *Calidore* 26 and *n* (p. 37 above), 'The bowery shore'.

i *432. fingering*] Elaboration. Cp. the web in Spenser's *Muiopotmos* 366,
                    . . . loupes of fingring fine . . .

i *435. minstrel memories*] Songs. The line suggests a recollection of Wordsworth's *The Solitary Reaper* (1807) 18–20,
                Perhaps the plaintive numbers flow
                For old, unhappy, far-off things,
                And battles long ago . . .

i *441.*   When last the Harvesters rich armfuls took.
        She tied a little bucket to a Crook,
        Ran some swift paces to a dark wells side,
        And in a sighing-time return'd, supplied
        With spar cold water; in which she did squeeze
        A snowy napkin, and upon her knees
        Began to cherish her poor Brother's face;
        Damping refreshfully his forehead's space,
        His eyes, his Lips: then in a cupped shell
        She brought him ruby wine; then let him smell,
        Time after time, a precious amulet,
        Which seldom took she from its cabinet . . .
                                 Fair copy (cancelled).
With '. . . tanned harvesters . . .' cp. *The Tempest* IV i 134, quoted in i 139 *n* above.

A patient watch over the stream that creeps
Windingly by it, so the quiet maid
Held her in peace—so that a whispering blade
450   Of grass, a wailful gnat, a bee bustling
Down in the blue-bells, or a wren light rustling
Among sere leaves and twigs, might all be heard.

O magic sleep! O comfortable bird,
That broodest o'er the troubled sea of the mind
455   Till it is hushed and smooth! O unconfined
Restraint! Imprisoned liberty! Great key
To golden palaces, strange minstrelsy,
Fountains grotesque, new trees, bespangled caves,
Echoing grottoes, full of tumbling waves
460   And moonlight—aye, to all the mazy world
Of silvery enchantment! Who, upfurled
Beneath thy drowsy wing a triple hour,
But renovates and lives? Thus, in the bower,
Endymion was calmed to life again.
465   Opening his eyelids with a healthier brain,

i *450. wailful gnat*] Cp. *To Autumn* 27 (p. 653 below),
          Then in a wailful choir the small gnats mourn . . .
i *452. sere*] Dry. Perhaps a reminiscence of *Macbeth* V iii 23, 'the sear, the
yellow leaf'. For K.'s earlier echo of Shakespeare's line see i 182 *n*.
i *453–60. O magic sleep . . . moonlight*] A passage singled out by Reynolds as
'. . . full of repose and feeling' (*Alfred, West of England Journal* 6, Oct. 1818;
repr. *Forman* (1883) iii 378). For celebrations of sleep elsewhere in K. see
Sleep and Poetry 11–18 *n* (p. 70 above).
i *453–5. O comfortable bird . . . smooth*] Perhaps suggested by the halcyons
resting on the sea in Milton's *Nativity Ode* 66–8,
                    . . . the milde Ocean,
     Who now hath quite forgot to rave,
     While Birds of Calm sit brooding on the charmed wave . . .
For K.'s earlier references to halcyons see *To Charles Cowden Clarke* 57 *n*,
To the Ladies who Saw Me Crowned 7 (pp. 56 and 110 above). The word
'comfortable' is an archaism for 'consolatory'. See, for example, *Romeo and
Juliet* V iii 148, 'O comfortable friar!'
i *455–6. unconfined . . . liberty*] Paradoxes expressing the notion that the con-
finement of the body and the stilling of the surface processes of the mind
give a free rein to the fancy.
i *460. mazy*] Suggesting the magical intricacy of the dream world.
i *461. upfurled*] See i 153–4 *n*.
i *465*. Followed in the fair copy by the cancelled lines,
               A cheerfuller resignment, and a smile
               For his fair Sister flowing like the Nile
               Through all the channels of her piety . . .

He said: 'I feel this thine endearing love
All through my bosom: thou art as a dove
Trembling its closèd eyes and sleekèd wings
About me; and the pearliest dew not brings
470 Such morning incense from the fields of May
As do those brighter drops that twinkling stray
From those kind eyes, the very home and haunt
Of sisterly affection. Can I want
Aught else, aught nearer heaven, than such tears?
475 Yet dry them up in bidding hence all fears
That, any longer, I will pass my days
Alone and sad. No, I will once more raise
My voice upon the mountain-heights; once more
Make my horn parley from their foreheads hoar;
480 Again my trooping hounds their tongues shall loll
Around the breathèd boar; again I'll poll
The fair-grown yew tree for a chosen bow,
And, when the pleasant sun is getting low,
Again I'll linger in a sloping mead
485 To hear the speckled thrushes, and see feed
Our idle sheep. So be thou cheerèd, sweet,
And, if thy lute is here, softly intreat
My soul to keep in its resolvèd course.'
    Hereat Peona, in their silver source,
490 Shut her pure sorrow-drops with glad exclaim,
And took a lute, from which there pulsing came
A lively prelude, fashioning the way
In which her voice should wander. 'Twas a lay

i 466. *I feel*] Dear Maid, may I this moment die
        If I feel not . . . *Fair copy (cancelled).*
See K.'s journal-letter of 23–4 Jan. 1818, 'Hunt . . . says the conversation is
unnatural and too high-flown for the Brother and Sister. Says it should be
simple forgetting . . . that they are both overshadowed by a Supernatural
Power and of force could not speak like Franchesca in the Rimini [Leigh
Hunt's *The Story of Rimini*, 1816]. He must first prove that Caliban's poetry
[in *A Midsummer Night's Dream*] is unnatural–This with me completely
overturns his objections' (L i 213–14).
i 470–2. From woodbine hedges, such a morning feel,
        As do those brighter drops, that twinkling steal
        Through those pressed lashes, from the blossom'd plant . . .
                                            Fair copy (cancelled).
i 470. *morning incense*] The fresh scent of the opening flowers. On this use
of 'incense' in K. see *Calidore* 155 *n* (p. 42 above).
i 493–7. *'Twas a lay . . . strange*] Probably suggested by the mournful lamenting of the nymph Dryope who was transformed into a tree while

More subtle cadencèd, more forest-wild
495 Than Dryope's lone lulling of her child;
And nothing since has floated in the air
So mournful strange. Surely some influence rare
Went, spiritual, through the damsel's hand,
For still, with Delphic emphasis, she spanned
500 The quick invisible strings, even though she saw
Endymion's spirit melt away and thaw
Before the deep intoxication.
But soon she came, with sudden burst, upon
Her self-possession—swung the lute aside,
505 And earnestly said: 'Brother, 'tis vain to hide
That thou dost know of things mysterious,
Immortal, starry; such alone could thus
Weigh down thy nature. Hast thou sinned in aught
Offensive to the heavenly powers? Caught
510 A Paphian dove upon a message sent?
Thy deathful bow against some deer-head bent
Sacred to Dian? Haply thou hast seen

---

nursing her child (Ovid's *Metamorphoses* ix 371–9). The other Dryope, Pan's
mother (see i 290 *n*), was frightened of her son and according to Chapman's
Homeric *Hymn to Pan* 70–1,

> . . . fled in feare
> The sight of so unsatisfying a Thing . . .

i *494–5.*   More forest-wild, more subtle-cadenced
> Than can be told by mortal: even wed
> The fainting tenors of a thousand Shells,
> To a million whisperings of Lilly bells;
> And, mingle too, the Nightingale's complain
> Caught in its hundredth echo; 'twould be vain . . .

Fair copy (cancelled).

i *499. Delphic*] Divinely inspired.

i *501.* See i 98–100 *n* above.

i *502. intoxication*] Six syllables.

i *510. Paphian dove*] From Venus's temple in Paphos. A standard reference
in the Elizabethans, for example, *The Tempest* IV i 92–4,

> . . . I met her deity
> Cutting the clouds towards Paphos and her son
> Dove-drawn with her . . .

i *511. deer-head*] In the fair copy either 'Deer-head' or 'Deer-herd' (the
reading of *1818*). Garrod's 'dear-head' is an error.

i *512–14. Haply . . . death*] Actaeon was changed into a stag and torn to
pieces by his own hounds because he saw Diana bathing (Ovid's *Metamorphoses* iii 173–252). K. also knew Spenser's account of Faunus watching
Diana bathing, *The Faerie Queene* VII vi 42–7.

Her naked limbs among the alders green—
And that, alas! is death. No, I can trace
515   Something more high-perplexing in thy face!'

Endymion looked at her, and pressed her hand,
And said, 'Art thou so pale, who wast so bland
And merry in our meadows? How is this?
Tell me thine ailment—tell me all amiss!
520   Ah, thou hast been unhappy at the change
Wrought suddenly in me. What indeed more strange?
Or more complete to overwhelm surmise?
Ambition is no sluggard—'tis no prize,
That toiling years would put within my grasp,
525   That I have sighed for; with so deadly gasp
No man e'er panted for a mortal love.
So all have set my heavier grief above
These things which happen. Rightly have they done.
I, who still saw the horizontal sun

i 513. *among the alders*] on flags and rushes *Fair copy (cancelled)*.
i 515. *high-perplexing*] One of K.'s many compounds with 'high', the
most familiar being *Ode on a Grecian Urn* 29 (p. 536 below) '. . . high-
sorrowful . . .'. Other examples in this poem at i 759, ii 437 below.
i 516–20. *Fair copy (cancelled)*,

     And I do pray thee by thy utmost aim
     To tell me all. No little fault or blame
     Canst thou lay on me for a teasing Girl;
     Ever as an unfathomable pearl
[5]   Hast been thy secrecy to me: but now
     I needs must hunger after it, and vow
     To be its jealous Guardian for aye.
       Uttering these words she got nigh and more nigh,
     And put at last her arms about his neck:
[10] Nor was there any tart, ungentle check,
     Nor any frown or stir dissatisfied,
     But smooth compliance and tender slide
     Of arm in arm, and what is written next.
       'Doubtless, Peona, thou hast been perplex'd,
[15] And pained oft, in thinking of the change . . .
  l. 12. *compliance*] Followed by an omission sign, presumably indicating
that the line wants a foot.
i 517. *bland*] Gentle.
i 523. *Ambition is no sluggard*] Perhaps a reminiscence of Milton's *Lycidas*
70,
     Fame is the spur that the clear spirit doth raise . . .
The word 'sluggard' means sluggish, slothful.

530 Heave his broad shoulder o'er the edge of the world,
Out-facing Lucifer, and then had hurled
My spear aloft, as signal for the chase—
I, who, for very sport of heart, would race
With my own steed from Araby; pluck down
535 A vulture from his towery perching; frown
A lion into growling, loth retire—
To lose, at once, all my toil-breeding fire,
And sink thus low! But I will ease my breast
Of secret grief, here in this bowery nest.

540 'This river does not see the naked sky
Till it begins to progress silverly
Around the western border of the wood,
Whence, from a certain spot, its winding flood
Seems at the distance like a crescent moon.
545 And in that nook, the very pride of June,
Had I been used to pass my weary eves;
The rather for the sun unwilling leaves
So dear a picture of his sovereign power,
And I could witness his most kingly hour,
550 When he doth tighten up the golden reins,
And paces leisurely down amber plains
His snorting four. Now when his chariot last

i 530. For the effect aimed at cp. *The Faerie Queene* II xii 23, 'sea-shoulder-ing Whales'. See *Cowden Clarke* '[K.] *hoisted* himself up, and looked burly and dominant, as he said, "What an image that is"' (126).

531. *Lucifer*] The morning star. See *Lemprière*: 'called Lucifer, when it appears in the morning before the sun; but when it follows it, and appears some time after its setting, it is called "Hesperus".' K. may be remembering Sandys's *Ovid, Metamorphoses* ii (p. 26. col. 2),

Cleare *Lucifer* the flying Stars doth chase;
And, after all the rest, resignes his place . . .

i 536. *growling*] grumbling *Fair copy (cancelled).*
i 538–9.   And come to such a Ghost as I am now!
        But listen, Sister, I will tell thee how . . .

Fair copy (cancelled).

i 539. *bowery*] See i 428 *n* (p. 139 above).
i 545.   And in that spot the most endowing boon
        Of balmy Air, sweet blooms, and coverts fresh
        Has been outshed; yes, all that could enmesh
        Our human senses—make us fealty sware
        To gadding Flora. In this grateful lair . . .

Fair copy (cancelled).

Its beams against the zodiac-lion cast,
There blossomed suddenly a magic bed
555 Of sacred ditamy and poppies red
At which I wondered greatly, knowing well
That but one night had wrought this flowery spell;
And, sitting down close by, began to muse
What it might mean. Perhaps, thought I, Morpheus,
560 In passing here, his owlet pinions shook;
Or, it may be, ere matron Night uptook
Her ebon urn, young Mercury, by stealth,
Had dipt his rod in it–such garland wealth
Came not by common growth. Thus on I thought,
565 Until my head was dizzy and distraught.
Moreover, through the dancing poppies stole
A breeze, most softly lulling to my soul,
And shaping visions all about my sight

i 552. *His snorting four*] The four horses which draw Apollo's chariot are
named in Ovid's *Metamorphoses* ii 153–5,

> . . . *volucres Pyrois et Eous et Aethon,*
> *Solis equi, quartusque Phlegon hinnitibus auras*
> *flammiferis inplent . . .*

('The sun's swift horses, Pyroïs, Eoüs, Aethon, and the fourth, Phlegon, fill
all the air with their fiery whinnying' [Loeb edn].)

i 553. *the zodiac-lion*] Leo, one of the constellations of the Zodiac. On K.'s
knowledge of the constellations see iv 581–605 *n* (p. 269 below).

i 555. *ditamy . . . poppies*] Emblems of Diana. See *Lemprière*: 'Among plants
the poppy and the ditamy were sacred to Diana.'

i 559–60. *Perhaps . . . shook*] For Morpheus's traditional association with
poppies see *Sleep and Poetry* 13–14 *n* (p. 70 above). 'Morpheus' is a dissyllable here.

i 561–2. *ere . . . urn*] During the night. The personification has an eighteenth-century flavour. The phrase 'ere matron Night' is substituted in the
fair copy for 'that, ere still Night'.

i 563. *his rod*] The *caduceus*, Mercury's magic wand. See *Lemprière*: '. . . a
rod entwined at one end by two serpents . . . the ensign of Mercury . . .
given him by Apollo in return for the lyre. . . With the caduceus Mercury
conducted to the infernal regions the souls of the dead, and, by its powerful
touch, he could lull mortals to sleep, and even raise to life a dead person.'

i 565. *dizzy*] A favourite word in K.'s early poetry. See, for example,
Sleep and Poetry 177, *On Seeing the Elgin Marbles* 11 (pp. 77, 105 above)
and also 'dizziness', 'dizzily' at iii 827, iv 904 below.

i 568. *shaping visions*] K.'s reference to the consoling 'breeze' in the preceding line may have called to his mind Coleridge's *Dejection Ode* (1802,
repr. 1817) 86,

> My shaping spirit of Imagination . . .

Of colours, wings, and bursts of spangly light,
570 The which became more strange, and strange, and dim,
And then were gulfed in a tumultuous swim—
And then I fell asleep. Ah, can I tell
The enchantment that afterwards befell?
Yet it was but a dream—yet such a dream
575 That never tongue, although it overteem
With mellow utterance like a cavern spring,
Could figure out and to conception bring
All I beheld and felt. Methought I lay
Watching the zenith, where the milky way
580 Among the stars in virgin splendour pours;
And travelling my eye, until the doors
Of heaven appeared to open for my flight,
I became loth and fearful to alight
From such high soaring by a downward glance,
585 So kept me steadfast in that airy trance,
Spreading imaginary pinions wide.
When, presently, the stars began to glide,
And faint away, before my eager view.
At which I sighed that I could not pursue,
590 And dropped my vision to the horizon's verge—
And lo! from opening clouds, I saw emerge
The loveliest moon, that ever silvered o'er
A shell for Neptune's goblet. She did soar
So passionately bright, my dazzled soul
595 Commingling with her argent spheres did roll
Through clear and cloudy, even when she went
At last into a dark and vapoury tent—
Whereat, methought, the lidless-eyèd train

i *569. bursts of spangly light*] Perhaps owed to *A Midsummer Night's Dream*
II i 29, 'spangled star-light sheen'; see below ii 207 *n*.
i *571. a tumultuous swim*] The phrasing follows Hunt. See *Calidore* 20 *n* (p.
37 above). On 'gulfed' (engulfed) see i 320 *n* (p. 134 above).
i *577. conception*] Probably clear formulation. Cp. i 294–6*n* above.
i *581. travelling*] Used transitively.
i *582. appeared*] seemed *Fair copy* (cancelled).
i *592–3. silvered . . . goblet*] K. appears to be suggesting that pearly shells
take their sheen from moonlight.
i *595. spheres*] In ancient astronomy the concentric, hollow, transparent
globes supposed to revolve round each planet.
i *596. Through clear and cloudy*] Echoes Thomson's *The Seasons* (1730),
Spring 332,

From clear to cloudy tossed . . .

Of planets all were in the blue again.
600 To commune with those orbs, once more I raised
My sight right upward; but it was quite dazed
By a bright something, sailing down apace,
Making me quickly veil my eyes and face.
Again I looked, and, O ye deities
605 Who from Olympus watch our destinies!
Whence that completed form of all completeness?
Whence came that high perfection of all sweetness?
Speak, stubborn earth, and tell me where, oh where,
Hast thou a symbol of her golden hair?
610 Not oat-sheaves drooping in the western sun;
Not—thy soft hand, fair sister, let me shun
Such follying before thee! Yet she had,
Indeed, locks bright enough to make me mad;
And they were simply gordianed up and braided,
615 Leaving, in naked comeliness, unshaded,
Her pearl-round ears, white neck, and orbèd brow;
The which were blended in, I know not how,
With such a paradise of lips and eyes,
Blush-tinted cheeks, half smiles, and faintest sighs,
620 That, when I think thereon, my spirit clings
And plays about its fancy, till the stings
Of human neighbourhood envenom all.
Unto what awful power shall I call?
To what high fane? Ah, see her hovering feet,
625 More bluely veined, more soft, more whitely sweet

i *598–9. lidless-eyèd . . . planets*] Perhaps suggesting that planets do not wink like stars, but see the *Bright star* sonnet 1–6 *n* (p. 737–8 below).
i *614–16.* Perhaps suggested by the simplicity of Phoebe's appearance in the gem engraving 'Endymion and Phoebe', reproduced in Spence's *Polymetis* 199 and Ian Jack's *Keats and the Mirror of Art* (Plate xv). Drayton's descriptions of Phoebe are highly ornate (see *Endimion and Phoebe* 105–32, *The Man in the Moone* 129–46).
i *614. gordianed*] Knotted. Derived from the Gordian knot, an intricate knot tied by the Phrygian king Gordius, which was eventually cut by Alexander. The epithet 'gordian' was common in the sixteenth and seventeenth centuries, but K.'s use of it as a verb is individual. Phoebe's simply dressed hair contrasts with Drayton's *The Man in the Moone* 77,
        Her Hayre tuck'd up in many a curious pleate . . .
i *621–2. the stings . . . envenom all*] On the painful return to daily life see i 681–705 *n* below.
i *621. plays*] fawns *Fair copy (cancelled)*.
i *624–32.* The resemblance of some of the descriptive details to Botticelli's 'Birth of Venus' is a coincidence, since the painting was not known in

Than those of sea-born Venus, when she rose
From out her cradle shell. The wind out-blows
Her scarf into a fluttering pavilion;
'Tis blue, and over-spangled with a million
630   Of little eyes, as though thou wert to shed,
Over the darkest, lushest blue-bell bed
Handfuls of daisies.' 'Endymion, how strange!
Dream within dream!' 'She took an airy range,
And then, towards me, like a very maid,
635   Came blushing, waning, willing, and afraid,
And pressed me by the hand. Ah, 'twas too much!
Methought I fainted at the charmèd touch,
Yet held my recollection, even as one
Who dives three fathoms where the waters run
640   Gurgling in beds of coral; for anon,
I felt upmounted in that region
Where falling stars dart their artillery forth,
And eagles struggle with the buffeting north
That balances the heavy meteor-stone—
645   Felt too, I was not fearful, nor alone,

England at the time and had not been engraved (see M. Levey's 'Botticelli and nineteenth-century England', *Journal of the Warburg and Courtauld Institutes*, 1960, xxiii 292). Ian Jack points out (*Keats and the Mirror of Art*, 1967, 154) that K.'s portrayal—especially in ll. 627–32—is in keeping with traditional representations of Diana which had been made familiar from various eighteenth-century works of classical reference.

i *624–8. her hovering feet . . . pavilion*] The engraving in Spence's *Polymetis* (see above i 614–16 *n*) shows Phoebe bare-foot and holding a scarf which arches over her head in the wind.

i *630. little eyes*] K. may have remembered the eyes scattered over the scarf held by the figure of Fame in Spence's *Polymetis* (Plate XXXIX, fig. iv). The context suggests his association of the 'eyes' with stars (see i 598–9 *n*, i 632 *n*).

i *632. daisies*] bud-stars *Fair copy (cancelled)*.

i *635. waning*] Drawing back. The word recalls the waxing and waning of the moon.

i *639–40. Who dives . . . coral*] Echoes *The Tempest* I ii 394–5,

Full fathom five thy father lies;
Of his bones are coral made . . .

K. marked the passage in his copy of Shakespeare (*Spurgeon* 71). See i 204 *n*.

i *641. region*] Trisyllabic.

i *643–4. the buffeting north*] Northern gales so strong that they can balance a heavy meteor in the air.

But lapped and lulled along the dangerous sky.
Soon, as it seemed, we left our journeying high,
And straightway into frightful eddies swooped,
Such as ay muster where grey time has scooped
650 Huge dens and caverns in a mountain's side.
There hollow sounds aroused me, and I sighed
To faint once more by looking on my bliss—
I was distracted. Madly did I kiss
The wooing arms which held me, and did give
655 My eyes at once to death—but 'twas to live,
To take in draughts of life from the gold fount
Of kind and passionate looks, to count and count
The moments, by some greedy help that seemed
A second self, that each might be redeemed
660 And plundered of its load of blessedness.
Ah, desperate mortal! I e'en dared to press
Her very cheek against my crownèd lip,
And, at that moment, felt my body dip
Into a warmer air—a moment more,
665 Our feet were soft in flowers. There was store
Of newest joys upon that alp. Sometimes
A scent of violets and blossoming limes
Loitered around us; then of honey cells,
Made delicate from all white-flower bells;
670 And once, above the edges of our nest,
An arch face peeped—an Oread as I guessed.

i 646. *along the dangerous sky*] in safe deliriousness *Fair copy* (*cancelled*). This is
followed in the fair copy by the cancelled lines,

>Sleepy with deep foretasting, that did bless
>My Soul from Madness, 'twas such certainty . . .

i 651. *sighed*] died *Fair copy* (*cancelled*).
i 654–5. *did give . . . death*] The overpowering ecstasy produced by gazing
at her; cp. i 652 above.
i 662. *crownèd lip*] So honoured by her touch that it becomes royal.
i 665–6. *There was . . . alp*]

>   Hurry o'er
>O sacrilegeous tongue the–best be dumb;
>For should one little accent from thee come
>On such a daring theme, all other sounds
>Would sicken at it, as would beaten hounds
>Scare the elysian Nightingales . . . *Fair copy* (*cancelled*).

i 666. *alp*] Upland pasture.
i 671. *Oread*] A mountain nymph. Oreads are associated with Phoebe in
Drayton's *The Man in the Moone* 426–8,

'Why did I dream that sleep o'er-powered me
In midst of all this heaven? Why not see,
Far off, the shadows of his pinions dark,
675 And stare them from me? But no, like a spark
That needs must die, although its little beam
Reflects upon a diamond, my sweet dream
Fell into nothing–into stupid sleep.
And so it was, until a gentle creep,
680 A careful moving, caught my waking ears,
And up I started. Ah, my sighs, my tears,
My clenchèd hands! For lo! the poppies hung
Dew-dabbled on their stalks, the ouzel sung
A heavy ditty, and the sullen day
685 Had chidden herald Hesperus away,
With leaden looks; the solitary breeze
Blustered, and slept, and its wild self did tease
With wayward melancholy and I thought,
Mark me, Peona, that sometimes it brought
690 Faint fare-thee-wells and sigh-shrillèd adieus!
Away I wandered–all the pleasant hues
Of heaven and earth had faded: deepest shades
Were deepest dungeons; heaths and sunny glades
Were full of pestilent light; our taintless rills
695 Seemed sooty, and o'er-spread with upturned gills
Of dying fish; the vermeil rose had blown

She the high Mountaynes actively assayes,
And there amongst the light *Oriades*,
That ride the swift *Roes* PHOEBE doth resort . . .

i *679. a gentle creep*] The phrasing follows Hunt. See *Calidore* 20 *n* (p. 37 above).

i *681–705. Ah, my sighs . . . disappointment*] With the mood of despair on awakening to actuality cp. *Sleep and Poetry* 157–9 *n* (p. 76 above),

A sense of real things comes doubly strong,
And, like a muddy stream, would bear along
My soul to nothingness . . .

See also i 919, iii 561–2, iv 614 below. The painful contrast between dream and reality is an experience shared by other romantic poets (cp. Emily Brontë, *Julian M. and A. G. Rochelle*, 1845, 69–88) and is of special importance to K. On the recurrent pattern of enchantment and awakening to disappointment in his poems, including the characteristic scenery in this passage, see M. Allott, ' "Isabella, "The Eve of St. Agnes" and "Lamia" ', *Reassessment* (1958), 49–62.

i *683. ouzel*] Blackbird.

i *685. herald Hesperus*] See i 531 *n*.

i *696. vermeil*] See i 50 *n*.

In frightful scarlet, and its thorns out-grown
Like spikèd aloe. If an innocent bird
Before my heedless footsteps stirred and stirred
700 In little journeys, I beheld in it
A disguised demon, missionéd to knit
My soul with under-darkness—to entice
My stumblings down some monstrous precipice.
Therefore I eager followed, and did curse
705 The disappointment. Time, that agèd nurse,
Rocked me to patience. Now, thank gentle heaven!
These things, with all their comfortings, are given
To my down-sunken hours, and with thee,
Sweet sister, help to stem the ebbing sea
Of weary life.'

710   Thus ended he, and both
Sat silent, for the maid was very loth
To answer, feeling well that breathèd words
Would all be lost, unheard, and vain as swords
Against the enchasèd crocodile, or leaps
715 Of grasshoppers against the sun. She weeps
And wonders, struggles to devise some blame,
To put on such a look as would say, *Shame*
On this poor weakness! But, for all her strife,
She could as soon have crushed away the life
720 From a sick dove. At length, to break the pause,
She said with trembling chance: 'Is this the cause?
This all? Yet it is strange and sad, alas!
That one who through this middle earth should pass
Most like a sojourning demi-god, and leave
725 His name upon the harp-string, should achieve
No higher bard than simple maidenhood,
Singing alone—and fearfully—how the blood

i 702. *under-darkness*] Darkness of the underworld. See i 723 n.
i 714. *enchasèd*] A poeticism for hunted.
i 722. *strange, and*]
                    wonderful—exceeding—
          And yet a shallow dream, for ever breeding
          Tempestuous Weather in that very Soul
          That should be twice content, twice smooth, twice whole,
          As is a double Peach. 'Tis . . . *Fair copy (cancelled)*.
i 723. *this middle earth*] Lying between heaven and the underworld.
i 724–5. *leave . . . harp-string*] i.e., to be sung by bards.
i 727–36. *how the blood . . . alas*] Perhaps owing something to Viola's
speech in *Twelfth Night* II iv 109–16,

Left his young cheek; and how he used to stray
He knew not where; and how he would say, *nay*,
730 If any said 'twas love—and yet 'twas love;
What could it be but love? How a ring-dove
Let fall a sprig of yew tree in his path;
And how he died; and then, that love doth scathe
The gentle heart as northern blasts do roses;
735 And then the ballad of his sad life closes
With sighs, and an 'alas!' Endymion!
Be rather in the trumpet's mouth–anon
Among the winds at large, that all may hearken!
Although, before the crystal heavens darken,
740 I watch and dote upon the silver lakes
Pictured in western cloudiness that takes
The semblance of gold rocks and bright gold sands,
Islands, and creeks, and amber-fretted strands
With horses prancing o'er them, palaces
745 And towers of amethyst; would I so tease
My pleasant days, because I could not mount
Into those regions? The Morphean fount
Of that fine element that visions, dreams,
And fitful whims of sleep are made of, streams
750 Into its airy channels with so subtle,
So thin a breathing, not the spider's shuttle,
Circled a million times within the space
Of a swallow's nest-door, could delay a trace,
A tinting of its quality—how light
755 Must dreams themselves be, seeing they're more slight
Than the mere nothing that engenders them!
Then wherefore sully the entrusted gem

... She never told her love,
But let concealment, like a worm i'the bud,
Feed on her damask cheek: she pin'd in thought,
And with a green and yellow melancholy,
She sat like Patience on a monument,
Smiling at grief. Was this not love indeed?

i 737. *in the trumpet's mouth*] Cp. *I stood tip-toe* 217 (p. 96 above),
Stepping like Homer at the trumpet's call ...
i 740–5. *silver lakes ... amethyst*] Shapes formed by the clouds at sunset.
i 741. *Pictured in*] Pight amid *Fair copy* (*cancelled*). See ii 60 n below.
i 747–9. *The Morphean fount ... made of*] Echoes *The Tempest* IV i 156–7,
... We are such stuff
As dreams are made on ...
K. marked the passage in his copy of Shakespeare (*Spurgeon* 81), which has
the folio reading 'of' for 'on' in the last line quoted.

Of high and noble life with thoughts so sick?
Why pierce high-fronted honour to the quick
760 For nothing but a dream?' Hereat the youth
Looked up. A conflicting of shame and ruth
Was in his pleated brow, yet his eyelids
Widened a little, as when Zephyr bids
A little breeze to creep between the fans
765 Of careless butterflies. Amid his pains
He seemed to taste a drop of manna-dew,
Full palatable, and a colour grew
Upon his cheek, while thus he lifeful spake.

'Peona, ever have I longed to slake
770 My thirst for the world's praises; nothing base,
No merely slumberous phantasm, could unlace
The stubborn canvas for my voyage prepared –
Though now 'tis tattered, leaving my bark bared
And sullenly drifting; yet my higher hope
775 Is of too wide, too rainbow-large a scope,

i *759. high-fronted*] Of noble bearing. An Elizabethanism. On compounds formed with 'high' in K. see *Ode on a Grecian Urn* 29 *n* (p. 536 below).
i *762. pleated*] Furrowed.
i *762-3. his eyelids / Widened*] Cp. *Hyperion* i 350-1 (pp. 414-15 below),
Hyperion arose, and on the stars
Lifted his curvèd lids, and kept them wide . . .
i *765. careless*] Free from care.
i *766. manna-dew*] Cp. the description of manna – the miraculous substance supplied to the Israelites in the wilderness – in *Exodus* xvii: 21, 'They gathered it every morning . . . and when the sun waxed hot it melted'. K. uses the phrase again in *La Belle Dame Sans Merci* 26 (p. 504 below), 'honey wild, and manna dew'. The compound may have been suggested by Coleridge's *Kubla Khan* (1816), 53, 'he on honey-dew hath fed'. For K.'s interest in Coleridge at this time see his letter to the Dilkes of Nov. 1817 requesting a copy of *Sibylline Leaves* (1817) (*L* i 183).
i *770-1. base . . . unlace*] mean . . . unseam *Fair copy (cancelled)*. The revised readings appear in Taylor's hand in the MS.
i *771. No merely slumbrous phantasm*] Repudiates the 'mere nothing' of i 754-6 above. Cp. i 857 below,
A hope beyond the shadow of a dream.
i *772-4.* With the image of travel cp. *To J. H. Reynolds Esq.* 72-3 *n* (p. 324 below),
. . . my flag is not unfurled
On the admiral staff . . .
and see *To Charles Cowden Clarke* 17 and *n* (p. 55 above),
With shattered boat, oar snapped, and canvas rent . . .

To fret at myriads of earthly wrecks.
Wherein lies happiness? In that which becks
Our ready minds to fellowship divine,
A fellowship with essence, till we shine
780   Full alchemized, and free of space. Behold
The clear religion of heaven! Fold

i 776. *myriads of earthly wrecks*] The wrecked hopes of other mortals. A rejected attempt at correction (written in Taylor's hand in the fair copy) was 'sight of this world's losses'.

i 777–842. K.'s 'pleasure-thermometer' (see following *n*) which measures happiness by its intensity and selfless absorption. The four gradations are, in ascending order, sensual enjoyment of the natural world, represented here by 'A rose leaf' (i 782); music and its associations (i 783–94); friendship (i 803–5); and passionate love (i 805–42).

i 778–81. *fellowship divine . . . religion of heaven*] blending pleasurable:

    And that delight is the most treasurable
    That makes the richest Alchymy. Behold
    Where in lies happiness Peona
    The clear Religion of Heaven! . . . *Fair copy (cancelled).*

For K.'s comment on the revised reading see his letter to Taylor of 30 Jan. 1818: 'You must indulge me by putting this in for setting aside the badness of the other, such a preface is necessary to the Subject . . . I assure you that when I wrote it, it was a regular stepping stone of the Imagination towards a Truth. My having written that Argument will perhaps be of the greatest Service to me of anything I ever did–It set before me at once the gradations of Happiness even like a kind of Pleasure Thermometer–and is my first Step towards the chief attempt in the Drama [i.e. *Endymion*]–the playing of different Natures with Joy and Sorrow' (*L* i 218–19). Critics have made heavy weather of the passage and K.'s comment on it, a major crux being the interpretation of 'fellowship with essence' (i 779), which is taken in a transcendental sense by Colvin, de Selincourt, Bridges, Middleton Murry and C. L. Finney who see K.'s 'pleasure-thermometer' variously as an idealistic or neo-Platonic hierarchy. For a full summary of such interpretations and counter-arguments see N. F. Ford's 'The meaning of "Fellowship with Essence" in *Endymion*', *PMLA* lxii (Dec. 1947) 1061–76 and *The Prefigurative Imagination of John Keats* (1951) 13–19, 46–8.

i 779. *essence*] See N. F. Ford's *The Prefigurative Imagination . . .*, 'Keats was almost unquestionably using the word "essence" as a synonym for "a thing of beauty" or "shape of beauty" [see i 1, 12 above]' (14). Cp. K.'s use of 'things' at i 795 below and the sensuous connotations of the word at iii 983–5 below,

    O sweetest essence! Sweetest of all minions!
    God of warm pulses and dishevelled hair
    And panting bosoms bare . . .

781. *religion*] Four syllables.

A rose leaf round thy finger's taperness
And soothe thy lips; hist, when the airy stress
Of music's kiss impregnates the free winds,
785   And with a sympathetic touch unbinds
Aeolian magic from their lucid wombs—
Then old songs waken from enclouded tombs,
Old ditties sigh above their father's grave,
Ghosts of melodious prophesyings rave
790   Round every spot where trod Apollo's foot;
Bronze clarions awake and faintly bruit
Where long ago a giant battle was;
And, from the turf, a lullaby doth pass
In every place where infant Orpheus slept.
795   Feel we these things? That moment have we stepped
Into a sort of oneness, and our state
Is like a floating spirit's. But there are
Richer entanglements, enthralments far
More self-destroying, leading, by degrees,
800   To the chief intensity: the crown of these
Is made of love and friendship, and sits high
Upon the forehead of humanity.
All its more ponderous and bulky worth
Is friendship, whence there ever issues forth

i *785–6.* A strained image. K. means that music impregnates the minds to produce music. 'Aeolian magic' was suggested by the music of the Aeolian lyre (see *Ode to Apollo* 34 *n*, p. 16 above). The word 'lucid' presumably means either translucent or transparent.

i *785. sympathetic touch*] sympathetically, unconfines *Fair copy* (*cancelled*).

i *787. enclouded*] Dim, obscure.

i *790. trod*] touch'd *Fair copy* (*cancelled*).

i *791. bruit*] Proclaim (usually 'noise abroad').

i *792. a giant battle*] The war of the Titans against the Olympian gods, K.'s theme in *Hyperion*. See iv 774 and *n* (p. 276 below).

i *794. place*] spot. *Fair copy* (*cancelled*).

i *795. Feel we these things?*–] The question mark is omitted in the fair copy. Garrod is probably right in suggesting that the original reading makes the sentence conditional.

i *796.* An unrhymed line.

i *799. self-destroying*] Subduing the sense of self (see i *777–842 n*). Cp. ii 275–6 below,

> And thoughts of self came on, how crude and sore
> The journey homeward to habitual self! . . .

and the *Ode to a Nightingale* 71–2 (p. 531 below),

> Forlorn! The very word is like a bell
> To toll me back from thee to my sole self!

i *802. forehead*) See *Addressed to the Same* ['Great spirits'] 10 *n* (p. 68 above).

805 A steady splendour; but at the tip-top
       There hangs by unseen film an orbèd drop
       Of light, and that is love. Its influence,
       Thrown in our eyes, genders a novel sense,
       At which we start and fret, till in the end,
810 Melting into its radiance, we blend,
       Mingle, and so become a part of it—
       Nor with aught else can our souls interknit
       So wingedly. When we combine therewith,
       Life's self is nourished by its proper pith,
815 And we are nurtured like a pelican brood.
       Aye, so delicious is the unsating food
       That men, who might have towered in the van
       Of all the congregated world, to fan
       And winnow from the coming step of time
820 All chaff of custom, wipe away all slime
       Left by men-slugs and human serpentry,
       Have been content to let occasion die,
       Whilst they did sleep in love's elysium.
       And, truly, I would rather be struck dumb
825 Than speak against this ardent listlessness,
       For I have ever thought that it might bless
       The world with benefits unknowingly,

i *808. genders*] Engenders. See i 320 *n* above.

i *813–15. when we . . . pelican brood*] Love as the vital sap of life nourishes and revivifies us as, in the fable, the pelican's blood nourishes and restores her young. The image may have been adapted from *King Lear* III iv 73, 'These pelican daughters'. K. has 'these Pelican duns' in his letter to Haydon of Aug. 1817 (*L* i 148).

i *813. combine*] amalgamate *Fair copy (cancelled)*.

i *816. unsating*] Never satisfying and never cloying. Cp. *Antony and Cleoprata* II ii 241–3,

> . . . other women cloy
> The appetites they feed, but she makes hungry
> Where most she satisfies . . .

i *818–21. to fan . . . chaff of custom*] Echoes *Troilus and Cressida* I iii 27–8,

> Distinction, with a broad and powerful fan,
> Puffing at all, winnows the light away . . .

The passage is marked by K. in his copy of Shakespeare (*Spurgeon* 152).

i *821. men-slugs . . . human serpentry*] Cp. K.'s use of animal images for enemies of liberty at iii 3 below, 'Their baaing vanities', and *Isabella* 221 (p. 339 below), 'break-covert blood-hounds'.

i *825. ardent listlessness*] Endymion is ardent in love, but listless in ambition. The phrase also expresses Keats's conception of the poetic state. Cp. *Sleep and Poetry* 19 *n* (p. 70 above).

As does the nightingale, up-perchèd high,
And cloistered among cool and bunchèd leaves—
830   She sings but to her love, nor e'er conceives
How tiptoe night holds back her dark-grey hood.
Just so may love, although 'tis understood
The mere commingling of passionate breath,
Produce more than our searching witnesseth—
835   What I know not, but who, of men, can tell
That flowers would bloom, or that green fruit would
    swell
To melting pulp, that fish would have bright mail,
The earth its dower of river, wood, and vale,
The meadows runnels, runnels pebble-stones,
840   The seed its harvest, or the lute its tones,
Tones ravishment, or ravishment its sweet,
If human souls did never kiss and greet?

    Now, if this earthly love has power to make
Men's being mortal, immortal; to shake
845   Ambition from their memories and brim
Their measure of content, what merest whim

i *828–31.* For other allusions to the nightingale and its song in K.'s early verse see *Calidore* 61, *Sleep and Poetry* 8 (pp. 31, 70 above), *To J. H. Reynolds Esq.* 85 (p. 325 below).

i *828. up-perched*] See i 154 *n.*

i *831.* A reminiscence of Milton's *Comus* 188–9,

            . . . the gray-hooded Eev'n
    Like a sad Votarist in Palmers weed . . .

The word 'tip-toe' is probably owed to *Romeo and Juliet* III v 9–10,

            . . . jocund day
    Stands tiptoe on the misty mountain tops . . .

i *833. commingling*] Intermingling. A seventeenth-century usage.

i *834–42.* The references to natural beauty (i 836–40) and music (i 840–1) recall the first two gradations in K.'s 'pleasure thermometer' (i 177–842 *n* above). Byron remarked of the passage, 'Keats says . . ."flowers would not blow, leaves bud" etc. if man and woman did not kiss. How sentimental' (Medwin's *Conversations of Lord Byron* (1824), repr. *Forman* (1883) iv 271). Cp. Bailey on *Endymion's* '. . . inclination to that abominable principle of *Shelley's*—that *Sensual Love* is the principle of *things*. Of this I believe him to be unconscious, and can see how by a process of the imagination he might arrive at so false, delusive, and dangerous conclusion' (*KC* i 34–5).

i *841.* The ravishing sound of the music and the intense delight of experiencing the ravishment.

i *843–4. make | Men's being mortal, immortal*] Make men's mortal being immortal.

i *845–6. brim . . . content*] See below iii 366 *n.*

Seems all this poor endeavour after fame
To one who keeps within his stedfast aim
A love immortal, an immortal too.
850 Look not so wildered, for these things are true,
And never can be born of atomies
That buzz about our slumbers, like brain-flies,
Leaving us fancy-sick. No, no, I'm sure
My restless spirit never could endure
855 To brood so long upon one luxury,
Unless it did, though fearfully, espy
A hope beyond the shadow of a dream.
My sayings will the less obscurèd seem
When I have told thee how my waking sight
860 Has made me scruple whether that same night
Was passed in dreaming. Hearken, sweet Peona!
Beyond the matron-temple of Latona,
Which we should see but for these darkening boughs,
Lies a deep hollow, from whose ragged brows
865 Bushes and trees do lean all round athwart
And meet so nearly, that, with wings outraught
And spreaded tail, a vulture could not glide
Past them, but he must brush on every side.
Some mouldered steps lead into this cool cell,
870 Far as the slabbèd margin of a well
Whose patient level peeps its crystal eye
Right upward, through the bushes, to the sky.
Oft have I brought thee flowers, on their stalks set
Like vestal primroses, but dark velvet

i 849. N. F. Ford suggests that the meaning 'would be clearer if Keats had
written, "A love everlasting, the love of *an* immortal"' (*The Prefigurative
Imagination of John Keats*, 1951, 125).
i 850. *wildered*] Bewildered. See i 320 *n* (p. 134 above).
i 851 *atomies*] Mites. Probably suggested by the 'Queen Mab' speech in
Romeo and Juliet I iv 58–9,

>   Drawn with a team of little atomies
>   Athwart men's noses as they lie asleep . . .

i 853–7. *I'm sure . . . dream*] Endymion believes that 'thinking makes it so'.
Cp. K.'s letter to Bailey of 22 Nov. 1817, 'The Imagination may be compared to Adam's dream (cp. *Paradise Lost* viii 452–90]–he awoke and found
it truth. . . . It is a "a Vision in the form of Youth" a shadow of reality to
come' (*L* i 185).
i 855. *luxury*] On K.'s use of this word see *Calidore* 92 *n* (p. 40 above).
i 857. See i 771 *n*.
i 862. *Beyond . . . the matron*] Behind . . . little *Fair copy* (*cancelled*). Latona
was the mother of Cynthia and Apollo.

875   Edges them round, and they have golden pits.
       'Twas there I got them, from the gaps and slits
       In a mossy stone, that sometimes was my seat
       When all above was faint with mid-day heat.
       And there in strife no burning thoughts to heed,
880   I'd bubble up the water through a reed;
       So reaching back to boy-hood make me ships
       Of moulted feathers, touchwood, alder chips,
       With leaves stuck in them; and the Neptune be
       Of their petty ocean. Oftener, heavily,
885   When love-lorn hours had left me less a child,
       I sat contemplating the figures wild
       Of o'er-head clouds melting the mirror through.
       Upon a day, while thus I watched, by flew
       A cloudy Cupid with his bow and quiver,
890   So plainly charactered no breeze would shiver
       The happy chance; so happy, I was fain
       To follow it upon the open plain,
       And, therefore, was just going, when, behold,
       A wonder, fair as any I have told—
895   The same bright face I tasted in my sleep,

i 887. *the mirror*] The crystal water of the well described at i 870–2 above.
He watches in it the reflections of clouds dissolving overhead.
i 888–9. A recollection of *A Midsummer Night's Dream* II i 155–7,

> That very time I saw, but thou couldst not,
> Flying between the cold moon and the earth,
> Cupid all arm'd . . .

The passage is marked by K. in his copy of Shakespeare (*Spurgeon* 92).
i 890. *Charactered*] Marked, clearly defined. So used this once by K.
i 895–905. Cp. the vision in the well in Shelley's *Alastor* (1815) 479–92,

> . . . A Spirit seemed
> To stand beside him—clothed in no bright robes
> Of shadowy silver or enshrining light,
> Borrowed from aught the visible world affords
> Of grace, or majesty, or mystery:—
> But, undulating woods, and silent well,
> And rippling rivulet, and evening gloom
> Now deepening the dark shades, for speech assuming,
> Held commune with him, as if he and it
> Were all that was,—only . . . when his regard
> Was raised by intense pensiveness . . . two eyes,
> Two starry eyes, hung in the gloom of thought,
> And seemed with their serene and azure smiles
> To beckon him . . .

Smiling in the clear well. My heart did leap
Through the cool depth. It moved as if to flee,
I started up—when lo! refreshfully,
There came upon my face in plenteous showers
900 Dew-drops and dewy buds and leaves and flowers,
Wrapping all objects from my smothered sight,
Bathing my spirit in a new delight.
Aye, such a breathless honey-feel of bliss
Alone preserved me from the drear abyss
905 Of death, for the fair form had gone again.
Pleasure is oft a visitant, but pain
Clings cruelly to us, like the gnawing sloth
On the deer's tender haunches; late, and loth,
'Tis scared away by slow returning pleasure.
910 How sickening, how dark the dreadful leisure

i *896-7. Smiling . . . cool depth*] Fair copy (*cancelled*),
       In the green opening smiling. Gods that keep,
       Mercifully, a little strength of heart
       Unkill'd in us by raving, pant and smart;
       And do preserve it, like a lilly root,
   [5] That, in another spring, it may outshoot
       From its wintry prison; let this hour go
       Drawling along its heavy weight of woe
       And leave me living! 'Tis not more than need –
       Your veriest help. Ah! how long did I feed
   [10] On that crystalline life of Portraiture!
       How long I hovered breathless round the tender lure!
       How many times dimpled the water glass
       With kisses maddest kisses; and, till they did pass
       And leave the liquid smooth again, how mad!
   [15] O 'twas as if the absolute sisters bad[e]
       My life into the compass of a Nut;
       Or all my breathing minished and shut
       To a scanty straw. To look above I fear'd
       Lest my hot eyeballs might be burnt and sear'd
   [20] By a blank naught . . .
l. [15]. *the absolute sisters bad[e]* The Fates ordained.
l. [17]. *minished*] Diminished. See i 320 *n* (p. 134 above).
i *906-12*. The mingling of pleasure, pain and languor is characteristically
Keatsian (cp. the *Ode to a Nightingale* 1 *n*, p. 525 below) and underlines the
painful contrast between the dream and everyday reality; see i 681-705 *n*
above.
i *907. the gnawing sloth*] Sloths are arboreal and fruit-eating. K. must have
in mind a carnivorous predator.

Of weary days, made deeper exquisite
By a fore-knowledge of unslumbrous night!
Like sorrow came upon me, heavier still
Than when I wandered from the poppy hill,
915 And a whole age of lingering moments crept
Sluggishly by, ere more contentment swept
Away at once the deadly yellow spleen.
Yes, thrice have I this fair enchantment seen,
Once more been tortured with renewèd life.
920 When last the wintry gusts gave over strife
With the conquering sun of spring and left the skies
Warm and serene, but yet with moistened eyes
In pity of the shattered infant buds—
That time thou didst adorn, with amber studs,
925 My hunting cap, because I laughed and smiled,
Chatted with thee, and many days exiled
All torment from my breast; 'twas even then,
Straying about, yet cooped up in the den
Of helpless discontent, hurling my lance
930 From place to place, and following at chance,
At last, by hap, through some young trees it struck,
And, plashing among bedded pebbles, stuck
In the middle of a brook, whose silver ramble
Down twenty little falls, through reeds and bramble,
935 Tracing along, it brought me to a cave,
Whence it ran brightly forth, and white did lave
The nether sides of mossy stones and rock,
'Mong which it gurgled blithe adieus to mock
Its own sweet grief at parting. Overhead
940 Hung a lush screen of drooping weeds, and spread
Thick, as to curtain up some wood-nymph's home.
'Ah, impious mortal, whither do I roam?'
Said I, low voiced: 'Ah, whither! 'Tis the grot

i *911. deeper exquisite*] Keener, more intense.
i *914.* See i 554–5, 681–705 above.
i *915. crept*] pass'd *Fair copy (cancelled)*.
i *919.* See i 681–705 *n* above.
i *924. amber studs*] Echoes Marlowe's *The Passionate Shepherd to his Love* 17–
18,

> A belt of straw and ivy buds,
> With coral clasps and amber studs . . .

i *933. silver ramble*] The phrasing follows Hunt. See *Calidore* 20 *n* (p. 37
above).
i *939. sweet grief at parting*] Echoes *Romeo and Juliet* II ii 184, 'parting is such
sweet sorrow'.

Of Proserpine, when Hell, obscure and hot,
945   Doth her resign, and where her tender hands
She dabbles on the cool and sluicy sands;
Or 'tis the cell of Echo, where she sits
And babbles thorough silence till her wits
Are gone in tender madness, and anon
950   Faints into sleep, with many a dying tone
Of sadness. Oh, that she would take my vows,
And breathe them sighingly among the boughs,
To sue her gentle ears for whose fair head
Daily I pluck sweet flowerets from their bed,
955   And weave them dyingly, send honey-whispers
Round every leaf, that all those gentle lispers
May sigh my love unto her pitying!
O charitable Echo! Hear, and sing
This ditty to her! Tell her—' So I stayed
960   My foolish tongue, and listening, half afraid,
Stood stupefied with my own empty folly,
And blushing for the freaks of melancholy.
Salt tears were coming, when I heard my name
Most fondly lipped, and then these accents came:
965   'Endymion! The cave is secreter
Than the isle of Delos. Echo hence shall stir
No sighs but sigh-warm kisses, or light noise

i *944. Proserpine*] The daughter of Ceres and Jupiter who was carried away
by Pluto to be his queen in the underworld (Ovid's *Metamorphoses* v 391–
571). Her introduction here may owe something to her identification in
various traditions with Hecate (on Diana and Hecate see main headnote
p. 117 above), but K. had a special fondness for her story. See his letter to
Bailey of July 1818, '. . . when I see you the first thing I shall do will be to
read that about Milton and Ceres and Proserpine [*Paradise Lost* iv 268–72]'
(*L* i 340).

i *947–51. Echo . . . sadness*] On the legend of Echo and Narcissus see *I stood
tip-toe*, 163–80 *n*, 171–4 *n*, 180 *n* (pp. 93–4 above).

i *964*. The line gave K. some difficulty. Earlier attempts in the fair copy
include,

    1. Again in passionatest syllables: saying . . .
    2. And thus again that voice's tender swells . . .

The word 'lipped' means murmured.

i *966. Delos*] An island of the Cyclades celebrated as the birthplace of Cynthia and Apollo (cp. i 862 *n*) and the site of the ancient temple to Apollo.
See *Lemprière*: 'The whole island . . . was held in such veneration, that the
Persians, who had pillaged all the temples of Greece, never offered violence
to the temple of Apollo.'

Of thy combing hand, the while it travelling cloys
And trembles through my labyrinthine hair.'
970 At that oppressed I hurried in. Ah, where
Are those swift moments? Whither are they fled?
I'll smile no more, Peona, nor will wed
Sorrow the way to death, but patiently
Bear up against it—so farewell, sad sigh,
975 And come instead demurest meditation,
To occupy me wholly, and to fashion
My pilgrimage for the world's dusky brink.
No more will I count over, link by link,
My chain of grief, no longer strive to find
980 A half-forgetfulness in mountain wind
Blustering about my ears. Aye, thou shalt see,
Dearest of sisters, what my life shall be,
What a calm round of hours shall make my days.
There is a paly flame of hope that plays
985 Where'er I look; but yet, I'll say 'tis naught—
And here I bid it die. Have not I caught,
Already, a more healthy countenance?
By this the sun is setting; we may chance
Meet some of our near-dwellers with my car.'

990   This said, he rose, faint-smiling like a star
Through autumn mists, and took Peona's hand;
They stepped into the boat, and launched from land.

i *968–9.* Probably a reminiscence of Milton's *Lycidas* 68–9,
                    To sport with *Amaryllis* in the shade,
                        Or with the tangles of *Neæra's* hair . . .
The verb 'cloys' is used to suggest the hand's pleasurably impeded movement through the 'labyrinthine hair'. For 'labyrinthine' the fair copy has
'labyrinthian'.
i *975.* Probably a half-conscious echo of Milton's *Il Penseroso* 31–2,
                    Come pensive Nun, devout and pure,
                        Sober, stedfast, and demure . . .
i *984. paly*] See i 341 *n.*
i *989.* They will have brought his chariot.
i *990.* See *The Eve of St Agnes* 318 and *n* (p. 475 below),
                    Ethereal, flushed, and like a throbbing star . . .

BOOK II

Exact period of composition unknown, but completed at Hampstead *c.* 28
Aug. 1817: see headnote to Book i (p. 120 above). For the view that the
opening lines (ii 1–130) were written on K.'s return to London early June

1817 and were influenced by his meeting with Mrs Isabella Jones at Bo Peep, near Hastings (end of May or beginning of June 1817), see *Gittings* (1968) 140.

> O sovereign power of love! O grief! O balm!
> All records, saving thine, come cool, and calm,
> And shadowy, through the mist of passèd years.
> For others, good or bad, hatred and tears
> 5 Have become indolent, but touching thine,
> One sigh doth echo, one poor sob doth pine,
> One kiss brings honey-dew from buried days.
> The woes of Troy, towers smothering o'er their blaze,
> Stiff-holden shields, far-piercing spears, keen blades,
> 10 Struggling, and blood, and shrieks—all dimly fades
> Into some backward corner of the brain;
> Yet, in our very souls, we feel amain
> The close of Troilus and Cressid sweet.
> Hence, pageant history! Hence, gilded cheat!
> 15 Swart planet in the universe of deeds!

ii *1–43*. K.'s defence of love as 'the chief intensity' (see i 777–842 *n*) and apologia for his present undertaking. Love stories are the only records of the past which move us deeply (ii 2–7); the love of Troilus and Cressida is more important than the fighting in the Trojan War (ii 8–13); history is a 'cheat' because it fails to record what is most valuable in human experience (ii 14–21); heroines of love stories matter more than men of action and the downfall of empires (ii 22–34); K. will hold to his purpose although discouraged by poetic inexperience and lack of inspiration, preferring to fail in love's cause than remain in discontented silence (ii 34–43).

ii *1. O grief! O balm*] See i 906–12 *n*, ii 773 *n*.

ii *4–5. others . . . indolent*] Records other than those of love have become too shadowy to cause either hatred or grief.

ii *6. pine*] Cause to pine.

ii *7. brings*] sends *Draft*. The word 'honey-dew' probably derives from Coleridge's *Kubla Khan* (1816) 53: see i 766 *n* above.

ii *8. smothering o'er their blaze*] Either suffocating in the smoke of their fire, or smothering the fire with their weight as they collapse.

ii *12. amain*] With full force. An Elizabethanism.

ii *13. Cressid sweet*] Cressida *Draft*. The word 'close' (embrace) echoes *Troilus and Cressida* III ii 51, 'an 'twere dark you'd close sooner'.

ii *14. gilded cheat*] proud dull feat *Fair copy* (*cancelled*); proud star *Draft*.

ii *15. swart*] Dark, black. A favourite word in K., perhaps owed in the first place to Milton's *Lycidas* 138,

> On whose fresh lap the swart Star sparely looks . . .

Other examples of its use at ii 376 below, *To the Nile* 5, *Hyperion* i 282, *The Eve of St Agnes* 241 (pp. 308, 412, and 469 below).

Wide sea, that one continuous murmur breeds
Along the pebbled shore of memory!
Many old rotten-timbered boats there be
Upon thy vaporous bosom, magnified
20 To goodly vessels; many a sail of pride,
And golden keeled, is left unlaunched and dry.
But wherefore this? What care, though owl did fly
About the great Athenian admiral's mast?
What care, though striding Alexander passed
25 The Indus with his Macedonian numbers?
Though old Ulysses tortured from his slumbers
The glutted Cyclops, what care? . . . Juliet leaning
Amid her window-flowers, sighing, weaning
Tenderly her fancy from its maiden snow,
30 Doth more avail than these. The silver flow
Of Hero's tears, the swoon of Imogen,
Fair Pastorella in the bandit's den,
Are things to brood on with more ardency
Than the death-day of empires. Fearfully
35 Must such conviction come upon his head

ii *22–3. owl . . . mast*] The incident is related in Plutarch's *Life of Themistocles*; K. probably remembered the account in J. Potter's *Antiquities of
Greece* (1697), 'Plutarch reports, that when Themistocles was consulting
with the other officers upon the uppermost deck of the ship, and most of
them opposed him, being unwilling to hazard a battle, an owl coming upon
the right side of the ship, and lighting upon the mast, so animated them,
that they unanimously concurred with him, and prepared themselves for
the fight' (1827 edn i 379–80).
ii *24–5*. Alexander crossed the Indus with his army 326 B.C.
ii *26–7. Ulysses . . . Cyclops*] For the blinding of the sleeping Cyclops by
Odysseus to make possible escape for himself and his men see Homer's
Odyssey ix. Cp. *Sleep and Poetry* 233–5 *n* (p. 79 above).
ii *27–30. leaning . . . snow*] leans

> Amid her window flowers, sighs,—and as she weans
> Her maiden thoughts from their young firstling snow,
> What sorrows from the melting whiteness grow . . .

Draft (cancelled).
See *Romeo and Juliet* II ii.
ii *31–2. Hero . . . Imogen . . . Pastorella*] Elizabethan heroines crossed in love.
'Hero's tears' probably refers to Marlowe's *Hero and Leander* rather than
Much Ado About Nothing IV i; for the 'swoon of Imogen' see *Cymbeline* IV
ii 195–291 and for Pastorella and the bandit *The Faerie Queene* VI xi.
ii *33–34. brood on . . . death-day*] With the phrasing cp. K.'s letter to Fanny
Browne of 25 July 1819, 'I have two luxuries to brood over . . . your loveliness and the hour of my death' (*L* ii 133).

7+K.

Who, thus far, discontent, has dared to tread,
Without one muse's smile or kind behest,
The path of love and poesy. But rest,
In chafing restlessness, is yet more drear
40 Than to be crushed in striving to uprear
Love's standard on the battlements of song.
So once more days and nights aid me along,
Like legioned soldiers.

                                    Brain-sick shepherd prince,
What promise hast thou faithful guarded since
45 The day of sacrifice? Or have new sorrows
Come with the constant dawn upon thy morrows?
Alas! 'tis his old grief. For many days
Has he been wandering in uncertain ways:
Through wilderness and woods of mossèd oaks,
50 Counting his woe-worn minutes by the strokes
Of the lone woodcutter, and listening still,
Hour after hour, to each lush-leavèd rill.
Now he is sitting by a shady spring,
And elbow-deep with feverous fingering
55 Stems the upbursting cold. A wild rose tree
Pavilions him in bloom, and he doth see
A bud which snares his fancy. Lo! but now
He plucks it, dips its stalk in the water—how
It swells, it buds, it flowers beneath his sight!
60 And, in the middle, there is softly pight
A golden butterfly, upon whose wings
There must be surely charactered strange things,
For with wide eye he wonders, and smiles oft.

        Lightly this little herald flew aloft,
65 Followed by glad Endymion's claspèd hands.

ii 36. *discontent*] halt and lame *Draft*.
ii 40. *uprear*] See i 153-4 *n* (p. 126 above).
ii 43. *legioned*] sturdy *Draft*. 'Brain-sick' was substituted for 'Fainting' in
the fair copy.
ii 49. *woods of*] brittle *Draft*.
ii 51. *lone*] distant *Draft*; lonely *Fair copy (cancelled)*.
ii 56. *Pavilions him in bloom*] Bends lightly over him *Draft*.
ii 57. *snares*] takes *Draft*.
ii 60. *pight*] Settled. Perhaps owed to *Troilus and Cressida* V x 23-4,
                                                            . . . tents
        Thus proudly pight upon our Phrygian plains . . .
ii 62. *charactered*] Inscribed. Cp. iii 762 and *n* below
                Nor masked with any sign or charactery . . .

Onward it flies. From languor's sullen bands
His limbs are loosed, and, eager, on he hies
Dazzled to trace it in the sunny skies.
It seemed he flew, the way so easy was,
70 And like a new-born spirit did he pass
Through the green evening quiet in the sun,
O'er many a heath, through many a woodland dun,
Through buried paths, where sleepy twilight dreams
The summer-time away. One track unseams
75 A wooded cleft and, far away, the blue
Of ocean fades upon him; then, anew,
He sinks adown a solitary glen
Where there was never sound of mortal men,
Saving, perhaps, some snow-light cadences
80 Melting to silence when upon the breeze
Some holy bark let forth an anthem sweet
To cheer itself to Delphi. Still his feet
Went swift beneath the merry-wingèd guide,
Until it reached a splashing fountain's side
85 That, near a cavern's mouth, for ever poured
Unto the temperate air. Then high it soared,
And downward suddenly began to dip,
As if, athirst with so much toil, 'twould sip
The crystal spout-head; so it did, with touch
90 Most delicate, as though afraid to smutch
Even with mealy gold the waters clear.
But, at that very touch, to disappear
So fairy-quick, was strange! Bewilderèd,
Endymion sought around and shook each bed

ii *67–8. eager . . . skies*] Earlier attempts in the draft were,
1.   . . . eagerly he paces
    With nimble feet beneath its airy traces . . .
2.   . . . eagerly he traces
    With nimble footsteps all its airy paces . . .
ii *79. snow-light cadences*] Faint echoes.
ii *80. Melting*] Thawing *Draft*.
ii *81–2. holy bark . . . Delphi*] Pilgrims voyaging across the Aegean Sea on
their way to Delphi, the inland town of Phocis, near Mount Parnassus,
which was celebrated for its temple of Apollo.
ii *90. smutch*] Smudge. So used in the seventeenth century.
ii *91. mealy gold*] The fine dust from the butterfly's wings. Cp. *Troilus and
Cressida* III iii 78–9,
                 . . . men, like butterflies,
      Show not their mealy wings but to the summer . . .

95 Of covert flowers in vain; and then he flung
    Himself along the grass. What gentle tongue,
    What whisperer disturbed his gloomy rest?
    It was a nymph uprisen to the breast
    In the fountain's pebbly margin, and she stood
100 'Mong lilies, like the youngest of the brood.
    To him her dripping hand she softly kissed,
    And anxiously began to plait and twist
    Her ringlets round her fingers, saying: 'Youth!
    Too long, alas, hast thou starved on the ruth,
105 The bitterness of love—too long indeed,
    Seeing thou art so gentle. Could I weed
    Thy soul of care, by heavens, I would offer
    All the bright riches of my crystal coffer
    To Amphitrite; all my clear-eyed fish,
110 Golden, or rainbow-sided, or purplish,
    Vermilion-tailed, or finned with silvery gauze;
    Yea, or my veinèd pebble-floor, that draws
    A virgin light to the deep; my grotto-sands
    Tawny and gold, oozed slowly from far lands
115 By my diligent springs; my level lilies, shells,
    My charming rod, my potent river spells;
    Yes, every thing, even to the pearly cup
    Meander gave me—for I bubbled up
    To fainting creatures in a desert wild.
120 But woe is me, I am but as a child
    To gladden thee; and all I dare to say
    Is that I pity thee; that on this day
    I've been thy guide; that thou must wander far
    In other regions, past the scanty bar
125 To mortal steps, before thou canst be ta'en
    From every wasting sigh, from every pain,
    Into the gentle bosom of thy love.

ii *95. covert*] Hidden in the grass.

ii *102. anxiously began to plait*] carelessly began to twine *Draft*.

ii *109. Amphitrite*] See *Lemprière*, '. . . daughter of Oceanus and Tethys, married Neptune. She became mother of Triton and shared the divine honours of her husband.'

ii *110. rainbow-sided*] K. uses this compound again in *Lamia* i 54 (p. 619 below).

ii *112–13. draws . . . deep*] The limpid reflections of light in a pebbled bed of clear water.

ii *116. charming*] Magical.

ii *118. Meander*] For this river in Asia Minor see *Sleep and Poetry* 74 *n* (p. 72 above).

Why it is thus, one knows in heaven above,
But, a poor naiad, I guess not. Farewell!
130   I have a ditty for my hollow cell.'

Hereat, she vanished from Endymion's gaze,
Who brooded o'er the water in amaze.
The dashing fount poured on, and where its pool
Lay, half asleep, in grass and rushes cool,
135   Quick waterflies and gnats were sporting still,
And fish were dimpling, as if good nor ill
Had fallen out that hour. The wanderer,
Holding his forehead, to keep off the burr
Of smothering fancies, patiently sat down,
140   And, while beneath the evening's sleepy frown
Glow-worms began to trim their starry lamps,
Thus breathed he to himself: 'Whoso encamps
To take a fancied city of delight,
Oh, what a wretch is he! And when 'tis his
145   After long toil and travailing, to miss
The kernel of his hopes, how more than vile.
Yet for him there's refreshment even in toil;
Another city doth he set about,
Free from the smallest pebble-bead of doubt
150   That he will seize on trickling honey-combs—
Alas, he finds them dry; and then he foams,
And onward to another city speeds.
But this is human life: the war, the deeds,
The disappointment, the anxiety,
155   Imagination's struggles, far and nigh,

ii *129. naiad*] Water nymph. See *To Charles Cowden Clarke* 6 *n* (p. 54 above)
and Drayton's *The Man in the Moone* 418–21,

> He follows PHOEBE, that him safely brings
> (As their great Queene) unto the nymphish Bowres,
> Wherein cleere Rivers beautified with Flowres,
> The silver *Naydes* bathe them in the bracke ...

ii *134. Lay, half asleep, in*] Crept smoothly by fresh *Draft*.
ii *136. dimpling*] Making ripples in the water as they rose to feed.
ii *138. burr*] Suggesting indistinctness and confusion. Derived from the
seventeenth-century use of the word meaning a nebulous dish of light
around the moon (*OED*).
ii *139. smothering*] drowning *Draft (cancelled)*.
ii *143. To take a fancied*] His soul to take a *Draft*. An unrhymed line.
ii *145. travailing*] The reading of the draft. *1818* has 'travelling', but the
draft reading shows the sense intended. For 'toil' the draft has 'siege'.
ii *153–6. But this ... All human*] Cp. *Sleep and Poetry* 122–54 *n* (p. 74 above).
ii *155. Imagination's struggles*] Imaginings and searchings *Draft*.

All human; bearing in themselves this good,
That they are still the air, the subtle food,
To make us feel existence, and to show
How quiet death is. Where soil is men grow,
160 Whether to weeds or flowers; but for me,
There is no depth to strike in. I can see
Naught earthly worth my compassing, so stand
Upon a misty, jutting head of land—
Alone? No, no; and, by the Orphean lute
165 When mad Eurydice is listening to't,
I'd rather stand upon this misty peak,
With not a thing to sigh for, or to seek,
But the soft shadow of my thrice-seen love,
Than be—I care not what. O meekest dove
170 Of heaven! O Cynthia, ten-times bright and fair!
From thy blue throne, now filling all the air,
Glance but one little beam of tempered light
Into my bosom that the dreadful might
And tyranny of love be somewhat scared!
175 Yet do not so, sweet queen; one torment spared
Would give a pang to jealous misery
Worse than the torment's self: but rather tie
Large wings upon my shoulders, and point out
My love's far dwelling. Though the playful rout

ii *164–5. Orphean lute . . . mad Eurydice*] The legend of Orpheus and Eurydice is related in Ovid's *Metamorphoses* x 1–63. K. may also have known the
description of Orpheus bewailing the loss of Eurydice in Virgil's *Georgics* iv
453–527.

ii *169–98. O meekest dove . . . morn*] Cp. Endymion's invocations to Diana
and Cynthia at ii 302–32, iii 142–87 below, and his puzzlement at iv 92–7
below over his divided allegiance to Cynthia, his unknown goddess and the
Indian maid.

ii *170–1. O Cynthia . . . air*] Perhaps echoing Ben Jonson's *Cynthia's
Revells* (1601), 'Hymn to Diana' 1–4,

>Queene, and *Huntresse*, chaste, and faire,
>Now the *Sunne* is laid to sleepe,
>Seated, in thy silver chaire,
>State in wonted manner keepe . . .

Cp. ii 302 below, 'O Haunter chaste . . .' and also iv 567 *n* (p. 268 below).
ii *172–4.* Suggested by *A Midsummer Night's Dream* II i 161–2,
>. . . young Cupid's fiery shaft
>Quench'd in the chaste beams of the watery moon . . .

K. marked the passage in his copy of Shakespeare (*Spurgeon* 92).
ii *179–80. Though . . . shun thee*] Cynthia's reputation for chastity is given
as a reason for the concealment of her love at ii 778–94, iv 751–4 below.

180 Of Cupids shun thee, too divine art thou,
       Too keen in beauty, for thy silver prow
       Not to have dipped in love's most gentle stream.
       Oh, be propitious, nor severely deem
       My madness impious; for, by all the stars
185 That tend thy bidding, I do think the bars
       That kept my spirit in are burst—that I
       Am sailing with thee through the dizzy sky!
       How beautiful thou art! The world how deep!
       How tremulous-dazzlingly the wheels sweep
190 Around their axle! Then these gleaming reins,
       How lithe! When this thy chariot attains
       Its airy goal, haply some bower veils
       Those twilight eyes? Those eyes!—my spirit fails.
       Dear goddess, help, or the wide-gaping air
195 Will gulf me. Help!' At this with maddened stare
       And lifted hands and trembling lips he stood,
       Like old Deucalion mountained o'er the flood,
       Or blind Orion hungry for the morn.
       And, but from the deep cavern there was borne
200 A voice, he had been froze to senseless stone;

ii *185–95.* Endymion rides through the air in Phoebe's chariot in Drayton's
The Man in the Moone 430–5,

> . . . there she stayes not; but incontinent,
> Calls downe the Dragons that her Chariot draw,
> And with ENDIMION pleased that she saw,
> Mounteth thereon, in twinkling of an eye,
> Stripping the winds, beholding from the Skye,
> The Earth in roundnesse of a perfect Ball . . .

ii *189. tremulous–dazzlingly*] Earlier attempts in the draft were,

1. silently and tremulous . . .
2. bright and tremulous . . .
3. tremulous and dazzling . . .

ii *192–3. Some bower . . . eyes*] haply thou veilst thine eyes
              In some fresh bower . . . *Draft (cancelled).*

ii *197–8. mountained o'er . . . hungry*] wondering at . . . waiting *Draft.* Deucalion longed for the flood to subside and Orion longed for the dawn. K. is probably combining memories of Ovid's account of Deucalion waiting above the waters on the summit of Mount Parnassus (*Metamorphoses* i 316–29) and Poussin's painting 'Landscape with Orion', which shows the blind Orion facing the dawn with Diana watching from the sky. Hazlitt used K.'s line as a motto for his essay of 1821, 'On a landscape of Nicolas Poussin' (*Works*, ed. P. P. Howe, viii (1931) 168–74); on the painting's being well-known at the time as a print see Ian Jack's *Keats and the Mirror of Art* (1967) 156.

Nor sigh of his, nor plaint, nor passioned moan
Had more been heard. Thus swelled it forth: 'Descend
Young mountaineer! Descend where alleys bend
Into the sparry hollows of the world!
205   Oft hast thou seen bolts of the thunder hurled
As from thy threshold; day by day hast been
A little lower than the chilly sheen
Of icy pinnacles, and dipp'dst thine arms
Into the deadening ether that still charms
210   Their marble being—now, as deep profound
As those are high, descend! He ne'er is crowned
With immortality who fears to follow
Where airy voices lead; so through the hollow,
The silent mysteries of earth, descend!'

215   He heard but the last words, nor could contend
One moment in reflection: for he fled
Into the fearful deep, to hide his head
From the clear moon, the trees, and coming madness.

'Twas far too strange and wonderful for sadness,
220   Sharpening, by degrees, his appetite
To dive into the deepest. Dark, nor light,
The region; nor bright, nor sombre wholly,
But mingled up; a gleaming melancholy;

ii *201. passioned*] Impassioned. See i 248 *n*.
ii *204. sparry*] Rich in crystalline minerals. The epithet was in common use
at the time. Cp. J. H. Reynolds's *The Eden of the Imagination* (1814), 'Some
sparry grot'.
ii *205-10. Oft . . . being*] Alludes to Endymion's mountain home (see i 63 *n*).
ii *207. sheen*] Brilliance. Perhaps owed to *A Midsummer Night's Dream* II i
29, 'spangled starlight sheen', since the line is marked by K. in his copy of
Shakespeare (*Spurgeon* 89).
ii *214. silent*] fearful *Draft*.
ii *220. Sharpening*] Upwinding *Draft*. See i 153-4 *n*.
ii *221-39. Dark nor light . . . crystal*] K.'s underground region owes something to his reading of eastern tales, including *The Arabian Nights* (cp. i
405-6 *n*) and William Beckford's *Vathek* (1786). K. refers to *Vathek* in his
letter to Reynolds of July 1818 (*L* i 324). Bailey commented in his letter
to Milnes of 7 May 1849, 'The subterranean scenery of the second Book
[of *Endymion*], and the submarine beauties of the third (cp. iii 119-36
n), do indeed display what an able Reviewer well describes to be "Giant
Imagination playing fancifully in building up Scenes of Magic, through
which the wanderer travels in amazement" [see *The Church of England
Quarterly Review* xxv, Jan. 1849, 158]' (*KC* ii 283-4).

A dusky empire and its diadems;
225 One faint eternal eventide of gems.
Aye, millions sparkled on a vein of gold,
Along whose track the prince quick footsteps told,
With all its lines abrupt and angular
Out-shooting sometimes, like a meteor-star,
230 Through a vast antre; then the metal woof,
Like Vulcan's rainbow, with some monstrous roof
Curves hugely; now, far in the deep abyss,
It seems an angry lightning, and doth hiss
Fancy into belief; anon it leads
235 Through winding passages where sameness breeds
Vexing conceptions of some sudden change,
Whether to silver grots, or giant range
Of sapphire columns, or fantastic bridge
Athwart a flood of crystal. On a ridge
240 Now fareth he that o'er the vast beneath
Towers like an ocean-cliff, and whence he seeth
A hundred waterfalls whose voices come
But as the murmuring surge. Chilly and numb
His bosom grew when first he far away
245 Descried an orbèd diamond, set to fray
Old darkness from his throne. 'Twas like the sun

ii *227.* Whose track the venturous Latmian follows bold . . . *Draft.*
ii *230. vast antre*] Echoes *Othello* I iii 140, 'antres vast and desarts idle'. An
antre is a cave (Latin *antrum*).
ii *230–1. metal woof / Like Vulcan's rainbow*] Interwoven with colours like a
rainbow; cp. *Lamia* ii 237 (p. 646 below),

Unweave a rainbow . . .

Vulcan was the blacksmith of the gods and patron of workers in iron and
metal. See *Lemprière*: 'His forges were supposed to be under Mount Aetna,
in the island of Sicily, as well as in every part of the earth where there were
volcanos.'
ii *233. hiss / Fancy into belief*] The sibilant echo in the cave is like the sound
of heavy rain.
ii *236. Vexing*] Dizzy *Draft.* See i *565 n.*
ii *240. vast*] Used as a noun. Cp. *The Tempest* I ii 327, 'at vast of night'. K.
quotes Shakespeare's line in his letter to Reynolds of April 1817 (see i *203 n*).
ii *245–8. an orbèd diamond . . . amazement*] Probably suggested by the 'Story
of Zobeide' in *The Arabian Nights*, 'What surprised me most was a sparkling light which came from above the bed . . . I ascended the steps, and . . .
saw a diamond as large as the egg of an ostrich lying on a low stool; it was
so pure, that I could not find the least blemish in it, and it sparkled with so
much brilliancy, that when I saw it by daylight I could not endure its
lustre' (1811 edn i 310). The word 'fray' (ii 245) is an archaism for frighten.
7*

Uprisen o'er chaos, and with such a stun
Came the amazement that, absorbed in it,
He saw not fiercer wonders—past the wit
250   Of any spirit to tell but one of those
Who, when this planet's sphering time doth close,
Will be its high remembrancers. Who they?
The mighty ones who have made eternal day
For Greece and England. While astonishment
255   With deep-drawn sighs was quieting, he went
Into a marble gallery, passing through
A mimic temple, so complete and true
In sacred custom that he well nigh feared
To search it inwards; whence far off appeared,
260   Through a long pillared vista, a fair shrine,
And just beyond, on light tiptoe divine,
A quivered Dian. Stepping awfully,
The youth approached, oft turning his veilèd eye
Down sidelong aisles and into niches old.
265   And when, more near against the marble cold
He had touched his forehead, he began to thread
All courts and passages, where silence dead,
Roused by his whispering footsteps, murmured faint.
And long he traversed to and fro, to acquaint
270   Himself with every mystery and awe,
Till, weary, he sat down before the maw
Of a wide outlet, fathomless and dim,
To wild uncertainty and shadows grim.
There, when new wonders ceased to float before
275   And thoughts of self came on, how crude and sore

ii 247. *such a stun*] The phrasing follows Hunt. See *Calidore* 20 *n* (p. 37 above).

ii 252. *Who they?*] An awkward ellipsis to preserve the metre.

ii 253. *who have made eternal day*] Who've shone athwart the day *Draft*. 'The mighty ones' are the major poets.

ii 260–2.   Thro' a long vist' of columns a fair shrine
                And just beyond lightly diminished
                A Dian quiver'd tiptoe, crescented . . . *Draft* (cancelled).

ii 262. *A quivered Dian*] Diana in her role of huntress. See Drayton's *The Man in the Moone* 75–6,

        . . . many a time apparelled in Greene,
        Arm'd with her Dart, she Huntress-like was seene . . .

ii 270–2.   Himself with every mystery, until
                His weary legs he rested on the sill
                Of some remotest chamber, outlet dim . . . *Draft*.

ii 274–6. See i 799 *n* above.

The journey homeward to habitual self!
A mad pursuing of the fog-born elf,
Whose flitting lantern, through rude nettle-briar,
Cheats us into a swamp, into a fire,
280 Into the bosom of a hated thing.
    What misery most drowningly doth sing
In lone Endymion's ear, now he has raught
The goal of consciousness? Ah, 'tis the thought,
The deadly feel of solitude; for lo!
285 He cannot see the heavens, nor the flow
Of rivers, nor hill-flowers running wild
In pink and purple chequer, nor, up-piled,
The cloudy rack slow journeying in the west,
Like herded elephants; nor felt, nor pressed
290 Cool grass, nor tasted the fresh slumberous air;
But far from such companionship to wear
An unknown time, surcharged with grief, away,
Was now his lot. And must he patient stay,
Tracing fantastic figures with his spear?
295 'No!' exclaimed he, 'why should I tarry here?'
'No!' loudly echoed times innumerable.
At which he straightway started, and 'gan tell
His paces back into the temple's chief,
Warming and glowing strong in the belief
300 Of help from Dian; so that when again
He caught her airy form, thus did he plain,
Moving more near the while: 'O Haunter chaste
Of river sides, and woods, and heathy waste,
Where with thy silver bow and arrows keen
305 Art thou now forested? O woodland Queen,
What smoothest air thy smoother forehead woos?
Where dost thou listen to the wide halloos
Of thy disparted nymphs? Through what dark tree

---

ii *277. fog-born elf*] Will-o'-the-wisp or *ignis fatuus*. On K.'s use of 'elf' see
ii 461 *n* below.
ii *282. raught*] Reached. An archaism much used by Spenser, for example
The Faerie Queene I vi 29, 'till ryper yeares he raught'.
ii *287. up-piled*] See i 153–4 *n* above.
ii *288. cloudy rack*] A mass of cloud driven by the wind.
ii *292. surcharged*] Weighed down. An Elizabethanism.
ii *298. chief*] Upper end, head. An Elizabethanism.
ii *301. plain*] Complain.
ii *302–32. O Haunter chaste . . . deep*] See ii 169–98 *n* above.
ii *305. now forested*] in covert hid *Draft*.
ii *308. Through what dark tree*] From what deep glen *Draft (cancelled)*. The

Glimmers thy crescent? Wheresoe'er it be,
310 'Tis in the breath of heaven. Thou dost taste
Freedom as none can taste it, nor dost waste
Thy loveliness in dismal elements,
But, finding in our green earth sweet contents,
There livest blissfully. Ah, if to thee
315 It feels Elysian, how rich to me,
An exiled mortal, sounds its pleasant name!
Within my breast there lives a choking flame—
Oh, let me cool it the zephyr-boughs among!
A homeward fever parches up my tongue—
320 Oh, let me slake it at the running springs!
Upon my ear a noisy nothing rings—
Oh, let me once more hear the linnet's note!
Before mine eyes thick films and shadows float—
Oh, let me 'noint them with the heaven's light!
325 Dost thou now lave thy feet and ankles white?
Oh, think how sweet to me the freshening sluice!
Dost thou now please thy thirst with berry-juice?
Oh, think how this dry palate would rejoice!
If in soft slumber thou dost hear my voice,
330 Oh, think how I should love a bed of flowers!
Young goddess, let me see my native bowers!
Deliver me from this rapacious deep!'

Thus ending loudly, as he would o'erleap
His destiny, alert he stood; but when
335 Obstinate silence came heavily again,
Feeling about for its old couch of space
And airy cradle, lowly bowed his face
Desponding, o'er the marble floor's cold thrill.
But 'twas not long; for, sweeter than the rill
340 To its old channel, or a swollen tide
To margin sallows, were the leaves he spied,
And flowers, and wreaths, and ready myrtle crowns

word 'disparted' (separated) is found in Spenser, for example *The Faerie
Queene* V iii 7, 'So they disparted were'.
ii *309. crescent*] Diana is usually represented in her role as huntress with a
small crescent moon bound to her head.
ii *318. zephyr-boughs*] waving boughs *Draft.*
ii *319. A homeward*] An endless *Draft.*
ii *332.* Lift me, oh lift me from this horrid deep . . . *Draft.*
ii *335–6.* The phrasing has an individual flavour. For 'about for' the draft
has 'its way to'.
ii *341. sallows*] Willows. See *I stood tip-toe* 67 *n* (p. 89 above).

Up-heaping through the slab. Refreshment drowns
Itself, and strives its own delights to hide—
345   Nor in one spot alone; the floral pride
In a long whispering birth enchanted grew
Before his footsteps, as when heaved anew
Old ocean rolls a lengthened wave to the shore,
Down whose green back the short-lived foam, all hoar,
350   Bursts gradual, with a wayward indolence.

    Increasing still in heart and pleasant sense,
Upon his fairy journey on he hastes,
So anxious for the end, he scarcely wastes
One moment with his hand among the sweets.
355   Onward he goes—he stops—his bosom beats
As plainly in his ear, as the faint charm
Of which the throbs were born. This still alarm,
This sleepy music, forced him walk tiptoe,
For it came more softly than the east could blow
360   Arion's magic to the Atlantic isles,
Or than the west, made jealous by the smiles
Of throned Apollo, could breathe back the lyre
To seas Ionian and Tyrian.

ii *343. Up-heaping*] Upswelling *Draft*. See i 153–4 *n* above.
ii *344.* Itself, lush tumbling on every side *Fair copy (cancelled).*
ii *349. Down . . . back . . . short-lived*] From . . . head . . . gentle *Draft (cancelled).*
ii *350. Bursts*] Runs *Draft.*
ii *357–60.* Perhaps inspired by *The Tempest* I ii 389–92,

    This music crept by me upon the waters,
    Allaying both their fury and my passion,
    With its sweet air: thence I have follow'd it,—
    Or it hath drawn me rather . . .

The passage is marked by K. in his copy of Shakespeare (*Spurgeon* 71).
ii *360. Arion*] See *Lemprière*: '. . . famous lyric poet and musician of Meth-
ymna in the island of Lesbos. He went into Italy with Periander, tyrant of
Corinth, where he obtained celebrity and acquired immense riches.' K. probably also knew the version of Arion's story in *The Faerie Queene* IV xi 23.
ii *363–72. To seas . . . miserable*]

    To seas Ionian and Tyrian. Dire
    Was the love lorn despair to which it wrought
    Endymion—for dire is the bare thought
    That among lovers things of tenderest worth
    Are swallow'd all, and made a blank—a dearth
    By one devouring flame: and far far worse
    Blessing to them become a heavy curse

Oh, did he ever live, that lonely man
365   Who loved—and music slew not? 'Tis the pest
Of love that fairest joys give most unrest,
That things of delicate and tenderest worth
Are swallowed all and made a searèd dearth
By one consuming flame—it doth immerse
370   And suffocate true blessings in a curse.
Half-happy, by comparison of bliss,
Is miserable. 'Twas even so with this
Dew-dropping melody in the Carian's ear;
First heaven, then hell, and then forgotten clear,
375   Vanished in elemental passion.

And down some swart abysm he had gone,
Had not a heavenly guide benignant led
To where thick myrtle branches, 'gainst his head
Brushing, awakened. Then the sounds again
380   Went noiseless as a passing noontide rain
Over a bower, where little space he stood,
For, as the sunset peeps into a wood,
So saw he panting light and towards it went
Through winding alleys—and lo, wonderment!
385   Upon soft verdure saw, one here, one there,
Cupids aslumbering on their pinions fair.

After a thousand mazes overgone,
At last, with sudden step, he came upon
A chamber, myrtle-walled, embowered high,

Half happy till comparisons of bliss
    To misery lead them . . . *Draft*.
The rhyme for ii 362 was lost in the revision.
ii *364–5. Oh, did he . . . slew not*] On K.'s feeling for music see *To Charles Cowden Clarke* 110–11 n, 113 n (p. 58 above).
ii *365–70. 'Tis the pest . . . curse*] Cp. i 816 and *n* above.
ii *373. the Carian*] Endymion.
ii *374. clear*] Unclouded sky.
ii *376. abysm*] Perhaps owed to *The Tempest* I ii 50, 'the dark backward and abysm of time'. K. quotes Shakespeare's line in his letter to Reynolds of April 1817 (see i 203 *n*).
ii *380–3.*   Came softly as a gentle evening rain
    Around a bower, where he stay'd harkening
    And through whose tufted shrubby darkening
    Bright starry glimmers came, towards which he went . . . *Draft*.
ii *389–427.* K. took some hints for his bower of Adonis from the Garden of Adonis in *The Faerie Queene* III vi 42–5.

390 Full of light, incense, tender minstrelsy,
    And more of beautiful and strange beside.
    For on a silken couch of rosy pride,
    In midst of all, there lay a sleeping youth
    Of fondest beauty, fonder, in fair sooth,
395 Than sighs could fathom, or contentment reach.
    And coverlids gold-tinted like the peach,
    Or ripe October's faded marigolds,
    Fell sleek about him in a thousand folds –
    Not hiding up an Apollonian curve
400 Of neck and shoulder, nor the tenting swerve
    Of knee from knee, nor ankles pointing light,
    But rather giving them to the fillèd sight
    Officiously. Sideway his face reposed
    On one white arm, and tenderly unclosed,
405 By tenderest pressure, a faint damask mouth
    To slumbery pout, just as the morning south
    Disparts a dew-lipped rose. Above his head,
    Four lily stalks did their white honours wed
    To make a coronal, and round him grew
410 All tendrils green, of every bloom and hue,
    Together intertwined and trammelled fresh:

ii *389*. See *The Faerie Queene* III vi 43, 44,

          . . . a gloomy grove of mirtle trees did rise . . .

      And in the thickest covert of that shade,
      There was a pleasant arbour, not by art,
      But of the trees owne inclination made . . .

ii *392–410*. K.'s 'sleeping Adonis' is a 'Titian-like picture' according to
Bailey (*KC* ii 284), but Ian Jack suggests a recollection of Poussin's 'Echo
and Narcissus' (reproduced as Plate XVII in his *Keats and the Mirror of Art*,
1967).

ii *394*. *fondest . . . fonder*] Finest . . . finer.

ii *397*. Foreshadowing K.'s more mature style. With his use of antithesis
cp. *To*—— ['*Time's sea* . . .'] 14 and *n* (p. 307 below).

ii *400–1*. *tenting swerve . . . knee*] 'Like the top of a tent' (Woodhouse's comment in his copy of *Endymion*).

ii *406*. *slumbery pout*] The phrasing follows Hunt. See *Calidore* 10 *n*, 20 *n*
(p. 37 above).

ii *407*. *Disparts*] Parts asunder, opens. Cp. ii 308 *n* above.

ii *409–18*. *round him . . . sisterhood*] Different varieties of climbing-plant
intertwine to make the bower. Cp. *The Faerie Queene* III vi 44,

      Which knitting their rancke braunches part to part,
      With wanton yvie twyne entrayld athwart,
      And Eglantine, and Caprifole emong . . .

The vine of glossy sprout; the ivy mesh,
Shading its Ethiop berries; and woodbine,
Of velvet leaves and bugle-blooms divine;
415   Convolvulus in streakèd vases flush;
The creeper, mellowing for an autumn blush;
And virgin's bower, trailing airily;
With others of the sisterhood. Hard by,
Stood serene Cupids watching silently.
420   One, kneeling to a lyre, touched the strings,
Muffling to death the pathos with his wings;
And, ever and anon, uprose to look
At the youth's slumber; while another took
A willow-bough, distilling odorous dew,
425   And shook it on his hair; another flew
In through the woven roof, and fluttering-wise
Rained violets upon his sleeping eyes.

At these enchantments, and yet many more,
The breathless Latmian wondered o'er and o'er,
430   Until, impatient in embarrassment,
He forthright passed, and lightly treading went
To that same feathered lyrist, who straightway,
Smiling, thus whispered: 'Though from upper day
Thou art a wanderer, and thy presence here
435   Might seem unholy, be of happy cheer!
For 'tis the nicest touch of human honour
When some ethereal and high-favouring donor
Presents immortal bowers to mortal sense—
As now 'tis done to thee, Endymion. Hence
440   Was I in no wise startled. So recline
Upon these living flowers. Here is wine,

ii 413. *Ethiop*] darkling *Draft*.
ii 414. *bugle blooms*] The bugle-shaped flowers of the woodbine.
ii 415. *streakèd vases*] The petals of the convolvulus. The word 'flush' means in full bloom.
ii 416. *mellowing for an autumn blush*] blushing deep at Autumn's blush *Draft*. The leaves of the Virginia creeper turn red in the autumn.
ii 417. *virgin's bower*] A species of clematis, also known as Traveller's Joy and Old Man's Beard.
ii 419.   Stood Cupids holding o'er an upward gaze
             Each a slim wand tipt with a silver blaze . . . *Draft*.
ii 421. *the pathos*] The pathetic sound.
ii 441–4. *Here is wine . . . purple*] Foreshadows *Ode to a Nightingale* 16–18 (p. 526 below),

Alive with sparkles—never, I aver,
Since Ariadne was a vintager,
So cool a purple; taste these juicy pears,
445 Sent me by sad Vertumnus, when his fears
Were high about Pomona; here is cream,
Deepening to richness from a snowy gleam,
Sweeter than that nurse Amalthea skimmed
For the boy Jupiter; and here, undimmed
450 By any touch, a bunch of blooming plums
Ready to melt between an infant's gums;
And here is manna picked from Syrian trees,
In starlight, by the three Hesperides.
Feast on, and meanwhile I will let thee know
455 Of all these things around us.' He did so,
Still brooding o'er the cadence of his lyre,
And thus: 'I need not any hearing tire

... the blushful Hippocrene,
With beaded bubbles winking at the brim,
And purple-stainèd mouth ...

On K.'s enjoyment of wine see *Hence burgundy, claret and port* 1–2 *n* (p. 299 below).

ii *443*. Bacchus consoled Ariadne when she was abandoned by Theseus on the island of Naxos; see *Sleep and Poetry* 335–6 *n* (p. 83 above).

ii *445–6. sad Vertumnus . . . Pomona*] Vertumnus, Roman deity of the spring, was at first rejected by Pomona, a wood-nymph associated in classical mythology with gardens and fruit-trees. See Ovid's *Metamorphoses* xiv 623–771.

ii *448–9. Sweeter . . . Jupiter*] Amalthea was a Cretan princess who nursed Jupiter in infancy on Mount Ida and fed him on goat's milk. See *Lemprière*: 'Some authors have called her a goat, and have maintained that Jupiter . . . gave one of her horns to the nymphs who had taken care of his infant years. This horn was called the horn of plenty.'

ii. *452. manna*] See i 766 *n*. With K.'s use of the word here to suggest exotic fruit cp. *The Eve of St Agnes* 268 (p. 471 below),

Manna and dates, in argosy transferred . . .

ii *453. the three Hesperides*] Daughters of Hesperus (see i 13 *n*), who guarded the tree with golden apples belonging to Atlas (Ovid's *Metamorphoses* iv 637–8, xi 113–14). K. sends them to Syria to pick their 'manna', but their home (Hesperis) was traditionally in Africa.

ii *456–7.*   Keeping a ravishing cadence with his lyre.
        And this it was 'I'll not thy knowing tire . . . *Draft*

ii *457–80. I need not . . . winter sleep*] K.'s account of Venus and Adonis draws chiefly on Shakespeare's *Venus and Adonis*, with some additional details from *The Faerie Queene* III i 34–8, vi 46–9, Ovid's *Metamorphoses* x 519–52, 708–39 and *Baldwin*.

By telling how the sea-born goddess pined
For a mortal youth, and how she strove to bind
460   Him all in all unto her doting self.
Who would not be so prisoned? But, fond elf,
He was content to let her amorous plea
Faint through his careless arms; content to see
An unseized heaven dying at his feet;
465   Content, oh fool, to make a cold retreat,
When on the pleasant grass such love, lovelorn,
Lay sorrowing, when every tear was born
Of diverse passion, when her lips and eyes
Were closed in sullen moisture, and quick sighs
470   Came vexed and pettish through her nostrils small.
Hush, no exclaim—yet, justly mightst thou call
Curses upon his head. I was half glad,
But my poor mistress went distract and mad

ii *458. sea-born goddess*] Venus arose from the sea near the coast of the island of Cythera (Cyprus in some traditions). See *Lemprière*: 'She was wafted by the zephyrs, and received on the sea-shore by the seasons, daughters of Jupiter and Themis.'

ii *459–60. how she strove . . . doting self*] K. is thinking here of Shakespeare's *Venus and Adonis*.

ii *461. prisoned? But, fond*] bound, but foolish *Draft*. The word 'elf', a favourite word in K. (who sometimes employs it for the convenience of the rhyme) is probably owed to its habitual use by Spenser when referring to his fairy knights. Other examples in K. include *Isabella* 453, *Read me a lesson* 11, *How fevered is the man* 7, *Ode to a Nightingale* 74, *Lamia* i 55 (pp. 350, 376, 514, 532, and 619 below).

ii *462–7. He was content . . . sorrowing*] See *Venus and Adonis* 811–14,

> . . . he breaketh from the sweet embrace
> Of those fair arms which bound him to her breast,
> And homeward through the dark lawnd runs apace;
> Leaves Love upon her back deeply distressed . . .

ii *462. her amorous plea*] Divinity *Draft*.

ii *466. love, lovelorn*] Cp. *Venus and Adonis* 328, 'love-sick love'.

ii *468–9. eyes . . . moisture*] See *Venus and Adonis* 956–7,

> She vail'd her eyelids, who, like sluices, stopp'd
> The crystal tide . . .

The passage is marked by K. in his copy of Shakespeare's (1806 edn) which is at Hampstead.

ii *468. diverse passion*] See *Venus and Adonis* 967–8,

> Variable passions throng her constant woe,
> As striving who should best become her grief . . .

ii *473–4. But my poor mistress . . . tusked him*] Related in Ovid's *Metamorphoses* x 708–23; see also *Venus and Adonis* 1027–62.

When the boar tusked him. So away she flew
475 To Jove's high throne, and by her plainings drew
Immortal tear-drops down the thunderer's beard,
Whereon it was decreed he should be reared
Each summer-time to life. Lo, this is he,
That same Adonis, safe in the privacy
480 Of this still region all his winter-sleep.
Aye, sleep: for when our love-sick queen did weep
Over his wanèd corse, the tremulous shower
Healed up the wound, and, with a balmy power,
Medicined death to a lengthened drowsiness,
485 The which she fills with visions and doth dress
In all this quiet luxury; and hath set
Us young immortals, without any let,
To watch his slumber through. 'Tis well nigh passed,
Even to a moment's filling up, and fast
490 She scuds with summer breezes, to pant through
The first long kiss, warm firstling, to renew

ii *474–8. So away . . . to life*] Venus does not plead with Jupiter in the versions of the story in Shakespeare, Spenser or Lemprière, but see *Baldwin*: 'Venus was inconsolable for his loss, and at length obtained from Jupiter that he should return to life for six months in every year; so that Adonis revives and dies in incessant succession' (chap. xxiii). According to some traditions it was Proserpine who revived him.

ii *474. tusked*] tushed *Fair copy*. See *To J. H. Reynolds, Esq.* 16 *n* (p. 321 below).

ii *475–6. drew . . . beard*] Perhaps a reminiscence of Milton's *Il Penseroso* 107,
                Drew Iron tears down *Pluto's* cheek . . .

On Jupiter as the 'thunderer' see *To Apollo* 13–14, 15–16 *n* (p. 111 above).

ii *482. Over this paly course, the crystal shower . . . Draft.*

ii *484.* Perhaps suggested by *Othello* III iii 331–3,
                . . . Not poppy, nor mandragora,
            Nor all the drowsy syrups of the world,
            Shall ever medicine thee to that sweet sleep . . .

ii *485. The which she fills with visions*] Suggesting a parallel with Endymion's dreams of Cynthia on Mount Latmos.

ii *486. luxury*] On K.'s use of this word see *Calidore* 92 *n* (p. 40 above).

ii *487. without any let*] Without break or interruption.

ii *488. slumber*] winter *Draft*. See i *474–8 n*.

ii *489. filling up*] complishing *Draft*.

ii *490. scuds*] An Elizabethanism. Shakespeare says of Adonis's horse in *Venus and Adonis* 301, 'Sometimes he scuds far off'. Used again by K. at ii 698, iii 956 below and *Hyperion* ii 236 *n* (p. 428 below).

ii *491. warm firstling*] sweet prologue *Draft*.

Embowered sports in Cytherea's isle.
Look, how those wingèd listeners all this while
Stand anxious! See! Behold!'—This clamant word
495 Broke through the careful silence, for they heard
A rustling noise of leaves, and out there fluttered
Pigeons and doves. Adonis something muttered
The while one hand, that erst upon his thigh
Lay dormant, moved convulsed and gradually
500 Up to his forehead. Then there was a hum
Of sudden voices, echoing, 'Come! Come!
Arise! Awake! Clear summer has forth walked
Unto the clover-sward, and she has talked
Full soothingly to every nested finch.
505 Rise, Cupids, or we'll give the blue-bell pinch
To your dimpled arms! Once more sweet life begin!'
At this, from every side they hurried in,
Rubbing their sleepy eyes with lazy wrists,
And doubling over head their little fists
510 In backward yawns. But all were soon alive.
For as delicious wine doth, sparkling, dive
In nectared clouds and curls through water fair,
So from the arbour roof down swelled an air
Odorous and enlivening, making all
515 To laugh and play and sing and loudly call
For their sweet queen—when lo! the wreathèd green
Disparted, and far upward could be seen
Blue heaven, and a silver car, air-borne,
Whose silent wheels, fresh wet from clouds of morn,
520 Spun off a drizzling dew, which falling chill
On soft Adonis' shoulders made him still
Nestle and turn uneasily about.
Soon were the white doves plain, with neck stretched
     out,
And silken traces lightened in descent;

ii 492. *Cytherea*] Venus. See ii 458 *n* and Sandys's gloss on 'Cythera', 'An
Iland in the *Aegean* Sea, whereof *Venus* was called *Cytherea*' (Sandys's *Ovid*,
p. 190, col. 1).
ii 497. *Pigeons and doves*] Emblems of Venus.
ii 505. Cupids awake! or black and blue we'll pinch . . . *Fair copy (cancelled)*.
ii 506. *Once more sweet life begin*] for lo! your Queen, your Queen *Draft*.
ii 511. *delicious wine*] See ii 441–4 *n* above.
ii 517. *Disparted*] See ii 308 *n*.
ii 520–2. Suggests reluctance at being awakened from his dream. Cp. i 681–
705 *n* above.

525 And soon, returning from love's banishment,
    Queen Venus leaning downward open-armed,
    Her shadow fell upon his breast and charmed
    A tumult to his heart and a new life
    Into his eyes. Ah, miserable strife,
530 But for her comforting! Unhappy sight,
    But meeting her blue orbs! Who, who can write
    Of these first minutes? The unchariest muse
    To embracements warm as theirs makes coy excuse.

    Oh, it has ruffled every spirit there
535 Saving Love's self, who stands superb to share
    The general gladness. Awfully he stands:
    A sovereign quell is in his waving hands;
    No sight can bear the lightning of his bow;
    His quiver is mysterious, none can know

ii 526–34.   Queen Venus bending downward, so o'ertaken,
              So suffering sweet, so blushing mad, so shaken
              That the wild warmth prob'd the young sleeper's heart
              Enchantingly; and with a sudden start
              His trembling arms were out in instant time
              To catch his fainting love.–O foolish rhyme
              What mighty power is in thee that so often
              Thou strivest rugged syllables to soften
              Even to the telling of a sweet like this.
              Away! let them embrace alone! that kiss
              Was far too rich for thee to talk upon.
              Poor wretch! mind not these sobs and sighs! begone!
              Speak not one atom of thy paltry stuff,
              That they are met is poetry enough.
                    O this has ruffled every spirit there . . . *Draft (cancelled)*.
ii 532. *unchariest*] Least bashful. The unusual superlative may be owed to
Hamlet I iii 36, 'The chariest maid . . .'.
ii 533. *coy excuse*] Echoes Milton's *Lycidas* 18–20,
              Hence with denial vain, and coy excuse,
              So may som gentle Muse
              With lucky words favour my destin'd Urn . . .
K.'s 'muse' is similarly bashful at ii 716–23 (p. 193 below).
ii 535. *Love's self*] Cupid, Venus's son, who caused her to fall in love with
Adonis when he accidentally wounded her with his arrow (Ovid's *Metamorphoses* x 525–32).
ii 537. *quell*] An archaism for the power or means to destroy, here referring
to Cupid's bow and arrow. Cp. *Spenser! A jealous honourer* 7 (p. 309 below),
              To rise like Phoebus with a golden quell . . .
ii 538. His bow can bear for lightning so . . . *Fair copy*.

540   What themselves think of it; from forth his eyes
There darts strange light of varied hues and dyes;
A scowl is sometimes on his brow, but who
Look full upon it feel anon the blue
Of his fair eyes run liquid through their souls.

545   Endymion feels it, and no more controls
The burning prayer within him; so, bent low,
He had begun a plaining of his woe.
But Venus, bending forward, said: 'My child,
Favour this gentle youth; his days are wild

550   With love—he—but alas! too well I see
Thou know'st the deepness of his misery.
Ah, smile not so, my son, I tell thee true
That when through heavy hours I used to rue
The endless sleep of this new-born Adon',

555   This stranger ay I pitied. For upon
A dreary morning once I fled away
Into the breezy clouds to weep and pray
For this my love, for vexing Mars had teased
Me even to tears. Thence, when a little eased,

560   Down-looking, vacant, through a hazy wood,
I saw this youth as he despairing stood,
Those same dark curls blown vagrant in the wind,
Those same full-fringèd lids a constant blind
Over his sullen eyes. I saw him throw

565   Himself on withered leaves, even as though
Death had come sudden; for no jot he moved,
Yet muttered wildly. I could hear he loved
Some fair immortal, and that his embrace

ii *541. varied*] changeful *Draft.* An earlier cancelled attempt was 'sundry'.
ii *548–79.* Venus encourages Endymion again at iii 903–21 below.
ii *552. my son*] sweet boy *Draft.* Probably altered to make it clear that Venus
is addressing Cupid.
ii *554. new-born*] mad-brain'd *Draft.*
ii *558–9. vexing Mars . . . tears*] The love of Mars and Venus is related in
Ovid's *Metamorphoses* iv 171–89. See also *Venus and Adonis* 97–102,

> I have been woo'd, as I entreat thee now,
> Even by the stern and direful god of war,
> Whose sinewy neck in battle ne'er did bow,
> Who conquers where he comes in every jar;
>   Yet he hath been my captive and my slave,
>   And begg'd for that which thou unask'd shall have . . .

ii *563. full fringèd lids*] See i 394 *n.*
ii *567. wildly*] madly *Draft.*
ii *569–72. There is . . . secretest*] See ii 179–80 *n.*

Had zoned her through the night. There is no trace
570   Of this in heaven. I have marked each cheek,
And find it is the vainest thing to seek,
And that of all things 'tis kept secretest.
Endymion, one day thou wilt be blest.
So still obey the guiding hand that fends
575   Thee safely through these wonders for sweet ends.
'Tis a concealment needful in extreme,
And if I guessed not so, the sunny beam
Thou shouldst mount up to with me. Now adieu!
Here must we leave thee.' At these words upflew
580   The impatient doves, uprose the floating car,
Up went the hum celestial. High afar
The Latmian saw them minish into naught,
And, when all were clear vanished, still he caught
A vivid lightning from that dreadful bow.
585   When all was darkened, with Aetnean throe
The earth closed, gave a solitary moan,
And left him once again in twilight lone.

He did not rave, he did not stare aghast,
For all those visions were o'ergone, and past,
590   And he in loneliness. He felt assured
Of happy times when all he had endured
Would seem a feather to the mighty prize.
So, with unusual gladness, on he hies
Through caves and palaces of mottled ore,
595   Gold dome and crystal wall and turquoise floor,
Black polished porticoes of awful shade,
And, at the last, a diamond balustrade,
Leading afar past wild magnificence,
Spiral through ruggedest loopholes, and thence
600   Stretching across a void, then guiding o'er
Enormous chasms, where, all foam and roar,

ii 578–81. Now adieu . . . celestial] See Cowden Clarke's letter to Milnes of
March 1846, 'I have often thought of that Sunday afternoon, when [K.] . . .
read to Mr. Severn and myself the description of the "Bower of Adonis";
and the conscious pleasure with which he looked up when he came to the
passage that tells the ascent of the car of Venus' (KC ii 151).
ii 582. minish] Diminish. See i 320 n.
ii 584–5.   Anon and ever gleams from that dread bow
      One lightning more–then with Oetnean throe . . . Draft.
For the 'dreadful bow' see ii 537 n.
ii 597. Then diamond steps and ruby balustrade . . . Draft.
ii 601–4. Enormous chasms . . . thousand fountains] Similar descriptions in Romantic poetry known to K. include Coleridge's Kubla Khan (1816) 17–19,

Streams subterranean tease their granite beds,
Then heightened just above the silvery heads
Of a thousand fountains, so that he could dash
605   The waters with his spear—but at the splash,
Done heedlessly, those spouting columns rose
Sudden a poplar's height, and 'gan to enclose
His diamond path with fretwork, streaming round
Alive, and dazzling cool, and with a sound,
610   Haply, like dolphin tumults when sweet shells
Welcome the float of Thetis. Long he dwells
On this delight, for, every minute's space,
The streams with changèd magic interlace:
Sometimes like delicatest lattices,
615   Covered with crystal vines; then weeping trees,
Moving about as in a gentle wind,
Which, in a wink, to watery gauze refined,
Poured into shapes of curtained canopies,
Spangled, and rich with liquid broideries
620   Of flowers, peacocks, swans, and naiads fair.
Swifter than lightning went these wonders rare,
And then the water, into stubborn streams
Collecting, mimicked the wrought oaken beams,
Pillars, and frieze, and high fantastic roof,

... from this chasm with ceaseless turmoil seething,
As if this earth in fast thick pants were breathing,
A mighty fountain momently was forced ...

and Shelley's *Alastor* (1816) 377–81,

... sound
That shook the everlasting rocks, the mass
Filled with one whirlpool all that ample chasm;
Stair above stair the eddying water rose,
Circling immeasurably fast ...

ii *602. tease*] wear *Draft*. An earlier cancelled attempt was 'rage'.
ii *608. diamond ... streaming*] mid-air ... quivering *Draft*.
ii *610. sweet*] loud *Draft*.
ii *611. Thetis*] A sea deity, mother of Achilles by Peleus. The story of Thesis and Peleus is related in Ovid's *Metamorphoses* xi 235–65.
ii *613–27.* K.'s 'founts Protean' (see ii 627 *n*) may owe something to the kaleidoscopic scenes representing 'the surface of a Sea and Land' depicted on Phoebe's cloak in Drayton's *The Man in the Moone* 145–220 (see iii 197–212 *n*), but the details suggest a recollection of spectacular stage effects popular at the time.
ii *615. weeping trees*] Weeping willows.
ii *620. naiads*] See ii 129 *n*.

625   Of those dusk places in times far aloof
        Cathedrals called. He bade a loth farewell
        To these founts Protean, passing gulf and dell
        And torrent, and ten thousand jutting shapes,
        Half seen through deepest gloom, and grisly gapes,
630   Blackening on every side, and overhead
        A vaulted dome like heaven's, far bespread
        With starlight gems. Aye, all so huge and strange,
        The solitary felt a hurried change
        Working within him into something dreary–
635   Vexed like a morning eagle, lost and weary
        And purblind amid foggy, midnight wolds.
        But he revives at once, for who beholds
        New sudden things, nor casts his mental slough?
        Forth from a rugged arch, in the dusk below,
640   Came mother Cybele! Alone, alone,

ii *625. dusk*] dim *Draft*.

ii *627. Protean*] Constantly changing. Proteus, the sea-god who was able to assume any shape he pleased, appears in Ovid's story of Thetis and Peleus (see ii 611 *n*).

ii *628. jutting*] Earlier attempts in the draft were 'massy', 'blackening' and 'bulging'.

ii *629. Half seen through deepest gloom*] Hid in the dim profound *Draft*. The 'grisly gapes' are presumably gaping holes in the rock.

ii *632. huge and*] monstrous *Draft*.

ii *633. hurried*] dizzy *Draft*. See i 565 *n*.

ii *635.* The eagle is a favourite image in K.'s early verse. Cp. *On First Looking into Chapman's Homer' 11, On Seeing the Elgin Marbles 5 n* (pp. 62 and 104 above) and ii 910–11 *n* below.

ii *636. wolds*] Uplands.

ii *639–49.* Bailey said of this passage in his letter to Milnes of May 1849, 'a more sublime imagining can hardly be found in English Poetry' (*KC* ii 284).

ii *639. rugged*] Earlier attempts included 'dismal', 'beetling' and 'gloomy.'

ii *640–7. mother Cybele . . . tawny brushes*] On Cybele, the mother of the gods, see *Hyperion* ii 4 *n* (p. 415 below) and Sandys's commentary on Ovid's *Metamorphoses* x, '. . . fained to be crowned with towers, in that taken for the Earth which supporteth so many: said to be the mother of the Gods; or rather the generall mother of all things. . . . She is said to be drawn by Lions, in regard of their heat and rapacitie, representing the Heavens, wherein the Ayre, which carrieth the Earth, or Cybel, is contained' (Sandys's *Ovid*, p. 201). According to Ovid, Cybele transformed Hippomenes and Atalanta into lions as a punishment for profaning her temple. The episode forms part of the legend of Atalanta related by Venus as a warning to Adonis in Ovid's *Metamorphoses* x 560–707.

In sombre chariot; dark foldings thrown
About her majesty; and front death-pale,
With turrets crowned. Four manèd lions hale
The sluggish wheels. Solemn their toothèd maws,
645 Their surly eyes brow-hidden, heavy paws
Uplifted drowsily, and nervy tails
Cowering their tawny brushes. Silent sails
This shadowy queen athwart, and faints away
In another gloomy arch.

Wherefore delay,
650 Young traveller, in such a mournful place?
Art thou wayworn, or canst not further trace
The diamond path? And does it indeed end
Abrupt in middle air? Yet earthward bend
Thy forehead, and to Jupiter cloud-borne
655 Call ardently! He was indeed wayworn.
Abrupt, in middle air, his way was lost.
To cloud-borne Jove he bowèd, and there crossed
Towards him a large eagle, 'twixt whose wings,

ii *641. foldings*] Folds of drapery.
ii *642–7. front death-pale . . . brushes*]

her pale brow
With turrets crown'd, which forward heavily bow
Weighing her chin to the breast. Four lions draw
The wheels in sluggish time—each toothed maw
Shut patiently—eyes hid in tawny veils—
Drooping about their paws, and nervy tails
Cowering their tufted brushes to the dust . . . *Draft (cancelled).*
With both versions cp. Sandys's *Ovid, Metamorphoses* x (p. 191, col. 2),
. . . The Mother, crownd
With towres, had Struck them to the *Stygian* Sound:
But that she thought the punishment too small.
When yellow maines on their smooth shoulders fall;
Their armes, to legs; their fingers turn to nailes:
Their brests of wondrous strength: their tufted tailes
Whisk up the dust; their looks are full of dread:
For speech, they rore: the woods become their bed.
These lions, fear'd by others, *Cybel* checks
With curbing bits; and yokes their stubborne necks . . .
ii *644. toothèd*] Earlier attempts in the draft were 'closed' and 'patient'.
ii *645. brow-hidden*] half-shut *Draft.*
ii *646. drowsily*] lazily *Draft.*
ii *647. Cowering their tawny brushes*] Vailing their tawny tufts *Draft.*

Without one impious word, himself he flings,
660 Committed to the darkness and the gloom,
Down, down, uncertain to what pleasant doom.
Swift as a fathoming plummet down he fell
Through unknown things, till exhaled asphodel
And rose, with spicy fannings interbreathed,
665 Came swelling forth where little caves were wreathed
So thick with leaves and mosses that they seemed
Large honey-combs of green, and freshly teemed
With airs delicious. In the greenest nook
The eagle landed him, and farewell took.

670   It was a jasmine bower, all bestrown
With golden moss. His every sense had grown
Ethereal for pleasure: 'bove his head
Flew a delight half-graspable; his tread
Was Hesperian; to his capable ears
675 Silence was music from the holy spheres;
A dewy luxury was in his eyes;
The little flowers felt his pleasant sighs
And stirred them faintly. Verdant cave and cell
He wandered through, oft wondering at such swell

ii *657–60. bowèd . . . gloom*]
                              bent: and there was tost
                    Into his grasping hands a silken cord
                    At which without a single impious word
                    He swung upon it off into the gloom . . . *Draft.*
ii *658. a large eagle*] The eagle was an emblem of Jupiter. Cp. *To Apollo*
15–16 *n* (p. 111 above).
ii *662. Swift as*] Dropt like *Draft.*
ii *664. fannings*] On K.'s use of participial nouns see *Calidore* 27 *n* (p. 38
above).
ii *668–71. In the . . . moss*]
                              Long he hung about
                    Before his nice enjoyment could pick out
                    The resting place: but at the last he swung
                    Into the greenest cell of all—among
                    Dark leaved jasmine: star flower'd and bestrown
                    With golden moss . . . *Draft.*
ii *672. Ethereal*] Fine-tuned. On K.'s various uses of this word see *To Hope*
5 *n* (p. 13 above).
ii *674. Hesperian*] Westward (from Hesperus, the western, or evening, star).
ii *676.* Cp. *Calidore* 88 (p. 40 above), 'tears of languishment'. On K.'s use
of 'luxury' see *Calidore* 92 *n* (p. 40 above).
ii *679. oft wondering at*] with still increasing *Draft.*

680 Of sudden exaltation, but, 'Alas!'
     Said he, 'will all this gush of feeling pass
     Away in solitude? And must they wane,
     Like melodies upon a sandy plain,
     Without an echo? Then shall I be left
685 So sad, so melancholy, so bereft!
     Yet still I feel immortal! O my love,
     My breath of life, where art thou? High above,
     Dancing before the morning gates of heaven?
     Or keeping watch among those starry seven,
690 Old Atlas' children? Art a maid of the waters,
     One of shell-winding Triton's bright-haired daughters?
     Or art–impossible!–a nymph of Dian's,
     Weaving a coronal of tender scions
     For very idleness? Where'er thou art,
695 Methinks it now is at my will to start
     Into thine arms; to scare Aurora's train,
     And snatch thee from the morning; o'er the main

ii *685*. For a similar grouping of epithets see *As Hermes once* 4 *n* (p. 499 below).

ii *687–94*. *My breath . . . idleness*] Endymion does not recognize his love as an Olympian goddess, but imagines that she may be one of the Horae (ii 688), one of the Pleiades (ii 689–90), a sea-nymph (ii 690–1), or a nymph attending Diana (ii 692–4).

ii *688*. She may be one of the three Horae who 'were the same as the seasons . . . and were represented by the poets as opening the gates of Heaven and Olympus, and yoking the horses of Phoebus at the approach of morning' (*Lemprière*).

ii *689–90*. *starry seven . . . children*] The Pleiades. See *Lemprière*: 'A name given to seven of the daughters of Atlas by Pleione or Aethra, one of the Oceanides. They were placed in the heavens after their death, where they formed a constellation'.

ii *690*. *maid*] nymph *Draft*. Cp. ii 692 *n* below.

ii *691*. *shell-winding Triton*] See i 206 *n* (p. 128 above).

ii *692*. *nymph*] maid *Draft*.

ii *693*. *scions*] Branches, twigs. An archaism **from Middle** English 'sioun' (*Oxford Dictionary of Etymology*). Cp. Shakespeare's use of 'scion' in *The Winter's Tale* IV iii 93, a passage quoted in *Ode to Psyche* 62–3 *n* (p. 520 below).

ii *695–700*. There are various things she may be, so there are various corresponding things he may do to claim her.

ii *697–8*. *the morning . . . off*] from among them; to attain,
     The starry heights and find thee ere a breath . . . *Draft* (*cancelled*).

ii *698*. *scud*] skim *Draft*. On 'scud' see ii 490 *n* above.

To scud like a wild bird, and take thee off
From thy sea-foamy cradle; or to doff
700 Thy shepherd vest, and woo thee 'mid fresh leaves.
No, no, too eagerly my soul deceives
Its powerless self. I know this cannot be.
Oh, let me then by some sweet dreaming flee
To her entrancements. Hither, sleep, awhile!
705 Hither most gentle sleep! And soothing foil
For some few hours the coming solitude.'
      Thus spake he, and that moment felt endued
With power to dream deliciously, so wound
Through a dim passage, searching till he found
710 The smoothest mossy bed and deepest, where
He threw himself, and just into the air
Stretching his indolent arms, he took–oh, bliss!–
A naked waist: 'Fair Cupid, whence is this?'
A well-known voice sighed, 'Sweetest, here am I!'
715 At which soft ravishment, with doting cry,
They trembled to each other. Helicon!
O fountained hill! Old Homer's Helicon,
That thou wouldst spout a little streamlet o'er
These sorry pages! Then the verse would soar
720 And sing above this gentle pair, like lark
Over his nested young. But all is dark
Around thine agèd top, and thy clear fount
Exhales in mists to heaven. Aye, the count

ii *699. doff*] Take off.
ii *700. shepherd vest*] The clothing she would wear as a nymph of Diana (see ii 692 above).
ii *702. powerless*] mortal *Draft*.
ii *706. For some few hours*] With thy quick magic *Draft*. Cp. i 453 above, 'O magic sleep!'
ii *709. searching*] feeling *Draft*.
ii *713. Fair Cupid*] Good heavens! *Draft*.
ii *715.* At which each uttering forth a wailful cry ... *Draft*. K.'s rejected correction for 'a wailful' was 'an anguished'.
ii *716–32.* K.'s poetic inspiration fails him at a similar crisis at ii 532–3 above. Here he relates his sense of inadequacy to the decline of poetry since the great ages of the past.
ii *717.* See *Lemprière*: 'Helicon ... a mountain of Boeotia ... was sacred to the Muses who had there a temple, and who were supposed to have selected this favourite spot for their residence. The fountain Hippocrene flowed from this mountain.' For K.'s earlier reference to Hippocrene see *To Charles Cowden Clarke* 27 *n* (p. 55 above).
ii *722. top*] green *Draft*.

Of mighty poets is made up; the scroll
725   Is folded by the Muses; the bright roll
Is in Apollo's hand; our dazèd eyes
Have seen a new tinge in the western skies.
The world has done its duty. Yet, oh yet,
Although the sun of poesy is set,
730   These lovers did embrace, and we must weep
That there is no old power left to steep
A quill immortal in their joyous tears.
Long time ere silence did their anxious fears
Question that thus it was; long time they lay
735   Fondling and kissing every doubt away;
Long time ere soft caressing sobs began
To mellow into words, and then there ran
Two bubbling springs of talk from their sweet lips.
'O known Unknown from whom my being sips
740   Such darling essence, wherefore may I not
Be ever in these arms? In this sweet spot
Pillow my chin for ever? Ever press
These toying hands and kiss their smooth excess?
Why not for ever and for ever feel
745   That breath about my eyes? Ah, thou wilt steal
Away from me again, indeed, indeed—
Thou wilt be gone away, and wilt not heed
My lonely madness. Speak, delicious fair!
Is—is it to be so? No! Who will dare
750   To pluck thee from me? And, of thine own will,
Full well I feel thou wouldst not leave me. Still
Let me entwine thee surer, surer—now
How can we part? Elysium! Who art thou?
Who, that thou canst not be for ever here,

ii *726. dazèd*] mortal *Draft.*

ii *727–8. a new tinge . . . duty*] The sun is setting: the world has completed its poetic task.

ii *733–4. Long time . . . it was*] i.e. 'It was a long time before their anxious fears did question the silence that they were really together. . . .'

ii *735. every*] dreaming *Draft.*

ii *736. soft*] few *Draft.*

ii *740. essence*] See i 779 *n* above.

ii *740–2. wherefore . . . for ever?*] Foreshadows the *Bright star* sonnet (p. 736 below).

ii *743. toying*] languid *Draft.*

ii *748. delicious*] Restored from the draft version. The fair copy has 'my kindest . . .'.

ii *751. Full well I feel*] I know—I feel *Draft.*

755   Or lift me with thee to some starry sphere?
      Enchantress! Tell me by this soft embrace,
      By the most soft completion of thy face,
      Those lips, O slippery blisses, twinkling eyes,
      And by these tenderest, milky sovereignties—
760   These tenderest—and by the nectar-wine,
      The passion——' 'O, doved Ida the divine!
      Endymion! Dearest! Ah, unhappy me!
      His soul will 'scape us—oh, felicity!
      How he does love me! His poor temples beat
765   To the very tune of love—how sweet, sweet, sweet.
      Revive, dear youth, or I shall faint and die;
      Revive, or these soft hours will hurry by
      In trancèd dullness; speak, and let that spell
      Affright this lethargy! I cannot quell
770   Its heavy pressure, and will press at least
      My lips to thine that they may richly feast
      Until we taste the life of love again.
      What! Dost thou move? Dost kiss? O bliss! O pain!
      I love thee, youth, more than I can conceive,
775   And so long absence from thee doth bereave
      My soul of any rest—yet must I hence.
      Yet, can I not to starry eminence
      Uplift thee, nor for very shame can own
      Myself to thee. Ah, dearest, do not groan

ii *756. soft*] mad *Draft.*

ii *757-9.* With the sentimental style cp. *Calidore* 80–108 *n* (p. 40 above). Robert Bridges remarks of K.'s 'idea of woman', 'His conception often offends taste without raising the imagination, and it reveals a plainly impossible foundation for dignified passion' ('Endymion', Introduction to *Poems of John Keats* ed. G. Thorn Drury (1896) xxviii).

ii *757.* By the moist languor of thy breathing face . . . *Draft.*

ii *760–1. nectar . . . divine*]

              breath—the love
     The passion—nectar—Heaven.'–'Jove above! . . .' *Draft.*

ii *761. Ida*] The mountain near Troy where Paris awarded the golden apple to Venus, here perhaps an invocation to Venus herself.

ii *768. trancèd dullness*] For this characteristic mood see *Ode to a Nightingale* 1 *n* (p. 525 below).

ii *773. O bliss! O pain!*] Cp. ii 822–4 below, 'I am pained . . . In the very deeps of pleasure . . .'. On the close relationship between pain and pleasure in K. see *Ode to a Nightingale* 1 *n* (p. 525 below and ii 823–4 *n* below).

ii *779–95. Ah, dearest . . . love*] K. may have taken a hint for Cynthia's relationship with her fellow-Olympians from Drayton's *The Man in the Moone* 59–66,

780   Or thou wilt force me from this secrecy,
      And I must blush in heaven. Oh, that I
      Had done it already; that the dreadful smiles
      At my lost brightness, my impassioned wiles,
      Had wanèd from Olympus' solemn height,
785   And from all serious Gods; that our delight
      Was quite forgotten, save of us alone!
      And wherefore so ashamed? 'Tis but to atone
      For endless pleasure by some coward blushes.
      Yet must I be a coward! Horror rushes
790   Too palpable before me—the sad look
      Of Jove, Minerva's start, no bosom shook
      With awe of purity, no Cupid pinion
      In reverence vailed, my crystalline dominion
      Half lost, and all old hymns made nullity!
795   But what is this to love? Oh, I could fly
      With thee into the ken of heavenly powers,
      So thou wouldst thus, for many sequent hours,
      Press me so sweetly. Now I swear at once
      That I am wise, that Pallas is a dunce—
800   Perhaps her love like mine is but unknown.
      Oh, I do think that I have been alone
      In chastity! Yes, Pallas has been sighing,
      While every eve saw me my hair uptying
      With fingers cool as aspen leaves. Sweet love,
805   I was as vague as solitary dove,
      Nor knew that nests were built. Now a soft kiss . . .

          But let them doe to cross her what they could,
          Down unto *Latmus* every Month shee would.
          So that in Heaven about it there was ods,
          And as a question troubled all the Gods,
          Whether without their generall consent,
          She might depart, but nath'lesse, to prevent
          Her Lawlesse course, they laboured all in vayne,
          Nor could their Lawes her liberty restraine . . .

K.'s emphasis on his goddess's troubled emotions is in keeping with his
attempt to show 'the playing of different Natures with Joy and Sorrow' (i
778–81 n).

ii *791. Minerva*] The goddess of wisdom, celebrated for her chastity.

ii *791–4. no bosom . . . nullity*] She bewails her loss of authority as the chaste
goddess.

ii *793. vailed*] Lowered.

ii *799. Pallas*] Minerva.

ii *800.* Does Pallas self not love? she must—she must! . . . *Draft*.

ii *803. uptying*] See i 153–4 n.

Aye, by that kiss I vow an endless bliss,
An immortality of passion's thine.
Ere long I will exalt thee to the shine
810   Of heaven ambrosial, and we will shade
Ourselves whole summers by a river glade,
And I will tell thee stories of the sky,
And breathe thee whispers of its minstrelsy.
My happy love will overwing all bounds!
815   Oh, let me melt into thee, let the sounds
Of our close voices marry at their birth.
Let us entwine hoveringly–Oh, dearth
Of human words! Roughness of mortal speech!
Lispings empyrean will I sometime teach
820   Thine honeyed tongue–lute-breathings, which I gasp
To have thee understand, now while I clasp
Thee thus, and weep for fondness. I am pained,
Endymion. Woe, woe! Is grief contained
In the very deeps of pleasure, my sole life?'
825   Hereat, with many sobs, her gentle strife
Melted into a languor. He returned
Entrancèd vows and tears.

                       Ye who have yearned
With too much passion will here stay and pity
For the mere sake of truth, as 'tis a ditty

ii 814. *My happy love*] Earlier attempts in the draft were 'My maddened love . . .' and 'O my mad love . . .'.
ii 818. *Of mortal words! I'll teach thee other speech . . . Draft.*
ii 819. *empyrean*] immortal *Draft.*
ii 820. *lute*] Gold *Fair copy (cancelled).*
ii 822. *weep for fondness*] shed these drops *Draft.*
ii 823–4. *grief . . . pleasure*] Foreshadows *Ode on Melancholy* 25–6 (p. 541 below),

     . . . in the very temple of Delight
        Veiled Melancholy has her sovran shrine . . .

For 'deeps' the draft has 'shrine'.
ii 825. *many*] fainting *Draft.*
ii 826. *Melted into a*] Died into passive *Draft.*
ii 827–53. *Ye who have . . . gusty deep*] Shelley praised this passage and iii 113–120, 197–212 below in the letter he drafted in defence of *Endymion* to the editor of the *Quarterly Review* (see *Forman* (1883) iii 385).
ii 827–9. Those who have felt such passionate longing will dwell compassionately on this part of the story because they will recognize its truth.
ii 827. *Entrancèd vows and . . . yearned*] No answer saving . . . burned *Draft.*
ii 828. *too much . . . stay*] over . . . exclaim *Draft.*

8 + K.

830   Not of these days, but long ago 'twas told
      By a cavern wind unto a forest old;
      And then the forest told it in a dream
      To a sleeping lake, whose cool and level gleam
      A poet caught as he was journeying
835   To Phoebus' shrine; and in it he did fling
      His weary limbs, bathing an hour's space,
      And after, straight, in that inspirèd place
      He sang the story up into the air,
      Giving it universal freedom. There
840   Has it been ever sounding for those ears
      Whose tips are glowing hot. The legend cheers
      Yon sentinel stars, and he who listens to it
      Must surely be self-doomed or he will rue it.
      For quenchless burnings come upon the heart,
845   Made fiercer by a fear lest any part
      Should be engulfèd in the eddying wind.
      As much as here is penned doth always find
      A resting place, thus much comes clear and plain.
      Anon the strange voice is upon the wane–
850   And 'tis but echoed from departing sound
      That the fair visitant at last unwound
      Her gentle limbs and left the youth asleep.
      Thus the tradition of the gusty deep.

ii 830–9. long ago . . . freedom] On the origin of myths and legends see *I stood tip-toe* 141–204 n (pp. 91–2 above).

ii 831. wind] mouth *Fair copy (cancelled).*

ii 833. sleeping] slumbering *Draft.* With 'cool and level gleam' cp. the lake in Collins's *Ode to Evening* (1747) 32,

                    . . . its last cool gleam.

ii 839–46. There . . . wind] The expression is obscure, but K. means that the legend arouses a restless ardour in the aspiring poet.

ii 840–1. those ears . . . glowing hot] Presumably ears glowing with passion (and thus sensitively attuned to the poet's song). Perhaps suggested by Milton's *Lycidas* 77,

          Phoebus replied and touch'd my trembling ears . . .

ii 842. sentinel stars] An image used by Lovelace in *To Lucasta* (1660) 1,

          Like to the Sent'nal Stars, I watch all Night . . .

and Campbell in *The Soldier's Dream* (1804), 2

          And the sentinel stars set their watch in the sky . . .

ii 847–8. The love of Endymion and Phoebe is one part of the legend which can be understood by everyone.

ii 850. echoed from] guessed from the *Draft.*

ii 852. gentle] prison'd *Draft.*

Now turn we to our former chroniclers.
855   Endymion awoke, that grief of hers
      Sweet paining on his ear. He sickly guessed
      How lone he was once more, and sadly pressed
      His empty arms together, hung his head,
      And most forlorn upon that widowed bed
860   Sat silently. Love's madness he had known.
      Often with more than tortured lion's groan
      Moanings had burst from him, but now that rage
      Had passed away. No longer did he wage
      A rough-voiced war against the dooming stars.
865   No, he had felt too much for such harsh jars.
      The lyre of his soul, Aeolian-tuned,
      Forgot all violence, and but communed
      With melancholy thought. Oh, he had swooned
      Drunken from pleasure's nipple, and his love
870   Henceforth was dove-like. Loth was he to move
      From the imprinted couch, and when he did,
      'Twas with slow, languid paces and face hid
      In muffling hands. So tempered, out he strayed
      Half seeing visions that might have dismayed
875   Alecto's serpents, ravishments more keen
      Than Hermes' pipe, when anxious he did lean

ii 853. gusty deep] Referring to the 'cavern wind' from which the legend
emanated (ii 830–1).

ii 854. our former chroniclers] Presumably all those who have attempted to
recreate the legend. With Endymion's grief in the subsequent lines (ii 855–60)
cp. Drayton's The Man in the Moone 114–16,

>   Now from the Splene the Melancholy deepe,
>   Pierceth the Veynes, and like a raging Floud,
>   Rudely it selfe extending through the Bloud,
>   Appaulls the spirits . . .

ii 860. Sat silently] Patiently sat Draft.

ii 862. Moanings] Passion Draft.

ii 866. Aeolian-tuned] Finely tuned like the strings of the Aeolian lyre which
respond harmoniously to the movements of the wind (see Ode to Apollo 34
n, p. 16 above).

ii 871. imprinted] dear Draft.

ii 874. Half] Scarce Draft.

ii 875. Alecto] One of the Furies. See Sandys's Ovid, Metamorphoses x (p. 188,
col. 1),

>   Alecto, with swolne snakes, and Stygian fire . . .

ii 875–7 more keen . . . eyes] Sweeter than the sound of Hermes's music
when he lulled to sleep the hundred-eyed monster Argus (see As Hermes once
1–2 n, 3–5 n, p. 499 below).

Over eclipsing eyes; and at the last
It was a sounding grotto, vaulted, vast,
O'er studded with a thousand, thousand pearls
880 And crimson-mouthèd shells with stubborn curls,
Of every shape and size, even to the bulk
In which whales arbour close to brood and sulk
Against an endless storm. Moreover, too,
Fish-semblances of green and azure hue,
885 Ready to snort their streams. In this cool wonder
Endymion sat down, and 'gan to ponder
On all his life: his youth, up to the day
When, 'mid acclaim and feasts and garlands gay,
He stepped upon his shepherd throne; the look
890 Of his white palace in wild forest nook,
And all the revels he had lorded there.
Each tender maiden whom he once thought fair,
With every friend and fellow-woodlander,
Passed like a dream before him. Then the spur
895 Of the old bards to mighty deeds; his plans
To nurse the golden age 'mong shepherd clans;
That wondrous night, the great Pan-festival;
His sister's sorrow, and his wanderings all,
Until into the earth's deep maw he rushed;
900 Then all its buried magic, till it flushed
High with excessive love. 'And now,' thought he,
'How long must I remain in jeopardy
Of blank amazements that amaze no more?
Now I have tasted her sweet soul to the core
905 All other depths are shallow. Essences,
Once spiritual, are like muddy lees,
Meant but to fertilize my earthly root
And make my branches lift a golden fruit
Into the bloom of heaven. Other light,

ii *880.* And shells outswelling their faint tinged curls . . . *Draft.*

ii *881. shape*] hue *Fair copy (cancelled).*

ii *884. azure*] golden *Draft.*

ii *885. snort their streams*] The spouting of whales.

ii *896. the golden age*] On the Golden Age in classical mythology see *Hyperion* i 107–10 n (pp. 402–3 below).

ii *897. That wondrous night*] Endymion's first encounter with Phoebe (i 552–671 above).

ii *899. deep*] dim *Draft.*

ii *905–6. Essences | Once spiritual*] Things which once seemed to transcend the earthly.

ii *908. a golden*] their ripen'd *Draft.*

910   Though it be quick and sharp enough to blight
      The Olympian eagle's vision, is dark,
      Dark as the parentage of chaos. Hark!
      My silent thoughts are echoing from these shells;
      Or they are but the ghosts, the dying swells
915   Of noises far away? List!'—Hereupon
      He kept an anxious ear. The humming tone
      Came louder, and behold, there as he lay,
      On either side outgushed, with misty spray,
      A copious spring, and both together dashed
920   Swift, mad, fantastic round the rocks, and lashed
      Among the conches and shells of the lofty grot,
      Leaving a trickling dew. At last they shot
      Down from the ceiling's height, pouring a noise
      As of some breathless racers whose hopes poise
925   Upon the last few steps, and with spent force
      Along the ground they took a winding course.
      Endymion followed—for it seemed that one
      Ever pursued, the other strove to shun—
      Followed their languid mazes, till well nigh
930   He had left thinking of the mystery,
      And was now rapt in tender hoverings
      Over the vanished bliss. Ah, what is it sings
      His dream away? What melodies are these?
      They sound as through the whispering of trees,
935   Not native in such barren vaults. Give ear!

         'O Arethusa, peerless nymph, why fear
      Such tenderness as mine? Great Dian, why,
      Why didst thou hear her prayer? Oh, that I

ii *910–11. quick . . . vision*] A flash of light so brilliant that it could dazzle even Jupiter's eagle (see ii 658 *n* above).

ii *912. Dark as the parentage of chaos*] See *Hyperion* ii 190, 191 and *nn* (p. 427 below).

ii *914. but the ghosts*] subtlest and *Draft*.

ii *931. hoverings*] On K.'s use of participial nouns see *Calidore* 27 *n* (p. 201 above).

ii *932. Over the vanished bliss*] Oe'r past and future *Draft*.

ii *936–1009*. An imaginative reworking of Ovid's legend concerning the love of the river Alpheus for Arethusa, a nymph attending Diana (*Metamorphoses* v 572–641).

ii *937–8. Great Dian . . . prayer*] Diana answered Arethusa's prayer for protection by transforming her into a river whose waters ran through underground caverns to Ortygia (Delos): see ii 1008–9 *n* below.

ii *938–49. Oh, that I . . . captured*] Alpheus fell in love with Arethusa when

Were rippling round her dainty fairness now,
940 Circling about her waist and striving how
To entice her to a dive, then stealing in
Between her luscious lips and eyelids thin!
Oh, that her shining hair was in the sun,
And I distilling from it thence to run
945 In amorous rillets down her shrinking form!
To linger on her lily shoulders, warm
Between her kissing breasts, and every charm
Touch raptured! See how painfully I flow!
Fair maid, be pitiful to my great woe.
950 Stay, stay thy weary course, and let me lead,
A happy wooer, to the flowery mead
Where all that beauty snared me.' 'Cruel god,
Desist, or my offended mistress' nod
Will stagnate all thy fountains—tease me not
955 With siren words. Ah, have I really got
Such power to madden thee? And is it true—
Away, away, or I shall dearly rue
My very thought. In mercy then away,

---

she bathed in his waters after hunting in the woods. See Sandys's *Ovid*,
Metamorphoses v (p. 92, col 2),

> In this coole Rivulet my foot I dipt;
> Then knee-deepe wade: nor so content, unstript
> My selfe forth-with; upon a Sallow stud
> My robe I hung, and leapt into the flood.
> Where, while I swim, and labour to and fro
> A thousand waies, with armes that swiftly row,
> I from the bottom heard an unknown tongue;
> And frighted to the hither margent sprung.
> Whither so fast, O *Arethusa*! twice
> Out-cry'd *Alpheus*, with a hollow voice . . .

The descriptive details also suggest a recollection of Neptune's toying with
Leander in Marlowe's *Hero and Leander* ii 183–92.

ii *945. In amorous rillets down*] Amorous and slow adown *Draft*. The word
'rillet' (rivulet) is an Elizabethanism revived by Keats and later used by
Tennyson in his *Recollections of the Arabian Nights* (1830) 47–8,

> . . . many a fall
> Of diamond rillets musical . . .

ii *947. kissing*] Earlier attempts in the draft were 'budding' and 'pouting'.
ii *948–9.*   Kiss, raptur'd, even to her milky toes.
        O foolish maid be gentle to my woes . . . *Draft*.
ii *952–75. Cruel god . . . cruel thing*] Arethusa is coldly hostile in the original.
ii *952. snared*] slew *Draft*.
ii *954. fountains*] waters *Fair copy (cancelled)*.

Kindest Alpheus, for should I obey
960   My own dear will, 'twould be a deadly bane.
        O Oread-Queen, would that thou hadst a pain
        Like this of mine, then would I fearless turn
        And be a criminal! Alas, I burn,
        I shudder—gentle river, get thee hence.
965   Alpheus, thou enchanter! Every sense
        Of mine was once made perfect in these woods.
        Fresh breezes, bowery lawns, and innocent floods,
        Ripe fruits, and lonely couch, contentment gave;
        But ever since I heedlessly did lave
970   In thy deceitful stream, a panting glow
        Grew strong within me. Wherefore serve me so,
        And call it love? Alas, 'twas cruelty.
        Not once more did I close my happy eye
        Amid the thrushes' song. Away! Avaunt!
975   Oh, 'twas a cruel thing.' 'Now thou dost taunt
        So softly, Arethusa, that I think
        If thou wast playing on my shady brink
        Thou wouldst bathe once again. Innocent maid!
        Stifle thine heart no more, nor be afraid
980   Of angry powers—there are deities
        Will shade us with their wings. Those fitful sighs
        'Tis almost death to hear. Oh, let me pour
        A dewy balm upon them! Fear no more,
        Sweet Arethusa! Dian's self must feel
985   Sometime these very pangs. Dear maiden, steal
        Blushing into my soul, and let us fly
        These dreary caverns for the open sky.
        I will delight thee all my winding course,
        From the green sea up to my hidden source
990   About Arcadian forests, and will show

ii *961. Oread-Queen*] Diana. See i 671 *n*.

ii *961–3. would . . . criminal*] If Diana were to suffer the same longings as
herself, Arethusa would have no fears about breaking her vow of chastity.

ii *964. gentle river*] for sweet mercy *Draft*.

ii *966. perfect*] happy *Draft*.

ii *968. lonely*] leafy *Draft*.

ii *973.* No longer could I close my wearied eye . . . *Draft*.

ii *984–5. Dian's self . . . pangs*] Cp. Phoebe's similar comment on Minerva
at ii 800–3 above.

ii *990. Arcadian forests*] Arcadia's Plains *Draft*. See *Lemprière*: 'Alpheus . . . a
river of Peloponnesus . . . rises in Arcadia, and, after passing through Elis,
falls into the sea below Olympia.'

The channels where my coolest waters flow
Through mossy rocks; where, 'mid exuberant green,
I roam in pleasant darkness, more unseen
Than Saturn in his exile; where I brim
995   Round flowery islands, and take thence a skim
Of mealy sweets which myriads of bees
Buzz from their honeyed wings, and thou shouldst
    please
Thyself to choose the richest, where we might
Be incense-pillowed every summer night.
1000   Doff all sad fears, thou white deliciousness,
And let us be thus comforted, unless
Thou couldst rejoice to see my hopeless stream
Hurry distracted from Sol's temperate beam,
And pour to death along some hungry sands.'
1005   'What can I do, Alpheus? Dian stands
Severe before me. Persecuting fate!
Unhappy Arethusa! thou wast late
A huntress free in—' At this, sudden fell
Those two sad streams adown a fearful dell.
1010   The Latmian listened, but he heard no more,
Save echo, faint repeating o'er and o'er
The name of Arethusa. On the verge
Of that dark gulf he wept, and said, 'I urge

ii *993–4. more unseen ... exile*] An allusion to Saturn's defeat by the Olympian gods. 'Saturn in his exile' is portrayed in *Hyperion* i 1–14 (pp. 396–7 below).

ii *996. mealy*] powdery *Draft*. Cp. ii 91 *n.*

ii *997. Buzz*] Shake *Fair copy (cancelled)*.

ii *998. richest*] freshest *Draft*.

ii *1004. some hungry*] hot Afric's *Draft*.

ii *1006. Persecuting*] cruel, cruel *Draft*.

ii *1008–9. At this ... fearful dell*] See Sandys's *Ovid, Metamorphoses* v (p. 93, col. 1),

>   ... sooner then I tell
> My destinie, into a Flood I grew,
> The River his beloved waters knew;
> And, putting off th'assumed shape of man,
> Resumes his own; and in my Current ran.
> Chaste *Delia* cleft the ground. Then through blind caves
> To loved *Ortygia* she conducts my waves ...

and also *Lemprière*: 'The fountain Arethusa is in Ortygia, a small island near Syracuse; and the ancients affirm, that the river Alpheus passes under the sea from Peloponnesus, rises again in Ortygia, and joins the stream of Arethusa.'

Thee, gentle Goddess of my pilgrimage,
1015   By our eternal hopes, to soothe, to assuage,
If thou art powerful, these lovers' pains,
And make them happy in some happy plains.'

He turned – there was a whelming sound. He
        stepped –
There was a cooler light; and so he kept
1020   Towards it by a sandy path, and lo!
More suddenly than doth a moment go,
The visions of the earth were gone and fled –
He saw the giant sea above his head.

ii *1023.* According to R. Gittings (*Gittings* (1968) 146) K.'s final line 'has
the sudden sharp isolated echo of the great single lines with which Dante
finishes each canto' and may owe something to Cary's *Dante, Inferno* xxvi
135 (marked by K. in his copy of Cary's *Dante*, 1814 edn, which he acquired 1818),
              And over us the booming billow clos'd . . .
K. may have possessed the 1805 edn of Cary in Sept. 1817, but his close
study of Dante belongs to a later date (see iv 14–16 *n* and headnote to *The
Fall of Hyperion*, pp. 245 and 656 below).

BOOK III

Written Sept. 1817 mainly at Oxford while K. was staying with Bailey at
Magdalen Hall (burnt down in 1822; abutted on Magdalen College): see
K.'s letter to Haydon from Oxford of 28 Sept. 1817, '. . . within these last
three weeks I have written 1000 lines – which are the third Book of my
Poem' (*L* i 168). Bailey records in his letter to Milnes of 7 May 1849, 'He
wrote, and I read, sometimes at the same table, and sometimes at separate
desks or tables, from breakfast to the time of our going out for exercise, –
generally two or three o'clock. He sat down to his task, – which was about
50 lines a day, – with his paper before him, and wrote with as much regularity, and apparently with as much ease, as he wrote his letters. . . . he
quite acted up to the principle . . . 'That if poetry comes not as naturally
as leaves [to] a tree, it had better not come at all' [See *L* i 238–9] . . . Sometimes he fell short of his allotted task, – but not often: and he would make it
up another day. But he never forced himself. When he had finished his
writing for the day, he usually read it over to me; and he read or wrote letters until we went out for a walk. This was our habit day by day. The rough
manuscript was written off daily, and with few erasures' (*KC* ii 270). K.'s
occasional use of Latin constructions and Miltonic phrasing hints at his
reading of *Paradise Lost* – see Bailey's comment later in the same letter, 'I
was a great student of Milton . . . I yet possess Todd's edition. . . . This
edition Keats saw when he visited me' (*KC* ii 283).

8*

There are who lord it o'er their fellow-men
With most prevailing tinsel, who unpen
Their baaing vanities to browse away
The comfortable green and juicy hay
5   From human pastures; or–oh, torturing fact–
Who, through an idiot blink, will see unpacked
Fire-branded foxes to sear up and singe
Our gold and ripe-eared hopes. With not one tinge
Of sanctuary splendour, not a sight
10   Able to face an owl's, they still are dight
By the blear-eyed nations in empurpled vests,
And crowns and turbans. With unladen breasts,
Save of blown self-applause, they proudly mount

iii *1–21*. K.'s attack on the reactionary régimes of the day, which had
gathered strength following the restoration of the monarchy in France (May
1814) and the Congress of Vienna (1814–15). Woodhouse notes in his copy
of *Endymion* (Berg Collection, New York Public Library), 'K. said, with
much simplicity, "It will easily be seen what I think of the present Ministers by the beginning of the 3d Book."' The passage is in keeping with the
tone of Hunt's articles for the *Examiner* Aug. 1817. With the mood and
style cp. also *Nebuchadnezzar's Dream* (p. 288 below). Bailey comments in
his letter to Milnes of 7 May 1849, 'I think he had written the few first introductory lines . . . before he became my guest. I did not then, and I cannot
now very much approve that introduction. The "baaing vanities" [iii 3]
have something of the character of what was called "the cockney school".
Nor do I like many of the forced rhymes, and the apparent effort, by breaking up the lines, to get as far as possible in the opposite direction of the Pope
school' (*KC* ii 269).
iii *5. torturing*] devilish *Draft*.
iii *7–8. Fire-branded . . . hopes*] See *Judges* 15: 4–5, 'Samson went and caught
three hundred foxes, and took firebrands, and turned tail to tail, and put a
firebrand in the midst between two tails. And when he had set the brands
on fire, he let them go into the standing corn of the Philistines, and burnt
up both the shocks, and also the standing corn, with the vineyards and
olives.'
iii *11. empurpled vests*] Hunt had recently ridiculed the French clergy for
accepting what he called 'the Roman purple' of Cardinal's hats, adding,
'The Roman purple . . . the garb of the Antonines,–and of the Neros!'
(*Examiner* 31 Aug. 1817, 550–1).
iii *12. crowns and turbans*] Cp. *On Receiving a Laurel Crown from Leigh Hunt*
10–12 (p. 109 above),

. . . I see
A trampling down of what the world most prizes,
   Turbans and crowns and blank regality . . .

To their spirit's perch, their being's high account,
15 Their tiptop nothings, their dull skies, their thrones,
Amid the fierce intoxicating tones
Of trumpets, shoutings, and belaboured drums,
And sudden cannon. Ah, how all this hums
In wakeful ears, like uproar past and gone—
20 Like thunder clouds that spake to Babylon,
And set those old Chaldeans to their tasks.
Are then regalities all gilded masks?
No, there are thronèd seats unscalable
But by a patient wing, a constant spell,
25 Or by ethereal things that, unconfined,
Can make a ladder of the eternal wind,
And poise about in cloudy thunder-tents
To watch the abysm-birth of elements.
Aye, 'bove the withering of old-lipped Fate
30 A thousand Powers keep religious state,
In water, fiery realm, and airy bourne,
And, silent as a consecrated urn,
Hold sphery sessions for a season due.
Yet few of these far majesties—ah, few!—
35 Have bared their operations to this globe—
Few, who with gorgeous pageantry enrobe
Our piece of heaven, whose benevolence

---

iii *17–18. trumpets . . . cannon*] Probably a recollection of the peace celebrations after Napoleon's abdication (6 April 1814), which culminated in the 'national jubilee' of 1 Aug. 1814, a date chosen as the centenary of the accession of the House of Brunswick. See under 1 Aug. in *Annual Register* 1814, 'the two last months had been distinguished in the metropolis by an almost constant succession of spectacles of grandeur and festivity . . . yet it was determined in the councils of the Prince Regent that the return of peace should be marked by displays of joy still more striking' (67). The festivities included a 'naumachia', or mock sea-fight (see *Nebuchadnezzar's Dream* 4 *n*, p. 288 below), between barges fitted up to represent the French and British fleets.

iii *20–1*. The storm-god Rammon was celebrated in Babylonia as a god of oracles; he and Shamash, the sun-god, were known as 'lords of divination'.

iii *22–3*.   Are then all regal things so gone, so murk?
                        No there are other thrones to mount . . . *Draft*.

iii *25. ethereal*] Spirit-like (see *To Hope* 5 *n*, p. 13 above).

iii *31–2*.   In the several vastnesses of air and fire;
                        And silent, as a corpse upon a pyre . . . *Draft*.

iii *31. bourne*] Domain (correctly 'boundary'—see i 295 *n*, above). So used this once by K.

Shakes hand with our own Ceres, every sense
Filling with spiritual sweets to plenitude,
40   As bees gorge full their cells. And, by the feud
'Twixt Nothing and Creation, I here swear,
Eterne Apollo, that thy Sister fair
Is of all these the gentlier-mightiest.
When thy gold breath is misting in the west,
45   She unobservèd steals unto her throne,
And there she sits most meek and most alone,
As if she had not pomp subservient;
As if thine eye, high Poet, was not bent
Towards her with the Muses in thine heart;
50   As if the ministering stars kept not apart,
Waiting for silver-footed messages.
O Moon! The oldest shades 'mong oldest trees
Feel palpitations when thou lookest in.
O Moon! Old boughs lisp forth a holier din
55   The while they feel thine airy fellowship.

iii *38–9*.   Salutes our native Ceres–and each sense
              With spiritual honey fills to plenitude . . . *Draft*.
Ceres was the goddess of plenty and mother of Proserpine. See i 944 *n*
above.

iii *40–1. the feud* / *'Twixt Nothing and Creation*] Cp. Ovid's account of the
beginning of the world, *Metamorphoses* i 7–21,

              . . . *rudis indigestaque moles*
       nec quicquam nisi pondus iners congestaque eodem
       non bene iunctarum discordia semina rerum.
       nullus adhuc mundo praebebat lumina Titan,
       nec nova crescendo reparabat cornua Phoebe . . .

('. . . a rough, unordered mass of things, nothing at all save lifeless bulk and
warring seeds of ill-matched elements heaped in one. No sun as yet shone
forth upon the world, nor did the waxing moon renew her slender horns'
[Loeb edn].)

iii *42. Eterne*] Probably a Shakespearian borrowing. See *Macbeth* III ii 38,
              But in them nature's copy's not eterne . . .

iii *42–71. thy Sister . . . load*] On K.'s romantic feeling for the moon see *I
stood tip-toe* 116–24 *n* (p. 90 above) and cp. iii 142–79 below.

iii *43. gentlier–mightiest*] Gentler than the other 'majesties' (see iii 34–5)
and also the most powerfully affecting. The word 'gentlier' is a coinage.

iii *44*. When thy gold hair falls thick about the west . . . *Draft*.

iii *46. meek*] Mild and gentle. A favourite word in K. when describing
women. See *I stood tip-toe* 204 and *n* (p. 95 above), 'gave meek Cynthia
her Endymion'.

iii *54. din*] See i 40 *n* above.

Thou dost bless everywhere, with silver lip
Kissing dead things to life. The sleeping kine,
Couched in thy brightness, dream of fields divine.
Innumerable mountains rise and rise,
60   Ambitious for the hallowing of thine eyes.
And yet thy benediction passeth not
One obscure hiding-place, one little spot
Where pleasure may be sent. The nested wren
Has thy fair face within its tranquil ken,
65   And from beneath a sheltering ivy leaf
Takes glimpses of thee. Thou art a relief
To the poor patient oyster, where it sleeps
Within its pearly house. The mighty deeps,
The monstrous sea is thine—the myriad sea!
70   O Moon! Far-spooming Ocean bows to thee,
And Tellus feels his forehead's cumbrous load.

Cynthia! Where art thou now? What far abode
Of green or silvery bower doth enshrine
Such utmost beauty? Alas, thou dost pine
75   For one as sorrowful. Thy cheek is pale
For one whose cheek is pale. Thou dost bewail
His tears, who weeps for thee. Where dost thou sigh?
Ah, surely that light peeps from Vesper's eye,
Or what a thing is love! 'Tis she, but lo!
80   How changed, how full of ache, how gone in woe!
She dies at the thinnest cloud, her loveliness

iii *56–7. Thou dost bless . . . life*]
        Thou dost bless all things—even dead things sip
        A midnight life from thee . . . *Draft.*
iii *63. sent*] wrought *Draft.*
iii *64. within its tranquil den*] Quiet behind dark ivy leaves *Draft.*
iii *70.* The effect of the moon on the tides. See *On the Sea* 3–4 *n* (p. 112 above). The epithet 'spooming' means foaming.
iii *71.* The weight of the incoming tides on the earth's shores. On Tellus (Earth) see *Hyperion* i 246 and ii 4 *n* (pp. 410, 415 below).
iii *77–8. Where dost thou . . . eye*]
                 Where art thou Ah
        Surely that light is from the Evening Star . . . *Draft.*
On 'Vesper' see *Lemprière*: '. . . a name applied to the planet Venus, when it was the evening-star . . .'.
iii *80.* The phrasing anticipates *The Eve of St Agnes* 311 (p. 474 below),
        How changed thou art! How pallid, chill, and drear . . .
See also *La Belle Dame Sans Merci* 6 *n* (p. 502 below),
        So haggard and so woe-begone . . .

Is wan on Neptune's blue. Yet there's a stress
Of love-spangles, just off yon cape of trees,
Dancing upon the waves, as if to please
85   The curly foam with amorous influence.
Oh, not so idle—for down-glancing thence
She fathoms eddies, and runs wild about
O'erwhelming water-courses, scaring out
The thorny sharks from hiding-holes and frightening
90   Their savage eyes with unaccustomed lightning.
Where will the splendour be content to reach?
O love! How potent hast thou been to teach
Strange journeyings! Wherever beauty dwells,
In gulf or eyrie, mountains or deep dells,
95   In light, in gloom, in star or blazing sun,
Thou pointest out the way, and straight 'tis won.
Amid his toil thou gav'st Leander breath;
Thou leddest Orpheus through the gleams of death;
Thou madest Pluto bear thin element;
100   And now, O wingèd chieftain, thou hast sent
A moonbeam to the deep, deep water-world,
To find Endymion.

On gold sand impearled
With lily shells and pebbles milky-white,
Poor Cynthia greeted him, and soothed her light
105   Against his pallid face. He felt the charm
To breathlessness, and suddenly a warm

---

iii *82–3. a stress . . . waves*] Reflections of moonlight on the water.
iii *86. Oh, not so idle*] Cancelled attempts in the draft include,

> 1. Nor there sleeps the idleness . . .
> 2. Nor cradled idly . . .
> 3. Yet not so idle . . .

iii *87.* It mingles and starts about unfathomed . . . *Draft (cancelled).*
iii *89. The thorny*] Enormous *Draft.*
iii *90. Their savage*] The whale's large . . . *Draft.*
iii *94–5. In gulf . . . star*]

> In air, or living flame–or magic shells,
> In earth, or mist, in star . . . *Draft.*

iii *97–9. Leander . . . Orpheus . . . Pluto*] Figures in classical mythology who
braved respectively the sea, the underworld and the upper air for the sake of
love. For K.'s earlier allusions to them see respectively *On a Leander Gem*
(p. 107 above), ii 164–5 *n* and i 944 *n* above.
iii *100. wingèd chieftain*] Cupid.
iii *106–7. a warm / Of his heart's blood*] See K.'s letter to Reynolds of 22

Of his heart's blood. 'Twas very sweet. He stayed
His wandering steps, and half-entrancèd laid
His head upon a tuft of straggling weeds
110 To taste the gentle moon and freshening beads
Lashed from the crystal roof by fishes' tails.
And so he kept until the rosy veils
Mantling the east by Aurora's peering hand
Were lifted from the water's breast and fanned
115 Into sweet air, and sobered morning came
Meekly through billows—when, like taper-flame
Left sudden by a dallying breath of air,
He rose in silence, and once more 'gan fare
Along his fated way.

               Far had he roamed,
120 With nothing save the hollow vast that foamed
Above, around and at his feet—save things
More dead than Morpheus's imaginings:
Old rusted anchors, helmets, breast-plates large
Of gone sea-warriors; brazen beaks and targe;
125 Rudders that for a hundred years had lost
The sway of human hand; gold vase embossed
With long-forgotten story, and wherein
No reveller had ever dipped a chin
But those of Saturn's vintage; mouldering scrolls

Sept. 1818, 'This morning Poetry has conquered. . . . There is an awful
warmth about my heart like a load of Immortality' (*L* i 370).

iii *113–20*. A passage admired by Shelley. See ii 827–53 *n*.

iii *119–36. Far had he roamed . . . monster*] Probably inspired by *Richard III*
I iv 22–8,

> What dreadful noise of waters in my ears!
> What ugly sights of death within my eyes!
> Methought I saw a thousand fearful wrecks;
> Ten thousand men that fishes gnaw'd upon;
> Wedges of gold, great anchors, heaps of pearl,
> Inestimable stones, unvalued jewels,
> All scattered in the bottom of the sea . . .

See Jeffrey's comment on the passage in his 1820 review (headnote to the
whole poem, p. 118 above), '. . . it comes of no ignoble lineage nor shames
its high descent'. Shelley's *Prometheus Unbound* iv 283–95 may be a half-
conscious tribute.

iii *120. vast*] The sea. See ii 240 *n*.

iii *124. brazen beaks*] The bronze beak-heads of the wrecked war-galleys.
The word 'targe' is a poeticism for shield.

iii *129. of Saturn's vintage*] From primeval times. Saturn was one of the
oldest gods. See *Hyperion* i 4 *n* (p. 396 below).

130 Writ in the tongue of heaven by those souls
       Who first were on the earth; and sculptures rude
       In ponderous stone, developing the mood
       Of ancient Nox; then skeletons of man,
       Of beast, behemoth, and leviathan,
135 And elephant, and eagle, and huge jaw
       Of nameless monster. A cold leaden awe
       These secrets struck into him, and unless
       Dian had chased away that heaviness,
       He might have died. But now, with cheerèd feel,
140 He onward kept, wooing these thoughts to steal
       About the labyrinth in his soul of love.

           'What is there in thee, Moon, that thou shouldst
               move
           My heart so potently? When yet a child
           I oft have dried my tears when thou hast smiled.
145   Thou seem'dst my sister. Hand in hand we went
           From eve to morn across the firmament.
           No apples would I gather from the tree
           Till thou hadst cooled their cheeks deliciously.
           No tumbling water ever spake romance
150   But when my eyes with thine thereon could dance.
           No woods were green enough, no bower divine,
           Until thou liftedst up thine eyelids fine.
           In sowing time ne'er would I dibble take,
           Or drop a seed, till thou wast wide awake,
155   And, in the summer-tide of blossoming,
           No one but thee hath heard me blithely sing
           And mesh my dewy flowers all the night.
           No melody was like a passing sprite

iii *133–4. ancient Nox*] Probably a Miltonic echo. See *Paradise Lost* ii 970,
'*Chaos* and *ancient Night*'.
iii *134. behemoth . . . leviathan*] Monsters referred to in the Bible (*Job* xl 15,
Isaiah xxvii 1) which may have been recalled to K. by his recent reading of
Milton. See *Paradise Lost* vii 471–2,

>   *Behemoth* biggest born of Earth upheav'd
>   His vastness . . .

and vii 412–14 (marked by K. in his copy of Milton),

>   . . . Leviathan
>   Hugest of living Creatures, on the Deep
>   Stretcht like a Promontorie . . .

iii *150. eyes*] soul *Draft*.
iii *157. mesh my dewy flowers*] Weave them into garlands.
iii *158. like a passing spright*] Delicate and pure like a fleeting spirit.

If it went not to solemnize thy reign.
160 Yes, in my boyhood, every joy and pain
     By thee were fashioned to the self-same end.
     And, as I grew in years, still didst thou blend
     With all my ardours. Thou wast the deep glen,
     Thou wast the mountain-top, the sage's pen,
165 The poet's harp, the voice of friends, the sun.
     Thou wast the river, thou wast glory won.
     Thou wast my clarion's blast, thou wast my steed,
     My goblet full of wine, my topmost deed.
     Thou wast the charm of women, lovely Moon!
170 Oh, what a wild and harmonizèd tune
     My spirit struck from all the beautiful!
     On some bright essence could I lean, and lull
     Myself to immortality. I pressed
     Nature's soft pillow in a wakeful rest.
175 But, gentle orb, there came a nearer bliss.
     My strange love came—felicity's abyss!
     She came, and thou didst fade and fade away—
     Yet not entirely. No, thy starry sway
     Has been an under-passion to this hour.
180 Now I begin to feel thine orby power
     Is coming fresh upon me. Oh, be kind,

iii 159. *went*] Earlier attempts in the draft were 'flew' and 'sought'.

iii 163–9. *deep glen . . . charm of women*] A catalogue of 'luxuries'. See *Sleep and Poetry* 1–10 n (p. 69 above).

iii 168. *topmost*] highest *Draft*.

iii 170. *harmonizèd*] harmonizing *Draft*.

iii 171. *struck*] Earlier attempts in the draft were 'sung' and 'made'.

iii 172. *essence*] See i 779 n.

iii 173–4. *I pressed . . . wakeful rest*] Anticipates the *Bright star* sonnet 10–12 (pp. 738–9 below),

> Pillowed upon my fair love's ripening breast,
> To feel for ever its soft fall and swell,
> Awake for ever in a sweet unrest . . .

Cp. ii 740–2 n above.

iii 175–87. *But, gentle orb . . . far beyond*] Hints at the identity of the moon with Endymion's 'strange love'. See ii 169–98 n.

iii 176. *felicity's abyss*] Pleasure so profound that it is unfathomable. For 'felicity's' the draft reading has 'dear pleasure's own'.

iii 179. *under-passion*] Passion for the moon accompanies all other emotions. A coinage by analogy from 'under-song' (see *Calidore* 61 n, p. 39 above).

iii 180. *orby*] orbed *Draft*. On K.'s fondness for epithets ending in '-y' see *Calidore* 10 n (p. 37 above).

Keep back thine influence, and do not blind
My sovereign vision. Dearest love, forgive
That I can think away from thee and live!
185   Pardon me, airy planet, that I prize
One thought beyond thine argent luxuries!
How far beyond!' At this a surprised start
Frosted the springing verdure of his heart,
For as he lifted up his eyes to swear
190   How his own goddess was past all things fair,
He saw far in the concave green of the sea
An old man sitting calm and peacefully.
Upon a weeded rock this old man sat,
And his white hair was awful, and a mat
195   Of weeds were cold beneath his cold thin feet,
And, ample as the largest winding-sheet,
A cloak of blue wrapped up his agèd bones,
O'erwrought with symbols by the deepest groans
Of ambitious magic. Every ocean-form
200   Was woven in with black distinctness. Storm,
And calm, and whispering, and hideous roar,
Quicksand, and whirlpool, and deserted shore,
Were emblemed in the woof, with every shape
That skims, or dives, or sleeps, 'twixt cape and cape.

iii *183*. *My sovereign vision*] The vision of my love *Draft*.
iii *186*. *luxuries*] On K.'s use of 'luxury' see *Calidore* 92 *n* (p. 40 above).
iii *188*. Blighted the flowing river of his heart . . . *Draft*.
iii *192*. *An old man*] Glaucus. See iii 318–638 *n*. Ian Jack suggests that the description in the subsequent lines owes something to Salvator Rosa's 'Glaucus and Scylla' (reproduced as Plate XVIII in his *Keats and the Mirror of Art*, 1967).
iii *197–212*. Inspired by the designs depicted on Phoebe's cloak in Drayton's *The Man in the Moone* 145–220, beginning,

> . . . her Mantle amorously did swell,
> From her straight Shoulders carelesly that fell.
> Now here, now there, now up and down that flew,
> Of sundry Coloures, wherein you might view
> A sea that somewhat straitned by the Land,
> Two furious Tydes raise their ambitious Hand,
> One 'gainst the other, warring in their Pride . . .

Cp. ii 613–27 *n* above. On Shelley's admiration for K.'s lines see ii 827–53 *n* above.
iii *200–2*. *storm . . . roar*] Cp. *The Man in the Moone* 159–60,

> Outragious Tempest, Shipwracks over-spread
> All the rude NEPTUNE . . .

205   The gulfing whale was like a dot in the spell,
      Yet look upon it, and 'twould size and swell
      To its huge self, and the minutest fish
      Would pass the very hardest gazer's wish
      And show his little eye's anatomy.
210   Then there was pictured the regality
      Of Neptune, and the sea nymphs round his state,
      In beauteous vassalage, look up and wait.
      Beside this old man lay a pearly wand,
      And in his lap a book, the which he conned
215   So stedfastly that the new denizen
      Had time to keep him in amazèd ken,
      To mark these shadowings, and stand in awe.

      The old man raised his hoary head and saw
      The wildered stranger—seeming not to see,
220   His features were so lifeless. Suddenly
      He woke as from a trance. His snow-white brows
      Went arching up, and like two magic ploughs
      Furrowed deep wrinkles in his forehead large,
      Which kept as fixedly as rocky marge,
225   Till round his withered lips had gone a smile.
      Then up he rose, like one whose tedious toil
      Had watched for years in forlorn hermitage,
      Who had not from mid-life to utmost age
      Eased in one accent his o'er-burdened soul
230   Even to the trees. He rose, he grasped his stole,

iii *205*. The whale engulfed in the deep seas was like a mere speck in the magical pattern. Perhaps suggested by Drayton's allusion to whales in *The Man in the Moone* 173–4,

               . . . the Monsters of the Maine,
      Their horrid Foreheads through the Billows straine . . .

iii *219. wildered*] See i 850 *n*.

iii *221–5*. See Bailey's letter to Milnes of 7 May 1849, 'I remember very distinctly . . . [K.'s] reading . . . of the fine and affecting story of the old man, Glaucus, which he read to me immediately after its composition. . . . The lines [iii 222–5, 'and like two magic ploughs . . . smile'] . . . are those which then . . . struck me as peculiarly fine. . . . I remember his upward look when he read of the "magic ploughs"' (*KC* ii 270–1). K.'s description suggests a recollection of Sandys's commentary on Glaucus, 'Philostratus describeth him to have a mossie beard, of colour blew, his haire shaggy and dishevel'd; thick and arched eye-browes which touch one another' (Sandys's *Ovid*, p. 252).

iii *226. tedious*] studious *Draft*.

iii *230. stole*] 'A long robe. Chiefly used in translation from Greek and Latin' (*OED*).

With convulsed clenches waving it abroad,
And in a voice of solemn joy, that awed
Echo into oblivion, he said:

'Thou art the man! Now shall I lay my head
235   In peace upon my watery pillow. Now
Sleep will come smoothly to my weary brow.
O Jove! I shall be young again, be young!
O shell-borne Neptune, I am pierced and stung
With new-born life! What shall I do? Where go
240   When I have cast this serpent-skin of woe?
I'll swim to the sirens, and one moment listen
Their melodies and see their long hair glisten;
Anon upon that giant's arm I'll be,
That writhes about the roots of Sicily;
245   To northern seas I'll in a twinkling sail,
And mount upon the snortings of a whale
To some black cloud; thence down I'll madly sweep
On forkèd lightning, to the deepest deep,
Where through some sucking pool I will be hurled
250   With rapture to the other side of the world!
Oh, I am full of gladness! Sisters three,
I bow full-hearted to your old decree!
Yes, every god be thanked and power benign,
For I no more shall wither, droop and pine.
255   Thou art the man!' Endymion started back
Dismayed; and, like a wretch from whom the rack

iii 234 (and ii 255 below). *Thou art the man*] 2 *Samuel* xii 7, 'And Nathan said to David, Thou art the man'.

iii 241. *the sirens*] See Homer's *Odyssey* xii 37–54, 165–200.

iii 243. *that giant*] Typhon. See *Hyperion* ii 20 *n* (p. 417 below) and Sandys's *Ovid, Metamorphoses* xiv (p. 253),

Now *Glaucus*, thron'd in tumid floods, had past
High *Aetna*, on the jaws of Typhon cast . . .

iii 245. *I'll in a twinkling sail*] Probably a half-conscious recollection of the witch in *Macbeth* I iii 8,

. . . in a sieve I'll thither sail . . .

See following *n* and iii 254 *n*. Cp. also Puck's magical speed in *A Midsummer Night's Dream* II i 175–6,

I'll put a girdle round about the earth
In forty minutes . . .

iii 251. *Sisters three*] The Fates, but K. may also be remembering the weird sisters in *Macbeth*.

iii 254. Echoing the first witch in *Macbeth* I iii 22–3,

Weary se'nnights nine times nine
Shall he dwindle, peak and pine . . .

Tortures hot breath and speech of agony,
Muttered: 'What lonely death am I to die
In this cold region? Will he let me freeze,
260   And float my brittle limbs o'er polar seas?
Or will he touch me with his searing hand,
And leave a black memorial on the sand?
Or tear me piece-meal with a bony saw,
And keep me as a chosen food to draw
265   His magian fish through hated fire and flame?
Oh, misery of hell! Resistless, tame,
Am I to be burnt up? No, I will shout,
Until the gods through heaven's blue look out!
Oh, Tartarus, but some few days agone
270   Her soft arms were entwining me, and on
Her voice I hung like fruit among green leaves.
Her lips were all my own, and–ah, ripe sheaves
Of happiness! Ye on the stubble droop,
But never may be garnered. I must stoop
275   My head, and kiss death's foot. Love, love, farewell!
Is there no hope from thee? This horrid spell
Would melt at thy sweet breath. By Dian's hind
Feeding from her white fingers, on the wind
I see thy streaming hair! And now, by Pan,
280   I care not for this old mysterious man!'

He spake, and, waking to that agèd form,
Looked high defiance. Lo! his heart 'gan warm
With pity, for the grey-haired creature wept.

iii *261–2.* i.e., 'Will he scorch me to a cinder?' The 'black memorial' is the mark left by lightning when it strikes. It is not clear why Endymion should associate Glaucus with 'fire and flame' (iii 265). Bridges maintains that 'the four books [of *Endymion*] correspond with the four elements', Book II being Fire, which has 'its proper home beneath the earth's crust', but this is the first substantial allusion to fire in the poem.

iii *265. magian*] Magical. Cp. *Not Aladdin magian* 1 *n* (p. 373 below).

iii *269. Tartarus*] See *Baldwin*: 'The Greeks . . . separated the infernal region into two principal divisions, Tartarus, or the abode of woe, and Elysium, or the mansions of the blest' (149).

iii *272–4. ripe sheaves . . . garnered*] Foreshadows K.'s more mature style. See *When I have fears* 3–4 (p. 297 below),

> Before high-pilèd books, in charactery,
>
>   Hold like rich garners the full ripened grain . . .

and the ode *To Autumn* (p. 650 below).

iii *282. Looked high defiance*] The phrasing is Miltonic. See, for example, *Paradise Lost* iv 873,

> Stand firm, for in his look defiance lours.

Had he then wronged a heart where sorrow kept?
285   Had he, though blindly contumelious, brought
Rheum to kind eyes, a sting to humane thought,
Convulsion to a mouth of many years?
He had in truth; and he was ripe for tears.
The penitent shower fell as down he knelt
290   Before that care-worn sage, who trembling felt
About his large dark locks and faltering spake:

'Arise, good youth, for sacred Phoebus' sake!
I know thine inmost bosom, and I feel
A very brother's yearning for thee steal
295   Into mine own. For why? Thou openest
The prison gates that have so long oppressed
My weary watching. Though thou know'st it not,
Thou art commissioned to this fated spot
For great enfranchisement. Oh, weep no more,
300   I am a friend to love, to loves of yore.
Aye, hadst thou never loved an unknown power,
I had been grieving at this joyous hour.
But even now, most miserable old,
I saw thee, and my blood no longer cold
305   Gave mighty pulses. In this tottering case
Grew a new heart, which at this moment plays
As dancingly as thine. Be not afraid,
For thou shalt hear this secret all displayed,
Now as we speed towards our joyous task.'

iii *282–8. Lo! his heart . . . tears*] Perhaps a recollection of Leander's pity for
Neptune in Marlowe's *Hero and Leander* ii 213–16,

When this fresh bleeding wound Leander viewd
His colour went and came, as if he rued
The grief which Neptune felt: in gentle breasts
Relenting thoughts, remorse and pity rests . . .

iii *285. contumelious*] Insolent. An Elizabethanism. See, for example, Chapman's note 'Agamemnon's contumelious repulse of Chryses' (Chapman's *Homer*, *Iliad* i 24–5).

iii *286. humane*] The reading of the fair copy. The *1818* reading 'human' is probably a misprint. 'Rheum' means tears, as in *Coriolanus* V v 46, 'drops of women's rheum'.

iii *291. About his*] The youth's *Draft*.

iii *294. brother's*] fathers *Fair copy* (*cancelled*). Probably altered because Glaucus is closer in age to Endymion than he appears (see iii 310, 590–99, 775–8 below). The correction also underlines the theme of fraternal sympathy in the episode.

iii *307. dancingly*] youthfully *Draft*.

iii *309. Now as*] The while *Draft*.

310 So saying, this young soul in age's mask
   Went forward with the Carian side by side,
   Resuming quickly thus, while ocean's tide
   Hung swollen at their backs, and jewelled sands
   Took silently their foot-prints:

            'My soul stands
315 Now past the midway from mortality,
   And so I can prepare without a sigh
   To tell thee briefly all my joy and pain.
   I was a fisher once upon this main,
   And my boat danced in every creek and bay.
320 Rough billows were my home by night and day,
   The sea-gulls not more constant, for I had
   No housing from the storm and tempests mad
   But hollow rocks—and they were palaces
   Of silent happiness, of slumberous ease.
325 Long years of misery have told me so.
   Aye, thus it was one thousand years ago.
   One thousand years! Is it then possible
   To look so plainly through them? To dispel
   A thousand years with backward glance sublime?
330 To breathe away as 'twere all scummy slime
   From off a crystal pool to see its deep,
   And one's own image from the bottom peep?
   Yes, now I am no longer wretched thrall,
   My long captivity and moanings all
335 Are but a slime, a thin-pervading scum,
   The which I breathe away, and thronging come
   Like things of yesterday my youthful pleasures.

   'I touched no lute, I sang not, trod no measures.
   I was a lonely youth on desert shores.

iii *315.* More than half recovered from death.
iii *318–638.* K.'s story of Glaucus and Scylla is freely adapted from the legend related in Ovid's *Metamorphoses* xiii 898–968, xiv 1–74.
iii *318–25.* See Sandys's *Ovid, Metamorphoses* xiii (p. 243, col. 2),
     Yet once a mortall; and did then frequent
     Th'affected Seas. On those my labour spent.
     Sometimes with nets I fishes hale to land:
     Sometimes the line directed with my wand ...
iii *329.* At one glance back the mistiness of time? . . . *Draft.*
iii *337. youthful*] first youth's *Draft.*
iii *338–42.* See Sandys's *Ovid, Metamorphoses* xiii (p. 243, col. 2),
     The shore a meadow bounds; whereof one side
     Is fring'd with weeds, the other with the tyde.

340   My sports were lonely, 'mid continuous roars,
        And craggy isles, and sea-mew's plaintive cry
        Plaining discrepant between sea and sky.
        Dolphins were still my playmates. Shapes unseen
        Would let me feel their scales of gold and green,
345   Nor be my desolation. And, full oft,
        When a dread waterspout had reared aloft
        Its hungry hugeness, seeming ready ripe
        To burst with hoarsest thunderings and wipe
        My life away like a vast sponge of fate,
350   Some friendly monster, pitying my sad state,
        Has dived to its foundations, gulfed it down,
        And left me tossing safely. But the crown
        Of all my life was utmost quietude.
        More did I love to lie in cavern rude,
355   Keeping in wait whole days for Neptune's voice,
        And if it came at last, hark and rejoice!
        There blushed no summer eve but I would steer
        My skiff along green shelving coasts, to hear
        The shepherd's pipe come clear from aery steep,
360   Mingled with ceaseless bleatings of his sheep.
        And never was a day of summer shine,
        But I beheld its birth upon the brine,
        For I would watch all night to see unfold
        Heaven's gates, and Aethon snort his morning gold

          On this nor horned cattle ever fed,
          Nor harmlesse sheepe, nor goats on mountaines bred.
          No bees from thence their thighes with hony lade;
          Those flowers no marriage garlands ever made:
          That grasse ne'r cut with sithes. Of mortals I
          First thither came . . .

iii *343–56.* An imaginative expansion of Ovid's reference to Glaucus's early love of the sea in *Metamorphoses* xiii 920–1,

                    ante tamen mortalis eram, sed scilicet altis
                    deditus aequoribus . . .

('I was mortal once, but even then devoted to the sea' [Loeb edn].)

iii *343*] *Dolphins were still my playmates*] Perhaps suggested by Sandys's reference to the Sicilian swimmer Colon in his commentary on Ovid's *Metamorphoses* xiii, '. . . he would swim like a Dolphin about five hundred furlongs together, even in a Tempest and against the rake of the billow, with incredible celeritie' (Sandys's *Ovid*, p. 252).

iii *353. utmost*] tip-top *Fair copy.*

iii *359–60* (and iii *368–71* below). Glaucus has no human company in Ovid's version of the story.

iii *364. Aethon*] One of Apollo's horses. See i 552 *n* above.

365   Wide o'er the swelling streams. And constantly
       At brim of day-tide, on some grassy lea,
       My nets would be spread out, and I at rest.
       The poor folk of the sea-country I blessed
       With daily boon of fish most delicate.
370   They knew not whence this bounty, and elate
       Would strew sweet flowers on a sterile beach.

           Why was I not contented? Wherefore reach
       At things which, but for thee, O Latmian!
       Had been my dreary death? Fool! I began
375   To feel distempered longings, to desire
       The utmost privilege that ocean's sire
       Could grant in benediction—to be free
       Of all his kingdom. Long in misery
       I wasted, ere in one extremest fit
380   I plunged for life or death. To interknit
       One's senses with so dense a breathing stuff
       Might seem a work of pain, so not enough
       Can I admire how crystal-smooth it felt,

iii *366. brim of day-tide*] When day was full. K. frequently uses this image, especially in his early poems; see, for example, i 421 (p. 138 above), 'brim-full and flush', i 845–6 (p. 157 above), 'brim / Their measure of content' and also *Calidore* 146, *Keen, fitful gusts* 9 (pp. 42 and 63 above).

iii *370. elate*] A favourite poeticism in K.'s early poems. Other examples in *To Chatterton* 5, *Written on the Day Mr Leigh Hunt left Prison* 4 (pp. 10 and 11 above).

iii *372–92*. In the original legend Glaucus is transformed into a sea-deity after eating a magic herb found on the sea-shore (Ovid's *Metamorphoses* xiii 936–63).

iii *374–80. I began . . . death*] K.'s lines are closer to the original than to Sandys. Cp. Ovid's *Metamorphoses* xiii 945–8,

> cum subito trepidare intus praecordia sensi
> alteriusque rapi naturae pectus amore;
> nec potui restare diu 'repetenda' que 'numquam
> terra, vale!' dixi corpusque sub aequora mersi . . .

('When suddenly I felt my heart trembling within me, and my whole being yearned with desire for another element. Unable long to stand against it, I cried aloud: "Farewell, O Earth, to which I shall never more return." And I plunged into the sea' [Loeb edn].)

iii *375. distempered*] Deranged.

iii *380–4. To interknit . . . limbs*] Illustrating K.'s theory of 'fellowship with essence' (i 779 *n* above). See i 795–6 above,

> . . . That moment have we stepped
> Into a sort of oneness, and our state
> Is like a floating spirit's . . .

And buoyant round my limbs. At first I dwelt
385   Whole days and days in sheer astonishment,
Forgetful utterly of self-intent,
Moving but with the mighty ebb and flow.
Then, like a new fledged bird that first doth show
His spreaded feathers to the morrow chill,
390   I tried in fear the pinions of my will.
'Twas freedom! And at once I visited
The ceaseless wonders of this ocean-bed.
No need to tell thee of them, for I see
That thou hast been a witness—it must be;
395   For these I know thou canst not feel a drouth,
By the melancholy corners of that mouth.
So I will in my story straightway pass
To more immediate matter. Woe, alas!
That love should be my bane! Ah, Scylla fair!
400   Why did poor Glaucus ever, ever dare
To sue thee to his heart? Kind stranger-youth!
I loved her to the very white of truth,
And she would not conceive it. Timid thing!
She fled me swift as sea-bird on the wing,
405   Round every isle, and point, and promontory,

iii *384–94.* Cp. Ovid's *Metamorphoses* xiii 958–63,

> quae postquam rediit, alium me corpore toto,
> ac fueram nuper, neque eundem mente recepi:
> hanc ego tum primum viridi ferrugine barbam
> caesariemque meam, quam longa per aequora verro,
> ingentesque umeros et caerula bracchia vidi
> cruraque pinnigero curvata novissima pisce . . .

('When my senses came back to me I was far different from what I was but
lately in all my body, nor was my mind the same. Then for the first time
I beheld this beard of dark green hue, these locks which sweep on the long
waves, these huge shoulders and bluish arms, these legs which twist and
vanish in a finny fish' [Loeb edn].)

iii *395. For these I know*] For such a drink *Draft.*

iii *402. to the very white of truth*] Completely or absolutely. The image may
be derived from archery, the 'white' being the bull's eye at the centre of
the target; cp. *The Taming of the Shrew* V ii 187,

> . . . I won the wager, though you hit the white . . .

iii *403–4. Timid thing . . . wing*] See Sandys's *Ovid, Metamorphoses* xiii (p.
244, col. 2), 'coy Scylla flys'. Scylla, the daughter of Typhon (Phorcys in
some traditions), was sought by many suitors but rejected all of them
(Ovid's *Metamorphoses* xiii 735–7).

iii *405–15.* An individual reworking of the original. See Sandys's *Ovid,
Metamorphoses* xiv (p. 253, col. 1),

From where large Hercules wound up his story
Far as Egyptian Nile. My passion grew
The more, the more I saw her dainty hue
Gleam delicately through the azure clear,
410 Until 'twas too fierce agony to bear.
And in that agony, across my grief
It flashed that Circe might find some relief–
Cruel enchantress! So above the water
I reared my head and looked for Phoebus' daughter.
415 Aeaea's isle was wondering at the moon.
It seemed to whirl around me, and a swoon
Left me dead-drifting to that fatal power.

When I awoke, 'twas in a twilight bower,
Just when the light of morn, with hum of bees,
420 Stole through its verdurous matting of fresh trees.
How sweet, and sweeter–for I heard a lyre,
And over it a sighing voice expire.
It ceased–I caught light footsteps, and anon
The fairest face that morn e'er look'd upon

Now *Glaucus*, thron'd in tumid floods, had past
High *Aetna*, on the jaws of *Typhon* cast;
Cyclopian fields, where never Oxen drew
The furrowing plough, nor ever tillage knew;
Crookt *Zancle*; *Rhegium* on the other side;
The wrackful Straights, whose double bounds divide
Sicilia from *Ausonia*: forward drives
Through spatious *Tyrrhen* Seas; at length arrives
At hearbie Hills, *Phoebean Circes* seat,
With sundry formes of monstrous beasts repleat...

iii *406.* Hercules burnt himself on a pyre on Oeta, a mountain lying between Thessaly and Macedonia (Ovid's *Metamorphoses* ix 199–272).
iii *414.* Phoebus' daughter] The enchantress Circe was the child of Sol and Perses. See Milton's *Comus* 50–1,

                    ... who knows not *Circe*
      The daughter of the Sun ...

iii *415.* Aeaea's isle] The island off the coast of Italy where Circe lived after she was expelled from Colchis. For 'wondering' the draft has 'looking'.
iii *416–22.* The 'swoon' and the music are individual details in keeping with K.'s customary descriptions of fatal enchantment, for example *La Belle Dame Sans Merci* 21–34, *Lamia* i 296–99 (pp. 503–5, 629 below).
iii *421–2. How sweet ... voice*]

      How sweet to me! and then I heard a Lyre
      With which a sighing voice ... *Fair copy (cancelled).*

425 Pushed through a screen of roses. Starry Jove!
     With tears and smiles and honey-words she wove
     A net whose thraldom was more bliss than all
     The range of flowered Elysium. Thus did fall
     The dew of her rich speech: 'Ah! Art awake?
430 Oh, let me hear thee speak, for Cupid's sake!
     I am so oppressed with joy! Why, I have shed
     An urn of tears, as though thou wert cold-dead.
     And now I find thee living, I will pour
     From these devoted eyes their silver store,
435 Until exhausted of the latest drop,
     So it will pleasure thee and force thee stop
     Here, that I too may live. But if beyond
     Such cool and sorrowful offerings, thou art fond
     Of soothing warmth, of dalliance supreme;
440 If thou art ripe to taste a long love-dream;
     If smiles, if dimples, tongues for ardour mute,
     Hang in thy vision like a tempting fruit,
     Oh, let me pluck it for thee.' Thus she linked
     Her charming syllables, till indistinct
445 Their music came to my o'er-sweetened soul.
     And then she hovered over me and stole
     So near, that if no nearer it had been
     This furrowed visage thou hadst never seen.

     Young man of Latmos, thus particular
450 Am I that thou may'st plainly see how far
     This fierce temptation went, and thou may'st not
     Exclaim, "How then, was Scylla quite forgot?"

     Who could resist? Who in this universe?
     She did so breathe ambrosia, so immerse
455 My fine existence in a golden clime.
     She took me like a child of suckling time,
     And cradled me in roses. Thus condemned,

iii 425. *Starry*] Mighty *Draft*.

iii 426–48. Expands the matter-of-fact account in Ovid's *Metamorphoses* xiv 25–36 (Sandys's *Ovid*, p. 253, col. 2).

iii 441. *ardour*] rapture *Draft*.

iii 445. *soul*] sense *Draft*.

iii 446–7.   And then I felt a hovering influence
                  A breathing on my forehead . . .*Draft*

iii 449–72. In the original legend Glaucus resists Circe who takes her revenge by transforming Scylla into a monster (Ovid's *Metamorphoses* xiv 37–74).

The current of my former life was stemmed,
And to this arbitrary queen of sense
460   I bowed a trancèd vassal. Nor would thence
Have moved, even though Amphion's harp had wooed
Me back to Scylla o'er the billows rude.
For as Apollo each eve doth devise
A new apparelling for western skies,
465   So every eve, nay every spendthrift hour,
Shed balmy consciousness within that bower.
And I was free of haunts umbrageous,
Could wander in the mazy forest-house
Of squirrels, foxes shy, and antlered deer,
470   And birds from coverts innermost and drear
Warbling for very joy mellifluous sorrow—
To me new born delights!
                    Now let me borrow,
For moments few, a temperament as stern
As Pluto's sceptre, that my words not burn
475   These uttering lips, while I in calm speech tell
How specious heaven was changed to real hell.

    One morn she left me sleeping. Half awake
I sought for her smooth arms and lips, to slake
My greedy thirst with nectarous camel-draughts.
480   But she was gone. Whereat the barbèd shafts
Of disappointment stuck in me so sore
That out I ran and searched the forest o'er.
Wandering about in pine and cedar gloom
Damp awe assailed me, for there 'gan to boom
485   A sound of moan, an agony of sound,

iii *459–60. to this arbitrary . . . vassal*] Probably suggested by Sandys's versified introduction to his translation of Ovid's *Metamorphoses*, 'The Minde
of the Frontispiece, and argument of this Worke' 11–15,

> . . . who forsake that faire *Intelligence*,
> To follow *Passion*, and voluptuous *Sence*;
> That sun the Path and Toyles of HERCULES;
> Such, charmèd by CIRCE's luxurie, and ease,
> Themselves deforme . . .

iii *461. Amphion*] See *Lemprière*: '. . . said to have been the inventor of music,
and to have built the walls of Thebes by the sound of his lyre.' The stones
were supposed to have been so affected by his playing that they moved into
position of their own accord.

iii *466. balmy consciousness*] nectarous Influence *Draft*.

iii *474. Pluto*] See i 944 *n* above.

iii *485. moan*] A Spenserianism. See *La Belle Dame Sans Merci* 20 *n* (p. 503
below).

Sepulchral from the distance all around.
Then came a conquering earth-thunder and rumbled
That fierce complain to silence, while I stumbled
Down a precipitous path as if impelled.
490   I came to a dark valley. Groanings swelled
Poisonous about my ears, and louder grew
The nearer I approached a flame's gaunt blue
That glared before me through a thorny brake.
This fire, like the eye of gordian snake,
495   Bewitched me towards, and I soon was near
A sight too fearful for the feel of fear.
In thicket hid I cursed the haggard scene—
The banquet of my arms, my arbour queen,
Seated upon an uptorn forest root,
500   And all around her shapes, wizard and brute,
Laughing, and wailing, grovelling, serpenting,
Showing tooth, tusk, and venom-bag, and sting!
Oh, such deformities! Old Charon's self,
Should he give up awhile his penny pelf,
505   And take a dream 'mong rushes Stygian,
It could not be so phantasied. Fierce, wan
And tyrannizing was the lady's look,
As over them a gnarlèd staff she shook.
Oft-times upon the sudden she laughed out,
510   And from a basket emptied to the rout
Clusters of grapes, the which they ravened quick

iii *488. complain*] Complaint.

iii *494. gordian*] Intricately looped. See i 614 *n* above, 'gordianed up'.

iii *495. Bewitched me towards*] Drew me towards it *Draft*.

iii *496. the feel of fear*] On K.'s use of 'feel' see *In drear-nighted December* 21 *n* (p. 288 below).

iii *498. The banquet of my arms*] My beautiful rose bud *Draft*.

iii *500–31.* Circe transformed her lovers into beasts by means of her magic drug (Homer's *Odyssey* x 210–43, Ovid's *Metamorphoses* xiv 276–87). K. is probably also recollecting the 'monstrous rout' led by Comus, Circe's son, in Milton's *Comus* 520–36.

iii *501. grovelling*] see Milton's *Comus* 51–3,

... Whose charmed Cup
Whoever tasted, lost his upright shape,
And downward fell into a groveling Swine ...

iii *504. penny pelf*] The obolus, Charon's charge for ferrying souls across the Styx and Acheron to the regions of the dead.

iii *511. Clusters of grapes*] Perhaps a reminiscence of Bacchus's union with Circe, see *Comus* 46–50,

And roared for more, with many a hungry lick
About their shaggy jaws. Avenging, slow,
Anon she took a branch of mistletoe,
515   And emptied on it a black dull-gurgling phial—
Groaned one and all, as if some piercing trial
Was sharpening for their pitiable bones.
She lifted up the charm. Appealing groans
From their poor breasts went sueing to her ear
520   In vain. Remorseless as an infant's bier
She whisked against their eyes the sooty oil.
Whereat was heard a noise of painful toil,
Increasing gradual to a tempest rage,
Shrieks, yells, and groans of torture-pilgrimage,
525   Until their grievèd bodies 'gan to bloat
And puff from the tail's end to stifled throat.
Then was appalling silence, then a sight
More wildering than all that hoarse affright,
For the whole herd, as by a whirlwind writhen,
530   Went through the dismal air like one huge Python
Antagonizing Boreas–and so vanished.
Yet there was not a breath of wind; she banished
These phantoms with a nod. Lo! from the dark
Came waggish fauns, and nymphs, and satyrs stark,
535   With dancing and loud revelry–and went
Swifter than centaurs after rapine bent.
Sighing, an elephant appeared and bowed
Before the fierce witch, speaking thus aloud
In human accent: "Potent goddess! Chief
540   Of pains resistless! Make my being brief,

Bacchus that first from out the purple Grape
Crush't the sweet poyson of mis–used Wine
After the *Tuscan* Mariners transform'd
Coasting the *Tyrrhene* shore, as the winds listed,
On *Circes* Iland fell . . .

iii *529. writhen*] Made to writhe.

iii *530–1. Python . . . Boreas*] For Python, the serpent generated from the slime after Deucalion's flood, see *Lamia* ii 80 *n* (p. 637 below). Boreas was the North Wind.

iii *534–5. Came waggish fauns . . . revelry*] Probably a reminiscence of *Comus* 103–4,

Midnight shout, and revelry,
Tipsie dance, and Jollity . . .

iii *537. Sighing, an*] For a large *Draft*

iii *540. pains*] Earlier attempts in the draft were 'spells' and 'charms'.

Or let me from this heavy prison fly—
Or give me to the air, or let me die!
I sue not for my happy crown again;
I sue not for my phalanx on the plain;
545 I sue not for my lone, my widowed wife;
I sue not for my ruddy drops of life,
My children fair, my lovely girls and boys!
I will forget them; I will pass these joys;
Ask nought so heavenward, so too, too high.
550 Only I pray, as fairest boon, to die,
Or be delivered from this cumbrous flesh,
From this gross, detestable, filthy mesh,
And merely given to the cold bleak air.
Have mercy, Goddess! Circe, feel my prayer!"

555   That curst magician's name fell icy numb
Upon my wild conjecturing. Truth had come
Naked and sabre-like against my heart.
I saw a fury whetting a death-dart,
And my slain spirit, overwrought with fright,
560 Fainted away in that dark lair of night.
Think, my deliverer, how desolate
My waking must have been! Disgust and hate
And terrors manifold divided me
A spoil amongst them. I prepared to flee
565 Into the dungeon core of that wild wood.

iii 542. Cp. Patrick Henry (1736–99) American statesman, in his speech in
the Virginia House of Delegates, 23 March 1775, '. . . but as for me, give
me liberty or give me death'. Henry's revolutionary speeches became
widely known from W. Wirt's enthusiastic *Life* (1817).

iii 545. *my lone, my widowed*] my lonely, my dear *Draft*.

iii 546. *ruddy drops*] The phrasing in the previous line has recalled to K.
Julius Caesar II i 288–90,

> . . . my true and honourable wife,
>
> As dear to me as are the ruddy drops
>
> That visit my sad heart . . .

For 'ruddy' the draft has 'hearts blood'.

iii 547. *children fair*] sweetest babes *Draft*.

iii 548. *I will forget them*] Ah, likely they are dead *Draft*.

iii 554.   Have mercy goddess! feel oh feel my prayer.
                Pity great Circe!'–Nor sight nor syllable
                Saw I or heard I more of this sick spell . . . *Draft*.

iii 560. *dark lair*] dull realm *Draft*.

iii 561–2. *how desolate | My waking*] See i 681–705 *n*.

iii 565. A reminiscence of *Comus* 349,

> In this close dungeon of innumerous bowes . . .

I fled three days—when lo! before me stood
Glaring the angry witch. O Dis! Even now,
A clammy dew is beading on my brow
At mere remembering her pale laugh and curse.
570 "Ha, ha! Sir Dainty! There must be a nurse
Made of rose leaves and thistledown, express,
To cradle thee, my sweet, and lull thee—yes,
I am too flinty-hard for thy nice touch,
My tenderest squeeze is but a giant's clutch.
575 So, fairy-thing, it shall have lullabies
Unheard of yet, and it shall still its cries
Upon some breast more lily-feminine.
Oh, no—it shall not pine, and pine, and pine
More than one pretty, trifling thousand years,
580 And then 'twere pity, but fate's gentle shears
Cut short its immortality. Sea-flirt!
Young dove of the waters! Truly I'll not hurt
One hair of thine. See how I weep and sigh
That our heart-broken parting is so nigh.
585 And must we part? Ah, yes, it must be so.
Yet ere thou leavest me in utter woe,
Let me sob over thee my last adieus,
And speak a blessing. Mark me! Thou hast thews
Immortal, for thou art of heavenly race,
590 But such a love is mine that here I chase

iii 567. *Dis*] Pluto. See i 944 *n*.
iii 568. Foreshadows *La Belle Dame Sans Merci* 9–10 (pp. 502–3 below),
. . . thy brow,
With anguish moist and fever dew . . .
iii 575. *fairy*] tender *Draft*.
iii 577. *lily*] zephyr *Draft*.
iii 579. *trifling*] little *Draft*.
iii 581–3. *Sea-flirt . . . sigh*]

Great Jove
What fury of the three could harm this dove
Dear youth! see how I weep, hear how I sigh . . . *Draft*
iii 590–9 (and see iii 636–8 below). Perhaps suggested by the transformation
of Endymion—resulting from Tellus's jealous anger at his fidelity to Cynthia—in Lyly's *Endymion* (1591) II iii 29–36, 'Thou that liest downe with
golden lockes shalt not awake untill thee bee turned to silver haires; and
that chin, on which scarcely appeareth soft downe shall be filled with
brissels as hard as broome, thou shalt sleep out thy youth and flowring
time, and become dry hay before thou knowest thy selfe greene grass, and
ready by age to step into the grave when thou wakest, that was youthfull
in the Court when thou laidst thee downe to sleepe. The malice of *Tellus*

9+K.

Eternally away from thee all bloom
Of youth, and destine thee towards a tomb.
Hence shalt thou quickly to the watery vast,
And there, ere many days be overpast,

595   Disabled age shall seize thee; and even then
Thou shalt not go the way of agèd men,
But live and wither, cripple and still breathe
Ten hundred years—which gone, I then bequeath
Thy fragile bones to unknown burial.

600   Adieu, sweet love, adieu!" As shot stars fall,
She fled ere I could groan for mercy. Stung
And poisoned was my spirit; despair sung
A war-song of defiance 'gainst all hell.
A hand was at my shoulder to compel

605   My sullen steps, another 'fore my eyes
Moved on with pointed finger. In this guise
Enforcèd, at the last by ocean's foam
I found me—by my fresh, my native home.
Its tempering coolness, to my life akin,

610   Came salutary as I waded in,
And, with a blind voluptuous rage, I gave
Battle to the swollen billow-ridge and drave
Large froth before me, while there yet remained
Hale strength, nor from my bones all marrow drained.

615   Young lover, I must weep—such hellish spite
With dry cheek who can tell? While thus my might
Proving upon this element, dismayed,
Upon a dead thing's face my hand I laid.
I looked—'twas Scylla! Cursèd, cursèd Circe!

---

hath brought this to passe. . . .' Lyly's play was included in the second
volume of C. Dilke's *Old English Plays* (6 vols. 1814–16); see i 294–69 *n*.
iii *600–1. As shot stars fall / She fled*] Probably a half-conscious echo of
Shakespeare's *Venus and Adonis* 815–16,

> Look, how a bright star shooteth from the sky
> So glides he in the night from Venus's eye . . .

iii *604–10.* See iii 372–92 *n* above.
iii *611–12. with a blind . . . billow-ridge*] Perhaps a reminiscence of Marlowe's
Hero and Leander ii 150–4,

> . . . pray'd the narrow toiling Hellespont
> To part in twain, that he might come and go,
> But still the rising billows answered 'No'.
> With that he stripped him to the ivory skin,
> And crying, 'Love, I come,' leapt lively in . . .

620   O vulture-witch, hast never heard of mercy?
      Could not thy harshest vengeance be content,
      But thou must nip this tender innocent
      Because I loved her? Cold, oh cold indeed
      Were her fair limbs, and like a common weed
625   The sea-swell took her hair. Dead as she was
      I clung about her waist, nor ceased to pass
      Fleet as an arrow through unfathomed brine,
      Until there shone a fabric crystalline,
      Ribbed and inlaid with coral, pebble, and pearl.
630   Headlong I darted, at one eager swirl
      Gained its bright portal, entered, and behold!
      'Twas vast, and desolate, and icy-cold.
      And all around—but wherefore this to thee
      Who in few minutes more thyself shalt see?
635   I left poor Scylla in a niche and fled.
      My fevered parchings-up, my scathing dread
      Met palsy half way. Soon these limbs became
      Gaunt, withered, sapless, feeble, cramped, and lame.

           Now let me pass a cruel, cruel space,
640   Without one hope, without one faintest trace
      Of mitigation, or redeeming bubble
      Of coloured phantasy—for I fear 'twould trouble
      Thy brain to loss of reason—and next tell
      How a restoring chance came down to quell
645   One half of the witch in me.

                              On a day,
      Sitting upon a rock above the spray,
      I saw grow up from the horizon's brink
      A gallant vessel. Soon she seemed to sink
      Away from me again, as though her course
650   Had been resumed in spite of hindering force—
      So vanished; and not long, before arose
      Dark clouds and muttering of winds morose.

iii 621–35. K. departs from the original—see iii 449–72 n above—by
making Scylla fall into a tranced sleep.

iii 621. Wast not thine harshest Avengeance content . . . Fair copy.

iii 624–5. like . . . hair] Cp. Sleep and Poetry 376–80 n (p. 84 above),
                                        . . . as when ocean
           Heaves calmly its broad swelling smoothness o'er
           Its rocky marge, and balances once more
           The patient weeds . . .

iii 650. Had been resumed . . . hindering] She would resume . . . adverse
Draft.

Old Aeolus would stifle his mad spleen,
But could not; therefore all the billows green
655 Tossed up the silver spume against the clouds.
The tempest came. I saw that vessel's shrouds
In perilous bustle, while upon the deck
Stood trembling creatures. I beheld the wreck;
The final gulfing; the poor struggling souls.
660 I heard their cries amid loud thunder-rolls.
Oh, they had all been saved but crazèd eld
Annulled my vigorous cravings. And thus quelled
And curbed, think on it, O Latmian, did I sit
Writhing with pity and a cursing fit
665 Against that hell-born Circe. The crew had gone,
By one and one, to pale oblivion;
And I was gazing on the surges prone,
With many a scalding tear and many a groan,
When at my feet emerged an old man's hand
670 Grasping this scroll and this same slender wand.
I knelt with pain—reached out my hand—had grasped
These treasures—touched the knuckles—they
      unclasped—
I caught a finger. But the downward weight
O'erpowered me—it sank. Then 'gan abate
675 The storm, and through chill aguish gloom outburst
The comfortable sun. I was athirst
To search the book, and in the warming air
Parted its dripping leaves with eager care.

iii 653. *Aeolus*] Aeolus was the god of the winds, which he kept shut up in
a cave in the Aeolian isles between Sicily and Italy.
iii 654–60. *all the billows . . . thunder-rolls*] A recollection of *The Tempest* I ii
3–9,

> The sky, it seems, would pour down stinking pitch,
> But that the sea, mounting to th'welkin's cheek,
> Dashes the fire out. O! I have suffer'd
> With those I saw suffer: a brave vessel,
> Who had, no doubt, some noble creatures in her,
> Dash'd all to pieces. O! the cry did knock
> Against my very heart. Poor souls, they perish'd . . .

For K.'s reading of *The Tempest* in 1817 see i 204 *n.*
iii 661. *eld*] Old age. An Elizabethanism.
iii 662–3. *quelled | And curbed*] Perhaps suggested by *Macbeth* III iv 24,
'cabin'd, cribb'd, confin'd, bound in'.
iii 675. *aguish*] See *The Eve of St Mark* 12 *n* (p. 482 below), 'the aguish
hills'.
iii 678. *Parted its dripping*] Unfolded its damp *Draft.*

Strange matters did it treat of, and drew on
680 My soul page after page, till well-nigh won
Into forgetfulness–when, stupefied,
I read these words, and read again, and tried
My eyes against the heavens, and read again.
Oh, what a load of misery and pain
685 Each Atlas-line bore off! A shine of hope
Came gold around me, cheering me to cope
Strenuous with hellish tyranny. Attend!
For thou hast brought their promise to an end.

In the wide sea there lives a forlorn wretch,
690 Doomed with enfeebled carcase to outstretch
His loathed existence through ten centuries,
And then to die alone. Who can devise
A total opposition? No one. So
One million times ocean must ebb and flow,
695 And he oppressed. Yet he shall not die,
These things accomplished. If he utterly
Scans all the depths of magic and expounds
The meanings of all motions, shapes and sounds,
If he explores all forms and substances
700 Straight homeward to their symbol-essences,
He shall not die. Moreover, and in chief,
He must pursue this task of joy and grief
Most piously: all lovers tempest-tossed,
And in the savage overwhelming lost,
705 He shall deposit side by side, until
Time's creeping shall the dreary space fulfil.
Which done, and all these labours ripened,

iii *685. Each Atlas-line*] Each line bears a burden as heavy as that of Atlas.
See *Lemprière*: 'This mountain [Atlas], which runs across the deserts of Africa
east and west, is so high that the ancients have imagined that the heavens
rested on its top, and that Atlas supported the world on his shoulders.'
iii *685–6. A shine . . . to cope*]
sweet rays of hope
Glanc'd round me cheering me at once to cope . . . *Draft.*
iii *695–6. he oppressed . . . These things accomplished*] Latin constructions which
may owe something to K.'s recent reading of Milton. See headnote to
Book III (p. 205 above).
iii *697. Scans*] Sounds *Draft.*
iii *699–700.* Recalling the 'fellowship with essence' aspired to in Book I.
See i 778–81 *n*, i 779 *n*.
iii *702. joy and*] heaviest *Draft.*
iii *706. Time's creeping*] Echoing *Macbeth* V v 19–21,
To-morrow, and to-morrow, and to-morrow,

A youth, by heavenly power loved and led,
Shall stand before him, whom he shall direct
710   *How to consummate all. The youth elect*
Must do the thing, or both will be destroyed.'

'Then,' cried the young Endymion, overjoyed,
'We are twin brothers in this destiny!
Say, I entreat thee, what achievement high
715   Is in this restless world for me reserved?
What! If from thee my wandering feet had swerved,
Had we both perished?' 'Look!' the sage replied,
'Dost thou not mark a gleaming through the tide,
Of diverse brilliances? 'Tis the edifice
720   I told thee of, where lovely Scylla lies,
And where I have enshrinèd piously
All lovers whom fell storms have doomed to die
Throughout my bondage.' Thus discoursing, on
They went till unobscured the porches shone,
725   Which hurryingly they gained and entered straight.
Sure never since king Neptune held his state
Was seen such wonder underneath the stars.
Turn to some level plain where haughty Mars
Has legioned all his battle, and behold
730   How every soldier, with firm foot, doth hold
His even breast. See, many steelèd squares
And rigid ranks of iron, whence who dares
One step? Imagine further, line by line,
These warrior thousands on the field supine—
735   So in that crystal place, in silent rows,
Poor lovers lay at rest from joys and woes.
The stranger from the mountains, breathless, traced
Such thousands of shut eyes in order placed;
Such ranges of white feet, and patient lips
740   All ruddy—for here death no blossom nips.
He marked their brows and foreheads, saw their hair
Put sleekly on one side with nicest care,
And each one's gentle wrists, with reverence,
Put cross-wise to its heart.

Creeps in this petty pace from day to day,
To the last syllable of recorded time . . .

iii *713. twin brothers*] See iii 294 *n.*
iii *728–44.* K.'s army of doomed lovers probably owes something to the account of Satan's host in *Paradise Lost* i 344–55 and i 544–71, but the magical atmosphere suggests *The Arabian Nights* and the Hall of Eblis in Beckford's *Vathek* (1816 edn, 206 ff).

'Let us commence,'
745   Whispered the guide, stuttering with joy, 'even now.'
He spake, and, trembling like an aspen-bough,
Began to tear his scroll in pieces small,
Uttering the while some mumblings funeral.
He tore it into pieces small as snow
750   That drifts unfeathered when bleak northerns blow,
And, having done it, took his dark blue cloak
And bound it round Endymion, then struck
His wand against the empty air times nine.
'What more there is to do, young man, is thine.
755   But first a little patience. First undo
This tangled thread and wind it to a clue.
Ah, gentle! 'Tis as weak as spider's skein,
And shouldst thou break it–what, is it done so clean?
A power overshadows thee! Oh, brave!
760   The spite of hell is tumbling to its grave.
Here is a shell; 'tis pearly blank to me,
Nor marked with any sign or charactery–
Canst thou read aught? Oh, read for pity's sake!
Olympus, we are safe! Now, Carian, break
765   This wand against yon lyre on the pedestal.'

'Twas done. And straight with sudden swell and fall
Sweet music breathed her soul away and sighed
A lullaby to silence. 'Youth, now strew
These mincèd leaves on me, and passing through
770   Those files of dead, scatter the same around,
And thou wilt see the issue.'
                     'Mid the sound
Of flutes and viols, ravishing his heart,
Endymion from Glaucus stood apart

iii *750. unfeathered*] Light feathery snow falls only when there is little or no wind. The draft reads 'all shattered'.
iii *752. struck*] So in 1818; the draft has 'stroke' (a Spenserian archaism).
iii *753. against the empty*] at something in the *Draft*.
iii *756. clue*] Nail.
iii *762. charactery*] See *When I have fears* 3 *n* (p. 297 below), 'high-piled books, in charactery'.
iii *766–806*. Perhaps, as H. Rollins suggests, written 20 Sept. 1817. See Bailey's letter to Reynolds of 21 Sept. 1817, 'There is one passage of Keats's 3d. Book which beats all he has written. It is on *death*. He wrote it last night' (*KC* i 7).
iii *769. mincèd*] Cut up finely. Shakespeare has *Hamlet* II iii 517–18,
        . . . she saw Pyrrhus make malicious sport
      In mincing with his sword her husband's limbs . . .

And scattered in his face some fragments light.
775   How lightning-swift the change! A youthful wight
Smiling beneath a coral diadem,
Out-sparkling sudden like an upturned gem,
Appeared, and, stepping to a beauteous corse,
Kneeled down beside it and with tenderest force
780   Pressed its cold hand and wept–and Scylla sighed!
Endymion, with quick hand, the charm applied–
The nymph arose. He left them to their joy,
And onward went upon his high employ,
Showering those powerful fragments on the dead.
785   And, as he passed, each lifted up his head
As doth a flower at Apollo's touch.
Death felt it to his inwards—'twas too much:
Death fell a-weeping in his charnel-house.
The Latmian persevered along, and thus
790   All were re-animated. There arose
A noise of harmony, pulses and throes
Of gladness in the air–while many, who
Had died in mutual arms devout and true,
Sprang to each other madly, and the rest
795   Felt a high certainty of being blest.
They gazed upon Endymion. Enchantment
Grew drunken and would have its head and bent.
Delicious symphonies, like airy flowers,
Budded and swelled, and, full-blown, shed full showers
800   Of light, soft, unseen leaves of sounds divine.
The two deliverers tasted a pure wine
Of happiness, from fairy-press oozed out.
Speechless they eyed each other, and about
The fair assembly wandered to and fro,
805   Distracted with the richest overflow
Of joy that ever poured from heaven.

'Away!'
Shouted the new-born god, 'Follow, and pay
Our piety to Neptunus supreme!'
Then Scylla, blushing sweetly from her dream,

iii *786. Apollo's touch*] The light of the sun.
iii *787. inwards*] Innermost being. An Elizabethanism.
iii *791. A noise of*] A hum, a *Draft*.
iii *795. high*] sweet *Draft*.
iii *796. Enchantment*] Ravishment *Fair copy (cancelled)*.
iii *802. from fairy-press oozed*] not from earthly grapes press'd *Draft*.
iii *810. meek*] See iii 46 *n*.

810   They led on first, bent to her meek surprise,
      Through portal columns of a giant size,
      Into the vaulted, boundless emerald.
      Joyous, all followed, as the leader called,
      Down marble steps, pouring as easily
815   As hour-glass sand—and fast, as you might see
      Swallows obeying the south summer's call,
      Or swans upon a gentle waterfall.

      Thus went that beautiful multitude, nor far
      Ere from among some rocks of glittering spar,
820   Just within ken, they saw descending thick
      Another multitude. Whereat more quick
      Moved either host. On a wide sand they met,
      And of those numbers every eye was wet,
      For each their old love found. A murmuring rose,
825   Like what was never heard in all the throes
      Of wind and waters. 'Tis past human wit
      To tell; 'tis dizziness to think of it.

      This mighty consummation made, the host
      Moved on for many a league, and gained and lost
830   Huge sea-marks, vanward swelling in array,
      And from the rear diminishing away,
      Till a faint dawn surprised them. Glaucus cried,
      'Behold! Behold, the palace of his pride!
      God Neptune's palaces!' With noise increased,
835   They shouldered on towards that brightening east.
      At every onward step proud domes arose
      In prospect—diamond gleams and golden glows
      Of amber 'gainst their faces levelling.
      Joyous, and many as the leaves in spring,
840   Still onward, still the splendour gradual swelled.
      Rich opal domes were seen, on high upheld
      By jasper pillars, letting through their shafts
      A blush of coral. Copious wonder-draughts
      Each gazer drank, and deeper drank more near.

iii *812*. Into the sea.
iii *816*. See *To Autumn* 33 *n* (p. 654 below), '. . . gathering swallows twitter
in the skies'.
iii *827*. *dizziness*] See i 565 *n*.
iii *832*. *down surprised them. Glaucus*] dawning bloom'd—and Glaucus *Draft*.
iii *835*. *shouldered*] Probably echoing Spenser. See i 530 *n*.
iii *836*. *At every onward step*] And as it moved along *Draft*.
iii *838–9*.   Of amber leveling against their faces.
                   With expectation high, and hurried paces . . . *Draft*

9*

845   For what poor mortals fragment up, as mere
       As marble was there lavish, to the vast
       Of one fair palace, that far, far surpassed,
       Even for common bulk, those olden three,
       Memphis and Babylon and Nineveh.

850   As large, as bright, as coloured as the bow
       Of Iris, when unfading it doth show
       Beyond a silvery shower, was the arch
       Through which this Paphian army took its march
       Into the outer courts of Neptune's state,
855   Whence could be seen, direct, a golden gate,
       To which the leaders sped—but not half raught
       Ere it burst open swift as fairy thought,
       And made those dazzled thousands veil their eyes
       Like callow eagles at the first sunrise.
860   Soon with an eagle nativeness their gaze
       Ripe from hue-golden swoons took all the blaze,
       And then, behold, large Neptune on his throne
       Of emerald deep—yet not exalt alone.
       At his right hand stood wingèd Love, and on
865   His left sat smiling Beauty's paragon.

           Far as the mariner on highest mast
       Can see all round upon the calmèd vast,

iii 845–9. Confused syntax, but K. means that all vast palaces built by mortals are surpassed by Neptune's palace, whose lavish marble makes our resources seem meagre and whose size surpasses that of our greatest cities.

iii 849. *Memphis . . . Babylon . . . Nineveh*] Cities of antiquity celebrated for their splendour. Shelley has in *Alastor* (1816) 110–12,

                    . . . the fallen towers
           Of Babylon, the enternal pyramids,
           Memphis and Thebes . . .

iii 850–1. *the bow / Of Iris*] Iris, the goddess of the rainbow, was also one of the Oceanides (sea-nymphs).

iii 853. *Paphian army*] An army of lovers. See i 510 n.

iii 856. *raught*] Reached. See ii 282 n.

iii 860. *Soon with an eagle nativeness*] But soon like eagles natively *Draft*.

iii 862–5. Ian Jack notes, '[K.] may . . . have remembered the portrayal of Neptune and Venus in Tooke's *Pantheon* and Poussin's "The Triumph of Neptune and Amphitrite" as well as the section "Of the Deities of the Waters" in Spence's *Polymetis*. Such images no doubt helped to inspire the Hymn to Neptune [iii 943–990 below]' (*Keats and the Mirror of Art*, 159).

iii 865. And on his left Love fairest mother sate . . . *Draft*. The revised reading may be owed to *The Faerie Queene* VII vii 51,

           So Venus eeke, that goodly Paragone . . .

So wide was Neptune's hall. And as the blue
Doth vault the waters, so the waters drew
870 Their doming curtains, high, magnificent,
Awed from the throne aloof, and when storm-rent
Disclosed the thunder-gloomings in Jove's air,
But soothed, as now, flashed sudden everywhere
Noiseless, sub-marine cloudlets, glittering
875 Death to a human eye. For there did spring
From natural west and east, and south and north,
A light as of four sunsets, blazing forth
A gold-green zenith 'bove the Sea-God's head.
Of lucid depth the floor, and far outspread
880 As breezeless lake on which the slim canoe
Of feathered Indian darts about, as through
The delicatest air—air verily
But for the portraiture of clouds and sky.
This palace floor breath-air but for the amaze
885 Of deep-seen wonders motionless and blaze
Of the dome pomp, reflected in extremes,
Globing a golden sphere.

      They stood in dreams
Till Triton blew his horn. The palace rang;
The Nereids danced; the Sirens faintly sang;
890 And the great Sea-King bowed his dripping head.
Then Love took wing and from his pinions shed
On all the multitude a nectarous dew.
The ooze-born Goddess beckonèd and drew
Fair Scylla and her guides to conference,
895 And when they reached the thronèd eminence
She kissed the sea-nymph's cheek, who sat her down
A-toying with the doves. Then, 'Mighty crown

iii *880–1. slim canoe / Of feathered Indian*] Perhaps a recollection from K.'s
early reading of William Robertson's *History of America* (1777).

iii *882–7. air verily . . . sphere*] The lake might be taken for the air, were it
not for its reflecting the clouds and sky; the palace floor might also be taken
for air, were it not for its reflecting the wonders of the palace and the blazing
dome, which is mirrored as far as the eye can see and creates the effect of an
encompassing golden sphere.

iii *888. Triton blew his horn*] See i 206 *n*, ii 691 *n*.

iii *889. Nereids . . . Sirens*] See *Lemprière*: 'Nereides, nymphs of the sea,
daughters of Nereus and Doris. They were fifty in number, according to
most mythologists', and iii 241 *n*, 'I'll swim to the sirens'. For 'faintly' the
draft reads 'sweetly'.

iii *893. ooze-born Goddess*] Venus. See ii 458 *n*.

iii *897. the doves*] Attending Venus. See i 510 *n*.

And sceptre of this kingdom!' Venus said,
'Thy vows were on a time to Naïs paid–
900   Behold!' Two copious tear-drops instant fell
From the God's large eyes; he smiled delectable,
And over Glaucus held his blessing hands.
'Endymion! Ah, still wandering in the bands
Of love? Now this is cruel. Since the hour
905   I met thee in earth's bosom, all my power
Have I put forth to serve thee. What, not yet
Escaped from dull mortality's harsh net?
A little patience, youth! 'Twill not be long,
Or I am skilless quite. An idle tongue,
910   A humid eye, and steps luxurious,
Where these are new and strange, are ominous.
Aye, I have seen these signs in one of heaven,
When others were all blind, and were I given
To utter secrets, haply I might say
915   Some pleasant words–but Love will have his day.
So wait awhile expectant. Prithee soon,
Even in the passing of thine honeymoon,
Visit thou my Cythera. Thou wilt find
Cupid well-natured, my Adonis kind.
920   And pray persuade with thee–ah, I have done,
All blisses be upon thee, my sweet son!'
Thus the fair goddess, while Endymion
Knelt to receive those accents halcyon.

Meantime a glorious revelry began
925   Before the water-monarch. Nectar ran
In courteous fountains to all cups outreached.
And plundered vines, teeming exhaustless, pleached

iii *899–902.* According to some traditions (recorded in *Lemprière*) Glaucus
was the child of Neptune by the sea-nymph Nais.
iii *901. he smiled delectable*] He smiled delightfully. The phrasing is Miltonic.
iii *904–5. Since . . . bosom*] See ii 548–79.
iii *907. harsh*] rough *Draft*.
iii *908–15.* Venus has guessed at Cynthia's love for Endymion. Cp. ii 569–
72 above.
iii *913. others were all*] others' sight was *Draft*.
iii *915. pleasant*] honey *Draft*.
iii *918. Cythera*] See ii 492 *n*.
iii *922. fair*] blithe *Draft*.
iii *927. pleached*] Interwove. See *Much Ado About Nothing* III i 7–9,
              . . . the pleached bower
        Where honey-suckles, ripened by the sun,
        Forbid the sun to enter . . .

New growth about each shell and pendent lyre,
The which, in disentangling for their fire,
930   Pulled down fresh foliage and coverture
For dainty toying. Cupid, empire-sure,
Fluttered and laughed, and oft-times through the
      throng
Made a delighted way. Then dance and song
And garlanding grew wild, and pleasure reigned.
935   In harmless tendril they each other chained,
And strove who should be smothered deepest in
Fresh crush of leaves.

              Oh, 'tis a very sin
For one so weak to venture his poor verse
In such a place as this. Oh, do not curse,
940   High Muses, let him hurry to the ending!

All suddenly were silent. A soft blending
Of dulcet instruments came charmingly;
And then a hymn.

              'King of the stormy sea!
Brother of Jove, and co-inheritor
945   Of elements! Eternally before
Thee the waves awful bow. Fast, stubborn rock,
At thy feared trident shrinking, doth unlock
Its deep foundations, hissing into foam.
All mountain-rivers, lost in the wide home
950   Of thy capacious bosom, ever flow.
Thou frownest, and old Aeolus thy foe
Skulks to his cavern, 'mid the gruff complaint
Of all his rebel tempests. Dark clouds faint

iii *929–31. The which . . . toying*] The syntax is confused, but K. means that
the lovers pull down the 'New growth' in their excitement. With 'coverture'
(shelter) cp. *Much Ado About Nothing* III i 30, '. . . couched in the woodbine
coverture . . .'

iii *934–5. pleasure . . . chained*]   and wildness reigns.
       They bound each other up in tendril chains . . . *Draft*.

iii *943–90.* On the pictorial influences possibly affecting K.'s 'Hymn to
Neptune' see iii 862–5 n above. For K.'s other lyrical interpolations in *Endymion* see the 'Hymn to Pan' (i 232–306 n), the 'Ode to Sorrow' and description of Bacchus's procession (iv 146–290) and Cynthia's marriage song (iv 563–611).

iii *944–5. Brother . . . elements*] See *Hyperion* i 147 n (p. 405 below).

iii *951. Aeolus*] See iii 653 n.

When from thy diadem a silver gleam
955 Slants over blue dominion. Thy bright team
Gulfs in the morning light and scuds along
To bring thee nearer to that golden song
Apollo singeth, while his chariot
Waits at the doors of heaven. Thou art not
960 For scenes like this. An empire stern hast thou,
And it hath furrowed that large front. Yet now,
As newly come of heaven, dost thou sit
To blend and interknit
Subduèd majesty with this glad time.
965 O shell-borne King sublime!
We lay our hearts before thee evermore—
We sing and we adore!

'Breathe softly, flutes,
Be tender of your strings, ye soothing lutes,
970 Nor be the trumpet heard! oh, vain, oh, vain—
Not flowers budding in an April rain,
Nor breath of sleeping dove, nor river's flow,
No, nor the Aeolian twang of Love's own bow,
Can mingle music fit for the soft ear
975 Of goddess Cytherea!
Yet deign, white Queen of Beauty, thy fair eyes
On our souls' sacrifice.

'Bright-wingèd Child!
Who has another care when thou hast smiled?
980 Unfortunates on earth, we see at last
All death-shadows, and glooms that overcast
Our spirits, fanned away by thy light pinions.
O sweetest essence! Sweetest of all minions!
God of warm pulses and dishevelled hair
985 And panting bosoms bare!

iii 954–5.   When thy bright diadem a silver gleam
            O'er blue dominion starts. Thy finny team . . . Draft.
iii 956. Gulfs] Rushes forward like a gulf (OED). The draft has ' Snorts'.
iii 961. front] Brow or forehead, as in Shakespeare and Milton.
iii 962. As newly come of] Like a young child of Draft.
iii 973. Aeolian twang] Like the sound of an Aeolian lyre. See Ode to Apollo
34 n (p. 16 above).
iii 975. Cytherea] Venus. See ii 492 n.
iii 978. Cupid.
iii 979. Who has another care] Who is not full of heaven Draft.
iii 983–5. See i 799 n.
iii 983. sweetest of all minions] essence of all sweetest minions Draft.

Dear unseen light in darkness! Eclipser
Of light in light! Delicious poisoner!
Thy venomed goblet will we quaff until
We fill—we fill!
990   And by thy Mother's lips——'
                              Was heard no more
For clamour when the golden palace door
Opened again, and from without in shone
A new magnificence. On oozy throne
Smooth-moving came Oceanus the old,
995   To take a latest glimpse at his sheep-fold
Before he went into his quiet cave
To muse for ever. Then a lucid wave,
Scooped from its trembling sisters of mid-sea,
Afloat and pillowing up the majesty
1000   Of Doris and the Aegean seer, her spouse.
Next, on a dolphin, clad in laurel boughs,
Theban Amphion leaning on his lute.
His fingers went across it—all were mute
To gaze on Amphitrite, queen of pearls,
1005   And Thetis pearly too.
                              The palace whirls
Around giddy Endymion, seeing he
Was there far strayèd from mortality.
He could not bear it—shut his eyes in vain.
Imagination gave a dizzier pain.

iii *986. unseen light in darkness*] Perhaps suggested by the legend of Cupid's
visiting Psyche in the dark. See *Ode to Psyche* 66–7 *n* (p. 521 below).
iii *993–7. On oozy throne . . . muse for ever*] For K.'s later interest in Oceanus
see *Hyperion* ii 163–6 *n*, (p. 425 below). 'Oceanus the old' recalls here *The
Faerie Queene* IV xi 18,

> Next came the aged *Ocean*, and his Dame,
> Old *Tethys*, th'oldest two of all the rest,
> For all the rest of those two parents came . . .

iii *1000. Doris*, the daughter of Oceanus and Tethys, married her brother
Nereus (cp. iii 889 *n*). See *Lemprière*: 'Nereus was generally represented as an
old man, with a long flowing beard, and hair of an azure colour. The chief
place of his residence was the Aegean Sea. . . . He was endowed with the
gift of prophecy to a remarkable degree. . . .'
iii *1002. Theban Amphion*] See iii 461 *n*.
iii *1004. Amphitrite*] See ii 109 *n*.
iii *1005. Thetis*] See ii 611 *n*.
iii *1007. far strayed*] a stray lamb *Draft*.
iii *1008–9*. Cp. *On Seeing the Elgin Marbles* 11 (p. 105 above), 'a most dizzy
pain'.

1010   'Oh, I shall die! Sweet Venus, be my stay!
        Where is my lovely mistress? Well-away!
        I die—I hear her voice—I feel my wing—'
        At Neptune's feet he sank. A sudden ring
        Of Nereids were about him in kind strife
1015   To usher back his spirit into life.
        But still he slept. At last they interwove
        Their cradling arms, and purposed to convey
        Towards a crystal bower far away.

        Lo! while slow carried through the pitying crowd,
1020   To his inward senses these words spake aloud,
        Written in star-light on the dark above:
        Dearest Endymion, my entire love,
        How have I dwelt in fear of fate! '*Tis done—*
        Immortal bliss for me too hast thou won.
1025   *Arise then! For the hen-dove shall not hatch*
        Her ready eggs, before I'll kissing snatch
        Thee into endless heaven. Awake! Awake!

        The youth at once arose. A placid lake
        Came quiet to his eyes, and forest green,
1030   Cooler than all the wonders he had seen,
        Lulled with its simple song his fluttering breast.
        How happy once again in grassy nest!

iii *1012. I hear her voice—I feel my wing*] love calls me hence—thus muttering *Draft.*

iii *1016–18.*   They gave him nectar—shed bright drops, and strove
               Long time in vain. At last they interwove
               Their cradling arms, and carefully conveyed
               His body towards a quiet bowery shade . . . *Draft.*

iii *1019. pitying*] parting *Draft (cancelled).*

iii *1024.* Cp ii 808 above, 'An immortality of passion's thine'.

iii *1026. kissing*] madly *Draft.*

BOOK IV

Written at Hampstead between *c.* 5 Oct.–*c.* 21 Nov. 1817 and Burford Bridge, Surrey, 22–8 Nov. 1817: K. returned to Hampstead 5 Oct. 1817 (*L* i 168) and informed Bailey 22 Nov. 1817, 'I am just arrived at Dorking to change the Scene—change the Air and give me a Spur to wind up my Poem, of which there are wanting 500 Lines. . . . Direct Burford Bridge near Dorking' (*L* i 187); for the date of completion see headnote to the whole poem (p. 116 above). K. had written only 300 lines by 30 Oct. 1817 (*L* i 175), but he appears to have written over 80 lines a day at Burford

Bridge–cp. his '50 lines a day' at Oxford (headnote to Book III, p. 205 above).

<blockquote>

Muse of my native land! Loftiest Muse!
O first-born on the mountains, by the hues
Of heaven on the spiritual air begot!
Long didst thou sit alone in northern grot
5   While yet our England was a wolfish den.
Before our forests heard the talk of men,
Before the first of Druids was a child,
Long didst thou sit amid our regions wild
Rapt in a deep prophetic solitude.
10   There came an eastern voice of solemn mood—
Yet wast thou patient. Then sang forth the Nine,
Apollo's garland–yet didst thou divine
Such home-bred glory, that they cried in vain,
'Come hither, Sister of the Island!' Plain
15   Spake fair Ausonia; and once more she spake

</blockquote>

iv *1–29*. An invocation to the muse in Milton's manner, probably owing someting to K.'s recent reading of *Paradise Lost* (see headnote to Book III, p. 205 above). The lines were copied out by K. in his letter to Bailey of 28 Oct. 1817 with the comment, '. . . you will see from the Manner I had not an opportunity of mentioning any Poets, for fear of spoiling the effect of the passage by particularising them' (*L* i 172–3). This outline of the major developments in poetry includes references to the Bible (iv 10), the classical poets (iv 11–14), Dante (iv 14–15) and Shakespeare (iv 16–20), and owes a distant debt to Gray's *The Progress of Poesy* (1759).

iv *6*. *talk*] voice *Draft*.

iv *7*. *Druids*] See *To George Felton Mathew* 39 *n* (p. 26 above).

iv *9*. Foreseeing England's poetic greatness. The phrasing suggests a recollection of Milton's *Il Penseroso* 40–2,

> Thy rapt soul sitting in thine eyes:
> There held in holy passion still,
> Forgetting thyself to Marble . . .

iv *10*. *eastern*] hebrew *Fair copy*. An allusion to the Bible.

iv *11*. *the Nine / Apollo's garland*] On Apollo and the muses see *Ode to Apollo* 42–7 *n* (p. 17 above).

iv *14–16*. *Plain . . . summons*] Ausonia is the ancient name for Italy. The two poets referred to are Virgil and Dante. K. began to read Cary's translation of Dante closely June 1818 (see *On Visiting the Tomb of Burns* 9 *n*, p. 358 below). The letter, now lost, allegedly written by K. to Haydon 20 Nov. 1817 expressing 'admiration of the memory and works of Dante' is a forgery; see C. Price's 'Six letters by Keats' and J. Stillinger's reply, *Neuphilologische Mitteilungen* 3 lix (1958) 192–7, lxi (1960) 387.

A higher summons—still didst thou betake
Thee to thy native hopes. Oh, thou hast won
A full accomplishment! The thing is done,
Which undone, these our latter days had risen
20   On barren souls. Great Muse, thou know'st what
             prison
Of flesh and bone curbs, and confines, and frets
Our spirit's wings. Despondency besets
Our pillows, and the fresh tomorrow morn
Seems to give forth its light in very scorn
25   Of our dull, uninspired, snail-pacèd lives.
Long have I said, how happy he who shrives
To thee! But then I thought on poets gone,
And could not pray—nor could I now. So on
I move to the end in lowliness of heart.

30   'Ah, woe is me that I should fondly part
From my dear native land! Ah, foolish maid!
Glad was the hour when, with thee, myriads bade
Adieu to Ganges and their pleasant fields!
To one so friendless the clear freshet yields
35   A bitter coolness, the ripe grape is sour.
Yet I would have, great gods, but one short hour
Of native air—let me but die at home.'
       Endymion to heaven's airy dome
Was offering up a hecatomb of vows
40   When these words reached him. Whereupon he bows

iv 16. *A higher*] In self-surpassing *Draft.*

iv 17. *native*] darling *K.'s letter copy.*

iv 19. Which wanting all these latter days had dawned . . . *Draft.*

iv 20–9. *Great Muse . . . heart*] K. turns despondently to his own poetic achievement.

iv 21. *curbs, and confines, and frets*] Perhaps a reminiscence of *Macbeth* III iv, 24, quoted in iii 662–3 *n* above.

iv 25. The disappointing contrast between poetic aspiration and ordinary everyday experience.

iv 26. *shrives*] Confesses, but the correct meaning of 'shrive' is 'to grant absolution'. Cp. Scott's poem *The Gray Brother* (1802) st. 30,
             . . . who art thou, thou Gray Brother,
       That I should shrive to thee . . .

iv 34. Where no friends are, the very freshet yields *Draft.* With 'freshet' cp. *Isabella* 212–13 and *n* (p. 338 below),
                       . . . the bream
             Keeps head against the freshets . . .

iv 36. *Yet I would have*] Then take my life *Draft.*

iv 39. *hecatomb*] A vast quantity.

His head through thorny-green entanglement
Of underwood, and to the sound is bent,
Anxious as hind towards her hidden fawn.

'Is no one near to help me? No fair dawn
45 Of life from charitable voice? No sweet saying
To set my dull and saddened spirit playing?
No hand to toy with mine? No lips so sweet
That I may worship them? No eyelids meet
To twinkle on my bosom? No one dies
50 Before me, till from these enslaving eyes
Redemption sparkles? I am sad and lost.'

Thou, Carian lord, hadst better have been tossed
Into a whirlpool. Vanish into air,
Warm mountaineer! For canst thou only bear
55 A woman's sigh alone and in distress?
See not her charms! Is Phoebe passionless?
Phoebe is fairer far–oh, gaze no more.

iv *41. thorny-green*] ever rough *Draft (cancelled).*
iv *49–54. No one dies . . . mountaineer*]   false! 'twas false
                They said how beautiful I was! who calls
                Me now divine? Who now kneels down and dies
                Before me till from these enslaving eyes
                Redemption sparkles. Ah me how sad I am!
                Of all the poisons sent to make us mad
                Of all death's overwhelmings'–Stay Beware
                Young Mountaineer! . . . *Draft.*
iv *55. alone and in*] in the luxury of *Draft.* With K.'s use of 'luxury' here
cp. *Isabella* 236 *n* (p. 339 below),
                She brooded o'er the luxury alone . . .
iv *56. Phoebe*] K.s first use of this name here in the poem, together with
his use of a disguise for Endymion's 'unknown goddess', has led some
readers to guess that he had recently read Drayton's *Endimion and Phoebe*
(see main headnote, p. 117 above).
iv. *57–66.* The contrasted attractions of the Indian maid and Phoebe may
owe something to the Poet's encounters with the dark-haired Cashmir maid
and the blue-eyed Spirit in Shelley's *Alastor* (1816) 178–82, 489–92,
                Her dark locks floating in the breath of night,
                Her beamy bending eyes, her parted lips
                Outstretched, and pale, and quivering eagerly.
                His strong heart sunk and sickened with excess
                Of love . . .
                            . . . two eyes
                Two starry eyes, hung in the gloom of thought,
                And seemed with their serene and azure smiles
                To beckon him . . .

Yet if thou wilt behold all beauty's store,
Behold her panting in the forest grass!
60 Do not those curls of glossy jet surpass
For tenderness the arms so idly lain
Amongst them? Feelest not a kindred pain,
To see such lovely eyes in swimming search
After some warm delight that seems to perch
65 Dovelike in the dim cell lying beyond
Their upper lids? Hist!

'Oh, for Hermes' wand,
To touch this flower into human shape!
That woodland Hyacinthus could escape
From his green prison and here kneeling down
70 Call me his queen, his second life's fair crown!
Ah me, how I could love! My soul doth melt
For the unhappy youth. Love! I have felt
So faint a kindness, such a meek surrender
To what my own full thoughts had made too tender,
75 That but for tears my life had fled away!
Ye deaf and senseless minutes of the day,
And thou, old forest, hold ye this for true,
There is no lightning, no authentic dew
But in the eye of love. There's not a sound,
80 Melodious howsoever, can confound
The heavens and earth in one to such a death
As doth the voice of love. There's not a breath

iv 63. *swimming*] fruitless *Draft*.
iv 66. *Hermes' wand*] See i 563 *n*.
iv 68. *Hyacinthus*] See i 326–31 *n*.
iv 70. *life's fair*] living's *Draft*.
iv 72. After some beauteous youth—Who, who hath felt . . . *Draft*.
iv 73. *So faint a kindness*] So warm a faintness *Draft*.
iv 74. *full*] fair *Draft*.
iv 76–7.   Sweet shadow, be distinct awhile and stay
                While I speak to thee—trust me it is true . . . *Draft*.
iv 78–85. Cp. the celebrations of love at i 797–842, ii 1–43 and *n* above. The
phrasing and cadence suggest the influence of Berowne's speech on love in
Love's Labour's Lost IV iii 287–362.
iv 79. *the eye of love*] a Lover's eye *Draft*. Cp. *Love's Labour's Lost* IV iii 331,
                A lover's eyes will gaze an eagle blind . . .
iv 79–82. *there's not a sound . . . voice of love*] Cp. *Love's Labour's Lost* IV iii
341–2,
                . . . when Love speaks, the voice of all the gods
                Makes heaven drowsy with the harmony . . .
iv 82. *As doth the voice of love*] As will a lover's voice *Draft*.

Will mingle kindly with the meadow air
Till it has panted round and stolen a share
85   Of passion from the heart!'

                                        Upon a bough
He leant, wretched. He surely cannot now
Thirst for another love. Oh, impious,
That he can even dream upon it thus!
Thought he, 'Why am I not as are the dead,
90   Since to a woe like this I have been led
Through the dark earth, and through the wondrous
            sea?
Goddess, I love thee not the less! From thee
By Juno's smile I turn not—no, no, no—
While the great waters are at ebb and flow.
95   I have a triple soul! Oh, fond pretence—
For both, for both my love is so immense,
I feel my heart is cut for them in twain.'

And so he groaned, as one by beauty slain.
The lady's heart beat quick, and he could see
100   Her gentle bosom heave tumultuously.
He sprang from his green covert. There she lay,
Sweet as a muskrose upon new-made hay,
With all her limbs on tremble, and her eyes

iv 85–7. Upon a bough . . . another love] '. . . Where love is not
                    Only is solitude—poor shadow! what
                    I say thou hearest not! away begone
                    And leave me prythee with my grief alone!'
                    The Latmian lean'd his arm upon a bough,
                    A wretched mortal: what can he do now?
                    Must he another Love? . . . Draft.
iv 92. Goddess] Mine own Draft.
iv 94–5. While . . . triple soul]
                    While the fair moon gives light, or rivers flow
                    My adoration of thee is yet pure
                    As infants prattling. How is this—why sure
                    I have a tripple soul! . . . Draft.
Endymion has a 'triple soul' because of his simultaneous devotion to the
moon, his unknown goddess and the Indian maid. See ii 169–98 n.
iv 96. both] The unknown goddess and the Indian maid.
iv 102. Sweet as a muskrose] On K.'s fondness for the muskrose see To a
Friend who Sent me Some Roses 6 n (p. 47 above).
iv 103–4. her eyes . . . alive] Inspired by Shakespeare's Venus and Adonis
1033–8,

Shut softly up alive. To speak he tries.
105 'Fair damsel, pity me! Forgive that I
Thus violate thy bower's sanctity!
Oh, pardon me, for I am full of grief—
Grief born of thee, young angel, fairest thief,
Who stolen hast away the wings wherewith
110 I was to top the heavens. Dear maid, sith
Thou art my executioner, and I feel
Loving and hatred, misery and weal,
Will in a few short hours be nothing to me
And all my story that much passion slew me,
115 Do smile upon the evening of my days.
And, for my tortured brain begins to craze,
Be thou my nurse, and let me understand
How dying I shall kiss that lily hand.
Dost weep for me? Then should I be content.
120 Scowl on, ye fates, until the firmament
Outblackens Erebus, and the full-caverned earth

. . . as the snail, whose tender horns being hit,
Shrinks backwards in his shelly cave with pain,
And there, all smother'd up, in shade doth sit,
Long after fearing to creep forth again;
So, at his bloody view his eyes are fled.
Into the deep dark cabins of her head . . .

K. quotes the passage in his letter to Reynolds of 22 Nov. 1817 (*L* i 189).

iv *104–5. To speak . . . pity me*]   Ye harmonies
Ye tranced visions—ye flights ideal
Nothing are ye to life so dainty real
O Lady pity me! . . . *Draft*.

Cp. *Lamia* i 330–2 *n* (p. 631 below).

iv *111. Thou art my executioner*] Echoing Phebe to Silvius in *As You Like It*
III v 8
I would not be thy executioner . . .

iv *118. that lily hand*] A detail lending some support to Colvin's suggestion
that a source for K.'s Indian Maid was *The Lay of Aristotle*, printed in G. L.
Way's translation (1800) of Le Grand's *Fabliaux*. Cp. K.'s early prose fragment, according to Colvin derived from *The Lay of Aristotle*: 'Whanne
Alexandre the Conquerore was wayfayringe in ye londe of Inde, there
mette hym a damoselle of marveillouse beautie slepynge uponne the herbes
and flourys . . . Her forhed was as whytte as . . . snowe whyche yᵉ talle hed
of a Norwegian pyne stelythe from yᵉ northerne wynde. One of her
fayre hondes was yplaced thereonne, and thus whytte wyth whytte was
ymyngld. . . .' For the rest of the fragment and accounts of its probable
source see *Colvin* (1917) 33, 551–3, *Finney* 276.

iv *121. Erebus*] A poetical commonplace for hell. Derived from a deity of

Crumbles into itself. By the cloud girth
Of Jove, those tears have given me a thirst
To meet oblivion.' As her heart would burst
125   The maiden sobbed awhile and then replied:
'Why must such desolation betide
As that thou speak'st of ? Are not these green nooks
Empty of all misfortune ? Do the brooks
Utter a gorgon voice? Does yonder thrush,
130   Schooling its half-fledged little ones to brush
About the dewy forest, whisper tales?
Speak not of grief, young stranger, or cold snails
Will slime the rose tonight. Though if thou wilt,
Methinks 'twould be a guilt–a very guilt–
135   Not to companion thee, and sigh away
The light, the dusk, the dark, till break of day!'
'Dear lady,' said Endymion, ''tis past.
I love thee—and my days can never last!
That I may pass in patience still speak.
140   Let me have music dying, and I seek
No more delight–I bid adieu to all.
Didst thou not after other climates call,
And murmur about Indian streams?' Then she,
Sitting beneath the midmost forest tree,
145   For pity sang this roundelay:

---

hell known by this name, who 'married Nox, by whom he had Lux and
Dies. . . . The poets often used the word to signify hell itself' (*Lemprière*).

iv *126. desolation*] Five syllables.

iv *129. gorgon*] Monstrous.

iv *136*. Followed in the draft by the lines,

        Canst thou do so ? Is there no balm, no cure
        Could not a beckoning Hebe soon allure
        Thee into Paradise ? What sorrowing
        So weighs thee down what utmost woe could bring
  [5] This madness–Sit thee down by me, and ease
        Thine heart in whispers–haply by degrees
        I may find out some soothing medecine.'–
        'Dear Lady,' said Endymion, 'I pine
        I die–the tender accents thou hast spoken
  [10] Have finish'd all–my heart is lost and broken . . .

l. [2]. *Hebe*] See iv 415 *n*.

iv *139. patience*] Trisyllabic.

iv *143. Then she*]   –now, now–
     I listen, it may save me–On my vow–
       Let me have music dying !' The ladye . . . *Draft.*

'O Sorrow,
Why dost borrow
The natural hue of health, from vermeil lips?
To give maiden blushes
150   To the white rose bushes?
Or is it thy dewy hand the daisy tips?

O Sorrow,
Why dost borrow
The lustrous passion from a falcon-eye?
155   To give the glow-worm light?
Or, on a moonless night,
To tinge, on siren shores, the salt sea-spry?

O Sorrow
Why dost borrow
160   The mellow ditties from a mourning tongue?
To give at evening pale
Unto the nightingale,
That thou mayst listen the cold dews among?

iv *146–81.* K. copied out his 'Ode to Sorrow' with some variants in his letters to Jane Reynolds and Bailey of 31 Oct. 1817 and 3 Nov. 1817 (*L* i 176–7, 181–2). (The letters are referred to below as *L1, L2*.) K. comments on the verses in his letter to Bailey of 22 Nov. 1817, 'I am certain of nothing but of the holiness of the Heart's affections and the truth of Imagination – What the Imagination siezes as Beauty must be truth – whether it existed before or not – for I have the same Idea of all our Passions as of Love they are all in their sublime, creative of essential Beauty – In a Word, you may know my favourite Speculation by my first Book [*Endymion* I] and the little song I sent in my last – which is a representation from the fancy of the probable mode of operating in these Matters – The Imagination may be compared to Adam's dream – he awoke and found it truth. . . . O for a Life of Sensations rather than of Thoughts! It is "a Vision in the form of Youth" a Shadow of reality to come' (*L* i 184–5). For a full discussion of this letter and its bearing on *Endymion* see Newell Ford, *The Prefigurative Imagination of John Keats* (1951) 20–38. The song expresses K.'s characteristic feelings about the connection between pain and joy, and although lacking the richness of his mature style foreshadows his linking of melancholy with the perception of beauty and its transience in the *Ode to Melancholy* (p. 538 below).

iv *148. vermeil*] See i 50 *n.*

iv *154. a falcon-eye*] a Lover's eye *Draft, L1*; an orbed eye *L2*.

iv *157. spry*] Spray. An Elizabethanism. See, for example, Sandys's *Ovid, Metamorphoses* xi (p. 207, col. 2),

Now tossing Seas appear to touch the sky,
And wrap their curles in clouds, frotht with their spry . . .

iv *160. mellow*] tender *L2*.

O Sorrow,
165   Why dost borrow
Heart's lightness from the merriment of May?
        A lover would not tread
        A cowslip on the head,
Though he should dance from eve till peep of day—
170   Nor any drooping flower
        Held sacred for thy bower,
Wherever he may sport himself and play.

        To Sorrow
        I bade good-morrow,
175 And thought to leave her far away behind.
        But cheerly, cheerly,
        She loves me dearly,
She is so constant to me, and so kind.
        I would deceive her
180   And so leave her,
But ah, she is so constant and so kind!

Beneath my palm trees, by the river side,
I sat a-weeping. In the whole world wide
There was no one to ask me why I wept—
185   And so I kept
Brimming the water-lily cups with tears
        Cold as my fears.

Beneath my palm trees, by the river side,
I sat a-weeping. What enamoured bride,
190 Cheated by shadowy wooer from the clouds,
        But hides and shrouds
Beneath dark palm trees by a river side?

iv 167–8. Echoes Sabrina's song in Milton's *Comus* 897–9,
                    Thus I set my printless feet
                    O're the Cowslips velvet head,
                    That bends not as I tread . . .
iv 172. *Wherever*] However *Draft*.
iv 178. *so constant to me*] to me so constant *L1, L2*.
iv 181. *so . . . so*] too . . . too *L1, L2*.
iv 186. Echoes Milton's *Lycidas* 150,
                    And Daffadillies fill their cups with tears . . .
iv 187. Chill'd with strange fears . . . *Draft*.
iv 190. *wooer*] lover *Draft*. Phoebe is thinking of her own treatment of
Endymion.

And as I sat, over the light blue hills
There came a noise of revellers. The rills
195   Into the wide stream came of purple hue—
      'Twas Bacchus and his crew!
The earnest trumpet spake, and silver thrills
From kissing cymbals made a merry din—
      'Twas Bacchus and his kin!
200   Like to a moving vintage down they came,
Crowned with green leaves, and faces all on flame—
All madly dancing through the pleasant valley,

iv *193–272.* K.'s account of Bacchus's triumphal progress is a re-working
of details from several sources, including Sandys's *Ovid*, Titian's painting
'Bacchus and Ariadne' (see *Sleep and Poetry* 335–6 *n*, p. 83 above), and
various works of classical reference. For a full discussion of the sources see
Finney 272–91 and on the influence of Poussin Ian Jack's *Keats and the Mirror
of Art* (1967) 159–60. The irregular stanzas and some pictorial details suggest
the influence of Milton's *Nativity Ode*. See *Lemprière*: 'Of all the achievements of Bacchus, his expedition into the East is the most celebrated. He
marched at the head of an army composed of men as well as women, all inspired with divine fury, and armed with thyrsi, cymbals, and other musical
instruments. The leader was drawn in a chariot by a lion and a tyger, and
was accompanied by Pan, Silenus, and all the Satyrs. His conquests were
easy and without bloodshed: the people cheerfully submitted and gratefully
elevated to the rank of a god the hero who taught them the use of the vine,
the cultivation of the earth, and the manner of making honey.'
iv *194–8.* Bacchus was traditionally associated with noise and music (one of
his names was Bromius, the noisy one). See Sandys's *Ovid*, *Metamorphoses*
iv (p. 65, col. 2),

>   What place so-e're thou entrest, sounding brasse,
>   Lowd Sac-buts, Tymbrels, the confused cryes
>   Of Youths and Women, pierce the marble skyes . . .

iv *195–6. rills . . . hue*] Purple rills of wine mingled with the waters of the
river.
iv *198. merry din*] Perhaps echoing Coleridge's *Ancient Mariner* (1798) 8,

>   May'st hear the merry din . . .

Wordsworth has *The White Doe of Rylstone* (1815) 43, 'the fervent din'.
Cp. i 40, iii 54 above.
iv *200–1. Like to a moving . . . leaves*] See *Lemprière*: '[Bacchus] is generally
represented crowned with vine and ivy leaves, with a thyrsus in his hand'.
Cp. Sandys's *Ovid*, *Metamorphoses* iv (p. 65, col. 1),

>   . . . wrapt in skins, their hair-laces unbound,
>   And dangling Tresses with wild Ivy crown'd,
>   They leafy Speares assume . . .

The phrase 'moving vintage' may owe something to *Macbeth* V v 38, 'a
moving grove'.

>   To scare thee, Melancholy!
>   Oh, then, oh, then, thou wast a simple name!
> 205   And I forgot thee, as the berried holly
>   By shepherds is forgotten, when, in June,
>   Tall chestnuts keep away the sun and moon—
>   I rushed into the folly!
>
>   Within his car, aloft, young Bacchus stood,
> 210   Trifling his ivy-dart, in dancing mood,
>   With sidelong laughing;
>   And little rills of crimson wine imbrued
>   His plump white arms and shoulders, enough white
>   For Venus' pearly bite;
> 215   And near him rode Silenus on his ass,
>   Pelted with flowers as he on did pass
>   Tipsily quaffing.
>
>   Whence came ye, merry Damsels, whence came ye?
>   So many, and so many, and such glee?

iv 203. thee] my Draft. Bacchus was also known as Lyaeus, the deliverer from care. See Sandys's gloss on Ovid's Metamorphoses iv 11, 'Lyaeus, because liberall cups exhalerate the heart, and free it from sorrow' (Sandys's Ovid, p. 73).

iv 207. Tall chestnuts] The Beeches Draft.

iv 209–14. K. follows tradition in describing Bacchus as young and effeminate. See Baldwin: 'Bacchus was ordinarily represented under the naked figure of a beautiful young man, but considerably plump in his face and limbs, as might seem best to befit the generous living of the patron of the vine, and his countenance expressed the merry and jovial cast of thought which wine inspires' (225-6).

iv 212. rills] streaks Draft.

iv 213–14. The lines have an Elizabethan flavour. See, for example, Marlowe's Hero and Leander i 63–5,

>   Even as delicious meat is to the taste,
>   So was his necke in touching, and surpast
>   The white of Pelops' shoulder . . .

iv 215–17. See Lemprière: 'Silenus, a demi-god, who became the nurse, the preceptor, and the attendant of the god Bacchus. . . . [He] is generally represented as a fat jolly old man riding on an ass, crowned with flowers and always intoxicated. . . .' Cp. Sandys's Ovid, Metamorphoses iv (p. 65, col. 2),

>   Whil'st old Sylenus, reeling still, doth hollow;
>   Who weakly hangs, upon his tardy Asse . . .

iv 219 (and see iv 229 below). So many, and so many] C. L. Finney suggests that K. is remembering Rabelais's humorous estimate of the vast number of Bacchus's followers during his Indian journey, 'Le nombre estoit octante cinq mille six vingtz et treize' (Pantagruel v, chap. 39). K. possessed a copy of Rabelais in the original French.

220   Why have ye left your bowers desolate,
            Your lutes and gentler fate?
        "We follow Bacchus! Bacchus on the wing,
            A-conquering!
        Bacchus, young Bacchus! Good or ill betide,
225   We dance before him thorough kingdoms wide—
        Come hither, lady fair, and joinèd be
            To our wild minstrelsy!"

        Whence came ye, jolly Satyrs, whence came ye?
        So many, and so many, and such glee?
230   Why have ye left your forest haunts, why left
            Your nuts in oak-tree cleft?
        "For wine, for wine we left our kernel tree;
        For wine we left our heath and yellow brooms;
235   For wine we follow Bacchus through the earth—
        Great God of breathless cups and chirping mirth!
        Come hither, lady fair, and joinèd be
            To our mad minstrelsy!"

        Over wide streams and mountains great we went,
240   And, save when Bacchus kept his ivy tent,
        Onward the tiger and the leopard pants,
            With Asian elephants.
        Onward these myriads—with song and dance,

iv 220–1. Perhaps suggested by Ovid's account of the Bacchanalian feast in his *Metamorphoses* iv 9–10. See Sandys's *Ovid, Metamorphoses* iv (p. 65, col. 1),

            The Matrons and new-married Wives obay:
            Their webs, their unspun Wooll aside they lay;
            Sweete odours burne; and sing: *Lyaeus, Bacchus* . . .
Line 221 is followed in the draft by,
            We follow Bacchus from a far country . . .
iv 225. *before*] beside *Draft*.
iv 228. *Satyrs*] See *Lemprière*: 'Demigods of the country . . . represented like men, but with the feet and the legs of goats, short horns on the head, and the whole body covered with thick hair. They chiefly attend Bacchus, and rendered themselves known in his orgies by their riotous demeanour and lasciviousness.' Cp. Sandys's *Ovid, Metamorphoses* iv (p. 65, col. 2),

            Light *Bacchides*, and skipping Satyrs follow . . .
iv 232. *kernel tree*] forest meat *Draft*.
iv 234. An individual detail.
iv 236. *chirping*] endless *Draft*.
iv 241. *leopard*] Bacchus's chariot is drawn by leopards in Titian's 'Bacchus and Ariadne'. K.'s enthusiasm for this painting and its influence on his description of Bacchus are recorded in W. Sharp's *Life of Severn* (1892) 32.

With zebras striped and sleek Arabians' prance,
245   Web-footed alligators, crocodiles,
Bearing upon their scaly backs, in files,
Plump infant laughers mimicking the coil
Of seamen and stout galley-rowers' toil—
With toying oars and silken sails they glide,
250   Nor care for wind and tide.

Mounted on panthers' furs and lions' manes,
From rear to van they scour about the plains—
A three days' journey in a moment done.
And always, at the rising of the sun,
255   About the wilds they hunt with spear and horn,
       On spleenful unicorn.

I saw Osirian Egypt kneel adown
       Before the vine-wreath crown!
I saw parched Abyssinia rouse and sing
260   To the silver cymbals' ring!
I saw the whelming vintage hotly pierce
       Old Tartary the fierce!
The kings of Inde their jewel-sceptres vail,
And from their treasures scatter pearlèd hail.

iv 244. *prance*] A favourite verb in K.'s early verse. Cp. i 744 above, *Calidore* 57, *To my Brother George* 26, *To Charles Cowden Clarke* 46 (pp. 152, 39, 50, and 56 above).

iv 245. *alligators*] Found in America and China, but not in India.

iv 247.   Arch infant crews in mimic of the coil . . . *Draft*.
'Plump infant laughters' are the *putti* of Renaissance paintings and sculpture. The word 'coil' (noisy bustle) is an Elizabethanism; cp. *Hamlet* III i 67, 'this mortal coil'.

iv 251. *panther's furs*] See *Lemprière*: 'The panther was sacred to [Bacchus], because he went on his expedition covered with the skin of that beast.'

iv 252. *scour about the plains*] The phrasing suggests a recollection of Pope's *An Essay on Criticism* (1711) 372, 'swift *Camilla* scours the plain'.

iv 256. *unicorn*] A detail not found in traditional accounts of Bacchus. C. L. Finney suggests (*Finney* 289) an echo of Chapman's *Hymnus in Cynthiam* 284–5,

        . . . in eager chase drew neare,
    Mounted on Lyons, Unicorns, and Bores . . .

iv 257. *Osirian Egypt*] Osiris was among the chief deities of the ancient Egyptian pantheon.

iv 263–4. See Rabelais, 'Es costéz du char estoient les roys indiens prins et lyés à grosses chesnes d'or. Toute la brigade marchoit . . .portans infiniz trophées, ferculles et despouilles des ennemys' (*Pantagruel* V, chap. 40).

iv 263. *vail*] See ii 793 *n*.

265   Great Brahma from his mystic heaven groans,
                And all his priesthood moans,
        Before young Bacchus' eye-wink turning pale.
        Into these regions came I following him,
        Sick hearted, weary–so I took a whim
270   To stray away into these forests drear
                Alone, without a peer.
        And I have told thee all thou mayest hear.

                Young stranger!
                I've been a ranger
275   In search of pleasure throughout every clime.
                Alas, 'tis not for me!
                Bewitched I sure must be,
        To lose in grieving all my maiden prime.

                Come then, Sorrow!
280   Sweetest Sorrow!
        Like an own babe I nurse thee on my breast.
                I thought to leave thee
                And deceive thee,
        But now of all the world I love thee best.

285   There is not one
                No, no, not one
        But thee to comfort a poor lonely maid.
                Thou art her mother,
                And her brother,
290   Her playmate, and her wooer in the shade.'

                Oh, what a sigh she gave in finishing,
        And look, quite dead to every worldly thing!
        Endymion could not speak, but gazed on her,
        And listened to the wind that now did stir
295   About the crispèd oaks full drearily,
        Yet with as sweet a softness as might be
        Remembered from its velvet summer song.

iv 265. *Great Brahma*] The supreme God in post-Vedic Hindu mythology.
Probably suggested by K.'s reading of oriental verse romances of the day,
for example Southey's *The Curse of Kehama* (1810).
iv 266. Bacchus's triumph over Osiris and Brahma probably called to K.'s
mind the passing of the old gods in Milton's *Nativity Ode* 189–1,

                In consecrated Earth,
                And on the holy Hearth,
                        The *Lars*, and *Lemures* moan with midnight plaint . . .

See *Ode to Psyche* 38–45 *n* (p. 518 below). This is followed in the draft by
the cancelled line, 'All the city gates were opened to his pomp'.

At last he said: 'Poor lady, how thus long
Have I been able to endure that voice?
300   Fair Melody! Kind Siren! I've no choice—
I must be thy sad servant evermore;
I cannot choose but kneel here and adore.
Alas, I must not think–by Phoebe, no!
Let me not think, soft Angel! Shall it be so?
305   Say, beautifullest, shall I never think?
Oh, thou could'st foster me beyond the brink
Of recollection, make my watchful care
Close up its bloodshot eyes, nor see despair!
Do gently murder half my soul and I
310   Shall feel the other half so utterly!
I'm giddy at that cheek so fair and smooth.
Oh, let it blush so ever, let it soothe
My madness, let it mantle rosy-warm
With the tinge of love, panting in safe alarm.
315   This cannot be thy hand, and yet it is.
And this is sure thine other softling–this
Thine own fair bosom, and I am so near!
Wilt fall asleep? Oh, let me sip that tear!
And whisper one sweet word that I may know
320   This is this world–sweet dewy blossom!' *Woe!*
Woe! Woe to that Endymion! Where is he?
Even these words went echoing dismally
Through the wide forest–a most fearful tone,
Like one repenting in his latest moan,
325   And while it died away a shade passed by
As of a thunder cloud. When arrows fly
Through the thick branches, poor ring-doves sleek forth
Their timid necks and tremble, so these both
Leant to each other trembling, and sat so
330   Waiting for some destruction–when lo,
Foot-feathered Mercury appeared sublime
Beyond the tall tree tops. And, in less time
Than shoots the slanted hail-storm, down he dropped
Towards the ground, but rested not, nor stopped

iv *311–14.*   That–oh how beautiful–how giddy smooth!
Blush so for ever! let those glances soothe
My madness for did I no mercy spy
Dear lady I should shudder and then die . . . *Draft.*
iv *318. let me sip that tear*] See *Isabella* 39 n (p. 329 below), 'I will drink her tears'.
iv *331. Foot-feathered Mercury*] See *I stood tip-toe* 24 n (p. 87 above).

335   One moment from his home. Only the sward
      He with his wand light touched, and heavenward
      Swifter than sight was gone—even before
      The teeming earth a sudden witness bore
      Of his swift magic. Diving swans appear
340   Above the crystal circlings white and clear,
      And catch the cheated eye in wide surprise
      How they can dive in sight and unseen rise—
      So from the turf outsprang two steeds jet-black,
      Each with large dark blue wings upon his back.
345   The youth of Caria placed the lovely dame
      On one and felt himself in spleen to tame
      The other's fierceness. Through the air they flew,
      High as the eagles. Like two drops of dew
      Exhaled to Phoebus' lips, away they are gone,
350   Far from the earth away—unseen, alone,
      Among cool clouds and winds, but that the free,
      The buoyant life of song can floating be
      Above their heads and follow them untired.
      Muse of my native land, am I inspired?
355   This is the giddy air, and I must spread
      Wide pinions to keep here. Nor do I dread
      Or height, or depth, or width, or any chance
      Precipitous. I have beneath my glance
      Those towering horses and their mournful freight.
360   Could I thus sail, and see, and thus await,
      Fearless for power of thought, without thine aid?

      There is a sleepy dusk, an odorous shade
      From some approaching wonder, and behold
      Those wingèd steeds with snorting nostrils bold
365   Snuff at its faint extreme and seem to tire,
      Dying to embers from their native fire!

      There curled a purple mist around them. Soon
      It seemed as when around the pale new moon

iv 336. *his wand*] The *caduceus*. See i 563 *n*.

iv 343. *jet-black*] coal black *Draft*. The horses were probably suggested by
K.'s reading of eastern tales: see, for example, the magical black horse depicted in the frontispiece to the 1811 edn. of *The Arabian Nights* (vol. i).

iv 346. *in spleen*] In a fiery resolute mood. See *Romeo and Juliet* III i 156–7,
                                          . . . the unruly spleen
                        Of Tybalt deaf to peace

iv 365. *snuff*] Cp. *Hyperion* i 167 *n* (p. 406 below), 'snuffed the incense'.

iv 366. Seeming but embers to their former fire . . . *Draft*.

iv 367. *curled*] comes *Draft*.

Sad Zephyr droops the clouds like weeping willow—
370 'Twas Sleep slow journeying with head on pillow.
For the first time, since he came nigh dead born
From the old womb of night, his cave forlorn
Had he left more forlorn. For the first time
He felt aloof the day and morning's prime—
375 Because into his depth Cimmerian
There came a dream, showing how a young man,
Ere a lean bat could plump its wintery skin,
Would at high Jove's empyreal footstool win
An immortality, and how espouse
380 Jove's daughter and be reckoned of his house.
Now was he slumbering towards heaven's gate,
That he might at the threshold one hour wait
To hear the marriage melodies, and then
Sink downward to his dusky cave again.
385 His litter of smooth semilucent mist,
Diversely tinged with rose and amethyst,
Puzzled those eyes that for the centre sought,
And scarcely for one moment could be caught
His sluggish form reposing motionless.
390 Those two on wingèd steeds with all the stress
Of vision searched for him, as one would look
Athwart the sallows of a river nook
To catch a glance at silver-throated eels;
Or from old Skiddaw's top, when fog conceals

iv 369. *Zephyr*] See i 326–31 *n*.

iv 370. *journeying*] voyaging *Draft*. With the whole line cp. Milton's *Comus* 553–4,

                    ... the drowsie frighted steeds
        That draw the litter of close-curtain'd sleep ...

iv 375. *Cimmerian*] Derived from Cimmerius, the ancient Asian town supposed to be perpetually shrouded in clouds. See Milton's *L'Allegro* 10,
                In dark *Cimmerian* desert ...

iv 376–80. Prophesying the happy outcome of Endymion's story.

iv 377. The bat is 'lean' after its winter sleep. K.'s colloquial use of 'plump' as a verb foreshadows *To Autumn* 7 (p. 651 below), 'plump the hazel-shells'.

iv 380 *Jove's daughter*] Phoebe was the daughter of Latona by Jupiter.

iv 384. *Sink downward to his dusky*] Betake him downward to his *Draft*.

iv 385. *smooth*] pale *Draft*.

iv 392. *sallows*] Willows. See *I stood tip-toe* 67 *n* (p. 89 above).

iv 394. *top*] front *Draft*. See iii 961 and *n*. Skiddaw was known to K. at this time through Wordsworth's poetry (see, e.g., *To Joanna*, 1800, 62 'old Skiddaw ...'). He first visited the Lakes in the summer of 1818.

10+K.

395   His rugged forehead in a mantle pale,
       With an eye-guess towards some pleasant vale
       Descry a favourite hamlet faint and far.

       These raven horses, though they fostered are
       Of earth's splenetic fire, dully drop
400   Their full-veined ears, nostrils blood-wide, and stop.
       Upon the spiritless mist have they outspread
       Their ample feathers, are in slumber dead—
       And on those pinions, level in mid air,
       Endymion sleepeth and the lady fair.

405   Slowly they sail, slowly as icy isle
       Upon a calm sea drifting, and meanwhile
       The mournful wanderer dreams. Behold, he walks
       On heaven's pavement; brotherly he talks
       To divine powers; from his hand full fain
410   Juno's proud birds are pecking pearly grain;
       He tries the nerve of Phoebus' golden bow
       And asketh where the golden apples grow;
       Upon his arm he braces Pallas' shield,
       And strives in vain to unsettle and wield

415   A Jovian thunderbolt; arch Hebe brings
       A full-brimmed goblet, dances lightly, sings
       And tantalizes long; at last he drinks,
       And lost in pleasure at her feet he sinks,
       Touching with dazzled lips her starlight hand.

420   He blows a bugle—an ethereal band
       Are visible above: the Seasons four—

iv 399. splenetic] See iv 346 n.
iv 400. blood-wide] Wide open and suffused with blood.
iv 407. The mournful wanderer] Endymion.
iv 410. proud birds] Peacocks, traditionally associated with the goddess Juno.
iv 413. Pallas' shield] Pallas Athene was the goddess of wisdom and war.
See Lemprière: 'Usually she was represented with a helmet on her head. . . .
In one hand she held a spear, and in the other a shield, with the dying head
of Medusa upon it.'
iv 415. Hebe] Juno's daughter and cup-bearer to the gods before the advent
of Ganymede (see i 170 n).
iv 418. With pleasure at her knees he swoons and sinks . . . Draft.
iv 420. He takes a bugle, blows it, an aerial band . . . Draft.
iv 420-6. an ethereal band . . . Hours] See Sandys's Ovid ii (p. 25, cols. 1-2),
       Sol, clothèd in purple, sits upon a Throne
       Which clerely with translucent Emralds shone.
       With equall-raigning Houres on either hand,
       The dayes, the Moneths, the Yeares, the Ages stand:
       The fragrant Spring with flowry chaplet crown'd:

Green-kirtled Spring, flush Summer, golden store
In Autumn's sickle, Winter frosty hoar –
Join dance with shadowy Hours; while still the blast,
425   In swells unmitigated, still doth last
To sway their floating morris. 'Whose is this?
Whose bugle?' he inquires. They smile. 'O Dis!
Why is this mortal here? Dost thou not know
Its mistress' lips? Not thou? 'Tis Dian's. Lo!
430   She rises crescented!' He looks, 'tis she,
His very goddess. Good-bye earth, and sea,
And air, and pains, and care, and suffering.
Good-bye to all but love! Then doth he spring
Towards her, and awakes – and, strange, o'erhead,
435   Of those same fragrant exhalations bred,
Beheld awake his very dream. The gods
Stood smiling, merry Hebe laughs and nods,
And Phoebe bends towards him crescented.
Oh, state perplexing! On the pinion bed,
440   Too well awake, he feels the panting side
Of his delicious lady. He who died
For soaring too audacious in the sun,
When that same treacherous wax began to run,
Felt not more tongue-tied than Endymion.
445   His heart leapt up as to its rightful throne,

Wheat-eares, the brows of naked Summer bound:
Rich Autumne smear'd with crusht *Lyaeus'* blood;
Next, hoary-headed Winter quivering stood ...
iv *426. their floating morris*] Their airy dance. See Milton's *Comus* 116,
Now to the Moon in wavering Morrice move ...
iv *427. Dis*] See iii 567 *n.*
iv *429–30. 'Tis Dian's ... she*] Ah, Ah, Ah, Ah!
   'Tis Dian's, here she comes, look out afar ... *Draft, Fair copy.*
iv *430–1. 'tis she ... goddess*] Endymion's unknown goddess and Phoebe
(Diana) are identified in his dream.
iv *436. Beheld awake his very dream*] See K.'s letter to Bailey of 22 Nov. 1817,
'The Imagination may be compared to Adam's dream – he awoke and
found it truth' (see iv 146–81 *n*).
iv *442–4.* Because in sunshine treacherous wax would melt.
   Even at the fatal melting thereof, felt
   Not more tongue-tied than did Endymion ... *Draft.*
Alludes to the legend of Icarus: see *Sleep and Poetry* 302–3 *n* (p. 82 above).
iv *445. His heart leapt up*] Perhaps echoing Wordsworth's *The Rainbow*
(1807) 1–2,
      My heart leaps up when I behold
      A rainbow in the sky ...

To that fair shadowed passion pulsed its way—
Ah, what perplexity! Ah, well-a-day!
So fond, so beauteous was his bed-fellow,
He could not help but kiss her. Then he grew
450 Awhile forgetful of all beauty save
Young Phoebe's, golden haired, and so 'gan crave
Forgiveness. Yet he turned once more to look
At the sweet sleeper—all his soul was shook;
She pressed his hand in slumber, so once more
455 He could not help but kiss her and adore.
At this the shadow wept, melting away.
The Latmian started up: 'Bright goddess, stay!
Search my most hidden breast! By truth's own tongue,
I have no daedal heart. Why is it wrung
460 To desperation? Is there nought for me,
Upon the bourne of bliss, but misery?'

These words awoke the stranger of dark tresses.
Her dawning love-look rapt Endymion blesses
With 'haviour soft. Sleep yawned from underneath.
465 'Thou swan of Ganges, let us no more breathe
This murky phantasm! Thou contented seem'st
Pillowed in lovely idleness, nor dream'st
What horrors may discomfort thee and me.
Ah, shouldst thou die from my heart-treachery!
470 Yet did she merely weep—her gentle soul
Hath no revenge in it. As it is whole
In tenderness, would I were whole in love!
Can I prize thee, fair maid, all price above,
Even when I feel as true as innocence?
475 I do, I do. What is this soul then? Whence

iv 453. *was shook*] A forced archaism for the sake of the rhyme.
iv 455. *kiss her*] kiss, kiss *Draft*.
iv 458. *truth's own tongue*] See iv 474 *n*.
iv 459. *daedal*] An epithet suggesting intricacy and cunning derived from Daedalus, the cunning artificer (see *Sleep and Poetry* 302–3 *n*, p. 82 above). Spenser has *The Faerie Queene* III, Prologue l.13,
His daedale hand would faile . . .
The word was also a favourite with Shelley, e.g., *Prometheus Unbound* (1820) iv 416, 'Daedal harmony'.
iv 462. *stranger*] lady *Draft*.
iv 463. *love-look*] love-glance *Draft*.
iv 465. *Thou swan of Ganges*] Thou wandering fair one *Draft*.
iv 474. Echoes *Troilus and Cressida* III ii 168–9 (marked by K. in his folio Shakespeare at Hampstead),

Came it? It does not seem my own, and I
Have no self-passion or identity.
Some fearful end must be. Where, where is it?
By Nemesis, I see my spirit flit
480   Alone about the dark. Forgive me, sweet—
Shall we away?' He roused the steeds. They beat
Their wings chivalrous into the clear air,
Leaving old Sleep within his vapoury lair.

The good-night blush of eve was waning slow,
485   And Vesper, risen star, began to throe
In the dusk heavens silverly when they
Thus sprang direct towards the Galaxy.
Nor did speed hinder converse soft and strange—
Eternal oaths and vows they interchange
490   In such wise, in such temper, so aloof
Up in the winds, beneath a starry roof,
So witless of their doom, that verily
'Tis well nigh past man's search their hearts to see,
Whether they wept, or laughed, or grieved, or toyed—
495   Most like with joy gone mad, with sorrow cloyed.

Full facing their swift flight, from ebon streak,

I am as true as truth's simplicity,
And simpler than the infancy of truth . . .
Cp. iv 458 above, 'truth's own tongue'.

iv 475–7. *What is this soul . . . my own*] Probably a reminiscence of Troilus on Cressida's duplicity in *Troilus and Cressida* V ii 134–5,
This she? no, this is Diomed's Cressida.
If beauty have a soul this is not she . . .

iv 479. *Nemesis*] See *Lemprière*: 'One of the infernal deities, daughter of Nox. She was the goddess of vengeance, and represented always prepared to punish impiety, and at the same time liberally to reward the good and virtuous.'

iv 483. *within*] to sail in *Draft*.

iv 484. *blush*] hush *Draft*.

iv 485. *Vesper, risen star*] Vesper's timid pulse *Draft*.

iv 492. *witless of their doom*] Perhaps a reminiscence of Gray's *Ode on a Distant Prospect of Eton College* (1747) 51–2,
Alas, regardless of their doom,
The little victims play . . .
For 'their doom' the draft reads 'all things'.

iv 495. *joy*] woe *Draft*. On 'cloyed' cp. *Sleep and Poetry* 178 n (p. 77 above), 'the Muses were nigh cloyed'.

iv 496–502. Perhaps written 22 Nov. 1817 on K.'s arrival at Burford Bridge. See his letter to Reynolds of this date, '. . . I like this place very

The moon put forth a little diamond peak,
No bigger than an unobservèd star,
Or tiny point of fairy scimitar,
500   Bright signal that she only stooped to tie
Her silver sandals ere deliciously
She bowed into the heavens her timid head.
Slowly she rose, as though she would have fled,
While to his lady meek the Carian turned,
505   To mark if her dark eyes had yet discerned
This beauty in its birth. Despair! Despair!
He saw her body fading gaunt and spare
In the cold moonshine. Straight he seized her wrist;
It melted from his grasp. Her hand he kissed,
510   And, horror, kissed his own–he was alone.
Her steed a little higher soared, and then
Dropped hawkwise to the earth.

There lies a den,
Beyond the seeming confines of the space
Made for the soul to wander in and trace
515   Its own existence, of remotest glooms.
Dark regions are around it, where the tombs
Of buried griefs the spirit sees, but scarce
One hour doth linger weeping, for the pierce
Of new-born woe it feels more inly smart.
520   And in these regions many a venomed dart
At random flies; they are the proper home
Of every ill; the man is yet to come
Who hath not journeyed in this native hell.
But few have ever felt how calm and well

much–There is Hill and Dale and a little River–I went up Box Hill this
Evening after the Moon–you 'a seen the Moon–came down–and wrote
some lines' (L i 188).

iv *506. This beauty in its birth*] Such beauty being born *Draft*.

iv *512–54. There lies a den ... high feast*] K.'s description of the 'Cave of
Quietude' (see below l. 548) is a characteristic statement about the necessary connection between suffering and creativity. An essay on the passage
and its significance in K.'s poetic development appears in *Murry* (1949)
118–50.

iv *513. Beyond*] Of misery beyond *Draft*.

iv *520. venomed*] random *Draft*.

iv *522. the man*] that soul *Draft*.

iv *524–48*. See *Murry* (1949) 127: 'There is a sudden passing sorrow and
joy which comes unsought for. If it is sought for, it is not found. It comes

525 Sleep may be had in that deep den of all.
    There anguish does not sting, nor pleasure pall.
    Woe-hurricanes beat ever at the gate,
    Yet all is still within and desolate.
    Beset with plainful gusts, within ye hear
530 No sound so loud as when on curtained bier
    The death-watch tick is stifled. Enter none
    Who strive therefore—on the sudden it is won.
    Just when the sufferer begins to burn,
    Then it is free to him, and from an urn,
535 Still fed by melting ice, he takes a draught—
    Young Semele such richness never quaffed
    In her maternal longing! Happy gloom!
    Dark paradise! Where pale becomes the bloom
    Of health by due; where silence dreariest
540 Is most articulate; where hopes infest;
    Where those eyes are the brightest far that keep
    Their lids shut longest in a dreamless sleep.
    O happy spirit-home! O wondrous soul!
    Pregnant with such a den to save the whole
545 In thine own depth. Hail, gentle Carian!
    For never since thy griefs and woes began
    Hast thou felt so content. A grievous feud
    Hath led thee to this Cave of Quietude.
    Aye, his lulled soul was there, although upborne

---

when misery has reached its extreme point; then the misery marvellously
changes into a profound content . . . in this calm ecstasy of despair, the
whole of the sufferer is bathed and renewed.'

iv 526–7.   There anguish stings not—sweetness cannot pall:
                Dark hurricanes of woe beat ever at the gate . . . *Draft*.

iv 531. *death-watch*] 'Any of various insects which make a noise like the
ticking of a watch, supposed by the superstitious to portend death' (*OED*).
The 'tick' is 'stifled' because death has taken place. For 'stifled' the draft
has 'muffled'.

iv 534. *Then it*] This den *Draft*.

iv 536. *Semele*] The mother of Bacchus by Jupiter.

iv 537–42. *Happy gloom . . . dreamless sleep*] A series of paradoxes. Cp. i
455–6 n,

                                    . . . O unconfined
                Restraint! Imprisoned liberty . . .

iv 539. *Of health by due*] An earlier attempt was 'A rightful tinge of
health . . .'

iv 542. *shut*] close *Draft*.

iv 546. *woes*] joys *Draft*.

550 With dangerous speed, and so he did not mourn
Because he knew not whither he was going.
So happy was he, not the aerial blowing
Of trumpets at clear parley from the east
Could rouse from that fine relish, that high feast.
555 They stung the feathered horse—with fierce alarm
He flapped towards the sound. Alas, no charm
Could lift Endymion's head, or he had viewed
A skyey masque, a pinioned multitude—
And silvery was its passing. Voices sweet
560 Warbling the while as if to lull and greet
The wanderer in his path. Thus warbled they,
While past the vision went in bright array.

'Who, who from Dian's feast would be away?
For all the golden bowers of the day
565 Are empty left? Who, who away would be
From Cynthia's wedding and festivity?
Not Hesperus—lo! upon his silver wings
He leans away for highest heaven and sings,
Snapping his lucid fingers merrily!

iv 554–6. *Could rouse ... sound*]

> Could rouse from inward feast–and yet to hear't
> 'Twas like a gift of Prophecy–alert
> The feather'd horse he snorted with alarm
> And towards it flapp'd away ... *Draft*.

iv 554. *fine relish ... high feast*] K.'s luxurious enjoyment of the psychological relief described.

iv 558. *masque*] mask *Draft, Fair copy*. K. was familiar with this kind of entertainment from his reading of Milton and the Elizabethans, but he may be recollecting in particular the masque celebrating the union of Ferdinand and Miranda in *The Tempest* IV i 60–138.

iv 567. *Hesperus*] See i 531 *n* (p. 144 above). Perhaps suggested here by Ben Jonson's *Hymn to Diana* 1–6,

> *Queene*, and *Huntresse*, chaste, and faire,
> Now the *Sunne* is laid to sleepe,
> Seated, in thy silver chaire,
> State in wonted manner keepe:
> HESPERUS intreats thy light,
> Goddesse, excellently bright ...

See ii 170–1 *n* above.

iv 569. Followed in the draft by the lines,

> He stay behind–he glad of lazy plea?
> Not he! not he! ...

The word 'lucid' here means shining.

570   Ah, Zephyrus, art here, and Flora too!
      Ye tender bibbers of the rain and dew,
      Young playmates of the rose and daffodil,
      Be careful, ere ye enter in, to fill
            Your baskets high
575   With fennel green, and balm, and golden pines,
      Savory, latter-mint, and columbines,
      Cool parsley, basil sweet, and sunny thyme—
      Yea, every flower and leaf of every clime,
      All gathered in the dewy morning. Hie
580   Away! Fly, fly,
      Crystalline brother of the belt of heaven,
      Aquarius, to whom king Jove has given
      Two liquid pulse streams 'stead of feathered wings,
      Two fan-like fountains—thine illuminings
585   For Dian play!
      Dissolve the frozen purity of air;
      Let thy white shoulders silvery and bare
      Show cold through watery pinions; make more bright

iv 570. *art here*] [Thou] art here. On Zephyrus see i 326–31 *n* and on Flora *Sleep and Poetry* 102 *n* (pp. 134 and 73 above). Their association is a poetical commonplace, for example *Paradise Lost* V 16,

       Milde, as when *Zephyrus* on *Flora* breathes . . .

iv 573. Mind ere ye enter in to oppress and fill . . . *Draft.*

iv 575. *balm*] A fragrant herb, for example Balm-mint, Balm Gentle.

iv 576. *latter-mint*] A coinage, perhaps meaning late-growing mint. For 'latter' the draft version has 'early'.

iv 581–605. Figures from the Zodiac and the constellations join in the masque celebrating Phoebe's wedding. K. may owe some details to his early reading of Spence's *Polymetis*, Dialogue xi, 'Of the Constellations; Planets: Times and Seasons'.

iv 581–90. Copied out by K. in his letter to Reynolds 22 Nov. 1817 with the comment, 'By the Whim King! I'll give you a Stanza . . . when I wrote it I wanted you to—give your vote, pro or con' (*L* i 189). See *Colvin* (1917), 'one of the weakest things in the poem: pity Reynolds had not been there indeed, to give his vote contra' (153).

iv 581. *the belt of heaven*] Cp. Drayton's *The Man in the Moone* 390, 'the bright Girdle of the Zodiake'.

iv 582. *Aquarius*] The Water-Carrier, sometimes identified with Jupiter's cup-bearer Ganymede (i 170 *n*). See Sandys's commentary on Ovid's *Metamorphoses* x, 'Ganymed . . . is . . . fained to have been converted into the winter figure of *Aquarius*; and because abundance of raine is powred upon the Earth from the clouds when the Sunne is in that signe, he is said to be Jupiter's cup-bearer' (Sandys's *Ovid*, p. 196).

The Star-Queen's crescent on her marriage night.
590   Haste, haste away!
Castor has tamed the planet Lion, see!
And of the Bear has Pollux mastery.
A third is in the race! Who is the third
Speeding away swift as the eagle bird?
595   The ramping Centaur!
The Lion's mane's on end, the Bear how fierce!
The Centaur's arrow ready seems to pierce
Some enemy—far forth his bow is bent
Into the blue of heaven. He'll be shent,
600   Pale unrelenter,
When he shall hear the wedding lutes a-playing.
Andromeda, sweet woman! Why delaying
So timidly among the stars? Come hither!
Join this bright throng and nimbly follow whither
605   They all are going.
Danae's Son, before Jove newly bowed,
Has wept for thee, calling to Jove aloud.
Thee, gentle lady, did he disenthral.
Ye shall for ever live and love, for all
610   Thy tears are flowing.
By Daphne's fright, behold Apollo!—'

iv 589. *Star-Queen*] Night-Queen *Draft*.
iv 591–2. *Castor . . . Pollux*] Twin sons of Jupiter by Leda. They were transformed into the constellation Gemini.
iv 593. *A third is*] Ay three are *Draft*.
iv 597–9. *The Centaur's arrow . . . heaven*] See Spence's commentary on the Farnese Globe, 'Arcitenens . . . was represented under the figure of a satyr. . . . He held his bow as just ready to shoot it off; and the arrow in it seems to aim at the tail of Scorpius. The artists in process of time substituted the form of a Centaur, instead of that of a satyr, for this sign of the Zodiac' (*Polymetis*, Dialogue xi).
iv 599. *shent*] Scolded. An Elizabethanism. See, for example, *Troilus and Cressida* II iii 79, 'He shent our messengers'.
iv 602. *Andromeda*] The story of Andromeda and her rescuer Perseus is related in Ovid's *Metamorphoses* iv 663–752.
iv 606. *Danae's son*] Perseus. See Spence's commentary on the Farnese Globe, 'We now come to a set of constellations, that have all some relation to one another . . . the person . . . with her arms extended is Andromeda herself: and next to her is her deliverer' (*Dialogue* xi 167).
iv 611. *Daphne . . . Apollo*] Daphne was saved from Apollo's amorous pursuit by being transformed into a laurel tree (Ovid's *Metamorphoses* i 452–57).

More
Endymion heard not. Down his steed him bore,
Prone to the green head of a misty hill.

His first touch of the earth went nigh to kill.
615   'Alas!' said he, 'were I but always borne
Through dangerous winds, had but my footsteps worn
A path in hell, for ever would I bless
Horrors which nourish an uneasiness
For my own sullen conquering. To him
620   Who lives beyond earth's boundary grief is dim,
Sorrow is but a shadow. Now I see
The grass, I feel the solid ground. Ah, me!
It is thy voice–divinest! Where? Who, who
Left thee so quiet on this bed of dew?
625   Behold upon this happy earth we are.
Let us ay love each other. Let us fare
On forest-fruits, and never, never go
Among the abodes of mortals here below,
Or be by phantoms duped. O destiny!
630   Into a labyrinth now my soul would fly,
But with thy beauty will I deaden it.
Where didst thou melt to? By thee will I sit
For ever. Let our fate stop here–a kid
I on this spot will offer. Pan will bid
635   Us live in peace, in love and peace among
His forest wildernesses. I have clung
To nothing, loved a nothing, nothing seen
Or felt but a great dream! Oh, I have been
Presumptuous against love, against the sky,
640   Against all elements, against the tie
Of mortals each to each, against the blooms
Of flowers, rush of rivers, and the tombs

iv 613. *the green head of a misty hill*] Foreshadows *Ode to Melancholy* 14
(p. 540 below), 'the green hill in an April shroud'.

iv 614. See i 681–705 *n*.

iv 616–21. '*Alas!* . . . *shadow*] Horrors in my imaginative flights were no
more than spurs to my spirit and ultimately unreal.

iv 621. *The grass*] The real grass *Draft, Fair copy*.

iv 623. *It is . . . divinest*] Phoebe has resumed her role as the Indian maid.

iv 636–8. *I have clung . . . great dream*] The phrasing suggests an echo of *A
Midsummer Night's Dream* IV i 206–9, 'I have had a most rare vision. I have
had a dream, past the wit of man to say what dream it was: man is but an
ass, if he go about to expound this dream.'

iv 641. *each to each*] to each other *Draft*.

iv 642. *flowers*] roses *Draft*.

Of heroes gone! Against his proper glory
Has my own soul conspired. So my story
645   Will I to children utter, and repent.
There never lived a mortal man who bent
His appetite beyond his natural sphere
But starved and died. My sweetest Indian, here,
Here will I kneel, for thou redeemèd hast
650   My life from too thin breathing. Gone and past
Are cloudy phantasms. Caverns lone, farewell,
And air of visions, and the monstrous swell
Of visionary seas! No, never more
Shall airy voices cheat me to the shore
655   Of tangled wonder, breathless and aghast.
Adieu, my daintiest dream, although so vast
My love is still for thee. The hour may come
When we shall meet in pure elysium.
On earth I may not love thee, and therefore
660   Doves will I offer up and sweetest store
All through the teeming year. So thou wilt shine
On me and on this damsel fair of mine
And bless our silver lives. My Indian bliss!
My river-lily bud! One human kiss!
665   One sigh of real breath—one gentle squeeze,
Warm as a dove's nest among summer trees,
And warm with dew at ooze from living blood!
Whither didst melt? Ah, what of that! All good

iv *643. his*] its *Draft.*

iv *646–55.* Perhaps a deliberate rejection of Shelley's visionary idealism in *Alastor* (1816).

iv *650. life . . . breathing*] spirit . . . a breath *Draft.*

iv *650–5. gone . . . aghast*] A recollection of Milton's *Comus* 205–9,

                . . . A thousand fantasies
      Begin to throng my memory
      Of calling shapes, and beckning shadows dire,
      And airy tongues, that syllable mens names
      On Sands, and Shoars, and desert Wildernesses . . .

iv *656. although so vast*] how vast, how vast *Draft.* The word 'daintiest' may be owed to *The Tempest* V i 95, 'my dainty Ariel! I shall miss thee'.

iv *663. silver lives*] Perhaps lives lived under the moon's dominion.

iv *664. human*] mortal *Draft.*

iv *665. one gentle squeeze*] A phrase illustrating what Colvin calls '. . . the simpering familiar mood which Keats at this time had caught from or naturally shared with Leigh Hunt' (*Colvin* (1917) 214).

iv *667.* An elegant periphrasis for the Indian maid's perspiration.

iv *668. Whither didst melt?*] The answer is supplied by the rising of the moon at iv 496–508 above.

We'll talk about—no more of dreaming. Now,
670 Where shall our dwelling be? Under the brow
Of some steep mossy hill, where ivy dun
Would hide us up, although spring leaves were none,
And where dark yew trees, as we rustle through,
Will drop their scarlet berry cups of dew?
675 Oh, thou wouldst joy to live in such a place,
Dusk for our loves, yet light enough to grace
Those gentle limbs on mossy bed reclined.
For by one step the blue sky shouldst thou find,
And by another, in deep dell below,
680 See, through the trees, a little river go
All in its mid-day gold and glimmering.
Honey from out the gnarlèd hive I'll bring,
And apples, wan with sweetness, gather thee,
Cresses that grow where no man may them see,
685 And sorrel untorn by the dew-clawed stag.
Pipes will I fashion of the syrinx flag
That thou mayst always know whither I roam
When it shall please thee in our quiet home
To listen and think of love. Still let me speak,
690 Still let me dive into the joy I seek—
For yet the past doth prison me. The rill,
Thou haply mayest delight in, will I fill
With fairy fishes from the mountain tarn,
And thou shalt feed them from the squirrel's barn.
695 Its bottom will I strew with amber shells
And pebbles blue from deep enchanted wells.
Its sides I'll plant with dew-sweet eglantine

iv *670–721.* K.'s 'pastoral fantasia' (*Colvin* (1917) 201) may be inspired by
Polyphemus's wooing of Galatea in Ovid's *Metamorphoses* xiii 810–39, with
some additional hints from Marlowe's *The Passionate Shepherd to his Love*
(1599). For an earlier echo of Marlowe's poem see i 924 *n.*
iv *682. hive*] nest *Draft.*
iv *685. dew-clawed*] Dappled with dew.
iv *686.* Recollecting the legend of Pan and Syrinx, the nymph who was
changed 'into a reed called Syrinx by the Greeks' (*Lemprière*); see *I stood tip
toe* 159–62 *n* (p. 93 above). The word 'flag' is used here to mean a reed-
like plant which grows in moist places.
iv *687. mayest always know*] by ear mayst know *Draft.*
iv *691. prison me*] weigh me down *Draft.*
iv *693. the mountain tarn*] A Wordsworthian detail. Cp. iv 394 *n.*
iv *694. barn*] Hoard.
iv *697. eglantine*] See *Ode to a Nightingale* 46 (p. 528 below), 'the pastoral
eglantine'.

And honeysuckles full of clear bee-wine.
I will entice this crystal rill to trace
700   Love's silver name upon the meadow's face.
I'll kneel to Vesta for a flame of fire;
And to god Phoebus for a golden lyre;
To Empress Dian for a hunting spear;
To Vesper for a taper silver-clear,
705   That I may see thy beauty through the night;
To Flora, and a nightingale shall light
Tame on thy finger; to the River-gods,
And they shall bring thee taper fishing-rods
Of gold and lines of naiad's long bright tress.
710   Heaven shield thee for thine utter loveliness!
Thy mossy footstool shall the altar be
'Fore which I'll bend, bending, dear love, to thee.
Those lips shall be my Delphos and shall speak
Laws to my footsteps, colour to my cheek,
715   Trembling or stedfastness to this same voice,
And of three sweetest pleasurings the choice.
And that affectionate light, those diamond things,
Those eyes, those passions, those supreme pearl springs,
Shall be my grief or twinkle me to pleasure.
720   Say, is not bliss within our perfect seizure?
Oh, that I could not doubt!'

                                    The mountaineer
Thus strove by fancies vain and crude to clear
His briared path to some tranquillity.

iv 698. *full of clear bee-wine*] See *Ode to a Nightingale* 49 (p. 528 below),
'full of dewy wine'.

iv 699. *entice*] make *Fair copy* (*cancelled*). The word 'trace' means 'to form
the letters of'. This is followed in the fair copy by,

> And by it shalt thou sit and sing, hey nonny!
> While doves coo to thee for a little honey . . .

iv 701. *Vesta*] The Roman goddess of the hearth. See Sandys's *Ovid*, *Metamorphoses* xv (p. 278, col. 2),

> Chast *Vesta*, with thy ever-burning fire . . .

iv 704. *Vesper*] See i 363 n.

iv 706. *Flora*] See *Sleep and Poetry* 102 n (p. 73 above).

iv 709. *naiad's*] See ii 129 n above.

iv 713. *my Delphos*] My oracle.

iv 716. And the most velvet peaches to my choice . . . *Draft*. The other
two 'sweet pleasurings' are left in a discreet obscurity.

iv 720. *Say, is not*] Is not, then *Draft*.

It gave bright gladness to his lady's eye,
725 And yet the tears she wept were tears of sorrow,
Answering thus, just as the golden morrow
Beamed upward from the valleys of the east:
'Oh, that the flutter of this heart had ceased,
Or the sweet name of love had passed away.
730 Young feathered tyrant, by a swift decay
Wilt thou devote this body to the earth.
And I do think that at my very birth
I lisped thy blooming titles inwardly,
For at the first, first dawn and thought of thee,
735 With uplift hands I blessed the stars of heaven.
Art thou not cruel? Ever have I striven
To think thee kind, but ah, it will not do!
When yet a child I heard that kisses drew
Favour from thee and so I kisses gave
740 To the void air, bidding them find out love.
But when I came to feel how far above
All fancy, pride, and fickle maidenhood,
All earthly pleasure, all imagined good,
Was the warm tremble of a devout kiss —
745 Even then, that moment, at the thought of this,
Fainting I fell into a bed of flowers,
And languished there three days. Ye milder powers,
Am I not cruelly wronged? Believe, believe
Me, dear Endymion, were I to weave
750 With my own fancies garlands of sweet life,
Thou shouldst be one of all. Ah, bitter strife!
I may not be thy love. I am forbidden,
Indeed I am — thwarted, affrighted, chidden
By things I trembled at and gorgon wrath.
755 Twice hast thou asked whither I went. Henceforth
Ask me no more! I may not utter it,
Nor may I be thy love. We might commit

iv 724. There was rejoicing in his Lady's eye . . . *Draft* (cancelled).
iv 726. *just as*] what time *Draft*.
iv 730–48. Addressed to Cupid.
iv 730. *Young feathered tyrant*] Cupid.
iv 739. An unrhymed line.
iv 744. The phrasing follows Hunt.
iv 748. *wronged*] served *Fair copy* (cancelled).
iv 751–4. *Ah, bitter strife . . . wrath*] See ii 179–80 n.
iv 750–1. *With . . . all*]

> My own imaginations to sweet life
> Thou would'st o'ertop them all . . . *Draft*.

Ourselves at once to vengeance; we might die;
We might embrace and die—voluptuous thought!
760   Enlarge not to my hunger or I'm caught
In trammels of perverse deliciousness.
No, no, that shall not be. Thee will I bless,
And bid a long adieu.'

The Carian

No word returned. Both lovelorn, silent, wan,
765   Into the valleys green together went.
Far wandering, they were perforce content
To sit beneath a fair lone beechen tree,
Nor at each other gazed, but heavily
Pored on its hazel cirque of shedded leaves.

770   Endymion! Unhappy! It nigh grieves
Me to behold thee thus in last extreme—
Enskied ere this but truly that I deem
Truth the best music in a first-born song.
Thy lute-voiced brother will I sing ere long,
775   And thou shalt aid—hast thou not aided me?
Yes, moonlight emperor! Felicity
Has been thy meed for many thousand years,
Yet often have I, on the brink of tears,

iv *759.* See *Ode to a Nightingale* 55 and *n* (p. 529 below),
       Now more than ever seems it rich to die . . .

iv *760. Enlarge not to my hunger*] Do not become too seductive a bait. The words are addressed to 'voluptuous thought'.

iv *764. lovelorn, silent, wan*] A grouping of epithets probably influenced by K.'s early reading of Chatterton. See *La Belle Dame Sans Merci* 6 *n* (p. 502 below).

iv *766. Far*] Long *Draft*.

iv *769. cirque of shedded*] carpet of shed *Draft*. The word 'cirque' (circle) may be a Wordsworthian echo. See *Hyperion* ii 34–5 and ii 34 *n* (p. 419 below),
       . . . like a dismal cirque
     Of Druid stones . . .

iv *770–5.* K.'s interpolation expressing his sense of poetic apprenticeship and faith in the legend of Endymion as a source of inspiration for *Hyperion* (p. 394 below).

iv *772.* That hadst been high ere this, but that I deem *Draft*. 'Enskied' is probably owed to *Measure for Measure* I iv 34,
       I hold you as a thing ensky'd and sainted . . .

iv *774. Thy lute-voiced brother*] Apollo, Diana's brother (and therefore also Endymion's), whom K. planned to celebrate as Hyperion's successor; see *Hyperion* ii 262–95, iii 28–136 (pp. 429–30 and 436–41 below).

iv *778. on the brink of*] mid some foolish *Draft*.

Mourned as if yet thou wert a forester,
Forgetting the old tale.

780   He did not stir
His eyes from the dead leaves or one small pulse
Of joy he might have felt. The spirit culls
Unfaded amaranth when wild it strays
Through the old garden-ground of boyish days.

785 A little onward ran the very stream
By which he took his first soft poppy-dream,
And on the very bark 'gainst which he leant
A crescent he had carved, and round it spent
His skill in little stars. The teeming tree

790 Had swollen and greened the pious charactery,
But not ta'en out. Why, there was not a slope
Up which he had not feared the antelope;
And not a tree, beneath whose rooty shade
He had not with his tamèd leopards played;

795 Nor could an arrow light or javelin
Fly in the air where his had never been—
And yet he knew it not.

                          Oh, treachery!
Why does his lady smile, pleasing her eye
With all his sorrowing? He sees her not.

800 But who so stares on him? His sister sure!
Peona of the woods! Can she endure—

iv *783. wild*] perchance *Draft*. The word 'amaranth' (an imaginary unfading flower) is probably owed to Milton's *Paradise Lost* iii 352–6,

> Thir Crowns inwove with Amarant and Gold,
> Immortal Amarant, a Flour which once
> In Paradise, fast by the Tree of Life
> Began to bloom, but soon for mans offence
> To Heav'n remov'd where first it grew, there grows,
> And flours aloft shading the Fount of Life ...

The last two lines are marked by K. in his copy of Milton.

iv *784.* The Eden-like world of childhood.

iv *786. his first soft poppy-dream*] See i 552–671.

iv *791. ta'en out*] effac'd *Draft*.

iv *792. feared*] Frightened. Frequently in the Elizabethans, e.g. *The Merchant of Venice* II i 8–9,

>   ... this aspect of mine
>   Hath fear'd the valiant ...

The draft reads 'chaced'.

iv *794. tamèd leopards*] jessied falcons *Draft*.

iv *801–2. Can she endure— / Impossible!*] The meaning is probably, 'How can she bear to see Endymion's unhappiness?'

Impossible! How dearly they embrace!
His lady smiles, delight is in her face—
It is no treachery.

'Dear brother mine!
805 Endymion, weep not so! Why shouldst thou pine
When all great Latmos so exalt will be?
Thank the great gods, and look not bitterly,
And speak not one pale word, and sigh no more.
Sure I will not believe thou hast such store
810 Of grief, to last thee to my kiss again.
Thou surely canst not bear a mind in pain,
Come hand in hand with one so beautiful.
Be happy both of you, for I will pull
The flowers of autumn for your coronals.
815 Pan's holy priest for young Endymion calls,
And when he is restored, thou, fairest dame,
Shalt be our queen. Now, is it not a shame
To see ye thus—not very, very sad?
Perhaps ye are too happy to be glad.
820 Oh, feel as if it were a common day,
Free-voiced as one who never was away.
No tongue shall ask, "Whence come ye?", but ye shall
Be gods of your own rest imperial.
Not even I, for one whole month, will pry

iv 808. *and sigh no more*] nor sigh once more *Draft.* Cp. Balthazar's song
Much Ado About Nothing II iii 61,

Sigh no more, ladies, sigh no more . . .

iv *811–13. Thou surely . . . of you*]

Were this sweet damsel like a long neck'd crane
Or an old rocking barn owl half asleep
Some reason would there be for thee to keep
So dull-eyed—but thou knowest she's beautiful
Yes, Yes! and thou dost love her well—I'll pull . . . *Draft.*

iv *815. Pan's holy priest*] Great Pan's high priest *Draft.*
iv *816. And when he is*] This Shepherd Prince *Draft.*
iv *819.* Earlier attempts in the draft were
    1. Perhaps ye feel too much joy—too overglad . . .
    2. Perhaps ye are too glad, too overglad . . .
iv *820.* Perhaps suggested by Wordsworth's *Excursion*, 'Prospectus' 52–5,
    . . . the discerning intellect of Man,
    When wedded to this goodly universe
    In love and holy passion, shall find these
    A simple produce of the common day . . .

Cp. I i *n* above.

825 Into the hours that have passed us by
  Since in my arbour I did sing to thee.
  O Hermes, on this very night will be
  A hymning up to Cynthia, queen of light
  For the soothsayers old saw yesternight

830 Good visions in the air, whence will befall,
  As say these sages, health perpetual
  To shepherds and their flocks; and furthermore,
  In Dian's face they read the gentle lore.
  Therefore for her these vesper-carols are.

835 Our friends will all be there from nigh and far.
  Many upon thy death have ditties made,
  And many, even now, their foreheads shade
  With cypress on a day of sacrifice.
  New singing for our maids shalt thou devise

840 And pluck the sorrow from our huntsmen's brows.
  Tell me, my lady-queen, how to espouse
  This wayward brother to his rightful joys!
  His eyes are on thee bent, as thou didst poise
  His fate most goddess-like. Help me, I pray,

845 To lure—Endymion, dear brother, say
  What ails thee?' He could bear no more, and so
  Bent his soul fiercely like a spiritual bow
  And twanged it inwardly, and calmly said:
  'I would have thee my only friend, sweet maid,

850 My only visitor! Not ignorant, though,
  That those deceptions which for pleasure go
  'Mong men are pleasures real as real may be.
  But there are higher ones I may not see
  If impiously an earthly realm I take.

855 Since I saw thee, I have been wide awake
  Night after night and day by day until
  Of the empyrean I have drunk my fill.
  Let it content thee, sister, seeing me
  More happy than betides mortality.

860 A hermit young, I'll live in mossy cave,
  Where thou alone shalt come to me and lave
  Thy spirit in the wonders I shall tell.
  Through me the shepherd realm shall prosper well,
  For to thy tongue will I all health confide.

865 And, for my sake, let this young maid abide

iv 827. *O Hermes . . . night*] Why! hark ye! . . . eve *Draft*.
iv 840. *sorrow*] cypress *Draft*.
iv 853. *there are*] I have *Draft*.
iv 859. *betides*] Befits.

With thee as a dear sister. Thou alone,
Peona, mayst return to me. I own
This may sound strangely. But when, dearest girl,
Thou seest it for my happiness, no pearl
870　Will trespass down those cheeks. Companion fair!
Wilt be content to dwell with her, to share
This sister's love with me?' Like one resigned
And bent by circumstance, and thereby blind
In self-commitment, thus that meek unknown:
875　'Aye, but a buzzing by my ears has flown
Of jubilee to Dian—truth I heard?
Well, then, I see there is no little bird,
Tender soever, but is Jove's own care.
Long have I sought for rest, and, unaware,
880　Behold I find it! So exalted too,
So after my own heart! I knew, I knew
There was a place untenanted in it.
In that same void white Chastity shall sit
And monitor me nightly to lone slumber.
885　With sanest lips I vow me to the number
Of Dian's sisterhood, and, kind lady,
With thy good help, this very night shall see
My future days to her fane consecrate.'
As feels a dreamer what doth most create
890　His own particular fright, so these three felt;
Or like one who, in after ages, knelt
To Lucifer or Baal, when he'd pine
After a little sleep; or, when in mine
Far underground, a sleeper meets his friends
895　Who know him not. Each diligently bends
Towards common thoughts and things for very fear,
Striving their ghastly malady to cheer
By thinking it a thing of yes and no
That housewives talk of. But the spirit-blow

iv 874. *meek*] mild *Draft*. On K.'s use of 'meek' see iii 46 *n.*
iv 877–8. See *Matthew* x 29–31, 'Are not two sparrows sold for a farthing?
and one of them shall not fall to the ground without your Father . . . Fear
ye not therefore, ye are of more value than many sparrows . . .'.
iv 882. *place*] void *Draft*.
iv 884. *monitor*] Guide, instruct. K.'s use of the word as a verb is individual.
iv 889–90. They seem to be living in a bad dream. For 'doth' the draft has
'can'.
iv 893–5. *or, when . . . him not*] The sense of loneliness and fear.
iv 898–9. *a thing . . . talk of*] A commonplace everyday affair.

900   Was struck, and all were dreamers. At the last
      Endymion said: 'Are not our fates all cast?
      Why stand we here? Adieu, ye tender pair!
      Adieu!' Whereat those maidens, with wild stare,
      Walked dizzily away. Painèd and hot
905   His eyes went after them until they got
      Near to a cypress grove whose deadly maw,
      In one swift moment would what then he saw
      Engulf for ever. 'Stay!' he cried, 'ah, stay!
      Turn, damsels! Hist! One word I have to say.
910   Sweet Indian, I would see thee once again.
      It is a thing I dote on. So I'd fain,
      Peona, ye should hand in hand repair
      Into those holy groves that silent are
      Behind great Dian's temple. I'll be yon
915   At vesper's earliest twinkle—they are gone—
      But once, once, once again.' At this he pressed
      His hands against his face and then did rest
      His head upon a mossy hillock green,
      And so remained as he a corpse had been
920   All the long day, save when he scantly lifted
      His eyes abroad to see how shadows shifted
      With the slow move of time—sluggish and weary
      Until the poplar tops, in journey dreary,
      Had reached the river's brim. Then up he rose,
925   And, slowly as that very river flows,
      Walked towards the temple grove with this lament:
      'Why such a golden eve? The breeze is sent
      Careful and soft that not a leaf may fall
      Before the serene father of them all
930   Bows down his summer head below the west.
      Now am I of breath, speech and speed possessed,
      But at the setting I must bid adieu
      To her for the last time. Night will strew

iv *904. dizzily*] patiently *Draft.*
iv *906. maw*] shade *Draft.*
iv *914. yon*] Yonder.
iv *918-19.*   His hands upon a pillow of green moss
                    And so remained without impatient toss ... *Draft.*
iv *922.* And note the weary time. Ah weary, weary ... *Draft.*
iv *926. with this lament*] lamenting O *Draft.*
iv *927. The breeze is sent*] The breezes blow *Draft.*
iv *929. serene father*] Apollo (here the summer sun).

On the damp grass myriads of lingering leaves,
935 And with them shall I die, nor much it grieves
To die when summer dies on the cold sward.
Why, I have been a butterfly, a lord
Of flowers, garlands, love-knots, silly posies,
Groves, meadows, melodies, and arbour roses.
940 My kingdom's at its death, and just it is
That I should die with it. So in all this
We miscall grief, bale, sorrow, heartbreak, woe,
What is there to plain of? By Titan's foe
I am but rightly served.' So saying, he
945 Tripped lightly on, in sort of deathful glee,
Laughing at the clear stream and setting sun
As though they jests had been. Nor had he done
His laugh at nature's holy countenance
Until that grove appeared, as if perchance,
950 And then his tongue with sober seemlihed
Gave utterance as he entered: 'Ha! I said
"King of the butterflies", but by this gloom,
And by old Rhadamanthus' tongue of doom,
This dusk religion, pomp of solitude,
955 And the Promethean clay by thief endued,
By old Saturnus' forelock, by his head

iv 943. *Titan's foe*] Jupiter. See *Hyperion* i 4 *n* (p. 396 below).
iv 945. *in sort of deathful glee*] For a similar mood see *Lamia* ii 135 (p. 640 below),

>   In pale contented sort of discontent . . .

iv 949–50. *Until . . . seemlihed*]

>   Until he saw that grove, as if perchance,
>   And then his soul was changed . . . *Draft (cancelled)*.

The word 'seemlihed' (seemliness) is an archaism probably owed to Spenser. See *The Faerie Queene* IV viii 14, 'his persons secret seemlyhed'.
iv 953. *Rhadamanthus*] Celebrated in classical mythology as a judge of the underworld. See *Lemprière*: 'The ancients have said he became one of the judges of hell, and that he was employed in the infernal regions in obliging the dead to confess their crimes, and in punishing them for their offences.'
iv 954. *dusk*] Used as an epithet.
iv 955. See *Lemprière*: 'According to Apollodorus, Prometheus made the first man and woman that ever were upon the earth, with clay, which he animated by means of the fire which he had stolen from heaven.'
iv 956–7. *By old . . . palsy*] Foreshadowing *Hyperion* i 89–90, 92–4 (p. 402 below),

>   . . . old Saturn lifted up
>   His faded eyes, and saw his kingdom gone . . .

Shook with eternal palsy, I did wed
Myself to things of light from infancy,
And thus to be cast out, thus lorn to die,
960   Is sure enough to make a mortal man
Grow impious.' So he inwardly began
On things for which no wording can be found,
Deeper and deeper sinking until drowned
Beyond the reach of music. For the choir
965   Of Cynthia he heard not, though rough briar
Nor muffling thicket interposed to dull
The vesper hymn, far swollen, soft and full,
Through the dark pillars of those sylvan aisles.
He saw not the two maidens, nor their smiles,
970   Wan as primroses gathered at midnight
By chilly-fingered spring. 'Unhappy wight!
Endymion!' said Peona, 'We are here!
What wouldst thou ere we all are laid on bier?'
Then he embraced her, and his lady's hand
975   Pressed, saying: 'Sister, I would have command,
If it were heaven's will, on our sad fate.'
At which that dark-eyed stranger stood elate
And said, in a new voice, but sweet as love,
To Endymion's amaze: 'By Cupid's dove,
980   And so thou shalt! And by the lily truth
Of my own breast thou shalt, beloved youth!'
And as she spake, into her face there came
Light, as reflected from a silver flame.
Her long black hair swelled ampler, in display

. . . then spake,
As with a palsied tongue, and while his beard
Shook horrid with such aspen-malady . . .

iv 959. *lorn*] Forlorn.
iv 967. *vesper*] prelude *Draft*.
iv 970-1. *wan as . . . spring*] Probably a remininiscence of *The Winter's Tale* IV iii 122-4,

. . . pale prime-roses,
That die unmarried, ere they can behold
Bright Phoebus in his strength . . .

The phrase 'chilly-fingered spring' has an eighteenth-century flavour. De
Selincourt notes a parallel with Collins's *How sleep the brave* (1746) 3, 'Spring
with dewy fingers cold'.
iv 977. *dark-eyed*] dark-tressed *Draft*.
iv 984-6. *in display . . . blue*]   while it turned
    Golden - and her eyes of jet dawned forth a brighter day
    Blue-blue- . . . *Draft*.

985 Full golden; in her eyes a brighter day
Dawned blue and full of love. Aye, he beheld
Phoebe, his passion! Joyous she upheld
Her lucid bow, continuing thus: 'Drear, drear
Has our delaying been. But foolish fear
990 Withheld me first; and then decrees of fate;
And then 'twas fit that from this mortal state
Thou shouldst, my love, by some unlooked-for change
Be spiritualized. Peona, we shall range
These forests, and to thee they safe shall be
995 As was thy cradle. Hither shalt thou flee
To meet us many a time.' Next Cynthia bright
Peona kissed and blessed with fair good night.
Her brother kissed her too and knelt adown
Before his goddess in a blissful swoon.
1000 She gave her fair hands to him, and, behold,
Before three swiftest kisses he had told,
They vanished far away! Peona went
Home through the gloomy wood in wonderment.

iv *988. Lucid*] Shining.
iv *1002–3.* Cp. the phrasing in *I stood tip-toe* 141–2 (p. 92 above),
                              . . . Psyche went
        On the smooth wind to realms of wonderment . . .
See Bailey's comment in his letter to Taylor of 20 May 1818, 'The 4th book
[of *Endymion*], which I at first thought inferior, I *now* think . . . perhaps
finer than any. . . . Nor do I think the abrupt conclusion so bad—it is *rather*,
but not *much* too abrupt. It is like the conclusion of Paradise Regained' (*KC*
i 25).

60 Lines Rhymed in a Letter from Oxford

Probably written Sept. 1817 at the beginning of K.'s visit to Bailey at Magdalen Hall, Oxford, *c.* 3 Sept.–*c.* 5 Oct. 1817: see K.'s undated letter to
Reynolds: 'Wordsworth sometimes, though in a fine way, gives us sen-
tences in the Style of School exercises . . . for Instance
                    The lake doth glitter
                    Small birds twitter etc.,
Now I think this is an excellent method of giving a very clear description
of an interesting place such as Oxford is' (*L* i 151–2). The couplet is a misquotation of Wordsworth's *Written in March while resting on the bridge at the*

foot of Brother's Water (1807) 3–4. For K.'s first impressions of Oxford see his letters to the Reynolds sisters 4 Sept. 1817, 'here am I among Colleges, Halls, Stalls, Plenty of Trees thank God' (L i 149), and to Fanny Keats 10 Sept. 1817, 'This Oxford I have no doubt is the finest City in the world' (*L* i 154).

Text from K.'s letter.
Published *Forman* (1883).

I

The Gothic looks solemn,
The plain Doric column
Supports an old bishop and crosier.
The mouldering arch,
5   Shaded o'er by a larch,
Stands next door to Wilson the Hosier.

II

Vicè—that is, by turns—
O'er pale faces mourns
The black tasselled trencher and common hat.
10   The chantry boy sings,
The steeple-bell rings,
And as for the Chancellor—*dominat*.

III

There are plenty of trees,
And plenty of ease,
15 And plenty of fat deer for parsons.
And when it is venison,
Short is the benison,
Then each on a leg or thigh fastens.

¶ 60. *9. black tasselled trencher*] Mortar-boards worn by commoners. Noble-men's caps had a gold tassel.
10. chantry boy] Choir boy.
12. dominat] He rules. Correctly 'dominatur'.
17. benison] Grace.

61 'Think not of it, sweet one, so'

Written *c.* 11 Nov. 1817, probably as a song for the Reynolds sisters: so dated in *Woodhouse* 2, 3 and *Reynolds*. The poem's light-hearted eroticism is in keeping with the style of K.'s early 1818 songs (see headnote to *Oh, blush*

not so, p. 298 below). For the view that the song was written spring 1817
see *Ward* (1963) 124, 424.
Text from K.'s MS (Morgan Library), with some variants noted from
Woodhouse's transcripts.
Published *1848*.

Think not of it, sweet one, so,
　　Give it not a tear.
Sigh thou mayst and bid it go
　　Any, any where.

5 Do not look so sad, sweet one—
　　Sad and fadingly.
Shed one drop, then it is gone,
　　Oh, 'twas born to die.

Still so pale? Then dearest, weep—
10　　Weep, I'll count the tears,
And each one shall be a bliss
　　For thee in after years.

Brighter has it left thine eyes
　　Than a sunny rill,
15 And thy whispering melodies
　　Are tenderer still.

Yet, as all things mourn awhile
　　At fleeting blisses,
E'en let us too! But be our dirge
20　　A dirge of kisses.

¶ 61. *1.* Preceded in K.'s MS by the cancelled stanza,
Think not of it gentle sweet
　　It is worth a tear ?
Will thy heart less warmly beat
　　Thy voice less dear . . .
3. and] but *Woodhouse*. Cp. Balthazar's song, *Much Ado About Nothing* II ii
65,
Then sigh not so but let them go . . .
K. echoes the song again in *Oh, blush not so* 9 (p. 298 below); see also *Endymion* iv 808 *n* (pp. 274, 278 above).
7. then it is gone] an only one *K.'s MS* (*cancelled*).
8. Sweetly did it die *K.'s MS* (*cancelled*).
9–10.　　　Wilt thou mourn and wilt thou sob
　　Art indeed so sad and wan . . . *K.'s MS* (*cancelled*).
11.　　　For each one will I invent a bliss. . . *K.'s MS* (*cancelled*).
14. rill] hill *Woodhouse.*
18. fleeting] dying *K.'s MS* (*cancelled*).

62 'In drear-nighted December'

Written Dec. 1817: so dated in *Woodhouse* 2 with note, '. . . the date from Miss Reynolds' Album'. The poem owes a metrical debt to Dryden's song, 'Farwell ungratefull Traytor' from *The Spanish Friar* (1681).

Text—except for l. 21—from K.'s holograph MS (Bristol University Library) which agrees in important respects with the three transcripts in *Woodhouse* 1, 2, 3. The variants in the three early printed versions are noted below. For a discussion of the various MSS and their relation to the early printed versions see A. Whitley, *Harvard Library Bulletin* v 1951.

Published *The Literary Gazette* 19 Sept. 1829; repr. *Galignani* (1829).

I

In drear-nighted December,
    Too happy, happy tree,
Thy branches ne'er remember
    Their green felicity.
5   The north cannot undo them
    With a sleety whistle through them,
    Nor frozen thawings glue them
    From budding at the prime.

II

In drear-nighted December,
10   Too happy, happy brook,
Thy bubblings ne'er remember
    Apollo's summer look.
But with a sweet forgetting,
They stay their crystal fretting,
15   Never, never petting
    About the frozen time.

¶ 62. *1–8.* Cp. the stanza in Dryden's *Farwell ungratefull Traytor*, for example, ll. 1–8,

Farwell ungratefull Traytor,
    Farwell my perjur'd Swain,
Let never injur'd Creature
    Believe a Man again.
The Pleasure of Possessing
Surpasses all Expressing,
But 'tis too short a Blessing,
    And Love too long a Pain . . .

1 (and *9* below). *In*] In a *Literary Gazette, Galignani, Gem.*
7. frozen thawings] Ice or snow which has melted and frozen again.
15. petting] Complaining.

III
Ah, would 'twere so with many
A gentle girl and boy!
But were there ever any
20   Writhed not of passèd joy?
The feel of not to feel it,
When there is none to heal it,
Nor numbèd sense to steel it,
Was never said in rhyme.

18. girl and boy] Perhaps suggested by Guiderius's song, *Cymbeline* IV ii
262–3,

Golden lads and girls all must,
As chimney-sweepers, come to dust . . .

20. of] at *Woodhouse's transcripts. Woodhouse* 2 has the note, '*Of* in Miss
R.'s copy in Keats's handwriting'.
21. The feel of not to] To know the change and *Literary Gazette, Galignani,
Gem.* The variant, which is also written above the line in K.'s MS in an
unidentified hand, is probably owed to Woodhouse. See his letter to Taylor
23 Nov. 1818, 'I have tried unsuccessfully to admire the 3d stanza. . . . I
plead guilty . . . of an utter abhorrence of the word "feel" for feeling. . . .
But Keats seems fond of it, and will ingraft it "in aeternum" in our language' (*KC* i 64). Woodhouse concludes his letter with his own revised
version of the third stanza (see *Garrod*). Cp. K.'s earlier use of the word
'feel' in *Endymion* iii 496 (p. 226 above),

A sight too fearful for the feel of fear . . .

The line is discussed at length in *Murry* (1930) 65–70.
23. steel] steal *K.'s MS.* The reading seems to be justified by the context
and is supported by Woodhouse's transcripts (in *Woodhouse* 1 the reading
'steal' is altered to 'steel').

63   Nebuchadnezzar's Dream

Date of composition unknown, but perhaps Dec. 1817 to celebrate the victory of liberal over Government interests in a current political controversy:
'1817' in Brown's transcript. There is no general agreement about the sonnet's meaning, but the 'Daniel' of the poem probably stands for the radical
journalist William Hone (1780–1842) who was tried three times in 1817 and
finally acquitted Dec. 1817 after satirizing Government policy in his parodies of the Catechism, Creed and Litany. For K.'s interest in Hone see his
journal letter of Dec. 1817 to George and Tom Keats, 'I send you . . . the
Examiner . . . Hone the publisher's trial [reported in *The Examiner* 21, 28
Dec. 1817], you must find very amusing; and as Englishmen very encouraging – his *Not Guilty* is a thing, which not to have been would have dulled

still more Liberty's Emblazoning' (*L* i 191). Aileen Ward has a detailed discussion of the poem as a comment on Hone, *PQ* xxxiv (1955) 177–88. The
interpretation (*Finney* 142–3) of the poem as reflecting an episode in K.'s
personal life is unconvincing.
Text from K.'s holograph draft (Huntington Library) which generally
agrees with the transcripts by Woodhouse and J. C. Stephens. Brown's
transcript has minor variants from the other MSS, some of which are noted
below.
Published *Literary Anecdotes of the Nineteenth Century*, ed. W. R. Nicoll and
T. J. Wise 1896.

> Before he went to feed with owls and bats,
>   Nebuchadnezzar had an ugly dream,
>   Worse than an housewife's when she thinks her cream
> Made a naumachia for mice and rats.
> 5 So scared, he sent for that 'Good King of Cats',
>   Young Daniel, who soon did pluck away the beam
>   From out his eye, and said he did not deem
> The sceptre worth a straw—his cushions old doormats.
> A horrid nightmare similar somewhat
> 10   Of late has haunted a most worthy crew

¶ 63. *1.* See *Daniel* iv 33, 'Nebuchadnezzar . . . was driven from men, and
did eat grass as oxen, and his body was wet with the dew of heaven, till his
hairs were grown like eagles' feathers, and his nails like birds' claws.' K.
substituted 'with owls and bats' for 'like Bottom on good dry hay' (see *A
Midsummer Night's Dream* iv i 35).

2. See *Daniel* ii 1: 'Nebuchadnezzar dreamed dreams, wherewith his spirit
was troubled.'

4. Naumachia] A mock sea-fight. The term was currently familiar after the
'Serpentine Naumachia' which formed part of the peace celebrations in
1814 (see *Endymion* iii 17–18, p. 207 above). An account of the aquatic
entertainment called by this name and inaugurated at Sadlers Wells Theatre
in 1804 appears in Dorothy Hewlett's *Adonais* (1937) 24–5.

5. '*Good King of Cats*'] Borrowed from *Romeo and Juliet* III i 76 and used as
a joking reference to Daniel in the lions' den (*Daniel* vi 16–23).

6–8. Refers to Daniel's fearless interpretation of Nebuchadnezzar's dream
(*Daniel* ii 31–45).

6–7. beam . . . eye] See *Luke* vi 42: 'Thou hypocrite, cast out first the beam
out of thine own eye, and then thou shalt see clearly to pull out the mote
that is in thy brother's eye.'

7–8. he did . . . door-mats]   . . . I do not deem
  Your sceptre worth a straw—your Cushions old door-mats . . .
                                             Brown's MS

10. worthy] valiant *Brown's MS*; motley *Woodhouse* 3. K. substituted
'worthy' for 'worshipful' in his draft.

Of loggerheads and chapmen–we are told
That any Daniel though he be a sot
Can make the lying lips turn pale of hue
By belching out, 'Ye are that head of gold.'

11. *loggerheads and chapmen*] Fools and money grubbers.
14. *belching*] drawling *Brown's MS.* Nebuchadnezzar had dreamed of an
idol with a head of gold and feet of clay and was told by Daniel, 'Thou art
this head of gold' (*Daniel* ii 38).

64 Apollo to the Graces

Probably written early Jan. 1818 as a song for the Reynolds sisters: Woodhouse notes, 'From the original in Miss Reynolds possession. . . . Written
to the tune of an air in Don Giovanni' (*Woodhouse* 2)–Woodhouse is referring to the Christmas pantomime, *Harlequin's Vision; or, The Feast of the
Statue*, produced at Drury Lane Theatre, Dec. 1817 and reviewed by K. in
'Don Giovanni: a Pantomime', *The Champion* 4 Jan. 1818. The review
appears in *Forman* (1939) v 252–6.
Text from *Woodhouse* 2.
Published *TLS* 16 April 1914; repr. *Colvin* (1915).

APOLLO
Which of the fairest three
Today will ride with me?
My steeds are all pawing at the threshold of the morn.
Which of the fairest three
5   Today will ride with me
Across the gold autumn's whole kingdom of corn?

THE GRACES *all answer.*
I will, I–I–I,
O young Apollo let me fly,
Along with thee.
10   I will, I–I–I,
The many wonders see—
I–I–I–I–
And thy lyre shall never have a slackened string.
I–I–I–I,
Thro' the golden day will sing.

¶ 64. 3. Cp. *Endymion* iii 957–9 (p. 242 above),
. . . that golden song
Apollo singeth, while his chariot
Waits at the doors of heaven . . .

65 To Aubrey George Spencer

Date of composition unknown, but late 1817 or early 1818: Woodhouse includes a copy of the poem—not in his own hand—in *Woodhouse 3* with the prefatory comment: 'To A.G.S. on reading his admirable verses in this (Miss Reynolds') album on either side of the following attempt to pay small tribute thereto.' 'A.G.S.' is Aubrey George Spencer (1795–1872), a contemporary of Benjamin Bailey at Magdalen Hall Oxford and later Bishop of Jamaica, whom K. may have met while staying with Bailey at Oxford Sept. 1817, and the 'admirable verses' are two sonnets (included in *Woodhouse 3*) dated 8 Oct. 1817 and 1 Nov. 1817, addressed to Spencer's great-aunt, the Countess Dowager of Pembroke. For further details concerning Spencer and arguments against C. L. Finney's attribution of the poem to Woodhouse (*Finney* 751) see H. W. Garrod's comments in *TLS* 27 Nov. 1937. The case for K.'s authorship is strengthened by the likelihood that the MS is in his hand and by the poem's resemblance in some respects to the preceding and following sonnets, *Nebuchadnezzar's Dream* and *To Mrs. Reynolds's Cat* (pp. 288 above, 292 below).

Text from *Woodhouse 3*.

Published *TLS* 27 Nov. 1937 and *Garrod* (1939 edn).

> Where didst thou find, young bard, thy sounding lyre?
>   Where the bland accent and the tender tone?
> A-sitting snugly by thy parlour fire?
>   Or didst thou with Apollo pick a bone?
> 5 The muse will have a crow to pick with me
>   For thus assaying in thy brightening path.
> Who that with his own brace of eyes can see,
>   Unthunderstruck beholds thy gentle wrath?
> Who from a pot of stout e'er blew the froth
> 10 Into the bosom of the wandering wind,
>   Light as the powder on the back of moth,
> But drank thy muse's with a grateful mind?
>   Yea, unto thee beldams drink metheglin,
>   And annisies and carraway and gin.

¶ 65. 5. *a crow to pick*] See *OED*: 'To have a crow to pluck or pull (rarely pick) with anyone: to have something awkward to settle, or some fault to find with him.'
12. *thy muse's*] Thy muse's health.
13. *metheglin*] A spiced or medicated form of mead, originally peculiar to Wales (OED).
14. *annisies . . . carraway*] Aniseed and caraway, spices presumably used by the 'beldams' to flavour their gin.

66 To Mrs. Reynolds's Cat

Written 16 Jan. 1818: so dated in K.'s holograph fair copy (Buffalo and
Erie County Library).
Text from K.'s MS.
Published *The Comic Annual* 1830.

<blockquote>

Cat, who hast passed thy grand climacteric,
   How many mice and rats hast in thy days
   Destroyed? How many titbits stolen? Gaze
With those bright languid segments green, and prick
5 Those velvet ears–but prithee do not stick
   Thy latent talons in me, and upraise
   Thy gentle mew, and tell me all thy frays
Of fish and mice, and rats and tender chick.
Nay, look not down, nor lick thy dainty wrists–
10   For all the wheezy asthma, and for all
Thy tail's tip is nicked off, and though the fists
   Of many a maid have given thee many a maul,
Still is that fur as soft as when the lists
   In youth thou enter'dst on glass-bottled wall.

</blockquote>

¶ 66. *1.* A man is said to have reached his 'grand climacteric' at the age of
sixty-three. The line parodies the opening invocation in Milton's sonnets,
for example *On the Lord Gen. Fairfax . . . 1*,

     Fairfax, whose name in armes through Europe rings . . .
9. dainty] tender *Woodhouse* 1; gentle *Woodhouse* 2.

67 On Seeing a Lock of Milton's Hair
Ode

Written 21 Jan. 1818: so dated in K.'s letter to Bailey 23 Jan. 1818, 'I was at
Hunt's the other day, and he surprised me with a real authenticated Lock of
Milton's Hair. I know you would like what I wrote thereon. . . . This I did
at Hunt's at his request–perhaps I should have done something better alone
and at home' (*L* i 210–12). The poem is an early expression of K.'s new
interest in Milton which had been stimulated by Bailey in late 1817; see
headnote to *Endymion* iii (p. 205 above).
Text from K.'s letter with some variants noted from his draft and his holograph copy (Hampstead).
Published *Plymouth and Devon Weekly Journal* 15 Nov. 1838; repr. *1848*.

Chief of organic numbers!
  Old scholar of the spheres!
Thy spirit never slumbers,
  But rolls about our ears,
5   For ever and for ever!
Oh, what a mad endeavour
    Worketh he,
Who to thy sacred and ennobled hearse
Would offer a burnt sacrifice of verse
10   And melody.

How heavenward thou soundest,
  Live temple of sweet noise,
And discord unconfoundest,
  Giving delight new joys,
15   And pleasure nobler pinions!
Oh, where are thy dominions?
    Lend thine ear
To a young Delian oath—aye, by thy soul,
By all that from thy mortal lips did roll,
20 And by the kernel of thine earthly love,
Beauty in things on earth and things above,
    [I swear]
  When every childish fashion

¶ 67. *Title*. 'Ode' omitted in other MSS.

1. *Chief*] Father of *Draft* (*cancelled*). The word 'organic' means organ-like (see *Ode to Apollo* 22 n, pp. 15–16 above). Its use here was perhaps suggested by Milton's *Nativity Ode* 130,

    And let the Base of Heav'n's deep Organ blow . . .

2. Milton is an authority on the music of the spheres. K. may be remembering *Arcades* 62–73, beginning

    . . . then listen I
  to the celestial *Sirens* harmony
  That sit upon the nine enfolded Sphears . . .

11. *heavenward*] heavenly *Draft*. For 'soundest' K.'s letter has 'soundedst'.
12. O living fane of sounds . . . *Draft* (*cancelled*).
13. Milton creates harmony out of discord. The word 'unconfoundest' ('unconfoundedst' in K.'s letter) means 'dost disentangle'.
18. *Delian*] Poetic. K. is thinking of the isle of Delos, Apollo's birthplace. The word is substituted for 'phebean' in the draft.
22. *I swear*] The line is added in pencil in K.'s letter, possibly by Woodhouse who adds it in pencil in his two transcripts, one of which has the note, 'Should there not be a short line to rhyme with "ear" . . . such as "I swear"?' (*Woodhouse* 2).

11 + K.

Has vanished from my rhyme
25 Will I, grey-gone in passion,
Give to an after-time
Hymning and harmony
Of thee, and of thy works, and of thy life.
But vain is now the burning and the strife,
30 Pangs are in vain, until I grow high-rife
With old philosophy,
And mad with glimpses at futurity!

For many years my offering must be hushed.
When I do speak, I'll think upon this hour,
35 Because I feel my forehead hot and flushed,
Even at the simplest vassal of thy power—
A lock of thy bright hair.
Sudden it came,
And I was startled, when I caught thy name
40 Coupled so unaware,
Yet, at the moment, temperate was my blood.
Methought I had beheld it from the Flood.

26. Give] Leave *Draft*; *Hampstead MS.*

30–31. See K.'s letter to Taylor of 24 April 1818, 'I know nothing, I have read nothing. . . I mean to follow Solomon's directions of "get Wisdom-get understanding" [*Proverbs* iv 5] . . . the road lies through application, study and thought . . . I have been hovering . . . between an exquisite sense of the luxurious and a love for Philosophy . . . I shall turn all my soul to the latter' (*L* i 271).

32. at] of *Hampstead MS.* This is followed in the draft by the cancelled attempts

1. Till then . . .

2. And so presumptuous longer in Art . . .

33–4.   Then will I speak—but now my voice is hush'd
Then will I speak and think upon this hour . . . *Draft.*

37–8. A lock of thy bright hair—sudden it came. . . *Hampstead MS.* Woodhouse notes, 'In the copy from which I took this, these two lines were written in one: I have separated them on account of the rhyme to "unaware". They are written separate in B.B.'s [Bailey's] copy' (*Woodhouse* 2). For 'A lock . . .' the draft has 'One lock . . .'

39. Before me and I started at thy name . . . *Draft.*

41. temperate] unheated *Draft.*

42. Methought] It seem'd *Draft.* This is weak, but K. is trying to express a genuine sensation, namely that the expected gush of feeling was delayed and in the interval the lock of hair seemed to move him as little as if it had been familiar to him for a long time.

68 On Sitting Down to Read *King Lear* Once Again

Written 22 Jan. 1818: so dated in K.'s holograph fair copy (Hampstead), and see K.'s letter of 23 Jan. 1818 to George and Tom Keats at Teignmouth, 'I sat down yesterday to read King Lear once again the thing appeared to demand the prologue of a Sonnet, I wrote it and began to read' (*L* i 214). The contrast between 'Romantic' and Shakespearian poetry recognized in the poem was brought home to K. by his current task of preparing his 'Poetic Romance', *Endymion*, for the press. His letter to Bailey of 23 Jan. 1818, part quoted in the preceding headnote (p. 292 above), continues later, 'I have sent my first book [*Endymion* i] to the Press—and this afternoon shall begin preparing the second' (*L* i 212). The poem is a Petrarchan sonnet, but its concluding couplet points towards K.'s new preference for the Shakespearian rhyme-scheme (see headnote to the following poem, *When I have fears*, p. 296 below).

Text from K.'s fair copy, with some variants noted from his draft (Scottish National Library) and transcribed letter copy.

Published *Plymouth and Devonport Weekly Journal* 8 Nov. 1838; repr. *1848*.

> O golden-tongued Romance, with serene lute!
>   Fair plumèd Siren, Queen of far-away!
>   Leave melodizing on this wintry day,
> Shut up thine olden pages, and be mute.
> Adieu! For, once again, the fierce dispute

¶ 68. *1* (and *5–8* below). See K. to Sarah Jeffrey 9 June 1819, 'Boyardo [Matteo Maria Boiardo (1434–94)] . . . was a noble Poet of Romance; not a miserable and mighty Poet of the human Heart. The middle age of Shakespeare was all clouded over; his days were not more happy than Hamlet's' (*L* ii 115–16).

2. of] if *1848*. Romance is pictured as a Spenserian heroine wearing the knightly panache which K. associated with chivalric romance. See *Specimen of an Induction* 1–2 (p. 33 above),

>   Lo! I must tell a tale of chivalry,
>   For large white plumes are dancing in my eye . . .

and K.'s description of Mary Frogley as the Spenserian warrior-heroine Britomartis in *To Mary Frogley* 52–3 (p. 31 above),

>   Thy locks in knightly casque are rested,
>   O'er which bend four milky plumes . . .

4. pages] Books *Draft* (cancelled); volume *Letter*.

5. once again] For K.'s early reading of *King Lear* see *Imitation of Spenser* 22 and headnote to *On the Sea* (pp. 4, 112 above).

Betwixt damnation and impassioned clay
Must I burn through, once more humbly assay
The bitter-sweet of this Shakespearian fruit.
Chief Poet, and ye clouds of Albion,
10   Begetters of our deep eternal theme!
When through the old oak forest I am gone,
Let me not wander in a barren dream,
But, when I am consumèd in the fire,
Give me new Phoenix wings to fly at my desire.

6. *damnation*] Hell torment *Letter*; *1848*. For 'impassioned clay' see *Genesis*
ii 7: 'And the Lord God formed man of the dust of the ground, and breathed
into his nostrils the breath of life; and man became a living soul.'

7. *assay*] Test.

9. Chief! what a gloom thine old oak forest hath! *Draft (cancelled)*.

11. K. means, 'After I have finished reading the play' (see l. 9 *n* above). The
phrase 'old oak forest' reinforces 'clouds of Albion' (l. 9) in suggesting both
the sombre nature and the native English origin of Shakespeare's themes in
King Lear.

13. *in*] with *Letter*.

14. K. will be reborn as a poet through the fiery experience of reading
Shakespeare. On his hopes for his own poetic development from unreflect-
ing delight in nature to a deeper understanding of human life see *Sleep and
Poetry* 122–54 *n* (p. 74 above).

69 'When I have fears that I may cease to be'

Written between 22–31 Jan. 1818: see K.'s letter to Reynolds 31 Jan. 1818
where the poem is copied out as 'my last sonnet' (*L* i 222); K. had written
the sonnet *On Sitting Down to Read* King Lear *Once Again* 22 Jan. 1818 (see
preceding headnote, p. 295 above). The poem marks K.'s preference from
Jan. 1818 for the Shakespearian over the Petrarchan sonnet form and is a
Keatsian reflection of Shakespeare's concern in his sonnets with love, poetic
ambition and the passage of time. For Woodhouse's comments on the
poem see ll. 7–8 *n* below and for a possible echo of Cowper's *Stanza sub-
joined to the yearly bill of mortality* . . . (1788) T. O. Mabbott's 'Keats and
Cowper: A Reminiscence?' *N and Q* 3 Sept 1938, 170.

Text from *1848*, as largely agreeing with the various transcripts; the minor
variants in K.'s letter are noted below.
Published *1848*.

When I have fears that I may cease to be
   Before my pen has gleaned my teeming brain,
Before high-pilèd books, in character,
   Hold like rich garners the full ripened grain;
5   When I behold, upon the night's starred face,
   Huge cloudy symbols of a high romance,
And think that I may never live to trace
   Their shadows with the magic hand of chance;
And when I feel, fair creature of an hour,
10   That I shall never look upon thee more,

¶ 69. *1*. Cp. the opening of Shakespeare's sonnet 12,

     When I do count the clock that tells the time . . .

and sonnet cvii 1–2,

     Not mine own fears, nor the prophetic soul
     Of the wide world, dreaming on things to come . . .

Both sonnets are marked by K. in his copy of Shakespeare's *Poems* (1806 edn) at Hampstead.

2–4. gleans . . . teeming . . . garners] A sustained figure expressing K.'s sense of the fecundity of his imagination and his hopes for a rich ripening of his poetic powers. On his poetic aspirations see also *On Sitting Down to Read King Lear Once Again* 14 and *n* (p. 296 above),

     Give me new Phoenix wings to fly at my desire . . .

3. charactery] Handwriting or printing. Cp. *Endymion* iii 762 (p. 235 above),

     Nor marked with any sign or charactery . . .

4. rich] full *Letter copy.* The word 'garners' means granaries.

5–6. Cp. K.'s letter of 19 Feb. 1818 to Reynolds, '. . . man should . . . weave a tapestry empyrean—full of Symbols for his spiritual eye' (*L* i 232).

7–8. Woodhouse notes (MS fragment dated by H. Rollins 'July (?) 1820'), 'These lines give some insight into K.'s mode of writing Poetry. He has repeatedly said . . . that he never sits down to write, unless he is full of ideas—and then thoughts come about him in troops . . . one of his Maxims is that if Poetry does not come naturally, it had better not come at all [see *L* i 238–9]. . . . "My judgment, (he says), is as active while I am actually writing as my imagination. In fact all my faculties are strongly excited and in their full play—And shall I afterwards . . . sit down coldly to criticise when in possession of only one faculty, what I have written, when almost inspired." . . . He has said, that he has often not been aware of the beauty of some thought until after he has composed and written it down—It has then struck him with astonishment—and seemed rather the production of another person than his own. . . It is probable that this is what he meant, and has expressed in these lines so happily that they are in illustration of the very thing itself' (*KC* i 128–9).

9. fair creature of an hour] According to Woodhouse the same woman celebrated by K. in his early poem, *Fill for me* (p. 6 above) and again in *To*–['Time's sea'] (p. 306 below).

Never have relish in the fairy power
  Of unreflecting love; then on the shore
Of the wide world I stand alone and think
Till love and fame to nothingness do sink.

9–14. The realization that he will never see the 'fair creature' again compels K. to ponder the nature of time. The 'distancing' of ordinary life that this reflection produces causes thoughts of love and fame, usually so important in K.'s early poems, to dwindle into insignificance.

70 'Oh, blush not so, oh, blush not so'

Written 31 Jan. 1818 in K.'s letter of this date to J. Reynolds, '. . . inward innocence is like a nested dove; or as the old song says . . .' (*L* i 219–20). The poem is an erotic *jeu d'esprit* in the manner of an Elizabethan song and may have some autobiographical connection with *Think not of it, sweet one* (p. 285 above). It pleased K.'s friends (see *Finney* 357), but was considered unfit for publication by some Victorian readers, including even Swinburne (*L* i 219 *n*) and D. G. Rossetti (*John Keats: Criticism and Comment* (1919) 16–17).
Text from K.'s letter with some variants noted from *Woodhouse* 3.
Published *Forman* (1883).

    Oh, blush not so, oh, blush not so,
      Or I shall think ye knowing.
    And if ye smile the blushing while,
      Then maidenheads are going.

5   There's a blush for won't, and a blush for shan't—
      And a blush for having done it.
    There's a blush for thought, and a blush for naught,
      And a blush for just begun it.

    Oh, sigh not so, oh, sigh not so,

¶ 70. *1–4.* Probably suggested by Pandarus's innuendoes in *Troilus and Cressida* III ii, for example III ii 39, 'Come, come, what need you blush?' and III ii 100, 'What! blushing still?' The scene is marked by K. in his copy of Shakespeare (*Spurgeon* 164–5).
4. Echoes *Troilus and Cressida* IV ii 23,
        How now, how now! how go maidenheads . . .
9 sigh . . . sigh] say . . . say *Woodhouse* 3 (*written above the letter readings*). Cp.
Balthazar's song, *Much Ado About Nothing* II iii 61,
        Sigh no more, ladies, sigh no more . . .
and II iii 65,
        Then sigh not so but let them go . . .
For K.'s earlier echoes of this song see *Think not of it* 3 and *n* (p. 286 above).

10   For it sounds of Eve's sweet pippin.
      By those loosened hips you have tasted the pips
            And fought in an amorous nipping.

      Will you play once more at nice-cut-core,
            For it only will last our youth out?
15 And we have the prime of the kissing time,
            We have not one sweet tooth out.

      There's a sigh for yes, and a sigh for no,
            And a sigh for I can't bear it!
      Oh, what can be done, shall we stay or run?
20   Oh, cut the sweet apple and share it!

10–13 (and *20* below). See K.'s Feb.–May 1819 journal letter, 'On going he leaves her three pips of eve's apple – and some how – she, having liv'd a virgin all her life, begins to repent of it' (*L* ii 61).
11. hips] lips *Woodhouse 3 (written above the letter reading)*.
13. nice-cut-core] Dividing the apple. Perhaps the name of a real game, or of an imaginary game invented by K.
14–15. Cp. *Twelfth Night* II iii 50–2,
            In delay there lies no plenty;
            Then come kiss me, sweet and twenty,
            Youth's a stuff will not endure . . .
16. Cp. *All's Well that Ends Well* II iii 45: 'I'll like a maid the better, whilst I have a tooth in my head.'
17. yes . . . no] aye . . . nay *Woodhouse 3*.

71 'Hence burgundy, claret and port'

Written 31 Jan. 1818 in K.'s letter of this date to Reynolds, 'Now I purposed to write you a serious poetic letter. . . . Yet I cannot write in prose, It is a sun-shiny day and I cannot so here goes' (*L* i 220–1).
Text from K.'s letter.
Published *1848*.

            Hence burgundy, claret, and port,
                  Away with old hock and madeira,

¶ 71. *1–2.* On K.'s attendance at drinking-parties in Jan. 1818 see his letter to George and Tom Keats 5 Jan. 1818: 'Wells and Severn dined with me yesterday. . . . I pitched upon another bottle of claret – Port – we . . . were all very witty and full of Rhyme . . . at Redhall's . . . drank deep' (*L* i 196–7, 200). K. expresses his special fondness for claret in his Feb.–May 1819

Too couthly ye are for my sport—
There's a beverage brighter and clearer!
5   Instead of a pitiful rummer,
My wine overbrims a whole summer.
    My bowl is the sky,
    And I drink at my eye,
    Till I feel in the brain
10   A Delphian pain—
Then follow, my Caius, then follow!
    On the green of the hill
    We will drink our fill
    Of golden sunshine,
15   Till our brains intertwine
With the glory and grace of Apollo!

God of the meridian,
    And of the East and West,
    To thee my soul is flown,
20   And my body is earthward pressed.
It is an awful mission,
A terrible division,
And leaves a gulf austere
To be filled with worldly fear.
25   Aye, when the soul is fled
To high above our head,

---

journal-letter to George and Georgiana Keats, '. . . 'tis so fine–it fills . . .
one's mouth with a gushing freshness–then goes down cool and feverless–
then you do not feel it quarrelling with your liver. . . . Other wines of a
heavy and spirituous nature transform a Man into a Silenus; this makes him
a Hermes–and gives a Woman the soul and immortality of Ariadne for
whom Bacchus always kept a good celler of claret' (*L* ii 64). For an earlier
expression of K.'s liking for wine see *Fill for me* (p. 6 above).

3. couthly] An archaism for well-known or familiar. Milnes's attempted
emendation in *1848* was 'earthy'.

4. Cp. *Ode to a Nightingale* 32–3 (p. 527 below),

    Not charioted by Bacchus and his pards,
    But on the viewless wings of Poesy . . .

5. rummer] 'A large drinking glass' (*OED*).

10. Delphian] Poetic.

11. Caius] Reynolds sometimes used this signature for his articles in *The
Yellow Dwarf*.

17–41. Omitted in the transcripts by George Keats and Brown, and printed
as a separate poem in *Garrod*, but the lines lead on from the reference to
Apollo.

17. God of the noonday (as well as of sunrise and sunset).

Affrighted do we gaze
After its airy maze,
As doth a mother wild
30   When her young infant child
Is in an eagle's claws—
And is not this the cause
Of madness? God of Song,
Thou bearest me along
35   Through sights I scarce can bear.
Oh, let me, let me share
With the hot lyre and thee
The staid Philosophy.
Temper my lonely hours,
40   And let me see thy bowers
More unalarmed!

38. the staid Philosophy] Cp. *On Seeing a Lock of Milton's Hair* 30–1 *n* (p. 294 above),

Pangs are in vain, until I grow high-rife
With old philosophy . . .

40–1. For the feverish excitement often associated by K. with poetic activity see his Sept. 1819 journal-letter, 'I want to compose without this fever' (*L* ii 209) and *The Fall of Hyperion* i 168–9 (p. 668 below),

. . . Thou art a dreaming thing,
A fever of thyself . . .

72 Robin Hood

To a friend

Written *c.* 3 Feb. 1818 and copied out in K.'s letter of this date to Reynolds with the comment, 'Your . . . sonnets gave me more pleasure than will the 4th Book of Byron's Childe Harold [published April 1818] and the whole of anybody's life and opinions. . . . I hope you will like them [the present lines] they are at least written in the Spirit of Outlawry' (*L* i 225)–Reynolds's sonnets were *The trees in Sherwood Forest are old and good* and *With coat of Lincoln green and mantle too* (published *The Yellow Dwarf* 21 Feb. 1818; repr. *The Garden of Florence* 1821). K.'s seven-syllable couplets probably owe a metrical debt to Fletcher's *The Faithful Shepherdess*; Fletcher is one of the 'old Poets' celebrated in the following companion poem, *Lines on the Mermaid Tavern* (p. 304 below).

Text from *1820*, which has minor variants from K.'s draft (in the possession of S. R. Townshend Meyer), some of which are noted below.
Published *1820*.

11*

No, those days are gone away,
And their hours are old and gray,
And their minutes buried all
Under the down-trodden pall
5   Of the leaves of many years.
Many times have winter's shears,
Frozen north and chilling east,
Sounded tempests to the feast
Of the forest's whispering fleeces,
10   Since men knew nor rent nor leases.

No, the bugle sounds no more,
And the twanging bow no more.
Silent is the ivory shrill
Past the heath and up the hill.
15   There is no mid-forest laugh,
Where lone Echo gives the half
To some wight, amazed to hear
Jesting, deep in forest drear.

On the fairest time of June
20   You may go with sun or moon
Or the seven stars to light you,
Or the polar ray to right you.
But you never may behold
Little John, or Robin bold,
25   Never one, of all the clan,

¶ 72. *8–9.* The trees are stripped of their foliage in winter as sheep are stripped of their fleece at the spring ceremony of sheepshearing in spring.
10. Since Men paid no Rent and Leases . . . *Draft.* Since men lived freely like Robin Hood in Sherwood Forest. Reynolds had recently begun to study law to become a solicitor.
13. ivory] Hunting horn.
16. No old hermit with his . . . *Draft (cancelled).*
18. forest drear] Cp. Milton's *Il Penseroso* 119,

        Of Forests and inchantments drear . . .

19.   No more barbed arrows fly
                Through one's own roof to the sky . . . *Draft (cancelled).*
21. seven stars] Planets seven *Draft (cancelled).*
22. ray] Beam *Draft (cancelled).* The pole star is always visible in the northern hemisphere. K. probably owed his knowledge of the stars in part to Bonnycastle's *Introduction to Astronomy* (see *To Charles Cowden Clarke* 67 *n*, p. 57 above).
25–7.   Never meet one of all the clan
                Rattling on an empty can
                An old hunting ditty . . . *Draft (cancelled).*

Thrumming on an empty can
Some old hunting ditty, while
He doth his green way beguile
To fair hostess Merriment,
30   Down beside the pasture Trent,
For he left the merry tale,
Messenger for spicy ale.

Gone, the merry morris din;
Gone, the song of Gamelyn;
35   Gone, the tough-belted outlaw
Idling in the 'grenè shawe';
All are gone away and past!
And if Robin should be cast
Sudden from his turfèd grave,

30. pasture] Pastoral, running through pastures.

33. merry morris din] The music of the morris dancers. Cp. *All's Well that Ends Well* II ii 24, 'a morris for May-day' and see *Endymion* iv 198 *n* (p. 254 above), 'merry din'.

34. the song of Gamelyn] *The Tale of Gamelyn*, a verse romance (*c.* 1350) in which the hero takes to the forest and becomes king of the outlaws. It was used by Thomas Lodge in his *Rosalynde. Euphues' Golden Legacy* (1590), the source of Shakespeare's *As You Like It*.

36. 'grenè shawe'] A quotation from Chaucer's *The Friar's Tale* 88,
        Wher rydestow under this grene shawe?

37. away and] and all is *Draft*

38–41.   No those times are flown and past
        What if Robin should be cast
        Sudden from his turfed grave?
        How would Marian behave
        In the forest now a days? . . . *Draft (cancelled).*

38–9. K. was probably remembering the account of Robin Hood's death in the ballad 'Robin Hood's Death and Burial', included in J. Ritson's *Robin Hood, A Collection of all the ancient Poems, Songs and Ballads now extant* . . . (1795), sts 16–17,
        . . . give me my bent bow in my hand,
           And a broad arrow I'll let flee;
    And where this arrow is taken up,
        There shall my grave digg'd be.

    Lay me a greed sod under my head,
        And another at my feet;
    And lay my bent bow by my side,
        Which was my music sweet;
    And make my grave of gravel and green,
        Which is most right and meet . . .

40   And if Marian should have
       Once again her forest days,
       She would weep, and he would craze.
       He would swear, for all his oaks,
       Fallen beneath the dockyard strokes,
45   Have rotted on the briny seas.
       She would weep that her wild bees
       Sang not to her—strange that honey
       Can't be got without hard money!

       So it is—yet let us sing,
50   Honour to the old bow-string!
       Honour to the bugle-horn!
       Honour to the woods unshorn!
       Honour to the Lincoln green!
       Honour to the archer keen!
55   Honour to tight little John,
       And the horse he rode upon!
       Honour to bold Robin Hood,
       Sleeping in the underwood!
       Honour to maid Marian,
60   And to all the Sherwood-clan!
       Though their days have hurried by
       Let us two a burden try.

44. *dockyard*] Woodman's *Draft*.
45. The ships built from the oaks in Sherwood Forest have now rotted away.
55. *tight*] Skilful. Perhaps incorporating a playful reference to his size, since the word also means trim, compact; Little John was one of Robin Hood's most skilled archers and won his nick-name because he was so tall.
61. *days*] Pleasures *Draft (cancelled)*.
62. You and I a stave will try *Draft*. On 'burden' see *Endymion* i 136 *n* (p. 125 above).

73 Lines on the Mermaid Tavern

Written *c.* 3 Feb. 1818 and copied out after the preceding poem *Robin Hood* (p. 301 above) in K.'s letter of this date to Reynolds (L i 225). According to E. F. Madden K. explained (in a letter now lost) that he wrote the poem after spending an evening at the Mermaid Tavern, Cheapside, traditionally the former meeting-place of Beaumont, Fletcher and other Elizabethan dramatists (*Harper's New Monthly Magazine* lv (1877) 361, repr. L i 225 *n*; on the uncertain evidence concerning the regular meeting of Elizabethan

writers at the Mermaid Tavern see I. A. Shapiro's 'The "Mermaid Club"'
MLR xlv Jan 1950 6–17). The poem owes something to Beaumont's description of the Mermaid Tavern in his *Letter to Ben Jonson* and indicates K.'s
enthusiasm for Elizabethan poetry, which is elsewhere expressed in his letter
to Reynolds, 'It may be said that . . . Wordsworth etc. should have their
due from us. . . . I don't mean to deny Wordsworth's grandeur and Hunt's
merit, but . . . we need not be teazed with grandeur and merit–when we
can have them uncontaminated and unobtrusive. Let us have the old Poets'
(*L* i 223–5).
Text from *1820*, with some variants noted from K.'s undated holograph
MS.
Published *1820*.

Souls of Poets dead and gone,
What Elysium have ye known,
Happy field or mossy cavern,
Choicer than the Mermaid Tavern?
5 Have ye tippled drink more fine
Than mine host's Canary wine?
Or are fruits of Paradise
Sweeter than those dainty pies
Of venison? Oh, generous food,
10 Dressed as though bold Robin Hood
Would, with his Maid Marian,
Sup and bowse from horn and can.

I have heard that on a day
Mine host's sign-board flew away,
15 Nobody knew whither, till
An astrologer's old quill

¶ 73. 2. 'Elysium or Elysii Campi, a place or island in the infernal regions,
where, according to the mythology of the ancients, the souls of the virtuous were placed after death' (*Lemprière*).
4. *Choicer*] Fairer *MS*. On the Mermaid Tavern see headnote above.
5–6. Cp. Beaumont's *Letter to Ben Jonson* 5–6,
     . . . In this warm shine
  I lie, and dream of your full Mermaid wine . . .
9. *Oh*] Old *MS*.
10–12. A reference to Reynolds's Robin Hood sonnets–see headnote to
Robin Hood (p. 301 above).
12. *bowse*] A colloquialism for 'drink'. K. would also have known the
Elizabethan use of the word, e.g. Sandys's commentary on Ovid's *Metamorphoses* v (Sandys's *Ovid*, p. 95),
  I of the horses spring did never bowse . . .
13. *I have heard*] The story is K.'s own invention.

To a sheepskin gave the story,
Said he saw you in your glory,
Underneath a new old sign
20   Sipping beverage divine,
And pledging with contented smack
The Mermaid in the Zodiac.

Souls of Poets dead and gone,
What Elysium have ye known,
25   Happy field or mossy cavern,
Choicer than the Mermaid Tavern?

18. *Said*] Says *MS*.
19. *new old sign*] A newly arrived old sign-board.
22. *in the Zodiac*] In the skies.
24-6.   Are the winds a sweeter home,
                          Richer is uncellar'd cavern
                          Than the merry Mermaid Tavern . . . *MS*.

74 To —— ['Time's sea']

Written 4 Feb. 1818: so dated in three transcripts (*Reynolds; Woodhouse* 1,
2). For the subject see headnote to *Fill for me* and *When I have fears* 9 n (pp.
6 and 297 above). The poem is K.'s second Shakespearian sonnet and
shows the influence of his new close study of Shakespeare's manner in the
sonnets.
Text from *1848*, with some variants noted from the version in *Hood's
Magazine*.
Published *Hood's Magazine* Sept. 1844 and *1848*.

Time's sea hath been five years at its slow ebb,
     Long hours have to and fro let creep the sand,

¶ 74. 1. *Time's . . . years*] Life's . . . times *Hood's Magazine*. K.'s first poem
celebrating the unknown woman he had once briefly caught sight of was
written less than four years before this—see headnote to *Fill for me* (p. 306
above). The phrasing in this and the following line suggests the influence
of Shakespeare's statements about the passing of time in his sonnets, for
example Sonnet civ 3-6,
                          . . . Three winters cold
          Have from the forests shook three summers' pride,
          Three beauteous springs to yellow autumn turn'd
          In process of the seasons have I seen . . .
and Sonnet lx 1-2,
          Like as the waves make towards the pebbled shore,
          So do our minutes hasten to their end . . .
Both sonnets are marked by K. in his copy of Shakespeare's *Poems* (1806
edn) at Hampstead.

Since I was tangled in thy beauty's web,
   And snared by the ungloving of thine hand.
5 And yet I never look on midnight sky,
   But I behold thine eyes' well-memoried light.
I cannot look upon the rose's dye,
   But to thy cheek my soul doth take its flight.
I cannot look on any budding flower,
10   But my fond ear, in fancy at thy lips
And hearkening for a love-sound, doth devour
   Its sweets in the wrong sense. Thou dost eclipse
Every delight with sweet remembering,
And grief unto my darling joys dost bring.

6. well-memoried] The phrase has a Shakespearian flavour. See, for example,
Sonnet xxxii 1 (marked by K. in his copy of Shakespeare's *Poems*), 'my
well-contented day'.
7. cannot look] never gaze *Hood's Magazine*.
7–12. Perhaps suggested by Shakespeare's Sonnet xcviii 9–12 (marked by
K. in his copy of Shakespeare's *Poems*),

      Nor did I wonder at the lily's white,
      Nor praise the deep vermilion in the rose;
      They were but sweet, but figures of delight,
      Drawn after you, you pattern of all those . . .

11–12. doth devour / Its sweets in the wrong sense] The 'budding flower' re-
minds K. of the girl's mouth, so he listens 'for a love sound' from it instead
of enjoying its scent and colour. The use of the word 'devour' in this context foreshadows *Ode on Melancholy* 15 (p. 540 below), 'glut thy sorrow on
a morning rose'.
13–14.   Other delights with thy remembering
      And sorrow to my darling joys dost bring . . .
               Hood's Magazine
14. A Shakespearian antithesis. See, for example, Sonnet l 14,
      My grief lies onward, and my joy behind.
The word 'darling' is probably a Shakespearian echo. Cp. Sonnet xviii 3
(marked by K. in his copy of Shakespeare's *Poems*), 'the darling buds of
May'.

75 To the Nile

Written 4 Feb. 1818: see K.'s letter to George and Tom Keats 14 Feb. 1818,
'The Wednesday before last [4 Feb.] Shelley, Hunt and I wrote each a son-
net on the River Nile' (*L* i 227–8). Woodhouse records that K. and
Shelley finished within the set period of fifteen minutes (*Woodhouse* 2);
Shelley's sonnet was published in 1876, Hunt's in 1818. For K.'s contribu-
tions to similar poetry contests see headnote to *On the Grasshopper* (p. 97

above). The poem is one of the few Petrarchan sonnets written by K. after Jan. 1818.

Text from *1848*, which follows Brown's transcript corrected in K.'s hand. Published *Plymouth and Devonport Weekly Journal* 19 July 1838; repr. *1848*.

Son of the old moon-mountains African!
   Chief of the pyramid and crocodile!
   We call thee fruitful, and, that very while,
A desert fills our seeing's inward span.
5 Nurse of swart nations since the world began,
   Art thou so fruitful? Or dost thou beguile
   Such men to honour thee, who, worn with toil,
Rest for a space 'twixt Cairo and Decan?
Oh, may dark fancies err! They surely do.
10   'Tis ignorance that makes a barren waste
Of all beyond itself. Thou dost bedew
   Green rushes like our rivers, and dost taste
The pleasant sunrise. Green isles hast thou too,
   And to the sea as happily dost haste.

¶ 75. *1. moon-mountains African*] The mountains at the source of the Nile were sometimes known as the Mountains of the Moon. See, for example, Thomson's *The Seasons* (1730) *Autumn*, 801–2,

        Of Abyssinia's cloud-compelling cliffs,
        And of the bending Mountains of the Moon!

3–4. The Nile's annual flooding makes Egypt 'fruitful', but its course flows through the desert.

5. swart] Dark or black. A Miltonic word. See *Endymion* ii 15 *n* (p. 164 above).

6–7.   Art thou so beautiful, or a wan smile
        Pleasant but to those men, who sick with toil . . .

                          Reynolds; Woodhouse, 1, 2.
The lines are written out, with l. 8 below, in K.'s hand in a space left blank in Brown's transcript.

8. Englishmen on their way to India landed at Alexandria and sailed up the Nile to Cairo before travelling across the desert to Suez and the Red Sea.

11–14. K.'s countryside suggests England rather than Africa.

76 'Spenser! A jealous honourer of thine'

Written 5 Feb. 1818: so dated in K.'s draft (Dumbarton Oaks Library) and holograph fair copy (Morgan Library). K. wrote the poem for Reynolds after visiting him 4 Feb. 1818 (*L* i 225).

Text from K.'s fair copy, with some variants noted from his draft.
Published *1848*.

> Spenser! A jealous honourer of thine,
>   A forester deep in thy midmost trees,
> Did last eve ask my promise to refine
>   Some English that might strive thine ear to please.
> 5 But, Elfin Poet, 'tis impossible
>   For an inhabitant of wintry earth
> To rise like Phoebus with a golden quell
>   Fire-winged and make a morning in his mirth.
> It is impossible to escape from toil
> 10 O' the sudden and receive thy spiriting—
> The flower must drink the nature of the soil
>   Before it can put forth its blossoming.
> Be with me in the summer days and I
> Will for thine honour and his pleasure try.

¶ 76. *1. jealous honourer*] Reynolds. See his *Sonnet to a Friend* [? Bailey] (1817) 1–2,

> We are both lovers of the poets old!
> But Milton hath your heart,–and Spenser mine . . .

2. forester] An allusion to Reynolds's Robin Hood sonnets. See headnote to *Robin Hood* (p. 301 above).

5. Elfin Poet] Poet of Elfin or Fairy land. The phrase 'Elfin knight' occurs frequently in *The Faerie Queene*.

7–8. like Phoebus . . . Fire-winged] Like Phoebus Apollo whose fiery light dispels the wintry darkness. For K.'s earlier use of 'quell' (the power to subdue or destroy) see *Endymion* ii 537 and *n* (p. 185 above),

> A sovereign quell is in his waving hands . . .

9. escape from toil] leave this world *Draft*. K.'s 'toil' was the preparation of *Endymion* for the press. He was still revising *Endymion* ii on 5 Feb. 1818–see his letter of this date to J. Taylor (*L* i 226)–and did not finish copying out the poem until *c.* 14 March 1818 (*L* i 246). Another reason for K.'s desertion of Spenser is suggested by his renewed interest in Shakespeare and Milton.

77 'Blue! 'Tis the life of heaven'

Answer to a sonnet ending thus:

> Dark eyes are dearer far
> Than those that mock the hyacinthine bell

J. H. REYNOLDS

Written 8 Feb. 1818 as a reply to Reynold's sonnet, *Sweet poets of the gentle antique line*: so dated in five of the seven transcripts.

Text from *1848*, as generally agreeing with Woodhouse's transcripts
(*Woodhouse* 1, 2), with some variants noted from K.'s draft and the tran-
script in Reynolds's copy of *The Garden of Florence* (1821).
Published *1848*.

> Blue! 'Tis the life of heaven, the domain
>   Of Cynthia, the wide palace of the sun,
> The tent of Hesperus and all his train,
>   The bosomer of clouds, gold, grey and dun.
> 5   Blue! 'Tis the life of waters. Ocean
>   And all its vassal streams, pools numberless,
> May rage, and foam, and fret, but never can
>   Subside, if not to dark blue nativeness.
> Blue! Gentle cousin of the forest-green,
> 10   Married to green in all the sweetest flowers—
> Forget-me-not, the blue bell, and that queen
>   Of secrecy, the violet! What strange powers
> Hast thou as a mere shadow! But how great,
> When in an eye thou art alive with fate!

¶ 77. *1. life*] hue *Reynolds MS.*

2. wide] bright *Reynolds MS.*

3. Hesperus and all his train] The stars. Hesperus, the evening star, is the
first to appear.

6. its vassel] his tributary *Reynolds MS.* K. substituted 'Pools numberless'
for 'Lakes, Pools and Sea' in his draft.

7-8.   And Waterfalls and Fountains never ran
                     Or swell'd or slept . . . still *Draft (cancelled)*.

8. Subside, if not to] Subside but to a *Draft*.

12. secrecy] Hiddenness *Draft (cancelled)*.

14. art alive] The reading of K.'s draft, *Woodhouse* 1, *1848*; art, alive
Reynolds, Woodhouse 2. K. substituted 'When' for 'Trembling' in his draft.

78 'O thou whose face hath felt the winter's wind'

Written 19 Feb. 1818 in K.'s letter of this date to Reynolds with the following introduction, 'I have not read any Books-the Morning said I was right—
I had no idea, but of the Morning and the Thrush said I was right—seeming
to say-' (*L* i 232–3). The poem is an unrhymed sonnet and restates in
Keatsian terms the theme of 'wise passiveness' in Wordsworth's *Expostulation and Reply* (1798).

Text from K.'s letter.
Published *1848*.

O thou whose face hath felt the winter's wind,
   Whose eye has seen the snow-clouds hung in mist,
   And the black elm tops 'mong the freezing stars,
   To thee the spring will be a harvest-time.
5 O thou, whose only book has been the light
   Of supreme darkness which thou feddest on
   Night after night when Phoebus was away,
   To thee the spring shall be a triple morn.
  Oh, fret not after knowledge—I have none,
10   And yet my song comes native with the warmth.
  Oh, fret not after knowledge—I have none,
   And yet the evening listens. He who saddens
  At thought of idleness cannot be idle,
  And he's awake who thinks himself asleep.

¶ 78. *1* (and *5* below). *O thou*] The repetitions in the poem—see also ll. 9 and 11 below—compensate for its absence of rhyme and may be the result of K.'s half-conscious attempt to imitate the melodic repetitions of the thrush's song.

3. the freezing stars] Cp. *Keen, fitful gusts* 3 (p. 63 above),

        The stars look very cold about the sky . . .

4 (and *8* below). On K.'s special feeling for the return of spring after winter see *After dark vapours* 1–4 *n* (p. 101 above).

5–6. Whose only book . . . supreme darkness] The paradox was probably suggested by the phrasing in Wordsworth's *Expostulation and Reply* 5–6,

       Where are your books?—that light bequeathed
       To Beings else forlorn and blind . . .

8. triple] Threefold. Used for emphasis.

9–11. Cp. Wordsworth's *The Tables Turned* 9–10,

       Books! 'tis a dull and endless strife:
       Come hear the woodland linnet . . .

and *13–16*,

         . . . how blithe the throstle sings!
       He, too, is no mean preacher:
       Come forth into the light of things,
       Let Nature be your Teacher . . .

and see another part of K.'s letter to Reynolds of 19 Feb. 1818, '. . . let us not therefore go . . . buzzing here and there impatiently from a knowledge of what is to be arrived at . . . let us open our leaves like a flower and be passive and receptive' (*L* i 232).

10. The thrush's song is a natural spontaneous response to the new warmth of spring.

12–14. To reflect regretfully about one's own idleness and to think of oneself as asleep are really forms of activity. K. recognizes the mixture of truth and disingenuousness in this argument in his letter to Reynolds, 'Now I am sensible all this is mere sophistication, however it may be neighbour to any truths, to excuse my own indolence' (*L* i 233).

79 'Four seasons fill the measure of the year'

Written between 7 and 13 March 1818: K. arrived at Teignmouth *c.* 6–7 March 1818 and copied out the poem in his letter to Bailey from Teignmouth 13 March 1818 with the prefatory comments, 'I am sometimes so very sceptical as to think Poetry itself a mere Jack a lanthorn ... probably every mental pursuit takes its reality and worth from the ardour of the pursuer–being in itself a nothing–Ethereal thing[s] may at least be thus real, divided under three heads–Things real–things semireal–and no things–Things real–such as existences of Sun Moon & Stars and passages of Shakespeare–Things semireal such as Love, the Clouds etc. which require a greeting of the Spirit to make them wholly exist–and Nothings which are made Great and dignified by an ardent pursuit ...I have written a Sonnet here [i.e. at Teignmouth] of a somewhat collateral nature' (*L* i 242–3). The parallel in the poem between human life and the seasons is a poetic commonplace (for example, Ovid's *Metamorphoses* xv 199–213), but K. gives a marked Shakespearian ring to his celebration of poetic receptiveness, passivity and reflection.

Text from the first printed version with some variants noted from K.'s letter.

Published Leigh Hunt's *Literary Pocket Book* (1819); repr. *Galignani* (1829).

> Four seasons fill the measure of the year;
>   There are four seasons in the mind of man.
> He has his lusty spring, when fancy clear
>   Takes in all beauty with an easy span.
> 5 He has his summer, when luxuriously
>   Spring's honeyed cud of youthful thought he loves
> To ruminate, and by such dreaming nigh
>   His nearest unto heaven. Quiet coves
> His soul has in its autumn, when his wings
> 10   He furleth close, contented so to look

¶ 79. 2. *There are four seasons*] Four seasons are there ... *Letter.*
3–12. Spring, summer and autumn represent states of fruitful passivity.
6–10.   He chews the honied cud of fair spring thoughts,
        Till, in his Soul dissolv'd they come to be
          Part of himself. He hath his Autumn ports
        And Havens of repose, when his tired wings
          Are folded up, and he content to look ... *Letter copy.*
7–8. nigh | His nearest unto heaven] By such dreaming he comes as near as he can in this life to heaven.

On mists in idleness—to let fair things
    Pass by unheeded as a threshold brook;
He has his winter, too, of pale misfeature,
Or else he would forego his mortal nature.

11. mists] Cp. *To Autumn* 1 (p. 651 below),
                Season of mists and mellow fruitfulness . . .
12. threshold brook] A brook that runs by a cottage.
13. misfeature] Haggardness. The word is a fine coinage with a Shakespearian flavour.
14. forego] forget *Letter*.

80 Extracts from an Opera

Probably written spring 1818: dated '1818' by Woodhouse, who tran-
scribes the six short pieces (printed together in *1848*) under the general title
given above: see K. to George and Tom Keats 14 (?) Feb. 1818, 'I have been
writing at intervals many songs and Sonnets' (*L* i 228). For the view that K.
attempted an opera at Brown's instigation see *Finney* 370. Brown's comic
opera, *Narensky, or the road to Yaroslaff*, was first performed at Drury Lane
11 Jan. 1814.
Published *1848*.

I

Oh, were I one of the Olympian twelve,
Their godships should pass this into a law—
That when a man doth set himself in toil
After some beauty veilèd far away,
5 Each step he took should make his lady's hand
More soft, more white, and her fair cheek more fair.
And for each briar-berry he might eat,
A kiss should bud upon the tree of love,
And pulp and ripen richer every hour,
10 To melt away upon the traveller's lips.

¶ 80. i *1. the Olympian twelve*] The twelve gods who ruled on Mount
Olympus.
i *9. pulp*] Cp. *Hush, hush! Tread softly* 16 (p. 450 below), 'her lips pulped
with bloom'.

II. Daisy's Song

The poem is similar in style to K.'s Teignmouth songs, *For there's Bishop's
Teign* and *Where be ye going* (pp. 316 and 318 below).

I

The sun, with his great eye,
Sees not so much as I;

And the moon, all silver-proud,
Might as well be in a cloud.

II

5   And oh, the spring, the spring!
I lead the life of a king!
Couched in the teeming grass,
I spy each pretty lass.

III

I look where no one dares,
10   And I stare where no one stares,
And when the night is nigh,
Lambs bleat my lullaby.

ii 5. Cp. *For there's Bishops Teign* 31-2(p. 317 below),
And oh, and oh,
The daisies blow . . .
ii 7-10. Cp. *Where be ye going* 15-16 (p. 319 below),
And we will sigh in the daisy's eye
And kiss on a grass-green pillow.
and *Over the hill and over the dale* 19-20 (p. 319 below),
Oh, who would not rumple the daisies there
And make the wild fern for a bed do?

III. Folly's Song

When wedding fiddles are a-playing,
Huzza for folly O!
And when maidens go a-maying,
Huzza, &c.
5   When a milk-pail is upset,
Huzza, &c.
And the clothes left in the wet,
Huzza, &c.
When the barrel's set abroach,
10   Huzza, &c.
When Kate Eyebrow keeps a coach,
Huzza, &c.
When the pig is over-roasted,
Huzza, &c.
15   And the cheese is over-toasted,
Huzza, &c.
When Sir Snap is with his lawyer,
Huzza, &c.
And Miss Chip has kissed the sawyer,
20   Huzza, &c.

IV

Oh, I am frightened with most hateful thoughts!
Perhaps her voice is not a nightingale's,
Perhaps her teeth are not the fairest pearl.
Her eye-lashes may be, for aught I know,
5   Not longer than the may-fly's small fan-horns.
There may not be one dimple on her hand.
And freckles many! Ah, a careless nurse,
In haste to teach the little thing to walk,
May have crumped up a pair of Dian's legs,
10   And warped the ivory of a Juno's neck.

iv 2–7. *Perhaps . . . freckles many*] K.'s ironical version of Shakespeare's sonnet cxxx 1–8 (marked by K. in his copy of Shakespeare's *Poems*, 1806 edn, at Hampstead).

> My mistress' eyes are nothing like the sun;
> Coral is far more red than her lips' red:
> If snow be white, why then her breasts are dun;
> If hairs be wires, black wires grow on her head.
> I have seen roses damask'd, red and white,
> But no such roses see I in her cheeks;
> And in some perfumes there is more delight
> Than in the breath that from my mistress reeks . . .

iv 9. *crumped*] Bent. 'Crump' was used at the time to mean 'bend into a curve, crook, curl up' (*OED*).

V

K.'s first attempt to imitate ballad style; for his later attempts see *Old Meg she was a gipsy* and *La Belle Dame Sans Merci* (pp. 358 and 500 below).

I

The stranger lighted from his steed,
    And ere he spake a word
He seized my lady's lily hand,
    And kissed it all unheard.

II

5   The stranger walked into the hall,
    And ere he spake a word
He kissed my lady's cherry lips,
    And kissed 'em all unheard.

III

The stranger walked into the bower—
10   But my lady first did go;

Aye, hand in hand into the bower,
　　Where my lord's roses blow.

IV

My lady's maid had a silken scarf,
　　And a golden ring had she,
15　And a kiss from the stranger, as off he went
　　Again on his fair palfrey.

VI

Asleep! Oh, sleep a little while, white pearl!
And let me kneel, and let me pray to thee,
And let me call Heaven's blessing on thine eyes,
And let me breathe into the happy air,
5　That doth enfold and touch thee all about,
Vows of my slavery, my giving up,
My sudden adoration, my great love!

81 'For there's Bishop's Teign'

Written 21 March 1818 in K.'s letter of this date to Haydon from Teignmouth, with the prefatory comment, 'I have enjoyed the most delightful Walks these three fine days beautiful enough to make me content here all the summer could I stay' (*L* i 249). The poem is one of three light-hearted songs–the others being *Where be you going, you Devon maid* and *Over the hill and over the dale* (pp. 318 and 319 below)–written by K. at Teignmouth while he was completing the preparation of *Endymion* for the press and also working on *Isabella* (headnote p. 326 below).
Text from K.'s letter.
Published in T. Taylor's *Autobiography of Haydon* (1853) and *Forman* (1883).

I

For there's Bishop's Teign
　　And King's Teign
And Coomb at the clear Teign head –
　　Where close by the stream
5　　You may have your cream
All spread upon barley bread.

¶ 81. *1–3. Bishop's Teign . . . King's Teign . . . Coomb*] Bishopsteignton and Kingsteignton are on the north side of the Teign estuary, both within about five miles from Teignmouth. Combinteignhead is across the ferry on the south side, less than four miles from Teignmouth. K. would have encountered the other places mentioned in the poem in his 'most delightful walks' in the neighbourhood.

II

There's arch Brook
And there's Larch Brook,
Both turning many a mill,
10   And cooling the drouth
Of the salmon's mouth,
And fattening his silver gill.

III

There is Wild Wood,
A Mild hood
15 To the sheep on the lea o' the down,
Where the golden furze,
With its green, thin spurs,
Doth catch at the maiden's gown.

IV

There is Newton march
20   With its spear grass harsh,
A pleasant summer level
Where the maidens sweet
Of the Market Street
Do meet in the dusk to revel.

V

25   There's the barton rich
With dyke and ditch
And hedge for the thrush to live in,
And the hollow tree
For the buzzing bee,
30 And a bank for the wasp to hive in.

VI

And oh, and oh,
The daisies blow
And the primroses are wakened,
And violets white
35   Sit in silver plight,
And the green bud's as long as the spike end.

VII

Then who would go
Into dark Soho,

25. *barton*] Farm-land.
35. *plight*] Attire. Cp. *The Faerie Queene* III xii 8,

> . . . *Indians* do aray
> Their tawnye bodies, in their proudest plight . . .

36. *spike*] Ear of corn. The rhyme suggests a cockney pronunciation.

And chatter with dacked-haired critics,
40   When he can stay
For the new-mown hay
And startle the dappled prickets?

39. dacked-haired] Short haired. The suggestion that K. is referring to
Hazlitt (*L* i 250 *n*) is unconvincing.
42. prickets] Deer.

82 'Where be ye going, you Devon maid'

Written 21 March in K.'s letter of this date to Haydon after the preceding
poem, 'Here's some doggrel for you—Perhaps you would like a bit of
B...hrell ["Bitchrell", K.'s coinage from "doggerel"]' (*L* i 250). K.
adapted the metre for his song from Chatterton (see *1–4 n*).
Text from K.'s letter.
Published, without stanza 2, *1848* and reprinted T. Taylor's *Autobiography
of Haydon* (1853); Forman (1883) is the first accurate version.

I

Where be ye going, you Devon Maid?
    And what have ye there i' the basket?
Ye tight little fairy, just fresh from the dairy,
    Will ye give me some cream if I ask it?

II

5   I love your meads and I love your flowers,
        And I love your junkets mainly,
    But 'hind the door I love kissing more,
        Oh, look not so disdainly!

III

    I love your hills and I love your dales,
10   And I love your flocks a-bleating—

¶ 82. *1–4.* Cp. the Minstrel's song *As Elynour bie the greene lesselle was syt-
tynge* in Chatterton's *Aella* (1777) 212–15,

Mie husbande, Lord Thomas, a forrester boulde,
    As ever clove pynne, or the baskette,
Does no cherysauncys from Elynour houlde,
    I have ytte as soon as I aske ytte . . .

K. wrote the first version of his dedication of *Endymion* to Chatterton
March 1818 (*Endymion* i, *n* to Title, p. 120 above). Bailey records K.'s enjoyment of Chatterton's songs, 'Methinks I now hear him recite, or *chant* in his
peculiar manner . . . the "Roundelay sung by the minstrels of Ella [*Aella*
844–903]"' (*KC* ii 276).

But oh, on the heather to lie together,
With both our hearts a-beating!

IV
I'll put your basket all safe in a nook,
Your shawl I hang up on this willow,
15 And we will sigh in the daisy's eye
And kiss on a grass-green pillow.

83 'Over the hill and over the dale'

Written 23 March 1818 in K.'s letter of this date to James Rice after visiting Dawlish Fair (*L* i 256–7); the fair was held on Easter Monday, which in 1818 fell on 23 March.
Text from K.'s letter.
Published *Lowell* (1925). Milnes gave the first quatrain only in *1848*.

Over the hill and over the dale,
And over the bourn to Dawlish,
Where gingerbread wives have a scanty sale
And gingerbread nuts are smallish.

5 Rantipole Betty she ran down a hill,
And kicked up her petticoats fairly.
Says I, 'I'll be Jack if you will be Jill.'
So she sat on the grass debonairly.

'Here's somebody coming, here's somebody coming!'
10 Says I, ''Tis the wind at a parley.'
So without any fuss, any hawing and humming,
She lay on the grass debonairly.

'Here's somebody here and here's somebody *there*!'
Says I, 'Hold your tongue you young gipsy.'
15 So she held her tongue and lay plump and fair
And dead as a Venus tipsy.

Oh, who wouldn't hie to Dawlish fair,
Oh, who wouldn't stop in a meadow?
Oh, who would not rumple the daisies there
20 And make the wild fern for a bed do?

¶ 83. *1–2.* Dawlish, a town near the mouth of the river Exe, is about three miles from Teignmouth.
2. bourn] Stream.
5. Rantipole] Used in the eighteenth century to mean 'wild, disorderly, rakish' (*OED*).

84 To J. H. Reynolds, Esq.

Written 25 March 1818 as a verse letter to Reynolds, who was ill at the
time: 'In hopes of cheering you through a Minute or two I was determined
to send you some lines so you will excuse this unconnected subject and
careless verse—You know, I am sure, Claude's Enchanted Castle and I wish
you may be pleased with my remembrance of it' (*L* i 259). K. probably
knew Claude's painting 'The Enchanted Castle' from the engraving of
1782 by William Woollett (1735–85), reproduced as Plate VI in Colvin
(1917) and as Plate XII in Ian Jack's *Keats and the Mirror of Art* (1967), which
also records (pp. 67–8, 127–30) the interest expressed by K.'s contemporaries, including Hazlitt, in this and other paintings by Claude. The first
half of the poem mixes uneasily jocose elements with romantic verse, but
ll. 67–105 express more urgently than any of K.'s work before this time his
awareness of the perplexities and cruelties of existence, from which he turns
away impatiently at the end. Commentaries on the poem include *Murry*
(1926) 65–7, *Bate* (1963) 306–9, D. Bush's *John Keats* (1966) 73–5, M.
Visick's '"Tease us out of thought": Keats's *Epistle to Reynolds* and the
Odes', *KShJ* xv (Winter 1966) 87–98.
Text from K.'s letter.
Published (without the last four lines) *1848*.

> Dear Reynolds, as last night I lay in bed,
> There came before my eyes that wonted thread
> Of shapes, and shadows, and remembrances,
> That every other minute vex and please.
> 5   Things all disjointed come from north and south,
> Two witch's eyes above a cherub's mouth,
> Voltaire with casque and shield and habergeon,
> And Alexander with his night-cap on,
> Old Socrates a-tying his cravat,

¶ 84. *5–12*. K.'s incongruities and 'Things all disjointed' recall Horace's
Ars Poetica 1–5,

> Humano capiti cervicem pictor equinam
> iungere si velit, et varias inducere plumas
> undique collatis membris, ut turpiter atrum
> desinat in piscem mulier formosa superne,
> spectatum admissi risum teneatis, amici? . . .

('If a painter chose to join a human head to the neck of a horse, and to
spread feathers of many a hue over limbs picked up now here now there, so
that what at the top is a lovely woman ends below in a black and ugly fish,
could you, my friends, if favoured with a private view, refrain from
laughing?' [Loeb edn].)
7. K. had been reading Voltaire in Feb. 1818 (*L* i 237).

10   And Hazlitt playing with Miss Edgeworth's cat,
     And Junius Brutus pretty well so so,
     Making the best of his way towards Soho.
       Few are there who escape these visitings–
     Perhaps one or two, whose lives have patient wings,
15   And through whose curtains peeps no hellish nose,
     No wild boar tushes, and no mermaid's toes;
     But flowers bursting out with lusty pride,
     And young Aeolian harps personified;
     Some, Titian colours touched into real life.
20   The sacrifice goes on; the pontiff knife
     Gleams in the sun, the milk-white heifer lows,
     The pipes go shrilly, the libation flows;

10. Maria Edgeworth (1767–1849) liked cats and was disliked by Hazlitt. See Hazlitt's *On the English Comic Writers* (1819), 'Mrs. Edgeworth's Tales . . . are a kind of pedantic, pragmatical common sense, tinctured with the pertness and pretensions of the paradoxes to which they are so self-complacently opposed' ('On the English Novelists', *Works* ed. P. P. Howe (1930–34) vi 123), and cp. K. to Haydon 21 March 1818, 'Hazlitt has damned the bigotted and the blue stockin[g]ed' (*L* i 252). K.'s early familiarity with Maria Edgeworth's novels is recorded in *Cowden Clarke* (1878) 124.

11. Junius Brutus] It is not certain whom K. had in mind, but probably Lucius Junius Brutus, founder of the Roman Republic (created consul 509 B.C.), celebrated for his part in defeating the Tarquins and for his strict moral sense. For 'so so' (tipsy) see also K. to Bailey May 1815, 'Rice . . . got a little so so at a Party of his' (*L* i 288).

14. patient] patent K.'s letter (*preserved in Woodhouse's transcript*). The reading follows the emendation suggested by S. R. Swaminathan who comments 'Keats uses the word "patient" about thirty times in his poems, while "patent" does not occur elsewhere . . . [K.'s] failure to dot his i might have misled the copyist' (*N & Q* Aug. 1967, 307). See also *Endymion* iii 24 (p. 207 above), 'patient wing'.

15–16. no hellish . . . mermaid's toes] A monster made up of incongruities.
16. tushes] An archaism for tusks.
17–18. One of the fanciful but harmonious 'visitings' experienced by the untroubled in spirit.
18. Aeolian harps] See *Ode to Apollo* 34 *n* (p. 16 above).
19. Titian colours] Rich colours.
20–2. The details suggest Claude's 'Landscape with the Father of Psyche sacrificing at the Milesian Temple of Apollo', exhibited at the British Institution in 1816 (reproduced as Plate XXXV in Ian Jack's *Keats and the Mirror of Art* (1967); for other indications of K.'s familiarity with this painting see *Sleep and Poetry* 354–91 *n* (pp. 83–4 above) and cp. *Ode on a Grecian Urn* 31–40 and *n* (p. 536 below).

A white sail shews above the green-head cliff,
Moves round the point, and throws her anchor stiff.
25 The mariners join hymn with those on land.
You know the Enchanted Castle–it doth stand
Upon a rock on the border of a lake
Nested in trees, which all do seem to shake
From some old magic like Urganda's sword.
30 O Phoebus, that I had thy sacred word
To show this castle in fair dreaming wise
Unto my friend, while sick and ill he lies.
    You know it well enough, where it doth seem
A mossy place, a Merlin's Hall, a dream.
35 You know the clear lake, and the little isles,
The mountains blue, and cold, near-neighbour rills.
All which elsewhere are but half animate
Here do they look alive to love and hate,
To smiles and frowns. They seem a lifted mound
40 Above some giant, pulsing underground.
    Part of the building was a chosen see
Built by a banished Santon of Chaldee;
The other part two thousand years from him
Was built by Cuthbert de Saint Aldebrim;
45 Then there's a little wing, far from the sun,

26–66. K.'s description of 'The Enchanted Castle' incorporates details found in Claude's 'Landscape with the Father of Psyche . . .' with others of his own invention.

29. Urganda's sword] Urganda the Unknown, the enchantress in the fifteenth-century romance *Amadis of Gaul* (abridged version published by Southey 1803), gave Amadis a lance, not a sword,

34. Merlin's Hall] A place which a magician like Merlin might have built.
40. some giant] Such as Enceladus or Typhon, Titans who were buried underground by Jupiter. See *Hyperion* ii 22–8 *n*, 66 *n* (pp. 417 and 420–1 below).

41. see] Place of abode.
41–54. Fanciful associations suggested by the mixed Roman, medieval and Palladian architectural styles of the building in 'The Enchanted Castle'.
42. Santon] A Mohammedan holy man. The word is found in 'Eastern' tales of the romantic period. See Beckford's *Vathek*, '. . . the multitude of Calendars, Santons and Dervishes, who were continually coming and going' (1816 edn. 114) and cp. Byron's *Childe Harold* ii 56,
    Slaves, eunuchs, soldiers, guests and santons wait . . .
According to Woodhouse this was followed by the cancelled line, 'Poor Man he left the Terrace walls of Ur'. See *Genesis* xi 31, 'They went forth from Ur of the Chaldees, to go into the land of Canaan . . .'.
44. Cuthbert de Saint Aldebrim] An invented name.

Built by a Lapland witch turned maudlin nun—
And many other juts of agèd stone
Founded with many a mason-devil's groan.
    The doors all look as if they oped themselves,
50 The windows as if latched by fays and elves—
And from them comes a silver flash of light
As from the westward of a summer's night;
Or like a beauteous woman's large blue eyes
Gone mad through olden songs and poesies.
55   See what is coming from the distance dim!
A golden galley all in silken trim.
Three rows of oars are lightening moment-whiles
Into the verdurous bosoms of those isles.
Towards the shade under the castle wall
60 It comes in silence—now tis hidden all.
The clarion sounds, and from a postern grate
An echo of sweet music doth create
A fear in the poor herdsman who doth bring
His beasts to trouble the enchanted spring.
65 He tells of the sweet music and the spot
To all his friends—and they believe him not.
    Oh, that our dreamings all of sleep or wake
Would all their colours from the sunset take,
From something of material sublime,
70 Rather than shadow our own soul's daytime
In the dark void of night. For in the world

46. *Lapland witch*] Associated with black magic. K. echoes Milton, *Paradise Lost* ii 664–5,

> Lur'd with the smell of infant blood, to dance
> With *Lapland* witches . . .

50. Foreshadows *Ode to a Nightingale* 69–70 (p. 530 below),

> . . . magic casements, opening on the foam
> Of perilous seas in fairy lands forlorn . . .

57. *lightening moment-whiles*] Flashing light from their blades as they are lifted from the water.

67–109] K. forgets his playful tone and becomes impassioned as he turns to the complexities of real life, confessing his distress at their bewildering effect on him (ll. 67–85) and his pain at the cruelty which he finds in Nature (ll. 86–109).

68–9. Echoes Wordsworth's *Tintern Abbey* (1798) 95–7,

> . . . a sense sublime
> Of something far more deeply interfused,
> Whose dwelling is the light of setting suns . . .

70–1. *shadow . . . night*] The incongruous elements of our dreams are connected with daytime experience.

>   We jostle . . . but my flag is not unfurled
>   On the admiral staff—and to philosophize
>   I dare not yet. Oh, never will the prize,
> 75   High reason and the lore of good and ill,
>   Be my award. Things cannot to the will
>   Be settled, but they tease us out of thought.
>   Or is it that imagination brought
>   Beyond its proper bound, yet still confined,
> 80   Lost in a sort of Purgatory blind,
>   Cannot refer to any standard law
>   Of either earth or heaven?
>   It is a flaw
>   In happiness to see beyond our bourn—

72–3. my flag . . . admiral staff] K. is still on the threshold of experience and
has not yet proved his powers. The image was suggested by North's translation of Plutarch's *Lives* (1676), 'The Life of Alcibiades', '. . . Alcibiades
setting up a Flag in the top of his Admiral Galley, to show what he was'
(178). For K.'s other references to Alcibiades see his letter to Reynolds 8
April 1818, '. . . Alcibiades leaning on his Crimson Couch in his Galley'
(*L* i 265).

73–4. to philosophise / I dare not yet] Cp. *Lines on Seeing a Lock of Milton's
Hair* 30–1 and *n* (p. 294 above),

>   Pangs are in vain, until I grow high-rife
>   With old Philosophy . . .

75. lore of good and ill] love of good and ill *1848*. Middleton Murry bases his
interpretation of the phrase on the *1848* reading; see *Murry* (1926) 66, 228–9.

76. to the will] To our wishes.

77. tease us out of thought] K. uses this expression again in *Ode on a Grecian
Urn* 44–5 (p. 537 below),

>   Thou, silent form, dost tease us out of thought
>   As doth eternity . . .

but he is chiefly concerned here with the limits of his own intellectual
powers, and the thought and feeling are closer to *Endymion* i 294–6 (p. 133
above),

>   . . . solitary thinkings—such as dodge
>   Conception to the very bourne of heaven,
>   Then leave the naked brain . . .

78–82. Or is it that imagination . . . heaven?] Imagination is lost in a half
world, since it is brought beyond its 'proper bound', which is heaven, and
yet cannot adjust itself to the laws of everyday reality which belong to
earth.

83. to see beyond our bourn] To become aware of complexities which are
beyond one's understanding. Expresses K.'s sense of his own immaturity—
his imagination is precociously active, but his knowledge of life is limited.
See his letter to Reynolds of 3 May 1818, 'An extensive knowledge is need-

It forces us in summer skies to mourn;
85   It spoils the singing of the nightingale.
        Dear Reynolds, I have a mysterious tale
    And cannot speak it. The first page I read
    Upon a lampit rock of green sea weed
    Among the breakers. 'Twas a quiet eve;
90   The rocks were silent; the wide sea did weave
    An untumultuous fringe of silver foam
    Along the flat brown sand. I was at home,
    And should have been most happy, but I saw
    Too far into the sea—where every maw
95   The greater on the less feeds evermore . . .
    But I saw too distinct into the core
    Of an eternal fierce destruction,
    And so from happiness I far was gone.
    Still am I sick of it; and though today
100   I've gathered young spring-leaves, and flowers gay
    Of periwinkle and wild strawberry,
    Still do I that most fierce destruction see:
    The shark at savage prey, the hawk at pounce,
    The gentle robin, like a pard or ounce,
105   Ravening a worm. . . . Away ye horrid moods,
    Moods of one's mind! You know I hate them well,

---

ful to thinking people—it takes away the heat and fever; and helps by widening speculation, to ease the Burden of the Mystery [see Wordsworth's
Tintern Abbey 38]. . . . The difference of high Sensations with and without
knowledge appears to me this—in the latter case we are falling continually
ten thousand fathoms deep and being blown up again without wings . . . in
the former case, our shoulders are fledge[d], and we go through the same
air and space without fear' (*L* i 277).

88. *lampet*] Limpet.

93–105. A mood of Romantic despair at the cruelty of Nature. For K.'s
cooler reflections on the 'fierce destruction' in the natural world see his
journal-letter of Feb.–May 1819, '. . . disinterestedness [i.e. unselfishness] . . .
ought to be carried to its highest pitch, as there is no fear of its ever injuring
society—which it would do I fear pushed to an extremity—For in wild
nature the Hawk would lose his Breakfast of Robins and the Robin his of
Worms. The Lion must starve as well as the swallow' (*L* ii 79).

94–5. *where . . . evermore*] Cp. *Pericles* II i 27–30: 'I marvel how the fishes
live in the sea. . . . Why, as men do a-land; the great ones eat up the little
ones.'

106. *Moods of one's mind*] Echoes Wordsworth's phrase, 'Moods of my own
mind', used as a title for thirteen poems in his *Poems* (1807). K. had imitated
one of these poems (*Written in March*) in *Lines Rhymed . . . from Oxford*
(headnote, p. 284 above).

You know I'd sooner be a clapping bell
To some Kamschatkan missionary church,
Than with these horrid moods be left in lurch.

110 Do you get health–and Tom the same–I'll dance,
And from detested moods in new romance
Take refuge. . . . Of bad lines a centaine dose
Is sure enough, and so 'here follows prose'.

108. Kamschatka missionary church] K. knew about the bleak landscape of
the Kamschatka peninsula, which is in the far east of Russia and is washed
by the Pacific Ocean and the Bering Sea, and about the conversion of its
inhabitants to Christianity, from accounts in Buffon's *Histoire Naturelle*
(English translation 1792), Robertson's *History of America* (1777) and various
records of Captain Cook's voyages; for a detailed discussion of these
sources see A. D. Atkinson, *N & Q* Aug 4 (1951) 343–5.

111. new romance] A reference to *Isabella*, which K. was currently writing;
see following headnote.

112. centaine dose] A dose of one hundred lines.

113. 'here follows prose'] See *Twelfth Night* II v 147, 'Soft! here follows
prose'.

85 Isabella; or, The Pot of Basil

Begun late Feb. or early March 1818 and completed by 27 April 1818: see
K.'s letter to Reynolds from Teignmouth 27 April 1818, 'I have written
for my folio Shakespeare in which there is the first few stanzas of my "Pot
of Basil": I have the rest here finish'd and will copy out the whole fair
shortly' (*L* i 274); K. left Hampstead for Teignmouth 4 March 1818. The
poem was intended as a contribution to a collection of verse tales based on
Boccaccio, which was projected as a joint venture by K. and Reynolds: see
Reynolds's letter to K. 14 Oct. 1818, 'I am of all things anxious that you
should publish it ['Isabella']. . . . I give over all intention and you ought to
be alone' (*L* i 376). The idea of translating Boccaccio was probably suggested by Hazlitt's lecture on 3 Feb. 1818, 'On Dryden and Pope' (published in *Lectures on the English Poets*, 1818), which K. attended (*L* i 39),
'[Dryden's] Tales have been the most popular of his works. . . . I should
think that a translation of some of the other serious tales in Boccaccio . . .
as that of Isabella . . . if executed with taste and spirit, could not fail to succeed in the present day' (*Works* ed. P. P. Howe (1930–4) v 82).

K.'s source for the story was the fifth novel of the fourth day in Boccaccio's *Decameron*, which he read in the fifth edition (1684) of the first English
translation of 1620. His treatment of the story shows the influence of the
translation, which differs in minor details from the original, but the poem

is a romantic expansion of Boccaccio's swiftly paced narrative and incorporates various interpolations and descriptive details of K.'s own invention.
For Matthew Arnold's censure of K.'s handling of the story see the preface
to *Poems* (1853). The poem is written in *ottava rima*, a metre frequently used
by the Italian poets and familiar to K. from his Elizabethan reading; his
handling of it, which is usually adroit in spite of stylistic lapses, suggests in
particular the influence of Fairfax's translation of Tasso's *Gerusalemme
Liberata* (1600), which he read early–see *On Receiving a Curious Shell* 8 *n*
(p. 20 above)–and of which he possessed a copy of the fourth edn (1749).
His choice of the metre is unlikely to have been guided by its current revival
as a medium for satire and burlesque in William Tennant's *Anster Fair*
(1812), Hookham Frere's *The Monk and the Giants* (1818) and Byron's
Beppo (published 28 Feb. 1818). Edward Thomas noted in his *Keats* (1916,
p. 49): 'The verse form was a discipline that exhibits the poet's choiceness
of detail better than the couplets of *Endymion* and . . . each stanza being complete in itself gave more excuse for it . . . *Isabella* became with the help
of the adagio stanza a very still poem.'

K. was dissatisfied with *Isabella* (see l. 54 *n* below), but Charles Lamb
praised it as the 'finest thing in the volume' in his review of *1820* (*The New
Times* 19 July 1820). For other critical commentaries on the poem see
Ridley (1933) 18–56, *Bate* (1945) 32–42, H. Wright's *Boccaccio in England*
(1957) 397–407, M. Allott's "Isabella", "The Eve of St. Agnes" and
"Lamia" in *Reassessment* (1958) 50–4.

Text from *1820*, with some variants noted from K.'s fair copy (British
Museum), draft and attempted revisions in the transcripts of his fair copy in
Woodhouse 1, 2. For the location of the various fragments of the draft see
Garrod.

Published *1820*.

¶ 85. *Title*. The Pot of Basil *Fair copy*. K. follows the English translation in
calling his heroine Isabella. The original has Lisabetta.

1–104. K. departs from Boccaccio by opening his narrative with the love
between Lorenzo and Isabella. Cp. Boccaccio's matter-of-fact beginning,
'In Messina there dwelt three young men, Brethren . . . Merchants by their
common profession, who becomming very rich by the death of their
Father, lived in very good fame and repute . . . they had a Sister named
Isabella, young beautiful, and well condition'd . . . as yet . . . unmarried. A
proper youth . . . a Gentleman borne in Pisa . . . named Lorenzo, as a trusty
factor or servant, had the mangaging of the brethrens businesse and affaires
. . . Lorenzo . . . of comely personage, affable, and excellent in his behaviour, grew so gracious in the eyes of Isabella, that she affoorded him
many very respective looks, yea kindnesses of no common quality. Which
Lorenzo . . . observing by degrees . . . gave over all other beauties in the
City, which might allure any affection from him, and . . . fixed his heart
on her . . . their love grew to a mutuall embracing, both . . . respecting

I

Fair Isabel, poor simple Isabel!
   Lorenzo, a young palmer in Love's eye!
They could not in the self-same mansion dwell
   Without some stir of heart, some malady;
5   They could not sit at meals but feel how well
   It soothed each to be the other by;
They could not, sure, beneath the same roof sleep
But to each other dream, and nightly weep.

II

With every morn their love grew tenderer,
10   With every eve deeper and tenderer still;
He might not in house, field, or garden stir,
   But her full shape would all his seeing fill;
And his continual voice was pleasanter
   To her than noise of trees or hidden rill;
15   Her lute-string gave an echo of his name,
She spoilt her half-done broidery with the same.

III

He knew whose gentle hand was at the latch
   Before the door had given her to his eyes;
And from her chamber-window he would catch
20   Her beauty farther than the falcon spies;

one another, and entertaining kindnesses, as occasion gave leave' (Shakespeare Head edn, 1934–35, i. 234). K. postpones reference to Isabella's
brothers until l. 105 and does not indicate the story's locality until l. 129.
2. *palmer in love's eye*] Pilgrim in search of love. Perhaps suggested by
Romeo and Juliet I v 103–4,

> And palm to palm is holy palmer's kiss.
> Have not saints lips, and holy palmers too?

Lorenzo's rejecting 'all other beauties in the City' for Isabella may have
reminded K. of Romeo's abandoning Rosaline for Juliet.
3 (and 5 below). They could not] K.'s use of repetition for rhetorical effect is
influenced by Spenser and probably also by Fairfax's *Tasso*, for example
i st. 72,

> Some shirts of mail, some coats of plate put on,
> Some donn'd a curace, some a corslet bright,
> And halbert some, and some a haberion . . .

and i st. 47,

> Sight, wonder; wonder, love; love bred his care.
> O love, O wonder; love new born, new bred,
> Now grown, now arm'd, this champion captive led . . .

For other examples in the poem see ll. 9–10, 81–4, 90–4, 169–70, 417–20,
433–6 below.

And constant as her vespers would he watch,
  Because her face was turned to the same skies;
And with sick longing all the night outwear,
To hear her morning-step upon the stair.

IV

25   A whole long month of May in this sad plight
      Made their cheeks paler by the break of June:
  'Tomorrow will I bow to my delight,
    Tomorrow will I ask my lady's boon.'
  'Oh, may I never see another night,
30   Lorenzo, if thy lips breathe not love's tune.'
So spake they to their pillows; but, alas,
Honeyless days and days did he let pass—

V

Until sweet Isabella's untouched cheek
  Fell sick within the rose's just domain,
35   Fell thin as a young mother's, who doth seek
    By every lull to cool her infant's pain.
  'How ill she is,' said he, 'I may not speak,
    And yet I will, and tell my love all plain.
If looks speak love-laws, I will drink her tears,
40 And at the least 'twill startle off her cares.'

VI

So said he one fair morning, and all day
  His heart beat awfully against his side;
And to his heart he inwardly did pray
  For power to speak; but still the ruddy tide
45   Stifled his voice and pulsed resolve away—
    Fevered his high conceit of such a bride,
Yet brought him to the meekness of a child.
Alas! when passion is both meek and wild!

21. *vespers*] Evening prayers.
30. *lips breathe*] tongue speak *Fair copy*.
39. *I will drink her tears*] A sentimental flourish perhaps borrowed from the eighteenth-century novel of sensibility. See, for example, Henry Brooke's *The Fool of Quality* (1766–70) Chap. 18, '. . . seeing some drops on her Harry's cheeks, she drew them in with her lips, crying—Precious pearls be these!'
40. *least*] worst *Fair copy*.
45 (and 244–5 below). So punctuated in K.'s fair copy and *1820* (which generally agree over the punctuation), but K.'s doubts are expressed in his notes on these lines in *Woodhouse* 1 which read respectively, 'Stop [i.e. punctuate] this as you please' and 'Please point this as you like'.

VII

So once more he had waked and anguishèd
50   A dreary night of love and misery,
If Isabel's quick eye had not been wed
    To every symbol on his forehead high.
She saw it waxing very pale and dead,
    And straight all flushed; so lispèd tenderly,
55 'Lorenzo!'–here she ceased her timid quest,
But in her tone and look he read the rest.

54. *lispèd tenderly*] K.'s love scenes recall the sentimental style of *Calidore* (headnote p. 36 above) and help to account for his later dislike of *Isabella*. See his letter to Woodhouse 22 Sept. 1819, 'I shall persist in not publishing The Pot of Basil–It is too smokeable [see *Cap and Bells* 615 *n*, p. 730 below] . . . There is too much inexperience of life, and simplicity of knowledge in it–which might do very well after one's death–but not while one is alive. . . . Isabella is what I should call were I a reviewer "A weak-sided Poem" with an amusing sober-sadness about it . . . in my dramatic capacity I enter fully into the feeling: but in Propria Persona I should be apt to quiz it myself' (*L* ii 174). See also Woodhouse's letter to Taylor 19 Sept. 1819, '[K.] said he could not bear [*Isabella*] now. It appeared to him mawkish' (*L* ii 162).

55–6. K.'s dissatisfaction with the couplet is indicated by the number of fragmentary corrections attempted in *Woodhouse* 1, 2 (see *Garrod*) and by the two following attempted expansions of Isabella's speech in K.s fair copy:

(a) Lorenzo, I would clip my ringlet hair
     To make thee laugh again and debonair

     'Then should I be,' said he 'full deified;
     And yet I would not have it, clip it not;
[5] For Lady I do love it where 'tis tied
     About the Neck I dote on; and that spot
     That anxious dimple it doth take a pride
     To play about.–Aye Lady I have got
     Its shadow in my heart and ev'ry sweet
[10] Its Mistress owns there summed all complete

(b) ['] Lorenzo in the twilight Morn was wont
     To rouse the clamorous Kennel to the hunt;

     And then his cheek inherited the Ray
     Of the outpouring Sun; and ere the Horn
[5] Could call the Hunter to the Chase away
     His Voice more softly woke the sun: Many a Morn
     From sweetest Dreams it drew me to a Day

VIII

'O Isabella, I can half perceive
 That I may speak my grief into thine ear.
If thou didst ever anything believe,
60 Believe how I love thee, believe how near
My soul is to its doom. I would not grieve
 Thy hand by unwelcome pressing, would not fear
Thine eyes by gazing, but I cannot live
Another night and not my passion shrive.

IX

65 Love, thou art leading me from wintry cold,
 Lady, thou leadest me to summer clime,
And I must taste the blossoms that unfold
 In its ripe warmth this gracious morning time.'
So said, his erewhile timid lips grew bold,
70 And poesied with hers in dewy rhyme.
Great bliss was with them, and great happiness
Grew like a lusty flower in June's caress.

X

Parting they seemed to tread upon the air,
 Twin roses by the zephyr blown apart
75 Only to meet again more close, and share
 The inward fragrance of each other's heart.
She, to her chamber gone, a ditty fair
 Sang, of delicious love and honeyed dart;
He with light steps went up a western hill,
80 And bade the sun farewell, and joyed his fill.

XI

All close they met again, before the dusk
 Had taken from the stars its pleasant veil,
All close they met, all eves, before the dusk

   More sweet; but now Lorenzo holds in scorn
   His Hunting [? Health] and all those by-gone Joys are
   Dreams
 [*10*] To me–to him, somehow–so chang'd he seems–[']
Ll. 3 to 10 of (*b*) are printed for the first time.
61. *My soul is*] This moment's *Draft*.
62. *fear*] Make afraid. See Woodhouse's note, 'i.e. alarm' (*Woodhouse 2*).
63–4. *Fair copy (written beside the 1820 reading)*,
    Thine eyes by gazing, nor sh[oul]d thy hand fear
    Unwelcome pressing: but I cannot live . . .
Garrod's reading of the last four words above is 'that it cannot bear'.
64. *shrive*] Confess. See *Endymion* iv 26 *n* (p. 246 above).

Had taken from the stars its pleasant veil,
85   Close in a bower of hyacinth and musk,
Unknown of any, free from whispering tale.
Ah, better had it been for ever so,
Than idle ears should pleasure in their woe.

XII

Were they unhappy then? It cannot be.
90   Too many tears for lovers have been shed,
Too many sighs give we to them in fee,
Too much of pity after they are dead,
Too many doleful stories do we see,
Whose matter in bright gold were best be read,
95   Except in such a page where Theseus' spouse
Over the pathless waves towards him bows.

XIII

But, for the general award of love,
The little sweet doth kill much bitterness.

87. O that unto the end it had been so . . . Draft (cancelled).

89–104. The first of four Keatsian 'insertions' in the narrative – the other three being ll. 121–60, 385–92, 433–48 below. For the view that they may have been suggested by Mirabeau's Nouvelles de Jean Boccacce, Traduction libre (Paris 1802) see Ridley (1933) 55–6. K. quotes the lines together with ll. 233–40 below in his letter to Reynolds 27 April 1818, 'Perhaps a Stanza or two will not be too foreign to your Sickness' (L i 274).

94. in bright gold were best be read] Should be celebrated for its happiness.

95. Theseus' spouse] Ariadne. See Sleep and Poetry 335–6 n (p. 83 above).

96. pathless] See Addressed to Haydon 4 n (p. 66 above).

98. An image deriving originally from Petrarch's Triumphus Cupidinis iii 186,

Ché poco dolce molto amaro appaga . . .

and probably known to K. from Spenser's version in The Faerie Queene I iii 30,

A dram of sweet is worth a pound of sowre . . .

99. A reference to Virgil's Aeneid vi 440–74, particularly vi 442–51,

hic, quos durus amor crudeli tabe peredit,
secreti celant calles et myrtea circum
silva tegit; curae non ipsa in morte relinquunt

. . .

inter quas Phoenissa recens a volnere Dido
errabat silva in magna . . .

('Here those whom stern Love has consumed with cruel wasting are hidden in walks withdrawn, embowered in a myrtle grove; even in death the pangs leave them not. . . . Among them, with wound still fresh, Phoenician Dido was wandering in the great forest' [Loeb edn].) For K.'s early familiarity with Dido's story, see Imitation of Spenser 21 n (p. 4 above).

Though Dido silent is in under-grove,
100   And Isabella's was a great distress,
Though young Lorenzo in warm Indian clove
        Was not embalmed, this truth is not the less –
Even bees, the little almsmen of spring-bowers,
Know there is richest juice in poison-flowers.

XIV

105 With her two brothers this fair lady dwelt,
        Enrichèd from ancestral merchandise,
And for them many a weary hand did swelt
        In torchèd mines and noisy factories,
And many once proud-quivered loins did melt
110   In blood from stinging whip. With hollow eyes
Many all day in dazzling river stood,
To take the rich-ored driftings of the flood.

XV

For them the Ceylon diver held his breath,
        And went all naked to the hungry shark;
115 For them his ears gushed blood; for them in death

103. almsmen] The buzzing of the bees is like the sound of prayers murmured by almsmen (men endowed to pray for others; see *The Eve of St. Agnes* 5 n, p. 453 below).

104. For later expressions of K.'s feeling for the close association of pain and pleasure see *Ode to Melancholy* 23–4 (p. 540 below),

    . . . aching Pleasure nigh,
        Turning to poison while the bee-mouth sips . . .

and *Lamia* i 192 (p. 625 below),

        To unperplex bliss from its neighbour pain . . .

105–44. K. gives Isabella two brothers instead of three, but expands Boccaccio's brief characterisation of them—quoted in ll. 1–104 n above—by dwelling on their greedy commercialism. His description introduces an element of social criticism into the poem for which he apologises in ll. 145–60.

107. swelt] Swelter. A Spenserianism, e.g. *The Faerie Queene* I vii 6,

    . . . like a fever fit through all his body swelt . . .

K. may be recollecting Mammon in *The Faerie Queene* II vii 8,

        . . . all this worldes good,
    For which men swinck and sweat incessantly . . .

Cp. 451 n below.

109. proud-quivered] K.'s compounds—see also l. 112 below, 'rich-ored'—point towards the concentrated style of his later verse.

113–20. Probably echoing Dryden's *Annus Mirabilis* (1667) 9–12,

        For them alone the Heav'ns had kindly heat,
            In Eastern Quarries ripening precious Dew:

12*

The seal on the cold ice with piteous bark
Lay full of darts; for them alone did seethe
   A thousand men in troubles wide and dark.
Half-ignorant, they turned an easy wheel
120   That set sharp racks at work to pinch and peel.

XVI

Why were they proud? Because their marble founts
   Gushed with more pride than do a wretch's tears?
Why were they proud? Because fair orange-mounts
   Were of more soft ascent than lazar stairs?
125   Why were they proud? Because red-lined accounts
   Were richer than the songs of Grecian years?
Why were they proud? Again we ask aloud,
Why in the name of glory were they proud?

XVII

Yet were these Florentines as self-retired
130   In hungry pride and gainful cowardice,
As two close Hebrews in that land inspired,
   Paled in and vineyarded from beggar-spies.
The hawks of ship-mast forests, the untired
   And panniered mules for ducats and old lies,
135   Quick cat's-paws on the generous stray-away,
Great wits in Spanish, Tuscan, and Malay.

For them the *Idumaean* Balm did sweat,
      And in hot *Ceilon* Spicy Forrests grew ...
K. follows Dryden in accenting the first syllable in 'Ceylon' (l. 113).
116. Cp. Buffon's *Natural History* (English translation 1792), 'The voice of
the seal may be compared to the barking of an angry dog' (ix 68); for K.'s
March 1818 references to Buffon see *To J. H. Reynolds Esq.* 108 *n* (p. 326
above).
117. alone] in woe *Draft (cancelled).*
121–60. See ll. 89–104 *n* above.
124. lazar stairs] Stairs in a lazar-house, occupied by the poor and diseased.
129. Florentines] Boccaccio sets the story in Messina but there are frequent
references to Florence and its neighbourhood in the *Decameron.* For their
probable influence on K.'s setting see H. G. Wright's *Boccaccio in England*
402–3.
131. that land inspired] Palestine.
136. Followed in the fair copy by the stanza:
      Two young Orlandos far away they seem'd,
         But on a near inspect their vapid Miens—
      Very alike,—at once themselves redeem'd
         From all suspicion of Romantic spleens—
   [5] No fault of theirs, for their good Mother dream'd

XVIII

How was it these same ledger-men could spy
    Fair Isabella in her downy nest?
How could they find out in Lorenzo's eye
140   A straying from his toil? Hot Egypt's pest
Into their vision covetous and sly!
    How could these money-bags see east and west?
    Yet so they did—and every dealer fair
    Must see behind, as doth the hunted hare.

XIX

145 O eloquent and famed Boccaccio!
    Of thee we now should ask forgiving boon,
And of thy spicy myrtles as they blow,
    And of thy roses amorous of the moon,
    And of thy lilies, that do paler grow
150   Now they can no more hear thy ghittern's tune,
For venturing syllables that ill beseem
The quiet glooms of such a piteous theme.

XX

Grant thou a pardon here, and then the tale
    Shall move on soberly, as it is meet;
155 There is no other crime, no mad assail
    To make old prose in modern rhyme more sweet.
But it is done—succeed the verse or fail—
    To honour thee, and thy gone spirit greet,

      In the longing time of Units[,] in their teens
    Of proudly bas'd addition and of net—
      And both their backs were mark'd with tare and tret . . .

The stanza, rightly rejected by K. for its inappropriate satirical tone, makes use of commercial references: the brothers' mother dreamed of money when she was pregnant and later whipped her sons into a proper respect for trade—'tare and tret' are the normal deductions made in calculating the weight of goods sold by retail.

140-1. Hot Egypt's pest / Into their vision] Alludes to the plague of darkness visited upon the Egyptians (*Exodus* x 21-3).

145. and famed Boccaccio!] Boccace of Green Arno! *Fair copy.* Dryden refers to Boccaccio as 'Boccace' in his *Fables* (1700).

146. forgiving boon] The boon of forgiveness.

150. ghittern's] guittern's *Fair copy.* A ghittern was a form of guitar. See Boccaccio's *Decameron*, fifth novel of the ninth day, '. . . carrying his Gitterne . . . with him . . . hee both played and sung' (Shakespeare Head edn ii 174).

151-2.   For venturing one word unseemly mean
        In such a place on such a daring theme . . . *Fair copy.*

To stead thee as a verse in English tongue,
160 An echo of thee in the north wind sung.

XXI

These brethren having found by many signs
    What love Lorenzo for their sister had,
And how she loved him too, each unconfines
    His bitter thoughts to other, well nigh mad
165 That he, the servant of their trade designs,
    Should in their sister's love be blithe and glad,
When 'twas their plan to coax her by degrees
To some high noble and his olive-trees.

XXII

And many a jealous conference had they,
170 And many times they bit their lips alone,
Before they fixed upon a surest way
    To make the youngster for his crime atone.
And at the last, these men of cruel clay

161–4. In Boccaccio the eldest brother made the discovery: 'Long time
continued this amorous league of love . . . at the length, the secret meeting
of Lorenzo and Isabella . . . was discovered by the eldest of the Brethren . . .
being a man of great discretion . . . he kept it to himselfe till the next
morning, labouring his braine what might best be done . . . When day was
come, he resorted to his other Brethren, and told them what he had seen'
(Shakespeare Head edn i 234).

164. well nigh mad] Cp. Boccaccio: '. . . this sight was highly displeasing . . .
their stolne love . . . was altogether against their liking' (Shakespeare Head
edn i 234).

165–8. The brothers' motives for murdering Lorenzo–his inferior status
and their schemes for Isabella's marriage–are not found in Boccaccio, but
are in keeping with their characterisation in ll. 105–44 above.

168. olive] Forest *Fair copy (cancelled)*. The 'high noble' was perhaps suggested by Boccaccio's wealthy 'ancient knight . . . Signior Neri degli
Uberti' who 'bought a parcel of ground plentifully stored with variety of
Trees, bearing Olives . . . and other excellent frutages' (*Decameron*, sixth
novel of the tenth day, Shakespeare Head edn ii 217–18).

169–70. Cp. Boccaccio, 'Many deliberations passed on this case' (Shakespeare Head edn i 234).

173–6. Cp. Boccaccio, '. . . they concluded . . . to let [the meeting between
Lorenzo and Isabella] . . . proceede on with patient supportance, that no
scandall might ensue to them, or their Sister, no evill acte being (as yet)
committed. And seeming, as if they knew not of their love, had a wary eye
upon her secret walkes, awaiting for some convenient time, when . . . they
might safely breake off this their stolne love' (Shakespeare Head edn i 234).

Cut Mercy with a sharp knife to the bone,
175   For they resolvèd in some forest dim
To kill Lorenzo, and there bury him.

XXIII

So on a pleasant morning, as he leant
Into the sunrise, o'er the balustrade
Of the garden-terrace, towards him they bent
180   Their footing through the dews, and to him said,
'You seem there in the quiet of content,
Lorenzo, and we are most loth to invade
Calm speculation, but if you are wise,
Bestride your steed while cold is in the skies.

XXIV

185   Today we purpose, aye, this hour we mount,
To spur three leagues towards the Apennine.
Come down, we pray thee, ere the hot sun count
His dewy rosary on the eglantine.'
Lorenzo, courteously as he was wont,
190   Bowed a fair greeting to these serpents' whine,
And went in haste, to get in readiness,
With belt and spur and bracing huntsman's dress.

XXV

And as he to the court-yard passed along,
Each third step did he pause, and listened oft
195   If he could hear his lady's matin-song,
Or the light whisper of her footstep soft.
And as he thus over his passion hung,
He heard a laugh full musical aloft,
When, looking up, he saw her features bright
200   Smile through an indoor lattice, all delight.

174. Imitates Chaucer's *Canterbury Tales*, *The Prioress' Tale* 197,
      My throte is cut unto my nekke-boon . . .
177–232. Expanding Boccaccio's brief account, 'So, shewing no worse
countenance to Lorenzo, then formerly they had done, but imploying and
conversing with him in kinde manner; it fortuned, that riding (all three) to
recreate themselves out of the City, they tooke Lorenzo in their company,
and when they were come to a solitarie place, such as suited with their vile
purpose: they ran sodainly upon Lorenzo, slew him, and afterward enterred
his body, where hardly it could be discovered by any one' (Shakespeare
Head edn i 234).
199–200. bright . . . all delight] fair . . . debonair *Woodhouse* 1 (*cancelled*)–K.
notes on 'debonair': 'As I have used this word before in the poem you may
use your judgment between your lines and mine. I think my last alteration

XXVI

'Love, Isabel!' said he, 'I was in pain
    Lest I should miss to bid thee a good morrow.
Ah, what if I should lose thee, when so fain
    I am to stifle all the heavy sorrow
205 Of a poor three hours' absence? But we'll gain
    Out of the armorous dark what day doth borrow.
Good bye! I'll soon be back.' 'Good bye!' said she,
And as he went she chanted merrily.

XXVII

So the two brothers and their murdered man
210   Rode past fair Florence, to where Arno's stream
Gurgles through straitened banks, and still doth fan
    Itself with dancing bulrush, and the bream
Keeps head against the freshets. Sick and wan
    The brothers' faces in the ford did seem,
215 Lorenzo's flush with love. They passed the water
Into a forest quiet for the slaughter.

XXVIII

There was Lorenzo slain and buried in,
    There in that forest did his great love cease.
Ah, when a soul doth thus its freedom win,

[i.e. the *1820* readings] will do.' The word does not appear elsewehere in
the poem. The opposite leaf in *Woodhouse* 1 has the variant (in Taylor's
hand?),

When lo an indoor lattice met his view,
And her fair features smiling playful through . . .

207–8. Bathetic in Hunt's manner.

209. their murdered man] A proleptic phrase praised by Charles Lamb ('The
anticipation of the assassination is wonderfully conceived in one epithet')
and by Leigh Hunt, who cites it in his 'What is Poetry' (prefixed to *Imagination and Fancy*, 1844) to illustrate the poetic imagination 'concentrating
into a word the main history of any person or thing' (World's Classics
Nineteenth Century Critical Essays 306).

210–13. Arno's stream . . . freshets] The Arno appears to be an English river
here. Cp. *I stood tip-toe* 70–3 (p. 89 above),

. . . the hurrying freshnesses ay preach
A natural sermon o'er their pebbly beds,
Where swarms of minnows show their little heads,
Staying their wavy bodies 'gainst the streams . . .

219–21. The soul of a murdered man is as uneasy as the conscience of his
murderer. The image 'break-covert blood-hounds' suggests a recollection
of the hounds belonging to Guido's ghost in Boccaccio's *Decameron*, eighth

220 It aches in loneliness—is ill at peace
  As the break-covert blood-hounds of such sin.
   They dipped their swords in the water, and did tease
  Their horses homeward with convulsèd spur,
  Each richer by his being a murderer.

XXIX

225 They told their sister how, with sudden speed,
   Lorenzo had ta'en ship for foreign lands,
  Because of some great urgency and need
   In their affairs, requiring trusty hands.
  Poor girl! Put on thy stifling widow's weed,
230 And 'scape at once from Hope's accursèd bands.
  To-day thou wilt not see him, nor to-morrow,
  And the next day will be a day of sorrow.

XXX

  She weeps alone for pleasures not to be,
   Sorely she wept until the night came on,
235 And then, instead of love, O misery!
   She brooded o'er the luxury alone.
  His image in the dusk she seemed to see,
   And to the silence made a gentle moan,

---

tale of the fifth day: 'out of a little thicket of bushes and briars . . . ingirt
with spreading trees . . . a young Damosell come running . . . and crying
out for mercy. . . . Two fierce Blood-Hounds also followed swiftly after,
and . . . did most cruelly bite her' (Shakespeare Head edn i 303).
223. with convulsèd spur] The convulsive spurring of their horses. Cp. *Hyperion* ii 27–8 (p. 418 below),

    . . . horribly convulsed
  With sanguine feverous boiling gurge of pulse . . .

225–8. Boccaccio, 'They . . . gave it forth (as a credible report) that they
had sent him abroad about their affaires, as formerly they were wont to do:
which everyone verily beleeved because they knew no reason why they
should conceite any otherwise' (Shakespeare Head edn i 235).
229–56. Contrast Boccaccio's bald account of Isabella's first reactions to
Lorenzo's absence, 'Isabella, living in expectation of his returne, and per-
ceiving his stay to her was so offensive long: made many importunate demands to her Brethren, into what parts they had sent him' (Shakespeare
Head edn i 235).
229. stifling] doleful *Draft*.
236. Suggesting Isabella's excessive indulgence of rather than delight in her
grief. On K.'s use of the word 'luxury' see *Calidore* 92 *n* (p. 40 above).
237. What might have been too plainly did she see . . . *Draft*.

Spreading her perfect arms upon the air,
240   And on her couch low murmuring,'Where? Oh, where?'

XXXI

But Selfishness, Love's cousin, held not long
    Its fiery vigil in her single breast.
She fretted for the golden hour, and hung
    Upon the time with feverish unrest–
245   Not long, for soon into her heart a throng
    Of higher occupants, a richer zest,
Came tragic—passion not to be subdued,
And sorrow for her love in travels rude.

XXXII

In the mid days of autumn, on their eves,
250   The breath of winter comes from far away
And the sick west continually bereaves
    Of some bold tinge, and plays a roundelay
Of death among the bushes and the leaves,
    To make all bare before he dares to stray
255   From his north cavern. So sweet Isabel
By gradual decay from beauty fell,

XXXIII

Because Lorenzo came not. Oftentimes
    She asked her brothers, with an eye all pale,
Striving to be itself, what dungeon climes
260   Could keep him off so long? They spake a tale
Time after time, to quiet her. Their crimes
    Came on them, like a smoke from Hinnom's vale,

242. single breast] native mind Draft (cancelled).

244–5. See l. 45 n above.

248. And sorrow] A yearning Draft. K.'s first attempt at the line was 'Exalt-
ing her to patient Fortitude . . .'.

251. the sick west] For K.'s regarding winter as a sickness see After dark
vapours 1–4 n (p. 101 above).

260–1. They spake . . . to quiet her] Modifies Boccaccio's account, 'Such was
her importunate speeches to them, that . . . one of them returned her this
frowning answer. What is your meaning, Sister, by so many questionings
after Lorenzo? What urgent affaires have you with him, that makes you so
impatient upon his absence? If hereafter you make any more demands for
him, we shall shape you such a reply, as will be but little to your liking. At
these harsh words, Isabella fell into abundance of teares . . . she durst not
question any more after him' (Shakespeare Head edn i 235).

261. Time after time] Month after month Fair copy; Draft.

261–4. Their crimes . . . shroud] Not in Boccaccio.

262. smoke from Hinnom's vale] 2 Chronicles xxviii 3: 'He burnt incense in

And every night in dreams they groaned aloud
To see their sister in her snowy shroud.

XXXIV

265 And she had died in drowsy ignorance,
    But for a thing more deadly dark than all.
It came like a fierce potion, drunk by chance,
    Which saves a sick man from the feathered pall
For some few gasping moments; like a lance,
270   Waking an Indian from his cloudy hall
With cruel pierce, and bringing him again
Sense of the gnawing fire at heart and brain.

XXXV

It was a vision. In the drowsy gloom,
    The dull of midnight, at her couch's foot
275 Lorenzo stood, and wept. The forest tomb
    Had marred his glossy hair which once could shoot

the valley of the son of Hinnom, and burnt his children in the fire, after the abominations of the heathen. . . .'

265–96. Boccaccio has 'In the silence of darke night, as she lay afflicted in her bed, oftentimes would she call for Lorenzo. . . . One night amongst the rest . . . having a long while wept . . . her senses and faculties utterly spent and tired, that she could not utter any more complaints, she fell into a trance or sleepe; and dreamed, that the ghost of Lorenzo appeared unto her, in torne and unbefitting garments, his lookes pale, meager, & staring: & (as she thought) thus spake to her' (Shakespeare Head edn i 235).

268. feathered pall] Death. The vision is like a sharp medecine which momentarily revives a dying man.

269–72. K. is remembering William Robertson's account of the methods of torture and the tests of physical endurance practised by the American Indians, for example (on the torture of prisoners), 'Some burn their limbs with red-hot irons, some mangle their bodies with knives . . . they often prolong this . . . anguish for several days . . .' and (on the trial of a warrior), 'A fire of . . . herbs is kindled . . . so as he may feel its heat, and be involved in its smoke. Though scorched and almost suffocated, he must continue to endure with . . . patient insensibility' (History of America ii 156–7, 163).

272. Echoing Southey's The Curse of Kehama (1810) V ii 30, IX x 139,
    A fire was in his heart and brain . . .
and see the same poem xix i 3–6,
    . . . his own redoubled agony,
    Which now through heart and brain
      With renovated pain
    Rush'd to its seat . . .

273. drowsy] heavy Draft.

Lustre into the sun, and put cold doom
    Upon his lips, and taken the soft lute
From his lorn voice, and past his loamèd ears
280 Had made a miry channel for his tears.

XXXVI

Strange sound it was, when the pale shadow spake,
    For there was striving, in its piteous tongue,
To speak as when on earth it was awake,
    And Isabella on its music hung.
285 Languor there was in it, and tremulous shake,
    As in a palsied Druid's harp unstrung.
And through it moaned a ghostly under-song,
Like hoarse night-gusts sepulchral briars among.

XXXVII

Its eyes, though wild, were still all dewy bright
290   With love, and kept all phantom fear aloof
From the poor girl by magic of their light,
    The while it did unthread the horrid woof
Of the late darkened time—the murderous spite
    Of pride and avarice, the dark pine roof
295 In the forest, and the sodden turfèd dell,
Where, without any word, from stabs he fell.

XXXVIII

Saying moreover, 'Isabel, my sweet!
    Red whortle-berries droop above my head,
And a large flint-stone weighs upon my feet;

277. put cold] stamped his *Draft (cancelled).*
278. taken the soft] took the mellow *Draft (cancelled).*
281. pale] poor *Fair copy; Draft.*
285. Languor] Passion *Draft.*
286. Druid] See *To George Felton Matthew* 39 *n* (p. 26 above).
287–8. Suggesting the hollow echoing sound of a ghostly voice.
288. sepulchral briars] Briars growing in a graveyard.
289–320. Lorenzo's speech in Boccaccio runs: 'My deere love Isabella,
thou dost nothing but torment thy selfe, with calling on me, accusing me
for overlong tarrying from thee: I am come therefore to let thee know, that
thou canst not enjoy my company any more, because the very same day
when last thou sawest me, thy brethren most bloodily murthered me. And
acquainting her with the place where they had buried his mangled body: he
strictly charged her, not to call him at any time afterward, and so vanished
away' (Shakespeare Head edn i 235).
298–303. The details belong to an English landscape.

300   Around me beeches and high chestnuts shed
    Their leaves and prickly nuts; a sheep-fold bleat
      Comes from beyond the river to my bed.
    Go, shed one tear upon my heather-bloom,
    And it shall comfort me within the tomb.

XXXIX

305   I am a shadow now, alas! alas!
    Upon the skirts of human-nature dwelling
      Alone. I chant alone the holy mass,
      While little sounds of life are round me knelling,
    And glossy bees at noon do fieldward pass,
310   And many a chapel bell the hour is telling,
    Paining me through. Those sounds grow strange to me,
    And thou art distant in humanity.

XL

    I know what was, I feel full well what is,
      And I should rage, if spirits could go mad.
315   Though I forget the taste of earthly bliss,
      That paleness warms my grave, as though I had
    A seraph chosen from the bright abyss
      To be my spouse. Thy paleness makes me glad;
      Thy beauty grows upon me, and I feel
320   A greater love through all my essence steal.'

XLI

    The spirit mourned 'Adieu!'–dissolved and left
      The atom darkness in a slow turmoil,

---

304. And it shall turn a diamond in my tomb *Fair copy.*

305–12. H. G. Wright notes, 'the spot . . . though solitary, is not . . . far . . . from the haunts of men . . . within reach of fields and a chapel. The essence of this passage is found in the Induction to the eighth day' (*Boccaccio in England* 404). Local details in Boccaccio's *Decameron*, introduction to the first novel of the eighth day, include, 'The Queen and her Companie . . . having walked a while abroad, in the goodly greene Meadowes . . . re-turned . . . into the Palace. . . . Afterward . . . they went to heare Masse, in a faire Chappell neere at hand, and thence returned to their Lodgings' (Shakespeare Head edn ii 85).

315. taste of earthly bliss] heaven of a kiss *Fair copy*; what pleasure was a kiss *Draft.*

319–20. K. quoted these lines in his letter to Fanny Brawne of Feb. (?) 1820, 'In my present state of Health I feel too much separated from you and could almost speak to you in the words of Lorenzo's Ghost to Isabella' (*L* ii 256).

320. essence] Being. Cp. *Endymion* i 99 (p. 124 above), 'his essence fine' and *Hyperion* i 232 *n* (p. 410 below).

As when of healthful midnight sleep bereft,
    Thinking on rugged hours and fruitless toil
325 We put our eyes into a pillowy cleft,
    And see the spangly gloom froth up and boil.
It made sad Isabella's eyelids ache,
And in the dawn she started up awake—

XLII

'Ha! ha!' said she, 'I knew not this hard life,
330   I thought the worst was simple misery.
I thought some Fate with pleasure or with strife
    Portioned us—happy days, or else to die.
But there is crime—a brother's bloody knife!
    Sweet spirit, thou has schooled my infancy.
335 I'll visit thee for this and kiss thine eyes,
And greet thee morn and even in the skies.'

XLIII

When the full morning came, she had devised
    How she might secret to the forest hie;
How she might find the clay, so dearly prized,
340   And sing to it one latest lullaby;
How her short absence might be unsurmised,
    While she the inmost of the dream would try.
Resolved, she took with her an agèd nurse,
And went into that dismal forest-hearse.

XLIV

345 See, as they creep along the river side,
    How she doth whisper to that agèd dame,
And, after looking round the champaign wide,
    Shows her a knife. 'What feverous hectic flame
Burns in thee, child? What good can thee betide,
350   That thou should'st smile again?' The evening
        came,
And they had found Lorenzo's earthy bed—
The flint was there, the berries at his head.

337–44. Boccaccio has 'The young Damosell awaking . . . sighed and wept
exceedingly . . . she resolutely determined, to go see the place . . . onely to
make triall, if that which she seemed to see in her sleepe, should carry any
likely-hood of truth . . . [she] obtained favour of her brethren, to ride a dayes
journey from the City, in company of her trusty Nurse' (Shakespeare Head
edn 8 235).

344. forest-hearse] Place of burial. The expression was forced on K. by the
need to rhyme.

348. a knife] Boccaccio's 'having brought a keen razor with her' (Shakespeare Head edn i 235).

XLV

Who hath not loitered in a green church-yard,
      And let his spirit, like a demon-mole,
355 Work through the clayey soil and gravel hard,
      To see skull, coffined bones, and funeral stole,
      Pitying each form that hungry Death hath marred,
         And filling it once more with human soul?
      Ah, this is holiday to what was felt
360 When Isabella by Lorenzo knelt.

XLVI

She gazed into the fresh-thrown mould, as though
      One glance did fully all its secrets tell.
Clearly she saw, as other eyes would know
      Pale limbs at bottom of a crystal well.
365 Upon the murderous spot she seemed to grow,
      Like to a native lily of the dell—
      Then with her knife, all sudden, she began
      To dig more fervently than misers can.

XLVII

Soon she turned up a soilèd glove, whereon
370 Her silk had played in purple phantasies,
She kissed it with a lip more chill than stone,
      And put in in her bosom, where it dries
      And freezes utterly unto the bone
      Those dainties made to still an infant's cries.

354. *demon-mole*] This curious compound was probably suggested by *Hamlet* I v 162,

      Well said, old mole! canst work in the ground so fast . . .

361–84. Expanded from Boccaccio: '. . . they rode directly to the designed place, which being covered with dried leaves, & more deeply sunke then any other part of the ground therabout, they digged not farre, but they found the body of the murthered Lorenzo, as yet very little corrupted or impaired' (Shakespeare Head edn i 235). The passage is one of the descriptive climaxes of the poem: Charles Lamb wrote enthusiastically, '. . . there is nothing more awfully simple in diction, more nakedly grand and moving in sentiment, in Dante, in Chaucer, or in Spenser' (*The New Times* 19 July 1820). See, however, K.'s comment in ll. 385–92 below.

373. *unto the bone*] 'Love's sighful throne'–K.'s rejected revision in *Woodhouse* 1.

374. *dainties*] Perhaps suggested by Marlowe's *Hero and Leander* ii 269–70,

               . . . he greedily assay'd
      To touch those dainties . . .

Here the expression has the un-Elizabethan coyness which K. caught from Hunt. Cp. *Ah, who can e'er forget* 2 (p. 44 above), 'her half-retiring sweets'.

375 Then 'gan she work again, nor stayed her care,
     But to throw back at times her veiling hair.

XLVIII

     That old nurse stood beside her wondering,
        Until her heart felt pity to the core
     At sight of such a dismal labouring,
380   And so she kneelèd, with her locks all hoar,
     And put her lean hands to the horrid thing—
        Three hours they laboured at this travail sore.
     At last they felt the kernel of the grave,
     And Isabella did not stamp and rave.

XLIX

385 Ah, wherefore all this wormy circumstance?
        Why linger at the yawning tomb so long?
     Oh, for the gentleness of old romance,
        The simple plaining of a minstrel's song!
     Fair reader, at the old tale take a glance,
390   For here, in truth, it doth not well belong
     To speak—Oh, turn thee to the very tale,
     And taste the music of that vision pale.

L

     With duller steel than the Persean sword
        They cut away no formless monster's head,
395 But one, whose gentleness did well accord
        With death, as life. The ancient harps have said,
     Love never dies, but lives, immortal Lord.

384. stamp and] 'weep or'–an unadopted alternative reading in the fair copy.

385–92. K. regards his description in ll. 361–84 as a departure from the narrative simplicity which he associates with 'old Romance'. See his address to Boccaccio in ll. 145–52 above.

393–4. Boccaccio is more circumstantial: 'Gladly would she have carried the whole body with her . . . but it exceeded . . . her ability . . . by helpe of the Nurse, she divided the head from the body . . . wrapped it up in a Napkin, which the Nurse conveyed into her lap, & then laide the body in the ground againe' (Shakespeare Head edn i 235).

393–4.   With duller silver than the persean sword
                    They cut away no foul Medusa's head . . . *Fair copy.*

Perseus cut off the Gorgon's head with the scythe-shaped sword given to him by Mercury (Vulcan in some sources). See Ovid's *Metamorphoses* iv 666, 772–86.

396. ancient harps] Poets of long ago. K. is thinking of the 'old Romance' referred to in l. 387 above.

If Love impersonate was ever dead,
Pale Isabella kissed it, and low moaned.
400   'Twas Love—cold, dead indeed, but not dethroned.

LI

In anxious secrecy they took it home,
   And then the prize was all for Isabel.
She calmed its wild hair with a golden comb,
   And all around each eye's sepulchral cell
405   Pointed each fringèd lash. The smearèd loam
   With tears, as chilly as a dripping well,
She drenched away—and still she combed, and kept
Sighing all day—and still she kissed, and wept.

LII

Then in a silken scarf—sweet with the dews
410   Of precious flowers plucked in Araby,
And divine liquids come with odorous ooze
   Through the cold serpent-pipe refreshfully—
She wrapped it up, and for its tomb did choose
   A garden-pot, wherein she laid it by,

398. If ever any piece of love was dead *Fair copy. Woodhouse* 1 has the following unadopted alternatives to *1820*:
   1. With fond caress as if it were not dead
   2. The ghastly features of her lover dead . . .

401–8. Dramatizes Boccaccio's brief account: '. . . they departed thence, and arrived home in convenient time, where alone by themselves in the Chamber: she washed the head over and over with her tears, and bestowed infinite kisses thereon' (Shakespeare Head edn i 236).

403. calmed its wild hair] Cp. *Sleep and Poetry* 180 *n* (p. 77 above), 'soothe their wavy hair . . .'

409–32. K. takes more details than usual from Boccaccio who is expansive at this point: 'Not long after, the Nurse having brought her large earthen pot, such as we use to set Basile, Marjerom, Flowers, or other sweet hearbes in, and shrowding the head in a silken Scarfe, put it into the pot, covering it with earth, and planting divers rootes of excellent Basile therein, which she never watered but either with her teares, Rose water, or water distilled from the Flowers of Oranges. This pot she used continually to sitte by, either in her chamber, or any where else: for she carried it alwaies with her, sighing and breathing foorth sad complaints thereto, even as if they had beene uttered to her Lorenzo, and day by day this was her continuall exercise, to the no meane admiration of her bretheren, and many other friends that beheld her.

So long she held on in this mourning manner, that, what by the continuall watering of the Basile, and the putrifaction of the head, so buried in the pot of earth; it grew very flourishing, and most oderifferous to such as scented it, that as no other Basile could possibly yeeld so sweete a savour' (Shakespeare Head edn i 236).

415   And covered it with mould, and o'er it set
       Sweet basil, which her tears kept ever wet.

LIII

       And she forgot the stars, the moon, and sun,
           And she forgot the blue above the trees,
       And she forgot the dells where waters run,
420   And she forgot the chilly autumn breeze.
       She had no knowledge when the day was done,
           And the new morn she saw not, but in peace
       Hung over her sweet basil evermore,
       And moistened it with tears unto the core.

LIV

425   And so she ever fed it with thin tears,
           Whence thick and green and beautiful it grew,
       So that it smelt more balmy than its peers
           Of basil-tufts in Florence, for it drew
       Nurture besides, and life, from human fears,
430   From the fast mouldering head there shut from view.
       So that the jewel, safely casketed,
       Came forth, and in perfumèd leafits spread.

LV

       O Melancholy, linger here awhile!
       O Music, Music, breathe despondingly!
435   O Echo, Echo, from some sombre isle,
           Unknown, Lethean, sigh to us—Oh, sigh!
       Spirits in grief, lift up your heads, and smile.
       Lift up your heads, sweet spirits, heavily,

417–20. Perhaps prompted by Wordsworth's *The Thorn* (1798) 69–74,
                    And she is known to every star,
                    And every wind that blows;
                    And there, beside the Thorn, she sits
                    When the blue daylight's in the skies,
                    And when the whirlwind's on the hill,
                    Or frosty air is keen and still . . .

432. leafits] Currently used for 'leaflets'.

433–48. See ll. 89–104 *n* above.

435–50. The personifications have an eighteenth-century flavour but K.'s
repetitions in ll. 433–5 (which occur again with slight variations in ll. 481–4
below) owe something to Spenser's elegiac effects, for example the refrain
closing each section in *Daphnaida*,
                    Weepe Sheapherd weepe to make my undersong . . .

435. sombre] lonely *Draft.*

436. Unknown, Lethean] Ionian—unknown *Draft.*

438. heads] eyes *Draft.*

And make a pale light in your cypress glooms,
440   Tinting with silver wan your marble tombs.

LVI

Moan higher, all ye syllables of woe,
   From the deep throat of sad Melpomene!
Through bronzèd lyre in tragic order go,
   And touch the strings into a mystery.
445   Sound mournfully upon the winds and low,
   For simple Isabel is soon to be
Among the dead. She withers, like a palm
Cut by an Indian for its juicy balm.

LVII

Oh, leave the palm to wither by itself,
450   Let not quick winter chill its dying hour!
It may not be–those Baälites of pelf,
   Her brethren, noted the continual shower

442. Melpomene] The muse of Tragedy.
443. bronzèd] large *Draft (cancelled).*
451. Baälites] Worshippers of false gods; the brothers worshipped money.
With the use of 'pelf' cp. in *The Faerie Queene* II vii 7 Mammon's
'heapes of pretious pelfe . . .'
452–504. K.'s conclusion keeps fairly closely to Boccaccio: 'The neigh-
bours noting . . . how . . . her bright beauty was defaced, and the eyes sunke
into her head by incessant weeping, made many kinde and friendly motions, to understand the reason . . . but could not by any means prevaile
with her, or win any discovery by her Nurse. . . . Her brethren also waxed
wearie of this carriage in her; and having . . . often reproved her . . . they
. . . stole . . . the potte of Basile . . . for which she made infinite . . . lamen-
tations . . . avouching that she could not live without it. . . . Her brethren
grew greatly amazed thereat . . . and . . . were . . . desirous to ransacke the
pot to the . . . bottome. Having emptied out the earth, they found the
Scarfe of silke, wherein the head . . . was wrapped; which was as yet not so
much consumed, but by the lockes of haire, they knew it to be Lorenzoes
. . . whereat they became confounded with amazement . . . least their
offence might come to open publication, they buried it . . . and . . .departed
from Messina . . . to dwell in Naples, Isabella crying and calling still for her
pot of Basile, being unable to give over mourning, dyed within a few days.
. . . Within no long while after, when this . . . came to be publikely
knowne, an excellent ditty was composed thereof beginning thus,
   Cruell and unkinde was the Christian,
   That robd me of my Basiles blisse, etc.' (Shakespeare Head edn i 236).
For versions of the traditional 'ditty' in Italian and in an English translation
by John Payne see *Forman* (1883) ii 552–7.
450. quick winter chill] hot lightning sear *Draft.*

From her dead eyes, and many a curious elf,
   Among her kindred, wondered that such dower
455 Of youth and beauty should be thrown aside
By one marked out to be a noble's bride.

LVIII

And, furthermore, her brethren wondered much
   Why she sat drooping by the basil green,
And why it flourished, as by magic touch.
460   Greatly they wondered what the thing might mean.
They could not surely give belief that such
   A very nothing would have power to wean
Her from her own fair youth, and pleasures gay,
And even remembrance of her love's delay.

LIX

465 Therefore they watched a time when they might sift
   This hidden whim, and long they watched in vain.
For seldom did she go to chapel-shrift,
   And seldom felt she any hunger-pain.
And when she left, she hurried back, as swift
470   As bird on wing to breast its eggs again,
And, patient as a hen-bird, sat her there
Beside her basil, weeping through her hair.

LX

Yet they contrived to steal the basil-pot,
   And to examine it in secret place.
475 The thing was vile with green and livid spot,
   And yet they knew it was Lorenzo's face.
The guerdon of their murder they had got,
   And so left Florence in a moment's space,
Never to turn again. Away they went,
480 With blood upon their heads, to banishment.

LXI

O Melancholy, turn thine eyes away!
   O Music, Music, breathe despondingly!
O Echo, Echo, on some other day,
   From isles Lethean, sigh to us—Oh, sigh!
485 Spirits of grief, sing not your 'Well-a-way!'
   For Isabel, sweet Isabel, will die—
Will die a death too lone and incomplete,
Now they have ta'en away her basil sweet.

457. wondered] marvel'd *Draft.*
482. breathe despondingly] slumber silently *Draft.*
484. Lethean] hesperrian *Draft.*

LXII
Piteous she looked on dead and senseless things,
490   Asking for her lost basil amorously.
And with melodious chuckle in the strings
      Of her lorn voice, she oftentimes would cry
After the pilgrim in his wanderings,
      To ask him where her basil was, and why
495 'Twas hid from her: 'For cruel 'tis,' said she,
'To steal my basil-pot away from me.'

LXIII
And so she pined, and so she died forlorn,
      Imploring for her basil to the last.
No heart was there in Florence but did mourn
500   In pity of her love, so overcast.
And a sad ditty of this story born
      From mouth to mouth through all the country
            passed.
Still is the burthen sung: 'Oh, cruelty,
To steal my basil-pot away from me!'

490. lost] sweet *Draft.*
492. Of her dissolving accent would she cry *Draft.*
500. of] at *Draft.*

86 To James Rice

Written *c.* 20 April 1818, the date of the inscription in James Rice's gift
copy to K. of the Spanish romance *Guzman D'Alfarache* (1634): K. was in
Teignmouth at this date and Rice presumably gave the book to him during
the short visit to what K. called 'your favourite Devon' (*L* i 254) celebrated
in the poem. K. met Rice through Reynolds in 1817 and remained warmly
attached to him: see K.'s journal-letter of Sept. 1819. 'He is the most sensible, and even wise Man I know' (*L* ii 187) and Charles Dilke's comment in
his copy of *1848* (Hampstead): 'dear generous noble James Rice–the best,
and in his quaint way one of the wittiest and wisest men I ever knew.'
Text from *1848* which substantially agrees with K.'s undated holograph
draft and the three transcripts.
Published *1848* (with incorrect title 'To J. H. Reynolds').

Oh, that a week could be an age, and we
      Felt parting and warm meeting every week!
Then one poor year a thousand years would be,
      The flush of welcome ever on the cheek.

¶ 86. *Title.* To J. R. *K.'s MS*

5   So could we live long life in little space,
        So time itself would be annihilate,
     So a day's journey in oblivious haze
        To serve our joys would lengthen and dilate.
     Oh, to arrive each Monday morn from Ind!
10   To land each Tuesday from the rich Levant!
     In little time a host of joys to bind,
        And keep our souls in one eternal pant!
     This morn, my friend, and yester-evening taught
     Me how to harbour such a happy thought.

5. *long life in little space*] The antithesis is influenced by Shakespeare's sonnet
style. Cp. *To*—— ['Time's sea'] 14 *n* (p. 307 above),
                And grief unto my darling joys dost bring.
13.   This morn and yester eve my friend has taught
                Such greediness of Pleasure . . . *Draft* (*cancelled*).

87 To Homer

Probably written April/May 1818 at Teignmouth: '1818' in the four transcripts; see K. to Reynolds 27 April 1818, 'I have written to George [Keats]
for some Books—shall learn Greek. . . . I long to feast upon old Homer as
we have upon Shakespeare and as I have lately upon Milton' (*L* i 274).
Text from Brown's transcript as corrected in K.'s hand.
Published *1848*.

     Standing aloof in giant ignorance,
        Of thee I hear and of the Cyclades,
     As one who sits ashore and longs perchance
        To visit dolphin-coral in deep seas.

¶ 87. *1. giant ignorance*] K. had known Chapman's translation of Homer
since Oct. 1816—see headnote to *On First Looking into Chapman's Homer* (p.
60 above)—but knew no Greek.
2. Cyclades] Islands of the Greek archipelago.
3. sits ashore and longs perchance] An earlier reading was 'stands against a level
glance'. The line is altered by K. in Brown's transcript.
4. dolphin-coral] K. associated dolphins with coral. Cp. *To my Brother George*
50–2 and *n* (p. 50 above),
                Like silver streaks across a dolphin's fin
                When he upswimmeth from the coral caves . . .
The image of travel recalls *On First Looking into Chapman's Homer* 1 (p. 61
above),
                Much have I travelled in the realms of gold . . .

5   So wast thou blind. But then the veil was rent,
        For Jove uncurtained Heaven to let thee live,
    And Neptune made for thee a spumy tent,
        And Pan made sing for thee his forest-hive.
    Aye, on the shores of darkness there is light,
10   And precipices show untrodden green;
    There is a budding morrow in midnight,
        There is a triple sight in blindness keen;
    Such seeing hadst thou, as it once befell
    To Dian, Queen of Earth and Heaven and Hell.

5. So wast thou blind] K. compares his disability of ignorance with Homer's
blindness. The sentence 'the veil was rent' is a reference to *Matthew* xxvii
51: 'And, behold, the veil of the temple was rent in twain from top to the
bottom.'

7. spumy] Milnes's 'spermy' in *1848* is probably an error.

8. K. had a special fondness for the Homeric *Hymn to Pan* which he knew
in Chapman's translation. See *Endymion* i 89–392 *n* (pp. 123–4 above).

10. untrodden green] Grass growing in the patches of soil on inaccessible
ledges.

11. Thought by D. G. Rossetti to be 'the greatest line in Keats' (see G.
Milner's 'On some marginalia made by D. G. Rossetti in a copy of Keats'
Poems', *The Manchester Quarterly* v, Jan. 1883, 8).

12. K. is speculating about the effects of Homer's blindness on his creative
imagination. See his comment on Milton's *Paradise Lost* i 56–76, '. . . it can
scarcely be conceived how Milton's Blindness might here aid the magnitude
of his conceptions' (K.'s copy of Milton at Hampstead). The word 'triple'
refers to Homer's writing about the gods of the upper world, the sea and
the earth (ll. 6–8) and leads by association to the recollection of Diana's
three spheres of influence in l. 14.

13. once] Formerly.

14. On Diana's threefold powers see headnote to *Endymion* (p. 117 above).

88 Ode to May

Fragment

Written 1 May 1818 and copied out in K.'s letter to Reynolds 3 May 1818
with the prefatory comment, 'With respect to the affections and Poetry you
must know by a sympathy my thoughts that way; and I dare say these few
lines will be but a ratification: I wrote them on May-day–and intend to
finish the ode all in good time' (*L* i 278)–but the ode was never completed. K.'s
irregular fourteen-line stanza looks forward to his 'attempt to find a better
sonnet stanza than we have' in spring 1819 (*L* ii 108)–see headnote to *If by*

dull rhymes (p. 521 below) – and helps to prepare the way for his major 1819 odes.

Text from K.'s letter.

Published *1848*.

> Mother of Hermes! And still youthful Maia!
>   May I sing to thee
> As thou wast hymnèd on the shores of Baiae?
>   Or may I woo thee
> 5   In earlier Sicilian? Or thy smiles
> Seek, as they once were sought in Grecian isles
> By bards who died content in pleasant sward,
>   Leaving great verse unto a little clan?
> Oh, give me their old vigour, and unheard,
> 10   Save of the quiet primrose and the span
>   Of Heaven and few ears,
> Rounded by thee, my song should die away
>   Content as theirs,
> Rich in the simple worship of a day.

¶ *88. 1. Mother of Hermes*] 'Maia, a daughter of Atlas and Pleione, mother of Mercury by Jupiter. She was one of the Pleiades, and the most luminous of the seven sisters' (*Lemprière*).

3. the shores of Baiae] The bay of Naples. In Italy Maia was celebrated as the mother of Mercury and also as a goddess associated with Vulcan.

9–14. Cp. K. to Reynolds 3 Feb. 1818, 'Poetry should be great and unobtrusive, a thing which enters into one's soul, and does not startle it or amaze it with itself but with its subject' (*L* i 224).

11–14. In K.'s letter, which is preserved in Woodhouse's transcript, the lines are divided as shown below; the slanting lines were added by Woodhouse with the note, 'Perhaps the lines sho^d be divided as shown . . .'

> Of Heaven, and few ears // rounded by thee
> My song should die away // content as theirs //
> Rich in the simple worship of a day. – //

Woodhouse's arrangement has been generally adopted since Milnes's use of it in *1848*.

89 Acrostic

Written 27 June 1818 and revised 18 Sept. 1819: see under 27 June in K.'s journal-letter of 27–8 June 1818 from the 'Foot of Helvellyn', where the lines follow the question, 'Ha! my dear Sister George, I wish I knew what humour you were in that I might accommodate myself to any one of your Amiabilities – Shall it be a Sonnet or a Pun or an Acrostic, a Riddle or a

Ballad [?]' (*L* i 303); K. copied out the poem with some variants on 18
Sept. in his journal-letter of 17–27 Sept. 1819, with the comments: 'On
looking over some letters I found the one . . . from the foot of Helvellyn to
Liverpool–but you had sail'd [to America] and therefore it was returned to
me. It contained . . . an Acrostic of my Sister's name–and a pretty long
name it is. I wrote it in a great hurry which you will see' (*L* ii 195). The
initial letters spell out the name of K.'s sister-in-law. This and the following
thirteen poems were written by K. during his walking-tour with Brown in
the Lakes and Scotland June–Aug. 1818.
Text from K.'s journal-letter of Sept. 1819, with some variants noted from
the earlier version.
Published *New York World* 25 June 1877; *Forman* (1883).

> Give me your patience, sister, while I frame
> Exact in capitals your golden name,
> Or sue the fair Apollo and he will
> Rouse from his heavy slumber and instil
> 5 Great love in me for thee and poesy.
> Imagine not that greatest mastery
> And kingdom over all the realms of verse
> Nears more to Heaven in aught than when we nurse,
> And surety give, to love and brotherhood.
>
> 10 Anthropophagi in Othello's mood,
> Ulysses stormed and his enchanted belt
> Glow with the Muse, but they are never felt

¶ 89. *2. Exact in Capitals*] Enitials verse-wise *1818*.
5. love in me for thee] On K.'s affection for Georgiana Keats see headnote to
To Georgiana Augusta Wylie (p. 98 above).
9. And surety give to] In its vast safety *1818* (*cancelled*).
10. An allusion to *Othello* I iii 143–4,

> . . . the Cannibals that each other eat,
> The Anthropophagi . . .

11. stormed] Tempest-tossed. Acrostic rules have put a strain on K.'s syntax.
The phrase 'his enchanted belt' probably refers to the magic 'veil', a gift
from the goddess Leucothea, which Odysseus tied round himself before
diving into the sea and which saved him from drowning (*Odyssey* v 346–
47).
12. Glow with the Muse] Are full of poetic power; the reading 'Glowed' in
Garrod is an unnecessary emendation. A cancelled attempt at the line in *1818*
was 'By the sweet Muse are never felt . . .' (obviously altered because it
disobeyed acrostic rules).
12–16. but they . . . sister mine] Comic exaggeration awkwardly expressed:
his own lines are more moving in their expression of feeling than Shake-

Unbosomed so and so eternal made,
Such tender incense in their laurel shade
15 To all the regent sisters of the Nine,
As this poor offering to you, sister mine.

Kind sister! Aye, this third name say you are.
Enchanted has it been the Lord knows where.
And may it taste to you like good old wine,
20 Take you to real happiness and give
Sons, daughters and a home like honeyed hive.

---

speare's and Homer's; they will endure longer and are a more tender tribute
to the muses.
14. *tender*] selfsame *1818*.
15. *sisters of the Nine*] The nine muses.
18. *Enchanted*] Enhanced *1818*.
19. *good old wine*] For K.'s enjoyment of wine see *Hence burgundy, claret and
port* 1-2 *n* (pp. 299-300 above).

90 'Sweet, sweet is the greeting of eyes'

Written 28 June 1818 for George and Georgiana Keats: see under this date
in K.'s journal-letter of 27-8 June 1818, where the lines follow his statement, 'I shall drop like a Hawk on the Post Office at Carlisle to ask for some
letter from you and Tom' (*L* i 304).
Text from K.'s letter.
Published *Lowell* (1925).

Sweet, sweet is the greeting of eyes,
And sweet is the voice in its greeting,
When adieus have grown old and goodbyes
Fade away where old Time is retreating.

5 Warm the nerve of a welcoming hand,
And earnest a kiss on the brow,
When we meet over sea and o'er land
Where furrows are new to the plough.

¶ 90. *8.* i.e. in America. See K. to Bailey July 1818, 'I intend to pass a whole
year with George [in America] if I live to the completion of the three next'
(*L* i 343). For K.'s change of mind later see his Sept. 1819 journal-letter,
'. . . it is quite out of my interest to come to America—What could I do
there? How could I employ myself? Out of the reach of Libraries' (*L* ii
210).

91 On Visiting the Tomb of Burns

Written at Dumfries 1 July 1818 in a mood of disenchantment at the first
sight of Scotland: see under this date in K.'s journal-letter to Tom Keats 29
June–2 July 1818, 'Burns' tomb is in the Churchyard corner [the south-east
corner of the churchyard at St. Michael's Church, Dumfries] not very much
to my taste. . . . This Sonnet I have written in a strange mood, half asleep. I
know not how it is, the Clouds, the sky, the Houses, all seem anti Grecian
and anti Charlemagnish' (L i 309). On K.'s being out of love with things
Scottish see further Brown to Dilke July 1818, 'Keats has been these five
hours abusing the Scotch and their country. He says that the women have
large splay feet . . . and . . . thanks Providence he is not related to a Scot,
nor any way connected with them' (L i 309 n).

Text from the only known MS of the poem, an imperfect transcript by
John Jeffrey. For discussions of the poem's meaning and various conjectural
readings see Murry (1939); J. C. Maxwell, KShJ iv 1955 77–80; G. Yost,
JEGP lvii (1958) 220–9.

Published 1848.

> The town, the churchyard, and the setting sun,
>   The clouds, the trees, the rounded hills all seem,
>   Though beautiful, cold—strange—as in a dream
> I dreamèd long ago. Now new begun
> 5 The short-lived, paly summer is but won
>   From winter's ague for one hour's gleam.
>   Through sapphire warm their stars do never beam;

¶ 91. 4. *now new begun*] now new begun. *1848, Garrod*. There is no full-
stop in Jeffrey's transcript. Milnes's emendation in *1848* is not required,
since the phrase refers to the late starting Scottish summer (l. 5) and not to
K.'s 'dream' (l. 3).

5. *paly*] On K.'s use of adjectives ending in '-y' see *Calidore* 10 n (p. 37
above).

7. *Through*] Though *1848, Garrod*. The emendation is unnecessary as K. is
clearly contrasting the chilly northern sky with the warm sky of a 'Grecian'
landscape; see his letter to Tom Keats (headnote). K. again uses the image of
stars shining in a 'sapphire' sky in *Ode to Psyche* 26 (p. 517 below),

>   Fairer than Phoebe's sapphire-regioned star . . .

8–12. K.'s syntax is hard to follow, but the passage obviously expresses his
romantic disappointment at not finding the scene more inspiring and recalls the despondent mood of his March 1818 verse letter to Reynolds 67–9
(p. 323 above),

>   Oh, that our dreamings all of sleep or wake
>   Would all their colours from the sunset take . . .

13+K.

All is cold beauty; pain is never done
   For who has mind to relish, Minos-wise,
10   The real of beauty, free from that dead hue
   Sickly imagination and sick pride
Cast wan upon it! Burns! With honour due
   I have oft honoured thee. Great shadow, hide
Thy face; I sin against thy native skies.

8. pain is never done] pain is never done: *1848, Garrod.* The colon converts
the following clause, 'For who . . . upon it!' (ll. 9–11) into a question–Garrod substitutes ' ?' for the ' !' of the transcript–and K. from one who is trying to face reality into one who seeks illusion.
9. For who . . .] The meaning is 'For him who . . .'. The phrase 'Minos-wise' was probably suggested by Dante's reference to Minos, judge of the underworld, in his *Inferno* v. K. took to Scotland with him Henry Cary's three-volume translation (1814) of Dante's *Divina Commedia*; see his letter to Bailey 22 July 1818, '. . . the only Books I have with me are those three little Volumes' (*L* i 343).
10–12. The real . . . upon it] Echoing *Hamlet* III i 84–5,
     . . . the native hue of resolution
   Is sicklied o'er with the pale cast of thought . . .
11. Sickly] Jeffrey's 'Fickly' is almost certainly a slip or a mis-reading. For a different view see J. C. Maxwell, *KShJ* iv (1955) 78.
12. Cast] Milnes's conjectural reading in *1848.* Jeffrey leaves a blank space with the note, 'An illegible word occurs here'.

92 'Old Meg she was a gipsy'

Written on the way to Kirkcudbright via Auchencairn 2 July 1818 at the beginning of K.'s letter to Fanny Keats of 2–5 July 1818, with the comment, 'We are in the midst of Meg Merrilies' country. . . . If you like these sort of Ballads I will now and then scribble one for you' (*L* i 311–12). K. had not read Scott's *Guy Mannering* (1814), which contains the character of Meg Merrilies, but Brown records of himself that he 'chatted half the way' to Auchencairn about the novel (*L* i 437).
Published *Plymouth and Devonport Weekly Journal* 22 Nov. 1838 and *1848.*

I
Old Meg she was a gipsy,
   And lived upon the moors,
Her bed it was the brown heath turf,
   And her house was out of doors.

II
5 Her apples were swart blackberries,
   Her currants pods o' broom,

Her wine was dew of the wild white rose,
    Her book a churchyard tomb.

III

Her brothers were the craggy hills,
10   Her sisters larchen trees–
Alone with her great family
    She lived as she did please.

IV

No breakfast had she many a morn,
    No dinner many a noon,
15   And 'stead of supper she would stare
    Full hard against the moon.

V

But every morn of woodbine fresh
    She made her garlanding,
And every night the dark glen yew
20   She wove, and she would sing.

VI

And with her fingers old and brown
    She plaited mats o' rushes,
And gave them to the cottagers
    She met among the bushes.

VII

25   Old Meg was brave as Margaret Queen
    And tall as Amazon,
An old red blanket cloak she wore,
    A chip hat had she on.
God rest her agèd bones somewhere–
30   She died full long agone!

¶ 92. 25. *Margaret Queen*] Perhaps Henry VII's belligerent daughter Margaret (married James IV of Scotland 1503).
28. *a chip hat*] A hat made of thin strips of wood.

93 A Song about Myself

Written 3 July 1818 to entertain Fanny Keats: K.'s letter to her, part quoted in preceding headnote, continues under this date, '. . . since I scribbled the Song [*Old Meg, she was a gipsy* . . ., No. 92 above] we have walked through a beautiful Country to Kirkudbright–at which place I will write you a song about myself' (*L* i 312).
Text from K.'s letter.
Published *Forman* (1883).

I

There was a naughty boy,
  A naughty boy was he,
He would not stop at home,
  He could not quiet be—
5   He took
      In his knapsack
      A book
      Full of vowels
      And a shirt
10   With some towels,
      A slight cap
      For night-cap,
      A hair brush,
      Comb ditto,
15   New stockings,
      For old ones
      Would split O!
      This knapsack
      Tight at's back
20   He rivetted close
  And followed his nose
      To the north,
      To the north,
  And followed his nose
25   To the north.

II

There was a naughty boy,
  And a naughty boy was he,
For nothing would he do
  But scribble poetry—
30   He took
      An inkstand
      In his hand,
      And a pen
      Big as ten
35   In the other.
      And away
      In a pother
      He ran
      To the mountains
40   And fountains
      And ghostès
      And postès
      And witches

	And ditches,
45	And wrote
	In his coat
	When the weather
	Was cool—
	Fear of gout—
50	And without
	When the weather
	Was warm.
	Och, the charm
	When we choose
55	To follow one's nose
	To the north,
	To the north,
	To follow one's nose
	To the north!

III

	There was a naughty boy,
60	And a naughty boy was he,
	He kept little fishes
	In washing tubs three.
	In spite
65	Of the might
	Of the maid,
	Nor afraid
	Of his granny-good,
	He often would
70	Hurly burly
	Get up early
	And go,
	By hook or crook,
	To the brook
75	And bring home
	Miller's thumb,

¶ 93. *42. postès*] Posts. Possibly chosen for the convenient rhyme, but K. could be referring to the rocky landscape since the word 'post' was used in the early nineteenth century to mean 'a vertical mass or stack of stratified rock between two "joints" or fissures' (*OED*).

62–93. Cp. K. to Fanny Keats 13 March 1819, '. . . remembering how fond I used to be of Goldfinches, Tomtits, Minnows, Mice, Ticklebacks, Dace, Cock salmons, and all the whole tribe of the Bushes and the Brooks' (*L* ii 46).

68. Granny-good] On K.'s affection for his grandmother, Alice Jennings, see headnote to *As from the darkening gloom* (p. 8 above).

76. Miller's thumb] A small freshwater fish.

Tittlebat
Not over fat,
Minnows small
80 As the stall
Of a glove,
Not above
The size
Of a nice
85 Little baby's
Little finger–
Oh, he made
('Twas his trade)
Of fish a pretty kettle—
90 A kettle,
A kettle,
Of fish a pretty kettle,
A kettle!

IV
There was a naughty boy,
95 And a naughty boy was he,
He ran away to Scotland
The people for to see–
Then he found
That the ground
100 Was as hard,
That a yard
Was as long,
That a song
Was as merry,
105 That a cherry
Was as red,
That lead
Was as weighty,
That fourscore
110 Was as eighty,
That a door
Was as wooden
As in England–
So he stood in his shoes
115 And he wondered,
He wondered,
He stood in his shoes
And he wondered.

118. Followed in K.'s letter by the comment, 'My dear Fanny I am ashamed
of writing you such stuff, nor would I if it were not for being tired after my

day's walking . . . so fatigued that when I am asleep you might sew my nose to my great toe and trundle me round the town like a Hoop without waking me' (*L* i 315–16).

94 'Ah, ken ye what I met the day'

Written 9 July at Ballantrae: see under 10 July in K.'s journal-letter to Tom Keats 10–14 July 1818, 'The reason for my writing these lines was that Brown wanted to impose a galioway song on dilke [Charles Dilke] – but it wont do – the subject I got from meeting a wedding just as we came down into this place' (*L* i 328). Brown and K. arrived at Ballantrae, Ayrshire, 9 July 1818. The poem captures something of Burns's characteristic song rhythms and perhaps owes a debt to *Remains of Nithsdale and Galloway Song* ed. R. H. Cromek (1810), but its diction is a combination of Scottish dialect with modern and archaic English. See K. to Reynolds 13 July 1818, 'One song of Burns's is of more worth to you than all I could think of for a year in his native country' (*L* i 325).

Text from K.'s letter.

Published *Forman* (1883).

Ah, ken ye what I met the day
    Out oure the mountains,
A-coming down by craggies grey
    An mossie fountains?
5   Ah, goud-haired Marie yeve I pray
    Ane minute's guessing,
For that I met upon the way
    Is past expressing.
As I stood where a rocky brig
10   A torrent crosses,
I spied upon a misty rig
    A troup o' horses,
And as they trotted down the glen
    I sped to meet them
15 To see if I might know the men
    To stop and greet them.
First Willie on his sleek mare came
    At canting gallop—
His long hair rustled like a flame
20   On board a shallop.
Then came his brother Rab and then
    Young Peggy's mither,

¶ 94 . 2. *oure*] O'er.
5. *yeve*] Give. An English archaism.
20. *shallop*] See *Calidore* 67 *n* (p. 39 above), 'his light shallop'.

And Peggy too—adown the glen
    They went togither.

25 I saw her wrappit in her hood
    Fra wind and raining—
Her cheek was flush wi' timid blood
    Twixt growth and waning.
She turned her dazèd head full oft,
30   For thence her brithers
Came riding with her bridegroom soft
    And mony ithers.
Young Tam came up an' eyed me quick
    With reddened cheek—
35 Braw Tam was daffèd like a chick,
    He coud na speak.
Ah, Marie, they are all gane hame
    Through blustering weather,
An' every heart is full on flame
40   An' light as feather.
Ah, Marie, they are all gone hame
    Fra happy wedding,
Whilst I—ah, is it not a shame?—
    Sad tears am shedding.

27. There was a blush upon her . . . *Letter (cancelled).*
35. daffèd] From 'daff', an early northern dialect word meaning 'daunt'.
39. full] light *Letter (cancelled).*

95 To Ailsa Rock

Written 10 July 1818 after travelling from Stranraer through Ballantrae to
Girvan and copied out on the same day in K.'s journal-letter to Tom Keats
10–14 July 1818: '. . . we had a gradual ascent and got among the tops of the
Mountains . . . I descried in the Sea Ailsa Rock 940 feet high [Ailsa Crag
rises to 1097 feet]–it was 15 Miles distant and seemed close upon us–The
effect . . . with the peculiar perspective of the Sea . . . and the misty rain
. . . gave me a complete Idea of a deluge–Ailsa struck me very suddenly
. . . I was a little alarmed. . . . This is the only Sonnet of any worth I have
of late written' (*L* i 329–30)–K. wrote five sonnets during his Scottish tour,
the others being *On Visiting the Tomb of Burns* (p. 357 above), *This mortal
body, Of late two dainties* and *Read me a lesson, Muse* (pp. 365, 369 and 375
below). Brown notes that K. wrote the poem 'At our inn in Girvan' (*KC*
ii 62).
Text from K.'s letter, which largely agrees with the version in Leigh Hunt's
Literary Pocket Book (1819). Reprinted A. A. Watt's *Poetical Album* 1828,
Plymouth and Devonport Weekly Journal 13 Sept. 1838, *1848.*

Hearken, thou craggy ocean pyramid!
  Give answer from thy voice, the sea-fowls' screams!
When were thy shoulders mantled in huge streams?
When from the sun was thy broad forehead hid?
5 How long is it since the mighty power bid
  Thee heave to airy sleep from fathom dreams—
  Sleep in the lap of thunder or sunbeams,
Or when grey clouds are thy cold coverlid?
Thou answer'st not, for thou art dead asleep.
10 Thy life is but two dead eternities—
The last in air, the former in the deep,
  First with the whales, last with the eagle-skies.
Drowned wast thou till an earthquake made thee steep,
  Another cannot wake thy giant size.

¶ 95. *Title.* To Ailsa Crag *Literary Pocket Book.*
6. *fathom dreams*] Dreams fathom-deep in the sea. The word 'fathom' is
used this once as an epithet by K.

96 'This mortal body of a thousand days'

Written 11 July 1818 in Burns's cottage at Ayr: see under this date in K.'s
11–13 July 1818 journal–letter to Reynolds: 'I am approaching Burns's
Cottage very fast . . .'; and under 13 July: 'We went to the Cottage and
took some Whiskey–I wrote a sonnet for the mere sake of writing some
lines under the roof–they are so bad I cannot transcribe them–the Man at
the Cottage was a great Bore with his Anecdotes . . .O the flummery of a
birth place! Cant! Cant! Cant! . . . The flat dog made me write a flat
sonnet' (*L* i 322, 324). K. also refused to send a copy to Tom Keats (*L* i 332),
but the poem was preserved in a transcript by Brown, who notes, '[the
cottage's] conversion into a whiskey-shop, together with its drunken land-
lord, went far towards the annihilation of . . . [K.'s] poetic power' (*KC* ii
62). D. G. Rossetti told H. Buxton Forman that the sonnet, ' . . . for all
Keats says of it himself is a good thing' (letter of 13 June 1881, *John Keats,
Criticism and Comment*, 1919, p. 20).
Text from *1848* as following Brown's transcript.

This mortal body of a thousand days
  Now fills, O Burns, a space in thine own room,
Where thou didst dream alone on budded bays,
  Happy and thoughtless of thy day of doom!

¶ 96. *3. budded bays*] Poetic fame.
13*

5 My pulse is warm with thine own barley-bree,
  My head is light with pledging a great soul,
My eyes are wandering and I cannot see,
  Fancy is dead and drunken at its goal.
Yet can I stamp my foot upon thy floor,
10 Yet can I ope thy window-sash to find
The meadow thou hast trampèd o'er and o'er,
  Yet can I think of thee till thought is blind,
Yet can I gulp a bumper to thy name—
  Oh, smile among the shades, for this is fame!

12. Some of K.'s thoughts are in his journal-letter to Reynolds: '[Burns's] Misery is a dead weight upon the nimbleness of one's quill – I tried to forget it – to drink Toddy without any Care – to write a merry Sonnet – it wont do – he talked with Bitches – he drank with Blackguards, he was miserable – We can see horribly clear in the works of such a man his whole life, as if we were God's spies [see *King Lear* V iii 17]' (*L* i 325).

13. a bumper] A toast.

5. barley-bree] Ale.

97 'All gentle folks who owe a grudge'

Written 17 July 1818 to fill up space under this date in K.'s journal-letter to Tom Keats 17–21 July 1818 and introduced by the following comment, 'I have just been bathing in Loch fine [Fyne] a salt-water Lake opposite the Window – quite pat and fresh but for the cursed Gad flies – damn 'em they have been at me ever since I left the Swan and two necks [properly 'The Swan with Two Necks', London coaching inn]' (*L* i 334).

Text from K.'s letter.

Published *Forman* (1883).

I

All gentle folks who owe a grudge
 To any living thing,
Open your ears and stay your trudge
 Whilst I in dudgeon sing.

II

5 The gadfly he hath stung me sore—
 Oh, may he ne'er sting you!
But we have many a horrid bore
 He may sting black and blue.

III

Has any here an old grey mare
10 With three legs all her store?

Oh, put it to her buttocks bare
And straight she'll run on four.

IV

Has any here a lawyer suit
Of 1743?
15 Take lawyer's nose and put it to 't
And you the end will see.

V

Is there a man in Parliament
Dumb-foundered in his speech,
Oh, let his neighbour make a rent
20 And put one in his breech.

VI

O Lowther, how much better thou
Hadst figured t'other day,
When to the folks thou mad'st a bow
And hadst no more to say,

VII

25 If lucky gadfly had but ta'en
His seat upon thine a–e,
And put thee to a little pain
To save thee from a worse.

VIII

Better than Southey it had been,
30 Better than Mr. D——

¶ 97. *13–14*. A long-drawn-out legal case (like the Chancery suit in Dickens's *Bleak House*) supposedly begun 1743.

21. Lowther] William Lowther (1787–1872), second earl of Lonsdale, became Tory M.P. for Westmorland in 1818. See K. to Tom Keats from Endmoor 26 June 1818, 'I enquired ... for Wordsworth ... he had been here a few days ago, canvassing for the Lowthers ... Wordsworth versus Brougham!! Sad–sad–sad–' (*L* i 299). Lord Brougham was the Whig candidate.

29. Southey] See K. on himself in his March 1819 journal-letter, 'the undersigned ... doth not admire ... Bob Southey' (*L* ii 69).

30 (and *32* below). *Mr D—— ... Mr V——*] Mr D—— may be Burridge Davenport, the Keats brothers' irritating Hampstead neighbour (*L* ii 76–7, 83). Mr V—— is perhaps the 'Vincent' whom K. refers to perfunctorily in a letter of Oct. 1818 (*L* i 376 *n*). M. Buxton Forman suggests Nicholas Vansittart (1766–1851), Chancellor of the Exchequer 1812–22 (cp. *The Cap and Bells* 145 *n*, p. 709 below), and Robert Dundas, Viscount Melville (1771–1851), referred to in Wordsworth's 'Two Addresses to the Freeholders of Westmoreland' (1818); see *The Letters of John Keats*, ed. M. Buxton Forman (1935) 186–7 *n*.

Better than Wordsworth too, I ween,
   Better than Mr. V——.

IX

Forgive me pray, good people all,
   For deviating so.
35 In spirit sure I had a call—
   And now I on will go.

X

Has any here a daughter fair
   Too fond of reading novels,
Too apt to fall in love with care
40   And charming Mister Lovels?

XI

Oh, put a gadfly to that thing
   She keeps so white and pert—
I mean the finger for the ring,
   And it will breed a Wert.

XII

45 Has any here a pious spouse
   Who seven times a day
Scolds as King David prayed, to chouse
   And have her holy way?

XIII

Oh, let a gadfly's little sting
50   Persuade her sacred tongue
That noises are a common thing,
   But that her bell has rung.

XIV

And as this is the *summum bo-
   num* of all conquering,
55 I leave withouten wordës mo
   The gadfly's little sting.

40. Mister Lovels] A reference to Lovel, the hero of Scott's *The Antiquary* (1816), a novel well known to K. (*L* i 200).

41–4. In key with Brown's enjoyment of bawdy jokes, of which K. gives some examples at the beginning of his letter to Tom Keats.

44. Wert] Wart.

46–7. seven times . . . prayed] See *Psalms* cxix 164, 'Seven times a day do I praise thee . . .'. The word 'chouse' means cheat (fairly common in the late eighteenth century).

53–4. And as this is the greatest of all conquests.

55. withouten wordës mo] A Chaucerian tag.

98 'Of late two dainties were before me placed'

Written 18 July 1818 in K.'s journal-letter to Tom Keats 17–21 July 1818 with the following explanation, '— On entering Inverary [17 July] we saw a Play Bill—Brown was knock'd up from new shoes—so I went to the Barn alone where I saw the Stranger [see *nn.* below] accompanied by a bag-pipe' (*L* i 336).

Text from K.'s letter.

Published *The Athenaeum* 7 June 1873 and *Forman* (1883).

Of late two dainties were before me placed,
    Sweet, holy, pure, sacred and innocent,
    From the ninth sphere to me benignly sent
That Gods might know my own particular taste.
5   First the soft bag-pipe mourned with zealous haste,
    The Stranger next with head on bosom bent
    Sighed; rueful again the piteous bag-pipe went,
Again the Stranger sighings fresh did waste.
O bag-pipe, thou didst steal my heart away—
10   O Stranger thou my nerves from Pipe didst charm
O Bag-pipe, thou didst re-assert thy sway—
    Again thou, Stranger, gav'st me fresh alarm!
Alas! I could not choose. Ah, my poor heart,
Mumchance art thou with both obliged to part!

¶ 98. *3. From the ninth sphere*] From remotest space—there were nine spheres in Ptolomaic astronomy.

6. The Stranger] *The Stranger*, a play by the German dramatist Augustus von Kotzebue (1761–1819), first performed in England at Drury Lane Theatre 24 March 1798. It was parodied by James Smith in *Rejected Addresses* (1812) and attacked by Reynolds in *The Champion* 2 March 1817.

7–8. K.'s letter to Tom Keats continues, 'There they went on about "interesting creaters" and "human nater"—till the Curtain fell and then Came the Bag pipe—When Mrs. Haller fainted [end of Act IV] down went the Curtain and out came the Bagpipe—at the heartrending, shoemaking reconciliation the Piper blew amain—I never read or saw this play before; not the Bag pipe nor the wretched players themselves were little in comparison with it—thank heaven it has been scoffed at lately' (*L* i 336–7).

8. sighings fresh did] sighed in discontent *Letter* (*cancelled*).

14. Mumchance] An archaism for 'silent' or 'tongue-tied'.

99 Lines Written in the Highlands after a Visit to Burns's Country

Written *c.* 18 July 1818 (so dated in *Woodhouse* 3) and copied out with this comment 22 July on the island of Mull in K.'s letter to Bailey 18–22 July 1818, 'One of the pleasantest bouts we have had was our walk to Burns's Cottage, over the Doon and past Kirk Alloway–I had determined to write a Sonnet in the Cottage. I did but ... it was ... wretched ... a few days afterwards I wrote some lines cousin-german to the Circumstance' (*L* i 343–5). K. tries to compensate in this poem for his 'wretched' sonnet–see headnote to *This mortal body* (p. 365 above)–by recording the intense excitement which he had experienced when approaching Burns's cottage on 11 July. The poem is set out as rhyming fourteeners in K.'s letter, but in George Keats's undated transcript (British Museum) is copied out as quatrains consisting of lines alternately of 4 and 3 stresses.
Text from the letter with some variants noted from K.'s holograph draft. Published *The Examiner* 14 July 1822; *1848*.

> There is a joy in footing slow across a silent plain
> Where patriot battle has been fought, where glory had
>   the gain;
> There is a pleasure on the heath where Druids old have
>   been,
> Where mantles grey have rustled by and swept the
>   nettles green;
> 5   There is a joy in every spot made known by times of old,
> New to the feet, although the tale a hundred times be
>   told.
> There is a deeper joy than all, more solemn in the heart,
> More parching to the tongue than all, of more divine a
>   smart,
> When weary feet forget themselves upon a pleasant turf,
> 10   Upon hot sand, or flinty road, or sea-shore iron scurf,
> Toward the castle or the cot where long ago was born
> One who was great through mortal days and died of
>   fame unshorn.
> Light heatherbells may tremble then, but they are far
>   away;

¶ 99. *1. joy*] charm *1848*. K. substituted 'silent plain' in his draft for the false start 'grand camp[aign]'.
5. by times] in days *Examiner*.
9. See K. to Reynolds 11 July 1818, 'One of the pleasantest means of annulling self is approaching such a shrine' (*L* i 323).
10. scurf] A forced rhyme.

Wood-lark may sing from sandy fern, the sun may hear
    his lay;
15   Runnels may kiss the grass on shelves and shallows clear,
    But their low voices are not heard though come on
       travels drear;
    Blood-red the sun may set behind black mountain peaks;
    Blue tides may sluice and drench their time in caves and
       weedy creeks;
    Eagles may seem to sleep wingwide upon the air;
20   Ring-doves may fly convulsed across to some high-
       cedared lair;
    But the forgotten eye is still fast wedded to the ground –
    As palmer's that with weariness mid-desert shrine hath
       found.
    At such a time the soul's a child, in childhood is the
       brain;
    Forgotten is the worldly heart – alone, it beats in vain.
25   Aye, if a madman could have leave to pass a healthful
       day
    To tell his forehead's swoon and faint when first began
       decay,
    He might make tremble many a man whose spirit had
       gone forth
    To find a bard's low cradle-place about the silent north!
    Scanty the hour and few the steps beyond the bourn of
       care,
30   Beyond the sweet and bitter world – beyond it unaware;

17. A foot short.
18. Cp. *On the Sea* 2–4 (p. 112 above),

             . . . its mighty swell
     Gluts twice ten thousand caverns, till the spell
     Of Hecate leaves them their old shadowy sound . . .

19. 'We have also seen an Eagle or two. They move about without the least motion of Wings when in an indolent fit . . .', K. to Tom Keats 21 July 1818 (*L* i 338).
20. convulsed] Agitated – the doves are terrified by the eagles.
22. palmer] Pilgrim.
24. Ordinary everyday claims are forgotten.
25–8. To be in this stage of intense abstraction is like being on the verge of insanity. Cp. K.'s 'prayer' not to 'lose his mind' in ll. 45–6 below.
29. bourn] Boundary. Cp. *To J. H. Reynolds Esq.* 83 *n* (p. 324 above), 'to see beyond our bourn'.
30. sweet and bitter world] On the close relationship between pain and pleasure elsewhere in K. see *Isabella* 104 *n* (p. 333 above).

Scanty the hour and few the steps, because a longer stay
Would bar return, and make a man forget his mortal
        way.
Oh, horrible to lose the sight of well-remembered face,
Of brother's eyes, of sister's brow, constant to every place,
35 Filling the air, as on we move, with portraiture intense,
More warm than those heroic tints that fill a painter's
        sense
When shapes of old come striding by and visages of old,
Locks shining black, hair scanty grey, and passions
        manifold.
No, no, that horror cannot be, for at the cable's length
40 Man feels the gentle anchor pull and gladdens in its
        strength–
One hour, half-idiot, he stands by mossy waterfall,
But in the very next he reads his soul's memorial.
He reads it on the mountain's height, where chance he
        may sit down
Upon rough marble diadem, that hill's eternal crown.
45 Yet be the anchor e'er so fast, room is there for a prayer
That man may never lose his mind on mountains bleak
        and bare;
That he may stray league after league some great
        birthplace to find,
And keep his vision clear from speck, his inward sight
        unblind.

31. Scanty the] Short is *Draft* (*cancelled*).
38. Locks] Hair *Draft* (*cancelled*).

100 'Not Aladdin magian'

Written 26 July 1818 in K.'s journal-letter to Tom Keats of 23–26 July 1818
from the Isle of Mull, and introduced by the following comment, 'I am
puzzled to give you an Idea of Staffa. . . . The finest thing is Fingal's Cave
. . . it is impossible to describe it' (*L* i 348–51); Brown records, 'Keats wrote
some lines on this cave . . . which I never could induce him to finish'
(*KC* ii 63).
Text for ll. 1–42 from K.'s Sept. 1819 copy (*L* ii 199–200), which has minor
variants from the first version and omits ll. 43–55, and for ll. 43–55 from his
July 1818 letter, with some variants noted from Brown's transcript; the
MSS are referred to below as *1818, 1819, Brown's MS.*
Published *1848.*

Not Aladdin magian
Ever such a work began;
Not the wizard of the Dee
Ever such a dream could see;
5   Not St. John in Patmos' Isle,
In the passion of his toil,
Gazed on such a rugged wonder.
As I stood its roofing under,
Lo! I saw one sleeping there
10 On the marble cold and bare,
While the surges washed his feet
And his garments white did beat,
Drenched, about the sombre rocks.
On his neck his well-grown locks,
15 Lifted dry above the main,
Were upon the curl again.
'What is this? and who art thou?'
Whispered I, and touched his brow.
'What art thou and what is this?'
20 Whispered I, and strove to kiss
The spirit's hand to wake his eyes.
Up he started in a trice.
'I am Lycidas,' said he,
'Famed in funeral minstrelsy!
25 This was architected thus

¶ 100. *Title. Brown's MS* has 'On Fingal's Cave. A Fragment'.

1. magian] Magical. Cp. *Endymion* iii 265 (p. 217 above), 'His magian fish'.

3. wizard of the Dee] Merlin.

5–6. St. John is said to have written the Apocalypse on Patmos.

6. Followed in *1818* by the lines,

>When he saw the churches seven
>Golden aisled built up in heaven . . .

See K.'s adaptation of the couplet in *The Eve of St. Mark* 33–4 and *n* (p. 483 below),

>. . . the seven
>Candlesticks John saw in heaven . . .

The allusion is to *Revelation* i 9–12.

7. on] at *1818*.

17. who art] what art *1818*.

22. trice] thrice *1818, 1819*; trice *Garrod*.

23–4. An allusion to Milton's *Lycidas*, especially 156–8,

>. . . beyond the stormy *Hebrides*,
>Where thou perhaps under the whelming tide
>Visit'st the bottom of the monstrous world . . .

25–36. Cp. K.'s prose account of the cave in his letter to Tom Keats (head-

By the great Oceanus!
Here his mighty waters play
Hollow organs all the day;
Here by turns his dolphins all,
30   Finny palmers great and small,
Come to pay devotion due,
Each a mouth of pearls must strew.
Many mortals of these days
Dare to pass our sacred ways,
35   Dare to see audaciously
This Cathedral of the sea.
I have been the pontiff-priest
Where the waters never rest,
Where a fledgy sea-bird quire
40   Soars for ever; holy fire
Have I hid from mortal man;
Proteus is my sacristan.
But the stupid eye of mortal

---

note), '. . . entirely a hollowing out of Basalt Pillars. Suppose . . . the Giants
who rebelled against Jove had taken a whole Mass of black Columns and
bound them together like bunches of matches – and then with immense Axes
had made a cavern in the body of these columns – of course the roof and the
floor must be composed of the broken ends of the Columns . . . the roof
is arched somewhat gothic wise . . . the colour of the columns is a sort of
black with a lurking gloom of purple therin – For solemnity and grandeur
it far surpasses the finest Cathedrall' (*L* i 348–9). K.'s allusion to the Titans
foreshadows *Hyperion* (headnote p. 394 below).

26. *Oceanus*] One of the Titans. See *Hyperion* ii 163–6 *n* (p. 425 below).

28. *Hollow organs*] See K.'s prose account of the cave's hollow 'basalt pillars', quoted in 25–36 *n* above.

29. Here his dolphins, one and all . . . *Brown's MS.*

30. *palmers*] Pilgrims.

33–4.   Many a mortal comes to see
                        This Cathedrall of the S[ea] . . . *1818 (cancelled).*

36. Cp. *Hyperion* i 86 (p. 401 below),
                        Like natural sculpture in cathedral cavern . . .

37. *pontiff-priest*] High priest. Cp. *To J. H. Reynolds* 20–1 (p. 321 above),
                        The sacrifice goes on; the pontiff knife
                        Gleams . . .

39. *quire*] See *As from the darkening gloom* 9 *n* (p. 9 above).

42. *Proteus*] A sea deity. Cp. *Endymion* ii 627 *n* (p. 189 above). K. breaks off
after this line in *1819.*

43. *stupid*] dulled *Brown's MS.* The correction was probably suggested by
l. 48 below ('stupid face') which K. did not include in his Sept. 1819 copy
(see headnote).

Hath passed beyond the rocky portal,
45 So for ever will I leave
Such a taint and soon unweave
All the magic of the place—
'Tis now free to stupid face,
To cutters and to fashion boats,
50 To cravats and to petticoats.
The great sea shall war it down
For its fame shall not be blown
At every farthing quadrille dance.'
So saying with a spirit's glance
55 He dived ...

46–7. *unweave* / *All the magic*] Cp. *Lamia* ii 367 (p. 646 below), 'Unweave a rainbow ...'
48–50. 'Staffa ... is a fashionable place ... everyone concerned with it ... are what you call up'–K. to Tom Keats 21 July 1818 (*L* i 339). Cp. K. on Windermere 26 June 1818, '... contaminated with bucks and soldiers, and women of fashion. ... The border inhabitants are quite out of keeping with the romance about them, from a continual intercourse with London rank and fashion' (*L* i 299).
55. After breaking off the line in *1818* K.'s letter continues, 'I am sorry I am so indolent as to write such stuff as this' (*L* i 351).

101 'Read me a lesson, Muse, and speak it loud'

Written 2 Aug. 1818 at the top of Ben Nevis: see K.'s letter (which contains the sonnet) to Tom Keats from Inverness-shire 3 Aug. 1818, 'yesterday ... we went up Ben Nevis' (*L* i 352); Brown records, 'on the summit of this mountain, we were enveloped in a cloud and, waiting till it was slowly wafted away ... [K.] sat on the stones, a few feet from the edge of that fearful precipice, fifteen hundred feet perpendicular from the valley below, and wrote this sonnet' (*KC* ii 63). D. G. Rossetti called the sonnet, 'perhaps the most thoughtful in Keats, and greatly superior in execution to the draft of Ailsa Crag [p. 364 above]' (letter to H. Buxton Forman 13 June 1881, John Keats, *Criticism and Comment*, 1919, p. 19].
Text from K.'s letter.
Published *Plymouth and Devonport Weekly Journal* 6 Sept. 1838; *1848*.

Read me a lesson, Muse, and speak it loud
    Upon the top of Nevis, blind in mist!
I look into the chasms, and a shroud
    Vaporous doth hide them; just so much I wist
5 Mankind do know of Hell. I look o'erhead
    And there is sullen mist; even so much
Mankind can tell of heaven. Mist is spread
    Before the earth beneath me; even such,
Even so vague is man's sight of himself.
10   Here are the craggy stones beneath my feet—
Thus much I know, that, a poor witless elf,
    I tread on them, that all my eye doth meet
Is mist and crag, not only on this height,
    But in the world of thought and mental might.

¶ 101. 2. See K.'s letter to Tom Keats, 'We gained . . . the height of what in the Valley we had thought the top and saw still above us another huge crag which still . . . was not the top–to that we made with an obstinate fag and having gained it there came on a Mist . . . from that part to the verry top we walked in a Mist' (*L* i 353).

3. chasms] See K.'s letter, 'Talking of chasms they are the finest wonder of the whole–they appear great rents in the very heart of the mountain though they are not . . . but other huge crags arising round it give the appearance to Nevis of a shattered heart or Core in itself–These Chasms are 1500 feet in depth and are the most tremendous places I have ever seen' (*L* i 353).

3–4. a shroud . . . doth hide them] See K.'s letter, 'Sometimes these chasms are tolerably clear, sometimes there is a misty cloud which seems to steam up . . . sometimes they are entirely smothered with clouds' (*L* i 353).

11. elf] A Spenserian word often used by K. (see *Endymion* ii 461 *n*, p. 182 above). Here suggested by the smallness of human beings against the immensity of nature.

12–13. all that my eye doth meet / Is mist] Cp. *The Fall of Hyperion* i 84–5 *n* (p. 662 below), 'ending in mist / Of nothing'.

102 'Upon my life, Sir Nevis, I am piqued'

Written 3 Aug. 1818 in K.'s letter of this date to Tom Keats and prefaced by the following remarks '. . . there was one Mrs Cameron of 50 years of age and the fattest woman in all invernesshire who got up this Mountain [Ben Nevis] some few years ago. . . . 'Tis said a little conversation took place between the mountain and the Lady–After taking a glass of Wiskey as she was tolerably seated at her ease she thus begun——' (*L* i 354).
Text from K.'s letter.
Published *Forman* (1883).

MRS. C.

Upon my life, Sir Nevis, I am piqued
That I have so far panted, tugged and reeked
To do an honour to your old bald pate
And now am sitting on you just to bate,
5   Without your paying me one compliment.
Alas, 'tis so with all, when our intent
Is plain and in the eye of all mankind
We fair ones show a preference too blind!
You gentlemen immediately turn tail.
10   Oh, let me then my hapless fate bewail!
Ungrateful baldpate, have I not disdained
The pleasant valleys, have I not, madbrained,
Deserted all my pickles and preserves,
My china closet too—with wretched nerves
15   To boot. Say, wretched ingrate, have I not
Left my soft cushion chair and caudle pot?
'Tis true I had no corns—no, thank the fates,
My shoemaker was always Mr. Bates.
And if not Mr. Bates, why I'm not old!
20   Still dumb, ungrateful Nevis—still so cold!

BEN NEVIS

What whining bit of tongue and mouth thus dares
Disturb my slumber of a thousand years?
Even so long my sleep has been secure
And to be so awaked I'll not endure.
25   Oh, pain—for since the eagle's earliest scream
I've had a damned confounded ugly dream,
A nightmare sure. What, Madam, was it you?
It cannot be! My old eyes are not true!

¶ 102. 2. See K.'s description of climbing Ben Nevis: 'I have said nothing
yet of our getting among the loose stones large and small sometimes on two
sometimes on three, sometimes four legs—sometimes two and stick, sometimes three and stick, then four again, then two, then a jump, so that we
kept ringing changes on foot, hand, Stick, jump, boggle, stumble, foot,
hand, foot, (very gingerly) stick again, and then again a game at all fours'
(L i 354).
4. bate] Rest.
9. gentlemen] 'Gentleman' in K.'s letter is probably a slip.
16. caudle] Gruel. For 'Left' K.'s letter has 'Let'.
20. Followed in K.'s letter by this 'stage direction': 'Here the Lady took
some more wiskey and was putting even more to her lips when she dashed
[it] to the Ground, for the Mountain began to grumble which continued
for a few Minutes before he thus began. . . .'

Red-Crag, my spectacles! Now let me see!
30 Good Heavens, Lady, how the gemini
Did you get here? Oh, I shall split my sides!
I shall earthquake–

MRS. C.

Sweet Nevis, do not quake, for though I love
Your honest countenance all things above,
35 Truly I should not like to be conveyed
So far into your bosom. Gentle maid
Loves not too rough a treatment, gentle Sir–
Pray thee be calm and do not quake nor stir,
No, not a stone, or I shall go in fits–

BEN NEVIS

40 I must, I shall! I meet not such tit bits–
I meet not such sweet creatures every day
By my old night-cap, night-cap night and day,
I must have one sweet buss–I must and shal
Red-Crag! What, Madam, can you then repent
45 Of all the toil and vigour you have spent
To see Ben Nevis and to touch his nose?
Red-Crag, I say! Oh, I must have you close!
Red-Crag, there lies beneath my farthest toe
A vein of sulphur–go, dear Red-Crag, go
50 And rub your flinty back against it. Budge!
Dear Madam, I must kiss you, faith I must!
I must embrace you with my dearest gust!
Blockhead, d'ye hear? Blockhead, I'll make her feel.
There lies beneath my east leg's northern heel
55 A cave of young earth dragons. Well, my boy,
Go thither quick and so complete my joy.
Take you a bundle of the largest pines
And, when the sun on fiercest phosphor shines,
Fire them and ram them in the dragons' nest,
60 Then will the dragons fry and fizz their best,
Until ten thousand now no bigger than
Poor alligators–poor things of one span–
Will each one swell to twice ten times the size
Of northern whale. Then for the tender prize,
65 The moment then–for then will Red-Crag rub
His flinty back and I shall kiss and snub

29. *Red-Crag*] K. adds the note 'A domestic of Ben's'.
48–67. A fantastication of current ideas about the causes of volcanic eruption.
52. *gust*] A pun. Gust means 'blast' and 'taste'.

And press my dainty morsel to my breast.
Blockhead, make haste!
                                O Muses, weep the rest—
The Lady fainted and he thought her dead,
70   So pulled the clouds again about his head,
And went to sleep again. Soon she was roused
By her affrighted servants. Next day, housed
Safe on the lowly ground, she blessed her fate
That fainting fit was not delayed too late.

103 Stanzas on some Skulls in Beauley Abbey, near Inverness

Written in collaboration with Brown, *c.* 6 Aug. 1818 just before K. broke
off his Scottish tour: see under this date in K.'s journal-letter to Tom Keats
of 3, 6 Aug. 1818, 'We have just entered Inverness' (*L* i 357), and Brown's
letter to Dilke 7 Aug. 1818, 'Keats . . . is too unwell for fatigue and priva-
tion. I am waiting here to see him off in the Smack for London. He caught
a violent cold in the Island of Mull, which . . . has become worse, and the
Physician here thinks him too thin and fevered to proceed on our journey'
(*L* i 362). According to Woodhouse only the lines italicized in the text are
by K. (*Woodouse* 3). The verses, which owe something to the gravedigging
scene in *Hamlet* (V i 77–224), are written in the Burns stanza.
Text from *Woodhouse* 3, with some variants noted from Brown's transcript.
Published *The New Monthly Magazine* 1822; *Colvin* (1917).

> *I shed no tears;*
> *Deep thought, or awful vision, I had none;*
> *By thousand petty fancies I was cross'd;*
>
>   WORDSWORTH
> *And mock'd the dead bones that lay scatter'd by*
>
>   SHAKESPEARE

¶ 103. *Title.* So given in *The New Monthly Magazine.*
Mottoes. The first motto is a misquotation of Wordsworth's sonnet, *Beloved
Vale* (1807) 7–9,
> . . . from mine eyes escaped no tears;
> Deep thought, or dread remembrance, had I none.
> By doubts and thousand petty fancies crost . . .
The second motto correctly quotes *Richard III* I iv 33.

I

In silent barren Synod met
Within these roofless walls, where yet
The shafted arch and carvèd fret
    Cling to the ruin,
5 The brethren's skulls mourn, dewy wet,
    Their creed's undoing.

II

The mitred ones of Nice and Trent
Were not so tongue-tied. No, they went
Hot to their Councils, scarce content
10   With orthodoxy.
But ye, poor tongueless things, were meant
    To speak by proxy.

III

Your chronicles no more exist,
Since Knox, the revolutionist,
15 Destroyed the work of every fist
    That scrawled black letter.
Well! I'm a craniologist
    And may do better.

IV

This skull-cap wore the cowl from sloth,
20 Or discontent, perhaps from both.
And yet one day, against his oath,
    He tried escaping,
For men, though idle, may be loth
    To live on gaping.

V

25 A toper this! He plied his glass
More strictly than he said the Mass,
And loved to see a tempting lass
    Come to confession,
Letting his absolution pass
30   O'er first transgression.

6. *Their creed's undoing*] The Reformation.
7. *Nice and Trent*] The First Council of Nicaea (A.D. 325) was concerned with the Arian Controversy, and the Second Council of Nicaea (A.D. 787) with the Iconoclastic Controversy. The Council of Trent was the great council which inaugurated the Counter-Reformation.
14. *Knox, the revolutionist*] John Knox, Scottish religious reformer.
17. *craniologist*] A phrenologist or reader of bumps.

VI

This crawled thro' life in feebleness,
Boasting he never knew excess,
Cursing those crimes he scarce could guess,
      Or feel but faintly,
35 With prayers that Heaven would cease to bless
      Men so unsaintly.

VII

Here's a true Churchman! He'd affect
Much charity and ne'er neglect
To pray for mercy on th' elect,
40   But thought no evil
In sending Heathen, Turk and Sect
      All to the Devil!

VIII

Poor skull, thy fingers set ablaze
With silver Saint in golden rays
45 *The holy missal; thou did'st craze*
      'Mid bead and spangle,
While others passed their idle days
      In coil and wrangle.

IX

Long time this sconce a helmet wore,
50 But sickness smites the conscience sore.
He broke his sword and hither bore
      His gear and plunder,
Took to the cowl—then raved and swore
      At his damn'd blunder!

X

55 *This lily-coloured skull, with all*
The teeth complete, so white and small,
Belonged to one whose early pall
      A lover shaded.
He died ere superstition's gall
60   *His heart invaded.*

41. Sect] Scot *Brown.*
43–8. K.'s monk illuminated missals while other monks quarrelled (or indulged in controversy).
43. Poor skull] Perhaps suggested by *Hamlet* V i 190–1, 'Alas! poor Yorick . . .'.
48. coil] Fuss, bother. Cp. *Hamlet* III i 67, 'this mortal coil'.
53. there] then *Brown.*

XI

Ha! Here is 'undivulgèd crime!'
Despair forbade his soul to climb
Beyond this world, this mortal time
        Of fevered sadness,
65   Until this Monkish Pantomime
        Dazzled his madness!

XII

A younger brother this! A man
Aspiring as a Tartar Khan,
But, curbed and baffled, he began
70   The trade of frightening.
It smacked of power! And here he ran
        To deal Heaven's lightning.

XIII

This idiot-skull belonged to one,
A buried miser's only son,
75   Who, penitent ere he'd begun
        To taste of pleasure,
And hoping Heaven's dread wrath to shun,
        Gave Hell his treasure.

XIV

Here is the forehead of an ape,
80   A robber's mask—and near the nape
That bone, fie on't, bears just the shape
        Of carnal passion.
Ah, he was one for theft and rape,
        In monkish fashion!

XV

85   This was the Porter! He could ring,
Or dance, or play, do any thing,
And what the Friars bade him bring,
        They ne'er were balk'd of
(Matters not worth remembering
90   And seldom talked of).

XVI

Enough! Why need I further pore?
This corner holds at least a score,
And yonder twice as many more
        Of Reverend Brothers.
95   'Tis the same story o'er and o'er—
        They're like the others!

104 Translated from Ronsard

Written *c.* 21 Sept. 1818 at Hampstead while K. was nursing Tom Keats in his last illness: see K.'s copying out l. 12 of the poem on this date in his letter to Dilke 20–21 Sept. 1818 (*L* i 369) and his letter to Reynolds *c.* 22 Sept. 1818. 'Here is a free translation of a Sonnet by Ronsard. . . . I have the loan of his works–they have great Beauties' (*L* i 371). K.'s letter to Reynolds is preserved in a transcript by Woodhouse, who also records 'In the middle of Sept. 1818 I lent Keats Ronsard' (*Woodhouse* 3). The original poem is Ronsard's *Nature ornant Cassandre . . .*, the second sonnet in his *Les Amours de Cassandre* (1552), which K. knew in the text of 1584: see *Oeuvres Complètes de P. de Ronsard*, ed. P. Laumonier (1914–19) iv 6,

> Nature ornant Cassandre qui devoyt
> De sa douceur forcer les plus rebelles,
> La composa de cent beautez nouvelles
> Que dès mille ans en espargne elle avoyt.
> De tous les biens qu' Amour-oiseau couvoit
> Au plus beau ciel cherement sous ses ailes,
> Elle enrichit les graces immortelles
> De son bel oeil, qui les Dieux emouvoyt.
> Du ciel a peine elle etoyt descendue,
> Quand je la vi, quand mon ame esperdue
> En devint folle, et d'un si poignant trait,
> Amour coula ses beautez en mes veines,
> Qu'autres plaisirs je ne sens que mes peines,
> Ny autre bien qu'adorer son pourtrait.

For K.'s knowledge of Ronsard see further *Hyperion* ii 19–81 *n*, 70 *n* (pp. 417 and 421 below).
Text from *Woodhouse* 3 with some variants noted from K.'s holograph MS at Hampstead.
Published *1848*.

> Nature withheld Cassandra in the skies,
>   For more adornment, a full thousand years;
>   She took their cream of Beauty's fairest dyes,
>   And shaped and tinted her above all peers.
> 5 Meanwhile Love kept her dearly with his wings,
>   And underneath their shadow filled her eyes
>   With such a richness that the cloudy Kings

¶ 104. 2. *more*] meet *K.'s MS.*
3. *Beauty's fairest dyes*] Beauty,–fairest dies *K.'s MS.*
5. *Meanwhile Love kept her*] Love meanwhile held her *K.'s MS.*
6. *filled*] charm'd *K.'s MS.*
7. *With*] To *K.'s MS.*

> Of high Olympus uttered slavish sighs.
> When from the heavens I saw her first descend,
> 10   My heart took fire, and only burning pains . . .
> They were my pleasures – they my Life's sad end;
> Love poured her beauty into my warm veins . . .

*   *   *   *

9–10.   When I beheld her on the Earth descend
                    My heart began to burn – and only pains . . . *K.'s MS.*
The last three words are substituted for 'my head to daze'. See K.'s letter to Reynolds, quoted in headnote, 'I never was in love – Yet the voice and the shape of a woman has haunted me these two days' (*L* i 370) – the woman was probably Reynolds's cousin Jane Cox (see *L* i 394–5); Guy Murchie (in *The Spirit of Place*, 1955) believes that K. had by now met Fanny Brawne and was referring to her (see headnote to *The Eve of St. Agnes*, p. 451 below).

11. Life's sad end] sad Life's end *K.'s MS.*

12. K. probably did not complete the translation. See his letter to Reynolds, 'I had not the original by me when I wrote it, and did not recollect the purport of the last lines' (*L* i 371). Milnes supplies a concluding couplet in *1848*,

> So that her image in my soul upgrew,
> The only thing adorable and true.

105 "'Tis the "witching time of night""

Written 14 Oct. 1818 as a lullaby for George and Georgiana Keats's first child (born Feb. 1819): see under this date in K.'s journal-letter of 14–31 Oct. 1818 where the poem appears after the following remarks, 'If I had a prayer to make for any great good, next to Tom's recovery [see headnote to preceding poem, p. 383 above], it should be that one of your Children should be the first American Poet. I have a great mind to make a prophecy . . . they say prophecies work out their own fulfilment' (*L* i 398). John Howard Payne (1781–1852), American actor, playwright and diplomatist, liked the poem, but remarked in a letter to Milnes of 1847, 'The writer does not seem to have known that we have had, and then possessed, many poets in America' (*KC* ii 224–5).

Text from K.'s letter. Variants from this text in *1848* are Milnes's errors or emendations.

Published *1848*.

'Tis the 'witching time of night',
Orbèd is the moon and bright,
And the stars they glisten, glisten,
Seeming with bright eyes to listen—
5   For what listen they?
For a song and for a charm,
See they glisten in alarm,
And the moon is waxing warm
To hear what I shall say.
10   Moon, keep wide thy golden ears!
Hearken, stars, and hearken, spheres!
Hearken, thou eternal sky!
I sing an infant's lullaby,
A pretty lullaby!
15   Listen, listen, listen, listen,
Glisten, glisten, glisten, glisten,
And hear my lullaby!
Though the rushes that will make
Its cradle still are in the lake;
20   Though the linen then that will be
Its swathe is on the cotton tree;
Though the woollen that will keep
It warm is on the silly sheep;
Listen, stars' light, listen, listen,
25   Glisten, glisten, glisten, glisten,
And hear my lullaby!
Child, I see thee! Child, I've found thee
Midst of the quiet all around thee!
Child, I see thee! Child, I spy thee!
30   And thy mother sweet is nigh thee!
Child, I know thee! Child no more,
But a Poet evermore!
See, see, the lyre, the lyre,
In a flame of fire,
35   Upon the little cradle's top
Flaring, flaring, flaring,
Past the eyesight's bearing—
Awake it from its sleep,
And see if it can keep
40   Its eyes upon the blaze.

¶ 105. 1. *time*] hour *1848, Garrod.* Echoes *Hamlet* III ii 394,
'Tis now the very witching time of night . . .
20–1. K.'s error in identifying linen and cotton was noticed by J. H. Payne
(*KC* ii 225).
20. *then*] Omitted in *1848, Garrod.*
24. *stars' light*] starlight *1848, Garrod.*

Amaze, amaze!
It stares, it stares, it stares,
It dares what no one dares!
It lifts its little hand into the flame
45 Unharmed, and on the strings
Paddles a little tune, and sings,
With dumb endeavour sweetly!
Bard art thou completely!
Little child
50 O' the western wild,
Bard art thou completely!
Sweetly with dumb endeavour—
A Poet now or never!
Little child
55 O' the western wild,
A Poet now or never!

41. Amaze] A poeticism for amazement.

106 'Welcome joy and welcome sorrow'

Probably written Oct. 1818: '1818' in four MSS (of which one—in the possession of Miss Dorothy Withey—is conjecturally in K.'s hand); the month is suggested by K.'s use of a similar manner and metre in the preceding poem, *'Tis the 'witching time of night'* (No. 105 above) and by the poem's congruity with K.'s letter of 27 Oct. 1818 to Woodhouse:

'The poetical Character . . . has no self—it is every thing and nothing . . . it enjoys light and shade; it lives in gusto, be it foul or fair, high or low, rich or poor, mean or elevated.—It has as much delight in conceiving an Iago as an Imogen. What shocks the virtuous philosopher, delights the camelion Poet. It does no harm from its relish for the dark side of things any more than from its taste for the bright one; because they both end in speculation' (*L* i 386–7).

For other hints of the date see 16–17 *n*, 21 *n* below.

Text from *1848* as agreeing with Woodhouse's transcript and Miss Withey's MS, with some variants noted from Brown's transcript.

Published *1848*.

¶ 106. *Title*. 'Song' *Brown's MS.*

Motto. A misquotation. See Milton's *Paradise Lost* ii 898–903,

For hot, cold, moist, and dry, four Champions fierce
Strive here for Maistrie, and to Battel bring
Their embryon Atoms; they around the flag
Of each his faction, in their several Clanns,
Light-arm'd or heavy, sharp, smooth, swift or slow,
Swarm populous . . .

The passage is underlined in K.'s copy of Milton at Hampstead.

'*Under the flag
Of each his faction, they to battle bring
Their embryon atoms.*'

MILTON

Welcome joy and welcome sorrow,
  Lethe's weed and Hermes' feather;
Come today and come tomorrow,
  I do love you both together!
5   I love to mark sad faces in fair weather,
And hear a merry laugh amid the thunder.
  Fair and foul I love together:
Meadows sweet where flames burn under,
And a giggle at a wonder;
10 Visage sage at pantomime;
Funeral and steeple-chime;
Infant playing with a skull;
Morning fair and shipwrecked hull;
Nightshade with the woodbine kissing;
15 Serpents in red roses hissing;
Cleopatra regal-dressed
With the aspic at her breast;
Dancing music, music sad,
Both together, sane and mad.
20 Muses bright and Muses pale,
Sombre Saturn, Momus hale,
Muses bright and Muses pale,
Bare your faces of the veil!

1. K. is recalling Milton's separate celebrations of these moods in *L'Allegro* and *Il Penseroso*.

8. burn] are Brown's MS.

10–15. K.'s pleasure in opposites contrasts with his sense of 'Things all disjointed . . .' in *To J. H. Reynolds Esq.* 5–12 (p. 320 above).

16–17. See *Antony and Cleopatria* V ii 278,

    Give me my robe, put on my crown . . .

and V ii 291,

    Have I the aspic in my lips . . .

K. refers to the play in his 14–31 Oct. 1818 journal-letter, 'She is not a Cleopatra; but she is at least a Charmian. . . . She has faults–the same as Charmian and Cleopatra might have had' (L ii 395).

21. Sombre Saturn] Hints at K.'s preoccupation with *Hyperion*; see his description of Saturn in *Hyperion* i 1–21 (p. 396–8 below) and his 27 Oct. 1818 letter to Woodhouse 'Might I not . . . have been cogitating on . . . Saturn . . .?' (L i 387). Momus was 'the god of pleasantry among the ancients' (*Lemprière*).

>   Laugh and sigh, and laugh again!
> 25   Oh, the sweetness of the pain!
>   Let me see and let me write
>   Of the day and of the night—
>   Both together. Let me slake
>   All my thirst for sweet heart-ache!
> 30   Let my bower be of yew,
>   Interwreathed with myrtles new,
>   Pines and lime-trees full in bloom,
>   And my couch a low grass tomb.

25. K. repeats this characteristic phrase in *To [Fanny]* 54 (p. 689 below).
33. The line has the ring of an Elizabethan song, e.g. *Hamlet* IV v 31–2.

>   At his head a grass-green turf;
>   At his heels a stone . . .

107 Song ['Spirit here that reignest']

Probably written *c.* Oct. 1818, the date conjectured for the preceding poem, which has a similar theme. K. wrote out the verses in his copy of Beaumont and Fletcher at Hampstead.
Text from K.'s MS.
Published *Plymouth and Devonport Weekly Journal* 25 Oct. 1838; *1848*.

> I
>   Spirit here that reignest!
>   Spirit here that painest!
>   Spirit here that burnest!
>   Spirit here that mournest!
> 5   Spirit, I bow
>   My forehead low,
>   Enshaded with thy pinions.
>   Spirit, I look
>   All passion-struck
> 10   Into thy pale dominions.

> II
>   Spirit here that laughest!
>   Spirit here that quaffest!
>   Spirit here that dancest!
>   Noble soul that prancest!

¶ 107. 3. (*and 13–14 below*) *burnest . . . dancest . . . prancest*] *1848*; *burneth . . . danceth . . . pranceth K.'s MS.* K.'s use of the third person, corrected by Milnes in *1848*, was probably a slip made in the rapidity of composition. He uses the second person forms correctly in ll. 1–2, 4, 11–12.

<pre>
15   Spirit, with thee
            I join in the glee
            A-nudging the elbow of Momus.
            Spirit, I flush
            With a bacchanal blush
20   Just fresh from the banquet of Comus.
</pre>

17. *A-nudging*] While nudging *1848*. On Momus see *Welcome joy and welcome sorrow* 21 and *n* (p. 387 above), 'Momus hale'.
19–20. Cp. Milton's *Comus* 102–4,

> . . . welcom Joy, and Feast,
> Midnight shout, and revelry,
> Tipsie dance, and Jollity . . .

For K.'s earlier echo of these lines see *Endymion* iii 534–5 *n* (p. 227 above). The sombre and the laughing spirits in the two stanzas probably owe something to Milton's *L'Allegro* and *Il Penseroso*.

108 'Where's the Poet? Show him, Show him'

Probably written *c*. Oct. 1818: '1818' in the three transcripts; the fragment can be linked with what K. wrote on 27 Oct. 1818 to Woodhouse, 'A Poet is the most unpoetical of any thing in existence; because he has no Identity–he is continually . . . filling some other Body' (*L* i 387); the letter is further quoted in headnote to *Welcome joy and welcome sorrow* (p. 386 above), which the present poem resembles in style.
Text from *1848* as generally agreeing with the three transcripts.
Published *1848*.

<pre>
            Where's the poet? Show him, show him,
            Muses nine, that I may know him!
            'Tis the man who with a man
            Is an equal, be he king,
5   Or poorest of the beggar-clan,
            Or any other wondrous thing
            A man may be 'twixt ape and Plato.
            'Tis the man who with a bird,
            Wren or eagle, finds his way to
10   All its instincts. He hath heard
            The lion's roaring and can tell
            What his horny throat expresseth,
</pre>

¶ 108. *Title.* 'Fragment' in the three transcripts.
8–15. Cp. K.'s letter to Woodhouse (headnote), 'When I am in a room
14+K.

And to him the tiger's yell
Comes articulate and presseth
15   On his ear like mother-tongue.

with People ... then not myself goes home to myself ... the identity of
every one ... begins ... to press upon me' (*L* i 387), and to Bailey 22 Nov.
1817, '. . . if a Sparrow come before my Window I take part in its existence
and pick about the Gravel' (*L* i 186).

109 Fragment of the 'Castle Builder'

Probably written late Oct. 1818 as part of an unfinished satire on fashionable Romantic taste: '1818' in *Woodhouse* 2; the poem contains several
parallels with K.'s journal-letter of 14–31 Oct. 1818 (for which see notes
below). Composition earlier in 1818 at various dates is suggested in *Finney*
351–2, *Ward* (1963) 151, *Bate* (1963) 302 *n*.
Text from Woodhouse's transcript.
Published *1848* (ll. 24–71 only). The introductory lines (ll. 1–23) were first
printed in *TLS* 16 April 1914.

CASTLE BUILDER

In short, convince you that however wise
You may have grown from convent libraries,
I have, by many yards at least, been carding
A longer skein of wit in Convent garden.

BERNARDINE

5   A very Eden that same place must be!
Pray what demesne? Whose lordship's legacy?
What, have you convents in that Gothic isle?
Pray pardon me, I cannot help but smile.

CASTLE BUILDER

Sir, Convent Garden is a monstrous beast:
10   From morning, four o'clock, to twelve at noon,
It swallows cabbages without a spoon;
And then, from twelve till two, this Eden made is
A promenade for cooks and ancient ladies;

¶ 109. *Title*. So given by Woodhouse.
4. *Convent garden*] Covent Garden, a district in the West End of London,
famous for its Market (see ll. 10–11 below) and for Covent Garden Theatre.
K.'s journal-letter of Oct. 1818 mentions, '. . . On thursday [22 Oct.] I
walked with Hazlitt as far as covent Garden' (*L* i 402).
6. *demesne*] See 'On First Looking into Chapman's Homer' 6 *n* (p. 61
above).

And then for supper, 'stead of soup and poaches,
15 It swallows chairmen, damns, and Hackney coaches.
In short, Sir, 'tis a very place for monks,
For it containeth twenty thousand punks,
Which any man may number for his sport,
By following fat elbows up a court . . .

20 In such like nonsense would I pass an hour
With random friar, or rake upon his tour,
Or one of few of that imperial host
Who came unmaimèd from the Russian frost.
To-night I'll have my friar—let me think
25 About my room. I'll have it in the pink.
It should be rich and sombre, and the moon,
Just in its mid-life in the midst of June,
Should look through four large windows and display
Clear, but for golden vases in the way,
30 Their glassy diamonding on Turkish floor.
The tapers keep aside an hour and more
To see what else the moon alone can show,
While the night-breeze doth softly let us know
My terrace is well bowered with oranges.
35 Upon the floor the dullest spirit sees
A guitar-ribband and a lady's glove
Beside a crumple-leavèd tale of love;
A tambour-frame, with Venus sleeping there,

14. *poaches*] Lightly cooked food.
15. Crowds arrive in sedan chairs and hired coaches for the evening performance at the theatre.
16–17. Cp. the satirical comments on monks in *Stanzas on some Skulls* (p. 379 above).
22–3. A survivor from Napoleon's army after his retreat from Moscow (1812). K. has several references to Napoleon in his Oct. 1818 journal-letter; see L i 395, 397, 402.
25–69. K.'s imaginary room is filled with stock romantic furniture and its setting recalls the Italian background in Gothic stories. On K.'s interest in interior furnishings as an index to fashionable taste cp. his playful description of Mrs Jones's sitting-room 24 Oct. 1818, '. . . a very tasty sort of place with Books, Pictures, a bronze statue of Buonaparte, Music, aeolian Harp; a Parrot a Linnet–A Case of choice Liquers etc etc' (L i 402).
25. *in the pink*] Perfect.
28. *large windows*] Presumably casement windows with leaded diamond panes (see l. 30 below).
29. *golden vases*] gold-fish vases *1848*.
30. *Turkish floor*] Covered with Turkish carpets.

All finished but some ringlets of her hair;
40   A viol-bow, strings torn, cross-wise upon
A glorious folio of Anacreon;
A skull upon a mat of roses lying,
Inked purple with a song concerning dying;
An hour-glass on the turn, amid the trails
45   Of passion-flower ... just in time there sails
A cloud across the moon – the lights bring in!
And see what more my fantasy can win.
It is a gorgeous room, but somewhat sad.
The draperies are so, as though they had
50   Been made for Cleopatra's winding-sheet,
And opposite the steadfast eye doth meet
A spacious looking-glass, upon whose face,
In letters raven-sombre, you may trace
Old 'Mene, Mene, Tekel, Upharsin.'
55   Greek busts and statuary have ever been
Held, by the finest spirits, fitter far
Than vase grotesque and Siamesian jar.
Therefore 'tis sure a want of Attic taste
That I should rather love a Gothic waste
60   Of eyesight on cinque-coloured potter's clay
Than on the marble fairness of old Greece.
My table-coverlits of Jason's fleece

40. A viol, bowstrings torn] Emblem of romantic melancholy – cp. l. 42 below, 'skull upon a mat of roses'.

41. Anacreon] Sixth-century Greek lyric poet. A translation of his odes was published by Thomas Moore in 1800; for his early influence on K. see *Fill for me* 7–8 *n* (p. 7 above).

43. Inked purple] The manuscript of the 'song' is still wet, and the skull is lying on it.

50. For K.'s references to Cleopatra in his Oct. 1818 journal-letter see *Welcome joy and welcome sorrow* 16–17 *n* (p. 387 above).

54. From *Daniel* v 25. K. has an earlier reference to *Daniel* in *Nebuchadnezzar's Dream* (p. 289 above).

57. Siamesian] Siamese.

58. Attic] Grecian. Cp. *Ode on a Grecian Urn* 41 (p. 537 below),
              O Attic shape! Fair attitude ...

59–61. The multicoloured Siamese jar is contrasted with the whiteness of Greek statuary.

60. cinque-coloured] The Siamese jar is decorated in five different colours. The compound probably derives from *Cymbeline* II ii 38, 'A mole cinque-spotted'.

62. Jason's fleece] The golden fleece brought back by the Argonauts from Colchis (Ovid's *Metamorphoses* vii).

And black Numidian sheep-wool should be wrought,
Gold, black and heavy, from the Lama brought.
65 My ebon sofa should delicious be
With down from Leda's cygnet progeny.
My pictures all Salvator's, save a few
Of Titian's portraiture, and one, though new,
Of Haydon's in its fresh magnificence.
70 My wine—Oh, good! 'tis here at my desire
And I must sit to supper with my friar.

63. Numidian] African.
64. Lama] A pun may be intended on 'llama'.
65–6. '. . . the chairs and Sofa stuffed with Cygnet's down . . .' is part of
K.'s 24 Oct. 1818 fantasia–prompted by his visit to Mrs Jones–on the comforts of married life (*L* i 403). Cp. *Troilus and Cressida* I i 59–60,

> . . . to whose soft seizure
> The cygnet's down is harsh . . .

The passage is marked in K.'s Shakespeare (*Spurgeon* 150); K.'s frequent
references to the play in Oct. 1818 are listed in *Gittings* (1956) 172–3.
66. Leda] Wife of the Spartan King, Tyndareus, raped by Jupiter in the
shape of a swan (Ovid's *Metamorphoses* vi 109).
67. Salvator] Salvator Rosa (1615–73), Italian landscape painter popular in
England during the eighteenth century and the Romantic period. For some
indications of his influence on K. and his friends see Ian Jack's *Keats and the
Mirror of Art* (1967) 38–9, 68, 82, 158–60.
68. Titian. Frequently referred to by K. See, for example, *To J. H. Reynolds, Esq.* 19 (p. 321 above), 'Titian colours touched into real life' and
Sleep and Poetry 335–6 *n*, 354–91 *n* (pp. 83–4 above).
68–9. one . . . magnificence] A reference to Haydon's still unfinished 'Christ's
triumphal entry into Jerusalem', first exhibited March 1820. See K.'s Oct.
1818 journal-letter, 'Poor Haydon's eyes will not suffer him to proceed
with his picture' (*L* i 394).

110 'And what is love? It is a doll dressed up'

Probably written late Oct. 1818 with the preceding poem, *Fragment of the
'Castle Builder'* which follows it in *1848*: '1818' in the single transcript
(*Woodhouse* 2), from which the text is taken. Some influence from the
Epilogue to J. H. Payne's *Brutus; or, The Fall of Tarquin* (1818) is suggested
in *Gittings* (1968) 265.
Published *1848*.

¶ *110. Title.* 'Modern Love' (*1848*) is an editorial addition by Milnes.

And what is love? It is a doll dressed up
For idleness to cosset, nurse, and dandle.
A thing of soft misnomers, so divine
That silly youth doth think to make itself
5   Divine by loving, and so goes on
Yawning and doting a whole summer long,
Till Miss's comb is made a pearl tiara,
And common Wellingtons turn Romeo boots;
Then Cleopatra lives at Number Seven,
10   And Antony resides in Brunswick Square.
Fools! If some passions high have warmed the world,
If queens and soldiers have played high for hearts,
It is no reason why such agonies
Should be more common than the growth of weeds.
15   Fools! Make me whole again that weighty pearl
The Queen of Egypt melted, and I'll say
That ye may love in spite of beaver hats.

9 (and *16* below). For K.'s Oct. 1818 allusions to Cleopatra see *Welcome joy
and welcome sorrow* 16–17 *n* (p. 387 above).

15–16. pearl . . . melted] Cleopatra was supposed to have dissolved a pearl
in acid, which she drank as a toast to Antony.

III Hyperion. A Fragment

Begun autumn 1818 and abandoned April 1819: for the first date see K.'s
letter to Woodhouse 27 Oct. 1818: 'Might I not at that very instant have
been cogitating on the Characters of saturn and Ops?' (*L* i 387)—K. is
answering Woodhouse's allusion of 21 Oct. 1818 to 'our late conversation'
(*L* i 380); for the second date see Woodhouse's notes, 'Copied 20 Apl 1819
from JK's manuscript written in 1818/19' (*Woodhouse* 3) and under 'April
1819', 'K. lent me the fragment . . . abt 900 lines in all. . . . He said he was
dissatisfied . . . and should not complete it' (Woodhouse's copy of *Endymion*). For Woodhouse's account of the intended course of the poem see iii
136 *n* (p. 441 below). K.'s difficulty in completing the poem is indicated by
his references to it in his 16 Dec. 1818–4 Jan. 1819 journal-letter, for example:
'[18 Dec.] . . . I went on a little . . . last night–but it will take some time to
get in the vein again [Tom Keats died 1 Dec. 1818] . . . [22 Dec.] Just now I
took out my poem to go on with it–but . . . I could not . . . [31 Dec.] my
large poem . . . is scarce began' (*L* ii 12, 14–15, 18); see also his letter to
Haydon 8 March 1819, 'I am . . . in a sort of cui bono temper, not exactly

¶ III. *Title*. So given in *1820*, but K. was already referring to the poem as
'the fall of Hyperion' in Dec. 1818 (*L* ii 12). On the identity of Hyperion in
classical mythology see i 166 *n* (p. 405 below).

on the road to an epic poem' (*L* ii 42). On K.'s attempt to reconstruct the poem in the form of a vision later in 1819 see headnote to *The Fall of Hyperion. A Dream* (p. 655 below). K.'s interest in the subject dates from the middle of 1817: see the hints and anticipations in *Endymion* iii 993–7 *n*, iv 774 (pp. 243 and 276 above), K.'s preface to *Endymion*: 'I hope I have not in too late a day touched the beautiful mythology of Greece . . . I wish to try once more, before I bid it farewell' (p. 119 above), and his letter to Haydon 23 Jan. 1818 (in reply to the request for a passage from *Endymion* to illustrate as a frontispiece), '. . . wait for a choice out of *Hyperion*–when that Poem is done there will be a wide range for you . . . the nature of *Hyperion* will lead me to treat it in a more naked and grecian Manner–and the march of passion and endeavour will be undeviating. . . . Apollo in Hyperion being a fore-seeing God will shape his actions like one' (*L* i 207). K.'s 'mythology of Greece' derives as in earlier poems chiefly from Elizabethan sources and from studied works of classical reference in his possession, together with Hesiod's *Theogony*, which he probably knew from Cooke's translation (1728) in Chalmer's *English Poets* (1810), and Hyginus's *Fabulae*, printed in *Auctores Mythographi Latini* (1742), which he acquired in 1819 (*KC* i 260, ii 280), as additional sources for his fresh subject matter–the defeat of the Titans by the new race of Olympian gods. The treatment and adaptation of the material and the affirmation of the law of progress in the poem are K.'s own inventions, but the poem's style and imagery were strongly influenced by his reading of Cary's translation (1814 edn) of Dante's *Divina Commedia* in summer 1818 and by his close study of Milton's *Paradise Lost* during 1818–19 (for his later 'repudiation' of Milton as a model in Sept. 1819 see headnote to *The Fall of Hyperion*, p. 656 below). Substantial evidence of K.'s close reading of Milton is offered by the marginalia–first printed in *Forman* (1883)–and numerous markings in his copy of *Paradise Lost* (now lodged at Keats House, Hampstead).

Hyperion was highly praised on its appearance in *1820* by Hunt, Byron and Shelley (see *Forman* (1883) ii 536–9, iv 248–50, 269–70) and later by Matthew Arnold and D. G. Rossetti (see G. H. Ford, *Keats and the Victorians* (1944) 64, 143). Indications of its growing reputation in the 1850s are recorded in E. V. Lucas's *The Colvins and their Friends* (1928) 326–7. Modern opinion is probably best represented by W. J. Bate's description of the poem as an 'imposing fragment', remarkable for its bold attempts at an 'imitation' of the Miltonic blank-verse epic and its marked falling off in style–after a fine opening and the sustaining of considerable poetic qualities in Books I and II–in Book III. Critical commentaries appear in Edward Thomas's *Keats* (1916) 61–7; *Murry* (1926) 79–83; *Ridley* (1933) 57–95; R. Gittings's 'Keat's debt to Dante' in *Gittings* (1956) 5–44; K. Muir's 'The meaning of Hyperion' in *Reassessment* (1958) 102–22; *Bate* (1963) 388–417; Douglas Bush, *John Keats* (1966) 95–108. The publishers' Advertisement to the poem and K.'s repudiation of it are printed in Appendix D (p. 764 below). For K.'s original intention to publish *Hyperion* jointly with poems by Hunt see Severn's letter to Monckton Milnes 22 June 1848 (*KC* ii 234).

Text from *1820*. K.'s holograph MS (British Museum) and the transcripts in *Woodhouse* 1, 2 have some variants; a number in K.'s MS (referred to below as MS), including some which coincide with readings in *The Fall of Hyperion*, are noted below. For a detailed commentary on the variant readings see de Selincourt's *Hyperion* (1905).
Published *1820*.

BOOK I

Deep in the shady sadness of a vale
Far sunken from the healthy breath of morn,
Far from the fiery noon, and eve's one star,
Sat grey-haired Saturn, quiet as a stone,
5   Still as the silence round about his lair;

i *1–14*. Quoted by Edward Thomas in his *Keats* (1916) with the comment 'Hyperion . . . seldom quite matches even where it equals the opening lines . . . which are . . . perfect were it not for the rhymes [i 5, 7], and "shady", "healthy", "fiery", in successive lines [i 1–3]' (63). K.'s Oxford friend Bailey cites i 1–7 ('Deep . . . cloud on cloud') to illustrate K.'s 'theory' of melody in verse 'particularly in the management of open and close vowels . . . [which] should . . . not clash one with another so as to mar the melody . . . yet . . . should be interchanged, like differing notes of music to prevent monotony' (*KC* ii 277: for the 'theory' see further *Bate* (1945) 51–6, 65 and *Bate* (1963) 413–17). On the Miltonic 'stationing' in the passage cp. i 85–8 *n* below.

i *1*. *shady sadness of a vale*] Cp. Milton, *Paradise Lost* i 65,
                Regions of sorrow, doleful shades . . .
The passage is marked in K.'s copy of Milton, which is at Hampstead. K. expresses his fondness for the word 'vale' in his marginal note on *Paradise Lost* i 321 ('To slumber here, as in the vales of heaven . . .'), 'There is a cool pleasure in the very sound of vale. The English word is of the happiest chance. Milton has put vales in heaven and hell with the . . . affection and yearning of a great Poet. It is a sort of Delphic Abstraction–a beautiful thing made more beautiful by being reflected and put in a mist. . . .' The rhythm and phrasing of the whole line suggest a recollection of Thomson's 'Miltonic' cadence in *The Castle of Indolence* (1748) ii 6,
                Deep in the winding bosom of a lawn . . .
i *2–4*. Cp. Zeus's speech in Chapman's *Homer, Iliad* viii 421–4,
                . . . where endlesse night confounds
        Japet and my dejected Sire, who sit so far beneath
        They never see the flying Sunne, nor hear the winds that breathe . . .
i *3*. *Eve's one star*] Evening *MS* (*cancelled*).
i *4*. *grey-haired Saturn*] Saturn–Hyperion's brother, leader of the Titans (for whom see ii 19–81 *n*, p. 417 below), and father of the rebellious Jupiter–was among the oldest deities in classical mythology. K. draws freely on the various traditional stories about him; see further i 107–10 *n* (pp. 402–3 below).

Forest on forest hung about his head
Like cloud on cloud. No stir of air was there,
Not so much life as on a summer's day
Robs not one light seed from the feathered grass,
10   But where the dead leaf fell, there did it rest.
A stream went voiceless by, still deadened more
By reason of his fallen divinity
Spreading a shade; the Naiad 'mid her reeds
Pressed her cold finger closer to her lips.

15   Along the margin-sand large foot-marks went,
No further than to where his feet had strayed,
And slept there since. Upon the sodden ground
His old right hand lay nerveless, listless, dead,
Unsceptred; and his realmless eyes were closed,

i *6–10*. Cp. Wordworth's *The Excursion* (1814) iv 1280–2,
                                   . . . hushed
              As the unbreathing air, when not a leaf
              Stirs in the mighty woods . . .
i *6*. Cp. *Ode to Psyche* 54–5 *n* (p. 520 below),
              Far, far around shall those dark-clustered trees
              Fledge the wild-ridgèd mountains steep by steep . . .
i *8–9*. The *MS* version is preceded by the cancelled lines,
     Not so much Life as what an eagles [young vulture's *cancelled above*] wing
     Would spread upon a field of green ear'd corn . . .
and followed by an uncancelled but rejected further variant (in the margin),
              Not so much life as on a summer's day
              Robs not at all the dandelion's fleece . . .
See K.'s comment in his copy of Shakespeare (recorded in *Spurgeon* 157) on
Troilus and Cressida I iii 316–17 ('the seeded pride / That hath to this maturity blown up'), '"Blowne up" etc. One's very breath while leaning over
these Pages is held for fear of blowing this line away – as easily as the gentlest
breeze – Robs dandelions of their fleecy Crowns.'
i *13–14*. *the Naiad . . . lips*] Edward Thomas notes in his *Keats* (1916), 'The
consummate style makes of these thirteen words something more visible
and alive than all "The Eve of St. Agnes" and "The Eve of St. Mark"'
(65). The 'Naiad' is the tutelary nymph of the stream.
i *16*. *strayed*] stay'd *MS*. Cp. Cary's *Dante*, *Inferno* xiv 12–13.
                     . . . on the very edge
              Our steps we stay'd . . .
i *18*. For a similar grouping of epithets earlier in K. see *Endymion* iv 764 and
n (p. 276 above). Perhaps suggested here by *Paradise Lost* vi 852 (marked by
K. in his copy of Milton),
              Exhausted, spiritless, afflicted, fall'n . . .
i *19*. *realmless*] Rejected first attempts in the *MS* are 'ancient' and 'white-
browd'.

14*

20   While his bowed head seemed listening to the Earth,
        His ancient mother, for some comfort yet.

            It seemed no force could wake him from his place;
        But there came one, who with a kindred hand
        Touched his wide shoulders, after bending low
25   With reverence, though to one who knew it not.
        She was a Goddess of the infant world;
        By her in stature the tall Amazon
        Had stood a pigmy's height; she would have ta'en
        Achilles by the hair and bent his neck,
30   Or with a finger stayed Ixion's wheel.
        Her face was large as that of Memphian sphinx,
        Pedestalled haply in a palace court,

i 21. This is followed in the MS by the passage,

            Thus the old Eagle drowsy with great grief
            Sat moulting his weak Plumage never more
            To be restored or soar against the Sun
            Whilst his three Sons upon Olympus stood ...

For the 'three Sons' see i 147 n below.

i 24–5. bending low ... knew it not]. Perhaps suggested by Dante's attitude
to Brunetto Latini, Cary's Dante, Inferno xv 44–5,

                            ... held my head
        Bent down, as one who walks in reverent guise ...

i 28. pigmy's height] little child MS (cancelled). Cp. Paradise Lost i 777–81,

                        ... they but now who seemd
            In bigness to surpass Earth's Giant Sons
            Throng numberless, like that Pigmean Race ...

The last four words are underlined in K.'s copy of Milton.

i 30. stayed Ixion's wheel] eased Ixion's toil MS. See Lemprière: 'The father
of the gods, displeased with the insolence of Ixion, banished him from
heaven ... and ordered Mercury to tie him to a wheel in hell. This wheel
was perpetually in motion, and ... the punishment ... was eternal.'

i 31–51. K.'s portrayal of suffering in Hyperion's wife Thea prepares the
way for his description of the priestess Moneta in The Fall of Hyperion i; for
his shortened treatment of Thea in the revised version see The Fall of
Hyperion i 335–8 n (p. 677 below).

i 31–2. Reflects contemporary interest in Egyptian antiquities after Napoleon's Egyptian expedition in 1798 (see also i 277–83, ii 373–5, pp. 412 and
433–4 below). The British Museum acquired some Egyptian sculptures in
1818, but K. may not have visited them until early 1819–see under 3 (?)
March in his journal-letter of Feb.–May 1819, 'Severn and I took a turn
round the Museum. There is a Sphinx there of a giant size, and most volup-
tous Egyptian expression. I had not seen it before' (L ii 68). For a discussion
of books about Egypt available at the time see Barbara Garlitz, 'Egypt and
"Hyperion"', PQ XXXIV (1955) 189–96.

When sages looked to Egypt for their lore.
But oh, how unlike marble was that face!
35   How beautiful, if sorrow had not made
Sorrow more beautiful than Beauty's self.
There was a listening fear in her regard,
As if calamity had but begun;
As if the vanward clouds of evil days
40   Had spent their malice, and the sullen rear
Was with its storèd thunder labouring up.
One hand she pressed upon that aching spot
Where beats the human heart, as if just there,
Though an immortal, she felt cruel pain;
45   The other upon Saturn's bended neck
She laid, and to the level of his ear
Leaning with parted lips some words she spake
In solemn tenour and deep organ tone—
Some mourning words, which in our feeble tongue
50   Would come in these like accents (O how frail
To that large utterance of the early Gods!):
'Saturn, look up!—though wherefore, poor old King?
I have no comfort for thee, no, not one:

i 34–6. Foreshadows the description of Moneta's 'wan face' in *The Fall of Hyperion* i 256–63 (pp. 673–4 below). Cp. Sandys's *Ovid, Metamorphoses* vii 730–1 (Sandys's *Ovid* p. 129, col. 2),

> She still was sad: yet lovelier none than she,
>
> Even in that sadnesse . . .
>
> How excellent . . . was that face,
>
> Which could in griefe retaine so sweet a grace . . .

and Southey's *Thalaba* (1801) xi 31 383-4,

> Her face was sorrowful, but sure
>
> More beautiful for sorrow . . .

i 37. The phrasing suggests an echo of Landor's *Gebir* (1798) i 68,

> There was a brightening paleness in his face . . .

i 39–41. Calamity is compared to the clouds building up before a storm and to an invading army. The 'stored thunder' of the main cloud mass is like the artillery being brought into position for use behind the advanced troops.

i 46. *his ear*] his hollow ear *MS*. The *MS* reading is hypermetrical, but it is retained in *The Fall of Hyperion* i 348 (p. 678 below). For a similar instance of extra syllables to provide the proper stress-weight in a decasyllabic scheme see *Ode to a Nightingale* 20 (p. 526 below).

i 50. *these like accents*] A clumsy attempt at compression. See K.'s correction in *The Fall of Hyperion* i 352 (p. 678 below), 'this-like accenting . . .'

i 52–71. Thea's speech expresses the finality of the Titans' fate.

i 52. *poor old King*] K.'s conception of the fallen Saturn is partly influenced by *King Lear*; see i 98–103 below.

I cannot say, "Oh, wherefore sleepest thou?"
55 For heaven is parted from thee, and the earth
Knows thee not, thus afflicted, for a God;
And ocean too, with all its solemn noise,
Has from thy sceptre passed; and all the air
Is emptied of thine hoary majesty.
60 Thy thunder, conscious of the new command,
Rumbles reluctant o'er our fallen house;
And thy sharp lightning in unpractised hands
Scorches and burns our once serene domain.
O aching time! O moments big as years!
65 All as ye pass swell out the monstrous truth,
And press it so upon our weary griefs
That unbelief has not a space to breathe.
Saturn, sleep on! Oh, thoughtless, why did I
Thus violate thy slumbrous solitude?
70 Why should I ope thy melancholy eyes?
Saturn, sleep on, while at thy feet I weep!'

As when, upon a trancèd summer night,

i *60–1.* Jupiter, the new ruler of the gods, is now the Thunderer. See i 249 below, 'that infant thunderer, rebel Jove', and cp. *To Apollo* 13–14 (p. 111 above).

i *61. Rumbles reluctant*] A Miltonic construction. The word 'reluctant', although used by K. in a different sense, may derive from *Paradise Lost* vi 56–9,

　　　　　　　　　　　　　. . . Clouds began
　　　　　To darken all the Hill, and smoak to rowl
　　　　　In duskie wreathes, reluctant flames . . .

K. marked the passage in his copy of Milton with the note, '"Reluctant" with its original and modern meaning combined and woven together, with all its shades of signification has a powerful effect'.

i *62. unpractised*] impetuous *MS* (*cancelled*).

i *63. once serene domain*] A reference to the Saturnian Golden Age (see i 107–10 *n* below).

i *65. monstrous*] rebel *MS* (*cancelled*).

i *67.* Followed in *MS* by the cancelled line,
　　　　　Or a brief dream to find its way to heaven . . .

i *72–78.* Thea's words break the silence like a single gust of wind rising among the trees on a still summer night. K. follows Milton in introducing an extended simile into his 'epic', but the passage has an individual flavour and illustrates K.'s growing command of his own poetic style. For his revision of the passage in *The Fall of Hyperion* i 372–7 see p. 679 below.

i *72. trancèd*] Enchanted.

Those green-robed senators of mighty woods,
Tall oaks, branch-charmèd by the earnest stars,
75 Dream, and so dream all night without a stir,
Save from one gradual solitary gust
Which comes upon the silence, and dies off,
As if the ebbing air had but one wave;
So came these words and went, the while in tears
80 She touched her fair large forehead to the ground,
Just where her falling hair might be outspread
A soft and silken mat for Saturn's feet.
One moon, with alteration slow, had shed
Her silver seasons four upon the night,
85 And still these two were postured motionless,
Like natural sculpture in cathedral cavern:
The frozen God still couchant on the earth,

i 73-4. For an earlier expression of K.'s romantic feeling for forests see
Happy is England 3-4 (p. 100 above),

> To feel no other breezes than are blown
> Through its tall woods with high romances blent . . .

i 73. *green-robed senators*] The oak is one of the longest-lived of English
trees.

i 74. An earlier attempt was 'The oakes stand charmed . . .'. K. may be
recollecting Milton's *Arcades* 89, 'branching Elm Star-proof'. The stars are
earnest because their gaze is fixed and steady on such a night.

i 75. An earlier attempt in the MS was,

> And thus all night without a stir they rest . . .

i 76. *gradual solitary*] sudden momentary MS (*cancelled*).

i 78. *ebbing*] Sea of MS (*cancelled*).

i 81. *be outspread*] make MS (*cancelled*). For 'falling' MS and *The Fall of
Hyperion* i 380 (p. 679 below) have 'fallen'.

i 83-8. The slow passage of time heightens the sense of hopelessness.

i 85-8. One of K.'s attempts in the poem to imitate the quality described
in his marginal note on *Paradise Lost* vii 420-4: 'Milton in every instance
pursues his imagination to the utmost . . . in no instance is this . . . more
exemplified, than in what may be called his *stationing* or *statuary* [i.e. group-
ing]. He is not content with simple description, he must station. . . .'

i 86. Rocks so eroded by the sea that we recognize human features in their
forms—note that Saturn is 'quiet as a stone' in i 4 above. K. is thinking of
Fingal's Cave, which he saw in July 1818 during his Scottish tour. See *Not
Aladdin magian* 25-36 n, and 36 (pp. 373-4 above), 'This Cathedral of the
sea'. For K.'s later alteration of the image see *The Fall of Hyperion* i 383-4
(p. 679 below).

i 87. *earth*] sand MS (*cancelled*). Milton has the heraldic 'couchant' of Satan
in *Paradise Lost* iv 405, 'His couchant watch'. The passage is marked in K.'s
copy of Milton.

>   And the sad Goddess weeping at his feet;
>   Until at length old Saturn lifted up
>   90   His faded eyes, and saw his kingdom gone,
>   And all the gloom and sorrow of the place,
>   And that fair kneeling Goddess; and then spake,
>   As with a palsied tongue, and while his beard
>   Shook horrid with such aspen malady:
>   95   'O tender spouse of gold Hyperion,
>   Thea, I feel thee ere I see thy face;
>   Look up, and let me see our doom in it;
>   Look up, and tell me if this feeble shape
>   Is Saturn's; tell me, if thou hear'st the voice
>   100   Of Saturn; tell me, if this wrinkling brow,
>   Naked and bare of its great diadem,
>   Peers like the front of Saturn. Who had power
>   To make me desolate? Whence came the strength?
>   How was it nurtured to such bursting forth,
>   105   While Fate seemed strangled in my nervous grasp?
>   But it is so; and I am smothered up,
>   And buried from all godlike exercise

i 90. *faded ... kingdom*] faint blue ... royal *MS* (*cancelled*). 'His faded eyes ...' echoes the fallen Satan in *Paradise Lost* i 601–2,

>   ... care
>   Sat on his faded cheek ...

The passage is marked in K.'s copy of Milton.

i 94. *aspen malady*] The aspen shakes in the lighest breeze.

i 95–134. Saturn's speech expresses his bewildered sense of the loss of his personal identity–cp. Thea's more impersonal statement in i 52–71 above.

i 95. *gold Hyperion*] On Hyperion as the sun see i 166 *n* below.

i 98–103. Echoing *King Lear* I iv 226–9,

>   Does any here know me? This is not Lear:
>   Does Lear walk thus? speak thus? Where are his eyes?
>   Either his notion weakens, his discernings
>   Are lethargied. Ha! waking? 'tis not so.
>   Who is it that can tell me who I am? ...

K. reread *King Lear* in Oct. 1818 during Tom Keats's last illness–his folio Shakespeare at Hampstead has the note, 'Sunday evening Oct. 4 1818' against the phrase 'Poor Tom' (*King Lear* III iv 37).

i 102. *front*] Forehead. See *Endymion* iii 961 *n* (p. 242 above).

i 105. *nervous*] Vigorous. Cp. *Ode to Apollo* 7 (p. 14 above), 'Homer with his nervous arms'.

i 107–10. According to some traditions Saturn fled to Italy after his banishment by Jupiter and shared the throne with Janus. His reign, the *Saturnia regna* of the Roman poets, was known in classical mythology as the Golden Age because of its serenity and order. See Ovid's *Metamorphoses* i 89–90,

Of influence benign on planets pale,
Of admonitions to the winds and seas,
110 Of peaceful sway above man's harvesting,
And all those acts which Deity supreme
Doth ease its heart of love in.
                              I am gone
Away from my own bosom; I have left
My strong identity, my real self,
115 Somewhere between the throne and where I sit
Here on this spot of earth. Search, Thea, search!
Open thine eyes eterne, and sphere them round
Upon all space—space starred, and lorn of light;
Space regioned with life-air, and barren void;
120 Spaces of fire, and all the yawn of hell.
Search, Thea, search! And tell me, if thou seest

Aurea prima sata est aetas, quae vindice nullo,
    Sponte sua, sine lege fidem rectumque colebat . . .
('Golden was that first age, which, with no one to compel, without a law,
of its own will, kept faith and did the right' [Loeb edn].) K. identifies the
'Golden Age' with Saturn's period of power in heaven to heighten the
tragedy of his downfall and emphasize the poem's major theme summarized
in ii 228–9, below, "'tis the eternal law / That first in beauty should be first
in might . . .'.

i *108. planets*] sun *MS* (cancelled).

i *111. acts*] arts *1820*. Probably a misprint, since 'acts' is the reading in *The
Fall of Hyperion* (i 416, p. 681 below).

i *112.* Must do to ease itself lest two [*sic*] hot grown . . . *MS* (cancelled).
Between 'love in' and 'I am gone' the *MS* has the cancelled passage,
              . . . just as tears
    Leave a calm pleasure in the human breast—
    O Thea I must burn—my Spirit gasps . . .

i *113–16. I have left . . . earth*] Titans are men of identity and power. Their
successors, the Olympians, whose qualities are epitomised in Apollo, have
no identity and express K.'s idea of the poetical character. See his letter to
Woodhouse of 27 Oct. 1818, '. . . the poetical Character . . . that sort distinguished from the wordsworthian or egotistical sublime; which is a thing
per se and stands alone . . . is not itself—it has no self. . . . It has no character. . . . A poet . . . has no Identity—he is continually . . . filling some other
body' (*L* i 386–7). The letter is further quoted in headnote to *Welcome joy
and welcome sorrow* (p. 386 above). See also K.'s earlier statement in Nov.
1817, '. . . Men of Genius are great as certain ethereal Chemicals operating
on the Mass of neutral intellect . . . they have not any individuality, any
determined Character. I would call the top and head of those who have a
proper self Men of Power' (*L* i 184).

i *118–20.* K.'s cosmic topography derives from *Paradise Lost*.

A certain shape or shadow, making way
With wings or chariot fierce to repossess
A heaven he lost erewhile: it must—it must
125   Be of ripe progress: Saturn must be King.
Yes, there must be a golden victory;
There must be Gods thrown down, and trumpets blown
Of triumph calm, and hymns of festival
Upon the gold clouds metropolitan,
130   Voices of soft proclaim, and silver stir
Of strings in hollow shells; and there shall be
Beautiful things made new, for the surprise
Of the sky-children. I will give command:
Thea! Thea! Thea! Where is Saturn?'

135   This passion lifted him upon his feet,
And made his hands to struggle in the air,
His Druid locks to shake and ooze with sweat,
His eyes to fever out, his voice to cease.
He stood, and heard not Thea's sobbing deep;
140   A little time, and then again he snatched
Utterance thus: 'But cannot I create?
Cannot I form? Cannot I fashion forth
Another world, another universe,
To overbear and crumble this to naught?
145   Where is another chaos? Where?' That word
Found way unto Olympus, and made quake

i *122–5.* Saturn's 'real self' would not have accepted defeat and is imagined
as carrying on the battle.

i *125. of ripe progress*] going on MS (*cancelled*).

i *129. gold clouds metropolitan*] Miltonic word-order. See, for example,
Paradise Lost iii 72, 'the dun Air sublime', and iv 870, 'faded splendor
wan'. Both phrases occur in passages marked by K. in his copy of Milton.
For the later revised version see *The Fall of Hyperion* i 434 (p. 681 below).

i *130. silver stir*] A reversion to Hunt's style; see *Calidore* 20 n (p. 37 above).

i *134. Where is*] am I MS (*cancelled*).

i *135–8.* Saturn's renewal of his old strength and his second speech are
omitted in the revised version—see *The Fall of Hyperion* i 438–51 (pp. 681–2
below).

i *137. Druid locks*] Long haired like a Druid. The adjective suggests that K.
is recalling Gray's *The Bard* 17–20,

        Robed in the sable garb of woe,
        With haggard eyes the Poet stood;
        (Loose his beard, and hoary hair
        Stream'd, like a meteor, to the troubled air) . . .

i *138. fever out*] Start out of his head feverishly.

i *145. word*] sound MS (*cancelled correction*).

The rebel three. Thea was startled up,
And in her bearing was a sort of hope,
As thus she quick-voiced spake, yet full of awe:
150 'This cheers our fallen house. Come to our friends,
O Saturn, come away, and give them heart!
I know the covert, for thence came I hither.'
Thus brief; then with beseeching eyes she went
With backward footing through the shade a space;
155 He followed, and she turned to lead the way
Through agèd boughs, that yielded like the mist
Which eagles cleave upmounting from their nest.

Meanwhile in other realms big tears were shed,
More sorrow like to this, and such-like woe,
160 Too huge for mortal tongue or pen of scribe.
The Titans fierce, self-hid, or prison-bound,
Groaned for the old allegiance once more,
And listened in sharp pain for Saturn's voice.
But one of the whole mammoth-brood still kept
165 His sovereignty, and rule, and majesty—
Blazing Hyperion on his orbèd fire

i *147. The rebel three*] Saturn's sons, Jupiter, Neptune and Pluto, who eventually divided his kingdom between themselves, ruling heaven, the sea and the underworld respectively. The *MS* has 'started' for 'startled'.

i *148–57*. Thea remains silent at this point in *The Fall of Hyperion*.

i *150. our friends*] The rest of the Titans, introduced in ii 2–81 (pp. 415–22 below).

i *152. covert*] Hiding-place. Cp. *Paradise Lost* iii 39, 'in shadiest Covert hid'; see *Ode to a Nightingale* 51 m (p. 529 below).

i *154. With backward footing*] Retiring from a royal presence. K. substituted 'shade' for 'gloom' in his MS.

i *156. yielded like the mist*] gave to them like mist *MS*. A first attempt was 'to them gave like Air'.

i *158–212*. K. breaks off his account of Saturn and Thea, devoting the rest of Book I to Hyperion, whom he introduces here as still commanding his power as a divinity although full of foreboding.

i *162. allegiance*] Four syllables.

i *166. Hyperion*] 'Son of Coelus and Terra, who married Thea, by whom he had Aurora, Sol, and Luna . . . often taken by the poets for the sun itself' (*Lemprière*); cp. *Timon of Athens* IV iii 184–5,

. . . crisp heaven

Whereon Hyperion's quickening fire doth shine . . .

See Apollo in *Baldwin*, 'often called by the poets Hyperion . . . having been according to some accounts the God of the sun, before . . . that province was conferred on Apollo' (56). Unlike Apollo, Hyperion held no other offices and was not identified with poetry or music.

Still sat, still snuffed the incense, teeming up
From man to the sun's God—yet unsecure:
For as among us mortals omens drear
170 Fright and perplex, so also shuddered he—
Not at dog's howl, or gloom-bird's hated screech,
Or the familiar visiting of one
Upon the first toll of his passing-bell,
Or prophesyings of the midnight lamp;
175 But horrors portioned to a giant nerve
Oft made Hyperion ache. His palace bright,

i *167. snuffed the incense*] Cp. *Paradise Lost* x 272–3,

> . . . with delight he snuff'd the smell
>   Of mortal change on Earth . . .

The passage is marked in K.'s copy of Milton.
i *170. Fright and perplex*] See Milton's description of an eclipse of the sun
by the moon in *Paradise Lost* i 597–9,

> . . . disastrous twilight sheds
>   On half the Nations, and with fear of change
>   Perplexes Monarchs . . .

The passage is marked in K.'s copy of Milton (with note, 'How noble and
collected an indignation against kings').
i *171. gloom-bird's hated screech*] The hooting of an owl, traditionally por-
tending death. Cp. *Macbeth* II ii 4–5,

> It was the owl that shriek'd, the fatal bellman,
>   Which gives the stern'st good-night . . .

i *172–3*. Relatives and friends attending a death-bed. The word 'familiar'
is used here for 'familial' (fairly common in the eighteenth century).
i *173*.   Just at the tolling of his passing-bell . . . *MS (cancelled)*.
The 'passing-bell' was rung to call for prayers on behalf of a Christian *in
articulo mortis*.
i *174*. Perhaps suggested by Thomson's paraphrase of Virgil's *Georgics* i
390–2 in *The Seasons* (1730) *Winter* 134–7,

> Even as the matron, at her nightly task,
>   With pensive labour draws the flaxen thread,
>   The wasted taper and the crackling flame
>   Foretell the blast . . .

i *175. horrors . . . nerve*] warnings . . . sense *MS (cancelled)*. The word 'portioned' is a neologism for 'proportionate'.
i *176. made Hyperion ache*] Earlier attempts were 'made his Chin' and
'pressed his curly chin upon his Breast'.
i *176–82. His palace bright . . . Flush'd angerly*] Hyperion's cloud-palace as
dawn flushes the sky in the east. K.'s description—see also i 217–24 below—
—has no specific source but was probably inspired by the account of Mulciber's palace in *Paradise Lost* i 702–30 (the passage is underlined throughout
in K.'s copy of Milton) and by other descriptions of palaces incorporating

Bastioned with pyramids of glowing gold,
And touched with shade of bronzèd obelisks,
Glared a blood-red through all its thousand courts,
180 Arches, and domes, and fiery galleries;
And all its curtains of aurorian clouds
Flushed angerly, while sometimes eagle's wings,
Unseen before by Gods or wondering men,
Darkened the place, and neighing steeds were heard,
185 Not heard before by Gods or wondering men.
Also, when he would taste the spicy wreaths
Of incense, breathed aloft from sacred hills,
Instead of sweets, his ample palate took
Savour of poisonous brass and metal sick.

---

oriental details, notably Wordsworth's *The Excursion* ii 830–69 (in which clouds 'Molten together . . .', compose 'that marvellous array / Of temple, palace, citadel . . .' [ii 856–8]), Southey's *Thalaba* i sts. 12–13, 29–34, and Beckford's *Vathek* (1816 edn 202, 206–7).

i *178. touched with shade*] with chequer black *MS* (*cancelled*). Cp. Leila's flame-lit grove in Southey's *Thalaba* X xiv 246,

Chequer'd with blacker shade . . .

The 'bronzed obelisks' may derive from J. Potter's *Antiquities of Greece* (1697), '. . . the foundation [of the oracle of Trophonius] . . . supporting brazen obelisks, encompassed round with ligaments of brass . . .' (1828 edn i 341).

i *181. aurorian*] Rose-coloured like the dawn.

i *182. angerly*] Angrily. Cp. *Macbeth* III v i,

Why, how now, Hecate! you look angerly . . .

i *182–4. while sometimes . . . were heard*] Omens of disaster. Cp. the prodigies on the downfall of Duncan and Caesar in *Macbeth* and *Julius Caesar*. See *Macbeth* II iv 12–16,

A falcon, towering in her pride of place,
Was by a mousing owl hawk'd at and kill'd.
And Duncan's horses,–a thing most strange and certain,–
Beauteous and swift, the minions of their race
Turn'd wild in nature . . .

and *Julius Caesar* II ii 23,

Horses did neigh, and dying men did groan . . .

i *183. Unseen before*] Darkened the place *MS* (*cancelled*).

i *185. by Gods or wondering men*] by either Gods or men *MS* (*cancelled*) Altered to afford a Miltonic repetition.

i *186. Also . . . taste*] Sometimes . . . take *MS* (*cancelled*).

i *189. Savour of poisonous brass*] A poison feel of brass *MS*. Woodhouse notes, 'The alteration is the most felicitous of K.'s changes' (*Woodhouse 2*). K. wrote to Fanny Brawne Aug. 1820, 'The last two years taste like brass upon my Palate' (*L* ii 312).

190   And so, when harboured in the sleepy west,
         After the full completion of fair day,
         For rest divine upon exalted couch
         And slumber in the arms of melody,
         He paced away the pleasant hours of ease
195   With stride colossal, on from hall to hall;
         While far within each aisle and deep recess
         His wingèd minions in close clusters stood,
         Amazed and full of fear; like anxious men
         Who on wide plains gather in panting troops,
200   When earthquakes jar their battlements and towers.
         Even now, while Saturn, roused from icy trance,
         Went step for step with Thea through the woods,
         Hyperion, leaving twilight in the rear,
         Came slope upon the threshold of the west;
205   Then, as was wont, his palace-door flew ope
         In smoothest silence, save what solemn tubes,
         Blown by the serious Zephyrs, gave of sweet
         And wandering sounds, slow-breathèd melodies—

i *192*.   Instead of rest upon exalted couch . . . *MS (cancelled)*.
i *195*. *With stride colossal*] Cp. Landor's *Gebir* (1798) iii 18,
                    The parting Sun's gigantic strides . . .
The word 'colossal' was probably suggested by *Julius Caesar* I ii 134–5,
                    . . . he doth bestride the narrow world
              Like a Colossus . . .
i *196–200*. Suggested by the troops of fallen angels in the hall of Pandaemonium, *Paradise Lost* i 767–71,
              Thick swarm'd, both on the ground and in the air,
              Brusht with the hiss of russling wings. As Bees
              In spring time, when the Sun with *Taurus* rides,
              Poure forth thir populous youth about the Hive
              In clusters . . .
The passage is underlined in K.'s copy of Milton.
i *196. each . . . deep*] deep . . . wide *MS (cancelled)*.
i *198*.   In fear and sad amaze like men at gaze . . . *MS (cancelled)*.
i *200*.   When Earthquake hath shook their city towers . . . *MS*.
i *203*.   He of the Sun just lighted from the Air . . . *MS (cancelled)*.
i *204*. Cp. *Paradise Lost* iv 591,
              Bore him slope downward to the Sun now fall'n . . .
The line is marked in K.'s copy of Milton.
i *205–12*. Miltonic phrasing. The passage is omitted in *The Fall of Hyperion*.
i *205*. Followed in *MS* by the cancelled line,
              Most like a rose bud to a faerae's lute . . .
i *206–8*. Suggested by the musical sounds uttered by the statue of Memnon (see ii 374–6 *n*, pp. 433–4 below).

And like a rose in vermeil tint and shape,
210 In fragrance soft, and coolness to the eye,
That inlet to severe magnificence
Stood full blown, for the God to enter in.

He entered, but he entered full of wrath;
His flaming robes streamed out beyond his heels,
215 And gave a roar, as if of earthly fire,
That scared away the meek ethereal Hours
And made their dove-wings tremble. On he flared,
From stately nave to nave, from vault to vault,
Through bowers of fragrant and enwreathèd light,
220 And diamond-pavèd lustrous long arcades,
Until he reached the great main cupola.
There standing fierce beneath he stamped his foot,
And from the basements deep to the high towers
Jarred his own golden region; and before
225 The quavering thunder thereupon had ceased,
His voice leapt out, despite of godlike curb,
To this result: 'O dreams of day and night!
O monstrous forms! O effigies of pain!

i 213–50. Hyperion's obdurate pride owes something to Milton's portrayal of Satan.

i 214. *flaming*] fiery MS (*cancelled*).

i 216. *Hours*] The nymphs attendant on the sun. See *Endymion* iv 420–6 n (p. 262 above).

i 217. *flared*] went MS (*cancelled*).

i 218. From gorgeous vault to vault, from space to space MS (*cancelled*). Cp. Beckford's description of the afflicted Caliph and Nouronihar in the halls of Eblis, '. . . they went wandering on from chamber to chamber, hall to hall, and gallery to gallery, all without bounds or limit' (*Vathek*, 1816 edn, 217).

i 219. *fragrant and enwreathèd light*] Wreathed fragrant light MS (*cancelled*).

i 220–1. Echoes the cloud palace in Wordsworth's *The Excursion* ii 839–40,
    Fabric it seemed of diamond and of gold,
    With alabaster domes . . .
and the halls of Eblis in *Vathek*, 'rows of columns and arcades, which gradually diminished in a point, radiant as the sun' (1816 edn 206).

i 222. *There standing fierce beneath*] And there he stood beneath MS (*cancelled*).

i 223. *basements*] foundations MS (*cancelled*).

i 227–30. *O dreams . . . black-weeded pools*] Images of disaster (see i 169–75 above). A reminiscence of Elizabethan dramatic rhetoric.

i 228–9. K. may be thinking of the figures in the halls of Eblis in Beckford's *Vathek*, 'a vast multitude . . . incessantly passing, who . . . kept their right

O spectres busy in a cold, cold gloom!
230   O lank-eared phantoms of black-weeded pools!
Why do I know ye? Why have I seen ye? Why
Is my eternal essence thus distraught
To see and to behold these horrors new?
Saturn is fallen, am I too to fall?
235   Am I to leave this haven of my rest,
This cradle of my glory, this soft clime,
This calm luxuriance of blissful light,
These crystalline pavilions and pure fanes
Of all my lucent empire? It is left
240   Deserted, void, nor any haunt of mine.
The blaze, the splendour and the symmetry
I cannot see—but darkness, death and darkness.
Even here, into my centre of repose,
The shady visions come to domineer,
245   Insult, and blind, and stifle up my pomp.
Fall? No, by Tellus and her briny robes!
Over the fiery frontier of my realms
I will advance a terrible right arm
Shall scare that infant thunderer, rebel Jove,
250   And bid old Saturn take his throne again.'
He spake, and ceased, the while a heavier threat
Held struggle with his throat but came not forth;
For as in theatres of crowded men

hands on their hearts . . . they all had the livid paleness of death. . . . Some
stalked slowly on . . . some, shrieking in agony, ran furiously about . . .
each wandered . . . unheedful of the rest' (1816 edn, 208).

i *232. essence*] Being. The word is used in this sense again at ii 331, iii 104
below. See further *Endymion* i 779 *n* (p. 154 above).

i *235–42.* Suggested by Satan's speech in *Paradise Lost* i 242–5,

        Is this the Region, this the Soil, the Clime,
        Said then the lost Arch Angel, this the seat
        That we must change for Heav'n, this mournful gloom
        For that celestial light? . . .

i *236–9. this soft clime . . . empire*] An afterthought: l. 236 originally read,
                    This cradle of my glory. It is left . . .

i *239. lucent*] Shining.

i *243. centre*] sanctuary *MS (cancelled)*.

i *246. Tellus*] See ii 4 *n* (p. 415 below).

i *253–4.* K. is echoing J. and H. Smith's *Rejected Addresses* (1812), *The Theatre*
50–1,

        He who, in quest of quiet, 'Silence!' hoots,
        Is apt to make the hubbub he imputes . . .

and possibly may also be thinking of the 'Old Price' riots of 1809 at Covent

Hubbub increases more they call out 'Hush!',
255 So at Hyperion's words the phantoms pale
Bestirred themselves, thrice horrible and cold;
And from the mirrored level where he stood
A mist arose, as from a scummy marsh.
At this, through all his bulk an agony
260 Crept gradual, from the feet unto the crown,
Like a lithe serpent vast and muscular
Making slow way, with head and neck convulsed
From over-strainèd might. Released, he fled
To the eastern gates, and full six dewy hours
265 Before the dawn in season due should blush,
He breathed fierce breath against the sleepy portals,
Cleared them of heavy vapours, burst them wide
Suddenly on the ocean's chilly streams.
The planet orb of fire, whereon he rode
270 Each day from east to west the heavens through,
Spun round in sable curtaining of clouds;
Not therefore veilèd quite, blindfold, and hid,

Garden Theatre, to which there is a reference elsewhere in *Rejected Addresses* (see *The Rebuilding* 71–3). With i 253 cp. *Richard II* V ii 23,

As in a theatre, the eyes of men . . .

i 258–63. Probably inspired by the account, marked in K.'s copy of Milton, of Satan entering the serpent in *Paradise Lost* ix 180–90,

Like a black mist low creeping, he held on
His midnight search, where soonest he might finde
The Serpent: him fast sleeping soon he found
In Labyrinth of many a round self-rowld,
His head the midst, well stor'd with suttle wiles:
Not yet in horrid Shade or dismal Den,
Not nocent yet, but on the grassie Herbe
Fearless unfeard he slept: in at his Mouth
The Devil enterd, and his brutal sense,
In heart or head, possessing soon inspir'd
With act intelligential . . .

K. comments marginally, '. . . no passage of poetry ever can give a greater pain of suffocation'.

i 258. *scummy*] stagnant *MS (cancelled)*.

i 271–83. Spun at his round in darkest curtaining of clouds
Not therefore hidden up and muffled quite
But ever and anon the glancing spheres
Glow'd through and still about the sable shroud
Made sweet-shap'd light: Wings this orb . . . *MS (cancelled)*.

But ever and anon the glancing spheres,
Circles, and arcs, and broad-belting colure,
275   Glowed through, and wrought upon the muffling dark
Sweet-shapèd lightnings from the nadir deep
Up to the zenith—hieroglyphics old
Which sages and keen-eyed astrologers
Then living on the earth with labouring thought
280   Won from the gaze of many centuries—
Now lost, save what we find on remnants huge
Of stone, or marble swart, their import gone,
Their wisdom long since fled. Two wings this orb
Possessed for glory, two fair argent wings,
285   Ever exalted at the God's approach;
And now from forth the gloom their plumes immense
Rose, one by one, till all outspreaded were;
While still the dazzling globe maintained eclipse,
Awaiting for Hyperion's command.
290   Fain would he have commanded, fain took throne
And bid the day begin, if but for change.
He might not. No, though a primeval God,
The sacred seasons might not be disturbed.
Therefore the operations of the dawn
295   Stayed in their birth, even as here 'tis told.
Those silver wings expanded sisterly,
Eager to sail their orb; the porches wide

The reconstruction appears with further corrections on the preceding page in
MS. K.'s revisions suggest a conscious effort to heighten the Miltonic effect.
i *274. colure*] An astronomical term borrowed from *Paradise Lost* ix 66,
              From Pole to Pole, traversing each Colure . . .
The four preceding lines marked in K.'s copy of Milton. The colures are
the two circles, intersecting each other at the poles, which divide the
equinoctial and the ecliptic into four equal parts (OED).
i *277. hierglyphics old*] The zodiacal signs.
i *281–2. remnants huge . . . fled*] Ancient monuments covered with hieroglyphics—such as the Rosetta stone (discovered 1799, deciphered 1821–2)—
which cannot now be understood.
i *282. swart*] A Miltonic word. Cp. *Endymion* ii 15 *n* (p. 164 above), 'swart
planet'.
i *283–7. Two wings . . . outspreaded were*] The winged solar disc was the
regular emblem of the sun god Horus.
i *292. primeval*] Of the first and golden age of the world.
i *296. sisterly*] Like twin sisters. The MS cancelled reading of the line is
'Those silver wings of the Sun were full outspread . . .'.
i *297. Eager*] Ready MS (*cancelled*).

Opened upon the dusk demesnes of night;
And the bright Titan, frenzied with new woes,
300   Unused to bend, by hard compulsion bent
His spirit to the sorrow of the time;
And all along a dismal rack of clouds,
Upon the boundaries of day and night,
He stretched himself in grief and radiance faint.
305   There as he lay, the heaven with its stars
Looked down on him with pity, and the voice
Of Coelus, from the universal space,
Thus whispered low and solemn in his ear:
'O brightest of my children dear, earth-born
310   And sky-engenderèd, son of mysteries
All unrevealèd even to the powers
Which met at thy creating; at whose joys
And palpitations sweet, and pleasures soft,
I, Coelus, wonder how they came and whence;
315   And at the fruits thereof what shapes they be,
Distinct, and visible—symbols divine,

i *298. demesnes*] domain *MS (cancelled)*.

i *299. bright*] enraged *MS (cancelled)*.

i *300. hard*] stern *MS (cancelled)*.

i *302-3*. See *Endymion* ii 288 and *n* (p. 175 above),

> The cloudy rack slow journeying in the west . . .

i *304. stretched . . . in grief*] laid . . . supine *MS (cancelled)*.

i *305-8*. K. deliberately breaks with tradition in suppressing the savagely
hostile relationship between Coelus and his sons.

i *311. the powers*] Tellus and Coelus.

i *316-18. symbols divine . . . eternal space*] See Baldwin's account of the festival of Ceres, 'to these were appropriated the Mysteries . . . it has been
conjectured that the doctrine revealed by the high-priest was . . . the unity
of the great principle of the universe . . . the enlightened were satisfied . . .
secretly to worship one God under the emblems of the various manners and
forms in which he operates' (*Baldwin* 19–20). The tone and cadence suggest
Wordsworth's influence, e.g. *The Excursion* ix 1–9,

> To every Form of being is assigned
>
> .   .   .
>
> An *active* Principle:–howe'er removed
> From sense and observation, it subsists
> In all things, in all natures; in the stars
> Of azure heaven, the unenduring clouds,
> In flower and tree, in every pebbly stone
> That paves the brooks, the stationary rocks,
> The moving waters and the invisible air . . .

i *317. beauteous life*] Life and Beauty *MS (cancelled)*.

Manifestations of that beauteous life
Diffused unseen throughout eternal space.
Of these new-formed art thou, O brightest child!

320 Of these, thy brethren and the Goddesses!
There is sad feud among ye, and rebellion
Of son against his sire. I saw him fall,
I saw my first-born tumbled from his throne!
To me his arms were spread, to me his voice

325 Found way from forth the thunders round his head!
Pale wox I, and in vapours hid my face.
Art thou, too, near such doom? Vague fear there is:
For I have seen my sons most unlike Gods.
Divine ye were created, and divine

330 In sad demeanour, solemn, undisturbed,
Unruffled, like high Gods, ye lived and ruled.
Now I behold in you fear, hope, and wrath;
Actions of rage and passion—even as
I see them, on the mortal world beneath,

335 In men who die. This is the grief, O son,
Sad sign of ruin, sudden dismay, and fall!
Yet do thou strive; as thou art capable,
As thou canst move about, an evident God,
And canst oppose to each malignant hour

340 Ethereal presence. I am but a voice;
My life is but the life of winds and tides,
No more than winds and tides can I avail.
But thou canst. Be thou therefore in the van
Of circumstance; yea, seize the arrow's barb

345 Before the tense string murmur. To the earth!
For there thou wilt find Saturn, and his woes.
Meantime I will keep watch on thy bright sun,
And of thy seasons be a careful nurse.'
Ere half this region-whisper had come down,

350 Hyperion arose, and on the stars

---

i *323. my first-born*] Saturn. K. substituted 'tumbled' for 'hurled' in his MS.

i *326. wox*] waxed. A Spenserian archaism.

i *329-31*. The Epicurean calm which Lucretius attributes to the gods. See *De Rerum Natura* ii 646-51.

i *331. Unruffled*] Passionless *MS (cancelled).*

i *334*. In widest speculation I do see *MS (cancelled)*. See *I stood tip-toe* 189 n (p. 94 above).

i *341-2*. Coelus, like the winds and tides, is at the mercy of unalterable natural laws. See also i 290-5 above.

i *349. region-whisper*] Whisper from the sky.

Lifted his curvèd lids, and kept them wide
Until it ceased; and still he kept them wide;
And still they were the same bright, patient stars.
Then with a slow incline of his broad breast,
355 Like to a diver in the pearly seas,
Forward he stooped over the airy shore,
And plunged all noiseless into the deep night.

BOOK II

Just at the self-same beat of Time's wide wings
Hyperion slid into the rustled air,
And Saturn gained with Thea that sad place
Where Cybele and the bruisèd Titans mourned.
5 It was a den where no insulting light

i 351. *Lifted*] Opened *MS* (*cancelled*).

i 353. *they were the same bright, patient stars*] Cp. i 74 and *n* (p. 401 above),

Tall oaks, branch-charmèd by the earnest stars . . .

Earlier attempts in *MS* were 'they all were the same patient stars . . .', 'he
saw they were the same patient stars . . .'.

i 354–7. A re-working of similar passages in Milton and Dante, such as
Raphael's flight in *Paradise Lost* v 266–8 (marked in K.'s copy of Milton),

. . . Down thither prone in flight
He speeds, and through the vast Ethereal Skie
Sailes between worlds and worlds . . .

and Geryon's in Cary's *Dante, Inferno* xvii,

. . . He slowly sailing wheels
His downward motion . . .

ii *Title*] Canto 2nd *MS*.

ii *1*.   Upon the very point of wingèd time . . . *MS* (*cancelled*).

ii *2. Hyperion slid*] That saw Hyperion *MS* (*cancelled*).

ii *4. the . . . Titans*] her . . . Children *MS* (*cancelled*). The correction reflects
the confusion over Cybele's role in classical mythology where she is sometimes identified with her mother Tellus. See *Baldwin*, 'The wife of Saturn is
variously called Ops and Rhea, and Cybele . . . she also sometimes bears the
names of her mother . . . like her she seems likewise to be the Earth, and . . .
was invoked by the appellations of . . . *Magna Mater* . . . and . . . Mother of
the Gods' (40–1). K. seems to distinguish Ops from Tellus in ii 54, 78 below,
but see ii 389 below, 'Saturn sat near the Mother of the Gods . . .' K. scans
Cybele as a dissyllable, as in *The Fall of Hyperion* i 425 (p. 681 below),

Moan, Cybele, moan, for thy pernicious babes . . .

ii *5. den*] place *MS* (*uncancelled rejected reading*).

ii *5–6. where no insulting light | Could glimmer*] Echoing *Paradise Lost* i 181–3
(marked in K.'s copy of Milton),

Could glimmer on their tears; where their own groans
They felt, but heard not, for the solid roar
Of thunderous waterfalls and torrents hoarse,
Pouring a constant bulk, uncertain where.
10 Crag jutting forth to crag, and rocks that seemed
Ever as if just rising from a sleep,
Forehead to forehead held their monstrous horns;
And thus in thousand hugest fantasies
Made a fit roofing to this nest of woe.
15 Instead of thrones, hard flint they sat upon,
Couches of rugged stone, and slaty ridge
Stubborned with iron. All were not assembled,
Some chained in torture, and some wandering.

The seat of desolation, voyd of light,
Save what the glimmering of these livid flames
Casts pale and dreadful . . .

The word 'insulting' here means assailing, intruding.

ii 7–9. *the solid roar . . . where*] A grandiose recollection of the waterfalls in
the Lake District which K. saw June 1818. He had described Stock Ghyll
Force at Ambleside, '. . . we . . . saw it streaming down . . . to the depth of
near fifty feet . . . the water was divided by a sort of cataract island on whose
other side burst out a glorious stream–then the thunder and freshness' (*L* i
300).

ii 9. *uncertain where*] A Miltonic echo. See *Paradise Lost* iii 75–6 (marked in
K.'s copy of Milton),

Firm land imbosom'd without Firmament,
Uncertain which, in Ocean or in Air . . .

ii 10–12. *Crag jutting forth to crag . . . horns*] A recollection of craggy mountain landscapes in the Lake District and Scotland. For K.'s account of the
crags surrounding Ben Nevis which he visited Aug. 1818 see *Read me a
lesson, Muse* 3 *n* (p. 376 above).

ii 11. Cp. *To Ailsa Rock* 5–6 (p. 365 above),

How long is it since the mighty power bid
Thee heave to airy sleep from fathom dreams . . .

ii 16. *Couches of rugged stone . . . slaty ridge*] Rough stones . . . edge of slate
MS (cancelled). The second attempt in the MS was,

Couches of rugged stone and sharp-edged ridge . . .

K. commented on the landscape at Ambleside, 'What astonishes me more
than any thing is the tone, the colouring, the slate, the stone' (*L* i 301).

ii 17. *All were not assembled*] All were not hidden here *MS (cancelled)*. 'Stubborned with iron' may have been suggested by the description of Malebolge
in Cary's *Dante*, *Inferno* xviii,

. . . all of rock dark-stain'd
With hue ferruginous . . .

Coeus, and Gyges, and Briareüs,
20   Typhon, and Dolor, and Porphyrion,
      With many more, the brawniest in assault,
      Were pent in regions of laborious breath;

ii *19–81.* K.'s use of the Titans' sounding names in this passage is Miltonic.
The assembly of Titans is inspired by Milton's description of the fallen
angels in Hell (*Paradise Lost* i 376–521), but his details are selected from various accounts of the Titans in *Lemprière*, *Baldwin*, Sandys's *Ovid*, Hesiod's
Theogony (Cooke's translation 1728), Hyginus's *Fabulae* (1742 edn) and possibly from Ronsard's description of the Titans and Giants warring with the
Olympian gods in *A Michel de l'Hospital* (1550, revised 1584). Woodhouse
quotes ll. 259–62, 289–96 of Ronsard's poem opposite the opening lines of
this passage in his transcript of *Hyperion* (*Woodhouse* 2); for K.'s reading of
Ronsard Sept. 1818 see *Translated from Ronsard* (p. 383 above). See *Lemprière*, 'Titanes, a name given to the sons of Coelus and Terra. They were
45 in number, according to the Aegyptians. Apollodorus mentions 13,
Hyginus 6, and Hesiod 20. The most known are Saturn, Hyperion,
Oceanus, Japetus, Cottus and Briareus, to whom Horace adds, Tiphoes
[Typhon], Mimas, Porphyrion, Rhoetus and Enceladus, who are by other
mythologists reckoned among the giants. They were all of gigantic stature,
and with proportionate strength . . .'; and *Baldwin*, 'the Titans were Oceanus, Coeus, Creus, Hyperion, Iapetus, Cottus, Gyges and Briareus: they
had an equal number of sisters with whom they married, Oceanus to Tethys,
Coeus to Phoebe, Hyperion to Thea, and Iapetus to Clymene' (45–6).
ii *19. Coeus*] Woodhouse's note 'Coeus 108' (*Woodhouse* 2) is a reference to
Sandys's *Ovid*, *Metamorphoses* vi, '*Coeus*, one of the *Titans*' (p. 108, col. 1).
ii *20. Typhon . . . Dolor . . .*] Woodhouse notes 'Typhon or Typhoes 90'
(*Woodhouse* 2), a reference to the note in Sandys's *Ovid*, *Metamorphoses* v,
'The son of *Tellus* and *Tartarus*, called also Typhoeus' (p. 90, col. 2). Typhon, traditionally one of the most violent Titans, supplies several details
for K.'s portrayal of Enceladus (see ii 66 *n*, pp. 420–1 below). K.'s source for
Dolor is Hyginus, who records his birth as 'Ex Aethere et Terra' (*Fabulae*,
1781 edn, 3) but does not classify him as a Titan. K. probably chose the
name for its sound and meaning.
ii *21. brawniest*] hugest *MS* (*cancelled*). Woodhouse quotes Ronsard's
account of Typhon and Porphyrion in *A Michel de l'Hospital* 267–9,

              Typhé hochoit arraché
              Un grand sapin esbranché
              Comme une lance facile.

and 295–6,

              Là Porfyre luy feit broncher
              Hors des poings l'arc et la sagette . . .

ii *22–8.* Typhon was imprisoned by Jupiter under the island of Sicily; the
volcanic eruptions of Mount Aetna were supposed to be caused by his

Dungeoned in opaque element, to keep
Their clenchèd teeth still clenched, and all their limbs
25   Locked up like veins of metal, cramped and screwed;
Without a motion, save of their big hearts
Heaving in pain, and horribly convulsed
With sanguine feverous boiling gurge of pulse.
Mnemosyne was straying in the world;
30   Far from her moon had Phoebe wanderèd;
And many else were free to roam abroad,
But for the main, here found they covert drear.

---

struggles and by the release of his pent-up breath. See Sandys's *Ovid, Meta-morphoses* v (p. 90, col. 2),

>   *Trinacria* [Sicily] was on wicked *Typhon* throwne;
>   Who underneath the Ilands waight doth grone;
>   That durst affect the Empire of the skyes:
>   Oft he attempteth, but in vaine, to rise.
>   *Ausonian Pelorus* his right hand
>   Down waighs; *Pachyne* on the left doth stand;
>   His legs are under *Lilybaeus* spred;
>   And *Aetna's* bases charge his horrid head:
>   Where, lying on his back, his jawes expire
>   Thick clouds of dust, and vomit flakes of fire . . .

ii *23–8*. A later insertion. The passage is written on the back of the preceding page in the MS.

ii *23*. *Dungeoned in opaque element*] Buried beneath the sea.

ii *25*. *cramped and screwed*] with cramp and screw MS (*cancelled*).

ii *27*. *Heaving*] Labouring MS (*cancelled*).

ii *28*. *boiling*] whelming MS (*cancelled*). The 'boiling gurge' refers to volcanic eruptions of lava. Cp. *Paradise Lost* xii 41–2,

>   . . . a black bituminous gurge
>   Boiles out from under ground, the mouth of Hell . . .

ii *29*. *Mnemosyne*] Mother of the Muses by Jupiter and included among the Titans in Hesiod's *Theogony* (Cooke's translation 81–4). She is 'straying in the world' because she is seeking Apollo–see iii 45–136 (pp. 436–41 below). K. identifies her with the priestess Moneta in *The Fall of Hyperion*.

ii *30*. *Phoebe*] Linked with Mnemosyne in Hesiod's *Theogony*–see Cooke's translation 221–2,

>   And thou Mnemosyne and Phoebe crown'd
>   With gold . . .

ii *31*. A later insertion. The line is written on the back of the preceding page in the MS.

ii *32*. *they covert drear*] grief and sad respite MS (*cancelled*). For 'covert' see i 152 *n* (p. 405 above).

Scarce images of life, one here, one there,
Lay vast and edgeways; like a dismal cirque
35   Of Druid stones upon a forlorn moor,
When the chill rain begins at shut of eve
In dull November, and their chancel vault,
The heaven itself, is blinded throughout night.
Each one kept shroud, nor to his neighbour gave
40   Or word, or look, or action of despair.
Creüs was one; his ponderous iron mace
Lay by him, and a shattered rib of rock
Told of his rage, ere he thus sank and pined.
Iäpetus another; in his grasp,
45   A serpent's plashy neck; its barbèd tongue
Squeezed from the gorge, and all its uncurled length
Dead – and because the creature could not spit
Its poison in the eyes of conquering Jove.
Next Cottus; prone he lay, chin uppermost,
50   As though in pain, for still upon the flint
He ground severe his skull, with open mouth
And eyes at horrid working. Nearest him

ii *33–8.* K. wrote to Tom Keats from Keswick 29 June 1818, 'we . . . set forth . . . on the Penrith road, to see the Druid temple [the prehistoric stone circle at Castlerigg]. We had a fag up hill . . . near dinner time, which was rendered void, by the gratification of seeing those aged stones, on a gentle rise in the midst of Mountains, which at that time darkened all round' (*L* i 306). With ii 33–6 cp. the comment in ii 116–24 *n* below on K.'s descriptive power in *Hyperion*.

ii *34. cirque*] Probably suggested by Wordsworth's *Excursion* iii 50–2,

Upon a semicirque of turf-clad ground,
The hidden nook discovered to our view
A mass of rock . . .

ii *35. stones*] temple *MS* (*cancelled*).

ii *36. at shut of eve*] Echoing *Paradise Lost* ix 278 (marked in K.'s copy of Milton), 'at shut of Evening Flours'.

ii *37. their chancel vault*] The gloom of a Gothic church is suggested by the stones and the November evening.

ii *39. shroud*] Shrouded.

ii *44. Iäpetus*] Pronounced as a quadrisyllable.

ii *47. and because*] i.e., and all this because.

ii *50. As though in pain*] Pain'd he seem'd *MS* (*cancelled*).

ii *51. severe*] Harshly.

ii *52. at horrid working*] Moving in a terrifying manner. The word 'horrid' is Miltonic. See, for example, Satan in *Paradise Lost* ii 710–11 (marked in K.'s copy of Milton),

. . . from his horrid hair
Shakes Pestilence and Warr . . .

Asia, born of most enormous Caf,
Who cost her mother Tellus keener pangs,
55   Though feminine, than any of her sons.
More thought than woe was in her dusky face,
For she was prophesying of her glory;
And in her wide imagination stood
Palm-shaded temples and high rival fanes,
60   By Oxus or in Ganges' sacred isles.
Even as Hope upon her anchor leans,
So leant she, not so fair, upon a tusk
Shed from the broadest of her elephants.
Above her, on a crag's uneasy shelve,
65   Upon his elbow raised, all prostrate else,
Shadowed Enceladus—once tame and mild

ii *53–5*. Asia's parentage is K.'s invention. In Hesiod she is the child of Oceanus and Tethys, and in Hyginus one of the Nereids. K. presents her as the child of Earth and the 'most enormous' mountain Caf to make her origins accord with the vast region bearing her name. He derived Caf from his reading of various eastern tales, for example, 'The History of Abdul Motallub, the Sage' in the English version of the Comte de Caylus's *Contes Orientaux* (1749), repr. H. Weber's *Tales of the East* (1812), 'the mountain of Kaf . . . surrounds the world, and . . . is composed wholly of one entire piece of emerald. . . . It is placed . . . between the horns of a white ox . . . the distance . . . between his horns may be compared to a journey that may be performed in the course of a hundred thousand years' (ii 621). K. was also familiar with 'horrible Kaf' in Beckford's *Vathek*—see Beckford's note, '. . . This mountain, which in reality is no other than Caucasus, was supposed to surround the earth like a ring encompassing a finger; the sun was supposed to rise from one of its eminences . . . and to set on the opposite, whence from Kaf to Kaf signified from one extremity of the world to the other' (*Vathek*, 1816 edn, 248–9).

ii *54*. Echoing *Paradise Lost* iv 271 (marked in K.'s copy of Milton), 'which cost *Ceres* all that pain . . .' On K.'s fondness for this passage in Milton see *Endymion* i 944 *n* (p. 162 above).

ii *60*. From Tigris unto Ganges, and far north *MS (cancelled)*. Altered to heighten the Milton effect. With the revised reading cp., for example, *Paradise Lost* iii 436,

        Of *Ganges* or *Hydaspes, Indian* streams . . .

ii *61*. *anchor*] A traditional emblem of hope, as in *Hebrews* vi 19, 'Which hope we have as an anchor of the soul, both sure and stedfast.' K. probably remembered Spenser's description of Speranza, *The Faerie Queene* I x 14,

        Upon her arme a silver anchor lay,
        Whereon she leaned . . .

ii *64. shelve*] Slope.

ii *66. Enceladus*] Included among the Titans in *Lemprière* (see ii 19–81 *n*, p.

As grazing ox unworried in the meads;
Now tiger-passioned, lion-thoughted, wroth,
He meditated, plotted, and even now
70   Was hurling mountains in that second war,
Not long delayed, that scared the younger Gods
To hide themselves in forms of beast and bird.
Not far hence Atlas; and beside him prone
Phorcus, the sire of Gorgons. Neighboured close
75   Oceanus, and Tethys, in whose lap
Sobbed Clymene among her tangled hair.
In midst of all lay Themis, at the feet

---

417 above), which also has in a separate entry, 'the most powerful of the
giants who conspired against Jupiter. He was struck with Jupiter's lightning
and overwhelmed by the god under mount Aetna. Some suppose that he is
the same as Typhon' (for Jupiter's punishment of Typhon see ii 22–8 n, pp.
417–18 above). K. singles him out as the spokesman for the most belligerent
Titans in ii 308–45 (pp. 431–2 below).

ii 69. *even now*] In his imagination.

ii 70. Woodhouse quotes Ronsard's *A Michel de l'Hospital* 270–2,

> Encelade un mont avoit
> Qui bien tost porter devoit
> Le fardeau de la Sicile . . .

ii 71–2. *the younger Gods . . . bird*] A reference to the muse's description of Typhon and the Olympians in Sandys's *Ovid, Metamorphoses* v (p. 90, col. 1),

> . . . earth-born *Typhon* them pursu'd:
> When as the Gods concealing shapes indu'd.
> *Jove* turn'd himself, she said, into a Ram:
> From whence the hornes of *Libyan Hammon* came.
> *Bacchus* a Goat, *Apollo* was a Crow,
> *Phoebe* a Cat, *Jove's* wife a Cow of snow:
> *Venus* a fish, a Stork did *Hermes* hide . . .

ii 73. *Atlas*] 'One of the Titans, son of Iapetus and Clymene' (*Lemprière*).

ii 74. *Phorcus*] 'A sea deity, son of Pontus and Terra [Sea and Earth], who
married his sister Ceto, by whom he had the Gorgons, the dragon that kept
the apples of the Hesperides, and other monsters' (*Lemprière*).

ii 75. *Oceanus . . . Tethys*] See ii 19–81 n (p. 417 above).

ii 76. *Clymene*] In Hyginus's *Fabulae* one of the Nereids. K. follows Hesiod
in associating her with the Titans—see Cooke's translation of *Theogony*
769–70,

> Clymene, ocean born, with beauteous feet,
> And Japhet, in the bands of wedlock meet . . .

–but his reference to her 'tangled hair' seems to derive from Milton's
Lycidas 69, 'the tangles of *Neæra's* hair'.

ii 77. *Themis*] One of the Titans in Hesiod's *Theogony* (Cooke's translation
220); in *Lemprière*, 'a daughter of Coelus and Terra'.

15+K.

Of Ops the queen all clouded round from sight,
No shape distinguishable, more than when
80   Thick night confounds the pine-tops with the clouds;
And many else whose names may not be told.
For when the Muse's wings are air-ward spread,
Who shall delay her flight? And she must chant
Of Saturn and his guide, who now had climbed
85   With damp and slippery footing from a depth
More horrid still. Above a sombre cliff
Their heads appeared, and up their stature grew
Till on the level height their steps found ease;
Then Thea spread abroad her trembling arms
90   Upon the precincts of this nest of pain,
And sidelong fixed her eye on Saturn's face.
There saw she direst strife—the supreme God
At war with all the frailty of grief,
Of rage, of fear, anxiety, revenge,
95   Remorse, spleen, hope, but most of all despair.
Against these plagues he strove in vain; for Fate
Had poured a mortal oil upon his head,
A disanointing poison, so that Thea,
Affrighted, kept her still, and let him pass
100   First onwards in among the fallen tribe.

As with us mortal men, the laden heart
Is persecuted more, and fevered more,
When it is nighing to the mournful house
Where other hearts are sick of the same bruise;

ii 78. *Ops the queen*] See ii 4 *n* (p. 415 above).

ii 81. *else*] more *MS (cancelled)*.

ii 83. *chant*] trill *MS (cancelled)*.

ii 86. *Above a sombre cliff*] and now was slowly come *MS (cancelled)*.

ii 90. A later insertion. The line is added in the MS on the back of the preceding page.

ii 92–5. Echoing Milton's description of Satan, *Paradise Lost* iv 114–16 (marked in K.'s copy of Milton),

> . . . each passion dimm'd his face
> Thrice chang'd with pale ire, envie and despair,
> Which marrd his borrow'd visage . . .

ii 92. *direst strife*] A Miltonic phrase—'dire' is a favourite epithet of Milton. Cp. *Paradise Lost* i 623–5,

> . . . that strife
> Was not inglorious, though th'event was dire,
> As this place testifies, and this dire change . . .

ii 98. *A disanointing poison*] i.e., loss of majesty.

105 So Saturn, as he walked into the midst,
Felt faint and would have sunk among the rest,
But that he met Enceladus's eye,
Whose mightiness, and awe of him, at once
Came like an inspiration; and he shouted,
110 'Titans, behold your God!' At which some groaned;
Some started on their feet; some also shouted;
Some wept, some wailed, all bowed with reverence.
And Ops, uplifting her black folded veil,
Showed her pale cheeks and all her forehead wan,
115 Her eye-brows thin and jet, and hollow eyes.
There is a roaring in the bleak-grown pines
When winter lifts his voice; there is a noise
Among immortals when a God gives sign,
With hushing finger, how he means to load
120 His tongue with the full weight of utterless thought,
With thunder, and with music, and with pomp.
Such noise is like the roar of bleak-grown pines,
Which, when it ceases in this mountained world,
No other sound succeeds; but ceasing here,
125 Among these fallen, Saturn's voice therefrom
Grew up like organ, that begins anew
Its strain, when other harmonies, stopped short,
Leave the dinned air vibrating silverly.
Thus grew it up: 'Not in my own sad breast,
130 Which is its own great judge and searcher-out,
Can I find reason why ye should be thus;
Not in the legends of the first of days,
Studied from that old spirit-leavèd book

ii *112. wailed*] sat up *MS (cancelled).*

ii *115.* $\left\{ \begin{array}{cc} & 2 \qquad\quad 1 \\ & \text{Her hollow eyes and eyebrows thin and jet ...} \ MS. \end{array} \right.$

ii *116–24. There is a roaring ... succeeds.*] Quoted by Edward Thomas in his *Keats* (1916) to illustrate K.'s success in the poem, 'Wherever there is no action, but only an inanimate scene, or the effects of action or preparation for it, to be described ...' Thomas continues, 'The succeeding philosophic speeches ... are but the gentlest of flights' (66).

ii *120. utterless*] Unutterable. The line has an extra syllable.

ii *128. vibrating silverly*] vibrations silver in the roof *MS (cancelled).*

ii *129–345.* The speeches by Saturn (ii 129–66), Oceanus (ii 173–243), Clymene (ii 252–99) and Enceladus (ii 309–45) are modelled on the 'Stygian council' in *Paradise Lost* ii 11–505, but see *Ridley* (1933), '... the moment Oceanus begins to speak .. the Miltonic influence becomes less dominant' (83).

ii *133–8. spirit-leavèd book ... footstool*] An imaginary book existing from

Which starry Uranus with finger bright
135 Saved from the shores of darkness, when the waves
Low-ebbèd still hid it up in shallow gloom—
And the which book ye know I ever kept
For my firm-basèd footstool—ah, infirm!
Not there, nor in sign, symbol, or portent
140 Of element, earth, water, air, and fire—
At war, at peace, or inter-quarrelling
One against one, or two, or three, or all
Each several one against the other three,
As fire with air loud warring when rain-floods
145 Drown both, and press them both against earth's face,
Where, finding sulphur, a quadruple wrath
Unhinges the poor world; not in that strife,
Wherefrom I take strange lore and read it deep,
Can I find reason why ye should be thus.

---

the beginning of time and recording the first stages of the evolution of the world. The description 'spirit-leavèd' probably derives from allusions to the Sibylline prophetic books encountered in K.'s reading, for example, Virgil's *Aeneid* iii 443–4,

> *insanam vatem aspicies, quae rupe sub ima*
> *fata canit foliisque notas et nomina mandat . . .*

('. . . thou shalt look on an inspired prophetess, who deep in a rocky cave sings the Fates and entrusts to leaves signs and symbols . . .' [Loeb edn].)

ii *134. starry*] starr'd *MS*. Uranus was another name for Coelus or Heaven; see *Paradise Lost* viii 66–8,

>   . . . Heav'n
> Is as the Book of God before thee set,
> Wherein to read his wondrous Works . . .

ii *135. shores of darkness*] Cp. *To Homer* 9 (p. 353 above),

> Aye, on the shores of darkness there is light . . .

ii *136. hid it up*] Scantly touch'd *MS* (cancelled).

ii *141–3.* Suggested by *Paradise Lost* ii 898–900 (marked in K.'s copy of Milton),

> . . . hot, cold, moist, and dry, four Champions fierce
> Strive here for Maistrie, and to Battel bring
> Thir embryon Atoms . . .

The passage supplies the motto for *Welcome joy and welcome sorrow* (p. 386 above).

ii *144. loud warring*] engaging *MS* (cancelled).

ii *147. Unhinges the poor world*] Echoing Milton's *Nativity Ode* 120–2,

> . . . the Creator Great
> His constellations set,
> And the well-ballanc't world on hinges hung . . .

150   No, nowhere can unriddle, though I search,
      And pore on Nature's universal scroll
      Even to swooning, why ye Divinities,
      The first-born of all shaped and palpable Gods,
      Should cower beneath what, in comparison,
155   Is untremendous might. Yet ye are here,
      O'erwhelm'd, and spurned, and battered, ye are here!
      O Titans, shall I say, "Arise!"? Ye groan;
      Shall I say "Crouch!"? Ye groan. What can I then?
      O Heaven wide! O unseen parent dear!
160   What can I? Tell me, all ye brethren Gods,
      How we can war, how engine our great wrath?
      Oh, speak your counsel now, for Saturn's ear
      Is all a-hungered. Thou, Oceanus,
      Ponderest high and deep; and in thy face
165   I see, astonied, that severe content
      Which comes of thought and musing. Give us help!'

      So ended Saturn; and the God of the Sea,
      Sophist and sage from no Athenian grove
      But cogitation in his watery shades,
170   Arose, with locks not oozy, and began,

ii *150. unriddle*] discover *MS (cancelled)*.

ii *161. engine our great wrath*] Transform our wrath into an instrument of war. Cp. Moloch's speech in *Paradise Lost* ii 60–2, 64–6,

>   . . . let us rather choose
> Arm'd with Hell flames and fury all at once
> O're Heav'ns high Towrs to force resistless way. . .
> . . . when to meet the noise
> Of his Almighty Engin he shall hear
> Infernal Thunder . . .

ii *163–6. Oceanus . . . Give us help*] Oceanus was one of the oldest gods – he is preceded only by Earth and Heaven in Hesiod's *Theogony* (Cooke's translation 206–16) – and was traditionally revered for his wisdom by his fellow-deities. For his 'thought and musing' see also *Endymion* iii 993–7 (p. 243 above),

>   . . . On oozy throne
> Smooth-moving came Oceanus the old,
> To take a latest glimpse at his sheep-fold
> Before he went into his quiet cave
> To muse for ever . . .

ii *165. astonied*] astonished *MS (cancelled)*. The archaism occurs only once in Milton (*Paradise Lost* ix 890), but is frequent in Spenser.

ii *169. in his . . . shades*] beneath watry . . . glooms *MS (cancelled)*.

ii *170. with locks not oozy*] The epithet echoes Milton's *Lycidas* 175,

> With *Nectar* pure his oozy Locks he laves . . .

In murmurs which his first-endeavouring tongue
Caught infant-like from the far-foamed sands:
'O ye, whom wrath consumes, who, passion-stung,
Writhe at defeat, and nurse your agonies!
175 Shut up your senses, stifle up your ears,
My voice is not a bellows unto ire.
Yet listen, ye who will, whilst I bring proof
How ye, perforce, must be content to stoop;
And in the proof much comfort will I give,
180 If ye will take that comfort in its truth.
We fall by course of Nature's law, not force
Of thunder, or of Jove. Great Saturn, thou
Hast sifted well the atom-universe;
But for this reason, that thou art the King,
185 And only blind from sheer supremacy,
One avenue was shaded from thine eyes,
Through which I wandered to eternal truth.
And first, as thou wast not the first of powers,

ii *176*. Tradition dissociated Oceanus from active engagement in the war against the Olympians.

ii *179*. *will I give*] may be felt *MS (cancelled)*. K.'s rejected false start to the line was 'Healthy content . . .'.

ii *181–243*. Oceanus's belief in the law of progress is partly determined by his dramatic function in the poem, but the tenor of his argument corresponds with the movement of K.'s ideas during 1818–19. See K.'s views on individual development in his May 1818 letter to Reynolds and in *Sleep and Poetry* 101–21 *n*, 122–54 *n* (pp. 73 and 74 above), and his further comments in the same letter, '. . . there is really a grand march of intellect . . . a mighty providence subdues the mightiest Minds to the service of the time being' (*L* i 282). K. extends his view to politics in Sept. 1819, 'All civilized countries become gradually more enlighten'd . . . the french Revolution put a temporry stop to this . . . change. . . . Now it is in progress again' (*L* ii 193–4). According to K. Muir's 'The meaning of Hyperion' (*Reassessment* (1958) 104): 'As [K.] brooded on his subject it began to acquire a contemporary significance'.

ii *183*. Alludes to Saturn's searching 'earth, water, air, fire . . .' (ii 140 above). For the Miltonic echo in 'atom-universe' see ii 141–3 *n* above.

ii *185*. *only*] being *MS (cancelled)*.

ii *188–90*. See *King Lear* V ii 9–11,

                    . . . Men must endure
        Their going hence, even as their coming hither:
        Ripeness is all . . .

and ii 194 below, 'The ripe hour came . . .'.

So art thou not the last; it cannot be.
190   Thou art not the beginning nor the end.
From chaos and parental darkness came
Light, the first fruits of that intestine broil,
That sullen ferment, which for wondrous ends
Was ripening in itself. The ripe hour came,
195   And with it light, and light, engendering
Upon its own producer, forthwith touched
The whole enormous matter into life.
Upon that very hour, our parentage,
The Heavens and the Earth, were manifest;
200   Then thou first-born, and we the giant race,
Found ourselves ruling new and beauteous realms.
Now comes the pain of truth, to whom 'tis pain—
O folly! for to bear all naked truths,
And to envisage circumstance, all calm,
205   That is the top of sovereignty. Mark well!
As Heaven and Earth are fairer, fairer far
Than chaos and blank darkness, though once chiefs;

ii *190.* See *Revelation* i 8, 'I am Alpha and Omega, the beginning and the ending, saith the Lord'. The biblical tone is sustained in the cancelled passage following this line in the *MS*,

> Darkness was first and then a light there was;
> From Chaos came the Heavens and the Earth
> The first grand Parent . . .

which reflects *Genesis* i 1–4.

ii *191. chaos and parental darkness*] Cp. *Paradise Lost* ii 969–70,

> . . . Spirits of this nethermost Abyss,
> *Chaos* and *ancient Night* . . .

ii *192. intestine broil*] Civil war. Borrowed from Chaos's speech, *Paradise Lost* ii 1001–2,

> . . . our intestine broiles
> Weakning the Scepter of old Night . . .

ii *193. which for wondrous ends*] grown into its height *MS* (*cancelled*).

ii *194. ripening*] at strange boil *MS* (*cancelled*).

ii *196. its own producer*] The darkness of chaos.

ii *202. to whom 'tis pain*] For those to whom it is a pain.

ii *203–5.* See under 19 March in K.'s Feb.–May 1819 journal-letter 'This is the world. . . . Circumstances are like Clouds continually gathering and bursting—While we are laughing the seed of some trouble is put into the wide arable land of events . . . it sprouts . . . and suddenly bears a poison fruit which we must pluck—Even so we have leisure to reason on the misfortunes of our friends; our own touch us too nearly for words. Very few men have ever arrived at a complete disinterestedness of Mind' (*L* ii 79).

ii *207. chiefs*] kings *MS* (*cancelled*).

And as we show beyond that Heaven and Earth
In form and shape compact and beautiful,
210 In will, in action free, companionship,
And thousand other signs of purer life;
So on our heels a fresh perfection treads,
A power more strong in beauty, born of us
And fated to excel us, as we pass
215 In glory that old darkness; nor are we
Thereby more conquered than by us the rule
Of shapeless chaos. Say, doth the dull soil
Quarrel with the proud forests it hath fed,
And feedeth still, more comely than itself?
220 Can it deny the chiefdom of green groves?
Or shall the tree be envious of the dove
Because it cooeth, and hath snowy wings
To wander wherewithal and find its joys?
We are such forest-trees, and our fair boughs
225 Have bred forth, not pale solitary doves,
But eagles golden-feathered, who do tower
Above us in their beauty, and must reign
In right thereof. For 'tis the eternal law
That first in beauty should be first in might;
230 Yea, by that law, another race may drive
Our conquerors to mourn as we do now.
Have ye beheld the young God of the Seas,
My dispossessor? Have ye seen his face?
Have ye beheld his chariot, foamed along
235 By noble wingèd creatures he hath made?
I saw him on the calmèd waters scud,
With such a glow of beauty in his eyes,
That it enforced me to bid sad farewell

ii *209–10*. The phrasing was probably suggested by *Hamlet* II ii 309–11:
'What a piece of work is a man! . . . in form, in moving, how express and
admirable! in action how like an angel! in apprehension how like a god!
the beauty of the world. . . .'

ii *210*. *free*] voice MS (*cancelled*).

ii *217*. *Say, doth the dull soil*] Strife indeed there was MS (*cancelled*).

ii *229*. The source of the 'beauty' and 'might' is indicated in Apollo's
speech iii 113 (p. 440 below), 'Knowledge enormous makes a God of me'.

ii *232*. Neptune.

ii *234–6*. Suggested by traditional pictorial representations of Neptune driv-
ing his chariot. Spence describes Neptune in *Polymetis* (1747) as 'passing
over the calm surface of the sea in his chariot drawn by sea-horses' (219).

ii *236*. *scud*]. See *Endymion* ii 490 *n* (p. 183 above).

To all my empire: farewell sad I took,
240 And hither came to see how dolorous fate
Had wrought upon ye, and how I might best
Give consolation in this woe extreme.
Receive the truth, and let it be your balm.'

Whether through posed conviction, or disdain,
245 They guarded silence when Oceanus
Left murmuring, what deepest thought can tell?
But so it was; none answered for a space,
Save one whom none regarded, Clymene;
And yet she answered not, only complained,
250 With hectic lips, and eyes up-looking mild,
Thus wording timidly among the fierce:
'O Father, I am here the simplest voice,
And all my knowledge is that joy is gone,
And this thing woe crept in among our hearts,
255 There to remain for ever, as I fear.
I would not bode of evil, if I thought
So weak a creature could turn off the help
Which by just right should come of mighty Gods;
Yet let me tell my sorrow, let me tell
260 Of what I heard, and how it made me weep,
And know that we had parted from all hope.
I stood upon a shore, a pleasant shore,
Where a sweet clime was breathèd from a land
Of fragrance, quietness, and trees, and flowers.
265 Full of calm joy it was, as I of grief;
Too full of joy and soft delicious warmth;
So that I felt a movement in my heart
To chide, and to reproach that solitude
With songs of misery, music of our woes;
270 And sat me down, and took a mouthèd shell
And murmured into it, and made melody.
Oh, melody no more! For while I sang,
And with poor skill let pass into the breeze
The dull shell's echo, from a bowery strand
275 Just opposite, an island of the sea,
There came enchantment with the shifting wind,
That did both drown and keep alive my ears.

ii 239. took] gave MS (cancelled).
ii 244. posed] pos'd MS. Pretended, assumed. The Titans are silent either
from a polite wish to appear convinced or from contempt.
ii 250. hectic] Feverish.
ii 263. was breathèd from a land] came breathing from inland MS (cancelled).
ii 271. made melody] what till then MS (cancelled).
15*

I threw my shell away upon the sand,
And a wave filled it, as my sense was filled
280   With that new blissful golden melody.
A living death was in each gush of sounds,
Each family of rapturous hurried notes,
That fell, one after one, yet all at once,
Like pearl beads dropping sudden from their string;
285   And then another, then another strain,
Each like a dove leaving its olive perch,
With music winged instead of silent plumes,
To hover round my head, and make me sick
Of joy and grief at once. Grief overcame,
290   And I was stopping up my frantic ears,
When, past all hindrance of my trembling hands,
A voice came sweeter, sweeter than all tune,
And still it cried, "Apollo! Young Apollo!
The morning-bright Apollo! Young Apollo!"
295   I fled, it followed me, and cried "Apollo!"
O Father, and O Brethren, had ye felt
Those pains of mine—O Saturn, hadst thou felt,
Ye would not call this too indulgèd tongue
Presumptuous in thus venturing to be heard.'

300   So far her voice flowed on, like timorous brook
That, lingering along a pebbled coast,
Doth fear to meet the sea; but sea it met,
And shuddered. For the overwhelming voice
Of huge Enceladus swallowed it in wrath:
305   The ponderous syllables, like sullen waves
In the half-glutted hollows of reef-rocks,

ii *280–9. golden melody . . . at once*] According to Joseph Severn, 'a beautifull
air of Glucks . . . furnished the groundwork of the coming of Apollo in
Hyperion' (letter to Monckton Milnes, 6 Oct. 1845, *KC* ii 133).
ii *281.* Cp. *The Eve of St. Agnes* 56 (p. 457 below),
              The music, yearning like a God in pain . . .
ii *286–8. Each like a dove . . . my head*] Cp. K.'s early sonnet, *As from the
darkening gloom* 1–3 (p. 8 above),
              As from the darkening gloom a silver dove
              Upsoars, and darts into the Eastern light,
              On pinions that naught moves but pure delight . . .
ii *289.* Joy at the music. Grief that her own music is surpassed.
ii *294. morning-bright Apollo*] bright Apollo *MS (cancelled)*.
ii *301. lingering along*] Meandering towards.
ii *306.* Cp. *On the Sea* 2–3 (p. 112 above),

Came booming thus, while still upon his arm
He leaned – not rising, from supreme contempt.
'Or shall we listen to the over-wise,
310 Or to the over-foolish, Giant-Gods?
Not thunderbolt on thunderbolt, till all
That rebel Jove's whole armoury were spent,
Not world on world upon these shoulders piled
Could agonize me more than baby-words
315 In midst of this dethronement horrible.
Speak! Roar! Shout! Yell, ye sleepy Titans all!
Do ye forget the blows, the buffets vile?
Are ye not smitten by a youngling arm?
Dost thou forget, sham Monarch of the Waves,
320 Thy scalding in the seas? What, have I roused
Your spleens with so few simple words as these?
O joy! for now I see ye are not lost:
O joy! for now I see a thousand eyes
Wide-glaring for revenge!' As this he said,
325 He lifted up his stature vast and stood,
Still without intermission speaking thus:
'Now ye are flames, I'll tell you how to burn,
And purge the ether of our enemies;
How to feed fierce the crooked stings of fire,
330 And singe away the swollen clouds of Jove,

... its mighty swell
Gluts twice ten thousand caverns ...

ii *308–45.* K.'s characterization of Enceladus owes something to Moloch,
the 'fiercest Spirit' in the council at Pandaemonium (*Paradise Lost* ii 43–
105), and also draws on Sandys's account of Typhon, 'the type of Ambition
... said to have reached Heaven with his hands, in regard of his aspiring
thoughts ... This horrid figure ... agrees with rebellion' (Sandys's *Ovid*,
commentary on *Metamorphoses* v, pp. 96–7).

ii *311–13.* For the rhetorical style see *Titus Andronicus* IV ii 94–7,

I tell you, younglings, not Enceladus,
With all his threatening band of Typhon's brood,
Nor great Alcides, nor the god of war,
Shall seize this prey ...

ii *313. piled*] poure'd MS (*substituted for* lain *cancelled*).

ii *323. thousand*] hundred MS (*cancelled*).

ii *323–4. eyes* / *Wide-glaring*] Like those of a lion. See *Paradise Lost* iv 402
(marked in K.'s copy of Milton),

A Lion now he stalkes with fierie glare ...

ii *325. lifted*] arose MS (*cancelled*).

ii *326.* And stood [standing *cancelled*], continuing thus MS (*cancelled*).

ii *330. singe ... swollen clouds*] lick ... cloudy tent MS (*cancelled*).

Stifling that puny essence in its tent.
O let him feel the evil he hath done;
For though I scorn Oceanus's lore,
Much pain have I for more than loss of realms.
335 The days of peace and slumberous calm are fled;
Those days, all innocent of scathing war,
When all the fair Existences of heaven
Came open-eyed to guess what we would speak –
That was before our brows were taught to frown,
340 Before our lips knew else but solemn sounds;
That was before we knew the wingèd thing,
Victory, might be lost, or might be won.
And be ye mindful that Hyperion,
Our brightest brother, still is undisgraced –
345 Hyperion, lo! his radiance is here!'

All eyes were on Enceladus's face,
And they beheld, while still Hyperion's name
Flew from his lips up to the vaulted rocks,
A pallid gleam across his features stern –
350 Not savage, for he saw full many a God
Wroth as himself. He looked upon them all,
And in each face he saw a gleam of light,
But splendider in Saturn's, whose hoar locks
Shone like the bubbling foam about a keel
355 When the prow sweeps into a midnight cove.
In pale and silver silence they remained,
Till suddenly a splendour, like the morn,
Pervaded all the beetling gloomy steeps,
All the sad spaces of oblivion,

ii *331. essence*] See i 232 *n* above.
ii *341–2. the wingèd thing, / Victory*] 'The goddess of Victory . . . was represented with wings' (*Lemprière*). Cp. *Paradise Lost* vi 762–3 (marked in K.'s
copy of Milton),

> . . . at his right hand Victorie
> Sate Eagle-wing'd . . .

ii *355. sweeps*] turns *MS* (*cancelled*).
ii *357–71.*

> Till suddenly a full-blown Splendour fill'd
> Those native spaces of oblivion
> And every gulph [*sic*] was seen and chasm old
> And every height and every sullen depth
> [*5*] Voiceless or filled with hoarse tormented Streams;
> And all the everlasting Cataracts
> And all the headlong Torrents far and near,
> And all the Caverns soft with moss and weed

360   And every gulf, and every chasm old,
      And every height, and every sullen depth,
      Voiceless, or hoarse with loud tormented streams;
      And all the everlasting cataracts,
      And all the headlong torrents far and near,
365   Mantled before in darkness and huge shade,
      Now saw the light and made it terrible.
      It was Hyperion: a granite peak
      His bright feet touched, and there he stayed to view
      The misery his brilliance had betrayed
370   To the most hateful seeing of itself.
      Golden his hair of short Numidian curl,
      Regal his shape majestic, a vast shade
      In midst of his own brightness, like the bulk
      Of Memnon's image at the set of sun
375   To one who travels from the dusking east;
      Sighs, too, as mournful as that Memnon's harp,

                Or blazon'd with clear spar and barren gems
        [10]   And all the Gods. It was Hyperion:
                He stood upon a granite peak aloof
                With golden hair of short numidian curl
                Rich as the colchian fleece . . . MS (cancelled).

l. [3]. was seen and] and every (cancelled).

l. [9]. blazon'd . . . spar] dazzling . . . bright (cancelled).

l. [13]. the colchian fleece] The Golden Fleece. See Fragment of the 'Castle
Builder' 62 n (p. 392 above). De Selincourt comments, '. . . The reconstruction . . . [makes] the situation . . . more familiar and more vivid to
the imagination, as an actual sunrise among the mountains (de Selincourt
511).

ii 360–5. Suggests some influence from Wordsworth's references to the
cataracts and waterfalls of the Lake District, for example Not 'mid the
World's vain objects (1815) 5–8,

                . . . dark wood and rocky cave,
            And hollow vale which foaming torrents fill
            With omnipresent murmur as they rave
            Down the steep beds, that never shall be still . . .

ii 366. saw] showed MS (cancelled).

ii 369–70. Hyperion's radiance throws the misery of his fellow-Titans into
stronger relief.

ii 371. Numidian curl] Like the mane of an African lion.

ii 372. Regal his shape majestic] Miltonic construction.

ii 373. bulk] shade MS (cancelled).

ii 374–6. Refers to the ancient Egyptian statue of Memnon–cp. i 31–2 n
(p. 398 above)–which was supposed to utter a melodious sound when struck

He uttered, while his hands contemplative
He pressed together, and in silence stood.
Despondence seized again the fallen Gods
380 At sight of the dejected King of Day,
And many hid their faces from the light.
But fierce Enceladus sent forth his eyes
Among the brotherhood; and, at their glare,
Uprose Iapetus, and Creüs too,
385 And Phorcus, sea-born, and together strode
To where he towered on his eminence.
There those four shouted forth old Saturn's name;
Hyperion from the peak loud answered, 'Saturn!'
Saturn sat near the mother of the Gods,
390 In whose face was no joy, though all the Gods
Gave from their hollow throats the name of 'Saturn!'

BOOK III

Thus in alternate uproar and sad peace,
Amazèd were those Titans utterly.
Oh, leave them, Muse! Oh, leave them to their woes;

---

by the rays of the rising and setting sun. See *Lemprière*, where the sound is
compared to '. . . the breaking of the string of a harp when it is wound
up . . .'. Other references to the legend known to K. include Sandys's commentary on Ovid's *Metamorphoses* xiii (pp. 247–8) and Hazlitt's 'On Shakespeare and Milton' (*Works*, ed. P. P. Howe (1933–4 v 60). On the connection in the eighteenth and early nineteenth centuries with the Aeolian
Harp see G. Grigson's *The Harp of Aeolus* (1947) 41–2.

ii *376. mournful*] melodious *MS* (*cancelled*).

ii *383–6*. Cp. *Paradise Lost* ii 473–5,

> . . . But they
> Dreaded not more th'adventure then his voice
> Forbidding; and at once with him they rose . . .

ii *385. Phorcus, sea-born*] See ii 74 *n* above.

ii *387*. There whispered they bewildered while [?] despair . . . *MS* (*cancelled*). Garrod reads the last word as 'despise[d]'.

ii *389. sat*] stood *MS* (*cancelled*).

iii *Title*] Canto 3 *MS*.

iii *2. Amazèd*] Perplexed *MS* (*cancelled*).

iii *3–28*. An invocation to the Muse in imitation of Milton's invocations in
Paradise Lost, but 'surely the weakest in any poem of comparable quality . . .
suggests how numb [K.'s] usually perceptive faculties were as he continued
to force himself' (*Bate* (1963) 403–4).

iii *3. Oh, leave them to their woes*] for they have succour none *MS* (*cancelled*).

For thou art weak to sing such tumults dire;
5   A solitary sorrow best befits
Thy lips, and antheming a lonely grief.
Leave them, O Muse! for thou anon wilt find
Many a fallen old Divinity
Wandering in vain about bewildered shores.
10   Meantime touch piously the Delphic harp,
And not a wind of heaven but will breathe
In aid soft warble from the Dorian flute;
For lo! 'tis for the father of all verse.
Flush every thing that hath a vermeil hue,
15   Let the rose glow intense and warm the air,
And let the clouds of even and of morn
Float in voluptuous fleeces o'er the hills;
Let the red wine within the goblet boil

iii *5–6. solitary sorrow . . . lonely grief*] K. may be thinking of his celebration of Saturn's grief in i 1–21 (pp. 396–7 above).

iii *6. Thy lips*] Thine anthem'd lips *MS (cancelled)*.

iii *7. O Muse*] for many *MS (cancelled)*.

iii *8. fallen*] mateless *MS (cancelled)*. The rejected first reading was 'lonely'.

iii *10. piously*] deftly *MS (cancelled)*. On 'Delphic' see *Endymion* i 499 *n* (p. 142 above).

iii *12. the Dorian flute*] Echoing *Paradise Lost* i 550–1,

              . . . the *Dorian* mood
    Of Flute and soft Recorders . . .

K. marked the passage in his copy of Milton with the marginal note: 'The light and shade . . . the sorrow, the pain, the sad-sweet melody. . .'.

iii *13. 'tis for*] thou singst *MS (cancelled)*. The line heralds the advent of Apollo.

iii *14–28*. Contrasting with the angry sunrise in i 176–82 (pp. 406–7 above). For the style see W. J. Bate on *Hyperion* iii, 'The imagery, frequently the idiom, even the conception of Apollo himself, begin to remind us disturbingly of *Endymion*' (Bate (1963) 403). This is true. The inferiority of Book III is marked.

iii *14*.   Let a warm rosy hue distain . . . *MS (cancelled)*.

K. uses 'distain' to mean imbue with colour. The idea is sustained by his use of 'vermeil' for rose-coloured in the revised version. The word 'vermeil' is used earlier by K. only in *Endymion* i 50, 696 and iv 148 (pp. 122, 150 and 252 above).

iii *16*. And the corn-haunting poppy *MS (cancelled)*.

iii *18–19. red wine . . . bubbling well*] Faintly anticipates *Ode to a Nightingale* 15–17 (p. 526 below),

        Oh, for a beaker full of the warm South,
        Full of the true, the blushful Hippocrene,
        With beaded bubbles winking at the brim . . .

Cold as a bubbling well; let faint-lipped shells,
20   On sands, or in great deeps, vermilion turn
Through all their labyrinths; and let the maid
Blush keenly, as with some warm kiss surprised.
Chief isle of the embowered Cyclades,
Rejoice, O Delos, with thine olives green,
25   And poplars, and lawn-shading palms, and beech
In which the zephyr breathes the loudest song,
And hazels thick, dark-stemmed beneath the shade.
Apollo is once more the golden theme.
Where was he, when the Giant of the Sun
30   Stood bright, amid the sorrow of his peers?
Together had he left his mother fair
And his twin-sister sleeping in their bower,
And in the morning twilight wandered forth
Beside the osiers of a rivulet,
35   Full ankle-deep in lilies of the vale.
The nightingale had ceased, and a few stars
Were lingering in the heavens, while the thrush
Began calm-throated. Throughout all the isle
There was no covert, no retirèd cave,
40   Unhaunted by the murmurous noise of waves,
Though scarcely heard in many a green recess.
He listened, and he wept, and his bright tears
Went trickling down the golden bow he held.
Thus with half-shut suffusèd eyes he stood,
45   While from beneath some cumbrous boughs hard by

iii *19. faint*] red *MS* (*cancelled*).
iii *24. Delos*] Apollo's birthplace.
iii *28.* See the reference to Apollo in *Endymion* iv 774 (p. 276 above),
              Thy lute-voiced brother will I sing ere long . . .
Apollo affords a 'golden theme' since he is the god of the sun and of poetry.
For K.'s early association of poetry with gold see *On First Looking into Chapman's Homer* 1 and *n* (p. 61 above).
iii *29. Giant of the Sun*] Hyperion.
iii *31–2. mother . . . twin-sister*] Latona and Diana (Artemis). See *Endymion*
i 862 *n* (p. 158 above).
iii *33. wandered*] roamed *MS* (*cancelled*).
iii *36–8. The nightingale . . . calm-throated*] The dawn is only just beginning.
iii *37. heavens*] Scanned as a monosyllable. The word is marked with an
asterisk in the *MS*, presumably because K. was doubtful about its scansion.
iii *39. covert*] Cp. i 152 *n* (p. 405 above), 'I know the covert'.
iii *41.* Cp. *Lamia* i 144 (p. 622 below), 'the green-recessèd woods'.
iii *44.* So kept his with his eyes suffus'd half-shut *MS* (*cancelled*).
iii *45. boughs*] oaks *MS* (*cancelled*). The first attempt in the MS was 'shade'.

With solemn step an awful Goddess came,
And there was purport in her looks for him,
Which he with eager guess began to read
Perplexed, the while melodiously he said:
50 'How cam'st thou over the unfooted sea?
Or hath that antique mien and robèd form
Moved in these vales invisible till now?
Sure I have heard those vestments sweeping o'er
The fallen leaves, when I have sat alone
55 In cool mid-forest; surely I have traced
The rustle of those ample skirts about
These grassy solitudes, and seen the flowers
Lift up their heads, as still the whisper passed.
Goddess! I have beheld those eyes before,
60 And their eternal calm, and all that face,
Or I have dreamed.' 'Yes,' said the supreme shape,
'Thou hast dreamed of me; and awaking up
Didst find a lyre all golden by thy side,
Whose strings touched by thy fingers all the vast
65 Unwearied ear of the whole universe
Listened in pain and pleasure at the birth

iii 46. *an awful Goddess*] Mnemosyne. See ii 29 *n* (p. 418 above).
iii 50. *unfooted*] pathless *MS* (*cancelled*).
iii 52. *Moved*] Walked *MS* (*cancelled*).
iii 53. *o'er*] by *MS* (*cancelled*).
iii 56. *about*] along *MS* (*cancelled*).
iii 57. These solitudes and seeing the grass and flowers *MS* (*cancelled*).
iii 58. *passed*] went *MS* (*cancelled*).
iii 60. *their eternal calm*] Cp. ii 203–5 *n* (p. 427 above),

        . . . to bear all naked truths,
    And to envisage circumstance, all calm,
    That is the top of sovereignty . . .

For K.'s later description of Mnemosyne as the priestess Moneta see *The
Fall of Hyperion* i 256–71 (pp. 673–5 below).
iii 62–79. Mnemosyne's address lacks the austere authority of Moneta's
speeches in *The Fall of Hyperion* i 107–17, 141–81 (pp. 664 and 666–9 below).
iii 62. *hast dreamed*] dreamedst *MS* (*cancelled*).
iii 64. *touched*] swept *MS* (*cancelled*).
iii 66. *Listened in pain and pleasure*] Cp. ii 288–99 (p. 430 above),

                        . . . sick
    Of joy and grief at once. Grief overcame,
    And I was stopping up my frantic ears,
    When, past all hindrance of my trembling hands,
    A voice came sweeter, sweeter than all tune,

Of such new tuneful wonder. Is't not strange
That thou shouldst weep, so gifted? Tell me, youth,
What sorrow thou canst feel; for I am sad
70   When thou dost shed a tear. Explain thy griefs
To one who in this lonely isle hath been
The watcher of thy sleep and hours of life,
From the young day when first thy infant hand
Plucked witless the weak flowers, till thine arm
75   Could bend that bow heroic to all times.
Show thy heart's secret to an ancient Power
Who hath forsaken old and sacred thrones
For prophecies of thee, and for the sake
Of loveliness new born.' Apollo then,
80   With sudden scrutiny and gloomless eyes,
Thus answered, while his white melodious throat
Throbbed with the syllables: 'Mnemosyne!
Thy name is on my tongue, I know not how;
Why should I tell thee what thou so well seest?
85   Why should I strive to show what from thy lips
Would come no mystery? For me, dark, dark,
And painful, vile oblivion seals my eyes.
I strive to search wherefore I am so sad,

And still it cried, "Apollo! Young Apollo!
The morning-bright Apollo! Young Apollo"...'
See also iii 113–20 *n* below.

iii *76. Show*] Develop *MS* (*cancelled*).

iii *77.* Mnemosyne has deserted her fellow Titans for Apollo's sake.

iii *79. Apollo then*] To whom the God *MS* (*cancelled*). Probably altered because Apollo is not yet a god; his transfiguration occurs in iii 113–36 below

iii *80. gloomless eyes*] Apollo's melancholy appears to lift at Mnemosyne's
address.

iii *81. white melodious throat*] Woodhouse records that K. quoted the phrase
in explaining 'that he [Keats] has often not been aware of the beauty of
some thought or expression until after he has composed and written it
down—It has then struck him with astonishment—and seemed rather the
production of another person than his own' (*KC* i 129). It seems an odd
choice of phrase for K.'s purpose.

iii *83. Thy name*] That sound *MS* (*cancelled*).

iii *84.* Thou knowest better *MS* (*cancelled*).

iii *86–7. dark, dark ... eyes*] Echoing Milton's *Samson Agonistes* 80–1,

O dark, dark, dark, amid the blaze of noon,
Irrecoverably dark ...

iii *88 ff.* See Leigh Hunt's review of *1820*, 'The fragment [of *Hyperion*]
ends with the deification of Apollo ... there is something too effeminate

Until a melancholy numbs my limbs;
90   And then upon the grass I sit and moan,
     Like one who once had wings. Oh, why should I
     Feel cursed and thwarted, when the liegeless air
     Yields to my step aspirant? Why should I
     Spurn the green turf as hateful to my feet?
95   Goddess benign, point forth some unknown thing.
     Are there not other regions than this isle?
     What are the stars? There is the sun, the sun!
     And the most patient brilliance of the moon!
     And stars by thousands! Point me out the way
100 To any one particular beauteous star,
     And I will flit into it with my lyre,
     And make its silvery splendour pant with bliss.
     I have heard the cloudy thunder. Where is power?
     Whose hand, whose essence, what Divinity,
105 Makes this alarum in the elements,
     While I here idle listen on the shores
     In fearless yet in aching ignorance?
     Oh, tell me, lonely Goddess, by thy harp,
     That waileth every morn and eventide,
110 Tell me why thus I rave, about these groves.
     Mute thou remainest—mute! Yet I can read
     A wondrous lesson in thy silent face:

---

and human in the way in which Apollo receives the exaltation which his
wisdom is giving him. He weeps and wonders somewhat too fondly; but
his powers gather nobly on him as he proceeds' (*The Indicator* 2 and 9 Aug.
1820); and also W. J. Bate, 'The evolution of Apollo into godhood, so
crucial to this new poetic exploration of the passages that open from the
Chamber of Maiden-Thought [see *Sleep and Poetry* 101-21 *n* p. 73 above]
is suddenly condensed into a few lines' (*op. cit.* 403).

iii *92. liegeless*] Owing no service.

iii *93. step aspirant*] Miltonic phrasing.

iii *98.* Cp. i 353 *n* (p. 415 above),
            And still they were the same bright patient stars . . .

iii *100.* Echoing *All's Well that Ends Well* I i 91,
            That I should love a bright particular star . . .
The line foreshadows K.'s *Bright star* sonnet (p. 736 below).

iii *102. Silvery*] panting *MS* (*cancelled*). With the cancelled reading cp.
Lamia i 300 *n* (p. 629 below), 'the stars drew in their panting fires'.

iii *104. essence* See i 232 *n* above.

iii *107. aching*] Longing.

iii *108. by thy harp*] *Woodhouse* 2 has note, 'i.e. the harp which thou gavest
me'. See iii 63 above.

Knowledge enormous makes a God of me.
Names, deeds, grey legends, dire events, rebellions,
115   Majesties, sovran voices, agonies,
Creations and destroyings, all at once
Pour into the wide hollows of my brain,
And deify me, as if some blithe wine
Or bright elixir peerless I had drunk,
120   And so become immortal.' Thus the God,
While his enkindled eyes, with level glance
Beneath his white soft temples, steadfast kept
Trembling with light upon Mnemosyne.
Soon wild commotions shook him, and made flush
125   All the immortal fairness of his limbs—

iii *113–20*. Apollo becomes a god through his knowledge of human suffering. See K.'s 3 May 1818 letter to Reynolds, 'Until we are sick, we understand not . . . as Byron says "Knowledge is Sorrow" [see *Manfred* I i 10, 'Sorrow is Knowledge . . .']; and I go on to say that "Sorrow is Wisdom"' (*L* i 279); for K.'s views in the same letter on the understanding of human life as essential to individual development see *Sleep and Poetry* 101–21 *n*, 122–54 *n* (pp. 73 and 74 above). The dependence of poetic power upon insight into human suffering is a major theme in *The Fall of Hyperion*.

iii *114–16*. *Names . . . destroyings*] K.'s catalogue is perfunctorily Miltonic.

iii *114*. *rebellions*] loud voices *MS* (*cancelled*).

iii *115*. *sovran*] Sovereign. The spelling is Miltonic (cp. *Paradise Lost* vi 56, 'So spake the Sovran voice').

iii *116*. *all at once*] and calm peace *MS* (*cancelled*).

iii *119*. *bright elixir peerless*] A Miltonic construction—see i 129 *n* (p. 404 above). The word 'elixir' combines associations of gold and immortality as a term in alchemy and as the name of a drug to prolong life.

iii *121–3*.   While level glanced beneath his temple soft
                    His eyes were stedfast on Mnemosyne . . . *MS* (*cancelled*).

iii *124*. K.'s difficulty with this line is suggested by the number of corrections in the MS. His first rejected attempt was,
              And while through all his frame [limbs *cancelled*] . . .
Another cancelled attempt reads,
                    and wild commotion throughout . . .

iii *125*. *the immortal*] his white *MS* (*cancelled*). This is followed in the MS by the lines,
              Into a hue more roseate than sweet pain
              Gives to ravish'd Nymph when her warm tears
              Gush luscious with no sob. Or more severe;—

l. [1] Roseate and pained as a [any *cancelled*] nymph . . . *MS* (*cancelled*).

l. [3] *luscious*] K.'s only other use of this word is in *Endymion* ii 942 (p. 202 above), 'her luscious lips'. The passage reverts to the erotic style of

Most like the struggle at the gate of death;
Or liker still to one who should take leave
Of pale immortal death, and with a pang
As hot as death's is chill, with fierce convulse
130 Die into life. So young Apollo anguished;
His very hair, his golden tresses famed,
Kept undulation round his eager neck.
During the pain Mnemosyne upheld
Her arms as one who prophesied. At length
135 Apollo shrieked—and lo! from all his limbs
Celestial . . .

K.'s earlier poems—see iii 14–28 *n* (p. 435 above)—and was probably rejected for this reason.

iii *126. Most*] More *MS*.

iii *129. convulse*] Convulsion.

iii *131–2*. Contrasts with Hyperion's 'hair of short Numidian curl' in ii 371 (p. 433 above). Cp. the Archangel Uriel in *Paradise Lost* iii 626–8 (marked in K.'s copy of Milton),

> . . . his Locks behind
> Illustrious on his Shoulders fledge with wings
> Lay waving round . . .

ii *131. His very hair*] Even his hair *MS (cancelled)*.

ii *132. undulation*] graceful *MS (cancelled)*.

iii *135. Apollo . . . from all his limbs*] Phoebus . . . he was the God *MS (cancelled)*.

iii *136. Celestial*] And godlike *MS (cancelled)*. Woodhouse's note in his copy of *Endymion* runs: 'The poem, if completed, would have treated of the dethronement of Hyperion, the former God of the Sun, by Apollo,—and incidentally of those of Oceanus by Neptune, of Saturn by Jupiter etc., and of the war of the Giants for Saturn's reestablishment—with other events, of which we have but very dark hints in the mythological poets of Greece and Rome. In fact the incidents would have been pure creations of the Poet's brain.' For the view that the poem would probably not have exceeded 1200–1500 lines see *de Selincourt* 486–9.

112 Fancy

Probably written Dec. 1818 and copied out 2 Jan. 1819 with its companion poem *Ode* 'Bards of Passion' (p. 446 below) in K.'s journal-letter of 16 Dec. 1818–4 Jan. 1819 with the comment, '[the Poems] . . . are specimens of a sort of rondeau which I think I shall become partial to—because you have one idea amplified with greater ease and more delight and freedom than in the sonnet' (*L* ii 26). The two poems have little in common with the conventional rondeau, but derive their trochaic four-stressed rhyming couplets

-also used by K. in *Robin Hood* and *Lines on the Mermaid Tavern* (pp. 301, 304 above)–from Milton's *L'Allegro* and *Il Penseroso* and Fletcher's *The Faithful Shepherdess* (K. wrote out the *Ode* in his copy of Beaumont and Fletcher which is at Hampstead). Allusions to the pleasures of 'fancy' which may have affected the poem include Burton's prefatory verses to *The Anatomy of Melancholy* (1621), 'The Author's Abstract of Melancholy' 1–6, and Fuller's comments under 'Fancy' in his *Holy and Profane State* (1642; repr. by Charles Lamb 1818).

Text from *1820*, with some variants noted from K.'s letter.
Published *1820*.

<blockquote>

Ever let the fancy roam,
Pleasure never is at home,
At a touch sweet Pleasure melteth,
Like to bubbles when rain pelteth.

5   Then let wingèd Fancy wander
Through the thought still spread beyond her;
Open wide the mind's cage-door,
She'll dart forth and cloudward soar.
Oh, sweet Fancy, let her loose!

10 Summer's joys are spoilt by use,
And the enjoying of the spring
Fades as does its blossoming.
Autumn's red-lipped fruitage, too,
Blushing through the mist and dew,

15 Cloys with tasting. What do then?
Sit thee by the ingle, when
The sere faggot blazes bright,
Spirit of a winter's night;
When the soundless earth is muffled,

</blockquote>

¶ 112. *Title*. So *1820*. Brown's transcript has 'Ode to Fancy'.
1–2 (and *93–4*). K.'s repetition of lines with slight modifications–see also ll. 3–4, 77–8, 9–10, 67–7 below–probably prompted his description, 'a sort of rondeau' (headnote). Of the handling of the metre de Selincourt notes: 'Keats is hardly at home with the four accent verse. . . . He is . . . troubled with the weight of his unaccented syllables . . . and was never completely successful with the metre till . . . the *Eve of St. Mark* [p. 480 below].'
6. Through the thought] Towards heaven *Letter*.
13–15. Autumn . . . tasting] Autumn is personified as a girl whose kisses lose their savour; K.'s letter has 'kissing' for 'tasting'. Cp. the rejected line later in the poem (l. 68 *n* below), 'Not a Mistress but doth cloy'. On K.'s use of 'cloy' see *Sleep and Poetry* 178 *n* (p. 77 above). The word may have been suggested here by *Antony and Cleopatra* II ii 241–2, quoted in *Endymion* i 816 *n* (p. 156 above).
17–18. The blazing fire is like the tutelary spirit of the winter night.

20   And the cakèd snow is shuffled
      From the ploughboy's heavy shoon;
      When the night doth meet the noon
      In a dark conspiracy
      To banish even from her sky.

25   Sit thee there and send abroad,
      With a mind self-overawed,
      Fancy—high-commissioned send her!
      She has vassals to attend her.
      She will bring, in spite of frost,

30   Beauties that the earth hath lost.
      She will bring thee, all together,
      All delights of summer weather;
      All the buds and bells of May,
      From dewy sward or thorny spray;

35   All the heapèd autumn's wealth,
      With a still, mysterious stealth.
      She will mix these pleasures up
      Like three fit wines in a cup,
      And thou shalt quaff it. Thou shalt hear

40   Distant harvest-carols clear;
      Rustle of the reapèd corn;
      Sweet birds antheming the morn;
      And, in the same moment—hark!
      'Tis the early April lark,

45   Or the rooks with busy caw
      Foraging for sticks and straw.
      Thou shalt, at one glance, behold
      The daisy and the marigold,
      White-plumed lilies and the first

50   Hedge-grown primrose that hath burst,
      Shaded hyacinth, alway

22–4. A reference to the short winter day.

24. *even*] vesper *Letter.*

26. *self-overawed*] Awed by its own imaginative powers.

33–4.   All the faery buds of May
                   On Spring turf or scented spray . . . *Letter.*

33. Cp. *Ode to Psyche* 61–2 (p. 520 below),
                   With buds, and bells . . .
                   With all the gardener Fancy e'er could feign . . .

42. Perhaps suggested by *Paradise Lost* v 7–8 (marked by K. in his copy of
Milton),

                   . . . the shrill Matin Song
                   Of Birds on every bough . . .

Sapphire queen of the mid-May,
And every leaf and every flower
Pearlèd with the self-same shower.
55 Thou shalt see the field-mouse peep
Meagre from its cellèd sleep,
And the snake all winter-thin
Cast on sunny bank its skin.
Freckled nest-eggs thou shalt see
60 Hatching in the hawthorn tree,
When the hen-bird's wing doth rest
Quiet on her mossy nest.
Then the hurry and alarm
When the bee-hive casts its swarm,
65 Acorns ripe down-pattering,
While the autumn breezes sing.

Oh, sweet Fancy! Let her loose;
Every thing is spoilt by use.
Where's the cheek that doth not fade,
70 Too much gazed at? Where's the maid
Whose lip mature is ever new?
Where's the eye, however blue,
Doth not weary? Where's the face
One would meet in every place?
75 Where's the voice, however soft,
One would hear so very oft?
At a touch sweet Pleasure melteth,
Like to bubbles when rain pelteth.
Let, then, wingèd Fancy find
80 Thee a mistress to thy mind,
Dulcet-eyed as Ceres' daughter,

52. *mid-May*] Cp. *Ode to a Nightingale* 48 (p. 528 below),
. . . mid-May's eldest child
The coming musk-rose . . .
and *The Fall of Hyperion* i 97 *n* (p. 664 below), 'in mid-May'.
66. Followed in the letter by the couplet,
For the same sleek-throated mouse
To store up its winter house . . .
68. *thing*] joy *Letter*. This is followed in the letter by the lines,
Every pleasure, every joy—
Not a Mistress but doth cloy . . .
See 13–15 *n* above. Perhaps rejected because of K.'s feelings about Fanny
Brawne with whom he probably came to an 'understanding' 25 Dec. 1818;
see headnote to *The Eve of St. Agnes* (p. 451 below).
81. *Ceres' daughter*] Proserpine. On her story and K.'s fondness for it see
Endymion i 944 *n* (p. 162 above).

Ere the God of Torment taught her
How to frown and how to chide,
With a waist and with a side
85   White as Hebe's, when her zone
Slipped its golden clasp, and down
Fell her kirtle to her feet,
While she held the goblet sweet,
And Jove grew languid.
                              Break the mesh
90   Of the Fancy's silken leash,

82. *God of Torment*] Pluto.
84–7. Perhaps suggested by Coleridge's *Christabel* (1816) 248–52,

                    . . . she unbound
        The cincture from beneath her breast:
        Her silken robe, and inner vest,
        Dropt to her feet, and full in view,
        Behold! her bosom and half her side– . . .

Hebe was the goddess of youth and cup-bearer to the gods.
89. Between 'And Jove grew languid' and 'Break the mesh' the letter has
the following,

                    . . . Mistress fair,
        Thou shalt have that tressed hair,
        Adonis tangled all for spite;
        And the mouth he would not kiss,
[5]   And the treasure he would miss,
        And the hand he would not press,
        And the warmth he would distress,
        O the Ravishment–the Bliss!
        Fancy has her there she is–
[10]   Never fulsome, ever new,
        There she steps! and tell me who
        Has a Mistresss so divine?
        Be the palate ne'er so fine
        She cannot sicken . . .

ll. [2–7]. Suggested by the description of Venus in Shakespeare's *Venus
and Adonis*.
l. [10]. Cp. *Ode on a Grecian Urn* 24 (p. 535 below),
        For ever piping songs for ever new . . .
ll. [13–14]. See l. 68 and *n* above.
89–92. *Break . . . bring*] Fancy is seen as a cage-bird lightly tethered by a
silken leash; cp. *I had a dove* 3–4 (p. 448 below),
                    . . . Its feet were tied
        With a silken thread of my own hand's weaving . . .

> Quickly break her prison-string
> And such joys as these she'll bring.
> Let the wingèd Fancy roam,
> Pleasure never is at home.

K. recognizes the limits of fancy's power in the *Ode to a Nightingale* 73–5 (pp. 531–2 below),

> ... The fancy cannot cheat so well
> As she is famed to do, deceiving elf ...

94. 'I did not think this had been so long a Poem ...'–K.'s comment after copying out the poem in his letter (*L* ii 24).

113 Ode ['Bards of passion and of mirth']

Probably written Dec. 1818: see headnote to preceding poem; K.'s 2 Jan. 1819 entry in his journal-letter of 16 Dec. 1818–4 Jan. 1819 continues later, '... now I will copy the other Poem–it is on the double immortality of Poets' (*L* ii 25). The poem expands the theme in *Lines on the Mermaid Tavern* (p. 304 above), which is printed with it in 1820.
Text from *1820*, with some variants noted from K.'s letter and his holograph MS at Hampstead.
Published *1820*.

> Bards of passion and of mirth,
> Ye have left your souls on earth!
> Have ye souls in heaven too,
> Double-lived in regions new?
> 5 Yes, and those of heaven commune
> With the spheres of sun and moon;
> With the noise of fountains wondrous,
> And the parle of voices thund'rous;
> With the whisper of heaven's trees,
> 10 And one another, in soft ease
> Seated on Elysian lawns

¶ 113. *Title.* The poem is untitled in K.'s MSS.
1–4. Repeated at ll. 37–40 below. See *Fancy* 1–2 *n* (p. 442 above).
2. Cp. the reference to the poets of the past in *Sleep and Poetry* 206–7 (p. 78 above),

> ... O ye whose charge
> It is to hover round our pleasant hills ...

5. With the earth ones I am talking *Hampstead MS (cancelled).*
8. parle] Speech.

Browsed by none but Dian's fawns,
Underneath large blue-bells tented,
Where the daisies are rose-scented
15 And the rose herself has got
Perfume which on earth is not,
Where the nightingale doth sing
Not a senseless, trancèd thing,
But divine melodious truth,
20 Philosophic numbers smooth,
Tales and golden histories
Of heaven and its mysteries.

Thus ye live on high, and then
On the earth ye live again;
25 And the souls ye left behind you
Teach us, here, the way to find you,
Where your other souls are joying,
Never slumbered, never cloying.
Here, your earth-born souls still speak
30 To mortals of their little week;
Of their sorrows and delights;
Of their passions and their spites;
Of their glory and their shame;
What doth strengthen and what maim.
35 Thus ye teach us, every day,
Wisdom, though fled far away.

Bards of passion and of mirth,
Ye have left your souls on earth!
Ye have souls in heaven too,
40 Double-lived in regions new!

19–20.   But melodious truth divin[e]
                    Philosophic numbers fine . . . *Letter.*
Suggested by Milton's *Comus* 476–8,
        How charming is divine Philosophy!
        Not harsh, and crabbed as dull fools suppose,
        But musical as is *Apollo's* lute . . .
K. quotes the passage in his journal-letter 19 March 1819, 'I repeat Milton's
lines . . . feeling grateful . . . to have got into a state of mind to relish them
properly' (*L* ii 81).
21. Tales] Stories *Hampstead MS.*
28. slumbered] Dulled. With 'cloying' cp. *Fancy* 15 (p. 442 above), 'Cloys
with tasting . . .'
30. little week] Short lives. This is followed in the letter copy by the half
couplet,
        They must sojourn with their cares . . .

114 'I had a dove and the sweet dove died'

Probably written Dec. 1818: '1818' in *Woodhouse* 2; see under 3 Jan. in K.'s
Dec. 1818–Jan. 1819 journal-letter, 'there is just room . . . to copy a little
thing I wrote off to some music as it was playing' (*L* ii 27). The 'music' may
have been played by Charlotte Reynolds–see headnote to the following
poem, *Hush, hush! Tread softly! Hush, hush, my dear!* (No. 115 below).
Text from K.'s letter copy, with one correction noted from Woodhouse's
transcript in *Woodhouse* 2, which agrees with *1848*.
Published *1848*.

> I had a dove and the sweet dove died,
>   And I have thought it died of grieving.
> Oh, what could it grieve for? Its feet were tied
>   With a silken thread of my own hand's weaving.
> 5   Sweet little red feet! Why should you die–
>   Why would you leave me, sweet dove! Why?
> You lived alone on the forest-tree,
>   Why, pretty thing, could you not live with me?
> I kissed you oft and gave you white peas;
> 10   Why not live sweetly, as in the green trees?

¶ 114. *3. Its feet were*] *Woodhouse, 1848*, it was *Letter*. The reading is justified as leading up to l. 5 below.
4. Cp. the silken leash of the cage-bird Fancy in *Fancy* 90 (p. 445 above).
5. *would*] should *Woodhouse*.
6. *would . . . dove*] should . . . bird *Woodhouse*.
7. *on*] in *Woodhouse*.
8. *could*] would *Woodhouse*.

115 'Hush, hush! Tread softly! Hush, hush, my dear!'

Probably written Dec. 1818: '1818' in *Woodhouse* 2; the poem was copied
out by Fanny Brawne on the first blank page in K.'s gift copy to her of
Leigh Hunt's *The Literary Pocket Book* 1819, probably on 21 Jan. 1819 (the
note 'Written twenty-first January' is faintly pencilled on the opposite
page). H. Buxton Forman records: 'Miss Charlotte Reynolds tells me that
. . . [K.] was passionately fond of music, and would sit for hours while she
played the piano for him. It was to a Spanish air which she used to play that
the song . . . was composed' (*Forman* (1883) i xxix–xxx). The 'air' has not

been identified, but see *Athenaeum* 15 Oct. 1859, 'Steibelt . . . was a melodist
. . . as the tune to which Keats wrote the song . . . may remind those who
care to seek no further . . .'. David Steibelt (1765–1823), whose wife was
Spanish, was a prolific composer of popular melodies. For the view–likely
although vigorously repudiated by Middleton Murry–that K. was recollecting a recent encounter with Isabella Jones see *Gittings* (1954) 57–60
(Fanny Brawne's copy of the poem is reproduced pp. 59, 86) and *Gittings*
(1956) 45–53.

Text from K.'s MS with one correction added from the MS in *The Literary
Pocket Book* and some variants noted from the same source and from Woodhouse's transcripts.

Published *Hood's Magazine* March 1845 and *1848*.

I

Hush, hush! Tread softly! Hush, hush, my dear!
    All the house is asleep, but we know very well
That the jealous, the jealous old bald-pate may hear,
        Though you've padded his night-cap, O sweet Isabel!
5   Though your feet are more light than a fairy's feet,
        Who dances on bubbles where brooklets meet.
Hush, hush! Soft tiptoe! Hush, hush my dear!
For less than a nothing the jealous can hear.

II

No leaf doth tremble, no ripple is there
10   On the river; all's still, and the night's sleepy eye
Closes up, and forgets all its Lethean care,
        Charmed to death by the drone of the humming
            mayfly;
        And the moon, whether prudish or complaisant,
        Has fled to her bower, well knowing I want

¶ 115. *Title. Song Pocket Book, 1848.*
1. *Hush, hush, my dear*] breathe lightly my dear *K.'s MS (cancelled).*
2. *but we*] and you *Woodhouse 3.*
3. *jealous old bald-pate*] Supposed by R. Gittings to refer to Isabella Jones's
friend Donal O'Callaghan, who 'would be in or about' his seventies at this
time; see *Gittings* (1956) 233–5.
4. *O*] My *Woodhouse 2, 3.*
7. *Hush, hush! Soft tiptoe*] Yet hush! soft, tiptoe *Woodhouse 3*; hush hush
tread softly *Pocket Book.*
9. *doth tremble*] in the tree *K.'s MS (cancelled).*
10. *On . . . still*] In . . . hush'd *Woodhouse 3.*
11. *Lethean*] empire and *K.'s MS (cancelled).*

15   No light in the dusk, no torch in the gloom,
       But my Isabel's eyes, and her lips pulped with bloom.

                            III
       Lift the latch! Ah, gently! Ah, tenderly, sweet!
           We are dead if that latchet gives one little clink—
       Well done—now those lips, and a flowery seat;
20   The old man may sleep, and the planets may wink!
               The shut rose shall dream of our loves and awake
               Full blown, and such warmth for the morning's take;
       The stock-dove shall hatch her soft brace and shall coo,
       While I kiss to the melody, aching all through!

15. dusk] darkness *Pocket Book*. The words 'light' and 'torch' are transposed in *Woodhouse 3*.
17–18. Cp. the lovers in *The Eve of St. Agnes* 362, 367–9 (p. 478–9 below),
       Like phantoms, to the iron porch they glide
                            .   .   .
       By one, and one, the bolts full easy slide;
       The chains lie silent on the footworn stones;
       The key turns, and the door upon its hinges groans . . .
17. tenderly] softly *K.'s MS (cancelled)*.
18. clink] chink *Pocket Book*.
20. sleep] dream *Pocket Book*.
22. morning's] morning *Pocket Book*.
23. and shall coo] The reading of *Pocket Book*. Before 'coo' K.'s MS has
'and above our heads . . .' cancelled with nothing substituted.

116 The Eve of St. Agnes

Written 18 Jan.–2 Feb. 1819 at Bedhampton and Chichester, and revised at
Winchester Sept. 1819: see under 14 Feb. 1819 in K.'s journal-letter, 'I was
nearly a fortnight at Mr. John Snooks [Bedhampton 23 Jan.–1/2 Feb. 1819]
and a few days at old Mr. Dilke's [Chichester 18/19–23 Jan. 1819] . . . I took
down some thin paper and wrote on it a little Poem called "St. Agnes
Eve"' (*L* ii 58), and his 5 Sept. 1819 letter from Winchester to Taylor,
'. . . am now occupied in revising St. Agnes' Eve' (*L* ii 157).
    K. comments in his letter to Bailey 14 Aug. 1819, '. . . I have written two
Tales, one from Boccaccio call'd the Pot of Basil; and another call'd St.
Agnes' Eve on a popular superstition' (*L* ii 139). K.'s account of the rites of
St. Agnes' Eve was probably elaborated mainly from current oral tradition
with some additional information from Henry Ellis's edn (1813) of John
Brand's *Observations on Popular Antiquities* (1777) 32–4. Woodhouse notes
that the subject of the poem was proposed to K. by Mrs. Isabella Jones

(*Woodhouse* 2), but its romantic celebration of erotic fantasy was almost certainly inspired by the early stages of K.'s association with Fanny Brawne, whom he first met *c.* autumn 1818 and with whom he probably came to an 'understanding' 25 Dec. 1818 (see Aileen Ward's 'Christmas Day 1818' *KShJ* x (1961) 15–27).

K.'s treatment of the story in the poem, in particular the hostile setting for the lovers and the part played by the heroine's aged female attendant, is chiefly influenced by *Romeo and Juliet*, with some additional touches from Mrs. Radcliffe's Gothic tales and possibly from the version of the medieval romance of 'Florice and Blanchefleur' in George Ellis's *Specimens of Early English Romances in Metre* (1805) iii 101–41. For the conjectured influence of Boccaccio's *Il Filocolo*, which draws on the same romance, see *Finney* 541–3, *Ridley* (1933) 139–42. K. relies for his medieval colouring in the poem primarily on contemporary sources, notably Mrs Radcliffe's novels, Scott's *The Lay of the Last Minstrel* (1805) and Coleridge's *Christabel* (1816); for the possible additional influence of Lasinio's engraving (1812) of Orcagna's 'The triumph of Death', which K. had recently seen at Haydon's studio, see *Gittings* (1968) 279–81. The poem is written in Spenserian stanzas, used previously by K. only in the early poem *Imitation of Spenser* (p. 3 above). On the nature of the Spenserian influence see R. Mayhead's *John Keats* (1967), 'We note that Keats is once more using the Spenserian stanza; yet this poem is not simply a more mature imitation of Spenser. The gorgeousness is not there for its own sake, but has a particular function in the organisation of the whole work, a function that is mainly a matter of contrast with effects that are not gorgeous at all . . . the impression left is of a complex blend, in which the gorgeousness is one element' (48).

K.'s initial doubts about *The Eve of St. Agnes* are suggested by his linking it in Sept. 1819 with *Isabella* as displaying similar sentimental weaknesses 'only not so glaring' (*L* ii 174), but his intention expressed in March 1820 of placing it at the beginning of *1820* (*KC* i 105) instead of *Lamia* (p. 613 below), although not carried out, argues that he came to think of the poem more approvingly. For his further comments on his achievement in it in relation to his dramatic ambitions see headnote to *King Stephen* (p. 690 below). Hunt praised *The Eve of St. Agnes* in his review of *1820* (*The Indicator* 2 and 9 Aug. 1820) and reprinted the poem in *The London Journal* 21 Jan. 1835, adding a detailed commentary, which he later revised and incorporated in his *Imagination and Fancy* (1844) with the prefatory note: '"The Eve of St. Agnes" still appears to me the most delightful and complete specimen of . . . [K.'s] genius'–a view with which many modern readers still find themselves in sympathy. The poem is discussed at length, with special emphasis on its textural richness, by M. R. Ridley in *Ridley* (1933) 98–180 and by W. J. Bate in *Bate* (1945) 91–118 and *Bate* (1963) 438–51. Other discussions include R. Gittings's 'St. Agnes Eve and Chichester' and 'St. Agnes Eve and Stansted' in *Gittings* (1954) 64–82; M. Allott's '"Isabella", "The Eve of St. Agnes" and "Lamia"' in *Reassessment* (1958) 39–62; J. C. Stillinger's 'The Hoodwinking of Madeline', *Studies in Philology* lviii (1961)

533–55 (repr. in *Keats: A Collection of Critical Essays*, ed. W. J. Bate, 1964); and John Bayley's lecture, 'Keats and Reality', *Proceedings of the British Academy* 48, 1962, 117–25.

Text from *1820*, with some variants noted from K.'s holograph first draft (K1); from Woodhouse's transcript in *Woodhouse* 1 (K1W) for stanzas 1–7, missing in K.'s MS; and from the transcript in *Woodhouse* 2 which follows K.'s lost second draft (K2). (The bracketed symbols K1, K1W, K2 are used to designate these drafts in the footnotes.) George Keats's transcript, which differs in minor respects from *Woodhouse* 2, is given *in extenso* in Ridley (1933) 180–90. Woodhouse notes that K. altered his 'original MS for publication . . . [he] added some stanzas and omitted others . . . [he] left it to his Publishers to adopt which they pleased and to revise the whole' (*Woodhouse* 2). K.'s decision to reject some of these 'revisions' in *1820* may have been affected in the first place by his publishers' prudish objections (see 54 *n*, 314–22 *n* below), but a final if reluctant approval of the *1820* text seems to be implied in his insistence when overseeing the proofs of the poem on the restoration of a number of his MS readings (see ll. 57–9 *n* below). Some arguments for restoring to the text from Woodhouse's transcript of K2 the additional stanza following l. 54 and the revised version of ll. 314–22 are set out by Stillinger in 'The text of "The Eve of St. Agnes"', *Studies in Bibliography* (1963) 207–12.

Published *1820*.

I

St. Agnes' Eve—ah, bitter chill it was!
The owl, for all his feathers, was a-cold;

¶ 116. *Title. St. Agnes' Eve K1W, K2 (for K.'s habitual use of this form of the title see also L ii 58, 62, 139, 157, 174, 234, 294).* The *1820* version may well be owed to Woodhouse and Taylor (see their use of it in *L* ii 162, 182). K. comments in his 14 Feb.–3 May 1819 journal-letter, 'In my next Packet . . . I shall send you the Pot of Basil, St. Agnes eve, and if I should have finished it . . . the "eve of St. Mark" you see what fine mother Radcliff names I have' (*L* ii 62).

1–9. See Hunt's *Imagination and Fancy* (1844), '. . . how quiet and gentle, as well as wintry, are all these circumstances. . . . The breath of the pilgrim (ll. 6–9) . . . is . . . in admirable "keeping" as the painters call it . . . a complete feeling of winter-time is in this stanza' (331). On the atmosphere of the poem see further ll. 112–13 *n*, 218 *n*, 378 *n* below.

1. chill] cold *K1W, K2*. Altered 'to avoid the echo cold in the second line', K.'s letter to Taylor June 1820 (*L* ii 295). St. Agnes's Eve is celebrated 20 January. Various legends exist concerning the martyrdom of St. Agnes, venerated as a virgin in Rome since the fourth century, but K. probably used the account in John Brand's *Popular Antiquities* (1813 edn), 'a Roman virgin and martyr, who suffered in the tenth persecution under the Emperor Dioclesian A.D. 306. She was condemned to be debauched in the com-

The hare limped trembling through the frozen grass,
And silent was the flock in woolly fold.
5   Numb were the Beadsman's fingers, while he told
His rosary, and while his frosted breath,
Like pious incense from a censer old,
Seemed taking flight for heaven, without a death,
Past the sweet Virgin's picture, while his prayer he saith.

mon stews before her execution, but her virginity was miraculously preserved by lightning and thunder from Heaven. About eight days after her
execution, her parents going to lament and pray at her tomb, they saw a
vision of angels, among whom was their daughter, a lamb standing by her
as white as snow, on which account it is that in every graphic representation
of her, there is a lamb pictured by her side' (32–3). The Feast of St. Agnes is
celebrated annually 21 January in the basilica of St. Agnes fuori le mura at
Rome by the presentation and blessing at the altar of two white unshorn
lambs during the singing of the Agnus Dei. Their wool is woven by nuns
into the pallium–see ll. 115–17 below. Versified accounts of the annual
church festival–one of them a satirical piece published 1794–are quoted in
Brand's *Popular Antiquities* (1813 edn) 32–4.
2. *a-cold*] Echoing *King Lear* III iv 56, 'Tom's a-cold' (marked in K.'s folio
Shakespeare at Hampstead). K. read *King Lear* Oct. 1818 during Tom Keats's
last illness; see *Hyperion* i 98–103 *n* (p. 402 above).
4. *woolly*] sheltered *K1*.
5. *Numb were the Beadsman's fingers*] Cp. the personification of 'old January'
in *The Faerie Queene* VII vii 42,

> Yet did he quake and quiver like to quell,
> And blowe his nayles to warm them if he may:
> For they were numbd . . .

Spenser's stanza is quoted in Leigh Hunt's *Literary Pocket Book* (1819), of
which K. gave a copy to Fanny Brawne *c*. Jan. 1819; see headnote to *Hush,
hush! Tread Softly!* (p. 448 above). A beadsman was a pensioner endowed
to pay for the repose of his benefactor's family and friends. According to
R. Gittings, 'the sombre figure of the Beadsman, who begins and ends
"The Eve of St. Agnes" [see ll. 377–8 below]' derives from the hermit who
is portrayed in various situations in Orcagna's fresco 'The Triumph of
Death' (reproduced *Gittings* (1968) following p. 304: see headnote and also
ll. 372–5 *n* below)–an engraving of the fresco was seen by K. at Haydon's
studio Dec. 1816.
7. Possibly a recollection of Spenser's *Colin Clout's Come Home Againe*
608–9,

> . . . like the fume of Franckincence,
> Which from a golden Censer forth doth rise . . .

For K.'s earlier echo of this passage see *To Mary Frogley* 21–2 *n* (p. 30
above).
8. *without a death*] The beadsman's 'frosted breath' rising in the air resembles pictures of the spirit leaving the body of a dying man.

16+K.

II

10   His prayer he saith, this patient, holy man;
Then takes his lamp, and riseth from his knees,
And back returneth, meagre, barefoot, wan,
Along the chapel aisle by slow degrees.
The sculptured dead, on each side, seem to freeze,
15   Imprisoned in black, purgatorial rails.
Knights, ladies, praying in dumb orat'ries,
He passeth by; and his weak spirit fails
To think how they may ache in icy hoods and mails.

III

Northward he turneth through a little door,
20   And scarce three steps, ere music's golden tongue
Flattered to tears this agèd man and poor;
But no—already had his deathbell rung,
The joys of all his life were said and sung;

12. meagre, barefoot, wan] Cp. the similar groupings of epithets in *Endymion* iv 764 and *Hyperion* i 18 *n* (pp. 276 and 397 above). The word 'meagre' may echo Romeo's description of the apothecary in *Romeo and Juliet* V i 40, 'meagre were his looks'.

14–15. K. is likely to have seen the sculptured effigies on the tombstones in the cathedral during his visit to Chichester Jan. 1819, but Woodhouse notes, 'The stone figures of the Temple Church [in London] probably suggested these lines' (*Woodhouse* 2). Hunt praises the 'felicitous introduction of the Catholic idea in the word "purgatorial"' (*Imagination and Fancy* 332).

18. Hunt (*Imagination and Fancy* 331–2) finds a parallel in Cary's *Dante*, *Purgatorio* X 119–23,

> As, to support incumbent floor or roof,
> For corbel, is a figure sometimes seen,
> That crumples up its knees unto its breast;
> With the feign'd posture, stirring ruth unfeign'd
> In the beholder's fancy . . .

On K.'s later familiarity with Dante's *Purgatorio* see headnote to *The Fall of Hyperion* (p. 656 below).

20. music's golden tongue] Perhaps echoing *Troilus and Cressida* I ii 110 'Helen's golden tongue' (marked by K. in his copy of Shakespeare). The context also suggests a recollection of Milton's *Arcades* 68,

> Such sweet compulsion doth in musick ly . . .

21. Flattered] See Hunt's *Imagination and Fancy*, 'In this word . . . is the whole theory of the secret of tears; which are the tributes of self-pity to self-love . . . the . . . old man was moved, by the sweet music, to think that . . . the mysterious kindness of Heaven did not omit even his . . . sorry case . . . he . . . found himself deserving of tears . . . he shed them, and felt soothed' (332).

His was harsh penance on St. Agnes' Eve.
25   Another way he went, and soon among
Rough ashes sat he for his soul's reprieve,
And all night kept awake for sinners' sake to grieve.

IV

That ancient Beadsman heard the prelude soft,
And so it chanced for many a door was wide
30   From hurry to and fro. Soon, up aloft,
The silver, snarling trumpets 'gan to chide;
The level chambers, ready with their pride,
Were glowing to receive a thousand guests;
The carvèd angels, ever eager-eyed,
35   Stared, where upon their heads the cornice rests,
With hair blown back, and wings put cross-wise on
        their breasts.

26. *Rough*] Black *K1W*. See *Richard II* V i 49,
        And some will mourn in ashes, some coal-black . . .
The word 'reprieve' is used here to mean 'redemption'.
27. *sake*] souls *K1W*. This was followed in *K1W* by the stanza,

        But there are ears may hear sweet melodies,
        And there are eyes to heighten festivals,
        And there are feet for nimble minstrelsies,
        And many a lip that for the red wine calls,–
[5]   Follow, then follow to the illumined halls,
        Follow me youth–and leave the eremite–
        Give him a tear–then trophied banneral
        And many a brilliant tasseling of light,
Shall droop from arched ways this high baronial night.

l. [6]. *eremite*] See L.277 *n* below.
l. [7]. *banneral*] Cp. *Specimen of an Induction* 38 *n* (p. 35 above),
        Beneath the shade of stately banneral . . .
29–30. *many a door . . . to and fro*] Cp. the bustle as the Capulets prepare to
welcome their guests for the feast in *Romeo and Juliet* I v 1–31.
31. *snarling*] Hints at the high-pitched notes of the trumpets and perhaps at
the violent temper of the host and his friends. See l. 99 below,
        They are all here to-night, the whole blood-thirsty race! . . .
32. *level*] high lamped *K2*.
33. *Were glowing*] Seem'd anxious *K1W*. The correction emphasises the
contrast between the coldness outside and the warmth and light within;
see ll. 112–13 *n* below.
34–6. Cherubs as found on the canopies of tombs, or on organ cases. Cp.
Browning, *Transcendentalism: a Poem in Twelve Books* (1855) 49–51,

V

At length burst in the argent revelry,
With plume, tiara, and all rich array,
Numerous as shadows haunting fairily

40   The brain, new stuffed in youth, with triumphs gay
Of old romance. These let us wish away,
And turn, sole-thoughted, to one Lady there,
Whose heart had brooded, all that wintry day,
On love, and winged St. Agnes' saintly care,

45   As she had heard old dames full many times declare.

VI

They told her how, upon St. Agnes' Eve,
Young virgins might have visions of delight,
And soft adorings from their loves receive
Upon the honeyed middle of the night,

50   If ceremonies due they did aright;
As, supperless to bed they must retire,
And couch supine their beauties, lily white,

    . . . your own boy-face o'er the finer chords
    Bent, following the cherub at the top
    That points to God with his paired half-moon wings . . .

37. burst . . . revelry] step . . . revellers *K1.*

39–42.   Ah what are they ? The idle pulse scarce stirs
             The Muse should never make the spirits gay;
             Away, bright dulness, laughing fools away, –
             And let me tell of one sweet lady there . . . *K1*

39. fairily] Enchantedly.

40. The brain, new stuffed, in youth] The phrasing was probably suggested by *Romeo and Juliet* II iii 37, quoted in *52–4 n* below.

46–51. See Brand's *Popular Antiquities*, 'On the eve of . . . [St. Agnes's] day many kinds of divination are practised by virgins to discover their future husbands. . . . This is called fasting St. Agnes's Fast. The following lines of Ben Jonson allude to this:

           And in sweet St. Agnes' night
           Please you with the promis'd sight,
           Some of husbands, some of lovers
           Which an empty dream discovers.

. . . Burton in his *Anatomy of Melancholy* (edit. 1660, p. 538) speaks of *Maids fasting on St. Agnes' Eve*, to know who shall be their first husband' (1813 edn 33–4). The passage from Burton (*Anatomy of Melancholy* III 2 ii 4) is marked in K.'s copy of Burton at Hampstead. Hunt quotes Jonson's lines – derived from *The Satyr* (1603) 50–3 – in his commentary on *The Eve of St. Agnes* (*Imagination and Fancy* 330).

52–4. M. R. Ridley quotes the account in the undated chap-book, *Mother*

Nor look behind, nor sideways, but require
Of Heaven with upward eyes for all that they desire.

VII

55   Full of this whim was thoughtful Madeline.
The music, yearning like a God in pain,
She scarcely heard; her maiden eyes divine,
Fixed on the floor, saw many a sweeping train

Bunches Closet newly broke open, 'When thou liest down lie as straight as
thou canst, lay thy hands under thy head and say

Now St. Agnes play thy part,

And send to me, my own sweetheart;

And show me such a happy bliss,

This night of him to have a kiss . . .' (*Ridley* (1933) 110)

The word 'couched' was probably suggested by *Romeo and Juliet* II iii 37–8
(marked by K. in his folio Shakespeare),

. . . where unbruised youth with unstuff'd brain

Doth couch his limbs, there golden sleep doth reign . . .

See 40 *n* above.

54. Followed in *K2* by the stanza,

'Twas said her future lord would there appear

Offering as sacrifice–all in the dream–

Delicious food even to her lips brought near;

Viands and wine and fruit and sugar'd cream,

[5]   To touch her palate with the fine extreme

Of relish: then soft music heard; and then

More pleasure followed in a dizzy stream

Palpable almost: then to wake again

Warm in the virgin morn, no weeping Magdalen . . .

See Woodhouse's letter to Taylor 19 Sept. 1819, '[K.] has . . . inserted an
additional stanza early in the poem to make the *legend* more intelligible, and
correspondent with what afterwards takes place . . . with respect to the
supper and the playing on the Lute' (*L* ii 162). K.'s indication of the erotic
nature of Madeline's dream in ll. [7–9] is in keeping with his revision of sts.
35–6; see ll. 314–22 *n* below.

55. Madeline] See K.'s letter to Reynolds 14 March 1818: '. . . tell me you
are well: . . . or by the holy Beaucoeur,–which I suppose is the virgin Mary,
or the repented Magdalen, (Beautiful name, that Magdalen) I'll take to my
Wings and fly away' (*L* i 246). Note the reference to Mary Magdalen in the
rejected stanza above.

56. Cp. the music of Apollo in *Hyperion* ii 281–2 (p. 430 above),

A living death was in each gush of sounds,

Each family of rapturous hurried notes . . .

57. She scarcely heard] Touch'd not her heart . . . *K1.*

57–9. her maiden eyes . . . Pass by] See K.'s letter to Taylor 11 June 1820,

Pass by—she heeded not at all; in vain
60   Came many a tiptoe, amorous cavalier,
And back retired—not cooled by high disdain,
But she saw not; her heart was otherwhere.
She sighed for Agnes' dreams, the sweetest of the year.

VIII

She danced along with vague, regardless eyes,
65   Anxious her lips, her breathing quick and short.
The hallowed hour was near at hand. She sighs
Amid the timbrels and the thronged resort
Of whisperers in anger, or in sport;
'Mid looks of love, defiance, hate, and scorn,
70   Hoodwinked with fairy fancy—all amort,
Save to St. Agnes and her lambs unshorn,
And all the bliss to be before to-morrow morn.

IX

So, purposing each moment to retire,
She lingered still. Meantime, across the moors,
75   Had come young Porphyro, with heart on fire
For Madeline. Beside the portal doors,
Buttressed from moonlight, stands he and implores
All saints to give him sight of Madeline

'. . . reading over the proof of St. Agnes Eve . . . I was struck with . . . an alteration in the 7th Stanza very much for the worse: the passage I mean stands thus

> "her maiden eyes incline
> Still on the floor, while many a sweeping train
> Pass by—"

. . . My meaning is quite destroyed by the alteration. I do not use *train* for *concourse of passers by* but for *Skirts* sweeping along the floor' (*L* ii 294–5).
64. *regardless*] uneager *K1, K2.*
65. Her anxious mouth [lips *cancelled*] full pulp'd wth rosy thoughts *K1* (*cancelled*). Cp. *Hush, hush!* 16 (p. 450 above), 'her lips pulped with bloom'.
67. *timbrels*] Tambourines.
70. *all amort*] all a mort *K1*; à la mort *K2*. The phrase means listless. Cp. *The Taming of the Shrew* IV iii 36, 'what sweeting, all amort'.
71. *lambs unshorn*] See l. 1 *n* above.
75. *Porphyro*] Lionel *K1*. The hero is variously Lionel and Porphyro in *K1*, but is Porphyro throughout *K2*. The name, perhaps suggested by Burton's references to the neo-Platonist Porphyrius in *The Anatomy of Melancholy* I ii i 2, signifies 'nobly born' or 'born in the purple'.
77. *Buttressed from moonlight*] Porphyro is standing for concealment in the shadows of a buttress.

But for one moment in the tedious hours,
80   That he might gaze and worship all unseen;
Perchance speak, kneel, touch, kiss—in sooth such things
        have been.

X

He ventures in—let no buzzed whisper tell,
All eyes be muffled, or a hundred swords
Will storm his heart, love's feverous citadel.
85   For him, those chambers held barbarian hordes,
Hyena foemen, and hot-blooded lords,
Whose very dogs would execrations howl
Against his lineage; not one breast affords
Him any mercy, in that mansion foul,
90 Save one old beldame, weak in body and in soul.

XI

Ah, happy chance! The agèd creature came,
Shuffling along with ivory-headed wand,
To where he stood, hid from the torch's flame,
Behind a broad hall-pillar, far beyond
95   The sound of merriment and chorus bland.

82. buzz'd] damned *K1, K2*. An earlier attempt at the line was,
        He ventures in cloak'd up in dark disguise . . .
83. All eyes be muffled] Let no Man see him *K1 (cancelled)*. The phrase 'a
hundred swords' may be derived from Edmund Burke's celebrated passage
on Marie Antoinette in his *Reflections on the French Revolution in France*
(1790), 'I thought ten thousand swords must have leaped from their scab-
bards to avenge even a look that threatened her with insult' (*Works*, Bohn
edn, 1894–1902) ii 348.
84. love's feverous citadel] for all his amorous sighs *K1 (cancelled)*.
85–8. For him . . . his lineage] Cp. Romeo's situation in the Capulets' house,
Romeo and Juliet I v.
88. one breast] a soul *K1*. Altered when K. saw he had used soul in l. 90
below.
90. beldame] Used in the sixteenth century when addressing nurses (*OED*).
91–189. The portrait of Angela owes some details to descriptions of various
aged female attendants in Gothic romances, for example Dorothée in Mrs
Radcliffe's *The Mysteries of Udolpho* (1794), but her part in the story and the
flavour of caricature in K.'s treatment of her are reminiscent of the nurse in
Romeo and Juliet.
91. creature] Beldam *K1*.
92. Shuffling . . . wand] Tottering . . . staff *K1 (cancelled)*. Cp. the references
to the nurse's age and aching bones in *Romeo and Juliet* II v.
94. broad] huge *K1 (cancelled)*.

He startled her; but soon she knew his face,
And grasped his fingers in her palsied hand,
Saying, 'Mercy, Porphyro! Hie thee from this place;
They are all here to-night, the whole blood-thirsty race!

XII

100   Get hence! Get hence! There's dwarfish Hildebrand—
He had a fever late, and in the fit
He cursèd thee and thine, both house and land;
Then there's that old Lord Maurice, not a whit
More tame for his gray hairs. Alas me! Flit,
105   Flit like a ghost away!' 'Ah, gossip dear,
We're safe enough; here in this arm-chair sit,
And tell me how–' 'Good Saints! Not here, not here;
Follow me, child, or else these stones will be thy bier.'

XIII

He followed through a lowly archèd way,
110   Brushing the cobwebs with his lofty plume,
And as she muttered, 'Well-a–well-a-day!'

98. Porphyro] Jesu *K1, K2.* Similar expletives attributed to Angela in the
draft readings at ll. 107, 143 below are dropped in *1820,* possibly because
K.'s publishers disapproved of them (see 314–22 *n*). The nurse in *Romeo and
Juliet* is given to uttering such exclamations.
100. Hildebrand] Ferdinand *K1 (cancelled).*
103. Lord Maurice] Lord Maurice Lacey *K1 (cancelled).* K.'s earlier attempt
at the line was,
　　　　　There's old Francesco Mendez not a wit ...
104. More tame for his grey hairs] Tamer for all his palsy *K1 (cancelled).* K.
has already described Angela as palsied in l. 97 above.
105. Gossip] Originally god-sib (god-relation), used variously by the
Elizabethans for a talkative woman and a female friend. Cp. Capulet to the
nurse in *Romeo and Juliet* III v 172, 'smatter with your gossips, go'.
106. here in this arm-chair sit] Cp. *The Mysteries of Udolpho* IV chap. iv,
'[Emily] drew one of the massy armchairs ... and begged Dorothée would
sit down, and try to compose her spirits' (55).
107. Saints] God *K1 (cancelled).*
108. Follow me Child–hush, hush *K1 (cancelled).*
109–10. Perhaps a borrowing from Scott's *The Lay of the Last Minstrel*
(1805) ii st. 3,
　　　　　The arched cloister, far and wide,
　　　　　Rang to the warrior's clanking stride;
　　　　　Till, stooping low his lofty crest,
　　　　　He enter'd the cell of the ancient priest ...

He found him in a little moonlight room,
Pale, latticed, chill, and silent as a tomb.
'Now tell me where is Madeline,' said he,
115   'Oh, tell me, Angela, by the holy loom
Which none but secret sisterhood may see,
When they St. Agnes' wool are weaving piously.'

XIV

'St. Agnes? Ah! It is St. Agnes' Eve—
Yet men will murder upon holy days:
120   Thou must hold water in a witch's sieve,
And be liege-lord of all the elves and fays,
To venture so; it fills me with amaze
To see thee, Porphyro!—St. Agnes' Eve!
God's help! My lady fair the conjuror plays
125   This very night. Good angels her deceive!
But let me laugh awhile, I've mickle time to grieve.'

XV

Feebly she laugheth in the languid moon,
While Porphyro upon her face doth look,

112–13. K.'s pictorial details were derived from romantic literature of the day and from medieval buildings seen at Chichester. On the 'little moonlight room' being suggested by the Pulpitum in the Vicars' Hall at Chichester see *Gittings* (1954) 71. See also Hunt: 'All is still wintry. There is to be no comfort in the poem, but what is given by love' (*Imagination and Fancy* 333–4) and William Empson '. . . the contrast between cold weather and the heat of passion . . . is never forgotten throughout "St. Agnes' Eve"' (*Seven Types of Ambiguity* (1930) 272).
113. chill] high *K1, K2*. K.'s first attempt at the line was,
        Pale, casemented and silent as the tomb . . .
115. Angela] Goody *K1, K2*.
115–17. the holy loom . . . weaving piously] See l. 1 *n* above.
120–1. I hold water . . . fays] Be a master of impossibilities.
120. Cp. the witch in *Macbeth* I iii 8,
        But in a sieve I'll thither sail . . .
Holding water in a sieve was traditionally a magic practice.
122. To venture so about these stony ways . . . *K2*.
123. To see thee, Porphyro] Attempting Beelzebub *K2*.
124. The conjuror plays] Intends to conjure up visions by forbidden spells. Cp. Mercutio's pretence at conjuration in *Romeo and Juliet* II i 15–16,
        He heareth not, he stirreth not, he moveth not;
        The ape is dead, and I must conjure him . . .
125. good angels her deceive] Let angels send her instead good dreams.
126. mickle] Much. Cp. the Friar in *Romeo and Juliet* III iii 15–16 (marked by K. in his folio Shakespeare),

16*

Like puzzled urchin on an agèd crone
130   Who keepeth closed a wondrous riddle-book,
As spectacled she sits in chimney nook.
But soon his eyes grew brilliant, when she told
His lady's purpose, and he scarce could brook
Tears at the thought of those enchantments cold,
135 And Madeline asleep in lap of legends old.

XVI

Sudden a thought came like a full-blown rose,
Flushing his brow, and in his painèd heart
Made purple riot; then doth he propose
A stratagem that makes the beldame start:
140   'A cruel man and impious thou art—
Sweet lady, let her pray, and sleep, and dream
Alone with her good angels, far apart
From wicked men like thee. Go, go! I deem
Thou canst not surely be the same that thou didst seem.'

XVII

145   'I will not harm her, by all saints I swear,'
Quoth Porphyro: 'Oh, may I ne'er find grace

... mickle is the powerful grace that lies
    In herbs, plants, stones ...

127. languid] bright *K1*.

129–31. Perhaps suggested by an illustration to a fairy-tale.

132. But soon] Sudden *K1*.

133. brook] Curb. See, for example, Scott's *Marmion* (1808) i st. 10,
        Well dost thou brook thy gallant roan ...

135. And ... in lap of] Sweet ... among those *K1* (*cancelled*). Hunt remarks
K.'s 'fusing ... the imaginative and the spiritual, the remote and the near.
Madeline is alseep in her bed; but ... also asleep in accordance with the
legends of the season ... the bed becomes *their* lap as well as sleep's' (*Imagination and Fancy* 334).

136. came like a full-blown rose] came full blown like a rose *K2*. K.'s first
attempt at the line was,
        Sudden a thought more rosy than the rose ...

137.   Heated his brow and in his painfle head ... *K1*.

138. purple riot] riot fierce *K1* (*cancelled*).

140–62. Cp. the nurse's anxiety and Romeo's winning protestations in
Romeo and Juliet II iv 164–88.

143. Go, go] O Christ *K1, K2*. See l. 98 *n* above.

145. by all saints I swear] by the great St Paul *K1, K2*. See l. 98 *n* above. K.
and Brown attended the consecration of Stansted Chapel near Bedhampton
on the feast of the conversion of St Paul 25 Jan. 1819 (*L* ii 62–3).

146. Quoth] Swear'th *K1*; swearth *K2*.

When my weak voice shall whisper its last prayer,
If one of her soft ringlets I displace,
Or look with ruffian passion in her face—
150   Good Angela, believe me by these tears,
Or I will, even in a moment's space,
Awake with horrid shout my foemen's ears,
And beard them, though they be more fanged than
    wolves and bears.'

XVIII

'Ah, why wilt thou affright a feeble soul?
155   A poor, weak, palsy-stricken, churchyard thing,
Whose passing-bell may ere the midnight toll!
Whose prayers for thee, each morn and evening,
Were never missed.' Thus plaining doth she bring
A gentler speech from burning Porphyro,
160   So woeful, and of such deep sorrowing,
That Angela gives promise she will do
Whatever he shall wish, betide her weal or woe.

XIX

Which was to lead him, in close secrecy,
Even to Madeline's chamber, and there hide
165   Him in a closet, of such privacy
That he might see her beauty unespied,
And win perhaps that night a peerless bride,
While legioned fairies paced the coverlet

147. whisper its last prayer] unto heaven call *K1, K2.*
150. believe me by these tears] thou hearest how I swear *K1 (cancelled).*
156. Cp. *Hyperion* i 173 *n* (p. 406 above),
           Upon the first tolling of his passing-bell . . .
163–252. The situation (the hero in his mistress's room without her knowledge and his watching of her while she sleeps) is from stock. Forms in which K. may have known it include Mrs Radcliffe's *The Romance of the Forest* (1791) ii chap. xiv (*British Novelists* edn, 1810, xliv 73–4) and the tale of the Enchanted Horse in *The Arabian Nights* (1811 edn) v 215–16. K. probably also recalled *Cymbeline* II ii, where the watcher is the villain of the piece.
163.   Which was, as all who ever lov'd will guess . . . *K1 (cancelled).*
165. of such privacy] if such a one there be *K1.*
168. paced the coverlet] round her pillow flew *K1.* Perhaps owed in part to Milton's description of the 'Fairy Ladies' in *At a Vacation Exercise* 61–4,
        Thy drowsie Nurse hath sworn she did them spie
        Come tripping to the Room where thou didst lie;
        And sweetly round about thy Bed
        Strew all their blessings on thy sleeping Head . . .

And pale enchantment held her sleepy-eyed.
170   Never on such a night have lovers met
Since Merlin paid his Demon all the monstrous debt.

XX

'It shall be as thou wishest,' said the Dame,
'All cates and dainties shall be storèd there
Quickly on this feast-night; by the tambour frame
175   Her own lute thou wilt see. No time to spare,
For I am slow and feeble, and scarce dare
On such a catering trust my dizzy head.
Wait here, my child, with patience; kneel in prayer
The while. Ah! Thou must needs the lady wed,
180   Or may I never leave my grave among the dead.'

XXI

So saying, she hobbled off with busy fear.
The lover's endless minutes slowly passed;

The line may have been suggested in the first place by Mercutio's description of Queen Mab *Romeo and Juliet* I iv 55–95 (marked by K. in his folio Shakespeare).

169. pale enchantment] Emphasizing the contrast between the pallor of an imagined vision (cp. l. 134 above, 'enchantments cold . . .') and Porphyro's warm presence.

171. The allusion has puzzled readers, including Hunt ('What he means . . . I cannot say . . .', *Imagination and Fancy* 334), but K. is probably referring to the perpetual imprisonment of Merlin by his mistress, the Lady of the Lake, who repaid his love by deceit. K. could have found all he needed for this in *The Faerie Queene* III iii 7–11, but he may also have read the accounts in Malory's *Morte d'Arthur* iv chap. 1 and John Dunlop's *The History of Fiction* (1814) 69–73. Brown's list of K.'s books contains the item 'Hist. of K. Arthur' (*KC* i 259). Editions of Malory were published 1816 and 1817 (Southey's edn).

173. cates . . . dainties] Elizabethan terms for delicacies. Cp. *The Comedy of Errors* III i 21,

I hold your dainties cheap, sir . . .

and III i 28,

But though my cates be mean, take them in good part . . .

174. tambour frame] Embroidery frame. Cp. *Fragment of the 'Castle Builder'* 38–9 (pp. 391–2 above),

A tambour-frame, with Venus sleeping there,
All finished but some ringlets of her hair . . .

178. But wait an hour's passing–kneel in prayer . . . *K1*.

179. Thou must needs the lady wed] Cp. the Nurse's eagerness to see that Romeo marries Juliet in *Romeo and Juliet* II iv 164–88.

The dame returned, and whispered in his ear
To follow her; with agèd eyes aghast
185   From fright of dim espial. Safe at last,
Through many a dusky gallery, they gain
The maiden's chamber, silken, hushed, and chaste,
Where Porphyro took covert, pleased amain.
His poor guide hurried back with agues in her brain.

XXII

190   Her faltering hand upon the balustrade,
Old Angela was feeling for the stair,
When Madeline, St. Agnes' charmèd maid,
Rose, like a missioned spirit, unaware.
With silver taper's light, and pious care,
195   She turned, and down the agèd gossip led
To a safe level matting. Now prepare,
Young Porphyro, for gazing on that bed—
She comes, she comes again, like ring-dove frayed and
    fled.

XXIII

Out went the taper as she hurried in;
200   Its little smoke, in pallid moonshine, died.

182. slowly] quickly *K1, K2.* With Porphyro's sense of the slow passage of
time, cp. Juliet's impatience in *Romeo and Juliet* II v 1–17, III ii 1–35.
185. dim espial] any noise *K1 (cancelled)*. The word 'espial' may be taken
from the personification of Danger in *The Faerie Queene* IV x 17,

    . . . oftentimes faint hearts at first espiall

    Of his grim face, were from approaching scard . . .

186–9.   Through lonely oaken Galleries they reach

    Where he in panting covert will remain

    In purgatory sweet to view what may he attain . . . *K1.*

187. silken, hushed and chaste] Cp. l. 12 above 'meagre, barefoot, wan' and
n.
188. covert] Cp. K.'s use of this word in *Hyperion* i 152, ii 32, iii 39 (pp. 405,
418 and 436 above).
190–2.   Scarce had old Angela the Staircase found

    Ere Madeline like an affrighted Swan

    Flew past her . . . *K1 (cancelled).*

190–1. A good example of K.'s power to see his story dramatically.
193. like a missioned spirit] like a spirit to her *K1 (cancelled)*. The word
'missioned' means commissioned.
198. frayed] Frightened. Echoing *The Faerie Queene* V xii 5, 'like doves,
whom the Eagle doth affray'.
199–207. Hunt finds a 'Chaucerian' minuteness and delicacy of detail in
this stanza (*Imagination and Fancy* 335).

She closed the door, she panted, all akin
To spirits of the air, and visions wide—
No uttered syllable, or woe betide!
But to her heart, her heart was voluble,
205   Paining with eloquence her balmy side,
As though a tongueless nightingale should swell
Her throat in vain, and die, heart-stifled, in her dell.

XXIV
A casement high and triple-arched there was,
All garlanded with carven imageries
210   Of fruits, and flowers, and bunches of knot-grass,

203. If she speaks she will break the spell.
204–5. The loud beating of Madeline's heart has its own painful eloquence.
205. Paining] Rending *K1* (*cancelled*).
208–10.   There was a Casement triple archd and high
All garlanded with carven imageries
Of fruits and flowers and sunny corn ears parched . . .
                                    K1 (*cancelled*).
An earlier attempt was,
            A Casement triple archd and diamonded
            With many coloured glass fronted the moon
            In midst whereof a shielded scutcheon shed
            High blushing gules . . .
K. took some details for this stanza from buildings seen at Chichester and
Stansted; for resemblances to the windows of the neo-Gothic chapel at
Stansted see Gittings (1954) 79–80. The description has a Spenserian opul-
ence, but its romantic colouring suggests some additional influence from
contemporary literary sources. See, for example, Scott's *The Lay of the Last
Minstrel* (1805) ii st. 11,
            The moon on the east oriel shone
            Through slender shafts of shapely stone,
                By foliaged tracery combined;
            Thou would'st have thought some fairy's hand
            'Twixt poplars straight the ozier wand,
                In many a freakish knot had twined;
            Then framed a spell, when the work was done,
            And changed the willow-wreaths to stone . . .
On echoes and imitations of the rich pictorial effects in this and the following stanza by various nineteenth-century poets, including Hood,
Arnold, Tennyson and Rossetti, see G. H. Ford, *Keats and the Victorians*
(1944) 8, 85, 128–33.
209. imageries] Designs.
210. knot-grass] A plant with intricately branched creeping stems and a
small pink flower, commonly found in waste ground.

And diamonded with panes of quaint device
Innumerable of stains and splendid dyes,
As are the tiger-moth's deep-damasked wings;
And in the midst, 'mong thousand heraldries,
215   And twilight saints, and dim emblazonings,
A shielded scutcheon blushed with blood of queens and
    kings.

XXV

Full on this casement shone the wintry moon,
And threw warm gules on Madeline's fair breast
As down she knelt for heaven's grace and boon;
220   Rose-bloom fell on her hands, together pressed,
And on her silver cross soft amethyst,
And on her hair a glory, like a saint.
She seemed a splendid angel, newly dressed,
Save wings, for Heaven. Porphyro grew faint;
225   She knelt, so pure a thing, so free from mortal taint.

XXVI

Anon his heart revives; her vespers done,
Of all its wreathèd pearls her hair she frees;

211. diamonded with panes] Cp. the windows with diamond-shaped panes in
Fragment of the 'Castle Builder' 28–30 (p. 391 above).
213. As is the tiger-moth's deep sunset [damasked *cancelled*] wings . . . *K1*.
215. emblazonings] Heraldic devices.
216. A coat-of-arms. It 'blushed with blood' because it was 'on a field
gules' and also showed the quarterings of the family and their royal connection. Cp. *Specimen of an Induction* 39–40 (p. 35 above),
      . . . slung with shining cuirass, sword and shield
      Where ye may see a spur in bloody field . . .
218. The warm colours contrast with the cold light of the moon, thus
sustaining the contrasts between warmth and cold which operate throughout the poem: see ll. 112–13 *n* above. K. relied on a literary source for his
description since colours are not transmitted in moonlight. Scott makes a
similar mistake in *The Lay of the Last Minstrel* ii st. 11,
      The moon-beam kiss'd the holy pane,
      And threw on the pavement a bloody stain . . .
220. Rose-bloom fell on her hands] Tinging her pious hands *K1* (*cancelled*).
222. glory] Aureole or nimbus.
223. splendid] silvery *K1*. Altered because K. saw he had used 'silver' in
l. 221 above.
225. so . . . so] too . . . too *K1, K2*.
226–43. K.'s difficulty with these stanzas is indicated by the numerous corrections in *K1*, a few of which are given below; for a detailed account see

Unclasps her warmèd jewels one by one;
Loosens her fragrant bodice; by degrees
230   Her rich attire creeps rustling to her knees.
Half-hidden, like a mermaid in sea-weed,
Pensive awhile she dreams awake, and sees,
In fancy, fair St. Agnes in her bed,
But dares not look behind, or all the charm is fled.

XXVII

235   Soon, trembling in her soft and chilly nest,
In sort of wakeful swoon, perplexed she lay,
Until the poppied warmth of sleep oppressed
Her soothèd limbs, and soul fatigued—away
Flown, like a thought, until the morrow-day;
240   Blissfully havened both from joy and pain;

Ridley (1933) 153–6. K.'s description expands his earlier lines in *Fancy* 84–7
(p. 445 above),

> With a waist and with a side
> White as Hebe's, when her zone
> Slipped its golden clasp, and down
> Fell her kirtle to her feet . . .

and suggests a reworking of similar situations encountered in his reading,
such as William Browne's graphic account of a girl preparing for bed in
Britannia's Pastorals Book 1 Song 5 807–30 and the description of Imogen
in bed in *Cymbeline* II ii.

227.   Of all its wreathed pearl she strips her hair
            And twists it in one Knot upon her head . . . *K1* (*cancelled*).
228. *warmèd jewels*] bosom jewels *K1* (*cancelled*).
229. *her fragrant bodice*] Earlier attempts include,
    1. her bursting boddice . . .
    2. her Boddice lace . . .
    3. her Boddice string . . .
    4. her Boddice and her bosom bare . . .
231. *mermaid in sea-weed*] Syren of the sea *K1* (*cancelled*).
        232. She stands awhile in dreaming thought; and sees . . . *K1*.
234. *fled*] dead *K1*.
235–315. The stanzas follow a characteristically Keatsian movement from
falling into a 'swoon' or 'sleep' (ll. 235–43), through on ensuing state of
'enchantment' (ll. 244–93), to an awakening to colder reality (ll. 294–315):
see further M. Allott, ' "Isabella", "The Eve of St. Agnes" and "Lamia" ',
Reassessment 46–9.
        235. The charm fled not—she did not look behind . . . *K1* (*cancelled*).
237. *the poppied warmth of sleep*] Cp. *Sleep and Poetry*, 348 and *n* (p. 83
above),

> Sleep, quiet with his poppied coronet . . .

Clasped like a missal where swart Paynims pray;
Blinded alike from sunshine and from rain,
As though a rose should shut, and be a bud again.

XXVIII

Stol'n to this paradise, and so entranced,
245   Porphyro gazed upon her empty dress,
And listened to her breathing, if it chanced
To wake into a slumbrous tenderness;
Which when he heard, that minute did he bless,
And breathed himself, then from the closet crept,
250   Noiseless as fear in a wide wilderness—

241. Clasped] Shut *K1* (*cancelled*). The line is ambiguous. Either held protectively as by a believer among unbelievers; or shut (i.e. with clasps) as a missal would be in a muslim country. The latter interpretation receives some support from the cancelled reading which recalls *Romeo and Juliet* I iii 92 (marked in K.'s folio Shakespeare), 'that in gold clasps locks the golden story'. Hunt favours the former interpretation, '... that is to say, where Christian prayer-books must not be seen, and are, therefore, doubly cherished for the danger' (*Imagination and Fancy* 337). The reference to 'Paynims' was perhaps suggested by the monk's narrative in *The Lay of the Last Minstrel* ii st. 12,

    For Paynim countries I have trod,
    And fought beneath the Cross of God ...

For the rather unlikely view that K. was referring to a particular missal used by the Goths under Moorish rule and known to bibliographers of the day see *Lowell* (1924) ii 173–4.
242. Blinded] Dead to *K1* (*cancelled*).
243. shut] close *K1* (*cancelled*). Cp. *Romeo and Juliet* II ii 121–2,

    This bud of love, by summer's ripening breath,
    May prove a beauteous flower when next we meet ...

and I ii 28–3,

           ... such delight
    Among fresh female buds shall you this night
    Inherit at my house ...

Both passages are marked by K. in his folio Shakespeare.
244. paradise] Frequently used in both eastern and 'Gothick' tales when describing the delights of passionate love. Mrs Radcliffe has *The Italian* (1797) i chap ii, 'From this moment Vivaldi seemed to have arisen into a new existence; the whole world to him was Paradise' (1826 edn 34).
247. The gentle regular breathing of the undisturbed sleeper.
248. that minute did he bless] he breath'd himself *K1* (*cancelled*).
249–50. Another example of the vivid working of K.'s dramatic sense as he unfolds his narrative.

And over the hushed carpet, silent, stepped,
And 'tween the curtains peeped, where, lo!—how fast
    she slept.

XXIX

Then by the bed-side, where the faded moon
Made a dim, silver twilight, soft he set
255 A table and, half anguished, threw thereon
A cloth of woven crimson, gold, and jet.
Oh, for some drowsy Morphean amulet!
The boisterous, midnight, festive clarion,
The kettle-drum and far-heard clarionet,
260 Affray his ears, though but in dying tone;
The hall door shuts again, and all the noise is gone.

XXX

And still she slept an azure-lidded sleep,
In blanchèd linen, smooth and lavendered,
While he from forth the closet brought a heap

251. *carpet*] An anachronism addng to K.'s pictorial effects. Cp. ll. 285, 360 below.
254. *a dim, silver*] an illumined *K1*.
255. *half anguished, threw*] with anguish spread *K1*; with care quick spread *K2*.
257. *drowsy Morphean amulet*] A charm to induce sleep.
258–9. Probably a recollection of *Hamlet* I iv 8–12,

        The king doth wake tonight and takes his rouse,
        Keeps wassail, and the swaggering up-spring reels;
        And, as he drains his draughts of Rhenish down,
        The kettle-drum and trumpet thus bray out
        The triumph of his pledge . . .

258. *midnight*] braying *George Keats's transcript.*
259. *clarionet*] Used as a diminutive for clarion, a trumpet. The MSS have 'clarinet'.
260. *dying*] faintest *K1*.
261. See Cowden Clarke: 'When Keats was reading to me the manuscript of "The Eve of St. Agnes", upon the repeating of the passage when Porphyrio is listening to the midnight music in the hall below . . . "That line," said he, "came into my head when I remembered how I used to listen in bed to your music at school"' (*Cowden Clarke* (1878) 143).
262–75. Cp. the feast in K.'s Venus and Adonis episode, *Endymion* ii 440–53 (pp. 180–1 above) and M. Allott, 'While the tranced intoxication lasts every sense is indulged . . . [K.] introduces . . . fruit . . . music and perfume, the warmth and colour of summer are . . . suggested, and erotic experience is the supreme sensuous culmination [see ll. 314–22 *n*]' (*loc. cit.* 47).

265   Of candied apple, quince, and plum, and gourd,
        With jellies soother than the creamy curd,
        And lucent syrops, tinct with cinnamon;
        Manna and dates, in argosy transferred
        From Fez; and spicèd dainties, every one,
270   From silken Samarcand to cedared Lebanon.

XXXI

        These delicates he heaped with glowing hand
        On golden dishes and in baskets bright
        Of wreathèd silver; sumptuous they stand
        In the retired quiet of the night,
275   Filling the chilly room with perfume light.
        'And now, my love, my seraph fair, awake!
        Thou art my heaven, and I thine eremite.

265. *apple, quince*] fruits sweets *K1* (*cancelled*).
266. *creamy*] dairy *K1* (*cancelled*). Cp *Endymion* ii 446–7 (p. 181 above),
        . . . here is cream,
    Deepening to richness from a snowy gleam . . .
The word 'soother' means smoother. Cp. *Sleep and Poetry* 180 and *n* (p. 77 above), 'soothe their wavy hair'.
267. *tinct*] An Elizabethan poeticism for tinged. Hunt notes, '. . . [the] delicate modulation, and . . . epicurean nicety . . . make us read the line delicately, and at the tip-end, as it were, of one's tongue' (*Imagination and Fancy* 337).
268. *argosy*] Brigantine *K1* (*cancelled*). An earlier attempt at the line was,
    And sugar'd dates that o'er Euphrates far'd . . .
For K.'s other attempts see the reproduction of K.'s MS (ll. 259–97) and the accompanying commentary in *Ridley* (1933) 160–3. Manna is apparently used here to mean an exotic fruit; cp. *Endymion* ii 452 and *n* (p. 181 above),
    And here is manna picked from Syrian trees . . .
269. *From Fez*] In Brigantine from Fez *K1* (*cancelled*). A brigantine is a small sailing ship. Fez is in northern Morocco.
270. *silken*] glutted *K1*. The ancient Persian city of Samarkand was famous for its wealth and as a market for silks. For the epithet 'cedared' see *Psalms* civ 16: 'The trees of the Lord are full of sap; the cedars of Lebanon, which he hath planted. . . .'
272. *dishes*] salvers *K1, K2*.
273. *wreathèd*] twisted *K1* (*cancelled*).
274.   Amid the quiet of St. Agnes' night . . . *K1*.
277. *eremite*] A poeticism for hermit or anchoret, used twice again by K.; see *The Eve of St. Mark* 95, the *Bright Star* sonnet 4 (pp. 485 and 738 below). With the whole line cp. *Romeo and Juliet* II ii 113–14 (marked in K.'s folio Shakespeare),

        . . . thy gracious self
    Which is the god of my idolatry . . .

Open thine eyes, for meek St. Agnes' sake,
Or I shall drowse beside thee, so my soul doth ache.'

XXXII

280   Thus whispering, his warm, unnervèd arm
Sank in her pillow. Shaded was her dream
By the dusk curtains; 'twas a midnight charm
Impossible to melt as icèd stream.
The lustrous salvers in the moonlight gleam,
285   Broad golden fringe upon the carpet lies.
It seemed he never, never could redeem
From such a steadfast spell his lady's eyes;
So mused awhile, entoiled in woofèd phantasies.

XXXIII

Awakening up, he took her hollow lute,
290   Tumultuous, and, in chords that tenderest be,
He played an ancient ditty, long since mute,
In Provence called, 'La belle dame sans mercy',
Close to her ear touching the melody—

---

and also the religious imagery in K.'s poems to Fanny Brawne, for example
Ode to Fanny 51 (p. 742 below),

Let none profane my Holy See of love . . .

See further *To [Fanny]* 25–6 *n* (p. 688 below).

279. so my soul doth ache] With a delight that verges on pain. Perhaps
suggested here by *Othello IV* ii 67–8,

Who art so lovely fair and smell'st so sweet
That the sense aches at thee . . .

For the pleasure–pain equivalent elsewhere in K. see *Ode to Melancholy* 23–4
and *n* (p. 540 below),

. . . aching Pleasure nigh,
Turning to poison while the bee-mouth sips . . .

280. unnervèd] Weak (from excessive feeling).

282. 'twas a midnight charm] dreamless of alarms K1 (*cancelled*).

286. redeem] Set free.

288. woofèd] Woven.

289. lute] A standard piece of equipment for heroes and heroines in Gothic
tales.

291. ditty, long since mute] The phrasing suggests a distant reminiscence of
Milton's *Lycidas* 32,

Meanwhile the Rural ditties were not mute . . .

292. 'La belle dame sans mercy'] Borrowed from the title of Alain Chartier's
poem *La Belle Dame Sans Mercy* (1424); see *La Belle Dame sans merci* note
to *Title* (pp. 500–1 below).

Wherewith disturbed, she uttered a soft moan.
295   He ceased–she panted quick–and suddenly
Her blue affrayèd eyes wide open shone;
Upon his knees he sank, pale as smooth-sculptured stone.

XXXIV

Her eyes were open, but she still beheld,
Now wide awake, the vision of her sleep—
300   There was a painful change, that nigh expelled
The blisses of her dream so pure and deep.
At which fair Madeline began to weep,
And moan forth witless words with many a sigh,
While still her gaze on Porphyro would keep;
305   Who knelt, with joinèd hands and piteous eye,
Fearing to move or speak, she looked so dreamingly.

XXXV

'Ah, Porphyro!' said she, 'but even now
Thy voice was at sweet tremble in mine ear,
Made tuneable with every sweetest vow,

294–7. For a similar situation in Mrs Radcliffe see her *The Mysteries of Udolpho* (1794) ii chap. 6, 'She gazed at him for a moment in speechless affright, while he, throwing himself on his knee at the bedside, besought her to fear nothing' (164).

297. pale as smooth-sculptured stone] Suggested by the moonlight–cp. l. 169 above, 'pale enchantment'. K. may be recalling Mrs Ratcliffe's *The Mysteries of Udolpho* (1794) i chap. vi 190, 'his countenance became fixed, and touched as it now was by the silver whiteness of the moonlight, he resembled one of those marble statues of a monument which seem to bend, in hopeless sorrow, over the ashes of the dead, shewn

by the blunted light
That the dim moon through painted casements lends

[Charlotte Smith, *The Emigrants* (1793) ii 300–1]'
The passage is quoted in *Ridley* (1933) 166.

296. affrayèd] half-frayed *K1*. See l. 198 *n* above, 'like ring-dove frayed'.

297. smooth] fair *K2*.

300–2 (and *311* below). Reality is painful after the 'blisses of her dream'. Cp. *Sleep and Poetry* 157–9 *n* (p. 76 above),

A sense of real things comes doubly strong,
And, like a muddy stream, would bear my soul along
To nothingness . . .

and see ll. 235–315 *n* above.

303. Witless] little *K1*.

305.   Who with an aching brow and piteous eye . . . *K1, K2*.

309. Made tuneable] And tim'd devout *K2*. The word 'tuneable' is a Shakespearian borrowing. Cp. *A Midsummer Night's Dream* I i 183–4,

310   And those sad eyes were spiritual and clear.
        How changed thou art! How pallid, chill, and drear!
        Give me that voice again, my Porphyro,
        Those looks immortal, those complainings dear!
        Oh, leave me not in this eternal woe,
315 For if thou diest, my love, I know not where to go.'

                                    ... your tongue's sweet air
              More tuneable than lark to shepherd's ear ...
and IV i 126,

                                    A cry more tuneable
              Was never holla'd to ...
K. marked both passages in his copy of Shakespeare (*Spurgeon* 88, 102).
310. those sad] thy kind *K1*.
312. Perhaps suggested by *The Tempest* III ii 148-9,
                                    ... when I wak'd,
              I cried to dream again ...
The passage is marked in K.'s copy of Shakespeare (*Spurgeon* 77). In *Woodhouse* 2 the line reads,
              Give me that voice again sweet Prospero ...
314-22.   So while she speaks his arms encroaching slow
              Have zon'd her, heart to heart—loud the dark winds blow

              For on the midnight came a tempest fell
              More sooth for that his quick rejoinder flows
        [5] Into her burning ear:—and still the spell
              Unbroken guards her in serene repose.
              With her wild dream he mingled as a rose
              Marryeth its odour to a violet.
              Still, still she dreams.—louder the frost wind blows ... *K2*.
    l. [4]. *quick*] close *George Keats's transcript*.
K.'s decision to print his original version in *1820* has some aesthetic justification, but seems to have been influenced initially by Woodhouse and by K.'s publishers, Taylor and Hessey. See Woodhouse's 19 Sept. 1819 letter to Taylor, part quoted in l. *54 n* above, 'There was another alteration, which I abused for "a full hour by the *Temple* clock". . . . As the Poem was originally written, *we* innocent ones (ladies and myself) might very well have supposed that Porphyro, when acquainted with Madeline's love for him, and when "he arose, Etherial flushed" etc. etc. . . . set himself at once to persuade her to go off with him, and succeeded and went over the "Dartmoor black" (now changed for some other place [see l. *351 n* below]) to be married, in right honest chaste and sober wise. But, as it is now altered, as soon as M. has confessed her love, P. winds by degrees his arm round her, presses breast to breast, and acts all the acts of a bonâ fide husband, while she fancies she is only playing the part of a Wife in a dream ... tho' ... all is left to inference, and tho' profanely speaking, the Interest on

XXXVI

Beyond a mortal man impassioned far
At these voluptuous accents, he arose,
Ethereal, flushed, and like a throbbing star
Seen mid the sapphire heaven's deep repose;
320   Into her dream he melted, as the rose
Blendeth its odour with the violet,
Solution sweet—meantime the frost-wind blows
Like Love's alarum pattering the sharp sleet
Against the window-panes; St. Agnes' moon hath set.

XXXVII

325   'Tis dark; quick pattereth the flaw-blown sleet.

the reader's imagination is greatly heightened, yet I do apprehend it will render the poem unfit for ladies ... [K.] says he does not want ladies to read his poetry: that he writes for men—and that if in the former poem there was an opening for doubt what took place, it was his fault for not writing clearly and comprehensibly—that he should despise a man who would be such an eunuch in sentiment as to leave a maid, with that Character about her, in such a situation: and should despise himself to write about it, etc. etc.—and all this sort of Keats-like rhodomontade' (*L* ii 163). Taylor's reply, written 25 Sept. 1819 before seeing the text, contains among other disapproving comments, '... This Folly of Keats is the most stupid piece of Folly I can conceive.—He does not bear the ill opinion of the World calmly, and yet he will not allow it to form a good Opinion of him and his Writings ... I don't know how the Meaning of the new Stanzas is wrapped up, but I will not be accessory (I can answer also for H. [Hessey] I think) towards publishing any thing which can only be read by Men, since even on their Minds a bad Effect must follow the Encouragement of those Thoughts which cannot be raised without Impropriety ... if ... [K.] will not so far concede to my Wishes as to leave the passage as it originally stood, I must be content to admire his Poems with some other Imprint' (*L* ii 182–3).

318–19. like ... repose] Perhaps suggested by *Romeo and Juliet* III ii 22–4,

    ... cut him out in little stars,
And he will make the face of heaven so fine
That all the world will be in love with night ...

318. throbbing] Cp. *Lamia* i 300 *n* (p. 629 below),

    ... the stars drew in their panting fires ...

320. Into her dream] With her bright dream *K1* (*cancelled*).

322. Solution sweet] A Miltonic construction. 'Solution' means fusion.

323. Like Love's alarum] The rising wind warns the lovers of their danger in remaining where they are.

324. window-panes] windows dark *K1*. An earlier attempt at the line was,

    Against the Casement gloom—St. Agnes' moon hath set ...

325. flaw-blown sleet] Sleet driven by the wind. Cp. Cary's *Dante, Inferno* vi 9, quoted in *As Hermes once* 9–11 *n* (p. 500 below).

'This is no dream, my bride, my Madeline!'
'Tis dark; the icèd gusts still rave and beat.
'No dream, alas! alas! and woe is mine!
Porphyro will leave me here to fade and pine.
330   Cruel! What traitor could thee hither bring?
I curse not, for my heart is lost in thine,
Though thou forsakest a deceivèd thing—
A dove forlorn and lost with sick, unprunèd wing.'

XXXVIII

'My Madeline! Sweet dreamer! Lovely bride!
335   Say, may I be for ay thy vassal blest?
Thy beauty's shield, heart-shaped and vermeil dyed?
Ah, silver shrine, here will I take my rest
After so many hours of toil and quest,
A famished pilgrim—saved by miracle.
340   Though I have found, I will not rob thy nest
Saving of thy sweet self; if thou think'st well
To trust, fair Madeline, to no rude infidel.

333. dove forlorn and lost] silent mateless dove *K1 (cancelled)*. Cp. l. 198
above, 'like ring-dove frayed'. The bedraggled dove is betrayed innocence;
'unpruned' means unpreened.
334. Sweet dreamer! Lovely bride!] Dark is the wintry night *K1 (cancelled)*.
335. See K.'s letter to Fanny Brawne 25 July 1819, '. . . the very first week
I knew you I wrote myself your vassal' (*L* ii 132). The knightly protector
in this and the following line, the 'pilgrim' (l. 339) and the 'infidel' (l. 342),
all belong to the medieval world.
336. vermeil] On K.'s use of this word see *Hyperion* iii 14 *n* (p. 435 above).
337. here will I take my rest] Echoing *Romeo and Juliet* V iii 109–10,

. . . here
Will I set up my everlasting rest

With K.'s use of 'shrine' cp. *Romeo and Juliet* I v 96–7 (marked by K. in his
folio Shakespeare),

If I profane with my unworthiest hand
This holy shrine . . .

339. Pale featured and in weeds of pilgrimage . . . *K1*. An earlier attempt
was,

With features pale and mournful Pilgrim's weeds . . .

Probably suggested by the references to Romeo as a pilgrim at his first
meeting with Juliet, *Romeo and Juliet* I v 98–105 (marked by K. in his Folio
Shakespeare).
341–2.   Soft Nightingale, I'll keep thee in a cage

To sing to me—but hark! the blended tempests' rage . . . *K1*.
Cp. l. 206 above, 'tongueless nightingale'.
342. infidel] Cp. in l. 241 above, 'swart Paynims'.

XXXIX

Hark! 'Tis an elfin-storm from fairy land,
Of haggard seeming, but a boon indeed.
345   Arise—arise! The morning is at hand;
The bloated wassailers will never heed.
Let us away, my love, with happy speed—
There are no ears to hear, or eyes to see,
Drowned all in Rhenish and the sleepy mead.
350   Awake! Arise, my love, and fearless be!
For o'er the southern moors I have a home for thee.'

XL

She hurried at his words, beset with fears,
For there were sleeping dragons all around,
At glaring watch, perhaps, with ready spears;
355   Down the wide stairs a darkling way they found.
In all the house was heard no human sound;
A chain-drooped lamp was flickering by each door;
The arras, rich with horseman, hawk, and hound,

343. elfin] Frequent in Spenser.
344. haggard] Wild, fierce.
346 (and *349* below). Echoing *Hamlet* I iv 8–12, quoted in ll. 258–9 *n*
above.
349. Rhenish] Wine from the region of the Rhine.
350–1. Similar proposals are made in Mrs Radcliffe's *The Mysteries of
Udolpho* (1794) ii chap. vi, 'I have bribed a servant . . . to open the gates,
and before tomorrow's dawn you shall be far on the way to Venice' (267)
and her *The Sicilian Romance* (1790) chap. iii 'Come my love, the keys are
ours . . . we have not a moment to lose . . .'.
350.   Put on warm clothing sweet, and fearless be . . . *K1*.
See K.'s letter to Fanny Keats 19 Feb. 1820, 'Mind my advice . . . be very
careful to wear warm cloathing in a thaw' (*L* ii 261).
351.   Over the dartmoor black I have a home for thee . . . *K1*.
352–69. K. may have taken some hints for this part of the narrative from
Scott's *The Lay of the Last Minstrel* ii st. 26,
                Why does she stop, and look often around,
                As she glides down the secret stair;
                And why does she pat the shaggy bloodhound,
                As he rouses him up from his lair;
                And, though she passes the postern alone,
                Why is not the watchman's bugle blown? . . .
355. darkling] Dark. For K.'s later use of this word see *Ode to a Nightingale*
51 *n* (p. 529 below),
                        Darkling I listen . . .
357–60. Perhaps suggested by Byron's *Siege of Corinth* (1816) 620–27,

Fluttered in the besieging wind's uproar;
360   And the long carpets rose along the gusty floor.

XLI

They glide, like phantoms, into the wide hall;
Like phantoms, to the iron porch they glide;
Where lay the Porter, in uneasy sprawl,
With a huge empty flagon by his side.
365   The wakeful bloodhound rose and shook his hide,
But his sagacious eye an inmate owns.
By one, and one, the bolts full easy slide;

Like the figures on arras, that gloomily glare,
Stirred by the breath of the wintry air
So seen by the dying lamp's fitful light,
Lifeless, but life-like, and awful to sight . . .
Fearfully flitting to and fro,
As the gusts on the tapestry come and go . . .

357.   A drooping lamp was flickering here and there . . . *K1 (cancelled)*,
K.'s difficulty at this point is suggested by the number of earlier cancelled
readings in his *MS* which include,

1. But noise of winds beseiging the high doors . . .
2. The Lamps were flickering with death shad[e]s on the wall . . .
3. Without, the Tempest kept a hollow roar . . .
4. But here and there a lamp was flickering out . . .

The lamp as finally described may derive from the description of Christabel's room in Coleridge's *Christabel* (1816) i 182–4,

The lamp with twofold silver chain
Is fastened to an angel's feet . . .

The silver lamp burns dead and dim . . .

360.   See l. 251 *n* above.
361–2.   Like Spirits into the wide-paved hall
                    They glide and to the porch in haste . . . *K1 (cancelled)*.
The chiasmus with variations in the revised reading may have been influenced by the repetitions in Coleridge's *Christabel* i 184–6,

The silver lamp burns dead and dim;
But Christabel the lamp will trim,
She trimmed the lamp, and made it bright . . .

364. *flagon*] beaker *K1, K2*.
366.   But with a calmed eye his Mistress owns . . . *K1 (cancelled)*.
K.'s earlier attempt was,
                    And paced round Madeline all angerless . . .
The phrasing in the revised version has an incongruous eighteenth-century
flavour.
367. *the bolts full easy slide*] the easy bolts back slide *K1 (cancelled)*.

The chains lie silent on the footworn stones;
The key turns, and the door upon its hinges groans.

XLII

370   And they are gone—aye, ages long ago
These lovers fled away into the storm.
That night the Baron dreamt of many a woe,
And all his warrior-guests, with shade and form
Of witch and demon, and large coffin-worm,
375   Were long be-nightmared. Angela the old
Died palsy-twitched, with meagre face deform;

368.   Upon the pavement lie the heavy chains . . . *K1* (*cancelled*).
370–1. Cp. the similar distancing of the story in the concluding lines of
medieval romances, for example *Florice and Blanchfleur*, quoted in George
Ellis's *Specimens of Early English Metrical Romances* (1805) iii 141,

> Now ben they both dead,
> Christ of heaven home their spirits led.
> Now is this tale brought to an end
> Of Florice and of his leman hend.

371. fled away into the storm] fled into a night of storm *K1* (*cancelled*).
372–5. the Baron . . . be-nightmared] Perhaps owing something to the night-
marish details, including coffins and coffin-worms, which alarm the festive
hunting party in Orcagna's 'The Triumph of Death' (see l. 5 *n* above).
373. warrior-guests] warrior sons *K1* (*cancelled*).
375–7. Angela the old . . . ashes cold]

> . . . Angela went off
> Twitch'd with the Palsy; and with face deform
> The beadsman stiffen'd, 'twixt a sigh and laugh
> Ta'en sudden from his beads by one weak little cough. *K2*.

See Woodhouse's Sept. 1819 letter to Taylor '[K.] has altered the last 3 lines
to leave on the reader a sense of pettish disgust, by bringing Old Angela in
dead stiff and ugly.—He says he likes that the poem should leave off with
this Change of Sentiment—it was what he aimed at, and was glad to find
from my objections to it that he had succeeded' (*L* ii 162–3). The revised
reading is at variance with the tone of the poem, but is in keeping with
some effects in *Lamia* (see headnote, p. 616 below) and with the satirical
temper of K.'s last poems, also written in Spenserian stanzas. See *The Cap
and Bells, In after-time, a sage* (pp. 701 and 742 below). Woodhouse's note,
'Altered 1820', refers to the printing of the original version in *1820*. Cp.
ll. 314–22 *n* above.
376. meagre face deform] The phrasing and use of 'deform' are Miltonic.
Perhaps owed to a half-conscious recollection of the vision of disease and
death afflicting mankind when Adam and Eve depart from Paradise,
Paradise Lost xi 480–92 (marked by him in his copy of Milton).

> The Beadsman, after thousand aves told,
> For ay unsought for slept among his ashes cold.

> . . . all maladies
> Of gastly Spasm, or racking torture, qualmes
> Of heart-sick Agonie, all feavorous kinds,
> Convulsions, Epilepsies, fierce Catarrhs,
> Intestin Stone and Ulcer, Colic pangs,
> Dropsies, and Asthma's and Joint-racking Rheums
>
> .   .   .
>
> Sight so deform what heart of Rock could long
> Drie-ey'd behold? . . .

The recollection would be in keeping with the movement of feeling towards the close of the poem.

378. K. closes with the effect of encompassing cold. The last word 'cold' picks up the coldness at the beginning of the poem and applies now to all the warmth of the lovers who fled 'ages long ago'.

117 The Eve of St. Mark

[Fragment]

Written 13–17 Feb. 1819 shortly after K.'s return from Chichester and Bedhampton: so dated by Woodhouse, whose transcript contains the extra lines (101–16) probably written by K. after 20 Sept. 1819; K. copied out the shorter version of the poem 20 Sept. in his Sept. 1819 journal-letter with the comment, 'Some time since I began a Poem call'd "the Eve of St. Mark" quite in the spirit of Town quietude. I think it will give you the sensation of walking about an old county Town in a coolish evening. I know not yet whether I shall ever finish it' (*L* ii 201). For D. G. Rossetti's speculation about K.'s plan for completing the poem in Aug. 1820 see l. 137 *n* below.

K.'s interest in the superstition concerning St. Mark's Eve may be owed to Mrs Isabella Jones, who suggested the subject of the preceding poem, *The Eve of St. Agnes*, also based on 'a popular superstition' (headnote p. 450 above). See the references to meeting Mrs Jones early Feb. 1819 in K.'s 14 Feb.–3 May journal-letter (*L* ii 65). For additional information about the superstition K. probably relied, as in his description of the rites of St. Agnes, on John Brand's *Popular Antiquities* (1813 edn), which records (166),

St. Mark's Day [*April the Twenty-fifth*] *or Eve*

'It is customary in Yorkshire, as a gentleman of that county informed me, for the common people to sit and watch in the church porch on St. Mark's Eve, from eleven o'clock at night till one in the morning. The third year (for this must be done thrice), they are supposed to see the ghosts of all those who are to die next year, pass by into the church. When anyone sickens that is thought to have been seen in this manner, it is presently whispered about that he will not recover, for that such, or such an one, who has watched St. Mark's Eve, says so.

'This superstition is in such force, that, if the patients themselves hear of it, they almost despair of recovery. Many are said to have actually died by their imaginary fears on the occasion; a truly lamentable, but by no means incredible, instance of human folly.'

K.'s 'spirit of Town quietude' in the poem reflects his impressions of Chichester; the pictorial details derive from recollections of Stansted Chapel near Bedhampton, with possibly some additional suggestions from the interior furnishings of Mrs Jones's rooms in London. For a detailed discussion of these influences see R. Gittings's 'St. Valentine and St. Mark', Gittings (1954) 83–92. K. probably intended *The Eve of St. Mark* as a companion to *The Eve of St. Agnes*, but its attempted imitation of Middle English brings it closer than *The Eve of St. Agnes* to Chaucer and Chatterton. K.'s use in the poem of octosyllabic couplets freely interspersed with sevensyllabled lines has several precedents in his early work (see headnote to *Fancy*, p. 441 above), but was probably influenced here by Coleridge's *Christabel* (1816), which also supplied some hints for *The Eve of St. Agnes*. Edward Thomas notes of *The Eve of St. Mark* in his *John Keats* (1916), 'It anticipates the pre-Raphaelites, but with a fresh early savour. It might have grown to a poem as much like "Christabel" as another poem could be' (59). Pre-Raphaelite admirers included D. G. Rossetti, who told H. Buxton Forman in his letter of 11 Feb. 1880, '[K.'s] unfinished poem is perhaps, with *La Belle Dame Sans Merci* [p. 500 below] . . . the chastest and choicest example of his maturing manner, and shows astonishingly real medievalism for one not bred as an artist' (*John Keats: Criticism and Comment*, 1919, 9). For some echoes and imitations of the poem in Rossetti and Morris see G. H. Ford, *Keats and the Victorians* (1944) 122–3, 132, 159.

Text from *Woodhouse 2*, with some variants noted from K.'s letter and the earlier draft (British Museum, except for ll. 101–16 of which the draft is in the Morgan Library).

Published *1848* (without ll. 101–16, which were first printed in the addenda to *de Selincourt*, 1926 edn).

> Upon a Sabbath day it fell;
> Twice holy was the Sabbath bell
> That called the folk to evening prayer.
> The city streets were clean and fair

¶ 117. *1*. It was on a twice holiday . . . *Draft (cancelled)*.
2 (and *13* below). *Twice*] Thrice *Letter*. 'Twice holy' because this Sunday is the vigil of St. Mark.

5   From wholesome drench of April rains,
    And, on the western window panes,
    The chilly sunset faintly told
    Of unmatured green valleys cold,
    Of the green thorny bloomless hedge,
10 Of rivers new with spring-tide sedge,
    Of primroses by sheltered rills,
    And daisies on the aguish hills.
    Twice holy was the Sabbath-bell;
    The silent streets were crowded well
15 With staid and pious companies,
    Warm from their fireside orat'ries,
    And moving with demurest air
    To even-song and vesper prayer.
    Each archèd porch and entry low
20 Was filled with patient folk and slow,
    With whispers hush and shuffling feet,
    While played the organ loud and sweet.

    The bells had ceased, the prayers begun,
    And Bertha had not yet half done
25 A curious volume patched and torn,

5. *Wholesome drench of April rains*] The feast-day was 25 April (see headnote).
K. is probably remembering in this line Chaucer's opening to *The Canter-bury Tales* 1–2,

> Whan that Aprille with his shoures sote
> The droghte of Marche hath perced to the rote . . .

8. *unmatured*] immatured *Letter.*

12. *aguish hills*] The cold hills are likely to give one ague, or perhaps the
grasses on the windy hills shiver as with an ague.

14–22. With the quiet atmosphere of the country town cp. K.'s picture of
the city of Corinth in *Lamia* i 352–61 (p. 632 below).

17. *moving*] pacing *Draft (cancelled).*

20. *folk*] crowd *Letter.*

22. *organ*] organs *Letter, Draft.*

24. *Bertha*] Birtha is the name of Chatterton's heroine in *Aella, a Tragic
Interlude* (1777). K. uses the name Bertha again in *The Cap and Bells* (p. 701
below).

25–38. The decorations in the 'curious volume'—notably the stars and
winged angels, the seven candlesticks and the Ark of the Covenant—were
suggested by the stained glass windows of Lewis Way's Stansted Chapel,
which K. visited when it was consecrated Jan. 1819 (see *The Eve of St.
Agnes* 145 *n*, p. 462 above). For a detailed description and photograph of
the windows see *Gittings* (1954) 87–9. Way's self-appointed mission to
convert the Jews explains the biblical symbolism in his design for the
chapel windows.

That all day long from earliest morn
Had taken captive her two eyes
Among its golden broideries,
Perplexed her with a thousand things—
30 The stars of Heaven and angels' wings,
Martyrs in a fiery blaze,
Azure saints 'mid silver rays,
Aaron's breast plate, and the seven
Candlesticks John saw in heaven,
35 The wingèd Lion of Saint Mark,
And the Covenantal Ark
With its many mysteries,
Cherubim and golden mice.

Bertha was a maiden fair,
40 Dwelling in the old Minster Square;
From her fireside she could see,
Sidelong, its rich antiquity
Far as the Bishop's garden-wall,
Where sycamores and elm-trees tall,
45 Full-leaved, the forest had outstripped,

28. golden broideries] K. is thinking of the illuminated MS.

31-2. Silver rays of light and a burning brazier appear in the Stansted Chapel windows.

33. Aaron's breastplate] Moses's breastplate *1848*, *Woodhouse* 2 (marginally). The breastplate, worn by the high priest of the Israelites, was a square of rich embroidery, folded to contain the Urim and Thummim and set with precious stones, each engraved with one of the names of the tribes of Israel. Aaron's investiture with the breastplate by Moses is recorded in *Leviticus* viii 8.

33-4. seven Candlesticks . . . heaven] See *Revelation* i 20: 'The seven stars are the angels of the seven churches: and the seven candlesticks which thou sawest are the seven churches. . . .'

35. The lion as a traditional emblem of St. Mark derives from the apocalyptic vision in *Revelation* iv 6-9 of the four winged beasts before the throne of God, one of which was shaped like a lion.

36-7. See *Hebrews* ix 4-5: '. . . the ark of the covenant overlaid round about with gold, wherein was the golden pot that had manna, and Aaron's rod that budded and the tables of the covenant. And over it the cherubims of glory shadowing the mercy seat.'

38. golden mice] Five golden mice were sent by the Philistines as a trespass offering when returning the Ark of the Covenant to the Israelites (I *Samuel* vi 4).

45. the forest had outstripped] Come earlier into leaf than trees in the forest.

By no sharp north-wind ever nipped,
So sheltered by the mighty pile.
Bertha arose and read awhile
With forehead 'gainst the window-pane.
50   Again she tried, and then again,
Until the dusk eve left her dark
Upon the legend of St. Mark.
From pleated lawn-frill, fine and thin,
She lifted up her soft warm chin,
55   With aching neck and swimming eyes,
And dazed with saintly imageries.

All was gloom, and silent all,
Save now and then the still foot-fall
Of one returning homewards late,
60   Past the echoing Minster gate.

The clamorous daws, that all the day
Above tree tops and towers play,
Pair by pair had gone to rest,
Each in its ancient belfry nest,
65   Where asleep they fall betimes
To music of the drowsy chimes.

All was silent, all was gloom,
Abroad and in the homely room.
The maiden, lost in dizzy maze,
70   Turned to the fire and made a blaze;
Down she sat, poor cheated soul,
And struck a lamp from the dismal coal,

53. *pleated*] wide *Draft* (*cancelled*). *Woodhouse* 2 has the marginal note
'plaited'. See 120 *n* below.
56. *imageries*] Pictures. Cp. *The Eve of St. Agnes* 209 (p. 466 above), 'garlanded with carven imageries'.
57 (and 67 below). The repetitions suggest the influence of Coleridge's
Christabel (1816). Cp. *The Eve of St. Agnes* 357 *n* (p. 478 above).
61–6. See *Gittings* (1954). 'In the poem the beauty of old Chichester still
lives, as some of its surrounding circumstances do to this day – the jackdaws
that still nest in the separate bell-tower of the Cathedral . . . the echoing
steps which still ring out under the hollow arch . . .' (90).
63. Were gone long ago *Draft* (*cancelled*).
69–70. Omitted in the letter.
71. *poor cheated soul*] Bertha is deprived of the pleasure of reading by the
fading light – see ll. 48–52 above.
72.   And struck a swart lamp from the coal . . . *Letter*.

Leaned forward, with bright drooping hair,
And slant book full against the glare.
75 Her shadow, in uneasy guise,
Hovered about, a giant's size,
On ceiling beam and old oak chair,
The parrot's cage and panel square,
And the warm angled winter screen
80 On which were many monsters seen
Called doves of Siam, Lima mice,
And legless birds of Paradise,
Macaw and tender Av'davat,
And silken-furred Angora cat.
85 Untired she read, her shadow still
Glowered about, as it would fill
The room with wildest forms and shades;
As though some ghostly queen of spades
Had come to mock behind her back
90 And dance and ruffle her garments black.
Untired she read the legend page
Of holy Mark from youth to age,
On land, on sea, in pagan chains,
Rejoicing for his many pains.
95 Sometimes the learned eremite
With golden star or dagger bright
Referred to pious poesies

79–84. The screen is a modern detail, but the date of the setting of the poem is left vague. This appears to be a Coromandel screen (made in China seventeenth to nineteenth centuries) with exotic oriental motifs romantically appreciated by K., but see *Gittings* (1954) 90–1, for the view that K. is describing a screen in Mrs Jones's sitting-room and that the 'Lima mice' are really Lemur mice, small native mammals native to Madagascar. Note the 'parrot's cage' in l. 78 above and K.'s reference to Mrs Jones's parrot in his description of her room in his Sept. 1818 journal-letter (quoted in *Fragment of the 'Castle-builder'* 25–69 n, p. 391 above).

81.   Java Pheasants, Doves of Siam . . . *Draft* (*cancelled*).

83. *Av'davat*] The Avadavat or Amadavat is an Indian song bird.

88–9. The Queen of Spades is the death card.

91–4. Little is known of the life of St. Mark, author of the Second Gospel, but as an evangelist he became the subject of numerous legends; his death and burial at Alexandria are first found in St. Jerome (*c.* 342–420), who also claims that he was martyred.

95. *eremite*] For K.'s use of this word see *The Eve of St. Agnes* 277 n (p. 471 above).

96. *star . . . dagger*] Conventional signs used to indicate footnotes.

17+K.

Written in smallest crow-quill size
Beneath the text; and thus the rhyme
100   Was parcelled out from time to time:
'Gif ye wol stonden, hardie wight,
Amiddës of the blackë night,
Righte in the churchë porch, pardie,
Ye wol behold a companie
105   Approchen thee full dolourouse.
For sooth to sain, from everich house,
Be it in city or village,
Wol come the phantom and image
Of ilka gent and ilka carle,
110   Whom coldë Deathë hath in parle,
And wol some day that very year
Touchen with foulë venime spear,
And sadly do them all to die:
Hem all shalt thou see verilie.
115   And everichon shall by thee pass,
All who must die that year, alas...

98. *crow-quill*] Used for very fine writing.

101–16. Written out in *Woodhouse* 2 as an additional fragment at the end of the poem. K. may have intended to incorporate the lines later in the narrative. Their insertion here follows Garrod's arrangement, which is probably justified by the effect of continuity with ll. 117–32. K. breaks off at l. 100 in his Sept. 1819 journal-letter and resumes at l. 117 after commenting 'What follows [ll. 117–32] is an imitation of the Authors in Chaucer's time–'tis more ancient than Chaucer himself and perhaps between him and Gower' (*L* ii 204). K.'s 'imitation' owes most to Chatterton's 'medieval' poems, but was doubtless also affected by his reading of Chaucer and of George Ellis's *Early English Metrical Romances* (1805). For details of the superstition see headnote. See also 137 *n* below.

103. *Righte*] Full *Draft (cancelled)*.

105. *Approchen*] Garrod reads 'Appouchen', but this is obviously a slip of the pen in K.'s holograph of the lines in the Morgan Library.

108. *Phantom*] Feature *Draft (cancelled)*.

109. *carle*] Common fellow, churl.

110. *in parle*] At his mercy. The word normally means to discourse or hold in parley: so used by K. in *He is to weet a melancholy carle* 3 (p. 497 below) and *Ode* ['Bards of passion'] 8 (p. 446 above).

114. Followed in the draft by the cancelled attempts
1. And shall passe thee beside
2. The [e ?] in the dark

115–16.   And everichon shall ny thee go
Truly mine Auctour sayeth so ... *Draft (cancelled)*.

Als writith he of swevenis
Men han beforne they wake in blis,
Whanne that hir friendës thinke hem bound
120 In crimpede shroude farre under grounde;
And how a litling childe mote be
A saint er its nativitie,
Gif that the modre (God her blesse!)
Kepen in solitarinesse,
125 And kissen devoute the holy croce.
Of Goddis love, and Sathan's force,
He writith; and thinges many mo.
Of swichë thinges I may not show.
Bot I must tellen verilie
130 Somdel of Saintë Cicilie,
And chieflie what he auctorith
Of Saintë Markis life and dethe.'

At length her constant eye had come
Upon the fervent martyrdom,
135 Then lastly to his holy shrine,
Exalt amid the tapers' shine
At Venice . . .

117. *Swevenis*] Dreams.
120. *crimpede*] To crimp is to compress or pinch into minute parallel plaits or folds (*OED*).
124. *solitarinesse*] Frequently in Burton, who has a section 'Solitariness' in his *Anatomy of Melancholy* I 3 i 2. K. quotes the line in his letter to Reynolds of 21 Sept. 1819, 'I "kepen in solitarinesse" . . . I am surprised myself at the pleasure I live alone in' (*L* ii 166). Later in this letter K. refers to Chatterton as 'The purest writer in the English language'.
130. *Saintë*] Scainte *Letter*. Chaucer had told the legend of 'Seint Cecilie' in the *Second Nonne's Tale*.
131. *auctorith*] Writes. A coinage derived from the archaism 'auctor' (cp. K.'s 'Auctor' in ll. 115–16 *n* above).
135. *his holy shrine*] At St. Mark's, Venice.
137. D. G. Rossetti suspected that K. was considering the completion of the poem in his letter to Fanny Brawne of Aug. 1820, 'I could write a Poem which I have in my head, which . . . would show some one in Love as I am, with a person living in such Liberty as you do' (*L* ii 312). See Rossetti's letter to H. B. Forman of 9 May 1880, 'I judge that the heroine–remorseful after trifling with a sick and now absent lover–might make her way to the minster porch to learn his fate by the spell, and perhaps see his figure enter but not return. Watts [Theodore Watts-Dunton (1832–1914)], to whom I showed this passage [from K.'s letter] . . . was at once convinced of the great probability' (*John Keats: Criticism and Comment*, 1919, 13–14).

118 'Why did I laugh to-night?'

Written before 19 March 1819, the date of its inclusion in K.'s journal-
letter of 14 Feb.–3 May 1819, and possibly shortly before 8 March from the
parallel between a phrase in K.'s letter of this date to Haydon and l. 7 of the
poem (see *n* below). The journal-letter has the following comments, 'I did
not intend to have sent you the following sonnet . . . it was written with no
Agony but that of ignorance; with no thirst of any thing but knowledge
. . . the first steps to it were through my human passions–they went away,
and I wrote with my Mind–and perhaps I must confess a little bit of my
heart. . . . I went to bed, and enjoyed an uninterupted sleep–Sane I went
to bed and sane I arose' (*L* ii 81–2).
Text from K.'s letter.
Published *1848*.

      Why did I laugh to-night? No voice will tell;
         No God, no Demon of severe response,
      Deigns to reply from Heaven or from Hell.
         Then to my human heart I turn at once—
5   Heart, thou and I are here sad and alone;
         Say wherefore did I laugh? Oh, mortal pain!
      Oh, darkness, darkness! Ever must I moan,
         To question Heaven and Hell and Heart in vain!
      Why did I laugh? I know this being's lease
10   My fancy to its utmost blisses spreads;
      Yet could I on this very midnight cease,
         And the world's gaudy ensigns see in shreds.

¶ 118. *6. mortal*] Human. In *1848* the line begins, 'I say, why did I
laugh . . .'.
7. Oh, darkness, darkness!] Cp. K.'s letter to Haydon of 8 March 1819 in
which he resolves 'never to write for the sake of writing . . . I will not spoil
my love of gloom by writing an ode to darkness' (*L* ii 43). The repetitions
suggest an echo of Milton's *Samson Agonistes* 80–1, quoted in *Hyperion* iii
86–7 *n* (p. 438 above).
9–10. K.'s imaginative grasp of all that life has to offer does not make him
less despondent. The phrase 'this being's lease' means 'the terms on which I
hold the lease of life'. Cp. *Mabeth* IV i 98–100,

                                                    . . . Macbeth
              Shall live the lease of nature, pay his breath
              To time and mortal custom . . .
11. Foreshadowing *Ode to a Nightingale* 56 (p. 529 below),
                    To cease upon the midnight . . .
For 'could' *1848* reads 'would'.
12. ensigns] Banners.

Verse, fame, and beauty are intense indeed,
But Death's intenser–Death is Life's high meed.

14. Death's intenser] Death intenser *1848*.

119 'Shed no tear–oh, shed no tear'

Date of composition unknown, but probably before 15 April 1819 when K.
wrote *When they were come unto the Fairy's court* (p. 491 below), which seems
to be indebted to Brown's unpublished and unfinished fairy-story, 'The
Fairies' Triumph' for which this song was written: see Brown's note
attached to K.'s holograph MS, 'A faery Song–written for a particular purpose at the request of C.B.'. Brown copied out the poem at the end of chap.
4 of 'The Fairies' Triumph' in his MS Notebook at Hampstead and also
preserved the poem in a second transcript (used in *1848*). Brown's story relates the trials visited by King Boulimar, with the help of his Dwarf Glob-
dod and the Dwarf's companion the Ape, upon King Pensarvan of Cordi-
land and members of Pensarvan's family, including the Princess Floramente
and the Princes Elmy, Azameth and Selrik. The song refers to events following the Princess's disappearance while in captivity to King Boulimar.
The drift of Brown's story indicates that King Boulimar will eventually be
frustrated by good fairies, represented in the present poem by the singing
bird. Chap. 4 of 'The Fairies' Triumph' ends with the grief of Elmy and
Azameth when the flower, Hope's Love, into which their brother Selrik
has been magically transformed, shrivels into dust as they pluck it, '. . . neither could find words which might console the other, they stood there like
statues of grief. At length immediately above their heads they heard a most
enchanting melody breathed forth; and looking up they saw, perched upon
a slender bough, a bird of lovely form and brilliant plumage, and it gazed
down on them with its mild dove-like eyes, and warbled its song to them'.
For a commentary on the poem, including further details of Brown's story,
see J. Stillinger's 'The Context of Keats's "Fairy Song"', *KShJ* x (1961) 6–8.
Text from K.'s MS with the variant in l. 7 noted from Brown's Notebook
copy. A facsimile of K.'s MS appears as the frontispiece in *1848* ii.
Published *Plymouth and Devonport Weekly Journal* 18 Oct. 1838 and *1848*.

> Shed no tear–oh, shed no tear!
> The flower will bloom another year;
> Weep no more–oh, weep no more!
> Young buds sleep in the root's white core.
> 5 Dry your eyes–oh, dry your eyes!
> For I was taught in Paradise

¶ 119. *Title.* Fairy's Song *1848*; Fairy Bird's Song *Plymouth and Devonport
Weekly Journal*.

To ease my breast of melodies—
        Shed no tear.

Overhead, look overhead
10 'Mong the blossoms white and red.
Look up, look up—I flutter now
On this flush pomegranate bough.
See me—'tis this silvery bill
Ever cures the good man's ill.
15 Shed no tear—oh, shed no tear!
The flower will bloom another year.
Adieu, adieu—I fly, adieu,
I vanish in the heaven's blue.
        Adieu, adieu!

7. *my breast of*] the heart in *Brown's MS.*
17–19. D. G. Rossetti noted a parallel with Glycine's reference to the bird's song in Coleridge's *Zapolya* (1817) Part II, II ii 74–81,

              . . . Adieu! adieu!
      Love's dreams prove seldom true.
      The blossoms they make no delay:
      The sparkling dew-drops will not stay.
              Sweet month of May,
                  We must away;
                  Far, far away!
                  To-day! to-day!

See S. Milner's 'On some marginalia made by D. G. Rossetti, in a copy of Keats's Poems', *The Manchester Quarterly* V, Jan. 1883, 7.
19. After copying out the poem in 'The Fairies' Triumph' Brown takes up the narrative in the next chapter, beginning, 'Our youths were awakened from their trance of sleep by this song . . .'

120 'Ah, woe is me, poor silver-wing'

Probably written before 15 April 1819 with the preceding poem *Shed no tear* (No. 119 above) for Brown's 'The Fairies' Triumph'. The consoling singer in the poem may be one of the good fairies in Brown's story and the lady may be Princess Floramente.
Text from Brown's transcript (used in 1848).
Published *Plymouth and Devonport Weekly Journal* 18 Oct. 1838 (Brown sent several poems by K. to this periodical) and *1848*.

    Ah, woe is me, poor silver-wing,
        That I must chant thy lady's dirge,

¶ 120. *Title*] Faery Song *Brown*; Faery Dirge *Plymouth and Devonport Journal*.

And death to this fair haunt of spring,
    Of melody, and streams of flowery verge.
5 Poor silver-wing! Ah, woe is me!
      That I must see
These blossoms snow upon thy lady's pall!
    Go, pretty page, and in her ear
    Whisper that the hour is near!
10   Softly tell her not to fear
Such calm Favonian burial!
    Go, pretty page, and soothly tell.
    The blossoms hang by a melting spell,
And fall they must, ere a star wink thrice
15   Upon her closèd eyes,
That now in vain are weeping their last tears,
    At sweet life leaving and these arbours green –
Rich dowry from the spirit of the spheres.
      Alas, poor queen!

1. *poor silver-wing*] The fairy page of the unknown lady.
11. *Favonian*] Gentle. Favonius is the west wind.
12. *soothly*] Truly.

121 'When they were come unto the Fairy's court'

Written 15 April 1819, as an unfinished comic narrative: see under this date in K.'s 14 Feb.–3 May 1819 journal-letter where it appears with the prefatory comment, 'Shall I treat you with a little extempore' (*L* ii 85). The princess, dwarf and ape in the poem may have been suggested by characters in Brown's fairy-story, 'The Fairies' Triumph', for which K. wrote *Shed no tear* (p. 489 above). The poem was probably intended as a humorous fantasy with satirical touches in Brown's manner; see his versified satirical version of 'The Fairies' Triumph' in his notebook at Hampstead. For the view – possible, though not finally convincing – that the poem was meant as a family joke, with the ape and princess as George and Georgiana Keats and the fool and dwarf as Tom Keats and K. see *Gittings* (1954) 107–9. F. Page argues less probably (*Dublin Review* cci (1937) 97–9) that K., represented by the dwarf, is weighing his poetic conscience and that the princess is poetry, the ape Wordsworth and the fool Coleridge. For the suggestion that K. may have been remembering 'The Mule without a Bridle' in G. L. Way's translation (1796) of Le Grand's *Fabliaux* see Phyllis Mann, 'Keats's

Reading', *Keats-Shelley Memorial Bulletin* xiii (1962) 41–3. K.'s use of heroic
couplets hints at his recent reading of Dryden. For further evidence of K.'s
interest in Dryden in 1819 see headnotes to *Fame like a wayward girl* and
Lamia (pp. 512 and 613 below).
Text from K.'s letter.
Published *Macmillan's Magazine* August 1888; in full *Forman* (1890).

When they were come unto the Fairy's Court
They rang—no one at home; all gone to sport
And dance and kiss and love as fairies do,
For fairies be as humans, lovers true.
5 Amid the woods they were, so lone and wild,
Where even the robin feels himself exiled
And where the very brooks as if afraid
Hurry along to some less magic shade.
'No one at home!' the fretful princess cried,
10 'And all for nothing such a dreary ride,
And all for nothing my new diamond cross,
No one to see my Persian feathers toss,
No one to see my ape, my dwarf, my fool,
Or how I pace my Otaheitan mule.
15 Ape, dwarf and fool, why stand you gaping there?
Burst the door open, quick—or I declare
I'll switch you soundly and in pieces tear.'
The Dwarf began to tremble and the Ape
Stared at the Fool, the Fool was all agape,
20 The Princess grasped her switch, but just in time
The dwarf with piteous face began to rhyme.
'O mighty Princess, did you ne'er hear tell
What your poor servants know but too, too well?
Know you the three 'great crimes' in fairy land?
25 The first—alas, poor Dwarf!—I understand:
I made a whipstock of a fairy's wand.
The next is snoring in their company.
The next, the last, the direst of the three,
Is making free when they are not at home.
30 I was a Prince, a baby prince—my doom

¶ 121. *12. Persian feathers*] Headdresses made like oriental turbans and
decorated with feathers were fashionable wear for ladies at the time.
'Persian' here may mean outlandish. See Horace's *Odes* I 38 1,

Persicos odi, puer, apparatus . . .

('Persian elegance, my lad, I hate' [Loeb edn]). On K. and Horace see *Ode
to a Nightingale* 1–4 *n* and 36 *n* (pp. 524–5 and 527–8 below).
14. Otaheitan] Tahiti was in the news because of the activities of the London
Missionary Society. Pomare II, King of Tahiti, became a Christian in 1812.
See l. 79 below, 'O King of Otaheitè . . .'.

You see—I made a whipstock of a wand.
My top has henceforth slept in fairy land.
He was a Prince, the Fool, a grown-up Prince,
But he has never been a King's son since
35   He fell a-snoring at a fairy Ball.
Your poor Ape was a Prince and he, poor thing,
Picklocked a fairy's boudoir—now no king,
But ape. So pray your highness stay awhile;
'Tis sooth indeed, we know it to our sorrow—
40   Persist and *you* may be an ape to-morrow.'
While the Dwarf spake the Princess all for spite
Peeled the brown hazel twig to lily white,
Clenched her small teeth, and held her lips apart,
Tried to look unconcerned with beating heart.
45   They saw her Highness had made up her mind,
A-quavering like three reeds before the wind—
And they had had it, but—oh, happy chance!—
The Ape for very fear began to dance
And grinned as all his ugliness did ache.
50   She stayed her vixen fingers for his sake,
He was so very ugly; then she took
Her pocket mirror and began to look
First at herself and then at him and then
She smiled at her own beauteous face again.
55   Yet for all this, for all her pretty face,
She took it in her head to see the place.
Women gain little from experience
Either in lovers, husbands or expense.
The more the beauty, the more fortune too,
60   Beauty before the wide world never knew—
So each Fair reasons, though it oft miscarries.
She thought *her* pretty face would please the fairies.
'My darling Ape, I won't whip you to-day—
Give me the picklock, sirrah, and go play.'
65   They all three wept—but counsel was as vain
As crying 'C'up, biddy' to drops of rain.

33–5. R. Gittings's suggestion that this is an allusion to Tom Keats's early death is difficult to accept.

46. A-quavering] Earlier attempts were 'They quaver'd . . .' and 'And quavered . . .'.

47. they had had it] They would have been whipped.

53. and then at him] at him *K.'s letter*. The reading follows Garrod's emendation.

66. As telling the rain to stop. 'C'up biddy' (Come up, biddy) follows Garrod's correction of 'cup biddy' in K.'s letter.

17*

Yet lingeringly did the sad Ape forth draw
The picklock from the pocket in his jaw.
The Princess took it and, dismounting straight,
70   Tripped in blue silvered slippers to the gate
And touched the wards; the door full courteously
Opened—she entered with her servants three.
Again it closed and there was nothing seen
But the mule grazing on the herbage green.

End of Canto xii

Canto the xiii

75   The mule no sooner saw himself alone
Than he pricked up his ears and said, 'Well done;
At least, unhappy Prince, I may be free—
No more a Princess shall side-saddle me.
O King of Otaheitè—though a Mule,
80   "Aye every inch a King"; though "Fortune's fool",
Well done—for by what Mr. Dwarfy said
I would not give a sixpence for her head.'
Even as he spake he trotted in high glee
To the knotty side of an old pollard tree
85   And rubbed his sides against the mossèd bark
Till his girths burst and left him naked stark
Except his bridle—how get rid of that,
Buckled and tied with many a twist and plait?
At last it struck him to pretend to sleep
90   And then the thievish monkeys down would creep
And filch the unpleasant trammels quite away.
No sooner thought of than adown he lay,

67–8. K. may be remembering *Hamlet* IV ii 17–19, 'such officers do the king best service in the end: he keeps them, like an ape, in the corner of his jaw . . .'.

71. *touched the wards*] Possibly recollected from Cary's *Dante, Inferno* xiii 60–2, quoted in *To Sleep* 13 *n* (p. 512 below).

74. See Wordsworth's *The White Doe of Rylstone* (1815) 973–4,

The same who quietly was feeding
On the green herb, and nothing heeding . . .

80. The mule is quoting *King Lear* IV vi 108 and *Romeo and Juliet* III i 135.

90 (and 93 below). For the view that K.'s reference to Otaheite recalled to him Captain Cook's descriptions of the Tahitians' adroit thievishness see A. D. Atkinson *N and Q* 4 Aug. (1951) 383. K. refers to monkeys on 16 April in his journal-letter, '. . . now you might easily distill some whiskey—and going into the woods set up a whiskey shop for the Monkeys' (*L* ii 92).

Shammed a good snore–the Monkey-men descended
And whom they thought to injure they befriended.
95   Thy hung his bridle on a topmost bough,
And off he went, run, trot, or anyhow ...

96. K. comments in his journal-letter, after breaking off the line, 'Brown is gone to bed–and I am tried of rhyming' (*L* ii 88).

122   'The House of Mourning written by Mr. Scott'

Date uncertain, but perhaps mid–April 1819 as an extempore *jeu d'esprit* in the light-hearted style of the preceding and the following poem: some support for the date is found in the personal allusions in ll. 8–14 (see the notes below). The sonnet is aimed at and partly parodies Wordsworth's catalogue of delights in his *Composed in the Valley near Dover, on the Day of Landing* (1807). R. Gittings suggests that ll. 1–7 may have been written by Woodhouse as reflecting 'the special hates of ... a publisher's reader, as Woodhouse was' (*Gittings* (1954) 112). The poem is preserved in Woodhouse's transcript in *Woodhouse* 3 (reproduced *Finney* 652), from which the text is taken.
Published *Finney* (1936).

The House of Mourning written by Mr. Scott,
   A sermon at the Magdalen, a tear
   Dropped on a greasy novel, want of cheer
After a walk uphill to a friend's cot,
5   Tea with a maiden lady, a cursed lot
   Of worthy poems with the author near,
   A patron lord, a drunkenness from beer,

¶ 122. *1.* John Scott's *The House of Mourning: A Poem; with some smaller pieces* was published 1817 by Taylor and Hessey.
2. the Magdalen] Magdalen Hospital, a home for reformed prostitutes, was instituted 1758 and situated 1772–1863 in St George's Fields at the south end of Blackfriars Road, London.
2–3. a tear ... novel] Cp. K.'s satire on fashionable romantic taste in *Pensive they sit* (p. 649 below).
4. uphill] Suggesting the steep streets and paths at Hampstead.
5–6. a cursed lot ... near] Gittings conjectures an allusion to unsold copies of John Scott's book lying on the shelves at Taylor and Hessey's publishing house (*Gittings* (1954) 112).
7. drunkenness from beer] K. preferred wine.

> Haydon's great picture, a cold coffee pot
> At midnight when the muse is ripe for labour,
> 10   The voice of Mr. Coleridge, a French bonnet
> Before you in the pit, a pipe and tabour,
> A damned inseparable flute and neighbour—
>   All these are vile. But viler Wordsworth's sonnet
> On Dover. Dover! Who *could* write upon it?

8. Haydon's great picture] 'Christ's triumphal entry into Jerusalem'. K. refers to Haydon's 'little progress' with this painting on 15 April in his Feb.–May 1819 journal-letter (*L* ii 83). K.'s feelings for Haydon were probably soured by the latter's recent demands for money—see K.'s 13 April 1819 letter in reply, 'I am doubly hurt at the slightly reproachful tone of your note and at the occasion of it' (*L* ii 55).

10. The voice of Mr. Coleridge] Cp. K.'s account of his meeting with Coleridge on Hampstead Heath 11 April 1819, 'I heard his voice as he came towards me—I heard it as he moved away—I had heard it all the interval' (*L* ii 89). See headnote to *Ode to a Nightingale* (p. 524 below).

11. a pipe . . . and tabour] Perhaps alluding to Brown's noisy nephews who were staying at Wentworth Place. See under 15 April in K.'s Feb.–May 1819 journal-letter, '. . . we have had the Boys here lately—they make a bit of a racket—I shall not be sorry when they go' (*L* ii 83).

13–14. See headnote. K. may have passed through Dover when travelling from the Isle of Wight to Margate in April 1817.

123 'He is to weet a melancholy carle'

Written 16 April 1819 as an ironical extempore encomium on Brown: see under this date in K.'s 14 Feb.–3 May journal-letter, 'Brown this morning is writing some spenserian stanzas against Mrs Miss Brawne and me; so I shall amuse myself with him a little: in the manner of Spenser' (*L* ii 89). The Brawnes moved in next door to K. and Brown at Wentworth Place in Hampstead 3 April 1819. The verses are probably modelled on Wordsworth's poem in Spenserians on himself and Coleridge, published 1815 under the heading, 'Written in my pocket-copy of Thomson's *Castle of Indolence*' and beginning 'Within our happy Castle there dwelt One . . .' Text from K.'s letter.
Published *1848*.

I

> He is to weet a melancholy carle:
> Thin in the waist, with bushy head of hair,

¶ *123. 1. Carle*] Churl. Cp. *The Eve of St. Mark* 109 (p. 486 above), 'ilka gent and ilka carle'.

As hath the seeded thistle when in parle
It holds the Zephyr, ere it sendeth fair
5   Its light balloons into the summer air;
Thereto his beard had not begun to bloom,
No brush had touched his chin or razor sheer;
No care had touched his cheek with mortal doom,
But new he was and bright as scarf from Persian loom.

II

10   Ne cared he for wine, or half-and-half,
Ne cared he for fish or flesh or fowl,
And sauces held he worthless as the chaff.
He 'sdained the swine-head at the wassail-bowl,
Ne with lewd ribbalds sat he cheek by jowl,
15   Ne with sly lemans in the scorner's chair,
But after water-brooks this pilgrim's soul
Panted, and all his food was woodland air
Though he would oft-times feast on gilliflowers rare.

III

The slang of cities in no wise he knew,
20   *Tipping the wink* to him was heathen Greek.

3. parle] Discourse. K. uses the same rhyme in *The Eve of St. Mark* 110 (p. 486 above).

9. Persian] Cp. K.'s reference to 'Persian feathers' in *When they were come unto the Fairy's court* 12 and see *n* (p. 492 above).

10. half-and-half] A mixture of light and dark ale.

13. 'sdained] scorn'd *Letter (cancelled)*.

14. lewd ribalds] Echoing *The Faerie Queene* II i 10,

    When that lewd ribauld with vile lust advaunst . . .

15. sly lemans . . . in the scorner's chair] Echoes *The Faerie Queene* VI viii 21,

    Thus I triumphed long in lovers paine,
    And sitting carelesse on the scorners stoole,
    Did laugh at those that did lament and plaine . . .

('lemans' means lovers). Brown's stanzas may have contained joking references to some attachment between K. and Fanny Brawne (Brown was kept in ignorance of their real feelings until 1820). On Browne's flirtatiousness see K.'s comments in his July 1820 letter to Fanny Brawne, 'When you were in the habit of flirting with Brown you would have left off, could your own heart have felt one half of one pang mine did . . . [he] did not know he was doing me to death by inches' (*L* ii 303).

16–17. after water-brooks . . . Panted] *Psalms* xlii 1: 'As the hart panteth after the water brooks, so panteth my soul after thee, O God.'

18. gilliflowers] Sweet scented flowers.

20. Tipping the wink] Slang for giving a private signal.

He sipped no olden Tom or ruin blue,
Or nantz or cheery-brandy drank full meek
By many a damsel hoarse and rouge of cheek.
Nor did he know each agèd watchman's beat,
25   Nor in obscured purlieus would he seek
For curlèd Jewesses with ankles neat,
Who as they walk abroad make tinkling with their feet.

21. *olden Tom or ruin blue*] Different terms for gin. Blue ruin was the current slang for cheap gin.
22. *cheery*] Garrod reads 'cherry', but the pun was probably intended; 'nantz' is brandy (derived from Nantes, one of the towns in France where it is made).
24. Playing practical jokes on the London watchmen, or 'Charlies', was a favourite past-time of young bucks on their way home after a night's drinking; see, for example, Tom and Jerry in Pierce Egan's *Life in London* (1821).
26–7. See *Isaiah* iii 6: 'The daughters of Zion . . . walking and mincing as they go, and making a tinkling with their feet.' K. marked Burton's quotation of this passage in his copy of Burton's *Anatomy of Melancholy* (1813 edn ii 245).

124 'As Hermes once took to his feathers light'

Written *c.* 16 April 1819 after reading Cary's *Dante, Inferno* v: see under 16 April in K.'s 14 Feb–3 May 1819 journal-letter, 'The fifth canto of Dante pleases me more and more–it is that one in which he meets with Paulo [sic] and Francesca–I had passed many days in rather a low state of mind and in the midst of them I dreamt of being in that region of Hell. The dream was one of the most delightful enjoyments I ever had in my life–I floated about the whirling atmosphere as it is described with a beautiful figure to whose lips mine were joined as it seem'd for an age–and in the midst of all this cold and darkness I was warm–even flowery tree tops sprung up and we rested on them sometimes with the lightness of a cloud till the wind blew us away again–I tried a Sonnet upon it–there are fourteen lines but nothing of what I felt in it–o that I could dream it every night' (*L* ii 91). The poem is associated emotionally with Fanny Brawne. K.'s draft appears in *Inferno* i of his gift copy to her of Cary's *Dante* (Ashley Library), which also contains her transcript of the *Bright star* sonnet (p. 736 below). D. G. Rossetti thought *As Hermes once* 'By far the finest of [K.'s] sonnets . . . besides that on Chapman's Homer' (letter of 11 Feb. 1880, *John Keats: Criticism and Comment*, 1919, 6).
Text from K.'s letter (referred to in the notes as *L*), with some variants noted from his draft and from the faulty version in *The Indicator*.
Published *The Indicator* 28 June 1820 (signed 'Caviare') and *1848*.

As Hermes once took to his feathers light,
   When lullèd Argus, baffled, swooned and slept,
So on a Delphic reed, my idle sprite
   So played, so charmed, so conquered, so bereft
5 The dragon-world of all its hundred eyes;
   And, seeing it asleep, so fled away—
Not to pure Ida with its snow-cold skies,
   Nor unto Tempe where Jove grieved that day;

¶ 124. *Title.* A dream, after reading Dante's Episode of Paolo and Francesca *Indicator*; On a dream *Charles Brown's transcript.*
1. Preceded in the draft by the cancelled lines,

> Full in the midst of bloomless hours my spright [soul *cancelled*].
> Seeing one night the dragon world asleep
> Arose like Hermes . . .

1–2. Hermes rescued Io, the nymph beloved by Jupiter, by lulling to sleep with his music her hundred-eyed guardian Argus. The legend is related in Ovid's *Metamorphoses* i 668–720.
3–5. K. means that poetry allayed his anxieties about everyday-life; that he stayed up reading it until other people were asleep; and that once they were asleep he was free from the sense of being spied upon and escaped on the wings of his imagination. Cp. his June 1820 letter to Fanny Brawne, 'My friends have behaved well to me in every instance but one . . . they have become tattlers, and inquisitors into my conduct: spying on a secret I would rather die than share. . . . Good gods what a shame it is our loves should be so put into the microscope of a Coterie' (*L* ii 292–3). The phrasing suggests a recollection of *Paradise Lost* xi 129–3 (marked by K. in his copy of Milton),

>   . . . all thir shape
> Spangl'd with eyes more numerous then those
> Of *Argus,* and more wakeful than to drouze,
> Charm'd with *Arcadian* Pipe, the Pastoral Reed
> Of *Hermes,* or his opiate Rod . . .

4. Cp. the arrangement of epithets in *Endymion* ii 685 (p. 192 above),

>   So sad, so melancholy, so bereft . . .

Rossetti noted this parallel and also 'the singular defect' of a misrhyme [ll. 3/5 above, "slept/bereft"]' (*John Keats: Criticism and Comment* 6).
7. Snow-cold] Snow-clad *L* (*cancelled*). The *Indicator* reading 'unto' for 'to' (probably a misprint) makes the line hypermetrical. On Ida, the mountain near Troy, see *Endymion* ii 761 *n.* (p. 195 above). K.'s first attempt at the line in his draft was

>   But not olympus-ward to serene skies . . .

8. that] a *Indicator.* Tempe was Io's home in Thessaly. Ovid refers to Jove's distress when he lost Io (*Metamorphoses* i 615–21), but sets Jove's union with Io in Arcadia. K. may be thinking of Ovid's earlier description of Io's grief-stricken father Inachus (*Metamorphoses* i 583–7).

But to that second circle of sad hell,
10   Where in the gust, the whirlwind, and the flaw
Of rain and hail-stones, lovers need not tell
     Their sorrows. Pale were the sweet lips I saw,
Pale were the lips I kissed, and fair the form
I floated with, about that melancholy storm.

9–11. But to that . . . hailstones] K. conflates details from the second and
third circles of hell in Cary's *Dante*, *Inferno* v 32–4,

> . . . The stormy blast of hell
> With restless fury drives the spirits on
> Whirl'd round and dash'd amain with sore annoy . . .

and vi 9,

> Large hail, discolour'd water, sleety flaw . . .

10. in . . . whirlwind] 'mid . . . world-wind' *Indicator*. K. obviously intended 'whirlwind'–see the third line quoted from Cary's *Dante* above–
and his journal-letter, 'whirling atmosphere'.
11–12. lovers . . . sorrows] Either their sad situation speaks for them or, although sad, it ensures their protection from needless questioning. The latter
interpretation is supported by the pleasurable associations of the dream and
by the worry over the 'dragon-world' expressed in ll. 3–5.
13. Pale were the lips I kissed] See Cary's *Dante*, *Inferno* v 131–3,

> . . . he, who ne'er
> From me shall separate, at once my lips
> All trembling kiss'd . . .

The use of the word 'pale' in this and the preceding line anticipates the
description of the sufferers in the following poem, *La Belle Dame Sans Merci*
2 and 46 (pp. 501 and 506 below), 'alone and palely loitering', and 37–8 (p.
505 below),

> I saw pale kings, and princes too,
> Pale warriors, death-pale were they all . . .

125 La Belle Dame Sans Merci

Written 21 April 1819: see under this date in K.'s 14 Feb.–3 May 1819
journal–letter, where the poem appears without prefatory comment and
with corrections suggesting a first draft (*L* ii 95–6). The poem is obviously
connected with K.'s feelings about Fanny Brawne and is strongly influenced by memories of Spenser's fatal enchantresses in *The Faerie Queene* and
by various traditional ballads expressing the destructiveness of love, which
are also the chief models for its diction and metrical style–K. was probably
familiar with such ballads from Percy's *Reliques of Ancient English Poetry*
(1765) and other later collections (see ll. 13–16 *n*). See also Robert Graves,
The White Goddess (1948), 'That the Belle Dame represented Love, Death

¶ 125. *Title.* According to Leigh Hunt (*Indicator* 10 May 1820) derived from
the title of Alain Chartier's poem *La Belle Dame Sans Merci* (1424). K. prob-

by Consumption . . . and Poetry all at once can be confirmed by a study of the romances from which Keats developed the poem' (378). For details of some of the major influences and echoes from K.'s recent reading of Cary's *Dante, Inferno* y and Burton's *Anatomy of Melancholy* see the notes below. Discussions of the poem and its sources appear in *Finney* 593–9; Robert Graves *op. cit.* 374–80 and earlier in *English Poetry* (1922) 50–5; and 'La Belle Dame and the False Florimel', *Gittings* (1954) 113–23. For commentaries on Gittings's findings by K. Muir and F. W. Bateson see *Essays in Criticism* iv (1954) 432–40. On the poem's special appeal for the Pre-Raphaelites see D. G. Rossetti's comment quoted in headnote to *The Eve of St. Mark* (p. 481 above) and William Morris's testimony in Feb. 1894, recorded in *Colvin* (1917) 470, 'that it was the germ from which all the poetry of his group had sprung'.

Text from K.'s letter; variants from the revised version in *The Indicator*– with some representative criticisms of the revisions–are given in the notes, *The Indicator* text being given in Appendix B (p. 757 below).

Published *The Indicator* 10 May 1820 (signed 'Caviare') and *1848* (which follows the version in K.'s letter).

I

Oh, what can ail thee, knight-at-arms,
Alone and palely loitering?

---

ably first knew the poem from the English translation included in the 1782 edn of *The Poetical Works of Geoffrey Chaucer* (see headnote to *Written on a blank space at the end of Chaucer's tale ' The Floure and the Leafe'*, p. 103 above) X 133–67. Cp. *The Eve of St. Agnes* 291–2 (p. 472 above),

He played an ancient ditty, long since mute,
In Provence called 'La belle dame sans mercy' . . .

Woodhouse's transcripts add the sub-title, 'A Ballad'.

1–2. Perhaps suggested by the rendering in Burton's *Anatomy of Melancholy* III 2 iv 1 (1813 edn 292) of Chaucer's *The Knightes Tale* 1364–6,

His hew pale and ashen to unfold,
And solitary he was ever alone,
And waking all the night making mone . . .

The lines are marked by K. in his copy of Burton at Hampstead.

1 (and *5* below). *knight-at-arms*] wretched wight *Indicator*. Perhaps altered by K. to avoid specifically medieval associations, but see *Colvin* (1917), 'I should say, that the changes [in *The Indicator* version], which are all in the direction of the slipshod and the commonplace, were made on Hunt's suggestion and that Keats acquiesced from fatigue or indifference' (469) and *Bate* (1963), 'One can only suppose that Hunt–possibly Woodhouse– thought . . . that the magic, dreamlike quality of the poem would be considered sentimental'. On William Morris's indignation at the corrections (first known to him in 1894) see *Colvin* (1917) 470.

> The sedge has withered from the lake,
> And no birds sing!

II

> 5 Oh, what can ail thee, knight-at-arms,
> So haggard and so woe-begone?
> The squirrel's granary is full,
> And the harvest's done.

III

> I see a lily on thy brow,

3-4 (and *7-8* below). The sadness of winter is deepened by memories of spring and summer. Cp. Dante's *Inferno* v 121-3,

> *Nessun maggior dolore*
> *che ricordarsi del tempo felice*
> *nella miseria . . .*

(Cary's *Dante, Inferno* v 118-19,

> No greater grief than to remember days
> Of joy, when mis'ry is at hand . . .)

3. Cp. *The Eve of St. Mark* 10 (p. 482 above), 'rivers new with spring-tide sedge'.

4. Possibly echoing William Browne's *Britannia's Pastorals* Book 2 Song 1 244,

> Within the shady woods
> Let no birds sing! . . .

but the mood is closer to Shakespeare's sonnet lxxiii 4,

> Bare ruin'd choirs, where late the sweet birds sang . . .

6. Cp. Chatterton's *An Excelente Balade of Charitie* (1777) 22-3,

> Look in his glommed face, his sprighte there scanne;
> How woe-be-gone, how withered, forwynd, deade . . .

(Chatterton glosses 'glommed' = clouded, dejected, and 'forwynd' = dry, sapless).

9-12. The lily and the rose as emblems of physical beauty are literary commonplaces, but their use here may owe something to Drayton's *England's Heroicall Epistles*, 'Matilda to King John' 157-60, of which the 1597 reading is quoted in Burton's *Anatomy of Melancholy* III 2 vi 3 (1813 edn 375),

> I am not now as when thou sawst me last,
> That favour soone is vanished and past;
> That Rosie-blush, lappèd in a Lilly-vale,
> Now with the Morphew over-growne, and pale . . .

The last two lines are marked by K. in his copy of Burton. K.'s lines suggest a recollection of Tom Keats's last illness. See also Coleridge's record of meeting K. 11 April 1819, '"There is death in that hand," I said . . . when Keats was gone' (*Table Talk* 14 Aug. 1832).

9 (and *11* below). a] death's L (*cancelled*).

10   With anguish moist and fever-dew,
And on thy cheek a fading rose
Fast withereth too.

IV

I met a lady in the meads
Full beautiful, a fairy's child,
15   Her hair was long, her foot was light,
And her eyes were wild.

V

I made a garland for her head,
And bracelets too, and fragrant zone;
She looked at me as she did love,
20   And made sweet moan.

VI

I set her on my pacing steed,
And nothing else saw all day long;

13–16. The lady resembles enchantresses known to K. from *The Faerie Queene* and from various ballads and poems in the ballad tradition, for example, *Thomas the Rhymer*, included in Scott's *Border Minstrelsy* (1802–3) and Robert Jamieson's *Popular Ballads* (1806), and Allan Cunningham's *The Mermaid of Galloway*, included in R. H. Cromek's *Remains of Nithsdale and Galloway Song* (1810). See R. Graves on Thomas the Rhymer, 'an early thirteenth-century poet who claimed to have been given poetic insight by the Queen of Elfland ... who appeared suddenly to him as he lay on Huntlie Bank and chose him as her lover' (*The White Goddess* (1948) 379). 'The Mermaid', a painting by William Hilton (1786–1839) based on Cunningham's poem, was being exhibited at Sir John Leicester's gallery, visited by K. 'a few days' before 15 April 1819 (*L* ii 83). Hilton's painting (now at the City Art Gallery, Manchester) shows the knight of the poem lying dead in the mermaid's lap with a water-lily on his brow.

13. meads] Wilds *L* (*cancelled*).

17–24. Stanzas v and vi are transposed in the *Indicator* version.

17. K. is remembering the garlands made for the false Fidessa and the false Florimel in *The Faerie Queene* I ii 30, III vii 17. His review of Reynolds's parody of Wordsworth's *Peter Bell*, copied out in his journal-letter 21 April 1819, has "This false florimel has hurried from the press' (*L* ii 93).

18. fragrant zone] A girdle of flowers. K. refers to the true Florimel's lost girdle in his review of Reynolds's *Peter Bell* (*L* ii 93).

20. made sweet moan] Murmured or sang sweetly. Cp. *Ode to Psyche* 30 (p. 517 below),

Nor virgin choir to make delicious moan ...

'To make moan' is a poetic archaism familiar to K. from Spenser and Chaucer (see ll. 1–2 *n* above).

For sidelong would she bend, and sing
  A fairy's song.

VII

25 She found me roots of relish sweet,
  And honey wild, and manna dew;
  And sure in language strange she said,
   'I love thee true'.

VIII

She took me to her elfin grot,
30 And there she wept, and sighed full sore,
  And there I shut her wild wild eyes
   With kisses four.

23. sidelong would she bend] sideways would she lean *Indicator*.
26. Cp. Coleridge's *Kubla Khan* (1816) 53, for which, as for the Biblical origin of 'manna', see *Endymion* i 766 *n* (p. 153 above); 'manna' also suggests in this context a recollection of *Paradise Lost* ii 112–13 (marked by K. in his copy of Milton),

   But all was false and hollow; though his Tongue
   Dropt Manna . . .

29. Cp. *Thomas the Rhymer* 49–52,

   And see ye not yon bonny road
    That winds about the fernie brae?
   That is the road to fair Elfland,
    Where thou and I this night maun gae . . .

30. and sighed full sore] and there she sighed full sore *L* (*cancelled*); gazed and sighed deep *Indicator*. Cp. Alain Chartier's *La Belle Dame sans Merci* (*ed. cit.*) 197,

   I herd the lovir sighying wondir sore . . .

and *The Faerie Queene* IV viii 64,

   And sigh full sore, to heare the miserie . . .

31. wild wild] wild sad *Indicator*. Perhaps an echo of the haunting opening of Wordsworth's poem, *Her eyes are wild* (1798). See also 32 *n* below.
32. With kisses four] So kiss'd to sleep *Indicator*. K. commented in his journal-letter, '. . . Why four kisses—you will say—why four because I wish to restrain the headlong impetuosity of my Muse—she would have fain said 'score' without hurting the rhyme—but we must temper the Imagination as the Critics say with Judgment. I was obliged to choose an even number that both eyes might have fair play: and to speak truly I think two a piece quite sufficient—Suppose I had said seven; there would have been three and a half a piece—a very awkward affair—and well got out of on my side' (*L* ii 97). For an early example of K.'s fondness for pseudo-specific numerals see *To George Felton Mathew* 58 (p. 26 above). See *Colvin* (1917), '. . . the whimsical particularity . . . gives the poem an essential part of its savour' (469–70) and cp. D. G. Rossetti's opposite view in his letter to H. Buxton Forman 9 May 1880. 'a suggestiveness of undermeaning which is no gain'

IX

And there she lullèd me asleep,
   And there I dreamed–Ah! woe betide!—
35 The latest dream I ever dreamed
   On the cold hill side.

X

I saw pale kings, and princes too,
   Pale warriors, death-pale were they all;
They cried–'La belle Dame sans merci
40   Hath thee in thrall!'

(*John Keats: Criticism and Comment*, 1919, 13). R. Graves in *English Poetry* (1922) associates the 'undermeaning' with memories of Tom Keats's death and asks 'was it extravagant to suppose that two of the kisses were . . . pennies laid on the eyes of death?' (54); he further suggests that K.'s explanation in his journal-letter and revision of the line in the *Indicator* version were unconscious attempts to limit the 'painful doubleness of the tragic vision' and that 'the change of "wild wild eyes" [l. 31 *n* above] . . . meaning . . . elf-wild and horror-wild . . . would have the same effect'.

33. *she lullèd me asleep*] we slumbered on the moss *Indicator*.

37–42. K. head read about the doomed lovers in the second circle of hell in Cary's *Dante, Inferno* v 64–8,

        . . . there the great
Achilles, who with love fought to the end.
Paris I saw, and Tristan; and beside,
A thousand more he show'd me, and by name
Pointed them out, whom love bereav'd of life . . .

but the deathly appearance and 'horrid warning' of his 'kings and princes' may owe a debt to *Pericles* I i 34–40,

Yon sometime famous princes, like thyself,
Drawn by report, famous by desire,
Tell thee with speechless tongues and semblance pale,
That without covering, save yon field of stars,
They here stand martyrs, slain in Cupid's wars;
And with dead cheeks advise thee to desist
For going on death's net, whom none resist . . .

37–8. Cp. the pale figure in the 'second circle of sad hell' in the preceding poem, *As Hermes once* 12–13 (p. 500 above),

        . . . Pale were the sweet lips I saw,
Pale were the lips I kissed . . .

39. *They*] Who *Indicator*.

40. *thrall*] Perhaps suggested by Cary's *Dante, Inferno* V 124–5,

        . . . we read of Lancelot,
How him love thrall'd . . .

The passage may also have recalled to K. Spenser's frequent use of 'thrall'

XI

I saw their starved lips in the gloam
   With horrid warning gapèd wide,
And I awoke, and found me here
   On the cold hill side.

XII

45   And this is why I sojourn here,
   Alone and palely loitering,
Though the sedge is withered from the lake,
   And no birds sing.

---

when describing the destructiveness of passion, e.g. *The Faerie Queene* II i
54, 'him that witch hath thralled to her will'.
41. *gloam*] Twilight. A Keatsian derivation from 'gloaming'. *The Indicator*
has 'gloom'.
42. With horrid warning wide agape . . . *L* (*cancelled*). The first attempt at
the line was 'All tremble . . .'.
45. *sojourn*] wither *L* (*cancelled*).
47. *is*] Garrod reads 'has', for which there is no authority.

126 Song of Four Fairies

Written 21 April 1819: see under this date in K.'s journal-letter of 14 Feb.–
3 May 1819 where the poem appears without comment and with alterations
suggesting a first draft (*L* ii 97–100). The four fairies are a compound of the
elves of popular tradition and the spirits of the elements. K.'s use of them to
represent contrasts of heat and cold may derive from Burton's 'Division of
the Body, Humours, Spirits', *Anatomy of Melancholy* I 2 ii 2 (1813 edn 80–4).
With the poem's metrical style cp. *The Eve of St. Mark* (p. 480 above).
Text from K.'s holograph copy, with some variants noted from his letter
(referred to below as *L*).
Published *1848*.

FIRE, AIR, EARTH, AND WATER
SALAMANDER, ZEPHYR, DUSKETHA, AND BREAMA

SALAMANDER
Happy, happy glowing fire!

ZEPHYR
Fragrant air! Delicious light!

¶ 126. *Title.* Chorus of Faries 4 Fire, air, earth and water–
       Salamander, Zephyr, Dusketha, Breama– . . . *L.*
The last two names are made up by K. from 'dusk' and 'bream' (a freshwater fish).

DUSKETHA

Let me to my glooms retire!

BREAMA

I to green-weed rivers bright!

SALAMANDER

5   Happy, happy glowing fire,
    Dazzling bowers of soft retire!
    Ever let my nourished wing,
    Like a bat's, still wandering,
    Nimbly fan your fiery spaces,
10   Spirit sole in deadly places.
    In unhaunted roar and blaze,
    Open eyes that never daze,
    Let me see the myriad shapes
    Of men and beasts and fish and apes,
15   Portrayed in many a fiery den
    And wrought by spumy bitumen
    On the deep intenser roof.
    Archèd every way aloof.
    Let me breathe upon their skies,
20   And anger their live tapestries;
    Free from cold, and every care
    Of chilly rain and shivering air.

ZEPHYR

    Spirit of Fire! Away! Away!
    Or your very roundelay
25   Will sear my plumage newly budded
    From its quillèd sheath, all studded
    With the self-same dews that fell
    On the May-grown asphodel.
    Spirit of Fire! Away! Away!

6. *retire*] Retirement. Cp. l. 51 below 'the cherish . . .'
9. *Nimbly*] Faintless *L*.
15–16. Cp. Thomson's *The Seasons* (1730), *Summer* 1108–9,
                . . . the fiery spume
        Of fat bitumen . . .
and see K.'s use of 'spumy' in *To Homer* 7 (p. 353 above).
19. *their*] my *L*.
20. *live tapestries*] Shapes formed by the flames.
23. *Spirit*] K. writes 'spright' for 'spirit' throughout *L*. In *As Hermes once*
he uses this spelling for 'sprite' (see, for example, 1 *n*, p. 449 above).
28. *asphodel*] The immortal flower which was supposed to cover the
Elysian Fields.

BREAMA

30 Spirit of Fire! Away! Away!
    Zephyr, blue-eyed fairy, turn
    And see my cool sedge-buried urn,
    Where it rests its mossy brim
    'Mid water-mint and cresses dim;
35 And the flowers, in sweet troubles,
    Lift their eyes above the bubbles,
    Like our Queen, when she would please
    To sleep and Oberon will tease.
    Love me, blue-eyed fairy true,
40 Soothly I am sick for you.

ZEPHYR

    Gentle Breama! By the first
    Violet young nature nursed,
    I will bathe myself with thee,
    So you sometime follow me
45 To my home, far, far in west,
    Beyond the nimble-wheelèd quest
    Of the golden-presenced sun.
    Come with me, o'er tops of trees,
    To my fragrant palaces,
50 Where they ever floating are
    Beneath the cherish of a star

32–4. Perhaps suggested by the invocation to Sabrina in Milton's *Comus* 860–1,

> Listen where thou art sitting
> Under the glassie, cool, translucent wave . . .

See Severn's notes on K. written Oct. 1845, 'He intended to write a long Poem on the story of Sabrina as left by Milton, and often spoke of it at Rome but never wrote a line' (*KC* ii 138).

32. *sedge*] Used by K. in *La Belle Dame Sans Merci* 3, 47 and *The Eve of St. Mark* 10 (pp. 502, 506 and 482 above). For 'sedge-buried . . .' *L* has 'sedge shaded . . .'.

35. *in*] amid *L* (*cancelled*).

37–8. Breama is seen as one of Titania's attendants in *A Midsummer Night's Dream* II ii 1–26.

40. *Soothly*] For in sooth *L* (*cancelled*).

46.   Far beyond the search and quest . . .*L*.

47. *presenced*] browed *L*. Woodhouse supplies the following line to complete the couplet (*Woodhouse* 2),

> When his arched course is done . . .

51. *the cherish*] The cherishing. Cp. l. 6 *n* above.

Called Vesper, who with silver veil
Ever hides his brilliance pale,
Ever gently-drowsed doth keep
55   Twilight for the fays to sleep.
Fear not that your watery hair
Will thirst in drouthy ringlets there;
Clouds of storèd summer rains
Thou shalt taste, before the stains
60   Of the mountain soil they take,
And too unlucent for thee make.
I love thee, crystal fairy true!
Sooth I am as sick for you!

SALAMANDER
Out, ye aguish fairies, out!
65   Chilly lovers, what a rout
Keep ye with your frozen breath,
Colder than the mortal death.
Adder-eyed Dusketha, speak,
Shall we leave these, and go seek
70   In the earth's wide entrails old
Couches warm as theirs are cold?
Oh, for a fiery gloom and thee,
Dusketha, so enchantingly
Freckle-winged and lizard-sided!

DUSKETHA
75   By thee, sprite, will I be guided!
I care not for cold or heat—
Frost and flame, or sparks, or sleet,
To my essence are the same;
But I honour more the flame.
80   Sprite of Fire, I follow thee

52. *Vesper*] The evening star.
53. *brilliance*] brightness *L (cancelled)*.
61. *unlucent*] Dull.
64. *aguish*] Damp and chilly. Cp. *The Eve of St. Mark* 12 (p. 482 above) 'the aguish hills'.
65.   Chillier than the water . . . *L (cancelled)*.
68. *Adder-eyed*] Dark and gleaming like the eyes of a snake.
70. *earth's wide entrails*] Perhaps echoing *Paradise Lost* vi 516–17,
        Part hidd'n veins digged up (nor hath this Earth
        Entrails unlike) of Mineral and Stone . . .
74. *lizard-sided*] Dusketha has properties in common with the salamander, a lizard-like creature supposed by the ancients to be at home in fire.

Wheresoever it may be,
To the torrid spouts and fountains,
Underneath earth-quakèd mountains;
Or, at thy supreme desire,
85   Touch the very pulse of fire
With my bare unlidded eyes.

SALAMANDER

Sweet Dusketha! Paradise!
Off, ye icy spirits, fly!
Frosty creatures of the sky!

DUSKETHA

90   Breathe upon them, fiery sprite!

ZEPHYR AND BREAMA

Away! Away to our delight!

SALAMANDER

Go, feed on icicles, while we
Bedded in tonguèd flames will be.

DUSKETHA

Lead me to those feverous glooms,
Sprite of Fire!

95   BREAMA
Me to the blooms,
Blue-eyed Zephyr, of those flowers
Far in the west where the May-cloud lowers;
And the beams of still Vesper, when winds are all
        whist,
Are shed through the rain and the milder mist,
100   And twilight your floating bowers.

82. *torrid spouts*] very fire *L* (*cancelled*).
98. *whist*] Silent. Milton has *Nativity Ode* 64,
            The Windes with wonder whist . . .
100. *twilight*] Used as a verb.

127 To Sleep

Probably written April 1819: K. drafted *La Belle Dame Sans Merci* and *Song of Four Fairies* (pp. 500 and 506 above) on 21 April in his 14 Feb.–3 May journal-letter and copied out this poem on 30 April in the same journal-letter as one of 'two or three lately written' sonnets (*L* ii 105–6)–the other sonnets referred to may include *The House of Mourning written by Mr. Scott* and *As Hermes once* (pp. 495 and 498 above), both probably written earlier in the same month. *To Sleep* is the first and most successful of K.'s spring 1819 experimental sonnets (for the others see *How fevered is the man* and *If by dull rhymes*, pp. 513 and 521 below) and suggests in style and diction his increased independence of literary models. Its metrical structure—two Shakespearian quatrains followed by the sestet (*abab cdcd bcefef*)—indicates his new dissatisfaction with the Shakespearian rhyme-scheme. The draft version (in K.'s copy of Milton at Hampstead) consists of three Shakespearian quatrains and may have been abandoned in this form because of his distaste for the concluding Shakespearian couplet. For this criticism of the couplet and comments on the general weaknesses of both the Shakespearian and the Petrarchan sonnet see headnote to *If by dull rhymes* (p. 521 below). Discussions of K.'s experimental sonnets and their bearing on the metrical structure of his odes appear in H. W. Garrod's *Keats* (1926) 83–90, *Ridley* (1933) 195–210 and *Bate* (1945) 125–33.

Text from Woodhouse's transcript (*Woodhouse* 2), which has corrections in K.'s hand, with some variants noted from the draft. Published *1848*.

> O soft embalmer of the still midnight,
>   Shutting with careful fingers and benign
> Our gloom-pleased eyes, embowered from the light,
>   Enshaded in forgetfulness divine:
> 5   O soothest Sleep! If so it please thee, close,
>   In midst of this thine hymn, my willing eyes,
> Or wait the 'Amen', ere thy poppy throws
>   Around my bed its lulling charities.
> Then save me, or the passèd day will shine

¶ 127. 4. As wearisome as darkness is divine . . . *Draft*. The cancelled false start in the draft was 'Of sun or teasing candles . . .'
5. *soothest*] Softest. Cp. *The Eve of St. Agnes* 266 (p. 471 above).
              . . . soother than the creamy curd
6.   My willing eyes in midst of this thine hymn . . . *Draft*.
7. *wait the 'Amen'*] Wait until I have finished the poem (which is Sleep's 'hymn').
8.   Its sweet-death dews o'er every pulse and limb . . . *Draft*
K. substituted 'lulling' for 'dewy' in Woodhouse's transcript of the revised version. Woodhouse notes, 'The word "lulling" is in K.'s handwriting. The correction was made when he borrowed this book to select a small poem to write in an Album, intended to consist of original poetry, for a lady' (*Woodhouse* 2).
9–12.   Then shut the hushed Casket of my soul
          And turn the key round in the oiled wards
   [3]   And let it rest until the morn has stole

10   Upon my pillow, breeding many woes;
        Save me from curious conscience, that still hoards
     Its strength for darkness, burrowing like a mole;
        Turn the key deftly in the oilèd wards,
     And seal the hushèd casket of my soul.

     Bright tressed from the grey east's shuddering bourn ... *Draft*.
l. [3] *has stole*] Cancelled, but nothing substituted.
l. [4] *grey east's*] west's *cancelled*.
11. *curious conscience*] Conscience which probes with minute thoroughness.
The image is sustained by 'burrowing like a mole' in the subsequent line,
which suggests a reminiscence of the image in *Hamlet* I v 162,
        Well said, old mole! canst work i'the earth so fast?
In *Woodhouse* 2 'hoards' is written over the reading 'lords' (uncancelled).
K. wrote 'lords' in his letter copy but made the change in the obvious
interests of sense and syntax when he re-read the poem in *Woodhouse* 2
(cp. l. 8 *n* above).
13. The image may be derived from Cary's *Dante, Inferno* xiii 60–2,
                . . . I it was, who held
        Both keys to Frederick's heart, and turn'd the wards,
        Opening and shutting with a skill so sweet . . .
The passage is marked by K. in his copy of Cary's *Dante*; see *Gittings* (1956)
151.

128 'Fame like a wayward girl will still be coy'

Written 30 April 1819 as a half-serious, half-playful comment on the
inequalities of fame: see under this date in K.'s journal-letter of 14 Feb.–3
May 1819, 'Brown has been rummaging up some of my old sins—that is to
say sonnets . . . I have just written one on Fame' (*L* ii 104). The poem follows the Shakespearian rhyme-pattern and is K.'s single non-experimental
sonnet during this period (see headnote to the preceding poem *To Sleep*, pp.
510–11 above). The subject and style suggest a debt to Dryden's *The Conquest of Granada* (1672), Epilogue to Part I 5–22.
Text from K.'s letter.
Published *The Ladies' Companion* (New York) Aug. 1837 and *1848*.

     Fame, like a wayward girl, will still be coy
        To those who woo her with too slavish knees,

¶ 128. *1.* Cp. Dryden's *The Conquest of Granada*, Epilogue to Part I 5–6,
        Fame, like a little Mistriss of the town,
        Is gaind with ease; but then she's lost as soon . . .

But makes surrender to some thoughtless boy,
    And dotes the more upon a heart at ease.
5 She is a gipsy, will not speak to those
    Who have not learnt to be content without her;
A jilt, whose ear was never whispered close,
    Who thinks they scandal her who talk about her—
A very gipsy is she, Nilus-born,
10   Sister-in-law to jealous Potiphar.
Ye love-sick bards, repay her scorn for scorn;
    Ye lovelorn artists, madmen that ye are,
Make your best bow to her and bid adieu—
    Then, if she likes it, she will follow you.

3. Cp. Dryden's *The Conquest of Granada*, Epilogue 11–12.
      . . . Fame is false to all that keep her long:
      And turns up to the Fop that's brisk and young . . .
7. She remains aloof.
8. *scandal*] Defame.
9. *Nilus-born*] Gipsies, as the word implies, were formerly believed to come from Egypt.
10. *jealous Potiphar*] Potiphar was jealous of Joseph, who had caught the eye of Potiphar's wife. See *Genesis* xxxix.
12. *lovelorn artists*] Artists lovelorn! *1848, Garrod.*

129 'How fevered is the man who cannot look'

Written 30 April in K.'s journal-letter of 14 Feb.–3 May to fill in time before copying the preceding sonnet on Fame (No. 128 above), '. . . which Brown is transcribing and he has his book and mine I must employ myself perhaps in a sonnet on the same subject' (*L* ii 104). The metrical structure (*ababcdcd efeggf*) represents a further stage in K.'s experiments with the sonnet and is used again in the following poem, the *Ode to Psyche* (No. 130 below). Text from *Woodhouse 2* as following a lost later version by K., with some variants from K.'s letter (referred to in the notes as *L*).
Published *1848*.

          You cannot eat your cake and have it too   PROVERB

How fevered is the man who cannot look
    Upon his mortal days with temperate blood,
Who vexes all the leaves of his life's book,

¶ 129. 1. *How fevered is the man*] How is that Man misled *L (cancelled).*
3–4. The restless pursuit of fame vexes every moment of his life and deprives him of his youthful freshness.

And robs his fair name of its maidenhood:
5   It is as if the rose should pluck herself,
        Or the ripe plum finger its misty bloom,
      As if a Naiad, like a meddling elf,
        Should darken her pure grot with muddy gloom;
      But the rose leaves herself upon the briar,
10   For winds to kiss and grateful bees to feed,
      And the ripe plum still wears its dim attire,
            The undisturbèd lake has crystal space.
            Why then should man, teasing the world for grace,
      Spoil his salvation for a fierce miscreed?

7–8.   As if a clear Lake meddling with itself
             Should cloud its pureness with a muddy gloom . . . L.
The revised version is written marginally in *Woodhouse* 2 with note, 'The objection to these lines was probably that "itself" was thus made to rhyme to itself [see l. 5]. But the author . . . forgot that he left an allusion in the 12th line to those thus erased.' The correction upsets the balanced repetition of 'rose', 'plum', 'lake' in the letter version.

7. *elf*] See *Ode to a Nightingale* 73–4 *n* (pp. 531–2 below).

13–14. Why then should man, plaguing the world for favours, spoil his peace of mind for a fierce misbelief? The 'fierce miscreed' is the worship of fame.

13. *teasing the world for grace*] his own bright name deface L (*cancelled*). K. wrote 'leasing' when he corrected the line in L, but presumably substituted 'teasing' later to emphasize the restless plaguing of worldly ambition.

14.   And spoil our pleasures in his selfish fire . . . L (*cancelled*).

130 Ode to Psyche

Written between 21 and 30 April 1819 and the first of K.'s five spring 1819 odes: K. wrote *La Belle Dame Sans Merci* and *Song of Four Fairies* (pp. 500 and 506 above) on 21 April and referred to this poem as 'the last I have written' when copying it out on 30 April in his journal-letter of 14 Feb.–3 May 1819, in which he comments, '. . . [the poem] is the first and only one with which I have taken even moderate pains–I have for the most part dash'd off my lines in a hurry–this I have done leisurely–I think it reads the more richly for it and will I hope encourage me to write other things in even a more peaceable and healthy spirit. You must recollect that Psyche was not embodied as a goddess before the time of Apulieus [*sic*] the Platonist who lived after the Augustan age, and consequently the Goddess was never worshipped or sacrificed to with any of the ancient fervour–and perhaps never thought of in the old religion–I am more orthodox than to let a hethan Goddess be so neglected' (*L* ii 105–6). K.'s account of Psyche in his letter suggests that he consulted *Lemprière*: 'The word signifies the *soul*, and this personification of Psyche first mentioned by Apuleius is thus posterior to the Augustan age, though it is connected with ancient mythology.'

K.'s interest in the legend of Psyche should be associated with his view of the world as a 'vale of Soul-making'–see under 21 April in the same journal-letter, 'There may be intelligences or sparks of the divinity in millions–but they are not souls till they acquire identities. . . . Do you not see how necessary a world of Pains and troubles is to school an Intelligence and make it a soul? . . . It is pretty generally suspected that the christian scheme had been copied from the ancient persian and greek Philosophers. Why may they not have made this simple thing even more simple for common apprehension by introducing Mediators and Personages in the same manner as in the hethan mythology abstractions are personified–Seriously I think it probable that this system of Soul-making–may have been parent of all the more palpable and Personal schemes of Redemption . . . as one part of the human species must have their carved Jupiter; so another part must have the palpable and named Mediator and Saviour, their Christ, their Oromanes and their Vishnu' (*L* ii 102, 103).

For some pictorial details in *Ode to Psyche* K. drew on Apuleius's *Cupid and Psyche*, in William Adlington's translation (1566) of *The Golden Ass* (cited below in notes as Adlington's *Apuleius*). His 'more peaceable and healthy spirit' is revealed in the happy mood of the poem; thus the emphasis is laid at first on Psyche's reunion with Eros (strophe 1) and later on the tranquil 'region of my mind' (strophe 4). His 'pains' over composition are reflected in his devising for the poem a loose Pindaric form–consisting of irregular verse-paragraphs with lines of varying length–based on his recent experiments with the sonnet (see, for example, the similar rhyme scheme in *Fame like a wayward girl*, p. 512 above). K. divides the poem into three verse-paragraphs in his letter and four in *1820*. Style and diction are as usual affected by K.'s reading of the Elizabethans, but Milton and Wordsworth influence the poem's second and third strophes. Discussions of the *Ode to Psyche* appear in most commentaries on K.'s odes, for example in *Colvin* (1915) 411–23, *Bate* (1963) 487–98 and J. Stillinger, *Twentieth Century Interpretations of Keats's Odes* (1968). Separate critical commentaries on the poem include M. R. Ridley's 'Ode to Psyche' in *Ridley* (1933) 197–210 and K. Allott's 'The "Ode to Psyche"' in *Reassessment* (1958) 74–94.

Text from *1820*, with some variants noted from K.'s letter (referred to in the notes as *L*) and his draft (Morgan Library).
Published *1820*.

> O Goddess! Hear these tuneless numbers, wrung
>   By sweet enforcement and remembrance dear,

¶ 130. *2.* K. conflates Milton's *Lycidas* 4 and 6,
      . . . with forc'd fingers rude . . .
        Bitter constraint, and sad occasion dear . . .

And pardon that thy secrets should be sung
Even into thine own soft-conchèd ear.
5   Surely I dreamt to-day, or did I see
The wingèd Psyche with awakened eyes?
I wandered in a forest thoughtlessly,
And, on the sudden, fainting with surprise,
Saw two fair creatures, couchèd side by side
10   In deepest grass, beneath the whispering roof
Of leaves and trembled blossoms, where there ran
A brooklet, scarce espied.
'Mid hushed, cool-rooted flowers, fragrant-eyed,
Blue, silver-white and budded Tyrian,
15   They lay calm-breathing on the bedded grass;
Their arms embracèd, and their pinions too;
Their lips touched not, but had not bade adieu,
As if disjoinèd by soft-handed slumber,
And ready still past kisses to outnumber
20   At tender eye-dawn of aurorean love.

4. *soft-conchèd*] Shell-like.

5–6. A poetical commonplace probably recollected from K.'s reading of
the Elizabethans, perhaps from Spenser's *Amoretti* lxxvii,

Was it a dreame, or did I see it playne.

a goodly table of pure yvory . . .

For K.'s use of the figure again in spring 1819 see *Ode to a Nightingale* 79 *n*
(p. 532 below).

7. *thoughtlessly*] Indolently, in an unthinking mood.

8. *fainting*] Cp. K.'s earlier use of the word in connection with erotic romantic fantasy in *Endymion* iv 746 (p. 275 above),

Fainting I fell into a bed of flowers . . .

9. *two fair creatures*] K. postpones identifying the 'fair creatures' until the
end of the stanza to heighten the dramatic effect.

10–14. The setting owes something to Adlington's *Apuleius*, 'Psyches . . .
was blowne by the gentle aire . . . and brought . . . downe into a deepe
valley . . . Psyches being sweetly couched among the soft and tender hearbs,
as in a bed of sweet and fragrant floures . . . was now well reposed . . . [she]
fortuned to espy a pleasant wood . . . likewise a running river as cleare as
crystall' (C. Whibley's 1893 reprint of Adlington's *Apuleius* 102).

10. *roof*] fan *Draft, L.* The alteration leaves this unrhymed line. Other unrhymed lines are found at ll. 15, 44, 45 below.

14. *silver-white . . . Tyrian*] freckle-pink . . . syrian *Draft, L.*

20. *eye-dawn*] dawning *Draft (cancelled)*. Cp. Milton's *Lycidas* 26,

Under the opening eye-lids of the morn . . .

The renewal of their love each time they awake is like the daily rising of
the sun.

The wingèd boy I knew;
But who wast thou, O happy, happy dove?
His Psyche true!
O latest born and loveliest vision far
25   Of all Olympus' faded hierarchy!
Fairer than Phoebe's sapphire-regioned star,
Or Vesper, amorous glow-worm of the sky;
Fairer than these, though temple thou hast none,
Nor altar heaped with flowers;
30 Nor virgin-choir to make delicious moan

21. *the wingèd boy*] Spenser's regular phrase for Cupid; K. may be remembering especially his use of it when describing Cupid and Psyche, *The Faerie Queene* III vi 49–50.

24–67. Written as a single verse paragraph in *L*.

24–5. With the idea that the latest is the loveliest cp. *Hyperion* ii 228–9 (p. 428 above),

> . . . 'tis the eternal law
> That first in beauty should be first in might . . .

K. had abandoned *Hyperion* shortly before writing the *Ode to Psyche*.

26. *Phoebe's*] Night's full *Draft*. Earlier attempts in the draft were:
    1. Night's orbed . . .
    2. Night's wide . . .

With 'sapphire-regioned star' cp. *On Visiting the Tomb of Burns* 7 (p. 357 above)

> Through sapphire warm, their stars do never beam . . .

27. Cp. *Song of Four Fairies* 51–2 (pp. 508–9 above),

> Beneath the cherish of a star
> Called Vesper . . .

30–5. K.'s reference in l. 25 above to 'Olympus' faded hierarchy' probably recalled to him Milton's description, with its repeated negatives, of the disappearance of the ancient Greek deities at the birth of Christ in the *Nativity Ode* 173–80,

> The Oracles are dumm,
> No voice or hideous humm
> Runs through the arched roof in words deceiving.
> *Apollo* from his shrine
> Can no more divine,
> With hollow shreik the steep of *Delphos* leaving.
> No nightly trance, or breathed spell,
> Inspires the pale-ey'd Priest from the prophetic cell . . .

In the draft K. first wrote 'nor' for 'no' throughout this passage. (For K.'s earlier echo of Milton's Ode see *Endymion* iv 193–272 *n* (p. 254 above).

30. *make delicious moan*] Cp. *La Belle Dame Sans Merci* 20 and *n* (p. 503 above), 'made sweet moan'. See also l. 191 of Milton's *Nativity Ode* quoted in 38–45 *n* below. The draft has 'melodious' for 'delicious'.

18+K.

Upon the midnight hours—
No voice, no lute, no pipe, no incense sweet
   From chain-swung censer teeming;
No shrine, no grove, no oracle, no heat
35   Of pale-mouthed prophet dreaming.

O brightest, though too late for antique vows!
Too, too late for the fond believing lyre,
When holy were the haunted forest boughs,
   Holy the air, the water and the fire.
40   Yet even in these days so far retired
   From happy pieties, thy lucent fans,

32–3. incense . . . teeming] Cp. *Hyperion* i 167 and *n* (p. 406 above),
            . . . incense, teeming up
         From man to the Sun's god . . .
36. brightest] bloomiest *Draft, L.*
37. the fond believing lyre] Hymns written by those to whom the 'happy
pieties' of belief are natural and unquestioned. The word 'fond' means
'devoted' but probably also carries regret that the old beliefs should have
faded.
38–45. K.'s phrasing suggests a recollection, possibly unconscious, of Milton's *Nativity Ode* 184–91,

From haunted spring, and dale
Edg'd with poplar pale,
   The parting Genius is with sighing sent,
With flowre-inwov'n tresses torn
The Nimphs in twilight shade of tangled thickets mourn.

In consecrated Earth,
And on the holy Hearth,
   The *Lars,* and *Lemures* moan with midnight plaint . . .

With K.'s thinking in the passage cp. the Solitary's sympathy for Greek
paganism in Wordsworth's *Excursion* iv 735–44,

               . . . —a SPIRIT hung,
Beautiful region! o'er thy towns and farms,
Statues and temples, and memorial tombs;
And emanations were perceived; and acts
Of immortality, in Nature's course,
Exemplified by mysteries, that were felt
As bonds, on grave philosopher imposed
And armèd warrior; and in every grove
A gay or pensive tenderness prevailed,
   When piety more awful had relaxed . . .

41. lucent fans] Shining wings. See *Lemprière*: 'Psyche is generally represented with the wings of a butterfly, to intimate the lightness of the soil, of
which the butterfly is a symbol . . .'.

Fluttering among the faint Olympians,
I see, and sing, by my own eyes inspired.
So let me be thy choir and make a moan
45   Upon the midnight hours—
Thy voice, thy lute, thy pipe, thy incense sweet
From swingèd censer teeming;
Thy shrine, thy grove, thy oracle, thy heat
Of pale-mouthed prophet dreaming.

50   Yes, I will be thy priest, and build a fane
In some untrodden region of my mind,
Where branchèd thoughts, new grown with pleasant
pain,
Instead of pines shall murmur in the wind:

42. faint] The equivalent of 'faded' in l. 25 above.

44–9. Cp. K.'s journal-letter, 'I am more orthodox than to let a hethan Goddess be so neglected . . .'. The repetition with variations of ll. 30–5 above has a quasi-liturgical effect.

45. Followed in the draft by the uncancelled line (with which cp. l. 29 above),

Thy altar heap'd with flowers . . .

K. obviously first had it in mind to extend his repetition of the previous stanza.

50–1. Perhaps, as Edmund Blunden suggests, a recollection of Collins's *Ode to Pity* (1747) 25–7.

. . . by Fancy's Aid,
E'en now my thoughts, relenting Maid,
Thy Temple's Pride design . . .

52–61. K.'s mental region recalls in some details his setting for the sacrifice to Pan in *Endymion* i 63–106 (pp. 123–4 above), but its secluded Eden-like atmosphere is reminiscent of Psyche's resting-place in Adlington's *Apuleius*; see especially the description of the 'deepe valley' surrounded by 'great and mighty trees' where Psyche '. . . having qualified the thoughts and troubles of her restlesse mind was now well-reposed. And when she had refreshed herself sufficiently with sleepe, she rose with a more quiet and pacified minde' (1893 edn 102). Psyche's 'quiet and pacified minde' suggests K.'s 'peaceable and healthy spirit' in his journal-letter (headnote).

52. The labyrinthine intricacies of the poetic imagination; cp. l. 60 below,

. . . the wreathed trellis of a working brain . . .

The 'pleasant pain' is both the work involved in poetic composition and the intense experience which stimulates it. For the view that K.'s imagery derives from lectures on the structure of the brain given at St. Thomas's Hospital see C. W. Hagelman Jr, 'Keats's medical training and the last stanza of the "Ode to Psyche"', *KShJ* xi (1962) 73–82.

> Far, far around shall those dark-clustered trees
> 55   Fledge the wild-ridgèd mountains steep by steep;
> And there by zephyrs, streams, and birds, and bees,
>   The moss-lain Dryads shall be lulled to sleep;
> And in the midst of this wide quietness
> A rosy sanctuary will I dress
> 60 With the wreathed trellis of a working brain,
>   With buds, and bells, and stars without a name,
> With all the gardener Fancy e'er could feign,

54–5. Cp. *Endymion* i 63–4 (p. 123 above),

> Upon the sides of Latmos was outspread
> A mighty forest . . .

and i 85–6 (p. 123 above)

> . . . the space of heaven above,
> Edged round with dark tree tops . . .

'Fledge' (fringe) is a self-borrowing; see K.'s letter to Tom Keats from Keswick 29 June 1818, '. . . perpendicular Rocks, all fledged with Ash and other beautiful trees' (*L* i 306). K. had probably re-read the letter when looking over Tom's correspondence early in April 1819 (*L* ii 82). Ruskin praised the lines in his *Modern Painters* v (1860), 'Keats . . . puts all that may be said of the pine into one verse . . . I have come to that pitch of admiration for him now, that I dare not read him, so discontented he makes me with my own work; but others must not leave unread, in considering the influence of trees upon the human soul, that marvellous Ode to Psyche' (85).

56–7. Cp. the description in Adlington's *Apuleius* quoted in 10–14 *n* above.
59–61. Cp. *Endymion* i 89–91 (pp. 123–4 above),

> Full in the middle of this pleasantness
> There stood a marble altar, with a tress
> Of flowers budded newly . . .

62–3. Fancy as a gardener who aids and improves upon nature occurs in various Renaissance and neo-classical discussions of the imagination. See, for example, the comparison of art with a gardener in Puttenham's *The Arte of English Poesie* (1589) iii chap. 25: 'Arte is not only an aide and coadiutor to nature in all her actions, but an alterer of them . . . the Gardiner by his arte will not onely make an herbe or flowr, or fruite, come forth in his season without impediment, but will also embellish the same . . . that nature of herselfe would never have done.' See also *The Winter's Tale* IV iii 92–6,

> . . . we marry
> A gentler scion to the wildest stock,
> And make conceive a bark of baser kind
> By bed of nobler race: this is an art
> Which does mend nature, change it rather . . .

62. feign] Invent. The phrasing here and in l. 65 suggests that K. is echoing Spenser's *An Hymne in Honour of Love* 254–5,

Who breeding flowers will never breed the same:
And there shall be for thee all soft delight
65   That shadowy thought can win,
A bright torch, and a casement ope at night,
To let the warm Love in!

... to his fayning fansie represent
Sights never seene, and thousand shadowes vaine ...

65. *Shadowy thought*] Either musing thought that evolves obscurely or, perhaps, thought that is shadowy as the mere ghost of sensations.

66–7. Psyche will openly welcome Eros. In the legend Cupid was obliged to conceal his identity from Psyche and met her only in darkness; see *I stood tip-toe* 147–8 *n* (p. 92 above). The image may be connected with K.'s feelings for Fanny Brawne, as he would have been able to see her lighted window next door at Wentworth Place.

131 'If by dull rhymes our English must be chained'

Probably written between 30 April–3 May 1819 as the last of K.'s experimental sonnets: K. wrote the irregular sonnet on fame, *How fevered is the man* (p. 513 above) on 30 April in his journal-letter of 14 Feb.–3 May 1819 and copied out the present poem on 3 May in the same journal-letter with the comment, 'Incipit altera Sonneta – I have been endeavouring to discover a better sonnet stanza than we have. The legitimate [i.e. Petrarchan] does not suit the language over-well from the pouncing rhymes – the other kind [i.e. Shakespearian] appears too elegiac – and the couplet at the end of it has seldom a pleasing effect – I do not pretend to have succeeded – it will explain itself' (*L* ii 108). The poem seeks a sonnet–form 'more interwoven and complete' by adopting the economy of rhymes of the regular Petrarchan sonnet but disposing the rhyme words to avoid recalling the divisions of either the Shakespearian or the Petrarchan sonnet. K.'s feeling that he had not 'succeeded' may account for his three remaining sonnets being Shakespearian in form; see headnote to *The day is gone* (p. 685 below).
Text from K.'s letter.
Published *1848*.

If by dull rhymes our English must be chained,
And, like Andromeda, the Sonnet sweet
Fettered, in spite of painèd loveliness,

¶ 131. *2–3*. Andromeda was chained to a rock and exposed to a sea-monster as a punishment for praising her own beauty; see *Endymion* iv 602 *n* (p. 270 above).

Let us find out, if we must be constrained,
5   Sandals more interwoven and complete
To fit the naked foot of Poesy.
Let us inspect the lyre, and weigh the stress
Of every chord, and see what may be gained
By ear industrious, and attention meet;
10 Misers of sound and syllable, no less
Than Midas of his coinage, let us be
Jealous of dead leaves in the bay wreath crown;
So, if we may not let the Muse be free,
She will be bound with garlands of her own.

11. *Midas*] The Phrygian king, celebrated for his miserliness, to whom
Bacchus granted the gift of turning everything that he touched into gold.
His legend is related in Ovid's *Metamorphoses* xi 100–93.

132 'Two or three posies'

Written *c.* 1 May 1819: the verses appear in K.'s letter to Fanny Keats conjecturally ascribed to this date by H. Rollins (*L* ii 56). On 'Two or three . . .'
rhymes current at the time see *Forman* (1938–9) iv 204–5, *KShJ* ix (1960) 85.
Text from K.'s letter.
Published *Forman* (1883).

Two or three posies
With two or three simples—
Two or three noses
With two or three pimples—
5   Two or three wise men
And two or three ninnies—
Two or three purses
And two or three guineas—
Two or three raps
10 At two or three doors—
Two or three naps
Of two or three hours—
Two or three cats
And two or three mice—
15 Two or three sprats

¶ 132. 1. *Two or three posies*] Picks up the phrasing in K.'s letter, 'two or
three sensible people to chat with; two or three spiteful folks to spar with;
two or three odd fishes to laugh at and two or three numskulls to argue with,
(*L* ii 56).
2. *simples*] Medicinal herbs.

At a very great price—
Two or three sandies
And two or three tabbies—
Two or three dandies
20   And two Mrs —— mum!
Two or three smiles
And two or three frowns—
Two or three miles
To two or three towns—
25   Two or three pegs
For two or three bonnets—
Two or three dove's eggs
To hatch into sonnets.

20. Mrs.——] The missing word is 'Abbeys'. Richard Abbey had been appointed guardian of the four Keats children in 1810.

133 Ode to a Nightingale

Written May 1819 and probably the second of K.'s 'Spring' odes: 'May 1819' in *Woodhouse* 1, 2. The position of the poem in the sequence of K.'s odes is conjectural, but the metrical evidence suggests that it follows the *Ode to Psyche* and precedes the other odes: the regular ten-line stanza, consisting of one quatrain from a Shakespearian sonnet followed by the sestet of a Petrarchan sonnet, is used again in the remaining 'Spring' odes, but without the shortened line which was a feature of the irregular strophes in the *Ode to Psyche*. A date at the beginning of May may be suggested by the parallels in the second stanza with K.'s letter to Fanny Keats of 1 May 1819, quoted in ll. 12–13 *n* below. Brown's account of the poem's composition reads:

'. . . In the Spring of 1819 a nightingale had built her nest in my house. K. felt a continual and tranquil joy in her song; and one morning he took a chair from the breakfast-table to the grass-plot under a plum-tree where he sat for two or three hours. When he came into the house, I perceived he had some scraps of paper in his hand, and these he was quietly thrusting behind the books. On inquiry, I found these scraps, four or five in number, contained his poetic feeling on the song of the nightingale. The writing was not well legible; and it was difficult to arrange the stanzas on so many scraps. With his assistance I succeeded, and this was his "Ode to a Nightingale," a poem which has been the delight of everyone' (*KC* ii 65).

If Brown's account of the four or five scraps of paper is accurate, the only known MS in K.'s hand, which is on two sheets of writing-paper, is a later draft, and its corrections and cancellations are those of a second stage of composition. It is at least as likely that Brown's memory is at fault and that K.'s holograph, which has minor differences from the texts printed in *Annals* and *1820*, is the first and only draft of the poem.

The nightingale was a stock subject for celebration by pre-Romantic and Romantic poets, but K.'s treatment of the subject is individual. The poem traces the inception, nature and decline of the creative mood, and expresses K.'s attempt to understand his feelings about the contrast between the ideal and actual and the close association of pain with pleasure. Poems on the nightingale probably familiar to him include Charlotte Smith's *To a Nightingale* and *On the Departure of the Nightingale* in her *Elegiac Sonnets* (1784, 9th edn 1800) and Coleridge's *To the Nightingale* (1796) and *The Nightingale: A Conversation Poem* (1798). The suggestion of Coleridge's influence is strengthened by K.'s recent encounter with him on Hampstead Heath (11 April 1819), as the 'thousand things' broached by Coleridge during their two-mile walk included 'Nightingales, Poetry–on Poetical sensation' (*L* ii 88–9). K.'s thinking in the poem, especially in the two concluding stanzas, also points towards a recent re-reading of Wordsworth and Hazlitt. Style and diction show traces of these influences, but are chiefly notable for their condensation under the pressure of personal feeling of passages from K.'s earlier work recalled by association in the process of composition.

The *Ode to a Nightingale* has been widely discussed. Critics agree that it is among the greatest of K.'s odes, but have made heavy weather over the interpretation and value of ll. 61–2 in which the nightingale is described as immortal (see *nn* below). Janet Spens discusses the influence of Hazlitt and Wordsworth on the poem in her article on the *Ode to a Nightingale* in *RES* iii n.s. (1952) 234–43 and M. R. Ridley analyses the distillation in the poem of passages from K.'s earlier work in *Ridley* (1933) 218–31. Other commentaries appear in F. R. Leavis's *Revaluation* (1936) 244–52, G. Hough's *The Romantic Poets* (1953) 174–6, *Pettet* (1957) 251–81, D. Perkins's *The Quest for Permanence: the Symbolism of Wordsworth, Shelley and Keats* (1959) 244–57, R. Fogle's 'Keats's *Ode to a Nightingale*', *PMLA* lxvii (1953), and the general studies of the odes cited in the headnote to *Ode to Psyche* (p. 515 above). Haydon's professional relationship with James Elmes, who published the *Ode to a Nightingale* and the *Ode to a Grecian Urn* in his *Annals of the Fine Arts*, is traced by Ian Jack in his *Keats and the Mirror of Art* (1967) 46, 50–3.

Text from *1820*, with some variants noted from the draft and the version in *Annals*.

Published *Annals of the Fine Arts* July 1819: repr. *1820*.

I

My heart aches, and a drowsy numbness pains
    My sense, as though of hemlock I had drunk,
Or emptied some dull opiate to the drains
    One minute past, and Lethe-wards had sunk.
5 'Tis not through envy of thy happy lot,
    But being too happy in thine happiness–
        That thou, light-wingèd Dryad of the trees,
            In some melodious plot
    Of beechen green, and shadows numberless,
10   Singest of summer in full-throated ease.

II

Oh, for a draught of vintage that hath been
    Cooled a long age in the deep-delvèd earth,

¶ 133. *1–4.* Edmund Blunden adopts G. Greenwood's suggestion–see
Blunden's 'Keats and his Predecessors', *The London Mercury* xx (July 1929)
290–that K. was remembering Horace's *Epode* xiv 1–4, *Mollis inertia cur
tantam diffuderit imis /oblivionem sensibus, /Pocula Lethaeos ut si ducentia somnos/
arente fauce traxerim . . . /*('. . . why soft indolence has diffused as great forgetfulness over my inmost senses as if with parched throat I had drained the
bowl that brings Lethean sleep . . .' [Loeb edn]). K. possessed a copy of
Horace and refers to him several times in his letters (for example, *L* i 113,
141, ii 15, 268).

1. drowsy numbness pains] painful numbness falls *Draft (cancelled)*. On the
connection between K.'s 'drowsy numbness' and his creative moods see
John Holloway's 'The Odes of Keats' in his *The Charted Mirror* (1960) 40–
52. Allusions to the experience of a happiness so intense that it becomes
painful are frequent in K.'s 1819 poems. See, for example, *Ode to Melancholy*
23–4 (p. 540 below),

                . . . aching Pleasure nigh,
        Turning to poison while the bee-mouth sips . . .

2. as though of Hemlock I had drunk] Hemlock can be used as a sedative.
With the phrasing cp. Marlowe's trans. (*c.* 1597) of Ovid's *Amores* iii 6 13,
        Yet like as if cold Hemlock I had drunke . . .

3. emptied . . . to the drains] Drained to the dregs. A forced expression for
the sake of the rhyme.

7. light-wingèd Dryad] Small winged Dryad *Draft (cancelled)*.

10. full-throated ease] K. had frequently suffered from a sore throat during
the previous six months.

11–20. On K.'s enjoyment of wine see *Hence burgundy, claret and port 1–2 n*
(pp. 299–300 above).

11. vintage] A poeticism for wine used again in *Lamia* ii 203, *Otho the
Great* V v 123 (pp. 643 and 611 below).

12–13. See K.'s May 1819 letter to Fanny Keats, '. . . please heaven, a little
claret-wine cool out of a cellar a mile deep . . . a rocky basin to bathe in, a

Tasting of Flora and the country green,
    Dance, and Provençal song, and sunburnt mirth!
15 Oh, for a beaker full of the warm South,
    Full of the true, the blushful Hippocrene,
      With beaded bubbles winking at the brim,
        And purple-stainèd mouth,
    That I might drink, and leave the world unseen,
20   And with thee fade away into the forest dim—

III

Fade far away, dissolve, and quite forget
    What thou among the leaves hast never known,
The weariness, the fever, and the fret
    Here, where men sit and hear each other groan;
25 Where palsy shakes a few, sad, last gray hairs,

---

strawberry bed to say your prayers to Flora in' (*L* ii 56). On Flora cp. *Sleep and Poetry* 102 *n* (p. 73 above).

14. Merry-making at the annual grape-gathering.

15. warm South] Metonymy. Wine from the South.

16. the true, the blushful Hippocrene] Cp. Drayton's 'A Skeltoniad', *Odes* (1619), 10–12,

. . . Sacke
Which to the colder Braine
Is the true Hyppocrene . . .

Hippocrene was the spring on Mount Helicon sacred to the muses. Wine as blushing water has its origin in seventeenth-century allusions to the changing of wine into water at Cana (*John* ii 1–11); see, for example, Crashaw's individual version in his *Epigrammatum Sacrorum Liber* (1634), 'Joann. 4'

Nympha pudica Deum vidit, et erubuit.

17–18. Cp. *Endymion* ii 441–4 (pp. 180–1 above),

Here is wine,
Alive with sparkles—never, I aver,
Since Ariadne was a vintager,
So cool a purple . . .

17. beaded] cluster'd *Draft*. Probably altered when K. found he had to use the word later; see l. 37 *n* below, 'Clustered . . .'.

19. leave the world unseen] Unseen by the world and perhaps as a secondary meaning not seeing the world.

20. Hypermetrical. The word 'away' is found in the draft but is omitted in the four transcripts and *Annals* presumably in the interest of metrical regularity. See *Hyperion* i 46 *n* (p. 399 above).

21. dissolve] Vanish. Perhaps suggested by *Hamlet* I ii 29–30, quoted in *Endymion* i 98–100 *n* (p. 124 above).

23. Echoing Wordsworth's *Tintern Abbey* (1798) 52–3,

. . . the fretful stir
Unprofitable, and the fever of the world . . .

25–6. palsy . . . youth] Personifications, but not capitalized as are 'Beauty . . . Love' (ll. 29–30).

Where youth grows pale, and spectre-thin, and dies;
    Where but to think is to be full of sorrow
      And leaden-eyed despairs;
  Where Beauty cannot keep her lustrous eyes,
30   Or new Love pine at them beyond to-morrow.

IV

Away! away! For I will fly to thee,
    Not charioted by Bacchus and his pards,
  But on the viewless wings of Poesy,
    Though the dull brain perplexes and retards.
35 Already with thee! Tender is the night,
      And haply the Queen-Moon is on her throne,

26. pale, and spectre-thin, and dies] pale and thin and old and dies *Draft*
(*cancelled*). Tom Keats died of tuberculosis 1 Dec. 1818 aged 19. Cp. Wordsworth's *Excursion* iv 760,

    While man grows old, and dwindles, and decays . . .

27–8. Cp. K.'s May 1818 letter to Bailey, '. . . I have this morning such a
Lethargy that I cannot write . . . I have not an Idea to put to paper–my
hand feels like lead – and yet it is an unpleasant numbness it does not take
away the pain of existence' (*L* i 287). Cp. 'the dull brain perplexes and re-
tards' (l. 34).

27. sorrow] grief *Draft* (*cancelled*).

29–30. Cp. *Ode on Melancholy* 21–3 (p. 540 below),

    She dwells with Beauty–Beauty that must die;
      And Joy, whose hand is ever at his lips
    Bidding adieu . . .

31–4. Cp. *Endymion* ii 185–7 (p. 171 above),

         . . . I do think the bars
    That kept my spirit in are burst–that I
    Am sailing with thee through the dizzy sky . . .

32. Bacchus and his pards] A recollection of Titian's 'Bacchus and Ariadne',
See *Sleep and Poetry* 335–6 *n* (p. 83 above) and *Endymion* iv 240–1 (p. 256
above),

      . . . save when Bacchus kept his ivy tent,
    Onward the tiger and the leopard pants . . .

33. viewless] Invisible. Perhaps suggested here by Milton's *The Passion* 50,
'thence hurried on viewless wing'.

36. haply] Perhaps. With 'Queen-moon' cp. Coleridge's *To the Nightingale*
(1796) 187–8,

         . . . Bards address *thy* name,
  And hers, the full-orb'd Queen that shines above . . .

Edmund Blunden (*loc. cit*) suggests a recollection of Horace's *Epode* xv 1–2.

   Nox erat et caelo fulgebat Luna sereno
    inter minora sidera . . .

Clustered around by all her starry fays;
        But here there is no light,
Save what from heaven is with the breezes blown
40   Through verdurous glooms and winding mossy ways.

                              V

I cannot see what flowers are at my feet,
        Nor what soft incense hangs upon the boughs,
But, in embalmèd darkness, guess each sweet
        Wherewith the seasonable month endows
45 The grass, the thicket, and the fruit-tree wild—
        White hawthorn, and the pastoral eglantine;
                Fast-fading violets covered up in leaves;
                        And mid-May's eldest child,
        The coming musk-rose, full of dewy wine,
50   The murmurous haunt of flies on summer eves.

(''Twas night, and in a cloudless sky the moon was shining amid the lesser
lights . . .' [Loeb edn].)

37. Clustered] See l. 17 *n* above. 'Fays'= fairies; for another example see
ll. 69–70 *n* below.

38–50. Cp. the dark spring night and its association with growth and renewal in Coleridge's *The Nightingale: A Conversation Poem* (1798) 5–11,

        You see the glimmer of the stream beneath,
        But hear no murmurings: it flows silently,
        O'er its soft bed of verdure. All is still,
        A balmy night! and though the stars be dim,
        Yet let us think upon the vernal showers
        That gladden the green earth, and we shall find
        A pleasure in the dimness of the stars . . .

40. Through verdurous] Sidelong *Draft* (*cancelled*).

42. soft] blooms *Draft* (*cancelled*). On K.'s early use of 'incense' for the scent
of flowers see *Calidore* 155 *n* (p. 42 above).

43. embalmèd darkness] Darkness steeped in scents. The word 'embalmèd'
foreshadows the preoccupation with death in the following stanza. Cp.
To Sleep 1 (p. 511 above),

        O soft embalmer of the still midnight . . .

46–9. Cp. *A Midsummer Night's Dream* II i 249–52,

        I know a bank whereon the wild thyme blows,
        Where oxlips and the nodding violet grows
        Quite overcanopied with luscious woodbine,
        With sweet musk-roses and with eglantine . . .

49. On K.'s special fondness for the musk-rose see the early poem, *To a
Friend who Sent me Some Roses* 5–6 and 6 *n* (p. 47 above). For 'dewy' K.
first wrote 'sweetest'.

VI

Darkling, I listen; and, for many a time
   I have been half in love with easeful Death,
Called him soft names in many a musèd rhyme,
   To take into the air my quiet breath;
55 Now more than ever seems it rich to die,
   To cease upon the midnight with no pain,
      While thou art pouring forth thy soul abroad
         In such an ecstasy.
   Still wouldst thou sing, and I have ears in vain—
60   To thy high requiem become a sod.

VII

Thou wast not born for death, immortal bird!

51. Darkling] In the dark. Cp. *Paradise Lost* iii 38–40 (marked by K. in his
copy of Milton),

                              . . . the wakeful Bird
         Sings darkling, and in shadiest Covert hid
         Tunes her nocturnal Note . . .

52. half in love] F. R. Leavis comments, 'Keats is strictly only half in love
with death. . . . The desire not to die appears in the thought of becoming a
sod to the nightingale's high requiem and of having ears in vain [ll. 59–60],
and it swells into a strong revulsion against death in the opening lines of the
next stanza' (*Revaluation* (1936) 249).

54. quiet] painless *Draft.*

55. On death as a luxury in K. see *Endymion* ii 33–4 *n* (p. 165 above). With
K.'s colloquial use of 'rich' to describe intense experience cp. *Ode on Melancholy* 18 (p. 540 below), 'some rich anger'.

56. To cease upon the midnight] Cp. *Why did I laugh to-night?* 11 (p. 488
above),

         Yet would I on this very midnight cease . . .

57–8. Cp. the nightingale's song in Dryden's version (1700) of *The Floure
and the Leafe* 119–21,

         I stood intranc'd, and had no room for Thought.
         But all o'er-pour'd with Extasy of Bliss,
         Was in a pleasing Dream of Paradice . . .

60. The nightingale is imagined to be singing a mass for the dead. The cancelled false start to the line was 'But requiem'd . . .'.

61. Considered by Bridges to be '. . . fanciful or superficial,—man being as
immortal as the bird in every sense but that of sameness' (introduction to
The Poems of John Keats, ed. G. Thorn. Drury 1898, lxiv), but defended,
often at length, by subsequent writers; for some representative interpretations see *Pettet* (1957) 274–7. K. is obviously thinking of the nightingale's
song unchanged from age to age.

No hungry generations tread thee down;
The voice I hear this passing night was heard
In ancient days by emperor and clown:
65 Perhaps the self-same song that found a path
  Through the sad heart of Ruth, when, sick for home,
   She stood in tears amid the alien corn;
   The same that oft-times hath
  Charmed magic casements, opening on the foam
70 Of perilous seas in fairy lands forlorn.

62. Cp. Wordsworth's *Excursion* iv 760–2,

   While man grows old, and dwindles, and decays;
   And countless generations of mankind
   Depart; and leave no vestige where they trod . . .

See l. 26 *n* above for K.'s earlier echo of the first line of the quotation.
63. *passing night*] Points the contrast with 'immortal' in l. 61.
64. Cp. Shirley's closing dirge in *Ajax and Ulysses* (1659) 5–8,

    Sceptre and Crown
    Must tumble down
   And in the dust be equal made
   With the poor crooked scythe and spade . . .

65. *song*] voice *Draft (cancelled)*. Cp. Wordsworth's *To the Cuckoo* (1807)
3–4, 17–18,

   . . . shall I call thee Bird,
   Or but a wandering Voice?

   The same whom in my schoolboy days
   I listened to . . .

66–7. Ruth was driven by famine from her native land and had to work in
the fields of her kinsman Boaz (*Ruth* ii 3). With the image of the lonely
exile consoled by the nightingale's song cp. Wordsworth's *The Solitary
Reaper* (1807) 9–12,

   No Nightingale did ever chaunt
   More welcome notes to weary bands
   Of travellers in some shady haunt,
   Among Arabian sands . . .

and Hazlitt's reference in his 1818 lecture 'On Thomson and Cowper' to
the consoling effect of natural objects 'striking on the heart . . . like the music of one's native tongue heard in some far-off country' (*Works* ed P. P.
Howe 1930–34 v 103).
69–70. *magic casements . . . seas*] For K.'s romantic delight in windows looking out over water see his March 1819 letter to Fanny Keats, 'I should like
the window to open onto the Lake of Geneva–and there I'd sit and read all
day like the picture of somebody reading' (*L* ii 46) and his Oct. 1818
reference to the window of his ideal room 'opening on Winander mere'
(*L* i 403). See also his description of the magical windows opening on the

VIII

Forlorn! The very word is like a bell
    To toll me back from thee to my sole self!
Adieu! The fancy cannot cheat so well

sea in Claude's 'The Enchanted Castle', *To J. H. Reynolds Esq.* 50 (p. 323 above),

The windows as if latched by fays and elves . . .

For 'magic' K. first wrote 'wide'.

70. fairy lands forlorn] An admission that the romantic day-dream is at end. Cp. the repetition of 'forlorn' at l. 71. According to Cleanth Brooks, 'In the first instance, "forlorn" is being used primarily in its archaic sense of "utterly lost". The faery lands are those of a past which is remote and far away. But the meaning of "forlorn" is definitely shifted as the poet repeats the word . . . its meaning "pitiable; left desolate" . . . describes the poet's own state' (*Modern Poetry and the Tradition*, 1948, 40). The cancelled epithet for which 'perilous' was substituted is indecipherable: 'keelless', one reading, suggests the emptiness of the sea and looks forward to 'forlorn'; 'ruthless', another reading, has the sense of perilous but would have been cancelled at once to avoid the echo of Ruth's name. On the cancelled reading see *Ridley* (1933) 229–30 and N. Ford, 'Keats's romantic seas: "ruthless" or "keelless"', *KShJ* i (1952) 11–12.

71–2. like a bell . . . self] Suggests that the return to reality is a kind of death. See Cleanth Brooks on the theme of the poem, 'the world of the imagination offers a release from the painful world of actuality, yet at the same time it renders the world of actuality more painful by contrast' (*op. cit.* 41).

72. sole] Solitary.

73–8. K.'s farewell to the nightingale may owe something to Charlotte Smith's *Elegiac Sonnets* (1784), Sonnet vii, *On the Departure of the Nightingale* 4–8,

Sweet poet of the woods!—a long adieu!
Farewel, sweet minstrel of the year . . .

73–4. Fancy is like a will-o'-the-wisp; cp. *Endymion* ii 277–9 (p. 175 above),
. . . the fog-born elf,
Whose flitting lantern, through rude nettle-briar,
Cheats us into a swamp . . .

The 'elf' is 'deceiving' either because the fancy cheats or because it does not cheat well enough. The line has been criticised by various readers, including Bridges, '[K.'s] choosing *elf* [according to Bridges owed to William Browne] to rhyme with *self* turns out disastrously' (*The Poems of John Keats* ed G. Thorn Drury, 1896, lxiv), and Kingsley Amis in his discussion of K.'s 'weakness in handling rhyme', 'After the climax of the preceding stanza, and the vigour of the first two lines of this one, the elf's appearance here is doubly unwelcome . . . it [has] nothing to add in precision, it even hinders the reader from grasping how 'the fancy' appears in the poet's imagination' ('The Curious Elf, A Note on Rhyme in Keats', *Essays in*

As she is famed to do, deceiving elf.
75   Adieu! adieu! Thy plaintive anthem fades
       Past the near meadows, over the still stream,
         Up the hill-side; and now 'tis buried deep
           In the next valley-glades:
       Was it a vision, or a waking dream?
80·   Fled is that music . . . Do I wake or sleep?

Criticism I, April 1951, 191); other examples of K.'s use of 'elf' include *Endymion* ii 461, *Isabella* 453, *Read me a lesson* 11, *How fevered is the man* 7 (pp. 182, 350, 376 and 514 above), *Lamia* i 55 (p. 619 below).

75. *plaintive anthem*] The noun continues the religious associations of 'toll' (l. 72) and earlier 'requiem' (l. 60). The epithet recalls Wordsworth's *The Solitary Reaper* 18–20,

> Perhaps the plaintive numbers flow
> For old unhappy far-off things,
> And battles long ago . . .

77. *up the hillside*] Cp. *The Solitary Reaper* 30–31,

> And, as I mounted up the hill,
> The music in my heart I bore . . .

79. *Vision or a*] vision real or *Draft*. Cp. *Ode to Psyche* 5–6 and *n* (p. 516 above),

> Surely I dreamt to-day, or did I see
> The wingèd Psyche with awakened eyes?

The phrase 'waking dream' was probably suggested by Hazlitt's 1818 lecture, 'On Chaucer and Spenser', 'Spenser was the poet of our waking dreams; and he has invented not only a language, but a music of his own for them . . . lulling the senses into a deep oblivion of the jarring noises of the world from which we have no wish ever to be recalled' (*Works* 1930 edn v 44). F. W. Bateson suggests that K.'s use of 'vision' may owe something to a Wordsworthian influence, perhaps from the Immortality Ode (1807) 56–7,

> Whither is fled the visionary gleam?
> Where is it now, the glory and the dream? . . .

80. *Do I wake or sleep?*] K. is left wondering which has the greater truth— the happiness of romantic reverie or the colder experience of everyday reality.

134 Ode on a Grecian Urn

'May 1819': so dated in Dilke's transcript (Hampstead). The position of the poem in the sequence of K.'s 'Spring' odes is conjectural, but it probably follows the *Ode to a Nightingale* fairly closely since it shares with that ode both a preoccupation with the difference between ideal and actual experience and a poetic structure based on the flight from everyday reality and a return to it, yet metrically is closer to the remaining stanzaic odes in its abandonment of the shorter eighth line found in the 'Nightingale' stanza. Its position in *1820* suggests that K. may have intended it to provide an answer to the questions raised at the end of the *Ode to a Nightingale*.

K. probably had no single urn or vase in mind, but it is worth noting that: (1) Wedgwood reproductions of classical urns were fashionable at the time; (2) K. made a drawing of the outline of the Sosibios vase (then in the Museé Napoléon in Paris), probably from the engraving in Henry Moses's *A Collection of Antique Vases, Altars, Paterae . . . etc . . .*' (1814): see Noel Machin's 'The case of the empty-handed maenad', *Observer Colour Supplement* 28 Feb. 1965; (3) K.'s interest in Greek Art, the Elgin Marbles in particular, was always enthusiastic. Some illustrations of Greek vases accompany D. E. Robinson's 'Ode on a "New Etrurian Urn" (A Reflection of Wedgwood Ware in the Poetic Imagery of John Keats)', *KShJ* xii (1963) 11–35, the discussion of the poem in *Colvin* (1917) 416–19, and Ian Jack's commentary in *Keats and the Mirror of Art* (1967) 214–24.

The ode has been even more widely discussed than the *Ode to a Nightingale*. Critics differ on both the value of the last two lines of the poem and how they should be interpreted. T. S. Eliot and H. W. Garrod regard them as a blemish, but they have been defended, sometimes with more ingenuity than good sense, by subsequent writers. A summary of major interpretations of the poem appears in *Pettet* (1957) 375–81. Some notable commentaries, apart from those appearing in general surveys of K.'s odes, are Middleton Murry's 'Beauty is truth' in *Murry* (1930) 71–92, Cleanth Brooks's 'Keats's sylvan historian: History without footnotes' in *The Well Wrought Urn* (1949) 139–52, F. W. Bateson's study in 'The quickest way out of Manchester: four romantic odes' in *English Poetry: A Critical Introduction* (1950) 217–22, W. Empson's reply to Brooks in *The Structure of Complex Words* (1951) 368–74, H. T. Lyon's *Keats's Well-read Urn* (1958), and P. Hobsbaum's 'The "Philosophy" of the Grecian Urn: a concensus of readings,' *Keats–Shelley Memorial Bulletin* xv 1965.

Text from *1820*, with which the four transcripts largely agree; some variants noted from the earlier *Annals of the Fine Arts*.

Published *Annals of the Fine Arts* xv (Jan. 1820); *1820*.

I

Thou still unravished bride of quietness,
   Thou foster-child of silence and slow time,
Silvan historian, who canst thus express
   A flowery tale more sweetly than our rhyme!

¶ 134. *Title*] On a Grecian Urn *Annals*.
1. The urn is intact–a term applicable to pottery and virgins–which implies its lasting union with quiet. K. telescopes the notions of an 'unravished bride of time' and 'bride of quietness' at the risk of suggesting that quiet itself may be a ravisher. The pristine or virginal quality of the urn is linked below with the virgins on its frieze–'She cannot fade, though thou

5   What leaf-fringed legend haunts about thy shape
       Of deities or mortals, or of both,
           In Tempe or the dales of Arcady?
       What men or gods are these? What maidens loth?
   What mad pursuit? What struggle to escape?
10   What pipes and timbrels? What wild ecstasy?

II
Heard melodies are sweet, but those unheard

hast not thy bliss . . .' (l. 19) and 'still to be enjoyed' (l. 26). The image may
have been suggested in the first place by damaged Greek pottery and sculptures seen by K. at the British Museum or in illustrations. The comma after
'still' in *Annals* (not in the transcripts) converts the word into an epithet and
destroys a possible ambiguity.

2. The artist who made the urn died long ago, leaving it to be fostered by
time and silence. The line expresses paradoxically the perennial youthful-
ness of the urn together with its antique serenity.

3. *Silvan historian*] The urn is a historian because it tells a story. 'Silvan'
suggests that the pastoral existence depicted has happily no history in the
ordinary sense ('a flowery tale' l. 4) and also refers to the decorative border
of leaves which encloses the legend (l. 5).

4. *more sweetly*] Cp. 11–14 *n* below.

5. *leaf-fringed*] As on the Sosibios and Borghese Vases.

7. Tempe, a valley in Thessaly, and Arcadia were traditionally celebrated
in classical antiquity for their pastoral beauty and the happiness of their
inhabitants. The reference to Tempe suggests a recollection of Collins's
The Passions: an Ode for Music (1747) 86–8,

>   They saw in Tempe's Vale her native Maids,
>   Amidst the festal sounding Shades,
>   To some unwearied Minstrel dancing . . .

With the last line of Collins quoted cp. 'happy melodist, unwearièd' (l. 23
below).

8. *men or gods*] Gods or Men *Annals*. The general lack of information at the
time concerning the origin of ancient vases and the meaning of the figures
on them, in particular those on the Portland vase, is discussed by Henry
Moses in his *A Collection of Antique Vases* (1814) 1–14.

9. *what mad pursuit*] what love, what dance? *Annals*.

10. Cp. K. on the Elgin Marbles, 'I never cease to wonder at all that
incarnate Delight' (W. Sharp's *Life of Severn*, 1892, 29).

11–14. See K.'s Dec. 1818 comments in his journal-letter about engravings
from the frescoes in the Campo Santo at Pisa, '. . . even finer to me than
more accomplish'd works – as there was left so much room for Imagination'
(*L* ii 19) and also Wordsworth's *Excursion* ii 710–12,

>   Music of finer tone; a harmony
>   So I do call it, though it be the hand
>   Of silence, though there be no voice . . .

Are sweeter; therefore, ye soft pipes, play on;
Not to the sensual ear, but, more endeared,
Pipe to the spirit ditties of no tone.
15 Fair youth beneath the trees, thou canst not leave
Thy song, nor ever can those trees be bare;
Bold lover, never, never canst thou kiss,
Though winning near the goal—yet do not grieve:
She cannot fade, though thou hast not thy bliss,
20   For ever wilt thou love, and she be fair!

III

Ah, happy, happy boughs, that cannot shed
Your leaves, nor ever bid the spring adieu;
And, happy melodist, unwearièd,
For ever piping songs for ever new!
25 More happy love, more happy, happy love!
For ever warm and still to be enjoyed,
For ever panting, and for ever young—
All breathing human passion far above,

13. sensual] Of sense.
15–20. As K. realizes that the figures are frozen into immobility the ambivalance of his feelings begins to make itself felt. Love is the permanent possession of the lovers only by being unsatisfied.
18. yet do not grieve] O do not grieve *Annals.*
19–20. For the antithetical real world see *Ode to a Nightingale* 29–30 (p. 527 above),

    . . . Beauty cannot keep her lustrous eyes,
    Or new Love pine at them beyond to-morrow . . .

21–30. The repetitions show that it is the imperfections of ordinary human experience which are uppermost in this stanza and also suggest the urgency with which K. attempts to subdue the ambivalent feelings first apparent in ll. 15–20 above. With the reiterated word 'happy' cp. the undertone of longing in *Ode to Psyche* 22 (p. 517 above), 'O happy, happy dove', and *Ode to a Nightingale* 5–6 (p. 525 above),

    'Tis not through envy of thy happy lot,
    But being too happy in thine happiness . . .

28. Cp. Hazlitt on Greek statues in 'On Gusto' (1816, repr. *The Round Table* (1817), 'By their beauty they are raised above the frailties of pain or passion' (*Works*, ed. P. P. Howe 1930, iv 79) and his expansion of this in his 1818 lecture 'On Poetry in General', 'Greek statues are marble to the touch and to the heart . . .In their faultless excellence they appear sufficient to themselves. By their beauty they are raised above the frailties of passion or suffering' (*Works* ed. P. P. Howe 1930–4, v 11). See also Haydon's preferring Raphael to Michael Angelo, who 'seemed to disdain to imitate

That leaves a heart high-sorrowful and cloyed,
30   A burning forehead, and a parching tongue.

IV

Who are these coming to the sacrifice?
To what green altar, O mysterious priest,
Lead'st thou that heifer lowing at the skies,
And all her silken flanks with garlands dressed?
35   What little town by river or sea shore,
Or mountain-built with peaceful citadel,
Is emptied of this folk, this pious morn?

---

creatures who are weak enough to yield to passion and took refuge from the poverty of this world's materials in . . . imagining a higher order of beings and a world of his own' ('On the cartoon of the Sacrifice at Lystra', *The Examiner* 9 May 1819, 301). On the possible influence of Haydon's article on the whole poem see J. R. MacGillivray 'Ode on a Grecian Urn' *TLS* 9 July 1938, 465–6.

29–30. The feverishness of sexual passion. K. comments in Jan. 1819 in his journal-letter of 16 Dec. 1818–4 Jan. 1819 to George and Georgiana Keats, 'I never forget you except after seeing now and then some beautiful woman–but that is a fever' (*L* ii 21). With 'cloyed' cp. *To Fancy* 13–15 *n* (p. 442 above),

> Autumn's red-lipped fruitage, too,
> Blushing through the mist and dew,
> Cloys with tasting . . .

29. high-sorrowful] One of the best known of K.'s many compounds formed with the word 'high'. Others include *Endymion* i 759, 'high-fronted'; *When I have fears* 3, 'high-pilèd'; *Fancy* 27, 'high-commissioned' (pp. 153, 297 and 443 above).

31–40. The pictorial details suggest a recollection of Claude's 'Landscape with the Father of Psyche sacrificing at the Temple of Apollo', which inspired K.'s description of the Greek sacrifice in *To J. H. Reynolds Esq.* 20–2 (p. 321 above),

> The sacrifice goes on; the pontiff knife
> Gleams in the sun, the milk-white heifer lows,
> The pipes go shrilly, the libation flows . . .

The heifer 'lowing at the skies' (l. 33) may be a detail incoporated from the Elgin Marbles (see Plate xxxiii in Ian Jack's *Keats and the Mirror of Art*). On K.'s familiarity with Claude's paintings see *Sleep and Poetry* 354–91 *n* and headnote to *J. H. Reynolds Esq.* (pp. 83–4 and 320 above). With the word 'emptied' (l. 37) the other side of K.'s feelings–i.e. the sense of the thinness and lack of vitality in the ideal world–begins to impose itself more forcefully, finally becoming fully explicit in the following stanza with the paradox 'Cold Pastoral' (l. 45). With 'emptied' and 'desolate' cp. 'forlorn' in *Ode to a Nightingale* 71–2 and *n* (pp. 530–1 above).

34. flanks] sides *Annals*.

And, little town, thy streets for evermore
    Will silent be; and not a soul to tell
40   Why thou art desolate can e'er return.

v

O Attic shape! Fair attitude! With brede
    Of marble men and maidens overwrought,
With forest branches and the trodden weed—
    Thou, silent form, dost tease us out of thought
45 As doth eternity. Cold pastoral!
    When old age shall this generation waste,
        Thou shalt remain, in midst of other woe
    Than ours, a friend to man, to whom thou say'st,
        'Beauty is truth, truth beauty'—that is all
50   Ye know on earth, and all ye need to know.

41. brede] A poetical commonplace in the seventeenth and eighteenth centuries for anything interwoven or plaited, the best known example being Collins's *Ode to Evening* (1747) 7,

With brede etherial wove . . .

According to W. Empson the line is 'very bad . . . the half pun ['Attic . . . attitude'] suggesting a false Greek derivation and jammed up against an arty bit of Old English seems . . . affected and ugly'. See Bridges, 'The last stanza enters stumbling on a pun . . .'.

42. marble men and maidens] See l. 28 *n* above.

44. tease us out of thought] Baffle our attempts to think clearly, but also perhaps lift us into a state of vision. Cp. *To J. H. Reynolds Esq.* 76–7 and *n* (p. 324 above).

Thing cannot to the will

Be settled, but they tease us out of thought . . .

49–50.   Beauty is Truth, Truth Beauty.—That is all

Ye know on Earth, and all ye need to know. *Annals*.

The inverted commas of *1820* are omitted in *Garrod* on the grounds that they are missing in *Annals* and the four transcripts. Their inclusion in *1820* has led some critics, including Murry, to believe that only the words enclosed in them are spoken by the urn. It has been variously argued by other writers (1) that the two lines are addressed by the urn to man, (2) that the passage outside the inverted commas is addresssed by K. to the reader, (3) that this passage is addressed by K. to the urn. (1) is probably the correct interpretation in view of the aphoristic style, possibly deliberately emphasized by the inverted commas in *1820*, the use of 'Ye' (cp. 'us', 'ours' at ll. 45, 48) and the urn's consoling capacity as 'friend to man'; for additional support for this view based on the evidence of the punctuation of the two lines in the transcripts see Alvin Whitley's 'The message of the Grecian Urn', *Keats-Shelley Memorial Bulletin* v (1953) 1–3, and cp. also Henry

Moses's *A Collection of Antique Vases . . .*, 'On the painted vases inscriptions are often found . . . sometimes the inscription contains a moral sentiment' (7). Opinions about the meaning of the beauty-truth equivalent and its relevance to the rest of the poem can be roughly divided as follows: (1) philosophically defensible but of doubtful relevance (Murry); (2) a 'pseudo-statement', but emotionally relevant (I. A. Richards); (3) expressing the paradoxes in the poem and therefore dramatically appropriate (C. Brooks); (4) meaningless and therefore a blemish (T. S. Eliot); (5) an over-simplification, but attempting a positive synthesis of the oppositions expressed in the poem (F. W. Bateson); (6) emotionally and intellectually relevant when properly understood, but 'the effort to see the thing as Keats did is too great to be undertaken with pleasure' (W. Empson).

The passage is obviously a final, if not wholly convincing, attempt to subdue the disquieting feelings first appearing in the poem at ll. 15-20. The phrasing recalls K.'s tentative early discussion of the value of art in his Dec. 1817 letter, 'The excellence of every Art is in its intensity, capable of making all disagreeables evaporate, from their being in close relationship with Beauty and Truth' (*L* i 192). Other references to 'Beauty' and 'Truth' appear in *L* i 184, ii 19.

135   Ode on Melancholy

Probably written May 1819: '1819' in the three transcripts; the month is suggested by the references to spring and early summer in stanza 3 and by the correspondences in the poem with ideas expressed in the *Ode to a Nightingale* and the *Ode on a Grecian Urn*. The poem is a characteristic Keatsian statement about the necessary relationship between joy and sorrow. True Melancholy is not to be found among thoughts of oblivion, death and gloom (stanza 1); it descends suddenly and is linked with the perception of beauty and its transience (stanza 2); it is associated with beauty, joy, pleasure and delight and is felt only by those who can experience these intensely (stanza 3). Commentaries on the poem's structure, organisation and richness of texture occur in William Empson's *Seven Types of Ambiguity* (1930) 271-5, *Bate* (1963) 520-4 and Douglas Bush's *John Keats* (1966) 144-8. Text from *1820*, with some variants noted from K.'s MS (Stanzas 1 and 2, in the possession of R. H. Taylor, reproduced T. W. Higginson, *Book and Heart* 1897; facsimile of stanza 3 reproduced Sotheby's Catalogue 25 July 1931).
Published *1820*.

¶ 135. 1. *No, no, go not to Lethe*] Picks up the idea expressed in the last line of the cancelled opening stanza preserved in *Woodhouse* 2:

> Though you should build a bark of dead men's bones,
> And rear a phantom gibbet for a mast,
> Stitch creeds together for a sail, with groans

I

No, no, go not to Lethe, neither twist
    Wolf's-bane, tight-rooted, for its poisonous wine;
Nor suffer thy pale forehead to be kissed
    By nightshade, ruby grape of Proserpine;
5 Make not your rosary of yew-berries,
    Nor let the beetle, nor the death-moth be
        Your mournful Psyche, nor the downy owl
A partner in your sorrow's mysteries;
    For shade to shade will come too drowsily,
10   And drown the wakeful anguish of the soul.

II

But when the melancholy fit shall fall

            To fill it out, blood-stained and aghast;
            Although your rudder be a dragon's tail
            Long severed, yet still hard with agony,
            Your cordage large uprootings from the skull
            Of bald Medusa, certes you would fail
            To find the Melancholy—whether she
            Dreameth in any isle of Lethe dull . . .

K. obviously rejected the stanza as out of keeping with the mood he wished to express. The violent imagery suggests a recent reading of Burton's account—to which K.'s ode is in effect a reply—of the melancholy that leads to suicide in *The Anatomy of Melancholy* I 4 i (1814 edn i 317–26).

2. Wolf's bane] Aconite. An earlier attempt in *K.'s MS* was 'Herb'.

4. Proserpine was queen of the underworld; see *Endymion* i 944 *n* (p. 162 above). The nightshade has poisonous purple berries.

6–7. death-moth . . . mournful Psyche] The Death's Head moth has markings resembling a human skull. Psyche, or the soul, was formerly represented as a butterfly (see *Ode to Psyche* 41 *n*, p. 518 above).

9–10. Awareness, even if it is awareness of pain, is better than insentience. Cp. K.'s journal-letter 14 Feb.–3 May 1819, 'An indolent day–filled with speculations even of an unpleasant colour–is bearable and even pleasant' (*L* ii 77). See also *Ode to a Nightingale* 52 *n* (p. 529 above).

9. drowsily] Earlier attempts in *K.'s MS* were 'sleepily' and 'heavily'.

11–14. Melancholy appears to be associated with woe and death ('weeping', 'shroud'), but the cloud's tears revive the drooping flowers and the rain-shrouded hill will be greener for the rain. Melancholy is therefore revivifying and creative. With the phrasing cp. Thomson's *Seasons* (1730), *Spring* 1–4,

            Come, gentle Spring! etherial Mildness! come,
            And from the bosom of yon dropping cloud,
            While music wakes around, veil'd in a shower
            Of shadowing roses, on our plains descend . . .

Sudden from heaven like a weeping cloud,
That fosters the droop-headed flowers all,
And hides the green hill in an April shroud;
15　Then glut thy sorrow on a morning rose,
Or on the rainbow of the salt sand-wave,
Or on the wealth of globèd peonies;
Or if thy mistress some rich anger shows,
Imprison her soft hand, and let her rave,
20　　And feed deep, deep upon her peerless eyes.

III

She dwells with Beauty–Beauty that must die;
And Joy, whose hand is ever at his lips
Bidding adieu; and aching Pleasure nigh,
Turning to poison while the bee-mouth sips.

The lines are quoted in Hazlitt's lecture 'On Thomson and Cowper', *Lectures on the English Poets* (1818) (*Works* ed P. P. Howe 1930–4, v 86), which K. may recently have re-read (see *Ode to a Nightingale* 66–7 n, 79 n, pp. 530 and 532 above).

11. fall] come *K.'s MS* (*cancelled*).

15. glut . . . on] Enjoy to the full . . . by thinking of. This use of 'glut' – substituted in *K.'s MS* for 'feed' – is typically Keatsian; cp. *On the Sea* 3 n (p. 112 above).

16. salt sand] dashing *K.'s MS* (*cancelled*). The sun glints on the moisture in the sand-waves to make them appear like rainbows.

18. K. is not thinking of his mistress's feelings but of the pleasure to be found in their display. Cp. his journal-letter 14 Feb.–3 May, 'Though a quarrel in the streets is a thing to be hated, the energies displayed in it are fine' (*L* ii 80). On 'rich' see *Ode to a Nightingale* 55 n (p. 529 above).

20. deep, deep] Cp. the use of repetition in K.'s other odes, e.g. *Ode to Psyche* 22 (p. 517 above), 'happy, happy dove', and *Ode on a Grecian Urn* 25 (p. 535 above),

　　　　More happy love, more happy, happy love!

22–3. Joy . . . adieu] Joy cannot be separated from the awareness that it is momentary.

23. aching Pleasure] Cp. *Ode to a Nightingale*, 1 n and *The Eve of St. Agnes* 279 n (pp. 525, 472 above). The context suggests a recollection of Hazlitt's lecture of Jan. 1818 'On Poetry in General', 'The poetical impression of any subject is that uneasy, exquisite sense of beauty or power that . . . strives . . . to enshrine itself . . . in the highest forms of fancy, and to relieve the aching sense of pleasure by expressing it in the boldest manner' (*Works* ed. P. P. Howe 1930–4, v 3).

24. Recalls *Isabella* 103–4 (p. 333 above),

　　　　Even bees, the little almsmen of spring-bowers,
　　　　Know there is richest juice in poison flowers . . .

25   Aye, in the very temple of Delight
     Veiled Melancholy has her sovran shrine,
       Though seen of none save him whose strenuous
        tongue
     Can burst Joy's grape against his palate fine;
     His soul shall taste the sadness of her might,
30   And be among her cloudy trophies hung.

25–6. The imagery is sexual–*post coetum homo tristis*. 'Veiled' signifies the
melancholy that is the ode's subject, i.e., that which is connected with joy;
it may also imply a recollection of veiled statues of Isis (see *The Fall of
Hyperion* i 141 *n*, p. 666 below).

27–8. Douglas Bush suggests a recollection of *Troilus and Cressida* III ii
19–24,

>   . . . What will it be
> When that the wat'ry palates taste indeed
> Love's thrice-repured nectar? Death, I fear me;
> Sounding destruction; or some joy too fine,
> Too subtile-potent, tun'd too sharp in sweetness
> For the capacity of my ruder powers . . .

The passage is marked by K. in his copy of Shakespeare (*Spurgeon* 164). The
recollection supports the recognition of the sexual elements in the preceding
lines.

27. *him*] those *K.'s MS* (*cancelled*).

29. *sadness*] anguish *K.'s MS*.

30. Trophies of victory were hung up in Greek and Roman temples. See
J. Potter's *Antiquities of Greece* (1697), 'They had several methods of con-
secrating spoils . . . sometimes they made presents, which were dedicated and
hung up in temples' (1827 edn ii 110). K. may also be remembering Shakespeare's sonnet xxxi 9–10,

> Thou art the grave where buried love doth live,
> Hung with the trophies of my lovers gone . . .

The lines are marked by K. in his copy of Shakespeare's poems with the
marginal note 'conceit'.

136 Ode on Indolence

Probably written May 1819: '1819' in *Woodhouse* 2; from the adoption of
the stanza of the *Ode to a Grecian Urn* and *Ode to Melancholy* and the reference to May in l. 46, probably written in May after a re-reading, prior to
posting, of K.'s journal-letter of 14 Feb.–3 May 1819: see under 19 March
in the journal-letter, 'This morning I am in a sort of temper indolent and
supremely careless: I long after a stanza or two of Thomson's Castle of

Indolence. . . . Neither Poetry, nor Ambition, nor Love have any alertness
of countenance as they pass by me: they seem rather like three figures on a
greek vase–a Man and two women. . . . This is the only happiness . . .' (*L*
ii 78–9). K. refers to the poem in his letter of 9 June 1819 to Sarah Jeffrey,
'You will judge of my 1819 temper when I tell you that the thing I have
most enjoyed this year has been writing an ode to Indolence' (*L* ii 116). The
poem, which is stylistically inferior to the other odes and was omitted by K.
from *1820*, has an obvious relationship with the *Ode on a Grecian Urn*.
Text from *Woodhouse* 2, which is taken from Brown's transcript but introduces a different order for the stanzas. *1848* follows *Woodhouse* 2. The
order in Brown's transcript is 1, 2, 5, 6, 4, 3. Garrod's order for the
stanzas, which differs from *Woodhouse, Brown*, has no textual authority.
Published *1848*.

'They toil not, neither do they spin.'

I

    One morn before me were three figures seen,
        With bowèd necks, and joinèd hands, side-faced;
    And one behind the other stepped serene,
        In placid sandals, and in white robes graced;
5   They passed, like figures on a marble urn,
        When shifted round to see the other side;
          They came again; as when the urn once more
    Is shifted round, the first seen shades return;
        And they were strange to me, as may betide
10   With vases, to one deep in Phidian lore.

II

    How is it, Shadows, that I knew ye not?
        How came ye muffled in so hush a masque?
    Was it a silent deep-disguisèd plot
        To steal away, and leave without a task
15 My idle days? Ripe was the drowsy hour;
        The blissful cloud of summer indolence
          Benumbed my eyes; my pulse grew less and less;
    Pain had no sting, and pleasure's wreath no flower:

¶136. *Motto. Matthew* vi 28: 'Consider the lilies of the field, how they
grow; they toil not, neither do they spin.'
10. Phidian] Phidias (*c.* 490–*c.* 448 B.C.) was the sculptor of the Elgin
Marbles.
12. hush] Silent.
18. See K.'s journal-letter 14 Feb.–3 May, 'In this state of effeminacy the
fibres of the brain are relaxed in common with the rest of the body, and to
such a happy degree that pleasure has no show of enticement and pain no
unbearable frown' (*L* ii 78–9).

Oh, why did ye not melt, and leave my sense
20   Unhaunted quite of all but–nothingness?

III

A third time passed they by, and, passing, turned
Each one the face a moment while to me;
Then faded, and to follow them I burned
And ached for wings because I knew the three;
25 The first was a fair maid, and Love her name;
The second was Ambition, pale of cheek,
And ever watchful with fatiguèd eye;
The last, whom I love more, the more of blame
Is heaped upon her, maiden most unmeek,
30   I knew to be my demon Poesy.

IV

They faded, and, forsooth! I wanted wings.
Oh, folly! What is Love? And where is it?
And, for that poor Ambition–it springs
From a man's little heart's short fever-fit.
35 For Poesy! No, she has not a joy–
At least for me–so sweet as drowsy noons,
And evenings steeped in honeyed indolence.
Oh, for an age so sheltered from annoy
That I may never know how change the moons,
40   Or hear the voice of busy common-sense!

V

A third time came they by. Alas, wherefore?
My sleep had been embroidered with dim dreams;

20. See K.'s journal-letter, 'I do not know what I did on monday–nothing
–nothing–nothing–I wish this was anything extraordinary' (L ii 77).
33–4. Cp. K.'s two April 1819 sonnets on fame (pp. 512 and 513 above).
34. Men's passions are short-lived. The phrase 'fever-fit' may be suggested
by Macbeth (who was ambitious) on Duncan's death, Macbeth III ii 23,
            After life's fitful fever he sleeps well . . .
36–7. sweet . . . honeyed indolence] Cp. Four seasons fill, 5–8 (p. 312 above),
        He has his summer, when luxuriously
            Spring's honeyed cud of youthful thought he loves
        To ruminate . . .
41. A third time] 1848's emendation 'And once more' attempts to remove
an ambiguity caused by the re-arrangement of the stanzas: see the repetition
in l. 21 which originally followed the present stanza and was probably used
for emphasis.
52. Cp. Ode to Psyche 15 (p. 516 above),
        They lay calm-breathing on the bedded grass . . .

My soul had been a lawn besprinkled o'er
 With flowers, and stirring shades, and baffled beams.
45 The morn was clouded, but no shower fell,
  Though in her lids hung the sweet tears of May;
  The open casement pressed a new-leaved vine,
 Let in the budding warmth and throstle's lay;
 O Shadows, 'twas a time to bid farewell!
50 Upon your skirts had fallen no tears of mine.

VI

So, ye three Ghosts, adieu! Ye cannot raise
 My head cool-bedded in the flowery grass;
For I would not be dieted with praise,
 A pet-lamb in a sentimental farce!
55 Fade softly from my eyes, and be once more
  In masque-like figures on the dreamy urn.
  Farewell! I yet have visions for the night,
 And for the day faint visions there is store.
  Vanish, ye Phantoms, from my idle sprite
60 Into the clouds, and never more return!

53. Cp. K.'s letter to James Hessey of 8 Oct. 1818, 'Praise or blame has but a momentary effect on the man whose love of beauty in the abstract makes him a severe critic on his own Works. My own domestic criticism has given me pain without comparison beyond what Blackwood or the Quarterly could possibly inflict, and also when I feel I am right, no external praise can give me such a glow as my own solitary reperception and ratification of what is fine' (*L* i 373–4).

54. K. comments in his letter to Sarah Jeffrey, 'I hope I am a little more of a Philosopher than I was, consequently a little less of a versifying Pet-lamb' (*L* ii 116).

58. my idle sprite] The phrase is used in the April 1819 sonnet *As Hermes once* (p. 499 above).

137 Otho the Great

Written in collaboration with Charles Brown at Shanklin, Isle of Wight, and Winchester early July–*c.* 23 Aug. 1819 and revised *c.* 20 Dec. 1819–*c.* 13 Jan. 1820: see K.'s letter from Shanklin to Fanny Brawne 8 July 1819, 'I do not pass a day without sprawling some blank verse' (*L* ii 127)–K. settled in Shanklin 28 June–and his letter to Taylor from Winchester 23 Aug. 1819, 'We [K. and Brown] have together been engaged . . . in a Tragedy which I have just finish'd' (*L* ii 143). Brown joined K. at Shanklin *c* 22 July

¶ 137. *Title. Otho*] Otto the Great (912–973) became King of Germany 936 and ruler of the Holy Roman Empire 962.

and left with him for Winchester 12 Aug. Act I was completed and Act II begun by 11 July 1819 (*L* ii 128), Acts III and IV were finished by 14 Aug. (*L* ii 139). For the revisions see K.'s letter to Fanny Keats 20 Dec. 1819, '... very busy ... hightening the interest of our Tragedy' (*L* ii 237) and to Georgiana Keats 13 Jan. 1820, 'Not having succeeded at Drury Lane with our Tragedy, we have been making some alterations and are about to try Covent Garden—Brown has just done patching up the Copy, as it is altered' (*L* ii 241). Brown recorded in March 1841 (*KC* ii 66–7):

'At Shanklin [K.] undertook a difficult task: I engaged to furnish him with the fable, characters, and dramatic conduct of a tragedy, and he was to embody it into poetry ... while I sat opposite to him, he caught my description of each scene, entered into the characters to be brought forward, the events and everything connected with it. Thus he went on scene after scene, never knowing nor enquiring into the scene which was to follow, until four acts were completed. It was then he required to know, at once, all the events which were to occupy the fifth act ... he insisted on it that my incidents were too numerous and ... too melodramatic. He wrote the fifth act in accordance with his own view.... This tragedy ... was sent to Drury Lane Theatre.... It was ... accepted, with a promise to bring it forward during that very season. From what I could learn ... Kean ... desired to play the principal character [see below]. Afterwards I was told ... it was for the next season ... or for the season after the next ... I therefore ... sent it to Covent Garden Theatre, whence it was speedily returned with a note ... containing a negative....'

Brown's memory may have played him false, since his arrival in Shanklin nearly a month after K. suggests K.'s working alone on early drafts of Act I and Act II, probably using material discussed with Brown at Hampstead June 1819. On their collaboration after Brown's arrival in Shanklin see K. in their joint letter to Dilke 31 July 1819, 'Brown and I are pretty well harnessed again to our dog-cart. I mean the Tragedy' (*L* ii 135) and also I ii 1 *n*, III ii 1–3 *n*, IV ii 129–31 *n* below. K. described himself as 'Midwife' to Brown's plot in his letter to Taylor of 5 Sept. 1819 (*L* ii 157).

No specific source has been discovered for the play, which was an attempt to make money by following the popular taste for strongly flavoured tragedies based on German history—see, for example, the translations of German historical plays in Benjamin Thompson's *The German Theatre* (6 vols 1800, repr. 1801, 1811) and Coleridge's translation (1800) of Schiller's *Die Piccolomini* and *Wallensteins Tod* (1798–9). Schiller's plays may have affected the relationship between Otho and his son Ludolph in *Otho the Great*, but some elements in the relationship also suggest the influence of Scott's *Ivanhoe* (1819). The historical background—for which Brown's sources are unknown—is the suppression by Otto I (A.D. 936–73) of the Hungarian risings of 953–5 in which Ludolf and his brother-in-law Conrad, Duke of Franconia, were involved, but events covering some twenty years are compressed into the action of a single day, the historical details being freely adapted to serve a complicated Gothic drama of intrigue, written in quasi-Elizabethan style with numerous Shakespearian echoes, in which Ludolph emerges as the principal figure.

Otho the Great is K.'s first attempt to realize the dramatic ambitions which he confessed to Bailey 14 Aug. 1819, 'One of my Ambitions is to make as great a revolution in modern dramatic writing as Kean has done in acting' (*L* ii 139) and to Taylor 17 Nov. 1819 (see headnote to *King Stephen*, p. 691 below). His hopes for the play and his faith in Edmund Kean are expressed in his journal-letter Sept. 1819, 'Mine I am sure is a tolerable tragedy – it would have been a bank to me, if just as I had finish'd it I had not heard of Kean's resolution to go to America. . . . There is no actor can do the principal character besides Kean. . . . Were it to succeed . . . it would lift me out of the mire . . . of a bad reputation' (*L* ii 186). On Kean as Ludolph see I iii 24–9 *n* below, and for other references to Kean *L* ii 149 and K.'s 'On Edmund Kean as a Shakespearian Actor', *The Champion* 21 Dec. 1817, repr. *Forman* (1883) iii 3–6. Ludolph's speeches in the play are obviously influenced by recollections of Kean in his major Shakespearian roles. On the likelihood of their also reflecting something of K.'s feelings towards Fanny Brawne at the time of his separation from her in late summer 1819 see *Ward* (1963) 434.

Francis Jeffrey wrote of *Otho the Great* in his letter to Milnes of 15 Aug. 1848, 'The tragedy is a great failure. . . . There are brilliant images . . . but the . . . extravagance and . . . bombast of most of the passionate speeches – (Ludolph's especially) – appear . . . more humiliating, than even the palpable . . . weakness and absurdity of the dramatic conception' (*KC* ii 249). Subsequent readers have generally agreed that the play is a failure, though its dramatic promise is applauded by G. Wilson Knight in *The Starlit Dome* (1943) 306–7 and by Bernice Slote in *Keats and the Dramatic Principle* (1958) 104–20. The historical sources are discussed by Gál Istvan in 'Keats magyar vonat-kozázú drámája', *Filológai Közlöny* i–ii (Budapest 1965) 70–92. Notices of the first performance (26 Nov. 1950 by the Preview Theatre Club at St Martin's Theatre, London) appear in *The Times* 27 Nov. 1950, *The Christian Science Monitor* 6 Jan. 1951 and (by Dorothy Hewlett) *Keats–Shelley Memorial Bulletin* iv (1952). For Joseph Severn's attempt to mount an amateur production at Rome in 1834 see *The Letters of Charles Armitage Brown*, ed. J. Stillinger (1966), 331–2.

Text from Brown's transcript (used in *1848*), which has corrections in K.'s hand, with some variants noted from K.'s draft (I–IV i 1–184 at Texas University Library, Austin, and the rest at the Huntington Library; portions of a few pages missing from these sections of K.'s draft are at Harvard); I i 1–18, missing in the transcript, follows the draft reading with variants noted from *1848*. The transcript (*Brown's MS*) largely agrees with the draft (*K.'s MS*) except for I i 16–121, I i 137–55 which K. revised: fragments of his later draft of these passages (Harvard) agree with the readings of *Brown's MS*. For details of the *MSS*, including fragments of K.'s earlier drafts, see *Garrod* xliii–xlvi.

Published *1848*.

DRAMATIS PERSONAE

Otho the Great, *Emperor of Germany*.
Ludolph, *his Son*.
Conrad, *Duke of Franconia*.
Albert, *a Knight, favoured by Otho*.
Sigifred, *an Officer, friend of Ludolph*.
Theodore,⎫
Gonfred, ⎬ *Officers*.
Ethelbert, *an Abbot*.
Gersa, *Prince of Hungary*.
An Hungarian Captain.
Physician.
Page.
Nobles, Knights, Attendants, and Soldiers.

Erminia, *Niece of Otho*.
Auranthe, *Conrad's Sister*.
Ladies and Attendants.

Scene. *The Castle of Friedburg, its vicinity, and the Hungarian Camp.*

Time.–*One Day.*

ACT I

SCENE I

[*An Apartment in the Castle. Enter* Conrad]

Conrad. So, I am safe emergèd from these broils!
    Amid the wreck of thousands I am whole;
    For every crime I have a laurel-wreath,
    For every lie a lordship. Nor yet has
5   My ship of fortune struck her silken sails–

I i *Stage direction*. An Apartment in the Castle of Friedborg. Enter Conrad
bustling *K.'s MS* ('Conrad and Auranthe meeting' cancelled). Friedburg is
a town in Hesse near Frankfort-on-Main.
I i *1–15*. Establishing the villain of the piece in the style of the opening
soliloquy in *Richard III*. K. saw Kean in *Richard III* Dec. 1817. Conrad the
Red of Franconia, who married Otto's daughter Liutgard in 947 and joined
forces with Ludolf against Otto 953–5, was allowed to keep his estates after
Otto's victory at Regensburg 955. He died in the same year at the battle
of the Lechfeld while helping Otto to defeat the Magyars. His role in the
play as Auranthe's brother suggests a debt to Flamineo and Vittoria
Corombona in Webster's *The White Devil*.
I i *5. struck*] furled *1848*.

Let her sail on! This dangered neck is safe,
By dexterous policy, from the rebel's axe;
And of my ducal palace not one stone
Is bruised by the Hungarian petars.
10   Toil hard, ye slaves, and from the miser-earth
Bring forth once more my bullion, treasured deep,
With all my jewelled salvers, silver and gold,
And precious goblets that make sweet the wine.
But why do I stand babbling to myself?
15   Where is Auranthe? I have news for her
Shall—

Enter Auranthe

Auranthe. Conrad! What tidings? Good, if I may guess
From your alert eyes and high-lifted brows.
What tidings of the battle? Albert? Ludolph? Otho?
Conrad. You guess aright. And, sister, slurring o'er
20   Our by-gone quarrels, I confess my heart
Is beating with a child's anxiety,
To make our golden fortune known to you.
Auranthe. So serious?
Conrad.   Yes, so serious, that before
I utter even the shadow of a hint
25   Concerning what will make that sin-worn cheek
Blush joyous blood through every lineament,
You must make here a solemn vow to me.

I i 6. *sail . . . safe*] glide . . . saved *1848*.

I i 7. The omission of this line in *K.'s MS* may be a slip, since it appears in a fragment of an earlier holograph draft (see *Garrod*) and also in *1848*.

I i 9. *petars*] Petards were small engines of war used for firing breeches in walls and fortifications. See *Hamlet* III iv 207,

            Hoist with his own petar . . .

I i 13. *sweet*] rich *1848*.

I i 16–121. For the version in *K.'s MS*, omitting details of Conrad's duplicity towards Otho and Ludolph, see Appendix C (p. 759 below). I i 16–22, 32–42 agree with readings preserved in fragments of K.'s later draft at Harvard.

I i 16. *Auranthe*] An unhistorical character invented for the purposes of the plot. For K.'s original intention to incorporate naturalistic details into his Websterian portrait see Brown's letter to Dilke 12 Aug. 1819, 'I cannot endure his fancy of making the princess blow up her hairdresser, for smearing her cheek with pomatum, and spoiling her rouge. It may be natural, as he observes, but so might many things' (*The Letters of Charles Armitage Brown*, ed Jack Stillinger, 1966, 49). For other rejected attempts to add colourful details in the play see I ii 1 *n*, III ii 1–3 *n*, IV ii 129–31 *n* below.

Auranthe. I prithee, Conrad, do not overact
The hypocrite. What vow would you impose?

30 *Conrad.* Trust me for once—that you may be assured
'Tis not confiding to a broken reed,
A poor Court-bankrupt, outwitted and lost,
Revolve these facts in your acutest mood,
In such a mood as now you listen to me.

35 A few days since, I was an open rebel
Against the Emperor, had suborned his son,
Drawn off his nobles to revolt, and shown
Contented fools causes for discontent
Fresh hatched in my ambition's eagle nest.

40 So thrived I as a rebel, and behold
How I am Otho's favourite, his dear friend,
His right hand, his brave Conrad!
Auranthe.   I confess
You have intrigued with these unsteady times
To admiration; but to be a favourite!

45 *Conrad.* I saw my moment. The Hungarians,
Collected silently in holes and corners,
Appeared, a sudden host, in the open day.
I should have perished in our empire's wreck,
But, calling interest loyalty, swore faith

50 To most believing Otho; and so helped
His blood-stained ensigns to the victory
In yesterday's hard fight, that it has turned
The edge of his sharp wrath to eager kindness.
Auranthe. So far yourself. But what is this to me

55 More than that I am glad? I gratulate you.
Conrad. Yes, sister, but it does regard you greatly,
Nearly, momentously—aye, painfully!
Make me this vow—
Auranthe.   Concerning whom or what?
Conrad. Albert!
Auranthe.   I would inquire somewhat of him:

60 You had a letter from me touching him?
No treason 'gainst his head in deed or word!
Surely you spared him at my earnest prayer?
Give me the letter—it should not exist!

I i *36.* According to record Ludolf had quarrelled with Otho before Conrad joined the risings of 953–5. Ludolf was Otto's son by Edith, daughter of the English King, Aethelstan; he became disaffected after Otto's second marriage in 951 to Adelaide, widow of Lothair King of Italy, when the birth of their son threatened his succession.

I i *44. To admiration*] Wonderfully well.

19+K.

Conrad. At one pernicious charge of the enemy,
65   I, for a moment-whiles, was prisoner ta'en
And rifled. Stuff! The horses' hoofs have minced it!
Auranthe. He is alive?
Conrad.   He is! But here make oath
To alienate him from your scheming brain,
Divorce him from your solitary thoughts,
70   And cloud him in such utter banishment,
That when his person meets again your eye,
Your vision shall quite lose its memory,
And wander past him as through vacancy.
Auranthe. I'll not be perjured.
Conrad.   No, nor great, nor mighty;
75   You would not wear a crown, or rule a kingdom.
To you it is indifferent.
Auranthe.   What means this?
Conrad. You'll not be perjured! Go to Albert then,
That camp-mushroom—dishonour of our house.
Go, page his dusty heels upon a march,
80   Furbish his jingling baldric while he sleeps,
And share his mouldy ration in a siege.
Yet stay—perhaps a charm may call you back,
And make the widening circlets of your eyes
Sparkle with healthy fevers. The Emperor
85   Hath given consent that you should marry Ludolph!
Auranthe. Can it be, brother? For a golden crown
With a queen's awful lips I doubly thank you!
This is to wake in Paradise! Farewell,
Thou clod of yesterday—'twas not myself!
90   Not till this moment did I ever feel
My spirit's faculties! I'll flatter you
For this, and be you ever proud of it;
Thou, Jove-like, struck'dst thy forehead,
And from the teeming marrow of thy brain
95   I spring complete Minerva! But the prince—
His highness Ludolph—where is he?
Conrad.   I know not:
When, lackeying my counsel at a beck,
The rebel lords, on bended knees, received

I i *66. rifled*] Robbed.
I i *72–3.* Elizabethan for 'you will cut him dead'.
I i *93–5.* Minerva sprang fully armed from the head of her father Jupiter.
I i *97. lackeying . . . beck*] Servilely following my counsel at a nod. The
phrasing has a Shakespearian flavour. See, for example, *Antony and Cleo-
patra* IV x 34, quoted in I iii 82–3 *n* below.

The Emperor's pardon, Ludolph kept aloof,
100 Sole, in a stiff, fool-hardy, sulky pride;
Yet, for all this, I never saw a father
In such a sickly longing for his son.
We shall soon see him, for the Emperor–
He will be here this morning.
Auranthe.   That I heard
105 Among the midnight rumours from the camp.
Conrad. You give up Albert to me?
Auranthe.   Harm him not!
E'en for his highness Ludolph's sceptry hand,
I would not Albert suffer any wrong.
Conrad.   Have I not laboured, plotted?
Auranthe.   See you spare him:
110 Nor be pathetic, my kind benefactor,
On all the many bounties of your hand–
'Twas for yourself you laboured–not for me!
Do you not count, when I am queen, to take
Advantage of your chance discoveries
115 Of my poor secrets, and so hold a rod
Over my life?
Conrad.   Let not this slave–this villain–
Be cause of feud between us. See, he comes!
Look, woman, look, your Albert is quite safe!
In haste it seems. Now shall I be in the way,
120 And wished with silent curses in my grave,
Or side by side with 'whelmèd mariners.

Enter Albert

Albert. Fair on your graces fall this early morrow!
So it is like to do, without my prayers,
For your right noble names, like favourite tunes,
125 Have fallen full frequent from our Emperor's lips,
High commented with smiles.
Auranthe.   Noble Albert!
Conrad (aside).   Noble!
Auranthe. Such salutation argues a glad heart
In our prosperity. We thank you, sir.
Albert. Lady! Oh, would to Heaven your poor servant
130 Could do you better service than mere words!
But I have other greeting than mine own,

I i *105. rumours*] tidings *Brown's MS (cancelled).*
I i *109. See you spare him*] Touch him not *Brown's MS (cancelled).*
I i *124. like favourite tunes*] high commented *K.'s MS (cancelled).*
I i *125. fallen*] dwelt *K.'s MS (cancelled).* An earlier attempt was 'leaped'.

From no less man than Otho, who has sent
This ring as pledge of dearest amity;
'Tis chosen I hear from Hymen's jewellery,
135   And you will prize it, lady, I doubt not,
Beyond all pleasures past, and all to come.
To you, great duke—
Conrad.   To me! What of me, ha?
Albert. What pleased your grace to say?
Conrad.   Your message, sir!
Albert. You mean not this to me?
Conrad.   Sister, this way;
140   For there shall be no 'gentle Alberts' now,   [*Aside.*
No 'sweet Auranthes!'

                              [*Exeunt* Conrad *and* Auranthe.
Albert (solus). The duke is out of temper; if he knows
More than a brother of a sister ought,
I should not quarrel with his peevishness.
145   Auranthe—Heaven preserve her always fair!—
Is in the heady, proud, ambitious vein;
I bicker not with her—bid her farewell!
She has taken flight from me, then let her soar;
He is a fool who stands at pining gaze!
150   But for poor Ludolph, he is food for sorrow:
No levelling bluster of my licensed thoughts,
No military swagger of my mind,
Can smother from myself the wrong I've done him—
Without design, indeed—yet it is so—
155   And opiate for the conscience have I none!   [*Exit.*

SCENE II

[*The Court-yard of the Castle.*]

Martial music. Enter, from the outer gate, Otho, *Nobles,*
Knights, *and* Attendants. *The Soldiers halt at the*
gate, with Banners in sight.

Otho. Where is my noble herald?

I i *133–4.* Used by Trelawny as a motto for *Adventures of a Younger Son*
(1831) chap. 50.
I i *134–6.*   With every gratulation that can pass
                From friend to friend upon a happy day . . .
                                        K.'s MS (cancelled).
I i *136. Beyond*] Before *K.'s MS.*
I i *137–55.* For the version in *K.'s MS* see Appendix C (p. 761 below).

[*Enter* Conrad, *from the Castle, attended by two Knights
and Servants.* ALBERT *following.*]

　　　　　　　　　　　　　　　　Well, hast told
Auranthe our intent imperial?
Lest our rent banners, too o' the sudden shown,
Should fright her silken casements and dismay
5　Her household to our lack of entertainment.
A victory!
Conrad.　　God save illustrious Otho!
Otho. Aye, Conrad, it will pluck out all grey hairs;
It is the best physician for the spleen;
The courtliest inviter to a feast;
10　The subtlest excuser of small faults;
And a nice judge in the age and smack of wine.

　　[*Enter, from the Castle,* Auranthe, *followed by Pages
holding up her robes, and a train of Women. She kneels.*]

Hail my sweet hostess! I do thank the stars,
Or my good soldiers, or their ladies' eyes,
That, after such a merry battle fought,
15　I can, all safe in body and in soul,
Kiss your fair hand and lady Fortune's too.
My ring! Now, on my life, it doth rejoice
These lips to feel it on this soft ivory!
Keep it, my brightest daughter; it may prove
20　The little prologue to a line of kings.
I strove against thee and my hot-blood son,

I ii *1. Stage direction*] For 'Otho, Nobles, Knights, and Attendants' *K.'s MS*
has 'Otho and several officers'. The scene was obviously devised with an
eye to stage spectacle. Cp. K.'s joint letter with Brown to Dilke, 31 July
1819, 'We are thinking of introducing an Elephant but have not historical
reference within reach to determine us as to Otho's Menagerie. When
Brown first mention'd this I took it for a Joke; however he brings such
plausible reasons, and discoursed so eloquently on the dramatic effect that I
am giving it a serious consideration' (*L* ii 135). H. Rollins notes: 'On
elephants in drama see M. W. Disher's *Greatest Show on Earth* (1937), p. 76.'
I ii *6–11.* Used by Trelawny with I iii 5 below as one of his mottoes for
Adventures of a Younger Son (1831) chap. 33. The catalogue element has an
Elizabethan flavour.
I ii *6. illustrious*] the power of *Brown's MS* (*cancelled*); imperial *K.'s MS*.
I ii *20.* Echoes *Macbeth* III i 60,
　　　　They hail'd him father to a line of kings . . .
and I iii 128,
　　　　. . . happy prologues to the swelling act . . .

Dull blockhead that I was to be so blind,
But now my sight is clear; forgive me, lady.
Auranthe. My lord, I was a vassal to your frown,
25   And now your favour makes me but more humble;
In wintry winds the simple snow is safe,
But fadeth at the greeting of the sun:
Unto thine anger I might well have spoken,
Taking on me a woman's privilege,
30   But this so sudden kindness makes me dumb.
Otho. What need of this? Enough, if you will be
A potent tutoress to my wayward boy,
And teach him, what it seems his nurse could not,
To say, for once, I thank you. Sigifred!
35   *Albert.* He has not yet returned, my gracious liege.
Otho. What then! No tidings of my friendly Arab?
Conrad. None, mighty Otho.
                          [*To one of his Knights, who goes out.*
                                   Send forth instantly
An hundred horsemen from my honoured gates,
To scour the plains and search the cottages.
40   Cry a reward, to him who shall first bring
News of that vanishèd Arabian,
A full-heaped helmet of the purest gold.
Otho. More thanks, good Conrad; for, except my son's,
There is no face I rather would behold
45   Than that same quick-eyed pagan's. By the saints,
This coming night of banquets must not light
Her dazzling torches; nor the music breathe
Smooth, without clashing cymbal, tones of peace
And indoor melodies; nor the ruddy wine
50   Ebb spouting to the lees; if I pledge not,
In my first cup, that Arab!

I ii *24–30* (and see I ii *77–80* below). With Auranthe and Conrad welcoming
Otho cp. Lady Macbeth and Macbeth receiving Duncan, *Macbeth* I vi 14–28.
I ii *36. friendly Arab*] See I ii *58 n* below.
I ii *39. scour the plains*] Probably echoing Pope's *Essay on Criticism*; see
Endymion iv 252 *n* (p. 257 above).
I ii *42. purest*] brightest *K.'s MS (cancelled).*
I ii *45. By the saints*] By my crown *K.'s MS (cancelled).*
I ii *46. night*] day *K.'s MS (cancelled).*
I ii *47. breathe / Smooth, without*] nor the music sound / Softer than . . . *K.'s
MS (cancelled).*
I ii *51. Monarch*] Caesar *K.'s MS.* A reminder that Otto was a Roman
Emperor. Perhaps altered since Otto's crowning at Rome took place some
years after his victories at Regensburg and the Lechfeld.

Albert.   Mighty Monarch,
I wonder not this stranger's victor-deeds
So hang upon your spirit. Twice in the fight
It was my chance to meet his olive brow,
55   Triumphant in the enemy's shattered rhomb;
And, to say truth, in any Christian arm
I never saw such prowess.
Otho.   Did you ever?
O, 'tis a noble boy!—tut!—what do I say?
I mean a triple Saladin, whose eyes,
60   When in the glorious scuffle they met mine,
Seemed to say—'Sleep, old man, in safety sleep;
I am the victory!'
Conrad.   Pity he's not here.
Otho. And my son too, pity he is not here.
Lady Auranthe, I would not make you blush,
65   But can you give a guess where Ludolph is?
Know you not of him?
Auranthe.   Indeed, my liege, no secret—
Otho. Nay, nay, without more words, dost know of him?
Auranthe. I would I were so over-fortunate,
Both for his sake and mine, and to make glad
70   A father's ears with tidings of his son.
Otho. I see 'tis like to be a tedious day.
Were Theodore and Gonfred and the rest
Sent forth with my commands?
Albert.   Aye, my lord.
Otho. And no news! No news! 'Faith! 'tis very strange.
75   He thus avoids us. Lady, is 't not strange?
Will he be truant to you too? It is a shame.
Conrad. Will 't please your highness enter, and accept
The unworthy welcome of your servant's house?
Leaving your cares to one whose diligence
80   May in few hours make pleasures of them all.

I ii 55. *rhomb*] A lozenge-shaped formation. Cp. *Paradise Regained* iii 308–9,
                    See how in warlike muster they appear,
                    In Rhombs and wedges . . .
I ii 58. Otho has recognized his son in spite of his Arab disguise (see II i 126
below). Ludolph's use of a disguise and his eventual reconciliation with his
father may owe something to the hero of Scott's *Ivanhoe* (1819), who enters
his father's house disguised as a pilgrim and later, masquerading as 'The
Disinherited Knight', defeats his opponents in a tournament.
I ii 59. *Saladin*] An anachronism since Saladin lived 1138–93. His use here
as an example of chivalry and courage was probably suggested by Scott's
recent portrait of him in *Ivanhoe*.

Otho. Not so tedious, Conrad. No, no, no, no—
I must see Ludolph or the—What's that shout!
Voices without. Huzza! Huzza! Long live the Emperor!
Other Voices. Fall back! Away there!
Otho.   Say, what noise is that?
[Albert *advancing from the back of the Stage, whither
he had fastened on hearing the cheers of the soldiery.*

85   *Albert.* It is young Gersa, the Hungarian prince,
Picked like a red stag from the fallow herd
Of prisoners. Poor prince, forlorn he steps,
Slow in the demure proudness of despair.
If I may judge by his so tragic bearing,
90   His eye not downcast and his folded arm,
He doth this moment wish himself asleep
Among his fallen captains on yon plains.

Enter Gersa, *in chains, and guarded.*

Otho. Well said, Sir Albert.
Gersa.   Not a word of greeting,
No welcome to a princely visitor,
95   Most mighty Otho? Will not my great host
Vouchsafe a syllable, before he bids
His gentlemen conduct me with all care
To some securest lodging?—cold perhaps!
Otho. What mood is this? Hath fortune touched thy
brain?
100   *Gersa.* O kings and princes of this fev'rous world,
What abject things, what mockeries must ye be,
What nerveless minions of safe palaces!
When here a monarch, whose proud foot is used

I ii *82. the*—] Otho was about to say 'Arab'.
I ii *85. Gersa*] Variously 'Gersa' and 'Gerza' in *K.'s MS*; 'Gersa' throughout *Brown's MS*. The character is based on Géza, the first King of Hungary
(971–97), who did not meet Otto personally but made peace with him 972.
He was celebrated for the diplomacy which helped him to become the first
unifier of his country. Studies of Géza by János Pelcz appeared in German
(1759) and Latin (1769).
I ii *86. like a red stag*] Possibly suggested by Géza's conversion to Christianity (975) since the stag was a traditional emblem of Christ. Gál Istvan
points out that an illumination in an anonymous fourteenth-century Hungarian chronicle shows Géza and his brother on the banks of the Danube
with a stag standing on the spot where they are supposed to have founded a
church.
I ii *100. this fev'rous world*] Cp. *Macbeth* III ii 23, quoted in *Ode on Indolence*
34 *n* (p. 543 above).

To fallen princes' necks, as to his stirrup,
105 Must needs exclaim that I am mad forsooth,
Because I cannot flatter with bent knees
My conqueror!
Otho.   Gersa, I think you wrong me:
I think I have a better fame abroad.
Gersa. I prythee mock me not with gentle speech,
110 But, as a favour, bid me from thy presence;
Let me no longer be the wondering food
Of all these eyes; prythee command me hence!
Otho. Do not mistake me, Gersa. That you may not,
Come, fair Auranthe, try if your soft hands
115 Can manage those hard rivets to set free
So brave a prince and soldier.
Auranthe (sets him free).   Welcome task!
Gersa. I am wound up in deep astonishment!
Thank you, fair lady. Otho! Emperor!
You rob me of myself; my dignity
120 Is now your infant; I am a weak child.
Otho. Give me your hand, and let this kindly grasp
Live in our memories.
Gersa.   In mine it will.
I blush to think of my unchastened tongue;
But I was haunted by the monstrous ghost
125 Of all our slain battalions. Sire, reflect,
And pardon you will grant, that, at this hour,
The bruisèd remnants of our stricken camp
Are huddling undistinguished my dear friends,
With common thousands, into shallow graves.
130 *Otho.* Enough, most noble Gersa. You are free
To cheer the brave remainder of your host
By your own healing presence, and that too,
Not as their leader merely, but their king;
For, as I hear, your wily enemy,
135 Who eased the crownet from your infant brows,
Bloody Taraxa, is among the dead.

I ii *125. our slain battalions*] the hungarian *K.'s MS (cancelled)*. An earlier
attempt was 'my splendent Army'.

I ii *127. bruised . . . our*] poor . . . my *K.'s MS (cancelled)*.

I ii *128.* Are huddling unknown my dearest friends *K.'s MS, Brown's MS*
(*cancelled and corrected in K.'s hand*). Probably altered for the sake of the
metre.

I ii *136. Taraxa*] Perhaps derived from Taksony, the Hungarian ruler who
was defeated by Otto at the Lechfeld 955, but survived until 972 when he
was succeeded by Géza.

19*

Gersa. Then I retire, so generous Otho please,
Bearing with me a weight of benefits
Too heavy to be borne.
Otho.   It is not so;
140 Still understand me, King of Hungary,
Nor judge my open purposes awry.
Though I did hold you high in my esteem
For your self's sake, I do not personate
The stage-play emperor to entrap applause,
145 To set the silly sort o' the world agape,
And make the politic smile; no, I have heard
How in the Council you condemned this war,
Urging the perfidy of broken faith—
For that I am your friend.
Gersa.   If ever, sire,
150 You are mine enemy, I dare here swear
'Twill not be Gersa's fault. Otho, farewell!
Otho. Will you return, Prince, to our banqueting?
Gersa. As to my father's board I will return.
Otho. Conrad, with all due ceremony, give
155 The prince a regal escort to his camp;
Albert, go thou and bear him company.
Gersa, farewell!
Gersa.   All happiness attend you!
Otho. Return with what good speed you may; for soon
We must consult upon our terms of peace.
                    [*Exeunt* Gersa *and* Albert *with others.*
160 And thus a marble column do I build
To prop my empire's dome. Conrad, in thee
I have another stedfast one, to uphold
The portals of my state; and, for my own
Pre-eminence and safety, I will strive
165 To keep thy strength upon its pedestal.
For, without thee, this day I might have been
A show-monster about the streets of Prague,
In chains, as just now stood that noble prince:
And then to me no mercy had been shown,
170 For when the conquered lion is once dungeoned,

I ii *137. Otho*] Caesar *K.'s MS*. See I ii 51 *n* above.
I ii *142. did*] must *K.'s MS*.
I ii *164. I will strive*] it shall be my care *K.'s MS* (*cancelled*).
I ii *167.* Perhaps a recollection of *Antony and Cleopatra,* V ii 55–7,
                    . . . shall they hoist me up
              And show me to the shouting varletry
              Of censuring Rome ? . . .

Who lets him forth again? Or dares to give
An old lion sugar-cates of mild reprieve?
Not to thine ear alone I make confession,
But to all here, as, by experience,
175 I know how the great basement of all power
Is frankness, and a true tongue to the world;
And how intriguing secrecy is proof
Of fear and weakness, and a hollow state.
Conrad, I owe thee much.
Conrad.   To kiss that hand,
180 My emperor, is ample recompense
For a mere act of duty.
Otho.   Thou art wrong;
For what can any man on earth do more?
We will make trial of your house's welcome,
My bright Auranthe!
Conrad.   How is Friedburg honoured!

Enter Ethelbert *and six Monks*

185 *Ethelbert*. The benison of heaven on your head,
Imperial Otho!
Otho.   Who stays me? Speak! Quick!
Ethelbert. Pause but one moment, mighty conqueror,
Upon the threshold of this house of joy.
Otho. Pray, do not prose, good Ethelbert, but speak
190 What is your purpose.
Ethelbert. The restoration of some captive maids,
Devoted to Heaven's pious ministries,
Who driven forth from their religious cells,
And kept in thraldom by our enemy,
195 When late this province was a lawless spoil,
Still weep amid the wild Hungarian camp,
Though hemmed around by thy victorious arms.
Otho. Demand the holy sisterhood in our name
From Gersa's tents. Farewell, old Ethelbert.
200 *Ethelbert*. The saints will bless you for this pious care.

I ii *170. dungeoned*] caged *K.'s MS* (*cancelled*).
I ii *172. cates . . . reprieve*] plums . . . forgiveness *K.'s MS* (*cancelled*). On
'cates' (cakes) see *The Eve of St. Agnes* 173 *n* (p. 464 above).
I ii *175. basement*] Foundation.
I ii *179. To kiss*] To kneel and kiss *K.'s MS*. Probably altered for the sake of
the metre.
I ii *181. a mere act of duty*] my mere duty done *K.'s MS* (*cancelled*).
I ii *198–200*. In keeping with historical records of Otto's reputation for
piety.

Otho. Daughter, your hand; Ludolph's would fit it best.
Conrad. Ho! Let the music sound!

> [*Music.* Ethelbert *raises his hands, as in benediction of* Otho. *Exeunt severally. The scene closes on them.*

SCENE III

[*The Country, with the Castle in the distance*]

Enter Ludolph and Sigifred.

Ludolph. You have my secret; let it not be breathed.
Sigifred. Still give me leave to wonder that the Prince
Ludolph and the swift Arab are the same;
Still to rejoice that 'twas a German arm
5   Death doing in a turbaned masquerade.
Ludolph. The Emperor must not know it, Sigifred.
Sigifred. I prythee, why? What happier hour of time
Could thy pleased star point down upon from heaven
With silver index, bidding thee make peace?
10   *Ludolph.* Still it must not be known, good Sigifred;
The star may point oblique.
Sigifred.   If Otho knew
His son to be that unknown Mussulman
After whose spurring heels he sent me forth,
With one of his well-pleased Olympian oaths,
15   The charters of man's greatness, at this hour
He would be watching round the castle walls,
And, like an anxious warder, strain his sight
For the first glimpse of such a son returned—
Ludolph, that blast of the Hungarians,
20   That Saracenic meteor of the fight,
That silent fury, whose fell scimitar
Kept danger all aloof from Otho's head,
And left him space for wonder.
Ludolph.   Say no more.

I iii *1–63.* In *K.'s MS* this originally followed I iii 64–123: cp. I iii 64 *n*, I iii 123 *n*. K. obviously took pains over the scene as the occasion of Kean's first appearance in the play (see I iii 24–9 *n*).
I iii *4.* K.'s cancelled false starts were,

  1. And that a christian arm . . .
  2. And still let me rejoice . . .

I iii *5. doing*] giving *K.'s MS* (*cancelled*). For Trelawny's quoting this line see I ii 6–11 *n* above.
I iii *11. star*] planet *K.'s MS* (*cancelled*).
I iii *15. charters*] Privileges.
I iii *23. And left him space for wonder*] Like his good Angel *K.'s MS* (*cancelled*).

Not as a swordsman would I pardon claim,
25   But as a son. The bronzed centurion,
Long toiled in foreign wars, and whose high deeds
Are shaded in a forest of tall spears,
Known only to his troop, hath greater plea
Of favour with my sire than I can have.
30   *Sigifred.* My lord, forgive me that I cannot see
How this proud temper with clear reason squares.
What made you then, with such an anxious love,
Hover around that life, whose bitter days
You vexed with bad revolt? Was 't opium,
35   Or the mad-fumèd wine? Nay, do not frown,
I rather would grieve with you than upbraid.
Ludolph. I do believe you. No, 'twas not to make
A father his son's debtor, or to heal
His deep heart-sickness for a rebel child.
40   'Twas done in memory of my boyish days,
Poor cancel for his kindness to my youth,
For all his calming of my childish griefs,
And all his smiles upon my merriment.
No, not a thousand foughten fields could sponge
45   Those days paternal from my memory,
Though now upon my head he heaps disgrace.
Sigifred. My Prince, you think too harshly –
Ludolph.   Can I so?

I iii *24–9.* Quoted by K. in his journal-letter 27 Sept. 1819, 'The report
runs now more in favour of Kean stopping in England. . . . If he smokes
[see *The Cap and Bells* 615 *n*, p. 730 below] the hotblooded character of
Ludolph – and he is the only actor that can do it – He will add to my own
fame, and improve my fortune – I will give you a half dozen lines' (*L* ii 217).
K. underlines I iii 26–8 ('and whose . . . known only to his troop') in his
letter.
I iii *24.* K. cancelled the false start 'I would not buy my Pardon . . .' and
substituted 'claim' for 'crave' (the reading of his letter).
I iii *31.* Cancelled false starts in the draft were,
   1. What then could . . .
   2. Why then did you them [*sic*] so hover . . .
I iii *33. bitter*] painful *K.'s MS (cancelled).*
I iii *39.* Cancelled false starts in the draft were 'His bleeding . . .' and 'The
recent wounds . . .'.
I iii *41. cancel*] Repayment, i.e. cancellation of debt.
I iii *43.* Followed in *K.'s MS* by the cancelled passage,
             Ever will those bright days live in my heart
             Though he still . . .
I iii *47. think . . . harshly*] judge . . . sadly *K.'s MS (cancelled).*

Hath he not galled my spirit to the quick?
And with a sullen rigour obstinate
50   Poured out a phial of wrath upon my faults?
Hunted me as the Tartar does the boar,
Driven me to the very edge o' the world,
And almost put a price upon my head?
Sigifred. Remember how he spared the rebel lords.
55   *Ludolph.* Yes, yes, I know he hath a noble nature
That cannot trample on the fallen. But his
Is not the only proud heart in his realm.
He hath wronged me, and I have done him wrong;
He hath loved me, and I have shown him kindness;
We should be almost equal.
60   *Sigifred.*   Yet, for all this,
I would you had appeared among those lords,
And taken his favour.
Ludolph.   Ha! Till now I thought
My friend had held poor Ludolph's honour dear.
What! Would you have me sue before his throne
65   And kiss the courtier's missal, its silk steps?
Or hug the golden housings of his steed,
Amid a camp, whose steelèd swarms I dared
But yesterday? And, at the trumpet sound,
Bow like some unknown mercenary's flag,
70   And lick the soilèd grass? No, no, my friend,
I would not, I, be pardoned in the heap,
And bless indemnity with all that scum—
Those men I mean, who on my shoulders propped
Their weak rebellion, winning me with lies,
75   And pitying forsooth my many wrongs;
Poor self-deceivèd wretches, who must think
Each one himself a king in embryo,

I iii 50. *faults*] head *K.'s MS (cancelled)*.
I iii 52. *the very edge of the world*] Echoes *Antony and Cleopatra* II ii 119–21,
                    . . . if I knew
        What hoop should hold us stanch from edge to edge
        O' the world, I would pursue it . . .
I iii 55. *I know he hath a noble nature* well I know *K.'s MS (cancelled)*.
I iii 64. *What!*] K. broke off at this word in his MS, drew a line and continued at I iii 123 ('. . . to you I doubt not . . .').
I iii 65. *missal*] bible *K.'s MS (cancelled)*. At the opening of Pontifical mass the bishop kisses the missal before proceeding to his throne.
I iii 66. *golden . . . steed*] steeled . . . Horse *K.'s MS (cancelled)*. The word 'housings' is an Elizabethanism for trappings.
I iii 72. *bless indemnity*] be indemnified *K.'s MS (cancelled)*.

Because some dozen vassals cried '–My Lord!'
Cowards, who never knew their little hearts
80 Till flurried danger held the mirror up,
And then they owned themselves without a blush,
Curling, like spaniels, round my father's feet.
Such things deserted me and are forgiven,
While I, least guilty, am an outcast still,
85 And will be, for I love such fair disgrace.
Sigifred. I know the clear truth; so would Otho see,
For he is just and noble. Fain would I
Be pleader for you—
Ludolph.   He'll hear none of it;
You know his temper, hot, proud, obstinate;
90 Endanger not yourself so uselessly.
I will encounter his thwart spleen myself,
To-day, at the Duke Conrad's, where he keeps
His crowded state after the victory.
There will I be, a most unwelcome guest,
95 And parley with him, as a son should do
Who doubly loathes a father's tyranny;
Tell him how feeble is that tyranny;
How the relationship of father and son
Is no more valid than a silken leash
100 Where lions tug adverse, if love grow not
From interchangèd love through many years.
Aye, and those turreted Franconian walls,
Like to a jealous casket, hold my pearl—
My fair Auranthe! Yes, I will be there.
105 *Sigifred.* Be not so rash; wait till his wrath shall pass,

I iii *82–3.* Probably suggested by *Antony and Cleopatra* IV x 33–5,

>   ... The hearts
> That spaniel'd me at heels, to whom I gave
> Their wishes, do discandy, melt their sweets
> On blossoming Caesar ...

I iii *87. Fain would I*] Followed in *K.'s MS* by 'even though the sacred sense' (uncancelled, but written in a minute hand).

I iii *91.* I will break the matter to him myself *K.'s MS (cancelled)*. The phrase 'thwart spleen' (obstructing anger) echoes *King Lear* I iv 282–3,

> Create her a child of spleen, that it may live
> And be a thwart disnatur'd torment to her ...

K. also knew *Paradise Lost* viii 132 (marked by him in his copy of Milton),

> Mov'd contrarie with thwart obliquities ...

I iii *101. From interchangèd love*] Earlier attempts were 'Not from mutual benefits ...' and 'From mutual benefits interchanged ....'.

Until his royal spirit softly ebbs
Self-influenced; then, in his morning dreams
He will forgive thee, and awake in grief
To have not thy good morrow.
Ludolph.   Yes, to-day
110 I must be there, while her young pulses beat
Among the new-plumed minions of the war.
Have you seen her of late? No? Auranthe,
Franconia's fair sister, 'tis I mean.
She should be paler for my troublous days—
115 And there it is: my father's iron lips
Have sworn divorcement 'twixt me and my right.
Sigifred (*aside*). Auranthe! I had hoped this whim had
          passed.
Ludolph. And, Sigifred, with all his love of justice,
When will he take that grandchild in his arms?
120 That, by my love I swear, shall soon be his?
This reconcilement is impossible,
For see—but who are these?
Sigifred.   They are messengers
From our great emperor; to you, I doubt not,
For couriers are abroad to seek you out.
                Enter Theodore *and* Gonfred.
125 *Theodore.* Seeing so many vigilant eyes explore
The province to invite your highness back
To your high dignities, we are too happy.
Gonfred. We have no eloquence to colour justly
The emperor's anxious wishes.
Ludolph.   Go. I follow you.
                [*Exeunt* Theodore *and* Gonfred.
130 I play the prude: it is but venturing—
Why should he be so earnest? Come, my friend,
Let us to Friedburg castle.

I iii *109. To have not thy good morrow*] Followed in K.'s MS by the cancelled
passage,

                          Sigifred!
              Have you seen her of late . . .

I iii *115–16. it is . . . Have*] oppression again—my father's iron arm /
Weights . . . *K.'s MS* (*cancelled*).
I iii *121.* K.'s MS cancelled false start, 'Auranthe these hard times . . .'.
I iii *123.* K. drew a line under this in his MS and continued at I iii 1 (see I iii
1–64 n above).
I iii *124. are abroad to seek*] to that purpose are abroad *K.'s MS* (*cancelled*).
I iii *125–32.* For the draft reading see Appendix C (p. 762 below).

ACT II

SCENE I

[An Ante-chamber in the Castle.]

Enter Ludolph *and* Sigifred.

Ludolph. No more advices, no more cautioning:
I leave it all to fate–to any thing!
I cannot square my conduct to time, place,
Or circumstance; to me 'tis all a mist!
Sigifred. I say no more.
5   *Ludolph.*   It seems I am to wait
Here in the ante-room–that may be a trifle.
You see now how I dance attendance here,
Without that tyrant temper, you so blame,
Snapping the rein. You have medicined me
10 With good advices; and I here remain,
In this most honourable ante-room,
Your patient scholar.
Sigifred.   Do not wrong me, Prince.
By Heavens, I'd rather kiss Duke Conrad's slipper,
When in the morning he doth yawn with pride,
15 Than see you humbled but a half-degree!
Truth is, the Emperor would fain dismiss
The nobles ere he sees you.

Enter Gonfred *from the Council-room.*

Ludolph.   Well, sir! what?
Gonfred. Great honour to the Prince! The Emperor,

II i *1. cautioning*] cautions Sigifred *K.'s MS*. Brown's MS has 'Sigifred'
(cancelled) and the last three letters of 'cautioning' written in K.'s hand.
II i *4. 'tis all a mist*] Cp. K.'s letter to Reynolds of 3 May 1818, 'We see not
the ballance of good and evil. We are in a Mist' (*L* i 281). Perhaps suggested
here by Webster's *The White Devil* V vi 259–60,

                    . . . we confound
        Knowledge with knowledge. O, I am in a mist . . .

K. may have intended to expand Ludolph's speech: the line is followed in
his MS by the cancelled false start 'The Happy . . .'.
II i *9. You*] Certes *K.'s MS (cancelled)*. Cp. the use of 'certes' in *Lamia* ii 80
(p. 637 below). Verbal parallels with *Lamia*, some of which are noted below,
are increasingly frequent in the play after Act I. See K.'s letter to Reynolds
of 11 July 1819, 'I have finished the Act [of *Otho*], and in the interval of
beginning the 2d have proceeded pretty well with "Lamia"' (*L* ii 128).
The word 'medicined' is probably a Shakespearian echo; see *Endymion* ii
484 and *n* (p. 183 above).
II i *15. humbled*] so degraded *K.'s MS (cancelled)*.

Hearing that his brave son had re-appeared,
20   Instant dismissed the Council from his sight,
As Jove fans off the clouds. Even now they pass.

                                              [*Exit.*

Enter the Nobles from the Council-room. They cross the stage,
    bowing with respect to Ludolph, *he frowning on them.*
    Conrad *follows. Exeunt Nobles.*

Ludolph. Not the discoloured poisons of a fen,
Which he who breathes feels warning of his death,
Could taste so nauseous to the bodily sense
25   As these prodigious sycophants disgust
The soul's fine palate.
Conrad.   Princely Ludolph, hail!
Welcome, thou younger sceptre to the realm!
Strength to thy virgin crownet's golden buds,
That they, against the winter of thy sire,
30   May burst, and swell, and flourish round thy brows,
Maturing to a weighty diadem!
Yet be that hour far off; and may he live,
Who waits for thee as the chapped earth for rain.
Set my life's star! I have lived long enough,
35   Since under my glad roof, propitiously,
Father and son each other re-possess.
Ludolph. Fine wording, Duke! But words could never yet
Forestall the fates; have you not learnt that yet?
Let me look well: your features are the same,
40   Your gait the same, your hair of the same shade,
As one I knew some passèd weeks ago,
Who sung far different notes into mine ears.

II i *22–6. Not . . . fine palate*] Perhaps inspired by *Coriolanus* III iii 118–21,
                You common cry of curs! whose breath I hate
                As reek o' the rotten fens, whose love I prize
                As the dead carcases of unburied men
                That do corrupt my air . . .
II i *23.* Followed in *K.'s MS* by the cancelled line, 'Not the death watch
tickling a Beldam's ear . . .'.
II i *24. taste so nauseous*] nauseate me *K.'s MS* (*cancelled*).
II i *26. The soul's fine palate*] The relish of my soul's invisible **tongue** *K.'s
MS* (*cancelled*).
II i *28. virgin*] rounded *K.'s MS* (*cancelled*).
II i *29. against the*] in the last *K.'s MS* (*cancelled*).
II i *33. chapped*] Cracked.
II i *36. Father*] Meet *K.'s MS* (*cancelled*).

I have mine own particular comments on it;
You have your own, perhaps.
Conrad.   My gracious Prince,
45   All men may err. In truth I was deceived
In your great father's nature, as you were.
Had I known that of him I have since known,
And what you soon will learn, I would have turned
My sword to my own throat, rather than held
50   Its threatening edge against a good King's quiet:
Or with one word fevered you, gentle Prince,
Who seemed to me, as rugged times then went,
Indeed too much oppressed. May I be bold
To tell the Emperor you will haste to him?
55   *Ludolph.* Your Dukedom's privilege will grant so much.
                                        [*Exit* Conrad.
He's very close to Otho, a tight leech!
Your hand – I go. Ha! Here the thunder comes
Sullen against the wind! If in two angry brows
My safety lies, then Sigifred, I'm safe.

                    Enter Otho *and* Conrad.

60   *Otho.* Will you make Titan play the lackey-page
To chattering pigmies? I would have you know
That such neglect of our high Majesty
Annuls all feel of kindred. What is son –
Or friend, or brother, or all ties of blood –
65   When the whole kingdom, centred in ourself,
Is rudely slighted? Who am I to wait?
By Peter's chair! I have upon my tongue
A word to fright the proudest spirit here! –

II i *51. fevered you, gentle Prince*] put fever in your heart *K.'s MS* (*cancelled*).
II i *56. a tight leech*] Sigifred *K.'s MS* (*cancelled*). *K.'s MS* has the cancelled
stage-direction 'Aside'.
II i *57–8. the thunder ... the wind*] De Selincourt finds a parallel with Byron's
Childe Harold iv 98,
                    ... like a thunder cloud *against* the wind ...
(Byron's line was used by Shelley as a motto for his *Ode to Liberty*, 1820).
II i *60–1. Titan ... pigmies*] Cp. the Titan Thea in *Hyperion* i 27–8 and 28 *n*
(p. 398 above),
                    By her in stature the tall Amazon
                    Had stood a pigmy's height ...
For 'lackey-page' *K.'s MS* has the attempted correction 'lackey-boy'.
II i *67. By Peter's chair!*] By the authority of the Holy See. St Peter was the
first Pope.
II i *68. the proudest spirit here*] the Devil – Banishment! *K.'s MS, Brown's MS*
(*cancelled and corrected in K.'s hand*).

Death!—and slow tortures to the hardy fool
70   Who dares take such large charter from our smiles!
Conrad, we would be private. Sigifred!
Off! And none pass this way on pain of death!
                              [*Exeunt* Conrad *and* Sigifred.
Ludolph. This was but half expected, my good sire,
Yet I am grieved at it, to the full height,
75   As though my hopes of favour had been whole.
Otho. How you indulge yourself! What can you hope
        for?
Ludolph. Nothing, my liege; I have to hope for nothing.
I come to greet you as a loving son,
And then depart, if I may be so free,
80   Seeing that blood of yours in my warm veins
Has not yet mitigated into milk.
Otho. What would you, sir?
Ludolph.   A lenient banishment;
So please you let me unmolested pass
This Conrad's gates, to the wide air again.
85   I want no more. A rebel wants no more.
Otho. And shall I let a rebel loose again
To muster kites and eagles 'gainst my head?
No, obstinate boy, you shall be kept caged up,
Served with harsh food, with scum for Sunday-drink.
Ludolph. Indeed!
90   *Otho.*   And chains too heavy for your life:
I'll choose a gaoler, whose swart monstrous face
Shall be a hell to look upon, and she—
Ludolph.   Ha!

II i *76.* Hopes! what in your conscience can you hope for *K.'s MS* (*cancelled*). The revised reading is written by K. in a blank space left for this line in *Brown's MS.*

II i *80–1.* Probably suggested by Shakespeare's frequent use of 'milky' or 'milk-livered' for cowardice. Cp. *King Lear* IV ii 50, 'Milk-liver'd man'. The word 'mitigated' is used in *Lamia* ii 78 (p. 637 below), 'the mitigated fury'.

II i *89. scum for Sunday drink*] puddle for your drink *K.'s MS* (*cancelled*).

II i *91. swart*] Black. See *Endymion* ii 15 *n* (p. 164 above).

II i *93. Auranthe*] Followed in *K.'s MS* (*uncancelled*) and *Brown's MS* (*cancelled*) by

                    Oh! my Boy
              What will you say to that . . .

For K.'s view that Otho needed 'a spice of drollery' see III ii 1–3 *n* below. With the exclamation, 'Amaze! . . .' cp. ''*Tis the 'witching time of night*', 41 (p. 385 above).

Otho. Shall be your fair Auranthe.
Ludolph.   Amaze! Amaze!
Otho. To-day you marry her.
Ludolph.   This is a sharp jest!
95   *Otho.* No. None at all. When have I said a lie?
Ludolph. If I sleep not, I am a waking wretch.
Otho. Not a word more. Let me embrace my child.
Ludolph. I dare not. 'Twould pollute so good a father!
O heavy crime! that your son's blinded eyes
100 Could not see all his parent's love aright,
As now I see it. Be not kind to me—
Punish me not with favour.
Otho.   Are you sure,
Ludolph, you have no saving plea in store?
Ludolph. My father, none!
Otho.   Then you astonish me.
105 *Ludolph.* No, I have no plea. Disobedience,
Rebellion, obstinacy, blasphemy,
Are all my counsellors. If they can make
My crooked deeds show good and plausible,
Then grant me loving pardon, but not else,
110 Good Gods! not else, in any way, my liege!
Otho. You are a most perplexing, noble boy.
Ludolph. You not less a perplexing, noble father.
Otho. Well, you shall have free passport through the
        gates.
Farewell!
Ludolph. Farewell! And by these tears believe,
115 And still remember, I repent in pain
All my misdeeds!
Otho.   Ludolph, I will! I will!
But, Ludolph, ere you go, I would inquire
If you, in all your wandering, ever met
A certain Arab haunting in these parts.
120 *Ludolph.* No, my good lord, I cannot say I did.
Otho. Make not your father blind before his time;
Nor let these arms paternal hunger more
For an embrace, to dull the appetite
Of my great love for thee, my supreme child!
125 Come close, and let me breathe into thine ear.

II i *100. his parent's love aright*] the love your open nature clear *K.'s MS*
(cancelled).
II i *106. blasphemy*] Insult, Pride *K.'s MS (cancelled)*.
II i *124. supreme*] Last.

I knew you through disguise. You are the Arab!
You can't deny it.   [*Embracing him.*
Ludolph.   Happiest of days!
Otho. We'll make it so.
Ludolph.   'Stead of one fatted calf
Ten hecatombs shall bellow out their last.
130 Smote 'twixt the horns by the death-stunning mace
Of Mars, and all the soldiery shall feast
Nobly as Nimrod's masons, when the towers
Of Nineveh new kissed the parted clouds!
Otho. Large as a God speak out, where all is thine.
135 *Ludolph.* Aye, father, but the fire in my sad breast
Is quenched with inward tears! I must rejoice
For you, whose wings so shadow over me
In tender victory, but for myself
I still must mourn. The fair Auranthe mine!
140 Too great a boon! I prythee let me ask
What more than I know of could so have changed
Your purpose touching her?
Otho.   At a word, this:
In no deed did you give me more offence
Than your rejection of Erminia.
145 To my appalling, I saw too good proof
Of your keen-eyed suspicion—she is naught!
Ludolph. You are convinced?
Otho.   Aye, spite of her sweet looks.
O, that my brother's daughter should so fall!
Her fame has passed into the grosser lips
Of soldiers in their cups.
150 *Ludolph.*   'Tis very sad.
Otho. No more of her. Auranthe—Ludolph, come!
This marriage be the bond of endless peace!   [*Exeunt.*

II i *128. fatted calf*] See *Luke* xv 23–4: 'Bring hither the fattest calf, and kill
it; and let us eat, and be merry. For this my son was dead, and is alive again;
he was lost, and is found.'

II i *129. hecatombs*] See *Endymion* iv 39 *n* (p. 246 above),

            . . . a hecatomb of vows . . .

II i *132–3.* Refers to the building of the Tower of Babel (*Genesis* x 8–12, xi
1–9). With 'new kissed the parted clouds', cp. *Hamlet* III iv 59, 'a heaven-
kissing hill'.

II i *137–8. whose wings . . . tender victory*] Suggests a recollection of *Paradise
Lost* i 20–1 (marked by K. in his copy of Milton),

            . . . with mighty wings outspread
      Dove-like satst brooding . . .

SCENE II

[*The Entrance of* Gersa's *Tent in the Hungarian Camp.*]

Enter Erminia.

Erminia. Where, where, where shall I find a messenger?
A trusty soul? A good man in the camp?
Shall I go myself? Monstrous wickedness!
O cursed Conrad! Devilish Auranthe!
5   Here is proof palpable as the bright sun!
O for a voice to reach the Emperor's ears!

                             [*Shouts in the camp.*

Enter an Hungarian Captain.

Captain. Fair prisoner, hear you those joyous shouts?
The king—aye, now our king—but still your slave,
Young Gersa, from a short captivity
10 Has just returned. He bids me say, bright Dame,
That even the homage of his rangèd chiefs
Cures not his keen impatience to behold
Such beauty once again. What ails you, lady?
Erminia. Say, is not that a German, yonder? There!
15 *Captain.* Methinks by his stout bearing he should be—
Yes—'tis one Albert; a brave German knight,
And much in the Emperor's favour.
Erminia.   I would fain
Inquire of friends and kinsfolk; how they fared
In these rough times. Brave soldier, as you pass
20 To royal Gersa with my humble thanks,
Will you send yonder knight to me?
Captain.   I will.   [*Exit.*
Erminia. Yes, he was ever known to be a man
Frank, open, generous; Albert I may trust.
O proof! Proof! Proof! Albert's an honest man;
25 Not Ethelbert the monk, if he were here,
Would I hold more trustworthy. Now!

II ii. *Stage-direction.* Act 2nd—Scene 2nd. The Hungarian Camp—the entrance of Gerza's Tent—Erminia comes out with a letter in her hand *K.'s MS.*

II ii 5. *sun*] stars *K.'s MS (cancelled)*. K.'s cancelled false start to the line was 'An Emperor is no God ...'.

II ii 7. Preceded in *K.'s MS* by the cancelled line, 'Married to day! Oh O O ...'.

II ii 10. *Dame*] Lady *K.'s MS (cancelled)*. Probably altered to avoid the echo in II ii 13 below.

II ii 12. *keen*] hot *K.'s MS*, Brown's *MS (cancelled)*. Probably altered to avoid the chime with 'not'.

Enter Albert.

Albert.   Good Gods,
Lady Erminia! Are you prisoner
In this beleaguered camp? Or are you here
Of your own will? You pleased to send for me.
30   By Venus, 'tis a pity I knew not
Your plight before, and, by her Son, I swear
To do you every service you can ask.
What would the fairest–?
Erminia.   Albert, will you swear?
Albert. I have. Well?
Erminia.   Albert, you have fame to lose.
35   If men, in court and camp, lie not outright,
You should be, from a thousand, chosen forth
To do an honest deed. Shall I confide–?
Albert. Aye, anything to me, fair creature. Do;
Dictate my task. Sweet woman–
Erminia.   Truce with that.
40   You understand me not; and in your speech
I see how far the slander is abroad.
Without proof could you think me innocent?
Albert. Lady, I should rejoice to know you so.
Erminia. If you have any pity for a maid
45   Suffering a daily death from evil tongues;
Any compassion for that Emperor's niece,
Who, for your bright sword and clear honesty,
Lifted you from the crowd of common men
Into the lap of honour–save me, knight!
50   *Albert.* How? Make it clear; if it be possible,
I, by the banner of Saint Maurice, swear
To right you.
Erminia.   Possible!–Easy. O my heart!
This letter's not so soiled but you may read it–
Possible! There–that letter! Read–read it.
                                        [*Gives him a letter.*
55   *Albert (reading).* 'To the Duke Conrad.–Forget the threat
you made at parting, and I will forget to send the

II ii *27–8. are you . . . camp*] is your Nunnery emptied into this camp *K.'s
MS, Brown's MS (cancelled and corrected in K.'s hand)*. The word 'Nunnery'
(brothel) is probably owed to *Hamlet* III i 121, 'Get thee to a nunnery . . .'.
II ii *47. bright sword*] brave conduct *K.'s MS (cancelled)*.
II ii *51.* St Maurice, also known as St Mauritius and St Moritz, was an early
Christian martyr celebrated in Germany, Switzerland and Italy.
II ii *55. To the Duke Conrad*] Remember Conrad *K.'s MS (cancelled)*.

Emperor letters and papers of yours I have become
possessed of. His life is no trifle to me; his death you shall
find none to yourself.' (*Speaks aside.*) 'Tis me—my life
60   that's pleaded for! (*Reads.*) 'He, for his own sake, will be
dumb as the grave. Erminia has my shame fixed upon
her, sure as a wen. We are safe.

AURANTHE.'

A she-devil! A dragon! I her imp!
Fire of Hell! Auranthe—lewd demon!
65   Where got you this? Where? When?
Erminia. I found it in the tent, among some spoils
Which, being noble, fell to Gersa's lot.
Come in, and see.   [*They go in and return.*
Albert.   Villainy! Villainy!
Conrad's sword, his corslet, and his helm,
70   And his letter. Caitiff, he shall feel—
Erminia. I see you are thunderstruck. Haste, haste away!
Albert. O I am tortured by this villainy.
Erminia. You needs must be. Carry it swift to Otho;
Tell him, moreover, I am prisoner
75   Here in this camp, where all the sisterhood,
Forced from their quiet cells, are parcelled out
For slaves among these Huns. Away! Away!
Albert. I am gone.
Erminia.   Swift be your steed! Within this hour
The Emperor will see it.
Albert.   Ere I sleep:
80   That I can swear.   [*Hurries out.*
Gersa (*without*).   Brave captains! Thanks. Enough
Of loyal homage now!

Enter Gersa.

Erminia.   Hail, royal Hun!
Gersa. What means this, fair one? Why in such alarm?
Who was it hurried by me so distract?
It seemed you were in deep discourse together;
85   Your doctrine has not been so harsh to him

II ii *59–60*. Speaks . . . *for!*] Omitted in *K.'s MS*; added in K.'s hand in
Brown's MS.
II ii *60*. Reads] *1848*. Omitted in *K.'s MS, Brown's MS*.
II ii *62*. wen] Wart.
II ii *63*. imp] Familiar spirit (a demon supposed to attend at a call).
II ii *71*. are] Added in K.'s hand in *Brown's MS*.
II ii *81–2*.   I would be private in my tent awhile
                  Let me not be disturb'd . . . *K.'s MS, Brown's* (*cancelled*).

As to my poor deserts. Come, come, be plain.
I am no jealous fool to kill you both,
Or, for such trifles, rob the adornèd world
Of such a beauteous vestal.
Erminia.   I grieve, my Lord,
90   To hear you condescend to ribald phrase.
Gersa. This is too much! Hearken, my lady pure!
Erminia. Silence! and hear the magic of a name—
Erminia! I am she—the Emperor's niece!
Praised be the Heavens, I now dare own myself!
95   *Gersa.* Erminia! Indeed! I've heard of her.
Prythee, fair lady, what chance brought you here?
Erminia. Ask your own soldiers.
Gersa.   And you dare own your name.
For loveliness you may—and for the rest
My vein is not censorious.
Erminia.   Alas, poor me!
100   'Tis false indeed.
Gersa.   Indeed you are too fair:
The swan, soft leaning on her fledgy breast,
When to the stream she launches, looks not back
With such a tender grace; nor are her wings
So white as your soul is, if that but be
105   Twin-picture to your face. Erminia!
To-day, for the first day, I am a king,
Yet would I give my unworn crown away
To know you spotless.
Erminia.   Trust me one day more,
Generously, without more certain guarantee

II ii *87–9. I am . . . vestal*] Probably suggested by *Othello* III iii 323–5,
                              . . . trifles light as air
              Are to the jealous confirmations strong
              As proofs of holy writ . . .
II ii *95–100.* K.'s *MS*, Brown's *MS (cancelled and corrected in K.'s hand)*,
              Then you dare do no more than women dare
              Who dare the devil on his 'vantage ground
              Yet if some strange report I heard hold good
              You are in truth no coward. Ha! Erminia . . .
II ii *101–2. The swan . . . grace*] See *Imitation of Spenser* 14–15 and *n* (p. 4
above),
              There saw the swan his neck of archèd snow,
              And oared himself along with majesty . . .
II ii *101. fledgy*] Feathery. Cp. *Not Aladdin magian* 39 (p. 374 above), 'a
fledgy sea-bird quire'.
II ii *102. to the stream*] from the bank K.'s *MS (cancelled)*.

110 Than this poor face you deign to praise so much;
   After that, say and do whate'er you please.
   If I have any knowledge of you, sir,
   I think, nay I am sure, you will grieve much
   To hear my story. O be gentle to me,
115 For I am sick and faint with many wrongs,
   Tired out, and weary-worn with contumelies.
   Gersa. Poor lady!

   Enter Ethelbert.

   Erminia.   Gentle Prince, 'tis false indeed.
   Good morrow, holy father! I have had
   Your prayers, though I looked for you in vain.
120 *Ethelbert.* Blessings upon you, daughter! Sure you look
   Too cheerful for these foul pernicious days.
   Young man, you heard this virgin say 'twas false—
   'Tis false, I say. What! Can you not employ
   Your temper elsewhere, 'mong these burly tents,
125 But you must taunt this dove, for she hath lost
   The Eagle Otho to beat off assault?
   Fie! Fie! But I will be her guard myself;
   In the Emperor's name, I here demand of you
   Herself, and all her sisterhood. She false!
130 *Gersa.* Peace! peace, old man! I cannot think she is.
   Ethelbert. Whom I have known from her first infancy,
   Baptized her in the bosom of the Church,
   Watched her, as anxious husbandmen the grain,
   From the first shoot till the unripe mid-May,
135 Then to the tender ear of her June days,
   Which, lifting sweet abroad its timid green,
   Is blighted by the touch of calumny.
   You cannot credit such a monstrous tale.
   Gersa. I cannot. Take her. Fair Erminia,
140 I follow you to Friedburg—is 't not so?
   Erminia. Aye, so we purpose.
   Ethelbert.   Daughter, do you so?
   How's this? I marvel! Yet you look not mad.
   Erminia. I have good news to tell you, Ethelbert.
   Gersa. Ho! ho, there! Guards!

II ii *115–16.* Probably echoing *Hamlet* III i 71,
       The oppressor's wrong, the proud man's contumely . . .
II ii *134. unripe*] green *MS (cancelled)*. With 'mid-May' cp. *The Fall of
Hyperion* i 97 and *n* (pp. 663, 664 below).
II ii *136. sweet*] light *MS (cancelled)*.
II ii *137. Is blighted*] Was blasted *MS (cancelled)*.

145   Your blessing, father! Sweet Erminia,
         Believe me, I am well nigh sure—
         Erminia.   Farewell!
         Short time will show.   [*Enter Chiefs.*
                                Yes, father Ethelbert,
         I have news precious as we pass along.
         Ethelbert. Dear daughter, you shall guide me.
         Erminia.   To no ill.
150   *Gersa.* Command an escort to the Friedburg lines.
                                                [*Exeunt Chiefs.*
         Pray let me lead. Fair lady, forget not
         Gersa, how he believed you innocent.
         I follow you to Friedburg with all speed.   [*Exeunt.*

                        ACT III

                        SCENE I

                     [*The Country.*]

                     Enter Albert.

         Albert. O that the earth were empty, as when Cain
         Had no perplexity to hide his head!
         Or that the sword of some brave enemy
         Had put a sudden stop to my hot breath,
5   And hurdled me down the illimitable gulf
         Of times past, unremembered! Better so
         Than thus fast-limèd in a cursèd snare,
         The limbo of a wanton. This the end
         Of an aspiring life! My boyhood passed
10   In feud with wolves and bears, when no eye saw
         The solitary warfare, fought for love
         Of honour 'mid the growling wilderness.

III i *1–4.* The syntax and style are modelled on *Hamlet* I ii 129–32,
                    O! that this too too solid flesh would melt,
                    Thaw and resolve itself into a dew;
                    Or that the Everlasting had not fix'd
                    His canon gainst self-slaughter . . .
III i *2. no perplexity to hide*] No perplexity where to hide.
III i *5.* Cp. *Paradise Lost* i 44–7 (marked by K. in his copy of Milton),
                            . . . Him the Almighty Power
                Hurld headlong flaming from th' Etherial Skie
                To bottomless perdition . . .
III i *8. limbo*] Prison. Milnes's reading 'white limbs' in *1848* has no
authority.
III i *11. The solitary*] My restless K.'s MS (*cancelled*).

My sturdier youth, maturing to the sword,
Won by the siren-trumpets and the ring
15 Of shields upon the pavement, when bright-mailed
Henry the Fowler passed the streets of Prague.
Was 't to this end I louted and became
The menial of Mars, and held a spear
Swayed by command, as corn is by the wind?
20 Is it for this, I now am lifted up
By a well-judging Emperor, to see
My honour be my executioner–
My love of fame, my prided honesty
Put to the torture for confessional?
25 Then the damned crime of blurting to the world
A woman's secret! Though a fiend she be,
Too tender of my ignominious life.
But then to wrong the generous Emperor
In such a searching point, were to give up
30 My soul for foot-ball at Hell's holiday!
I must confess–and cut my throat–to-day?
To-morrow? Ho! some wine!

Enter Sigifred.

Sigifred.   A fine humour–
Albert. Who goes there? Count Sigifred? Ha! Ha!
Sigifred. What, man, do you mistake the hollow sky
35 For a thronged tavern–and these stubbèd trees
For old serge hangings–me, your humble friend,
For a poor waiter? Why, man, how you stare!
What gipsies have you been carousing with?
No, no more wine; methinks you've had enough.
40 *Albert.* You well may laugh and banter. What a fool
An injury may make of a staid man!
You shall know all anon.
Sigifred.   Some tavern brawl?

III i *16. Henry the Fowler*] Otho's father Henry I was known by this name.
III i *17. louted*] An archaism for bowed. Cp. *The Farie Queene* I x 44,
          He humbly louted in meeke lowlinesse . . .
III i *18–19. a spear . . . wind*] See *Paradise Lost* iv 980–3 (marked by K. in
his copy of Milton),
          With ported Spears, as thick as when a field
          Of *Ceres* ripe for harvest waving bends
          Her bearded Grove of ears, which way the wind
          Swayes them . . .
III i *21. a well-judging*] Europe's throned *1848.*
III i *36. serge hangings*] Coverings on the tavern walls.

Albert. 'Twas with some people out of common reach;
Revenge is difficult.
Sigifred.   I am your friend;
45 We meet again to-day, and can confer
Upon it. For the present I'm in haste.
Albert. Whither?
Sigifred.   To fetch King Gersa to the feast.
The Emperor on this marriage is so hot,
Pray Heaven it end not in apoplexy!
50 The very porters, as I passed the doors,
Heard his loud laugh, and answered in full choir.
I marvel, Albert, you delay so long
From those bright revelries; go, show yourself,
You may be made a duke.
Albert.   Aye, very like:
55 Pray, what day has his Highness fixed upon?
Sigifred. For what?
Albert.   The marriage. What else can I mean?
Sigifred. To-day! O, I forgot, you could not know;
The news is scarce a minute old with me.
Albert. Married to-day! To-day! You did not say so?
60 *Sigifred.* Now, while I speak to you, their comely heads
Are bowed before the mitre.
Albert.   O monstrous!
Sigifred. What is this?
Albert.   Nothing, Sigifred. Farewell!
We'll meet upon our subject. Farewell, count!   [*Exit.*
Sigifred. Is this clear-headed Albert? He brain-turned!
65 'Tis as portentous as a meteor.   [*Exit.*

SCENE II

[*An Apartment in the Castle.*]

Enter, as from the Marriage, Otho, Ludolph, Auranthe, Conrad,
Nobles, Knights, Ladies, etc., etc., etc. Music.

Otho. Now, Ludolph! Now, Auranthe! Daughter fair!
What can I find to grace your nuptial day

III i 43. *out of common reach*] of high consequence *K.'s MS, Brown's MS
(cancelled).*
III i 50. *porters*] Warders *K.'s MS (cancelled).*
III i 63. I long to greet the happy happy pair *K.'s MS (cancelled).*
III i 64-5. *K.'s MS. Brown's MS (cancelled and corrected in K.'s hand),*
          Farewell and nothing—but this nothing is
          Something I'll take my oath on—He is mad ...

More than my love, and these wide realms in fee?
Ludolph. I have too much.
Auranthe.   And I, my liege, by far.
5   *Ludolph.* Auranthe! I have! O, my bride, my love!
Not all the gaze upon us can restrain
My eyes, too long poor exiles from thy face,
From adoration and my foolish tongue
From uttering soft responses to the love
10   I see in thy mute beauty beaming forth!
Fair creature, bless me with a single word!
All mine!
Auranthe. Spare, spare me, my Lord; I swoon else.
Ludolph. Soft beauty! By to-morrow I should die,
Wert thou not mine.   [*They talk apart.*
First Lady.   How deep she has bewitched him!
15   *First Knight.* Ask you for her recipe for love philtres.
Second Lady. They hold the Emperor in admiration.
Otho. If ever king was happy, that am I!
What are the cities 'yond the Alps to me,
The provinces about the Danube's mouth,
20   The promise of fair soil beyond the Rhone;
Or routing out of Hyperborean hordes,
To these fair children, stars of a new age?
Unless perchance I might rejoice to win
This little ball of earth, and chuck it them
To play with!
25   *Auranthe.*   Nay, my Lord, I do not know.
Ludolph. Let me not famish.

III ii *Stage direction.* Act 3rd Scene 2nd. Enter as from a marriage – Otho,
Ludolph, Conrad, Auranthe and her train, Nobles, Knights, Ladies etc. etc.
etc. – Music playing – and cease *K.'s MS.*

III ii *1–3.* Otho's regal manner is preserved in this scene, but see Brown's
letter to Dilke of 12 Aug. 1819, 'Keats is very industrious, but . . . obstin-
ately monstrous. What think you of Otho's threatening cold pig to the new-
married couple? He says the Emperor must have a spice of drollery', (*Letters of Charles Armitage Brown*, ed. Jack Stillinger 1966, 48). 'Give cold pig'
is 'To awaken by sluicing with cold water or by pulling off the bed-clothes'
(Eric Partridge, *A Dictionary of Slang*, 1949, 169).

III ii *3. in fee*] In your full and rightful possession.

III ii *5–14. Auranthe . . . not mine*] For K.'s remarks on Ludolph as a lover
see III ii 38–45 *n*, IV ii 129–31 *n* below.

III iii *16.* Followed in *K.'s MS* by 'Devoted, made a slave to this day's
joy . . .'. The line is cancelled in *Brown's MS.*

III ii *21. Hyperborean*] Of the far North.

III ii *26. Ludolph*] *K.'s MS* has the stage direction 'talk aside'.

Otho (*to Conrad*).   Good Franconia,
You heard what oath I sware, as the sun rose,
That unless Heaven would send me back my son,
My Arab, no soft music should enrich
30   The cool wine, kissed off with a soldier's smack;
Now all my empire, bartered for one feast,
Seems poverty.
Conrad.   Upon the neighbour-plain
The heralds have prepared a royal lists;
Your knights, found war-proof in the bloody field,
Speed to the game.
35   *Otho.*   Well, Ludolph, what say you?
Ludolph. My lord!
Otho.   A tourney?
Conrad.   Or, if 't please you best—
Ludolph. I want no more!
First Lady.   He soars!
Second Lady.   Past all reason.
Ludolph. Though heaven's choir
Should in a vast circumference descend
40   And sing for my delight, I'd stop my ears!
Though bright Apollo's car stood burning here,
And he put out an arm to bid me mount,
His touch an immortality, not I!
This earth, this palace, this room, Auranthe!
45   *Otho.* This is a little painful; just too much.
Conrad, if he flames longer in this wise
I shall believe in wizard-woven loves
And old romances; but I'll break the spell.
Ludolph!

III ii 29. *enrich*] be heard *K.'s MS* (*cancelled*).
III ii 38–45 (and see III ii 76–99 below). K. may be referring to Ludolph's
behaviour in this scene in his letter to Fanny Brawne 5–6 Aug. 1819, 'I
leave this minute a scene in our Tragedy and see you . . . through the mist
of Plots speeches, counterplots and counter speeches–The Lover is madder
than I am–I am nothing to him–he has a figure like the statue of Meleager
and double distilled fire in his heart' (*L* ii 137)–Meleager, son of Oeneus,
King of Aetolia, and lover of Atalanta, was famed as an Argonaut and for
the slaying of the Calydonian boar; K. is referring to the statue in the
Museum of the Capitol.
III ii 42. *bid me mount*] help me in *K.'s MS.*
III ii 47. *wizard-woven loves*] K. was probably thinking of *Lamia*; see II i
9 *n* above.
III ii 48. Followed in *K.'s MS* by '*Otho.* Come, come, a little sober reason,
son . . .'

Conrad. He will be calm, anon.

Ludolph.   You called?

50   Yes, yes, yes, I offend. You must forgive me;
Not being quite recovered from the stun
Of your large bounties. A tourney, is it not?

                                        [*A sennet heard faintly.*

Conrad. The trumpets reach us.

Ethelbert (without).   On your peril, sirs,
Detain us!

First Voice (without). Let not the abbot pass.

Second Voice (without).   No,
On your lives!

55   *First Voice (without).* Holy father, you must not.

Ethelbert (without). Otho!

Otho.   Who calls on Otho?

Ethelbert (without).   Ethelbert!

Otho. Let him come in.

                    [*Enter* Ethelbert *leading in* Erminia.
                          Thou cursèd abbot, why
Hast brought pollution to our holy rites?
Hast thou no fear of hangman or the faggot?

60   *Ludolph.* What portent—what strange prodigy is this?

Conrad. Away!

Ethelbert.   You, Duke?

Erminia.   Albert has surely failed me!
Look at the Emperor's brow upon me bent!

Ethelbert. A sad delay!

Conrad.   Away, thou guilty thing!

Ethelbert. You again, Duke? Justice, most mighty Otho!

65   You—go to your sister there and plot again,
A quick plot, swift as thought to save your heads;
For lo! the toils are spread around your den,
The world is all agape to see dragged forth
Two ugly monsters.

Ludolph.   What means he, my lord?

Conrad. I cannot guess.

70   *Ethelbert.*   Best ask your lady sister,
Whether the riddle puzzles her beyond
The power of utterance.

Conrad.   Foul barbarian, cease;
The Princess faints!

III ii 59. Followed in *K.'s MS* by 'Mad Churchman, would'st thou be im-
pal'd alive . . .'.

III ii *67. toils*] Nets, snares. Used again by K. at IV i 61 below and *King
Stephen* I i 27 (p. 692 below).

20+K.

Ludolph.   Stab him! O sweetest wife!
                    [*Attendants bear off* Auranthe.
Erminia. Alas!
Ethelbert.   Your wife?
Ludolph.   Aye, Satan! Does that yerk ye?
Ethelbert. Wife! So soon!
75 *Ludolph.*   Aye, wife! O, impudence!
      Thou bitter mischief! Venomous bad priest!
      How dar'st thou lift those beetle brows at me?
      Me—the prince Ludolph, in this presence here,
      Upon my marriage-day, and scandalize
80   My joys with such opprobrious surprise?
      Wife! Why dost linger on that syllable,
      As if it were some demon's name pronounced
      To summon harmful lightning and make roar
      The sleepy thunder? Hast no sense of fear?
85   No ounce of man in thy mortality?
      Tremble! For, at my nod, the sharpened axe
      Will make thy bold tongue quiver to the roots,
      Those grey lids wink, and thou not know it, Monk!
      Ethelbert. Oh, poor deceivèd Prince! I pity thee!
      Great Otho! I claim justice—
90   *Ludolph.*   Thou shalt have 't!
      Thine arms from forth a pulpit of hot fire
      Shall sprawl distracted! Oh, that that dull cowl
      Were some most sensitive portion of thy life,
      That I might give it to my hounds to tear!
95   Thy girdle some fine zealous-painèd nerve
      To girth my saddle! And those devil's beads
      Each one a life, that I might every day
      Crush one with Vulcan's hammer!
      Otho.   Peace, my son;
      You far outstrip my spleen in this affair.

III ii *74. yerk*] Jolt, jerk (archaic form). Cp. *Othello* I ii 5,
        I had thought to have yerked him here under the ribs . . .
III ii *76. bad*] mad *K.'s MS.* The line is used by Trelawny as a motto for
Adventures of a Younger Son (1831) chap. 53.
III ii *82. some demon's name*] Cp. *Lamia* i 56 (p. 619 below),
              Some demon's mistress, or the demon's self . . .
See II i 9 *n* above.
III ii *83. To summon harmful lighting*] To rouse the sleepy thunder *K.'s MS*
(*cancelled*).
III ii *95. zealous-painèd*] Highly sensitive to pain.
III ii *96. girth*] lace *K.'s MS* (*cancelled*). The 'devil's beads' are the beads of
Ethelbert's rosary.

100   Let us be calm, and hear the abbot's plea
       For this intrusion.
       Ludolph.   I am silent, sire.
       Otho. Conrad, see all depart not wanted here.
                              [*Exeunt Knights, Ladies, &c.*
       Ludolph, be calm. Ethelbert, peace awhile.
       This mystery demands an audience
105   Of a just judge, and that will Otho be.
       Ludolph. Why has he time to breathe another word?
       Otho. Ludolph, old Ethelbert, be sure, comes not
       To beard us for no cause; he's not the man
       To cry himself up an ambassador
       Without credentials.
110   *Ludolph.*   I'll chain up myself.
       Otho. Old Abbot, stand here forth. Lady Erminia,
       Sit. And now, Abbot! What have you to say?
       Our ear is open. First we here denounce
       Hard penalties against thee, if 't be found
115   The cause for which you have disturbed us here,
       Making our bright hours muddy, be a thing
       Of little moment.
       Ethelbert.   See this innocent!
       Otho! Thou father of the people called,
       Is her life nothing? Her fair honour nothing?
120   Her tears from matins until even-song
       Nothing? Her burst heart nothing? Emperor!
       Is this your gentle niece—the simplest flower
       Of the world's herbal—this fair lily blanched
       Still with the dews of piety, this meek lady
125   Here sitting like an angel newly-shent,
       Who veils its snowy wings and grows all pale—
       Is she nothing?
       Otho.   What more to the purpose, abbot?
       Ludolph. Whither is he winding?

III ii *110. I'll chain up myself*] I will for Patience strive *K.'s MS (cancelled).*
III ii *119–26.* Modelled on the Friar's defence of Hero in *Much Ado About
Nothing* IV i 157–72; see III ii 140–7 *n* below.
III ii *122. This* guiltless sweet most innocent Niece *K.'s MS (cancelled).*
III ii *124–6. This meek lady . . . pale*] Cp. *Much Ado About Nothing* IV i
162–3,
                    . . . a thousand innocent shames
              In angel whiteness bear away those blushes . . .
III ii *125. newly-shent*] Scolded for the first time. Cp. *Lamia* i 198 *n* p. 625
below), 'a lovely graduate, still unshent'. See II i 9 *n* above. A cancelled
false start to the line was 'Who now sits here fo[r]lorn . . .'.

Conrad.   No clue yet!
Ethelbert. You have heard, my Liege, and so, no doubt,
                                                  all here,
130   Foul, poisonous, malignant whisperings;
       Nay open speech, rude mockery grown common,
       Against the spotless nature and clear fame
       Of the princess Erminia, your niece.
       I have intruded here thus suddenly,
135   Because I hold those base weeds with tight hand,
       Which now disfigure her fair growing stem,
       Waiting but for your sign to pull them up
       By the dark roots, and leave her palpable,
       To all men's sight, a lady, innocent.
140   The ignominy of that whispered tale
       About a midnight gallant, seen to climb
       A window to her chamber neighboured near,
       I will from her turn off and put the load
       On the right shoulders; on that wretch's head,
145   Who, by close stratagems, did save herself,
       Chiefly by shifting to this lady's room
       A rope-ladder for false witness.
       Ludolph.   Most atrocious!
       Otho. Ethelbert, proceed.
       Ethelbert.   With sad lips I shall:
       For, in the healing of one wound, I fear
150   To make a greater. His young highness here
       To-day was married.
       Ludolph.   Good.
       Ethelbert.   Would it were good!
       Yet why do I delay to spread abroad
       The names of those two vipers, from whose jaws
       A deadly breath went forth to taint and blast

III ii *136. fair*] clear *K.'s MS* (*cancelled*). Probably altered because the word
was used at III ii 132 above.
III ii *139.* Followed in *K.'s MS* by the cancelled passage,
                    Otho. I have wronged this man much
                    Ludolph. Have I not wrong'd this man
                    Conrad. Curs'd Priest
                    Ludolph. How! . . .
III ii *140–7.* Obviously borrowed from the plot to defame Hero in *Much
Ado About Nothing* II ii.
III ii *145. did save herself*] especially
                    By shifting a Rope ladder from her room
                    To this much injured Lady's has escap'd . . .
                                                  K.'s MS (*cancelled*)

This guileless lady?
155   *Otho.*   Abbot, speak their names.
    Ethelbert. A minute first. It cannot be—but may
    I ask, great judge, if you to-day have put
    A letter by unread?
    Otho.   Does 't end in this?
    Conrad. Out with their names!
    Ethelbert.   Bold sinner, say you so?
    Ludolph. Out, tedious monk!
160   *Otho.*   Confess, or by the wheel—
    Ethelbert. My evidence cannot be far away;
    And, though it never come, be on my head
    The crime of passing an attaint upon
    The slanderers of this virgin.
    Ludolph.   Speak aloud!
    Ethelbert. Auranthe, and her brother there.
165   *Conrad.*   Amaze!
    Ludolph. Throw them from the windows!
    Otho. Do what you will!
    Ludolph.   What shall I do with them?
    Something of quick dispatch, for should she hear,
    My soft Auranthe, her sweet mercy would
170   Prevail against my fury. Damnèd priest!
    What swift death wilt thou die? As to the lady
    I touch her not.
    Ethelbert.   Illustrious Otho, stay!
    An ample store of misery thou hast,
    Choke not the granary of thy noble mind
175   With more bad bitter grain, too difficult
    A cud for the repentance of a man
    Grey-growing. To thee only I appeal,
    Not to thy noble son, whose yeasting youth
    Will clear itself and crystal turn again.
180   A young man's heart, by Heaven's blessing, is
    A wide world, where a thousand new-born hopes
    Empurple fresh the melancholy blood:
    But an old man's is narrow, tenantless

III ii *159. sinner*] serpent *K.'s MS (cancelled).*
III ii *166.* Perhaps suggested by the Hussites' 'defenestration' of the burgo-master and town councillors of Prague in the religious conflicts of July 1419.
III ii *178–9. whose yeasting youth / Will clear itself*] Cp. K.'s description of the period between boyhood and manhood in his preface to *Endymion* (p. 119 above).
III ii *183. tenantless*] stagnated *K.'s MS (cancelled).*

Of hopes, and stuffed with many memories,
185   Which, being pleasant, ease the heavy pulse—
Painful, clog up and stagnate. Weigh this matter
Even as a miser balances his coin;
And, in the name of mercy, give command
That your knight Albert be brought here before you.
190   He will expound this riddle; he will show
A noon-day proof of bad Auranthe's guilt.
Otho. Let Albert straight be summoned.
                              [*Exit one of the Nobles.*
Ludolph.   Impossible!
I cannot doubt—I will not—no—to doubt
Is to be ashes!—withered up to death!
195   *Otho.* My gentle Ludolph, harbour not a fear;
You do yourself much wrong.
Ludolph.   O wretched dolt!
Now, when my foot is almost on thy neck,
Wilt thou infuriate me? Proof! Thou fool!
Why wilt thou teaze impossibility
200   With such a thick-skulled persevering suit?
Fanatic obstinacy! Prodigy!
Monster of folly! Ghost of a turned brain!
You puzzle me—you haunt me—when I dream
Of you my brain will split! Bald sorcerer!
205   Juggler! May I come near you? On my soul
I know not whether to pity, curse, or laugh.

Enter Albert, *and the Nobleman.*

Here, Albert, this old phantom wants a proof!
Give him his proof! A camel's load of proofs!
Otho. Albert, I speak to you as to a man
210   Whose words once uttered pass like current gold;
And therefore fit to calmly put a close
To this brief tempest. Do you stand possessed
Of any proof against the honourableness

III ii *194.* Is to be wither'd up to ashy death *K.'s MS* (*cancelled*).
III ii *202.* Cp. *Lamia* i 377 (p. 633 below),
          The ghost of folly haunting my sweet dreams . . .
See II i 9 *n* above.
III ii *204–5. Bald sorcerer! | Juggler*] Cp. *Lamia* ii 245 (p. 646 below), 'bald-
head philosopher', and ii 277 (p. 647 below),
          Shut, shut those juggling eyes, thou ruthless man . . .
See II i 9 *n* above.
III ii *210.* Whose word is ever counted trustworthy *K.'s MS, Brown's MS*
(cancelled and corrected in *K.'s* hand).

Of Lady Auranthe, our new-spoused daughter?

215 *Albert.* You chill me with astonishment. How's this?
My Liege, what proof should I have 'gainst a fame
Impossible of slur? [*Otho rises.*
Erminia.   O wickedness!
Ethelbert. Deluded monarch, 'tis a cruel lie.
Otho. Peace, rebel-priest!
Conrad.   Insult beyond credence!
Erminia. Almost a dream!

220 *Ludolph.*   We have awakened from
A foolish dream that from my brow hath wrung
A wrathful dew. O folly! Why did I
So act the lion with this silly gnat?
Let them depart. Lady Erminia!

225 I ever grieved for you, as who did not?
But now you have, with such a brazen front,
So most maliciously, so madly striven
To dazzle the soft moon, when tenderest clouds
Should be unlooped around to curtain her;

230 I leave you to the desert of the world
Almost with pleasure. Let them be set free
For me! I take no personal revenge
More than against a nightmare, which a man
Forgets in the new dawn. [*Exit* Ludolph.

235 *Otho.* Still in extremes! No, they must not be loose.
Ethelbert. Albert, I must suspect thee of a crime
So fiendish—
Otho.   Fear'st thou not my fury, monk?
Conrad, be they in your sure custody
Till we determine some fit punishment.

240 It is so mad a deed, I must reflect
And question them in private; for perhaps,
By patient scrutiny, we may discover
Whether they merit death, or should be placed
In care of the physicians.
                    [*Exeunt* Otho *and Nobles,* Albert *following.*
Conrad. My guards, ho!

245 *Erminia.*   Albert, wilt thou follow there?
Wilt thou creep dastardly behind his back,

III ii *222. wrathful*] moist *K.'s MS* (*cancelled*).
III ii *226. brazen*] shameless *K.'s MS* (*cancelled*).
III ii *228–9. the soft moon...curtain her*] Cp. K.'s early sonnet *To my Brother George* 10–11 (p. 48 above),

    Cynthia is from her silken curtains peeping
    So scantly, that it seems her bridal night ...

And slink away from a weak woman's eye?
Turn, thou court-Janus! Thou forget'st thyself;
Here is the Duke, waiting with open arms,

[*Enter Guards.*

250   To thank thee; here congratulate each other;
Wring hands; embrace; and swear how lucky 'twas
That I, by happy chance, hit the right man
Of all the world to trust in.
    Albert.   Trust! To me!
    Conrad (*aside*). He is the sole one in this mystery.
255   *Erminia.* Well, I give up, and save my prayers for
        Heaven!
You, who could do this deed, would ne'er relent,
Though, at my words, the hollow prison-vaults
Would groan for pity.
    Conrad.   Manacle them both!
Ethelbert. I know it—it must be—I see it all!
260   Albert, thou art the minion!
    Erminia.   Ah, too plain!—
Conrad. Silence! Gag up their mouths! I cannot bear
More of this brawling. That the Emperor
Had placed you in some other custody!
Bring them away.   [*Exeunt all but* Albert.
265   *Albert.* Though my name perish from the book of honour,
Almost before the recent ink is dry,
And be no more remembered after death
Than any drummer's in the muster-roll;
Yet shall I season high my sudden fall
270   With triumph o'er that evil-witted duke!
He shall feel what it is to have the hand
Of a man drowning, on his hateful throat.

Enter Gersa *and* Sigifred.

Gersa. What discord is at ferment in this house?
Sigifred. We are without conjecture; not a soul
275   We met could answer any certainty.

III ii *251.* Between 'embrace' and 'and swear how lucky 'twas . . .' K.'s
MS has the cancelled passage, 'the gale is over blown / And you are
safe . . .'.
III ii *253. Trust! To me!*] Trust to me? K.'s MS. The audience is kept in the
dark about Albert's true motives until IV i 136–49 below.
III ii *269. Season . . . sudden fall*] sweeten . . . evil hour K.'s MS (*cancelled*).
III ii *272.* Followed in K.'s MS by the lines,
    Erminia! dream tonight of better days
    Tomorrow makes them real—once more good morrow . . .

Gersa. Young Ludolph, like a fiery arrow, shot
By us.
Sigifred.   The Emperor, with crossed arms, in thought.
Gersa. In one room music, in another sadness,
Perplexity everywhere!
Albert.   A trifle mere!
280 Follow; your presences will much avail
To tune our jarrèd spirits. I'll explain.   [*Exeunt.*

ACT IV

SCENE I

[Auranthe's *apartment.*]

Auranthe and Conrad *discovered.*

Conrad. Well, well, I know what ugly jeopardy
We are caged in; you need not pester that
Into my ears. Prythee, let me be spared
A foolish tongue, that I may bethink me
5   Of remedies with some deliberation.
You cannot doubt but 'tis in Albert's power
To crush or save us?
Auranthe.   No, I cannot doubt.
He has, assure yourself, by some strange means
My secret; which I ever hid from him,
Knowing his mawkish honesty.
10   *Conrad.*   Cursed slave!
Auranthe. Ay, I could almost curse him now myself.
Wretched impediment! Evil genius!
A glue upon my wings, that cannot spread,
When they should span the provinces! A snake,
15   A scorpion, sprawling on the first gold step,
Conducting to the throne high canopied.
Conrad. You would not hear my council, when his life
Might have been trodden out, all sure and hushed;
Now the dull animal forsooth must be
20   Entreated, managed! When can you contrive
The interview he demands?
Auranthe.   As speedily
It must be done as my bribed woman can

IV i *12. Wretched impediment!*] O wretched woman! *K.'s MS (cancelled).*
IV i *15. sprawling*] threating on *K.'s MS (cancelled).*
IV i *22. woman*] minion *K.'s MS (cancelled).*

20*

Unseen conduct him to me; but I fear
'Twill be impossible, while the broad day
25   Comes through the panes with persecuting glare.
Methinks, if 't now were night I could intrigue
With darkness, bring the stars to second me
And settle all this trouble.
Conrad.   Nonsense! Child!
See him immediately; why not now?
30   *Auranthe.* Do you forget that even the senseless doorposts
Are on the watch and gape through all the house;
How many whisperers there are about,
Hungry for evidence to ruin me;
Men I have spurned, and women I have taunted?
35   Besides, the foolish prince sends, minute whiles,
His pages—so they tell me—to enquire
After my health, entreating, if I please,
To see me.
Conrad. Well, suppose this Albert here;
What is your power with him?
Auranthe.   He should be
40   My echo, my taught parrot! But I fear
He will be cur enough to bark at me;
Have his own say; read me some silly creed
'Bout shame and pity.
Conrad.   What will you do then?
Auranthe. What I shall do, I know not; what I would
45   Cannot be done; for see, this chamber-floor
Will not yield to the pick-axe and the spade—
Here is no quiet depth of hollow ground.
Conrad. Sister, you have grown sensible and wise,
Seconding, ere I speak it, what is now,
I hope, resolved between us.
50   *Auranthe.*   Say, what is 't?
Conrad. You need not be his sexton too: a man
May carry that with him shall make him die
Elsewhere—give that to him; pretend the while
You will to-morrow succumb to his wishes,
55   Be what they may, and send him from the Castle
On some fool's errand; let his latest groan
Frighten the wolves!
Auranthe.   Alas! He must not die!

IV i *30. senseless*] Inanimate. Cp. *Julius Caesar* I i 38,
       You blocks, you stones, you worse than senseless things . . .
IV i *43. What will you do then?*] You are a Cypher then *K.'s MS (cancelled).*

Conrad. Would you were both hearsed up in stifling lead!
Detested—
Auranthe. Conrad, hold! I would not bear
60   The little thunder of your fretful tongue,
        Though I alone were taken in these toils,
        And you could free me; but remember, sir,
        You live alone in my security:
        So keep your wits at work for your own sake,
        Not mine, and be more mannerly.
65   *Conrad.*   Thou wasp!
        If my domains were emptied of these folk,
        And I had thee to starve—
        Auranthe.   O, marvellous!
        But Conrad, now be gone; the host is looked for;
        Cringe to the Emperor, entertain the lords,
70   And, do ye mind, above all things, proclaim
        My sickness, with a brother's saddened eye,
        Condoling with Prince Ludolph. In fit time
        Return to me.
        Conrad.   I leave you to your thoughts.   [*Exit.*
        Auranthe (sola). Down, down, proud temper! Down,
              Auranthe's pride!
75   Why do I anger him when I should kneel?
        Conrad! Albert! Help! Help! What can I do?
        O wretched woman! Lost, wrecked, swallowed up,
        Accursèd, blasted! O thou golden Crown,

IV i 63. K.'s cancelled false start was 'You fall with me . . .'.

IV i 65. *Thou wasp*] Who knocks?
                        Auranthe. It may be Albert—hide yourself
                        You . . . *K.'s MS (cancelled).*
Albert's entrance was deferred to allow time for Auranthe's soliloquy (IV i
74–104 below).

IV i 66. *emptied of these folk*] Cp. *Ode on a Grecian Urn* 37 (p. 536 above),
'emptied of this folk'.

IV i 68–72. Perhaps suggested by *Macbeth* I v 63–5,
                        . . . To beguile the time,
              Look like the time; bear welcome in your eye,
              Your hand, your tongue: look like the innocent flower,
              But be the serpent under't . . .

IV i 69. *lords*] nobles *K.'s MS.*

IV i 73–4. *I leave . . . temper*] A sudden death light on you! / Auranthe.
'Twere well perhaps . . . *Brown's MS (cancelled and corrected in K.'s hand).*

IV i 78–90. Auranthe's grief at losing the crown probably owes something
to the abdication scene, *Richard II* IV i 181–205; cp. IV i 89–90 n and 96–8 n
below.

Orbing along the serene firmament
80 Of a wide empire, like a glowing moon;
And thou, bright sceptre! Lustrous in my eyes—
There—as the fabled fair Hesperian tree,
Bearing a fruit more precious! Graceful thing,
Delicate, godlike, magic! Must I leave
85 Thee to melt in the visionary air,
Ere, by one grasp, this common hand is made
Imperial? I do not know the time
When I have wept for sorrow; but methinks
I could now sit upon the ground and shed
90 Tears, tears of misery. O, the heavy day!
How shall I bear my life till Albert comes?
Ludolph! Erminia! Proofs! O heavy day!
Bring me some mourning weeds, that I may 'tire
Myself as fits one wailing her own death:
95 Cut off these curls and brand this lily hand,
And throw these jewels from my loathing sight—
Fetch me a missal and a string of beads—
A cup of bittered water and a crust—
I will confess, O holy Abbot!—How!
100 What is this? Auranthe! Thou fool, dolt,
Whimpering idiot! Up! Up! Act and quell!
I am safe! Coward! Why am I in fear?
Albert! He cannot stickle, chew the cud

Enter Albert.

IV i *82–3. the fabled . . . precious*] Echoing Milton's *Comus* 393–4,
                    . . . beauty like the fair Hesperian tree
              Laden with blooming gold . . .
IV i *85. melt in the visionary air*] Echoing *The Tempest* IV i 150–1,
                    . . . melted into air, into thin air
              And, like the baseless fabric of this vision . . .
Cp. V i 24 below,
                    Escaped—fled—vanished—melted into air . . .
IV i *89–90. I could now . . . misery*] Echoes *Richard II* III ii 155–6,
                    . . . let us sit upon the ground
              And tell sad stories of the death of kings . . .
IV i *96–8.* Cp. *Richard II* III iii 147–51,
              I'll give my jewels for a set of beads,
              My gorgeous palace for a hermitage,
              My gay apparel for an almsman's gown,
              My figured goblets for a dish of wood,
              My sceptre for a palmer's walking-staff . . .
IV i *103. stickle*] 'To hesitate, scruple, take offence at, 1819' (*OED*).

In such a fine extreme–impossible!

[*Goes to the door, listens, and opens it.*

105 Albert, I have been waiting for you here
With such an aching heart, such swooning throbs
On my poor brain, such cruel–cruel sorrow,
That I should claim your pity! Art not well?
Albert. Yes, lady, well.

110 *Auranthe.*   You look not so, alas!
But pale, as if you brought some heavy news.
Albert. You know full well what makes me look so pale.
Auranthe. No! Do I? Surely I am still to learn
Some horror; all I know, this present, is

115 I am near hustled to a dangerous gulf,
Which you can save me from–and therefore safe,
So trusting in thy love; that should not make
Thee pale, my Albert.
Albert.   It doth make me freeze.
Auranthe. Why should it, love?
Albert.   You should not ask me that

120 But make your own heart monitor and save
Me the great pain of telling. You must know.
Auranthe. Something has vexed you, Albert. There are
        times
When simplest things put on a sombre cast;
A melancholy mood will haunt a man

125 Until most easy matters take the shape
Of unachievable tasks; small rivulets
Then seem impassable.
Albert.   Do not cheat yourself
With hope that gloss of words, or suppliant action,
Or tears, or ravings, or self-threatened death,
Can alter my resolve.

130 *Auranthe.*   You make me tremble;
Not so much at your threats, as at your voice,
Untuned and harsh, and barren of all love.
Albert. You suffocate me! Stop this devil's parley
And listen to me; know me once for all.

135 *Auranthe.* I thought I did. Alas! I am deceived.
Albert. No, you are not deceived. You took me for
A man detesting all inhuman crime,
And therefore kept from me your demon's plot
Against Erminia. Silent? Be so still—

IV i *106. swooning throbs*] throbbing pains K.'s MS (*cancelled*).
IV i *133.*   Can Ludolph's wife hold such a devil's parley!
                Auranthe listen! know me once for all . . . K.'s MS (*cancelled*)

140   For ever! Speak no more, but hear my words,
      Thy fate. Your safety I have bought to-day
      By blazoning a lie, which in the dawn
      I'll expiate with truth.
      Auranthe.   O cruel traitor!
      Albert. For I would not set eyes upon thy shame;
145   I would not see thee dragged to death by the hair,
      Penanced, and taunted on a scaffolding!
      To-night, upon the skirts of the blind wood
      That blackens northward of these horrid towers,
      I wait for you with horses. Choose your fate.
      Farewell.
150   *Auranthe.* Albert, you jest; I'm sure you must.
      You, an ambitious soldier! I, a Queen,
      One who could say: Here, rule these Provinces!
      Take tribute from those cities for thyself!
      Empty these armouries, these treasuries,
155   Muster thy warlike thousands at a nod!
      Go! conquer Italy!
      Albert.   Auranthe, you have made
      The whole world chaff to me. Your doom is fixed.
      Auranthe. Out, villain! Dastard!
      Albert.   Look there to the door!
      Who is it?
      Auranthe.   Conrad, traitor!
      Albert.   Let him in.
                      [*Enter* Conrad.
160   Do not affect amazement, hypocrite,
      At seeing me in this chamber.
      Conrad.   Auranthe?
      Albert. Talk not with eyes, but speak your curses out
      Against me, who would sooner crush and grind
      A brace of toads than league with them to oppress
165   An innocent lady, gull an Emperor,
      More generous to me than autumn's sun
      To ripening harvests.
      Auranthe.   No more insult, sir!
      Albert. Aye, clutch your scabbard; but, for prudence'
         sake,

IV i *141–3. Your safety . . . truth*] Earlier attempts were,

  1.   . . . Tomorrow to the public ear
     I blazon out the truth . . . *K.'s MS, Brown's MS* (*cancelled*).
  2.   . . . To-day you are safe
     I have told a lie for you which in the dawn
     I'll expiate with truth . . . *Brown's MS* (in K.'s hand).

Draw not the sword; 'twould make an uproar, Duke,
170 You would not hear the end of. At nightfall
Your lady sister, if I guess aright,
Will leave this busy castle. You had best
Take farewell too of worldly vanities.
Conrad. Vassal!
Albert.   To-morrow, when the Emperor sends
175 For loving Conrad, see you fawn on him.
Good even!
Auranthe.   You'll be seen!
Albert.   See the coast clear then.
Auranthe (*as he goes*). Remorseless Albert! Cruel, cruel
    wretch!   [*She lets him out.*
Conrad. So, we must lick the dust?
Auranthe.   I follow him.
Conrad. How? Where? The plan of your escape?
Auranthe.   He waits
180 For me with horses by the forest-side,
Northward.
Conrad.   Good, good! He dies. You go, say you?
Auranthe. Perforce.
Conrad.   Be speedy, darkness! Till that comes,
Fiends keep you company!   [*Exit.*
Auranthe.   And you! And you!
And all men! Vanish!

          [*Retires to an inner apartment.*

SCENE II

[*An apartment in the Castle.*]

Enter Ludolph *and Page.*

Page. Still very sick, my Lord; but now I went
Knowing my duty to so good a Prince;
And there her women in a mournful throng
Stood in the passage whispering: if any
5 Moved 'twas with careful steps and hushed as death;
They bid me stop.
Ludolph.   Good fellow, once again
Make soft enquiry; prythee be not stayed

IV i *170–1. At nightfall / Your*] At shut / Of eve . . . *K.'s MS* (*cancelled*). Cp.
Lamia ii 107 and *n* (p. 639 below), 'at blushing shut of day'. See II i 9 *n*
above.
IV i *181. Good, good; he dies*] Substituted in *K's MS* for the cancelled passage, 'You go? Perforce . . .'

By any hindrance, but with gentlest force
Break through her weeping servants, till thou com'st
10 E'en to her chamber door, and there, fair boy—
If with thy mother's milk thou hast sucked in
Any diviner eloquence—woo her ears
With plaints for me more tender than the voice
Of dying Echo, echoed.
Page.   Kindest master!
15 To know thee sad thus, will unloose my tongue
In mournful syllables. Let but my words reach
Her ears and she shall take them coupled with
Moans from my heart and sighs not counterfeit.
May I speed better!   [Exit Page.
Ludolph.   Auranthe! My life!
20 Long have I loved thee, yet till now not loved:
Remembering, as I do, hard-hearted times
When I had heard even of thy death perhaps,
And thoughtless, suffered thee to pass alone
Into Elysium! Now I follow thee
25 A substance or a shadow, wheresoe'er
Thou leadest me—whether thy white feet press
With pleasant weight, the amorous-aching earth,
Or thro' the air thou pioneerest me,
A shade! Yet sadly I predestinate!
30 O unbenignest Love, why wilt thou let
Darkness steal out upon the sleepy world
So wearily; as if night's chariot wheels
Were clogged in some thick cloud. O changeful Love,
Let not her steeds with drowsy-footed pace
35 Pass the high stars, before sweet embassage
Comes from the pillowed beauty of that fair
Completion of all delicate nature's wit.
Pout her faint lips anew with rubious health

IV ii 23. *thee*] her *K.'s MS* (*cancelled*).
IV ii 24–5. *Now I . . . wheresoe'er*] Now I go with thee / When heaven
pleases: should it be tonight. . . . *K.'s MS* (*cancelled*).
IV ii 30. *unbenignest*] unpropitious *K.'s MS* (*cancelled*).
IV ii 32. *wearily*] heavily *K.'s MS* (*cancelled*).
IV ii 34. A reminiscence of Milton's *Comus* 553–4,

                    . . . the drowsie frighted steeds
          That draw the litter of close-curtain'd sleep . . .

For K.'s earlier echo of Milton's lines see *Endymion* iv 370 *n* (p. 261 above).
IV ii 37. *delicate nature's wit*] fairness and all form *K.'s MS* (*cancelled*).
IV ii 38. *rubious*] Red, rosy. Cp. *Lamia* i 163 (p. 623 below), 'rubious-
argent'.

And with thine infant fingers lift the fringe
40 Of her sick eyelids; that those eyes may glow
With wooing light upon me, ere the morn
Peers with disrelish, grey, barren and cold.

Enter Gersa *and courtiers.*

Otho calls me his Lion, should I blush
To be so tamed? so——
Gersa.   Do me the courtesy,
Gentlemen, to pass on.
45 *Courtier.*   We are your servants.
                                         [*Exeunt courtiers.*
Ludolph. It seems then, sir, you have found out the man
You would confer with—me?
Gersa.   If I break not
Too much upon your thoughtful mood, I will
Claim a brief while your patience.
Ludolph.   For what cause
Soe'er I shall be honoured.
50 *Gersa.*   I not less.
Ludolph. What may it be? No trifle can take place
Of such deliberate prologue, serious 'haviour.
But be it what it may I cannot fail
To listen with no common interest;
55 For though so new your presence is to me,
I have a soldier's friendship for your fame.
Please you explain.
Gersa.   As thus—for, pardon me,
I cannot in plain terms grossly assault
A noble nature; and would faintly sketch
60 What your quick apprehension will fill up,
So finely I esteem you.
Ludolph.   I attend.
Gersa. Your generous father, most illustrious Otho,
Sits in the banquet room among his chiefs:
His wine is bitter, for you are not there,
65 His eyes are fixed still on the open doors,
And every passer in he frowns upon
Seeing no Ludolph comes.
Ludolph.   I do neglect—

IV ii 41. *With wooing light upon me*] Earlier attempts in *K.'s MS* include
'Like ardent pensive planet . . .' and 'Like ardent planets through . . .'.
IV ii 42. *Peers*] Comes *K.'s MS* (*cancelled*).
IV ii 44-5. *Do me . . . pass on*] I sought you not / But as I chance to meet
you here alone . . . *K.'s MS* (*cancelled*).

Gersa. And for your absence, may I guess the cause?
Ludolph. Stay there! No! Guess? More princely you
      must be

70   Than to make guesses at me. 'Tis enough,
I'm sorry I can hear no more.
Gersa.   And I
As grieved to force it on you so abrupt;
Yet one day you must know a grief whose sting
Will sharpen more the longer 'tis concealed.

75   *Ludolph.* Say it at once, sir! Dead–dead–is she dead?
Gersa. Mine is a cruel task: she is not dead–
And would for your sake she were innocent–
Ludolph. Hungarian! Thou amazest me beyond
All scope of thought; convulsest my heart's blood

80   To deadly churning! Gersa, you are young,
As I am; let me observe you, face to face:
Not grey-browed like the poisonous Ethelbert,
No rheumèd eyes, no furrowing of age,
No wrinkles where all vices nestle in

85   Like crannied vermin–no, but fresh and young,
And hopeful featured. Ha! by heaven you weep
Tears, human tears! Do you repent you then
Of a cursed torturer's office! Why shouldst join–
Tell me–the league of Devils? Confess–confess
The lie!

90   *Gersa.*   Lie!–but begone all ceremonious points
Of honour battailous! I could not turn
My wrath against thee for the orbèd world.
Ludolph. Your wrath, weak boy? Tremble at mine,
      unless
Retraction follow close upon the heels

95   Of that late 'stounding insult: why has my sword
Not done already a sheer judgment on thee?
Despair, or eat thy words? Why, thou wast nigh
Whimpering away my reason! Hark ye, Sir,
It is no secret that Erminia,

100   Erminia, sir, was hidden in your tent–
O blessed asylum! Comfortable home!
Begone, I pity thee; thou art a gull–

IV ii *78. Hungarian*] Thou liest K.'s MS, Brown's MS (*cancelled and corrected in K.'s hand*).

IV ii *91. battailous*] Ready for battle. Frequently in Spenser, for example *The Faerie Queene* V xii 12,

                     . . . in battailous array
             Wayting his foe . . .

Erminia's last new puppet—
Gersa.   Furious fire!
Thou mak'st me boil as hot as thou canst flame!
105 And in thy teeth I give thee back the lie!
Thou liest! Thou, Auranthe's fool! A wittol!
Ludolph. Look! look at this bright sword;
There is no part of it to the very hilt
But shall indulge itself about thine heart!
110 Draw! but remember thou must cower thy plumes,
As yesterday the Arab made thee stoop—
Gersa. Patience! not here, I would not spill thy blood
Here, underneath this roof where Otho breathes,
Thy father—almost mine—
Ludolph.   O faltering coward—

Re-enter Page.

115 Stay, stay; here is one I have half a word with—
Well? What ails thee child?
Page.   My lord!
Ludolph.   What wouldst say?
Page. They are fled!
Ludolph.   They! Who?
Page.   When anxiously
I hastened back, your grieving messenger,
I found the stairs all dark, the lamps extinct,
120 And not a foot or whisper to be heard.
I thought her dead, and on the lowest step
Sat listening; when presently came by
Two muffled up—one sighing heavily,
The other cursing low, whose voice I knew
125 For the Duke Conrad's. Close I followed them
Thro' the dark ways they chose to the open air;
And, as I followed, heard my lady speak.
Ludolph. Thy life answer the truth!
Page.   The chamber's empty!
Ludolph. As I will be of mercy! So, at last,

IV ii *106. wittol*] Complaisant cuckold. Cp. *The Merry Wives of Windsor* II
ii 94–5: 'Wittol!–Cuckold! the devil himself hath not such a name.'
IV ii *129–31. As I will . . . I am*] K. may have intended to expand Ludolph's
reaction to Auranthe's treachery. See Brown's letter to Dilke of 12 Aug.
1819, written when the play had '. . . advanced nearly to the end of the
fourth Act,' 'K.'s introduction of Grimm's adventure, lying three days on
his back for love, though it spoils the unity of time is not out of the way for
the character of Ludolph, so I have consented to it' (*The Letters of Charles
Armitage Brown*, ed. Jack Stillinger 1966, 49). Stillinger notes that the allusion

This nail is in my temples!
130   *Gersa.*   Be calm in this.
Ludolph. I am.
Gersa.   And Albert too has disappeared;
Ere I met you, I sought him everywhere;
You would not hearken.
Ludolph.   Which way went they, boy?
Gersa. I'll hunt with you.
Ludolph.   No, no, no. My senses are
135   Still whole. I have survived. My arm is strong,
My appetite sharp—for revenge! I'll no sharer
In my feast; my injury is all my own,
And so is my revenge, my lawful chattels!
Terrier, ferret them out! Burn—burn the witch!
140   Trace me their footsteps! Away!

                                                    [*Exeunt.*

ACT V

SCENE I

[A part of the Forest.]

Enter Conrad *and* Auranthe.

Auranthe. Go no further; not a step more. Thou art
A master-plague in the midst of miseries.
Go—I fear thee! I tremble every limb,
Who never shook before. There's moody death
5   In thy resolvèd looks! Yes, I could kneel
To pray thee far away! Conrad, go! go!—

is to F. M. Grimm's account of his being jilted and falling 'into a sort of
catalepsy which continued for several days . . .' until he suddenly recovered
and '. . . never thought more of his chaste Lucretia' (*Historical and Literary
Memoirs . . . from the Correspondence of Baron de Grimm*, 1815, i viii). The
incident does not appear in the play.

IV ii *129–30. So . . . temples*] Alludes to Jael's slaying of Sisera, *Judges* iv
18–22. Cp. Milton, *Samson Agonistes* 989–90,

     Jael, who with inhospitable guile
     Smote *Sisera* sleeping through the Temples nail'd . . .

K.'s lines were used by Trelawny as a motto for *Adventures of a Younger Son*
(1831) chap. 124.

IV ii *138.* Followed in *K.'s MS* by 'Jackall, lead on: the lion preys to-
night . . .'. Probably omitted to avoid the incongruity in the following
line.

There! Yonder underneath the boughs I see
Our horses!
Conrad.   Aye, and a man.
Auranthe.   Yes, he is there.
Go, go—no blood! no blood! Go, gentle Conrad!
Conrad. Farewell!

10 *Auranthe.*   Farewell, for this Heaven pardon you!
                                      [*Exit* Auranthe.
Conrad. If he survive one hour, then may I die
In unimagined tortures—or breathe through
A long life in the foulest sink of the world!
He dies! 'Tis well she do not advertise

15 The caitiff of the cold steel at his back.
                                          [*Exit* Conrad.

              Enter Ludolph *and Page.*

Ludolph. Missed the way, boy? Say not that on your
      peril!
Page. Indeed, indeed I cannot trace them further.
Ludolph. Must I stop here? Here solitary die?
Stifled beneath the thick oppressive shade

20 Of these dull boughs—this oven of dark thickets—
Silent—without revenge? Pshaw!—bitter end—
A bitter death—a suffocating death—
A gnawing—silent—deadly-quiet death!
Escaped? Fled? Vanished? Melted into air?

25 She's gone!—I cannot clutch her! No revenge!
A muffled death, ensnared in horrid silence!
Suckled to my grave amid a dreamy calm!
O, where is that illustrious noise of war,
To smother up this sound of labouring breath,
This rustle of the trees!
                [Auranthe *shrieks at a distance.*

30 *Page.*   My Lord, a noise!
This way—hark!
Ludolph.   Yes, yes! A hope! A music!
A glorious clamour! Now I live again!   [*Exeunt.*

V i *14–15.* Used by Trelawny as a motto for *Adventures of a Younger Son*
(1831) chap. 61.
V i *18–32.* For the cancelled version in K.'s MS see Appendix C (p. 762
below).
V i *23–8.* Used by Trelawny as a motto for his *Adventures of a Younger Son*
(1831) chap. 62.
V i *24. melted into air*] See IV i 85 *n* above.

SCENE II

[*Another part of the Forest.*]

Enter Albert (*wounded*).

Albert. O, for enough life to support me on
To Otho's feet!

Enter Ludolph.

Ludolph.   Thrice villainous, stay there!
Tell me where that detested woman is,
Or this is through thee!
Albert.   My good Prince, with me
5   The sword has done its worst; not without worst
Done to another – Conrad has it home!
I see you know it all!
Ludolph.   Where is his sister?

Auranthe *rushes in.*

Auranthe. Albert!
Ludolph. Ha! There! There! – He is the paramour! –
There – hug him – dying! O thou innocence,
10   Shrine him and comfort him at his last gasp,
Kiss down his eyelids! Was he not thy love?
Wilt thou forsake him at his latest hour?
Keep fearful and aloof from his last gaze,
His most uneasy moments, when cold death
15   Stands with the door ajar to let him in?
Albert. Oh, that that door with hollow slam would close
Upon me sudden, for I cannot meet,
In all the unknown chambers of the dead,
Such horrors!
Ludolph.   Auranthe! What can he mean?
20   What horrors? Is it not a joyous time?
Am I not married to a paragon
'Of personal beauty and untainted soul'?
A blushing fair-eyed purity! A sylph,
Whose snowy timid hand has never sinned
25   Beyond a flower plucked, mild as itself?
Albert, you do insult my bride – your mistress –
To talk of horrors on our wedding night!

V ii *8. Auranthe* rushes in] Enter Auranthe *K.'s MS* (*cancelled*), *Browns' MS,*
1848.
V ii *22.* Ludolph is referring ironically to the general estimate of Auranthe's
character.

Albert. Alas, poor Prince, I would you knew my heart!
'Tis not so guilty–
Ludolph.   Hear you he pleads not guilty!
30   You are not? Or if so what matters it?
You have escaped me–free as the dusk air–
Hid in the forest–safe from my revenge.
I cannot catch you! You should laugh at me,
Poor cheated Ludolph! Make the forest hiss
35   With jeers at me! You tremble; faint at once,
You will come to again. O cockatrice,
I have you! Whither wander those fair eyes
To entice the devil to your help, that he
May change you to a spider, so to crawl
40   Into some cranny to escape my wrath?
Albert. Sometimes the counsel of a dying man
Doth operate quietly when his breath is gone:
Disjoin those hands–part–part, do not destroy
Each other–forget her! Our miseries
45   Are almost equal shared, and mercy is–
Ludolph.   A boon
When one can compass it. Auranthe, try
Your oratory–your breath is not so hitched–
Aye, stare for help–   [*Albert groans and dies.*
                There goes a spotted soul
Howling in vain along the hollow night!
50   Hear him! He calls you–sweet Auranthe, come!
Auranthe. Kill me!
Ludolph. No! What? Upon our marriage-night!
The earth would shudder at so foul a deed–
A fair bride! A sweet bride! An innocent bride!
55   No! We must revel it, as 'tis in use
In times of delicate brilliant ceremony.
Come, let me lead you to our halls again!
Nay, linger not–make no resistance sweet–
Will you? Ah wretch, thou canst not, for I have
The strength of twenty lions 'gainst a lamb!
60   Now–one adieu for Albert!–Come away!
                                        [*Exeunt.*

SCENE III

[*An inner Court of the Castle.*]
Enter Sigifred, Gonfred, *and* Theodore *meeting.*
Theodore. Was ever such a night?

V ii 47. *hitched*] Impeded, broken.
V iii *1–17.* Probably modelled on the scene following the discovery of
Duncan's murder, *Macbeth* II iv.

Sigifred.   What horrors more?
Things unbelieved one hour, so strange they are,
The next hour stamps with credit.
Theodore.   Your last news?
Gonfred. After the page's story of the death
Of Albert and Duke Conrad?
5   *Sigifred.*   And the return
Of Ludolph with the Princess.
Gonfred.   No more save
Prince Gersa's freeing Abbot Ethelbert,
And the sweet lady, fair Erminia,
From prison.
Theodore.   Where are they now? Hast yet heard?
10   *Gonfred.* With the sad Emperor they are closeted;
I saw the three pass slowly up the stairs,
The lady weeping, the old Abbot cowled.
Sigifred. What next?
Theodore.   I ache to think on 't.
Gonfred.   'Tis with fate.
Theodore. One while these proud towers are hushed as
        death.
15   *Gonfred.* The next our poor Prince fills the archèd rooms
With ghastly ravings.
Sigifred.   I do fear his brain.
Gonfred. I will see more. Bear you so stout a heart?
                          [*Exeunt into the castle.*

SCENE IV

[*A cabinet, opening towards a terrace.*]

Otho, Erminia, Ethelbert, *and a Physician, discovered.*

Otho. Oh, my poor boy! My son! My son! My Ludolph!
Have ye no comfort for me, ye physicians
Of the weak body and soul?
Ethelbert.   'Tis not the medicine

V iii *1–3.* Cp. *Macbeth* II iv 2–4,

                       . . . I have seen
    Hours dreadful and things strange, but this sore night
    Hath trifled former knowings . . .

V iv *2–5.* Cp. *Macbeth* V iii 40–6,

    Macbeth. Canst thou not minister to a mind diseas'd,
                Pluck from the memory a rooted sorrow,
                Raze out the written tablets of the brain,
                And with some sweet oblivious antidote

Either of heaven or earth can cure, unless
5   Fit time be chosen to administer–
Otho. A kind forbearance, holy abbot–come
Erminia; here sit by me, gentle girl;
Give me thy hand–hast thou forgiven me?
Erminia. Would I were with the saints to pray for you!
10 *Otho.* Why will ye keep me from my darling child?
Physician. Forgive me, but he must not see thy face.
Otho. Is then a father's countenance a Gorgon?
Hath it not comfort in it? Would it not
Console my poor boy, cheer him, heal his spirits?
15 Let me embrace him, let me speak to him;
I will! Who hinders me? Who's Emperor?
Physician. You may not, Sire; 'twould overwhelm him
       quite,
He is so full of grief and passionate wrath;
Too heavy a sigh would kill him–or do worse.
20 He must be saved by fine contrivances,
And most especially we must keep clear
Out of his sight a father whom he loves;
His heart is full, it can contain no more,
And do its ruddy office.
Ethelbert.   Sage advice;
25 We must endeavour how to ease and slacken
The tight-wound energies of his despair,
Not make them tenser.
Otho.   Enough! I hear, I hear.
Yet you were about to advise more. I listen.
Ethelbert. This learned doctor will agree with me,
30 That not in the smallest point should he be thwarted
Or gainsaid by one word; his very motions,
Nods, becks and hints, should be obeyed with care,
Even on the moment: so his troubled mind
May cure itself.
Physician.   There is no other means.
35 *Otho.* Open the door: let's hear if all is quiet.
Physician. Beseech you, Sire, forbear.
Erminia.   Do, do.
Otho.   I command!

Cleanse the stuff'd bosom of that perilous stuff
Which weighs upon the heart?
    Doctor.   Therein the patient
    Must minister to himself . . .
V iv 26. *despair*] hot soul *K.'s MS (cancelled).*

Open it straight—Sh! Quiet! My lost boy—
My miserable child!
Ludolph (*indistinctly without*). Fill full
My goblet—here, a health!
Erminia.   Oh, close the door!
40   *Otho.* Let, let me hear his voice; this cannot last;
And fain would I catch up his dying words,
Though my own knell they be! This cannot last—
Oh, let me catch his voice—for lo! I hear
This silence whisper me that he is dead!
It is so. Gersa?

Enter Gersa.

45   *Physician.*   Say, how fares the prince?
Gersa. More calm—his features are less wild and flushed;
Once he complained of weariness—
Physician.   Indeed!
'Tis good—'tis good; let him but fall asleep,
That saves him.
Otho.   Gersa, watch him like a child;
50   Ward him from harm,—and bring me better news!
Physician. Humour him to the height. I fear to go;
For should he catch a glimpse of my dull garb,
It might affright him, fill him with suspicion
That we believe him sick, which must not be.
55   *Gersa.* I will invent what soothing means I can.
                                        [*Exit* Gersa.
Physician. This should cheer up your Highness; weariness
Is a good symptom, and most favourable;
It gives me pleasant hopes. Please you, walk forth
Onto the terrace; the refreshing air
60   Will blow one half of your sad doubts away.
                                        [*Exeunt.*

SCENE V

[*A banqueting hall, brilliantly illuminated, and set forth with all
costly magnificence, with supper-tables, laden with services of
gold and silver. A door in the back scene, guarded by two soldiers.*

V iv *38. stage direction* Ludolph distant raving *K.'s MS.*
V iv *44.* A whisper in this silence that he's dead *K.'s MS* (*cancelled*).
V iv *51–60. K.'s MS* (*cancelled*),
          Physician. Honour him to the height. It shall be done—
          Gerza.   But for myself I keep me from his sight.
                                        [*exit. scene changes.*
V iv *57.* Is a most gentle symptom of the best *K.'s MS* (*cancelled*).

*Lords, ladies, knights, gentlemen, &c., whispering sadly, and
ranging themselves; part entering and part discovered.*]

First Knight. Grievously are we tantalized, one and all;
Swayed here and there, commanded to and fro,
As though we were the shadows of a dream
And linked to a sleeping fancy. What do we here?
5   *Gonfred.* I am no seer—you know we must obey
The prince from A to Z, though it should be
To set the place in flames. I pray, hast heard
Where the most wicked Princess is?
First Knight.   There, sir,
In the next room. Have you remarked those two
Stout soldiers posted at the door?
10   *Gonfred.*   For what?
                                     [*They whisper.*

First Lady. How ghast a train!
Second Lady. Sure this should be some splendid burial.
First Lady. What fearful whispering! See, see—Gersa
     there!

Enter Gersa.

Gersa. Put on your brightest looks; smile if you can;
15   Behave as all were happy; keep your eyes
From the least watch upon him; if he speaks
To any one, answer collectedly,
Without surprise, his questions, howe'er strange.
Do this to the utmost—though, alas! with me
20   The remedy grows hopeless! Here he comes—
Observe what I have said—show no surprise.

Enter Ludolph, *followed by* Sigifred *and Page.*

Ludolph. A splendid company! Rare beauties here!
I should have Orphean lips and Plato's fancy,
Amphion's utterance, toned with his lyre,
25   Or the deep key of Jove's sonorous mouth,

V v 1. K.'s MS omits the stage direction and throughout has 'lst Lord' for
'First Knight' and '2nd Lord' for 'Gonfred'. The stage direction indicates
that this was intended as a 'transformation' scene designed to meet the
popular taste for sumptuous stage effects. Cp. I ii *n* above.
V v 11. *ghast*] Ghastly (archaic form).
V v 19. *With me*] In my opinion.
V v 24. *Amphion*] see *Endymion* iii 461 *n* (p. 225 above).

To give fit salutation. Methought I heard,
As I came in, some whispers—what of that?
'Tis natural men should whisper; at the kiss
Of Psyche given by Love, there was a buzz
30   Among the gods!—and silence is as natural.
These draperies are fine, and, being a mortal,
I should desire no better; yet, in truth,
There must be some superior costliness,
Some wider-domèd high magnificence!
35   I would have, as a mortal I may not,
Hanging of heaven's clouds, purple and gold,
Slung from the spheres; gauzes of silver mist,
Looped up with cords of twisted wreathèd light,
And tasselled round with weeping meteors!
40   These pendent lamps and chandeliers are bright
As earthly fires from dull dross can be cleansed;
Yet could my eyes drink up intenser beams
Undazzled—this is darkness! When I close
These lids, I see far fiercer brilliances—
45   Skies full of splendid moons, and shooting stars,
And spouting exhalations, diamond fires,
And panting fountains quivering with deep glows!
Yes—this is dark—is it not dark?
Sigifred.   My Lord,
'Tis late; the lights of festival are ever
Quenched in the morn.
50   *Ludolph.*   'Tis not to-morrow then?
Sigifred. 'Tis early dawn.
Gersa.   Indeed full time we slept;
Say you so, Prince?
Ludolph.   I say I quarrelled with you;
We did not tilt each other—that's a blessing,
Good gods! No innocent blood upon my head!
Sigifred. Retire, Gersa!
55   *Ludolph.*   There should be three more here:
For two of them, they stay away perhaps,
Being gloomy-minded, haters of fair revels—

V v 43–7. *When I close . . . glows*] Cp. *Isabella* 323–6 (p. 344 above),
        As when of healthful midnight sleep bereft,
        Thinking on rugged hours and fruitless toil
        We put our eyes into a pillowy cleft,
        And see the spangly gloom froth up and boil . . .

They know their own thoughts best.
                                    As for the third,
Deep blue eyes, semi-shaded in white lids,
60 Finished with lashes fine for more soft shade,
Completed by her twin-arched ebon brows;
White temples of exactest elegance,
Of even mould, felicitous and smooth,
Cheeks fashioned tenderly on either side,
65 So perfect, so divine that our poor eyes
Are dazzled with the sweet proportioning,
And wonder that 'tis so–the magic chance!
Her nostrils, small, fragrant, fairy-delicate;
Her lips–I swear no human bones e'er wore
70 So taking a disguise. You shall behold her!
We'll have her presently; aye, you shall see her,
And wonder at her, friends, she is so fair–
She is the world's chief jewel, and by heaven
She's mine by right of marriage! She is mine!
75 Patience, good people, in fit time I send
A summoner. She will obey my call,
Being a wife most mild and dutiful.
First I would hear what music is prepared
To herald and receive her–let me hear!
80 *Sigifred.* Bid the musicians soothe him tenderly.
                                    [*A soft strain of music.*
Ludolph. Ye have none better? No–I am content;
'Tis a rich sobbing melody, with reliefs
Full and majestic; it is well enough,

V v *58. They ... best*] Followed in *Brown's MS* by the cancelled passage,
                        . . . Tis true indeed
            They fail in their allegiance to their Prince,
            But if they have more urgent business,
            I shall forgive them heartily . . .

V v *62–70.* See K.'s description of Fanny Brawne in his journal-letter Dec.
1818, '. . . a fine style of countenance of the lengthen'd sort . . . her nostrils
are fine–though a little painful . . . her full-face . . . is not full but pale and
thin without showing any bone–Her shape is very graceful and so are her
movements' (*L* ii 13).

V v *62. exactest elegance*] moulded even *K.'s MS* (*cancelled*).

V v *72. she is so fair*] See K.'s letter to Fanny Brawne of 1 July 1819, 'I
know not how to express my devotion to so fair a form: I want a brighter
word than bright, a fairer word than fair' (*L* ii 123).

V v *82. rich sobbing melody*] Cp. Apollo's song in *Lamia* i 75 (p. 620 below),
        . . . his throbbing throat's long, long melodious moan . . .
See II i *9 n* above.

And will be sweeter when ye see her pace
85   Sweeping into this presence, glistened o'er
With emptied caskets, and her train upheld
By ladies, habited in robes of lawn
Sprinkled with golden crescents, others bright
In silks, with spangles showered, and bowed to
90   By Duchesses and pearlèd Margravines!
Sad, that the fairest creature of the earth—
I pray you mind me not—'tis sad, I say,
That the extremest beauty of the world
Should so entrench herself away from me,
95   Behind a barrier of engendered guilt!
Second Lady. Ah! what a moan!
First Knight.   Most piteous indeed!
Ludolph. She shall be brought before this company,
And then—then—
First Lady.   He muses.
Gersa.   O, Fortune, where will this
end?
Sigifred. I guess his purpose! Indeed he must not have
100 That pestilence brought in—that cannot be,
There we must stop him.
Gersa.   I am lost! Hush, hush!
He is about to rave again.
Ludolph. A barrier of guilt! I was the fool,
She was the cheater! Who's the cheater now,
105 And who the fool? The entrapped, the cagèd fool,
The bird-limed raven? She shall croak to death
Secure! Methinks I have her in my fist,
To crush her with my heel! Wait, wait! I marvel
My father keeps away: good friend—ah! Sigifred!
110 Do bring him to me—and Erminia
I fain would see before I sleep—and Ethelbert,
That he may bless me, as I know he will
Though I have cursed him.
Sigifred.   Rather suffer me
To lead you to them—
Ludolph.   No, excuse me, no!
115 The day is not quite done. Go bring them hither.
                              [*Exit* Sigifred.
Certes, a father's smile should, like sunlight,

V v *90. Margravines*] Margrave is a German title.
V v *116. Certes*] See II i 9 *n* above.
V v *120. The strong Iberian juice*] Earlier attempts in *K.'s MS* include 'Mellow Greeks Sir . . .' and 'Purple Sicilian . . .'.

Slant on my sheafèd harvest of ripe bliss—
Besides, I thirst to pledge my lovely bride
In a deep goblet: let me see—what wine?
120 The strong Iberian juice, or mellow Greek?
Or pale Calabrian? Or the Tuscan grape?
Or of old Aetna's pulpy wine presses,
Black stained with the fat vintage, as it were
The purple slaughter-house, where Bacchus' self
125 Pricked his own swollen veins? Where is my Page?
Page.   Here, here!
Ludolph. Be ready to obey me; anon thou shalt
Bear a soft message for me; for the hour
Draws near when I must make a winding up
Of bridal mysteries. A fine-spun vengeance!
130 Carve it on my tomb, that when I rest beneath
Men shall confess—This Prince was gulled and cheated,
But from the ashes of disgrace he rose
More than a fiery dragon, and did burn
His ignominy up in purging fires!
135 Did I not send, sir, but a moment past,
For my father?
Gersa.   You did.
Ludolph.   Perhaps 'twould be
Much better he came not.
Gersa.   He enters now!

Enter Otho, Erminia, Ethelbert, Sigifred, *and Physician.*

Ludolph. O thou good man, against whose sacred head
I was a mad conspirator, chiefly too
140 For the sake of my fair newly wedded wife,
Now to be punished, do not look so sad!
Those charitable eyes will thaw my heart,
Those tears will wash away a just resolve,
A verdict ten times sworn! Awake, awake!
145 Put on a judge's brow, and use a tongue
Made iron-stern by habit! Thou shalt see
A deed to be applauded, 'scribed in gold!
Join a loud voice to mine, and so denounce
What I alone will execute!
Otho.   Dear son,

V v *122. pulpy wine-presses*] purple stained presses *K.'s MS (cancelled).* Cp.
Ode to a Nightingale 18 (p. 526 above), 'purple-stainèd mouth'.
V v *138–41. against . . . punished*] Added in K.'s hand in *Brown's MS* (in
which the first reading of V v 138 was, 'Oh! thou good Man, nay, do not
look so sad . . .').

150 What is it? By your father's love, I sue
       That it be nothing merciless!
       Ludolph.   To that demon?
       Not so! No! She is in temple-stall
       Being garnished for the sacrifice, and I,
       The Priest of Justice, will immolate her
155 Upon the altar of wrath! She stings me through!
       Even as the worm doth feed upon the nut,
       So she, a scorpion, preys upon my brain!
       I feel her gnawing here! Let her but vanish,
       Then, father, I will lead your legions forth,
160 Compact in steelèd squares, and spearèd files,
       And bid our trumpets speak a fell rebuke
       To nations drowsed in peace!
       Otho.   To-morrow, son,
       Be your word law; forget to-day—
       Ludolph.   I will
       When I have finished it! Now! now! I'm pight
       Tight-footed for the deed!
165 *Erminia.*   Alas! Alas!
       Ludolph. What Angel's voice is that? Erminia!
       Ah! gentlest creature, whose sweet innocence
       Was almost murdered; I am penitent,
       Wilt thou forgive me? And thou, holy man.
170 Good Ethelbert, shall I die in peace with you?
       Erminia. Die, my lord!
       Ludolph.   I feel it possible.
       Otho.   Physician?
       Physician. I fear me he is past my skill.
       Otho.   Not so!
       Ludolph. I see it—I see it—I have been wandering!
       Half-mad—not right here—I forget my purpose.
175 Bestir, bestir, Auranthe! Ha! Ha! Ha!
       Youngster! Page! Go bid them drag her to me!
       Obey! This shall finish it!   [*Draws a dagger.*
       Otho.   O my son! my son!
       Sigifred. This must not be—stop there!
       Ludolph.   Am I obeyed?
       A little talk with her—no harm—haste! haste!
                                              [*Exit Page.*
180 Set her before me—never fear I can strike.

V v *164. pight*] Fixed and settled. See *Endymion* ii 60 *n* (p. 166 above).
V v *176. drag her*] fetch her *K.'s MS* (*cancelled*).

Several Voices. My Lord! My Lord!
Gersa.   Good Prince!
Ludolph. Why do ye trouble me? Out–out–out away!
There she is! Take that! And that! No, no–
That's not well done. Where is she?

> [*The doors open. Enter Page. Several women are seen
> grouped about Auranthe in the inner room.*

185 *Page.* Alas! My Lord, my Lord! They cannot move her!
Her arms are stiff–her fingers clenched and cold!
Ludolph. She's dead!

> [*Staggers and falls into their arms.*

Ethelbert.   Take away the dagger.
Gersa.   Softly; so!
Otho. Thank God for that!
Sigifred.   It could not harm him now.
Gersa. No!–brief be his anguish!

190 *Ludolph.* She's gone–I am content. Nobles, good night!
Where is your hand, father? What sultry air!
We are all weary–faint–set ope the doors–
I will to bed!–To-morrow–   [*Dies.*

THE CURTAIN FALLS

V v *188. It could not harm him now*] I fear it could not harm him *K.'s MS.*
This half-line in *K.'s MS* originally read 'Ethelb . . I fear the dagger . . .'.
V v *191.* Added in K.'s hand on the opposite leaf in *Brown's MS*; omitted
in *K.'s MS*, 1848. Its position on the page and the movement of the lines
suggest that K. meant it to be inserted at this point, though Garrod prints
it as the final line of the play. K.'s first attempt was 'Give me your hand
father how sultry 'tis . . .'.

138 Lamia

Begun *c.* 28 June 1819 and completed *c.* 5 Sept. 1819: K. arrived at Shanklin 28 June and had finished Part I of the poem by 11 July–see his letter of
this date to Reynolds, 'I have . . . proceeded pretty well with Lamia,
finishing the 1st part which consists of about 400 lines' (*L* ii 128); he probably resumed work on the poem after his arrival at Winchester 12 Aug.–
when *Lamia* was still only 'half-finished' (letter to Bailey 14 Aug. 1819,
L ii 139)–and completed it *c.* 5 Sept. when he wrote to Taylor, 'I have
finish'd Lamia' (*L* ii 157); his delay in resuming the work is explained by his

¶ *138. Title.* K. follows Burton in omitting the vampirism associated with
the 'lamia' of legend and with the account in Burton's source, Philostratus's
life of Apollonius Tyana (see headnote and i *375 n* below).

21—K.

occupation with *Otho the Great* and the reconstruction of *Hyperion* (head-notes, pp. 544 above, 655 below). The poem was revised for publication March 1820; see Brown's letter to Taylor 13 March 1820, 'Keats . . . was occupied yesterday in revising Lamia' (*L* ii 276).

In his fair copy of *Lamia* K. indicates his source, 'The groundwork of the story will be found in Burton's *Anatomy of Melancholy* Part 3 Sect. 2 Memb. 1st. Subj. 1st.', and the passage referred to is printed at the end of the poem in *1820*:

'Philostratus in his fourth book *de vita Apollonii*, hath a memorable in-stance in this kind, which I may not omit, of one Mennipus Lycius, a young man twenty-five years of age, that going between Cenchreas and Corinth, met such a phantasm in the habit of a fair gentlewoman, which taking him by the hand carried him home to her house in the suburbs of Corinth, and told him she was a Phoenician by birth, and if he would tarry with her, "he would hear her sing and play, and drink such wines as never any drank, and no man should molest him; but she being fair and lovely would live and die with him that was fair and lovely to behold". The young man, a philo-sopher, otherwise staid and discreet, able to moderate his passions, though not this of love, tarried with her awhile to his great content, and at last married her, to whose wedding amongst other guests, came Apollonius, who, by some probable conjectures, found her out to be a serpent, a lamia, and that all her furniture was like Tantalus's gold described by Homer, no substance, but mere illusions. When she saw herself descried, she wept, and desired Apollonius to be silent, but he would not be moved, and thereupon she, plate, house, and all that was in it, vanished in an instant: "many thousands took notice of this fact, for it was done in the midst of Greece" (*Anatomy of Melancholy*, 1813 edn ii 196–7).'

In expanding the narrative K. drew for incidental details of Greek customs on Potter's *Antiquities of Greece* (1697); his episode of Hermes and the nymph (i 1–145) was probably influenced by Ovid's *Metamorphoses* ii 722–832 and Marlowe's *Hero and Leander* (1598) i 386–464; his handling of Lamia's 'metamorphosis' from a snake into a woman in i 146–64 and his description of her death scene probably also owe a general debt to Ovid, but the magical effects in the poem and some elements in his portrayal of Lamia as an en-chantress are strongly influenced by his recent reading of eastern tales, notably 'The Story of Prince Ahmed, and the Fairy Pari Banou' in *The Arabian Nights* (ed. John Scott 1811), 'The History of the Merchant Abudah, or the Talisman of Oromanes' in James Ridley's *Tales of the Genii* (1764), and the Comte de Caylus's 'L'Histoire de la Corbeille' in *Contes Orientaux* (1749), all of which appear in Henry Weber's *Tales of the East* (1812), which was probably K.'s source. His presentation of Lamia as a sympathetic figure recalls Coleridge's mysterious Geraldine in *Christabel* (1816) and also Peacock's enchantress in *Rhododaphne* (1818), who is a victim as well as an agent of fatal love, conjures up a magic palace for the hero, and is recognized for what she is by a 'seer' who warns the hero against her. K.'s treatment of the story is chiefly remarkable both for its expression of the conflicting ideas and feelings characteristic of his thinking in 1819 and for its attempt to combine vivid pictorial detail with the dramatic presentation of human relationships.

The different impulses at work in the poem are reflected in its unequal achievement – the uncertainty of direction is particularly noticeable in the management of Part II – and in its style and diction, which are often strongly Miltonic but also vary from an Elizabethan descriptive richness to quasi-Byronic satirical comment. For the versification see Woodhouse's letter to Taylor 19–20 Sept. 1819, 'The metre is Drydenian heroic – with many triplets, and many alexandrines. But this K. observed, and I agreed, was required, or rather quite in character with the language and sentiment in those particular parts. – K. has a fine feeling when and where he may use poetical licenses with effect' (L ii 165). K. follows Dryden in employing balance and antithesis and rejecting feminine rhymes, but makes less use than Dryden of the end-stopped line.

K.'s view of the importance of Lamia is indicated by its appearance as the opening poem in 1820. His care over its composition is recorded in his July 1819 letter to Reynolds, 'I have great hopes of success, because I make use of my Judgment more deliberately than I have yet done' (L ii 128). His hopes for the popular success of the poem were based on its avoidance of the sentimental weaknesses which he associated with Isabella and The Eve of St. Agnes; see his letter of 22 Sept. 1819 to Woodhouse, 'There is no objection of this kind to Lamia' (L ii 174) and his journal-letter of Sept. 1819, 'I am certain there is that sort of fire in it which must take hold of people in some way – give them either pleasant or unpleasant sensation. What they want is a sensation of some sort' (L ii 189). Lamia has usually aroused in readers 'a sensation of some sort', but the diversity of critical opinion points to K.'s uncertain intentions in the poem. Robert Bridges considered it to be 'the most perfect of the narratives' while regretting that 'Philosophy or Reason is made unamiable' (introduction to The Poems of Keats, ed. G. Thorn Drury 1898, lxi), but Colvin placed it below Isabella and The Eve of St. Agnes, noting 'the bewilderment in which it leaves us as to the effect intended to be made on our imaginative sympathies' (Colvin (1915) 408). Subsequent writers have differed as widely over the poem's meaning and value, but it is obvious that the narrative has some bearing on K.'s preoccupation with the destructiveness of love, the contrast between the ideal and the actual, and the relative importance of 'feeling' and 'thought' for the poetic imagination. A summary of representative allegorical and biographical interpretations appears in W. J. Bate's analysis of Lamia in Bate (1963) 547–61. Other critical readings appear in Murry (1926) 156–60; Ridley (1933) 250–65; Finney (1933) 667–703; Pettet (1957) 227–40; B. Slote, Keats and the Dramatic Principle (1958) 138–92; M. Allott's "Isabella", "The Eve of St. Agnes" and "Lamia", Reassessment (1958) 56–62; D. Perkin's The Quest for Permanence: the Symbolism of Wordsworth, Shelley and Keats (1959) 263–76. On the versification see de Selincourt lii–liv; Ridley

(1933) 241–50; *Bate* (1945) 146–71. A summary of the principal alterations made by K. when correcting the proofs of the poem appears in W. A. Coles's 'The Proof Sheets of Keats's "Lamia"', *Harvard Library Bulletin* viii (1954) 114–19. Text from *1820*, with some variants noted from K.'s fair copy. The draft readings are preserved in a few fragments of K.'s MS – two fragments for Part I, six for Part II (see *Garrod*) – and in K.'s 'sample' of Part II quoted in his letter of 5 Sept. 1819 (*L* ii 157–9). The evidence of the draft readings suggests some toning-down of the satirical elements in the poem.

Published *1820*.

PART I

Upon a time, before the fairy broods
Drove Nymph and Satyr from the prosperous woods,
Before king Oberon's bright diadem,
Sceptre, and mantle clasped with dewy gem,
5   Frighted away the Dryads and the Fauns
From rushes green, and brakes, and cowslipped lawns,

i *1–6*. The association of the fairies of English folk-lore with figures of classical mythology was common in Elizabethan and seventeenth-century literature. See, for example, the chronicle of the 'Elfin Emperours' in *The Faerie Queene* ii 10 sts. 70–6 and Burton's *Anatomy of Melancholy* I 2 i 2, 'Terrestial devils are those Lares, Genii, Fauns, Satyrs, Wood-nymphs, Foliots, Fairies, Robin Goodfellows, Trulli, etc.' (1813 edn i 67). H. Buxton Forman and de Selincourt find a parallel in Sandys's *Ovid, Metamorphoses* i (p. 3, col. 1),

Our Demi-gods, Nymphs, Sylvans, Satyres, Faunes,
Who haunt clear Springs, high Mountains, Woods and Lawnes,
(On whom since yet we please not to bestow
Celestial dwellings) must subsist below . . .,

but K. may be remembering here Dryden's *The Wife of Bath Her Tale* 1–4 (cited in *Gittings* (1954) 224),

In days of Old when *Arthur* filled the Throne,
Whose Acts and Fame to Foreign Lands were blown;
The King of Elfs and little Fairy Queene
Gamboll'd on Heaths, and danc'd on ev'ry Green . . .

i *2. prosperous woods*] More widespread than in these times.
i *6*. Perhaps a recollection of the pastoral setting in Milton's *Comus* 890–99,

By the rushy-fringed bank,
Where grows the Willow and the Osier dank,

. . .

O're the Cowslips Velvet head,
That bends not as I tread . . .

The ever-smitten Hermes empty left
His golden throne, bent warm on amorous theft.
From high Olympus had he stolen light,
10   On this side of Jove's clouds, to escape the sight
Of his great summoner, and made retreat
Into a forest on the shores of Crete.
For somewhere in that sacred island dwelt
A nymph to whom all hoofèd Satyrs knelt,
15   At whose white feet the languid Tritons poured
Pearls, while on land they withered and adored.
Fast by the springs where she to bathe was wont,
And in those meads where sometime she might haunt,
Were strewn rich gifts, unknown to any Muse,
20   Though Fancy's casket were unlocked to choose.
Ah, what a world of love was at her feet!
So Hermes thought, and a celestial heat
Burnt from his wingèd heels to either ear,
That from a whiteness, as the lily clear,
25   Blushed into roses 'mid his golden hair,
Fallen in jealous curls about his shoulders bare.

From vale to vale, from wood to wood, he flew,
Breathing upon the flowers his passion new,
And wound with many a river to its head
30   To find where this sweet nymph prepared her secret
        bed.
In vain; the sweet nymph might nowhere be found,

i 7-145. The episode of Hermes and the nymph suggests in some details a
recollection of Hermes's courtship of Herse in Ovid's *Metamorphoses* ii 708–
832, but K.'s use of the episode to indicate the contrast between ideal and
actual experience (i 126–8, 145) may owe something to Marlowe's use of
one of Hermes's amorous intrigues to underline the ill-fated destiny of the
lovers in *Hero and Leander* i 386–464.

i 7. *ever-smitten*] Hermes was celebrated for his love affairs. Cp. *Lemprière*,
'His children are also numerous as well as his amours.' K.'s portrayal of
Hermes is faintly sardonic throughout the episode.

i 11. *great summoner*] Cp. Sandys's *Ovid*, *Metamorphoses* ii (p. 31, col. 2),

                        He am I
        Who on *Jove's* errands (*Jove*, my father) flie . . .

i 13. *sacred island*] See *Lemprière*: 'Jupiter was secretly educated in a cave on
Mount Ida, in Crete.'

i 15. *languid*] Languishing.

i 16. *on land they withered*] The Tritons' natural element is water.

i 23. *wingèd heels*] See *I stood tip-toe* 24 n (p. 87 above).

And so he rested on the lonely ground,
Pensive, and full of painful jealousies
Of the Wood-Gods and even the very trees.
35   There as he stood, he heard a mournful voice,
Such as, once heard, in gentle heart destroys
All pain but pity; thus the lone voice spake:
'When from this wreathèd tomb shall I awake!
When move in a sweet body fit for life,
40   And love, and pleasure, and the ruddy strife
Of hearts and lips! Ah, miserable me!'
The God, dove-footed, glided silently
Round bush and tree, soft-brushing in his speed
The taller grasses and full-flowering weed,
45   Until he found a palpitating snake,
Bright, and cirque-couchant in a dusky brake.

She was a gordian shape of dazzling hue,
Vermilion-spotted, golden, green and blue;
Striped like a zebra, freckled like a pard,
50   Eyed like a peacock, and all crimson barred;

i 36–7. *Such as . . . pity*] Cp. Chaucer's *The Knightes Tale* 903,
                For pitee renneth soon in gentil herte . . .
The use of the phrase 'gentle heart' to suggest nobility, generosity and
chivalry is frequent in Chaucer and Spenser, who derived it from the Italian
poets; K. probably remembered Dante's use of it in *Inferno* v 100 (on
K.'s learning Italian in summer 1819 see headnote to *The Fall of Hyperion*,
p. 656 below),
                Amor ch'al cor gentil ratto s'apprende . . .
The version in Cary's *Dante*, *Inferno* v 99 runs,
                Love, that in gentle heart is quickly learned . . .
(Cary supplies an extensive gloss on the line.)
i 42. *dove-footed*] See i 23 *n* above.
i 46. *cirque-couchant*] A neologism. Lying in circular coils.
i 47–53. Probably inspired by the description of the serpent in *Paradise
Lost* ix 498–503 (marked by K. in his copy of Milton),
                . . . rising foulds, that tour'd
                Fould above fould a surging Maze, his Head
                Crested aloft, and Carbuncle his Eyes;
                With burnisht Neck of verdant Gold, erect
                Amidst his circling Spires, that on the grass
                Floted redundant . . .
i 47. *gordian*] Intricately interwoven. Cp. *Endymion* iii 494 (p. 226 above),
'like the eye of gordian snake'.
i 49–50. The balanced adjectival phrases suggest Dryden's influence, but
the cadence is not Augustan.

And full of silver moons, that, as she breathed,
Dissolved, or brighter shone, or interwreathed
Their lustres with the gloomier tapestries—
So rainbow-sided, touched with miseries,
55 She seemed, at once, some penanced lady elf,
Some demon's mistress, or the demon's self.
Upon her crest she wore a wannish fire
Sprinkled with stars, like Ariadne's tiar;
Her head was serpent, but ah, bitter-sweet!
60 She had a woman's mouth with all its pearls complete;
And for her eyes—what could such eyes do there
But weep, and weep, that they were born so fair,
As Proserpine still weeps for her Sicilian air?
Her throat was serpent, but the words she spake
65 Came, as through bubbling honey, for love's sake,
And thus—while Hermes on his pinions lay,
Like a stooped falcon ere he takes his prey:

    'Fair Hermes, crowned with feathers, fluttering light,
    I had a splendid dream of thee last night:
70 I saw thee sitting, on a throne of gold,
    Among the Gods, upon Olympus old,
    The only sad one; for thou didst not hear

i 55. *elf*] Fairy. The expression was probably forced by the rhyme (cp.
Endymion ii 461 *n*, p. 182 above), but K. may have known that Lamiae were
sometimes called fairies or elves—see Huloet's *Dictionarie* (revised John Hig-
gins 1572), 'fayres or Elves–Lamiae, Empusae, Larvae, Lemures, les
fées . . .'.
i 57–8. K. is remembering the circlet of stars above Ariadne's head in
Titian's 'Bacchus and Ariadne'. Lamia's crown may have been first suggested by the illustration in Sandys's *Ovid* (1632 edn, facing p. 113) showing
Hermione as half-serpent, half-woman and wearing a pointed crown on her
head. With 'wannish fire' cp. *Paradise Lost* x 412 (marked by K. in his copy
of Milton), 'the blasted Starrs lookt wan'.
i 63. On K.'s fondness for the legend of Proserpine see *Endymion* i 944 *n*
(p. 162 above).
i 64–5. Cp. *Lemprière*: 'Though [Lamiae] . . . were not endowed with the
faculty of speech, yet their hissings were said to be pleasant and agreeable . . .'.
i 67. *stooped falcon*] A falcon which is about to descend–Hermes is hovering. Cp. *The Faerie Queene* II xi 43,
        As when *Jove*'s harnesse-bearing Bird from hie
        Stoupes at a flying heron . . .
i 68. *crowned with feathers*] See *I stood tip-toe* 24 *n* (p. 87 above).
i 69. *splendid*] silver *Fair copy*.

The soft, lute-fingered Muses chanting clear,
Nor even Apollo when he sang alone,
75   Deaf to his throbbing throat's long, long melodious
              moan.
      I dreamt I saw thee, robed in purple flakes,
      Break amorous through the clouds, as morning breaks,
      And, swiftly as a bright Phoebean dart,
      Strike for the Cretan isle; and here thou art!
80   Too gentle Hermes, hast thou found the maid?'
      Whereat the star of Lethe not delayed
      His rosy eloquence, and thus inquired:
      'Thou smooth-lipped serpent, surely high inspired!
      Thou beauteous wreath, with melancholy eyes,
85   Possess whatever bliss thou canst devise,
      Telling me only where my nymph is fled—
      Where she doth breathe!' 'Bright planet, thou hast
              said,'
      Returned the snake, 'but seal with oaths, fair God!'
      'I swear,' said Hermes, 'by my serpent rod,
90   And by thine eyes, and by thy starry crown!'
      Light flew his earnest words, among the blossoms blown.
      Then thus again the brilliance feminine:
      'Too frail of heart! For this lost nymph of thine,
      Free as the air, invisibly, she strays
95   About these thornless wilds; her pleasant days

i 75. Cp. the description of Apollo in *Hyperion* iii 81–2 (p. 438 above),
                    . . . his white melodious throat
              Throbbed with the syllables . . .
i 76. *purple flakes*] Clouds reddened by the sunrise.
i 78. *a bright Phoebean dart*] A ray of sunshine. For 'bright' the fair copy
reads 'mission'd'; cp. *The Eve of St. Agnes* 193 (p. 465 above), 'like a missioned spirit'.
i 81. *star of Lethe*] Hermes in his role of psychopomp, or conductor of the
souls of the dead. See Charles Lamb's review of *1820*, '. . . one of those prodigious phrases which Mr. Keats abounds in' (*New Times*, 19 July 1820).
The construction 'not delayed' is Miltonic.
i 84. *wreath*] Referring to the coils of the lamia.
i 87–8. *thou hast said . . . oaths*] Hermes was renowned for his specious eloquence. Cp. *Lemprière*: 'He . . . not only presided over orators, merchants,
and declaimers, but was also the god of thieves, pick-pockets and all dishonest persons. . . .'
i 89. *serpent rod*] The caduceus. See *Lemprière*, '. . . a rod entwined at one
end by two serpents. . . . It was the ensign of Mercury, and the emblem of
power . . .'.
i 93. *Too frail*] Superb *Fair copy (cancelled)*.

She tastes unseen; unseen her nimble feet
Leave traces in the grass and flowers sweet;
From weary tendrils, and bowed branches green,
She plucks the fruit unseen, she bathes unseen;
100 And by my power is her beauty veiled
To keep it unaffronted, unassailed
By the love-glances of unlovely eyes
Of Satyrs, Fauns, and bleared Silenus' sighs.
Pale grew her immortality, for woe
105 Of all these lovers, and she grievèd so
I took compassion on her, bade her steep
Her hair in weird syrups, that would keep
Her loveliness invisible, yet free
To wander as she loves, in liberty.
110 Thou shalt behold her, Hermes, thou alone,
If thou wilt, as thou swearest, grant my boon!'
Then, once again, the charmèd God began
An oath, and through the serpent's ears it ran
Warm, tremulous, devout, psalterian.
115 Ravished, she lifted her Circean head,
Blushed a live damask, and swift-lisping said,
'I was a woman, let me have once more
A woman's shape, and charming as before.
I love a youth of Corinth—Oh, the bliss!
120 Give me my woman's form, and place me where he is.
Stoop, Hermes, let me breathe upon thy brow,
And thou shalt see thy sweet nymph even now.'
The God on half-shut feathers sank serene,
She breathed upon his eyes, and swift was seen

i *103. Satyrs, Fauns*] See *Lemprière*, 'Satyri . . . attended on Bacchus, and rendered themselves known in his orgies by their riotous demeanour and lasciviousness. . . . The Romans called them indifferently Fauni, Panes or Sylvani.' On Silenus, Bacchus's constant attendant, see *Endymion* iv 215–17 *n* (p. 255 above).

i *104. grew*] wox *Fair copy.*

i *105–6. she grieved . . . on her*] See i 56 *n* above.

i *107. weird*] Magic. Dissyllabic here.

i *112. charmèd*] Fascinated.

i *114.* Warm, devout, bright-toned, psalterian . . . *Fair copy.* The epithet 'psalterian' is derived from psaltery, an antique stringed instrument.

i *115. Circean*] Beautiful and fatally enchanting like Circe. Peacock's *Rhododaphne* (1818) iv i has 'spells Circean . . .'

i *116. swift-lisping*] Indicative of the Lamia's serpent nature. See i 64–5 *n* above.

i *119.* Explained at i 215–19 below.

21*

125   Of both the guarded nymph near-smiling on the green.
         It was no dream; or say a dream it was,
         Real are the dreams of Gods, and smoothly pass
         Their pleasures in a long immortal dream.
         One warm, flushed moment, hovering, it might seem
130   Dashed by the wood-nymph's beauty, so he burned;
         Then, lighting on the printless verdure, turned
         To the swooned serpent, and with languid arm,
         Delicate, put to proof the lithe Caducean charm.
         So done, upon the nymph his eyes he bent
135   Full of adoring tears and blandishment,
         And towards her stepped: she, like a moon in wane,
         Faded before him, cowered, nor could restrain
         Her fearful sobs, self-folding like a flower
         That faints into itself at evening hour.
140   But the God fostering her chillèd hand,
         She felt the warmth, her eyelids opened bland,
         And, like new flowers at morning song of bees,
         Bloomed, and gave up her honey to the lees.
         Into the green-recessèd woods they flew;
145   Nor grew they pale, as mortal lovers do.

         Left to herself, the serpent now began
         To change; her elfin blood in madness ran,

i *125. near-smiling*] Smiling close by.

i *126–8.* See i 7–145 *n* above.

i *132. swooned*] Overcome with love–see i 119 above, 'O the bliss . . .'.

i *133. lithe*] Suggested by the snakes entwined round the caduceus; see i 89
n above.

i *138–9. a flower . . . evening hour*] A recollection of *Paradise Lost* ix 278
(marked by K. in his copy of Milton), 'at shut of Evening Flours'. Milton's
line is echoed again at ii 107 below, 'shut of day'.

i *141. bland*] Mildly.

i *143. gave . . . to the lees*] Surrendered completely.

i *144. the green-recessèd woods*] Cp. the description of Delos in *Hyperion*
iii 41 (p. 436 above), 'many a green recess'.

i *146–70.* See Woodhouse's Sept. 1819 letter to Taylor, 'She is meta-
morphosed into a beautiful Woman, the Change is quite Ovidian, but better' (*L* ii 164). There are no close parallels in Ovid, though there are
references to the transformation of mortals into serpents (e.g. in the legend
of Cadmus and his wife, *Metamorphoses* iv 569–603). K.'s description may
remember the inspired Sibyl in Virgil's *Aeneid* vi 47–9,

               . . . *subito non voltus, non color unus,*
          non comptae mansere comae, sed pectus anhelum . . .

('. . . suddenly nor countenance, nor colour was the same, nor stayed her

Her mouth foamed, and the grass, therewith besprent,
Withered at dew so sweet and virulent;
150   Her eyes in torture fixed and anguish drear,
Hot, glazed, and wide, with lid-lashes all sear,
Flashed phosphor and sharp sparks, without one cooling
      tear.
The colours all inflamed throughout her train,
She writhed about, convulsed with scarlet pain.
155   A deep volcanian yellow took the place
Of all her milder-moonèd body's grace;
And, as the lava ravishes the mead,
Spoilt all her silver mail, and golden brede;
Made gloom of all her frecklings, streaks and bars,
160   Eclipsed her crescents, and licked up her stars,
So that, in moments few, she was undressed
Of all her sapphires, greens, and amethyst,
And rubious-argent; of all these bereft,
Nothing but pain and ugliness were left.
165   Still shone her crown; that vanished, also she
Melted and disappeared as suddenly;
And in the air, her new voice luting soft,

---

tresses braided; but her bosom heaves, her heart swells with wild frenzy'
[Loeb edn]).

i *148–9. grass . . . besprent . . . dew*] Echoing Milton's *Comus* 541–2,
             . . . the savoury Herb
     Of Knot-grass dew-besprent . . .

i *151. sear*] Scorched.

i *155. volcanian yellow*] The colour of sulphur.

i *157. ravishes the mead*] Lava shrivels and buries the vegetation as it pours
over the countryside.

i *158. brede*] See *Ode on a Grecian Urn* 41 *n* (p. 537 above).

i *160. licked up*] Destroyed. Cp. *Numbers* xxii 4: 'Now shall this company
lick up all that are round about us, as the ox licketh up the grass of the
field. . . .'

i *163. rubious-argent*] Silver with glints of red. Cp. the 'verdant gold' of
Milton's serpent (i 47–53 *n* above). K. uses 'rubious' in *Otho the Great*
IV ii 38 (p. 596 above),
     Pout her faint lips with rubious health . . .,

i *165. her crown*] See i 57–8 above.

i *167–8.*   And her new voice; soft luting in the air
     Cried 'Lycius! gentle Lycius, where, ah where! . . . *Fair copy*.
The passage may have given K. some trouble: in the proofs the last three
words are deleted and an exclamation point added after 'gentle Lycius'; see
also Woodhouse's June 1820 letter to Taylor (*KC* i 112) which contains the
further variant,

Cried, 'Lycius! Gentle Lycius!' Borne aloft
With the bright mists about the mountains hoar
170 These words dissolved; Crete's forests heard no more.

Whither fled Lamia, now a lady bright,
A full-born beauty new and exquisite?
She fled into that valley they pass o'er
Who go to Corinth from Cenchreas' shore;
175 And rested at the foot of those wild hills,
The rugged founts of the Peraean rills,
And of that other ridge whose barren back
Stretches, with all its mist and cloudy rack,
South-westward to Cleone. There she stood
180 About a young bird's flutter from a wood,
Fair, on a sloping green of mossy tread,
By a clear pool, wherein she passionèd
To see herself escaped from so sore ills,
While her robes flaunted with the daffodils.

And a soft voice was heard upon the air
Muttering, 'where art thou, Lycius! Ah where?...'
The words 'was heard'–presumably Woodhouse's emendation–are written above the uncancelled 'swell'd out'. Woodhouse comments, 'If the
above will not do, pray "hit off something better"... But... do not let
the poem be published incomplete. Rather... let it remain as he had
written it...' Woodhouse's letter is endorsed on the back in K.'s hand
with the inscription 'Shore Shore Shore Jane Jane' (Nicholas Rowe's
Jane Shore, 1714, was revived 13 April 1819 at Drury Lane).
i *173–9. She fled ... Cleone*] Cenchreas (or Cenchrea) was the port of
Corinth at the head of the Saronic gulf. Cleone was a village southward
from Corinth on the road to Argos. The rockiness of the landscape is also
referred to by Peacock in his *Rhododaphne* iii 322–3,
Along the rocky way, that led
Tow'rds the Corinthian isthmus...
i *173–4.* She fled into that valley they must pass
Who go from Corinth out to Cenchreas ... *Fair copy.*
Further attempts in the proof include,
She fled into that valley they must skirt
Who go from Corinth out to Cenchrea's por[t?]...
i *176.* The rugged paps of little Perea's rills ... *Fair copy.* Peraea has not
been identified.
i, *182. Wherein she passionèd*] The water reflects her excited gestures. For
K.'s earlier use of 'passion' as a verb see *Endymion* i 248 *n* (p. 131 above).
i *184. flaunted*] Waved gaily. This is followed in the fair copy by the lines,
Ah! never heard of, delight never known
Save of one happy mortal! only one...

185 Ah, happy Lycius!—for she was a maid
   More beautiful than ever twisted braid,
   Or sighed, or blushed, or on spring-flowered lea
   Spread a green kirtle to the minstrelsy;
   A virgin purest lipped, yet in the lore
190 Of love deep learnèd to the red heart's core;
   Not one hour old, yet of sciential brain
   To unperplex bliss from its neighbour pain,
   Define their pettish limits, and estrange
   Their points of contact and swift counterchange;
195 Intrigue with the specious chaos, and dispart
   Its most ambiguous atoms with sure art;
   As though in Cupid's college she had spent
   Sweet days a lovely graduate, still unshent,
   And kept his rosy terms in idle languishment.

200 Why this fair creature chose so fairily
   By the wayside to linger, we shall see;
   But first 'tis fit to tell how she could muse
   And dream, when in the serpent prison-house,
   Of all she list, strange or magnificent:
205 How, ever, where she willed, her spirit went;
   Whether to faint Elysium, or where
   Down through tress-lifting waves the Nereids fair

i *185.* Lycius the happy: for she was a Maid . . . *Fair copy.*

i *191. sciential*] Endowed with wisdom. Cp. *Paradise Lost* ix 837–8 (marked
by K. in his copy of Milton),

      . . . sciential sap, deriv'd
    From Nectar, drink of Gods . . .

i *192–6.* The close relationship of joy and sorrow is bewildering to ordinary mortals.

i *192. its*] her *Fair copy.*

i *193. pettish*] Irksome.

i *195. dispart*] Separate. For K.'s earlier use of the word see *Endymion* ii
308 *n* (pp. 175–6 above).

i *197–8. As though . . . graduate*] R. Gittings (*loc. cit.*) notes a parallel in Dryden's *The First Book of Ovid's Art of Love* 1–2,

    In *Cupid's* school whoe'er would take Degree,
    Must learn his Rudiments, by reading me . . .

i *198. unshent*] Unspoilt. Cp. *Sleep and Poetry* 379 and *n* (p. 84 above),
'unshent by foam'.

i *203–4.* Cp. K.'s marginal note on *Paradise Lost* ix 179–91 in his copy of
Milton: '. . . Whose head is not dizzy at the probable speculations of Satan
in the serpent prison. . . .'

i *206. faint*] Dimly discerned.

Wind into Thetis' bower by many a pearly stair;
Or where God Bacchus drains his cups divine,
210   Stretched out, at ease, beneath a glutinous pine;
Or where in Pluto's gardens palatine
Mulciber's columns gleam in far piazzian line.
And sometimes into cities she would send
Her dream, with feast and rioting to blend;
215   And once, while among mortals dreaming thus,
She saw the young Corinthian Lycius
Charioting foremost in the envious race,
Like a young Jove with calm uneager face,
And fell into a swooning love of him.
220   Now on the moth-time of that evening dim
He would return that way, as well she knew,
To Corinth from the shore; for freshly blew
The eastern soft wind, and his galley now
Grated the quaystones with her brazen prow
225   In port Cenchreas, from Egina isle
Fresh anchored; whither he had been awhile
To sacrifice to Jove, whose temple there
Waits with high marble doors for blood and incense
          rare.
Jove heard his vows, and bettered his desire;

i *208*. Cp. *Endymion* iii 1005 and *n* (p. 243 above), 'And Thetis pearly too . . .'
i *210*. *glutinous*] Resinous.
i *211*. *Pluto's gardens palatine*] The gardens of Pluto's palace in the underworld; the epithet 'palatine' is probably used here to mean palatial, splendid. The cadence is Miltonic.
i *212*. A recollection of the construction of Pandemonium by Mulciber
(Vulcan) in *Paradise Lost* i 713–15 (marked by K. in his copy of Milton),

Built like a Temple, where *Pilasters* round
Were set, and Doric pillars overlaid
With Golden Architrave . . .

The epithet 'piazzian', derived from piazza (a square or open space surrounded by buildings), is used here to suggest a colonnade.
i *215–19*. For a similar situation in *The Arabian Nights* see, e.g., 'Prince
Ahmed and the Fairy Pari Banou', where the enchantress watches the
Prince from afar and falls in love with him without his knowledge (H.
Weber's *Tales of the East* (1812) i 441).
i *220*. *moth-time*] Early evening.
i *225*. *port*] harbour *Fair copy*. The island of Egina lies at the head of the
Saronic Gulf.
i *229*. Lycius's 'vows' were presumably offered for a happy marriage; K.
would have known from Potter's *Antiquities* that Jupiter was one of 'the
gods that had the care of marriage' (ii 276).

230 For by some freakful chance he made retire
    From his companions, and set forth to walk,
    Perhaps grown wearied of their Corinth talk.
    Over the solitary hills he fared,
    Thoughtless at first, but ere eve's star appeared
235 His fantasy was lost, where reason fades,
    In the calmed twilight of Platonic shades.
    Lamia beheld him coming, near, more near—
    Close to her passing, in indifference drear,
    His silent sandals swept the mossy green;
240 So neighboured to him, and yet so unseen
    She stood. He passed, shut up in mysteries,
    His mind wrapped like his mantle, while her eyes
    Followed his steps, and her neck regal white
    Turned—syllabling thus, 'Ah, Lycius bright,
245 And will you leave me on the hills alone?
    Lycius, look back, and be some pity shown!'
    He did—not with cold wonder fearingly,
    But Orpheus-like at an Eurydice;
    For so delicious were the words she sung,
250 It seemed he had loved them a whole summer long.
    And soon his eyes had drunk her beauty up,
    Leaving no drop in the bewildering cup,
    And still the cup was full—while he, afraid
    Lest she should vanish ere his lip had paid
255 Due adoration, thus began to adore
    (Her soft look growing coy, she saw his chain so sure):

i *234–6.* Lycius sets out on his walk in an unthinking mood, but as evening comes on his thoughts are lost in high Platonic speculations.

i *236. Platonic*] platonian *Fair copy.*

i *238. drear*] Drear to Lamia.

i *244. syllabling*] Probably suggested by Milton's *Comus* 207–8,

> . . . calling shapes, and beckning shadows dire,
> And airy tongues, that syllable mens names . . .

For K.'s earlier echo of Milton's lines see *Endymion* iv 650–5 *n* (p. 272 above).

i *248.* With fated longing.

i *251.* Cp. Burton's *Anatomy of Melancholy* III 2 iii, '"They cannot look off whom they love", they will . . . be still gazing, staring . . . so she will . . . drink to him with her eyes, nay drink him up, devour him' (1813 edn ii 297). The passage is marked by K. in his copy with the marginal note 'Ben Jonson' (obviously a reference to Ben Jonson's *To Celia* 1–2,

> Drinke to me, onely, with thine eyes,
> And I will pledge with mine . . .)

i *256. chain*] Cp. the frequent use of this literary convention in Peacock's

'Leave thee alone! Look back! Ah, Goddess, see
Whether my eyes can ever turn from thee!
For pity do not this sad heart belie—
260   Even as thou vanishest so shall I die.
Stay! Though a naiad of the rivers, stay!
To thy far wishes will thy streams obey.
Stay! Though the greenest woods be thy domain,
Alone they can drink up the morning rain.
265   Though a descended Pleiad, will not one
Of thine harmonious sisters keep in tune
Thy spheres, and as thy silver proxy shine?
So sweetly to these ravished ears of mine
Came thy sweet greeting, that if thou shouldst fade
270   Thy memory will waste me to a shade—
For pity do not melt!' 'If I should stay,'

Rhododaphne (1818), for example vi 362–4,

> 'Now thou art mine!' again she cried;
> 'My love's indissoluble chain
> Has found thee . . .'

and ii 169–70,

> . . . him whose hapless steps around
> Thessalian spells their chains have bound . . .

i *257–67.* Cp. King Kemsarai's encounter with the enchanted princess in the Comte de Caylus's 'L'Histoire de la Corbeille' (1749), translated as 'The History of a Basket' in H. Weber's *Tales of the East* (1812), 'What then can you be, oh beauty of beauties? Are you an angel, or a celestial spirit? Are you a sun, or the shining star of the firmament?' (ii 671). K. refers to the story in his letter of 15 July 1819 to Fanny Brawne as 'of a . . . beautiful color–It is of a city of melancholy men . . . each one of them by turns reach some gardens of Paradise . . . they meet with a most enchanting Lady . . . just as they are . . . to embrace her, she bids them shut their eyes–they shut them–and on opening their eyes again find themselves descending to the earth in a magic basket. The remembrance of this Lady and their delights lost beyond all recovery render them melancholy ever after. How I applied this to you, my dear; how I palpitated at it' (L ii 130).

i *260.* Thou to Elysium gone, here for the vultures I . . . *Fair copy.*

i *261–70.* Cp. the hero's speculations about the identity of his love in *Endymion* ii 687–94 (p. 192 above).

i *265. Pleiad*] One of the seven daughters of Atlas transformed after their death into the constellation Pleiades. Perhaps suggested here by the 'History of a Basket', 'The princess retired and all the virgins of her train followed her like the Pleiades' (*Tales of the East* ii 671).

i *266–7. keep in tune / Thy spheres*] A fanciful allusion to the Pythagorean belief in the music of the spheres.

Said Lamia, 'here, upon this floor of clay,
And pain my steps upon these flowers too rough,
What canst thou say or do of charm enough
275   To dull the nice remembrance of my home?
Thou canst not ask me with thee here to roam
Over these hills and vales, where no joy is—
Empty of immortality and bliss!
Thou art a scholar, Lycius, and must know
280   That finer spirits cannot breathe below
In human climes, and live. Alas, poor youth,
What taste of purer air hast thou to soothe
My essence? What serener palaces,
Where I may all my many senses please,
285   And by mysterious sleights a hundred thirsts appease?
It cannot be. Adieu!' So said, she rose
Tiptoe with white arms spread. He, sick to lose
The amorous promise of her lone complain,
Swooned, murmuring of love, and pale with pain.
290   The cruel lady, without any show
Of sorrow for her tender favourite's woe,
But rather, if her eyes could brighter be,
With brighter eyes and slow amenity,
Put her new lips to his, and gave afresh
295   The life she had so tangled in her mesh;
And as he from one trance was wakening
Into another, she began to sing,
Happy in beauty, life, and love, and everything,
A song of love, too sweet for earthly lyres,
300   While, like held breath, the stars drew in their panting
       fires.
And then she whispered in such trembling tone,
As those who, safe together met alone
For the first time through many anguished days,
Use other speech than looks; bidding him raise

i 272. *here*] Omitted in the fair copy.
i 285. *sleights*] Artifices. Frequent in Spenser.
i 288. *complain*] Complaint. A forced poeticism for the sake of the rhyme.
i 290–9. 'The cruel lady' and her entrancing song recall *La Belle Dame Sans Merci* (p. 500 above). See also *The Eve of St. Agnes* 235–315 n (p. 468 above).
i 300. The stars are imagined to be so spell-bound that they stop twinkling. The epithet 'panting' carries erotic overtones in K. Cp. *Ode on a Grecian Urn* 27 (p. 535 above),

      For ever panting, and for ever young . . .

and *Endymion* iii 985 (p. 242 above), 'panting bosoms bare'.
i 302–4. *For the first time . . . looks*] K. may be thinking of the rare occasions when he was able to see Fanny Brawne alone.

305   His drooping head, and clear his soul of doubt,
      For that she was a woman, and without
      Any more subtle fluid in her veins
      Than throbbing blood, and that the self-same pains
      Inhabited her frail-strung heart as his.
310   And next she wondered how his eyes could miss
      Her face so long in Corinth, where, she said,
      She dwelt but half retired, and there had led
      Days happy as the gold coin could invent
      Without the aid of love; yet in content
315   Till she saw him, as once she passed him by,
      Where 'gainst a column he lent thoughtfully
      At Venus' temple porch, 'mid baskets heaped
      Of amorous herbs and flowers, newly reaped
      Late on that eve, as 'twas the night before
320   The Adonian feast; whereof she saw no more,
      But wept alone those days, for why should she adore?
      Lycius from death awoke into amaze,
      To see her still, and singing so sweet lays;
      Then from amaze into delight he fell

i *307. subtle*] Rarified.

i *313.* Days as happy as money could make them.

i *317–20. Till she saw . . . Adonian feast*] Cp. Marlowe's *Hero and Leander* i 91–3,

> The men of wealthy Sestos, every year,
> For his sake whom their goddess held so dear,
> Rose-cheek'd Adonis, kept a solemn feast . . .

and i 131–4,

> On this feast-day, O cursed day and hour,
> Went Hero through Sestos, from her tower
> To Venus' temple, where unhappily,
> As after chanc'd, they did each other spy . . .

R. Gittings cites (*Gittings* (1954) 224) Dryden's *The First Book of Ovid's Art of Love* 80–1,

> Or *Venus'* Temple; where, on Annual Nights,
> They mourn *Adonis* with *Assyrian* rites . . .

i *318. amorous herbs . . . newly reaped*] Cp. Potter's description of the festival of Adonis in *Antiquities*, 'There were also carried . . . shells filled with earth, in which grew several sorts of herbs, especially lettuces; in memory that Adonis was laid out by Venus upon a bed of lettuces . . . those herbs were only sown so long before the festival as to sprout forth and be green at that time' (i 422).

i *322. into amaze*] into an amaze *Fair copy*.

325   To hear her whisper woman's lore so well;
      And every word she spake enticed him on
      To unperplexed delight and pleasure known.
      Let the mad poets say whate'er they please
      Of the sweet Fairies, Peris, Goddesses,
330   There is not such a treat among them all,
      Haunters of cavern, lake, and waterfall,
      As a real woman, lineal indeed
      From Pyrrha's pebbles or old Adam's seed.
      Thus gentle Lamia judged, and judged aright,
335   That Lycius could not love in half a fright,
      So threw the goddess off, and won his heart
      More pleasantly by playing woman's part,
      With no more awe than what her beauty gave,
      That, while it smote, still guaranteed to save.
340   Lycius to all made eloquent reply,
      Marrying to every word a twinborn sigh;
      And last, pointing to Corinth, asked her sweet,
      If 'twas too far that night for her soft feet.
      The way was short, for Lamia's eagerness
345   Made, by a spell, the triple league decrease

i 327. *unperplexed delight*] See i 191–2 above.

i 328. *mad*] Wildly enthusiastic.

i 329. *Peris*] A Persian term for good fairies or genii. See Weber's note on the name Peri Banou, 'Two Persian words, which signify the same, i.e. a female fairy, or genie' (*Tales of the East* i 432).

i 330–2. *There is not . . . real woman*] Probably an attempt to imitate Byron's worldly manner in *Don Juan* ii st. 118,

> . . . she was one
> Fit for the model of a statuary
> (A race of mere imposters, when all's done—
> I've seen much finer women, ripe and real,
> Than all the nonsense of their stone ideal) . . .

i 333. *Pyrrha's pebbles*] After Deucalion's flood (see *Endymion* ii 197–8 *n*, p. 171 above), Deucalion and Pyrrha re-peopled the world by throwing stones behind them which turn into men. The pairing of Adam with Pyrrha may have been suggested here by the description of Adam and Eve in *Paradise Lost* xi 8–14,

> . . . thir port
> Not of mean suiters, nor important less
> Seem'd thir Petition, then when th'ancient Pair
> In Fables old, less ancient yet then these,
> *Deucalion* and chaste *Pyrrha* to restore
> The Race of Mankind drownd, before the Shrine
> Of *Themis* stood devout . . .

To a few paces; not at all surmised
By blinded Lycius, so in her comprised.
They passed the city gates, he knew not how,
So noiseless, and he never thought to know.

350   As men talk in a dream, so Corinth all,
Throughout her palaces imperial
And all her populous streets and temples lewd,
Muttered, like tempest in the distance brewed,
To the wide-spreaded night above her towers.
355   Men, women, rich and poor, in the cool hours
Shuffled their sandals o'er the pavement white,
Companioned or alone; while many a light
Flared, here and there, from wealthy festivals,
And threw their moving shadows on the walls,
360   Or found them clustered in the corniced shade
Of some arched temple door or dusky colonnade.

     Muffling his face, of greeting friends in fear,
Her fingers he pressed hard, as one came near
With curled gray beard, sharp eyes, and smooth bald
     crown,
365   Slow-stepped, and robed in philosophic gown.
Lycius shrank closer, as they met and passed,
Into his mantle, adding wings to haste,
While hurried Lamia trembled: 'Ah,' said he,
'Why do you shudder, love, so ruefully?
370   Why does your tender palm dissolve in dew?' –
'I'm wearied,' said fair Lamia, 'tell me who
Is that old man? I cannot bring to mind
His features. Lycius! Wherefore did you blind
Yourself from his quick eyes?' Lycius replied,
375   ''Tis Apollonius sage, my trusty guide

i *347. comprised*] Absorbed, wrapped up.
i *352.* See Burton's description of Corinth, *Anatomy of Melancholy* III 2 ii 1,
'. . . every day strangers came in, at each gate, from all quarters. In that one
temple of Venus a thousand whores did prostitute themselves . . . all nations
resorted thither as to a school of Venus' (1813 edn ii 212).
i *363.* And pressing hard her fingers, one came near . . . *Fair copy*.
i *373. blind*] Hide.
i *375. Apollonius*] The reference in Burton is to Apollonius of Tyana in
Asia Minor, the philosopher of the first century A.D. whose life was recorded
by Philostratus (b. 170). As a Pythagorean, Apollonius Tyana upheld strict
moral and religious reform and was also credited with magical powers. See
Woodhouse's reference to K.'s Apollonius in his Sept. 1819 letter to Taylor
'He is a Magician' (*L* ii 164). K. may have read the 1809 translation of

And good instructor; but to-night he seems
The ghost of folly haunting my sweet dreams.'

While yet he spake they had arrived before
A pillared porch, with lofty portal door,
380 Where hung a silver lamp, whose phosphor glow
Reflected in the slabbèd steps below,
Mild as a star in water; for so new,
And so unsullied was the marble hue,
So through the crystal polish, liquid fine,
385 Ran the dark veins, that none but feet divine
Could e'er have touched there. Sounds Aeolian
Breathed from the hinges, as the ample span
Of the wide doors disclosed a place unknown
Some time to any, but those two alone,
390 And a few Persian mutes, who that same year
Were seen about the markets. None knew where
They could inhabit; the most curious
Were foiled, who watched to trace them to their house.

Philostratus's *Life*, but could have found all he needed in *Lemprière*, '. . . a
Pythagorean philosopher, well skilled in magic, and thoroughly acquainted
with those arts which can captivate and astonish the vulgar . . . he aspired
to the name of the reformer of mankind. He was courted by kings and
princes, and commanded unusual attention by his numberless artifices. . . .'
i *379. A pillared porch, with*] A royal-squared *Fair copy*.
i *380. phosphor*] Phosphorescent.
i *383. was the marble hue*] did the marble show *Fair copy*.
i *386. Aeolian*] Like the music of an Aeolian harp; see *Ode to Apollo* 34 *n* (p.
161 above).
i *388–93. disclosed . . . to their house*] See Woodhouse's letter to Taylor,
'. . . they live together in a palace in the middle of Corinth . . . the entrance
of which no one can see (like the Cavern Prince Ahmed found in the Arabian Nights, when searching for his lost arrow)' (*L* ii 164) and 'The Story
of Prince Ahmed and the Fairy Pari Banou', 'At first [the Prince] . . .
thought he was going into a dark obscure place, but presently a quite different light succeeded . . . entering into a large spacious place, he perceived
a magnificent palace' (*Tales of the East* i 440).
i *390. Persian mutes*] An oriental touch recalling the *Arabian Nights*.
i *392–3. the most curious . . . to their house*] Cp. 'Prince Ahmed and the
Fairy Pari Banou', '. . . she could perceive no opening, not so much as the
iron gate which Prince Ahmed discovered, which was to be seen and
opened . . . only to such whose presence was agreeable to the fairy Pari-
banou' (*Tales of the East* i 446). For 'trace' (i 393) the fair copy has 'maze'.
i *393–4.* An earlier reading (preserved in the fragment of K.'s draft containing i 386–97) was,

And but the flitter-wingèd verse must tell,
395   For truth's sake, what woe afterwards befell,
'Twould humour many a heart to leave them thus,
Shut from the busy world, of more incredulous.

PART II

Love in a hut, with water and a crust,
Is—Love, forgive us!—cinders, ashes, dust;
Love in a palace is perhaps at last
More grievous torment than a hermit's fast.
5   That is a doubtful tale from fairy land,
Hard for the non-elect to understand.
Had Lycius lived to hand his story down,
He might have given the moral a fresh frown,
Or clenched it quite; but too short was their bliss
10   To breed distrust and hate, that make the soft voice hiss.
Beside, there, nightly, with terrific glare,
Love, jealous grown of so complete a pair,
Hovered and buzzed his wings, with fearful roar,

Were foild they knew not how—but what can foil
The winged verse? What Poesy not win . . .

The epithet 'flitter-wingèd' means fluttering here and there at will, like a
bird or a fairy.

i 396–7. Tender-hearted readers, unwilling to believe in the sad outcome
of the story, would prefer to leave Lycius and Lamia in their present happy
situation. The comma after 'world' in i 397 is omitted in *1820*, but the
reading is supported by the draft version,

'Twould humour many a heart to close the door
Upon their happy days, incredulous of more . . .

ii 1–4. Love does not last for anyone, no matter whether poor or rich.
With the worldly tone cp. i 330–2 above and see the cancelled lines quoted
in ii 213–20 *n* below.

ii 1–2. Cp. the proverbial saying, 'When poverty comes in at the door love
flies out of the window'.

ii 6. *the non-elect*] Ordinary folk. They find it hard to understand that 'Love
in a palace' must also come to grief.

ii 9. *clenched it quite*] Proved it conclusively.

ii 12. *Love, jealous grown*] Cupid is anxiously solicitous for them.

ii 13. *buzzed . . . fearful roar*] Cupid is imagined as warning off intruders by
the noisy beating of his wings. With the mocking tone cp. K.'s portrayal of
Hermes (see i 7 *n* above).

Above the lintel of their chamber door,
15   And down the passage cast a glow upon the floor.

For all this, came a ruin: side by side
They were enthronèd, in the even tide,
Upon a couch, near to a curtaining
Whose airy texture, from a golden string,
20   Floated into the room and let appear
Unveiled the summer heaven, blue and clear,
Betwixt two marble shafts. There they reposed,
Where use had made it sweet, with eyelids closed,
Saving a tithe which love still open kept,
25   That they might see each other while they almost slept;
When from the slope side of a suburb hill,
Deafening the swallow's twitter, came a thrill
Of trumpets—Lycius started—the sounds fled,
But left a thought a-buzzing in his head.
30   For the first time, since first he harboured in
That purple-linèd palace of sweet sin,
His spirit passed beyond its golden bourn
Into the noisy world almost forsworn.
The lady, ever watchful, penetrant,
35   Saw this with pain, so arguing a want

ii *16. For all this*] In spite of all this.
ii *22. marble shafts*] Small columns used in the jambs of a window.
ii *22–5. There they . . . slept*] Cp. *Ode to Psyche* 17–20 (p. 516 above),

Their lips touched not, but had not bade adieu,
As if disjoinèd by soft-handed slumber,
And ready still past kisses to outnumber
At tender eye-dawn of aurorean love . . .

ii *26.* See *Paradise Lost* iv 261 (marked by K. in his copy of Milton),
Down the slope hills . . .
The epithet 'suburb' for neighbouring is an archaism.
ii *29. a-buzzing in his head*] Cp. *Endymion* i 851–2 (p. 158 above),
. . . atomies
That buzz about our slumbers, like brain-flies . . .
ii *34. penetrant*] Acute.
ii *35–45.* Recalls the fears of Pari Banou on Prince Ahmed's request to
visit his father in the outside world, 'This discourse alarmed the fairy, and
made her fear it was only an excuse to leave her, and thereupon said to him,
"What disgust have I given, to oblige you to ask me this leave? Is it possible
you should have forgot that you have pledged your faith to me, and that
you no longer love one who is passionately fond of you?"' ('Prince Ahmed
and the Fairy . . .', *Tales of the East* i 442.)

Of something more, more than her empery
Of joys; and she began to moan and sigh
Because he mused beyond her, knowing well
That but a moment's thought is passion's passing-bell.
40   'Why do you sigh, fair creature?' whispered he;
'Why do you think?' returned she tenderly,
'You have deserted me—where am I now?
Not in your heart while care weighs on your brow—
No, no, you have dismissed me; and I go
45   From your breast houseless; aye, it must be so.'
He answered, bending to her open eyes,
Where he was mirrored small in paradise,
'My silver planet, both of eve and morn!
Why will you plead yourself so sad forlorn,
50   While I am striving how to fill my heart
With deeper crimson, and a double smart?
How to entangle, trammel up and snare
Your soul in mine, and labyrinth you there
Like the hid scent in an unbudded rose?
55   Aye, a sweet kiss—you see your mighty woes.
My thoughts! Shall I unveil them? Listen then!
What mortal hath a prize, that other men
May be confounded and abashed withal,

ii *36. empery*] Empire, as in *Cymbeline* I vi 119–21,

. . . A lady
So fair,—and fasten'd to an empery
Would make the great'st king double . . .

ii *39. passing-bell*] See *Hyperion* i 173 *n* (p. 406 above).

ii *45.* Followed in the fair copy by,

Too fond was I believing, fancy fed
In high deliriums, and blossoms never shed . . .

ii *47.* Cp. Burton's *Anatomy of Melancholy* III 2 ii 5 (marked by K. in his
copy of Burton), '. . . "they may then kiss and coll, lie and look babies into
one another's eyes"' (1813 edn ii 393).

ii *48. silver planet*] An oriental flourish. See, for example, Zahide to the princess in 'The History of the Basket', '. . . beauteous moon of the world'
(*Tales of the East* i 678).

ii *52. trammel*] Enmesh. Cp. *Macbeth* I vii 2–3,

. . . if the assassination
Could trammel up the consequence . . .

K. frequently echoes *Macbeth* in *Otho the Great* (see headnote to the present
poem, p. 613 above). With the use of the word here cp. K.'s letter to Fanny
Brawne 1 July 1819, '. . . you . . . have so entrammelled me, so destroyed
my freedom' (*L* ii 123).

But lets it sometimes pace abroad majestical,
60 And triumph, as in thee I should rejoice
Amid the hoarse alarm of Corinth's voice.
Let my foes choke, and my friends shout afar,
While through the throngèd streets your bridal car
Wheels round its dazzling spokes.' The lady's cheek
65 Trembled; she nothing said, but, pale and meek,
Arose and knelt before him, wept a rain
Of sorrows at his words; at last with pain
Beseeching him, the while his hand she wrung,
To change his purpose. He thereat was stung,
70 Perverse, with stronger fancy to reclaim
Her wild and timid nature to his aim.
Besides, for all his love, in self-despite,
Against his better self, he took delight
Luxurious in her sorrows, soft and new.
75 His passion, cruel grown, took on a hue
Fierce and sanguineous as 'twas possible
In one whose brow had no dark veins to swell.
Fine was the mitigated fury, like
Apollo's presence when in act to strike
80 The serpent–ha, the serpent! Certes, she
Was none. She burnt, she loved the tyranny,
And, all subdued, consented to the hour

ii *59. majestical*] K. may owe this form of 'majestic' to his recollection of
Hamlet I i 143, 'being so majestical', and II ii 307, 'this majestical roof'.
ii *73–4*. Cp. *Ode on Melancholy* 18–20 (p. 540 above),

> . . . if thy mistress some rich anger shows,
>
> Imprison her soft hand and let her rave,
>
> And feed deep, deep upon her peerless eyes . . .

ii *78. mitigated*] Moderated. Perhaps echoing *The Faerie Queene* III iii 37,

> Ne shall he yet his wrath so mitigate . . .

Cp. the use of the word in *Otho the Great* II i 80–1 (p. 568 above),

> . . . that blood of yours in my warm veins
>
> Has not yet mitigated into milk . . .

and see in the same play II i 9 *n* (p. 565 above).
ii *80. The serpent*] Python, the monster engendered from the mud left on the
earth after Deucalion's flood and slain by Apollo at Delphi (Ovid's *Metamorphoses* i 438–47). The repetition underlines the irony in the allusion,
since Lamia appears to have nothing of the 'serpent' left in her nature. The
Spenserian word 'certes' (assuredly) is used in *Otho the Great* V v 116 (p. 610
above).
ii *81–3*. *she burnt . . . paramour*] See K.'s comment, recorded in Woodhouse's letter to Taylor, 'Women love to be forced to do a thing, by a fine
fellow–*such as this*' (L ii 164).

When to the bridal he should lead his paramour.
Whispering in midnight silence, said the youth,
85   'Sure some sweet name thou hast, though, by my truth,
I have not asked it, ever thinking thee
Not mortal, but of heavenly progeny,
As still I do. Hast any mortal name,
Fit appellation for this dazzling frame?
90   Or friends or kinsfolk on the citied earth,
To share our marriage feast and nuptial mirth?'
'I have no friends,' said Lamia, 'no, not one;
My presence in wide Corinth hardly known:
My parents' bones are in their dusty urns
95   Sepulchred, where no kindled incense burns,
Seeing all their luckless race are dead, save me,
And I neglect the holy rite for thee.
Even as you list invite your many guests;
But if, as now it seems, your vision rests
100   With any pleasure on me, do not bid
Old Apollonius—from him keep me hid.'
Lycius, perplexed at words so blind and blank,
Made close inquiry; from whose touch she shrank,
Feigning a sleep; and he to the dull shade
105   Of deep sleep in a moment was betrayed.
    It was the custom then to bring away

ii *81–2.*   Became herself a flame–'twas worth an age
                Of minor joys to revel in such rage . . . *Fair copy.*
Cp. ii 73–4 *n* above.
ii *83.* Followed in the fair copy by the cancelled lines,
           After the hottest days comes languidest
           The colour'd Eve, half-hidden in the west;
           So they both look'd, so spake, if breathed sound,
           That almost silence is, hath ever found
           Compare with nature's quiet. Which lov'd most,
           Which had the weakest, strongest, heart so lost,
           So ruin'd, wreck'd, destroy'd; they could not guess
           Whether 'twas misery or happiness . . .
ii *84.* Spells are but made to break. Whisper'd the Youth . . . *Fair copy*
(cancelled).
ii *94.* Cp. Potter's *Antiquities*, 'The bones and ashes [of the dead] . . . were
deposited in urns' (ii 215–16).
ii *97.* Cp. Potter's *Antiquities*, '. . . they had anniversary days, on which
they paid their devotions to the dead' (ii 237).
ii *105. betrayed*] Tricked into. The 'deep sleep' is the result of a magic spell.
ii *106–10. It was . . . pageants*] Cp. Potter's *Antiquities*, 'The bride was
usually conducted in a chariot from her father's house to her husband's in

The bride from home at blushing shut of day,
Veiled, in a chariot, heralded along
By strewn flowers, torches, and a marriage song,
110 With other pageants; but this fair unknown
Had not a friend. So being left alone
(Lycius was gone to summon all his kin)
And knowing surely she could never win
His foolish heart from its mad pompousness,
115 She set herself, high-thoughted, how to dress
The misery in fit magnificence.
She did so, but 'tis doubtful how and whence
Came, and who were her subtle servitors.
About the halls, and to and from the doors,
120 There was a noise of wings, till in short space
The glowing banquet-room shone with wide-archèd
        grace.
A haunting music, sole perhaps and lone
Supportress of the fairy-roof, made moan
Throughout, as fearful the whole charm might fade.

---

the evening, that time being chosen to conceal her blushes . . . torches were
carried before her. These torches were usually carried by servants. They
were sometimes attended with singers and dancers' (ii 281–2).

ii *107. shut of day*] See i 138–9 *n* above.

ii *114. pompousness*] Love of magnificent display.

ii *118. subtle*] Of tenuous substance, invisible. Cp. ii 136 below, 'viewless
servants'. Probably suggested by the invisible attendants in oriental tales,
for example, 'The History of the Merchant Abudah . . .', 'Abudah and the
fair company began the banquet, while genii invisible administered to
them' (*Tales of the East* iii 434).

ii *122–62.* The draft version of this passage copied out by K. in his letter to
Taylor of 5 Sept. 1819 (*L* ii 157–9) has major variants from *1820*, some of
which are noted below; see especially ii 199–212 *n*, ii 213–20 *n*.

ii *122–41.* A sumptuous banquet-room magically supplied with music,
lighted lamps, rich decoration and exotic food is a constant feature of oriental stories. For similar descriptions in romantic poetry also inspired by
eastern tales see, for example, the magic palace in Peacock's *Rhododaphne* vi,
vii and Southey's *Thalaba* (1801) vi sts. 25, 12–13.

ii *122–4.* The roof appears to be supported solely by the agency of music.
Perhaps a recollection of *Paradise Lost* i 710–12 (marked by K. in his copy of
Milton),

> Anon out of the earth a Fabrick huge
> Rose like an Exhalation, with the sound
> Of Dulcet Symphonies and voices sweet . . .

On 'made moan' see *La Belle Dame Sans Merci* 20 *n* (p. 503 above).

125 Fresh carvèd cedar, mimicking a glade
       Of palm and plantain, met from either side,
       High in the midst, in honour of the bride;
       Two palms and then two plantains, and so on,
       From either side their stems branched one to one
130 All down the aislèd place; and beneath all
       There ran a stream of lamps straight on from wall to
              wall.
       So canopied lay an untasted feast
       Teeming with odours. Lamia, regal dressed,
       Silently paced about, and as she went,
135 In pale contented sort of discontent,
       Missioned her viewless servants to enrich
       The fretted splendour of each nook and niche.
       Between the tree-stems, marbled plain at first,
       Came jasper panels; then, anon, there burst
140 Forth creeping imagery of slighter trees,
       And with the larger wove in small intricacies.
       Approving all, she faded at self-will,
       And shut the chamber up, close, hushed and still,
       Complete and ready for the revels rude,
145 When dreadful guests would come to spoil her solitude.

       The day appeared, and all the gossip rout.

ii *128–30. Two palms . . . aislèd place*] The pairing of the trees 'to honour
the bride' may owe something to Burton's quotation of passages from
Claudian, Constantine, Galen and other early writers to illustrate the power
of love in 'vegetal creatures', especially various types of tree, in *Anatomy of
Melancholy* III 2 i 1 (marked by K. in his copy of Burton), for example,
'. . . palm-trees . . . are both he and she, and express not a sympathy but a
love-passion . . . the two trees bend, and of their own accords stretch out
their boughs to embrace and kiss each other' (1813 edn ii 193); the passages occur shortly before Burton's account of the story from Philostratus,
which is K.'s source for the present poem (see headnote, p. 614 above).
ii *133. with odours*] a perfume K.'s letter.
ii *134. Silently*] Silverly *Fair copy*. For K.'s earlier use of this word see *Endymion* i 541, iv 486, *Hyperion* ii 128 (pp. 144, 265 and 423 above).
ii *135.* Apathetic resignation.
ii *136. viewless*] A poeticism for invisible (see ii 118 *n* above); cp. *Ode to a
Nightingale* 33 *n* (p. 527 above).
ii *137. fretted*] Carved. For 'fretted splendour' K.'s letter has 'spendid cor-
nicing'.
ii *138. marbled plain*] wainscoted *Fair copy (cancelled)*.
ii *142. faded at self-will*] Caused herself to vanish.

O senseless Lycius! Madman! Wherefore flout
The silent-blessing fate, warm cloistered hours,
And show to common eyes these secret bowers?
150   The herd approached; each guest, with busy brain,
Arriving at the portal, gazed amain,
And entered marvelling—for they knew the street,
Remembered it from childhood all complete
Without a gap, yet ne'er before had seen
155   That royal porch, that high-built fair demesne.
So in they hurried all, mazed, curious and keen—
Save one, who looked thereon with eye severe,
And with calm-planted steps walked in austere.
'Twas Apollonius: something too he laughed,
160   As though some knotty problem that had daffed
His patient thought had now begun to thaw,
And solve and melt—'twas just as he foresaw.

He met within the murmurous vestibule
His young disciple. ''Tis no common rule,
165   Lycius,' said he, 'for uninvited guest
To force himself upon you, and infest
With an unbidden presence the bright throng
Of younger friends; yet must I do this wrong,
And you forgive me.' Lycius blushed, and led
170   The old man through the inner doors broad-spread;
With reconciling words and courteous mien
Turning into sweet milk the sophist's spleen.

Of wealthy lustre was the banquet-room,

ii *147–8.* Lycius! Dolt! Fool! Madman! Lout!
     Why would you murder happiness like yours?... *K.'s letter.*
ii *152–5.* See i 388–93 *n*, 392–3 *n* above.
ii *155. demesne*] Palace.
ii *157. with eye severe*] Cp. the seer who warns the hero against the enchantress in Peacock's *Rhododaphne* ii 58–9,
                    ... an aged man was near
               Of rugged brow, and eye severe ...
ii *160. daffed*] Resisted. See *Ah, ken ye what I met the day* 35 *n* (p. 364 above),
                    Tom was daffèd like a chick ...
ii *163–72.* The lines appear on an inserted leaf in the fair copy. K. may
have added them later to explain Apollonius's appearance at the feast in
spite of Lamia's objections at ii 100–1 above. With i 172 cp. *Otho the Great*
II i 80–1, quoted in ii 78 *n* above.
ii *173–90.* K. may have been influenced by the magic banquet in Peacock's
Rhododaphne vi 318–42, but there are no close verbal parallels.

Filled with pervading brilliance and perfume:
175   Before each lucid panel fuming stood
A censer fed with myrrh and spicèd wood,
Each by a sacred tripod held aloft,
Whose slender feet wide-swerved upon the soft
Wool-woofèd carpets; fifty wreaths of smoke
180   From fifty censers their light voyage took
To the high roof, still mimicked as they rose
Along the mirrored walls by twin-clouds odorous.
Twelve spherèd tables, by silk seats ensphered,
High as the level of a man's breast reared
185   On libbard's paws, upheld the heavy gold
Of cups and goblets, and the store thrice told
Of Ceres' horn, and, in huge vessels, wine
Come from the gloomy tun with merry shine.
Thus loaded with a feast the tables stood,
190   Each shrining in the midst the image of a God.

When in an antichamber every guest

ii *175. lucid*] Shining.

ii *176.* Cp. Potter's *Antiquities*, '. . . the room wherein the entertainment was made was sometimes perfumed by burning myrrh or frankincese, or with other odours' (ii 383). K. probably also remembered Southey's *Thalaba* vi st. 25 359–61,

> . . . the aloes and the sandal-wood,
>   From golden censers, o'er the banquet room
>   Diffuse their dying sweets . . .

ii *182. the mirrored walls*] Cp. 'The History of the Merchant Abudah . . .', '. . . an inner apartment . . . whose walls were one entire mirror' (*Tales of the East* iii 433).

ii *183–5. spherèd tables . . . paws*] Cp. Potter's *Antiquities* . . ., '. . . the Greeks made their tables . . . spherical, in imitation of the world. . . . The most common support of these tables was an ivory foot, cast in the form of a lion, a leopard or some other animal' (ii 376–7).

ii *183. ensphered*] Surrounded by.

ii *185. libbards*] An archaism for leopards.

ii *187. Ceres' horn*] The cornucopia, or horn of plenty.

ii *188. tun*] Cask.

ii *190.* Cp. Potter's *Antiquities*, 'It was customary to place the statues of the gods upon the table' (ii 376).

ii *191–6.* Cp. Potter's *Antiquities*, 'Before they went into an entertainment they washed and anointed themselves. . . . Those who came off a journey were washed and clothed with apparel suitable to the occasion' (ii 364–5). References to the habit of wearing white for a feast and the placing of guests according to their rank appear in *Antiquities* ii 374, 380.

Had felt the cold full sponge to pleasure pressed,
By ministering slaves, upon his hands and feet,
And fragrant oils with ceremony meet
195 Poured on his hair, they all moved to the feast
In white robes, and themselves in order placed
Around the silken couches, wondering
Whence all this mighty cost and blaze of wealth could
    spring.

Soft went the music the soft air along,
200 While fluent Greek a vowelled undersong
Kept up among the guests, discoursing low
At first, for scarcely was the wine at flow;
But when the happy vintage touched their brains,
Louder they talk, and louder come the strains
205 Of powerful instruments. The gorgeous dyes,
The space, the splendour of the draperies,
The roof of awful richness, nectarous cheer,
Beautiful slaves, and Lamia's self, appear,

ii *197. Around the silken couches*] The custom of eating meals while reclining is discussed in *Antiquities* ii 371–4.

ii *199–212.* Soft went the music, and the tables all
        Sparkled beneath the viewless banneral
        Of Magic; and dispos'd in double row
        Seem'd edged Parterres of white bedded snow,
  [5] Adorne'd along the sides with living flowers
        Conversing, laughing after sunny showers:
        And, as the pleasant appetite entic'd,
        Gush came the wine, and sheer the meats were slic'd.
        Soft went the Music; the flat salver sang
 [10] Kiss'd by the emptied goblet, – and again it rang . . .
                           K.'s letter

l. [2]. *banneral*] For K.'s early use of this word see *Specimen of an Induction* 38 *n* (p. 35 above).

l. [4]. *Parterres*] The level spaces in a garden occupied by flower-beds (from the French *par terre*, 'on or over the ground' [*OED*]).

ii *203–8.* Probably inspired by the nightly festivities in 'The History of a Basket', where the intoxicating atmosphere is heightened by lavish helpings of wine and by rich music, splendid surroundings and the beauty of the presiding princess and her attendants (see *Tales of the East* ii 670, 671, 673).

ii *208. Beautiful slaves*] Cp. Potter's *Antiquities*, '. . . it was usual to procure beautiful slaves to attend at entertainments, not so much for any service they were to do, as to gratify the eyes of the beholders' (ii 389). See also the 'young slaves' bearing wine in The 'History of a Basket' *loc. cit.* ii 670).

Now, when the wine has done its rosy deed,
210   And every soul from human trammels freed,
No more so strange; for merry wine, sweet wine,
Will make Elysian shades not too fair, too divine.
Soon was God Bacchus at meridian height;
Flushed were their cheeks, and bright eyes double
        bright.
215   Garlands of every green, and every scent
From vales deflowered, or forest-trees branch-rent,
In baskets of bright osiered gold were brought
High as the handles heaped, to suit the thought
Of every guest–that each, as he did please,
220   Might fancy-fit his brows, silk-pillowed at his ease.
      What wreath for Lamia? What for Lycius?
What for the sage, old Apollonius?
Upon her aching forehead be there hung

ii *211. merry wine, sweet wine*] On K.'s enjoyment of wine see *Hence burgundy, claret and port* 1–2 *n* (pp. 299–300 above).
ii 213–20. Cp. the satirical description of the inebriated guests in K.'s letter
(*L* ii 159),

> Swift bustled by the servants:–here's a health
> Cries one–another–then, as if by stealth,
> A Glutton drains a cup of Helicon,
> Too fast down, down his throat the brief delight is gone.
> "Where is that Music?" cries a Lady fair.
> "Aye, where is it my dear? Up in the air?"
> Another whispers "Poo!" saith Glutton "Mum!"
> Then makes his shiny mouth a napkin for his thumb . . .

Woodhouse comments in his letter to Taylor 19 Sept. 1819, '. . . the friends
are invited to the wedding feast–and K. wipes the Cits and the low-lived
ones' (*L* ii 164). Woodhouse's copying out on to the proof sheets this and
the earlier cancelled passage (ii 199–212 *n* above) suggests, as W. A. Coles
points out, that the lines were 'apparently being seriously considered up to
the time of the poem's publication' ('The Proof Sheets of Keats's "Lamia"',
Harvard Library Bulletin viii (1954) 115).
ii *212.* Wine makes ideal happiness seem less remote.
ii *213. at meridian height*] At the peak of his ascendancy.
ii *215–20.* Cp. Potter's *Antiquities*, 'It was also customary to deck themselves with flowers, or garlands composed of flowers, which were provided
by the master of the feast. . . . They not only adorned their heads, necks,
and breasts, but often bestrewed the beds whereon they lay' (ii 380).
ii *217. osiered*] Woven.
ii *218–19. to suit . . . guest*]   . . . of every sort
                              Of fragrant wreath . . . *Fair copy.*

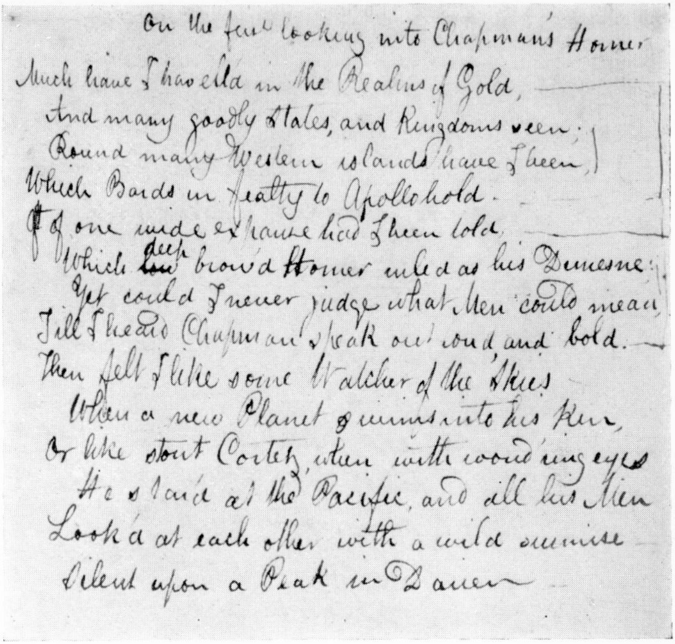
On the first looking into Chapman's Homer

Much have I travell'd in the Realms of Gold,
And many goodly States, and Kingdoms seen;
Round many Western islands have I been,
Which Bards in fealty to Apollo hold.
Oft of one wide expanse had I been told,
Which ~~low~~ deep brow'd Homer ruled as his Demesne;
Yet could I never judge what Men could mean,
Till I heard Chapman speak out loud, and bold.
Then felt I like some Watcher of the Skies
When a new Planet swims into his Ken,
Or like stout Cortez, when with wond'ring eyes
He star'd at the Pacific, and all his Men
Look'd at each other with a wild surmise
Silent upon a Peak in Darien—

Plate 2 The MS of *On First Looking into Chapman's Homer* written in 1816

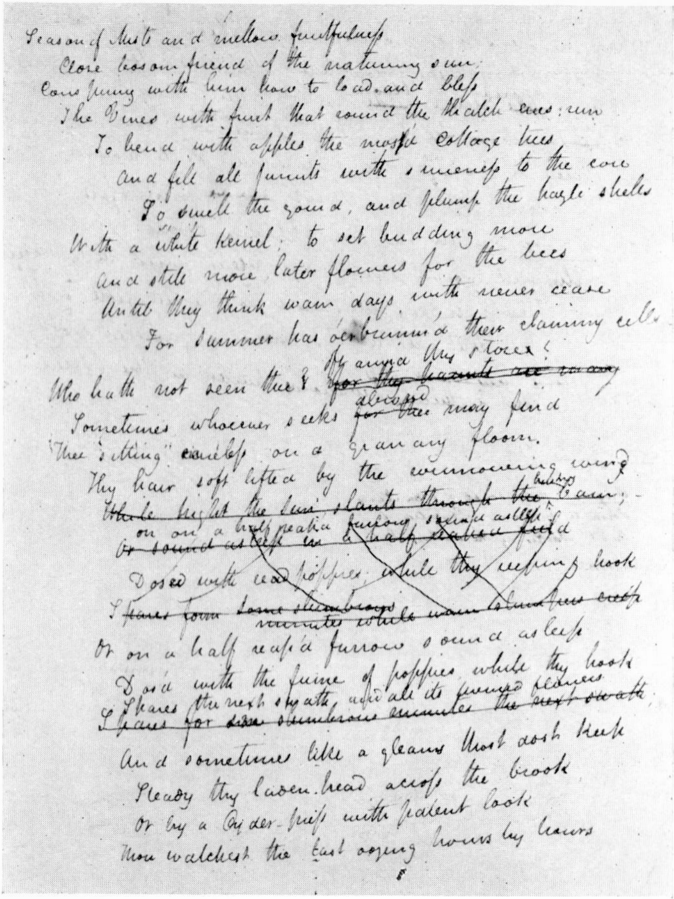

Season of Mists and mellow fruitfulness
Close bosom friend of the maturing sun;
Conspiring with him how to load and bless
The Vines with fruit that round the thatch eves run
To bend with apples the moss'd Cottage trees
And fill all fruits with sweetness to the core
To swell the gourd, and plump the hazle shells
With a white kernel; to set budding more
And still more later flowers for the bees
Until they think warm days with never cease
For Summer has o'erbrimm'd their clammy cells.

Who hath not seen thee? ~~for thy haunts are many~~ Oft amid thy stores!
Sometimes whoever seeks ~~for thee~~ abroad may find
Thee sitting careless on a granary floor,
Thy hair soft lifted by the winnowing wind;
~~While bright the Sun slants through the barn;~~
on on a half reaped furrow sound asleep
~~Or sound asleep in a half reaped field~~
Dosed with read poppies; while thy reeping hook
~~Spares form Some slumbrous~~ minutes while warm slumbers creep
Or on a half reap'd furrow sound asleep
Dos'd with the fume of poppies, while thy hook
Spares the next swath, and all its twined flowers
~~Spares for some slumbrous minutes the next swath~~;
And sometimes like a gleaner thou dost keep
Steady thy laden head across the brook
Or by a Cyder-press with patient look
Thou watchest the last oozing hours by hours

Plate 3 The MS of *To Autumn*, written in 1819

The leaves of willow and of adder's tongue;
225   And for the youth, quick, let us strip for him
The thyrsus, that his watching eyes may swim
Into forgetfulness; and, for the sage,
Let spear-grass and the spiteful thistle wage
War on his temples. Do not all charms fly
230   At the mere touch of cold philosophy?
There was an awful rainbow once in heaven:
We know her woof, her texture; she is given
In the dull catalogue of common things.

ii *224. willow ... adder's tongue*] Emblems of grief and sorrow. The Adder's Tongue is a species of fern formerly used in medicine for its soothing properties. K. obviously chose it for its appropriate name and probably also remembered Coleridge's use of it in *Melancholy* (1797, repr. 1817) 5–8,

> The fern was press'd beneath her hair,
> The dark green Adder's Tongue was there;
> And still as pass'd the flagging sea-gale weak,
> The long lank leaf bow'd fluttering o'er her cheek.

Coleridge notes of his own lines in *Sibylline Leaves* (1817): 'A botanical mistake. The plant I meant is called the Hart's Tongue, but this would ... spoil the poetical effect.'

ii *226. thyrsus*] Bacchus's staff, which was entwined with ivy and vine-leaves.

ii *228–9. wage / War on his temples*] Pierce him remorselessly. Cp. ii 276–86 below.

ii *229–37. Do not ... rainbow*] The question of scientific thinking and its effect on poetry was frequently discussed at the time. See Hazlitt's 1818 lecture 'On Poetry in General', 'It cannot be concealed ... that the progress of knowledge and refinement has a tendency to circumscribe the limits of the imagination, and to clip the wings of poetry' (*Works*, ed P. P. Howe 1930–34, v 9)–with the last five words quoted cp. ii 234 '... clip an Angel's wings ...'. For K.'s tentative individual exploration of the subject see his early agreement with Charles Lamb at Haydon's 'immortal dinner', 28 Dec. 1817, that Newton '... destroyed all the poetry of the rainbow by reducing it to the prismatic colours' (Taylor's *Autobiography of Haydon* (1853) 1926 edn i 269) and cp. his later ideas on poetry and philosophy in his Feb.–May 1819 journal-letter, '... our reasonings ... though er roneous ... may be fine–This is the very thing in which consists poetry and if so it is not so fine a thing as philosophy–For the same reason that an eagle is not so fine a thing as a truth' (*L* ii 80–1).

ii *231*. K. may be thinking here of the references to the rainbow in *Revela tion* iv 2–3, '... a throne was set in heaven ... and there was a rainbow round about the throne ...' and x 1, 'And I saw another mighty angel come down from heaven ... and a rainbow was upon his head ...' (cp. the allusion to 'Angel's wings' at ii 234 below).

22—K.

Philosophy will clip an Angel's wings,
235   Conquer all mysteries by rule and line,
Empty the haunted air and gnomèd mine—
Unweave a rainbow, as it erewhile made
The tender-personed Lamia melt into a shade.

By her glad Lycius sitting, in chief place,
240   Scarce saw in all the room another face,
Till, checking his love trance, a cup he took
Full brimmed, and opposite sent forth a look
'Cross the broad table, to beseech a glance
From his old teacher's wrinkled countenance,
245   And pledge him. The bald-head philosopher
Had fixed his eye, without a twinkle or stir
Full on the alarmèd beauty of the bride,
Brow-beating her fair form, and troubling her sweet
        pride.
Lycius then pressed her hand, with devout touch,
250   As pale it lay upon the rosy couch:
'Twas icy, and the cold ran through his veins;
Then sudden it grew hot, and all the pains
Of an unnatural heat shot to his heart.
'Lamia, what means this? Wherefore dost thou start?
255   Know'st thou that man?' Poor Lamia answered not.
He gazed into her eyes, and not a jot
Owned they the lovelorn piteous appeal;
More, more he gazed; his human senses reel;
Some hungry spell that loveliness absorbs;
260   There was no recognition in those orbs.
'Lamia!' he cried—and no soft-toned reply.
The many heard, and the loud revelry
Grew hush; the stately music no more breathes;
The myrtle sickened in a thousand wreaths.
265   By faint degrees, voice, lute, and pleasure ceased;
A deadly silence step by step increased,

ii 236–7. *Empty . . . rainbow*] A self-echo. See K.'s concluding address to
Kean in his 'On Edmund Kean as a Shakespearian Actor', 'Cheer us a little
in the failure of our days! for romance lives but in books. The goblin is
driven from the hearth, and the rainbow is robbed of its mystery' (*The
Champion* 21 Dec. 1817; repr. *Forman* (1883) iii 3–6).

ii 237. *unweave a rainbow*] For an early reference in K. to the 'interwoven'
colours of the rainbow see *Endymion* ii 230–1 *n* (p. 173 above).

ii 260. The phrasing and cadence suggest a half-conscious recollection of
Macbeth III iv 95,

        Thou hast no speculation in those eyes . . .

Until it seemed a horrid presence there,
And not a man but felt the terror in his hair.
'Lamia!' he shrieked; and nothing but the shriek
270   With its sad echo did the silence break.
'Begone, foul dream!' he cried, gazing again
In the bride's face, where now no azure vein
Wandered on fair-spaced temples; no soft bloom
Misted the cheek; no passion to illume
275   The deep-recessèd vision. All was blight;
Lamia, no longer fair, there sat a deadly white.
'Shut, shut those juggling eyes, thou ruthless man!
Turn them aside, wretch! Or the righteous ban
Of all the Gods, whose dreadful images
280   Here represent their shadowy presences,
May pierce them on the sudden with the thorn
Of painful blindness; leaving thee forlorn,
In trembling dotage to the feeblest fright
Of conscience, for their long offended might,
285   For all thine impious proud-heart sophistries,
Unlawful magic, and enticing lies.
Corinthians! Look upon that gray-beard wretch!
Mark how, possessed, his lashless eyelids stretch
Around his demon eyes! Corinthians, see!
290   My sweet bride withers at their potency.'
'Fool!' said the sophist, in an under-tone

ii *272–6. where now no azure vein . . . deadly white*] Cp. the transformation
of Aglauros in Sandys's *Ovid, Metamorphoses* ii (p. 32, col. 2),

> . . . lack of blood her veines blew branches pales.
> And as a Canker, slighting helplesse Arts,
> Creeps from th'infected to the sounder parts:
> So by degrees the winter of wan Death
> Congeales the path of life, and stops her breath:
> Nor strove she: had she strove to make her mone,
> Voice had no way; her neck and face now stone.
> There she a bloodless Statue sate . . .

Ovid's passage forms part of the story of Hermes and Herse (see i 7–145 *n*
above).

ii *275. deep-recessèd vision*] Sunken eyes.

ii *277. juggling*] Conjuring.

ii *285–90.* See i 375 *n* above. Cp. Rhododaphne's attack on the seer who
has recognized her as an enchantress in Peacock's *Rhododaphne* iii 177–8,

> Whose truth is lies, whose paths are error,
> Whose gods are fiends, whose heaven is terror . . .

ii *289. his demon eyes*] It is now Apollonius, not Lamia, who appears to be
a 'demon'; cp. i 55–6 above.

Gruff with contempt; which a death-nighing moan
From Lycius answered, as heart-struck and lost,
He sank supine beside the aching ghost.

295   'Fool! Fool!' repeated he, while his eyes still
Relented not, nor moved: 'From every ill
Of life have I preserved thee to this day,
And shall I see thee made a serpent's prey?'
Then Lamia breathed death-breath; the sophist's eye,

300   Like a sharp spear, went through her utterly,
Keen, cruel, perceant, stinging. She, as well
As her weak hand could any meaning tell,
Motioned him to be silent; vainly so,
He looked and looked again a level *No*!

305   'A serpent!' echoed he; no sooner said,
Than with a frightful scream she vanishèd:
And Lycius' arms were empty of delight,
As were his limbs of life, from that same night.
On the high couch he lay—his friends came round—

310   Supported him—no pulse, or breath they found,
And, in its marriage robe, the heavy body wound.

ii *293–4. as heart-struck . . . ghost*]   . . . as he sunk supine
              Upon the Couch where Lamia's beauties pine . . . *Fair copy.*
ii *297–8.*   That youth might suffer have I shielded thee
              Up to this very hour, and shall I see
              Thee married to a Serpent? Pray you Mark,
              Corinthians! A Serpent, plain and stark . . . *Fair copy.*
For other attempts, probably suggested by Woodhouse, see W. A. Coles,
'The Proof Sheets of Keats's "Lamia",' *Harvard Library Bulletin* viii (1954)
118–19. The passage recalls the seer's warning in Peacock's *Rhododaphne* ii
129–34,

        Beware! yet once again beware!
        Ere round thy inexperienced mind,
        With voice and semblance falsely fair
        A chain Thessalian magic bind,
        Which never more, oh youth! believe,
        Shall either earth or heaven unweave . . .

ii *301. perceant*] Piercing. An archaism used by Spenser, e.g. *The Faerie
Queene* II iii 23,

        In her faire eyes two living lamps did flame,

              . . .

        So passing persant, and so wondrous bright . . .

ii *308.* Apollonius preserves Lycius from Lamia, but destroys him in the
process. K. doubts both Apollonius's 'cold philosophy' and Lamia's magical enchantment; the poem poses his dilemma, but leaves it unresolved.

139 'Pensive they sit and roll their languid eyes'

Written 17 Sept. 1819 in K.'s journal-letter of 17–19 Sept. to George and Georgiana Keats with the prefatory comment, 'Nothing strikes me so forcibly with a sense of the rediculous as love–A Man in love I do think cuts the sorryest figure in the world. . . . Somewhere in the Spectator [6 May 1712] is related an account of a Man inviting a party of stutterers and squinters to his table. 'twould please me more to scrape together a party of Lovers, not to dinner–no to tea. There would be no fighting as among Knights of old–' (L ii 187–8). K. adds after writing the poem, 'You see I cannot get on without writing as boys do at school a few nonsense verses–I begin them and before I have written six the whim has pass'd' (L ii 188); for earlier unfinished pieces in a similar style see Fragment of the 'Castle Builder', And what is love (pp. 390 and 393 above).

Text from K.'s letter.

Published World (New York) 25 June 1877; repr. Forman (1883).

> Pensive they sit and roll their languid eyes,
> Nibble their toast and cool their tea with sighs;
> Or else forget the purpose of the night,
> Forget their tea, forget their appetite.
> 5   See, with crossed arms they sit. Ah, hapless crew!
> The fire is going out and no one rings
> For coals, and therefore no coals Betty brings.
> A fly is in the milk-pot–must he die
> Circled by a humane society?
> 10   No, no; there, Mr. Werter takes his spoon,
> Inserts it, dips the handle, and lo! soon
> The little straggler, saved from perils dark,
> Across the teaboard draws a long wet mark.
>   Romeo, arise! Take snuffers by the handle,
> 15   There's a large cauliflower in each candle,

¶ 139. *1. languid*] Languishing, as in *Lamia* i 15 (p. 617 above), 'languid Tritons . . .'

9. humane society] An allusion to the Royal Humane Society, founded 1774 to aid those in danger of drowning.

10–13. Mr. Werter] Goethe's *Die Leiden des jungen Werther* (1773) was translated by David Malthus as *The Sorrows of Werter: A German Story* (1783). K. is thinking of such passages as the following, 'Every moment I am myself a destroyer. The most innocent walk deprives of life thousands of poor insects; one step destroys the fabric of the industrious ant, and turns a little world into a chaos' (*The Sorrows of Werter* i 144–5).

15. cauliflower] Untrimmed wick.

A winding sheet . . . Ah, me! I must away
To No. 7, just beyond the Circus gay.
'Alas, my friend, your coat sits very well:
Where may your tailor live?' 'I may not tell.
20   Oh, pardon me–I'm absent now and then.
Where *might* my tailor live? I say again
I cannot tell. Let me no more be teased–
He lives in Wapping, *might* live where he pleased.'

16. *winding-sheet*] 'A mass of solidified drippings of grease clinging to the
side of a candle, resembling a sheet folded in creases, and regarded as an
omen of death or calamity, 1708' (*OED*).
17. *No. 7*] The context suggests either a fashionable tailoring establishment
or an undertaker's. The Circus is Piccadilly Circus in London.
23. *Wapping*] A district in East London near the docks.

140 To Autumn

Written *c.* 19 Sept. 1819 and the last of K.'s major 1819 odes; see K.'s letters
of (1) 21 Sept. 1819 to Reynolds from Winchester, 'How beautiful the
season is now–How fine the air. A temperate sharpness about it. Really,
without joking, chaste weather–Dian skies–I never lik'd stubble fields so
much as now–Aye better than the chilly green of the spring. Somehow a
stubble plain looks warm . . . this struck me so much in my sunday's walk
that I composed upon it' (*L* ii 167)–the Sunday in question fell on 19 Sept.
1819–and (2) 21–2 Sept. 1819 to Woodhouse, in which he copied out the
poem with the comment, 'You like Poetry . . . so you shall have some I
was going to give Reynolds' (*L* ii 170–1).

To Autumn differs from the Spring 1819 odes in mood. In stanzas 1 and 3
'ripeness is all' and Autumn is therefore a boundary between summer and
winter, between growth and decay. The personifications in stanza 2, which
suggest drowsiness and repose, lend some support to the theory that K.
added this stanza later (see ll. 12–22 *n* below). Metrically, the ode resembles
the four odes written *c.* May 1819, but K. adds an extra line to his earlier
ten-line stanza (stanza 1 rhymes *ababcdedcce*; stanzas 2 and 3 rhyme *ababc-
decdde*). *To Autumn* is usually seen as one of K.'s most poised achievements,
expressing a mood of calm acceptance although there is a characteristic
sense of the movement and processes of time at work throughout the poem.
Commentaries (apart from those included in general studies of the odes as a
group) include *Murry* (1925) 188–93; M. R. Ridley's ' "To Autumn" ' in
Ridley (1933) 281–90; F. R. Leavis's remarks in *Revaluation* (1936) 262–66;
A. Davenport's 'A Note on "To Autumn"' in *Reassessment* (1958) 95–101;
B. C. Southam's, 'The Ode "To Autumn"' in *KShJ* ix (Autumn 1960)
91–8; W. J. Bate's analysis in *Bate* (1963) 580–3; and Ian Jack's 'To Autumn'
in his *Keats and the Mirror of Art* (1967) 232–43.

Text from *1820*, with some variants noted from K.'s letter (referred to in the notes as *L*) and his earlier draft.
Published *1820*.

I

Season of mists and mellow fruitfulness,
    Close bosom friend of the maturing sun,
Conspiring with him how to load and bless
    With fruit the vines that round the thatch-eves run:
5   To bend with apples the mossed cottage-trees,
    And fill all fruit with ripeness to the core;
      To swell the gourd, and plump the hazel shells
    With a sweet kernel; to set budding more,
And still more, later flowers for the bees,
10 Until they think warm days will never cease,
      For summer has o'er-brimmed their clammy cells.

¶ 140. *1.* For these contradictory aspects of autumn K. may be drawing on Thomson's *The Seasons* (1730), *Autumn* 736–7,

      These roving mists that constant now begin
      To smoke along the hilly country . . .

and Wordsworth's *The Excursion* (1814) v 400,

    . . . mellow Autumn charged with bounteous fruit . . .

4. With fruit the vines] The vines with fruit *L*. With 'thatch-eves' cp. Coleridge's '. . . the nigh thatch . . .' and '. . . eave-drops . . .' in *Frost at Midnight* 69–70, quoted in 31–2 *n* below.
5–8. To bend . . . kernel] Images of ripeness and fulfilment. As Douglas Bush notes, 'In the first stanza the sense of fullness and heaviness is given through mainly tactile images; in the second they are mainly visual . . . in the last . . . the images are chiefly auditory' (*John Keats* (1967) 177).
5. Echoes Chatterton's *Aella* (1777) 184–5,

      When the fayre apple, rudde as even skie,
      Do bend the tree unto the fructyle ground . . .

See K.'s letter to Reynolds (headnote), 'I always somehow associate Chatterton with autumn' (*L* ii 167). With 'mossed cottage trees' cp. Coleridge's 'mossy apple-tree' in *Frost at Midnight* 69, quoted in ll. 31–2 *n* below.
6. ripeness] sweetness *Draft.* See K.'s 'Hymn to Pan', *Endymion* i 252–3 (p. 131 above),

      Broad leavèd fig trees even now foredoom
      Their ripened fruitage . . .

7. plump] Cp. K.'s earlier use of this colloquialism in *Endymion* iv 377 (p. 261 above),

      Ere a lean bat could plump its wintery skin . . .

8. sweet] white *Draft, L.*
11. Cp. *Enydmion* iii 38–40 (p. 208 above),

II
Who hath not seen thee oft amid thy store?
  Sometimes whoever seeks abroad may find
Thee sitting careless on a granary floor,
15   Thy hair soft-lifted by the winnowing wind;
Or on a half-reaped furrow sound asleep,
    Drowsed with the fume of poppies, while thy hook
      Spares the next swath and all its twinèd flowers;
And sometimes like a gleaner thou dost keep

. . . every sense
Filling with spiritual sweets to plenitude
As bees gorge full their cells . . .

12–22. Autumn is personified in this stanza. According to Ian Jack, the pictorial details are probably inspired by various paintings (see *nn* below) and 'about each of [the personifications] . . . there is even a slight suggestion of the classical figure of Ceres' (*Keats and the Mirror of Art*, 1967, 236). A. Davenport suggests that K. was recollecting the Biblical figure of Ruth ('A Note on "To Autumn"', *Reassessment*, 1958, 97). The numerous corrections in the draft suggest that the stanza may have been an afterthought. M. R. Ridley guesses, '. . . as Keats first wrote the poem it had only two stanzas . . . in copying it out he added what is now the second' (*Ridley* (1933) 282).

14–15. Ian Jack points out the similar pose in Giulio Romano's *Psyche asleep among the Grain* (*op. cit.* Plate xxxviii).

15. Followed in *Draft* by the cancelled line,
      While bright the Sun slants through the husky barn . . .

16–18. Ian Jack notes, 'A representation of harvesters resting during the heat of the day is a common feature of pictures of Autumn' and cites the engraving in Thomson's *Seasons* (1807 edn) of W. Hamilton's picture showing 'a boy-reaper asleep beside sheaves of grain, a rake, a basket, and a barrel. It is called the "Reaper's Repose"' (*op. cit.* 237).

17–18.   Dosed with red poppies; while thy reaping hook
      Spares for some slumbrous minutes the next swath . . .
Draft (cancelled).
For 'Drowsed' *L* has 'Dased'. Poppies, which even thirty years ago brightened cornfields, are traditionally associated with sleep (see *Sleep and Poetry* 13–14 *n*, p. 70 above).

19–20. Perhaps a recollection of the girl carrying a basket on her head in Poussin's painting 'Autumn, or The Grapes of the Promised Land' (Plate xxxix in *Keats and the Mirror of Art*). Ian Jack thinks it also possible that K. 'was influenced by Poussin's "Summer or Ruth and Boaz" [*op. cit.* Plate xl]', which shows Ruth pleading with Boaz among the 'alien corn' (see *Ode to a Nightingale* 66–7, *n* p. 530 above, and 12–22 *n* above). F. R. Leavis notes, 'In the step from the rime-word "keep", across . . . the pause en-

20   Steady thy laden head across a brook;
        Or by a cyder-press, with patient look,
           Thou watchest the last oozings hours by hours.

III

    Where are the songs of spring? Aye, where are they?
        Think not of them, thou hast thy music too—
25 While barrèd clouds bloom the soft-dying day,
        And touch the stubble-plains with rosy hue.
        Then in a wailful choir the small gnats mourn

---

forced by the line-division to "Steady", the balancing movement of the gleaner is enacted' (*Revaluation*, 1936, 263–4).

20. a] the *Draft.*

22. Cp. *Endymion* i 238 (p. 130 above),

    And through whole solemn hours dost sit, and hearken . . .

For 'oozings' the draft has 'oozing'.

23–33. A. Davenport comments: 'The music of Autumn which ends the poem is a music of living and dying, of staying and departure, of summer–winter' (*op. cit.*, p. 98).

25. barrèd . . . bloom] a gold . . . gilds *Draft (cancelled).* K.'s use of 'bloom' as a transitive verb is unusual; the suggestion is that the 'dying day' has paradoxically some of the characteristics of youth. The phrase '. . . barrèd clouds . . .' may derive from Coleridge's *Ode on Dejection* (1802, repr. *Sibylline Leaves*, 1817) 31,

    . . . those thin clouds above, in flakes and bars . . .

26. And touch] Touching the *Draft (cancelled).* See K.'s letter to Reynolds, 'Somehow a stubble plain looks warm . . .'. The phrase 'rosy hue' suggests dawn as well as sunset; cp. the use of 'bloom' in l. 25 above.

27–9. The phrasing suggests an echo of W. Kirby's and W. Spence's *An Introduction to Entomology* vol ii (1817), '. . . tribes of Tipulidae (usually, but improperly, called gnats) assemble . . . when the sun shines, and form themselves into choirs, that alternately rise and fall. . . . These little creatures may be seen at all seasons, amusing themselves with their choral dances' (4). See also the same authors' account of Ephemerae gnats (May-flies) swarming over a river at sunset in September, 'The choral dances consisted primarily of Ephemerae . . . alternately rising and falling' (*op. cit.* ii 6). The passages are noted in B. L. Woodruff's 'Keats's Wailful Choir of small Gnats', *MLN* (April 1953) 317–20.

27. See *Endymion* i 450 (p. 140 above), 'a wailful gnat' and Cowden Clarke (*Recollections* 126) on K.'s being much moved by *Cymbeline* I iii 20–1,

    . . . followed him, till he had melted from

    The smallness of a gnat to air . . .

The word 'mourn', obviously prompted here by the use of 'wailful', suggests that the gnats are lamenting for the shortness of their life and the lateness of the season.

22*

Among the river sallows, borne aloft
    Or sinking as the light wind lives or dies;
30 And full-grown lambs loud bleat from hilly bourn;
    Hedge-crickets sing; and now with treble soft
    The red-breast whistles from a garden-croft;
    And gathering swallows twitter in the skies.

28. sallows] Willows. On K.'s early fondness for this word see *I stood tip-
toe* 67 *n* (p. 89 above). Garrod's reading 'shallows' is an error.
29. or] and *Draft, L.*
30. hilly bourn] The downland bounding the horizon. See K.s description
of Winchester in his letter to Taylor of 5 Sept. 1819, '. . . there is on one
side of the city a dry chalky down where the air is worth six pence a pint'
(*L* ii 156).
31. Hedge-crickets sing] Carries associations of both summer and winter. See
On the Grasshopper and Cricket 3–5 (p. 98 above),

                    . . . a voice will run
        From hedge to hedge about the new-mown mead—
        That is the Grasshopper's . . .

and 10–12,

                        . . . when the frost
        Has wrought a silence, from the stove there shrills
        The cricket's song . . .

Cp. the dual associations (of maturity and immaturity) in the preceding
line's '. . . full-grown lambs . . .', i.e. the lambs of the previous spring.
31–2. and now . . . garden-croft] The context suggests a recollection of Coleridge's *Frost at Midnight* (1798, repr. *Sibylline Leaves*, 1817) 65–75,

        Therefore all seasons shall be sweet to thee,
        Whether the summer clothe the general earth
        With greenness, or the redbreast sit and sing
        Betwixt the tufts of snow on the bare branch
        Of mossy apple-tree, while the nigh thatch
        Smokes in the sun-thaw; whether the eave-drops fall
        Heard only in the trances of the blast,
        Or if the secret ministry of frost
        Shall hang them up in silent icicles,
        Quietly shining to the quiet Moon.

The lines may have been recalled to K. by association since he had echoed
Coleridge's poem in his sonnet *On the Grasshopper and Cricket* (see l. 31 *n*
above and ll. 10–11 *n* of the sonnet, p. 98 above), but some parallels in st. 1
with Coleridge's pictorial details (cp. ll. 4 *n*, 5 *n* above) hint that the lines
were working in his mind from the beginning.
33. gathering] now flock still *Draft* (*cancelled*); gather'd *L.* See Thomson's
Seasons (1730) *Autumn* 836–8, 846–8,

        When Autumn scatters his departing gleams,

> Warned of approaching Winter, gathered, play
> The swallow-people . . .
>
> They twitter cheerful, till the vernal months
> Invite them welcome back – for, thronging, now
> Innumerous wings are in commotion all . . .

The latter passage is quoted in A. Aiken's *Natural History of the Year* . . . (1815 edn), of which K. possessed a copy and which includes references to the 'softness and serenity of autumn' (135). K. may also have recollected Thomson's source in Virgil's *Aeneid* VI 309–12,

> *quam multa in silvis autumni frigore primo*
> *lapsa cadunt folia, aut ad terram gurgite ab alto*
> *quam multae glomerantur aves, ubi frigidus annus*
> *trans pontum fugat et terris immittit apricis* . . .

('. . . thick as the leaves of the forest that at autumn's first frost dropping fall, and thick as the birds that from the seething deep flock shoreward, when the chill of the year drives them overseas and sends them into sunny lands' [Loeb edn].)

141 The Fall of Hyperion. A Dream

Begun July 1819 in the Isle of Wight as a reconstruction of *Hyperion* (p. 394 above), largely completed in its present form by 21 Sept. 1819 when K. was at Winchester, and possibly further worked on Nov.–Dec. 1819 in London: for the first date see K.'s reference in his letter of 25 July 1819 to Fanny Brawne to his being '. . . all day employ'd in a very abstract Poem' (*L* ii 132)–*Hyperion* had been abandoned 21 April 1819 and K. was currently writing *Lamia* and *Otho the Great*, neither of which is 'abstract'–and his letter to Bailey of 14 Aug. 1819, 'I have also been writing parts of my Hyperion' (*L* ii 139); for the Sept. date see K.'s statement in his letter to Reynolds of 21 Sept. 1819, 'I have given up Hyperion' (*L* ii 167); evidence for K.'s attempt to work further on the poem in Nov.–Dec. 1819 is offered by Charles Brown, who records that K. was 'deeply engaged in remodelling his poem of "Hyperion" into a "vision" while also writing *The Cap and Bells* (see headnote, p. 701 below), but the fact that the 'few lines from Hyperion' (i 1–11, 61–86; ii 1–4, 6) which K. had copied out in his letter to Woodhouse of 21 Sept. 1819 (*L* ii 171–2) include a passage occurring towards the end of the poem–though not conclusively, since the passage in question could have originally occupied an earlier place in the narrative–that he had already carried out most of the 'remodelling' which he found it possible to complete.

Any work carried out by K. on the poem after Sept. 1819 presumably included attempts to reduce the effects of Milton's influence, which he no longer welcomed. His enthusiasm for Milton is expressed in his letter to Bailey of 14 Aug. 1819, 'Shakespeare and the paradise Lost every day become greater wonders to me–I look upon fine Phrases like a Lover' (*L* ii 139) and again in his letter to Reynolds of 24 Aug. 1819, '. . . the Paradise Lost becomes a greater wonder–The more I know what my diligence may in time probably effect; the more does my heart distend with Pride and Obstinacy [cp. *Paradise Lost* i 571–2]' (*L* ii 146).

K.'s reasons for abandoning *The Fall of Hyperion* are given in his letter to Reynolds of 21 Sept., '. . . there were too many Miltonic inversions in it– Miltonic verse cannot be written but in an artful or rather artist's humour. I wish to give myself up to other sensations. English ought to be kept up. It may be interesting to you to pick out some lines from Hyperion and put a mark X to the false beauty proceeding from art, and one // to the true voice of feeling' (*L* ii 167); cp. also his further comments in his Sept. 1819 journal-letter, 'I have but lately stood on my guard against Milton. Life to him would be death to me. Miltonic verse cannot be written but in the vein of art–I wish to devote myself to another sensation' (*L* ii 212).

Traces of Milton's influence are frequently apparent in the poem, but its reconstruction in the form of a vision, the cadence in a number of passages, and various incidental details are strongly affected–notably in the new introductory material (i 1–293)–by K.'s reading of Dante's *Divina Commedia*, especially the *Purgatorio*, both in Cary's translation and also in the original. K. was teaching himself Italian in the summer of 1819 and had made headway in reading Ariosto in the original by 5 Sept. (*L* ii 157); under 24 Sept. in his Sept. 1819 journal-letter he writes, 'In the course of a few months I shall be as good an Italian Scholar as I am a french one–I am reading Ariosto at present . . . I like to be acquainted with foreign languages. . . Also the reading of Dante is well worth the while' (*L* ii 212). K. may also have taken hints for re-casting his poem in the form of a vision from Coleridge's *Allegoric Vision* (1811, repr. *A Lay Sermon* 1817) and Addison's *Vision of Mirzah* (1710, quoted in *Baldwin* (1806)). For echoes of K.'s other reading in the poem, including Hyginus's *Fabulae* (1742 edn) and Potter's *Antiquities of Greece* (1697), see the notes below.

In reconstructing the poem as a vision in which the defeat of the Titans is related by the priestess Moneta K. lays stronger personal emphasis on the theme of suffering and its effect on the poetic imagination, which he had brought to a climax in *Hyperion* iii. The revised version opens with a short 'induction' (i 1–18) followed by an introduction on this theme, in which K. also faces the general question of the poet's value to humanity and the particular question of his own poetic achievement. The adaptation of the original narrative begins at i 294 with the appearance of Saturn and Thea, omits the description of their fallen fellow-Titans, and ends with the introduction of Hyperion (Canto ii 13–61). The poem was abandoned partly for the reasons given in K.'s letter to Reynolds, but other obvious reasons include failing health, the difficulty of sustaining the work both as a 'prophetic' vision and also as an exploratory personal statement, and the crucial fact that K. had already given dramatic expression to his major themes in the encounter with Moneta in the poem's first canto. K.'s decision to omit

The Fall of Hyperion from *1820* was probably based on his own dissatisfaction with his failure to complete it, but may also have been encouraged by the preference of his friends for the earlier unfinished *Hyperion*; the preference is referred to by Brown in his 1841 'Life of Keats' (*KC* ii 72). Critics are less divided than formerly over the relative merits of 'the two "Hyperions",' though they continue to differ over the degree of allegorical intention in the later poem. W. T. Arnold preferred the earlier version (Introduction to *The Poetical Works of John Keats*, 1888); Bridges–some of whose comments are recorded below–regarded the introduction to *The Fall of Hyperion* as K.'s 'most mature attempt . . . to express his own convictions concerning human life' (Introduction to *Poems of John Keats*, ed. G. Thorn Drury 1896, xlvi); de Selincourt saw the poem as on the whole an unsuccessful attempt at allegory showing evidence of K.'s declining poetic power (see the introduction to his 'Transliteration of the Manuscript of the Fall of Hyperion' in *Hyperion* (1905) and *de Selincourt* 515–16); and Colvin found value in the 'wholly new preamble or introduction', but felt that the 'de-Miltonizing and de-latinizing' of passages taken over from the earlier version were 'sometimes terribly to their disadvantage' (*Colvin* (1917) 447). Modern critics have generally recognized the strengthened promise of poetic maturity both in the new material and in the adaptation of passages from the earlier version. Substantial commentaries on the poem appear in *Murry* (1926) 169–87; J. L. Lowes's '"Hyperion' and the "Purgatorio"', *TLS* Jan. 11 1936, and his 'Moneta's Temple' *PMLA* li (1936) 1098–1113; *Ridley* (1936) 266–80; K. Muir's 'The Meaning of "Hyperion"', *Reassessment* (1958) 111–22; *Bate* (1963) 587–605; J. Saly's 'K.'s Answer to Dante: "The Fall of Hyperion",' *KShJ* XIV (1965) 65–78.

Text from *Woodhouse 2*, with some variants noted from *1856* and from the extracts copied out by K. in his letter of Sept. 1819 (referred to in the notes as *L*).

Published by Milnes in *Biographical and Historical Miscellanies of the Philobiblion Society* (1856).

CANTO I

Fanatics have their dreams, wherewith they weave
A paradise for a sect, the savage too
From forth the loftiest fashion of his sleep
Guesses at Heaven; pity these have not
5 Traced upon vellum or wild Indian leaf
The shadows of melodious utterance.

i *1–11. Fanatics . . . enchantment*] Copied out by K. in his Sept. 1819 letter to Woodhouse with the comment, 'Here is what I had written for a sort of induction' (*L* ii 172).
i *1. Fanatics*] Enthusiasts for a particular religious creed.
i *3.* Out of his noblest dreams.

But bare of laurel they live, dream, and die;
For Poesy alone can tell her dreams,
With the fine spell of words alone can save
10 Imagination from the sable charm
And dumb enchantment. Who alive can say,
'Thou art no poet; may'st not tell thy dreams'?
Since every man whose soul is not a clod
Hath visions, and would speak, if he had loved
15 And been well nurtured in his mother tongue.
Whether the dream now purposed to rehearse
Be poet's or fanatic's will be known
When this warm scribe my hand is in the grave.

Methought I stood where trees of every clime,

i 7. K. may be thinking of Gray's *Elegy in a Country Churchyard* (1751) 59,
Some mute inglorious Milton here may rest . . .

i 9–11. *With . . . enchantment*] Those who cannot express themselves are
like victims of an enchantment from which poetry alone has a magic strong
enough to release them.

i 10. *charm*] The reading 'chain' in *1856* is probably an error.

i 19–92. The opening stages of K.'s 'dream' recall his early commitment to
the idea of development from simple sensuous enjoyment to an understanding of the darker realities of existence (see *Sleep and Poetry* 96–154 *n*,
101–21 *n*, 122–54 *n*, pp. 73, 73–4 and 74–6 above): he experiences a period
of untroubled happiness in a garden which resembles Eden and also recalls
the Golden Age of Saturn's reign (i 19–40); falls reluctantly into a 'cloudy
swoon' after drinking from a vessel in the garden (i 41–57); awakens in an
austere temple whose black gates are 'shut against the sunrise evermore' (i
58–86); and begins to make his way painfully towards a shrine situated
'far off' at the western end of the sanctuary (i 87–92). According to Robert
Bridges, 'The garden and the feast represent the beauties of Nature, and the
drink is poetry, which is made from the fruits of the feast. The intoxication
which followed the draught represents that complete and excited absorption
by poetry which Keats describes himself as suffering when he was writing
Endymion, and the swoon would be that state of selfish isolation into which
he fell in his Miltonic period. His awakening in the temple is his recovery
from this to a sympathy with the miseries of the world [see i 147–9 below];
and the temple itself is the temple of Knowledge' (Introduction to *The
Poems of John Keats* ed. G. Thorn Drury 1896 (li–lii)).

i 19–27. K.'s paradise owes something to *Paradise Lost* v 377–9 (marked by
him in his copy of Milton),

. . . So to the Silvan Lodge
They came, that like *Pomona's* Arbour smil'd
With flourets deck't and fragrant smells . . .

but his phrasing is individual. With the arbour in i 25–7 cp., for example,
Ode to Psyche 59–61 (p. 520 above),

20   Palm, myrtle, oak, and sycamore, and beech,
      With plantain, and spice-blossoms, made a screen—
      In neighbourhood of fountains, by the noise
      Soft-showering in my ears, and, by the touch
      Of scent, not far from roses. Turning round,
25   I saw an arbour with a drooping roof
      Of trellis vines, and bells, and larger blooms,
      Like floral censers swinging light in air;
      Before its wreathèd doorway, on a mound
      Of moss, was spread a feast of summer fruits,
30   Which, nearer seen, seemed refuse of a meal
      By angel tasted, or our Mother Eve;
      For empty shells were scattered on the grass,
      And grape-stalks but half bare, and remnants more,
      Sweet-smelling, whose pure kinds I could not know.
35   Still was more plenty than the fabled horn
      Thrice emptied could pour forth at banqueting

      A rosy sanctuary will I dress
      With the wreathed trellis of a working brain,
        With buds, and bells, and stars without a name . . .

and with 'floral censers' cp. also *Ode to a Nightingale* 42 (p. 528 above),
        . . . soft incense hangs upon the boughs . . .

i *31*. K. is thinking of *Paradise Lost* v 303–7,
        And *Eve* within, due at her hour prepar'd
        For dinner savourie fruits, of taste to please
        True appetite, and not disrelish thirst
        Of nectarous draughts between, from milkie stream,
        Berrie or Grape . . .

See also v 326–8,
        . . . I will haste and from each bough and break,
        Each Plant and juciest Gourd will pluck such choice
        To entertain our Angel guest . . .

Both passages are marked by K. in his copy of Milton.

i *32–4*. Cp. *Paradise Lost* v 341–4 (marked by K. in his copy of Milton),
        . . . fruit of all kindes, in coate,
        Rough, or smooth rin'd, or bearded husk, or shell
        She gathers, Tribute large, and on the board
        Heaps with unsparing hand . . .

The 'remnants' have been left by other 'dreamers' who have been allowed
to experience a brief period of unalloyed happiness. See i 177–80 below.

i *35. fabled horn*] The cornucopia, an emblem of Proserpine's mother
Ceres, the goddess of corn. Cp. *Lamia* ii 186–7 (p. 642 above),
        . . . the store thrice told
      Of Ceres' horn . . .

For Proserpine returned to her own fields,
Where the white heifers low. And appetite
More yearning than on earth I ever felt
40   Growing within, I ate deliciously;
And, after not long, thirsted, for thereby
Stood a cool vessel of transparent juice,
Sipped by the wandered bee, the which I took,
And, pledging all the mortals of the world,
45   And all the dead whose names are in our lips,
Drank. That full draught is parent of my theme.
No Asian poppy, nor elixir fine
Of the soon-fading jealous Caliphat;
No poison gendered in close monkish cell,
50   To thin the scarlet conclave of old men,
Could so have rapt unwilling life away.
Among the fragrant husks and berries crushed,
Upon the grass I struggled hard against

i 37. On K.'s fondness for the legend of Proserpine see *Endymion* i 944 *n* (p. 162 above). Perhaps suggested here by Dante's *Purgatorio* xxviii 49–51,

> *Tu mi fai rimembrar, dove e qual era*
> *Proserpina nel tempo che perdette*
> *la madre lei, ed ella primavera . . .*

('I call to mind where wander'd and how look'd / Proserpine, in that season, when her child / The mother lost, and she the bloomy spring . . .' [Cary's translation]).

i 42. Cp *Paradise Lost* v 344–8,

> . . . for drink the Grape
> She crushes, inoffensive moust, and meathes
> From many a berrie, and from sweet kernels prest
> She tempers dulcet creams, nor these to hold
> Wants her fit vessels pure . . .

i 47–51. Suggested by K.'s reading of oriental and gothic tales. With the 'Elixir' of the 'jealous Caliphat' cp., for example, in 'The History of Ganem' in *The Arabian Nights*, the attempt by the Caliph's jealous wife Zobeide to do away with Fetnah, '. . . she . . . gave me a drug, which causes such a deep sleep, that it is easy to dispose of those who have taken it; and that sleep is so profound, that nothing can dispel it from the space of seven or eight hours' (Weber's *Tales of the East* i 280). The 'scarlet conclave' (i 50) is the college of cardinals who elect a new pope from their number when the pope dies: the poison from the monk's cell is presumably part of a 'Gothick' plot concerning the papal succession.

i 47. *soon-fading*] Woodhouse notes, 'originally death-doing'.

i 53–5. The phrasing recalls Cary's *Dante, Purgatorio* ix 9–10,

> When I, who had so much of Adam with me,
> Sank down upon the grass, o'ercome with sleep . . .

The domineering potion; but in vain—
55 The cloudy swoon came on, and down I sunk,
Like a Silenus on an antique vase.
How long I slumbered 'tis a chance to guess.
When sense of life returned, I started up
As if with wings; but the fair trees were gone,
60 The mossy mound and arbour were no more.
I looked around upon the carvèd sides
Of an old sanctuary with roof august,
Builded so high it seemed that filmèd clouds
Might spread beneath, as o'er the stars of heaven.
65 So old the place was, I remembered none
The like upon the earth: what I had seen
Of grey cathedrals, buttressed walls, rent towers,
The superannuations of sunk realms,
Or nature's rocks toiled hard in waves and winds,
70 Seemed but the faulture of decrepit things
To that eternal domèd monument.
Upon the marble at my feet there lay

i 56. *Silenus*] See *Endymion* iv 215–17 n (p. 255 above). K. may be recollecting here the drooping figure on the Borghese Vase (Plate XXXVII in Ian Jack's *Keats and the Mirror of Art*, 1967).

i 59–60. *the fair trees . . . no more*] K. awakens from his trance into a more sombre world. Cp. his May 1819 letter to Sarah Jeffrey, '. . . the world has taken on a quakerish look with me, which I once thought was impossible—

Nothing can bring back the hour
Of splendour in the grass and glory in the flower

I once thought this a Melancholist's dream' (*L* ii 113)–K. is misquoting Wordsworth's *Immortality Ode* 181–2.

i 64. *spread*] sail *L*.

i 65. *remembered*] remember *L*.

i 67. *grey cathedrals, buttressed walls*] A reference to the cathedrals and medieval buildings seen at Winchester, where K. was staying when he began to reconstruct *Hyperion* in July 1819 (headnote), and Chichester, which he visited Jan. 1819. The 'rent towers' are recollected from his walking-tour of the Lakes and Scotland in the summer of 1818.

i 68. *superannuations*] Obsolete remains. The effectiveness of the line depends on K.'s use of the abstract noun 'superannuation' (an archaism for infirmity or decay) as a concrete noun in the plural.

i 69. *toiled hard*] hard toil'd *L*. K. may be remembering in particular the rocks of Iona and Staffa which he saw in the summer of 1818. See *To Ailsa Rock, Not Aladdin magian, Read me a lesson, Muse* (pp. 364, 372 and 375 above).

i 70. *faulture*] Weakness. A neologism. K.'s letter copy has 'failing'.

i 72 (and i 91, 108, 214 below). *marble*] A descriptive detail perhaps owing

Store of strange vessels and large draperies,
Which needs had been of dyed asbestos wove,
75 Or in that place the moth could not corrupt,
So white the linen; so, in some, distinct
Ran imageries from a sombre loom.
All in a mingled heap confused there lay
Robes, golden tongs, censer and chafing-dish,
80 Girdles, and chains, and holy jewelleries.
Turning from these with awe, once more I raised
My eyes to fathom the space every way—
The embossed roof, the silent massy range
Of columns north and south, ending in mist
85 Of nothing, then to eastward, where black gates
Were shut against the sunrise evermore.
Then to the west I looked, and saw far off

---

something to Dante's frequent references to the marble steps and terraces of the Mount of Purgatory.

i 74. asbestos] A mineral of fibrous texture, capable of being woven into an incombustible fabric (OED). See also A. Adams's Roman Antiquities (1792), '. . . a species of incombustible cloth, made of what the Greeks called Asbestos' (483). K. owned a copy of Adams.

i 75. Or else woven in heaven. See Matthew vi 19–20: 'Lay not up for yourselves treasures upon earth, where moth and rust doth corrupt and where thieves break through and steal. But lay up for yourselves treasures in heaven, where neither moth nor rust doth corrupt.'

i 77. imageries] Embroidered designs. Cp. The Eve of St. Agnes 209 (p. 466 above), 'garlanded with carven imageries'.

i 79–80. Objects connected with religious ritual, most of which are mentioned in the directions given to the Israelites for the building of the tabernacle in Exodus. The 'chafing-dish' is a thurible or censer.

i 83–4. The embossed roof . . . south] K. is thinking of a Greek temple, but the phrasing recalls Milton's Il Penseroso 157–8,

                . . . the high embowed Roof,
        With antick Pillars massy proof . . .

For 'massy' L has 'massive'.

i 84–5. ending in mist / Of nothing] Perhaps suggested by the tide of eternity in Addison's The Vision of Mirzah (quoted in the chapter on Allegory in Baldwin 13), 'What is the reason, I asked, that the tide . . . rises out of a thick mist at the other? What thou seest, says he, is that portion of eternity which is called time' (Spectator no. 159, 1 Sept. 1710).

i 85–6. Eastwards . . . sunrise] See Potter's Antiquities of Greece, 'The way of building temples towards the east, so as the doors being opened, should receive the rising sun, was very ancient' (i 224).

i 87–9. Then to the west . . . slept] See Potter's Antiquities, 'Almost all the temples were then so contrived, that the entrance and statues should look

An image, huge of feature as a cloud,
At level of whose feet an altar slept,
90   To be approached on either side by steps,
And marble balustrade, and patient travail
To count with toil the innumerable degrees.
Towards the altar sober-paced I went,
Repressing haste as too unholy there;
95   And, coming nearer, saw beside the shrine
One ministering; and there arose a flame.
When in mid-May the sickening east wind

---

towards the east, and they who paid their devotion towards the west. . . .
The place of the images was in the middle of the temple, where they stood
on pedestals raised above the height of the altar' (i 224, 227).

i 88. *An image*] Of Saturn. See i 224–6 below.

i 90–2. Perhaps inspired by the steep ascent of the Mount of Purgatory, each
terrace of which is reached by a flight of steps; see, e.g., *Purgatorio* ix 94–
102,

> Là' ve venimmo, allo scaglion primaio,
> bianco marmo era sì pulito e terso,
> ch'io mi specchiai in esso quale io paio.

> Era il secondo tinto più che perso,
> d'una petrina ruvida ed arsiccia,
> crepata per lo lungo e per traverso . . .

('We straightway thither came. / The lowest stair was marble white, so
smooth / And polish'd, that therein my mirror'd form / Distinct I saw.
The next of hue more dark / Than sablest grain, a rough and singed block, /
Crack'd lengthwise and across' [Cary]). See also i 132–6 *n* below. Bridges
comments 'The steps to the altar are the struggle of a mind to reach truth'
(*op. cit.* lii).

i 93–4. Cp. *Purgatorio* iii 10–11,

> . . . li piedi suoi lasciàr la fretta,
> che l'onestade ad ogni atto dismaga . . .

('. . . his feet desisted (slack'ning pace) / From haste, that mars all decency of
act' [Cary]).

i 96. *One ministering*] Moneta, the priestess of the temple. See i 226 *n* below.

i 97–101. On winter as a sickness cured by spring see *After dark vapours* 1–4
n (p. 101 above). With the phrasing and cadence in i 97–9 cp. Dante's
Purgatorio xxiv 145–7,

> E quale, annunziatrice degli albori,
> l'aura di maggio movesi ed olezza,
> tutta l'impregnata dall'erba e da' fiori . . .

> tal mi sentii un vento dar per mezza
> la fronte . . .

Shifts sudden to the south, the small warm rain
Melts out the frozen incense from all flowers,
100 And fills the air with so much pleasant health
That even the dying man forgets his shroud.
Even so that lofty sacrificial fire,
Sending forth Maian incense, spread around
Forgetfulness of everything but bliss,
105 And clouded all the altar with soft smoke,
From whose white fragrant curtains thus I heard
Language pronounced: 'If thou canst not ascend
These steps, die on that marble where thou art.
Thy flesh, near cousin to the common dust,
110 Will parch for lack of nutriment—thy bones
Will wither in few years, and vanish so
That not the quickest eye could find a grain
Of what thou now art on that pavement cold.
The sands of thy short life are spent this hour,
115 And no hand in the universe can turn
Thy hourglass, if these gummed leaves be burnt
Ere thou canst mount up these immortal steps.'
I heard, I looked: two senses both at once,
So fine, so subtle, felt the tyranny
120 Of that fierce threat and the hard task proposed.

('As when, to harbinger the dawn, springs up / On freshen'd wing the air of May, and breathes / Of fragrance, all impregn'd with herb and flowers; / E'en such a wind I felt upon my front' [Cary].)

i *97. mid-May*] midway *Woodhouse* 2; midday *1856*. The emendation was suggested by A. E. Housman (*TLS* 4 May 1924). Cp. i 103 below, '. . . Maian incense . . .' and *Ode to a Nightingale* 48 (p. 528 above), 'mid-May's eldest child'.

i *98. the small warm rain*] Perhaps echoing the anonymous sixteenth-century lyric (first printed by Joseph Ritson in his introduction to *Ancient Songs and Ballads*, 1790),

Westron wynde, when wyll thow blow,
The smalle rayne downe can rayne . . .

i *103. Maian incense*] A perfume like that of spring flowers. The epithet 'Maian' derives from Maia, the goddess celebrated in the *Ode to May* (p. 353 above). Cp. K.'s use of 'incense' for the scent of flowers in *Ode to a Nightingale* 42, quoted in i 19–27 *n* above.

i *116. gummed leaves*] The leaves of aromatic trees. See Potter's *Antiquities*, '. . . broken fruits, leaves, or acorns, the only sacrifice of the ancients; whence in Suidas, Tà gúm . . . or incense . . . there were no sacrifices in primitive times . . . whereof trees or some parts of them were not made a considerable part of the oblation. These were chiefly oderiferous trees' (i 252–3).

Prodigious seemed the toil; the leaves were yet
Burning–when suddenly a palsied chill
Struck from the pavèd level up my limbs,
And was ascending quick to put cold grasp
125　Upon those streams that pulse beside the throat.
I shrieked; and the sharp anguish of my shriek
Stung my own ears. I strove hard to escape
The numbness, strove to gain the lowest step.
Slow, heavy, deadly was my pace; the cold
130　Grew stifling, suffocating, at the heart;
And when I clasped my hands I felt them not.
One minute before death, my iced foot touched
The lowest stair; and as it touched, life seemed
To pour in at the toes. I mounted up,
135　As once fair Angels on a ladder flew
From the green turf to Heaven. 'Holy Power,'
Cried I, approaching near the hornèd shrine,
'What am I that should so be saved from death?

i *122–31. a palsied chill . . . I felt them not*] Clinical signs of the approach of
death (cp. i 141–2 below, 'Thou hast felt / What 'tis to die and live
again . . .'). K. had been present at Tom's deathbed and had walked
hospital wards professionally.

i *125. those streams that pulse beside the throat*] The carotid arteries, which
carry the blood to the neck.

i *132–6. my iced foot . . . to Heaven*] The sudden change from the 'prodigious
toil' of crossing the 'paved level' to the easy ascent of the steps suggests a
debt to Dante's *Purgatorio* xii 115–26,

> Già montavam su per li scaglion santi,
>   ed esser mi parea troppo più lieve,
>   che per lo pian non mi parea davanti;

> ond' io: 'Maestro, di', qual cosa greve
>   levata s'è da me, che nulla quasi
>   per me fatica andando si receve?'

('We climb the holy stairs: / And lighter to myself by far I seem'd / Than
on the plain before; whence thus I spake: / "Say, master, of what heavy
thing have I / Been lighten'd; that scarce aught the sense of toil / Affects me
journeying?"' [Cary].)

i *135–6. As once . . . Heaven*] See *Genesis* xxviii 12: 'And [Jacob] . . .
dreamed, and behold a ladder set up on the earth, and the top of it reached
to heaven: and behold the angels of God ascending and descending on it.'

i *137. hornèd shrine*] See Potter's *Antiquities*, 'The most ancient altars were
adorned with horns' (i 229.)

i *138–210.* K. casts his attempt to assess the value of the poet to humanity
and also his own poetic position in the form of a dialogue with Moneta

What am I that another death come not
140 To choke my utterance sacrilegious here?'
Then said the veilèd shadow: 'Thou hast felt
What 'tis to die and live again before
Thy fated hour. That thou hadst power to do so
Is thy own safety; thou hast dated on

---

indicative of the urgent movements of his current debate with himself. The main points are roughly as follows: (1) only those who are aware of human suffering can reach 'this height', i.e. the spiritual and imaginative experience expressed in the preceding lines (i 138–49); (2) those who escape from the realities of life into selfish seclusion cannot attain the experience – if they suddenly perceive the cruelty of existence it breaks them (i 150–3); (3) those who not only feel for humanity but also labour in its service are superior to 'visionaries' and 'dreamers' and their fulfilment lies in human life and happiness (i 154–66); (4) K. thinks that he may be merely a 'dreamer' and, if so, can be of no use to the world or to himself, since dreamers are misfits and, unlike other men, are incapable of experiencing even brief moments of unclouded happiness (i 166–76); (5) the experiences in the garden and temple are offered to 'dreamers' as a compensation for their disabilities (i 177–85); (6) K. qualifies his statement about the uselessness of 'dreamers' –some are poets whose work is of service to their fellow-men (i 186–90); (7) K.'s doubts about his own claim to the title of poet heighten his sense of the sharp distinction between the 'poet' and the 'dreamer', a distinction seen primarily in terms not of their awareness but of the effects of their work on others (i 191–202); (8) K. is outraged by those writers–Byron in particular–whose pretensions to the title of poet seem to him to be flagrantly dishonest (i 202–210).

i *141–5. Then said . . . doom*] The knowledge of suffering and death brings its reward in the renewal and extension of life; the mood expressed recalls Oceanus's speech to the doomed Titans in *Hyperion* ii 203–5 (p. 427 above),

> . . . to bear all naked truths,
> And to envisage circumstance, all calm,
> That is the top of sovereignty . . .

i *141. veilèd shadow*] K.'s references to Moneta as a 'shade' (i 147, 155, 194, 216, 282 below) or a 'shadow' (i 187, 211 below) are probably owed to Dante's use of *ombra* (shade, shadow) throughout the *Purgatorio*. Moneta's being 'veiled'–cp. i 194, 216, 252–3 below–may be yet another detail affected by Dante, since the figure of Beatrice is veiled in *Purgatorio* xxx-xxxi, but the mysteriousness of K.'s veiled figure almost certainly owes something to traditional accounts of the ancient Egyptian goddess Isis as representing universal knowledge and truth; see *Lemprière*: 'The word *Isis*, according to some authors, signifies *antient*, and, on that account, the inscriptions on the statues of the goddess were often in these words: *I am all that has been, that shall be, and none among mortals has hitherto taken off my veil.*'

i *144. dated on*] Postponed.

145   Thy doom.' 'High Prophetess,' said I, 'purge off,
     Benign, if so it please thee, my mind's film.'
     'None can usurp this height,' returned that shade,
     'But those to whom the miseries of the world
     Are misery, and will not let them rest.
150   All else who find a haven in the world,
     Where they may thoughtless sleep away their days,
     If by a chance into this fane they come,
     Rot on the pavement where thou rotted'st half.'
     'Are there not thousands in the world,' said I,

i *145–6. purge off . . . my mind's film*] Help me to understand clearly. The phrasing 'purge off / Benign . . .' is Miltonic. Other examples of Miltonic inversion in the poem include i 184 'sickness not ignoble', i 215 'accent feminine', i 267 'visionless entire', i 283 'act adorant'.

i *147–59. None can usurp . . . mortal good?*] A. C. Bradley notes parallels with the thought, and occasionally the phrasing, of Shelley's attempt to distinguish the self-absorption of the poet from the self-centredness of other people in his preface to *Alastor* (1816): 'The Poet's self-centred seclusion was avenged by the furies of an irresistible passion pursuing him to speedy ruin. . . . Those [meaner spirits] who . . . keep aloof from sympathies with their kind, rejoicing neither in human joy nor mourning with human grief; these, and such as they, have their apportioned curse. . . . They are morally dead. They are neither friends, nor lovers, nor fathers, nor citizens of the world, nor benefactors of their country. Among those who attempt to exist without human sympathy, the pure and tender-hearted perish through the intensity and passion of their search after its communities, when the vacancy of their spirit suddenly makes itself felt. All else, selfish, blind, and torpid, are those unforeseeing multitudes who constitute, together with their own, the lasting misery and loneliness of the world. Those who love not their fellow-beings, live unfruitful lives, and prepare for their old age a miserable grave. . . .' Bradley felt that the reader could 'hardly doubt that some unconscious recollection of the Preface was at work in Keats's mind' ('The Letters of John Keats', *Oxford Lectures on Poetry*, 1909, 242).

i *147–9.* With the dependence of poetic power upon insight into human suffering cp. *Hyperion* iii 113–20 and *n* (p. 440 above),

     Knowledge enormous makes a God of me.
     Names, deeds, grey legends, dire events, rebellions,
     Majesties, sovran voices, agonies,
     Creations and destroyings, all at once
     Pour into the wide hollows of my brain,
     And deify me, as if some blithe wine
     Or bright elixir peerless I had drunk,
     And so become immortal . . .

i *154–9. Are there not . . . mortal good*] K. is less optimistic in his Feb.–May 1819 journal-letter, '. . . very few have been influenced by a pure desire ›

155   Encouraged by the sooth voice of the shade,
        'Who love their fellows even to the death;
        Who feel the giant agony of the world;
        And more, like slaves to poor humanity,
        Labour for mortal good? I sure should see
160   Other men here: but I am here alone.'
        'Those whom thou spak'st of are no visionaries,'
        Rejoined that voice. 'They are no dreamers weak,
        They seek no wonder but the human face;
        No music but a happy-noted voice—
165   They come not here, they have no thought to come—
        And thou art here, for thou art less than they.
        What benefit canst thou do, or all thy tribe,
        To the great world? Thou art a dreaming thing,
        A fever of thyself. Think of the earth;

---

the benefit of others—in the greater part of the Benefactors . . . to Humanity some meretricious motive has sullied their greatness—some melodramatic scenery has fascinated them' (*L* ii 79). For K.'s further views on 'disinterestedness' in the same journal-letter see *Hyperion* ii 203–5 *n*, *To J. H. Reynolds Esq.* 93–105 *n* (pp. 427 and 325 above).

i *155. sooth*] Smooth. On K.'s use of this word see *Sleep and Poetry* 180 *n* (p. 77 above).

i *157. the giant agony of the world*] Recalls *Sleep and Poetry* 122–5 (p. 74 above),

> And can I ever bid these joys farewell?
> Yes, I must pass them for a nobler life,
> Where I may find the agonies, the strife
> Of human hearts . . .

Cp. Shelley's *Julian and Maddalo* (1824) 449–50,

> *Me*—who am as a nerve o'er which do creep
> The else unfelt oppressions of this earth . . .

i *161–2. visionaries . . . dreamers*] The terms are used synonymously to refer to those who have been admitted to 'this height' (i 147–9). Bridges judges that 'the visionaries are those who neglect conduct for the pursuit of any ideal' and that 'it is death for a visionary' to enter the 'temple of knowledge' [see i 19–92 *n* above] if he lacks sympathy with human suffering (*op. cit.* li–lii).

i *163.* Cp. K.'s letter to Taylor of 17 Nov. 1819, 'Wonders are no wonders to me. I am more at home amongst Men and women. I would rather read Chaucer than Ariosto' (*L* ii 234).

i *166.* Followed in *Woodhouse* 2 by the cancelled lines,

> Mankind thou lovest; many of thine hours
> Have been distempered with their miseries . . .

i *169. fever*] On the feverish excitement associated by K. with poetic creativity see *Hence burgundy, claret and port* 40–1 and *n* (p. 301 above) and

170 What bliss even in hope is there for thee?
       What haven? Every creature hath its home;
       Every sole man hath days of joy and pain,
       Whether his labours be sublime or low—
       The pain alone; the joy alone; distinct:
175 Only the dreamer venoms all his days,
       Bearing more woe than all his sins deserve.
       Therefore, that happiness be somewhat shared,
       Such things as thou art are admitted oft
       Into like gardens thou didst pass erewhile,
180 And suffered in these temples; for that cause
       Thou standest safe beneath this statue's knees.'
       'That I am favoured for unworthiness,
       By such propitious parley medicined
       In sickness not ignoble, I rejoice—
185 Aye, and could weep for love of such award.'
       So answered I, continuing: 'If it please,
       Majestic shadow, tell me: sure not all

---

his Aug. 1819 letter to J. H. Reynolds, '. . . this state of excitement in me
. . . is the only state for the best sort of Poetry' (*L* ii 147). The dreamer is in
need of healing—his 'fever' is a sickness (cp. i 184 *n* below); the poet, on the
other hand, is a healer: see below i 190, 'physician', i 201, 'pours out balm
upon the world'. The context diffusely suggests a recollection of *Macbeth*
III ii 23, 'life's fitful fever'. Cp. *Ode on Indolence* 33–4 *n* (p. 543 above).

i *170. there*] On earth.

i *172–6.* Ordinary men are capable of experiencing moments of unalloyed
happiness, but the 'dreamer' is always haunted by 'the miseries of the
world' in the abstract—loss, change, transience, death.

i *172. sole*] Single, but the context suggests overtones of its further meaning
'solitary'.

i *180. suffered in*] Permitted to enter.

i *182–4.* Expressing gratitude for Moneta's gentle treatment of him in spite
of his unworthiness and for the gracious speech with which she ministers to
his 'sickness'. The word 'medicined' is probably a Shakespearian echo; see
Endymion ii 484 *n* (p. 183 above).

i *184. sickness not ignoble*] K. modifies the conception of the dreamer's sickness expressed in the preceding lines (see i 169, 'a fever of thyself' and i 175,
'the dreamer venoms all his days'); it is 'not ignoble' since it is incurred
through insight into suffering, which brings its own spiritual and imaginative rewards (cp. i 141–5 *n* above and i 175–81 above).

i *187–210.* Omitted in *1856*. Woodhouse notes in his second transcript,
'Keats seems to have intended to erase this [i 187–9] and the next twenty-
one lines'—note the repetitions at i 187 and i 211, and at i 194–8 and i 216–
20. K. may have wished either to omit or revise the passage as a personal
digression out of key with the tone and style of the rest of the poem (see,

Those melodies sung into the world's ear
Are useless; sure a poet is a sage,
190   A humanist, physician to all men.
That I am none I feel, as vultures feel
They are no birds when eagles are abroad.
What am I then? Thou spakest of my tribe:
What tribe?' The tall shade veiled in drooping white
195   Then spake, so much more earnest, that the breath
Moved the thin linen folds that drooping hung
About a golden censer from the hand
Pendent: 'Art thou not of the dreamer tribe?
The poet and the dreamer are distinct,
200   Diverse, sheer opposite, antipodes.
The one pours out a balm upon the world,
The other vexes it.' Then shouted I
Spite of myself, and with a Pythia's spleen:

---

for example, the aggressive critical temper of i 202–10), but the lines are included in the text because of their merit and as indicating the movement of his thought and feeling when composing the poem.

i *190. humanist*] Humanitarian. See i 154–9 *n*. With the poet's threefold role as 'sage . . . humanist . . . physician', cp. K.'s early description of poetry in *Sleep and Poetry* 246–7 *n* (p. 80 above),

> . . . a friend
> To soothe the cares and lift the thoughts of man . . .

i *191–2.* K.'s simile limits the distance which he places between himself and the 'poet', since vultures and eagles, if unequal in beauty and power, still belong to the same family. For K.'s reflections on his own poetry in 1819 see his views on the present poem (headnote and i 16–18 above); his comments on *Isabella, The Eve of St. Agnes* and *Lamia* (headnotes, pp. 327, 451 and 615 above); and his letter of 17 Nov. 1819 to Taylor, 'I have come to a determination not to publish any thing I have now ready written; but for all that to publish a Poem before long and that I hope to make a fine one' (*L* ii 234).

i *194.* (and see i *216* below). *veiled in drooping white*] See i 141 *n* above. The word 'drooping' may be a pictorial detail derived from the *Purgatorio* xxx 67–8,

> *il vel che le scendea di testa . . .*

('. . . from her brow the veil descending' [Cary]).

i *201–2. The one . . . vexes it*] The poet 'pours out a balm upon the world' because of his wisdom and understanding (see above, i 169 *n*, i 190 *n*). The dreamer 'vexes'–i.e. disturbs and troubles–mankind, because he dwells on the darker side of existence without suggesting a way of facing it (cp. i 175–6 above).

i *202. Then shouted I*] Apollo mine *Woodhouse 2 (cancelled).*

i *203. Pythia's spleen*] See Potter's *Antiquities*, 'The person that delivered

'Apollo! Faded, far-flown Apollo!
205 Where is thy misty pestilence to creep
Into the dwellings, through the door crannies,
Of all mock lyrists, large self-worshippers
And careless hectorers in proud bad verse.
Though I breathe death with them it will be life
210 To see them sprawl before me into graves.
Majestic shadow, tell me where I am,
Whose altar this; for whom this incense curls;
What image this whose face I cannot see,
For the broad marble knees; and who thou art,
215 Of accent feminine, so courteous?'

    Then the tall shade, in drooping linens veiled,
Spoke out, so much more earnest that her breath
Stirred the thin folds of gauze that drooping hung
About a golden censer from her hand
220 Pendent; and by her voice I knew she shed
Long-treasured tears: 'This temple, sad and lone,
Is all spared from the thunder of a war
Foughten long since by giant hierarchy
Against rebellion; this old image here,
225 Whose carvèd features wrinkled as he fell,

---

the oracles of the god [Apollo] was a woman, whom they called Pythia, Pythonissa, and Phoebas' (i 324) and also, 'The Pythia . . . was no sooner inspired but she began immediately to swell and foam at the mouth . . . if the spirit was in a kind and gentle humour, her rage was not very violent; but if sullen and malignant, she was thrown into extreme fury' (i 326).

i *205. misty pestilence*] See *Baldwin*, 'Apollo is the author of plagues and contagious diseases . . . in this character he is introduced by Homer in the first book of the Iliad [i 9–12], causing a plague among the Greeks' (57).

i *207–8*. Probably aimed chiefly at Byron, one of the poets whom K. had in mind in his early attack on contemporary poetry in *Sleep and Poetry* 233–5 (p. 79 above),

          . . . the themes
    Are ugly clubs, the poets Polyphemes
    Disturbing the grand sea . . .

For K.'s views on Byron in 1819 see his comment in his Feb.–May 1819 journal-letter on Reynolds's skit on Wordsworth's *Peter Bell*, 'It would be just as well to trounce Lord Byron in the same manner' (L ii 84) and his reference to *Don Juan* in his Sept. 1819 journal-letter as 'Lord Byron's last flash poem' (L ii 192).

i *222. all spared*] All that is spared.

i *222–4. a war . . . against rebellion*] The war of the Titans against the rebellious Olympian gods.

Is Saturn's; I, Moneta, left supreme,
Sole priestess of his desolation.'
I had no words to answer, for my tongue,
Useless, could find about its roofèd home
230 No syllable of a fit majesty
To make rejoinder to Moneta's mourn.
There was a silence, while the altar's blaze
Was fainting for sweet food. I looked thereon,
And on the pavèd floor, where nigh were piled
235 Faggots of cinnamon and many heaps
Of other crispèd spice-wood—then again
I looked upon the altar, and its horns
Whitened with ashes, and its languorous flame,
And then upon the offerings again;
240 And so by turns—till sad Moneta cried:
'The sacrifice is done, but not the less,
Will I be kind to thee for thy good will.
My power, which to me is still a curse,
Shall be to thee a wonder; for the scenes
245 Still swooning vivid through my globèd brain,
With an electral changing misery,
Thou shalt with these dull mortal eyes behold,
Free from all pain, if wonder pain thee not.'
As near as an immortal's spherèd words

i 226. *Moneta*] Another name for Mnemosyne, the mother of the muses (see *Hyperion* ii 29 *n*, p. 418 above). K.'s source was Hyginus's *Fabulae* (1742 edn), where the name appears after Saturn and Ops in the author's list of Titans with the editorial gloss, 'Illa est Mnemosyne Hesiodo et Apollodoro' (3). K. reverts to the name Mnemosyne twice in the poem (i 331, ii 50), but probably felt that Moneta was more appropriate to his new conception of the priestess's wisdom and prophetic power. He knew from the editorial commentary in his edition of Hyginus that some classical authorities associated Moneta with Minerva, the goddess of wisdom, and probably also recollected from *Lemprière* that Juno was worshipped as Juno Moneta after she had warned the Romans of the Gauls' approaching assault on the Capitol.

i 227. *priestess . . . his*] goddess . . . this *1856*.

i 231. *mourn*] Mourning. K.'s use of the word as a noun is individual.

i 235–6. *cinnamon . . . spiced wood*] See i 116 *n* above.

i 237. *horns*] See i 137 *n* above.

i 245. *globèd brain*] K. is thinking of the lobes of the brain. For a similar reference inspired by his medical studies see *Ode to Psyche* 52 *n* (p. 519 above).

i 246. *electral*] Electrical.

i 249–50. Cp. Beatrice's attitude to Dante in *Purgatorio* xxx 79–80,

250   Could to a mother's soften, were these last.
         But yet I had a terror of her robes,
         And chiefly of the veils, that from her brow
         Hung pale, and curtained her in mysteries,
         That made my heart too small to hold its blood.
255   This saw that Goddess, and with sacred hand
         Parted the veils. Then saw I a wan face,

> *Così la madre al figlio par superba,*
> *com' ella parve a me . . .*

('With a mien / Of that stern majesty, which doth surround / A mother's
presence to her awe-struck child, / She look'd' [Cary].)

i *251–71.* A passage illustrating T. S. Eliot's comment in 'The Meta-
physical Poets' (1921), '. . . in the second "Hyperion" . . . there are traces
of a struggle towards unification of sensibility' (*Selected Essays* 1917–32
(1932), 288).

i *252–3.* See i 141 *n* above.

i *254.* Cp. *Purgatorio* xxx 46–7,

> *. . . Men che dramma*
> *di sangue m'è rimaso, che non tremmi . . .*

('There is no dram of blood, / That doth not quiver in me' [Cary].)

i *256–62. Then saw I . . . that face*] Moneta's face records all the experience
of the world. Her awe-inspiring appearance is an imaginative expansion of
K.'s earlier descriptions of Mnemosyne and Thea in the first *Hyperion*. See
Hyperion iii 59–60 (p. 437 above),

> Goddess! I have beheld those eyes before,
> And that eternal calm, and all that face . . .

and i 34–6 (p. 399 above),

> But oh, how unlike marble was that face!
> How beautiful, if sorrow had not made
> Sorrow more beautiful than Beauty's self . . .

In reworking these passages K. may have recalled the reference in *Baldwin*
to statues of Minerva showing her countenance as 'composed and awful'
(53) – cp. i 226 *n* above – and K.'s expression of his awed sense of revelation
may have gathered inspiration from the unveiling of Beatrice in the *Purgatorio* xxxi 136–44,

> '. . . *Per grazia fa noi grazia che disvele*
> *a lui la bocca tua, sì che discerna*
> *la seconda bellezza che tu cele.'*

> *O isplendor di viva luce eterna,*
> *chi pallido si fece sotto l'ombra*
> *sì di Parnaso, o bevve in sua cisterna,*

> *Che non paresse aver la mente ingombra,*
> *tentando a render te qual tu paresti*
> *là dove armonizzando il ciel t'adombra . . .*

Not pined by human sorrows, but bright-blanched
By an immortal sickness which kills not.
It works a constant change, which happy death
260 Can put no end to; deathwards progressing
To no death was that visage; it had passed
The lily and the snow; and beyond these
I must not think now, though I saw that face–
But for her eyes I should have fled away.
265 They held me back, with a benignant light,
Soft-mitigated by divinest lids
Half-closed, and visionless entire they seemed
Of all external things–they saw me not,
But in blank splendour beamed like the mild moon,
270 Who comforts those she sees not, who knows not

("'Gracious at our pray'r, vouchsafe / Unveil to him thy cheeks; that he
may mark / Thy second beauty now concealèd." O splendor! / O sacred
light eternal! who is he, / So pale with musing in Pierian shades, / Or with
that fount so lavishly imbued, / Whose spirit should not fail him in the
essay / To represent thee such as thou didst seem"' [Cary].)

i *257. pined*] Wasted. Cp. Coleridge's *Christabel* (1816) i 205, 'Peak and
pine . . .'. The phrase 'bright blanched' suggests in context a recollection of
Coleridge's *The Ancient Mariner* (1798, rev. 1800) 192–4,

Her skin was white as leprosy,
And she was far liker Death than he;
Her flesh made the still air cold . . .

i *258. immortal sickness*] A pun on 'mortal sickness', which had special personal significance for K., and suggesting here the imaginative concentration
in his conception of the mystery and permanence of suffering.
i *262–72. beyond . . . upward cast*] Expressing acceptance of 'the burthen of
the mystery' (see *Sleep and Poetry* 122–54 n, p. 74 above). Moneta's power
to contemplate all and yet remain mild and benignant is dramatically introduced at i 263 by K.'s breaking off and switching attention from her 'wan
face' to her 'benignant' eyes.
i *263–5. I saw . . . light*] Cp. the brilliance and benignancy of Beatrice's
eyes in the *Purgatorio* xxxi.
i *266. Soft-mitigated*] Soft mitigated *Woodhouse 2*; soft, mitigated *1856*. The
reading follows de Selincourt's emendation.
i *267. visionless*] Unseeing. Moneta's gaze is concentrated on her own inward visions, which are an allegory of all experience.
i *269–71. But in . . . upward cast*] Cp. *All's Well That Ends Well* I iii 203–5,

. . . I adore
The sun, that looks upon his worshipper,
But knows of him no more . . .

i *269.* Cp. *Hyperion* iii 98 (p. 439 above)

. . . the most patient brilliance of the moon . .

What eyes are upward cast. As I had found
A grain of gold upon a mountain's side,
And twinged with avarice strainèd out my eyes
To search its sullen entrails rich with ore,
275 So at the view of sad Moneta's brow
I ached to see what things the hollow brain
Behind enwombed; what high tragedy
In the dark secret chambers of her skull
Was acting, that could give so dread a stress
280 To her cold lips, and fill with such a light
Her planetary eyes; and touch her voice
With such a sorrow. 'Shade of Memory!'
Cried I, with act adorant at her feet,
'By all the gloom hung round thy fallen house,
285 By this last temple, by the golden age,
By great Apollo, thy dear foster child.
And by thyself, forlorn Divinity,
The pale omega of a withered race,
Let me behold, according as thou said'st,
290 What in thy brain so ferments to and fro.'
No sooner had this conjuration passed
My devout lips than side by side we stood
(Like a stunt bramble by a solemn pine),

i 274. *sullen*] Gloomy. K.'s use of 'entrails' in this context suggests a Miltonic echo. See *Song of Four Fairies* 70 n (p. 509 above).

i 276–82. *I ached . . . sorrow*] The passage is a bridge to the story of the Titans in the first *Hyperion*, since Moneta eternally rehearses within her 'hollow brain' the 'high tragedy' of the Titans' war with the Olympians, which K. will now see through her eyes.

i 277. *enwombed*] environ'd 1856.

i 282]. *Shade of Memory*] Mnemosyne signifies 'memory'. The editorial gloss on Moneta in the 1741 edition of Hyginus describes her as the child of Jupiter 'ex Memoria uxore vel mente' ('by his wife Memory, or mind').

i 283. *adorant*] A neologism for adoring used this once by K.

i 285. *the golden age*] The *Saturnia regna*; see *Hyperion* i 107–10 n (pp. 402–3 above).

i 286. Cp. Mnemosyne to Apollo in *Hyperion* iii 72–5 (p. 438 above),

> The watcher of thy sleep and hours of life,
> From the young day when first thy infant hand
> Plucked witless the weak flowers, till thine arm
> Could bend that bow heroic to all times . . .

i 288. In this version Moneta is the last surviving representative of the Titans, whose war with the Olympians is now placed in the remote past.

i 293. *Like a stunt bramble*] K. is perhaps thinking of his own lack of height.

Deep in the shady sadness of a vale,
295   Far sunken from the healthy breath of morn,
Far from the fiery noon and eve's one star.
Onward I looked beneath the gloomy boughs,
And saw, what first I thought an image huge,
Like to the image pedestalled so high
300   In Saturn's temple. Then Moneta's voice
Came brief upon mine ear: 'So Saturn sat
When he had lost his realms.' Whereon there grew
A power within me of enormous ken
To see as a god sees, and take the depth
305   Of things as nimbly as the outward eye
Can size and shape pervade. The lofty theme
At those few words hung vast before my mind,
With half-unravelled web. I set myself
Upon an eagle's watch, that I might see,
310   And seeing ne'er forget. No stir of life
Was in this shrouded vale, not so much air
As in the zoning of a summer's day
Robs not one light seed from the feathered grass,
But where the dead leaf fell there did it rest.

i *294–6.* The first *Hyperion* opens at this point. See *Hyperion* i 1–3 (p. 396 above).

i *302–4. Whereon . . . God sees*] Cp. *Hyperion* iii 113 (p. 440 above),
      Knowledge enormous makes a God of me . . .
The revised version suggests the influence of Dante's *Paradiso* i 67–9,
     Nel suo aspetto tal dentro mi fei,
        qual si fe' Glauco nel gustar dell' erba,
        che il fe' consorto in mar degli altri dei . . .
('At her aspect, [I] such inwardly became / As Glaucus, when he tasted of the herb / That made him peer among the ocean gods' [Cary].)

i *304–6. take the depth . . . pervade*] Perceive the significance of things as readily as the eye discerns their size and shape.

i *306–8. The lofty theme . . . web*] The vision is only partly descried. By 'half unravelled web' K. may mean a fabric in which half the threads have become unknit or else one in which the intricate design is as yet only half perceived.

i *309. an eagle's watch*] Cp. Dante's *Paradiso* i 48,
      Aquila sì non gli s'afisse unquanco . . .
and Cary's *Dante, Paradiso* i 46,
      Gazing, as never eagle fix'd his ken . . .

i *310–30. No stir . . . knew it not*] Incorporates with some variants *Hyperion* i 7–25 (pp. 397–98 above).

i *310–12. No stir . . . summer's day*] Cp. *Hyperion* i 8–9 and *n* (p. 397 above).

i *312. zoning*] Compass.

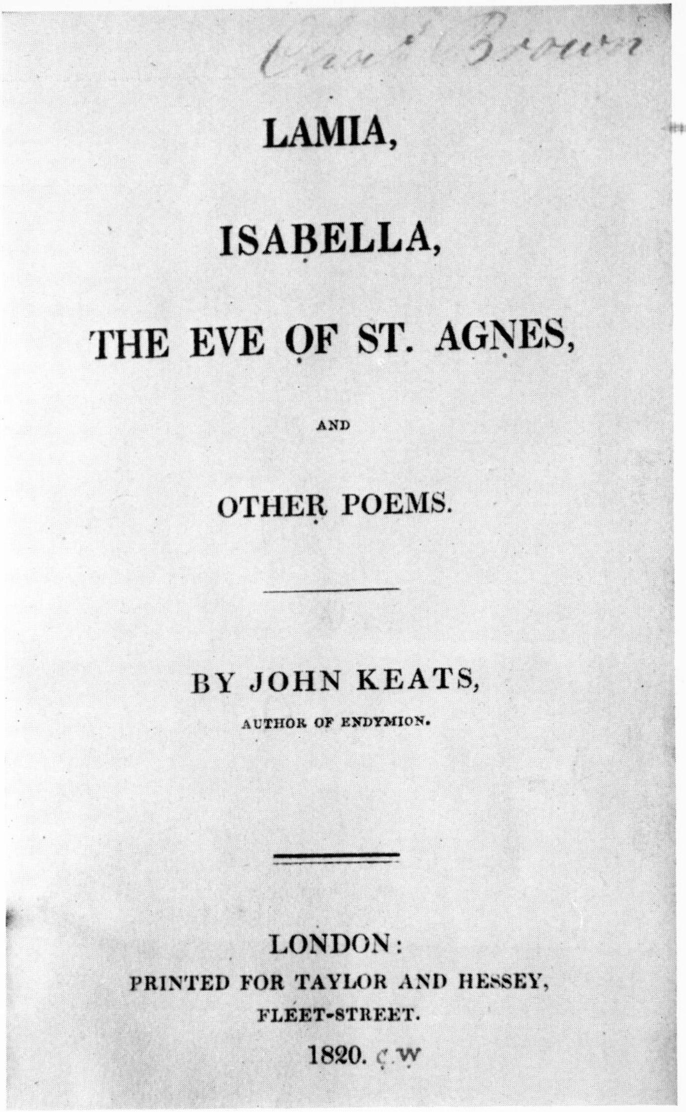

Charl Brown

LAMIA,

ISABELLA,

THE EVE OF ST. AGNES,

AND

OTHER POEMS.

BY JOHN KEATS,

AUTHOR OF ENDYMION.

===

LONDON:

PRINTED FOR TAYLOR AND HESSEY,

FLEET-STREET.

1820. C W

Plate 4 The title page of *Poems*, first published in 1820,
from the volume belonging to and signed by Keats'
friend, Charles Brown

28th Janr 3 O'clock mng. Drawn to keep me awake—a deadly sweat was on him all night.

Plate 5 Keats on his deathbed. Sketch by Joseph Severn

315   A stream went voiceless by, still deadened more
      By reason of the fallen Divinity
      Spreading more shade; the Naiad 'mid her reeds
      Pressed her cold finger closer to her lips.
      Along the margin-sand large footmarks went
320   No farther than to where old Saturn's feet
      Had rested, and there slept—how long a sleep!
      Degraded, cold, upon the sodden ground
      His old right hand lay nerveless, listless, dead,
      Unsceptred; and his realmless eyes were closed,
325   While his bowed head seemed listening to the Earth,
      His ancient mother, for some comfort yet.

         It seemed no force could wake him from his place;
      But there came one who, with a kindred hand,
      Touched his wide shoulders after bending low
330   With reverence, though to one who knew it not.
      Then came the grieved voice of Mnemosyne,
      And grieved I hearkened: 'That Divinity
      Whom thou saw'st step from yon forlornest wood,
      And with slow pace approach our fallen King,
335   Is Thea, softest-natured of our brood.'
      I marked the goddess in fair statuary
      Surpassing wan Moneta by the head,
      And in her sorrow nearer woman's tears.
      There was a listening fear in her regard,
340   As if calamity had but begun;
      As if the vanward clouds of evil days
      Had spent their malice, and the sullen rear
      Was with its storèd thunder labouring up.
      One hand she pressed upon that aching spot

i *320–1. to where . . . rested*] Cp. *Hyperion* i 16 and *n* (p. 397 above), 'to
where his feet had strayed'.
i *323. nerveless, listless, dead*] For this grouping of epithets cp. *Hyperion* i 17
and *n* (p. 397 above).
i *329–30 bending low . . . knew it not*] Probably echoing Cary's *Dante*. See
Hyperion i 24–5 *n* (p. 398 above).
i *335–8.* On Thea, Hyperion's wife, see *Hyperion* i 31–51 *n* (p. 398 above).
K. now wishes to emphasize that Thea's grief is nearer than Moneta's to
'human sorrows' (i 257) and consequently omits his earlier descriptions of
her superhuman size and strength (*Hyperion* i 26–33) and the dignified com-
posure of her suffering (*Hyperion* i 34–6)–K. uses the latter passage in de-
picting Moneta i 256–62 above.
i *336. statuary*] Stature.
i *341–3.* A military image. See *Hyperion* i 39–41 *n* (p. 399 above).

23＋K.

345   Where beats the human heart; as if just there,
       Though an immortal, she felt cruel pain;
       The other upon Saturn's bended neck
       She laid, and to the level of his hollow ear,
       Leaning with parted lips, some words she spake
350   In solemn tenor and deep organ tune—
       Some mourning words, which in our feeble tongue
       Would come in this-like accenting (how frail
       To that large utterance of the early Gods!):
       'Saturn! look up—and for what, poor lost king?
355   I have no comfort for thee, no, not one;
       I cannot cry, *Wherefore thus sleepest thou?*
       For heaven is parted from thee, and the earth
       Knows thee not, so afflicted, for a God;
       And ocean too, with all its solemn noise,
360   Has from thy sceptre passed, and all the air
       Is emptied of thine hoary majesty.
       Thy thunder, captious at the new command,
       Rumbles reluctant o'er our fallen house;
       And thy sharp lightning, in unpractised hands,
365   Scorches and burns our once serene domain.
       With such remorseless speed still come new woes
       That unbelief has not a space to breathe.
       Saturn, sleep on. Me thoughtless, why should I
       Thus violate thy slumbrous solitude?

i *348*. Hypermetrical; see *Hyperion* i 46 (p. 399 above).

i *350. tune*] tone *1856*. See *Hyperion* i 48 (p. 399 above).

i *352. this-like*] For the earlier version of this phrase see *Hyperion* i 50 and *n* (p. 399 above).

i *354–72*. On Thea's speech see *Hyperion* i 52–71 *n* (p. 399 above).

i *354. and for what, poor lost king*] For the earlier reading and the influence of *King Lear* on K.'s portrayal of Saturn see *Hyperion* i 52 and *n*, 98–103 *n* (pp. 399 and 402 above).

i *356. cry*] say *1856*. Cp. *Hyperion* i 54 (p. 400 above),

           I cannot say, 'Oh, wherefore sleepest thou? . . .'

i *362. captious*] Objecting querulously. Cp. *Hyperion* i 60 (p. 400 above).

i *363. rumbles reluctant*] A Miltonic borrowing; see *Hyperion* i 61 *n* (p. 400 above).

i *366–7*. Condenses *Hyperion* i 64–6 (p. 400 above),

           O aching time! O moments big as years!
           All as ye pass swell out the monstrous truth,
           And press it so upon our weary griefs . . .

The lines have a Shakespearian flavour.

i *368. Me thoughtless*] A Miltonic construction avoided in the first version. See *Hyperion* i 68 (p. 400 above), 'Oh, thoughtless . . .'.

370   Why should I ope thy melancholy eyes?
      Saturn, sleep on, while at thy feet I weep.'

      As when upon a trancèd summer night,
      Forests, branch-charmèd by the earnest stars,
      Dream, and so dream all night, without a noise,
375   Save from one gradual solitary gust,
      Swelling upon the silence; dying off;
      As if the ebbing air had but one wave.
      So came these words, and went; the while in tears
      She pressed her fair large forehead to the earth,
380   Just where her fallen hair might spread in curls,
      A soft and silken mat for Saturn's feet.
      Long, long these two were postured motionless,
      Like sculpture builded-up upon the grave
      Of their own power. A long awful time
385   I looked upon them: still they were the same;

i *372–7.* For comments on the first version of the passage see notes to
Hyperion i 72–8 (p. 400 above). K. curtails the pictorial effects in the simile
and varies its rhythm and phrasing in the interests of speed of movement
and descriptive economy.

i *372.* Followed in the first *Hyperion* by the line,
      Those green-robed senators of mighty woods . . .

i *373–4. Forests . . . a noise*] Substituted for 'Tall oaks, branch-charmèd by
the earnest stars, / Dream, and so dream all night without a stir' (*Hyperion*
i 74–5). See M. R. Ridley, 'The emphasis is to be transferred from the
motionless trees to a silence followed by the sound of the wind' (*Ridley*
(1936) 276–7).

i *376.* Cp. *Hyperion* i 77 (p. 401 above),
      Which comes upon the silence, and dies off . . .
K. Muir comments, 'The regular rhythm . . . is changed into one which
suggests what it describes' (*Reassessment* (1958) 116).

i *379–80. pressed . . . spread in curls*] Substituted for 'touched . . . be outspread' (*Hyperion* i 80–1, p. 401 above).

i *383–4. Like sculpture . . . power*] Replacing *Hyperion* i 86 (p. 401 above),
      Like natural sculpture in cathedral cavern . . .
With the revised version cp. the figures representing defeated pride sculptured on the pavement in Dante's *Purgatorio* xii 16–18,
      Come, perchè di lor memoria sia,
        spora i sepolti le tombe terragne
        portan segnato quel ch'elli eran pria . . .
and also Cary's version,
      As, in memorial of the buried, drawn
      Upon earth-level tombs, the sculptur'd form
      Of what was once appears . . .

i *384–99.* An expansion of *Hyperion* i 83–5 (p. 401 above),

The frozen God still bending to the earth,
And the sad Goddess weeping at his feet,
Moneta silent. Without stay or prop
But my own weak mortality, I bore
390   The load of this eternal quietude,
The unchanging gloom, and the three fixèd shapes
Ponderous upon my senses a whole moon.
For by my burning brain I measured sure
Her silver seasons shedded on the night,
395   And ever day by day methought I grew
More gaunt and ghostly. Oftentimes I prayed
Intense, that death would take me from the vale
And all its burthens. Gasping with despair
Of change, hour after hour I cursed myself—
400   Until old Saturn raised his faded eyes,
And looked around and saw his kingdom gone,
And all the gloom and sorrow of the place,
And that fair kneeling Goddess at his feet.
As the moist scent of flowers and grass and leaves
405   Fills forest dells with a pervading air
Known to the woodland nostril, so the words
Of Saturn filled the mossy glooms around,
Even to the hollows of time-eaten oaks,
And to the windings of the foxes' hole,
410   With sad low tones, while thus he spake, and sent
Strange musings to the solitary Pan:

> One moon, with alteration slow, had shed
> Her silver seasons four upon the night,
> And still these two were postured motionless . . .

The sense of hopelessness is now further heightened by K.'s 'proving on his own pulses' the paralysing weight of despair.

i *395. ever*] every *Woodhouse 2, 1856*. The emendation suggested by J. C. Maxwell was adopted by Garrod.

i *400–59.* Remodelled from *Hyperion* i 89–157 (pp. 402–5 above).

i *400. faded eyes*] For the Miltonic echo see *Hyperion* i 90 *n* (p. 402 above).

i *404–11.* Substituted for *Hyperion* i 92–4 (p. 402 above),

> . . . and then spake,
> As with a palsied tongue, and while his beard
> Shook horrid with such aspen malady . . .

The revised version avoids the Miltonic construction 'Shook horrid' and adds to the sense of desolation and decay—see 'mossy glooms' (i 407), 'time-eaten oaks' (i 408), 'solitary Pan' (i 411). The original passage is re-cast and incorporated into Saturn's speech at i 426–8 below.

i *411. the solitary Pan*] The precise meaning is obscure, but the phrase

'Moan, brethren, moan; for we are swallowed up
And buried from all godlike exercise
Of influence benign on planets pale,
415 And peaceful sway above man's harvesting,
And all those acts which deity supreme
Doth ease its heart of love in. Moan and wail.
Moan, brethren, moan; for lo, the rebel spheres
Spin round, the stars their ancient courses keep,
420 Clouds still with shadowy moisture haunt the earth,
Still suck their fill of light from sun and moon;
Still buds the tree, and still the sea-shores murmur.
There is no death in all the universe,
No smell of death—there shall be death. Moan, moan,
425 Moan, Cybele, moan; for thy pernicious babes
Have changed a god into an aching palsy.
Moan, brethren, moan, for I have no strength left,
Weak as the reed—weak—feeble as my voice—
Oh, oh, the pain, the pain of feebleness.
430 Moan, moan, for still I thaw—or give me help:
Throw down those imps, and give me victory.
Let me hear other groans, and trumpets blown
Of triumph calm, and hymns of festival
From the gold peaks of heaven's high-pilèd clouds—
435 Voices of soft proclaim, and silver stir
Of strings in hollow shells. And there shall be
Beautiful things made new for the surprise
Of the sky-children.' So he feebly ceased,
With such a poor and sickly sounding pause,
440 Methought I heard some old man of the earth
Bewailing earthly loss; nor could my eyes

suggests the loneliness and desolation of Nature after the passing of the
Golden Age (see i 285 n above).
i *412–30.* For the longer first version of Saturn's speech see *Hyperion* i 95–
134 and n (p. 402 above). The alterations are designed to increase Saturn's
pathetic weakness and loss of hope.
i *425. Cybele*] The mother of the gods. See *Hyperion* ii 4 n (p. 415 above).
i *431. those imps*] Saturn's rebellious sons. See *Hyperion* i 147 n (p. 405 above),
'The rebel three . . .'. The word 'imp' is an archaism for child or offspring.
i *434.* Cp. *Hyperion* i 129 (p. 404 above),
Upon the gold clouds metropolitan . . .
Obviously altered to avoid the 'Miltonic inversion' (see headnote).
i *438–51.* Cp. *Hyperion* i 135–8 and n (p. 404 above).
i *441–5. nor could . . . large-limbed visions*] There is no beauty or tragic
dignity in Saturn's pitiful lamenting, though when he falls silent his appearance is still awe-inspiring (see i 448–54 below).

And ears act with that pleasant unison of sense
Which marries sweet sound with the grace of form,
And dolorous accent from a tragic harp
445 With large-limbed visions. More I scrutinized:
Still fixed he sat beneath the sable trees,
Whose arms spread straggling in wild serpent forms,
With leaves all hushed; his awful presence there
(Now all was silent) gave a deadly lie
450 To what I erewhile heard; only his lips
Trembled amid the white curls of his beard.
They told the truth, though, round, the snowy locks
Hung nobly, as upon the face of heaven
A midday fleece of clouds. Thea arose,
455 And stretched her white arm through the hollow dark,
Pointing somewhither, whereat he too rose
Like a vast giant seen by men at sea
To grow pale from the waves at dull midnight.
They melted from my sight into the woods;
460 Ere I could turn, Moneta cried: 'These twain
Are speeding to the families of grief,
Where roofed in by black rocks they waste, in pain
And darkness, for no hope.' And she spake on,
As ye may read who can unwearied pass
465 Onward from the antichamber of this dream,
Where even at the open doors awhile
I must delay, and glean my memory
Of her high phrase—perhaps no further dare.

CANTO II

'Mortal, that thou may'st understand aright,
I humanize my sayings to thine ear,

i 442. Hypermetrical.
i 447. The bareness of the trees reveals their twisted branches.
i 454–6. Cp. Thea's purposiveness in *Hyperion* i 148–55 (p. 405 above).
i 458. *grow pale from the waves*] Rise from the sea like a ghost.
i 461. *families of grief*] Their fallen fellow-Titans.
i 462. Cp. the setting in *Hyperion* ii 10–14 (p. 416 above).
i 467–8. *glean . . . phrase*] Cp. *When I have fears* 2 (p. 297 above),
        Before my pen has gleaned my teeming brain . . .
ii 1–49. Recasts the narrative in *Hyperion* i 158–204 (pp. 405–8 above), alter-
ing the phrasing to accord with Moneta's role as historian and interpreter.
ii 1–6. Copied out by K. (omitting ii 5) in his letter of 21 Sept. 1819 to
Woodhouse with the comment, 'I will give you a few lines from Hyperion
on account of a word in the last line of a fine sound' (*L* ii 171). The 'word'
was 'legend-laden' (ii 6) With ii 1–3 cp. *Paradise Lost* v 571–74,

Making comparisons of earthly things;
Or thou might'st better listen to the wind,
5   Whose language is to thee a barren noise,
Though it blows legend-laden through the trees.
In melancholy realms big tears are shed,
More sorrow like to this, and such-like woe,
Too huge for mortal tongue, or pen of scribe;
10   The Titans fierce, self-hid or prison-bound,
Groan for the old allegiance once more,
Listening in their doom for Saturn's voice.
But one of our whole eagle-brood still keeps
His sovereignty, and rule, and majesty;
15   Blazing Hyperion on his orbèd fire
Still sits, still snuffs the incense teeming up
From man to the Sun's God—yet unsecure.
For as upon the earth dire prodigies
Fright and perplex, so also shudders he—
20   Nor at dog's howl or gloom-bird's even screech,
Or the familiar visitings of one
Upon the first toll of his passing-bell;
But horrors, portioned to a giant nerve,
Make great Hyperion ache. His palace bright,

... what surmounts the reach
Of human sense, I shall delineate so,
By lik'ning spiritual to corporal forms,
As may express them best ...

ii 12. *in their doom*] Cp. *Hyperion* i 163 (p. 405 above), 'in sharp pain'.

ii 13. *eagle-brood*] Cp. *Hyperion* i 164 (p. 405 above), 'mammoth-brood'.

ii 15. *Hyperion*] See *Hyperion* i 166 *n* (p. 405 above). The 'orbèd fire' is the sun.

ii 18. *upon the earth*] Cp. *Hyperion* i 169 (p. 406 above), 'among us mortals'.

ii 18–19. *dire prodigies ... perplex*] For the Miltonic echo see *Hyperion* i 170 *n* (p. 406 above).

ii 20. *gloom-bird's even screech*] For the earlier reading and the Shakespearian echo see *Hyperion* i 171 *n* (p. 406 above).

ii 20. *even*] Substituted for 'hated'. See *Hyperion* i 171 *n* (p. 406 above).

ii 21–2. See *Hyperion* i 172–3 *n* (p. 406 above). This is followed in the first *Hyperion* by the line (retained in *1856*),

Or prophesyings of the midnight lamp ...

On 'passing-bell' see *Hyperion* i 173 *n*.

ii 23. *portioned*] See *Hyperion* i 175 *n* (p. 406 above).

ii 24–30. *His palace bright ... Flush angerly*] For probable influences on K.'s description of Hyperion's cloud palace see *Hyperion* i 176–82 *n* (pp. 406–7 above).

25   Bastioned with pyramids of glowing gold,
      And touched with shade of bronzèd obelisks,
      Glares a blood-red through all the thousand courts,
      Arches, and domes, and fiery galleries;
      And all its curtains of aurorean clouds
30   Flush angerly: when he would taste the wreaths
      Of incense breathed aloft from sacred hills,
      Instead of sweets his ample palate takes
      Savour of poisonous brass and metals sick.
      Wherefore, when harboured in the sleepy west,
35   After the full completion of fair day,
      For rest divine upon exalted couch
      And slumber in the arms of melody,
      He paces through the pleasant hours of ease
      With strides colossal, on from hall to hall,
40   While far within each aisle and deep recess
      His wingèd minions in close clusters stand
      Amazed, and full of fear; like anxious men,
      Who on a wide plain gather in sad troops
      When earthquakes jar their battlements and towers.
45   Even now, while Saturn, roused from icy trance,
      Goes, step for step, with Thea from yon woods,
      Hyperion, leaving twilight in the rear,
      Is sloping to the threshold of the west.
      Thither we tend.' Now in clear light I stood,
50   Relieved from the dusk vale. Mnemosyne
      Was sitting on a square-edged polished stone,

ii 25. *glowing*] shining *1856*.

ii 26. *touched with shade*] See *Hyperion* i 178 *n* (p. 407 above).

ii 30. *when he . . . wreaths*] K. probably omitted the passage preceding this in the first version (*Hyperion* i 182–5) in the interests of economy and probably also to avoid the Miltonic repetitions: see *Hyperion* i 185 *n* (p. 407 above).

ii 33. *Savour of poisonous brass*] See *Hyperion* i 189 *n* (p. 407 above).

ii 34. *Wherefore*] Substituted for 'And so' (*Hyperion* i 190).

ii 39. *With strides colossal*] See *Hyperion* i 195 and *n* (p. 408 above).

ii 41–4. For the Miltonic echo see *Hyperion* i 196–200 *n* (p. 408 above).

ii 43. Cp. *Hyperion* i 199 (p. 408 above),

          Who on wide plains gather in panting troops . . .

Probably altered to accord with the tone of Moneta's speech.

ii 48. Cp. *Hyperion* i 204 and *n* (p. 408 above),

          Came slope upon the threshold of the west . . .

Altered to avoid the Miltonic phrasing.

ii 50. *Mnemosyne*] See i 226 *n* above.

ii 51–3. *square-edged . . . garments*] Cp. the polished marble stair in Cary's version of Dante's *Purgatorio* ix 94–6, quoted in i 90–2 *n* above.

That in its lucid depth reflected pure
Her priestess-garments. My quick eyes ran on
From stately nave to nave, from vault to vault,
55 Through bowers of fragrant and enwreathèd light
And diamond-pavèd lustrous long arcades.
Anon rushed by the bright Hyperion;
His flaming robes streamed out beyond his heels,
And gave a roar, as if of earthly fire,
60 That scared away the meek ethereal hours
And made their dove-wings tremble. On he flared . . .

ii *53–6. My quick eyes . . . arcades*] Reconstructs *Hyperion* i 213–20 (p. 409
above).

ii *54–6.* For parallels with the halls of Eblis in Beckford's *Vathek* and the
cloud palace in Wordsworth's *The Excursion* ii see *Hyperion* i 218 *n*, i 220–1 *n*
(p. 409 above).

ii *60. hours*] See *Hyperion* i 216 *n* (p. 409 above).

142 'The day is gone and all its sweets are gone'

Probably written 10 Oct. 1819 immediately after seeing Fanny Brawne for
the first time since June 1819: K. returned from Winchester to London *c.* 8
Oct. and visited Fanny at Hampstead 10 Oct.–see his letter to her 11 Oct.,
'My sweet Girl, I am living to-day in yesterday: I was in a complete fascina-
tion all day. I feel myself at your mercy. . . . You dazzled me–There is
nothing in the world so bright and delicate' (*L* ii 222–3); '1819' in the
transcripts by Brown and Woodhouse. K. returns to the use of the Shakespearian sonnet-form, rejected as a model in April 1819 (see headnotes to
To Sleep, If by dull rhymes, pp. 510 and 521 above), in this and the two
sonnets, *I cry your mercy* and *Bright star! Would I were steadfast* (pp. 689 and
736 below).
Text from Brown's transcript, which differs from K.'s draft (Morgan
Library) and Woodhouse's transcripts in *Woodhouse* 2, 3 in transposing the
second and third quatrains of the sonnet and adopting a new reading in l. 3,
and presumably follows a lost fair copy by K.
Published *Plymouth and Devonport Weekly Journal* 4 Oct. 1838; repr. *1848*.

The day is gone, and all its sweets are gone!
    Sweet voice, sweet lips, soft hand, and softer breast,
Warm breath, light whisper, tender semi-tone,
    Bright eyes, accomplished shape, and languorous waist!

¶ 142. *3. light*] tranc'd *Draft*.
4. accomplished] Finished, perfect.

23*

5   Faded the flower and all its budded charms,
     Faded the sight of beauty from my eyes,
   Faded the shape of beauty from my arms,
     Faded the voice, warmth, whiteness, paradise.
   Vanished unseasonably at shut of eve,
10   When the dusk holiday, or holinight,
   Of fragrant-curtained love begins to weave
     The woof of darkness thick, for hid delight;
   But, as I've read love's missal through to-day,
   He'll let me sleep, seeing I fast and pray.

5–8. Preceded by ll. 9–12 in K.'s draft.
8. *warmth, whiteness*] Cp. *I cry your mercy* 8 (p. 689 below),
       That warm, white, lucent, million-pleasured breast . . .
For 'paradise' the draft has the cancelled reading 'brilliance', with which
cp. the following poem *To [Fanny]* 3 (No. 143 below), 'my brilliant Queen'.
9. *shut of eve*] Cp. *Lamia* ii 107 and *n* (p. 639 above), 'at blushing shut of
day'.
12. *woof of darkness thick*] texture thick of darkness *Draft (cancelled)*.
13. Paid all due observances to love. With the religious imagery cp. the
following poem *To [Fanny]* 25–6 and *n* (p. 688 below).

143 To [Fanny]

Probably written between 15–31 Oct. 1819 after a meeting with Fanny
Brawne at Wentworth Place, Hampstead, following their reunion 10 Oct.
(see headnote to previous poem): K. visited the Brawnes at Wentworth
Place *c*. 15–17 Oct. and moved back to his old lodgings next door *c*. 21 Oct.;
the poem is dated 'Oct. 1819' in *1848*.

   To [Fanny] expresses the confused intensity of K.'s feelings for Fanny
when their relationship was renewed—see, for example, his letter to her 13
Oct. 1819 which like the poem manages to suggest a rueful element in his
emotional surrender, '. . . I can think of nothing else . . . I cannot exist
without you—I am forgetful of everything but seeing you again. . . . You
have ravish'd me away by a Power I cannot resist; and yet I could resist till
I saw you; and even since I have seen you I have endeavoured often "to
reason against the reasons of my Love" [K. is misquoting Ford's *'Tis Pity
She's a Whore* I ii 222]' (*L* i 223–4).
Text from *1848*.
Published *1848*.

     What can I do to drive away
     Remembrance from my eyes? For they have seen,
   Aye, an hour ago, my brilliant Queen!
   Touch has a memory. Oh, say, love, say,

```
 5   What can I do to kill it and be free
     In my old liberty?
     When every fair one that I saw was fair,
     Enough to catch me in but half a snare,
     Not keep me there;
10   When, howe'er poor or particoloured things,
     My muse had wings,
     And ever ready was to take her course
     Whither I bent her force,
     Unintellectual, yet divine to me.
15   Divine, I say! What sea-bird o'er the sea
     Is a philosopher the while he goes
     Winging along where the great water throes?

         How shall I do
         To get anew
20   Those moulted feathers, and so mount once more
         Above, above
         The reach of fluttering Love,
     And make him cower lowly while I soar?
     Shall I gulp wine? No, that is vulgarism,
25   A heresy and schism,
```

¶ 143. *5–14* (and *18–23* below). K.'s fear that his poetic ambition and passion for Fanny Brawne are at variance is expressed again in the following poem *I cry your mercy* 11–14 (p. 690 below),

> Or living on perhaps, your wretched thrall,
>> Forget, in the mist of idle misery,
>> Life's purposes—the palate of my mind
>> Losing its gust, and my ambition blind!

7–9. Cp. K.'s letter to Fanny Brawne 25 July 1819, '... I am indeed astonish'd to find myself so careless of all charms but yours—remembering as I do the time when even a bit of ribband was a matter of interest with me' (*L* ii 133).

10–13. Cp. K.'s letter to Fanny Brawne 16 Aug. 1819, '... I have had no idle leisure to brood over you–'t is well perhaps I have not ... I would feign, as my sails are set, sail on ... for a Brace of Months longer–I am in complete cue ... shall in these four months do an immense deal' (*L* ii 140–1).

10. particoloured] K. is thinking of his unequal poetic achievement.

17. throes] Is in throes, is convulsed. The verb is K.'s, formed from the common noun.

18. Cp. Chaucer's *Troilus and Criseyde* v 225,

> How shal I do? Whan shal she com ayeyn ...

K. ends his 11 Oct. 1819 letter to Fanny Brawne with the phrase, 'Ah hertè mine' (*L* ii 223), echoing *Troilus and Criseyde* v 228,

> O herte myn, Criseyde, O swete fo ...

Foisted into the canon law of love;
No—wine is only sweet to happy men;
More dismal cares
Seize on me unawares—
30 Where shall I learn to get my peace again?
To banish thoughts of that most hateful land,
Dungeoner of my friends, that wicked strand
Where they were wrecked and live a wretched life;
That monstrous region, whose dull rivers pour
35 Ever from their sordid urns unto the shore,
Unowned of any weedy-hairèd gods;
Whose winds, all zephyrless, hold scourging rods,
Iced in the great lakes, to afflict mankind;
Whose rank-grown forests, frosted, black, and blind,
40 Would fright a Dryad; whose harsh-herbaged meads
Make lean and lank the starved ox while he feeds.
There bud flowers have no scent, birds no sweet song,
And great unerring Nature once seems wrong.

25–6. *A heresy and schism . . . canon law*] See the religious imagery in K.'s letter to Fanny Brawne 13 Oct. 1819, 'Love is my religion. . . . My creed is Love and you are its only tenet' (*L* ii 223–4).

31–3. K. is thinking of George Keats's misfortunes in America. He ran into financial difficulties 1818–19 in Louisville, Kentucky, and was obliged to return to England Jan. 1820 to borrow money. See K.'s journal-letter 17 Sept. 1819, 'Your present situation I will not suffer myself to dwell upon. . . . In truth I do not believe you fit to deal with the world; or at least the American world' (*L* ii 185).

33. *wretched*] wrecked *1848*. The reading follows H. Buxton Forman's emendation.

34–43. K. probably derived his knowledge of the American landscape chiefly from descriptions in Buffon, Robertson's *History of America* and Morris Birkbeck's *Notes on a Journey through America* (1817) and *Letters from Illinois* (1818). K. refers to Birkbeck in his journal-letter Oct. 1818, '. . . the humanity of the United States can never reach the sublime—Birkbeck's mind is too much in the American Style—you must infuse a little Spirit of a different sort into the Settlement' (*L* i 398).

35. *urns*] Frequently used in eighteenth-century poetry and landscape gardening for the sources of rivers and streams.

36. *weedy-haired gods*] Sea deities. For K. the American countryside was the opposite of Arcadia (l. 37 'zephyrless', l. 40 'fright a Dryad').

42. *bud flowers*] bad flowers *1848*. H. B. Forman suspected that K. wrote 'bud' and then substituted 'flowers', leaving 'bud' uncancelled.

43. K is glancing lightly at Pope's *An Essay on Man* (1733) i 294,
        One truth is clear, 'Whatever is, is right' . . .

Oh, for some sunny spell
45 To dissipate the shadows of this hell!
Say they are gone—with the new dawning light
Steps forth my lady bright!
Oh, let me once more rest
My soul upon that dazzling breast!
50 Let once again these aching arms be placed,
The tender gaolers of thy waist!
And let me feel that warm breath here and there
To spread a rapture in my very hair—
Oh, the sweetness of the pain!
55 Give me those lips again!
Enough! Enough! It is enough for me
To dream of thee!

but 'great . . . Nature', an expression used again in *Ode to Fanny* 5 (p. 740 below), may be from Burns's *Second Epistle to J. Lapraik* 89,

'Tis he fulfils great Nature's plan . . .

since K. quotes this poem in his letter to Haydon 3 Oct. 1819 (*L* ii 219).
48–9. Cp. *Bright star!* 10 (p. 738 below),

Pillowed upon my fair love's ripening breast . . .

and also *The day is gone* 8 *n* (p. 686 above).
54. The phrase is used in *Welcome joy, and welcome sorrow* 25 (p. 388 above).

144 'I cry your mercy, pity, love'

Probably written Oct.–Nov. 1819: K.'s complete surrender to his passion for Fanny Brawne parallels that in his letter to her 19 Oct. 1819, 'I should like to cast the die for Love or death—I have no Patience with anything else—if you ever intend to be cruel to me as you say in jest now but may sometimes be in earnest be so now—as I will—my mind is in a tremble, I cannot tell what I am writing' (*L* ii 224).
Text from *1848* (which follows Brown's transcript).
Published *1848*.

I cry your mercy, pity, love—aye love!
    Merciful love that tantalizes not,
One-thoughted, never-wandering, guileless love,
    Unmasked, and being seen—without a blot!
5   Oh, let me have thee whole—all, all, be mine!
    That shape, that fairness, that sweet minor zest
Of love, your kiss—those hands, those eyes divine,
    That warm, white, lucent, million-pleasured breast;

¶ 144. *4. Unmasked*] Not concealing the real feeling behind a mask of pretence.
8. See the preceding poem *To [Fanny]* 48–9 and *n* above.

Yourself–your soul–in pity give me all,
10   Withhold no atom's atom or I die;
Or living on perhaps, your wretched thrall,
Forget, in the mist of idle misery,
Life's purposes–the palate of my mind
Losing its gust, and my ambition blind!

10. withhold] Garrod's 'without' is a misreading.
11–14. Cp. the same anxieties in *To* [*Fanny*] 5–14, 18–23 (p. 687 above).
11. wretched thrall] Enthralled slave. Cp. *La Belle Dame Sans Merci* 39–40
(p. 505 above),

> . . . La Belle Dame sans merci
> Hath thee in thrall . . .

145 King Stephen

A Fragment of a Tragedy

Begun late Aug. 1819 and probably completed in this fragmentary form
Nov. 1819: dated 'Nov. 1819' in the MS comprising Brown's transcript
of I i, I ii 1–19 and K.'s draft of the rest; for the earlier date see Brown on
K.'s writing 'two or three scenes' as soon as he had finished *Otho the Great*
(completed *c*. 23 Aug. 1819). Brown records (*KC* ii 67):

'I pointed out to him a subject for an English historical tragedy in the
reign of Stephen, beginning with his defeat by the Empress Maud, and
ending with the death of his son Eustace, when Stephen yielded the succession to the crown to the young Henry. He was struck with the variety of
events and characters which must necessarily be introduced; and I offered
to give, as before [i.e. in *Otho the Great*] their dramatic conduct. "The
play must open", I began, "with the field of battle, when Stephen's forces
are retreating"–"Stop!" he said, "stop! I have been already too long in
leading strings. I will do all this myself." He immediately set about it, and
wrote two or three scenes, about 130 lines' [i.e. the part of the play transcribed by Brown Nov. 1819].

K.'s and Brown's sources for the historical background are unknown,
but the narrative details in the fragment, which deals with Stephen's defeat
at Lincoln 1141, indicate that they were using material based for the most
part on Henry of Huntingdon's *Historia Anglorum*, which contains a circumstantial account of the battle, and William of Malmesbury's *Historia Novella*
(both first printed 1596). On K.'s intention to draw for some incidental details on John Selden's *Titles of Honour* (1614), bought by him in 1819, see
Lowell ii 361–2, *Finney* 728. The treatment of Stephen, which involves recollections of *Richard III* and *Macbeth*, indicates that K. again had Kean in
mind for the principal part. K.'s abandonment of the play was probably

influenced by Kean's departure to American in autumn 1819; it may also
be connected with the views stated in his letter to Taylor of 17 Nov. 1819,
'The little dramatic skill I may as yet have however badly it might show
in a Drama would I think be sufficient for a Poem–I wish to diffuse the
colouring of St. Agnes eve [p. 450 above] throughout a Poem in which
Character and Sentiment would be the figures to such drapery–Two or
three such Poems . . . written in the course of the next six years, would be a
famous gradus ad Parnassum altissimum . . . they would nerve me up to
the writing of a few fine Plays–my greatest ambition–when I do feel
ambitious. I am sorry to say that is very seldom' (L ii 234).

Readers have generally agreed over the fragment's poetic and dramatic
superiority to Otho the Great. Colvin saw Stephen as 'a real elemental force
and not a mere mouther of valiant rhetoric . . .' (Keats (1909) 179) and found
the scenes 'full of a spirit of heady action and the stir of battle' (Colvin
(1917) 443). De Selincourt adds, 'No writing . . . has reproduced with
greater success the spirit which pervades the martial scenes in the early historical plays of Shakespeare' (de Selincourt 555). See also Bernice Slote's
Keats and the Dramatic Principle (1958) 114–15.
Text from K.'s and Brown's MS.
Published 1848.

ACT I

SCENE I

[Field of Battle.]

Alarum. Enter King Stephen, *Knights, and Soldiers.*

Stephen. If shame can on a soldier's vein-swollen front
Spread deeper crimson than the battle's toil,
Blush in your casing helmets! For see, see!
Yonder my chivalry, my pride of war,
5   Wrenched with an iron hand from firm array,
Are routed loose about the plashy meads,
Of honour forfeit. Oh, that my known voice
Could reach your dastard ears, and fright you more!

I i *1. vein-swollen front*] Shakespearian phrasing. See also *Lamia* ii 77 (p. 637
above),
          . . . one whose brow had no dark veins to swell . . .
K. had been working on *Lamia* shortly before beginning *King Stephen* and
returned to it after writing his '130 lines'.
I i 6. *plashy meads*] The battle of Lincoln was fought on low-lying marshy
ground close to the Trent, which had overflowed its banks because of the
recent heavy rain (William of Malmesbury's *Historia Novella*, ed. K. R.
Potter 1955, 48).

Fly, cowards, fly! Gloucester is at your backs!
10 Throw your slack bridles o'er the flurried manes,
Ply well the rowel with faint trembling heels,
Scampering to death at last!
First Knight.   The enemy
Bears his flaunt standard close upon their rear.
Second Knight. Sure of a bloody prey, seeing the fens
Will swamp them girth-deep.
15 *Stephen*.   Over head and ears,
No matter! 'Tis a gallant enemy;
How like a comet he goes streaming on.
But we must plague him in the flank—hey, friends?
We are well breathèd—follow!

    Enter Earl Baldwin *and Soldiers, as defeated.*

Stephen.   De Redvers!
20 What is the monstrous bugbear that can fright
Baldwin?
Baldwin. No scare-crow, but the fortunate star
Of boisterous Chester, whose fell truncheon now
Points level to the goal of victory.
This way he comes, and if you would maintain
25 Your person unaffronted by vile odds,
Take horse, my Lord.
Stephen.   And which way spur for life?
Now I thank Heaven I am in the toils,
That soldiers may bear witness how my arm
Can burst the meshes. Not the eagle more

I i *9. Gloucester*] Variously 'Glocester' and 'Gloster' in K.'s MS. Robert,
Earl of Gloucester, the Empress's half-brother, joined forces with his son-
in-law Ranulf, Earl of Chester, to raise Stephen's siege of Lincoln Castle.
I i *13. flaunt*] Flaunted.
I i *17.* Used by E. J. Trelawny as a motto for his *Adventures of a Younger Son*
(1831) chap. ci.
I i *19–20. De Redvers . . . Baldwin*] Baldwin de Redvers was opposed to
Stephen, who banished him to Anjou 1136 and fought him again on his
return to England 1139–40. K. and Brown probably confused him with
Baldwin Fitz-Gilbert, whose address to the army on Stephen's behalf and
courage as a fighter are recorded in Henry of Huntingdon's *Historia Ang-
lorum* chaps. 16–17, 18 (T. Arnold's edn, 1879, 271–3).
I i *22. Chester*] See I i 9 *n*.
I i *29–33. Not . . . sepulchre*] Used by E. J. Trelawny as a motto for his
Adventures of a Younger Son chap. c.

30   Loves to beat up against a tyrannous blast,
      Than I to meet the torrent of my foes.
      This is a brag—be it so!—but if I fall,
      Carve it upon my 'scutcheoned sepulchre.
      On, fellow-soldiers! Earl of Redvers, back!
35   Not twenty Earls of Chester shall brow-beat
      The diadem.   [*Exeunt. Alarum.*

SCENE II

[*Another part of the Field.*]

Trumpets sounding a victory. Enter Gloucester, *Knights, and Forces.*

      Gloucester. Now may we lift our bruisèd vizors up,
      And take the flattering freshness of the air,
      While the wide din of battle dies away
      Into times past, yet to be echoed sure
5   In the silent pages of our chroniclers.
      First Knight. Will Stephen's death be marked there, my
            good Lord,
      Or that we gave him lodging in yon towers?
      Gloucester. Fain would I know the great usurper's fate.

Enter two Captains severally.

      First Captain. My Lord!
      Second Captain.   Most noble Earl!
      First Captain.   The King—
      Second Captain. The Empress greets—
      Gloucester. What of the King?
10   *First Captain.*   He sole and lone maintains
      A hopeless bustle mid our swarming arms,
      And with a nimble savageness attacks,
      Escapes, makes fiercer onset, then anew
      Eludes death, giving death to most that dare
15   Trespass within the circuit of his sword!
      He must by this have fallen. Baldwin is taken;

I ii *10–15.* Stephen's valour on the battlefield is stressed by the chronicles of the period.

I ii *10. sole and lone*] Cp. the phrasing in *Lamia* ii 122 (p. 639 above), 'sole perhaps and lone'.

I ii *12–15. with a . . . sword*] Used by E. J. Trelawny as a motto for his *Adventures of a Younger Son* chap. xi.

I ii *16. Baldwin is taken*] See Henry of Huntingdon's *Historia Anglorum* chap. 18 (ed. cit. 274), 'Capitur etiam Baldwinus . . .' ('Baldwin . . . was also taken . . .').

And for the Duke of Bretagne, like a stag
He flies, for the Welsh beagles to hunt down.
God save the Empress!
Gloucester.　　　　　　Now our dreaded Queen.
What message from her Highness?
20　*Second Captain.*　　　　　　Royal Maud
From the thronged towers of Lincoln hath looked down,
Like Pallas from the walls of Ilion,
And seen her enemies havocked at her feet.
She greets most noble Gloucester from her heart,
25　Entreating him, his captains, and brave knights,
To grace a banquet. The high city gates
Are envious which shall see your triumph pass;
The streets are full of music.

Enter Second Knight.

Gloucester.　　　　　　Whence came you?
Second Knight. From Stephen, my good Prince—Stephen!
　　Stephen!
30　*Gloucester.* Why do you make such echoing of his name?
Second Knight. Because I think, my lord, he is no man,
But a fierce demon, anointed safe from wounds,
And misbaptizèd with a Christian name.

I ii 17. *Duke of Bretagne*] Alan, Earl of Brittany, led Stephen's Breton followers at Lincoln. He heads the list of Stephen's allies in the Earl of Gloucester's exhortation to his army in *Historia Anglorum* (ed. cit. chap. 15, 269).
I ii 18. *the Welsh*] They fought on the wings of the army led by the Earls of Gloucester and Chester (*Historia Anglorum*, ed. cit. chap. 13, 268).
I ii 20. K.'s MS begins at this point with several cancelled false starts including,

　　　　　enter another captain
　　　Glocester. What ist you would say
　　　　　　　　　This to thee
　　Second Captain. Most noble Gloster . . .

I ii 20–5. *Royal Maud . . . banquet*] According to the records, including the *Historia Anglorum* and the *Historia Novella*, the empress was in Gloucester at the time of the battle.
I ii 22. *Pallas*] Pallas Athene, who aided the Greeks in their conquest of Troy.
I ii 28. *The streets are full of music*] An improbable detail. The city was sacked after the battle; see, for example, *Historia Anglorum* (ed. cit. chap. 18, 275), *Civitas ergo hostili lege direpta est* . . . ('The city was given up to plunder in accordance with the laws of war . . .').
I ii 31–2. *Because . . . wounds*] Used by E. J. Trelawny as a motto for his *Adventures of a Younger Son* chap. cii.

Gloucester. A mighty soldier!—Does he still hold out?

35 *Second Knight.* He shames our victory. His valour still
Keeps elbow-room amid our eager swords,
And holds our bladed falchions all aloof—
His gleaming battle-axe being slaughter-sick,
Smote on the morion of a Flemish knight,

40 Broke short in his hand; upon the which he flung
The heft away with such a vengeful force,
It paunched the Earl of Chester's horse, who then
Spleen-hearted came in full career at him.
Gloucester. Did no one take him at a vantage then?

45 *Second Knight.* Three then with tiger leap upon him flew,
Whom, with his sword swift-drawn and nimbly held,
He stung away again, and stood to breathe,
Smiling. Anon upon him rushed once more
A throng of foes, and in this renewed strife,

50 My sword met his and snapped off at the hilts.
Gloucester. Come, lead me to this Mars—and let us move
In silence, not insulting his sad doom
With clamorous trumpets. To the Empress bear
My salutation as befits the time.

[*Exeunt* Gloucester *and Forces.*

SCENE III

[*The Field of Battle. Enter* Stephen *unarmed.*]

Stephen. Another sword! And what if I could seize

I ii *35–50*. Probably modelled on the reported account of Macbeth's bravery in the field, *Macbeth* I ii. Cp. I iii 2 *n*.

I ii *36. keeps*] Maintains *K.'s MS (cancelled)*.

I ii *37–50*. A reworking of details originally derived from the narrative of Stephen's last stand in the *Historia Anglorum* (ed. cit. chap. 18, 274).

I ii *39. morion*] A visorless helmet. Frequently in Spenser, for example *The Faerie Queene* VII vii 28,

> And on his head (as fit for warlike stoures)
> A guilt engraven morion he did weare . . .

I iii *1. Another sword*] According to Henry of Huntingdon (*Historia Anglorum* ed. cit. chap. 18, 274) Stephen drew his sword after his battle-axe was broken and *rem mirabiliter agit, donec et gladius confractus est* ('wrought wonders until the sword too was broken').

I iii *1–13. And what . . . Come on*] *K.'s MS (cancelled)*,

> . . . for one short minute longer
> That I may pepper that De Kaimes and then
> Yield to this army some twenty squadrons—Stephen say

One from Bellona's gleaming armoury,
Or choose the fairest of her sheavèd spears!
Where are my enemies? Here, close at hand,
5   Here come the testy brood. Oh, for a sword!
I'm faint—a biting sword! A noble sword!
A hedge-stake—or a ponderous stone to hurl
With brawny vengeance, like the labourer Cain.
Come on! Farewell my kingdom, and all hail
10 Thou superb, plumed, and helmeted renown,
All hail! I would not truck this brilliant day
To rule in Pylos with a Nestor's beard—
Come on!

Enter De Kaims *and Knights, &c.*

De Kaims. Is 't madness, or a hunger after death,
That makes thee thus unarmed throw taunts at us?
15 Yield, Stephen, or my sword's point dip in

Wouldst thou exchange this helmeted renown
[5]   To rule in quiet Pylas Nestor-like?
No!—
        Enter De Kaims knights and soldiers dropping in
   l. [2]. *De Kaimes*] William of Kahaines (or Cahaignes); for his part in
seizing Stephen at the battle of Lincoln see l iii 14–17 *n* below.
   l. [3]. *this army*] A rejected correction was 'valiant'. 'Stephen say' is substituted for 'This is glory . . .'.
   l. [5]. See l. iii 12 *n*.
I iii 2. *Bellona*] The Roman goddess of war. Cp. *Macbeth* I ii 55,
        . . . Bellona's bridegroom, lapp'd in proof . . .
I iii 5–6. *Oh, for a sword . . . A noble sword*] Cp. *Richard III* vi 7,
        A horse! a horse! my kingdom for a horse!
I iii 7. *a ponderous stone*] According to William of Malmesbury Stephen fell
when one of Gloucester's knights struck him with a stone (*Historia Novella*,
ed. cit. 49). The detail is omitted in Henry of Huntingdon's *Historia Ang-
lorum*.
I iii 8. *Genesis* iv 8, '. . . when they were in the field . . . Cain rose up
against Abel his brother and slew him . . .'.
I iii 11. *truck*] Barter or exchange.
I iii 12. Nestor, King of Pylos and one of the oldest of the Greek leaders,
survived the Trojan War.
I iii 14–17. See *Historia Anglorum* (ed. cit. chap. 18, 274), *Guillemus de
Kahaines . . . irruit in regem, et eum galea arripiens voce magna clamavit:* 'Huc
omnes, huc! regem teneo' ('William of Kahaines . . . rushed upon the king,
and seizing him by the helmet cried in a loud voice: "Hither, all, hither! I
have the king"').
I iii 15. *dip in*] explore K.'s MS (*cancelled*). The word 'will' is understood.

The gloomy current of a traitor's heart.
Stephen. Do it, De Kaims, I will not budge an inch.
De Kaims. Yes, of thy madness thou shalt take the meed.
Stephen. Darest thou?
De Kaims.   How dare—against a man disarmed?
20   *Stephen.* What weapons has the lion but himself?
Come not near me, De Kaims, for by the price
Of all the glory I have won this day,
Being a king, I will not yield alive
To any but the second man of the realm,
25   Robert of Gloucester.
De Kaims.   Thou shalt vail to me.
Stephen. Shall I, when I have sworn against it, sir?
Thou think'st it brave to take a breathing king,
That, on a court-day bowed to haughty Maud;
The awèd presence-chamber may be bold
30   To whisper, there's the man who took alive
Stephen—me—prisoner. Certes, De Kaims,
The ambition is a noble one.
De Kaims.   'Tis true,
And, Stephen, I must compass it.
Stephen.   No, no,
Do not tempt me to throttle you on the gorge,
35   Or with my gauntlet crush your hollow breast,
Just when your knighthood is grown ripe and full
For lordship.
A Soldier.   Is an honest yeoman's spear
Of no use at a need? Take that.
Stephen.   Ah, dastard!
De Kaims. What, you are vulnerable! My prisoner!
40   *Stephen.* No, not yet. I disclaim it, and demand
Death as a sovereign right unto a king
Who 'sdains to yield to any but his peer,
If not in title, yet in noble deeds,
The Earl of Gloucester. Stab to the hilts, De Kaims,

I iii 22–6. *Come not . . . Gloucester*] Stephen's refusal to surrender to anyone except the Earl of Gloucester in person is recorded in Ordericus Vitalis's *Historia Ecclesiasticum* and John of Hexham's *Symeonis monachi*; *opera omnia*.
I iii 25. *vail*] Submit, yield. Cp. *Endymion* iv 263 (p. 257 above), 'The kings . . . their . . . sceptres vail . . .'
I iii 27. *a breathing king*] a king alive *K.'s MS* (cancelled).
I iii 31. Cancelled false starts in *K.'s MS* were,
   1. King . . .
   2. The Stubborn Reb[el].

45   For I will never by mean hands be led
    From this so famous field. Do ye hear! Be quick!
           [*Trumpets. Enter the Earl of* Chester *and Knights.*

SCENE IV

[*A Presence Chamber. Queen* Maud *in a Chair of State, the
    Earls of* Gloucester *and* Chester, *Lords, Attendants.*]

    Maud. Gloucester, no more; I will behold that Boulogne:
    Set him before me. Not for the poor sake
    Of regal pomp and a vain-glorious hour,
    As thou with wary speech, yet near enough,
    Hast hinted.
5   *Gloucester.*   Faithful counsel have I given;
    If wary, for your Highness' benefit.
    Maud. The Heavens forbid that I should not think so,
    For by thy valour have I won this realm,
    Which by thy wisdom I will ever keep.
10   To sage advisers let me ever bend
    A meek attentive ear, so that they treat
    Of the wide kingdom's rule and government,
    Not trenching on our actions personal.
    Advised, not schooled, I would be; and henceforth
15   Spoken to in clear, plain, and open terms,
    Not side-ways sermoned at.
    Gloucester.   Then, in plain terms,
    Once more for the fallen king–
    Maud.   Your pardon, brother,
    I would no more of that; for, as I said,
    'Tis not for worldly pomp I wish to see
20   The rebel, but as dooming judge to give

I iv 1. After the sacking of Lincoln Stephen was brought before the Empress
at Gloucester and imprisoned in Bristol Castle. 'Boulogne' was a title
acquired through his marriage to Matilda, daughter of Count Eustace of
Boulogne.

I iv 8–16. The Empress's forthright manner hints at the arrogance which
contributed to her downfall. Cp. *Historia Anglorum* (ed. cit. chap. 19, 275),
*Erecta est autem in superbiam, quia suis incerta belli prosperavissent, et omnium fere
corda a se alienavit* . . . ('But she was elated with insufferable pride at the success of her supporters in the uncertain fortunes of war, and alienated from
herself the hearts of most men . . .').

I iv 10. *let me ever bend*] ever will I bend K.'s MS (*cancelled*).

I iv 13. *trenching*] Encroaching.

I iv 15. *Spoken to in clear, plain*] I would be spoken with in plain K.'s MS
(*cancelled*).

A sentence something worthy of his guilt.
Gloucester. If 't must be so, I'll bring him to your presence.
            [*Exit* Gloucester.
Maud. A meaner summoner might do as well—
 My lord of Chester, is 't true what I hear
25 Of Stephen of Boulogne, our prisoner,
 That he, as a fit penance for his crimes,
 Eats wholesome, sweet, and palatable food
 Off Gloucester's golden dishes, drinks pure wine,
 Lodges soft?
Chester.   More than that, my gracious Queen,
30 Has angered me. The noble Earl, methinks,
 Full soldier as he is, and without peer
 In counsel, dreams too much among his books.
 It may read well, but sure 'tis out of date
 To play the Alexander with Darius.
35 *Maud.* Truth! I think so. By Heavens it shall not last!
 Chester. It would amaze your Highness now to mark
 How Gloucester overstrains his courtesy
 To that crime-loving rebel, that Boulogne—
 Maud. That ingrate!
Chester.   For whose vast ingratitude
40 To our late sovereign lord, your noble sire,
 The generous Earl condoles in his mishaps,
 And with a sort of lackeying friendliness,
 Talks off the mighty frowning from his brow,
 Woos him to hold a duet in a smile,
45 Or, if it please him, play an hour at chess—
 Maud. A perjured slave!

I iv *24–35.* Stephen's initially chivalrous reception by the Earl of Gloucester is stressed by William of Malmesbury, who attributes Stephen's subsequent imprisonment in fetters to his abuse of the privileges granted him (*Historia Novella* ed. cit. 49–50). K. and Brown agree with Henry of Huntingdon in attributing his changed treatment to the Empress's malice (*Historia Anglorum* ed. cit. chap. 19, 275).

I iv *32. too*] sometimes *K.'s MS* (*cancelled*).

I iv *33. out of date*] weak enough *K.'s MS* (*cancelled*).

I iv *34.* Alludes to Alexander's chivalrous treatment of the captive princesses after his victory over Darius at Issus (333 B.C.).

I iv *38.* K.'s cancelled false start was 'And finds for every one of all his . . .'

I iv *39–40. vast ingratitude . . . sire*] Henry I had persuaded his barons to accept his daughter as heir to England and Normandy in 1127. On his death in 1135 his nephew Stephen crossed to England and seized the crown.

I iv *42. lackeying friendliness*] See *Otho the Great* I i 97 *n* (p. 550 above), 'lackeying my counsel at a beck'.

Chester.   And for his perjury,
Gloucester has fit rewards—nay, I believe,
He sets his bustling household's wits at work
For flatteries to ease this Stephen's hours,
50   And make a heaven of his purgatory;
Adorning bondage with the pleasant gloss
Of feasts and music, and all idle shows
Of indoor pageantry; while siren whispers,
Predestined for his ear, 'scape as half-checked
55   From lips the courtliest and the rubiest
Of all the realm, admiring of his deeds.
Maud. A frost upon his summer!
Chester.   A queen's nod
Can make his June December. Here he comes . . .

I iv 55. *rubiest*] Cp. *Otho the Great* IV ii 38 (p. 596 above),
              Pout her faint lips anew with rubious health . . .
and *Lamia* i 163 *n* (p. 623 above), '*rubious-argent*'.
I iv 57–8. Perhaps suggested by *Richard III* I i 1–2,
              Now is the winter of our discontent
              Made glorious summer by this sun of York . . .
but de Selincourt notes a parallel with Matthew Prior's *English Ballad on the
Taking of Namur* (1707) 83–4,
              . . . that mighty year
              When you turn'd June into September . . .
I iv 58. *his June December*] cold Christmas *K.'s (cancelled)*.

146 'This living hand, now warm and capable'

Probably composed Nov. 1819: the fragment is written out on a sheet of
paper (reproduced *Finney* 740) containing st. 51 of K.'s comic poem *The Cap
and Bells* (No. 147 below), which he was writing Nov.–Dec. 1819. The belief shared by many of K.'s early readers that the lines were addressed to
Fanny Brawne is not now generally held. W. J. Bate comments, 'The
general feeling now is that the lines were a passage he might have intended
to use in some future poem or play' (*Bate* (1963) 626–7). For a hint of the
speaker's possible identity see K.'s letter to John Taylor of 17 Nov. 1819 in
which he speaks of 'The Earl of Leicester's histrory' as a 'promising' subject
for a play (*L* ii 234).
Text from K.'s MS.
Published *Forman* (1898).

This living hand, now warm and capable
Of earnest grasping, would, if it were cold
And in the icy silence of the tomb,
So haunt thy days and chill thy dreaming nights

5   That thou would wish thine own heart dry of blood
So in my veins red life might stream again,
And thou be conscience-calmed. See here it is—
I hold it towards you.

¶ 146. *1. This living hand ... cold*] Cp. *The Fall of Hyperion* i 18 (p. 658 above),

When this warm scribe my hand is in the grave ...

147 The Cap and Bells or, The Jealousies

A Fairy Tale–Unfinished

Written Nov.–Dec. 1819: see Brown's account of his association with K. during this period, 'By chance our conversation turned on the idea of a comic faery poem in the Spenser stanza, and I was glad to encourage it. He had not composed many stanzas before he proceeded with spirit. It was to be published under the feigned authorship of Lucy Vaughan Lloyd, and to bear the title of "The Cap and Bells", or , which he preferred, "The Jealousies". This occupied his mornings pleasantly. He wrote it with the greatest facility; in one instance I remember having copied (for I copied as he wrote) as many as twelve stanzas before dinner. In the evenings, at his own desire, he was alone in a sitting-room, deeply engaged in remodelling his poem of "Hyperion" into a "Vision" [see headnote to *The Fall of Hyperion*, p. 655 above]' (*KC* ii 71–2). There is no evidence of work on the poem after Dec. 1819: Brown records that K.'s personal anxieties obliged him to break off his '... morning and evening employment' (*KC* ii 72)– these anxieties were probably connected with his failing health in late December (*L* ii 238) and with George Keats's visit to England 9–28 Jan. 1820. K.'s references to the poem after he had suffered his first haemorrhage on 3 Feb. 1820 show that he hoped to complete the work when he had recovered his health (*L* ii 268, 299).

According to Brown, *The Cap and Bells* 'was written chiefly for amusement; it appeared to be a relaxation; and it was begun without framing laws in his [K.'s] mind for the supernatural. When I noticed certain startling

¶ 147. *Title.* So given in *1848* (in K.'s MS 'The Cap and Bells,' not in K.'s hand). *Woodhouse 2* has 'The Jealousies, A faery Tale by Lucy Vaughan Lloyd of China Walk, Lambeth'. China Walk was near Lambeth Road on the South bank of the Thames. On 'The Jealousies' see l. 64 *n* below.

contradictions, his answer used to be –"Never mind Brown; all these matters will be properly harmonized before we divide it into Cantos"' (*KC* ii 99). The poem's general conception suggests that K.'s chief 'amusement' in it was the invention of a romantic and fanciful 'eastern' fairy tale with a satirical flavour, but certain features of the style and manner–notably K.'s satirical glances at topical themes, such as the Prince Regent's matrimonial troubles, the invention of gaslighting and the discomforts of travelling by hackney-coach–indicate the influence of Byron's *Don Juan*, of which Cantos I and II were published July 1819.

Commentaries on the poem's literary echoes and topical allusions include *Finney* (732–7), Phyllis Mann's 'Keats's Indian Allegory', *KShJ* vi 1957 (4–9), which emphasizes K.'s use of details concerning Tipu Sultan (see ll. 190–3 *n* below), and R. Gittings's discussions in *Gittings* (1956) 115–43 and *Gittings* (1968) 368–73, which implausibly interpret the poem as an abortive satire on the rivalry between the Lake Poets and the Cockney School. *The Cap and Bells* has occasional life, as Jeffrey recognized in his letter to Milnes of Aug. 1848 ('. . . strange outbreaks of redundant fancy, and felicitous expression . . .,' *KC* ii 249), but the poem is an excursion into a field outside K.'s range and is generally regarded as one of his weakest performances.

Text from Woodhouse's transcript with some variants noted from the portions of K.'s MS (ll. 730–94 missing) now lodged at the Morgan Library, the Huntington Library and Harvard. For details concerning the MS *see Garrod* xlvi–xlviii, 395.

Published *1848*. An extract (ll. 226–65) was published in the *Indicator* 23 Aug. 1820; other extracts (ll. 390–6, 415–23) were used by E. J. Trelawny as mottoes for his *Adventures of a Younger Son* (1831), chaps. xii, xlviii.

I

In midmost Ind, beside Hydaspes cool,
There stood, or hovered, tremulous in the air,
A fairy city, 'neath the potent rule
Of Emperor Elfinan–famed ev'rywhere

1. Hydaspes] See *Paradise Lost* iii 436 (marked by K. in his copy of Milton), '*Ganges* or *Hydaspes, Indian* streams . . .'. K.'s Indian setting for his fairies was probably affected by Spenser (see following *n*) and *A Midsummer Night's Dream* (cp. ll. 389–96 *n* below).
4 Elfinan] Variously Elphinan and Elfinan in K.'s MS. The name is borrowed from Spenser's genealogy of the fairy race in *The Faerie Queene* II x 72,

> The first and eldest, which that sceptre swayd,
> Was *Elfin*; him all *India* obayd,
> And all that now *America* men call:
> Next him was noble *Elfinan* who layd
> *Cleopolis* foundation first of all . . .

5   For love of mortal women, maidens fair,
       Whose lips were solid, whose soft hands were made
       Of a fit mould and beauty, ripe and rare,
       To pamper his slight wooing, warm yet staid.
  He loved girls smooth as shades, but hated a mere shade.

II

10   This was a crime forbidden by the law,
       And all the priesthood of his city wept,
       For ruin and dismay they well foresaw,
       If impious prince no bound or limit kept,
       And fairy Zendervester overstepped.
15   They wept, he sinned, and still he would sin on,
       They dreamt of sin, and he sinned while they slept;
       In vain the pulpit thundered at the throne,
  Caricature was vain, and vain the tart lampoon.

III
Which seeing, his high court of parliament

K. borrowed the name of Elfinan's 'fairy city' (l. 3 above) from the same passage in Spenser: see l. 90 *n* below.

4–5. famed . . . fair] Elfinan's amorousness glances at the Prince Regent (see headnote). K. had seen the Prince yachting at Cowes in Aug. 1819 (*L* ii 142) and later described him as the 'fat Regent' (*L* ii 149). On Elfinan's love for 'mortal women' see l. 64 *n* below.

13. no bound or limit kept] religious limits overstept *Draft (cancelled).*

14. faery Zendervester] Fairy holy writ (from Zend-Avesta, the sacred book of the reglion of Zoroaster). R. Gittings suggests some influence from Burton's rendering of Ariosto's lines on jealousy, *Anatomy of Melancholy* III 3 iv 1 (1813 edn ii 455),

> This is the cruel wound against whose smart,
> No liquor's force prevails, or any plaister,
> No skill of stars, no depth of magic art,
> Devised by that great clerk Zoroaster . . .

K. had also recently come across references to Zoroaster when reading the entry on 'Cham' in Pierre Bayle's *Dictionnaire Historique* (see l. 403 *n* below).

17–18. An earlier attempt in the draft was,

> Until the faery City no more shone
> As it was wont, heaven's vengeance rubb'd its bloom . . .

18. tart] bold *Draft (cancelled).* Caricatures of the Prince Regent and lampoons on his behaviour–notably by William Hone (1780–1842) and 'Peter Pindar' [John Wolcot] (1738–1819)–had been common since the 'Delicate Investigation' of 1806 (see ll. 86–95 *n* below) and were increasingly popular in 1819–20 when the Prince was seeking grounds for divorce.

19–31. Negotiations were arranged in 1794 on the advice of George III

20   Laid a remonstrance at his Highness' feet,
        Praying his royal senses to content
        Themselves with what in fairy land was sweet,
        Befitting best that shade with shade should meet.
        Whereat, to calm their fears, he promised soon
25   From mortal tempters all to make retreat—
        Aye, even on the first of the new moon,
    An immaterial wife to espouse as heaven's boon.

IV

        Meantime he sent a fluttering embassy
        To Pigmio, of Imaus sovereign,
30   To half beg and half demand, respectfully,
        The hand of his fair daughter Bellanaine.
        And audience had, and speeching done, they gain
        Their point, and bring the weeping bride away;
        Whom, with but one attendant, safely lain
35   Upon their wings, they bore in bright array,
    While little harps were touched by many a lyric fay.

V

        As in old pictures tender cherubim
        A child's soul through the sapphired canvas bear,
        So, through a real heaven, on they swim
40   With the sweet princess on her plumaged lair,
        Speed giving to the winds her lustrous hair.
        And so she journeyed, sleeping or awake,

---

and his ministers for the Prince's marriage to Princess Caroline of Brunswick. The wedding took place April 1795.
29. Sovereign] Emperor *Draft (cancelled)*. Imaus, a mountain in Scythia, derives from *Paradise Lost* iii 431–2 (cp. l. 1 *n* above),

        As when a Vulture on *Imaus* bred . . .

31. Bellanaine] Probably derived, as R. Gittings suggests, from Italian
(*bella*) and French (*naine*) to mean 'beautiful dwarf'. Princess Caroline was
short and good-looking. C. L. Finney's view that the name is a partial ana-
gram of 'Annabella', otherwise Anne Isabella Milbank, who married Byron
1815 and separated from him 1816, is much less plausible but receives some
support from K.'s quoting Byron's poem to her at ll. 610–11 below.
37–8. As . . . soul]   As in old Pictures Cherubs bear aloft
        The Souls of Children . . . *Draft (cancelled)*.
38. sapphired] Painted blue to represent the sky. Cp. *On Visiting the Tomb of
Burns* 7 *n* (p. 357 above),

        Through sapphire warm . . .

42–5. Bellanaine's journey (described at length in sts. lxxii–lxxxiii below)
recalls the slow progress of Princess Caroline and her train from Brunswick
to England, Dec. 1794–April 1795.

Save when, for healthful exercise and air,
She chose to *promener à l'aile*, or take
45 A pigeon's somerset, for sport or change's sake.

VI

'Dear Princess, do not whisper me so loud,'
Quoth Corallina, nurse and confidant,
'Do you not see there, lurking in a cloud,
Close at your back, that sly old Crafticant?
50 He hears a whisper plainer than a rant.
Dry up your tears, and do not look so blue;
He's Elfinan's great state-spy militant,
His running, lying, flying foot-man too–
Dear mistress, let him have no handle against you!

VII

55 'Show him a mouse's tail, and he will guess,
With metaphysic swiftness, at the mouse;
Show him a garden, and, with speed no less,
He'll surmise sagely of a dwelling house,
And plot, in the same minute, how to chouse
60 The owner out of it; show him a—' 'Peace!
Peace! nor contrive thy mistress' ire to rouse!'

---

44. promener à l'aile] To take a turn in the air to stretch her wings. K.'s use of French words and phrases in the poem to suggest fashionable affectation– see ll. 283, 299, 369, 759 below–probably owes something to Byron's use of French and Italian in *Don Juan*, for example, I lxii,

And now I think on't, '*mi vien in mente . . .*'
See further ll. 292 *n*, 299 *n* below.

45. somerset] Somersault.

47. Corallina] The nurse's name derives from coral given to her charges when teething.

48. lurking in] coming through *Draft (cancelled)*.

49. Crafticant] Craft Cant *Draft (cancelled)*.

52-3. great . . . footman] state train and tail bearer,

His running and his flying footman . . . *Draft (cancelled)*.
The jingling invective in the revised reading has a Byronic flavour. The context suggests that K. was typifying Tory Ministers who sided with the Regent against Princess Caroline.

55-6. R. Gittings suggests an echo of Reynolds's parody of Wordsworth's *Peter Bell*, 'It has been my aim and my achievement to deduce moral thunder from butter-cups, daisies, celandines, and . . . "such small deer" [*King Lear* III iv 144]. Out of sparrows' eggs have hatched great truths.' (*Selected Prose of J. H. Reynolds*, ed. L. M. Jones, 1966, 259.)

59. chouse] Cheat. See *All gentle folks* 46-7 *n* (p. 368 above).

Returned the Princess, 'My tongue shall not cease
Till from this hated match I get a free release.

VIII

Ah, beauteous mortal!' 'Hush!' quoth Coralline,
65   'Really you must not talk of him, indeed.'
'*You* hush!' replied the mistress, with a shine
Of anger in her eyes enough to breed
In stouter hearts than nurse's fear and dread.
'Twas not the glance itself made nursey flinch,
70   But of its threat she took the utmost heed—
Not liking in her heart an hour-long pinch,
Or a sharp needle run into her back an inch.

IX

So she was silenced, and fair Bellanaine,
Writhing her little body with ennui,
75   Continued to lament and to complain
That Fate, cross-purposing, should let her be
Ravished away far from her dear country;
That all her feelings should be set at naught,
In trumping up this match so hastily,
80   With lowland blood. And lowland blood she thought
Poison, as every staunch true-born Imaian ought.

X

Sorely she grieved, and wetted three or four
White Provence rose-leaves with her fairy tears,
But not for this cause—alas! she had more
85   Bad reasons for her sorrow, as appears
In the famed memoirs of a thousand years,

64. *beauteous mortal*] Bellanaine, like Elfinan, is in love with a mortal (cp.
l. 711 below). C. L. Finney comments, 'K. took the plot of his poem—the
criss-cross loves of fairies and mortals—from *A Midsummer Night's Dream*'
(*Finney* 733). The 'jealousies' referred to in the poem's title were probably
intended to arise from this situation.

69. *'Twas not the glance itself*] Earlier attempts in the draft include,

    1. Not for themselves perhaps . . .
    2. Nor at the glance itself . . .

77. *country*] countrey *Draft*; countree *1848*. Milnes's correction in *1848* is
an attempt to emphasize the rhyme.

78. *That all her feelings*] That she a highland Princess *Draft (cancelled)*.

80–1. Bellanaine's home is in mountain country (see l. 29 *n*).

86–95. An allusion to the popular taste for candid memoirs and autobio-
graphies which probably aims at the style of Byron's attacks on current
fashions in literature (for example, *Don Juan* i ccv–cvi). K. may be thinking

Written by Crafticant, and publishèd
By Parpaglion and Co. (those sly compeers
Who raked up every fact against the dead)
90   In Scarab Street, Panthea, at the Jubal's Head.

XI

Where, after a long hypocritic howl
Against the vicious manners of the age,
He goes on to expose, with heart and soul,
What vice in this or that year was the rage,
95   Backbiting all the world in every page;
With special strictures on the horrid crime
(Sectioned and subsectioned with learning sage)
Of fairies stooping on their wings sublime
To kiss a mortal's lips, when such were in their prime.

XII

100   Turn to the copious index, you will find
Somewhere in the column, headed letter B,
The name of Bellanaine, if you're not blind.
Then pray refer to the text, and you will see
An article made up of calumny
105   Against this highland princess, rating her
For giving way, so over-fashionably,

---

especially of the 'Delicate Investigation' (1806) into Princess Caroline's
moral conduct. The documents in the case were prepared for publication
by Spenser Perceval (Prime Minister 1809-12) and printed with a substantial
historical preface in C. V. Williams's *The Book* (1813).

86. *memoirs*] memories *Draft*.

88. *Parpaglion*] An invented name with a Spenserian flavour, probably suggested by the Italian *paglia* meaning straw or chaff.

90. Parodies the style of the publishers' imprint on the title-pages of six-
teenth- and seventeenth-century books. Panthea derives from *The Faerie
Queene* II x 73 (see l. 4 *n* above),

　　　　　. . . *Elfant* was of most renowned fame
　　　Who all of Christall did *Panthea* build . . .

On Jubal see *Genesis* iv 21, '. . . the father of all such as handle the harp and
the organ . . .'.

91. *hypocritic*] hypercritic *Draft, 1848, Garrod*.

97. As in Burton's *Anatomy of Melancholy* (1621).

98. *on their wings sublime*] Cp. *Paradise Lost* ii 528-9 (marked by K. in his
copy of Milton),

　　　　　. . . in the Air sublime
　　　　Upon the wing . . .

To this new-fangled vice, which seemed a burr
Stuck in his moral throat, no coughing e'er could stir.

XIII

There he says plainly that she loved a man!
110   That she around him fluttered, flirted, toyed,
Before her marriage with great Elfinan;
That after marriage too, she never joyed
In husband's company but still employed
Her wits to 'scape away to Angle-land,
115   Where lived the youth who worried and annoyed
Her tender heart, and its warm ardours fanned
To such a dreadful blaze, her side would scorch her hand.

XIV

But let us leave this idle tittle-tattle
To waiting-maids and bedroom coteries,
120   Nor till fit time against her fame wage battle.
Poor Elfinan is very ill at ease—
Let us resume his subject if you please:
For it may comfort and console him much
To rhyme and syllable his miseries.
125   Poor Elfinan, whose cruel fate was such,
He sat and cursed a bride he knew he could not touch!

XV

Soon as, according to his promises,
The bridal embassy had taken wing,
And vanished, bird-like, o'er the suburb trees,
130   The Emperor, empierced with the sharp sting
Of love, retired, vexed and murmuring
Like any drone shut from the fair bee-queen,
Into his cabinet, and there did fling
His limbs upon a sofa, full of spleen,

---

107. seemed] seem *Draft*; seems *1848*.
110. That she with him would flutter flirt and toy . . . *Draft (cancelled)*.
114. Angle-land] England. See the references to Canterbury and Kent at
ll. 387, 527 below.
116. ardours] fires *Draft (cancelled)*.
118–19. Most of the evidence concerning Princess Caroline from the time
of the 'Delicate Investigation' to the divorce proceedings of 1820 was
gathered for the Prince Regent from servants and various other members of
the Princess's household staff.
129. suburb trees] Neighbouring trees; see *Lamia* ii 26 *n* (p. 635 above).
130. empierced] transfix'd *Draft (cancelled)*.

135 And damned his House of Commons, in complete
      chagrin.

XVI

    'I'll trounce some of the members,' cried the Prince,
    'I'll put a mark against some rebel names,
    I'll make the Opposition benches wince,
    I'll show them very soon, to all their shames,
140   What 'tis to smother up a Prince's flames.
    That ministers should join in it, I own,
    Surprises me!—They too at these high games!
    Am I an Emperor? Do I wear a crown?
Imperial Elfinan, go hang thyself or drown!

XVII

145   'I'll trounce 'em!—There's the square-cut chancellor,
    His son shall never touch that bishopric;
    And for the nephew of old Palfior,
    I'll show him that his speech has made me sick,
    And give the colonelcy to Phalaric;
150   The tiptoe marquis, moral and gallant,
    Shall lodge in shabby taverns upon tick;
    And for the Speaker's second cousin's aunt,

135–62. The Prince's relations with his Whig ministers had worsened since
his recently renewed attempts to divorce the Princess. Brown singled out
these stanzas as examples of 'failures in wit' (*KC* ii 99).

135. damned] curs'd *Draft*.

144. Followed in K.'s MS by the first line (erased) of st. xix. See following
n.

145–62. Probably an afterthought. The altered numbering of the stanzas in
K.'s MS suggest that the narrative originally continued without a break
from st. xvi to st. xix.

145. square-cut chancellor] K. may be glancing at Nicholas Vansittart (1706–
51), first Baron Bexley, who was Chancellor of the Exchequer 1812–22
and became extremely unpopular because of his taxation policies; he was
also known for his devotion to various Christian missions, such as the
British and Foreign Bible Mission and the Church Missionary Society. Cp.
All gentle folks 30 *n* (p. 367 above).

147 (and *149* below). *Palfior . . . Philaric*] Invented names. Earlier attempts
for Palfior in the draft were 'Belfior' and 'Palcolor'.

150. H. Buxton Forman suggests an allusion to the Marquis of Lansdowne
(who supported the Princess and '. . . whose refusal to sit upon the Green
Bay Committee in the House of Lords was both "moral" and "gallant"'
Forman (1883) ii 495).

151. upon tick] On credit. The phrase was in use in the eighteenth century.

152. second] Brothers *Draft* (*cancelled*).

24+κ.

She sha'n't be maid of honour, by heaven that she
    sha'n't!

XVIII

'I'll shirk the Duke of A., I'll cut his brother,
155   I'll give no garter to his eldest son;
I won't speak to his sister or his mother,
The Viscount B. shall live at cut-and-run;
But how in the world can I contrive to stun
That fellow's voice, which plagues me worse than any,
160   That stubborn fool, that impudent state-dun,
Who sets down every sovereign as a zany—
That vulgar commoner, Esquire Biancopany?

XIX

Monstrous affair! Pshaw! Pah! What ugly minx
Will they fetch from Imaus for my bride?
165   Alas, my wearied heart within me sinks
To think that I must be so near allied
To a cold dullard fay—ah, woe betide!
Ah, fairest of all human loveliness!
Sweet Bertha! What crime can it be to glide
170   About the fragrant pleatings of thy dress,
Or kiss thine eyes, or count thy locks, tress after tress?'

XX

So said, one minute's while his eyes remained
Half lidded, piteous, languid, innocent;
But, in a wink, their splendour they regained,
175   Sparkling revenge with amorous fury blent.
Love thwarted in bad temper oft has vent.
He rose, he stamped his foot, he rang the bell,
And ordered some death-warrants to be sent

155. garter] The Order of the Garter.
157. Viscount] Baron *Draft (cancelled)*. To 'cut-and-run' is to retreat in haste.
162. Biancopany] A play on the name Whitbread, from the Italian *bianco* (white) and *pane* (bread). Samuel Whitbread, radical member of the celebrated family of brewers, was among Princess Caroline's staunchest supporters.
169. Bertha] K. borrowed Bertha's name, her place of residence and various other details concerning her from his own *The Eve of St. Mark* (p. 480 above): see below 387, 447–50 *n*, 504 *n*, 512–18 *n*.
172. remained] were soft *Draft (cancelled)*.
178–80. Echoing Tom Moore's description of the Regent at breakfast in 1812, *The Insurrection of the Papers* 17–18,

For signature—somewhere the tempest fell,
180   As many a poor felon does not live to tell.

XXI

'At the same time Eban' (this was his page,
A fay of colour, slave from top to toe,
Sent as a present, while yet under age,
From the Viceroy of Zanguebar—wise, slow,
185   His speech, his only words were 'yes' and 'no,'
But swift of look, and foot, and wing was he),
'At the same time, Eban, this instant go
To Hum the soothsayer, whose name I see
Among the fresh arrivals in our empery.

XXII

190   Bring Hum to me! But stay—here, take my ring,
The pledge of favour, that he not suspect

_____

... plans for saddles, tea and toast,
Death warrants and the *Morning Post* ...
181. Cancelled false starts to the stanza include,
    1. 'At the same time Luscinnial' said he
      (This was his favourite Page, a negro Fay ...
    2. At the same time, Amorio, said he
    3. 'At the same time Eban' (This was his Page
      A Fay of Colour, sent from Zanguebar
      A Present from the Viceroy) ...
The name 'Eban' was obviously settled on because it suggests ebony.
Coloured servants became common in England during the eighteenth century after the Royal African Company was formed in 1672 with a mono-
poly of the slave trade.
182. slave from top to toe] lusty secret sure *Draft (cancelled).*
184. Zanguebar] A name perhaps owed to K.'s recollection of King Zanguebar in 'The History of the Princess of Deryabar', in *The Arabian Nights* (H.
Weber's *Tales of the East*, 1812, i 309).
185. To that old Fortunetellers whom I see ... *Draft (cancelled).* The word
'hum' was in use in the eighteenth and early nineteenth centuries as a slang
term for humbug; see, for example, Tom Moore's use of it as a name for the
Prince Regent in his satirical poem, 'Fum and Hum, the two Birds of
Royalty' (*Works*, ed A. D. Godley 1910, 452–3).
190–3. Phyllis Mann suggests in her 'Keats's Indian Allegory' (see headnote)
that K. is identifying Elfinan, who lives 'in midmost Ind', with Tipu Sultan whose sending of a valuable ring with his envoys to France and per-
forming of various acts of cruelty and treachery had been made generally
known from *Selected Letters of Tippoo Sultan to various Public Functionaries*,
transl. W. Kirkpatrick 1811 (Tipu fell at Seringapatam 1799).

Any foul play or awkward murdering,
Though I have bowstrung many of his sect.
Throw in a hint that if he should neglect
195   One hour, the next shall see him in my grasp,
And the next after that shall see him necked,
Or swallowed by my hunger-starvèd asp—
And mention ('tis as well) the torture of the wasp.'

XXIII
These orders given, the Prince, in half a pet,
200   Let o'er the silk his propping elbow slide,
Caught up his little legs, and, in a fret,
Fell on the sofa on his royal side.
The slave retreated backwards, humble-eyed,
And with a slave-like silence closed the door,
205   And to old Hum through street and alley hied.
He 'knew the city,' as we say, of yore,
And for short cuts and turns, was nobody knew more.

XXIV
It was the time when wholesale houses close
Their shutters with a moody sense of wealth,
210   But retail dealers, diligent, let loose
The gas (objected to on score of health),
Conveyed in little soldered pipes by stealth,
And make it flare in many a brilliant form,
That all the powers of darkness it repell'th,
215   Which to the oil-trade doth great scathe and harm,
And supersedeth quite the use of the glow-worm.

192. murdering] handling *Draft.*
193. bowstrung] Strangled; strangling with a bowstring was a common
punishment for offenders in Turkey during the seventeenth century. Other
examples of Elfinan's oriental despotism occur at ll. 196–8, 319, 333, below.
196. necked] Decapitated.
198. And mention ('tis as well)] Or at least put to the *Draft (cancelled).*
Phyllis Mann (*loc. cit.*) thinks that the wasp may have been intended as 'the
Indian fairy equivalent of a yellow, black-striped royal tiger' (see l. 333 *n*
below).
208. houses] *Draft;* dealers *Woodhouse* 2. Woodhouse's reading may be a
slip (see l. 210 below).
210–16. There were no restrictions on hours of work for the retail trade
until the first Shop Act (1912). Gas lighting was first introduced in London
c. 1807.
213. Make it flare] set to flaring *Draft (cancelled).*
215. scathe] Harm or damage. Frequently in Spenser.

XXV

Eban, untempted by the pastry-cooks
(Of pastry he got store within the palace),
With hasty steps, wrapped cloak, and solemn looks,
220   Incognito upon his errand sallies,
His smelling-bottle ready for the alleys.
He passed the hurdy-gurdies with disdain,
Vowing he'd have them sent aboard the galleys.
Just as he made his vow, it 'gan to rain,
225   Therefore he called a coach, and bade it drive amain.

XXVI

'I'll pull the string,' said he, and further said,
'Polluted Jarvey! Ah, thou filthy hack!
Whose springs of life are all dried up and dead,
Whose linsey-woolsey lining hangs all slack,
230   Whose rug is straw, whose wholeness is a crack;
And evermore thy steps go clatter-clitter;
Whose glass once up can never be got back,
Who prov'st, with jolting arguments and bitter,
That 'tis of modern use to travel in a litter.

XXVII

235   Thou inconvenience! Thou hungry crop

221. smelling bottle] Containing smelling salts or perfume, against the bad smells.

222. hurdy-gurdies] The hurdy-gurdy was the forerunner of the barrel-organ.

223. the galleys] A reference to the French custom, discontinued in the eighteenth century, of sentencing condemned criminals to row in the galleys.

226-65. Published by Leigh Hunt in his article 'On Coaches', *The Indicator* Aug. 1820. Brown commented to Milnes, 'What could be better than [K.'s] descrption of a London hackney-coach? – yet how much misplaced!' (*KC* ii 99).

226. the string] The check-string by which the occupant of the coach signalled the driver to stop.

227-52. The word 'jarvey' was used for the driver of a hackney-coach, but in these lines K. speaks of the driver, the horse and the coach as if they were a single entity.

227. In his heart Vile Jarvie! Ah thou filthy hack . . . *Draft (cancelled).*

229. linsey-wolsey] A mixture of wool and flax.

231. go clatter-clitter] are clattering *Draft.*

233-4.   Whose number stuck above my head a thing
Gives coldness to my heart and trembling to my wing . . .
Draft (cancelled).

234. in a litter] K. is playing on the two meanings of the word.

For all corn! Thou snail-creeper to and fro,
Who while thou goest ever seem'st to stop,
And fiddle-faddle standest while you go;
I' the morning, freighted with a weight of woe,
240　　Unto some lazar-house thou journeyest,
And in the evening tak'st a double row
Of dowdies, for some dance or party dressed,
Besides the goods meanwhile thou movest east and west.

XXVIII
By thy ungallant bearing and sad mien,
245　　An inch appears the utmost thou couldst budge.
Yet at the slightest nod, or hint, or sign,
Round to the curb-stone patient dost thou trudge,
Schooled in a beckon, learned in a nudge,
A dull-eyed Argus watching for a fare.
250　　Quiet and plodding, thou dost bear no grudge
To whisking tilburies, or phaetons rare,
Curricles, or mail-coaches, swift beyond compare.'

XXIX
Philosophizing thus, he pulled the check,
And bade the coachman wheel to such a street,
255　　Who, turning much his body, more his neck,
Louted full low and hoarsely did him greet:
'Certes, monsieur were best take to his feet,

236. corn] The horse's feed of oats.
238. fiddle-faddle] Fussing or wasting time. Cp. Wordsworth's *The Idiot Boy*
(1798) 13-14,

>Till she is tired, let Betty Foy
>With girt and stirrup fiddle-faddle . . .

240. lazar-house] Hospital for the diseased poor. See *Isabella* 124 *n* (p. 334
above),

>. . . of more soft ascent than lazar stairs . . .

241. evening tak'st a double row] Even takest in a glow *Draft*.
242. dowdies] Beauties *Draft*.
248. As courteous to a Cobler as a Judge *Draft*. The revised version has an
Augustan flavour.
249. As watchful as Argus, who had a hundred eyes and kept a sharp look
out (cp. *As Hermes once* 1-2 *n*, p. 499 above).
251-2. tilburies . . . phaetons . . . curricles] Light carriages fashionable in the
eighteenth and early nineteenth centuries. Mail coaches first came into use
in 1787.
253. check] String *Draft* (*cancelled*). See 226 *n* above.
256. Louted] Bowed, made obeisance. See *Otho the Great* III i 17 (p. 577
above),

>Was't to this end I louted . . .

Seeing his servant can no further drive
For press of coaches that to-night here meet
260 Many as bees about a straw-capped hive,
When first for April honey into faint flowers they dive.'

XXX

Eban then paid his fare, and tiptoe went
To Hum's hotel, and, as he on did pass
With head inclined, each dusky lineament
265 Showed in the pearl-paved street as in a glass.
His purple vest, that ever peeping was
Rich from the fluttering crimson of his cloak,
His silvery trousers, and his silken sash
Tied in a burnished knot, their semblance took
270 Upon the mirrored walls, wherever he might look.

XXXI

He smiled at self, and, smiling, showed his teeth,
And seeing his white teeth, he smiled the more;

261. Followed in the draft by the cancelled stanza,
       Ho! Ho thought Eban so this Signor Hum
       A Conversazione holds tonight
       Whene er he beats his literary drum
       The learned muster round all light and tight
       Drest in best black to talk by candle light
       E'en while he thought, for eighteen penny fare
       He paid a half penny by cu[n]ning sleight
       Made argent; then with self-contented Air
       Broke through the crowd to Hums, and all the world was
           there.
K. may have intended to continue the narrative with an account of Eban at
the Conversazione; see the cancelled lines (written upside down in the
draft after l. 338 below),
       His arms and wings rapt in a crimson cloak
       Incognito he makes important way
       Through the Court yard whose golden Portals look
       Full on a pearl–built Minster . . .
For the view that Hum and his Conversazione were intended as a satire on
Leigh Hunt see *Gittings* (1956) 125–9.
271. Cancelled openings for this stanza include,
    1. Past either ear half shown, his plenteous hair
       Went in a jetty wreath, and on his back
       Met in curl clusters, and ever shining there . . .
    2. Past either ear, half shown, his plenteous hair
       Went jetty, and in large curl-clusters fell
       Between his shoulders . . .

Lifted his eye-brows, spurned the path beneath,
Showed teeth again, and smiled as heretofore,
275   Until he knocked at the magician's door;
Where, till the porter answered, might be seen,
In the clear panel, more he could adore–
His turban wreathed of gold, and white, and green,
Mustachios, ear-ring, nose-ring, and his sabre keen.

XXXII

280   'Does not your master give a rout to-night?'
Quoth the dark page. 'Oh, no,' returned the Swiss,
'Next door but one to us, upon the right,
The *Magazin des Modes* now open is
Against the Emperor's wedding–and, sir, this
285   My master finds a monstrous horrid bore,
As he retired, an hour ago I wis,
With his best beard and brimstone, to explore
And cast a quiet figure in his second floor.

XXXIII

'Gad! he's obliged to stick to business!
290   For chalk, I hear, stands at a pretty price.
And as for aqua vitae–there's a mess!
The *dentes sapientiae* of mice,
Our barber tells me too, are on the rise.
Tinder's a lighter article, nitre pure
295   Goes off like lightning, grains of Paradise
At an enormous figure! Stars not sure!
Zodiac will not move without a sly douceur!

281–2. Quoth . . . but one] Quoth Eban, 'every Coach in all the Town / Methinks is here . . .' Draft (*cancelled*).
284–5. And who of all the gay world now would miss / To suit each shape . . . Draft (*cancelled*).
286. ago] Draft, *1848;* or more *Woodhouse* 2. Woodhouse's reading may be a slip since it echoes the rhyme in ll. 285, 287–8.
288. cast a quiet figure] Cast a horoscope.
290. chalk] For drawing magic signs (see l. 288 above).
291. aqua vitae] Originally a term in alchemy applied to unrectified alcohol.
292. dentes sapientiae] Wisdom teeth. Perhaps an imitation of Byron's use of Latin tags in *Don Juan,* for example I liii,

> I say that there's the place–but *'Verbum sat'* . . .

and I cci,

> The *Vade Mecum* of the true sublime . . .

293. Our barber tells me] Barbers still performed at the time the minor surgical operations of drawing teeth and blood-letting.
295. grains of Paradise] The seeds of an aromatic plant (*Amomum Meleguetta*) used since the thirteenth century in medicine and also as a spice.

XXXIV

Venus won't stir a peg without a fee,
And master is too partial, *entre nous*,
300   To—"'Hush, hush!' cried Eban, 'Sure that is he
Coming down stairs. By St. Bartholomew,
As backwards as he can! Is 't something new?
Or is 't his custom, in the name of fun?'
'He always comes down backward, with one shoe'—
305   Returned the porter, 'off, and one shoe on,
Like, saving shoe for sock or stocking, my man John.'

XXXV

It was indeed the great magician,
Feeling, with careful toe, for every stair,

297. douceur] Sweetener, bribe.
298–306. K. made several false starts to this stanza including,
        1. A ruddy fan . . .
        2. A bloodred fan of fire . . .
        3. A fan shap'd burst of fire . . .
Cp. l. 663 below.
298. a peg] an inch *Draft (cancelled).*
299. entre nous] 'Twixt you and me *Draft (cancelled).* See *Don Juan* I
lxxxiv,
              . . . *inter nos:*
(This should be *entre nous*, for Julia thought
In French, but then the rhyme would go for nought.) . . .
See l. 44 *n*, l. 292 *n* above.
301–3. Cancelled attempts in the draft include,
        1. Backwards . . .
        2. Coming down stairs, and by the Holyland . . .
304–6. one shoe . . . my man John] See the nursery rhyme,
        Diddle, diddle, dumpling, my son John,
        Went to bed with his trousers on;
        One shoe off, and one shoe on,
        Diddle, diddle, dumpling, my son John.
K. appears to have known a version in which 'sock' or 'stocking' replaces
'shoe', but the rhyme was commonly known at the time in the form given
above; see *The Oxford Dictionary of Nursery Rhymes*, 1952 edn, 245–6,
which also refers to Charles Lamb's quoting the rhyme at Haydon's 'immortal dinner' attended by K. and others 28 Dec. 1817 (Taylor's *Autobiography of Haydon* (1853) 1926 edn i 270).
305. porter] Swiss *Draft (cancelled).*
307. magician] Astrologer *Draft (cancelled).*
308. with careful toe] careful as he can *Draft.* An earlier cancelled attempt was
'like a careful Man'.

24*

And retrograding careful as he can,
310   Backwards and downwards from his own two pair:
'Salpietro!' exclaimed Hum, 'is the dog there?
He's always in my way upon the mat!'
'He's in the kitchen, or the Lord knows where',
Replied the Swiss, 'the nasty, yelping brat!'
315   'Don't beat him!' returned Hum, and on the floor
        came pat.

XXXVI

Then, facing right about, he saw the Page,
And said, 'Don't tell me what you want, Eban.
The Emperor is now in a huge rage–
'Tis nine to one he'll give you the rattan!
320   Let us away!' Away together ran
The plain-dressed sage and spangled blackamoor,
Nor rested till they stood to cool, and fan,
And breathe themselves at the Emperor's chamber
        door,
When Eban thought he heard a soft imperial snore.

XXXVII
325   'I thought you guessed, foretold, or prophesied
That 's Majesty was in a raving fit?'
'He dreams,' said Hum, 'or I have ever lied,
That he is tearing you, sir, bit by bit.'
'He's not asleep, and you have little wit,'
330   Replied the page, 'That little buzzing noise,
Whate'er your palmistry may make of it,
Comes from a play-thing of the Emperor's choice,
From a Man-Tiger-Organ, prettiest of his toys.'

310. From the last landing of his own two Pair . . . *Draft (cancelled).* The word 'two pair' means a room 'situated above two "pairs" or flights of stairs, i.e. on the second floor' (*OED*).
311. Salpietro!] By saltpetre! Salpetre is the chief constituent in gunpowder.
314. yelping] The draft reading 'whelping' was probably an error, as H. Buxton Forman suggests.
315. and on the floor came pat] or I will kill your Cat *Draft.*
319. give you the rattan] Give you a beating. A rattan is a switch cut from a palm tree.
333. prettiest of his toys] King of royal toys *Draft (cancelled).* The 'Man-Tiger-Organ', now at the Victoria and Albert Museum, is a mechanical tiger made for Tipu Sultan (see 190–3 *n* above) to symbolize his hatred of the English. When wound up the tiger would maul the figure of the English officer lying beneath him to the accompaniment of sounds resembling growls and cries. It had been sent to London after the fall of Seringapatam

XXXVIII

Eban then ushered in the learned seer.
335   Elfinan's back was turned, but, ne'ertheless,
Both, prostrate on the carpet, ear by ear,
Crept silently, and waited in distress,
Knowing the Emperor's moody bitterness.
Eban especially, who on the floor 'gan
340   Tremble and quake to death—he feared less
A dose of senna-tea or nightmare Gorgon
Than the Emperor when he played on his Man-Tiger-
      Organ.

XXXIX

They kissed nine times the carpet's velvet face
Of glossy silk, soft, smooth, and meadow-green,
345   Where the close eye in deep rich fur might trace
A silver tissue, scantly to be seen,
As daisies lurked in June-grass, buds in treen.
Sudden the music ceased, sudden the hand
Of majesty, by dint of passion keen,
350   Doubled into a common fist, went grand,
And knocked down three cut glasses and his best ink-
      stand.

XL

Then turning round, he saw those trembling two.
'Eban,' said he, 'as slaves should taste the fruits
Of diligence, I shall remember you
355   To-morrow, or the next day, as time suits,
In a finger conversation with my mutes—
Begone!—for you, Chaldean! here remain!

---

and had been housed since 1818 in the public reading-room of the East India
House in Leadenhall St. For the cancelled lines following this in the draft see
l. 261 *n* above.
335. ne'ertheless] for all that *Draft* (*cancelled*).
341. senna] Phisic *Draft* (*cancelled*).
343–7. Phyllis Mann suggests that K. was thinking of the 'small but rich
and beautiful carpet' used by Tipu on state occasions.
344. Cancelled attempts at the line were,
   1. Of green silk meadow . . .
   2. soft silk meadow green . . .
347. Treen] Trees.
349. by dint of passion keen] struck on the sofa Table *Draft* (*cancelled*).
356. finger conversation] Speaking by signs made with the fingers (the
London Asylum for the education and care of the deaf and dumb was
founded 1792).
357. Chaldean] Astrologer.

Fear not, quake not, and as good wine recruits
A conjurer's spirits, what cup will you drain?
360   Sherry in silver, hock in gold, or glassed champagne?'

XLI

'Commander of the Faithful!' answered Hum,
'In preference to these, I'll merely taste
A thimble-full of old Jamaica rum.'
'A simple boon!' said Elfinan, 'thou may'st
365   Have Nantz, with which my morning coffee's laced.'
'I'll have a glass of Nantz, then', said the Seer,
'Made racy (sure my boldness is misplaced)
With the third part (yet that is drinking dear!)
Of the least drop of *creme de citron*, crystal clear.'

XLII

370   'I pledge you, Hum, and pledge my dearest love,
My Bertha!' 'Bertha, Bertha!' cried the sage,
'I know a many Berthas!' 'Mine's above
All Berthas' sighed the Emperor. 'I engage,'
Said Hum, 'in duty and in vassalage,
375   To mention all the Berthas in the Earth.
There's Bertha Watson and Miss Bertha Page,
This famed for languid eyes, and that for mirth,
There's Bertha Blount of York and Bertha Knox of
Perth.'

XLIII

'You seem to know–''I do know,' answered Hum,
380   'Your Majesty's in love with some fine girl
Named Bertha, but her surname will not come
Without a little conjuring.' ''Tis Pearl,
'Tis Bertha Pearl what makes my brains so whirl,
And she is softer, fairer than her name!'
385   'Where does she live?' asked Hum. 'Her fair locks
curl
So brightly, they put all our fays to shame!–
Live?–Oh, at Canterbury, with her old grand-dame.'

361. Commander of the Faithful] The standard form of address for the Sultan
Haroun-al-Raschid in *The Arabian Nights*.
365. with which my morning coffee's laced] as clear as water and as chaste ..
Draft (cancelled). *Woodhouse 2* has the footnote, 'Mr. Nisby is of opinion
that laced coffee is bad for the head. Spectator.' On 'Nantz' see *He is to weet
a melancholy carle 22 n* (p. 498 above), 'nantz or cheery-brandy'.
369. crystal] bright and *Draft* (cancelled).
383. what] that *Draft* (cancelled).
387. at Canterbury] See 169 *n* above.

XLIV

'Good, good,' cried Hum, 'I've known her from a
    child!
She is a changeling of my management.
390 She was born at midnight in an Indian wild,
Her mother's screams with the striped tiger's blent
While the torch-bearing slaves a halloo sent
Into the jungles and her palanquin,
Rested amid the desert's dreariment,
395 Shook with her agony, till fair were seen
The little Bertha's eyes oped on the stars serene.'

XLV

'I can't say,' said the monarch, 'that may be
Just as it happened, true or else a bam.
Drink up your brandy, and sit down by me,
400 Feel, feel my pulse, how much in love I am;
And if your science is not all a sham,
Tell me some means to get the lady here.'
'Upon my honour,' said the son of Cham,
'She is my dainty changeling, near and dear,
405 Although her story sounds at first a little queer.'

XLVI

'Convey her to me, Hum, or by my crown,
My sceptre, and my cross-surmounted globe,
I'll knock you'—'Does your majesty mean—*down*?
No, no, you never could my feelings probe
410 To such a depth!' The Emperor took his robe
And wept upon its purple palatine,
While Hum continued, shamming half a sob,

389–96. Probably suggested by Titania's 'changeling boy' in *A Midsummer Night's Dream* II i 120–35, whose Indian mother died at his birth.
E. J. Trelawny used ll. 390–6 as a motto for his *Adventures of a Younger Son*
(1831) chap. xll.
392. halloo] screaming *Draft (cancelled).*
395. An earlier attempt was 'The little Bertha's face till fair were seen . . .'.
398. bam] Hoax. A slang term used twice by K. in his letters (*L* ii 40, 69).
403. Cham] See Pierre Bayle's *Dictionnaire Historique* (1695–97, rev. 1702)
'CHAM [Shem], le plus jeune des trois fils de Noé . . . On le fait l'inven-
teur de la magie . . .' *Woodhouse 2* has the footnote, 'Cham is said to have
been the inventor of Magic. Lucy learn'd from this Bayle's Dictonary, and
had copied a long Latin note from that work.' (Bayle's entry under 'Cham'
runs to nine columns and includes quotations from Latin authorities.)
411. palatine] Royal. Cp. *Lamia* i 211 *n* (p. 626 above).

'In Canterbury doth your lady shine?
But let me cool your brandy with a little wine.'

XLVII
Whereat a narrow Flemish glass he took,
That once belonged to Admiral de Witt,
Admired it with a connoisseuring look,
And with the ripest claret crownèd it,
And, ere one lively bead could burst and flit,
420   He turned it quickly, nimbly upside down,
His mouth being held conveniently fit
To catch 'the creature': 'Best in all the town'
He said, smacked his moist lips, and gave a pleasant
    frown.

XLVIII
'Ah, good my Prince, weep not!' And then again
425   He filled a bumper. 'Great Sire, do not weep.
Your pulse is shocking, but I'll ease your pain.'
'Fetch me that Ottoman and prithee keep
Your voice low,' said the Emperor, 'and steep
Some lady's-fingers nice in Candy wine;
430   And prithee, Hum, behind the screen do peep
For the rose-water vase, magician mine,
And sponge my forehead—so my love doth make me
    pine.'

XLIX
'Ah, cursèd Bellanaine!' 'Don't think of her,'
Rejoined the Mago, 'but on Bertha muse;
435   For, by my choicest best barometer,

415–23. Used by E. J. Trelawny as a motto for his *Adventures of a Younger Son* (1831) chap. xlviii.

415. Whereat he took a narrow flanders glass . . . *Draft* (*cancelled*).

416. Admiral] Pensioner *Draft* (*cancelled*). John de Witt (1625–72) was appointed grand pensionary of Dort in 1650 and led the Dutch fleet against the English in 1667.

419. Cp. *Ode to a Nightingale* 17 *n* (p. 526 above), 'beaded bubbles winking at the brim'.

422. creature] A colloquialism used in the nineteenth century for strong drink, and still current in Ireland.

427. Ottoman] Used at the time for a cushioned seat or footstool.

429. lady's fingers] Biscuits or small cakes. Candy wine is either sweet wine or wine from Kandy in Ceylon (Kandy had been in the news 1814–15 when it was brought under British control).

434. Mago] Magician.

You shall not throttled be in marriage noose.
I've said it, Sir. You only have to choose
Bertha or Bellanaine.' So saying, he drew
From the left pocket of his threadbare hose,
440   A sampler hoarded slyly, good as new,
Holding it by his thumb and finger full in view.

L

'Sire, this is Bertha Pearl's neat handy-work,
Her *name*, see here, *Midsummer, ninety-one*.'
Elfinan snatched it with a sudden jerk,
445   And wept as if he never would have done,
Honouring with royal tears the poor homespun,
Whereon were broidered tigers with black eyes,
And long-tailed pheasants, and a rising sun,
Plenty of posies, great stags, butterflies
450   Bigger than stags, a moon—with other mysteries.

LI

The monarch handled o'er and o'er again
These day-school hieroglyphics with a sigh;
Somewhat in sadness, but pleased in the main,
Till this oracular couplet met his eye
455   Astounded: *Cupid, I—do thee defy!*
It was too much! He shrunk back in his chair,
Grew pale as death, and fainted—very nigh.
'Pho! nonsense!' exclaimed Hum, 'now don't
    despair.
She does not mean it really. Cheer up, hearty – there!

LII

460   'And listen to my words. You say you won't,
On any terms, marry Miss Bellanaine;
It goes against your conscience—good! Well, don't!
You say you love a mortal. I would fain
Persuade your honour's highness to refrain

436. Perhaps echoing Burton on marriage, *Anatomy of Melancholy* III ii 6 v
(marked by K. in his copy of Burton), 'The band of marriage is adamantine,
no hope of loosing it, thou art undone' (1813 edn ii 417). K. substituted
'throttled' for 'confin'd' in his draft.

443. Midsummer] May 1392 *Draft (cancelled)*.

447–50. Cp. the oriental designs on Bertha's screen, *The Eve of St. Mark*
79–84 (p. 485 above).

449. great stags] a great stag *Draft (cancelled)*.

456. shrunk . . . in his chair] fell . . on the couch *Draft (cancelled)*.

459. Cheer up, hearty–there!] Cheer up–hearty there! *Draft;* cheer up,
hearty, there *Woodhouse 2*.

465   From peccadilloes. But, Sire, as I say,
           What good would that do? And, to be more plain,
           You would do me a mischief some odd day,
       Cut off my ears and hands—and head too, by my fay!

                              LIII
           'Besides, manners forbid that I should pass any
470   Vile strictures on the conduct of a prince
           Who should indulge his genius, if he has any,
           Not, like a subject, foolish matters mince.
           Now I think on 't, perhaps I could convince
           Your Majesty there is no crime at all
475   In loving pretty little Bertha, since
           She's very delicate, not over tall,
       A fairy's hand, and in the waist, why—very small.'

                              LIV
           'Ring the repeater, gentle Hum!' ''Tis five,'
           Said gentle Hum, 'The nights draw in apace;
480   The little birds I hear are all alive.
           I see the dawning touched upon your face.
           Shall I put out the candles, please your Grace?'
           'Do put them out, and, without more ado,
           Tell me how I may that sweet girl embrace—
485   How you can bring her to me.' 'That's for you,
       Great Emperor, to adventure, like a lover true.'

                              LV
           'I fetch her!'—'Yes, an't like your Majesty;
           And as she would be frightened wide awake
           To travel such a distance through the sky,
490   Use of some soft manoeuvre you must make,
           For your convenience, and her dear nerves' sake.
           Nice way would be to bring her in a swoon,
           Anon, I'll tell what course were best to take.
           You must away this morning.' 'Hum! So soon?'
495   'Sire, you must be in Kent by twelve o'clock at noon.'

468. *fay*] Faith (archaic form) and also fairy (see *Ode to a Nightingale* 37 *n*, p. 528 above).

472. *foolish matters mince*] Be precise and scrupulous about trifles.

478. *repeater*] A repeating watch or clock 1760 (*OED*). 'Ring' is substituted for 'Touch' in K.'s MS (probably because he saw that he had used 'touched' in l. 481 below).

486. *adventure*] fineagle *Draft* (*cancelled*). The word 'finagle' is slang for deceive by flattery, trick (derived from 'fainague, fainaguer' meaning to revoke at cards [*Websters Dictionary*]).

492. *Nice*] Best *Draft* (*cancelled*).

LVI

At this great Caesar started on his feet,
Lifted his wings, and stood attentive-wise.
'Those wings to Canterbury you must beat,
If you hold Bertha as a worthy prize.
500   Look in the Almanack—*Moore* never lies—
April the twenty-fourth, this coming day,
Now breathing its new bloom upon the skies,
Will end in St. Mark's Eve. You must away,
For on that eve alone can you the maid convey.'

LVII

505   Then the magician solemnly 'gan frown,
So that his frost-white eyebrows, beetling low,
Shaded his deep-green eyes, and wrinkles brown
Pleated upon his furnace-scorchèd brow.
Forth from the hood that hung his neck below,
510   He lifted a bright casket of pure gold,
Touched a spring-lock, and there in wool, or snow
Charmed into ever-freezing, lay an old
And legend-leavèd book, mysterious to behold.

LVIII

'Take this same book—it will not bite you, Sire.
515   There, put it underneath your royal arm.
Though it's a pretty weight it will not tire,
But rather on your journey keep you warm.
This is the magic, this the potent charm,

496. great Caesar] Cp. *Otho the Great* I ii 51 *n* (p. 554 above).
500. A reference to *Old Moore's Almanac*. Francis Moore (1657–1715 ?) published his first almanac in 1699.
501. April the twenty fifth this very morn . . . *Draft (cancelled)*.
502. breathing . . . new] spreading . . . young *Draft (cancelled)*.
503. Will end in St. Mark's eve] Ends in quiet St. Agnes E[ve] *Draft (cancelled)*. The cancelled reading was a slip, since K. knew that St. Agnes's Eve was 20 Jan. (see *The Eve of St. Agnes* 1 *n*, p. 452 above).
504. An invented variation on the popular superstition which K. had drawn on for his *The Eve of St. Mark* (headnote, p. 480 above).
506. frost] snow *Draft (cancelled)*.
508. furnace-scorchèd] weather beaten *Draft (cancelled)*. His brow was scorched from working at the furnace where he concocted brews for his spells and perhaps practised alchemy.
510. casket] book *Draft (cancelled)*.
512–13. an old . . . behold] Cp. Bertha's '. . . curious volume . . .' in *The Eve of St. Mark* (pp. 482ff above).
517. But rather] A Lover *Draft (cancelled)*.

That shall drive Bertha to a fainting fit!
520   When the time comes, don't feel the least alarm,
Uplift her from the ground, and swiftly flit
Back to your palace, where I wait for guerdon fit.'

LIX

'What shall I do with this same book?' 'Why merely
Lay it on Bertha's table close beside
525   Her work-box, and 'twill help your purpose dearly.
I say no more.' 'Or good or ill betide,
Through the wide air to Kent this morn I'll glide,'
Exclaimed the Emperor. 'When I return,
Ask what you will–I'll give you my new bride!
530   And take some more wine, Hum. Oh, Heavens, I burn
To be upon the wing! Now, now, that minx I spurn!'

LX

'Leave her to me,' rejoined the magian,
'But how shall I account, illustrious fay,
For thine imperial absence? Pho, I can
535   Say you are very sick, and bar the way
To your so loving courtiers for one day.
If either of their two archbishops' graces
Should talk of extreme unction, I shall say
You do not like cold pig with Latin phrases,
540   Which never should be used but in alarming cases.'

LXI

'Open the window, Hum; I'm ready now.'
'Zooks,' exclaimed Hum, as up the sash he drew,
'Behold, your Majesty, upon the brow
Of yonder hill, what crowds of people!' 'Whew!
545   The monster's always after something new,'
Returned his Highness, 'they are piping hot

519. That shall make swoon at once *Draft* (cancelled).
522. where I wait for guerdon fit] Draft. Omitted in *Woodhouse* 2, 1848.
526. I say] Ask me *Draft.*
531. that minx] my Bride *Draft.*
538. extreme unction] The sacrament administered in the Roman Catholic
Church to those *in extremis.*
539. You do not like being woken up with a wetting to the accompaniment
of Latin phrases (i.e. the form of words accompanying the Last Sacraments).
On 'cold pig' see *Otho the Great* III ii 1–3 *n*, p. 579 above.
540. alarming] extremest *Draft.*
544. Whew] Where *1848.* The word is not clear in K.'s MS.

To see my pigsney, Bellanaine. Hum, do
Tighten my belt a little–so, so–not
Too tight. The book–my wand–so, nothing is forgot.'

LXII

550   'Wounds, how they shout!' said Hum, 'and there–
        see, see
The Ambassador's returned from Pigmio!
The morning's very fine–uncommonly.
See, past the skirts of yon white cloud they go,
Tinging it with soft crimsons. Now below
555   The sable-pointed heads of firs and pines
They dip, move on, and with them moves a glow
Along the forest side. Now amber lines
Reach the hill top, and now throughout the valley
        shines!'

LXIII

'Why, Hum, you're getting quite poetical.
560   Those *nows* you managed in a special style.'
'If ever you have leisure, Sire, you shall
See scraps of mine will make it worth your while.
Tit-bits for Phoebus!–yes, you well may smile.
Hark, hark, the bells!' 'A little further yet,
565   Good Hum, and let me see this mighty coil.'

547. pigsney] A term of endearment derived from Burton's *Anatomy of Melancholy* III 2 iii (marked by K. in his copy of Burton), '. . . bird, mouse lamb, puss, pigeon, pigsney, kid, honey, love, dove, chicken' (1813 edn i 318).

549. so] no *Draft*.

551. The Ambassador] Your Embassy *Draft* (*cancelled*).

554–60. Now below . . . special style] Cp. Hunt's essay 'A Now, Descriptive of a Hot Day', to which K. contributed 'one or two of the passages' (*The Indicator* 28 June 1820, repr. *Forman* (1883) iii 33–9).

554. soft crimsons. Now below] purples crimsons and a glow *Draft* (*cancelled*).

556. move on, and with them moves a glow] and fill the forest with a glow *Draft* (*cancelled*).

560. you managed] are brought *Draft* (*cancelled*).

563–76. The atmosphere of a city *en fête*. Perhaps a recollection of the peace celebrations in London in 1814. See *Gittings* (1956), '. . . it is worth noting that such joyful descriptions come from a man whose letters at this time show the utmost despondence' (143).

565. see] view *Draft, 1848*. The word 'coil' means fuss, disturbance. See *Endymion* iv 247 *n* (p. 257 above).

Then the great Emperor full graceful set
His elbow for a prop, and snuffed his mignonnette.

LXIV

The morn is full of holiday: loud bells
With rival clamours ring from every spire;
570   Cunningly-stationed music dies and swells
In echoing places; when the winds respire,
Light flags stream out like gauzy tongues of fire;
A metropolitan murmur, lifeful, warm,
Comes from the northern suburbs; rich attire
575   Freckles with red and gold the moving swarm;
While here and there clear trumpets blow a keen alarm.

LXV

And now the fairy escort was seen clear,
Like the old pageant of Aurora's train,
Above a pearl-built minster, hovering near:
580   First wily Crafticant, the chamberlain,
Balanced upon his grey-grown pinions twain,
His slender wand officiously revealed;
Then black gnomes scattering sixpences like rain;
Then pages three and three; and next, slave-held,
585 The Imaian 'scutcheon bright—one mouse in argent
field.

LXVI

Gentlemen pensioners next; and after them,
A troop of wingèd Janizaries flew;

567. snuffed] Sniffed.
568. Cancelled false starts in the draft include,

        1. And sneering look'd upon the busy scene . . .
        2. The merry Bells with rival clamours rang . . .
        3. The flags talk withtheir gauzy tongues of fire . . .

With 3 cp. l 572 below.
572. Light flags stream out] Stream go the flags *Draft (cancelled).*
575. Freckled the moving populace an alarm *Draft (cancelled).*
576. While here and there trumpets] Of trumpets here and there *Draft
(cancelled).*
577. was seen clear] Earlier attempts were 'on splendid' and 'floated'.
580. First wily] Sagacious *Draft (cancelled).*
582. His slender wand official slant wise held *Draft (cancelled).*
583. Then black gnomes] The Pages fluttering two and two *Draft (cancelled).*
584. Then pages three and three] Upon the populace *Draft (cancelled).*
585. one mouse in argent] Six mice in silver *Draft (cancelled).*
586. Gentlemen pensioners] Gentlemen-at-arms. So used in the eighteenth
century.

Then slaves, as presents bearing many a gem;
Then twelve physicians fluttering two and two;
590   And next a chaplain in a cassock new;
Then lords in waiting; then (what head not reels
For pleasure?) the fair Princess in full view,
Borne upon wings—and very pleased she feels
To have such splendour dance attendance at her heels.

LXVII

595   For there was more magnificence behind.
She waved her handkerchief. 'Ah, very grand,'
Cried Elfinan, and closed the window-blind.
'And, Hum, we must not shilly-shally stand—
Adieu! adieu! I'm off for Angle-land!
600   I say, old Hocus, have you such a thing
About you—feel your pockets, I command—
I want, this instant, an invisible ring.
Thank you, old mummy! Now securely I take wing.'

LXVIII

Then Elfinan swift vaulted from the floor,
605   And lighted graceful on the window-sill.
Under one arm the magic book he bore,
The other he could wave about at will.
Pale was his face, he still looked very ill.
He bowed at Bellanaine, and said, 'Poor Bell!
610   *Farewell! Farewell! and if for ever, still*

587. *troop of wingèd*] swarm of flying *Draft (cancelled).* Janissaries were formerly soldiers of the Turkish Sultan's guard.

588. *slaves*] pages *Draft (cancelled).*

600. *Hocus*] Hocus-pocus was used in the eighteenth century as a name for a conjuror or trickster as well as for conjuring or trickery.

601. *feel your pockets, I command*] in your old jewish pocket *Draft (cancelled).*

602. *an invisible ring*] A ring which can make its wearer invisible is a traditional device in eastern legends and fairy-tales, one of the earliest references being the ring of Gyges, Plato's *Republic* ii 359.

604–5.   So saying he vaulted to the window sill
            And standing like a little Mercury . . . *Draft (cancelled).*

608–9.   Hum you must laugh with me, I know you will
            More wine, old Boy! well mind it doesn't spill . . .
                                              Draft (cancelled).

610–11. *Farewell . . . fare thee well*] From Byron's poem to his wife after their separation, *Fare Thee Well* (1816, repr. 1819) 1–2,
            Fare thee well! and if for ever,
                Still for ever fare thee well . . .
For the public controversy over the poem on its appearance in various

For ever fare thee well!'—and then he fell
A laughing, snapped his fingers—shame it is to tell.

LXIX

'By'r Lady, he is gone!' cries Hum, 'and I
(I own it) have made too free with his wine.
615   Old Crafticant will smoke me by the by!
This room is full of jewels as a mine—
Dear valuable creatures, how ye shine!
Sometime to-day I must contrive a minute,
If Mercury propitiously incline,
620   To examine his scrutoire and see what's in it,
For of superfluous diamonds I as well may thin it.

LXX

The Emperor's horrid bad—yes, that's my cue.'
Some histories say that this was Hum's last speech;
That, being fuddled, he went reeling through
625   The corridor and scarce upright could reach
The stair-head; that being glutted as a leech,
And used, as we ourselves have just now said,
To manage stairs reversely, like a peach
Too ripe, he fell, being puzzled in his head
630   With liquor and the staircase. Verdict—*found stone dead.*

LXXI

This as a falsehood Crafticanto treats,
And as his style is of strange elegance,
Gentle and tender, full of soft conceits

---

newspapers and periodicals 14–21 April 1816 see Byron's *Works*, ed E. H. Coleridge (1904) iii 531–5.

615. smoke] Smoke me out, drive into the open. Frequently used by K. in his letters 1819–20, for example 17 Jan. 1820, '. . . once a person has smok'd the vapidness of . . . Society he must have . . . self-interest or the love of some sort of distinction to keep him in good humour with it' (*L* ii 244). See also his reference on 22 Sept. 1819 to *Isabella* (p. 326 above) as 'too smokeable' (*L* ii 174).

619. On Mercury as the god of thieves and tricksters see *Lamia* i 87–8 *n* (p. 620 above).

620. scrutoire] Escritoire, writing-desk.

626. glutted] See 737–8 *n* below.

628. manage] descend *Draft (cancelled).*

631. Earlier attempts include

> 1. But Crafticant denies this out and out . . .
> 2. This Crafticanto out and out denies . . .

632. of strange elegance] pure and elegant *Draft (cancelled).*

633. and tender] imaginative *Draft (cancelled).*

(Much like our Boswell's), we will take a glance
635   At his sweet prose and, if we can, make dance
His woven periods into careless rhyme.
O little fairy Pegasus, rear—prance—
Trot round the quarto—ordinary time!
March, little Pegasus, with pawing hoof sublime!

LXXII

640   Well, let us see—*tenth book and chapter nine*—
Thus Crafticant pursues his diary:
'''Twas twelve o'clock at night, the weather fine,
Latitude thirty-six; our scouts descry
A flight of starlings making rapidly
645   Toward Thibet. Mem.—birds fly in the night.
From twelve to half-past—wings not fit to fly
For a thick fog—the Princess, sulky quite,
Called for an extra shawl and gave her nurse a bite.

LXXIII

Five minutes before one—brought down a moth
650   With my new double-barrel—stewed the thighs
And made a very tolerable broth.
Princess turned dainty; to our great surprise,
Altered her mind, and thought it very nice.
Seeing her pleasant, tried her with a pun.
655   She frowned. A monstrous owl across us flies
About this time—a sad old figure of fun.
Bad omen—this new match can't be a happy one.

LXXIV

From two till half-past, dusky way we made,
Above the plains of Gobi—desert, bleak;
660   Beheld afar off, in the hooded shade
Of darkness, a great mountain (strange to speak)

634. *Boswell's*] Cowley's *Draft*.
641. *diary*] History *Draft*.
642–720. See 42–5 n. The journey through the air suggests a burlesque of magical journeys familiar to K. from eastern tales by Landor, Southey and others (see headnote to *Endymion*, p. 116 above).
650. *thighs*] Earlier attempts were 'ribs', 'legs' and 'loin'.
655. *A monstrous owl across us flies*] and tried to beat my face and eyes *Draft* (*cancelled*).
658. *dusky*] darkling *Draft* (*cancelled*).
661. *great mountain (strange to speak)*] Earlier attempts in the draft include,
      1. Volcano vast and great . . .
      2. Volcano's smoke and reek . . .

Spitting, from forth its sulphur-baken peak,
A fan-shaped burst of blood-red, arrowy fire,
Turbaned with smoke, which still away did reek,
665   Solid and black from that eternal pyre,
Upon the laden wind that scantly could respire.

LXXV

Just upon three o'clock a falling star
Created an alarm among our troop,
Killed a man-cook, a page, and broke a jar,
670   A tureen, and three dishes, at one swoop,
Then passing by the Princess, singed her hoop.
Could not conceive what Coralline was at—
She clapped her hands three times and cried out
    'Whoop!'
Some strange Imaian custom. A large bat
675   Came sudden 'fore my face and brushed against my hat.

LXXVI

Five minutes thirteen seconds after three—
Far in the west a mighty fire broke out.
Conjectured, on the instant, it might be
The city of Balk—'twas Balk beyond all doubt.
680   A griffin, wheeling here and there about,
Kept reconnoitring us—doubled our guard—
Lighted our torches, and kept up a shout,
Till he sheered off. The Princess very scared,
And many on their marrow-bones for death prepared.

LXXVII

At half-past three arose the cheerful moon.
Bivouacked for four minutes on a cloud,

---

662. *sulphur-baken peak*] nitrous peak elate *Draft* (*cancelled*). Perhaps altered to avoid the Miltonic word order.
664. *smoke*] monstrous clouds *Draft* (*cancelled*). 'Turbaned' is a suitable image for Indian fairy lore.
665. A cancelled false start was 'Upon the heavy-laden wind . . .'.
671. *her hoop*] Her hoop-skirt.
674–5. *A large bat / Came sudden 'fore my face*] Saw a bat / He sheered off to the right *Draft* (*cancelled*).
679. *Balk*] Balkh was an ancient Persian city equal in importance to Baby-lon and Nineveh. According to one tradition it was the burial-place of Zoroaster (cp. l. 14 *n* above).
680. *griffin*] Dragon *Draft* (*cancelled*).
684. *on their marrow-bones*] On their knees.

Where from the earth we heard a lively tune
Of tambourines and pipes, serene and loud,
While on a flowery lawn a brilliant crowd
690 Cinque-parted danced, some half asleep reposed
Beneath the green-fanned cedars, some did shroud
In silken tents, and 'mid light fragrance dozed,
Or on the open turf their soothèd eyelids closed.

LXXVIII

Dropped my gold watch, and killed a kettledrum.
695 It went for apoplexy—foolish folks!
Left it to pay the piper—a good sum
(I've got a conscience, maugre people's jokes).
To scrape a little favour 'gan to coax
Her Highness' pug-dog—got a sharp rebuff.
700 She wished a game at whist, made three revokes,
Turned from myself, her partner, in a huff.
His majesty will know her temper time enough.

LXXIX

She cried for chess—I played a game with her.
Castled her king with such a vixen look,
705 It bodes ill to his Majesty (refer
To the second chapter of my fortieth book,
And see what hoity-toity airs she took).
At half-past four the morn essayed to beam—
Saluted, as we passed, an early rook.
710 The Princess fell asleep, and, in her dream,
Talked of one Master Hubert, deep in her esteem.

LXXX

About this time, making delightful way,
Shed a quill-feather from my larboard wing—

687. *we heard a lively*] a most melodious *Draft (cancelled)*.
690. *cinque-parted*] In groups of five (or perhaps dancing the cinque-pace).
Cp. K.'s use of a similar compound in *Fragment of the 'Castle-Builder'* 60 *n*
(p. 392 above), 'cinque-coloured potter's clay'.
694. *kettledrum*] Kettle-drummer (so used in the eighteenth century).
695. The 'foolish folks' think the drummer died of apoplexy.
696. *Left it to pay the piper*] Left the gold watch as compensation.
697 (and 705–7, 745 below). Probably modelled on Byron's parenthetical
style, for example *Don Juan* I vii,
        And therefore I shall open with a line
        (Although it cost me half an hour in spinning) . . .
701 When at poor Corraline she 'gan to huff . . . *Draft (cancelled)*.
707. *hoity-toity airs*] whim and vagaries *Draft*.
711. *deep in her esteem*] now what can this mean *Draft (cancelled)*. See l. 64 *n*
above.

Wished, trusted, hoped 'twas no sign of decay—
Thank heaven, I'm hearty yet!—'twas no such thing.
At five the golden light began to spring
With fiery shudder through the bloomèd east.
At six we heard Panthea's churches ring—
The city all her unhived swarms had cast,
720   To watch our grand approach and hail us as we passed.

LXXXI
As flowers turn their faces to the sun,
So on our flight with hungry eyes they gaze,
And, as we shaped our course, this, that way run,
With mad-cap pleasure, or hand-clasped amaze.
725   Sweet in the air a mild-toned music plays,
And progresses through its own labyrinth.
Buds gathered from the green spring's middle-days
They scattered—daisy, primrose, hyacinth—
Or round white columns wreathed from capital to
       plinth.

LXXXII
730   Onward we floated o'er the panting streets,
That seemed throughout with upheld faces paved.
Look where we will, our bird's eye vision meets
Legions of holiday: bright standards waved,
And fluttering ensigns emulously craved
735   Our minute's glance; a busy thunderous roar
From square to square among the buildings raved,
As when the sea, at flow, gluts up once more
The craggy hollowness of a wild-reefed shore.

LXXXIII
And "Bellanaine for ever," shouted they,
740   While that fair Princess, from her wingèd chair,
Bowed low with high demeanour, and, to pay
Their new-blown loyalty with guerdon fair,

717. through the bloomèd east] upward through the dark *Draft (cancelled)*. The word 'fiery' was substituted for the cancelled attempts 'tremulous' and 'gleaming'.
724. clasped] join'd *Draft (cancelled)*.
726. Refers to the form of the music neatly.
735. Our] Woodhouse notes marginally 'q[uery] one'.
737–8. Cp. *Hyperion* ii 305–6 and 306 *n* (p. 430 above),
                    . . . like sullen waves
        In the half-glutted hollows of reef-rocks . . .
K. was revising *Hyperion* at this time.

Still emptied, at meet distance, here and there,
A plenty-horn of jewels. And here I
745   (Who wish to give the devil her due) declare
Against that ugly piece of calumny
Which calls them Highland pebble-stones not worth
  a fly.

LXXXIV

Still "Bellanaine" they shouted, while we glide
'Slant to a light Ionic portico,
750   The city's delicacy, and the pride
Of our Imperial Basilic. A row
Of lords and ladies, on each hand, make show
Submissive of knee-bent obeisance,
All down the steps; and, as we entered, lo!
755   The strangest sight, the most unlooked-for chance,
All things turned topsy-turvy in a devil's dance.

LXXXV

'Stead of his anxious Majesty and court
At the open doors, with wide saluting eyes,
Congées and scape-graces of every sort,
760   And all the smooth routine of gallantries,
Was seen, to our immoderate surprise,
A motley crowd thick gathered in the hall,
Lords, scullions, deputy-scullions, with wild cries
Stunning the vestibule from wall to wall,
765   Where the Chief Justice on his knees and hands doth
  crawl.

LXXXVI

Counts of the palace and the state purveyor
Of moth's-down to make soft the royal beds,
The common council and my fool Lord Mayor
Marching a-row, each other slipshod treads.
770   Powdered bag-wigs and ruffy-tuffy heads

744. A plenty-horn] A cornucopia. See *The Fall of Hyperion* i 35–6 and 35 *n*
(p. 659 above),

   . . . more plenty than the fabled horn
   Thrice emptied could pour forth . . .

751. Basilic] Basilica (anciently a royal palace and thence an oblong colon-
naded building used as a place of public assembly). K. may be thinking of
St Paul's Cathedral.

759. Congées and scape-graces] Bowings and scrapings.

770. The well-to-do and the vulgar. Bag-wigs (wigs with a bag to enclose
the back hair) were worn in the eighteenth century; 'ruffy-tuffy' means
tousled.

Of cinder wenches meet and soil each other.
Toe crushed with heel ill-natured fighting breeds,
Frill-rumpling elbows brew up many a bother,
And fists in the short ribs keep up the yell and pother.

LXXXVII

775   A poet, mounted on the Court-Clown's back,
Rode to the Princess swift with spurring heels,
And close into her face, with rhyming clack,
Began a Prothalamion. She reels,
She falls, she faints! while laughter peals
780   Over her woman's weakness. "Where," cried I,
"Where is his Majesty?" No person feels
Inclined to answer; wherefore instantly
I plunged into the crowd to find him or to die.

LXXXVIII

Jostling my way I gained the stairs and ran
785   To the first landing, where, incredible!
I met, far gone in liquor, that old man,
That vile impostor Hum——'
                So far so well,
For we have proved the Mago never fell
Down stairs, on Crafticanto's evidence,
790   And therefore duly shall proceed to tell,
Plain in our own original mood and tense,
The sequel of this day, though labour 'tis immense!

LXXXIX

Now Hum, new fledged with high authority,
Came forth to quell the hubbub in the hall...

*   *   *   *

788–9. See ll. 623–31 above.
793–4. Preserved only in *Woodhouse* 2; first printed *Garrod* (1938 edn).

148 'Bright star! Would I were steadfast as thou art'

Written 1819: so dated in Charles Brown's transcript. A more precise dating of the sonnet must involve conjecture, but it can be placed most convincingly with K.'s poems to Fanny Brawne written Oct.–Nov. 1819 (see Nos. 142, 143, 144, pp. 685, 686 and 689 above) on the grounds of some resemblances in phrasing, K.'s adoption of the Shakespearian sonnet form (see headnote to *The day is gone*, p. 685 above), and the fact that Fanny Brawne transcribed it in the copy of Cary's *Dante* given to her by K. (see headnote to *As Hermes once*, p. 498 above). A date in Oct.–Dec. 1819 is supported by W. J. Bate (*Bate* (1963) 618).

Until the discovery of Brown's transcript—see *Colvin* (1917) 493–4—*Bright Star!* was believed to be K.'s last poem because he wrote it out for Severn in his copy of Shakespeare's poems (now at Hampstead) *c.* 1 Oct. 1820 during their voyage to Italy Sept.–Oct. 1820. Since 1924, when K.'s journal-letter to Tom Keats of 25–7 June 1818 was first published, the poem has been seen to parallel K.'s description of Windermere in this letter (see ll. 1–6 *n* below). K. re-read the letter Oct. 1818 before sending it on to George and Georgiana Keats in America (*L* i 401); R. Gittings's suggestion that K. wrote the poem at this date with the passage on Windermere 'before his eyes . . . the likeness [in ll. 1–8 of the sonnet] is so close that there is no question of memory', and that the sonnet is therefore addressed to Mrs Isabella Jones (see ll. 10–14 *n* below), is unconvincing because it ignores Brown's dating, which we have no reason to doubt, and disregards the poem's relationship to the other poems to Fanny Brawne written Oct.–Nov. 1819. Arguments by several critics for a date in July 1819 are based on K.'s remarks in his letter to Fanny Brawne of 25 July 1819, 'I am distracted with a thousand thoughts. I will imagine you Venus tonight and pray, pray, pray to your Star like a Hethan. Your's ever fair Star' (*L* ii 133), but see W. J. Bate's convincing rebuttal, 'The use of the star . . . is utterly different: Fanny is . . . associated with the evening star, Venus; in the sonnet Keats wishes to identify himself with the steadfastness of a star (a common image in Keats [see ll. 1–6 *n* below] . . .)' (*Bate* (1963) 539).

Commentaries on the poem include those in F. W. Bateson's *English Poetry* (1950) 11–12; *Gittings* (1954) 25–36 and *Gittings* (1956) 54–68; *Murry* (1955) 113–23; A. Ward in 'The Date of Keats's "Bright Star" Sonnet', *Studies in Philology* LII (1955) 75–85 and *Ward* (1963) 297–8; and *Bate* (1963) 359, 539, 618–19.

Text from K.'s MS, with some variants noted from Brown's transcript. Published *Plymouth and Devonport Weekly Journal* 27 Sept. 1838; repr. *1848*.

Bright star! Would I were steadfast as thou art–
Not in lone splendour hung aloft the night

¶ 148. *1–6.* Cp. Wordsworth's 'Chaldean shepherds' who in *Excursion* iv 697–9,

> Looked on the polar star, as on a guide
> And guardian of their course, that never closed
> His steadfast eye . . .

K. was probably thinking of Wordsworth's lines when describing Lake Windermere in his journal-letter of 25–7 June 1818 to his brother Tom, '. . . the two views we have had of it are of the most noble tenderness–they can never fade away–they make one forget the divisions of life; age, youth,

And watching, with eternal lids apart,
    Like nature's patient, sleepless eremite,
5 The moving waters at their priestlike task
    Of pure ablution round earth's human shores,
Or gazing on the new soft-fallen mask
    Of snow upon the mountains and the moors;
No—yet still steadfast, still unchangeable,
10   Pillowed upon my fair love's ripening breast,

---

poverty and riches; and refine one's sensual vision into a sort of north star
which can never cease to be open lidded and stedfast over the wonders of
the great Power' (*L* i 299). With 'eternal lids apart' (l. 3) cp. also *Endymion* i
598–9 (p. 146–7 above),

            . . . the lidless-eyèd train
      Of planets . . .

and for stars as an image of steadfastness elsewhere in K. see *Endymion* ii 842
(p. 198 above),

           Yon sentinel stars . . .

and *Hyperion* i 353 (p. 415 above),

          And still they were the same bright, patient stars . . .

2. *aloft*] amid *Brown's MS*.
3. *And*] Not *Brown's MS*.
4. *Eremite*] Cp. *The Eve of St. Agnes* 277 and *n* (p. 471 above),

        Thou art my heaven and I thine eremite . . .

K.'s use of the image here may owe something to his half-conscious
recollection of Byron's *Childe Harold* II 27 1–3,

            . . . godly eremite
      Such as on lonely Athos may be seen,
      Watching at eve upon the giant height,
      Which looks o'er waves . . .

For 'patient' Brown's transcript reads 'devout'.
5. *The moving waters*] Echoing Wordworth's *Excursion* ix 9,

      The moving waters, and the invisible air . . .

For 'moving' Brown's MS has 'morning'.
6. *pure ablution*] A religious cleansing. The word 'ablution' was suggested
by 'priestlike' in the previous line; K. sees the ebb and flow of the tides
twice daily as a ritual devotedly performed.
7–8. Perhaps pointing to the poem's composition in late October when
there was an unusually early fall of snow; see under 23 Oct. in *Annual
Register* (1819), 'Between one and two o'clock yesterday morning, a great
fall of snow commenced. . . . The roads at the entrance of London were in
several parts impassable . . . and the pathways in the fields were not passable
for foot-passengers' (79–80).
10–14.   Cheek-pillowed on my Love's white breast
            To touch for ever its warm sink and swell

To feel for ever its soft fall and swell,
  Awake for ever in a sweet unrest,
Still, still to hear her tender-taken breath,
And so live ever—or else swoon to death.

    Awake, for ever, in a sweet unrest,
    To hear, to feel her tender-taken breath
    Half passionless, and so swoon on to death. *Brown's MS.*
For the controversial view that the version preserved in Brown's transcript
was written for Mrs Isabella Jones see *Gittings* (1954) 25–36 and for counter-
arguments Murry (1955) 113–23, A. Ward's 'The Date of Keats's "Bright
Star" Sonnet', *Studies in Philology* LII (1955) 75–85 and *Bate* (1963) 359.
10. Cp. *To [Fanny]* 48–9 (p. 689 above),
        Oh, let me once more rest
        My soul upon that dazzling breast! . . .
14. swoon] For an early example of K.'s use of this word in connection with
erotic fantasy see *Endymion* i 398 (p. 137 above).

149 Ode to Fanny

Probably written Feb. 1820 when K. was living next door to Fanny Brawne
at Hampstead and was confined indoors after his haemorrhage on 3 Feb.
1820: the tone and subject-matter of the poem agree with such of K.'s letters to her as are conjecturally dated Feb.–July 1820, but the reference in
l. 8 points to a date in February. Passages in the letters which bear on the
poem include the following: 1. (Feb. 1820, *L* ii 257), 'According to all
appearances I am to be separated from you as much as possible. How I shall
be able to bear it, I cannot tell. . . .' 2. (May 1820, *L* ii 290), 'I am greedy of
you—Do not think of anything but me . . Your going to town alone . . .
was a shock to me—yet I expected it—*promise me you will not for some time,
till I get better.* . . .' 3. (5 July 1820, *L* ii 304), '. . . if you still behave in dancing
rooms and other societies as I have seen you—I do not want to live . . .'.
For other parallels in the poem with K.'s letters in 1820 see the notes below.
C. L. Finney's suggestion (*Finney* 560–2) that the *Ode to Fanny* was written
in Feb. 1819 during a much earlier stage of K.'s relationship with Fanny
Brawne is unconvincing.
Text from *1848*, which corrects K.'s undated fragmentary draft (containing
stanzas 2, 3, 5, 6, 7) and presumably follows a later revised version.
Published *1848*.

               I
  Physician Nature, let my spirit blood!
  Oh, ease my heart of verse and let me rest;

¶ *149. 1. let . . . blood*] Blood-letting was a regular medical practice at the
time. See Brown's account of K.'s Feb. 1820 haemorrhage, 'I ran for a
surgeon; my friend was bled' (*KC* ii 74).

Throw me upon thy tripod till the flood
   Of stifling numbers ebbs from my full breast.
5   A theme, a theme! Great Nature, give a theme;
       Let me begin my dream.
I come—I see thee, as thou standest there,
Beckon me out into the wintry air.

II

Ah, dearest love, sweet home of all my fears,
10   And hopes, and joys, and panting miseries,
To-night, if I may guess, thy beauty wears
       A smile of such delight,
       As brilliant and as bright,
  As when with ravished, aching, vassal eyes,
15   Lost in soft amaze,
       I gaze, I gaze!

III

Who now, with greedy looks, eats up my feast?
  What stare outfaces now my silver moon?
Ah, keep that hand unravished at the least;
20   Let, let, the amorous burn,
      But, prithee, do not turn

3. tripod] The three-legged vessel in the shrine of Apollo at Delphi on which the Sibyl sat to prophesy.

5. Great Nature] See *To [Fanny]* 43 *n* (pp. 688–9 above).

7–8. I see . . . air] Cp. K.'s letter to Fanny Brawne Feb. (?) 1820, '. . . I shall be in the front parlour watching to see you show yourself for a minute in the garden. How illness stands as a barrier betwixt me and you' (*L* ii 263).

8. out] The reading of Milnes's transcript and followed by Garrod. The reading 'not' in *1848* is a misprint.

9. My temples with hot jealous pulses beat . . . *Draft (cancelled).*

14. aching . . . eyes] Cp. K.'s letter to Fanny Brawne to May (?) 1820, '. . . I have been haunted with a sweet vision—I have seen you the whole time in your shepherdess dress. How my senses have ached at it [see *Othello* IV ii 68]' (*L* ii 290). For the use of 'ache' elsewhere in K. see *The Eve of St. Agnes* 279 *n*, *Ode on a Nightingale* 1 *n* (pp. 472 and 525 above). With 'vassal' cp. *The Eve of St. Agnes* 335 (p. 476 above), 'may I be for ay thy vassal blest'.

17–18. greedy looks . . . outfaces] The phrasing suggests that K. is recollecting the passage in Burton's *Anatomy of Melancholy* quoted in *Lamia* 1 251–2 *n* (p. 627 above).

18. silver moon] Cp. *Lamia* ii 48 and *n* (p. 636 above),
       My silver planet, both of eve and morn . . .

21–2. K. offered to release Fanny Brawne from her engagement to him *c.* Feb. 1820, but his jealousy was only temporarily lulled by her refusal to leave him. See his letter to her of Feb. 1820, 'How hurt I should have been

The current of your heart from me so soon.
    Oh, save, in charity,
    The quickest pulse for me!

IV

25 Save it for me, sweet love! Though music breathe
    Voluptuous visions into the warm air,
Though swimming through the dance's dangerous
        wreath,
    Be like an April day,
    Smiling and cold and gay,
30 A temperate lily, temperate as fair;
    Then, Heaven, there will be
    A warmer June for me.

V

Why, this–you'll say, my Fanny–is not true.
    Put your soft hand upon your snowy side
35 Where the heart beats; confess–'tis nothing new–
    Must not a woman be
    A feather on the sea,
    Swayed to and fro by every wind and tide?
    Of as uncertain speed
40   As a blow-ball from the mead?

VI

I know it, and to know it is despair
    To one who loves you as I love, sweet Fanny,

had you ever acceded. . . . My greatest torment since I have known you has been the fear of you being a little inclined to the Cressid' (L ii 255–6).

25–32. See K.'s letter to Fanny Brawne May (?) 1820, 'If you could really . . . enjoy yourself at a Party–if you can smile in people's faces, and wish them to admire you *now*, you never have nor ever will love me–I see *life* in nothing but the certainty of your Love' (L ii 291).

27. Probably suggested by Burton's references to dancing in *Anatomy of Melancholy* III 2 ii 4 (marked by K. in his copy of Burton), 'Many will not allow man and woman to dance together, because it is a provocation to lust . . . it was a pleasant sight to see those pretty knots and swimming figures' (1813 edn ii 277).

30. Cp. K.'s letter to Fanny Brawne of 5 July (?) 1820, 'I cannot live without you, and not only you but *chaste you*; *virtuous you*' (L ii 304).

31–2. Cp. K.'s letter to Fanny Brawne of March 1820, 'Take care of yourself dear that we may both be well in the Summer' (L ii 277).

40. blow-ball] 'The globular seeding head of the dandelion' (*OED*).

41–2. and to know . . . sweet Fanny] Earlier attempts in the draft were,

  1. . . . But sweet Fanny I would feign

Knell for a mercy on my lonely hours . . .

25—K.

Whose heart goes fluttering for you everywhere,
  Nor, when away you roam,
45   Dare keep its wretched home,
 Love, love alone, has pains severe and many:
   Then, loveliest, keep me free
   From torturing jealousy.

VII

 Ah, if you prize my subdued soul above
50 The poor, the fading, brief pride of an hour,
 Let none profane my Holy See of love,
   Or with a rude hand break
   The sacramental cake;
 Let none else touch the just new-budded flower.
55   If not—may my eyes close,
   Love, on their last repose.

---

2. I know it: yet sweet fanny I would feign
Cry you soft mercy for a . . .
With the last line quoted cp. *I cry your mercy* 1 (p. 689 above).
42. Fanny] girl *Draft (cancelled).*
45. Dare] Can *Draft.*
46. has] The reading of the draft. Milnes's 'his' in his transcript and *1848* are errors.
51–3. With the religious imagery cp. *The day is gone* 13, *To [Fanny]* 26 (pp. 686 and 688 above).
54. the just new-budded flower] Cp. *The day is gone* 5 (p. 686 above),
   . . . the flower and all its budded charms . . .
56. last] The reading of the draft. Milnes's 'lost' in his transcript and *1848* are errors.

150 'In after-time, a sage of mickle lore'

Probably written *c*. July 1820 when K. was 'marking the most beautiful passages' in his copy of Spenser for Fanny Brawne (*L* ii 302), since the lines were written out in this copy (now lost) according to Monckton Milnes (*1848* i 281); Brown described it as 'the last stanza of any kind that [K.] . . . wrote before his lamented death' (*Plymouth and Devonport Weekly Journal* 4 July 1830). K.'s Spenserian stanza is a reply to the 'undemocratic' views expressed in *The Faerie Queene* V ii 29–54 in which the 'Giant' appears as a revolutionary champion of equality who presumes 'to weigh the world anew'; K. was probably thinking especially of V ii 38,

  Tyrants that make men subject to their law,
  I will suppresse, that they no more may raine;
  And Lordlings curbe, that commons over-aw;
 And all the wealth of rich men to the poore will draw . . .

Milnes comments, '[K.] expressed this *ex post facto* prophecy, his conviction of the ultimate triumph of freedom and equality by the power of transmitted knowledge' (*1848* i 281).

Text from *1848*.

Published *Plymouth and Devonport Weekly Journal* 4 July 1830; repr. *1848*.

<blockquote>

In after-time, a sage of mickle lore
Ycleped Typographus, the Giant took
And did refit his limbs as heretofore,
And made him read in many a learned book,
5   And into many a lively legend look;
Thereby in goodly themes so training him,
That all his brutishness he quite forsook,
When, meeting Artegall and Talus grim,
The one he struck stone-blind, the other's eyes wox
    dim.

</blockquote>

¶ 150. *1. mickle lore*] Much learning.

2. Typographus] The power of the printed word.

8. Artegall . . . Talus grim] In *The Faerie Queene* the Giant is defeated by Sir Artegall (representing Justice) and his 'yron' squire Talus. His 'brutishness' is seen by K. as the result of ignorance.

DOUBTFUL ATTRIBUTIONS AND TRIVIA

151 'Can death be sleep, when life is but a dream'

Copied out by George Keats and dated '1814' in his Scrap-book containing transcripts of poems by K. and others, newspaper cuttings and 'other curiosities' (see 'The Keats–Wylie Scrap-book', Garrod xlviii–l). C. L. Finney guesses that K. '. . . composed the poem before the death of his grandmother in Dec. 1814' (cp. As from the darkening gloom, p. 8 above), but Garrod notes, 'The piece is unsigned, nor does anything in the book [i.e. the Scrap-book] indicate or suggest that Keats wrote these weak verses . . . in view of the complete want of attestation I should be disposed to rule it out of the canon' (Garrod xlix–l).
Published Forman (1883).

I

Can death be sleep, when life is but a dream,
    And scenes of bliss pass as a phantom by?
The transient pleasures as a vision seem,
    And yet we think the greatest pain's to die.

II

5   How strange it is that man on earth should roam,
    And lead a life of woe, but not forsake
His rugged path; nor dare he view alone
    His future doom which is but to awake.

152 Song

TUNE – 'Julia to the Wood-Robin'

Dated 'Abt 1815/16' in the first of two transcripts in Woodhouse 3: Woodhouse copied out the poem again as one of ten 'small pieces . . . copied for my cousin [Mary Frogley] . . . by Mr. Kirkman, and said to be by Keats. . . . They must have been all written before the year 18. . Some of them are perhaps among his earliest compositions . . .' (for references to Kirkman see L i 410 n, ii 7, 27, 29, 33 n), but the poem may have been written by George Keats; the initials 'G.K.' are attached in pencil to the transcript by Georgiana Wylie in the Keats–Wylie Scrap-book from which the text is taken.
Published 1876.

Stay, ruby-breasted warbler, stay,
    And let me see thy sparkling eye.
Oh, brush not yet the pearl-strung spray,
    Nor bow thy pretty head to fly!

5   Stay while I tell thee, fluttering thing,
        That thou of love an emblem art.
    Yes, patient plume thy little wing,
        Whilst I my thoughts to thee impart.

    When summer nights the dews bestow,
10   And summer suns enrich the day,
    Thy notes the blossoms charm to blow—
        Each opes delighted at thy lay.

    So when in youth the eye's dark glance
        Speaks pleasure from its circle bright,
15 The tones of love our joys enhance
        And make superior each delight.

    And when bleak storms resistless rove,
        And every rural bliss destroy,
    Nought comforts then the leafless grove
20   But thy soft note—its only joy.

    E'en so the words of love beguile
        When Pleasure's tree no flower bears,
    And draw a soft endearing smile
        Amid the gloom of grief and tears.

¶ 152. *Title. Woodhouse* 3 has the note, 'This song was written at the request of some young ladies who were tired of singing the words printed
with the air and desired fresh words to the same tune. . . .' In a similar note
in *Woodhouse* 2 the ladies are identified as the Mathew sisters (see *To Some
Ladies* p. 18 above).
19. leafless] hapless *Woodhouse* 3.
20. soft] sweet *Woodhouse* 3.

153 'See, the ship in the bay is riding'

Copied out in *Woodhouse* 3 as one of ten 'small pieces . . . said to be by
Keats' (see headnote to the preceding poem, 'Song') with the note: 'This
poem K. said had not been written by him. He did not see it; but I repeated
the first 4 lines to him.' Garrod prints it among K.'s poems, 'but with no
belief in its authenticity' (*Garrod* lxxii).
Text from *Woodhouse* 3.
Published *Garrod* (1939 edn).

See, the ship in the bay is riding,
Dearest Ellen, I go from thee—
Boldly go, in thy love confiding,
Over the deep and trackless sea.
5 When thy dear form no longer is near me,
This soothing thought shall at midnight cheer me:
'My love is breathing a prayer for me.'

When the thunder of war is roaring,
When the bullets around me fly,
10 When the rage of the tempest, pouring,
Bends the billowy sea and sky,
Yet shall my heart, to fear a stranger,
Cherish its fondest hopes for thee—
This dear reflection disarming danger,
15 'My love is breathing a prayer for me'.

154 The Poet

Preserved in a transcript in *Woodhouse* 3, which has some variants from the version in *The London Magazine* Oct. 1821, and included among K.'s poems by Amy Lowell, C. L. Finney and Garrod, but the poem was probably written by K.'s publisher John Taylor: the version in *The London Magazine* was copied out by Taylor's partner, J. A. Hessey, in *A Collection of English Sonnets*, ed. R. F. Housman (1835), as the first of a group of sonnets assigned by him to Taylor. For further evidence of Taylor's authorship see M. A. B. Steele, 'The Authorship of "The Poet" and other sonnets: Selections from a 19th century Manuscript Anthology', *KShJ* v (1956) 69–79.
Text from *The London Magazine* with variants noted from *Woodhouse* 3.
Published *The London Magazine* Oct. 1821 and *Lowell* (1925).

At morn, at noon, at eve, and middle night,
    He passes forth into the charmèd air,
    With talisman to call up spirits rare
From flow'r, tree, heath, and fountain. To his sight
5 The husk of natural objects opens quite
    To the core, and every secret essence there
    Reveals the elements of good and fair,
Making him see, where learning lacketh light.

¶ 154. *Title*. So given in *Woodhouse* 3
4. *flow'r, tree, heath*] plant, cave, rock *Woodhouse* 3.
8. *lacketh*] hath no *Woodhouse* 3.

The poet's sympathies are not confined
10   To kindred, country, climate, class, or kind,
And yet they glow intense. Oh, were he wise
Duly to commune with his destined skies,
Then, as of old, might inspiration shed
A visible glory round his hallowed head.

9–14. Woodhouse 3,

Sometimes above the gross and palpable things
Of this diurnal sphere, his spirit flies
On awful wing; and with its destined skies
Holds premature and mystic communings:
[5]   Till such unearthly intercourses shed
A visible halo round his mortal head.

l. [2]. *sphere*] ball *Woodhouse 3* (*cancelled*). An earlier attempt was 'Earth'.
l. [3]. *awful*] buoyant *Woodhouse 3* (*cancelled*).
l. [6]. *mortal*] living *Woodhouse 3* (*cancelled*).

155 To Woman (from the Greek)

Preserved in an undated transcript with the above title in *Woodhouse 3*. Two MS copies appear in the Album of Mary Mathew, the sister of George Felton Mathew, and a printed copy (from an unidentified source) appears in George and Georgiana Keats's Scrap-Book with the Greek motto from Meleager, ἠὰρ μῖ ἐμοὶ γράφειαι φεος ('For I describe her as one goddess', *Greek Anthology*, Amatory Epigrams, 137, Loeb edn vol. i 194). Garrod prints it in his Introduction with the comment, 'Keats knew no Greek ... the poem is clearly not ... a translation from the Greek – the sentiment of the concluding lines, for example, derives from some one familiar with the contribution to the Fall of Man made by Eve ... I do not credit, or debit, it to Keats ...'
Text from *Woodhouse 3*.
Published *Garrod* (1939 edn).

O thou, by Heaven ordained to be
Arbitress of man's destiny!
From thy sweet lip one tender sigh,
One glance from thine approving eye,
5   Can raise or bend him to thy will
To Virtue's noblest flights, or worst extreme of ill.
Be angel-minded and despise
Thy sex's little vanities;
And let not passion's lawless tide
10   Thy better purpose sweep aside,
For woe awaits the evil hour

That lends to man's annoy thy heaven-entrusted power.
Woman, 'tis thine to cleanse his heart
From every gross, unholy part;
15 Thine, in domestic solitude,
To win him to be wise and good;
His pattern guide and friend to be—
To give him back the heaven he forfeited for thee.

156 Gripus. A Fragment

Found among Woodhouse's papers (*Woodhouse* 3). No evidence exists as to date and authorship. For the view that it was written early 1819 and has some reference to Charles Brown, Fanny Brawne and K. see *Gittings* (1968) 285–6. The fragment seems to me unKeatsian. Text from *Garrod*, with title, punctuation and name of speakers supplied.
Published *Lowell* (1925).

Gripus. And gold and silver are but filthy dross.
Then seek not gold and silver which are dross,
But rather lay thy treasure up in heaven!—
Slim. Hem!
Gripus. And thou has meat and drink and lodging too,
5 And clothing too, what more can Man require?
And thou art single ...
But I must lay up money for my children,
My children's children and my great-grandchildren;
For, Slim, thy master will be shortly married—
Slim. Married!
10 *Gripus.*   Yea! married. Wherefore dost thou stare,
As though my words had spoke of aught impossible?
Slim. My lord, I stare not, but my ears played false—
Methought you had said married.
Gripus.   Married, fool!
Is it aught unlikely? I'm not very old,
15 And my intended has a noble fortune.
Slim. My lord, 'tis likely.
Gripus.   Haste, then, to the butchers,
And ere thou go, tell Bridget she is wanted.
Slim. I go—Gods! what a subject for an ode,
With Hymen, Cupids, Venus, Loves and Graces!   [*exit*
                              Gripus *solus*
20 *Gripus.* This matrimony is no light affair;
Tis downright venture and mere speculation.

Less risk there is in what the merchant trusts
To winds and waves and the uncertain elements,
25 For he can have assurance for his goods
And put himself beyond the reach of losses—
But who can e'er ensure to me a wife,
Industrious and managing and frugal,
Who will not spend far more than she has brought,
But be almost a saving to her husband?
30 But none can tell—the broker cannot tell
He is not cheated in the wares he buys,
And to judge well of women or the seas
Would oft surpass the wisest merchant's prudence;
For both are deep alike—capricious, too—
35 And the worst things that money can be sunk in.
But Bridget comes—
Bridget.   Your pleasure, Sir, with me?
Gripus. Bridget, I wish to have a little converse
Upon a matter that concerns us both
Of like importance both to thee and me.
40 *Bridget.* Of like importance and concerning both!
What can your Honour have to say to me?
Aside] Oh Lord! I would give all that I am worth
To know what 'tis—
Gripus.   Then prithee rein thy tongue
That ever battles with thine own impatience.
45 But to the point. Thou knows't, for twenty years
Together we have lived as man and wife,
But never hath the sanction of the Church
Stamped its legality upon our union.
Bridget. Well, what of that?
Gripus.   Why, when in wiser years
50 Men look upon the follies of their youth,
They oft repent, and wish to make amends,
And seek for happier in more virtuous days.
In such a case, and such is mine I own,
'Tis marriage offers us the readiest way
55 To make atonement for our former deeds.
And thus have I determined in my heart
To make amends—in other words to marry.
Bridget. Oh, lord! How overjoyed I am to hear it!
I vow that I have often thought myself,
60 What wickedness it was to live as we did!
But do you joke?
Gripus.   Not so upon my oath.
I am resolved to marry and beget
A little heir to leave my little wealth to.

I am not old, my hair is hardly grey,
65   My health is good—what hast thou to object?
     Bridget. Oh, dear! How close your honour puts the
         question!
     I've said as much already as was fit
     And incompatible with female modesty—
     But would your honour please to name a day?
70   *Gripus.* To name a day! But hark, I hear a knock—
     'Tis perhaps young Prodigal, I did expect him.
     Bridget. But Sir – a day?
     Gripus.   Zounds! dost thou hear the bell?
     Wilt thou not run? He was to bring me money!
                                        [*Exit* B. *and returns*
     Bridget. 'Tis he, I've shown him to the little study.
75   *Gripus.* Then stay thee here, and when I've settled him
     I will return and hold more converse with thee.   [*exit*
     Bridget [*solus*]. My head runs round! Oh, what a happy
         change!
     Now I shall be another woman quite.
     Dame Bridget, then, adieu! and don't forget
80   Your lady Gripus now that is to be;
     Great Lady Gripus—Oh, lord!—
     The Lady of the old and rich Sir Gripus!
     Oh, how will people whisper, as I pass,
     'There goes my lady'—'What a handsome gownd,
85   All scarlet silk embroidered with gold!'
     Or green and gold will perhaps become me better—
     'How vastly fine!' How handsome I shall be
     In green and gold! Besides, a lady too!
     I'll have a footman, too, to walk behind me.
90   Slim is too slender to set off a livery,
     I must have one more lustier than him,
     A proper man to walk behind his lady.
     Oh, how genteel! Methinks I see myself
     In green and gold and carrying my fan—
95   *Or perhaps I'd have a* ridicule *about me!*
     The lusty footman all so spruce behind me,
     Walking on tiptoe in a bran new livery;
     And he shall have a favour in his hat,
     As sure as ever I am Lady Gripus!

                          Enter Slim
100 *Slim.* Why how now, Bridget, you're turned actress sure!
     Bridget. An actor, fellow, no! To something better,

95. *ridicule*] A malapropism for reticule. Cp. l. 111 below, 'excard' (discard),
l. 132 below, 'allegolly' (allegory' and l. 173 below 'nonplush' (nonplus).

To something grander and more ladylike,
Know I am turned!
Slim.   A lunatic, 'tis plain.
But, lovee, leave this jesting for a while,
105 And hear thy servant, who thus pleads for favour.
Bridget. For favour Sirrah! But I must be kind,
I will forget your insolence this once,
And condescend to keep you in my service.
But no! I want a much more lustier man,
110 You are too slender to become my livery
I must excard you, you must suit yourself!
Slim. Why, how now, Bridget—
Bridget.   You forget me, sure!
Slim. Forget thee, Bridget? Never from my heart
115   Shall thy dear image part.
              Ah, no,
        I love you so
No language can impart!
Alas! 'Tis love that makes me thin,
I have a fiery flame within,
120   That burns and shrivels up my skin—
        'Tis Cupid's little dart,
        And by this kiss I swear—   [*attempts to kiss her*
Bridget. Ruffin, begone, or I will tell my lord.
Do you not care for difference of rank,
125 Nor make distinction between dirt and dignity?
Slim. Why, Bridget, once you did not treat me thus.
Bridget. No, times are altered, Fortune's wheel is turned,
You still are Slim, but, though I once was Bridget,
I'm Lady Gripus now that is to be.
130 Did not his Honour tell you he should marry?
Slim. Yea, to a lady of an ample fortune.
Bridget. Why, that, you fool, he said in allegolly.
A virtuous woman, is she not a crown,
A crown of gold and glory to her husband?
135 *Slim.* Heaven, is it possible? I pray forgive me
That I could doubt a moment of that fortune
Which is but due to your assembled merits.
Bridget. Well, Slim, I do not wish to harbour malice,
But while you show a proper due respect
140 You may be certain of my condescension.
But hark! I hear his lordship on the stairs,
And we must have some privacy together.   [*exit Slim*
Oh, lord, how overjoyed I am your honour—
Gripus. Bridget, I thank thee for thy friendly zeal,
145 That seems to glory in thy Master's bliss;

And much it grieves me that I can't requite it
Except by mere reciprocal good wishes.
For as a change in my domestic government
Will make thy place in future but a sinecure,
150 It grieves me much that I must warn you thus
To seek and get a situation elsewhere.
Bridget. Oh, dear! Oh, lord! Oh, what a shock! Oh, lord!
                                                              [*faints*]
Gripus. Ho! Slim—the devil's in the fool, to faint.
Halloo!—What shall I do? Halloo! Halloo!
155 Ho! Slim, I say—run, Sirrah, for the brandy!
Slim. The brandy, Sir? There is none in the house!
Gripus. No brandy! None! What, none at all, thou knave?
What, none at all? Thou rascal, thou hast drunk it.
Why, Bridget, Bridget—what, no brandy, knave?
160 Zounds, what a fit! Where is my brandy, wretch!
Thou toping villain, say, or I will slay thee!
                                       [*lets* Bridget *fall and collars* Slim
Slim. Oh, lord! Forgive me, Bridget had the wind,
And drank the brandy up to warm her stomach.
Gripus. A tipsy Bacchanal! Then let her lie!
165 I'll not be drunken out of house and home.
Zounds! Brandy for the wind—a cure indeed!
A little water had done just as well.
This is the way, then, when I want a drop,
I always find my cellar is stark naked.
170 But both shall go, yes, I discard ye. Thieves!
Begone, ye thieves!   [Bridget *jumps up*
Bridget.   No, not without my wages!
I'll have a month's full wages or my warning!
I'll not be left at nonplush for a place.
Gripus. A month's full warning! What, another month,
175 To sack, to ransack, and to strip the house,
And then depart in triumph with your booty!
Begone, I say!
Bridget.   No, not without my wages!
And I'll have damages, you cruel man!
I will convict you of a breach of marriage!
180 *Gripus.* Begone, I say! Deceitful thing, begone!—
Who ever dared to promise such a match
But thy own fancy, and thy lying tongue?
What, marry one as poor as a church mouse,
And equally devoid of rank and beauty!
185 Reason would sleep and prudence would be blind,
And Gripus then would be no longer Gripus,
But only fitting for more sober men
To lodge in Bedlam and to call a lunatic . . .

157 Fragments

The three scraps are written out in K.'s hand. Fragment I was probably written Feb. 1816, since the lines appear on the second sheet of K.'s MS containing *To Mary Frogley* (see headnote, p. 29 above), and was first published *Garrod* (1939 edn); II is from an undated MS (Harvard) and was published J. M. Murray, *The Poems and Verses of John Keats* (1930); III is from an undated holograph MS formerly in the possession of M. Buxton Forman and was first published *Garrod* (1939 edn).

I

I am as brisk
As a bottle of Wisk-
Ey and as nimble
As a Milliner's thimble.

II

Oh, grant that like to Peter I
May like to Peter B,
And tell me, lovely Jesus, Y
Old Jonah went to C.

III

They weren fully glad of their gude hap
And tasten all the pleasaunces of joy

¶ 157. ii 4. This Peter went to C *Earlier variant in K.'s MS.*

APPENDIX A

The rejected preface to *Endymion*

K. wrote his original preface to *Endymion* 19 March 1818, sent it to the publishers 21 March 1818 (*L* i 253), and replaced it with the second preface (p. 119 above) 10 April 1818 (*L* i 269) after hearing that John Reynolds and the publishers had disapproved of it. See his statement in his letter to Reynolds of 9 April 1818 (*L* i 266–7),

'Since you all agree that the thing is bad, it must be so–though I am not aware there is anything like Hunt in it, (and if there is, it is my natural way, and I have something in common with Hunt) look it over again and examine into the motives, the seeds from which any one sentence sprung–I have not the slightest feel of humility towards the Public–or to any thing in existence,–but the eternal Being, the Principle of Beauty,–and the Memory of great Men–When I am writing for myself for the mere sake of the Moment's enjoyment, perhaps nature has its course with me–but a Preface is written to the Public; a thing I cannot help looking upon as an Enemy, and which I cannot address without feelings of Hostility–If I write a Preface in a supple or subdued style, it will not be in character with me as a public speaker–I would be subdued before my friends, and thank them for subduing me–but among Multitudes of Men–I have no feel of stooping, I hate the idea of humility to them–

I never wrote one single Line of Poetry with the least Shadow of public thought.

Forgive me for vexing you and making a Trojan Horse of such a Trifle, both with respect to the matter in Question, and myself–but it eases me to tell you–I could not live without the love of my friends–I would jump down Ætna for any great Public good–but I hate a Mawkish Popularity.– I cannot be subdued before them–My glory would be to daunt and dazzle the thousand jabberers about Pictures and Books–I see swarms of Porcupines with their Quills erect "like lime-twigs set to catch my Winged Book" and I would fright 'em away with a torch–You will say my preface is not much of a Torch. It would have been too insulting "to begin from Jove" and I could not set a golden head upon a thing of clay–if there is any fault in the preface it is not affectation: but an undersong of disrespect to the Public.–if I write another preface, it must be done without a thought of those people–I will think about it. If it should not reach you in four–or five days–tell Taylor to publish it without a preface, and let the dedication simply stand "inscribed to the memory of Thomas Chatterton" [see *Endymion*, note to the Dedication, p. 120 above] . . .'

K.'s defensively worded preface expresses more openly than the revised version his mixed feelings about *Endymion* in early 1818 when he was preparing the poem for the press. There are further expressions of his views on

the poem in his letters to John Taylor of 27 Feb. 1818 and John Hessey of 8
Oct. 1818 (*L* i 238–9, 373–4).

PREFACE

In a great nation, the work of an individual is of so little
importance; his pleadings and excuses are so uninterest-
ing; his 'way of life' such a nothing; that a preface seems
a sort of impertinent bow to strangers who care nothing
5 about it.

A preface however should be down in so many words;
and such a one that, by an eye glance over the type, the
Reader may catch an idea of an Author's modesty, and
non opinion of himself–which I sincerely hope may be
10 seen in the few lines I have to write, notwithstanding
certain proverbs of many ages' old which men find a great
pleasure in receiving for gospel.

About a twelve month since, I published a little book of
verses; it was read by some dozen of my friends who lik'd
15 it; and some dozen who I was unacquainted with, who did
not. Now when a dozen human beings, are at words with
another dozen, it becomes a matter of anxiety to side with
one's friends;–more especially when excited thereto by a
great love of Poetry.

20 I fought under disadvantages. Before I began I had no
inward feel of being able to finish; and as I proceeded my
steps were all uncertain. So this Poem must rather be considered as an endeavour than a thing accomplish'd: a
poor prologue to what, if I live, I humbly hope to do. In
25 duty to the Public I should have kept it back for a year or
two, knowing it to be so faulty: but I really cannot do so:–
by repetition my favourite Passages sound vapid in my
ears, and I would rather redeem myself with a new Poem–
should this one be found of any interest.

30 I have to apologise to the lovers of simplicity for touching the spell of loveliness that hung about Endymion: if any
of my lines plead for me with such people I shall be proud.

It has been too much the fashion of late to consider men
biggotted and adicted to every word that may chance to
35 escape their lips: now I here declare that I have not any

3. *a preface*] the nearly *K.'s MS* (*cancelled*).
5. *about it*] Followed in *K.'s MS* by the cancelled passage, 'However self-
pride is the less offended where . . .'.
11. *old*] standing *K.'s MS* (*cancelled*).
26. [*do*] *so*] [do] it *K.'s MS* (*cancelled*).
29. *be found of any interest*] create any interest *K.'s MS* (*cancelled*).

particular affection for any particular phrase, word or
letter in the whole affair. I have written to please myself
and in hopes to please others, and for a love of fame; if I
neither please myself, nor others nor get fame, of what
40   consequence is Phraseology?

I would fain escape the bickerings that all works, not
exactly in chime, bring upon their begetters:—but this is
not fair to expect, there must be conversation of some sort
and to object shows a Man's consequence. In case of a
45   London drizzle or a Scotch Mist, the following quotation
from Marston may perhaps 'stead me as an umbrella for
an hour or so: 'let it be the Curtesy of my peruser rather
to pity my self hindering labours than to malice me'.

One word more:—for we cannot help seeing our own
50   affairs in every point of view—Should anyone call my
dedication to Chatterton affected I answer as followeth:

'Were I dead Sir I should like a Book dedicated to me'—
Teignmouth March 19th 1818—

Text from K.'s MS (Morgan Library).

37. *affair*] matter *K.'s MS (cancelled).*
47–8. '*let . . . me*'] From Marston's preface to *The Fawn* (1633), which was
included in Dilke's *Old English Plays* (1814–16): cp. *Endymion* i 294–6 *n* (p.
133 above).
51. *answer*] say *K.'s MS (cancelled).*

APPENDIX B

The Indicator version of 'La Belle Dame sans Merci'

Ah, what can ail thee, wretched wight,
    Alone and palely loitering;
The sedge is withered from the lake,
    And no birds sing.

Ah, what can ail thee, wretched wight,
    So haggard and so woe-begone?
The squirrel's granary is full,
    And the harvest's done.

I see a lily on thy brow,
    With anguish moist and fever dew;
And on thy cheek a fading rose
    Fast withereth too.

I met a Lady in the meads
    Full beautiful, a fairy's child;
Her hair was long, her foot was light,
    And her eyes were wild.

I set her on my pacing steed,
    And nothing else saw all day long;
For sideways would she lean, and sing
    A fairy's song.

I made a garland for her head,
    And bracelets too, and fragrant zone;
She looked at me as she did love,
    And made sweet moan.

She found me roots of relish sweet,
    And honey wild, and manna dew;
And sure in language strange she said,
    I love thee true.

She took me to her elfin grot,
    And there she gazed and sighèd deep,
And there I shut her wild sad eyes—
    So kissed to sleep.

And there we slumbered on the moss,
    And there I dreamed—ah, woe betide—

The latest dream I ever dreamed
  On the cold hill side.

I saw pale kings, and princes too,
  Pale warriors, death-pale were they all;
Who cried–'La belle Dame sans mercy
  Hath thee in thrall!'

I saw their starved lips in the gloom
  With horrid warning gapèd wide,
And I awoke, and found me here
  On the cold hill side.

And this is why I sojourn here
  Alone and palely loitering
Though the sedge is withered from the lake,
  And no birds sing.

APPENDIX C

Cancelled passages from
Otho the Great Act I

The following passages in K.'s draft (*K.'s MS*) are printed here rather than in the commentary for the sake of convenience. On the general agreement between *K.'s MS* and *Brown's MS* apart from the passages in Act I numbered 1 and 2 below see headnote to *Otho the Great* (p. 546 above). Passage 3 appears in both *K.'s MS* and *Brown's MS*, but is cancelled in the latter. The punctuation and spelling are uncorrected.

1. I i *16–121*
Auranthe. Ha! Brother Conrad welcome from the War:
I thought I heard your Trumpet at the Gates.
Conrad. And I so welcome Sister—sister no more
But my liege Lady—
Auranthe.   Liege Lady are you mad?
Conrad. My sovran Lady what would you give now
If I would clear the puzzle from your brows?
Auranthe. Good Brother speak—
Conrad.   Good Brother—will I not
Speak out since a fair sister and an almost Queen
Commands. The Emperor—
Auranthe.   What? Pray speak
Conrad. Hath given consent that you should marry Ludolph
Auranthe. What sudden change is here—how was it Conrad?
Conrad. Never mind how—but let your royal blood
Mount in your cheeks
Auranthe.   I feel it mounting warm
But is it so—Kind Brother tell me how?
Conrad. Thank me for this:—in yesterday's hard fight
I did the Emperor service, and so help'd
His bloodstain'd Ensign to the victory
That it hath turn'd the edge of his sharp wrath
To overflowing kindness—now he's mine
And we must take him sister in the mood.
Auranthe. Aye this sounds well and reasonable too
Conrad. He will be heare this morning
Auranthe.   That I heard
Among the midnight tidings from the Camp.
(*going*) *Conrad.* That is all well Good bye my gracious Queen
Within an hour—

Auranthe.   Conrad one word more
Conrad. Speak Empress!
Auranthe. That Letter!
Conrad. What Letter?
Auranthe. Do give it me that I may mince it up
Then there will be no shadow of a chance
Against my coming greatness.
Conrad. What dost mean—
Auranthe. You sure received that Letter touching Albert?
Conrad. No. Yes—
Auranthe.   Give it me
Conrad.   I have it not
Auranthe. Alas!
Conrad. At one pernicious charge of the Enemy
I for a moment whiles was Prisoner ta'en
And rifled-stuff! the horses hoofs have minc'd it
Auranthe. Still I have half a fear:
Conrad.   Perhaps for Albert
Auranthe. Surely you spar'd him at my earnest prayer
Conrad. Spar'd him! O would to Heaven I had not—
Auranthe. If you do ever touch a hair of his head
I swear in your despite, I will refuse
Even his Highness Ludolph's sceptry hand
Conrad. Impossible! refuse a Prince—a Prince!
No woman no—you dare not for yourself
You could not though it were to save your teeth
Complete for kissing, your eyes and your cheeks colour
Be but a Queen and at word you make
Pearl mouths fade out of fashion. ha ha ha,
Refuse the Prince! forgive me. I must laugh
Auranthe. Sir, you may laugh, but by my Life I swear—
Conrad. Yes yes I know you'll swear—do any thing
To gain so poor a point as Albert's life.
Why I have known a Lady do as much
And more, fall sprawling hectic on the floor
To frighten her poor lord to unstring his purse
For a new silver service.
Auranthe.   You may find
Yourself not quite so learned cunning Sir!
Conrad. Would you be then unqueen'd for such a dog
Auranthe. Aye for that word I could to torture you—
Conrad. And this is then the fruit of all my pains
And all my risques, and all my weary plots
To make thee mighty. Plot who will again
For others benefit, I'll no more of it—
The very sister of our ducal house

Will weigh a Brother and a royal Crown
Against a—
Auranthe. Keep the word within your lips
And let it choak you! But I will be calm
To our better understanding one another—
You know some secret coverts of my heart
I know perhaps yours better than you mine.
Why so pathetic my kind Benefactor
On all the many bounties of your hand—
Sure, you forgot Duke Conrad all this while?
Conrad. By heavens I could almost stop this match—
Auranthe. No, Brother, no you dare not for yourself—
Ha! ha! forgive me for I too must laugh—
Do you not count, when I am queen, to take
Advantage of your mean discoveries
Of my poor secrets, and so hold a rod
Over my life for your sly purposes?
Conrad. Now could I hear that villain—see he comes
Look, woman Look your Albert is quite safe
In haste it seems—Now shall I be in the way
And wish'd with silent curses in my grave
Or side by side with whelmed Mariners

Enter Albert

Whisper a Curse Auranthe in my ear
'Twill be sweet musick—Curse me far away!
For there can be no 'gentle Alberts' now
No 'sweet Auranthes'
Auranthe.   Peace thou devil Peace . . .

2. I i *137–55.*
Albert. The Emperor is no further from you
Than what my Charger in three minutes clear'd
Galloping his Pomp. To you great Duke
He—
Conrad. What of me ha?
Albert.   What please'd your grace to say?
Conrad. What matters that?
Albert.   You mean not this to me
Auranthe. My noble Brother you have grieved enough:
(*To Albert*) Lord Albert now you must not heed his words
The Duke has ever since the battle sorrow'd
For one of his brave Captains slain—his friend
He was—and a most valliant—
Conrad. Sister! would you thrust me on—
Auranthe.   Hearst thou!

Albert. The Emperor's Flourish! Germany is here!
I'm sorry for his grace ...

3. I iii *125–32.*
Sigifred. Pray What would you with us?
Theodore. (*To Ludolph*)   My Lord I come
To bring you to the presence all in haste
No doubt you will obey the Emperor's summons
Ludolph. (*To Sigifred*) D'ye hear this fellow how he braves his
        Prince?
I've a shrewd guess the court atmosphere
Is to fine for my Breathing, Sigifred
When such an ugly vermin dares so much
Theodore. Yeeld up your sword My Lord and come away
Ludolph. Give him some answer Sigifred–or blows
Theodore. The Emperor's Commands!
Sigifred.   Insolent slave!
Gonfred. Nay my good Prince we are not warranted
Beyond a civil Message to request
Your Hinehess would obey great Otho's call
Ludolph. This is another tune. (*To Theodore*) fellow avaunt!
Theodore. I trust your Highness anger will not fall
On one whose fault, if such it was arose
From ignorance
Ludolph. Thou art right–thy place is good
Thou hast forgot the nature of an insult
By constant suffrance for a small preferment–
Let me not see thee more–come Sigifred
I will to Friedburg Castle on the spur
And feel the Dragon's paws ...

4. V i *18–32*
Ludolph. What here! here solitary must I die
Without revenge, here stifled in the shade
Of these dull Boughs? Pshaw bitter bitter end–
A bitter death! a suffocating death!
A gnawing, silent deadly quiet death!
Must she escape me? Can I not clutch her fast?
She's gone——, away, away, away–and now
Each moment brings its poison–I must die
As near a Hermit's death as patience–Oh!
War! War! War! where is that illustrious noise
To gasp away my life
To smother up this sound of labouring breath
This death song of the trees. Blow Trumpeters!
(*sinks*) O curs'd Auranthe!

Enter Albert wounded

Albert! here is hope!
(starts up) Of Glorious clamour yet; Thrice villainous
Tell me where that detested woman is
Or this through thee.
Albert.   My good Prince with me
The sword [h]as done its worst— *(Auranthe shrieks)*
Page   My Lord—a noise
This way—Hark!
Ludolph. Yes a glorious clamour yet—   *exeunt*

[*Scene changes to another part of the wood*]

Enter Albert wounded and Ludolph

APPENDIX D

The Publishers' Advertisement to *1820*

The Advertisement is dated 'Fleet Street, June 26, 1820', and according to
Hyder Rollins was written by John Taylor (*KC* ii 115). K. crossed out the
Advertisement in his presentation copy of *1820* for his Hampstead neighbour, Burridge Davenport, and commented, 'This is none of my doing – I
was ill at the time. This is a lie' – the last four words appear at the end of the
Advertisement and obviously refer to the reason given by the publishers
for K.'s abandoning *Hyperion*. The page from Davenport's presentation copy
containing the Advertisement and K.'s comments on it is reproduced in
Lowell (1925) 424. Woodhouse's draft of the Advertisement, which has
substantial variants in the wording, is printed in *KC* ii 115–16.

If any apology be thought necessary for the appearance of the
unfinished poem of HYPERION, the publishers beg to state
that they alone are responsible, as it was printed at their
particular request, and contrary to the wish of the author. The
poem was intended to have been of equal length with EN-
DYMION but the reception given to that work discouraged
the author from proceeding.

APPENDIX E

The order of the poems in *1817* and *1820*

1817

1. Dedication. To Leigh Hunt, Esq ('Glory and loveliness have passed away')
2. 'I stood tip-toe upon a little hill'
3. Specimen of an Induction to a Poem ('Lo! I must tell a tale of chivalry')
4. Calidore. A Fragment
5. To Some Ladies
6. On Receiving a Curious Shell and a Copy of Verses from the Same Ladies
7. To Mary Frogley
8. To Hope
9. Imitation of Spenser
10. 'Woman! When I behold thee flippant, vain'
11. 'Light feet, dark violet eyes, and parted hair'
12. 'Ah, who can e'er forget so fair a being'

EPISTLES

13. To George Felton Mathew
14. To my Brother George ('Full many a dreary hour have I past')
15. To Charles Cowden Clarke

SONNETS

16. To my Brother George ('Many the wonders I this day have seen')
17. To . . . ('Had I a man's fair form, then might my sighs')
18. Written on the Day that Mr. Leigh Hunt left Prison
19. 'How many bards gild the lapses of time'
20. To a Friend who Sent me Some Roses
21. To Georgiana Augusta Wylie
22. 'O Solitude, if I must with thee dwell'
23. To my Brothers
24. 'Keen, fitful gusts are whispering here and there'
25. 'To one who has been long in city pent'
26. On First Looking into Chapman's Homer
27. On Leaving Some Friends at an Early Hour
28. Addressed to Haydon ('Highmindedness, a jealousy for good')
29. Addressed to the Same ('Great spirits now on earth are sojourning')

30. On the Grasshopper and Cricket
31. To Kosciusko
32. 'Happy is England! I could be content'
33. Sleep and Poetry

1820

1. Lamia
2. Isabella
3. The Eve of St. Agnes
4. Ode to a Nighingale
5. Ode on a Grecian Urn
6. Ode to Psyche
7. Fancy
8. Ode ('Bards of passion and of mirth')
9. Lines on the Mermaid Tavern
10. Robin Hood
11. To Autumn
12. Ode on Melancholy
13. Hyperion. A Fragment

Index of Titles and First Lines

Titles are given in italic type. First lines commonly accepted as titles are in italic with an asterisk prefixed.